PHILIP'S

STREET ATLAS Edinburgh

and East Central Scotland

Contents

II	Major administrative and Postcode boundaries
III	**Key to map symbols**
IV	**Key to map pages**
VI	**Route planning**
1	**Street maps** at 3½ inches to 1 mile
218	**Street maps** at 1¾ inches to 1 mile
228	**Street map of Edinburgh city centre** at 7 inches to 1 mile
230	**Index** of towns, villages, streets, hospitals, industrial estates, railway stations, schools, shopping centres, universities and places of interest

www.philips-maps.co.uk
First published in 1995 by
Philip's, a division of
Octopus Publishing Group Ltd
www.octopusbooks.co.uk
Endeavour House, 189 Shaftesbury Avenue
London WC2H 8JY
An Hachette UK Company
www.hachette.co.uk

Fourth colour edition 2010
Second impression 2013
EDIDA

ISBN 978-1-84907-130-7 (spiral)

Speed camera data provided by
PocketGPSWorld.com Ltd

Post Office is a trade mark of Post Office Ltd in the UK and other countries.

Printed in China

Major administrative and Postcode boundaries

County and unitary authority boundaries
Postcode boundaries
Area covered by this atlas
Scale
0 5 10 15 km
0 5 10 miles
NN NO
NO
NT
NS NT
Stirling
Clackmannanshire
Perth and Kinross
Fife
Falkirk
West Lothian
City of Edinburgh
Midlothian
East Lothian
North Lanarkshire
South Lanarkshire
Scottish Borders
Bridge of Allan
FK9
FK11
FK12
Alva
FK8
Stirling
Alloa
Clackmannan
Bannockburn
FK10
FK7
Airth
Kincardine
Culross
FK2
FK6
Denny
Stenhousemuir
FK5
Grangemouth
FK3
Bo'ness
Bonnybridge
FK4
Falkirk
FK1
Slamannan
Lochgelly
KY5
KY1
Kirkcaldy
Cowdenbeath
KY2
KY4
Oakley
Dunfermline
KY12
KY3
Burntisland
Kinghorn
KY11
Rosyth
Dalgety Bay
Inverkeithing
Queensferry
Linlithgow
EH49
Winchburgh
EH30
EH4
EH29
EH52
Broxburn
EH12
EH28
EH15
EH48
Bathgate
Armadale
Livingston
EH54
East Calder
EH53
Currie
EH13
EH10
EH17
EH18
Dalkeith
EH20
EH22
Balerno
EH14
EH25
Roslin
Bonnyrigg and Lasswade
EH19
Rosewell
EH24
Whitburn
EH47
Fauldhouse
West Calder
EH27
EH55
Penicuik
EH26
EH23
EH46
ML6
Harthill
ML7
Shotts
ML2
ML11
ML8
Cockenzie and Port Seton
Prestonpans
Musselburgh
EH21
Tranent
EH33
Ormiston
Pencaitland
EH35
EH34
Pathhead
EH36
EH37
EH38
EH31
Gullane
North Berwick
EH39
EH32
Haddington
EH40
East Linton
EH41
Gifford
Dunbar
EH42
Cockburnspath
TD13
TD11
TD2
Granton
EH5
Leith
EH6
EH4
EH3
Drylaw
EH2
EH7
Edinburgh
EH1
EH8
Murrayfield
EH11
Stenhouse
The Grange
EH9
The Inch
Slateford
EH10
EH16
700
300
80
90
10
20
30
40
50
60
70

Key to map symbols

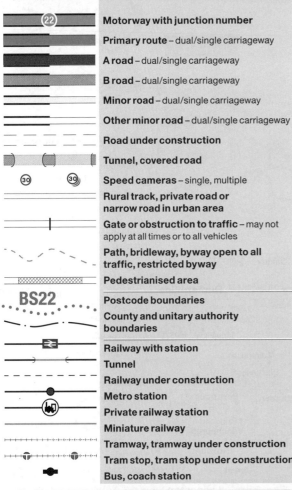

- **Motorway with junction number**
- **Primary route** – dual/single carriageway
- **A road** – dual/single carriageway
- **B road** – dual/single carriageway
- **Minor road** – dual/single carriageway
- **Other minor road** – dual/single carriageway
- **Road under construction**
- **Tunnel, covered road**
- **Speed cameras** – single, multiple
- **Rural track, private road or narrow road in urban area**
- **Gate or obstruction to traffic** – may not apply at all times or to all vehicles
- **Path, bridleway, byway open to all traffic, restricted byway**
- **Pedestrianised area**
- **Postcode boundaries** (BS22)
- **County and unitary authority boundaries**
- **Railway with station**
- **Tunnel**
- **Railway under construction**
- **Metro station**
- **Private railway station**
- **Miniature railway**
- **Tramway, tramway under construction**
- **Tram stop, tram stop under construction**
- **Bus, coach station**

- **Ambulance station**
- **Coastguard station**
- **Fire station**
- **Police station**
- **Accident and Emergency entrance to hospital**
- **Hospital**
- **Place of worship**
- **Information centre** – open all year
- **Shopping centre**
- **Parking**
- **Park and Ride**
- **Post Office**
- **Camping site**
- **Caravan site**
- **Golf course**
- **Picnic site**
- Church – **Non-Roman antiquity**
- ROMAN FORT – **Roman antiquity**
- Univ – **Important buildings, schools, colleges, universities and hospitals**
- **Built-up area**
- **Woods**
- River Medway – **Water name**
- **River, weir**
- **Stream**
- **Canal, lock, tunnel**
- **Water**
- **Tidal water**
- 112, 58, 87 – **Adjoining page indicators**

The small numbers around the edges of the maps identify the 1-kilometre National Grid lines

The dark grey border on the inside edge of some pages indicates that the mapping does not continue onto the adjacent page

Abbreviations

Acad	**Academy**	Meml	**Memorial**
Allot Gdns	**Allotments**	Mon	**Monument**
Cemy	**Cemetery**	Mus	**Museum**
C Ctr	**Civic centre**	Obsy	**Observatory**
CH	**Club house**	Pal	**Royal palace**
Coll	**College**	PH	**Public house**
Crem	**Crematorium**	Recn Gd	**Recreation ground**
Ent	**Enterprise**	Resr	**Reservoir**
Ex H	**Exhibition hall**	Ret Pk	**Retail park**
Ind Est	**Industrial Estate**	Sch	**School**
IRB Sta	**Inshore rescue boat station**	Sh Ctr	**Shopping centre**
Inst	**Institute**	TH	**Town hall / house**
Ct	**Law court**	Trad Est	**Trading estate**
L Ctr	**Leisure centre**	Univ	**University**
LC	**Level crossing**	W Twr	**Water tower**
Liby	**Library**	Wks	**Works**
Mkt	**Market**	YH	**Youth hostel**

The map scale on the pages numbered in blue is 1¾ inches to 1 mile
2.76 cm to 1 km • 1:36206

0 – ½ mile – 1 mile – 1½ miles – **2 miles**
0 – 500m – 1 km – 1½ km – **2km**

The map scale on the pages numbered in blue is 3½ inches to 1 mile
5.52 cm to 1 km • 1:18103

0 – ¼ mile – ½ mile – ¾ mile – **1 mile**
0 – 250m – 500m – 750m – **1km**

The map scale on the pages numbered in red is 7 inches to 1 mile
11.04 cm to 1 km • 1:9051

0 – 220yds – 440yds – 660yds – **½ mile**
0 – 125m – 250m – 375m – **500m**

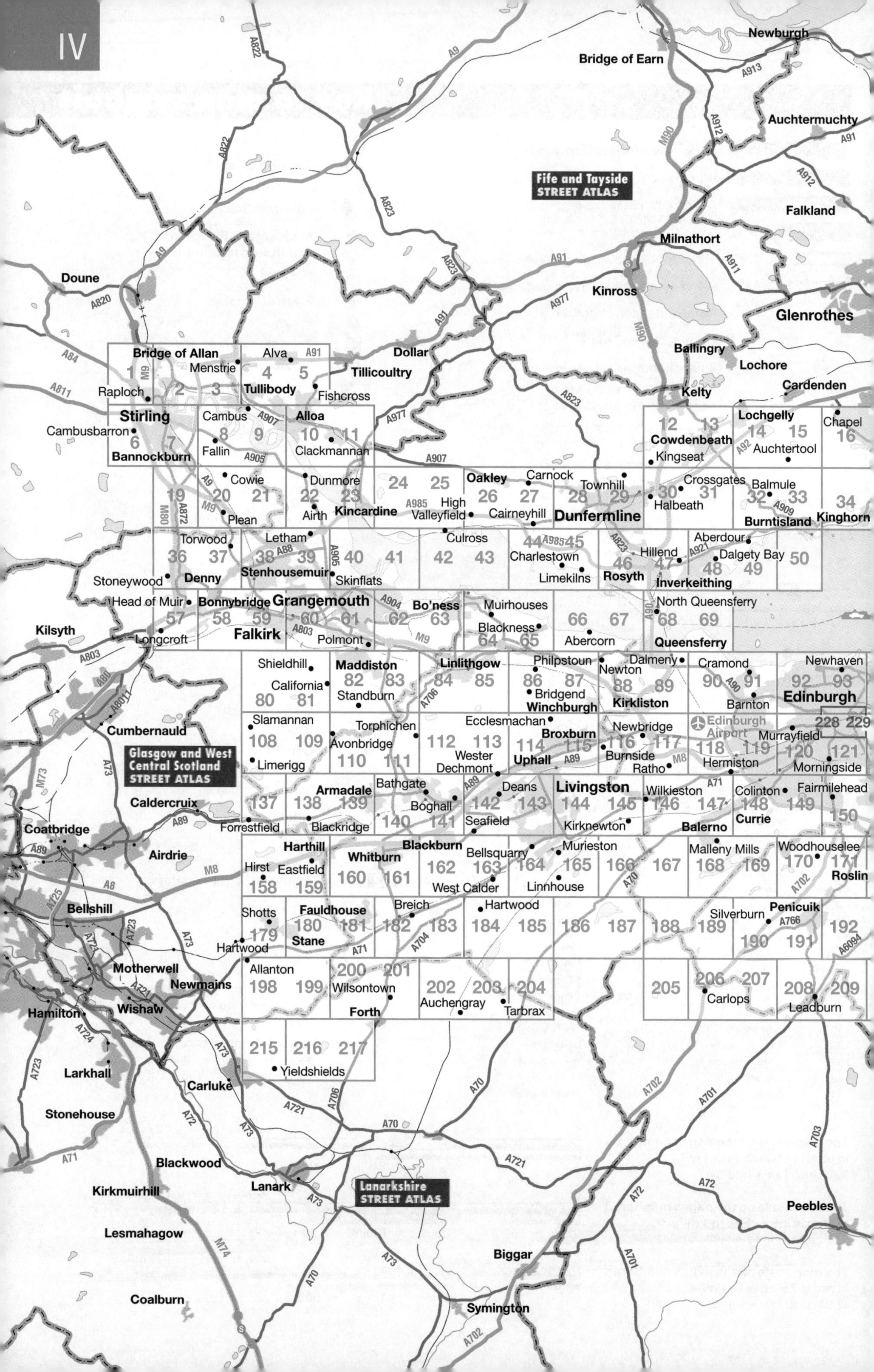
Newburgh
Bridge of Earn
A9
A822
A913
A912
Auchtermuchty
A91
M90
Fife and Tayside
STREET ATLAS
A823
Falkland
Milnathort
A911
Doune
A820
A91
Kinross
A977
Glenrothes
Ballingry
Lochore
Cardenden
Kelty
A84
A811
Bridge of Allan
Menstrie
Alva
Raploch
Tullibody
Fishcross
Dollar
Tillicoultry
Stirling
Cambusbarron
Cambus
Alloa
Clackmannan
Fallin
Bannockburn
A907
A905
A977
A823
Lochgelly
Chapel
Cowdenbeath
Kingseat
Auchtertool
A92
Cowie
Dunmore
Airth
Plean
Kincardine
High Valleyfield
Oakley
Carnock
Cairneyhill
Townhill
Dunfermline
Crossgates
Halbeath
Balmule
Burntisland
Kinghorn
A909
A985
M80
A872
M9
Torwood
Letham
Stoneywood
Denny
Stenhousemuir
Skinflats
Culross
Charlestown
Limekilns
Rosyth
Hillend
Aberdour
Dalgety Bay
Inverkeithing
A921
A88
A905
Head of Muir
Bonnybridge
Grangemouth
Bo'ness
Muirhouses
North Queensferry
Kilsyth
Longcroft
Falkirk
Polmont
Blackness
Abercorn
Queensferry
A904
A803
A90
Shieldhill
California
Maddiston
Standburn
Linlithgow
Philpstoun
Bridgend
Winchburgh
Newton
Dalmeny
Kirkliston
Cramond
Barnton
Newhaven
Edinburgh
A706
A80
A8011
Cumbernauld
Slamannan
Limerigg
Torphichen
Avonbridge
Ecclesmachan
Broxburn
Uphall
Wester Dechmont
Newbridge
Burnside
Ratho
Edinburgh Airport
Murrayfield
Hermiston
Morningside
Glasgow and West Central Scotland
STREET ATLAS
M73
A73
Caldercruix
Armadale
Bathgate
Boghall
Forrestfield
Blackridge
Deans
Seafield
Livingston
Kirknewton
Wilkieston
Balerno
Colinton
Currie
Fairmilehead
A89
A71
Coatbridge
Airdrie
M8
A8
Harthill
Hirst
Eastfield
Whitburn
Blackburn
Bellsquarry
West Calder
Murieston
Linnhouse
Malleny Mills
Woodhouselee
Roslin
A70
A702
A725
Bellshill
A723
Shotts
Fauldhouse
Stane
Hartwood
Breich
Hartwood
Silverburn
Penicuik
A766
A6094
A721
A704
Motherwell
Newmains
Allanton
Wilsontown
Forth
Auchengray
Tarbrax
Carlops
Leadburn
Hamilton
Wishaw
A724
Yieldshields
Larkhall
Carluke
A723
Stonehouse
A72
A721
A706
A70
A702
A701
A703
A71
Blackwood
Kirkmuirhill
Lanark
Lanarkshire
STREET ATLAS
A73
Peebles
Lesmahagow
M74
Biggar
Coalburn
Symington
1 2 3 4 5 6 7 8 9 10 11 12 13 14 15 16
19 20 21 22 23 24 25 26 27 28 29 30 31 32 33 34
36 37 38 39 40 41 42 43 44 45 46 47 48 49 50
57 58 59 60 61 62 63 64 65 66 67 68 69
80 81 82 83 84 85 86 87 88 89 90 91 92 93
108 109 110 111 112 113 114 115 116 117 118 119 120 121 228 229
137 138 139 140 141 142 143 144 145 146 147 148 149 150
158 159 160 161 162 163 164 165 166 167 168 169 170 171
179 180 181 182 183 184 185 186 187 188 189 190 191 192
198 199 200 201 202 203 204 205 206 207 208 209
215 216 217

Key to map pages

223	Map pages at 1¾ inches to 1 mile
145	Map pages at 3½ inches to 1 mile
229	Map pages at 7 inches to 1 mile

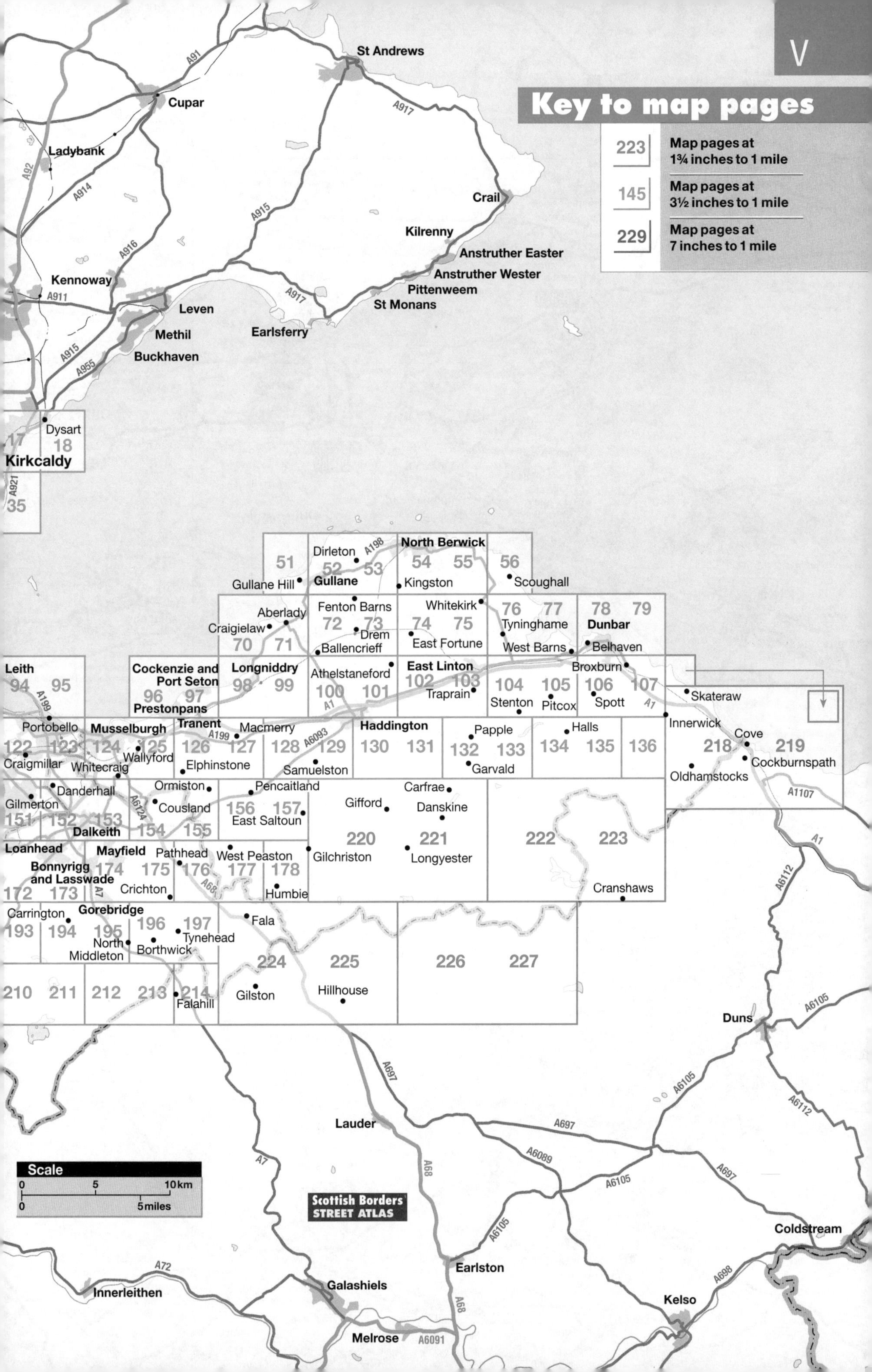

Clackmannanshire
Falkirk
North Lanarkshire
West Lothian
Stirling
ALLOA
Dunblane
Doune
Bridge of Allan
Menstrie
Tillicoultry
Alva
Tullibody
Dollar
Glendevon
Glendevon Resvrs.
Castle Hill Reservoir
Burnfoot
Pool o' Muckhart
Yetts o' Muckhart
BEN CLEUCH
KING'S SEAT HILL
BLAIRDENON HILL
STEEL'S KNOWE
INNERDOUNY HILL
Craigow
Dalqueich
Carnbo
South Queich
Crook of Devon
Drum
Coldrain
Rumbling Bridge
Powmill
Cleish
Blairingone
Hill End
Balgonar
KNOCK HILL
Loch Glow
Saline
Cowstrandburn
Devonside
Coalsnaughton
Forest Mill
Fishcross
Branshill
Sauchie
Keilarsbrae
Cambus
Cambuskenneth
Causewayhead
Blairlogie
Raploch
Cambusbarron
Torbrex
St Ninians
Bannockburn
Fallin
Throsk
Clackmannan
South Alloa
Kennet
Kilbagie
Cowie
Dunmore
Airth
Plean
STIRLING SERVICES
Devilla Forest
Kincardine
Kincardine Bridge
Blairhall
Oakley
Carnock
Comrie
Gowkhall
Milesmark
Wellwood
DUNFERMLINE
High Valleyfield
Low Torry
Torryburn
Cairneyhill
Crossford
Culross
Torry Bay
Charlestown
Limekilns
Kinbuck
Ashfield
Balhaldie
Burn of Cambus
Deanston
Blair Drummond
Easter Row
Pisgah
Sunnylaw
Gargunnock
Glentirranmuir
CARLEATHERAN
Earlsburn Reservoirs
Craigend
Loch Coulter
Easter Cringate
Muirmill
Carron Valley Forest
Carron Valley Res.
Carron Bridge
TOMTAIN
Fankerton
Stoneywood
Dunipace
DENNY
Torwood
Letham
Antonshill
Stenhousemuir
Skinflats
Larbert
Carron
Carronshore
Bainsford
GRANGEMOUTH
Head of Muir
Bonnybridge
Dennyloanhead
High Bonnybridge
Longcroft
Banknock
Banton
Greenhill
FALKIRK
Laurieston
Redding
Glen Village
Reddingmuirhead
Polmont
Brightons
Bo'ness
Grangepans
Carriden
Muirhouses
St. Margaret's Hope
Blackness
Mannerston
Grougfoot
Linlithgow
Linlithgow Bridge
Newton
Philpstoun
Old Philpstoun
Bridgend
Threemiletown
Winchburgh
Ecclesmachan
Broxburn
Uphall
Uphall Station
Pumpherston
Dechmont
Wester Dechmont
Kilsyth
Queenzieburn
Dullatur
Croy
Cumbernauld Village
Twechar
Balloch
Castlecary
Abronhill
CUMBERNAULD
KIRKINTILLOCH
Westfield
Waterside
Condorrat
Luggiebank
Moodiesburn
Bridgend
Chryston
Mollinsburn
Muirhead
Riggend
Greengairs
Wattston
Longriggend
Limerigg
Slamannan
Jawcraig
Shieldhill
California
Maddiston
Whitecross
Loan
Standburn
Avonbridge
Westfield
Torphichen
Crossburn
Binniehill
Black Loch
Hillend Res.
Caldercruix
Stand
Plains
Marnock
Glenboig
Gartcosh
Garnkirk
Stepps
Glenmavis
Gartsherrie
Thrashbush
Easterhouse
COATBRIDGE
AIRDRIE
Coatdyke
Craigneuk
Gartness
Chapelhall
Old Monkland
Baillieston
Calderbank
Birkenshaw
Viewpark
Uddingston
Bothwell
Bellshill
Mossend
Holytown
New Stevenston
Newarthill
Forgewood
MOTHERWELL
HAMILTON SERVICES
BOTHWELL SERVICES
Stonefield
Blantyre
Burnbank
Craigneuk
Knowetop
Cleland
HAMILTON
Udston
Ferniegair
WISHAW
Coltness
Newmains
Bonkle
Allanton
Hartwood
Shotts
Dykehead
Stane
Salsburgh
Newhouse
Hareshaw
Kirk of Shotts
Hirst
Eastfield
West Benhar
Harthill
HARTHILL SERVICES
Whitburn
East Whitburn
Croftmalloch
Stoneyburn
Longridge
Fauldhouse
Greenburn
Bents
Addiewell
Loganlea
Breich
West Calder
Polbeth
Forrestfield
Forrestburn Res.
Roughrigg Res.
Westrigg
Blackridge
Armadale
Windyknowe
Bathgate
Boghall
Bathville
Mayfield
Whiteside
Blackburn
Seafield
LIVINGSTON
Deans
Mid Calder
East Calder
Livingston Village
Oakbank
Bellsquarry
Linhouse Water
Woodmuir Plantation
Cobbinshaw Reservoir
Crosswood Reservoir
Woolfords Cottages
Tarbrax
WHITE CRAIG
Auchengray
Rootpark
Wilsontown
Forth
Climpy
HARE HILL
Kingshill Plantation
Morningside
Bogside
Waterloo
Overtown
Law
Cadzow
Meikle Earnock
Quarter
Larkhall
Millheugh
Limekilnburn
Shawtonhill
Shawton
Chapelton
Struthernill
Ashgill
Dalserf
Rosebank
Carluke
Yieldshields
Roadmeetings
Kilncadzow
Braehead
BLEAK LAW
Mouse Water
North Medwin
Braidwood
Netherburn
Heads
Udstonhead
Glassford
Stonehouse
Strathaven
Avon Water
Crossford
Hazelbank
Nemphlar
Cartland
Draffan
Auchenheath
Kirkfieldbank
Lanark
New Lanark
Sandford
Blackwood
Kirkmuirhill
Boghead
Dillarburn
Hyndford Bridge
Carstairs
Carstairs Junction
West End
Ravenstruther
Pettinain
Libberton
Carnwath
Kaimend
Newbigging
South Medwin
Walston
BLACK MOUNT
Dolphinton
Dunsyre
Melbourne
Elsrickle
Whitecastle
Candy Mill
Clyde

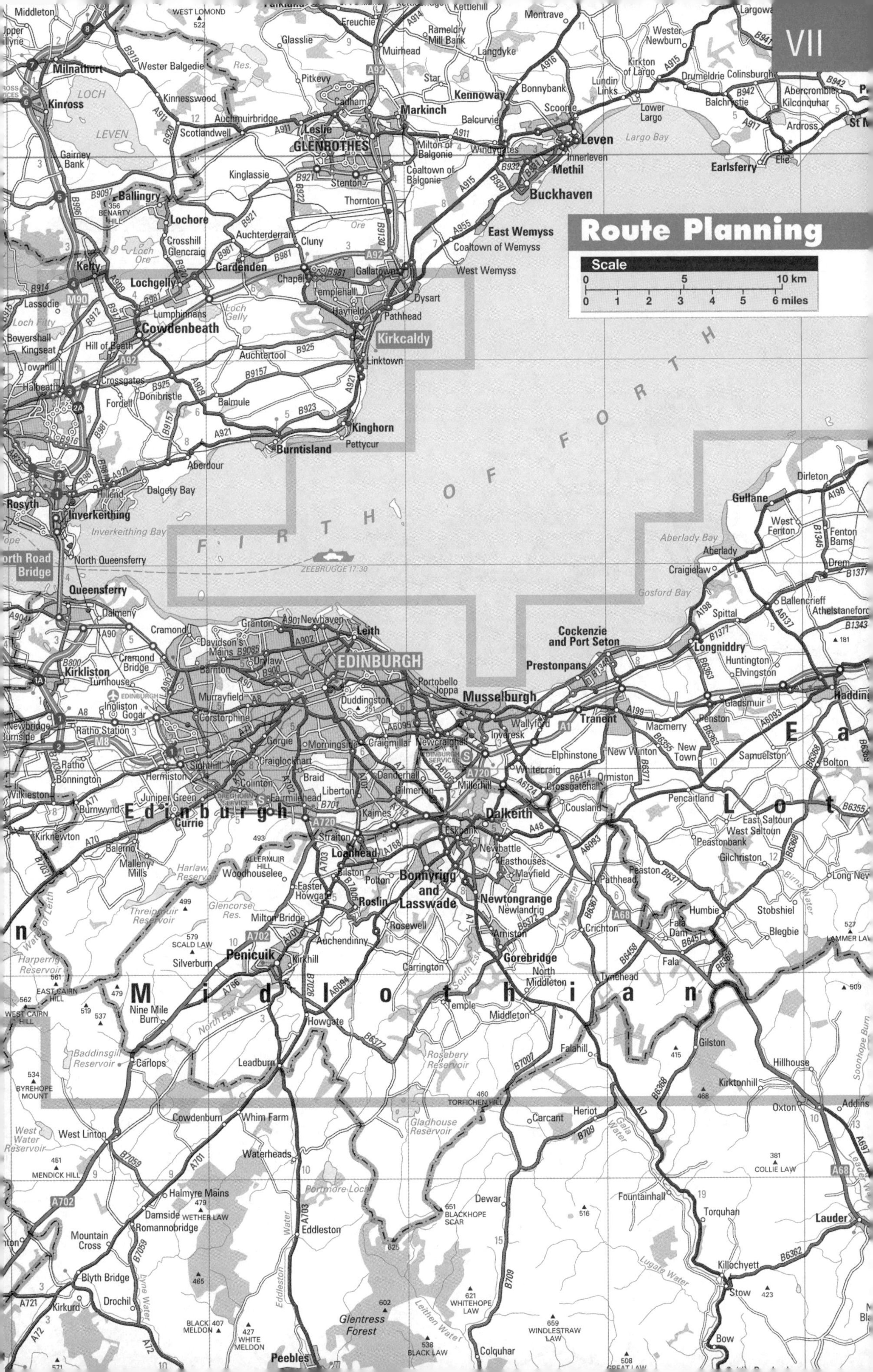
Route Planning
Scale
0 5 10 km
0 1 2 3 4 5 6 miles
FIRTH OF FORTH
ZEEBRUGGE 17:30
Forth Road Bridge
Middleton
WEST LOMOND
Freuchie
Kettlehill
Montrave
Largoward
Rameldry Mill Bank
Glasslie
Muirhead
Wester Newburn
Milnathort
Wester Balgedie
Langdyke
Kirkton of Largo
Drumeldrie
Colinsburgh
Kinross
LOCH LEVEN
Kinnesswood
Pitkevy
Star
Lundin Links
Kennoway
Bonnybank
Abercrombie
Kilconquhar
Balchrystie
Cadham
Markinch
Scoonie
Lower Largo
Ardross
Auchmuirbridge
Scotlandwell
Leslie
GLENROTHES
Balcurvie
Milton of Balgonie
Windygates
Leven
Largo Bay
Innerleven
Methil
Earlsferry
Elie
Gairney Bank
Kinglassie
Stenton
Coaltown of Balgonie
Buckhaven
Ballingry
BENARTY HILL
Thornton
Lochore
Crosshill
Glencraig
Auchterderran
Cluny
East Wemyss
Coaltown of Wemyss
Loch Ore
Kelty
Cardenden
Chapel
Gallatown
West Wemyss
Lochgelly
Templehall
Dysart
Lassodie
Hayfield
Pathhead
Loch Fitty
Lumphinnans
Loch Gelly
Cowdenbeath
Kirkcaldy
Bowershall
Kingseat
Hill of Beath
Auchtertool
Linktown
Townhill
Crossgates
Halbeath
Donibristle
Fordell
Balmule
Kinghorn
Aberdour
Pettycur
Burntisland
Dalgety Bay
Hillend
Rosyth
Inverkeithing
Inverkeithing Bay
North Queensferry
Queensferry
Dalmeny
Cramond
Granton
Newhaven
Leith
Davidson's Mains
Drylaw
Barnton
EDINBURGH
Kirkliston
Cramond Bridge
Turnhouse
Portobello
Joppa
Duddingston
Musselburgh
Ingliston
Gogar
Murrayfield
Corstorphine
Ratho Station
Newbridge
Burnside
Ratho
Bonnington
Gorgie
Morningside
Craigmillar
Newcraighall
Inveresk
Wallyford
Tranent
Sighthill
Craiglockhart
Hermiston
EDINBURGH SERVICES
Whitecraig
Elphinstone
New Winton
Braid
Colinton
Juniper Green
DREGHORN SERVICES
Fairmilehead
Liberton
Danderhall
Gilmerton
Millerhill
Crossgatehall
Ormiston
Wilkieston
Burnwynd
Edinburgh
Currie
Kaimes
Dalkeith
Cousland
Kirknewton
Straiton
Loanhead
Eskbank
Newbattle
Easthouses
Mayfield
Balerno
Malleny Mills
ALLERMUIR HILL
Harlaw Reservoir
Woodhouselee
Bilston
Polton
Bonnyrigg and Lasswade
Easter Howgate
Roslin
Newtongrange
Newlandrig
Threipmuir Reservoir
Glencorse Res.
Milton Bridge
Rosewell
Arniston
Crichton
Pathhead
SCALD LAW
Penicuik
Auchendinny
Gorebridge
Kirkhill
Silverburn
Carrington
North Middleton
Tynehead
Harperrig Reservoir
EAST CAIRN HILL
WEST CAIRN HILL
Midlothian
Nine Mile Burn
Temple
Middleton
Howgate
Baddinsgill Reservoir
Carlops
Leadburn
Rosebery Reservoir
Falahill
Gilston
BYREHOPE MOUNT
TORFICHEN HILL
Carcant
Heriot
Hillhouse
Kirktonhill
Oxton
Addinston
Cowdenburn
Whim Farm
West Water Reservoir
West Linton
Gladhouse Reservoir
Gala Water
MENDICK HILL
Waterheads
COLLIE LAW
Halmyre Mains
Portmore Loch
WETHER LAW
Dewar
BLACKHOPE SCAR
Fountainhall
Torquhan
Damside
Romannobridge
Lauder
Mountain Cross
Eddleston
Killochyett
Blyth Bridge
Lugate Water
Stow
Kirkurd
Drochil
WHITEHOPE LAW
Glentress Forest
BLACK MELDON
WHITE MELDON
WINDLESTRAW LAW
BLACK LAW
Peebles
Colquhar
Bow
Gullane
Dirleton
West Fenton
Fenton Barns
Aberlady Bay
Aberlady
Craigielaw
Drem
Gosford Bay
Ballencrieff
Athelstaneford
Spittal
Cockenzie and Port Seton
Longniddry
Prestonpans
Huntington
Elvingston
Haddington
Gladsmuir
Macmerry
Penston
New Town
Samuelston
Bolton
Pencaitland
East Saltoun
West Saltoun
Peastonbank
Gilchriston
Peaston
Long Newton
Humbie
Stobshiel
Fala Dam
Blegbie
Fala
LAMMER LAW
East Lothian
Birns Water
Tyne Water
South Esk
North Esk
Leithen Water
Lyne Water
Eddleston Water
Leader Water
Water of Leith
M90
M8
A92
A702
A720
A68
A7
A1
B709
B7007

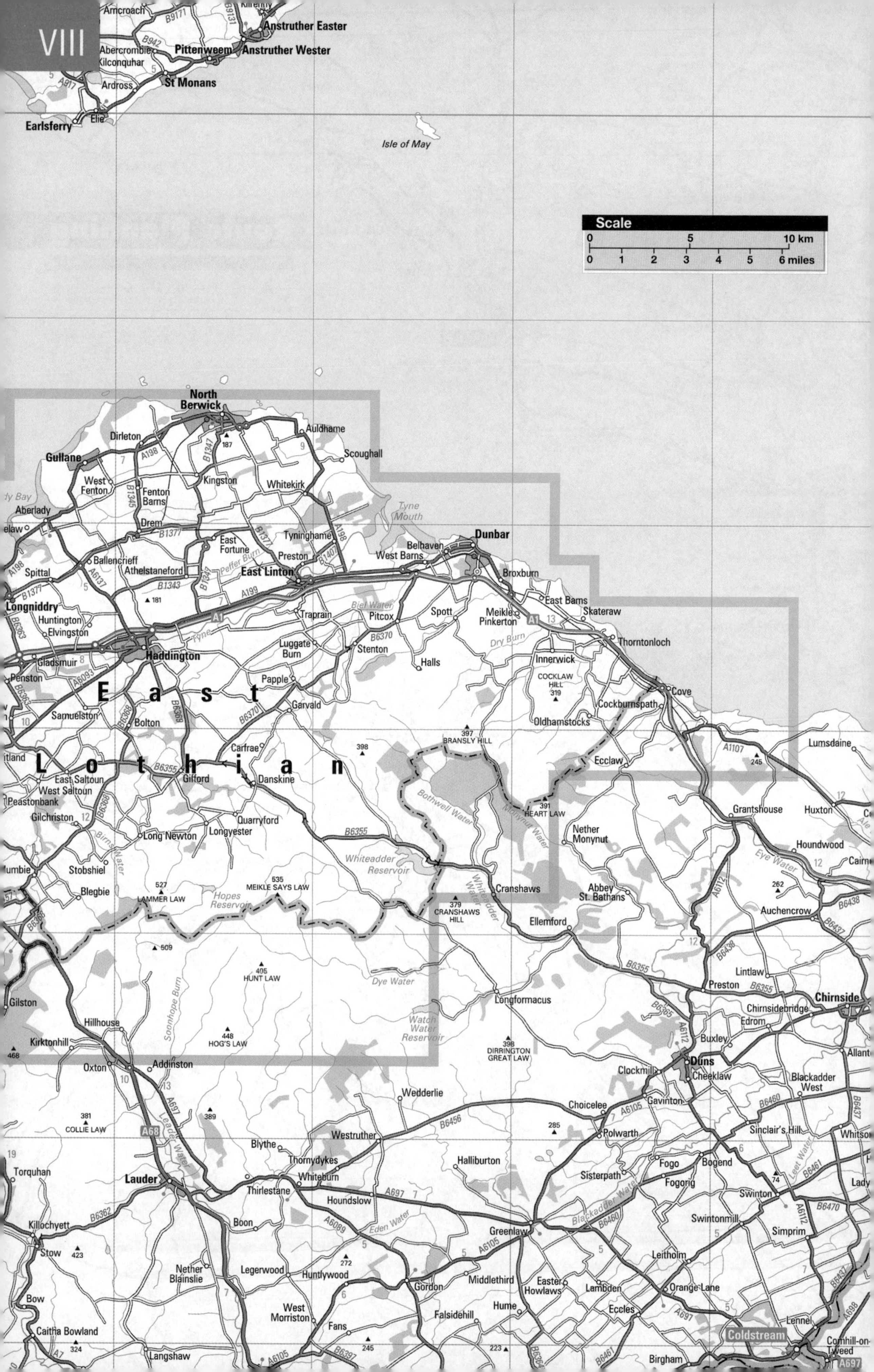
Scale
0 5 10 km
0 1 2 3 4 5 6 miles
Arncroach
Anstruther Easter
Anstruther Wester
Pittenweem
Abercrombie
Kilconquhar
Ardross
St Monans
Elie
Earlsferry
Isle of May
North Berwick
Dirleton
Gullane
West Fenton
Fenton Barns
Kingston
Whitekirk
Auldhame
Scoughall
Aberlady
Drem
East Fortune
Tyninghame
Tyne Mouth
Preston
Belhaven
West Barns
Dunbar
Ballencrieff
Athelstaneford
East Linton
Spittal
Broxburn
East Barns
Skateraw
Longniddry
Huntington
Elvingston
Traprain
Pitcox
Spott
Meikle Pinkerton
Thorntonloch
Haddington
Gladsmuir
Luggate Burn
Stenton
Halls
Innerwick
Penston
Papple
COCKLAW HILL 319
Cove
Samuelston
Bolton
Garvald
Cockburnspath
Oldhamstocks
397 BRANSLY HILL
398
East Lothian
Carfrae
Gifford
Danskine
Ecclaw
Lumsdaine
East Saltoun
West Saltoun
Peastonbank
Gilchriston
391 HEART LAW
Grantshouse
Huxton
Bothwell Water
Monynut Water
Nether Monynut
Long Newton
Longyester
Quarryford
Houndwood
Eye Water
Stobshiel
Blegbie
527 LAMMER LAW
535 MEIKLE SAYS LAW
Hopes Reservoir
Whiteadder Reservoir
Cranshaws
Abbey St. Bathans
379 CRANSHAWS HILL
Whiteadder Water
Ellemford
Auchencrow
509
405 HUNT LAW
Dye Water
Lintlaw
Preston
Chirnside
Chirnsidebridge
Edrom
Gilston
Hillhouse
Longformacus
Buxley
Kirktonhill
448 HOG'S LAW
Watch Water Reservoir
398 DIRRINGTON GREAT LAW
Oxton
Addinston
Duns
Clockmill
Cheeklaw
Blackadder West
Wedderlie
Choicelee
Gavinton
381 COLLIE LAW
389
285
Polwarth
Sinclair's Hill
Westruther
Blythe
Thornydykes
Halliburton
Fogo
Bogend
Torquhan
Lauder
Whiteburn
Thirlestane
Sisterpath
Fogorig
Swinton
Houndslow
Leader Water
Eden Water
Blackadder Water
Killochyett
Boon
Greenlaw
Swintonmill
Simprim
Stow
423
272
Leitholm
Nether Blainslie
Legerwood
Huntlywood
Gordon
Middlethird
Easter Howlaws
Lambden
Orange Lane
Bow
West Morriston
Hume
Eccles
Falsidehill
Lennel
Caitha Bowland
Fans
Coldstream
324
245
223
Langshaw
Birgham
Cornhill-on-Tweed
A1
A68
A697
A199
A198
A1107
A6112
A6105
A6089
A6093
A6137
B6355
B6370
B6456
B6460
B6437
B6438
B6362
B1377
B1343
B1345
B1347

2

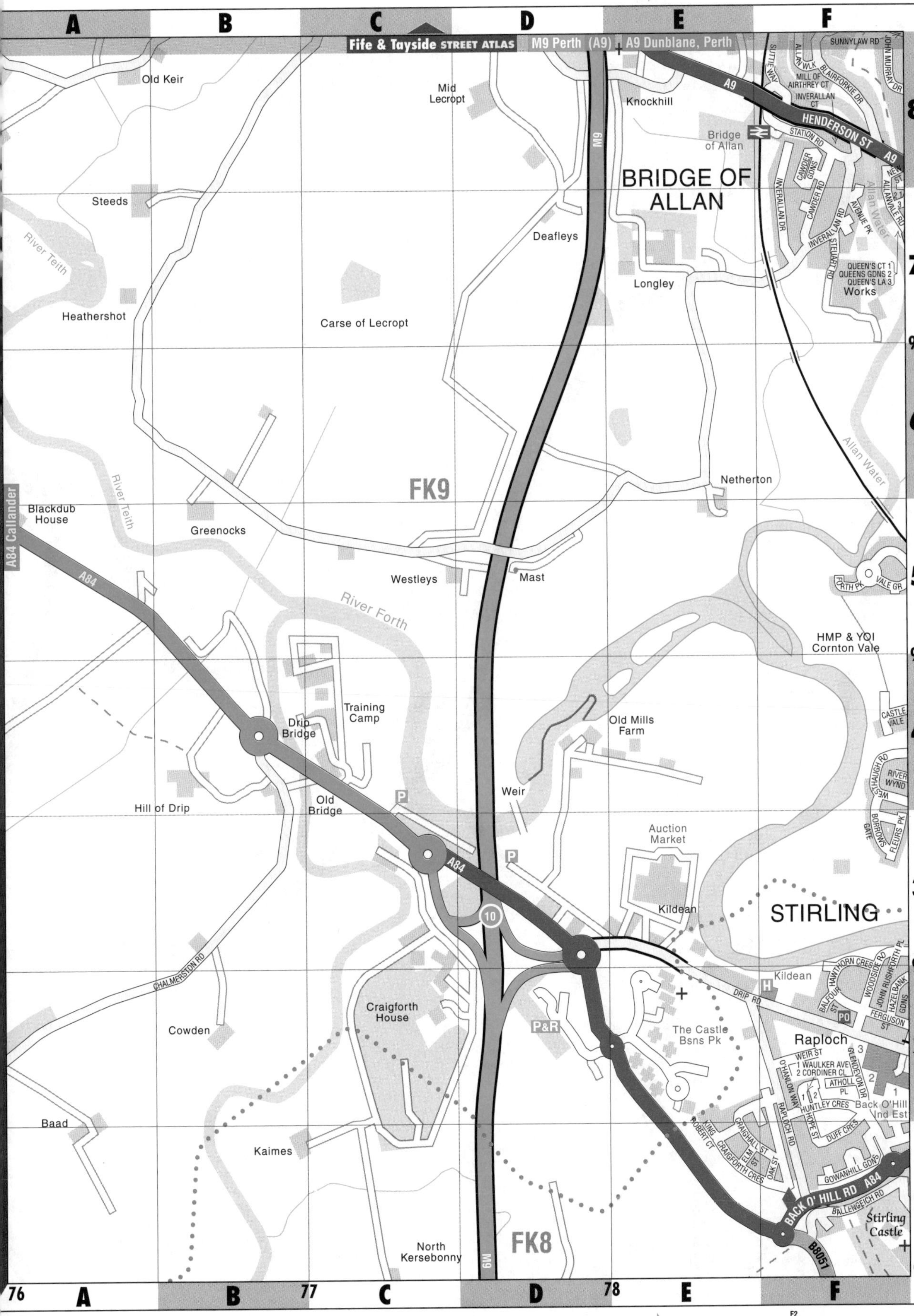
A
B
C
D
E
F
Fife & Tayside STREET ATLAS
M9 Perth (A9)
A9 Dunblane, Perth
Old Keir
Mid Lecropt
Knockhill
Bridge of Allan
BRIDGE OF ALLAN
SUNNYLAW RD
JOHN MURRAY DR
SUTTIE WAY
ALLAN WLK
MILL OF AIRTHREY CT
BLAIRFORKIE DR
INVERALLAN CT
HENDERSON ST
STATION RD
A9
CAWDER GDNS
CAWDER RD
INVERALLAN DR
INVERALLAN RD
AVENUE PK
STEUART RD
ALLANVALE RD
Allan Water
QUEEN'S CT 1
QUEENS GDNS 2
QUEEN'S LA 3
Works
Steeds
River Teith
Heathershot
Carse of Lecropt
Deafleys
Longley
M9
8
7
97
6
Netherton
FK9
Blackdub House
Greenocks
A84 Callander
A84
Westleys
Mast
River Forth
FORTH PK
VALE GR
5
HMP & YOI Cornton Vale
96
Training Camp
Drip Bridge
Old Mills Farm
CASTLE VALE
4
WESTHAUGH RD
RIVER WYND
BORROWS GATE
FLEURS PK
Hill of Drip
Old Bridge
Weir
P
Auction Market
3
Kildean
STIRLING
10
CHALMERSTON RD
Craigforth House
P&R
The Castle Bsns Pk
Kildean
DRIP RD
HAWTHORN CRES
WOODSIDE RD
JOHN RUSHFORTH PL
HAZELBANK GDNS
BALFOUR ST
FERGUSON ST
PO
95
Cowden
Raploch
WEIR ST
1 WAULKER AVE
2 CORDINER CL
ATHOLL PL
GLENDEVON DR
O'HANLON WAY
HUNTLEY CRES
HOPE ST
DUFF CRES
Back O'Hill Ind Est
2
Baad
Kaimes
KING ROBERT CT
CRAIGHALL ST
ELM ST
CRAIGFORTH CRES
OAK ST
RAPLOCH RD
GOWANHILL GDNS
BACK O' HILL RD
BALLENGEICH RD
Stirling Castle
1
North Kersebonny
FK8
B8051
94
76
77
78

6

2

F2
1 Our Lady's Prim Sch
2 Castleview Sch
3 Raplock Prim Sch

1

Fife & Tayside STREET ATLAS
A
B
C
D
E
F
8
7
97
6
5
96
4
3
95
2
1
94
79
80
81
BRIDGE OF ALLAN
Mine Wood
ALLANWATER APARTMENTS
Drumbrae
White Hill
Parkhead
Yellow Craig
Carlie Craig
Hermitage Wood
Beaconhurst Sch
Strathallan Games Park
Bridge of Allan Prim Sch
Forglen Burn
University of Stirling
Airthrey Castle
Cemy
Standing Stone
MCROBERT CTR
Works
FK9
Innovation Pk
Spittal Hill
HMP & YOI Cornton Vale
Wallace High Sch
Wester Cornton
Causewayhead
Cornton Prim Sch
Craigton
Hotel
Visitor Ctr
Wallace Monument
Powis Mains
Abbey Craig
Wallace's Pass
Cornton
Factory
Craigmill
Cornton Bsns Pk
Queenshaugh
River Forth
Forth Valley Coll
West Grange
Broom
Back O' Hill Ind Est
STIRLING
FK8
Gowanhill
Orchard House Day
Riverside
Haugh of West Grange
Cambuskenneth
FK7
Cemy
Castle
HENDERSON ST
AIRTHREY RD
Old Military Road
CORNTON RD
CAUSEWAYHEAD RD
ALLOA RD
HILLFOOTS RD
LOGIE RD
SHERIFFMUIR RD
BACK O' HILL RD
UNION ST
A9
A91
A907
A84
B823
B998
B8052
Logie Burn
1 CHALTON CT
2 KENILWORTH CT
1 QUEEN'S LA
2 QUEEN'S TERR
1 MEADOWLAND RD
2 ROUGHBURN RD
3 CHARLES RODGER PL
4 PATERSON PL
1 DONNELLY HO
2 FRASER OF ALLANDER HO
3 POLWARTH HO
4 ANDREW STEWART HALL
1 SCION HO
2 BETA CTR
1 ABBEYVIEW
2 LOGIE LA
3 HANOVER CT
1 OLD BRIDGE WYND
2 WESTHAUGH RD
3 RIVER WYND
4 SUNNYSIDE PL
5 DE MORAY CT
1 THISTLE PL
2 DUNCAN BUCHANAN CT
1 SHERIFFMUIRLANDS
2 BLENHEIM CT
BROOMHILL CT
FERNBANK
MONTGOMERY WAY
1 FORTH CT
2 OLIPHANT CT
3 Riverside Prim Sch
1 ABBOTSFORD PL
2 RIVERBANK VIEW
1 UPPER CASTLEHILL
2 LOWER CASTLEHILL

1
7

4

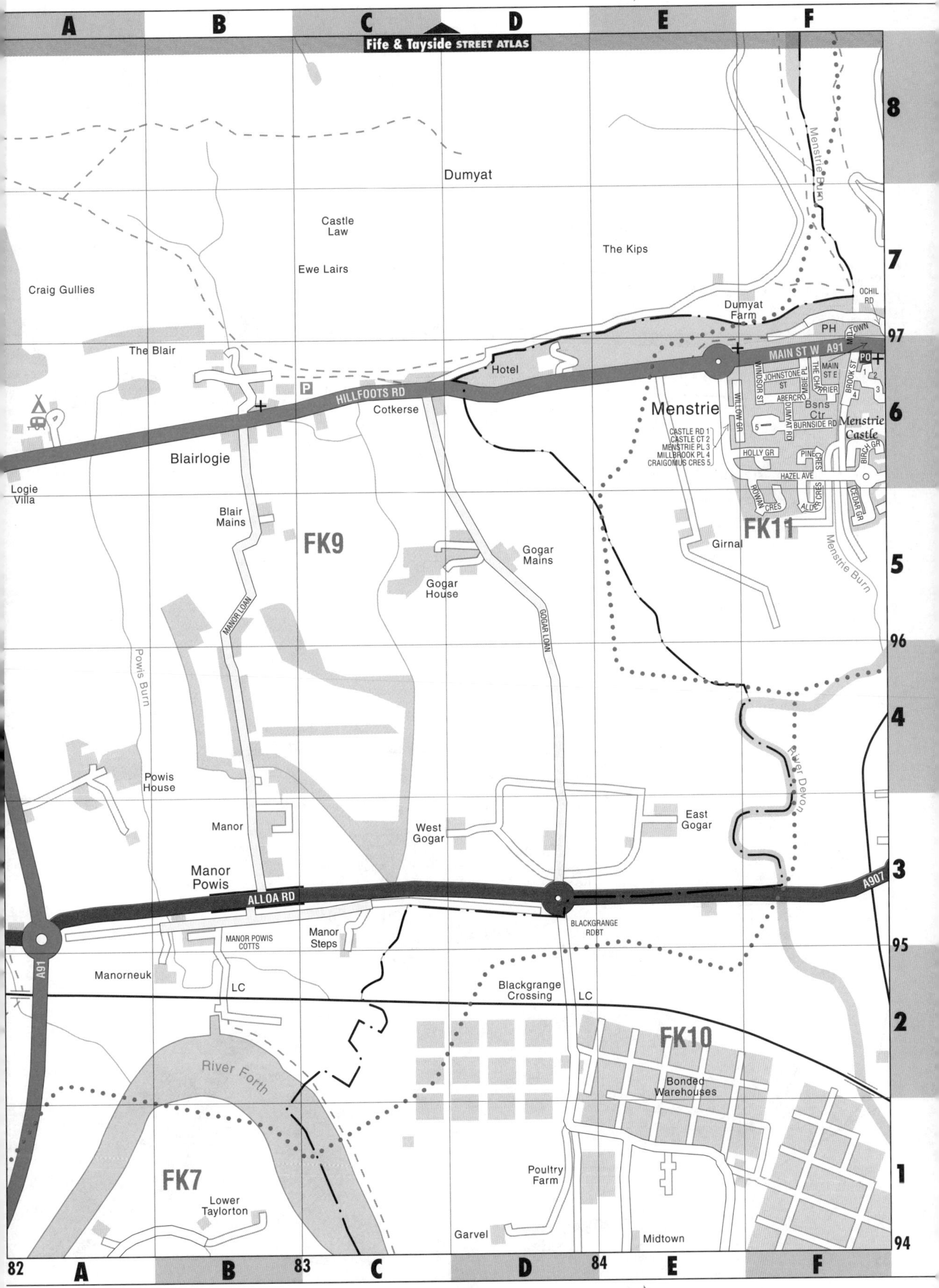

A
B
C
D
E
F
Fife & Tayside STREET ATLAS
8
7
6
5
4
3
2
1
97
96
95
94
82
83
84
Dumyat
Castle Law
Ewe Lairs
The Kips
Craig Gullies
Menstrie Burn
OCHIL RD
Dumyat Farm
PH
MILTOWN
The Blair
Hotel
MAIN ST W A91
PO
HILLFOOTS RD
Cotkerse
Menstrie
WINDSOR ST
JOHNSTONE ST
ABERCRO
DUMYAT RD
THE CHARRIER
MAIN ST E
BROOK ST
Bsns Ctr
BURNSIDE RD
Menstrie Castle
WILLOW GR
CASTLE RD 1
CASTLE CT 2
MENSTRIE PL 3
MILLBROOK PL 4
CRAIGOMUS CRES 5
HOLLY GR
PINE
BIRCH GR
HAZEL AVE
ROWAN CRES
ALDER CRES
CEDAR GR
Blairlogie
Logie Villa
Blair Mains
FK9
Gogar Mains
Gogar House
FK11
Girnal
MANOR LOAN
GOGAR LOAN
Powis Burn
River Devon
Powis House
Manor
West Gogar
East Gogar
Manor Powis
ALLOA RD
A907
BLACKGRANGE RDBT
MANOR POWIS COTTS
Manor Steps
Manorneuk
A91
LC
Blackgrange Crossing
FK10
River Forth
Bonded Warehouses
FK7
Lower Taylorton
Poultry Farm
Garvel
Midtown

8

4

3

A B C D E F
Fife & Tayside STREET ATLAS
8 7 97 6 5 96 4 3 95 2 1 94
85 86 87
Myreton Hill
Craig Leith
Carnaughton Burn
Barnaigh
Balquharn
BALQUHARN COTTS
The Myretoun
Loaningbank
Craigomish
1 SCHOOL LA
2 SCHOOL MEWS
Dams
FK12
FK11
FK10
BACK RD
BEAUCLERC ST
CLEUCH DR
TORRY DR
BROICH
THE GROWELL DR
COCHRANE CRES
WHARRY RD
GLENWINNEL RD
Mill Trail Visitor Ctr
Hall
PARK ST
PL
COPLAND
OCHIL RD
LONG ROW
CLIFFORD PK
HOLBOURNE PL
VICTORIA TERR
A91 WEST STIRLING ST
MAIN ST E A91
PARK RD
FORTHVALE
BROOMPARK W
BROOMPARK E
Dumyat L Ctr
MENSTRIE PL
ELMBANK
EAST MAINS
THE CAIRNS
LOSSHILL
GLENVIEW
Menstrie Prim Sch
COLSNAUR
INCHNA
MYRETON
LIPNEY
MIDDLETON
CRAIGHORN
THE CLOVES
BLACKTHORN GR
Factory
Warehouses
DUMYAT RD
MYRETOUNGATE
STIRLING RD
ST SERF'S WLK
CRAIGHORN RD
THE NEBIT
DALMORE DR
CARNAUGHTON
PARKGATE
THE NETHERGATE
CAROLINE CRES
COBLECROOK
VIEWFIELD DR
GDNS
CRAIGTON CRES
1 BLAIRDENON RD
COBLECROOK LA
BLINDWELLS 2
SOUTHCROFT 3
WEST JOHNSTONE ST 4
WEST JAMES ST 5
HOGGAN WAY 6
Sewage Works
River Devon
HM Prison Glenochil
Tullibody Bridge
Knowfaulds
Muirpark
GLENOCHIL TERR
DEVON DR
GLENOCHIL PK
MUIRPARK GDNS
KING O' MUIRS AVE
KING O' MUIRS RD
KING O' MUIRS FARM STEADING
FINGLEN CRES
B9140
St Serf's Prim Sch
Ditch
MARSHALL WAY
LETHEN VW
KING O' MUIRS DR
ROSE ST
GLENTYE DR
Muirside
MUIRSIDE AVE
THE GLEN
AULDKIRK RD
MACALPINE CT
KIDLAW CRES
ST SERF'S RD
DOVECOT PL
DOVECOT RD
ST SERFS PL
KNOWEFAULDS RD
REDLANDS RD
LADYWELL PL
LADYWELL DR
CROFTS RD
MENSTRIE RD
Tullibody
North Wood
Blackmuir Wood
Mast
CHESTNUT LA
ACORN DR
B9096
STIRLING RD
OCHIL CT
BANCHORY PL
NEWLAN DS
BANCHORY PL
MUIRSIDE RD
WALLACE VIEW
CRAIGLEITH VIEW
BROOMIEKNOWE
BLACKMUIR PL
THE BRAES
CARSEVIEW
BAINGLE BRAE
BAINGLE CRES
NEWMILLS
PO
ALLOA RD
BOND ST
A907
St Bernadette's RC Prim Sch
THE ORCHARD
TRON CT
MAIN ST
DELPH RD
Banchory Prim Sch
WESTVIEW CRES
FIRS RD
NORTHWOOD RD
Abercromby Prim Sch
CRAIGAMMORE
GLEN WICHIE
DEVON CT
TALISKER
OLD SCHOOL CT
SCHOOL RD
MANOR CRES
BRAEHEAD AVE
BARNHILL DR
COCHRIE PL
DELPH WYND
DELPHWOOD CRES
Lornshill Acad
LYCHGATE RD
LEDI AVE
DUMYAT AVE
CLEUCH AVE
C Ctr
Liby
ABERCROMBY PL
NEWBIGGIN CRES
ROBERT KINMOND AVE
ROBERT DICK CT
Delph Wood
HIGHLANDER WAY
RANKINE WYND
KING JAMES DR
ROBERT KNOX AVE
Fore Brae
Lornshill
Lornshill Cottages
BRIAR
ORMISTON DR
WOODSIDE RD
THE CEDARS
RAMSEY TULLIS DR
TULLIBODY RD
ROSE ST
THORNIE RD
LOMOND ST
Gubber Hill
LC
PARK TERR
THE BRAMBLES
THE WILLOWS
THE LAURELS
THE POPLARS
THE SYCAMORES
THE CLEAVES
WOOD AVENS
DONALDSON AVE
COATS CRES
BRAEHEAD
CLAREMONT
DUMYAT ST
GAVINS RD
WOODBURN DR
BROWN AVE
WOODSIDE
FORESTER GR
Inglewood House
River Devon
THE SHEILINGS
LC
STATION RD
MOWBRAY GDNS
DEVON PL
CH
A907
DUNMAR CRES
DUNMAR DR
FAIRYBURN RD
GEAN RD
B9096

3
9

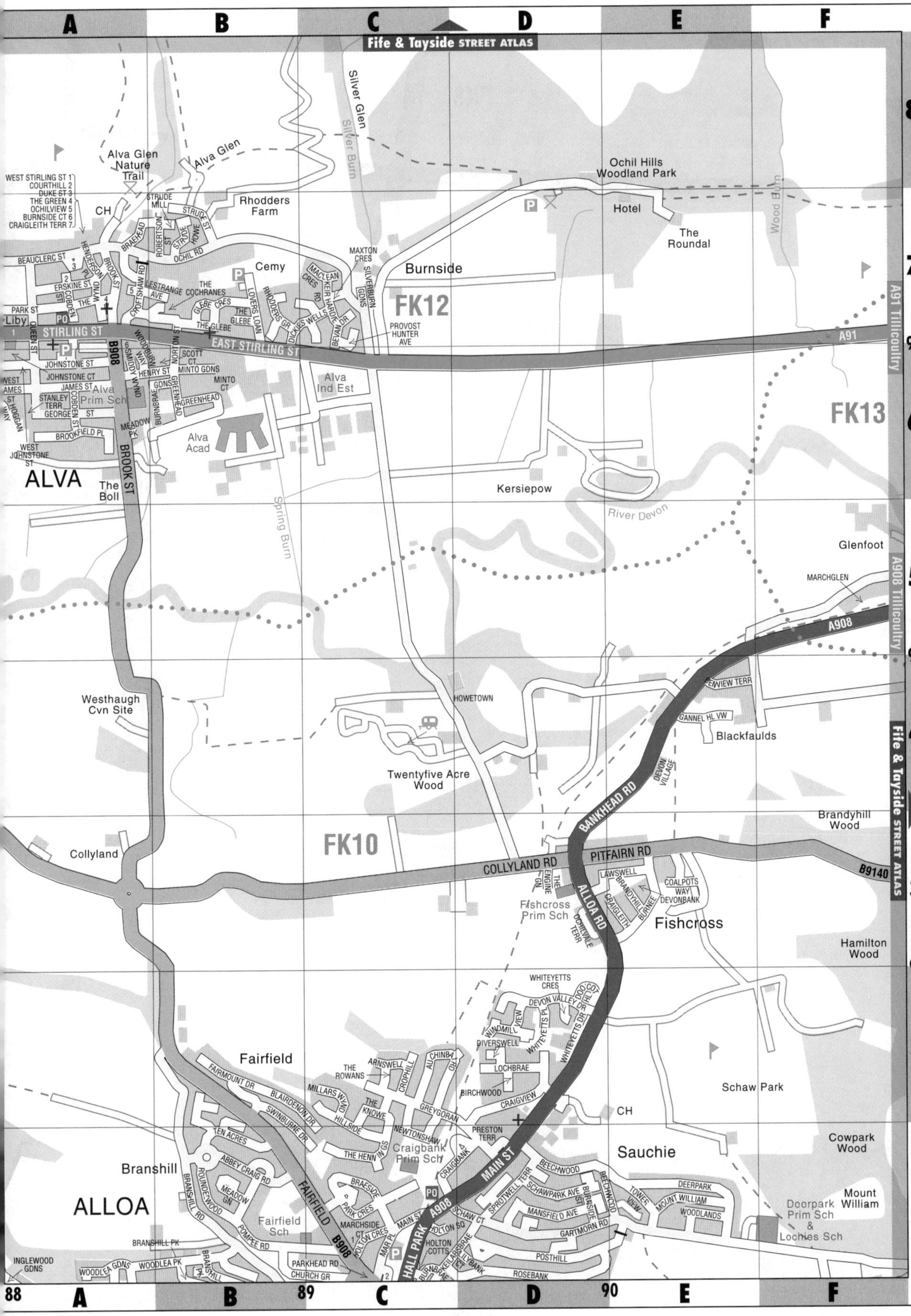

Fife & Tayside STREET ATLAS
A
B
C
D
E
F
8
7
97
6
5
96
4
3
95
2
1
94
88
89
90
Silver Glen
Silver Burn
Alva Glen Nature Trail
Alva Glen
Ochil Hills Woodland Park
Hotel
The Roundal
Wood Burn
Rhodders Farm
CH
WEST STIRLING ST 1
COURTHILL 2
DUKE ST 3
THE GREEN 4
OCHILVIEW 5
BURNSIDE CT 6
CRAIGLEITH TERR 7
STRUDE MILL
STRUDE ST
ROBERTSON ST
STRUDE HOWE
BRAEHEAD
OCHIL RD
BEAUCLERC ST
HENDERSON PL
BROOK ST
ERSKINE ST
COBDEN ST
CROFTSHAW RD
LESTRANGE AVE
THE COCHRANES
Cemy
GLEBE CRES
THE GLEBE
LOVERS LOAN
RHODDERS GR
DICKIES WELLS
MACLEAN CRES
KEIR HARDIE RD
BEVAN DR
MAXTON CRES
SILVERBURN GDNS
Burnside
FK12
PROVOST HUNTER AVE
PARK ST
Liby
PO
STIRLING ST
EAST STIRLING ST
A91
A91 Tillicoultry
QUEEN ST
P
B908
WOODBURN WAY
SMIDDY WYND
NORTON ST
SCOTT CT
MINTO GDNS
MINTO CT
HENRY ST
JOHNSTONE ST
JOHNSTONE CT
JAMES ST
WEST JAMES ST
HOGGAN WAY
STANLEY TERR
GEORGE ST
Alva Prim Sch
BURNBRAE GDNS
GREENHEAD
MEADOW PK
BROOKFIELD PL
WEST JOHNSTONE ST
Alva Ind Est
Alva Acad
ALVA
The Boll
BROOK ST
FK13
Kersiepow
River Devon
Spring Burn
Glenfoot
MARCHGLEN
A908 Tillicoultry
A908
PENNIEW TERR
GANNEL HL VW
Blackfaulds
HOWETOWN
Westhaugh Cvn Site
Twentyfive Acre Wood
DEVON VILLAGE
BANKHEAD RD
Brandyhill Wood
FK10
Collyland
COLLYLAND RD
PITFAIRN RD
B9140
THE ENGINE GN
LAWSWELL
BRANDYHILL
CRAIGLEITH
BURNEE
COALPOTS WAY
DEVONBANK
ALLOA RD
Fishcross Prim Sch
OCHILVALE TERR
Fishcross
Hamilton Wood
WHITEYETTS CRES
DEVON VALLEY DR
DOOCOT HL
WINDMILL VIEW
WHITEYETTS PL
WHITEYETTS DR
DIVERSWELL
LOCHBRAE
BIRCHWOOD
CRAIGVIEW
Fairfield
FAIRMOUNT DR
BLAIRDENON DR
SWINBURNE DR
THE ROWANS
ARNSWELL
CROPHILL
AILCHINBAD
MILLARS WYND
THE KNOWE
HILLSIDE
GREYGORAN
NEWTONSHAW
PRESTON TERR
Schaw Park
CH
Sauchie
Cowpark Wood
TEN ACRES
ABBEY CRAIG RD
THE HENNINGS
Craigbank Prim Sch
CRAIGBANK
MAIN ST
BEECHWOOD
SCHAWPARK AVE
SPROTWELL TERR
BURNSIDE ST
MANSFIELD AVE
TOWER VIEW
DEERPARK
MOUNT WILLIAM
WOODLANDS
GARTMORN RD
Mount William
Branshill
MEADOW GN
BRAESIDE
PARK CRES
ROUNDELWOOD
BRANSHILL RD
ALLOA
FAIRFIELD
Fairfield Sch
MARCHSIDE CT
HOLTON CRES
MAIN ST
A908
SCHAW CT
HOLTON SQ
HOLTON COTTS
HALL PARK
POMPEE RD
BRANSHILL PK
MAR PL
KEILARSBRAE
VALLEYBANK
POSTHILL
Doorpark Prim Sch & Lochies Sch
INGLEWOOD GDNS
WOODLEA GDNS
WOODLEA PK
BRANSHILL PK
PARKHEAD RD
CHURCH GR
ROSEBANK
B908

1

A
B
C
D
E
F
FK9
FK8
FK7
River Forth
Falleninch
KERSEBONNY RD
M9
B8051
RAPLOCH RD
King's Knot
DUMBARTON RD
King's Park Farm
A811
A811 Alexandria, Loch Lomond
Polrogan Bridge
Bankend
White House
The Homestead Bungalow
CH
BALMORAL PL
QUEEN'S RD
SOUTH KERSEBONNY STEADING
THE HOMESTEADS
King's Park
ST THOMAS'S WELL
Raploch Burn
Cemy
Hollandbush
Hayford House
BROOMHILL PL
DOUGLAS TERR
DOWAN PL
ST THOMAS'S PL
WOOLCARDERS CT
HAYFORD MILLS
Johnny's Bridge
Hillhead
PARKDYKE
SNOWDON PLACE LA 1
SNOWDON PL 2
PARK AVE
KING'S PK RD
BOBBIN WYND
PARK PL
MILL RD
NORTH END
DONALDSON PL
STEWART ST
BIRKHILL RD
CONEY PARK
DALMORGLEN PK
Cambusbarron
GRIERSON CRES
BATTERFLATTS HO
BEECH GDNS
Laurelhill Bsns Pk
TOUCH RD
BARONY CT
MILL HILL
THE BRAE
CHAPELCROFT
HAYFORD PL
GRAMPIAN RD
BATTERFLATTS GDNS
Johnny's Burn
MAIN ST
PO
SMIDDY VIEW
Torbrex
LAURELHILL GDNS
QUARRY RD
FIRPARK TERR
CAULDHAME CRES
THE YETTS
MURRAY PL
Liby
Abbey Kings Park (Private)
SPRINGWOOD
SPRINGWOOD AVE
OLD DROVE RD
THOMSON PL
WOODSIDE CT
UNDERWOOD COTTS
CLAYHILLS DR
HOME FARM RD
KENNINGKNOWES RD
POLMAISE RD
DERORAN PL
Cambusbarron Prim Sch
BRUCE TERR
ST NINIANS RD
H
LABURNUM GR
SYCAMORE PL
GILLIES HILL
WALLACE PL
Gartur
Polmaise Farm
BIRCH AVE
CEDAR AVE
ASH TERR
1 AULD SCHOOL WYND
2 UNDERWOOD RD
TORBREX LA
TORBREX FARM RD
ST VALERY DR
TORBREX RD
TOWN BURN
MOSSYOUSE
WELLPARK CRES
Murray's Wood
Gillies Hill
CRUCKBURN WYND
Bearside
Polmaise Castle
Touchadam Craig
WORDIE RD
CULTENHOVE RD
CAMPBELL CT
Coxet Hill
PAT KELLY AVE
Murrayshall Quarry
Fir Park
THE KIRKLANDS
POLMAISE RD
CULTENHOVE CRES
RINGANS LA
Haggs Wood
CULTENHOVE PL
GATESIDE RD
Castlehill
Murrayshall Farm
GRAYSTALE RD
Mast
Graystale
Wallstale
Sauchie Craig
Moor Burn
Bannock Burn
Middlethird Wood
Chartershall House
Cultenhove
Chartershall Farm
CHARTERSHALL RD
8
7
93
6
5
92
4
3
91
2
1
90
76
77
78

A8
1 ESPLANADE
2 UPPER CASTLEHILL
3 KINGSTABLES LA
4 CASTLE WYND
5 ST MARY'S WYND
6 BANK ST
7 Old Town Jail Mus

B7
1 CORN EXCHANGE RD
2 BACK WLK
3 STIRLING ARC
4 THISTLE CHAMBERS
5 ORCHARDCROFT
6 CASTLEGAIT
7 BASTION WYND
8 THE MARCHES
9 CAMERONIAN ST
10 ALLAN PARK HO
11 WELLGREEN LA

B8
1 WALLACE ST
2 COWANE ST
3 VIEWFIELD PL
4 VIEWFIELD ST
5 SEAFORTH PL
6 MAXWELL PL

2
8

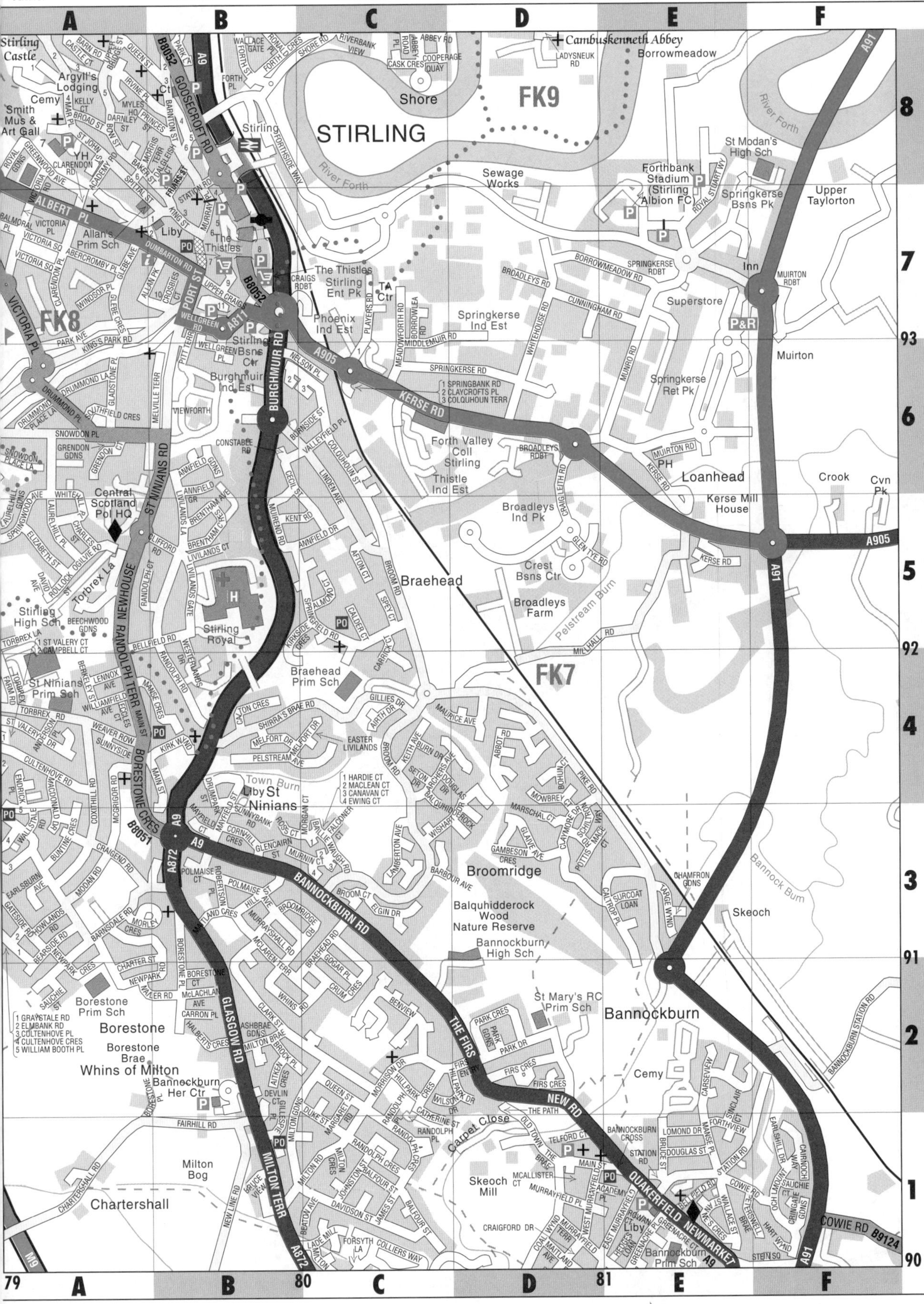

19
8

7
3

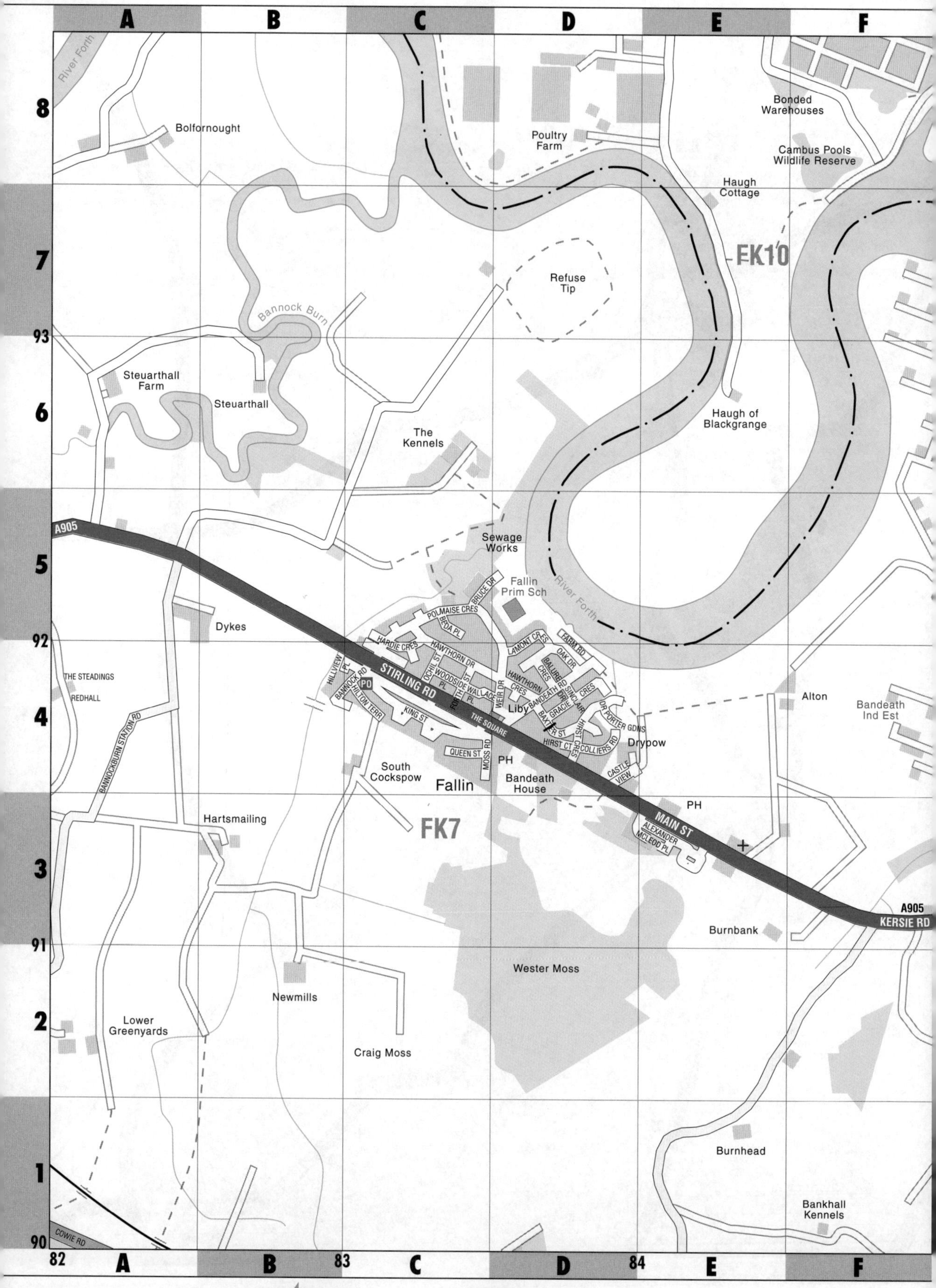
A
B
C
D
E
F
8
7
93
6
5
92
4
3
91
2
1
90
82
83
84
River Forth
Bolfornought
Poultry Farm
Bonded Warehouses
Cambus Pools Wildlife Reserve
Haugh Cottage
FK10
Refuse Tip
Bannock Burn
Steuarthall Farm
Steuarthall
Haugh of Blackgrange
The Kennels
A905
Sewage Works
Fallin Prim Sch
River Forth
Dykes
POLMAISE CRES
BRUCE DR
BEDA PL
HARDIE CRES
HAWTHORN DR
LAMONT CRES
FARM RD
OAK DR
HILLVIEW PL
STIRLING RD
THE STEADINGS
REDHALL
BANNOCK RD
PO
HILTON TERR
OCHIL ST
WOODSIDE PL
WALLACE PL
FORTH ST
WEIR DR
HAWTHORN CRES
BANDEATH RD
BALURE CRES
SINCLAIR DR
GRACIE CRES
Liby
KING ST
THE SQUARE
BAXTER ST
HIRST CT
HIRST CRES
COLLIERS RD
PORTER GDNS
DR
Drypow
Alton
Bandeath Ind Est
BANNOCKBURN STATION RD
QUEEN ST
MOSS RD
PH
South Cockspow
Fallin
Bandeath House
CASTLE VIEW
PH
Hartsmailing
FK7
MAIN ST
ALEXANDER
MCLEOD PL
A905
KERSIE RD
Burnbank
Wester Moss
Newmills
Lower Greenyards
Craig Moss
Burnhead
Bankhall Kennels
COWIE RD
82
A
B
83
C
D
84
E
F

7
20

4
10

A
B
C
D
E
F
MOUBRAY GDNS
STATION RD
MAIN ST
Cambus Farm
PH
FORTH ST
SOUTH ST
DEVON PL
Cambus
A907
Arnsbrae
DUNMAR DR
Gean House
ARNS GR
GEAN RD
KENT RD
B9096
TULLIBODY RD
WEST LOWER GDNS
CROWN GDNS
FAIRBURN RD
WINDSOR GDNS
LORNSHILL CRES
INGLEWOOD RD
ANNE ST
CHARLES ST
OBERON
DAWSON AVE
TITANIA
PAVILION VIEW
CHURCHILL ST
EDEN RD
CLAREMONT
ACADEMY ST
Claremont Prim Sch
STIRLING RD
CARSE TER
NORWOOD GR
NORWOOD AVE
REDWELL PL
NORWOOD CRES
ALEXANDRA DR
ALLOA
Pavilions Bsns PK
THE PAVILIONS
THE PLEASURES
Orchard Farm
FK10
Orchard House
Pier
Smart Village Bsns Campus
New Struan Sch
LC
A907
MITCHELL CRES
DIRLETON LA
DIRLETON GDNS
St John's Prim Sch
GRANGE RD
SMITHFIELD LOAN
THE HARLANDS
SMITHFIELD MDWS
Works
BELLEVUE RD
FORBES ST
MEDWYN PL
GRANT ST
BELLEVUE PK
STANTON AVE
SHIRE WAY
CARPENTERS WYND
KELLIEBANK
CALEDONIAN RD
DOWNS CRES
KEVERKAE
MUNRO PL
Tullibody Inch
Longcarse
KELLIEBANK
CRAIGWARD
Works
Bandeath Ind Est
Kelliebank Ind Est
Longcarse Reach
Rhind
Inch
Throsk House
FERRY RD
Works
Pier
THE HAVEN
South Alloa
Bandeath Ind Est
River Forth
KERSIE RD
Throsk
KERSIE RD
Kersie Mains
KERSIE TERR
FK7
Poppletrees
Mains of Throsk
Kersie Bridge
South Kersie
Willowbank
Meadowfield
SOUTH MAINS
FK2
A905
8
7
93
6
5
92
4
3
91
2
1
90
85
86
87

21
10

B6
1 BURGH MEWS
2 MERCAT WYND
3 STRIPEHEAD
4 UNION ST
5 BREWHOUSE CT
6 WEST VENNEL
7 CANDLERIGGS CT
8 THE CROSS
9 TOWNHEAD APARTMENTS
10 MAPLE CT
11 OLD BRIDGE ST
12 JUNCTION PL
13 BRIDGE TERR

9
5

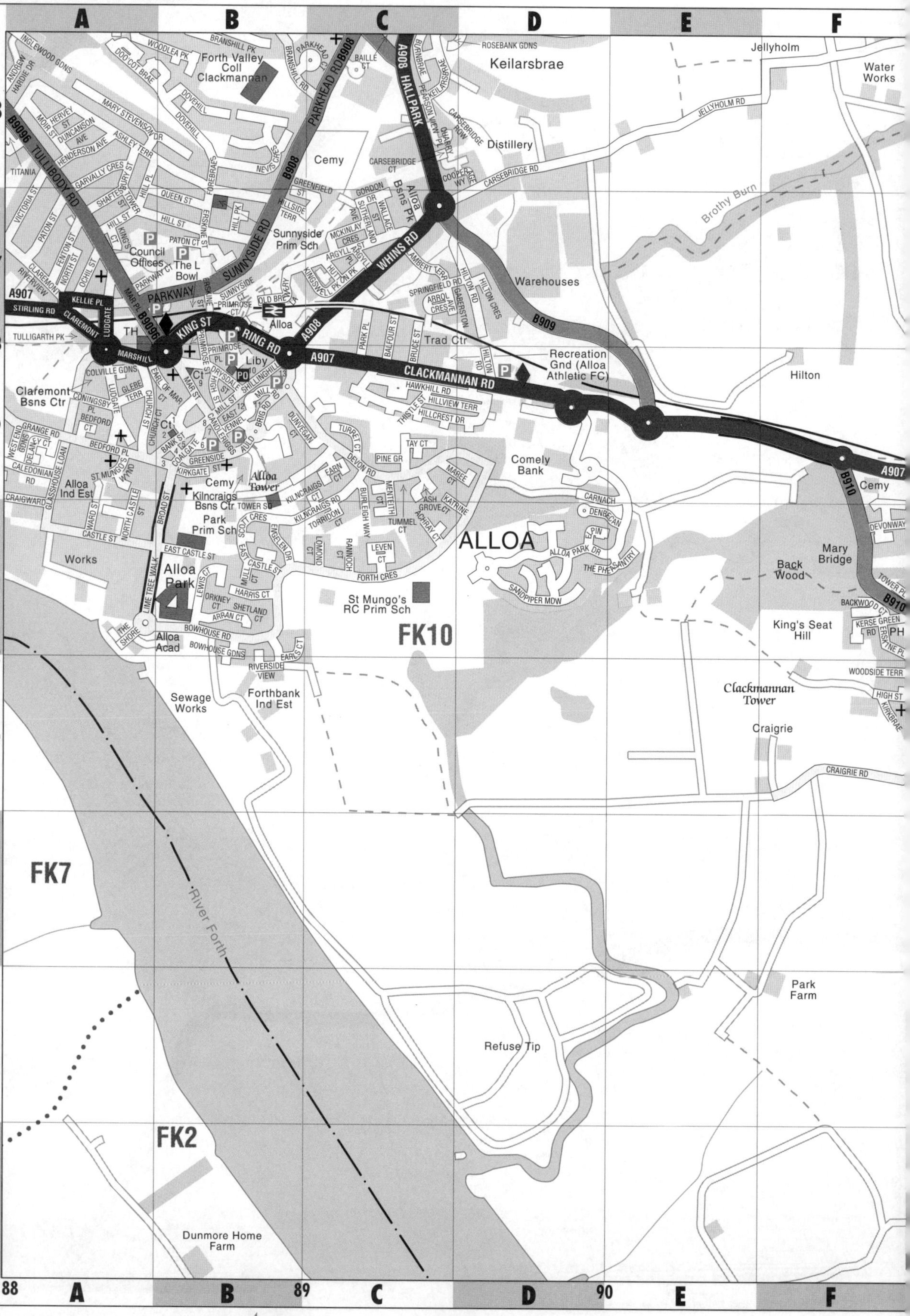

9
22

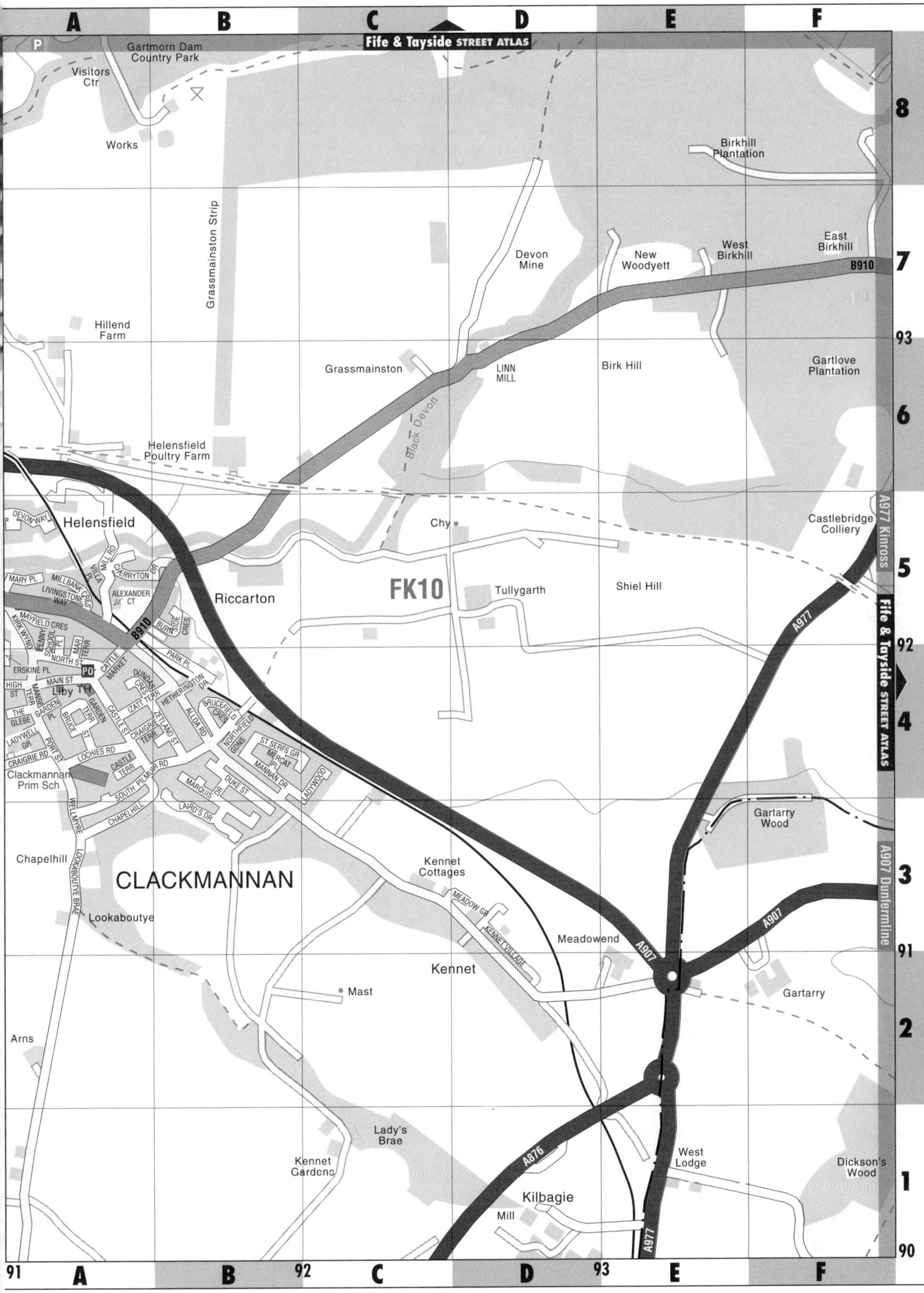
Fife & Tayside STREET ATLAS
Gartmorn Dam Country Park
Visitors Ctr
Works
Grassmainston Strip
Hillend Farm
Birkhill Plantation
Devon Mine
New Woodyett
West Birkhill
East Birkhill
B910
Grassmainston
LINN MILL
Birk Hill
Gartlove Plantation
Black Devon
Helensfield Poultry Farm
Helensfield
Chy
Castlebridge Colliery
A977 Kinross
Riccarton
FK10
Tullygarth
Shiel Hill
A977
Fife & Tayside STREET ATLAS
DEVON WAY
MILL RD
VILLA PL
CHERRYTON DR
MARY PL
MILLBANK CRES
LIVINGSTONE WAY
ALEXANDER CT
MAYFIELD CRES
KIRK WYND
PENNY SCHOOL PL
MAR TERR
NORTH ST
CATTLE MARKET
BURNSIDE CRES
PARK PL
ERSKINE PL
PO
MAIN ST
HIGH ST
Liby
TH
DUNDAS CRES
HETHERINGTON DR
THE GLEBE
MANSE TERR
GARDEN PL
BRUCE ST
GARDEN TERR
IZATT TERR
CASTLE ST
CRAIGRIE TERR
ZETLAND ST
ALLOA RD
BRUCEFIELD CRES
NORTHFIELD GDNS
ST SERFS GR
MERCAT PL
MANNAN DR
LADYWELL GR
PORT ST
CRAIGRIE RD
LOCHIES RD
CASTLE TERR
PILMUIR RD
SOUTH PILMUIR RD
MARQUIS DR
DUKE ST
LADYWOOD
Clackmannan Prim Sch
WELLMYRE
CHAPELHILL
LAIRD'S DR
Gartarry Wood
Chapelhill
CLACKMANNAN
LOOKABOUTYE BRAE
Kennet Cottages
MEADOW GR
KENNET VILLAGE
A907 Dunfermline
Lookaboutye
Meadowend
A907
Kennet
Mast
Gartarry
Arns
Lady's Brae
A876
West Lodge
Dickson's Wood
Kennet Gardens
Kilbagie
Mill
A977
A B C D E F
8 7 93 6 5 92 4 3 91 2 1 90
91 92 93

23

A
B
C
D
E
F
Fife & Tayside STREET ATLAS
M90 Kinross, Perth
A909 Cowdenbeath
A909 Junc.4 M90
BLAIR DR
COCKLAW ST
BLAIR ST
MOIR CT
WATSON CT
Works
B917
Drumnagoil Burn
Whitehouse Wood
South Lodge
B914
A909
M90
4
Kelty
Cocklaw Mains Farm
OAKFIELD ST
FLOWER PL
Lassodie Mine
CANTSDAM RD
Thornton Wood
Cantsdam
B912
Cantsdam Bridge
Lassodie Mill
Windyedge
OLD PERTH RD
Muirton
8
7
93
6
5
92
4
3
91
2
1
90
12
13
14
KY4
Kirkton Farm
Opencast Workings
Hanging Stone
KY12
Lassodie Piggery
Meml
Dalbeath Marsh Nature Reserve
Loch Fitty
Mast
Lochend
The Fishing Lodge
CUDDYHOUSE RD
Dalbeath
Loch View
KEIRSBEATH CT
Lochgelly Burn
PO
HENDERSON ST
Hotel
MAIN ST
CHURCH ST
Kingseat
FREW PL
PALMER PL
JONES ST
WALLACE PL
SLAYER DR
GREENACRES
NAGLE RD
LOCHWOOD PK
KEIRSBEATH RISE
KINGSEAT RD
Keirsbeath Ridge
Hill of Beath
Hillend
Hill of Beath Prim Sch
Opencast Workings
TORBEITH GDNS
DALBEATH
HAWTHORN CRES
GDNS
SWINTONS
MAIN ST

30

14

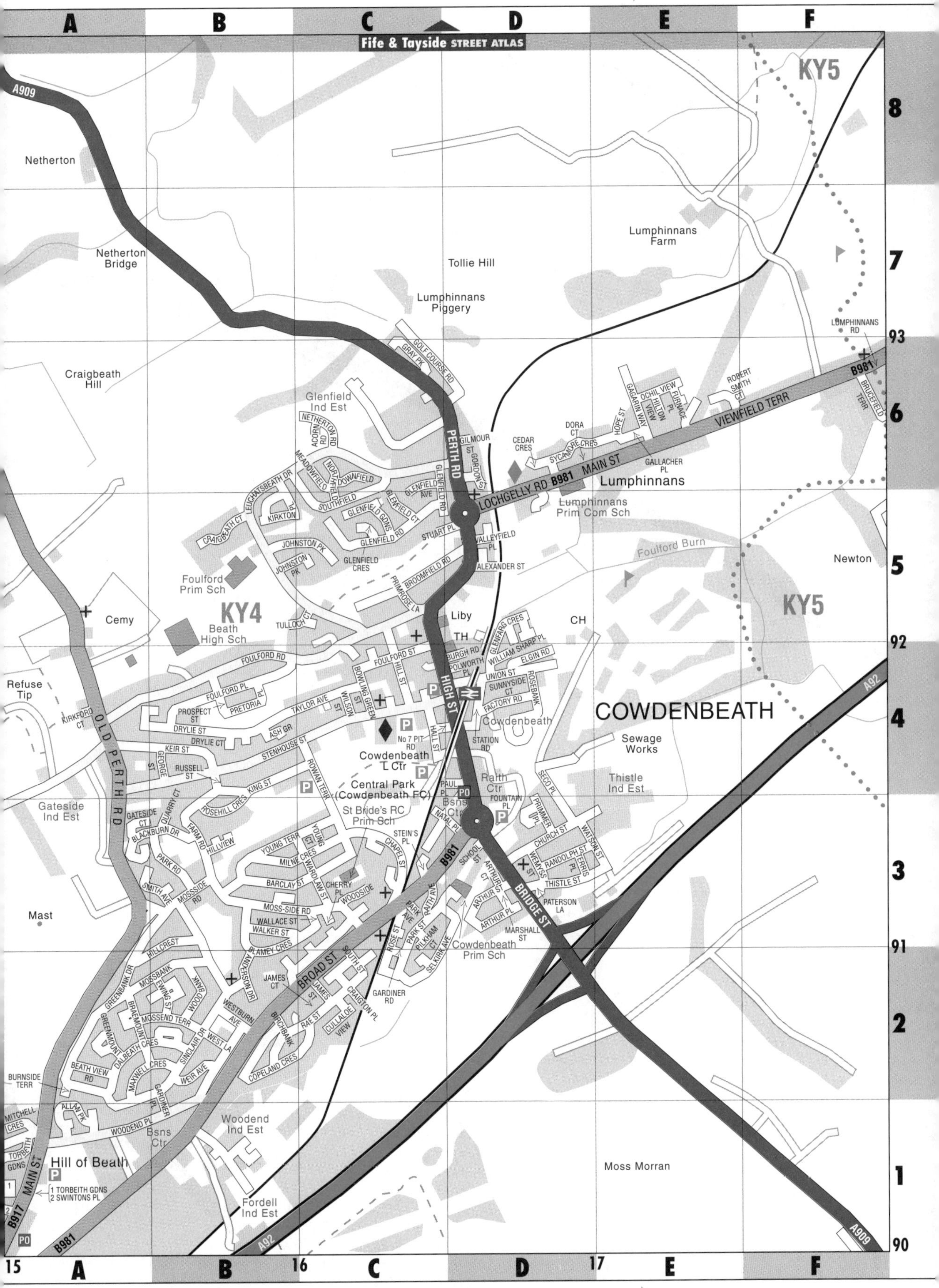
Fife & Tayside STREET ATLAS
A
B
C
D
E
F
8
7
93
6
5
92
4
3
91
2
1
90
15
16
17
KY5
KY4
A909
Netherton
Netherton Bridge
Craigbeath Hill
Tollie Hill
Lumphinnans Piggery
Lumphinnans Farm
Glenfield Ind Est
Lumphinnans
Lumphinnans Prim Com Sch
Foulford Prim Sch
Foulford Burn
Newton
Cemy
Beath High Sch
Liby
TH
CH
Refuse Tip
COWDENBEATH
Sewage Works
Thistle Ind Est
Gateside Ind Est
Cowdenbeath L Ctr
Central Park (Cowdenbeath FC)
St Bride's RC Prim Sch
Raith Ctr
Bsns Ctr
Cowdenbeath Prim Sch
Mast
Woodend Ind Est
Bsns Ctr
Hill of Beath
Fordell Ind Est
Moss Morran
PERTH RD
HIGH ST
BRIDGE ST
LOCHGELLY RD
B981
MAIN ST
VIEWFIELD TERR
OLD PERTH RD
BROAD ST
A92
B917 MAIN ST
LUMPHINNANS RD
BRUCEFIELD TERR
ROBERT SMITH CT
DORA CT
CEDAR CRES
SYCAMORE CRES
GALLACHER PL
HOPE ST
GAGARIN WAY
OCHIL VIEW
HILTON VIEW
FURNACE PL
GOLF COURSE RD
GRAY PK
GILMOUR ST
GORDON ST
NETHERTON RD
ACORN RD
MEADOWFIELD
NORTHFIELD
DOWNFIELD
SOUTHFIELD
GLENFIELD AVE
GLENFIELD RD
GLENFIELD GDNS
GLENFIELD CT
GLENFIELD CRES
LEUCHATSBEATH DR
CRAIGBEATH CT
KIRKTON
JOHNSTON PK
STUART PL
VALLEYFIELD PL
ALEXANDER ST
BROOMFIELD RD
PRIMROSE LA
TULLOCH CT
GLENFARG CRES
WILLIAM SHARP PL
ELGIN RD
BURGH RD
POLWORTH PL
UNION ST
SUNNYSIDE CT
ROSEBANK
FACTORY RD
FOULFORD RD
FOULFORD ST
HILL ST
BOWLING GREEN
WILSON ST
TAYLOR AVE
FOULFORD PL
PRETORIA PL
PROSPECT ST
KIRKFORD CT
DRYLIE ST
DRYLIE CT
ASH GR
STENHOUSE ST
KEIR ST
GEORGE ST
RUSSELL ST
KING ST
No 7 PIT RD
HALL ST
STATION RD
ROWAN TERR
PAUL PL
FOUNTAIN PL
SECO PL
PRIMMER PL
GATESIDE CT
QUARRY CT
BLACKBURN DR
FARM RD
ROSEHILL CRES
HILLVIEW
YOUNG TERR
YOUNG CT
MILNE CRES
WARDLAW ST
NAVAL PL
STEIN'S PL
CHAPEL ST
SCHOOL ST
ARTHUR CT
CHURCH ST
WEMYSS ST
RANDOLPH ST
FERRIS PL
WATSON ST
THISTLE ST
PATERSON LA
ARTHUR ST
ARTHUR PL
MARSHALL ST
PARK RD
SMITH AVE
MOSSSIDE RD
BARCLAY ST
CHERRY PL
WOODSIDE
MOSS-SIDE RD
WALLACE ST
WALKER ST
BLAMEY CRES
PARK AVE
RAITH AVE
PARK ST
PILKHAM CT
SELKIRK AVE
ROSE ST
SOUTH ST
HILLCREST
GREENBANK DR
MOSSBANK
EWING ST
WOOD BANK
ANDERSON DR
JAMES CT
JAMES ST
CRAIGTON PL
GARDINER RD
BRAEMOUNT DR
MOSSEND TERR
GREENMOUNT
DALBEATH CRES
WESTBURN AVE
WEST LA
SINCLAIR DR
RAE ST
CULLALOE VIEW
BIRCHBANK
COPELAND CRES
BEATH VIEW RD
MAXWELL CRES
WEIR AVE
GARDINER PL
BURNSIDE TERR
MITCHELL CRES
ALLAN PK
WOODEND PL
TORBEITH GDNS
1 TORBEITH GDNS
2 SWINTONS PL
PO

31
14

13

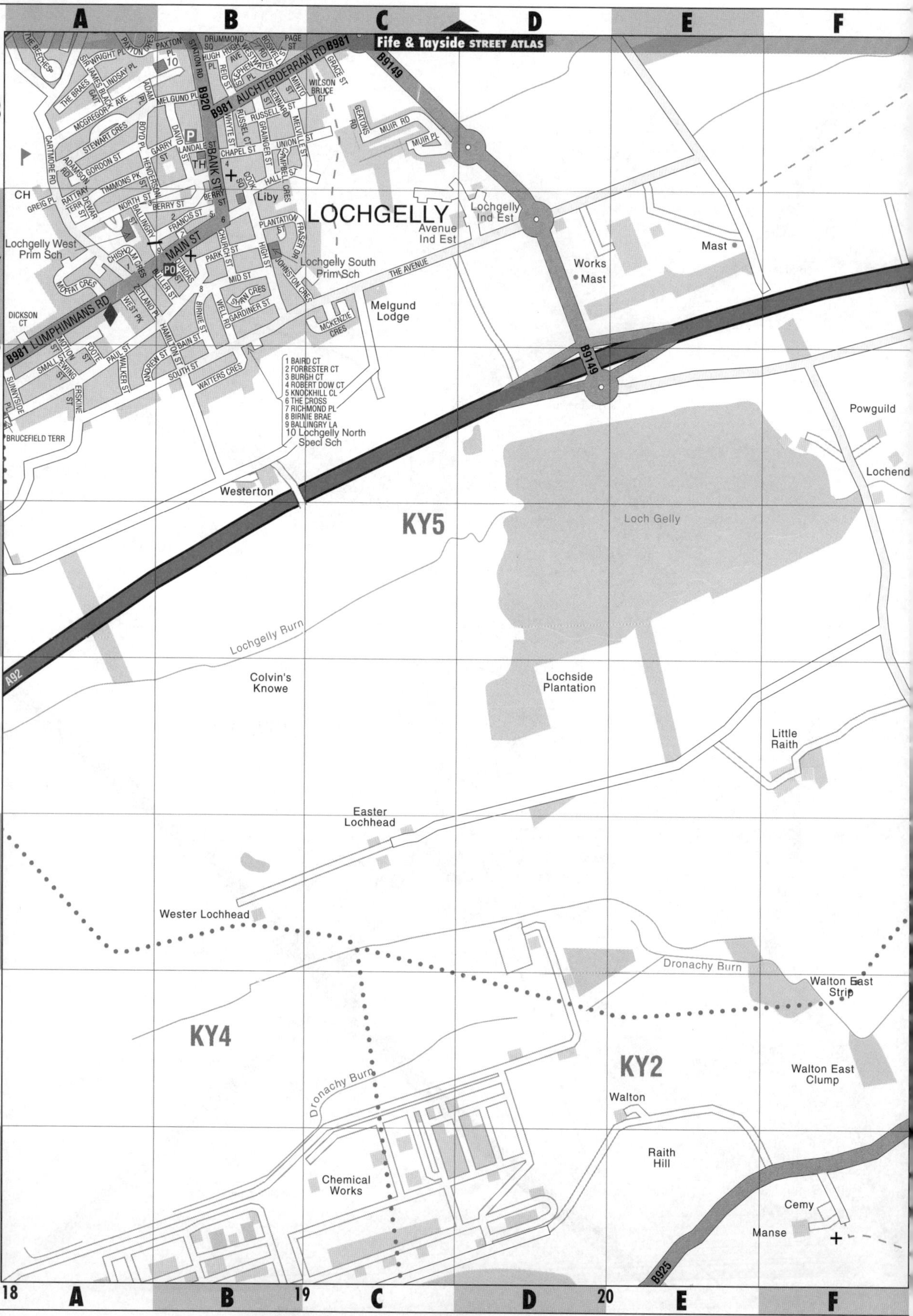

Fife & Tayside STREET ATLAS
A
B
C
D
E
F
8
7
93
6
5
92
4
3
91
2
1
90
18
19
20
LOCHGELLY
KY5
KY4
KY2
THE BEECHES
PAXTON CRES
PAXTON PL
STATION RD
DRUMMOND SQ
HUGH PL
HUGH AVE
REID ST
STEPHEN PL
WESTWATER RD
BOSWELL CT
PAGE ST
B981 AUCHTERDERRAN RD B981
GRACE ST
WILSON
BRUCE CT
B9149
SIR JAMES BLACK GAIT
WRIGHT PL
LINDSAY PL
THE BRAES
ADAM PL
MELGUND PL
B920
B981
MINTO ST
KENNARD ST
RUSSELL ST
RUSSEL CT
WHYTE ST
GRAINGER ST
MELVILLE ST
GEATONS RD
MUIR RD
MUIR PL
MCGREGOR AVE
STEWART CRES
BOYD PL
DAVID ST
CARTMORE RD
ADAMSON RD
GORDON ST
GARRY ST
LANDALE ST
CHAPEL ST
UNION ST
CAMPBELL ST
TH
BANK ST
SQ
COOK ST
HALL CRES
CH
GREIG PL
RATTRAY TERR
DEWAR ST
TIMMONS PK
HENDERSON ST
NORTH ST
BERRY ST
Liby
PLANTATION ST
FRASER DR
Lochgelly Ind Est
Avenue Ind Est
FRANCIS ST
BALLINGRY LA
Lochgelly West Prim Sch
CHISHOLM CRES
MAIN ST
CHURCH ST
HIGH ST
JOHNSTON CRES
PARK ST
Lochgelly South Prim Sch
THE AVENUE
Works
Mast
Mast
PO
DUNDAS ST
MOFFAT CRES
BULLER ST
ZETLAND PL
MID ST
SHAW CRES
GARDINER ST
WELL RD
BIRNIE ST
Melgund Lodge
MCKENZIE CRES
DICKSON CT
B981 LUMPHINNANS RD
WEST PK
HAMILTON ST
BAIN ST
MOTION ST
SMALL ST
EWING ST
FOOTE ST
PAUL ST
WALKER ST
ANDREW ST
SOUTH ST
WATTERS CRES
SUNNYSIDE PL
ERSKINE ST
1 BAIRD CT
2 FORRESTER CT
3 BURGH CT
4 ROBERT DOW CT
5 KNOCKHILL CL
6 THE CROSS
7 RICHMOND PL
8 BIRNIE BRAE
9 BALLINGRY LA
10 Lochgelly North Specl Sch
BRUCEFIELD TERR
Powguild
Lochend
Westerton
Loch Gelly
Lochgelly Burn
A92
Colvin's Knowe
Lochside Plantation
Little Raith
Easter Lochhead
Wester Lochhead
Dronachy Burn
Walton East Strip
Walton East Clump
Walton
Dronachy Burn
Raith Hill
Chemical Works
Cemy
Manse
B925

13

32

16

A B C D E F
Fife & Tayside STREET ATLAS
A92 Glenrothes, Dundee
A92
Carden Den
Tullylumb Plantation
Torbain Moss
LADY HELEN COTTS
Woodside Cottages
Twr
Den Burn
Dundonald Muir Plantation
South Dundonald
Bairns Bridge
Bairns Bridge Wood
Beaton's Wood
Braehead
Shawsmill Farm
Shawsmill Bridge
Bankhead Wood
Muirhead
Shawsmill Plantation
KY5
Gelly Burn
Bankhead of Raith
Haughbrae Wood
Knockbathy Wood
Glenniston
Target Wood
Lambswell Wood
Hallyards Castle
Camilla Loch
Clentrie Farm
West Balbarton
KY2
New Cottoun
Dronachy Burn
B925
CAMILLA RD
Camilla
SANDERSON TERR
HALYARD TERR
MORAY CT
MILTON PK
Auchtertool
MAIN ST
THE MALTINGS
NEWBIGGING TERR
NEWBIGGING
CAMILLA GR
Kinuny Plantation
Refuse Tip
PH
Auchtertool House
Auchtertool Prim Sch
Newbigging
Bottom Burn
Tiel Burn
Castle Hill
Mourn House
Lambert's Mill
Kirkton
8 7 93 6 5 92 4 3 91 2 1 90
21 22 23

33

16

15

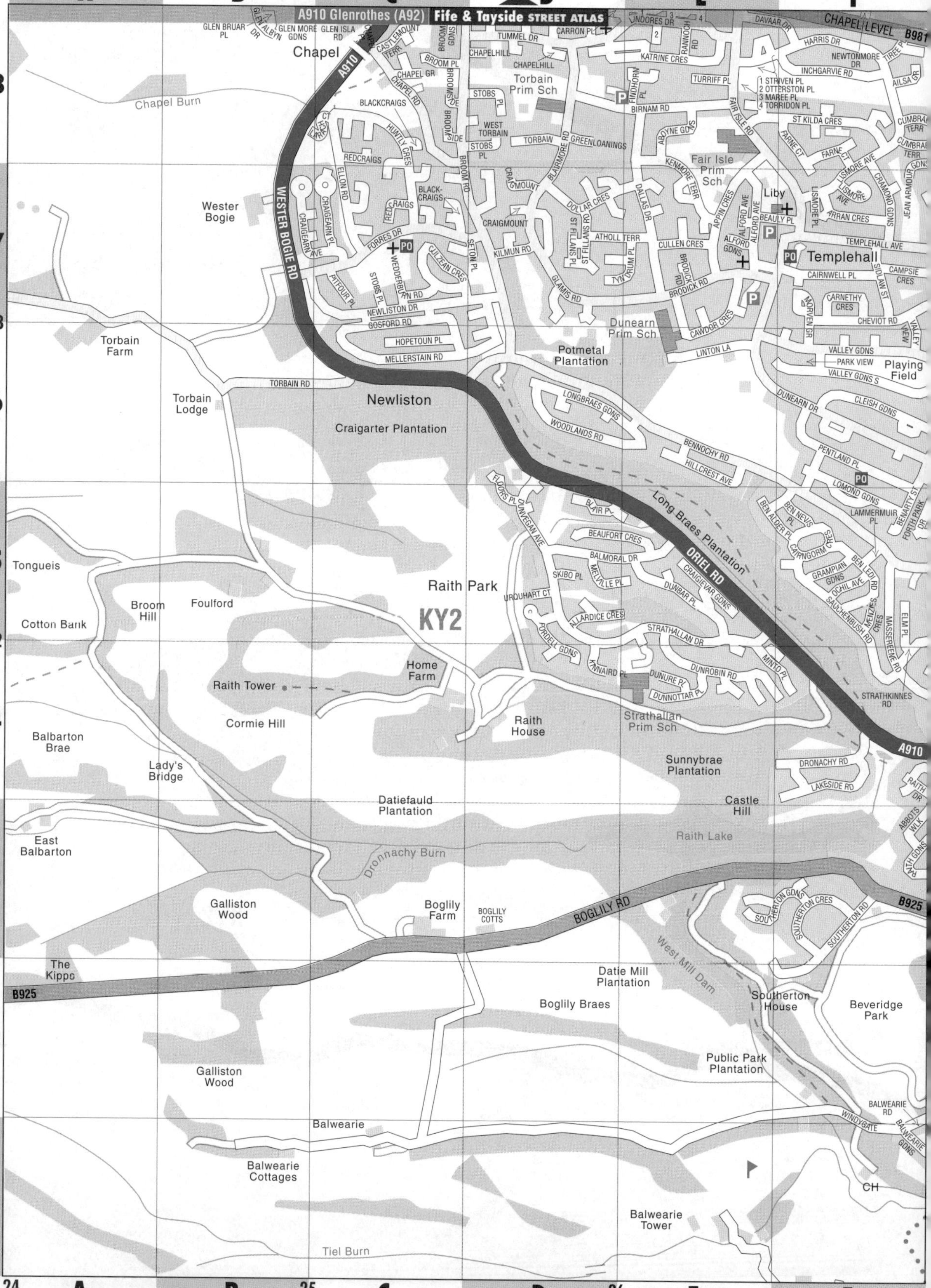
A910 Glenrothes (A92)
Fife & Tayside STREET ATLAS
A B C D E F
8 7 6 5 4 3 2 1
93 92 91 90
24 25 26
Chapel
Chapel Burn
Wester Bogie
WESTER BOGIE RD
Torbain Farm
Torbain Lodge
TORBAIN RD
Newliston
Craigarter Plantation
Torbain Prim Sch
Fair Isle Prim Sch
Liby
Templehall
Dunearn Prim Sch
Potmetal Plantation
Playing Field
Long Braes Plantation
ORIEL RD
Tongueis
Cotton Bank
Broom Hill
Foulford
Raith Park
KY2
Home Farm
Raith Tower
Cormie Hill
Raith House
Strathallan Prim Sch
Sunnybrae Plantation
Balbarton Brae
Lady's Bridge
Datiefauld Plantation
Castle Hill
Raith Lake
East Balbarton
Dronnachy Burn
Galliston Wood
Boglily Farm
BOGLILY COTTS
BOGLILY RD
B925
The Kippo
Datie Mill Plantation
West Mill Dam
Southerton House
Beveridge Park
Boglily Braes
Public Park Plantation
Balwearie
Balwearie Cottages
Balwearie Tower
Tiel Burn
CH
A910
CHAPEL LEVEL
B981

15
34

18

Fife & Tayside STREET ATLAS
A921 Glenrothes (A92)
KIRKCALDY
KY1
KY2
Gallatown
Smeaton
Pathhead
Hayfield
Sinclairtown
Linktown
Dunnikier Park
Playing Field
Kirkcaldy High Sch
St Andrew's RC High Sch
St Marie's RC Prim Sch
Middle Den
Den Burn
Whytemans Brae
Hayfield Ind Est
Cemy
Valley Prim Sch
Crem
Smeaton Ind Site
Pathhead Prim Sch
Rosslyn Sch
Sinclairtown Cemy
Sinclairtown Prim Sch
Viewforth High Sch
Liby
Victoria
Kirkcaldy North Prim Sch
Forth Park Maternity
Dunnikier Prim Sch
Ravenscraig Park
Ravenscraig Castle
Adam Smith Coll (Priory Campus)
Pathhead Sands
Coal Wynd Ind Est
Adam Smith Coll
Harbour
East Pier
South Pier
Port Brae
Mus, Gall & Liby
Adam Smith Theatre
Kirkcaldy
Forth Ave Ind Est
Mercat
The Postings
Fife Coastal Path
Kirkcaldy Sands
Boating Lake
Beveridge Park
Kirkcaldy West Prim Sch
Link Sands
Balwearie High Sch
Stark's Park (Raith Rovers)
Tiel Burn
DUNNIKIER WAY
ROSSLYN ST
ST CLAIR ST
DYSART RD
NAIRN ST
NETHER ST
THE PATH
VICTORIA RD
HIGH ST
ESPLANADE
NICOL ST
ORIEL RD
PRATT ST
ABBOTSHALL RD
BOGLILY RD
WINDMILL RD
A921
A955
A910
B925
B981
B928
B9157
C5
1 RUSSEL PL
2 YOUNG'S TERR
3 SMITH'S TERR
D6
1 PATHHEAD CT
2 MITCHELL PL
3 HAWKSMUIR
4 CITRON GLEBE
5 BIRRELL CL
6 CHIEF'S CL
7 BROAD WYND
8 BRANNING CT
9 BOGIES WYND
10 RAVENS CRAIG
11 FLESH WYND
12 WEST WYND
1 PATTERSON PL
2 NELSON ST
3 MARINERS ST
4 MURRAY TERR
5 WHYTEBANK GDNS
1 JEAN ARMOUR GDNS
2 TARBOLTON CT
1 BIRRELL'S LA
2 CAITHNESS CT
3 SUTHERLAND PL
1 CHARLOTTE ST
2 GLASSWORK ST
3 GLADNEY SQ
4 BUTE WYND
5 AITKEN CT
6 HENDRY'S WYND
7 BUCHANAN CT
A B C D E F
8 7 6 5 4 3 2 1
93 92 91 90
27 28 29

A4
1 Univ of Dundee Sch of Nursing & Midwifery Fife Campus

35

18

17

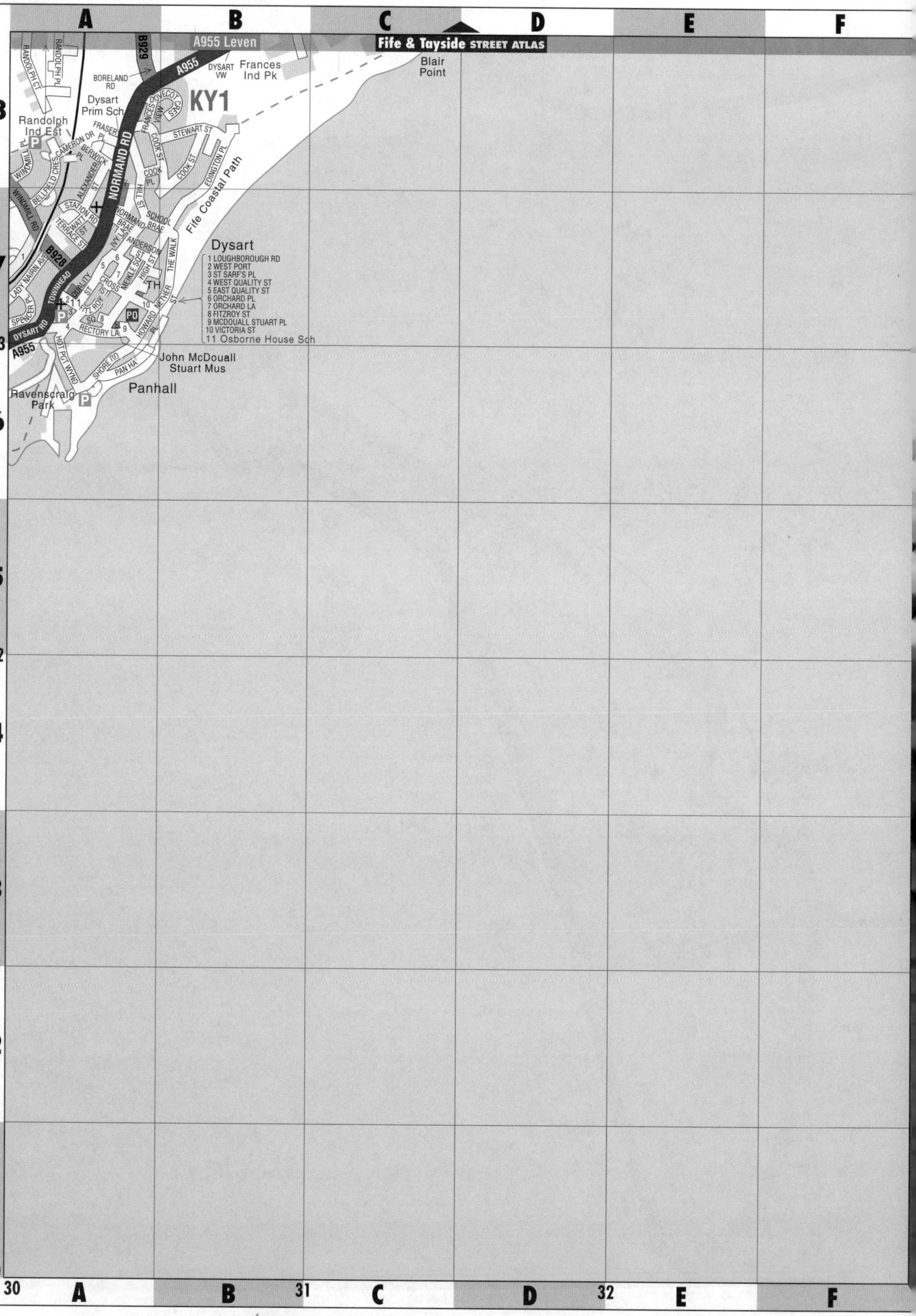
A
B
C
D
E
F
A955 Leven
Fife & Tayside STREET ATLAS
Blair Point
B929
A955
DYSART VW
Frances Ind Pk
BORELAND RD
Dysart Prim Sch
KY1
DOVECOT CRES
FRANCES VIEW
Randolph Ind Est
RANDOLPH CT
RANDOLPH PL
FRASER PL
NORMAND RD
STEWART ST
COOK ST
COOK PL
EDINGTON PL
CAMERON DR
BERWICK PL
WINDMILL PL
BELLFIELD CRES
ALEXANDER ST
HILL ST
Fife Coastal Path
WINDMILL RD
STATION RD
SCHOOL BRAE
NORMAND BRAE
TERRACE ST
IVY LA
ANDERSON ST
B928
THE WALK
Dysart
1 LOUGHBOROUGH RD
2 WEST PORT
3 ST SARF'S PL
4 WEST QUALITY ST
5 EAST QUALITY ST
6 ORCHARD PL
7 ORCHARD LA
8 FITZROY ST
9 MCDOUALL STUART PL
10 VICTORIA ST
11 Osborne House Sch
LADY NAIRN AVE
TOWNHEAD
QUALITY ST
CROSS ST
MEIKLE SQ
HIGH ST
TH
NETHER ST
SPENCER PL
FITZ ROY ST
SQ
PO
HOWARD PL
DYSART RD
RECTORY LA
A955
HOT POT WYND
SHORE RD
PAN HA'
John McDouall Stuart Mus
Panhall
Ravenscraig Park
8
7
93
6
5
92
4
3
91
2
1
90
30
31
32

17

7
20

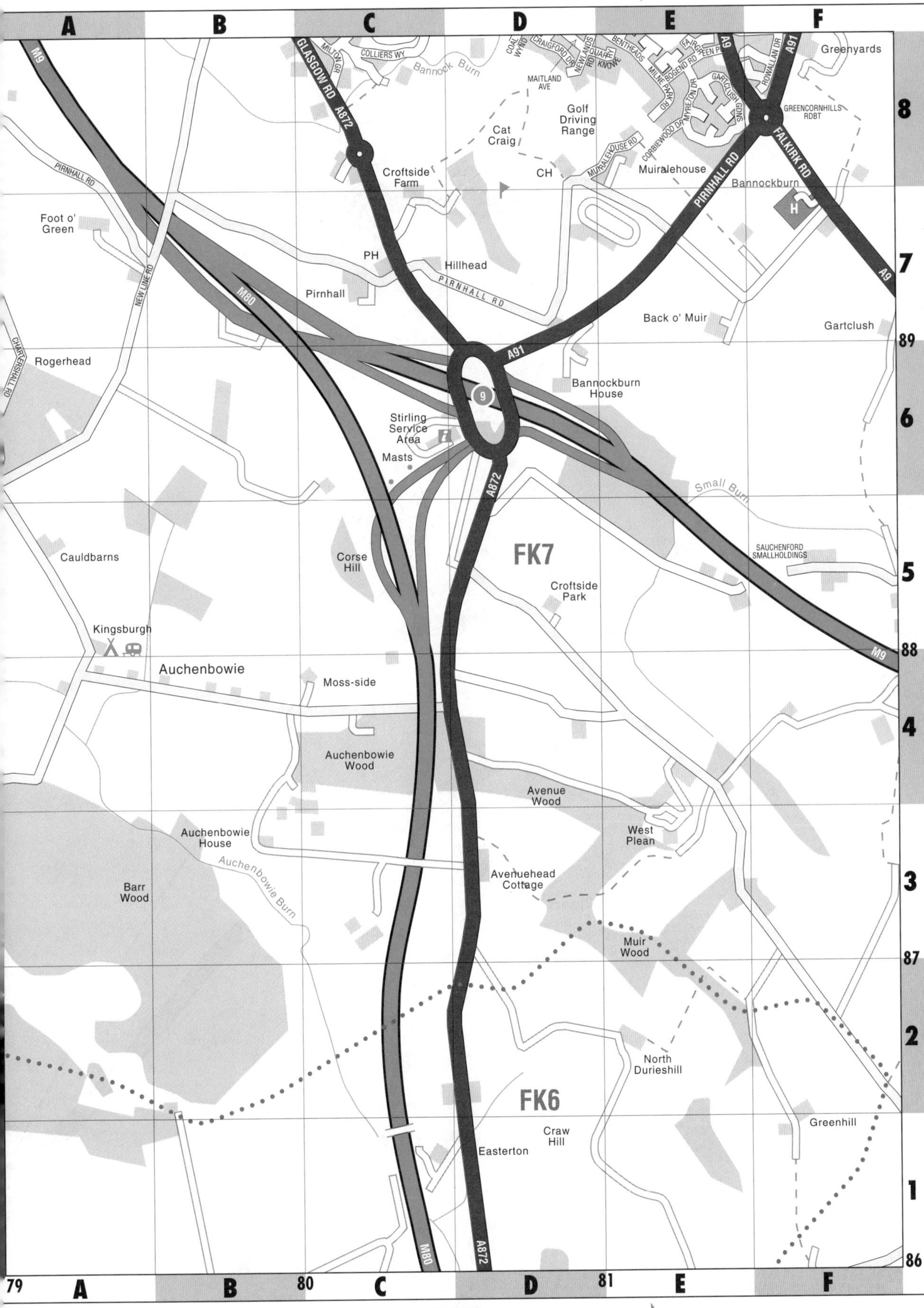
A
B
C
D
E
F
M9
GLASGOW RD
A872
MILTON GR
COLLIERS WY
Bannock Burn
MAITLAND AVE
CRAIGFORD DR
NEWLANDS RD
QUARRY KNOWE
BENTHEADS
MILNE PARK RD
MYRETON DR
GARTCLUSH GDNS
ROWALLAN DR
A9
A91
Greenyards
GREENCORNHILLS RDBT
Golf Driving Range
Cat Craig
Croftside Farm
CH
MUIRALEHOUSE RD
CORBIEWOOD DR
Muiralehouse
PIRNHALL RD
FALKIRK RD
Bannockburn
H
PIRNHALL RD
Foot o' Green
NEW LINE RD
PH
Hillhead
Pirnhall
M80
Back o' Muir
Gartclush
CHARTERSHALL RD
Rogerhead
A91
Bannockburn House
9
Stirling Service Area
Masts
Small Burn
A872
FK7
SAUCHENFORD SMALLHOLDINGS
Cauldbarns
Corse Hill
Croftside Park
Kingsburgh
Auchenbowie
Moss-side
M9
Auchenbowie Wood
Avenue Wood
West Plean
Auchenbowie House
Auchenbowie Burn
Barr Wood
Avenuehead Cottage
Muir Wood
North Durieshill
FK6
Craw Hill
Easterton
Greenhill
M80
A872
8
7
89
6
5
88
4
3
87
2
1
86
79
80
81

36
20

19
8

A
B
C
D
E
F
8
7
89
6
5
88
4
3
87
2
1
86
82
83
84
COWIE RD
B9124
Easter Greenyards
Westerton of Cowie
RICHARD QUINN ST
DA CAMPBELL AVE
FINCASTLE PL
ARDGOWAN PL
TIBBIES LOAN
OCHRE CRES
HOLMHOUSE
FLINT CRES
FARM RD
WESTERTON
CARNOCK ST
HILTON
COWIEHALL RD
PARK ST
SCOTSTOUN RD
BANNOCKBURN RD
St Margaret's RC Prim Sch
Cowie Prim Sch
Cowiehall
Hilton Farm
Sewage Works
Berry Hills
PO
PH
MAIN ST
Cowie
BERRYHILL
MOUNT OLIPHANT
EASTERTON DR
EASTERTON CRES
EASTERTON GR
ALLOWAY DR
TAM O'SHANTER DR
BURNS TERR
ARMOUR AVE
BRIG-O-DOON GR
KYLE AVE
OCHILVIEW
Gartclush
A9
Sink
P
Liby
MAIN ST
STATION RD
Works
FALKIRK RD
Plean Farm
Plean Junction
FK7
Gallamuir Wood
SAUCHENFORD SMALLHOLDINGS
B9124
GALLAMUIR RD
Gallamuir
M9
Pleanbank Wood
MCCANN CT
CAREY CT
Sauchinford Burn
HENDERSON PL
LOANFOOT GDNS
BURNSIDE CRES
PO
Liby
Pleanbank Farm
WALLACE CRES
PARKSIDE CT
PRESIDENT KENNEDY DR
KIRKBRIDE TERR
BRUCE CRES
BRUCE ST
OAK CRES
CARBROOK DR
BEECH AVE
GALLAMUIR DR
FK2
PLEANBANK COTTS
TOUCHHILL CRES
PH
Plean
STIRLING PL
BALFOUR CT
BALFOUR CRES
WILLOW BRAE
CUSHENQUARTER DR
Works
THORNYCROFT TERR
MCAULAY BRAE
MAIN ST
TORBURN AVE
Sewage Works
Gartwhinnie Farm
Plean Country Park Wlk
East Plean Prim Sch
CADGERS LOAN
P
CHURCH LA
Cushenquarter
Plean House
NEWLANDS CT
GILLESPIE TERR
Plean Country Park
Plean Burn
CARDROWAN RD
GLEN RD
Plean Ind Est
FK5
Muirmailing
Carbrook Mains

19
37

9
22

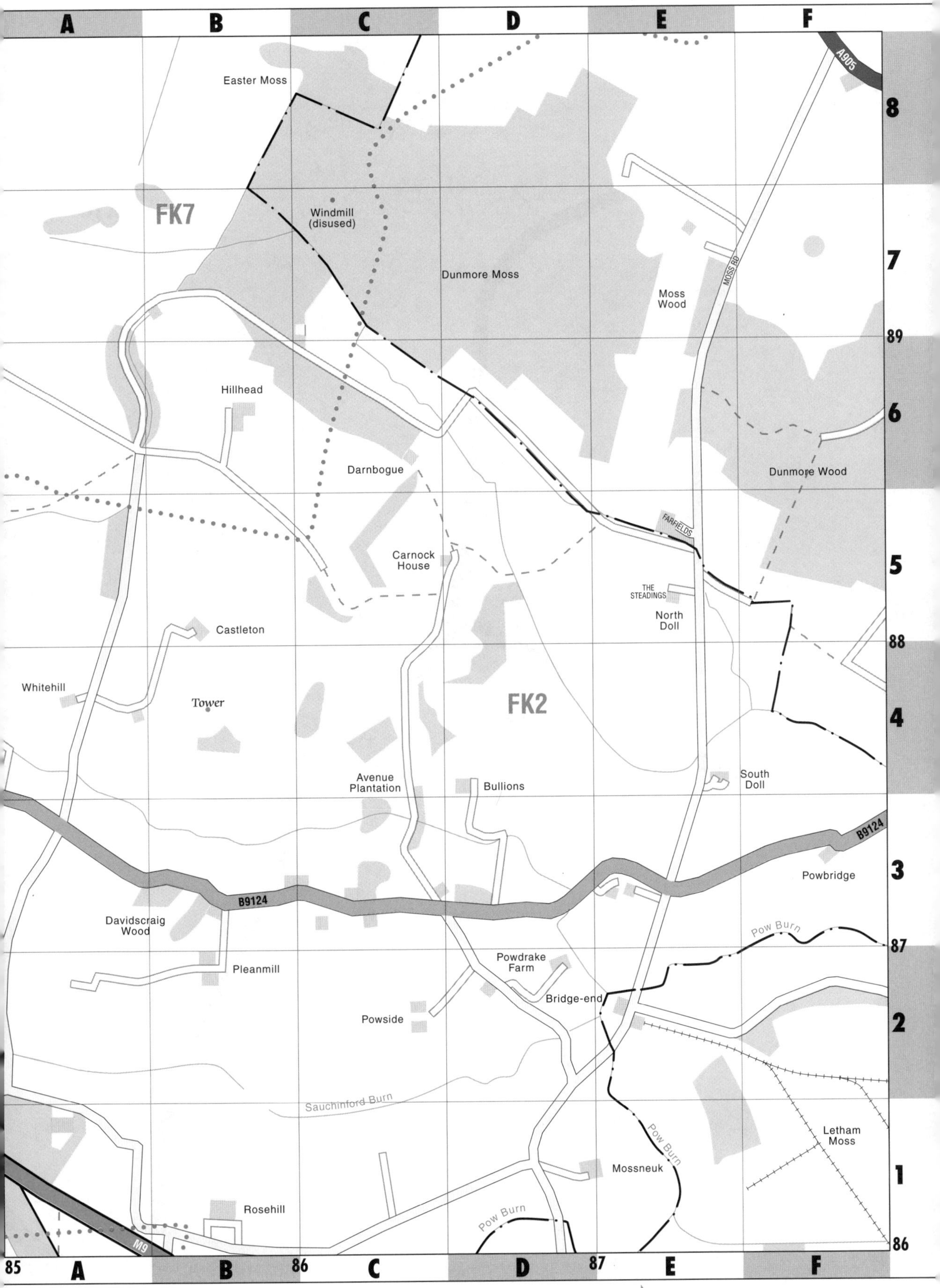
A
B
C
D
E
F
A905
8
Easter Moss
FK7
Windmill (disused)
Dunmore Moss
7
Moss Wood
MOSS RD
89
Hillhead
6
Darnbogue
Dunmore Wood
FARFIELDS
Carnock House
5
THE STEADINGS
North Doll
Castleton
88
Whitehill
Tower
FK2
4
Avenue Plantation
Bullions
South Doll
B9124
3
Powbridge
B9124
Davidscraig Wood
Pow Burn
87
Pleanmill
Powdrake Farm
Bridge-end
2
Powside
Sauchinford Burn
Pow Burn
Letham Moss
1
Mossneuk
Rosehill
Pow Burn
M9
86
85
A
B
86
C
D
87
E
F

38
22

21
10

A
B
C
D
E
F
8
7
89
6
5
88
4
3
87
2
1
86
88
89
90
A905
Pyetrees
Cottages
Inch of
Ferryton
Loanside
Dunmore
FK10
ST ANDREW'S DR
Dunmore
Park
Farm
Dunmore
Park
River Forth
Hill of
Dunmore
Tower
The
Pineapple
Dunmore
Wood
Sewage
Works
East
Lodge
B9724
SHIERLAW GDNS
NORTH GREEN DR
North
Greens
CRAWFORD SQ
NETHERBY RD
NETHERBY RD
THE WILDERNESS
SHORE RD
BANKS VIEW
GRAHAM TERR
FK2
Westfield
Dougalshill
Farm
PAUL DR
CARSE VIEW
MILLER PL
SHORE RD
PO
MAIN ST
THE PATH
KIRKWAY
DOWER PL
HIGH ST
ELPHINSTONE CRES
Airth
Prim Sch
Eastfield
Farm
B9124
Airth
FORRESTER PL
SOUTH GREEN DR
LINN PL
Hill of Airth
SNEDDON PL
CASTLE DR
Airth
Mains
DOUGLAS AVE
KENNEDY WAY
CASTLE AVE
BRUCE GATE
CASTLE VIEW
Airth
Castle
Pow Burn
Linkfield
Letham
Moss
Waterslap
LETHAM TERRS
Bowtrees
A905
A876
SOUTH APP RD

21
39

11
24

A
B
C
D
E
F
8
7
89
6
5
88
4
3
87
2
1
86
91
92
93
Kilbagie
Mill
A876
A977
Broadcarse
Canal Burn
Craigton
Kennet Pans
Dulquhamie Toll
Broomknowe
Crosshill
FK10
Tulliallan Castle
Hawkhill
KILDUTHIE PL
BROOMKNOWE DR
WINDYHILL AV
CASTLEPK
CH
River Forth
Tulliallan Castle
Scottish Pol Coll
Tulliallan Wood
MANSE RD
GLEBE RD
KIRK BRAE
TULLIALLAN TERR
WOOD LEA
HAWKHILL RD
CHAPELHILL ST
BRIDGE
FEREGAIT
KILBAGIE ST
Tulliallan Prim Sch
KIRK ST
RAMSAY CT
1 KINCAIRNE CT
2 SANDEMAN CT
3 SIVEWRIGHT CT
4 SIR ROBERT MAULE PL
ELPHINSTONE ST 1
COOPER'S LA 2
EXCISE ST 3
PARADISE LA 4
EXCISE LA 5
PRIMROSE LA 6
CHAPEL ST 7
Jetty
OCHIL VIEW
ASH BRAES
RAMSAY LA
HIGH ST
LANSDOWNE CRES
ROANHEAD TERR
DEWAR AVE
OSBORNE DR
JAMES WYLIE PL
WAR AVE
ANDERSON LA
Kincardine
LC
STATION RD
Liby
Firth of Forth
FORTH ST
ST JOHN ST
BANK ST
KEITH ST
PO
NORTH APPROACH RD
MERCER ST
REGENT ST
DONALDSON
TOLL RD
BURN BRAE PK
ROSEBANK GDNS
KELLYWOOD CRES
FORTH VIEW
PRIORY SQ
Pier
MILL LA
RIVERSIDE TERR
TARBERT TERR
Cemy
A977
P
SILVER ST
ORCHARD GR
GEORGE ST
STANDALANE
Pier
Kincardine on Forth Bridge
WALKER ST
DOCTOR'S PK
Football Ground
FK2
PH
Higgins' Neuck
A985
Inch House
WALKER ST
Pow Burn
SOUTH APPROACH RD
Inch Farm
Haughs of Airth

40
24

23

A
B
C
D
E
F
Fife & Tayside STREET ATLAS
Peathill Wood
North Wood
Mausoleum
Glasgow Moss
Peppermill Dam
Windyhill
Keir Plantation
Praybrae Wood
Moor Loch
Tulliallan Wood
Devilla Forest
Keir
FK10
Keir Burn
Keir Dam
Culross Moor
Sawmill Plantation
Bordie Moor
Standard Stone
NEW ROW
WESTFIELD
A977
A985
A985
Castle
LONGANNET RDBT
Bordie
KY12
WALKER ST
Lurg
STONY BRAE
Newpans
Lurg Farm
Mine
LONGANNET COTTS
Sands Farm
Caverns
8
7
89
6
5
88
4
3
87
2
1
86
94
95
96

23
41

26

A
B
C
D
E
F
Fife & Tayside STREET ATLAS
A907 Alloa
A907
8
Mine
Sight Hill
Overton
West
Grange
House
Burrowine
Alloa To Dunfermline Cycle Path
Blinkeerie
7
FK10
Middle
Grange
Launchout Burn
89
Balgownie
Mains
Bluther Burn
East
Grange
Oneford Burn
6
Righead
Thornyhaw
Balgownie Wood
Park
Plantation
5
KY12
88
Muirhead
Shires
Mill
4
B9037
Blairhall
Gallowridge
Blairhall
Wood
Kirkton Wood
Keir Burn
Couston
Wood
Kirkton
Blairhall
Mains
3
Cemy
B9037
Ashes
87
Waas
Plantation
A985
B9037
GALLOWS LOAN
2
Mast
WOODHEAD FARM RD
CATHERINES
WYND
DALY GDNS
B9037
Kirkbrae
Wood
FORTHBANK
PL
1
Dean Burn
MAIN ST
Culross
Abbey
The Park
KIRK ST
LOW CSWY
VEERE PK
ERSKINE BRAE
86
97
98
99

42

26

25

Fife & Tayside STREET ATLAS
A B C D E F
8 7 6 5 4 3 2 1
89 88 87 86
00 01 02
A907
B9037
Blairhall
Blairhall Prim Sch
Mains of Comrie
Tapitlaw Farm
Tapitlaw Cottage
Blair
Blair House
Oakley Ind Est
Oakley
Comrie
MAIN ST
PH
Liby
Inzievar Prim Sch & Holy Name RC Prim Sch
Mill
Comrie Dean Viaduct
Comrie Dean
Comrie Burn
Alloa To Dunfermline Cycle Path
East Grange
Grange Burn
Over Inzievar
KY12
Birch Cottages
Inzievar Wood
THE COURTYARD
INZIEVAR HO
Shires Mill
Pitsoulie
Langleas
Old Inzievar House
Bluther Burn
Valleyfield Woodland Park
Devilla Forest
Skiddy Hill
Couston Wood
Shawhill Plantation
Shaw Hill
CLINKUM BANK
High Valleyfield
A985
Drum Plantation
St Serf's RC Prim Sch
Loch Roy
Torrie House
Tuilyies
Standing Stones
Tuilyies Park
Newmills
Low Valleyfield
Forth View Ind Est
Torryburn Prim Sch
Torryburn
Low Torry
Back Burns Plantation
1 ORCHARD TERR
2 EILEAN LA
3 CRAIGFLOWER CT
4 CRAIGFLOWER HO
5 CRAIGFLOWER GDNS
6 CAUSEWAY LA

25
43

28

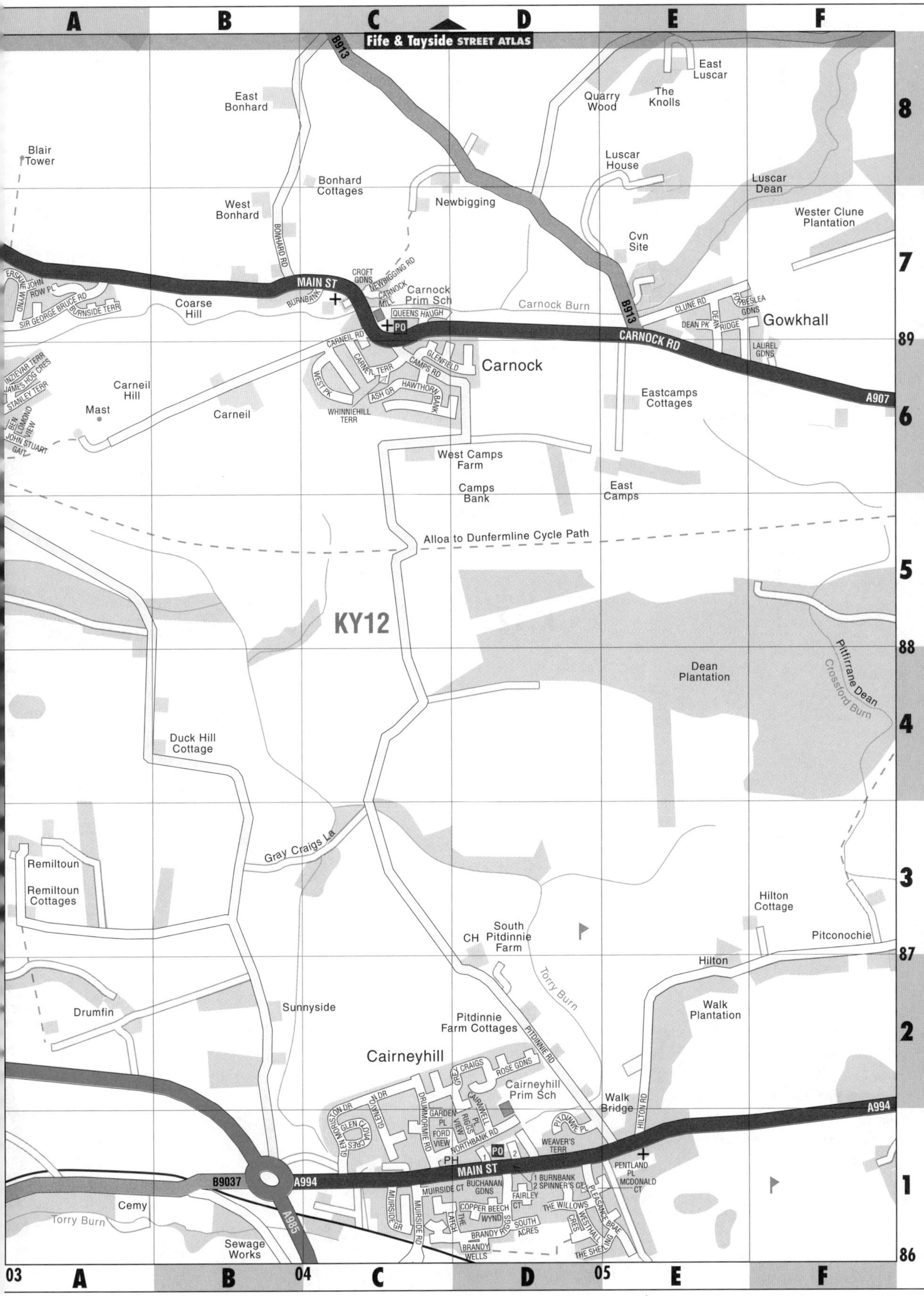
Fife & Tayside STREET ATLAS
A
B
C
D
E
F
8
7
89
6
5
88
4
3
87
2
1
86
03
04
05
East Bonhard
Blair Tower
Bonhard Cottages
West Bonhard
Newbigging
Quarry Wood
East Luscar
The Knolls
Luscar House
Luscar Dean
Wester Clune Plantation
Cvn Site
BONHARD RD
MAIN ST
CROFT GDNS
NEWBIGGING RD
CARNOCK MILL
Carnock Prim Sch
QUEENS HAUGH
BURNBANK
PO
Carnock Burn
B913
CLUNE RD
BESLEA GDNS
DEAN PK
DEAN RIDGE
Gowkhall
LAUREL GDNS
CARNOCK RD
ERSKINE WYND
JOHN ROW PL
SIR GEORGE BRUCE RD
BURNSIDE TERR
Coarse Hill
CARNEIL RD
CARNEIL TERR
GLENFIELD
CAMPS RD
Carnock
WEST PK
ASH GR
HAWTHORN BANK
WHINNIEHILL TERR
JAMES HOG CRES
STANLEY TERR
BEN LOMOND VIEW
JOHN STUART GAIT
Carneil Hill
Mast
Carneil
Eastcamps Cottages
A907
West Camps Farm
Camps Bank
East Camps
Alloa to Dunfermline Cycle Path
KY12
Dean Plantation
Pitfirrane Dean
Crossford Burn
Duck Hill Cottage
Gray Craigs La
Remiltoun
Remiltoun Cottages
South Pitdinnie Farm
CH
Hilton Cottage
Pitconochie
Hilton
Torry Burn
Walk Plantation
Drumfin
Sunnyside
Pitdinnie Farm Cottages
PITDINNIE RD
Cairneyhill
CRAIGS
ROSE GDNS
Cairneyhill Prim Sch
Walk Bridge
HILTON RD
A994
GARDEN PL
FORD VIEW
RIGGS VIEW
CAIRNWELL PL
NORTHBANK RD
DRUMMORMIE RD
GLEN CLOVA CRES
PITDINNIE PL
WEAVER'S TERR
PH
PO
MAIN ST
PENTLAND PL
MCDONALD CT
1 BURNBANK
2 SPINNER'S CT
B9037
A985
MUIRSIDE CT
BUCHANAN GDNS
FAIRLEY CT
COPPER BEECH WYND
THE WILLOWS
WESTHALL CRES
PLEASANCE BRAE
MUIRSIDE GR
MUIRSIDE RD
BRANDY RIGGS
SOUTH ACRES
BRANDY WELLS
THE SHEILING
Cemy
Torry Burn
Sewage Works

44
28

27

E5
1 CARLYLE LA
2 DOLLAR CT
3 JOHN CONNELLY CT
4 BARRIE PL
5 DAVID MILLAR PL

A B C D E F

A B C D E F

27

45

F4
1 HOUSTON CT
2 CASTLEBLAIR
3 CLAY ACRES CT
4 DAVID HENDERSON CT
5 FOUNDRY ST
6 WINTERTHUR LA
7 CHAPEL ST
8 QUEEN ANNE ST
9 PARK LA

F5
1 MID BRAE
2 CASTLEBLAIR LA
3 CASTLEBLAIR MEWS

30

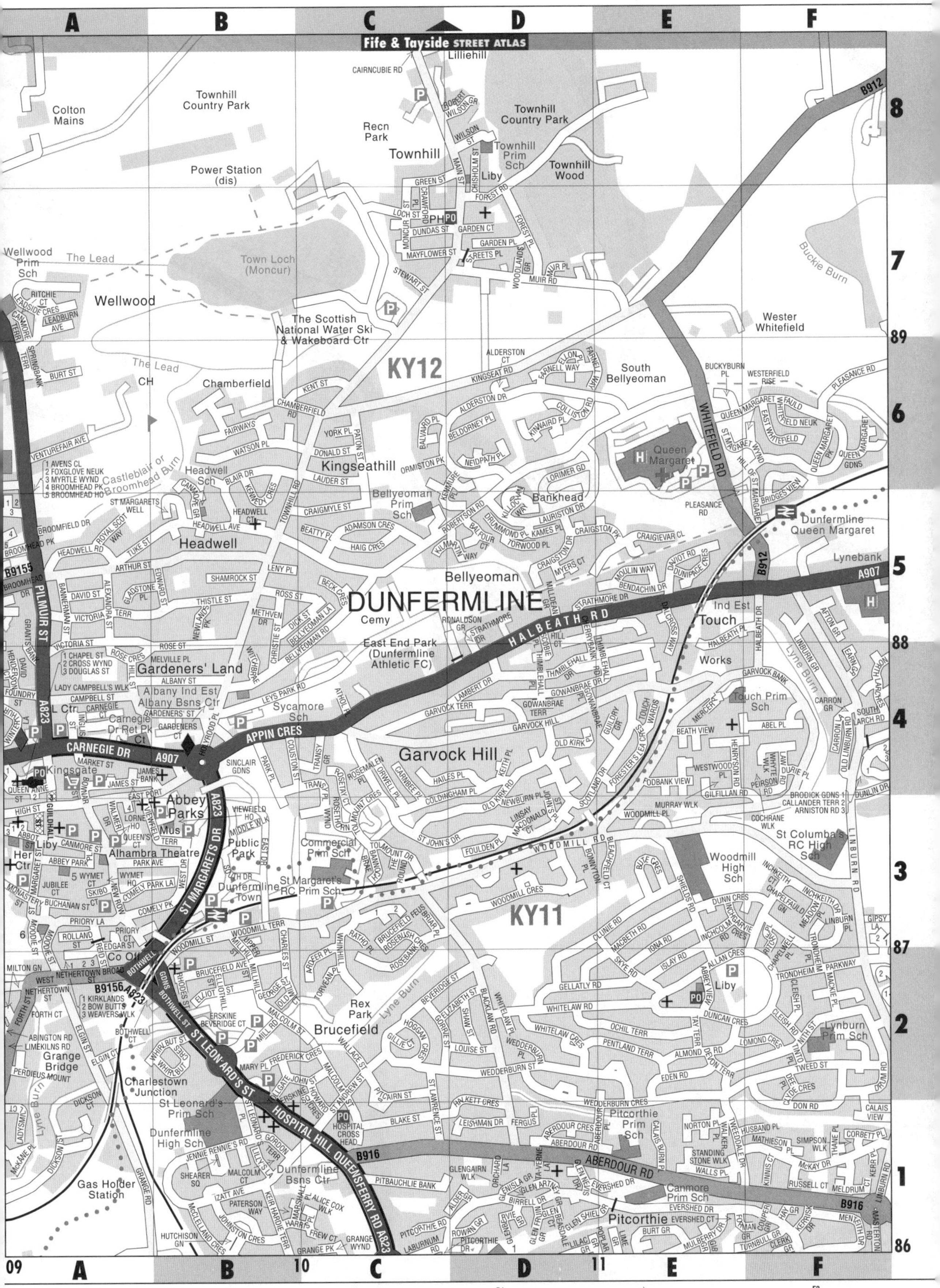

A3
1 WILSON'S CL
2 MUSIC HALL LA
3 MAYGATE
4 COMMERCIAL SCHOOL LA
5 Dunfermline Support Ctr
6 Andrew Carnegie Birthplace Mus

C3
1 BROOMIEKNOWE
2 HAILES PL

D1
1 Pitreavie Prim Sch

F2
1 NORWAY GDNS
2 SEA EAGLE CRES
F3
1 OSPREY CRES
2 WHEATEAR CT

46

30

29
12

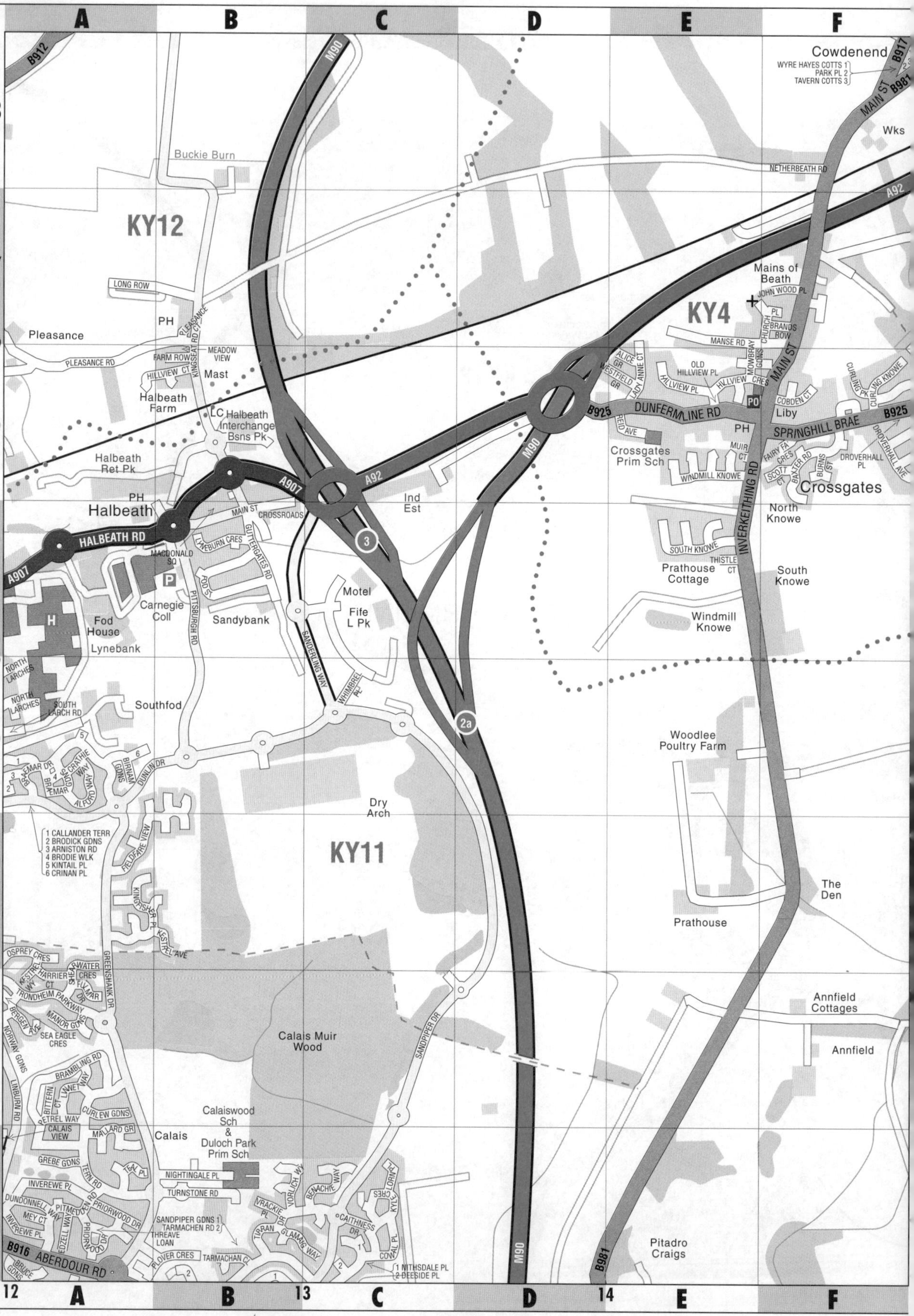
A
B
C
D
E
F
8
7
89
6
5
88
4
3
87
2
1
86
12
13
14
Cowdenend
WYRE HAYES COTTS 1
PARK PL 2
TAVERN COTTS 3
B917
B981
MAIN ST
Wks
NETHERBEATH RD
A92
B912
M90
Buckie Burn
KY12
LONG ROW
PH
PLEASANCE CT
KINGSEAT RD
Pleasance
PLEASANCE RD
FARM ROW
MEADOW VIEW
HILLVIEW CT
Mast
Halbeath Farm
LC
Halbeath Interchange Bsns Pk
Halbeath Ret Pk
PH
Halbeath
HALBEATH RD
A907
MAIN ST
CROSSROADS
LYNEBURN CRES
GUTTERGATES RD
MACDONALD SQ
P
FOD ST
PITTSBURGH RD
Carnegie Coll
Sandybank
H
Fod House
Lynebank
NORTH LARCHES
SOUTH LARCH RD
Southfod
DUNLIN DR
BIRNAM GDNS
BRAEMAR DR
CRATHIE WAY
ALFORD WAY
1 CALLANDER TERR
2 BRODICK GDNS
3 ARNISTON RD
4 BRODIE WLK
5 KINTAIL PL
6 CRINAN PL
FIELDFARE VIEW
KINGFISHER PL
KESTREL AVE
OSPREY CRES
HARRIER CT
SHEARWATER CRES
FULMAR DR
TRONDHEIM PARKWAY
BERGEN AVE
MANOR GDNS
SEA EAGLE CRES
NORWAY GDNS
GREENSHANK DR
BRAMBLING RD
BITTERN CT
LAPWING WAY
CURLEW GDNS
PETREL WAY
CALAIS VIEW
MALLARD GR
Calais
GREBE GDNS
TEAL PL
TERN RD
LINBURN RD
INVEREWE PL
DUNDONNELL WAY
PITMEDDEN RD
PRIORWOOD DR
MEY CT
EDZELL WAY
INVEREWE PL
B916
ABERDOUR RD
BRUCE GDNS
NIGHTINGALE PL
TURNSTONE RD
SANDPIPER GDNS 1
TARMACHEN RD 2
THREAVE LOAN
PLOVER CRES
TARMACHAN CT
Calaiswood Sch & Duloch Park Prim Sch
VRACKIE PL
VORLICH WAY
BENACHIE WAY
LORNE CRES
TIRRAN DR
GLAMAIS WAY
CAITHNESS DR
COVAL PL
1 NITHSDALE PL
2 DEESIDE PL
Calais Muir Wood
SANDPIPER DR
KY11
Dry Arch
Motel
Fife L Pk
SANDERLING WAY
WHIMBREL PL
3
2a
Ind Est
KY4
Mains of Beath
JOHN WOOD PL
CHURCH PL
BRANDS ROW
MANSE RD
ALICE GR
WESTFIELD GR
LADY ANNE CT
OLD HILLVIEW PL
HILLVIEW PL
HILLVIEW CRES
MOWBRAY GDNS
MAIN ST
PO
COBDEN CT
B925
DUNFERMLINE RD
REID AVE
Crossgates Prim Sch
PH
Liby
SPRINGHILL BRAE
CURLING PK
CURLING KNOWE
DROVERHALL AVE
DROVERHALL PL
FAIRY FA
SCOTT CT
BAXTER RD
BURNS ST
MUIR CT
WINDMILL KNOWE
Crossgates
INVERKEITHING RD
North Knowe
SOUTH KNOWE
THISTLE CT
Prathouse Cottage
South Knowe
Windmill Knowe
Woodlee Poultry Farm
The Den
Prathouse
Annfield Cottages
Annfield
Pitadro Craigs
B981

29
47

13
32

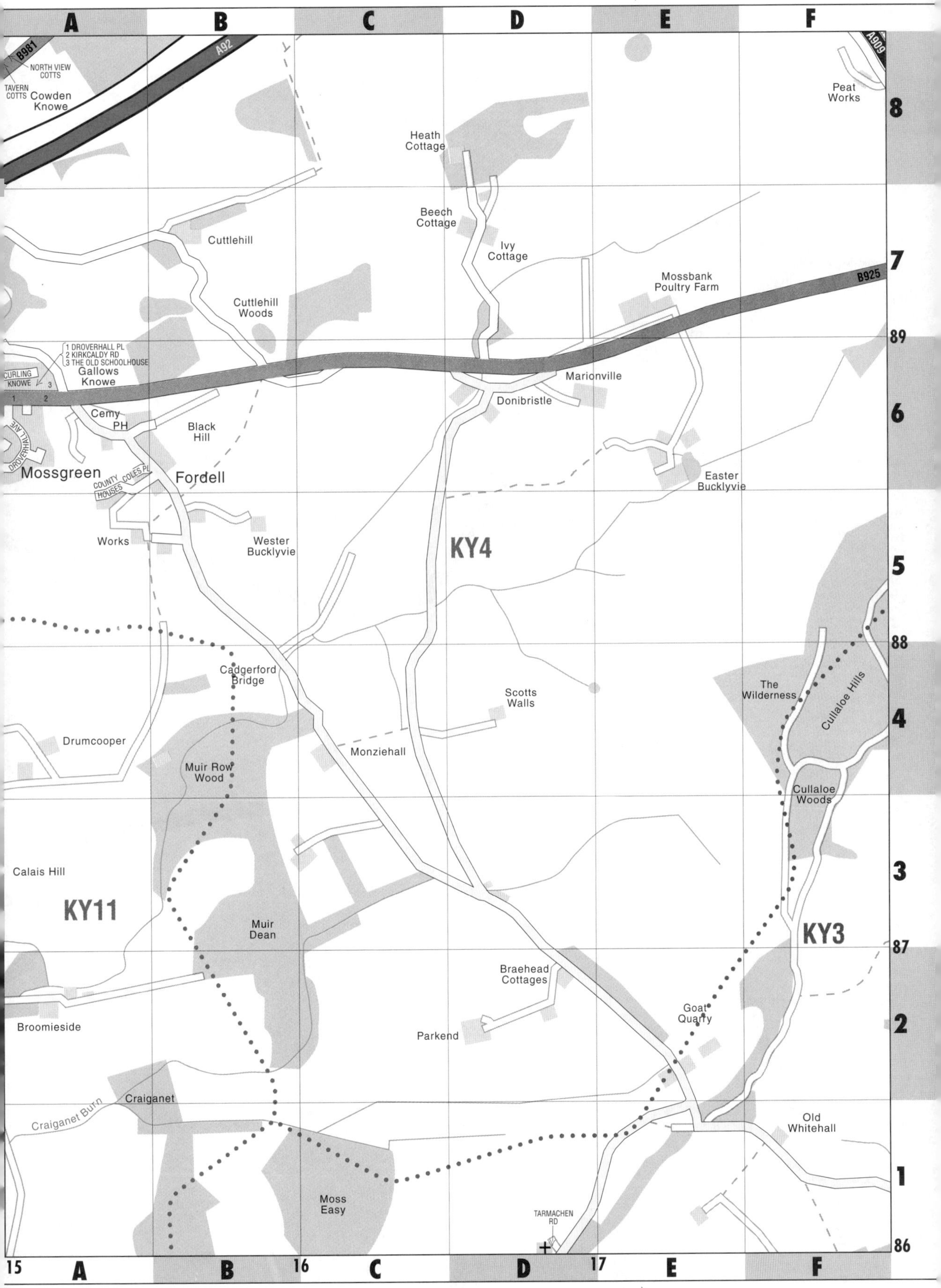
A
B
C
D
E
F
B981
A92
A909
NORTH VIEW COTTS
TAVERN COTTS
Cowden Knowe
Peat Works
Heath Cottage
Beech Cottage
Ivy Cottage
Cuttlehill
Cuttlehill Woods
Mossbank Poultry Farm
B925
1 DROVERHALL PL
2 KIRKCALDY RD
3 THE OLD SCHOOLHOUSE
Gallows Knowe
CURLING KNOWE
Marionville
Donibristle
Cemy
PH
Black Hill
DROVERHALL AVE
Mossgreen
COUNTY HOUSES
COLES PL
Fordell
Easter Bucklyvie
Works
Wester Bucklyvie
KY4
Cadgerford Bridge
Scotts Walls
The Wilderness
Cullaloe Hills
Drumcooper
Monziehall
Muir Row Wood
Cullaloe Woods
Calais Hill
KY11
Muir Dean
KY3
Braehead Cottages
Goat Quarry
Broomieside
Parkend
Craiganet
Craiganet Burn
Old Whitehall
Moss Easy
TARMACHEN RD
8
7
89
6
5
88
4
3
87
2
1
86
15
16
17

48
32

31
14

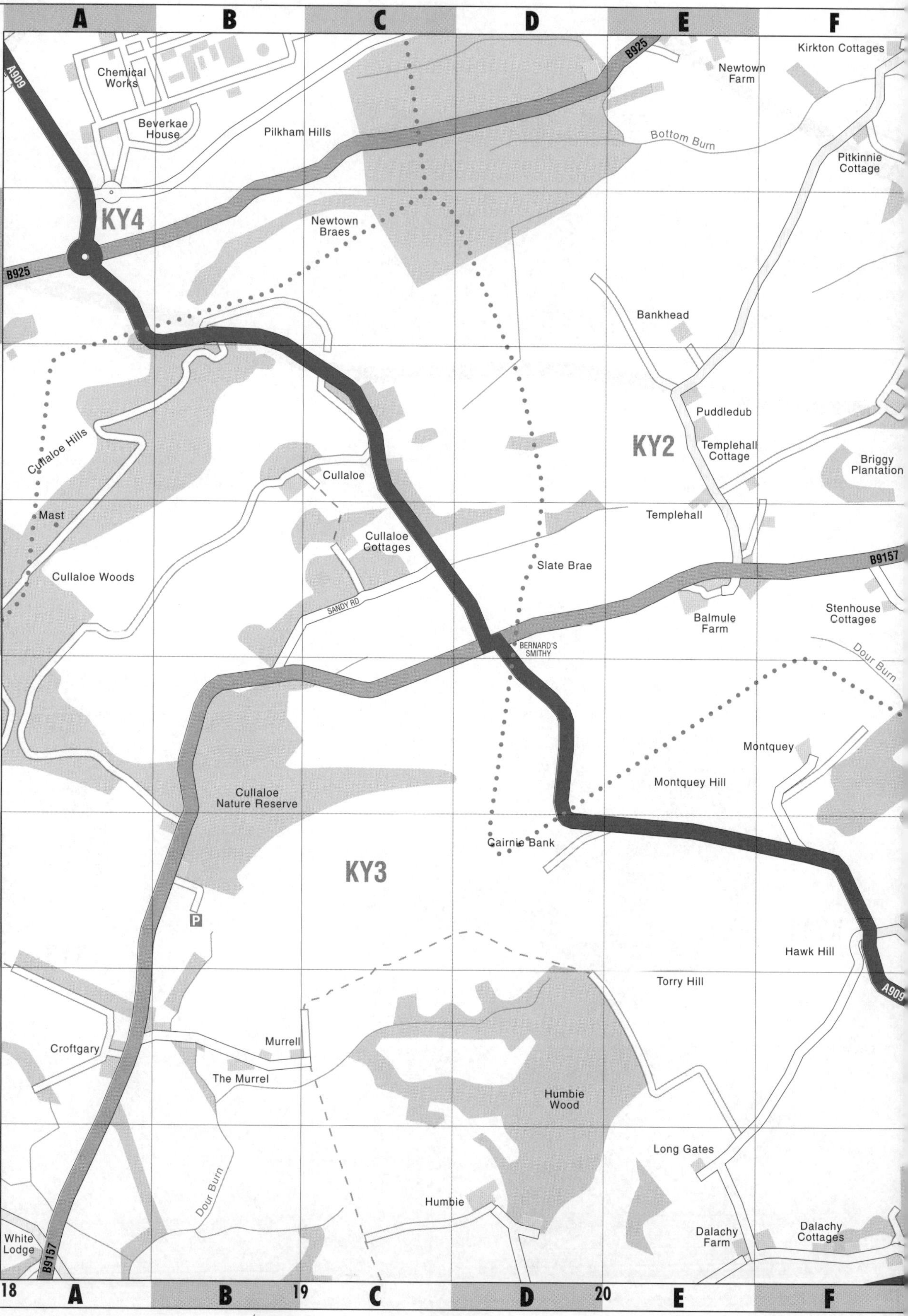
A
B
C
D
E
F
8
7
89
6
5
88
4
3
87
2
1
86
18
19
20
Chemical Works
Beverkae House
Pilkham Hills
A909
B925
KY4
Newtown Braes
Kirkton Cottages
Newtown Farm
Bottom Burn
Pitkinnie Cottage
Bankhead
Puddledub
KY2
Templehall Cottage
Briggy Plantation
Cullaloe Hills
Cullaloe
Mast
Templehall
Cullaloe Cottages
Cullaloe Woods
Slate Brae
B9157
SANDY RD
Balmule Farm
Stenhouse Cottages
BERNARD'S SMITHY
Dour Burn
Montquey
Montquey Hill
Cullaloe Nature Reserve
Cairnie Bank
KY3
P
Hawk Hill
Torry Hill
Croftgary
Murrell
The Murrel
Humbie Wood
Long Gates
Humbie
White Lodge
Dalachy Farm
Dalachy Cottages

31
49

15
34

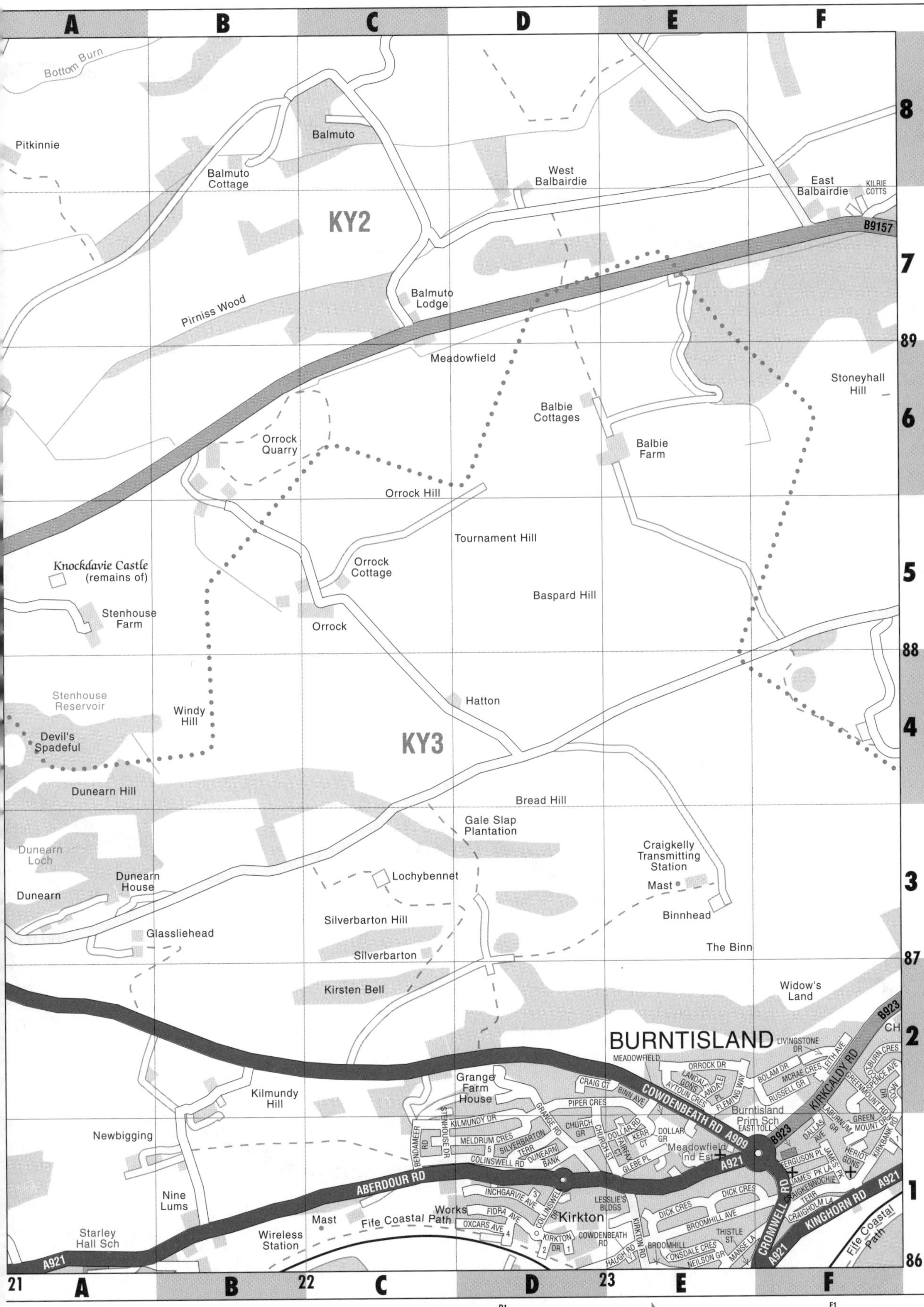

50
34

D1
1 BURNSIDE GDNS
2 SEAMILL GDNS
3 LITTLE CRAIGS VW
4 SEALS CRAIG VW
5 KINNONMONTH AVE

F1
1 GREENMOUNT RD S

33
16

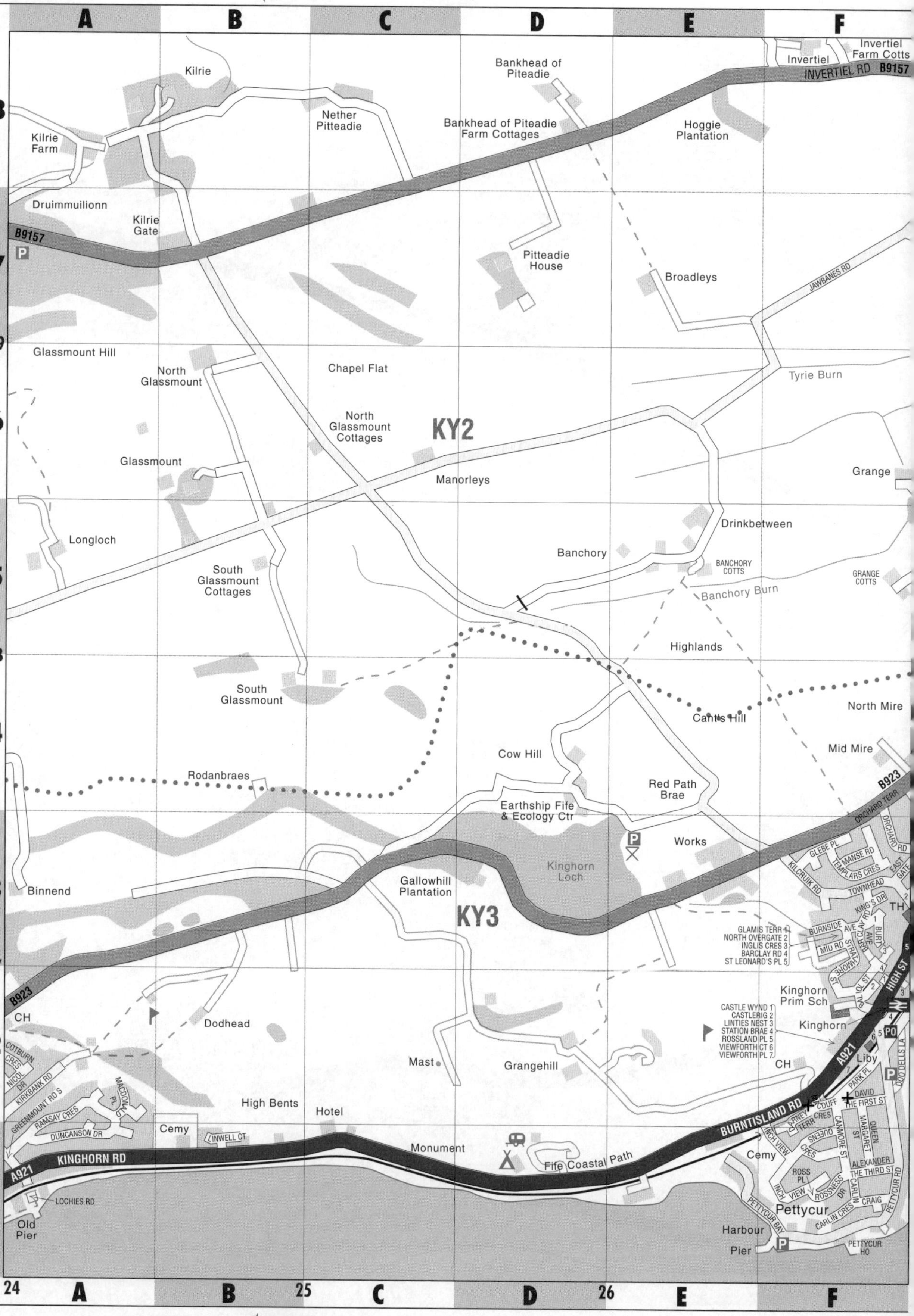
A
B
C
D
E
F
8
7
89
6
5
88
4
3
87
2
1
86
24
25
26
Kilrie
Kilrie Farm
Nether Pitteadie
Bankhead of Piteadie
Bankhead of Piteadie Farm Cottages
Invertiel
Invertiel Farm Cotts
INVERTIEL RD
B9157
Hoggie Plantation
Druimmuilionn
Kilrie Gate
B9157
Pitteadie House
Broadleys
JAWBANES RD
Glassmount Hill
North Glassmount
Chapel Flat
Tyrie Burn
North Glassmount Cottages
KY2
Glassmount
Manorleys
Grange
Longloch
Drinkbetween
Banchory
BANCHORY COTTS
GRANGE COTTS
South Glassmount Cottages
Banchory Burn
Highlands
South Glassmount
Cant's Hill
North Mire
Mid Mire
Cow Hill
Rodanbraes
Red Path Brae
B923
Earthship Fife & Ecology Ctr
ORCHARD TERR
Works
Kinghorn Loch
Binnend
Gallowhill Plantation
KY3
GLEBE PL
MANSE RD
TEMPLARS CRES
KILCRUIK RD
TOWNHEAD
EAST GATE
KING'S DR
TH
BURNSIDE AVE
GLAMIS TERR 1
NORTH OVERGATE 2
INGLIS CRES 3
BARCLAY RD 4
ST LEONARD'S PL 5
MIU RD
B923
Dodhead
Kinghorn Prim Sch
HIGH ST
CASTLE WYND 1
CASTLERIG 2
LINTIES NEST 3
STATION BRAE 4
ROSSLAND PL 5
VIEWFORTH CT 6
VIEWFORTH PL 7
Kinghorn
CH
COTBURN CRES
NICOL DR
KIRKBANK RD
Mast
Grangehill
CH
A921
Liby
PO
GREENMOUNT RD S
RAMSAY CRES
MACDONALD PL
High Bents
Hotel
PARK PL
DAVID
THE FIRST ST
DUNCANSON DR
Cemy
LINWELL CT
Monument
BURNTISLAND RD
CUFF
DARNEY TERR
CRES
CANMORE ST
MARGARET ST
QUEEN
KINGHORN RD
Fife Coastal Path
INCH VIEW
Cemy
QUEENS CRES
ALEXANDER
THE THIRD ST
A921
ROSS PL
VIEW
ROSSNESS DR
CARLIN
PETTYCUR RD
LOCHIES RD
INCH
CRAIG
Old Pier
Pettycur
CARLIN CRES
PETTYCUR BAY
Harbour
Pier
P
PETTYCUR HO

33

17

A
B
C
D
E
F
B9157
INVERTIEL RD
SEAFIELD VIEW
PEEBLES ST
LESLIE ST
SEAFIELD RD
Factory
A921
SEAFIELD CRES
SEAFIELD GDNS
BRANKTON WYND
LONG CRAIG WLK
BOWHOUSE RD
BOWHOUSE DR
JAWBANES RD
KY1
SEAFIELD TWRS
KINGHORN RD
BOWHOUSE GDNS
EAST VOWS WLK
CRAIGFOOT PL
Tyrie
TYRIE PL
TYRIE AVE
TYRIE CT
CRAIGFOOT WLK
SANDWELL CRES
WEST VOWS WLK
CRAIGFOOT CT
INCHKEITH CRES
KY2
Seafield House
Seafield Tower
Fife Coastal Path
KY3
LINTON CT
Abden Farm
KIRKCALDY RD
1 ORCHARD CT
2 ORCHARD GDNS
BRUCE TERR
MYRE CRES
LONG CRAIGS TERR
SEAFIELD VIEW
ABDEN AVE
ABDEN PL
BOSWELL DR
1 GLOVER'S CT
2 BRUCE ST
3 ST LEONARD'S PL
4 ST LEONARD'S CT
5 STATION YD
6 TRONGATE
7 SOUTH OVERGATE
8 BIRREL'S WYND
9 ABDEN CT
10 CHURCH WLK
BARTON BLDGS
NETHERGATE
KINGHORN
ST JAMES PL
LB Sta
11 HARBOUR RD
12 ST CLAIRS ENTRY
13 ST CLAIRS CT
Kinghorn Ness
8
7
89
6
5
88
4
3
87
2
1
86
27
28
29

19

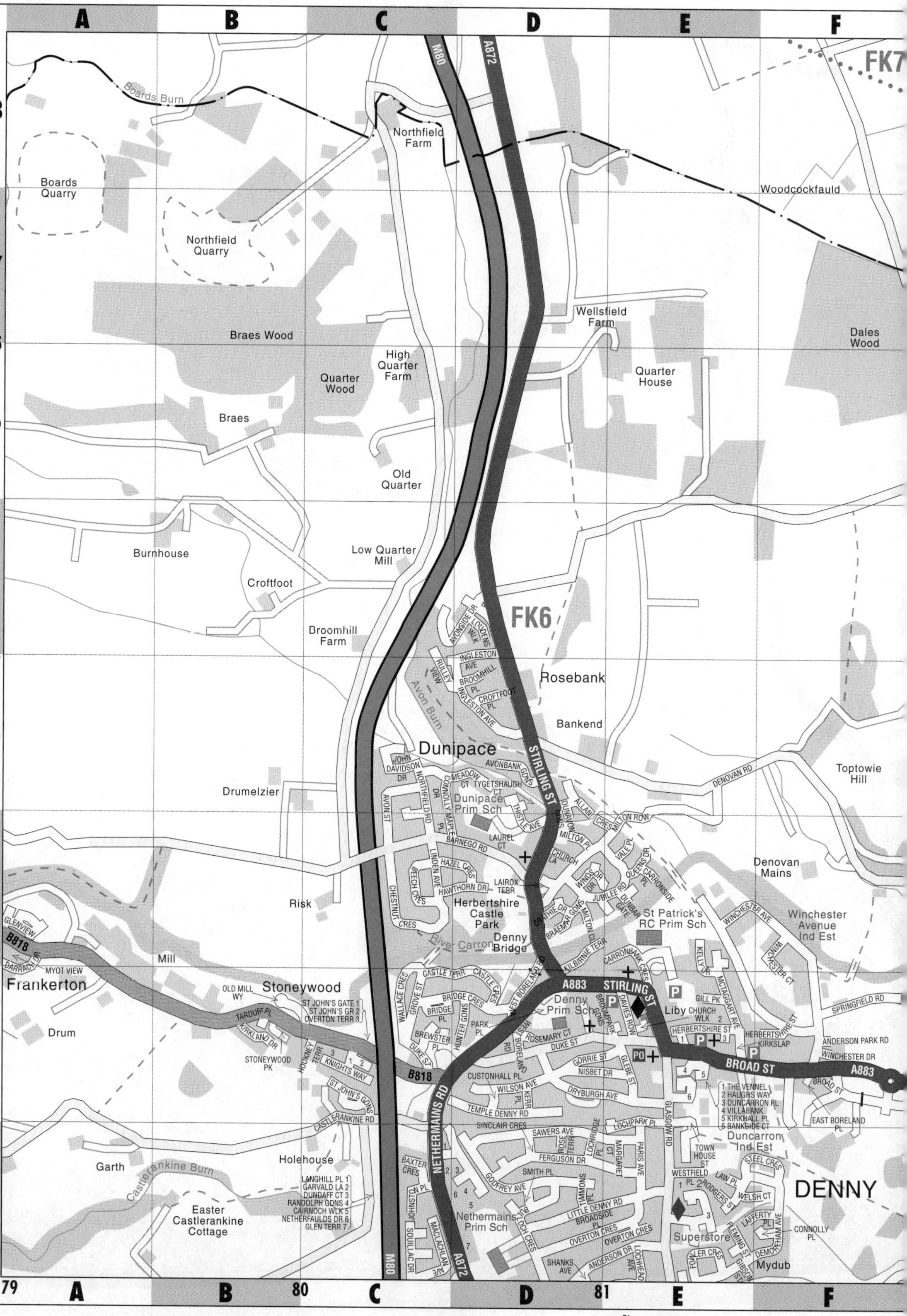

57

E1
1 CONROY CT
2 Westfield Trad Est
3 CRUIKSHANK'S CT

20
38

A
B
C
D
E
F
8
7
85
6
5
84
4
3
83
2
1
82
A9
FK7
GLEN RD
Tor Burn
Glenside
Hollings
BOGEND RD
Langlands
GLEN RD
CASTLE CRES
NEWINGTON LA
FORRESTER GAIT
The Rocks
Tappoch
Torwood
Whinnie Muir
Tor Wood
Torwood Castle
Torwoodhead
STIRLING RD
FK5
CH
Doghillock
Tod Hill
M876
Pamphellgoat Wood
FK6
A9
STIRLING RD
2
M876
Baxter Wood
Denovan
OLD DENNY RD
DENOVAN RD
Oakbank Wood
Sewage Works
Big Wood
H
Forth Valley Royal
Kirkland
River Carron
Evergreen Trailer Ct
BEECH TREE PARK
PH
Works
Larbert House
Househill Farm
Cemy
Headswood house
DENNY RD
B905
M876
A883
B905
82
A
B
83
C
D
84
E
F

58
38

37
21

A B C D E F
8 7 85 6 5 84 4 3 83 2 1 82
85 86 87
M9
Pow Burn
Bogend
BOGEND RD
Blairs
FK2
Kersebrock
Drum of Kinnaird
Hill of Kinnaird
8
M876
North Inches
Titlandhill
HAMILTON RD
Glenbervie House
Shiels Farm
Kinnaird Prim Sch
Bellsdyke
ANTONSHILL RDBT
A88
B902
BELLSDYKE RD
Central Park Bsns Pk
CENTRAL BVD
Hotel
North Broomage
Glenbervie Bsns Pk
STIRLING RD
A9
INCHES RDBT
ROBERT KAY PL
FK5
Stenhousemuir
Antonshill
Cemy
KING ST
Ochilview Park (Stenhousemuir FC & E Stirlingshire FC)
Stenhousemuir Prim Sch
Larbert
MAIN ST
CH
Liby
Crownest Park
Carron Hill
Carrongrange Sch
Larbert High Sch
Carron Dams
Works
Lochside House
Larbert Village Prim Sch
B2
1 EARDLEY PL
2 CRAWHALL PL
3 PEPLOE AVE
4 ERSKINE LA
5 ELLIOT PL
6 TURPIE DR
SIR JOHN GRAHAM CT 1
RUSSELL HILL CT 2
THE BUNGALOWS
DENNY RD
B905
River Carron
ASHCROFT HO
South Broomage
Ladeside Prim Sch
DOBBIE AVE
STENHOUSE RD
LADYWELL CT
NORTH BROOMAGE RDBT
TAPPOCH PL
OLD BELLSDYKE RD
OLD DENNY RD
GRAHAM AVE
SIR WILLIAM WALLACE CT
CHARLOTTE HILL CT
MARION WILSON VIEW
BURNHEAD RD
QUEEN'S DR
BALFOUR CRES
ALLANBANK RD
ELIZABETH AVE
ADAM GROSSERT CT
GLADSTONE RD
TRYST RD
JAMIESON AVE
CARRONGRANGE AVE
CARRONGRANGE GDNS
LAMOND VIEW
HILLARY RD
CEDAR GR
SOUTH BROOMAGE AVE
TAYLOR'S RD
BROOMHILL AVE
EDWARD AVE
BLENHEIM PL
HOLYROOD PL
WESTMINSTER PL
STRATHMIGLO PL
ALLOA RD
DUNBAR AVE
NEIDPATH DR

37
59

22
40

A B C D E F
8 7 85 6 5 84 4 3 83 2 1 82
88 89 90
Letham
Lochs of Airth
Motel
A905
M876
LETHAM COTTS
Letham Farm
North Langdyke
Southfield
North Bellsdyke
Kinnaird House
M876
South Bellsdyke
BRACKENLEES RD
A88
BELLSDYKE RD
Muirdyke Burn
FK2
Bensfield
Howkerse
Kirkton
Carronshore Prim Sch
BRACKENLEES RD
Roughlands
Carronshore
Westertown
Bothkennar Prim Sch
PH
Skinflats
BOTHKENNAR RD
NEW CARRON RD
B905
FK5
Carron Prim Sch
Carrongrove Bsns Pk
Carron
Carron House
Backrow Farm
PO
River Carron
Yonderhaugh
FALKIRK
Langlees
Sewage Works
FK3
M9
A905
B902
CORONATION PL
POTTER PL
ZETLAND PL
NEWTON AVE
EDWARD PL
CAMPIE TERR
BINNIE PL
1 BARRA PL
2 ROXBURGH PL
3 NEIDPATH DR
4 CRATHES AVE
CHURCH ST 1
WADDELL ST 2
MONTGOMERY WELL
MONTGOMERY CRES
MONTGOMERY PL

60
40

39
23

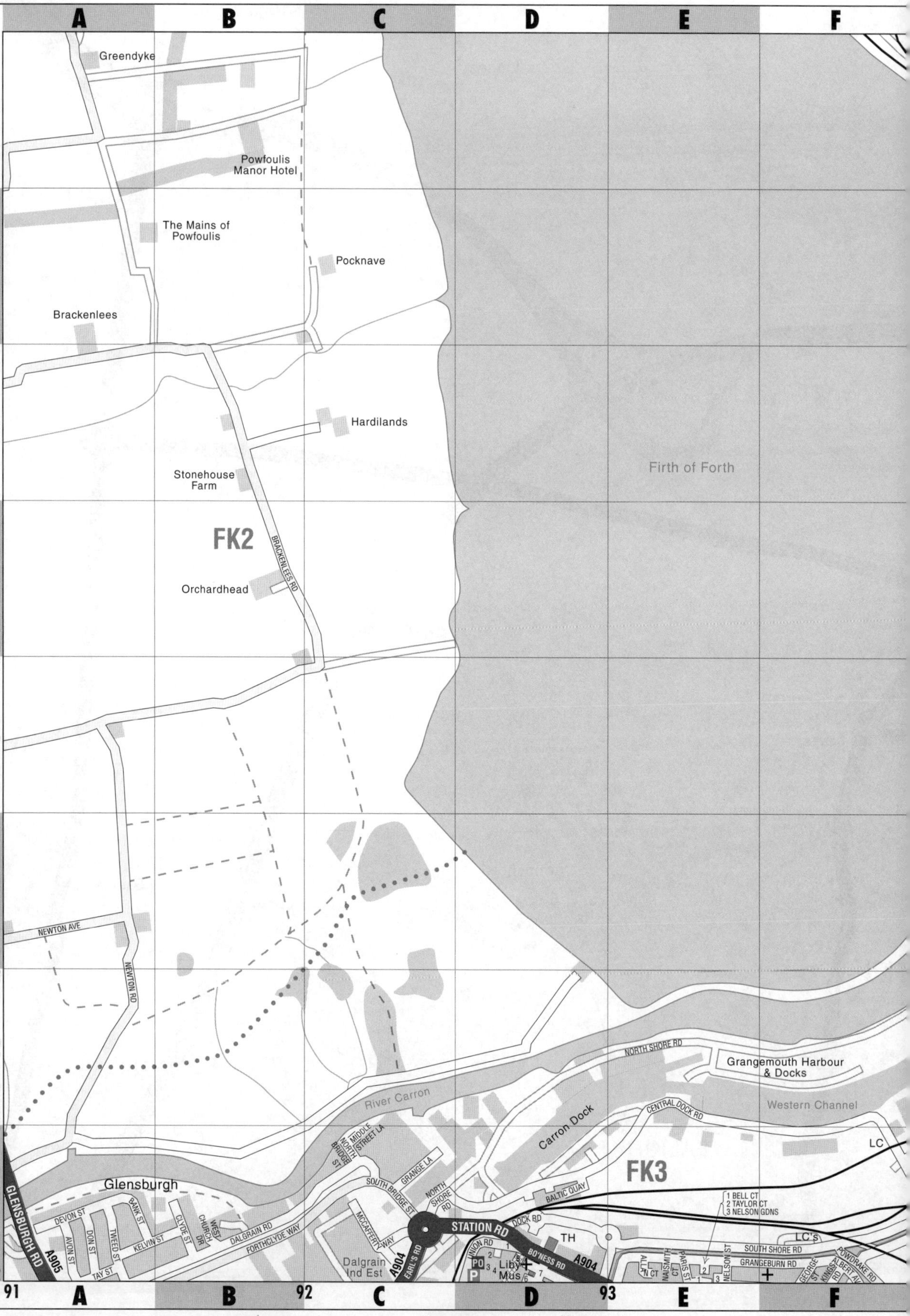
A
B
C
D
E
F
8
7
85
6
5
84
4
3
83
2
1
82
91
92
93
Greendyke
Powfoulis
Manor Hotel
The Mains of
Powfoulis
Pocknave
Brackenlees
Hardilands
Firth of Forth
Stonehouse
Farm
FK2
BRACKENLEES RD
Orchardhead
NEWTON AVE
NEWTON RD
River Carron
NORTH SHORE RD
Grangemouth Harbour
& Docks
Western Channel
Carron Dock
CENTRAL DOCK RD
LC
FK3
MIDDLE ST
NORTH BRIDGE ST
STREET LA
GRANGE LA
SOUTH BRIDGE ST
NORTH SHORE RD
BALTIC QUAY
Glensburgh
GLENSBURGH RD
A905
DEVON ST
BANK ST
AVON ST
DON ST
TWEED ST
KELVIN ST
CLYDE ST
CHURCH DR
WEST
DALGRAIN RD
FORTHCLYDE WAY
TAY ST
MCCAFFERTY WAY
Dalgrain
Ind Est
A904
EARL'S RD
STATION RD
DOCK RD
UNION RD
BO'NESS RD
A904
TH
PO
P
Liby
Mus
1 BELL CT
2 TAYLOR CT
3 NELSON GDNS
LC's
SOUTH SHORE RD
GRANGEBURN RD
ALLAN CT
NAISMITH CT
PARIS ST
NELSON ST
GEORGE ST
KINGS RD
ALBERT AV
POWDRAKE RD

39
61

D1
1 CHARING CROSS
2 YORK LA
3 YORK SQ
4 YORK ARC
5 LA PORTE PREC
6 ANNFIELD PL
7 LIBRARY LA

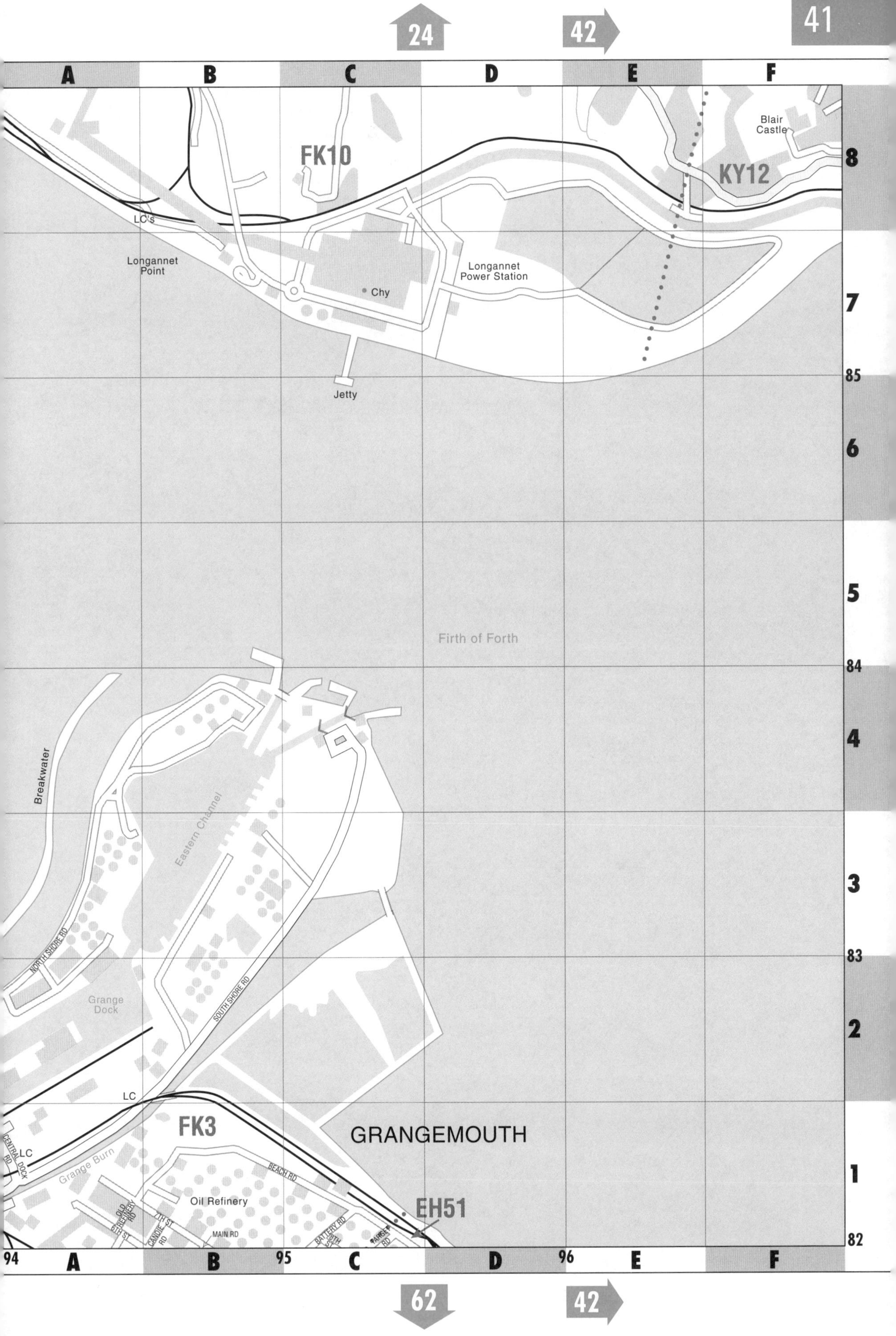
24
42
A
B
C
D
E
F
FK10
Blair Castle
KY12
8
LC's
Longannet Point
Longannet Power Station
Chy
7
85
Jetty
6
5
Firth of Forth
84
4
Breakwater
Eastern Channel
3
NORTH SHORE RD
83
Grange Dock
SOUTH SHORE RD
2
LC
FK3
GRANGEMOUTH
CENTRAL DOCK RD
LC
Grange Burn
BEACH RD
1
Oil Refinery
EH51
OLD REFINERY RD
7TH ST
CANDIE RD
MAIN RD
BATTERY RD
82
94
95
96
62
42

41
25

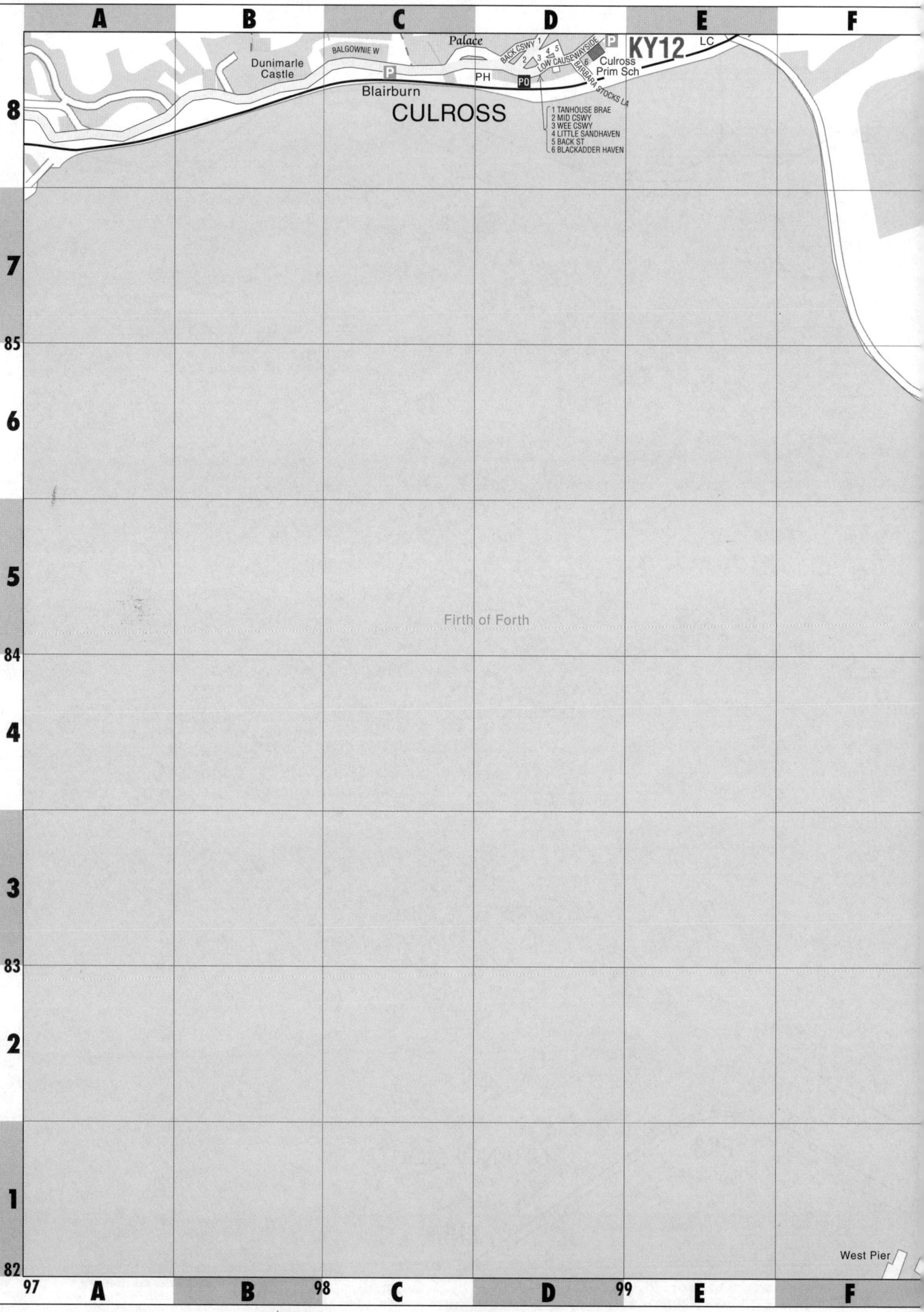
A
B
C
D
E
F
Dunimarle Castle
BALGOWNIE W
Palace
BACK CSWY
LOW CAUSEWAYSIDE
BARBARA STOCKS LA
KY12
LC
Culross Prim Sch
PH
PO
Blairburn
CULROSS
1 TANHOUSE BRAE
2 MID CSWY
3 WEE CSWY
4 LITTLE SANDHAVEN
5 BACK ST
6 BLACKADDER HAVEN
Firth of Forth
West Pier
8
7
85
6
5
84
4
3
83
2
1
82
97
98
99

41
63

26
44

A
B
C
D
E
F
CRAIGFLOWER VIEW
LOGAN RD
KAY RD
ADIA RD
GOLLET WAY
The Craig
KY12
Windmill Cottage
8
Torry Bay Nature Reserve
Church
KY12
Preston Island
Torry Bay
7
85
6
5
84
Firth of Forth
4
3
83
2
1
82
00
A
B
01
C
D
02
E
F

64
44

43
27

A
B
C
D
E
F
8
7
85
6
5
84
4
3
83
2
1
82
03
04
05
Muirside Cottage
MUIRSIDE LA
A985
Muirside
Mire End
Bankhead Farm
KY11
CRAIGWELL PATH
Crombie
Crombie Prim Sch
KY12
CENTRAL RD
MAIN RD
Shoreside
Bullions Farm Cottages
FARM RD
LINK RD
ORCHARD GR
LITTLE FOOTHORN
Stripeside
Bullions
Crombie Farm
ORDNANCE RD
Waukmill Cottages
A985
Kiln Hill
Crombie Point
Waulkmill
Crombie Pier
CAMP RD
DM Crombie
KY11
Kinniny Braes
Ironmill Bay
Crombie Pier
Jetty
Firth of Forth

43
65

28
46
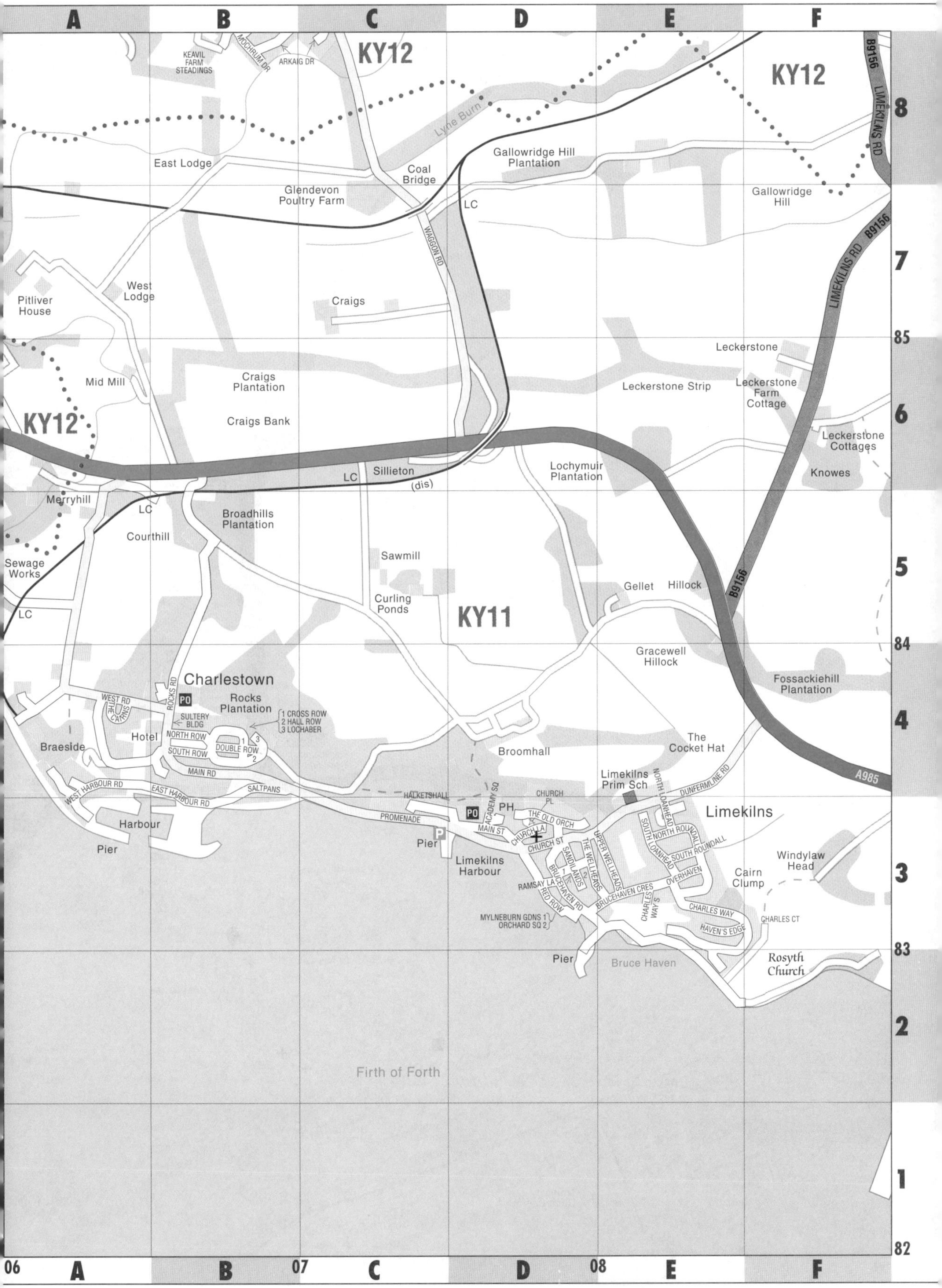
A
B
C
D
E
F
KY12
KEAVIL FARM STEADINGS
MOCHRUM DR
ARKAIG DR
KY12
B9156
LIMEKILNS RD
Lyne Burn
East Lodge
Gallowridge Hill Plantation
Coal Bridge
Glendevon Poultry Farm
LC
Gallowridge Hill
WAGGON RD
LIMEKILNS RD
B9156
West Lodge
Pitliver House
Craigs
Leckerstone
Mid Mill
Craigs Plantation
Leckerstone Strip
Leckerstone Farm Cottage
KY12
Craigs Bank
Leckerstone Cottages
Lochymuir Plantation
Knowes
Sillieton
(dis)
LC
Merryhill
LC
Broadhills Plantation
Courthill
Sawmill
Sewage Works
Gellet
Hillock
B9156
Curling Ponds
KY11
LC
Gracewell Hillock
Charlestown
Fossackiehill Plantation
WEST RD
THE CAIRNS
ROCKS RD
PO
Rocks Plantation
SULTERY BLDG
1 CROSS ROW
2 HALL ROW
3 LOCHABER
Braeside
Hotel
NORTH ROW
DOUBLE ROW
SOUTH ROW
Broomhall
The Cocket Hat
MAIN RD
Limekilns Prim Sch
A985
WEST HARBOUR RD
EAST HARBOUR RD
SALTPANS
HALKETSHALL
ACADEMY SQ
CHURCH PL
NORTH LOANHEAD
DUNFERMLINE RD
PH
Limekilns
PROMENADE
PO
THE OLD ORCH
Harbour
MAIN ST
CHURCH LA
NORTH ROUNDALL
Pier
P
Pier
CHURCH ST
SOUTH LOANHEAD
SOUTH ROUNDALL
UPPER WELLHEADS
THE WELLHEADS
SANDILANDS
Limekilns Harbour
Windylaw Head
Cairn Clump
OVERHAVEN
RAMSAY LA
BRUCEHAVEN RD
BRUCEHAVEN CRES
RED ROW
CHARLES WAY
CHARLES WAY
MYLNEBURN GDNS 1
ORCHARD SQ 2
CHARLES CT
HAVEN'S EDGE
Pier
Bruce Haven
Rosyth Church
Firth of Forth
8
7
85
6
5
84
4
3
83
2
1
82
06
07
08
66
46

45
29

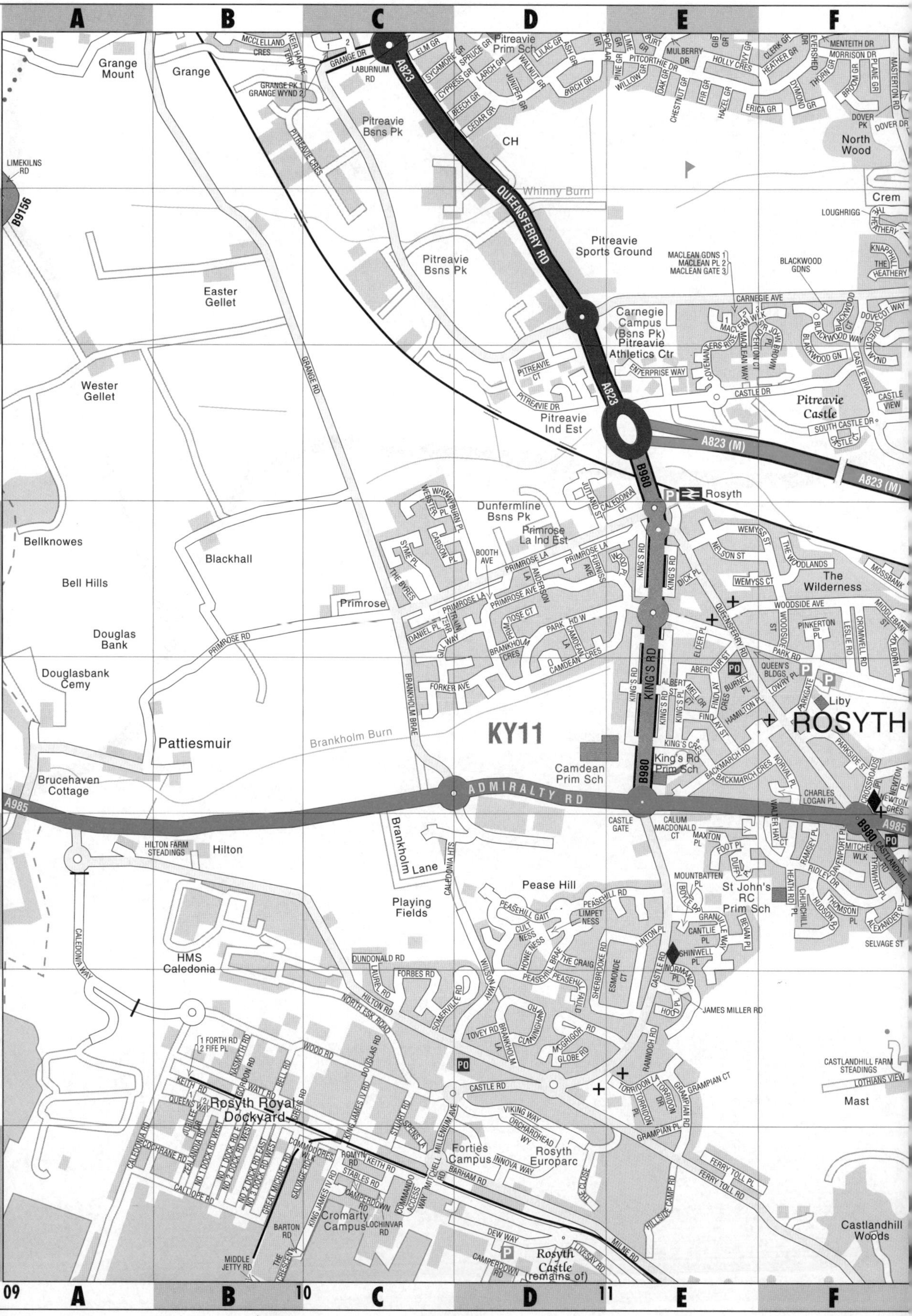
A
B
C
D
E
F
8
7
85
6
5
84
4
3
83
2
1
82
09
10
11
Grange Mount
Grange
MCCLELLAND CRES
KEIR HARDIE TERR
GRANGE DR
LABURNUM RD
GRANGE PK 1
GRANGE WYND 2
PITREAVIE CRES
A823
Pitreavie Prim Sch
Pitreavie Bsns Pk
CH
ELM GR
SYCAMORE GR
CYPRESS GR
BEECH GR
CEDAR GR
SPRUCE GR
LARCH GR
JUNIPER GR
WALNUT GR
LILAC GR
ASH GR
BIRCH GR
POPLAR
PINE GR
LIME GR
WILLOW GR
PITCORTHIE DR
BURT
MULBERRY DR
OAK GR
CHESTNUT GR
FIR GR
HAZEL GR
HOLLY CRES
GIB GR
IVY GR
CLERK GR
HEATHER GR
ERICA GR
DYMOND GR
EVERSHED DR
MENTEITH DR
MORRISON DR
THORN GR
BROOM GR
PLANE GR
MASTERTON RD
DOVER PK
DOVER DR
North Wood
Crem
LOUGHRIGG
THE HEATHERY
KNAPPHILL
LIMEKILNS RD
B9156
Whinny Burn
QUEENSFERRY RD
Pitreavie Sports Ground
Pitreavie Bsns Pk
Easter Gellet
MACLEAN GDNS 1
MACLEAN PL 2
MACLEAN GATE 3
BLACKWOOD GDNS
CARNEGIE AVE
Carnegie Campus (Bsns Pk)
Pitreavie Athletics Ctr
MACLEAN WLK
MACLEAN WAY
COVENANTERS RISE
VERTON CT
JOHN BROWN
BLACKWOOD CT
BLACKWOOD WAY
BLACKWOOD GN
DOVECOT WAY
DOVECOT WYND
CASTLE BRAE
ENTERPRISE WAY
CASTLE DR
Pitreavie Castle
CASTLE VIEW
SOUTH CASTLE DR
CASTLE
PITREAVIE CT
PITREAVIE DR
Wester Gellet
GRANGE RD
Pitreavie Ind Est
A823 (M)
B980
Rosyth
JUTLAND ST
CALEDONIA CT
WEBSTER PL
WHINNYBURN PL
CARSON PL
SYME PL
THE BYRES
Dunfermline Bsns Pk
Primrose La Ind Est
BOOTH AVE
PRIMROSE LA
ANDERSON LA
PRIMROSE AVE
FURNISS AVE
WOOD PL
KING'S RD
WEMYSS ST
NELSON ST
DICK PL
WEMYSS CT
THE WOODLANDS
The Wilderness
MOSSBANK
Bellknowes
Blackhall
Bell Hills
Primrose
DANIEL PL
TRAIN TERR
GILL WAY
BRANKHOLM CRES
ROSE CT
PARK HD W
CAMDEAN LA
CAMDEAN CRES
FORKER AVE
Douglas Bank
PRIMROSE RD
Douglasbank Cemy
WOODSIDE AVE
QUEENSFERRY RD
ELDER PL
PINKERTON PL
LESLIE RD
CROMWELL RD
MIDDLEBANK ST
KYLBORN PL
PARK RD
ABERLOUR ST
QUEEN'S BLDGS
LOWRY PL
PARKGATE
Liby
ALBERT ST
MELLOR CT
FINDLAY CRES
BURNEY PL
HAMILTON PL
KING'S PL
KING'S CRES
ROSYTH
BRANKHOLM BRAE
Brankholm Burn
KY11
Pattiesmuir
Camdean Prim Sch
King's Rd Prim Sch
BACKMARCH RD
BACKMARCH CRES
NORVAL PL
PARKSIDE ST
CROSSROADS
NEWTON PL
NEWTON CRES
Bruceaven Cottage
ADMIRALTY RD
A985
CHARLES LOGAN PL
CASTLE GATE
CALUM MACDONALD CT
MAXTON PL
FOOT PL
WALKER HAY
WALTER HAY CT
RAMSEY PL
DAVENPORT PL
MITCHELL WLK
RIDLEY DR
CASTLANDHILL
HILTON FARM STEADINGS
Hilton
Brankholm Lane
CALEDONIA HTS
Pease Hill
Playing Fields
PEASEHILL RD
PEASEHILL GAIT
LIMPET NESS
CULT NESS
HOWE NESS
THE CRAIG
PEASEHILL BRAE
MOUNTBATTEN PL
BOYLE PL
DUFFY PL
St John's RC Prim Sch
HEATH RD
CHURCHILL PL
HUDSON RD
THOMSON PL
ALEXANDER PL
SELVAGE ST
CANTLIE PL
GRANVILLE WAY
BEJAN PL
SHINWELL PL
NORMAND PL
CASTLE RD
SHERBROOKE RD
ESMONDE CT
LINTON PL
HMS Caledonia
CALEDONIA WAY
DUNDONALD RD
LAUREL RD
FORBES RD
HILTON RD
NORTH ESK ROAD
SOMERVILLE RD
WILSON WAY
CUNNINGHAM RD
TOVEY RD
BRANKHOLM LA
MCGREGOR RD
GLOBE RD
RANNOCH RD
JAMES MILLER RD
HOOD PL
1 FORTH RD
2 FIFE PL
NASMYTH RD
GORDON RD
WATT RD
BELL RD
WOOD RD
DOUGLAS RD
KEITH RD
QUEENS WAY
Rosyth Royal Dockyard
CASTLE RD
TORRIDON LA
TORRIDON PL
TORRIDON DR
GRAMPIAN CT
GRAMPIAN RD
GRAMPIAN PL
CASTLANDHILL FARM STEADINGS
LOTHIANS VIEW
Mast
CALEDONIA RD
COCHRANE RD
ZEALANDIA RD
JUBILEE
NO 1 DOCK RD WEST
NO 1 DOCK RD EAST
NO 2 DOCK RD WEST
NO 2 DOCK RD EAST
NO 3 DOCK RD WEST
CALLIOPE RD
GREAT MICHAEL RD
SALVAGE RD
COMMODORES WLK
KING JAMES IV RD
STUART RD
SPENS LA
MILLENNIUM AVE
VIKING WAY
ORCHARDHEAD WY
Forties Campus
Rosyth Europarc
INNOVA WAY
ROMYN RD
KEITH RD
STABLES RD
CAMPERDOWN RD
COMMANDO ACCESS WAY
MITCHELL RD
BARHAM RD
FERRY TOLL PL
FERRY TOLL RD
HILLSIDE CAMP RD
Cromarty Campus
LOCHINVAR RD
BARTON RD
THE CRESCENT
MIDDLE JETTY RD
DEW WAY
CAMPERDOWN RD
Rosyth Castle (remains of)
LIVESAY RD
MILNE RD
Castlandhill Woods

45
67

30
48

C8
1 MIDDLEBANK AVE
2 MIDDLEBANK CRES
3 PINKERTON ST
4 PINKERTON AVE

A
B
C
D
E
F
8
7
85
6
5
84
4
3
83
2
1
82
12
13
14
KY11
INVERKEITHING
B916
ABERDOUR RD
Masterton Prim Sch
Dover Heights
Mid Duloch
Old Duloch
Annfield Cottage
ANNFIELD FARM RD
Annfield
Duloch Home Farm
Pinkerton Burn
Perniehall Plantation
Castle Hill
Strawberry Bank
Fordell Burn
Fordell Castle
FORDELL GDNS
Clockluine Wood
Balbougie Glen
CLOCKLUINE RD
Fordell Glen
Balbougie
M90
B981
Mastertown
MIDDLEBANK HOLDINGS
Middlebank Welfare Ctr (SSPCA)
1 SPRINGWOOD
2 WINDLEBROOK
3 LOUGHRIGG
CARNEGIE AVE
DOVECOT WAY
MASTERTON ROAD
CASTLE BRAE
A823 (M)
Dales Farm Cottages
The Dales
Keithing Burn
Pargillis Bridge
Cemy
Dalgety Bay
A921
Hillend
WOODEND GDNS
PH
MAIN ST
SCHOOL LA
SCOTS MILL PL
MAIN ST W
LETHAM HILL AVE
Inverkeithing North Junc
East Junc
NORTH RD
MOSSBANK
Park Rd Prim Sch
PARK RD
Belleknowes Ind Est
KIRKGATE
Central Junc
Burnside Bsns Ct
Bois Bridge
A921 ADMIRALTY RD
ADMIRALTY RD
A985
NEWTON CRES
Inverkeithing
Inverkeithing High Sch
HILLEND RD
THE AVENUE
SPENCERFIELD STEADINGS
Inverkeithing Prim Sch & Carnegie Prim Sch
Letham Farm
Letham Hill Wood
FARMSTEAD RD
WAYFARERS WAY
CROFTAN RIGG
ROODS CRES
BINNING RD
Fairy Kirk
HILLWOOD TERR
B980
ALEXANDER PL
CHURCH ST
HIGH ST
KING ST
TOWNHALL ST
ALMA ST
GRAY PL
BORELAND RD
EGLINTON PL
COCHRANE AVE
Castlandhill
CASTLANDHILL RD
DUNFERMLINE WYND
LOTHIANS VIEW
Mast
Muckle Hill
MANSE PL
FRIARY CT
Civic Ctr, Liby & Her Ctr
HAMILTON TERR 1
MERCHANTS WAY 2
PRESTON CRES
Preston Hill
Seafield House
Fife Coastal Path
SPINNAKER WY
HALYARD RISE
SPINNAKER WAY
THE MOORINGS
St David's Harbour
South Pier
ROSEBERY CT
LINK RD
Mill
GLEBE TERR
GLEBE PK
Cemy
Little Hill
HOPE ST
Inner Bay
Pier
Pier
East Ness
Inverkeithing Bay
FERRYHILL RD
Whinny Hill
A90
P&R
CRUICKNESS RD
West Ness

68
48

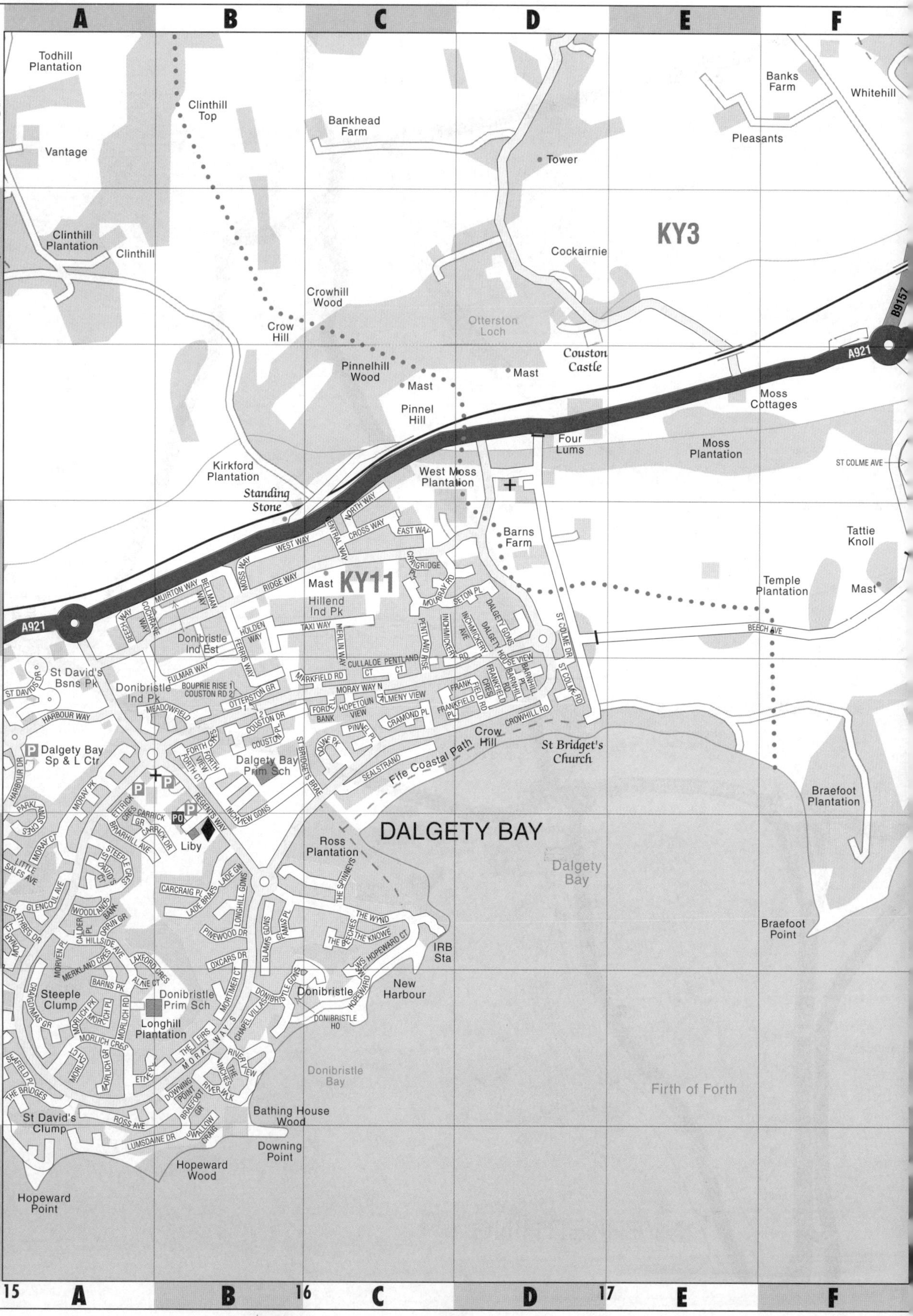
A
B
C
D
E
F
8
7
85
6
5
84
4
3
83
2
1
82
15
16
17
Todhill Plantation
Clinthill Top
Bankhead Farm
Banks Farm
Whitehill
Pleasants
Vantage
Tower
KY3
Clinthill Plantation
Clinthill
Cockairnie
Crowhill Wood
Crow Hill
Otterston Loch
Couston Castle
Mast
B9157
A921
Pinnelhill Wood
Pinnel Hill
Moss Cottages
Four Lums
Moss Plantation
ST COLME AVE
Kirkford Plantation
West Moss Plantation
Standing Stone
Barns Farm
Tattie Knoll
KY11
Hillend Ind Pk
Temple Plantation
BEECH AVE
ST COLME DR
St David's Bsns Pk
Donibristle Ind Est
Donibristle Ind Pk
HARBOUR WAY
Dalgety Bay Sp & L Ctr
Dalgety Bay Prim Sch
Fife Coastal Path
St Bridget's Church
Braefoot Plantation
Liby
DALGETY BAY
Ross Plantation
Dalgety Bay
Braefoot Point
IRB Sta
New Harbour
Donibristle
Steeple Clump
Donibristle Prim Sch
Longhill Plantation
Donibristle Bay
Firth of Forth
Bathing House Wood
St David's Clump
Downing Point
Hopeward Wood
Hopeward Point

32
50

A
B
C
D
E
F
B9157
A921
Inch Marton Plantation
Black Lodge
Hillside Sch
Easter Aberdour
Aberdour
Mill Farm
ST FILLANS CRES
ST FILLANS GR
CULLALO CRES
THE GLEBE
LOWER GLEBE
MURRELL RD
HUMBIE TERR
1 MURREL TERR
2 CASTLE VIEW
3 MURRAY PL
MORAYVALE
MAIN ST
Aberdour Prim Sch
The Heughs
MILL FARM RD
Nether Bouprie
KY3
Cemy
Hotel
Aberdour Castle
HOME PK
HAWKCRAIG RD
Long Haugh
Silversands Bay
TELNY PL
LIVINGSTON LA
4 HEWITT PL
5 STATION PL
ST COLME CRES
MANSE PL
Birkhill Wood
HIGH ST
PO
PARK LA
Liby
Aberdour
Harbour
Pier
INVERKEITHING RD
McLAUCHLAN RISE
COUNTESS OF MORAY HOSPITAL
SHORE RD
MANSE ST
SEASIDE PL
BELLHOUSE RD
DOVECOT PK
INCH AVE
Wester Aberdour
Forth View
Hawkcraig Point
ST COLME AVE
Skellies Plantation
Downans Plantation
CH
Cauldback Hill
Fife Coastal Path
Port Haven
Bell Rock
BEECH AVE
Primrose Wood
St Colme House
ST COLME AVE
Barnhill Bay
Charleshill Clump
Firth of Forth
Charles Hill
Oil Terminal
Ferny Hill
Braefoot Bay
Piers
Mortimer's Deep
Car Craig
St Colm's Abbey
(remains of)
Inchcolm
KY3
8
7
85
6
5
84
4
3
83
2
1
82
18
19
20

49
33

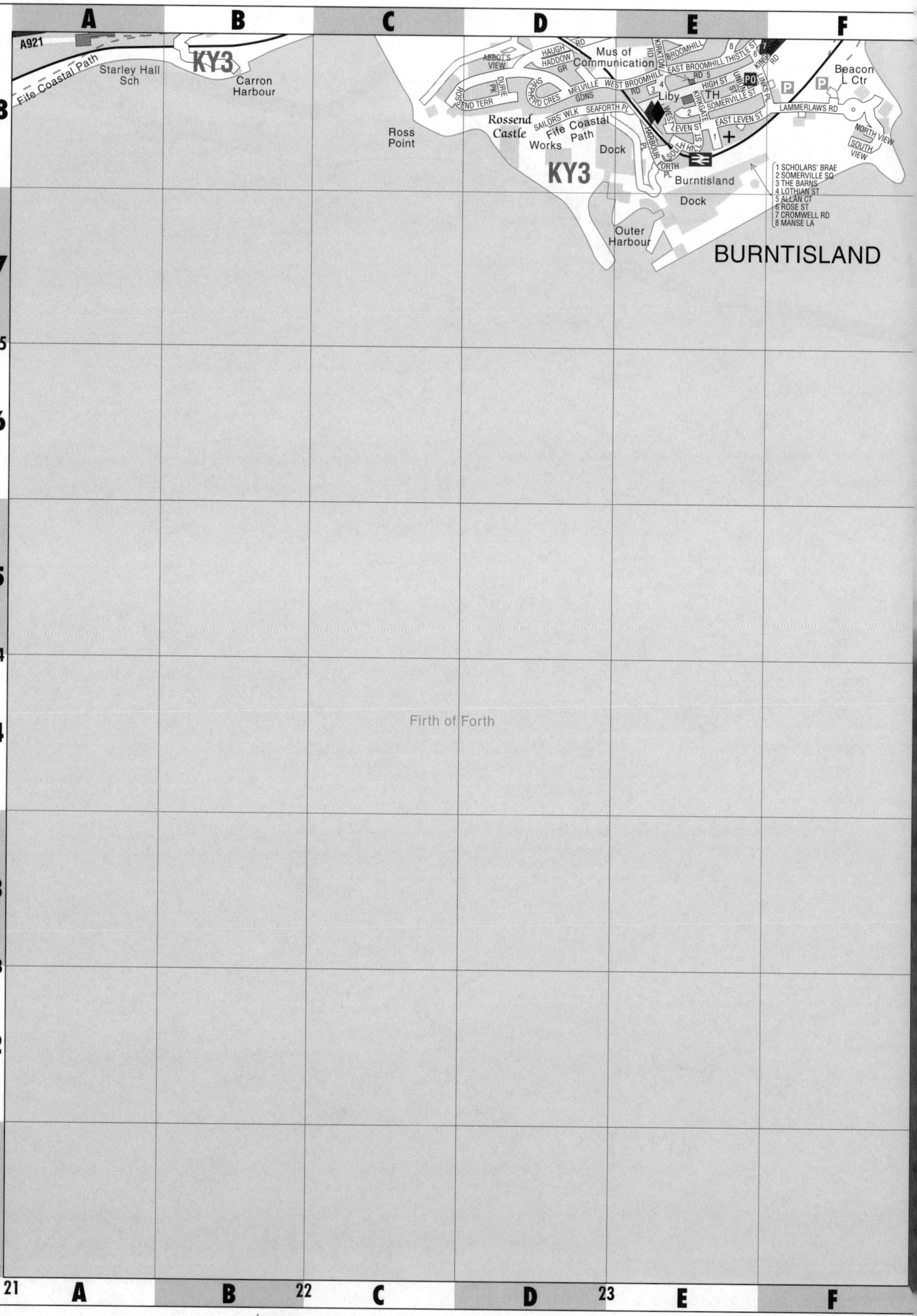
A
B
C
D
E
F
A921
Fife Coastal Path
Starley Hall
Sch
KY3
Carron
Harbour
Ross
Point
ABBOT'S
VIEW
HAUGH
HADDOW
GR
RD
Mus of
Communication
KIRKTON
RD
BROOMHILL
EAST BROOMHILL
RD
THISTLE ST
KINGHORN
RD
ROSSEND TERR
PK
DURIE
SHEPHERD CRES
MELVILLE
GDNS
WEST BROOMHILL
RD
HIGH ST
UNION
ST
PO
LINKS PL
Beacon
L Ctr
Liby
TH
KIRKGATE
SOMERVILLE ST
LAMMERLAWS RD
Rossend
Castle
SAILORS' WLK
SEAFORTH PL
Fife Coastal
Path
Works
WEST
LEVEN ST
EAST LEVEN ST
NORTH VIEW
SOUTH
VIEW
Dock
HARBOUR
PL
SOUTH HILL ST
FORTH
PL
KY3
Burntisland
Dock
Outer
Harbour
BURNTISLAND
1 SCHOLARS' BRAE
2 SOMERVILLE SQ
3 THE BARNS
4 LOTHIAN ST
5 ALLAN CT
6 ROSE ST
7 CROMWELL RD
8 MANSE LA
8
7
85
6
5
84
4
Firth of Forth
3
83
2
1
82
21
22
23

49

52

A
B
C
D
E
F
8
7
85
6
5
84
4
3
83
2
1
82
45
46
47
Firth of Forth
Gullane Bay
Gullane Bents
Gullane Point
The Old Man
Jophies Neuk
Maggie's Loop
MARINE TERR
SANDY LOAN
SANDY LA
HILL RD
WARREN HILL
NISBET RD
HUMMEL RD
Gullane Hill
WHIM RD
WEST LINKS RD
EH31
Gullane Links
A198

71

52

51

A
B
C
D
E
F
8
7
85
6
5
84
4
3
83
2
1
82
48
49
50
Firth of Forth
Hanging Rocks
Marina Villa
White Knowe
Eldbotle Wood
Sandy Knowe
North Links
Strabauchlinn Knowe
West Links
CH
Eldbotle Park
Duncan's Plantation
Freshwater Haven
Black Rocks
Rabbit Warren
Mast
Yapin Hill
Jamie's Neuk
Broad Wood
Archerfield
Home Farm
EH39
West Strip
Hotel
Halfmoon Plantation
Gullane Bents
EH31
Muirfield
A198
B1345
QUEENSTONBANK
MAIN ST
Scottish Fire Service Coll
WEST FENTON GAIT
Gullane Prim Sch
Liby
PO
Gullane
Saltcoats
Mill Burn
SALTCOATS FARM COTTS
1 LAMMERVIEW TERR
2 MAULE TERR
3 WAVERLEY HO N
4 WAVERLEY HO S
5 LAMMERMUIR CT
6 BOWHILL CT
7 MUIRFIELD APARTMENTS
THE HAWTHORNS
THE FINCHES
THE FALCONS
VARDON RD
DUNCUR RD
ERSKINE LOAN
ERSKINE RD
HOPETOUN PK
MUIRFIELD PK
MUIRFIELD HO
THE BEECHES
THE ROWANS
THE PINES
BROADGAIT CT
BROADGAIT
BROADGAIT GN
MIDDLESHOT RD
MIDDLE SHOT RD
MARINE TERR
MARINE RD
HOPETOUN TERR
THE PADDOCK
GOOSE GREEN RD
SANDY LOAN
ROSEBERY PL
TEMPLAR LA
TEMPLAR PL
SALTCOATS RD
STANLEY RD
EAST LINKS RD
ARCHERS CT
HALL CRES
HAMILTON RD
HAMILTON CRES
STATION RD
MUIRFIELD STATION
MUIRFIELD TERR
MUIRFIELD CRES
MUIRFIELD DR
MUIRFIELD GDNS
MUIRFIELD GR
GARLETON CT
MUIRFIELD STEADING
FENTOUN GAIT

51

72

54

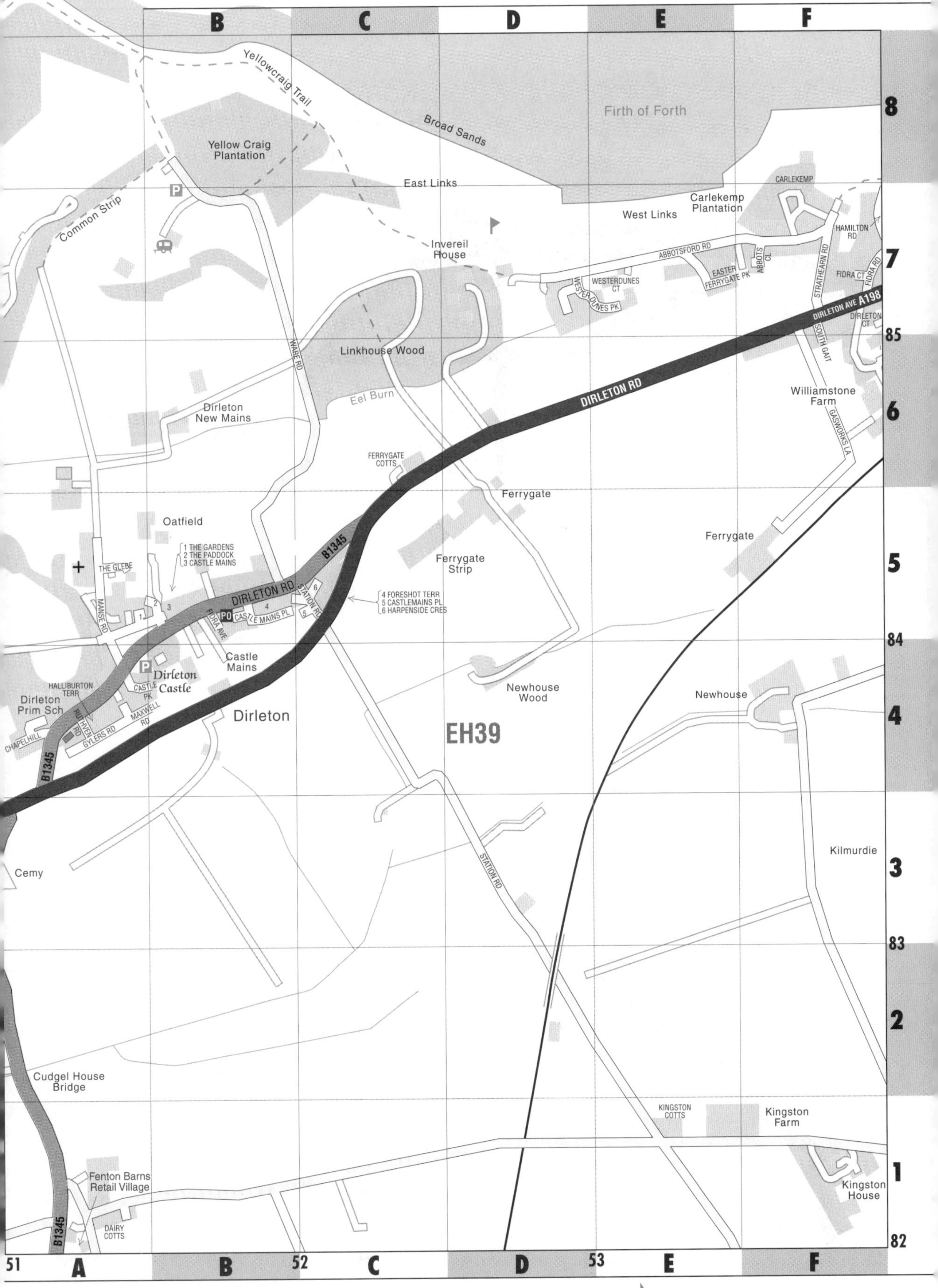
B
C
D
E
F
8
7
85
6
5
84
4
3
83
2
1
82
51
A
B
52
C
D
53
E
F
Yellowcraig Trail
Broad Sands
Firth of Forth
Yellow Craig Plantation
East Links
Common Strip
P
Invereil House
West Links
Carlekemp Plantation
CARLEKEMP
HAMILTON RD
ABBOTSFORD RD
WESTERDUNES CT
WESTER DUNES PK
EASTER FERRYGATE PK
ABBOTS CL
STRATHEARN RD
FIDRA CT
FIDRA RD
DIRLETON AVE A198
DIRLETON CT
SOUTH GAIT
Linkhouse Wood
WARE RD
Eel Burn
DIRLETON RD
Williamstone Farm
GASWORKS LA
Dirleton New Mains
FERRYGATE COTTS
Ferrygate
Oatfield
Ferrygate
1 THE GARDENS
2 THE PADDOCK
3 CASTLE MAINS
THE GLEBE
B1345
Ferrygate Strip
DIRLETON RD
4 FORESHOT TERR
5 CASTLEMAINS PL
6 HARPENSIDE CRES
MANSE RD
PO
CASTLE MAINS PL
FIDRA AVE
STATION RD
Castle Mains
P
Dirleton Castle
HALLIBURTON TERR
CASTLE PK
Newhouse Wood
Newhouse
Dirleton Prim Sch
MAXWELL RD
Dirleton
RUTHVEN RD
GYLERS RD
CHAPELHILL
EH39
B1345
Cemy
Kilmurdie
STATION RD
Cudgel House Bridge
KINGSTON COTTS
Kingston Farm
Fenton Barns Retail Village
Kingston House
B1345
DAIRY COTTS

73

54

53

A
B
C
D
E
F
8
7
85
6
5
84
4
3
83
2
1
82
54
55
56
Firth of Forth
NORTH BERWICK
A7
1 SOUTH HAMILTON RD
2 SPRINGFIELD GDNS
3 SPRINGFIELD CRES
4 DIRLETON CT
B7
1 CRAIGLEITH VIEW
2 WESTGATE CT
3 ABBEY MEWS
4 MARMION CT
Scottish Seabird Ctr
1 BALDERSTONE'S WYND
2 MARKET PL
3 FORTH STREET LA
4 CREEL CT
5 MILSEY CT
6 BRODIE CT
7 QUADRANT LA
West Links
North Berwick Bay
OLD GRANARY
Milsey Bay
CH
Liby
HAMILTON CT
CROMWELL RD
HYNDFORD HO
FIDRA RD
YORK RD
LINKS RD
WEST BAY RD
POINTGARRY RD
STATION HILL
B1346
BEACH RD
FORTH ST
HIGH ST
WESTGATE
DIRLETON AVE
A198
North Berwick
KIRK PORTS
MARINE PAR
TANTALLON TERR
HAUGH RD
EAST RD
East Links
Castle Hill
RHODES COTTS
ST ANDREW ST
MARMION RD
LAW RD
B1347
Edington Cottage
ST BALDRED'S CT
ST BALDRED'S CRES
GLASCLUNE GDNS
GREENHEADS RD
REDHOLM PK
REDHOLM
GLASCLUNE CT
CLIFFORD RD
ST BALDRED'S RD
DUNBAR RD
TANTALLON RD
RHODES PK
LIME GR
BEN SAYERS PK
Cemy
Mill Walk Bsns Pk
Marly Knowe
North Berwick Sp Ctr
MACNAIR AVE
DUNDAS AVE
LADY JANE GDNS
BRODIE AVE
COUPER AVE
CRAIGLEITH AVE
GILBERT AVE
LOCHBRIDGE RD
GLENBURN RD
WISHART AVE
1 QUIDENHAM CT
2 CUNNINGHAM CT
3 DUNCAN CT
MARLY GN
GRANGE RD
North Berwick High Sch
Law Prim Sch
HADDINGTON RD
Gilsland
THE HEUGH
HEUGH BRAE
Heugh
HEUGH STUDY
North Berwick Law
Bonnington
EH39
Thorntree
Wamphray
Highfield
Windmill
BALGONE BARNS COTTS
Balgone Barns
Balgone Heughs
Balgone House
Kingston
Twr (remains of)
CARPERSTANE

53
74

56

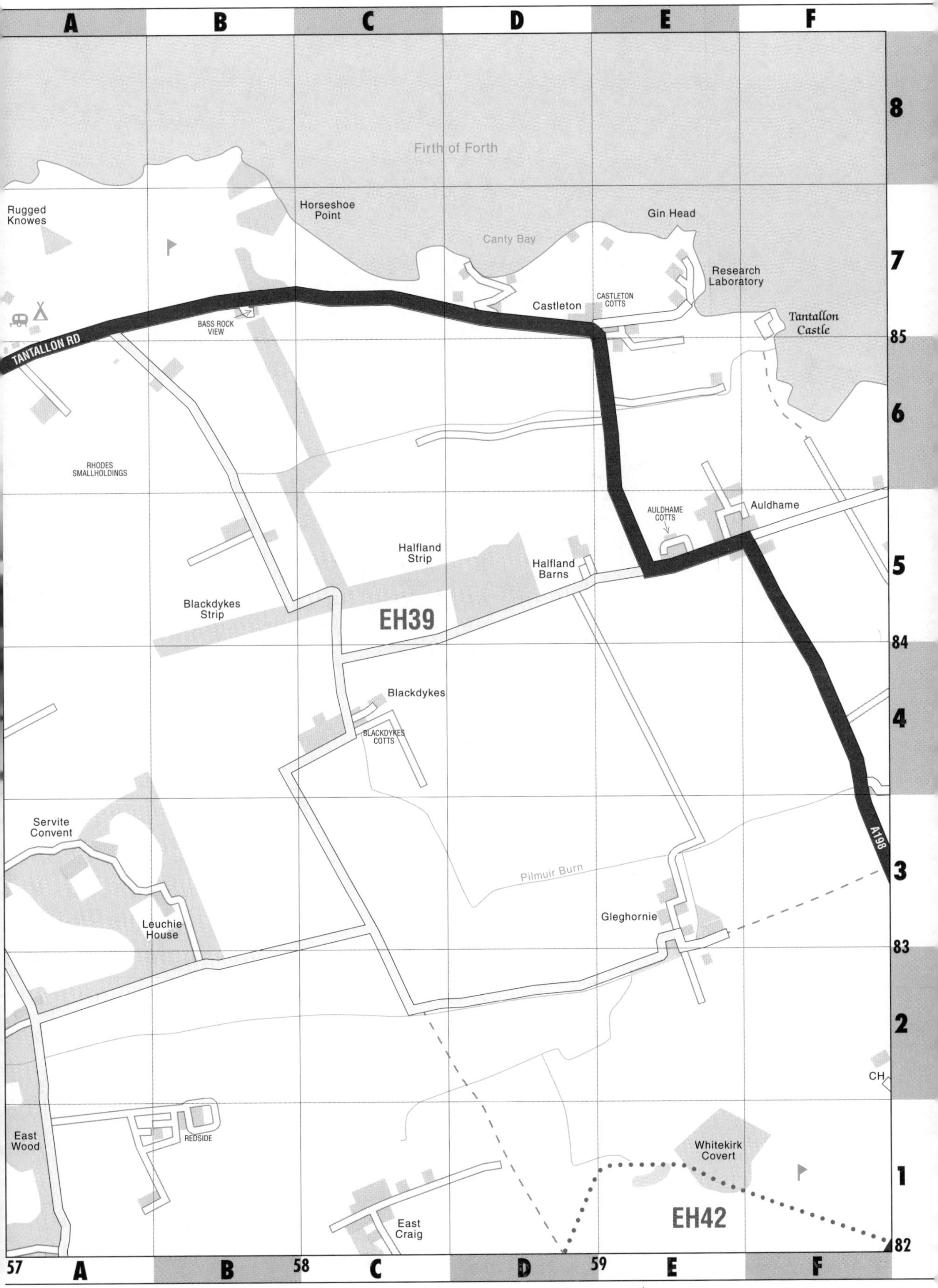
A
B
C
D
E
F
8
7
85
6
5
84
4
3
83
2
1
82
Firth of Forth
Rugged Knowes
Horseshoe Point
Canty Bay
Gin Head
Research Laboratory
Castleton
CASTLETON COTTS
Tantallon Castle
TANTALLON RD
BASS ROCK VIEW
RHODES SMALLHOLDINGS
AULDHAME COTTS
Auldhame
Halfland Strip
Halfland Barns
Blackdykes Strip
EH39
Blackdykes
BLACKDYKES COTTS
A198
Servite Convent
Pilmuir Burn
Gleghornie
Leuchie House
CH
East Wood
REDSIDE
Whitekirk Covert
EH42
East Craig
57
58
59

75

56

55

A
B
C
D
E
F
8
7
85
6
5
84
4
3
83
2
1
82
60
61
62
Auldhame
Cave
SEACLIFF COTTS
Seacliff
Chapel Brae
Crow Wood
Pilmuir Burn
EH39
Scoughall
SCOUGHALL COTTS
A198
Coastguard Lookout
New Mains
Scoughall Links
Peffer Burn
Pefferside
Peffer Sands
EH42

55
76

36
58

A
B
C
D
E
F
8
7
81
6
5
80
4
3
79
2
1
78
Blaefaulds
SOUILLAC DR
SCLANDERSBURN RD
LITHGOW PL
FLEMING CT
OCHIL VIEW
BRAES VIEW
BRAES VIEW
WOODLAND WAY
REEDLANDS DR
BLAEFAULDS CRES
BULLOCH CRES
SHANKS AVE
LONEY CRES
SHANKS AVE
LOCHHEAD AVE
ANDERSON DR
BLAEFAULDS CRES
SUTHERLAND DR
ARGYLL PATH
NETHERMAINS RD
Denny High Sch
DEMOREHAM AVE
GLASGOW RD
KARRIES CT
Little Denny Reservoir
GIBBDUN PL
HEATHERDALE GDNS
HILL HOUSE RD
AFTON DR
GLENBO DR
HILL HO RD
CHACEFIELD WOOD
GLOWRORUM DR
FK6
MYOTHILL RD
HILLCREST PL
LAXDALE DR
LEITH PL
GARVALD RD
SOLWAY DR
HAYFIELD TERR
HAYFIELD TERR
PO
DROVE LOAN CRES
DROVE LOAN
HOME FARM COTTS
Whitehill
LAXDALE DR
ENDRICK DR
EARN PL
Head of Muir
Head of Muir Prim Sch
HAYPARK RD
SPENCE ST 1
CLAREMONT ST 2
HOPEPARK TERR 3
M876
Easter Kelt
KELT RD
LOMOND WAY
ANNET RD
BANKHEAD CRES
LOANHEAD AVE
PARK AVE
BANKVIEW TERR
DENNY RD
Bankhead
BALFOUR ST
ASHLEY ST
DUNCAIRN AVE
MORRISON AVE
GLENMORE DR
ALLOWAY CRES
DUNVEGAN PL
DUNCAN ST
ARBERT RD
KATRINE PL
CRERAN DR
ELMBANK CRES
Mast
Easter Banknock
M80
M876
5
Wester Bankhead
PEARSON AVE
MOCHRAY CT
SINGERS PL
HOGAN PL
DICKBURN CRES
BONNYFIELD RD
A803
BONNYMUIR CRES
Banknock
GLEN VIEW
MONTROSE WAY
RANKIN CRES
RUSSELL PL
BELMONT AVE
WALKER DR
PEARSON PL
BY-PASS RD
BONNYBRIDGE RD
BONNYVALE PL
WOODLEA GDNS
CORONA CRES
EMMA'S WAY
Wester Banknock
Dennyloanhead
A872
A803
CALEDONIA TERR 1
JUBILEE WAY 2
VALE OF BONNY VIEW 3
STEWART ST 4
BOWLING GREEN PL 5
BROOMBRIDGE PL
LIND PL
WATSON PL
LYONCROSS
GLASGOW RD
Bonded Warehouses
SEABEGS CRES
SEABEGS RD
B816
M80
STATION RD
MCVEAN PL
Parkfoot
Longcroft
ANDERSON TERR
MAYFIELD DR
No 1 Holding
FK4
JOHN ST
A803
KILSYTH RD
CROFT EST
PH
Longcroft Farm
Bonny Water
Seabegs Wood Antonine Wall
GRAHAMSDYKE RD 1
ANTONINE GR 2
GRAHAMSDYKE CRES 3
SEABEGS PL
GREENHILL RD
MANNFIELD AVE
WOODBURN CRES
WOODBURN CRES
JAMES ST
CASTLEVIEW TERR
MARGARET AVE
CUMBERNAULD RD
Haggs
LONGCROFT HOLDINGS
Underwood Farm
LEAPARK DR
LAUREL GR
LAUREL PL
GARNGREW RD
Underwood House
Forth & Clyde Canal
Dalnair
Castlecary Mill Farm
THORNDALE GDNS
ALLANDALE COTTS
Allandale
Skipperton
OCHIL GDNS
GLENYARDS RD
DUNDAS COTTS
Woodend
Greenhill Upper Junction
B816
ANTONINE GATE
South Woodend
Forresterquarter
Clayfolds
Castlecary Low Wood
Lochdrum
79
80
81
A803 Kilsyth,Glasgow
M80 Glasgow (A80)
Glasgow STREET ATLAS

58

57
37

A
B
C
D
E
F
8
7
81
6
5
80
4
3
79
2
1
78
82
83
84
Cuthelton
FK6
FK5
FK4
FK1
M876
A883
A8004
B905
A803
B816
Cemy
Hills of
Dunipace
Nursery
River Carron
CHECKBAR
RDBT
Chacefield
Wood
Bogton
CH
Sewage
Works
Wester
Carmuirs
Works
Bonny Water
WEST CARMUIRS LOAN
Rowan Tree Burn
Bonnybridge
Park
Forth and Clyde Canal
FALKIRK RD
HIGH ST
MAIN ST
Bonnybridge
Cowden Hill
Liby
Bonnyside
Farm
Chattan
Ind Est
Bonnyfield
Nature Reserve
MOUNT
BARTHOLOMEW
VALE OF
BONNY VIEW
SEABEGS RD
Canal Bank
Ind Est
Murnin
Road
Ind Est
Antonine
Prim Sch
Bonnybridge
Ind Est
BROOMHILL RD
St Joseph's
RC Prim Sch
Milnquarter
ANTONINE WALL
Rough Castle
ROMAN FORT
Works
Works
BONNYHILL RD
HILLVIEW RD
BROOMSIDE RD
High
Bonnybridge
Greenhill
GLENYARDS RD
Margreta
Bonnyhill
Farm
Howierig
Drum
Farm
Drum
Wood
Greenrig
Bonnybridge
Prim Sch
BALFOUR ST
SPENCE ST
SKENE ST
COWAN ST
HOPEPARK
TERR
DUNURE ST
DUNURE CRES
URE CRES
CHACEFIELD ST
WHEATLANDS AVE
LARBERT RD
HIGHLAND DYKES CRES
HIGHLAND DYKES DR
BONNYVIEW GDNS
ROBERTSON AVE
FERGUSON GR
DRUMMOND PL
NORWOOD CT
NORWOOD PL
PRIMROSE ST
ROSE ST
FAIRWAYS PL
BONNYWOOD AVE
GREENFIELD ST
PEATHILL RD
FAIRFIELD AVE
MARGARET DR
WELLPARK TERR
FORD RD
PEATHILL TERR
THORNTON GDNS
THORNTON AVE
GATESIDE AVE
COWDEN HILL GDNS
ANDERSON ST
BARLEYHILL
PRINCESS ST
PATERSON PL
WELLSTOOD CT
BRIDGE ST
HUNTER PL
FOUNDRY RD
BONNYSIDE RD
BONNYMUIR PL
BONNYMILL
HARLEY GDNS
MURNIN RD
SEABEGS CRES
MANNFIELD AVE
GRAHAMSDYKE RD
ROMAN RD
ATRIUM WAY
ALLAN PL
MOFFAT PL
ARDGAY TERR
ARDGAY RD
ARDGAY CRES
ARDGAY DR
GREENACRE DR
GREENACRE PL
MILNQUARTER RD
FOXDALE DR
LEAPARK DR
GREENHILL RD
LAUREL GR
REILLY RD
REILLY GDNS
WAVERLEY CRES
MILLAR PL
CHURCH ST
PARK ST
WILSON PL
LOCHINVAR PL
1 GRAHAMSDYKE CRES
2 WOODBURN CRES
3 BANTON PL
4 LAURELBANK AVE
5 GREENACRE DR
6 FOXDALE CT
7 FOXDALE AVE
Glasgow STREET ATLAS

57

38
60

A
B
C
D
E
F
8
7
6
5
4
3
2
1
81
80
79
78
85
86
87
FK5
FK2
FK1
FK4
Lochlands
Lochlands Ind Est
Lochlands Bsns Pk
Ladeside Prim Sch
Carronvale House
South Broomage
Mill
STIRLING RD
River Carron
Dorrator
Longdales
Mungal Farm
Crem
Cauldhame
Cemy
CH
Works
Camelon
THREE BRIDGES RDBT
A883
A803
A9
GLASGOW RD
MAIN ST
CAMELON RD
Carmuirs
Easter Carmuirs Prim Sch
Carmuirs Prim Sch
Camelon
The Falkirk Wheel
Forth and Clyde Canal
Football Gd
LOCK SIXTEEN
Tamfourhill
Tamfourhill Ind Est
TAMFOURHILL RD
BONNYHILL RD
GLENFUIR RD
WESTBURN AVE
B8080
B816
Falkirk High Sch
Bantaskin Prim Sch
Windsor Park Sch
Bantaskin
Falkirk & District Royal
Summerford
Union Canal
FALKIRK
Tamfourhill Wood
Greenbank
Greenbank Farm
South Bantaskine Estate
Mon
Canada Wood
SLAMANNAN RD
B803
LOCHGREEN RDBT
Princes Park
Greenrig Strip
Craigburn Wood
Seafield
Craigieburn
Glen Burn
Fox Covert
BROWNIEKNOWE PL 1
GOOSEDUBS PL 2
MCINALLY CRES 3
WESTPARK CT 4
MUNGAL MILL CT 5
SKYTHORN WAY 1
GLENTYE GDNS 2
MELLOCK GDNS 3
CLANRANALD PL 1
FARQUHARSON WAY 2
KEPPOCK PL 3
MACINTOSH PL 4
BRACKLINN PL 5
STRATHYRE PL 6

80
60

E5
1 Camelon Ed Ctr

F2
1 HILLCREST RD
2 THORNDENE CT
3 SEAFIELD CT
4 CRAIGBURN CT
5 FORTHVIEW CT
6 MACPHERSON PL
7 MCKENZIE PL

F3
1 GREENHORN'S WELL CRES
2 GREENHORN'S WELL DR
3 GREENHORN'S WELL AVE
4 GARTCOWS CRES

F4
1 ARNOTHILL LA
2 MAYFIELD MEWS
3 WINDSOR GDNS
4 GARTCOWS DR
5 GARTCOWS GDNS

A8
1 MULLOCH AVE
2 ANDERSON AVE
3 NEWCARRON CT
4 WILLIAMSON AVE
5 DUNDEE CT
6 JARVIE PL
7 JOHNSTON CT
8 GASCOIGNE CT

59
39

B4
1 BURNFOOT LA
2 KIRK WYND
3 TOLBOOTH ST
4 WOOER ST
5 Callendar Square
6 The Mall
7 KINGS CT
8 MISSION LA
9 MELROSE PL
10 ST ANDREWS PL
11 PLEASANCE SQ
12 PLEASANCE CT
13 ST MODANS CT
14 COMELY PARK TERR
15 BLUEBELL CL
16 WILSON'S CL
17 COMELY PARK GDNS

59
81

B5
1 SILK HO
2 MELVILLE ST
3 MELVILLE LA
4 SOUTH MELVILLE LA
5 Superstore
6 UPPER NEWMARKET ST
7 NEWMARKET ST

40
62
E6
1 Sacred Heart
RC Prim Sch

A1
1 BEVERIDGE PL
2 NORTH MUIR AVE
3 MUIRHEAD PL

82
62

61
41

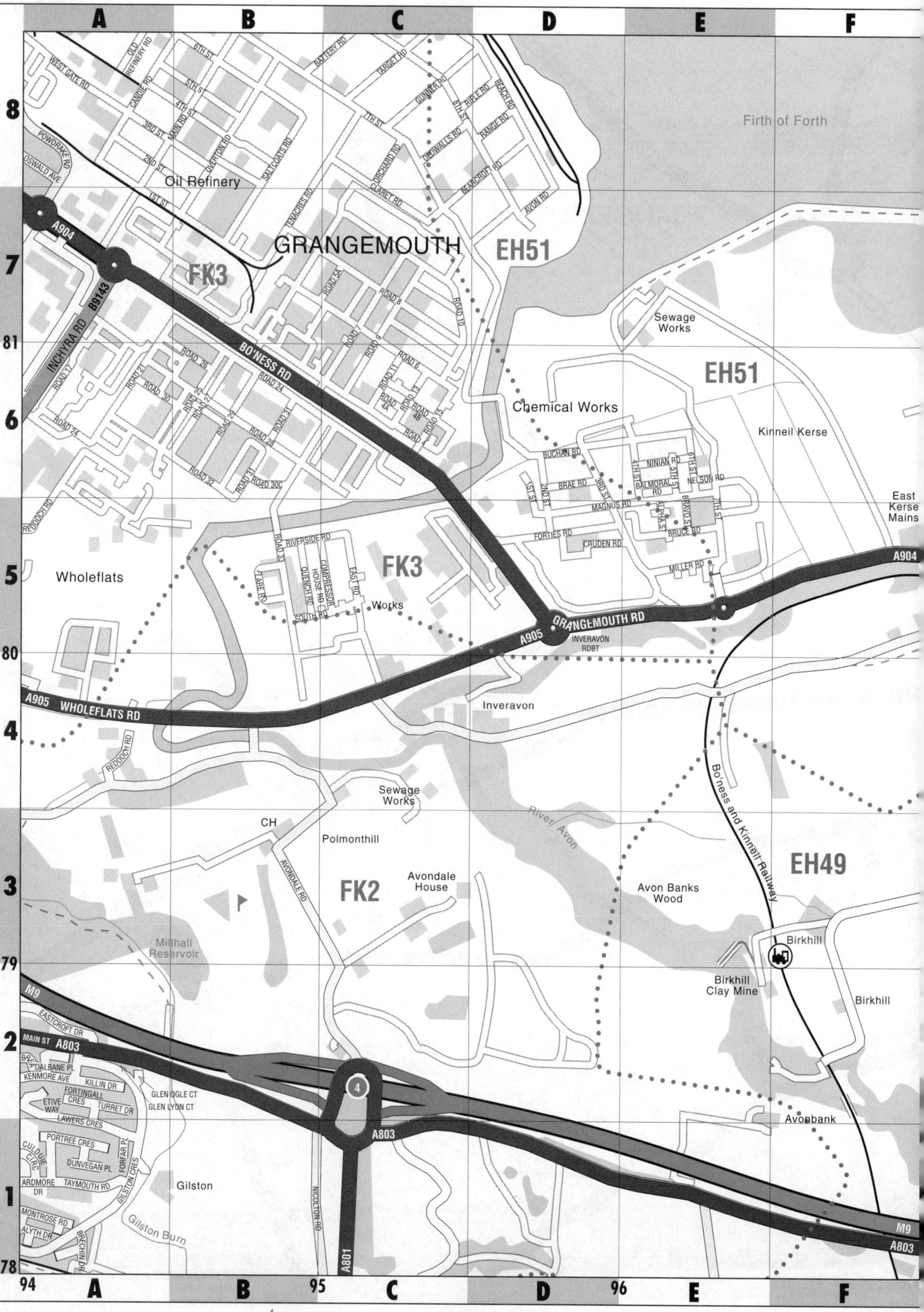
A
B
C
D
E
F
8
7
81
6
5
80
4
3
79
2
1
78
94
95
96
GRANGEMOUTH
Oil Refinery
FK3
EH51
Firth of Forth
Sewage Works
EH51
Chemical Works
Kinneil Kerse
East Kerse Mains
A904
BO'NESS RD
B9143
INCHYRA RD
WEST GATE RD
OLD REFINERY RD
CANDIE RD
6TH ST
5TH ST
4TH ST
3RD ST
MAIN RD
2ND ST
1ST ST
OVERTON RD
SALTCOATS RD
POWDRAKE RD
OSWALD AVE
BATTERY RD
TARGET RD
GUNNER RD
7TH ST
8TH ST
RIFLE RD
BEACH RD
RANGE RD
ORCHARD RD
DROWALLS RD
CLARET RD
BEARCROFT RD
AVON RD
TEMACRES RD
ROAD 5A
ROAD 8
ROAD 10
ROAD 7
ROAD 9
ROAD 6
ROAD 11
ROAD 13
ROAD 4A
ROAD 4B
ROAD 15
ROAD 4
ROAD 17
ROAD 21
ROAD 26
ROAD 30
ROAD 22
ROAD 27
ROAD 24
ROAD 29
ROAD 28
ROAD 31
ROAD 32
ROAD 30C
ROAD 24
REDDOCH RD
BUCHAN RD
1ST ST
2ND ST
BRAE RD
3RD ST
4TH ST
NINIAN RD
5TH ST
6TH ST
NELSON RD
BALMORAL RD
MAGNUS RD
ALPHA ST
BRAVO ST
7TH ST
FORTIES RD
BRUCE RD
CRUDEN RD
MILLER RD
Wholeflats
FK3
RIVERSIDE RD
ROAD 33
FLARE RD
QUENCH RD
COMPRESSOR HOUSE RD
EAST RD
SOUTH RD
Works
GRANGEMOUTH RD
A905
INVERAVON RDBT
A905 WHOLEFLATS RD
Inveravon
REDDOCH RD
Sewage Works
CH
Polmonthill
River Avon
Bo'ness and Kinneil Railway
EH49
AVONDALE RD
FK2
Avondale House
Avon Banks Wood
Millhall Reservoir
Birkhill
Birkhill Clay Mine
Birkhill
M9
EASTCROFT DR
MAIN ST A803
BREA
DALBANE PL
KENMORE AVE
KILLIN DR
FORTINGALL
ETIVE WAY
CRES
TURRET DR
LAWERS CRES
GLEN OGLE CT
GLEN LYON CT
4
A803
Avonbank
PORTREE CRES
CULDUIE CIRC
DUNVEGAN PL
FORFAR PL
GILSTON CRES
ARDMORE DR
TAYMOUTH RD
Gilston
NICOLTON RD
MONTROSE RD
ALYTH DR
Gilston Burn
BRECHIN DR
A801
M9
A803

61
83

42
64

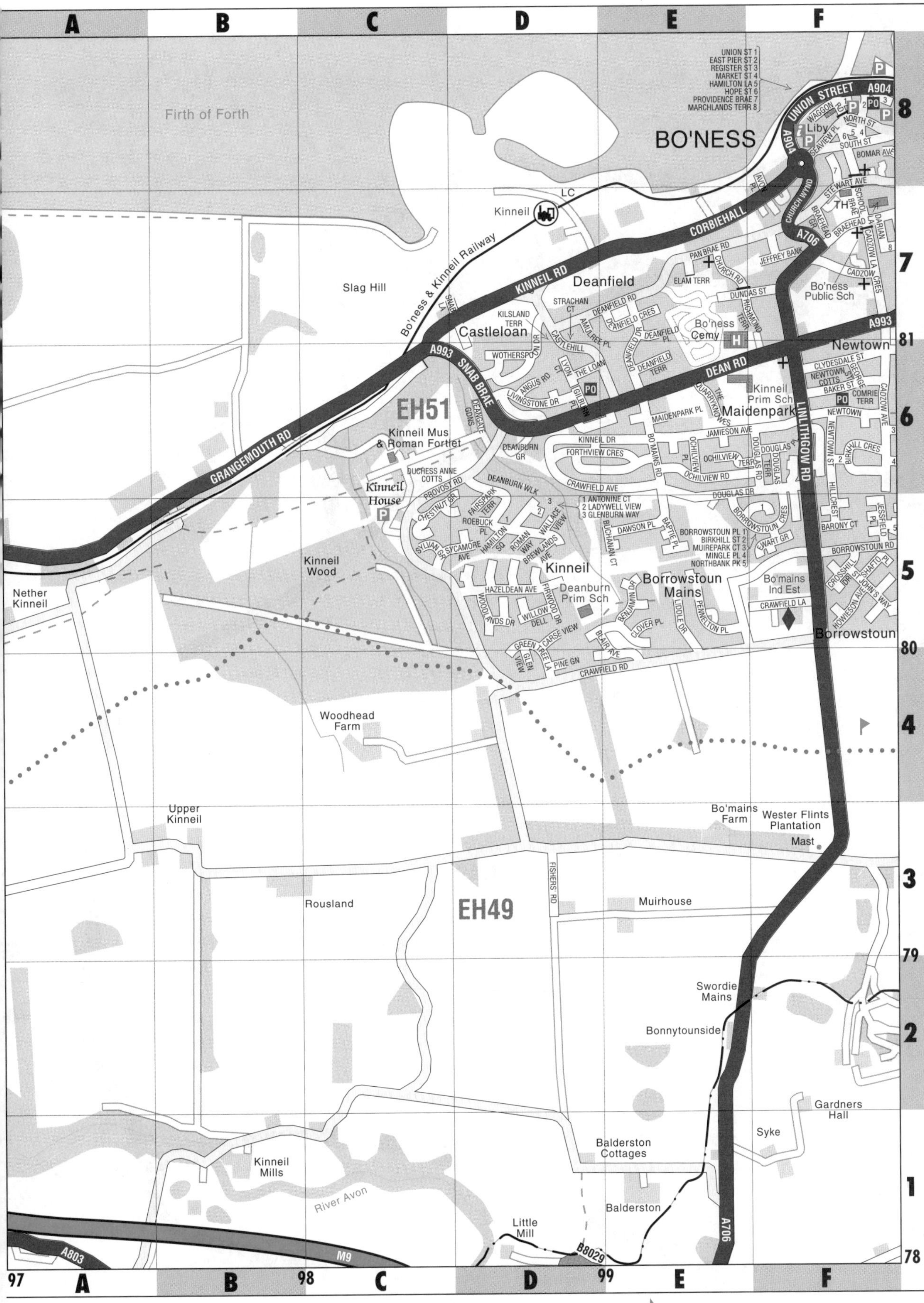
A
B
C
D
E
F
8
7
81
6
5
80
4
3
79
2
1
78
97
98
99
Firth of Forth
BO'NESS
UNION ST 1
EAST PIER ST 2
REGISTER ST 3
MARKET ST 4
HAMILTON LA 5
HOPE ST 6
PROVIDENCE BRAE 7
MARCHLANDS TERR 8
UNION STREET
A904
WAGGON RD
NORTH ST
SOUTH ST
SEAVIEW PL
Liby
BOMAR AVE
STEWART AVE
SCHOOL BRAE
CHURCH WYND
TH
BRAEHEAD GR
BRAEHEAD
DARIAN
CADZOW LA
CADZOW CRES
A706
JEFFREY BANK
Bo'ness Public Sch
AVON PL
LC
Kinneil
Bo'ness & Kinneil Railway
CORBIEHALL
KINNEIL RD
Deanfield
PAN BRAE RD
CHURCH RD
ELAM TERR
DUNDAS ST
RICHMOND TERR
Slag Hill
SNAB LA
STRACHAN CT
DEANFIELD RD
DEANFIELD CRES
DEANFIELD PL
DEANFIELD DR
DEANFIELD TERR
AMULREE PL
Bo'ness Cemy
KILSLAND TERR
Castleloan
CASTLEHILL
WOTHERSPOON DR
LYON CT
THE LOAN
ANGUS RD
LIVINGSTONE DR
GILBURN PL
PO
A993
SNAB BRAE
DEAN RD
Newtown
CLYDESDALE ST
NEWTOWN COTTS
GEORGE PL
BAKER ST
COMRIE TERR
CADZOW AVE
NEWTOWN
Kinneil Prim Sch
Maidenpark
THE QUARRYKNOWES
MAIDENPARK PL
JAMIESON AVE
LINLITHGOW RD
EH51
GRANGEMOUTH RD
DEANGATE GDNS
Kinneil Mus & Roman Fortlet
DEANBURN GR
KINNEIL DR
FORTHVIEW CRES
BO MAINS RD
OCHILVIEW PL
OCHILVIEW TERR
OCHILVIEW RD
DOUGLAS PL
DOUGLAS TERR
DOUGLAS RD
NEWTOWN ST
BIRKHILL CRES
DUCHESS ANNE COTTS
PROVOST RD
DEANBURN WLK
CRAWFIELD AVE
DOUGLAS DR
HILLCREST
JESSFIELD PL
Kinneil House
CHESTNUT GR
FAIRSPARK TERR
ROEBUCK PL
HAMILTON SQ
ROMAN WAY
WALLACE VIEW
BREWLANDS AVE
1 ANTONINE CT
2 LADYWELL VIEW
3 GLENBURN WAY
DAWSON PL
BUCHANAN CT
BAPTIE PL
BORROWSTOUN PL 1
BIRKHILL ST 2
MUIREPARK CT 3
MINGLE PL 4
NORTHBANK PK 5
BORROWSTOUN CRES
EWART GR
BARONY CT
BORROWSTOUN RD
SYLVAN GR
SYCAMORE AVE
Kinneil Wood
Kinneil
Borrowstoun Mains
Bo'mains Ind Est
CROSSHILL DR
SHAFTO PL
ST JOHN'S WAY
HOWIESON AVE
Nether Kinneil
HAZELDEAN AVE
WOODLANDS DR
WILLOW DELL
FIRWOOD DR
Deanburn Prim Sch
BENJAMIN DR
CLOVER PL
LIDDLE DR
PENNELTON PL
CRAWFIELD LA
CARSE VIEW
GREENTREE LA
GLEN VIEW
BLAIR AVE
PINE GN
CRAWFIELD RD
Borrowstoun
Woodhead Farm
Upper Kinneil
Bo'mains Farm
Wester Flints Plantation
Mast
FISHERS RD
Rousland
EH49
Muirhouse
Swordie Mains
Bonnytounside
Gardners Hall
Syke
Balderston Cottages
Kinneil Mills
River Avon
Balderston
Little Mill
A803
M9
B8029
A706

84
64

63
43

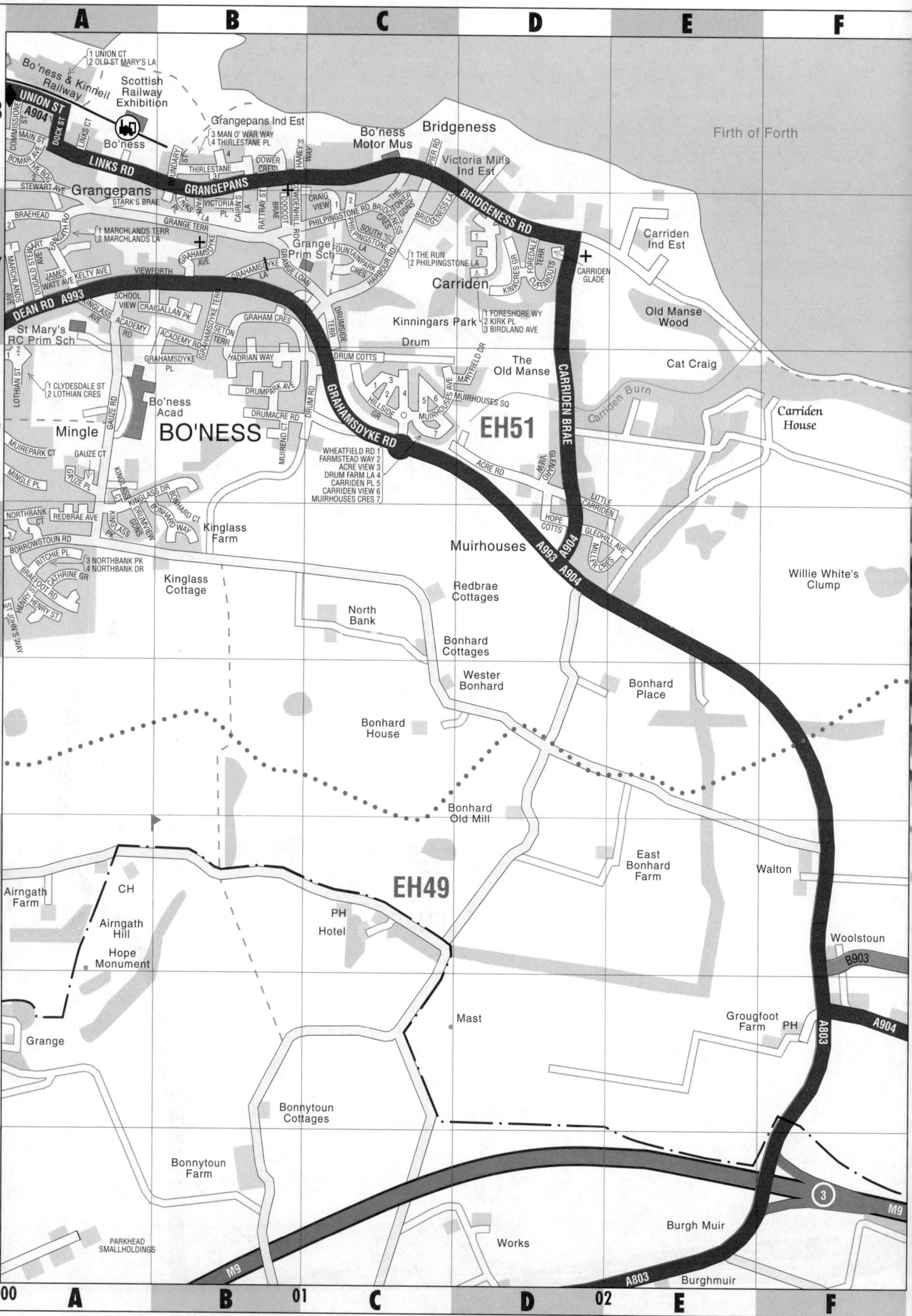
A
B
C
D
E
F
8
7
81
6
5
80
4
3
79
2
1
78
00
01
02
1 UNION CT
2 OLD ST MARY'S LA
Bo'ness & Kinneil Railway
Scottish Railway Exhibition
UNION ST
A904
COMMISSIONER ST
DOCK ST
LINKS CT
MAIN ST
BOMAR AVE
THE BOG
Bo'ness
Grangepans Ind Est
3 MAN O' WAR WAY
4 THIRLESTANE PL
BOUNDARY ST
THIRLESTANE
DOWER CRES
HANEY'S WAY
Bo'ness Motor Mus
Bridgeness
PIER RD
Victoria Mills Ind Est
Firth of Forth
LINKS RD
GRANGEPANS
STEWART AVE
Grangepans
STARK'S BRAE
VICTORIA PL
CAIRN'S LA
RATTRAY ST
DOOCOT BRAE
DOWDENHILL RD
CRAIG VIEW
PHILPINGSTONE RD
BRIDGENESS CRES
THE TOWERS GDNS
BRIDGENESS LA
BRIDGENESS RD
BRAEHEAD
CRAIGATH RD
1 MARCHLANDS TERR
2 MARCHLANDS LA
GRANGE TERR
GRAHAMSDYKE AVE
Grange Prim Sch
PHILPINGSTONE LA
SOUTH LA
FOUNTAINPARK CRES
HARBOUR RD
1 THE RUN
2 PHILPINGSTONE LA
Carriden Ind Est
CARRIDEN GLADE
FOREDALE TERR
CUFFABOUTS
KINNCRES GR
MARCHLANDS AVE
DUGALD STEWART AVE
JAMES WATT AVE
KELTY AVE
VIEWFORTH
GRAHAMSDYKE LA
GRANGE LOAN
Carriden
DEAN RD
A993
SCHOOL VIEW
KINGLASS AVE
CRAIGALLAN PK
GRAHAM CRES
DRUMSIDE TERR
Kinningars Park
1 FORESHORE WY
2 KIRK PL
3 BIRDLAND AVE
Old Manse Wood
St Mary's RC Prim Sch
ACADEMY RD
ACADEMY RD
SETON TERR
GRAHAMSDYKE TERR
GRAHAMSDYKE PL
HADRIAN WAY
DRUM COTTS
Drum
MAYFIELD DR
The Old Manse
Cat Craig
CARRIDEN BRAE
LOTHIAN ST
1 CLYDESDALE ST
2 LOTHIAN CRES
GAUZE RD
Bo'ness Acad
DRUMPARK AVE
DRUMACRE RD
DRUM RD
HILLSIDE GR
MUIRHOUSES AVE
MUIRHOUSES SQ
Carriden Burn
Carriden House
Mingle
BO'NESS
MUIREND CT
GRAHAMSDYKE RD
EH51
MUIREPARK CT
GAUZE CT
GAUZE PL
WHEATFIELD RD 1
FARMSTEAD WAY 2
ACRE VIEW 3
DRUM FARM LA 4
CARRIDEN PL 5
CARRIDEN VIEW 6
MUIRHOUSES CRES 7
ACRE RD
GLENARD VIEW
MINGLE PL
KINGLASS CT
KINGLASS DR
BONHARD CT
DRUMVIEW GDNS
BONHARD WAY
LITTLE CARRIDEN
NORTHBANK CT
REDBRAE AVE
KINGLASS PK
Kinglass Farm
HOPE COTTS
GLEDHILL AVE
MILLER CRES
BORROWSTOUN RD
Muirhouses
A993
A904
A904
RITCHIE PL
3 NORTHBANK PK
4 NORTHBANK DR
CATHRINE GR
BRAEFOOT RD
HENRY ST
HENRY ST
Kinglass Cottage
Redbrae Cottages
Willie White's Clump
North Bank
ST JOHN'S WAY
Bonhard Cottages
Wester Bonhard
Bonhard Place
Bonhard House
Bonhard Old Mill
CH
EH49
East Bonhard Farm
Walton
Airngath Farm
PH
Hotel
Airngath Hill
Hope Monument
Woolstoun
B903
Grange
Mast
Grougfoot Farm
PH
A803
A904
Bonnytoun Cottages
Bonnytoun Farm
3
M9
Burgh Muir
PARKHEAD SMALLHOLDINGS
Works
M9
A803
Burghmuir

63
85

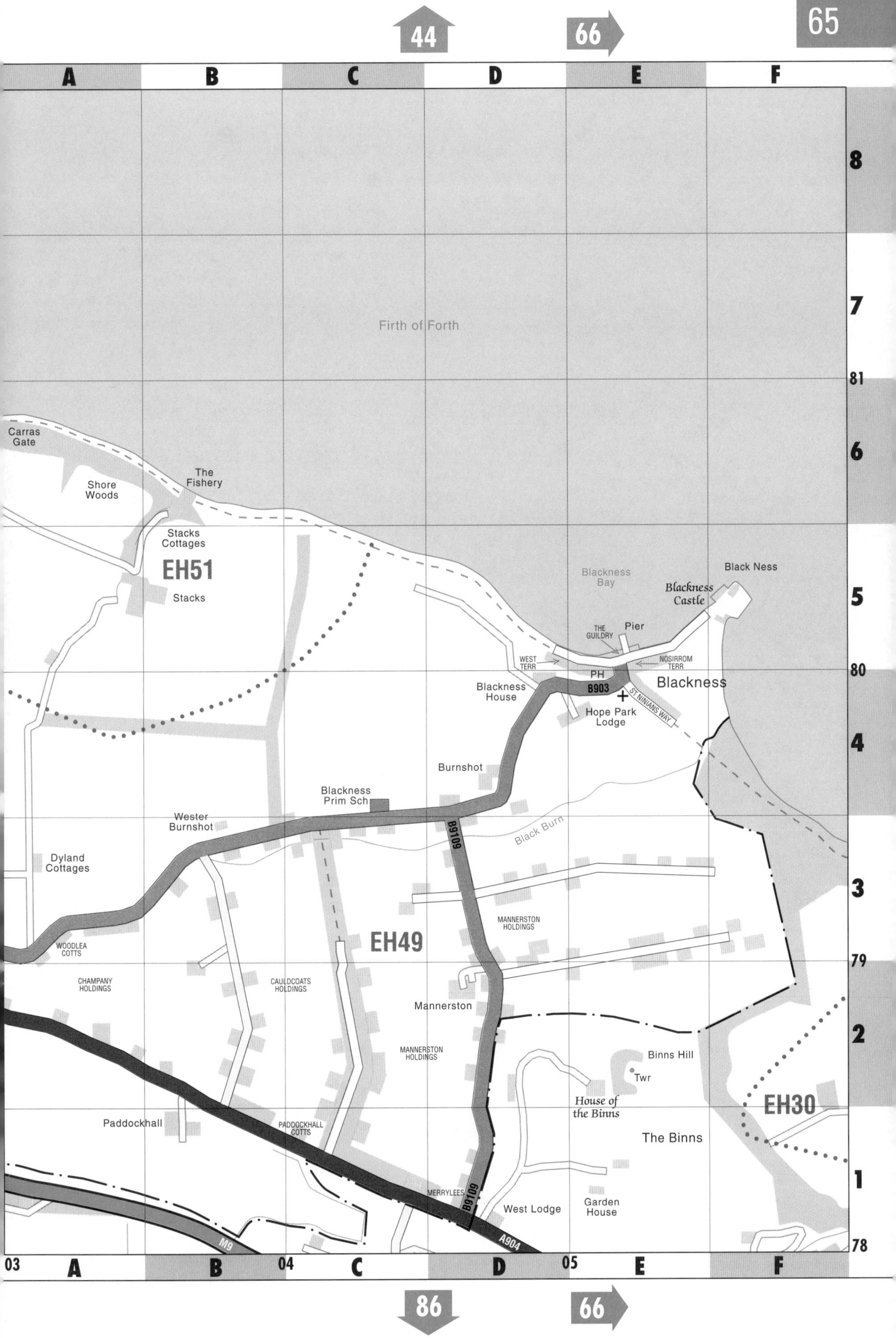
44
66
A
B
C
D
E
F
8
7
81
6
5
80
4
3
79
2
1
78
03
04
05
Firth of Forth
Carras Gate
Shore Woods
The Fishery
Stacks Cottages
EH51
Stacks
Blackness Bay
Black Ness
Blackness Castle
THE GUILDRY
Pier
WEST TERR
NOSIRROM TERR
PH
B903
Blackness
Blackness House
ST NINIANS WAY
Hope Park Lodge
Burnshot
Blackness Prim Sch
Wester Burnshot
B9109
Black Burn
Dyland Cottages
MANNERSTON HOLDINGS
EH49
WOODLEA COTTS
CHAMPANY HOLDINGS
CAULDCOATS HOLDINGS
Mannerston
MANNERSTON HOLDINGS
Binns Hill
Twr
House of the Binns
EH30
The Binns
Paddockhall
PADDOCKHALL COTTS
MERRYLEES
West Lodge
Garden House
M9
A904
86
66

65
45

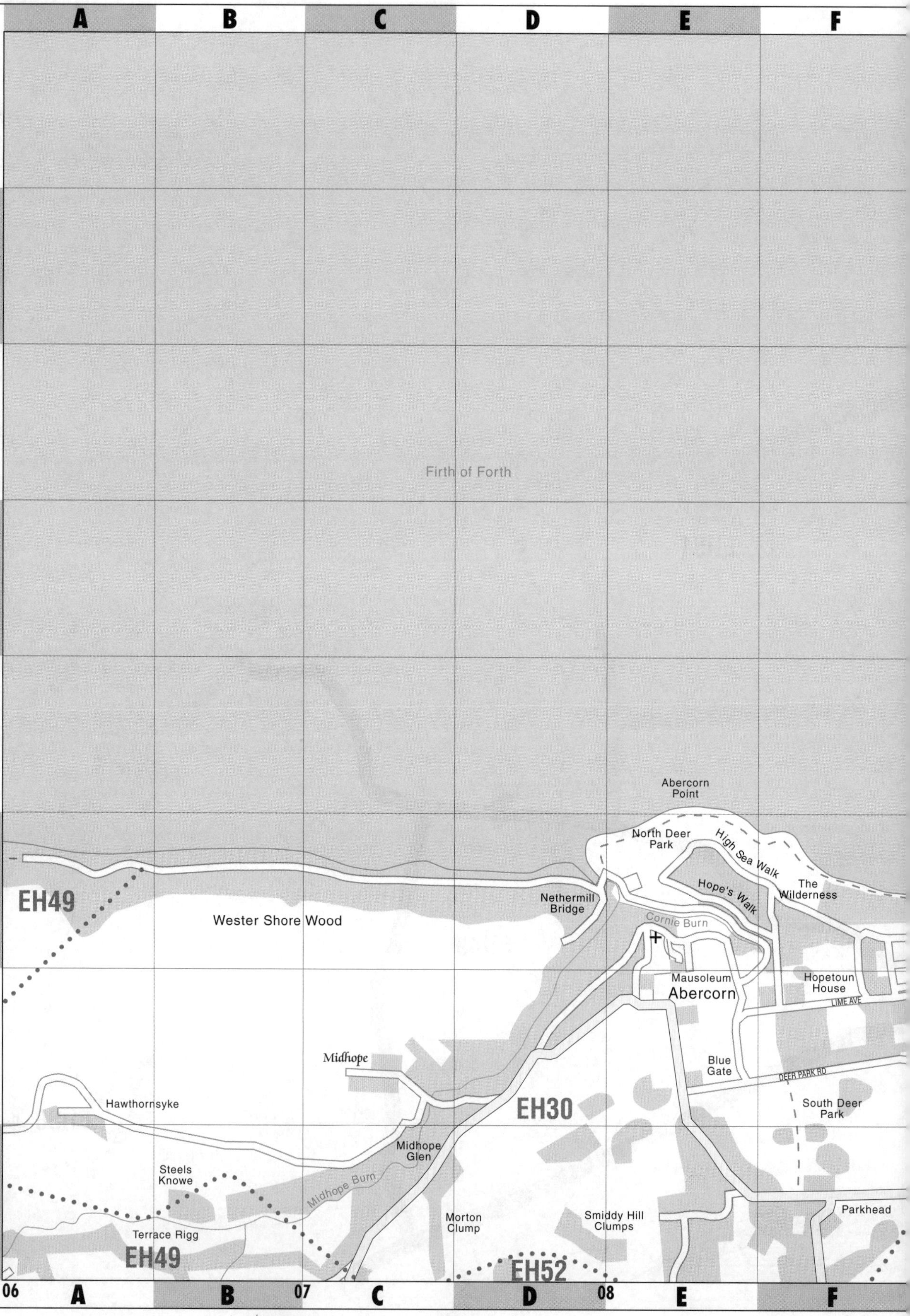
A
B
C
D
E
F
8
7
81
6
5
80
4
3
79
2
1
78
06
07
08
Firth of Forth
Abercorn Point
North Deer Park
High Sea Walk
The Wilderness
Hope's Walk
Nethermill Bridge
Cornie Burn
EH49
Wester Shore Wood
Mausoleum
Abercorn
Hopetoun House
LIME AVE
Midhope
Blue Gate
DEER PARK RD
South Deer Park
Hawthornsyke
EH30
Midhope Glen
Steels Knowe
Midhope Burn
Morton Clump
Smiddy Hill Clumps
Parkhead
Terrace Rigg
EH49
EH52

65
87

46
68

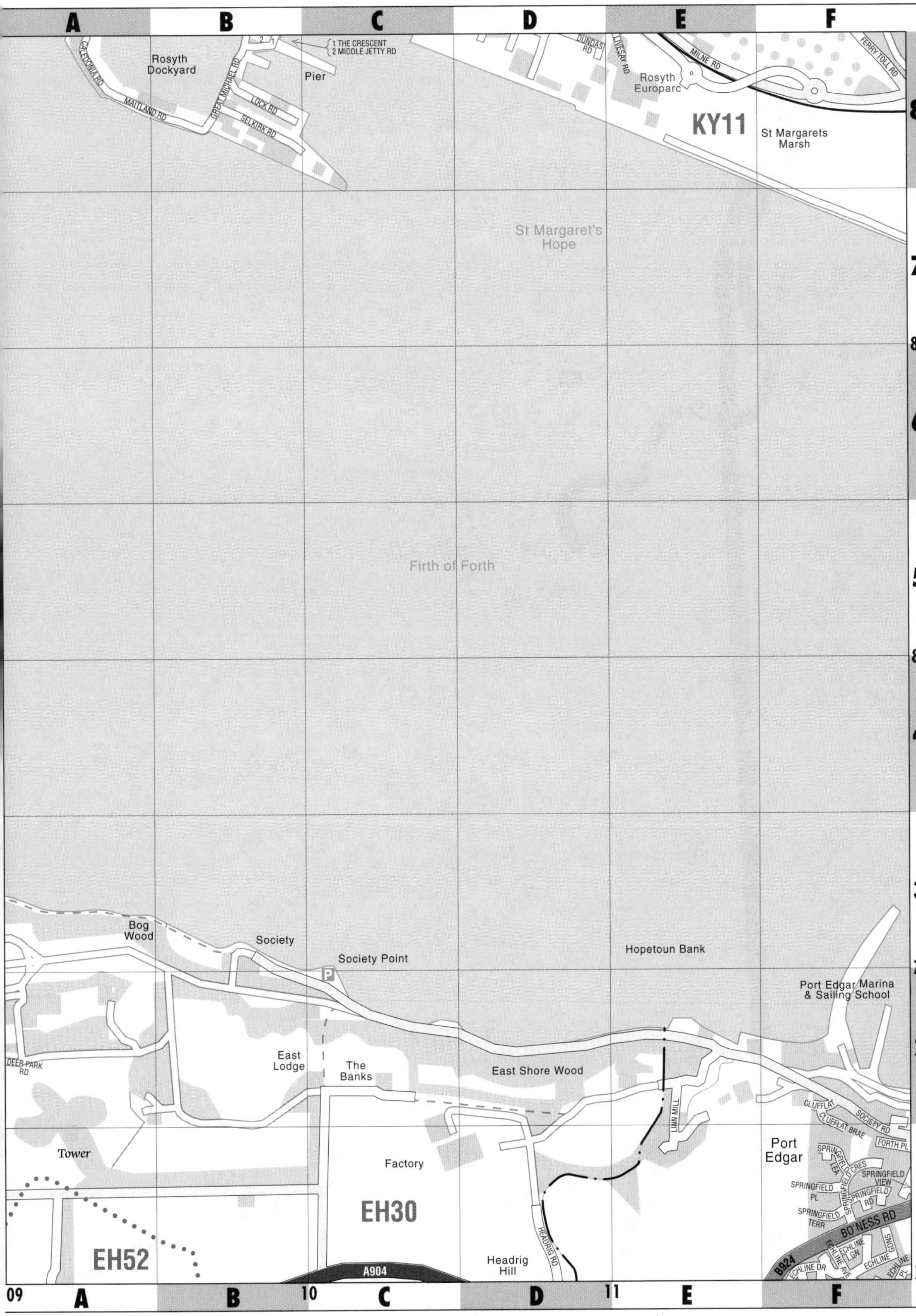
A
B
C
D
E
F
8
7
81
6
5
80
4
3
79
2
1
78
09
10
11
Rosyth Dockyard
CALEDONIA RD
MAITLAND RD
GREAT MICHAEL RD
LOCK RD
SELKIRK RD
1 THE CRESCENT
2 MIDDLE JETTY RD
Pier
DUNDAS RD
LIVESAY RD
MILNE RD
FERRY TOLL RD
Rosyth Europarc
KY11
St Margarets Marsh
St Margaret's Hope
Firth of Forth
Bog Wood
Society
Society Point
Hopetoun Bank
Port Edgar Marina & Sailing School
East Lodge
The Banks
East Shore Wood
LINN MILL
Tower
Factory
EH30
EH52
A904
HEADRIG RD
Headrig Hill
Port Edgar
CLUFFLAT
CLUFFLAT BRAE
SOCIETY RD
FORTH PL
SPRINGFIELD LEA
SPRINGFIELD CRES
SPRINGFIELD VIEW
SPRINGFIELD PL
SPRINGFIELD RD
SPRINGFIELD TERR
BO'NESS RD
B924
ECHLINE DR
ECHLINE AVE
ECHLINE GN
ECHLINE
ECHLINE PL

88
68

67
47

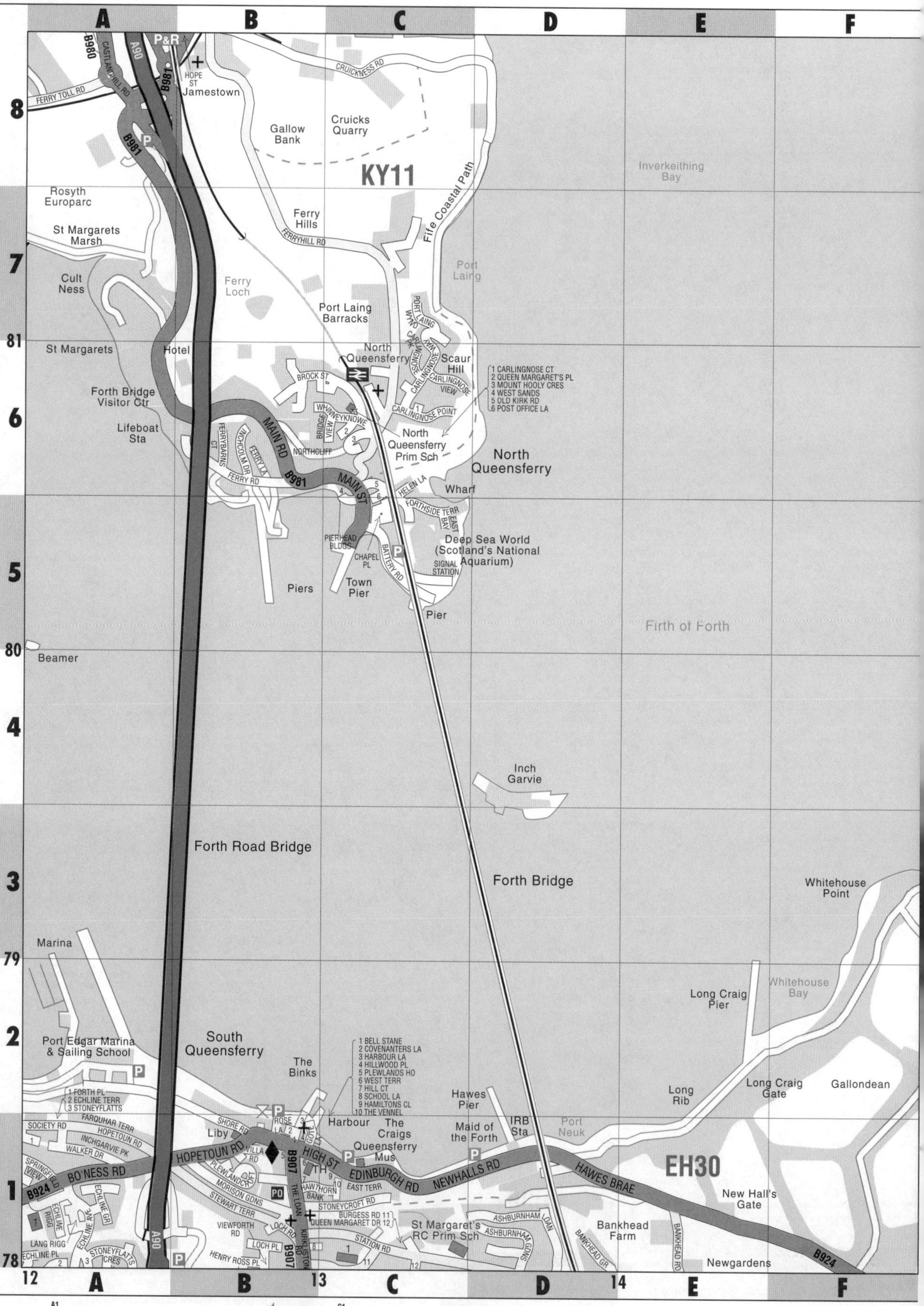
A
B
C
D
E
F
8
7
81
6
5
80
4
3
79
2
1
78
12
13
14
P&R
B980
A90
B981
HOPE ST
Jamestown
CASTLANDHILL RD
FERRY TOLL RD
CRUICKNESS RD
Gallow Bank
Cruicks Quarry
KY11
Inverkeithing Bay
Rosyth Europarc
St Margarets Marsh
Ferry Hills
FERRYHILL RD
Fife Coastal Path
Cult Ness
Ferry Loch
Port Laing
Port Laing Barracks
PORT LAING WYND
CARLINGNOSE PK
CARLINGNOSE WAY
St Margarets
Hotel
North Queensferry
Scaur Hill
BROCK ST
CARLINGNOSE VIEW
1 CARLINGNOSE CT
2 QUEEN MARGARET'S PL
3 MOUNT HOOLY CRES
4 WEST SANDS
5 OLD KIRK RD
6 POST OFFICE LA
Forth Bridge Visitor Ctr
WHINNEYKNOWE
BRIDGE VIEW
CARLINGNOSE POINT
Lifeboat Sta
MAIN RD
FERRYBARNS CT
INCHCOLM DR
FERRY LA
NORTHCLIFF
North Queensferry Prim Sch
North Queensferry
FERRY RD
B981
MAIN ST
HELEN LA
Wharf
FORTHSIDE TERR
EAST BAY
PIERHEAD BLDGS
CHAPEL PL
BATTERY RD
P
SIGNAL STATION
Deep Sea World (Scotland's National Aquarium)
Piers
Town Pier
Pier
Firth of Forth
Beamer
Inch Garvie
Forth Road Bridge
Forth Bridge
Whitehouse Point
Marina
Whitehouse Bay
Long Craig Pier
Port Edgar Marina & Sailing School
South Queensferry
The Binks
1 BELL STANE
2 COVENANTERS LA
3 HARBOUR LA
4 HILLWOOD PL
5 PLEWLANDS HO
6 WEST TERR
7 HILL CT
8 SCHOOL LA
9 HAMILTONS CL
10 THE VENNEL
Hawes Pier
Long Rib
Long Craig Gate
Gallondean
1 FORTH PL
2 ECHLINE TERR
3 STONEYFLATTS
SOCIETY RD
FARQUHAR TERR
HOPETOUN RD
INCHGARVIE PK
WALKER DR
SHORE RD
Liby
ROSE LA
Harbour
The Craigs
Queensferry Mus
Maid of the Forth
IRB Sta
Port Neuk
SPRINGFIELD VIEW
BO'NESS RD
HOPETOUN RD
VILLA RD
B907
HIGH ST
EDINBURGH RD
NEWHALLS RD
HAWES BRAE
EH30
B924
ECHLINE GR
ECHLINE RIGG
ECHLINE AVE
PLEWLANDS CT
MORISON GDNS
STEWART TERR
THE LOAN
PO
HAWTHORN BANK
EAST TERR
STONEYCROFT RD
BURGESS RD
QUEEN MARGARET DR
St Margaret's RC Prim Sch
ASHBURNHAM LOAN
ASHBURNHAM GDNS
Bankhead Farm
BANKHEAD GR
BANKHEAD RD
New Hall's Gate
Newgardens
VIEWFORTH RD
LOCH RD
LOCH PL
KIRKLISTON RD
STATION RD
LANG RIGG
ECHLINE PL
STONEYFLATTS CRES
HENRY ROSS PL

A1
1 Echline
Prim Sch

C1
1 Queensferry
Prim Sch

67
89

48

A B C D E F
8 7 81 6 5 80 4 3 79 2 1 78
15 16 17
Firth of Forth
Tanker Berths
Hound Point
Peatdraught Bay
The Warrens
Fishery Cottage
Leuchold
Leuchold Wood
EH30
Castle Craig Clump
Castle Craig
Midlothian Clump
Crow Thickets
Barnbougle Castle
Mons Hill
New England
Dalmeny Park
Peacock Ride
Livingston Clump
Dalmeny House

90

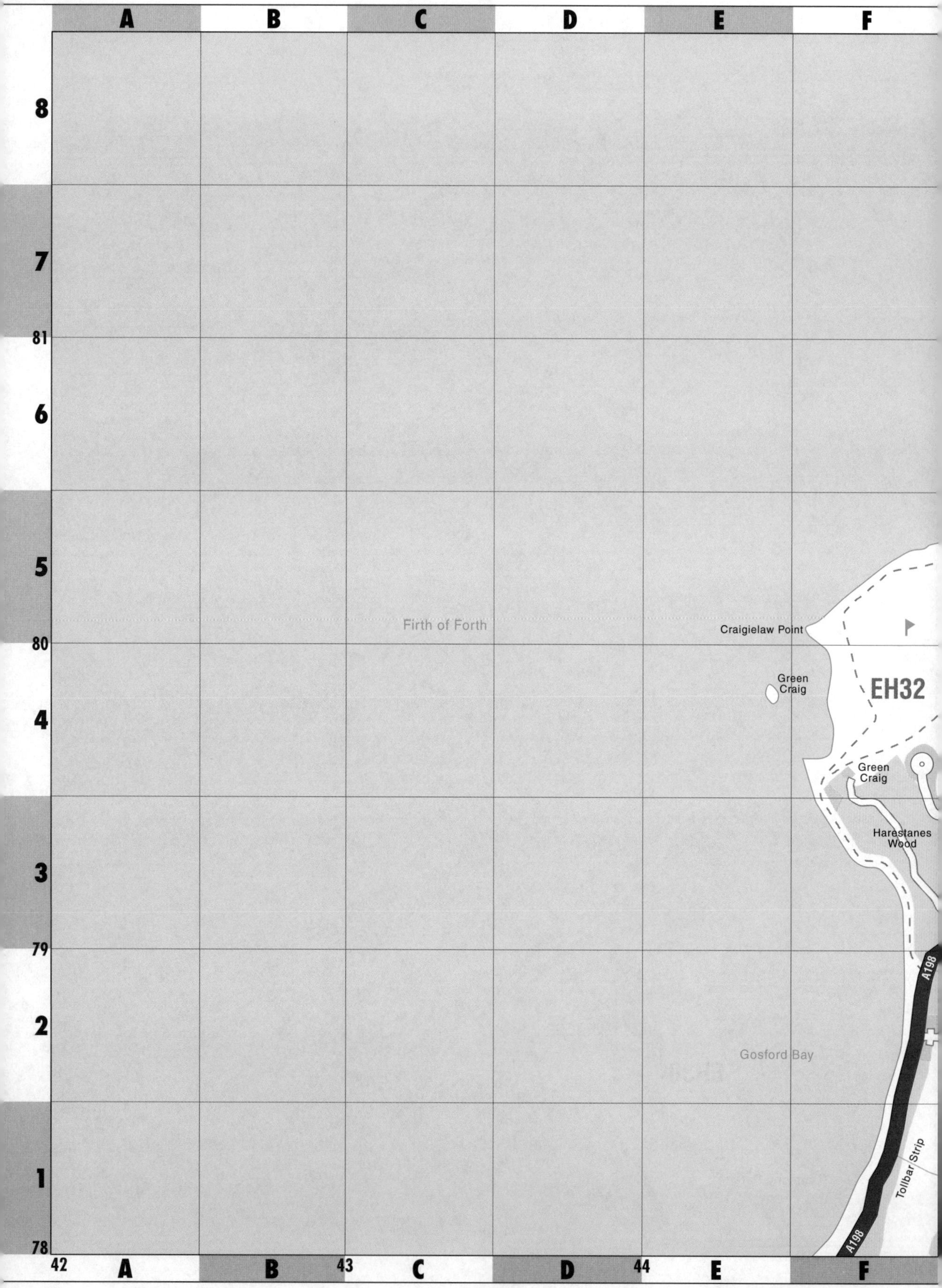
A
B
C
D
E
F
8
7
81
6
5
Firth of Forth
Craigielaw Point
80
Green Craig
EH32
4
Green Craig
Harestanes Wood
3
79
A198
2
Gosford Bay
1
Tollbar Strip
A198
78
42
43
44

98

51
72
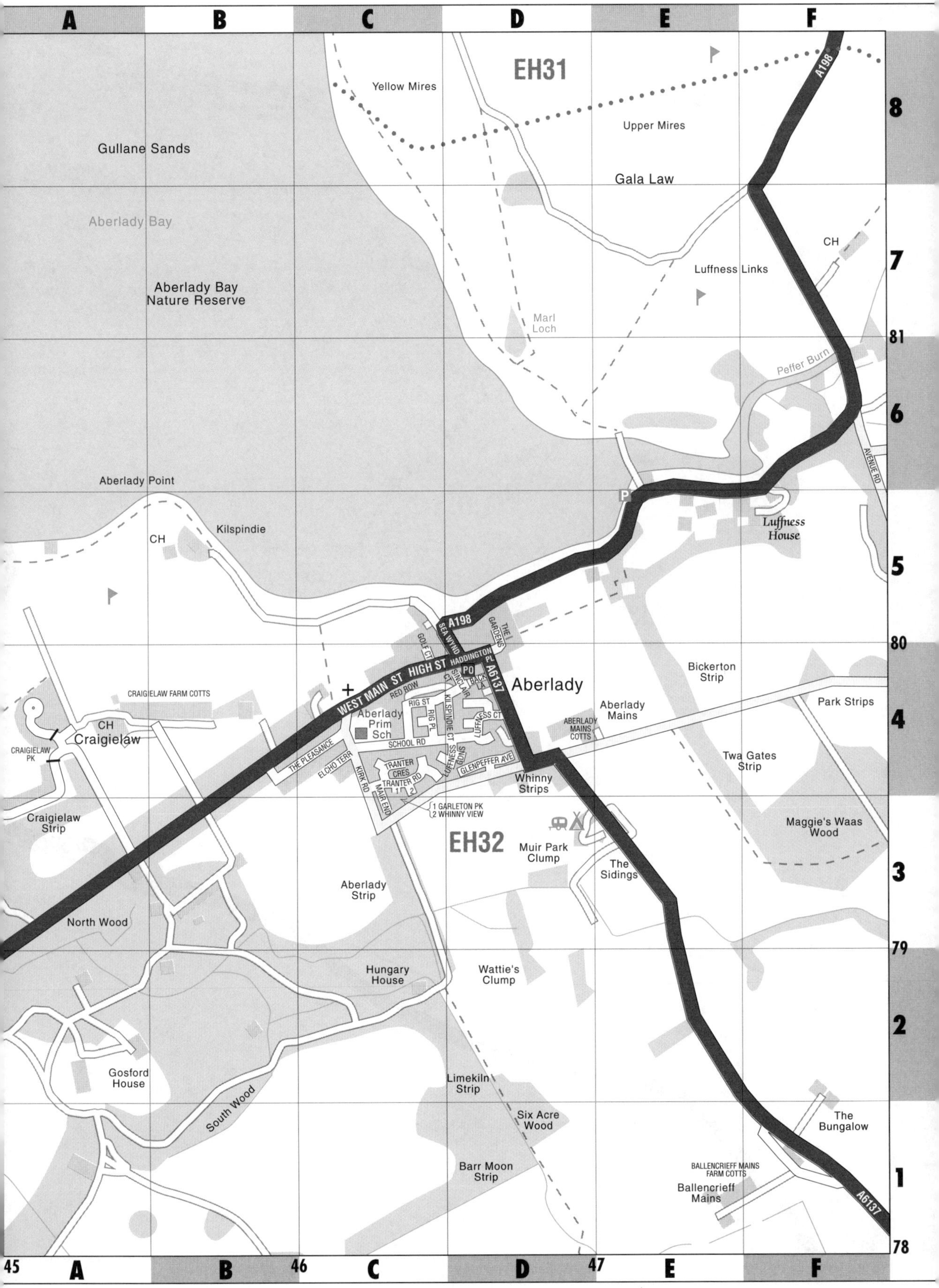
A
B
C
D
E
F
8
7
81
6
5
80
4
3
79
2
1
78
45
46
47
EH31
Yellow Mires
Upper Mires
Gala Law
Gullane Sands
Aberlady Bay
Aberlady Bay
Nature Reserve
CH
Luffness Links
Marl
Loch
Peffer Burn
AVENUE RD
Aberlady Point
Kilspindie
CH
Luffness
House
P
A198
SEA WYND
THE GARDENS
GOLF CT
HADDINGTON PL
PO
WEST MAIN ST
HIGH ST
A6137
Aberlady
RED ROW
SINCLAIR CT
BACK LA
RIG ST
RIG PL
KILSPINDIE CT
LUFFNESS CT
Aberlady
Prim
Sch
SCHOOL RD
THE PLEASANCE
ELCHO TERR
KIRK RD
TRANTER CRES
TRANTER RD
LUFFNESS GDNS
GLENPEFFER AVE
MAIR END
1 GARLETON PK
2 WHINNY VIEW
CRAIGIELAW FARM COTTS
CH
Craigielaw
CRAIGIELAW PK
Craigielaw
Strip
Bickerton
Strip
Aberlady
Mains
ABERLADY MAINS COTTS
Park Strips
Twa Gates
Strip
Whinny
Strips
EH32
Muir Park
Clump
The
Sidings
Maggie's Waas
Wood
Aberlady
Strip
North Wood
Hungary
House
Wattie's
Clump
Gosford
House
South Wood
Limekiln
Strip
Six Acre
Wood
Barr Moon
Strip
The
Bungalow
BALLENCRIEFF MAINS
FARM COTTS
Ballencrieff
Mains
A6137
99
72

71
52

EH31
EH32
EH39
John Muir Way
West Fenton
WEST FENTON CT
WEST FENTON COTTS
Craighead Cottage
New Mains
Depot
Peffer Bank Wood
Luffness Mill House
Hatty's Plantation
Park Hills
Drem Ride
Peffer Burn
Floors Strip
AVENUE RD
Coldhame Wood
B1345
LUFFNESS MAINS COTTS
Luffness Mains
Mungoswells Rough Strip
THE CHESTERS
Drem Farm
B1377
Myreton Motor Museum
LC
Poultry Farm
Mungoswells
MUNGOSWELLS COTTS
Bridgend
Sixpence Strip
Foster Law
Tighnablair
Dalvreck Farm
The Chesters (Fort)
BALLENCRIEFF COTTS
Ballencrieff House
Camptoun Holdings
A6137
B1377
Ballencrieff
A B C D E F
8 7 81 6 5 80 4 3 79 2 1 78
48 49 50
71
100

53
74

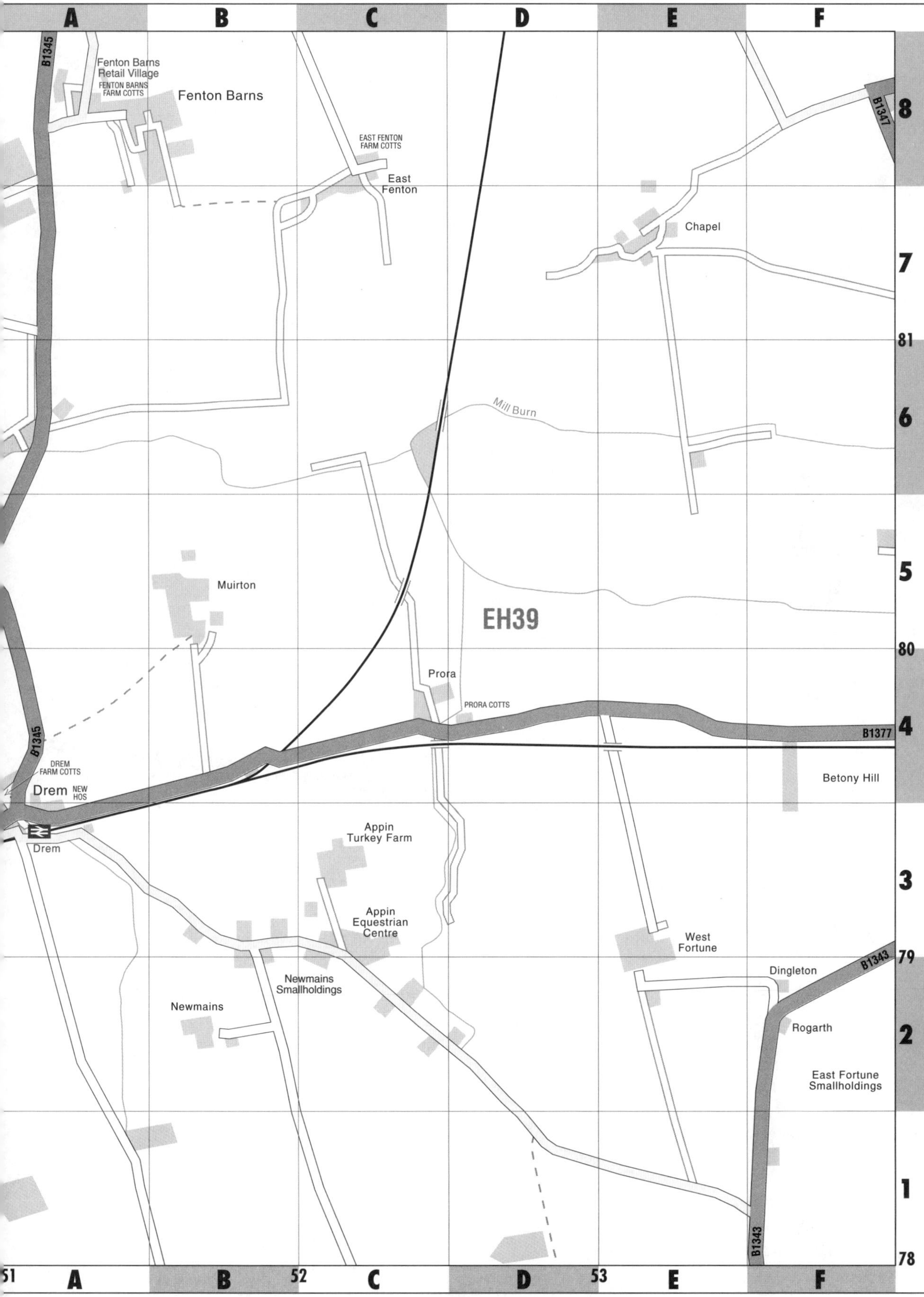
Fenton Barns
Retail Village
FENTON BARNS
FARM COTTS
Fenton Barns
B1345
EAST FENTON
FARM COTTS
East
Fenton
Chapel
B1347
Mill Burn
Muirton
EH39
Prora
PRORA COTTS
B1377
Betony Hill
DREM
FARM COTTS
Drem
NEW
HOS
Drem
Appin
Turkey Farm
Appin
Equestrian
Centre
West
Fortune
Dingleton
B1343
Rogarth
East Fortune
Smallholdings
Newmains
Smallholdings
Newmains

101
74

73
54

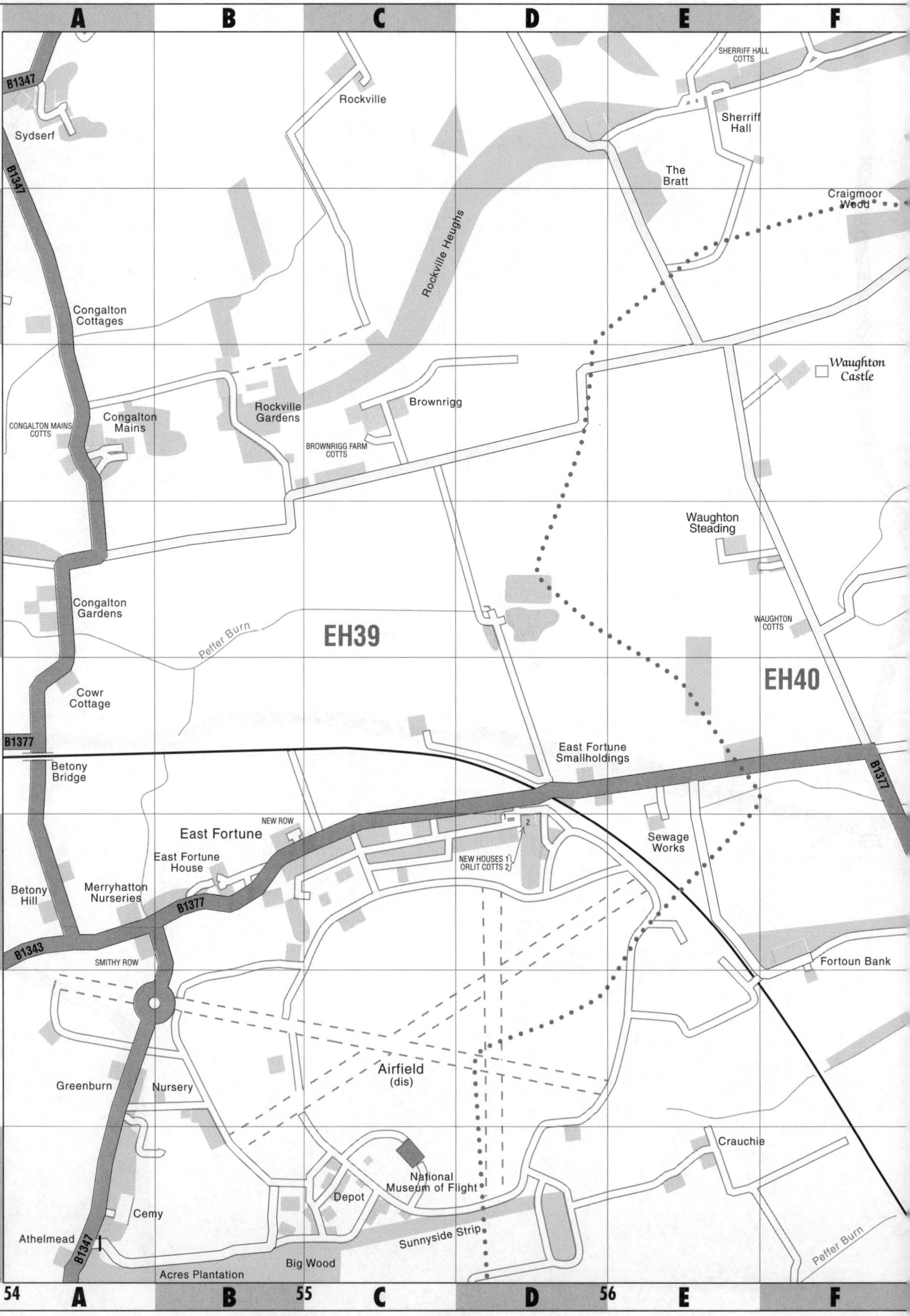
A
B
C
D
E
F
8
7
81
6
5
80
4
3
79
2
1
78
54
55
56
B1347
Sydserf
Rockville
SHERRIFF HALL COTTS
Sherriff Hall
The Bratt
Craigmoor Wood
Rockville Heughs
Congalton Cottages
Waughton Castle
Brownrigg
Rockville Gardens
CONGALTON MAINS COTTS
Congalton Mains
BROWNRIGG FARM COTTS
Waughton Steading
Congalton Gardens
WAUGHTON COTTS
Pefter Burn
EH39
EH40
Cowr Cottage
B1377
East Fortune Smallholdings
Betony Bridge
NEW ROW
East Fortune
East Fortune House
NEW HOUSES 1
ORLIT COTTS 2
Sewage Works
Betony Hill
Merryhatton Nurseries
B1343
SMITHY ROW
Fortoun Bank
Airfield
(dis)
Greenburn
Nursery
Crauchie
National Museum of Flight
Depot
Cemy
Athelmead
Sunnyside Strip
Big Wood
Acres Plantation
Peffer Burn

73
102

55
76

A
B
C
D
E
F
EH39
Whitekirk Hill
8
Craig
Wood
Pleasants
THE PADDOCK
WEST RD
Whitekirk
Whitekirk
Mains
A198
BINNING WOOD RD
A198
7
EH42
Old
Stonelaws
Merrylaws
81
John Muir Way
BANKHEAD
COTTS
STONELAWS
COTTS
Bankhead
Duncanson's
Wood
Gildswell
Wood
6
Stonelaws
Angus Wood
Newbyth
5
Crow
Wood
Newbyth
Steading
Howden
Old Mansion
House
NEWBYTH
STABLES
Inch
Wood
Howden Burn
80
4
Kamehill
Ashfield House
Birkhill
Peffer Burn
Oak Wood
Black's Park
Wood
EH40
3
LAWHEAD
COTTS
79
Cauldside
Smeaton
Farm
2
Smeaton
House
Nursery
1
Preston
Mains
Drylaw
Hill
B1377
DRYLAWHILL
THE DEAN
B1407
78
57
A
B
58
C
D
59
E
F

103
76

75
56

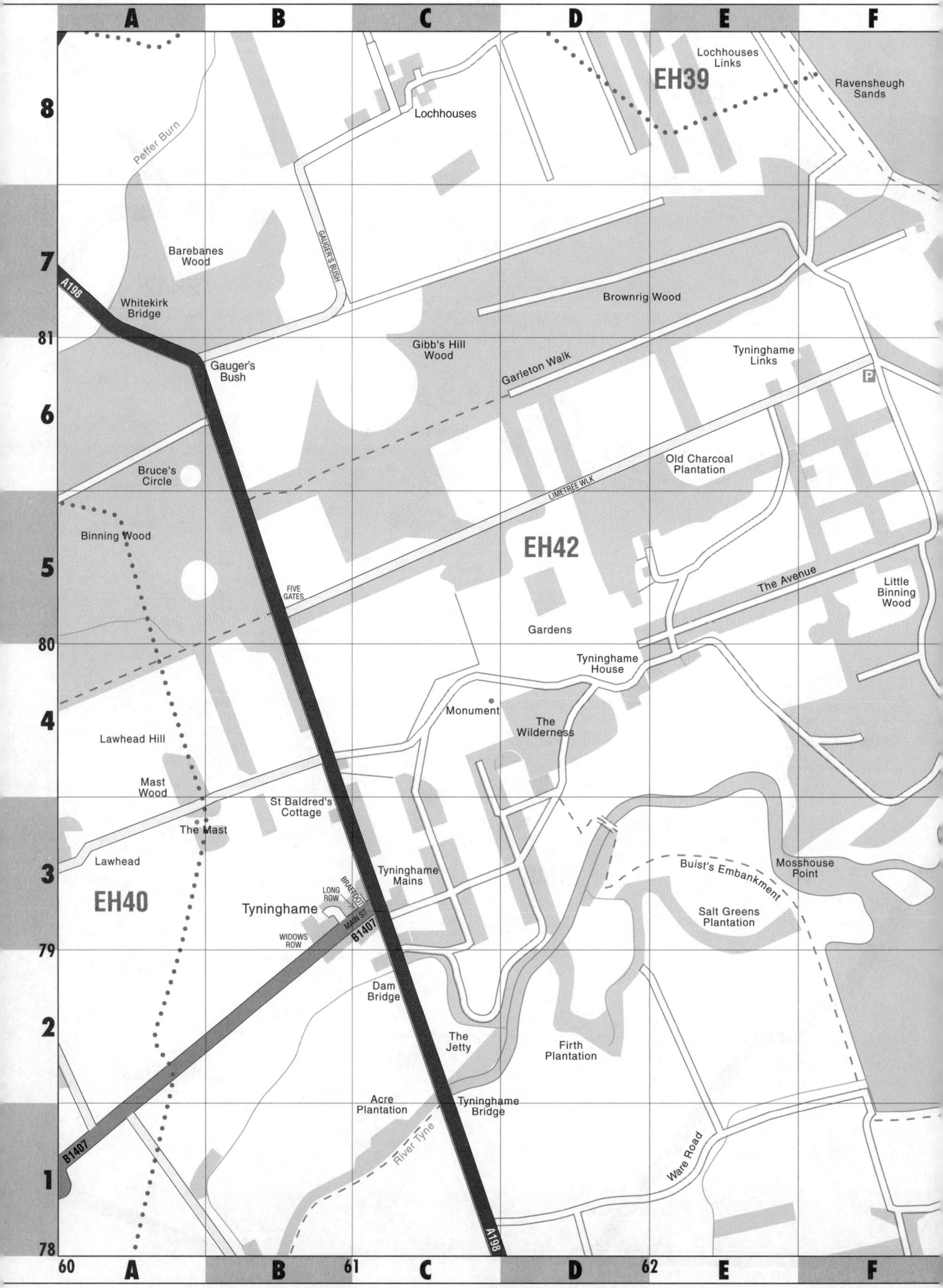
A
B
C
D
E
F
8
7
81
6
5
80
4
3
79
2
1
78
60
61
62
Lochhouses Links
EH39
Ravensheugh Sands
Lochhouses
Peffer Burn
GAUGER'S BUSH
Barebanes Wood
A198
Whitekirk Bridge
Brownrig Wood
Gibb's Hill Wood
Gauger's Bush
Garleton Walk
Tyninghame Links
P
Bruce's Circle
Old Charcoal Plantation
LIMETREE WLK
Binning Wood
EH42
FIVE GATES
The Avenue
Little Binning Wood
Gardens
Tyninghame House
Monument
The Wilderness
Lawhead Hill
Mast Wood
St Baldred's Cottage
The Mast
Lawhead
Tyninghame Mains
Buist's Embankment
Mosshouse Point
EH40
BRAEFOOT
LONG ROW
Tyninghame
MAIN ST
B1407
WIDOWS ROW
Salt Greens Plantation
Dam Bridge
The Jetty
Firth Plantation
Acre Plantation
Tyninghame Bridge
River Tyne
B1407
Ware Road
A198

75
104

78

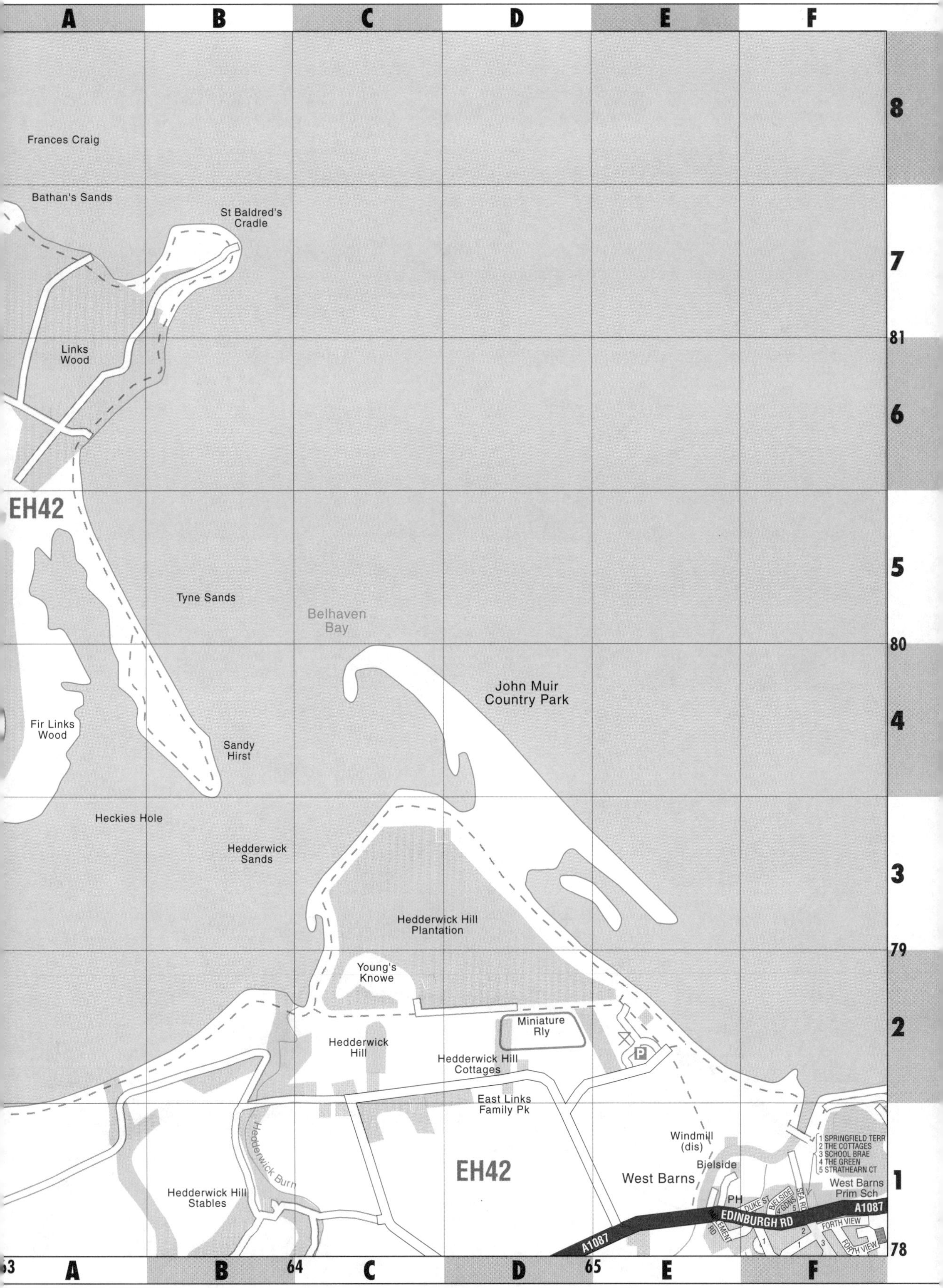
A
B
C
D
E
F
8
7
81
6
5
80
4
3
79
2
1
78
63
64
65
Frances Craig
Bathan's Sands
St Baldred's Cradle
Links Wood
EH42
Tyne Sands
Belhaven Bay
John Muir Country Park
Fir Links Wood
Sandy Hirst
Heckies Hole
Hedderwick Sands
Hedderwick Hill Plantation
Young's Knowe
Miniature Rly
Hedderwick Hill
Hedderwick Hill Cottages
East Links Family Pk
P
Hedderwick Burn
Hedderwick Hill Stables
EH42
Windmill (dis)
Bjelside
West Barns
PH
DUKE ST
BJELSIDE GDNS
SEA RD
EDINBURGH RD
A1087
A1087
FORTH VIEW
FORTH VIEW
1 SPRINGFIELD TERR
2 THE COTTAGES
3 SCHOOL BRAE
4 THE GREEN
5 STRATHEARN CT
West Barns Prim Sch

105

78

77
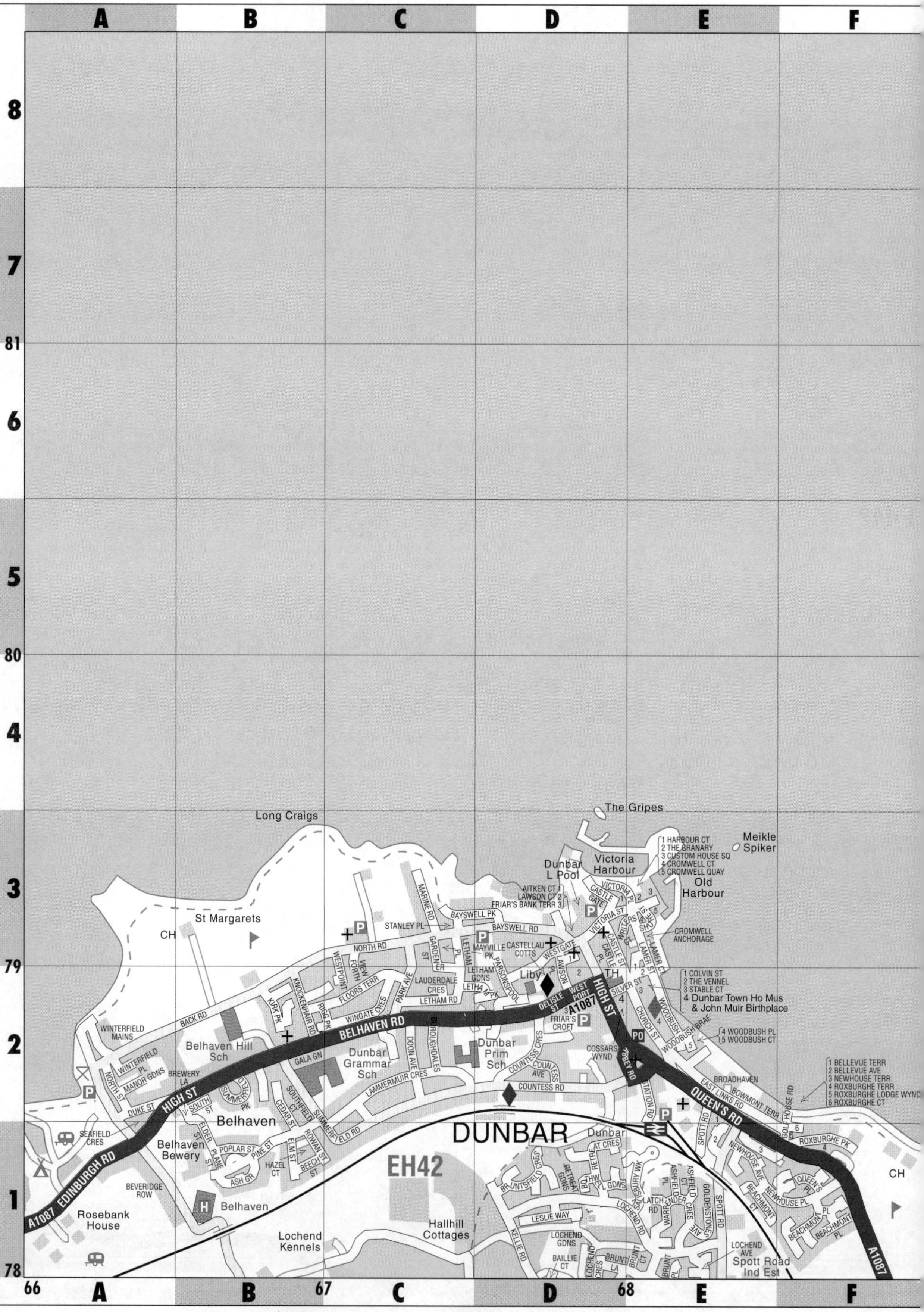

A
B
C
D
E
F
8
7
81
6
5
80
4
3
79
2
1
78
66
67
68
Long Craigs
The Gripes
Meikle Spiker
1 HARBOUR CT
2 THE GRANARY
3 CUSTOM HOUSE SQ
4 CROMWELL CT
5 CROMWELL QUAY
Victoria Harbour
Dunbar L Pool
Old Harbour
AITKEN CT 1
LAWSON CT 2
FRIAR'S BANK TERR 3
CROMWELL ANCHORAGE
St Margarets
CH
STANLEY PL
BAYSWELL PK
BAYSWELL RD
MARINE RD
NORTH RD
CASTELLAU COTTS
MAYVILLE PK
WESTGATE
VICTORIA PL
VICTORIA ST
CASTLE GATE
CASTLE ST
CASTLE PL
LAMER ST
TH
1 COLVIN ST
2 THE VENNEL
3 STABLE CT
4 Dunbar Town Ho Mus & John Muir Birthplace
SILVER ST
CHURCH ST
WOODBUSH BRAE
4 WOODBUSH PL
5 WOODBUSH CT
HIGH ST
A1087
WEST PORT
DELISLE ST
Liby
FRIAR'S CROFT
LETHAM RD
LAUDERDALE CRES
FLOORS TERR
WESTPOINT
PARK AVE
WINGATE CRES
BELHAVEN RD
BACK RD
WINTERFIELD MAINS
WINTERFIELD PL
MANOR GDNS
BREWERY LA
NORTH ST
Belhaven Hill Sch
KIRK PK
GALA GN
Dunbar Grammar Sch
DOON AVE
ROUGHDALES
LAMMERMUIR CRES
Dunbar Prim Sch
COUNTESS CRES
COUNTESS AVE
COUNTESS RD
COSSARS WYND
ABBEY RD
STATION RD
1 BELLEVUE TERR
2 BELLEVUE AVE
3 NEWHOUSE TERR
4 ROXBURGHE TERR
5 ROXBURGHE LODGE WYND
6 ROXBURGHE CT
BROADHAVEN
EAST LINKS RD
BOWMONT TERR
GOLF HOUSE RD
QUEEN'S RD
ROXBURGHE PK
DUKE ST
SOUTH ST
SUMMERFIELD PK
Belhaven
SEAFIELD CRES
Belhaven Bewery
POPLAR ST
PINE ST
ELM ST
HAZEL CT
BEECH ST
ASH GR
CEDAR ST
SOUTHFIELD CT
ROWAN ST
DUNBAR
Dunbar
EH42
SPOTT RD
NEWHOUSE AVE
BEACHMONT CT
NEWHOUSE PL
QUEEN'S PL
BEACHMONT PL
CH
EDINBURGH RD
A1087
BEVERIDGE ROW
Rosebank House
Belhaven
Lochend Kennels
Hallhill Cottages
BRUNTSFIELD CRES
RETREAT GDNS
RETREAT CRES
LESLIE WAY
KELLIE RD
LOCHEND GDNS
BAILLIE CT
LOCHEND CRES
BRUNT LA
BRUNT CT
BRUNT PL
LOCHEND RD
SALISBURY WK
LATCH RD
WARRENDER CRES
ASHFIELD CT
ASHFIELD PL
GOLDENSTONES AVE
LOCHEND AVE
Spott Road Ind Est
A1087

77
106

A
B
C
D
E
F
8
7
81
6
5
80
4
3
79
2
1
78
Lawrie's Den
The Vaults
John Muir Way
West Links
Sports & Social Centre
Fluke Dub
EH42
Vaults Wood
Mill Stone Neuk
69
70
71

107

59

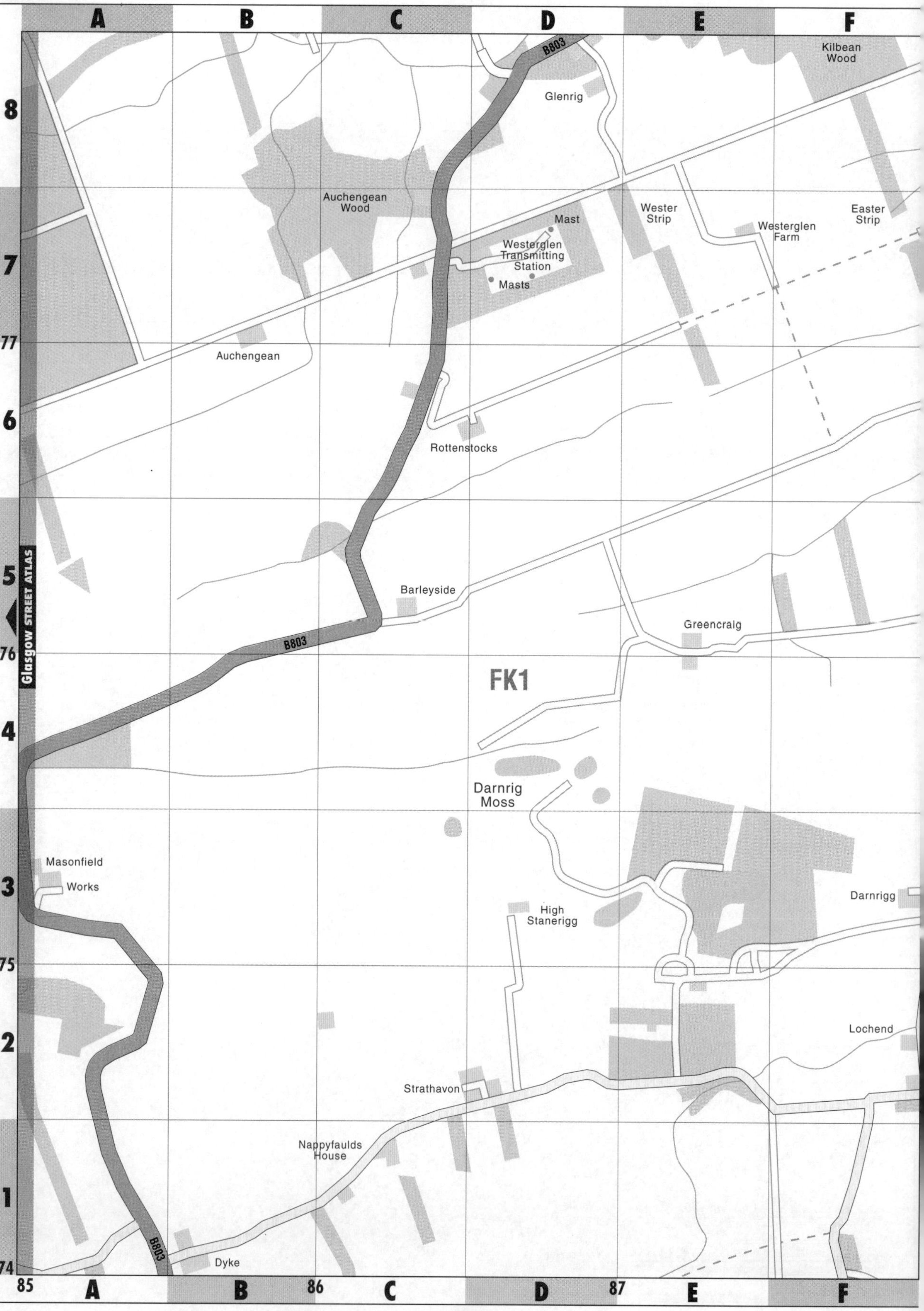
A
B
C
D
E
F
8
7
77
6
5
76
4
3
75
2
1
74
85
86
87
Kilbean Wood
B803
Glenrig
Auchengean Wood
Mast
Wester Strip
Westerglen Farm
Easter Strip
Westerglen Transmitting Station
Masts
Auchengean
Rottenstocks
Barleyside
Greencraig
FK1
Darnrig Moss
Masonfield
Works
High Stanerigg
Darnrigg
Lochend
Strathavon
Nappyfaulds House
Dyke
Glasgow STREET ATLAS

108

60
82

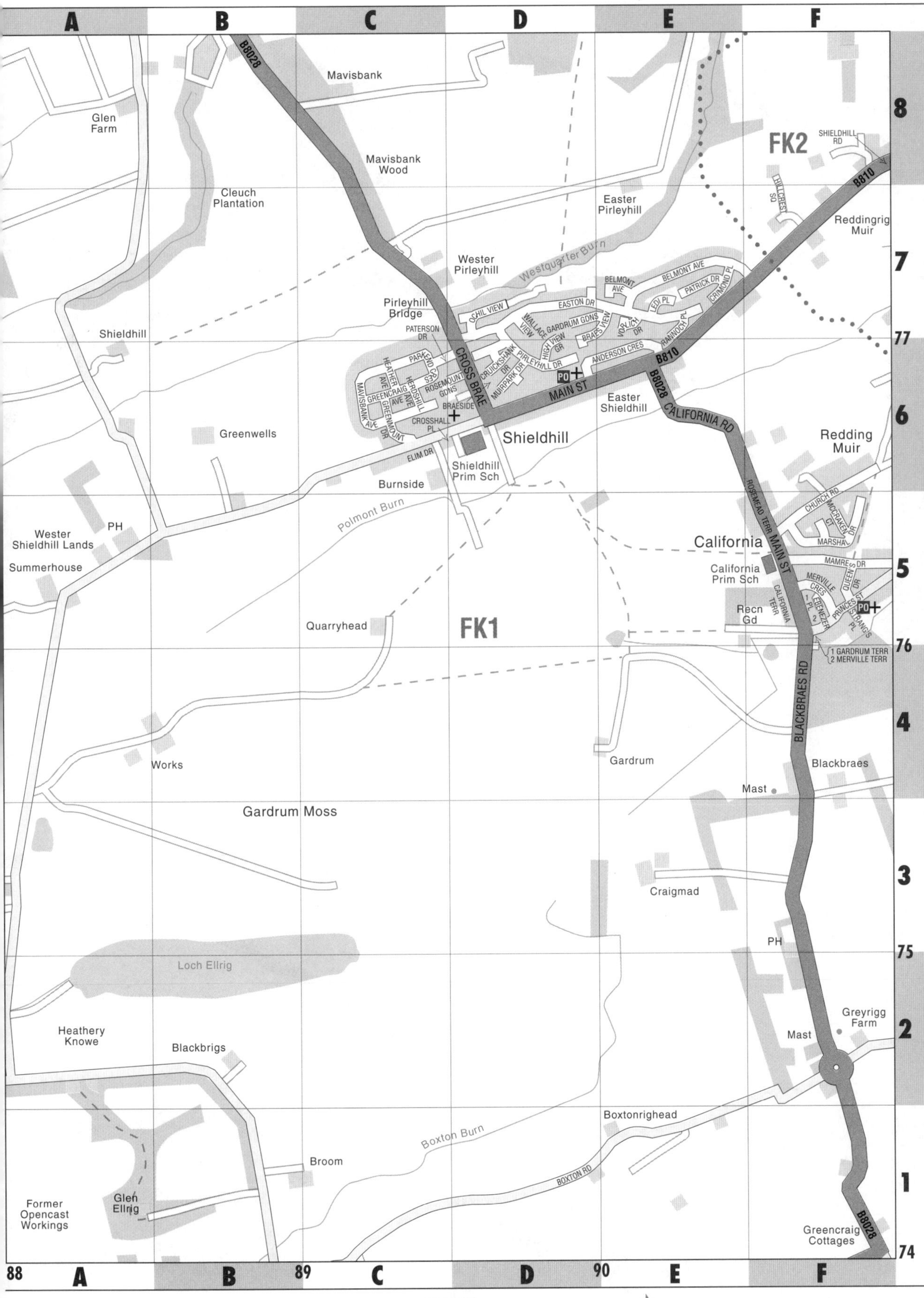
A
B
C
D
E
F
8
7
77
6
5
76
4
3
75
2
1
74
88
89
90
B8028
Mavisbank
Glen
Farm
Mavisbank
Wood
Cleuch
Plantation
FK2
SHIELDHILL
RD
B810
HILLCREST
SQ
Easter
Pirleyhill
Reddingrig
Muir
Wester
Pirleyhill
Westquarter Burn
BELMONT AVE
BELMONT
AVE
PATRICK DR
CRIMOND PL
LEDI PL
EASTON DR
OCHIL VIEW
Pirleyhill
Bridge
GARDRUM GDNS
WALLACE
VIEW
HIGH VIEW
GR
BRAES VIEW
VORLICH
DR
RANNOCH PL
PATERSON
DR
Shieldhill
PARK
LEND CT
CROSS BRAE
CRUICKSHANK
DR
PIRLEYHILL DR
ANDERSON CRES
B810
HEATHER
AVE
GREENCRAIG
AVE
HEADSHILL
AVE
ROSEMOUNT
GDNS
MUIRPARK DR
PO
MAIN ST
B8028
MAVISBANK
AVE
GREENMOUNT
DR
BRAESIDE
CROSSHALL
PL
Easter
Shieldhill
CALIFORNIA RD
Greenwells
ELIM DR
Shieldhill
Shieldhill
Prim Sch
Redding
Muir
Burnside
ROSEMEAD TERR
MAIN ST
CHURCH RD
McCRACKEN
DR
Polmont Burn
PH
Wester
Shieldhill Lands
California
MARSHALL
Summerhouse
MAMRES DR
California
Prim Sch
MERVILLE
CRES
QUEENS DR
EBENEZER
PRINCES ST
STRANG'S
PL
Recn
Gd
CALIFORNIA
TERR
Quarryhead
FK1
1 GARDRUM TERR
2 MERVILLE TERR
BLACKBRAES RD
Works
Gardrum
Blackbraes
Mast
Gardrum Moss
Craigmad
PH
Loch Ellrig
Greyrigg
Farm
Heathery
Knowe
Mast
Blackbrigs
Boxtonrighead
Boxton Burn
Broom
BOXTON RD
Former
Opencast
Workings
Glen
Ellrig
Greencraig
Cottages
B8028

109
82

81
61

C8
1 WALLACE BRAE CT
2 WALLACE BRAE GR
3 WALLACE BRAE PL
4 WALLACE BRAE GDNS
5 NEWLANDS ROAD RDBT
6 Scottish Prison Service Coll

D8
1 BRUCE GDNS
2 HOLMLEA AVE
3 CRAIGLAW TERR
4 PARK GDNS
5 HILLVIEW RD

F7
1 RAINHILL CT
2 NICOLTON CT
3 AILSA CT
4 MILLBANK TERR

A
B
C
D
E
F
8
7
77
6
5
76
4
3
75
2
1
74
91
92
93
HM Young Offenders Inst Polmont Brightons
NEWLANDS RD
SHIELDHILL RD
B810
B805
B825
Union Canal
Reddingmuirhead
Brightons
Braes High Sch
Wallacestone Prim Sch
Wallacestone
Middlerig
Rumford
Maddiston Prim Sch
MADDISTON RD
MAIN ST
Greenwells
Gardrum Burn
Polmont Burn
FK2
Whitesiderig Muir
Burnside
Central Scotland Fire & Rescue Service HQ
Manuel Burn
Glenhead
CH
FK1
Works
Craigend
Whiterigg
Snabhead
Easter Blackrig
Wester Blackrig
Opencast Workings
BOXTON RD
IRENE TERR
Standburn
Drumbowie Prim Sch
Windyrigg
Gateside
Drumbroider Moss
Easter Drumbroider
Coxhill
Candie House
Candie

81
110

62
84

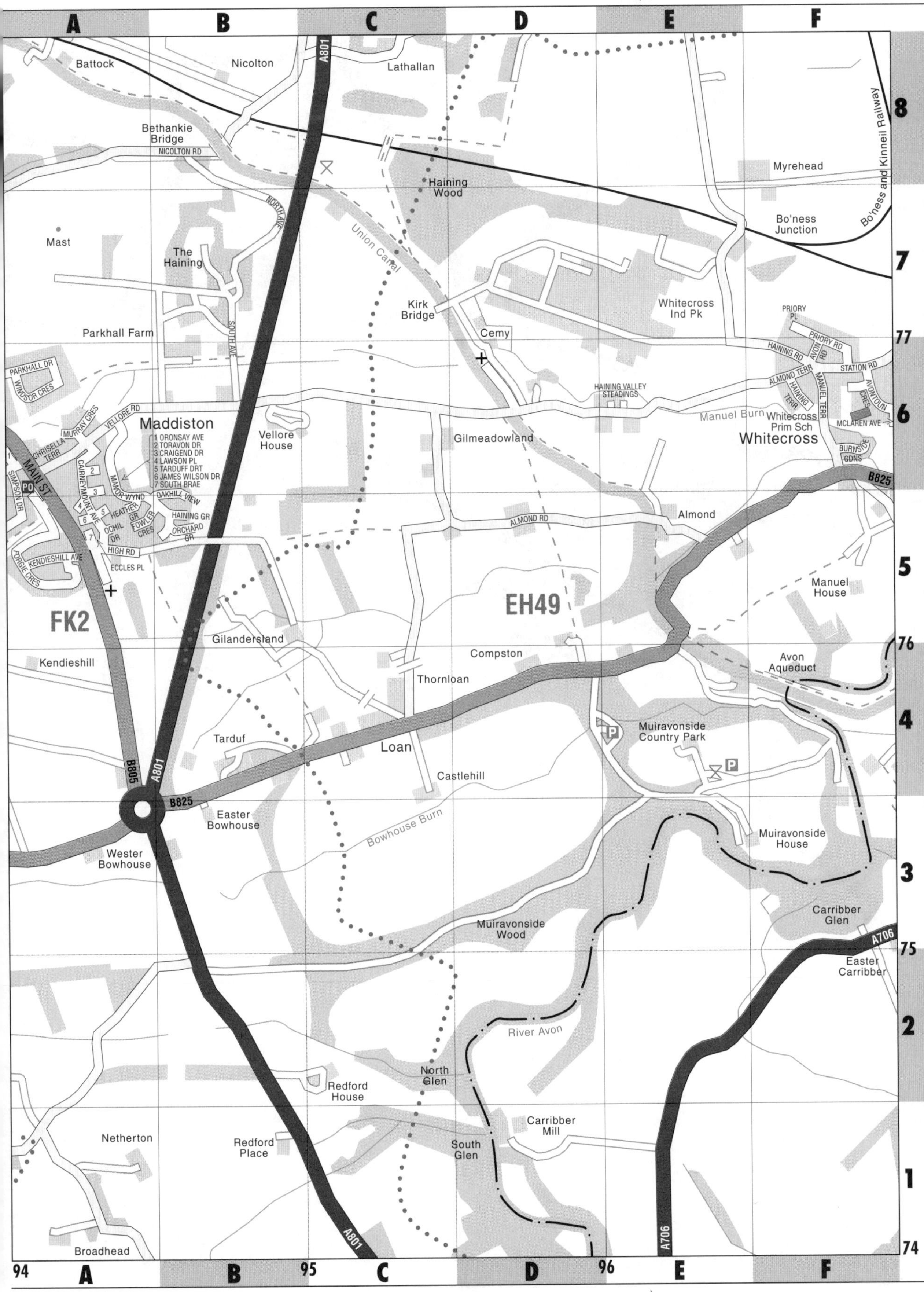
A
B
C
D
E
F
8
7
77
6
5
76
4
3
75
2
1
74
94
95
96
Battock
Nicolton
Lathallan
A801
Bethankie Bridge
NICOLTON RD
Haining Wood
Myrehead
Bo'ness and Kinneil Railway
Bo'ness Junction
NORTH AVE
Mast
The Haining
Union Canal
Kirk Bridge
Whitecross Ind Pk
PRIORY PL
PRIORY RD
HAINING RD
AVON RD
Parkhall Farm
SOUTH AVE
Cemy
PARKHALL DR
WINDSOR CRES
STATION RD
ALMOND TERR
HAINING TERR
MANUEL TERR
AVONTOUN CRES
HAINING VALLEY STEADINGS
Manuel Burn
Whitecross Prim Sch
MCLAREN AVE
Maddiston
VELLORE RD
MURRAY CRES
CHRISELLA TERR
MAIN ST
1 ORONSAY AVE
2 TORAVON DR
3 CRAIGEND DR
4 LAWSON PL
5 TARDUFF DRT
6 JAMES WILSON DR
7 SOUTH BRAE
Vellore House
Gilmeadowland
Whitecross
BURNSIDE GDNS
B825
SIMPSON DR
PO
CAIRNEYMOUNT AVE
MANOR WYND
OAKHILL VIEW
HEATHER GR
OCHIL DR
FOWLER CRES
HAINING GR
ORCHARD GR
HIGH RD
ALMOND RD
Almond
KENDIESHILL AVE
FORGIE CRES
ECCLES PL
Manuel House
FK2
EH49
Gilandersland
Kendieshill
Compston
Thornloan
Avon Aqueduct
Muiravonside Country Park
Tarduf
Loan
Castlehill
B805
A801
B825
Easter Bowhouse
Bowhouse Burn
Muiravonside House
Wester Bowhouse
Carribber Glen
Muiravonside Wood
A706
Easter Carribber
River Avon
North Glen
Redford House
Netherton
Redford Place
Carribber Mill
South Glen
A801
A706
Broadhead

111
84

83
63

E6
1 OLD SCHOOL CT
2 PRESTONFIELD GDNS

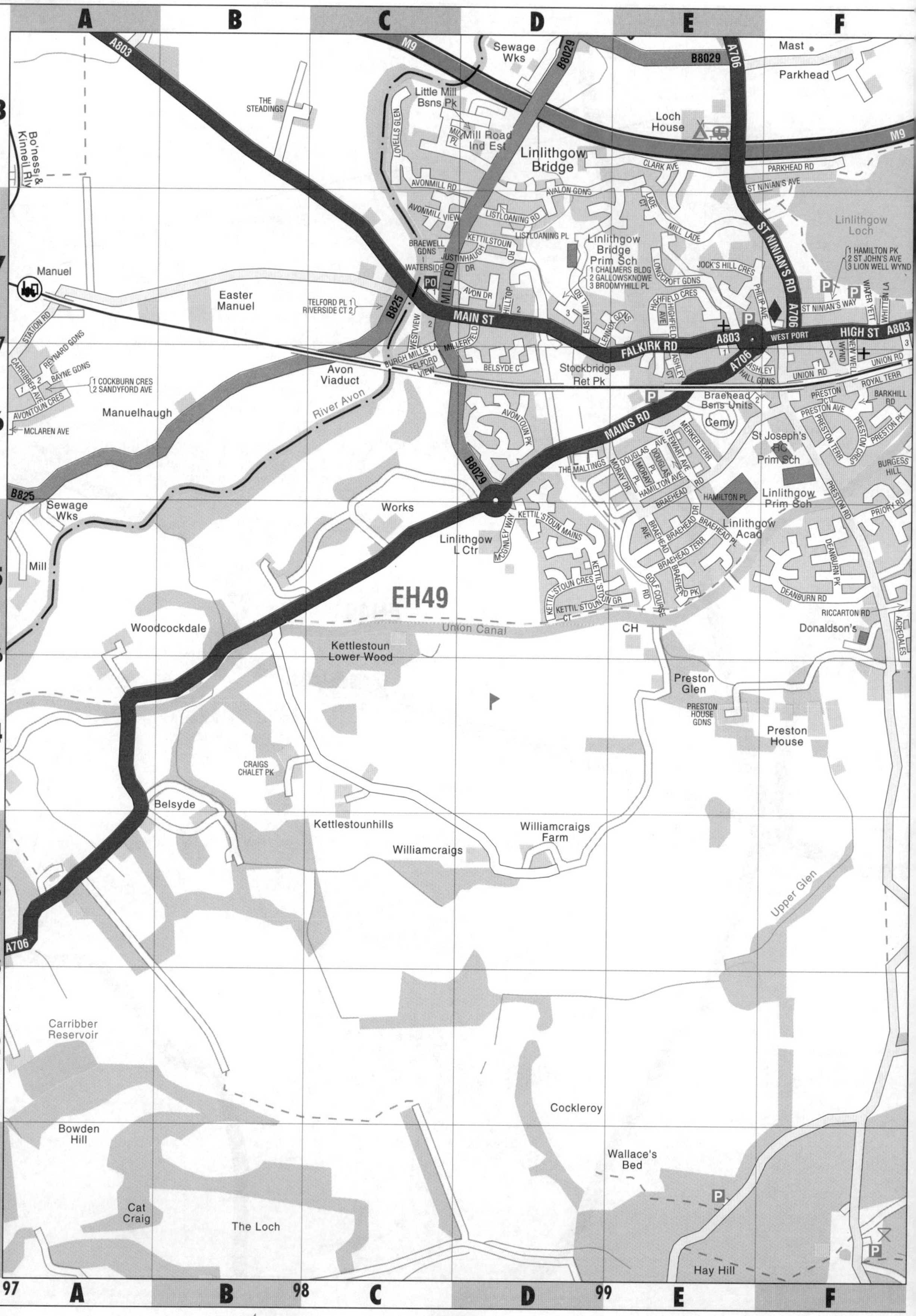
A
B
C
D
E
F
8
7
77
6
5
76
4
3
75
2
1
74
97
98
99
Sewage Wks
Mast
Parkhead
THE STEADINGS
Little Mill Bsns Pk
Mill Road Ind Est
Loch House
Bo'ness & Kinneil Rly
Linlithgow Bridge
CLARK AVE
PARKHEAD RD
ST NINIAN'S AVE
AVONMILL RD
AVALON GDNS
LISTLOANING RD
AVONMILL VIEW
MILL LADE
Linlithgow Loch
Linlithgow Bridge Prim Sch
1 CHALMERS BLDG
2 GALLOWSKNOWE
3 BROOMYHILL PL
KETTILSTOUN RD
LISTLOANING PL
BRAEWELL GDNS
JUSTINHAUGH DR
WATERSIDE
MILL RD
JOCK'S HILL CRES
1 HAMILTON PK
2 ST JOHN'S AVE
3 LION WELL WYND
Manuel
Easter Manuel
TELFORD PL 1
RIVERSIDE CT 2
AVON DR
HILLTOP
LONGCROFT GDNS
ST NINIAN'S RD
ST NINIAN'S WAY
WATER YETT
WHITTEN LA
MAIN ST
HIGHFIELD CRES
PHILIP AVE
STATION RD
REYNARD GDNS
CARRIBBER AVE
BAYNE GDNS
AVONTOUN CRES
1 COCKBURN CRES
2 SANDYFORD AVE
BURGH MILLS LA
WESTVIEW
MILLERFIELD
TELFORD VIEW
FALKIRK RD
WEST PORT
HIGH ST
NEW WELL WYND
UNION RD
Avon Viaduct
BELSYDE CT
Stockbridge Ret Pk
ASHLEY HALL GDNS
ROYAL TERR
BARKHILL RD
Manuelhaugh
River Avon
MCLAREN AVE
AVONTOUN PK
MAINS RD
Braehead Bsns Units
Cemy
St Joseph's RC Prim Sch
PRESTON CT
PRESTON AVE
PRESTON TERR
PRESTON CRES
PRESTON PK
BURGESS HILL
THE MALTINGS
MORAY DR
DOUGLAS AVE
STEWART AVE
MERKER TERR
HAMILTON AVE
Sewage Wks
Works
KETTILSTOUN MAINS
BRAEHEAD
HAMILTON PL
Linlithgow Prim Sch
PRESTON RD
PRIORY RD
Linlithgow Acad
Linlithgow L Ctr
MCGINLEY WAY
BRAEHEAD TERR
BRAEHEAD PL
BRAEHEAD PK
Mill
DEANBURN PK
KETTILSTOUN CRES
KETTILSTOUN GR
KETTILSTOUN CT
GOLF COURSE RD
DEANBURN RD
EH49
RICCARTON RD
Union Canal
CH
Donaldson's
ACREDALES
Woodcockdale
Kettlestoun Lower Wood
Preston Glen
PRESTON HOUSE GDNS
Preston House
CRAIGS CHALET PK
Belsyde
Kettlestounhills
Williamcraigs Farm
Williamcraigs
Upper Glen
Carribber Reservoir
Cockleroy
Bowden Hill
Wallace's Bed
Cat Craig
The Loch
Hay Hill
M9
B8029
A706
A803
B825

83
112

64
86

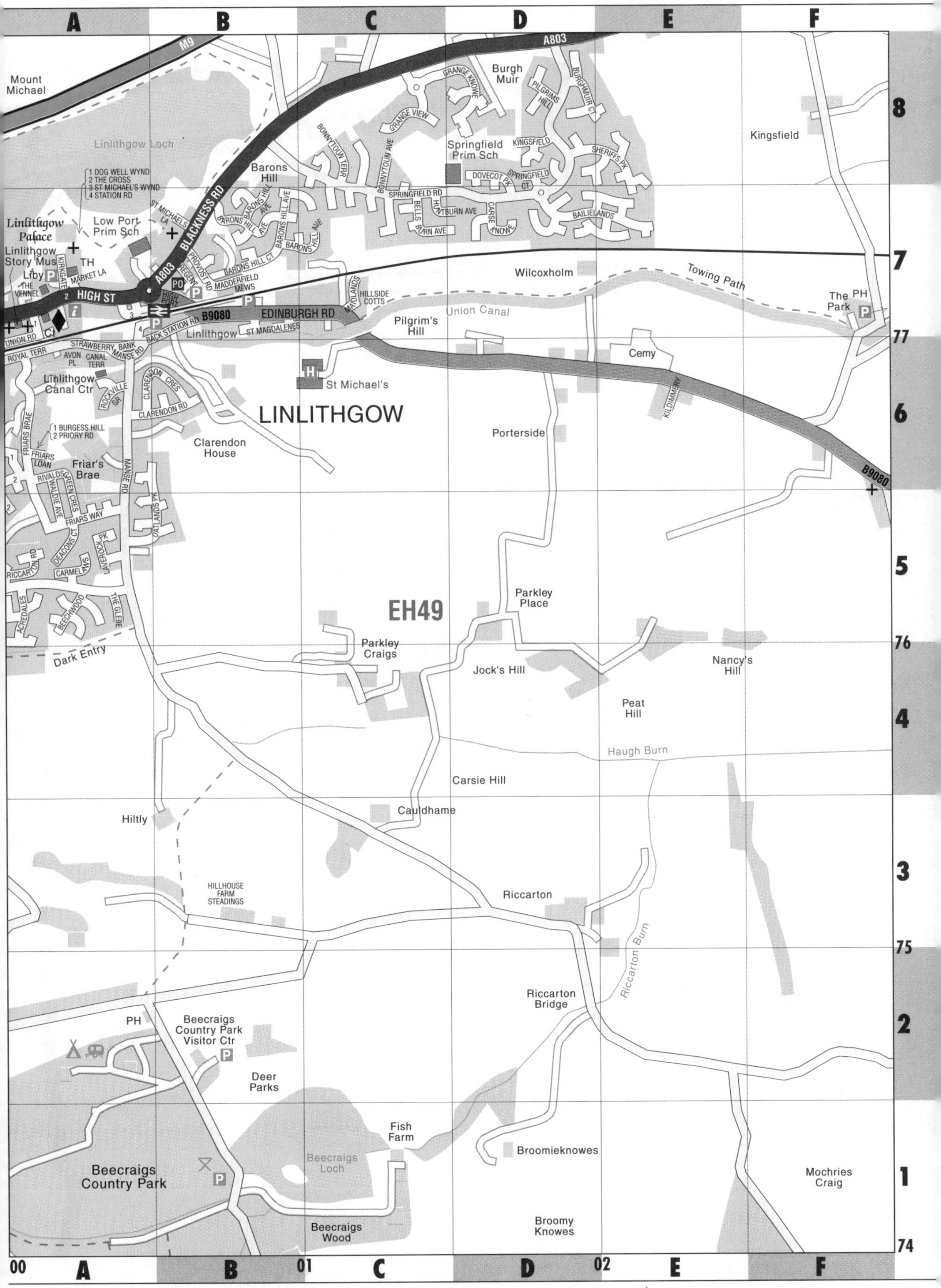
A
B
C
D
E
F
M9
A803
Mount Michael
Linlithgow Loch
Burgh Muir
Kingsfield
Barons Hill
Springfield Prim Sch
1 DOG WELL WYND
2 THE CROSS
3 ST MICHAEL'S WYND
4 STATION RD
Linlithgow Palace
Low Port Prim Sch
Linlithgow Story Mus
TH
Liby
THE VENNEL
HIGH ST
KIRKGATE
MARKET LA
BLACKNESS RD
ST MICHAEL'S LA
BARONS HILL AVE
BARONS HILL CT
PROVOST RD
REGENT
MADDERFIELD MEWS
HIGH PORT
PO
GRANGE KNOWE
GRANGE VIEW
BONNYTOUN TERR
BONNYTOUN AVE
PILGRIMS HILL
BURGHMUIR CT
KINGSFIELD
SHERIFFS PK
DOVECOT PK
SPRINGFIELD CT
SPRINGFIELD RD
BELLS BURN AVE
HUNTBURN AVE
CARSE KNOWE
BAILIELANDS
Wilcoxholm
Towing Path
The PH
Park
MAYLANDS
HILLSIDE COTTS
Union Canal
Pilgrim's Hill
EDINBURGH RD
B9080
Linlithgow
ST MAGDALENES
BACK STATION RD
UNION RD
ROYAL TERR
STRAWBERRY BANK
MANSE RD
AVON PL
CANAL TERR
Linlithgow Canal Ctr
ROCKVILLE GR
CLARENDON CRES
CLARENDON RD
St Michael's
LINLITHGOW
Cemy
KILDIMMERY
Porterside
1 BURGESS HILL
2 PRIORY RD
FRIARS BRAE
FRIARS LOAN
Friar's Brae
RIVALDSGREEN CRES
WALDIE AVE
FRIARS WAY
DEACONS CT
LAVEROCK PK
OATLANDS PK
Clarendon House
RICCARTON RD
CARMELAWS
ACREDALES
BEECHWOOD
THE GLEBE
EH49
Parkley Place
Parkley Craigs
Dark Entry
Jock's Hill
Nancy's Hill
Peat Hill
Haugh Burn
Carsie Hill
Cauldhame
Hiltly
HILLHOUSE FARM STEADINGS
Riccarton
Riccarton Burn
Riccarton Bridge
PH
Beecraigs Country Park Visitor Ctr
Deer Parks
Fish Farm
Beecraigs Loch
Broomieknowes
Beecraigs Country Park
Mochries Craig
Beecraigs Wood
Broomy Knowes
8
7
77
6
5
76
4
3
75
2
1
74
00
01
02

113
86

85
65

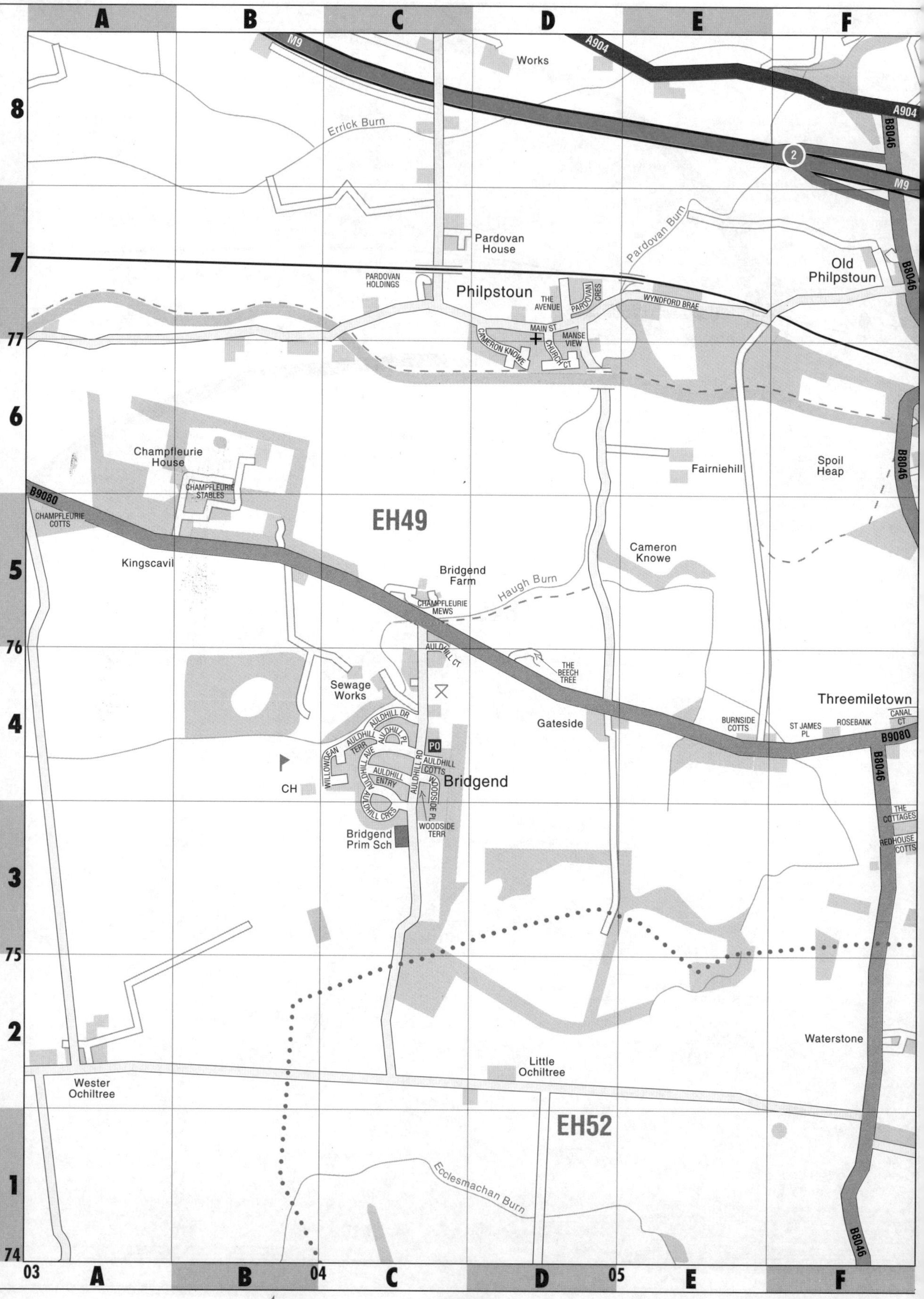
A
B
C
D
E
F
8
7
77
6
5
76
4
3
75
2
1
74
03
04
05
M9
A904
Works
Errick Burn
B8046
2
Pardovan House
Pardovan Burn
Old Philpstoun
PARDOVAN HOLDINGS
Philpstoun
THE AVENUE
PARDOVAN CRES
WYNDFORD BRAE
MAIN ST
CAMERON KNOWE
CHURCH CT
MANSE VIEW
Champfleurie House
CHAMPFLEURIE STABLES
B9080
CHAMPFLEURIE COTTS
Fairniehill
Spoil Heap
EH49
Kingscavil
Cameron Knowe
Bridgend Farm
Haugh Burn
CHAMPFLEURIE MEWS
AULDHILL CT
THE BEECH TREE
Sewage Works
Threemiletown
Gateside
BURNSIDE COTTS
ST JAMES PL
ROSEBANK
CANAL CT
AULDHILL DR
AULDHILL PL
AULDHILL TERR
WILLOWDEAN
AULDHILL AVE
PO
AULDHILL COTTS
AULDHILL RD
AULDHILL ENTRY
Bridgend
CH
AULDHILL CRES
WOODSIDE PL
WOODSIDE TERR
Bridgend Prim Sch
THE COTTAGES
REDHOUSE COTTS
Waterstone
Little Ochiltree
Wester Ochiltree
EH52
Ecclesmachan Burn

85
114

66
88

A
B
C
D
E
F
EH30
8
Philpstoun House
Hopetoun Wood
The Manse
Woodville
A904
Whitequarries Ind Est
Mast
B8020
Woodend
East Philpstoun
WYNDFORD BRAE
Galascrook
7
Duntarvie
77
Philpstoun Mill
Craigton
Bailies Muir
P
Philpstoun Muir
Craigton House
6
Fawnspark
EH49
M9
5
Union Canal
The Den
EH52
Mounthooly
Myre
76
B8046
4
THE COTTAGES
REDHOUSE COTTS
Trinlaymire
STATION RD
3
BENNET WOOD TERR 1
MIDHOPE PL 2
CRAIGTON CT 3
Reservoir
TIPPET KNOWES CT
AULDCATHIE PL
Lampinsdub
TIPPET KNOWES PK
MAIN ST
B9080
75
TIPPET KNOWES RD
DUNN PL
SYCAMORE GR
NIDDRY VIEW
Winchburgh Prim Sch
MILLGATE
CHESTNUT GR
ABERCORN PL
Glendevon
CRAIGTON PL
2
GLENDEVON PK
GLENDEVON
WINCHBURGH COTTS
NIDDRY RD
GLENDEVON COTTS
Holy Family RC Prim Sch
Winchburgh
PO
GLASS RD
BELL'S MILL TERR
GLASS CRES
GLASS PL
Tippet Knowes
Millcraig
Cemy
OLD GLENDEVON FARM COTTS
Niddry Burn
1
Kirklands
NIDDRY
Faucheldean
B8020
74
06
07
08

117
88

87
67

A
B
C
D
E
F
8
7
77
6
5
76
4
3
75
2
1
74
09
10
11
A904
B924
BO'NESS RD
Icehouse Hill
HEADRIG RD
ECHLINE DR
ECHLINE AVE
ECHLINE PK
BUILYEON RD
ECHLINE PL 1
ECHLINE 2
PH
MAIN ST
DUDDINGSTON CRES
GALLOW VIEW
DUDDINGSTONE TERR
Newton
Lawflat
Duddingston
Duddingston Wood
Linn Mill Burn
White Lodge
Echline Strip
Gallow Hill
Dundas Mains
Burn Craigs
EH30
Chapel Acre
B8020
Totleywells Cottages
Westfield Farm
Dundas Castle
Duntarvie Castle
EH52
Barrencraig Wood
Dundas Hill
M9
Swineburn Wood
Hopetoun Fishery
Swineburn
Dundas Loch
Swine Burn
Carmelhill Wood
Muiriehall Wood
Carmelhill Cottage
HUMBIE COTTS
Humbie Reservoir
Niddry Mains House
Humbie
Beatlie Wood
STATION RD
PH
BEATLIE RD
Niddry Mains
EH29
KIRKLANDS PARK GR 1
GLENDINNING DR 2
GLENDINNING PL 3
KIRKLANDS PARK RIGG 4
KIRKLANDS PARK GDNS 5
STIRLING RD 6
OAKBANK PL
CASTLE RD
CASTLE TERR
Hawk Hill Wood
1 NIDDRY VIEW
2 ABERCORN CT
3 ABERCORN PL
4 MIDHOPE PL
CRAIGTON PL
CH
Kirkliston L Ctr
KIRKLANDS PARK ST
GLENDINNING RD
KIRKLANDS PARK CRES
B9080
BUIE RIGG
BLIE BRAE
BUIE HAUGH
Cemy
Charles's Bridge
Ross's Plantation
Niddry Castle
Niddry Burn
1a
Union Canal
Lindsay's Craigs
COTLAWS
GATESIDE RD
Overton
KING EDWARDS WAY

87
116

68
90

A
B
C
D
E
F
8
7
77
6
5
76
4
3
75
2
1
74
12
13
14
QUEENSFERRY
EH30
EH29
EH12
BUILYEON RD
A904
A90
M9
B800
B924
B9080
B800 NEWLISTON RD
KIRKLISTON RD B907
FERRYMUIR RD
FERRYMUIR GAIT
FERRYMUIR LA
STONEYFLATTS CRES
STONEYFLATTS PK
ECHLINE TERR
ECHLINE AVE
LONG CROOK
CANMORE ST
PLEWLANDS PL
HUGH RUSSELL PL
VIEWFORTH PL
PRIORY GR
HOPE ST
CARMELITE RD
INCHCOLM TERR
Cemy
Hotel
Masts
Ferry Muir
BURGESS RD
LAWSON CRES
ROSEBERY AVE
ROSEBERY CT
DUNDAS AVE
WILLIAM BLACK PL
JOHN MASON CT
INCHKEITH AVE
KEMPSTON PL
PRIMROSE GDNS
CLARK AVE
ARROL PL
OCHIL CT
ALMOND GR
STEWART GR
LOVERS LA
FERRYBURN GN
MOUBRAY GR
SCOTSTOUN GN
SCOTSTOUN PK
SCOTSTOUN AVE
SOUTH SCOTSTOUN
ATHELING GR
WELLHEAD CL
PROVOST MILNE GR
SOMMERVILLE GDNS
WHITEHEAD GR
ASHBURNHAM RD
QUEEN MARGARET DR
STATION RD
STATION VIEW
Queensferry High Sch
Queensferry Recn Ctr
Works
Dalmeny
BANKHEAD GR
ROSSHILL TERR
FORTH TERR
FORTH PK
Bankhead Cottages
BANKHEAD RD
Crossall Hill
Wester Dalmeny Steading
MAIN ST
Mast
Easter Dalmeny
CARLOWRIE AVE
CARLOWRIE CRES
THE GLEBE
Dalmeny Prim Sch
DUNDAS HOME FARM
North Lodge
CH
Sewage Works
Oil Storage Depot
Dolphington Burn
STANDINGSTANE RD
Milton
Craigend
Craigbrae
Carlowrie Cottages
CARLOWRIE FARM COTTS
Carlowrie Farm
1 GLENDINNING DR
2 GLENDINNING WAY
LOANHEAD COTTS
Almondhill
ALMONDHILL COTTS
ALMONDHILL STEADING
ALMONDHILL RD
ALLISON PL
STEWART PL
DUNDAS PL
DUDGEON PL
JUMBIE RD
NEWMAINS RD
ALLAN PK
MAITLAND RD
STIRLING RD MAIN ST
QUEENSFERRY RD
STATION RD
LISTON DR
CARMEL AVE
LISTON PL
PENTLAND VIEW
CARMEL RD
MARSHALL RD
LISTON RD
MANSE RD
THE GLEBE
TODDSHILL RD
BOWLING GREEN RD
ALMONDSIDE
AULDGATE
KIRKSTYLE GDNS
HIGH ST
PATH BRAE
THE SQUARE
WELLFLATS RD
STATION TERR
MAIN ST
PO
PH
Liby
Kirkliston Prim Sch
COTLAWS
GATESIDE RD
KING EDWARDS WAY
MAITLAND HOG LA
CLERICS HILL
River Almond
Kirkliston
Foxhall
Wheatlands
Carlowrie
Cat Stone
Twr
Boathouse Bridge

117
90

89
69

A B C D E F
8
7
77
6
5
76
4
3
75
2
1
74
15 16 17
Shepherds Bog
Dunter Hill
Chapel Gate
B924
Royal Clump
Chapel Coppice
Mansion Hill
Mouse Wood
Dalmeny Park
Easter Dalmeny
Long Green Wood
Long Green
Barnbougle Gate
Mansion Hill Wood
Home Farm
Dolphington Burn
A90
BARNBOUGLE RIDE
Cockle Burn
HOME FARM COTTS
Dolphington House
Burnshot Wood
Dolphington
Dolphington Cottages
EH30
Craigie Hill
West Craigie Farm
EH4
East Craigie
New Burnshot
Craigiehill Quarry (dis)
Lowood
Burnshot Gate
Glenpunty Wood
HILLSIDE TERR
HILLSIDE RD
Edinburgh Gate
Clove Quarry (dis)
RIVER ALMOND WK
DOWIE'S MILL COTTS
Carlowrie Farm
Clove Craig
DOWIE'S MILL LA
CRAMOND BRIDGE COTTAGES
RIVERSIDE RD
Craigiehall
Cramond Bridge
QUEENSFERRY RD
PRIMROSE DR
Grotto Bridge
BRAEPARK RD
River Almond
EH29
STRATHALMOND RD
STRATHALMOND GN
STRATHALMOND CT
STRATHALMOND PK
Nether Lennie
Craigiehall Temple
CAMMO RD
EH12
Cammo Home Farm
CAMMO HILL
CAMMO GR
Lennie Gate
Cammo
Bughtlin Burn
Lennie Mains
CAMMO WLK
Turnhouse
Lennie Hill
LENNYMUIR
Tower
Edinburgh Airport
TURNHOUSE FARM RD
MASEFIELD WAY
TURNHOUSE RD

89
118

92

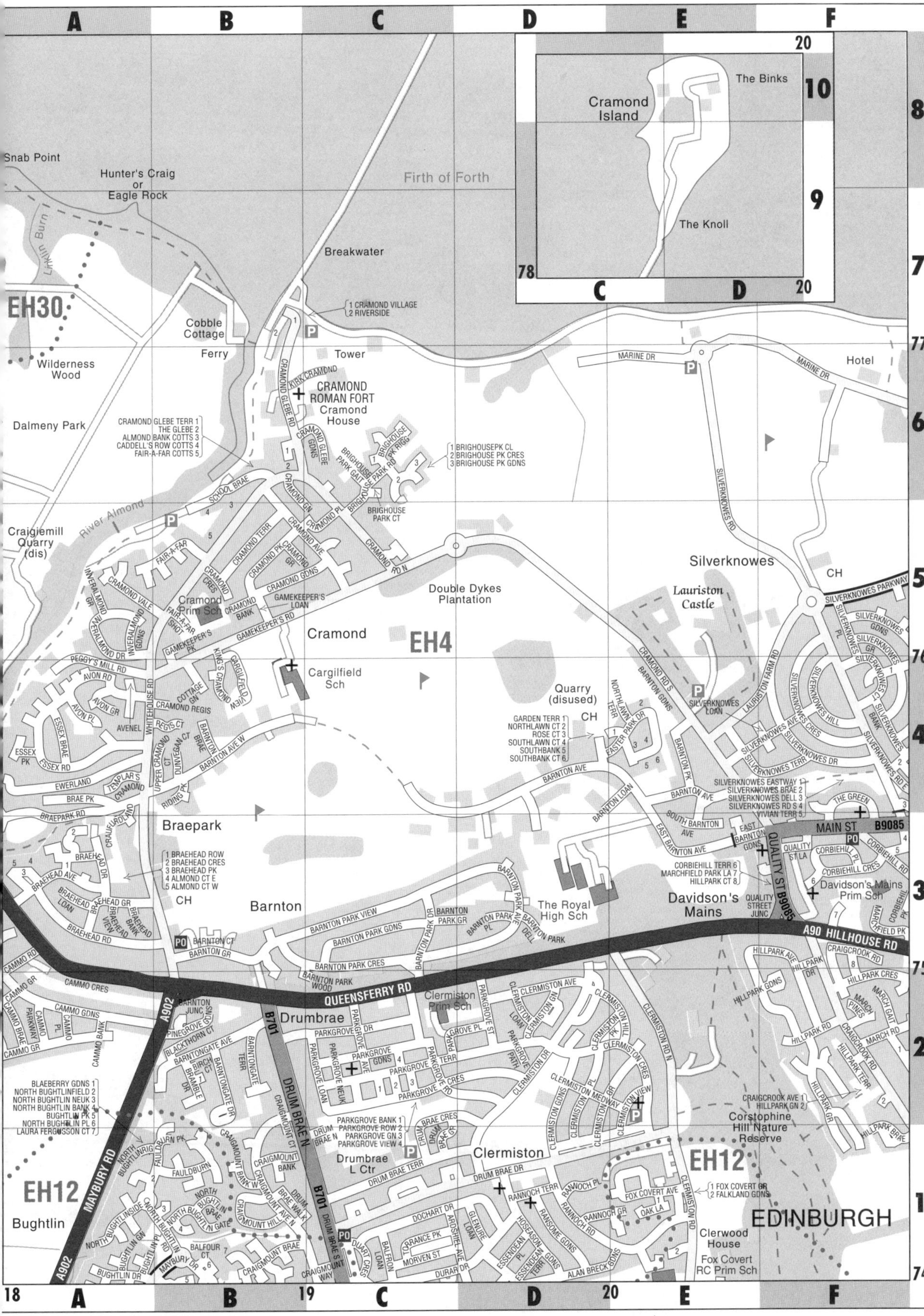

Cramond Island
The Binks
The Knoll
Firth of Forth
Snab Point
Hunter's Craig or Eagle Rock
Linkin Burn
Breakwater
EH30
Cobble Cottage
Ferry
Tower
Wilderness Wood
Dalmeny Park
1 CRAMOND VILLAGE
2 RIVERSIDE
KIRK CRAMOND
CRAMOND ROMAN FORT
Cramond House
CRAMOND GLEBE RD
CRAMOND GLEBE TERR 1
THE GLEBE 2
ALMOND BANK COTTS 3
CADDELL'S ROW COTTS 4
FAIR-A-FAR COTTS 5
1 BRIGHOUSEPK CL
2 BRIGHOUSE PK CRES
3 BRIGHOUSE PK GDNS
BRIGHOUSE PARK CT
BRIGHOUSE PARK GAIT
BRIGHOUSE PARK RD
BRIGHOUSE PK RIGG
SCHOOL BRAE
River Almond
Craigiemill Quarry (dis)
CRAMOND GN
CRAMOND PL
CRAMOND TERR
CRAMOND PK
CRAMOND AVE
CRAMOND GR
CRAMOND GDNS
CRAMOND RD N
CRAMOND CRES
CRAMOND BANK
FAIR-A-FAR
FAIR-A-FAR SHOT
GAMEKEEPER'S LOAN
GAMEKEEPER'S RD
GAMEKEEPER'S PK
Cramond Prim Sch
Cramond
Double Dykes Plantation
EH4
MARINE DR
Hotel
SILVERKNOWES RD
Silverknowes
CH
SILVERKNOWES PARKWAY
Lauriston Castle
INVERALMOND GR
INVERALMOND DR
INVERALMOND GDNS
CRAMOND VALE
PEGGY'S MILL RD
AVON RD
AVON GR
AVON PL
ESSEX BRAE
ESSEX PK
ESSEX RD
AVENEL
WHITEHOUSE RD
KING'S CRAMOND
CARGILFIELD VIEW
Cargilfield Sch
COTTAGE GN
CRAMOND REGIS
REGIS CT
UPPER CRAMOND CT
DUNVEGAN CT
BARNTON BRAE
BARNTON AVE W
EVERLAND
TEMPLAR'S CRAMOND
BRAE PK
RIDING PK
BRAEPARK RD
CRAUFURDLAND
Braepark
Quarry (disused)
CRAMOND RD S
BARNTON GDNS
NORTHLAWN TERR
EASTER PARK DR
GARDEN TERR 1
NORTHLAWN CT 2
ROSE CT 3
SOUTHLAWN CT 4
SOUTHBANK 5
SOUTHBANK CT 6
SILVERKNOWES LOAN
LAURISTON FARM RD
SILVERKNOWES GDNS
SILVERKNOWES GR
SILVERKNOWES CT
SILVERKNOWES HILL
SILVERKNOWES CRES
SILVERKNOWES AVE
SILVERKNOWES BANK
SILVERKNOWES TERR
SILVERKNOWES DR
SILVERKNOWES PL
SILVERKNOWES RD E
SILVERKNOWES EASTWAY 1
SILVERKNOWES BRAE 2
SILVERKNOWES DELL 3
SILVERKNOWES RD S 4
VIVIAN TERR 5
THE GREEN
BARNTON AVE
BARNTON PK
BARNTON LOAN
SOUTH BARNTON AVE
EAST BARNTON AVE
EAST BARNTON GDNS
MAIN ST
B9085
QUALITY ST
QUALITY ST LA
CORBIEHILL PL
CORBIEHILL RD
CORBIEHILL CRES
CORBIEHILL TERR 6
MARCHFIELD PARK LA 7
HILLPARK CT 8
Davidson's Mains Prim Sch
Davidson's Mains
QUALITY STREET JUNC
MARCHFIELD PK
1 BRAEHEAD ROW
2 BRAEHEAD CRES
3 BRAEHEAD PK
4 ALMOND CT E
5 ALMOND CT W
BRAEHEAD DR
BRAEHEAD AVE
BRAEHEAD LOAN
BRAEHEAD GR
BRAEHEAD VIEW
BRAEHEAD BANK
BRAEHEAD RD
CH
Barnton
BARNTON CT
BARNTON GR
BARNTON PARK VIEW
BARNTON PARK GDNS
BARNTON PARK DR
BARNTON PARK GR
BARNTON PARK PL
BARNTON PARK AVE
BARNTON PARK DELL
BARNTON PARK
BARNTON PARK CRES
BARNTON PARK WOOD
The Royal High Sch
A90 HILLHOUSE RD
HILLPARK AVE
HILLPARK DR
CRAIGCROOK RD
HILLPARK CRES
MARCH GAIT
MARCH PINES
HILLPARK GDNS
HILLPARK RD
HILLPARK TERR
MARCH RD
CAMMO RD
CAMMO GR
CAMMO CRES
CAMMO GDNS
CAMMO BRAE
CAMMO PARKWAY
CAMMO PL
CAMMO BANK
QUEENSFERRY RD
A902
BARNTON JUNC
PINEGROVE GDNS
BLACKTHORN CT
BARNTONGATE AVE
BARNTONGATE TERR
BARNTONGATE DR
BIRCH CT
BRAMBLE DR
Drumbrae
B701
DRUM BRAE N
Clermiston Prim Sch
PARKGROVE DR
PARKGROVE AVE
PARKGROVE GDNS
PARKGROVE PL
PARKGROVE ST
PARKGROVE TERR
PARKGROVE LOAN
PARKGROVE NEUK
PARKGROVE CRES
PARKGROVE PATH
PARKGROVE RD
PARKGROVE BANK 1
PARKGROVE ROW 2
PARKGROVE GN 3
PARKGROVE VIEW 4
CLERMISTON AVE
CLERMISTON LOAN
CLERMISTON GN
CLERMISTON DR
CLERMISTON GR
CLERMISTON HILL
CLERMISTON PK
CLERMISTON CRES
CLERMISTON PL
CLERMISTON MEDWAY
CLERMISTON GDNS
CLERMISTON VIEW
CLERMISTON RD N
CLERMISTON RD
BLAEBERRY GDNS 1
NORTH BUGHTLINFIELD 2
NORTH BUGHTLIN NEUK 3
NORTH BUGHTLIN BANK 4
BUGHTLIN PK 5
NORTH BUGHTLIN PL 6
LAURA FERGUSSON CT 7
CRAIGMOUNT CT
CRAIGMOUNT BANK
CRAIGMOUNT BANK W
CRAIGMOUNT AVE N
CRAIGMOUNT HILL
CRAIGMOUNT BRAE
CRAIGMOUNT WAY
DRUM BRAE CRES
DRUM BRAE WALK
DRUM BRAE DR
DRUM BRAE TERR
DRUM BRAE S
Drumbrae L Ctr
Clermiston
Corstophine Hill Nature Reserve
CRAIGCROOK AVE 1
HILLPARK GN 2
HILLPARK BRAE
EH12
MAYBURY RD
NORTH BUGHTLINRIG
FAULDBURN PK
FAULDBURN
NORTH BUGHTLIN GATE
NORTH BUGHTLIN BRAE
BUGHTLIN GN
BUGHTLIN DR
BALFOUR CT
MAYBURY DR
Bughtlin
RANNOCH TERR
RANNOCH PL
RANNOCH GR
RANNOCH RD
RANSOME GDNS
HOSEASON GDNS
ESSENDEAN PL
ESSENDEAN TERR
ALAN BRECK GDNS
DOCHART DR
TORRANCE PK
MORVEN ST
DURAR DR
BALFRON LOAN
GLENURE LOAN
ARDSHIEL AVE
QUARRY CRES
1 FOX COVERT GR
2 FALKLAND GDNS
FOX COVERT AVE
OAK LA
Clerwood House
Fox Covert RC Prim Sch
EDINBURGH

91

C5
1 St David's RC Prim Sch
2 Pirniehall Prim Sch

Firth of Forth
Western Breakwater
Granton Harbour
Middle Pier
Granton Point
West Shore Road Trad Est
Forth Ind Est
Granton
EH5
Caroline Park
Recn Gd
West Shore Bsns Ctr
Craigroyston
Mast
National Mus Collection Ctr
Edinburgh's Telford Coll
Muirhouse
Royston Prim Sch
Liby Granton Prim Sch
West Pilton
Pilton
Ainslie Park L Ctr
Superstore
Works
Forthview Prim Sch
Craigroyston Prim Sch
Oaklands Sch
Craigroyston High Sch
EH4
EH3
Fettes Coll Prep Sch
Fettes Coll
Western General
Ferryhill Prim Sch
Drylaw
Rowanfield Sch
Blackhall
Craigleith Ret Pk
Craigleith
Royal Victoria
Napier Univ
Cemy
Lothian & Borders Pol HQ
Broughton High Sch
Comely Bank
Superstore
Orchard Brae
Blackhall Prim Sch
Ravelston Woods Nature Reserve
The Mary Erskine Sch
Craigcrook Castle
Stewart's Melville Coll
Cemy Dean
A902
A90
B9085
B900
A901
A903
FERRY RD
TELFORD RD
QUEENSFERRY RD
CRAIGLEITH RD
COMELY BANK RD
HILLHOUSE RD
WEST GRANTON RD
PILTON AVE
MARINE DR
WEST SHORE RD

A4
1 FERRY GAIT WK
2 FERRY GAIT GDNS
3 FERRY GAIT PL

91

C1
1 EAST CT
2 CRAIGLEITH AVENUE N
3 RAVELSTON HOUSE GR

120

C2
1 GROATHILL GARDENS W
2 GROATHILL GARDENS E
3 QUEEN'S AVENUE S
4 SEAFORTH TERR
5 CRAIGCROOK TERR
6 CRAIGCROOK PL
7 MARISCHAL PL

E1
1 The Mary Erskine & Stewart's Melville Jun Sch

F1
1 LEARMONTH GARDENS LA
2 SOUTH LEARMONTH GDNS
3 LEARMONTH TERR LA
4 SOUTH LEARMONTH AVE
5 BUCKINGHAM TERR
6 BELGRAVE CRESCENT LA
7 BELGRAVE CRES
8 BELGRAVE MEWS
9 BACK DEAN

F2
1 ORCHARD BRAE W
2 LEARMONTH PK
3 LEARMONTH PL
4 Flora Stevenson Prim Sch

For full street detail of the highlighted area see pages 228 and 229

B2
1 ST BERNARD'S ROW
2 VEITCH'S SQ
3 GLENOGLE HO
4 GLENOGLE PL
5 PATRIOTHALL
6 NORTH EAST CIRCUS PL
7 GLANVILLE PL
8 BAKER'S PL
9 MILLHOUSE

C2
1 WEST SCOTLAND STREET LA
2 SUTHERLAND HO

D2
1 EAST SCOTLAND STREET LA
2 DUBLIN STREET LANE N
3 OLD BROUGHTON
4 NEW BROUGHTON

121

D2
5 BARONY PL
6 GAYFIELD STREET LA
7 ALBANY ST LA
8 EAST BROUGHTON PL
9 St Marys RC Prim Sch
10 Drummond Com High Sch

94

E2
1 LEOPOLD PL
2 ANTIGUA ST
3 SOUTH GAYFIELD LA
4 GAYFIELD CL
5 ALBERT PL
6 CROALL PL
7 BRUNSWICK PL
8 GAYFIELD PL

F3
1 SOUTH LORNE PL
2 CRIGHTON PL
3 PILRIG GLEBE

F4
1 CONSTITUTION ST
2 GORDON ST
3 SPRINGFIELD LA

93

A1	A2	B1	C1	C1	D1	E1
1 MONTROSE TERR	1 MARYFIELD	1 CAMBUSNETHAN ST	1 MEADOWBANK PL	10 PIERSHILL PL	1 PIERSHILL TERR	1 MOUNTCASTLE GN
2 BRAND PL	2 MARYFIELD PL	2 SUNNYBANK TERR	2 PARSONS GREEN TERR	11 ABERCORN RD		2 MOUNTCASTLE PL
3 EARLSTON PL	3 LADY MENZIES PL	3 SUNNYBANK PL	3 CONSIDINE TERR			3 MOUNTCASTLE PK
4 SALMOND PL	4 PITLOCHRY PL	4 ROYAL PARK PL	4 CONSIDINE GDNS			4 MOUNTCASTLE CRES
5 COMELY GREEN PL		5 MEADOWBANK TERR	5 LISMORE AVE			
6 COMELY GREEN CRES		6 MEADOWBANK AVE	6 WILFRID TERR			
7 WHYTE PL			7 WOLSELEY TERR			
8 TAYLOR PL			8 JOCK'S LODGE			
9 Abbeyhill Prim Sch			9 PIERSHILL LA			

93
122

A
B
C
D
E
F
8
7
77
6
5
76
4
3
75
2
1
74
Firth of Forth
PROMENADE
EH15
1 ELECTRA PL
2 HILLCOAT LOAN
3 WESTBANK PL
4 WESTBANK LOAN
5 HILLCOAT PL
6 GREAT CANNON BANK
1 HARBOUR PL
2 WILLIAM JAMESON PL
3 BRICKFIELD
4 LAW PL
5 THE POTTERY
6 SPA PL
7 SHRUB MOUNT
8 AITCHISON'S PL
9 WHINS PL
10 RAMSAY PL
11 MENTONE AVE
KING'S RD
WESTBANK ST
Portobello L Ctr
PORTOBELLO HIGH ST
B6415
BRIDGE ST
BRIDGE STREET LA
PIPE ST
PIPE LA
RATHBONE PL
NEW TOWER PL
Towerbank Prim Sch
FIGGATE LA
FIGGATE BANK
BATH PL
BEACH LA
MARY FIELD
WILSON'S PK
FIGGATE ST
ADELPHI PL
ADELPHI GR
FISHWIVES' CSWY
BAILEYFIELD CRES
REGENT ST
BATH ST
STRAITON PL
30
31
32

123

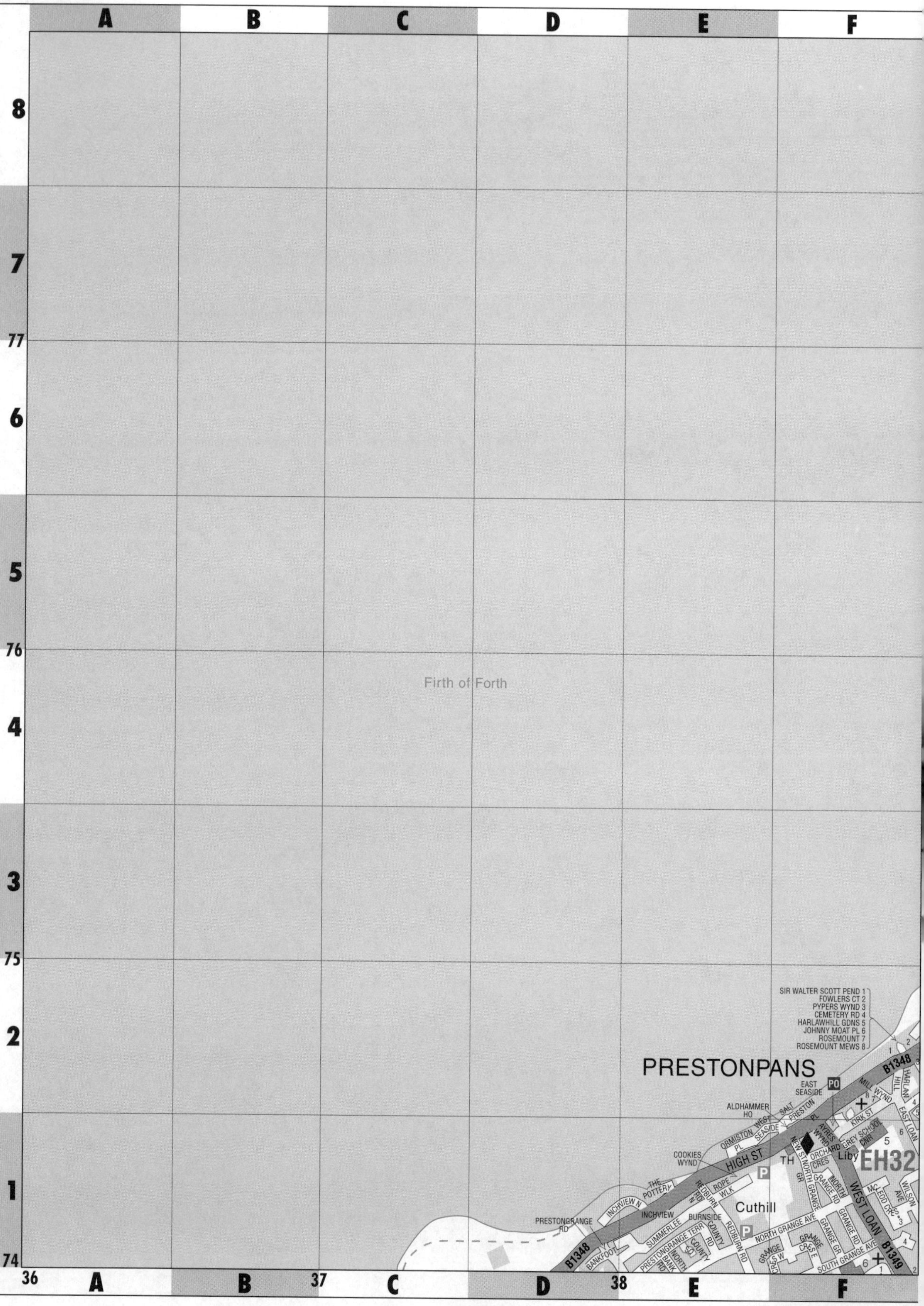

F1
1 NORTHFIELD CT
2 PRESTON TOWER
3 GLEBE GDNS
4 LABURNUM ARCH CT
5 Prestonpans Inf Sch
6 St Gabriel's RC Prim Sch

125

98

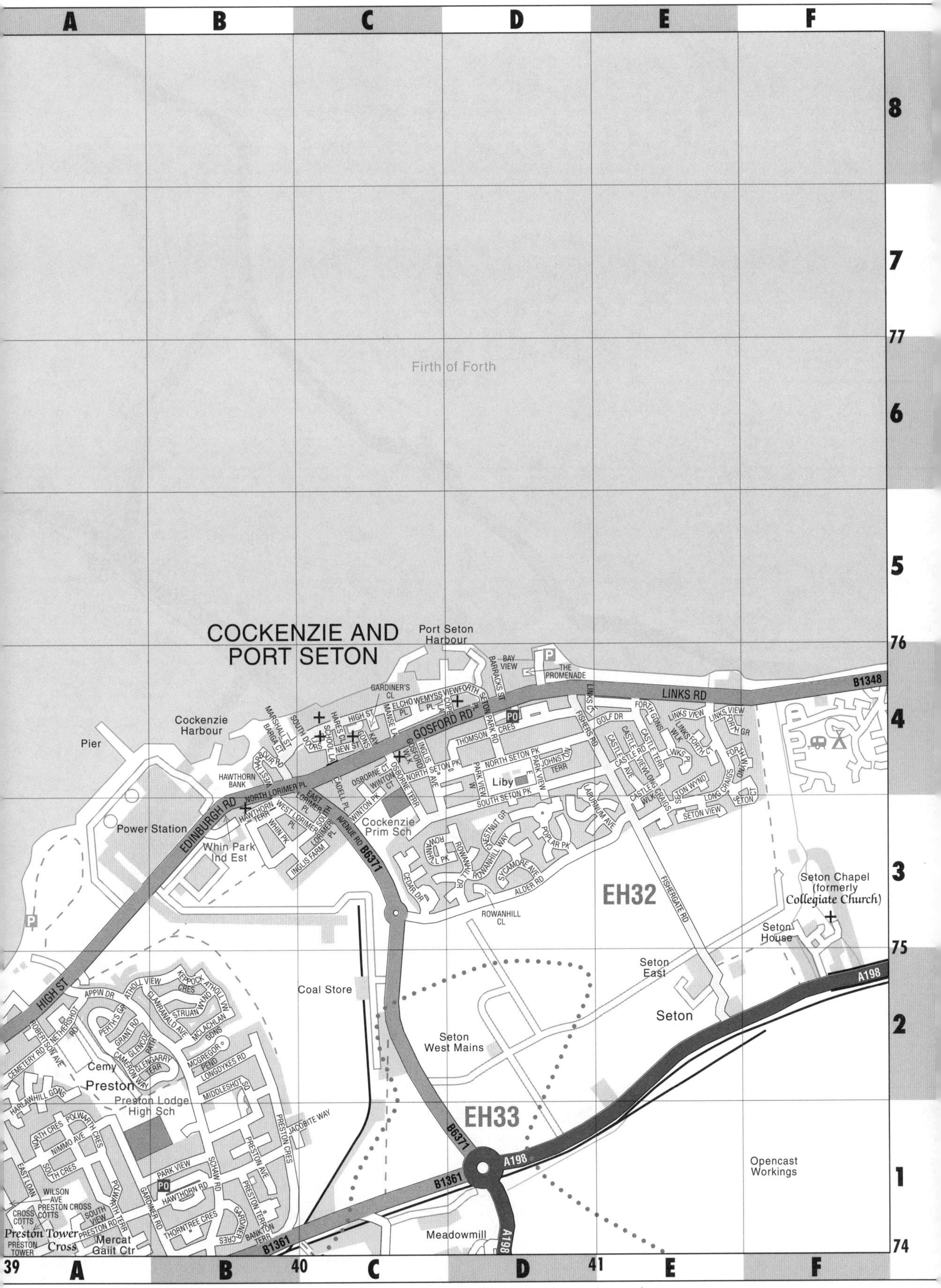
A
B
C
D
E
F
8
7
77
6
5
76
4
3
75
2
1
74
39
40
41
Firth of Forth
COCKENZIE AND
PORT SETON
Port Seton
Harbour
Cockenzie
Harbour
Pier
Power Station
Whin Park
Ind Est
Cockenzie
Prim Sch
Liby
BAY
VIEW
THE
PROMENADE
LINKS RD
B1348
GOSFORD RD
EDINBURGH RD
HIGH ST
AVENUE RD
B6371
EH32
EH33
Seton Chapel
(formerly
Collegiate Church)
Seton
House
Seton
East
Seton
Seton
West Mains
Coal Store
Cemy
Preston
Preston Lodge
High Sch
Opencast
Workings
Meadowmill
A198
B1361
Mercat
Gaiit Ctr
Preston Tower
Cross
PRESTON
TOWER
ROWANHILL
CL
FISHERGATE RD
FISHERS RD
JACOBITE WAY
PRESTON CRES
PRESTON AVE
SCHAW RD
PARK VIEW
HAWTHORN RD
THORNTREE CRES
GARDINER RD
POLWARTH TERR
NIMMO AVE
SOUTH VIEW
PRESTON RD
EAST LOAN
WILSON AVE
PRESTON CROSS
CROSS COTTS
HARLAWHILL GDNS
CEMETERY RD
ROBERTSON AVE
NETHERSHOT RD
APPIN DR
ATHOLL VIEW
KEPPOCK CRES
STRUAN WYND
MCLACHLAN GDNS
MCGREGOR PEND
LONGDYKES RD
MIDDLESHOT SQ
GRANT RD
GLENCOE PATH
GLENGARRY TERR
CAMERON WAY
CLANRANALD AVE
HAWTHORN BANK
NORTH LORIMER PL
WEST LORIMER PL
WHIN PK
INGLIS FARM
HAWTHORN TERR
MARSHALL ST
BARGA CT
SOUTH DOORS
SCHOOL LA
HARES CL
HIGH ST
NEW ST
GARDINER'S CL
ELCHO PL
WEMYSS PL
VIEWFORTH
MANSE LA
SETON PARK RD
BARRACKS ST
THOMSON CRES
NORTH SETON PK
SOUTH SETON PK
JOHNSTON TERR
PARK VIEW
OSBORNE CT
OSBORNE TERR
WINTON PK
WINTON CT
CADELL PL
CEDAR DR
ROWANHILL DR
ROWANHILL WAY
CHESTNUT GR
SYCAMORE AVE
POPLAR PK
ALDER RD
LABURNUM AVE
GOLF DR
LINKS CT
FORTH GDNS
CASTLE TERR
CASTLE RD
CASTLE AVE
CASTLE WLK
LINKS VIEW
LINKS PL
LINKS WLK
LONG CRAIGS
SETON VIEW
SETON CT
SETON WYND

126
98

97
70

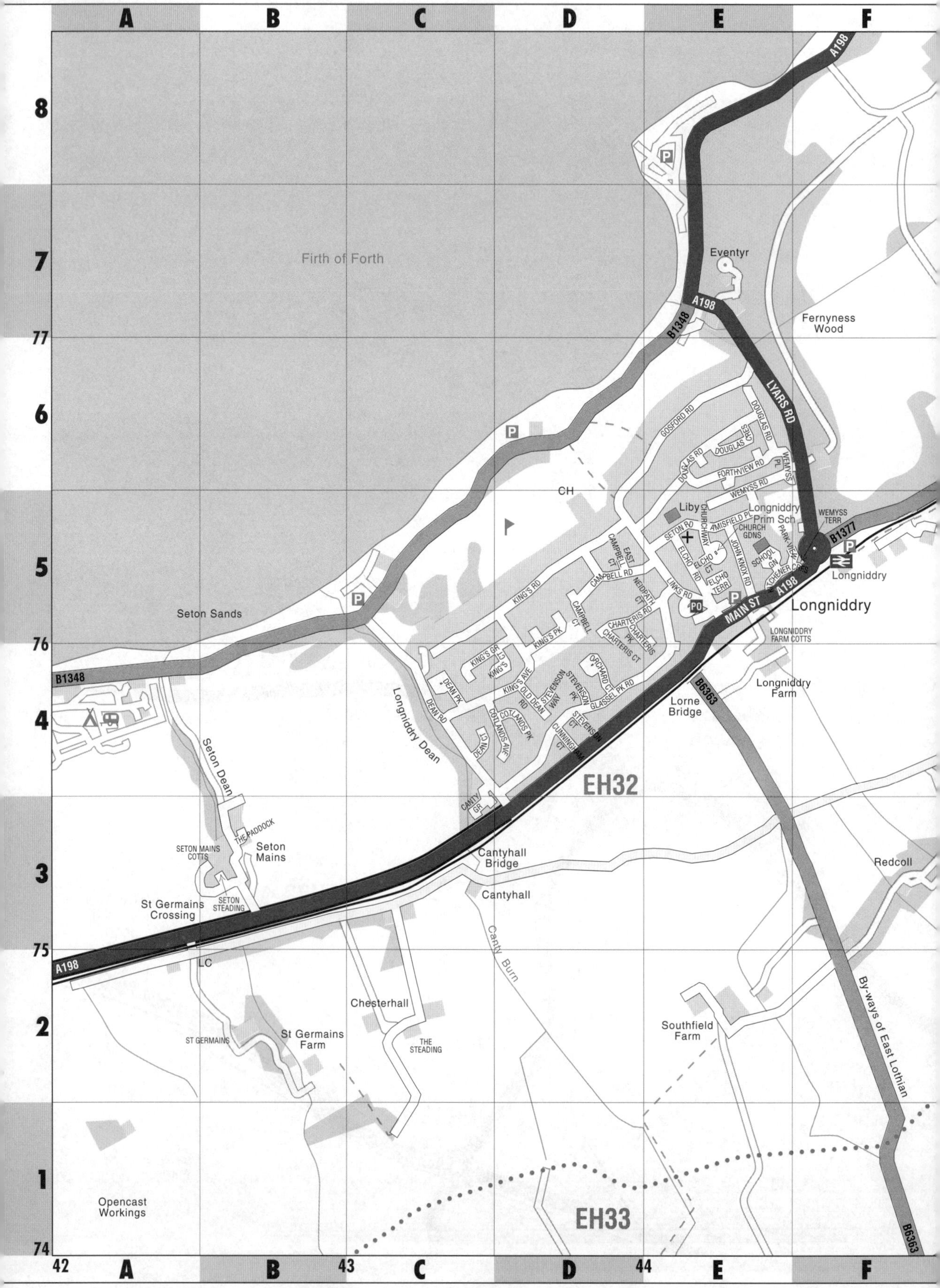

A
B
C
D
E
F
8
7
77
6
5
76
4
3
75
2
1
74
42
43
44
Firth of Forth
Eventyr
A198
B1348
Fernyness
Wood
LYARS RD
GOSFORD RD
DOUGLAS RD
DOUGLAS CRES
FORTHVIEW RD
WEMYSS PL
WEMYSS RD
CH
Liby
Longniddry
Prim Sch
WEMYSS
TERR
B1377
CHURCHWAY
AMISFIELD PL
CHURCH
GDNS
PARK VIEW
SETON RD
ELCHO RD
ELCHO CT
ELCHO TERR
JOHN KNOX RD
SCHOOL GN
KITCHENER CRES
Longniddry
EAST CAMPBELL CT
CAMPBELL RD
NEIDPATH CT
LINKS RD
PO
MAIN ST
A198
Longniddry
KING'S RD
CAMPBELL CT
CHARTERIS RD
CHARTERIS PK
CHARTERIS CT
KING'S PK
KING'S GR
KING'S CT
KING'S AVE
ORCHARD CT
GLASSEL PK RD
STEVENSON PK
STEVENSON WAY
OLD DEAN RD
STEVENSON GN
CUNNINGHAM CT
DEAN PK
DEAN RD
COTLANDS PK
COTLANDS AVE
DEAN CT
LONGNIDDRY
FARM COTTS
Longniddry
Farm
Lorne
Bridge
B6363
Seton Sands
B1348
Longniddry Dean
Seton Dean
EH32
CANTY GR
THE PADDOCK
SETON MAINS
COTTS
Seton
Mains
Cantyhall
Bridge
Redcoll
Cantyhall
St Germains
Crossing
SETON
STEADING
A198
LC
Canty Burn
By-ways of East Lothian
Chesterhall
ST GERMAINS
St Germains
Farm
THE
STEADING
Southfield
Farm
Opencast
Workings
EH33
B6363

97
127

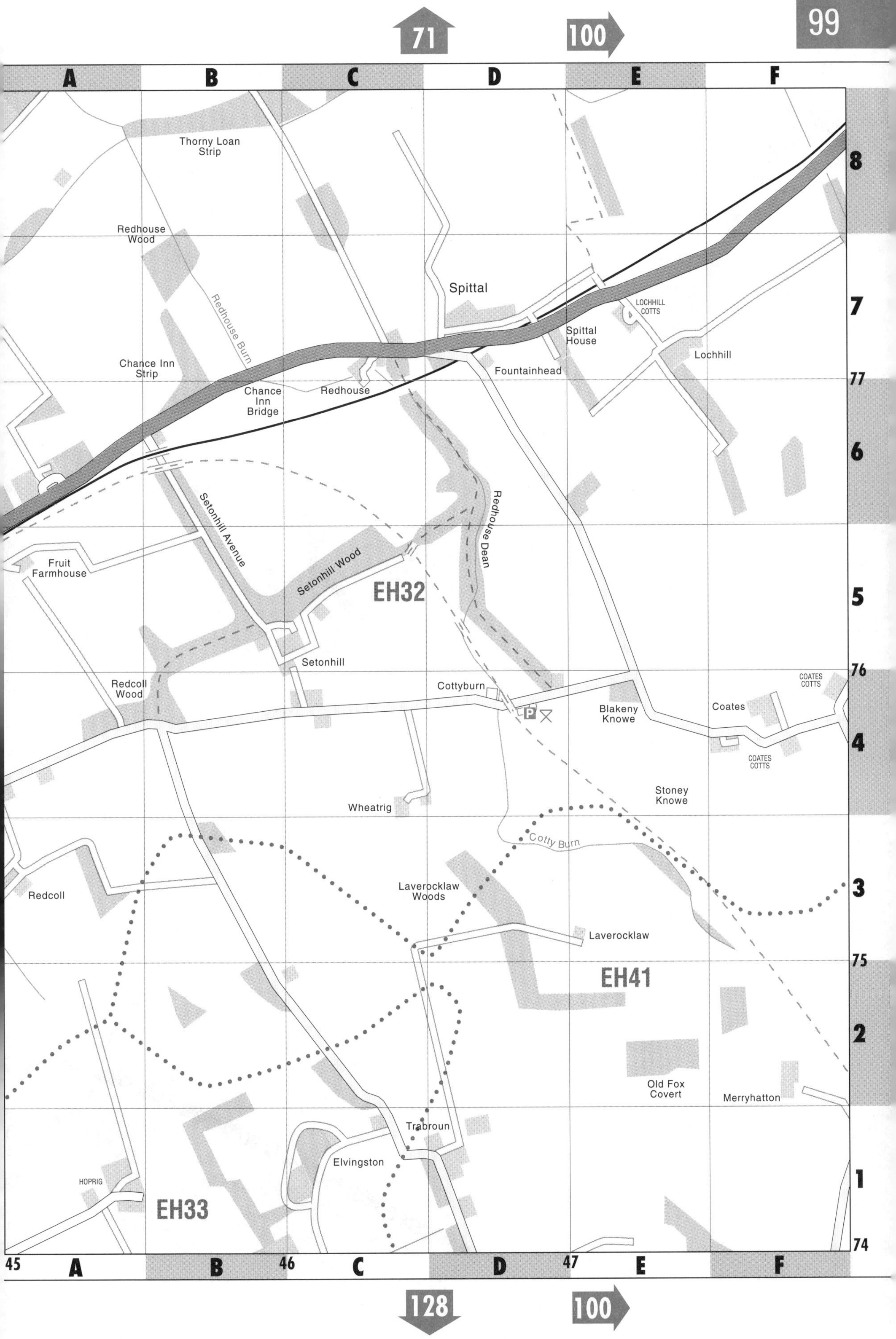
71
100
A
B
C
D
E
F
Thorny Loan Strip
Redhouse Wood
Redhouse Burn
Spittal
LOCHHILL COTTS
Spittal House
Lochhill
Chance Inn Strip
Chance Inn Bridge
Redhouse
Fountainhead
Setonhill Avenue
Redhouse Dean
Fruit Farmhouse
Setonhill Wood
EH32
Setonhill
Redcoll Wood
Cottyburn
COATES COTTS
Blakeny Knowe
Coates
COATES COTTS
Stoney Knowe
Wheatrig
Cotty Burn
Laverocklaw Woods
Redcoll
Laverocklaw
EH41
Old Fox Covert
Merryhatton
Trabroun
Elvingston
HOPRIG
EH33
8
7
77
6
5
76
4
3
75
2
1
74
45
46
47
128
100

99
72

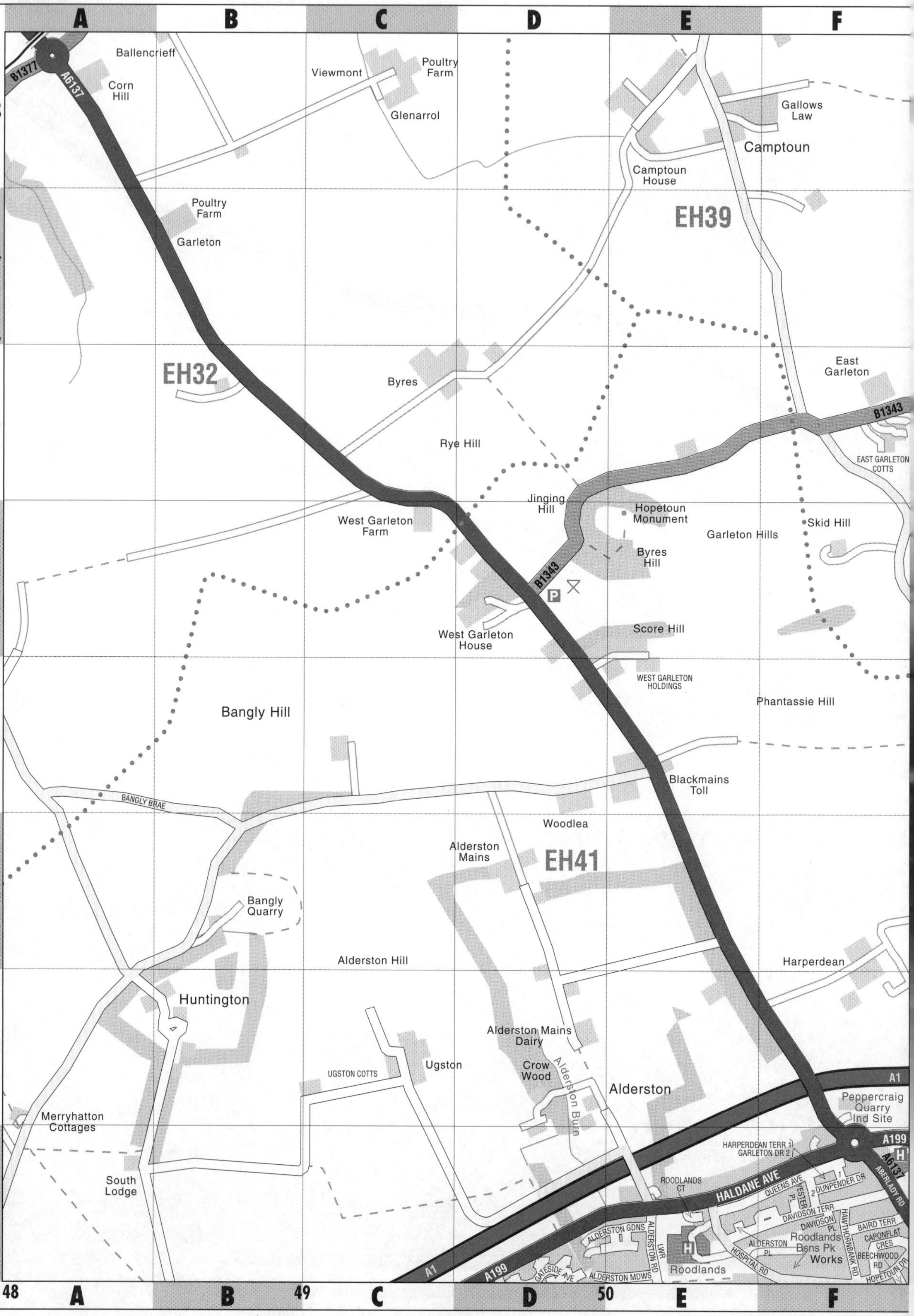
A
B
C
D
E
F
8
7
77
6
5
76
4
3
75
2
1
74
48
49
50
Ballencrieff
Corn Hill
B1377
A6137
Viewmont
Poultry Farm
Glenarrol
Gallows Law
Camptoun
Camptoun House
EH39
Poultry Farm
Garleton
EH32
Byres
East Garleton
B1343
Rye Hill
EAST GARLETON COTTS
Jinging Hill
Hopetoun Monument
West Garleton Farm
Garleton Hills
Skid Hill
Byres Hill
B1343
West Garleton House
Score Hill
WEST GARLETON HOLDINGS
Phantassie Hill
Bangly Hill
Blackmains Toll
BANGLY BRAE
Woodlea
Alderston Mains
EH41
Bangly Quarry
Alderston Hill
Harperdean
Huntington
Alderston Mains Dairy
Crow Wood
Alderston Burn
Ugston
UGSTON COTTS
Alderston
A1
Peppercraig Quarry Ind Site
Merryhatton Cottages
HARPERDEAN TERR 1
GARLETON DR 2
A199
A6137
ABERLADY RD
South Lodge
ROODLANDS CT
HALDANE AVE
QUEENS AVE
DUNPENDER DR
YESTER PL
DAVIDSON TERR
DAVIDSON PL
HAWTHORNBANK RD
BAIRD TERR
CAPONFLAT CRES
ALDERSTON GDNS
ALDERSTON RD
LWR
ALDERSTON PL
Roodlands Bsns Pk
Works
BEECHWOOD RD
HOSPITAL RD
HOPETOUN DR
Roodlands
GATESIDE AVE
ALDERSTON MDWS
A199
A1

99
129

73
102

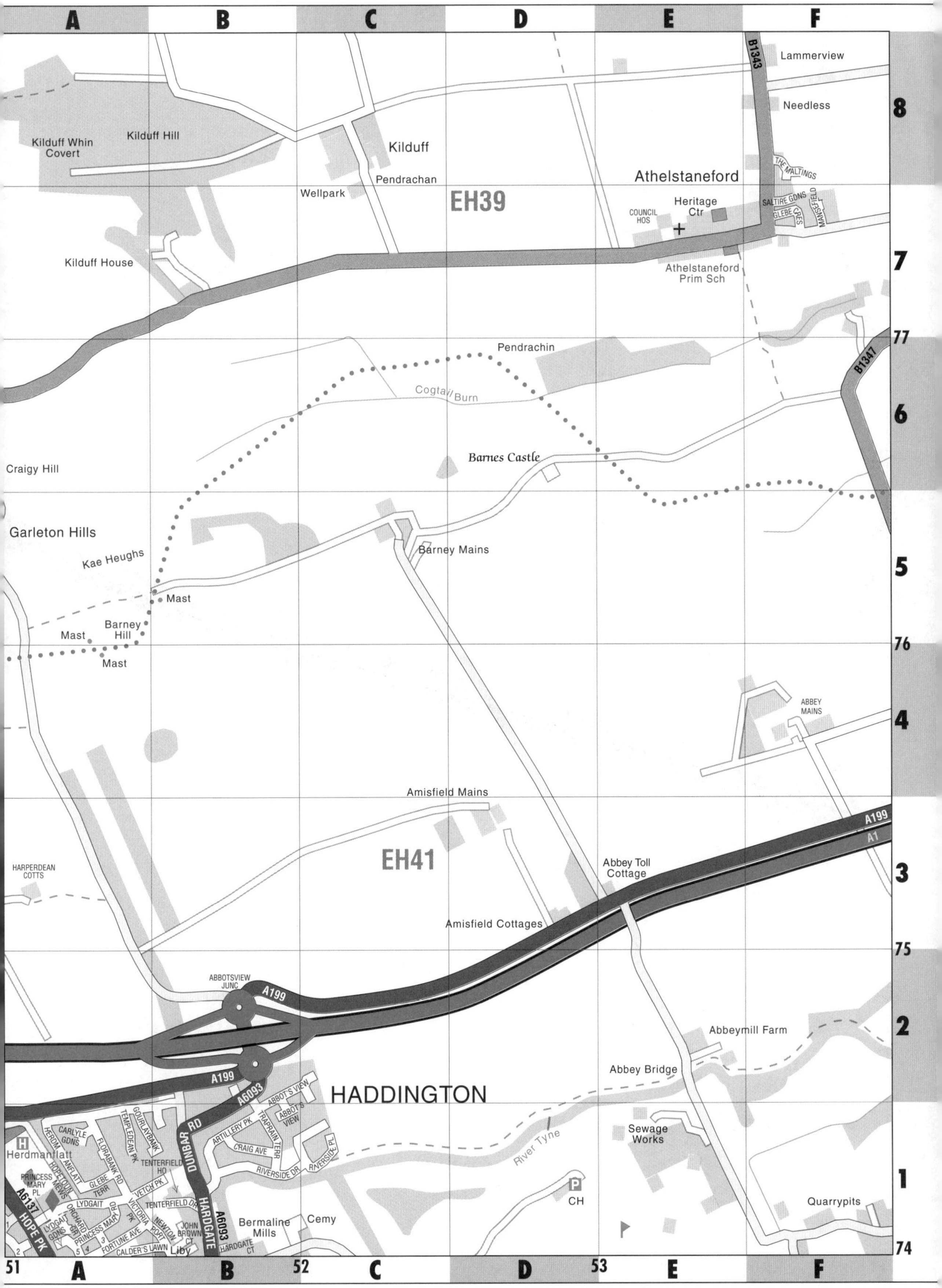

A1
1 HOPETOUN DR
2 HOPE PARK CRES
3 HEPBURN RD
4 AUCTION MART
5 MARKET CT

130
102

101
74

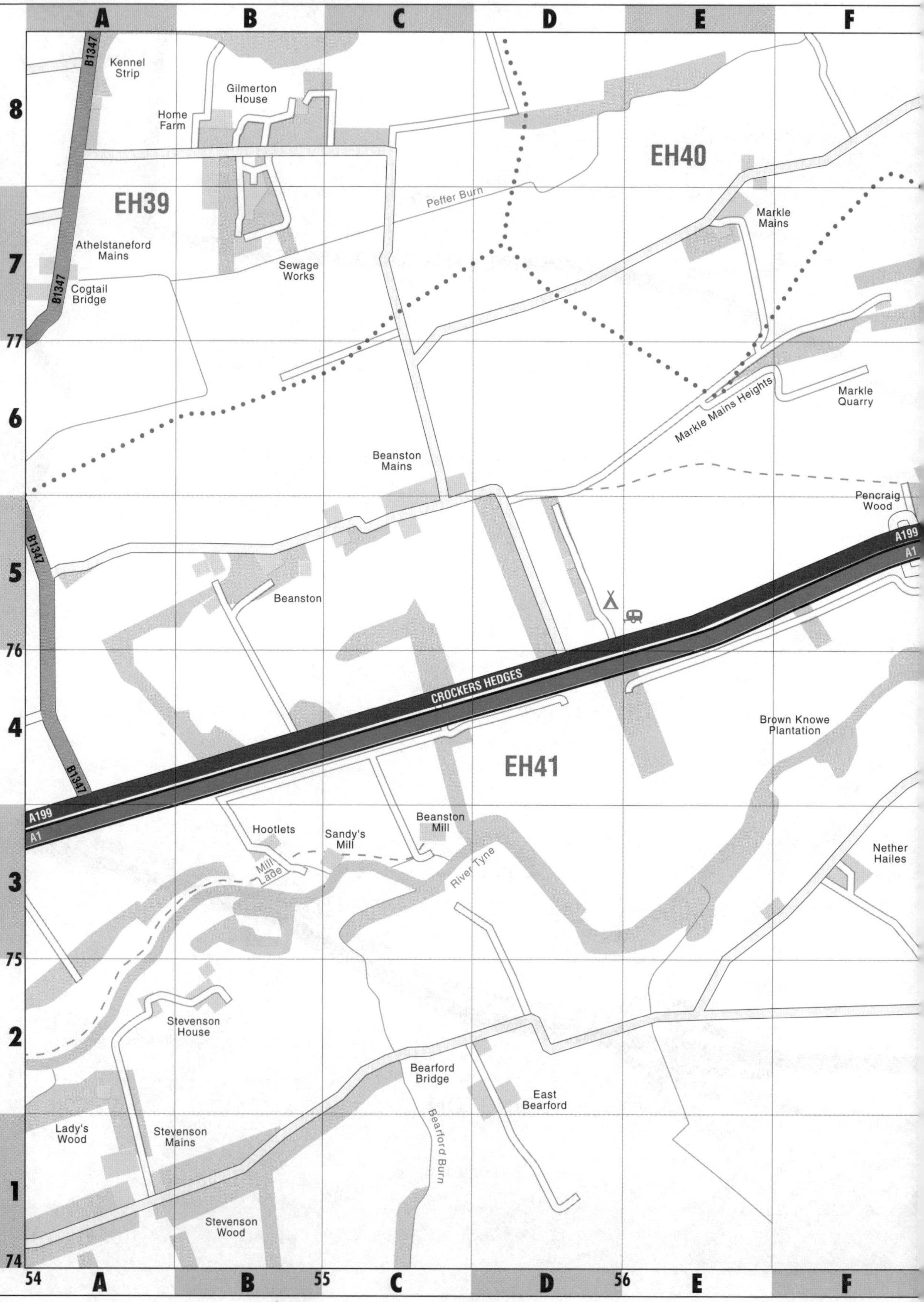
A
B
C
D
E
F
8
7
77
6
5
76
4
3
75
2
1
74
54
55
56
B1347
Kennel Strip
Gilmerton House
Home Farm
EH39
EH40
EH41
Peffer Burn
Markle Mains
Athelstaneford Mains
Sewage Works
Cogtail Bridge
Markle Mains Heights
Markle Quarry
Beanston Mains
Pencraig Wood
A199
A1
Beanston
CROCKERS HEDGES
Brown Knowe Plantation
Hootlets
Sandy's Mill
Beanston Mill
Mill Lade
River Tyne
Nether Hailes
Stevenson House
Bearford Bridge
East Bearford
Bearford Burn
Lady's Wood
Stevenson Mains
Stevenson Wood

101
131

75
104

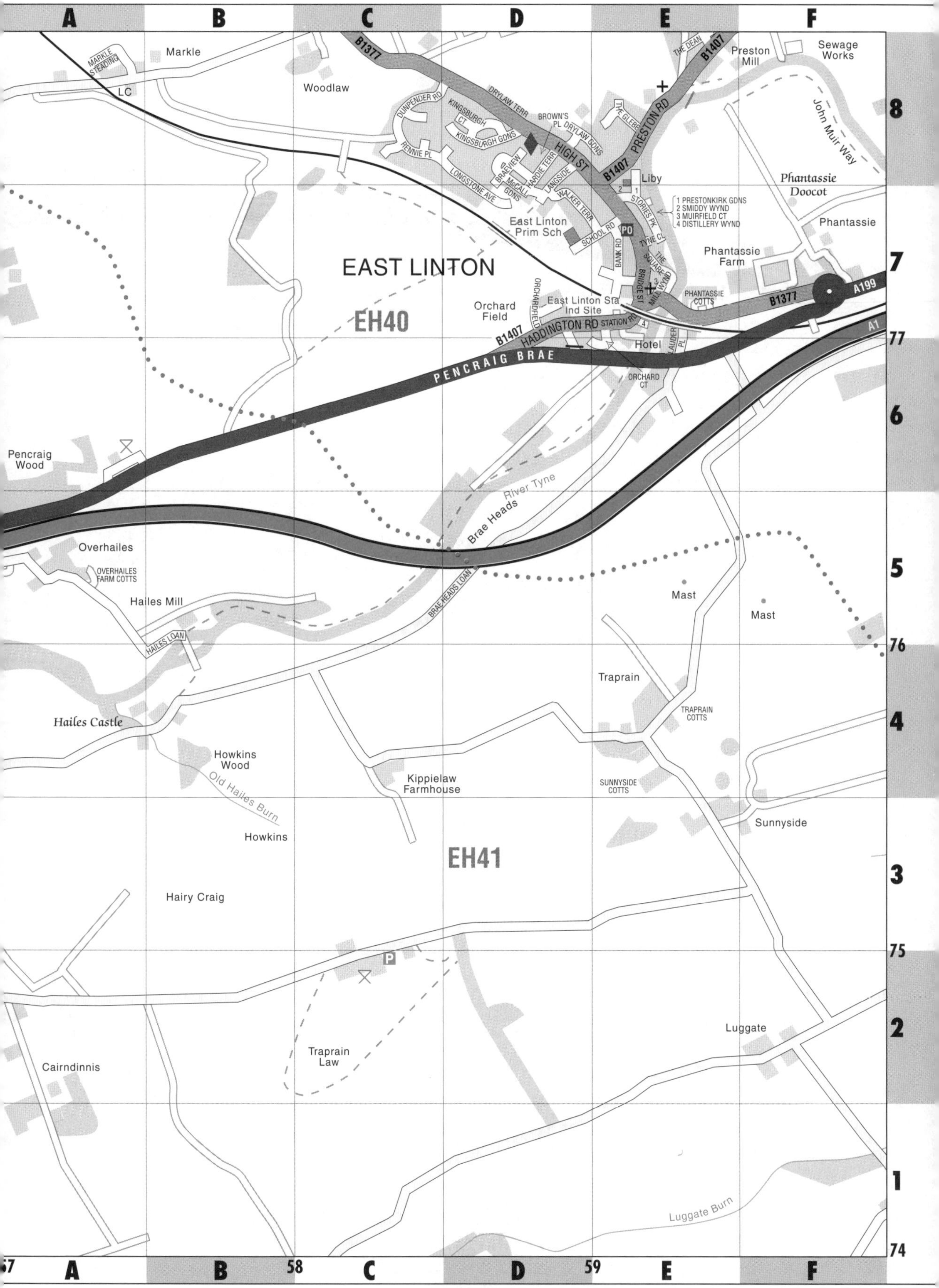
A
B
C
D
E
F
Markle
MARKLE STEADING
LC
Woodlaw
B1377
THE DEAN
B1407
Preston Mill
Sewage Works
John Muir Way
DUNPENDER RD
DRYLAW TERR
KINGSBURGH CT
KINGSBURGH GDNS
BROWN'S PL
DRYLAW GDNS
THE GLEBE
PRESTON RD
RENNIE PL
BRAEVIEW
McCALL GDNS
HARDIE TERR
HIGH ST
LANGSIDE
LONGSTONE AVE
WALKER TERR
Liby
Phantassie Doocot
1 PRESTONKIRK GDNS
2 SMIDDY WYND
3 MUIRFIELD CT
4 DISTILLERY WYND
STORIES PK
East Linton Prim Sch
SCHOOL RD
PO
Phantassie
TYNE CL
Phantassie Farm
EAST LINTON
BANK RD
BRIDGE ST
THE SQUARE
MILL WYND
PHANTASSIE COTTS
A199
ORCHARDFIELD
Orchard Field
East Linton Sta Ind Site
EH40
B1407
HADDINGTON RD
STATION RD
LAUDER PL
Hotel
A1
PENCRAIG BRAE
ORCHARD CT
Pencraig Wood
River Tyne
Brae Heads
Overhailes
OVERHAILES FARM COTTS
BRAE HEADS LOAN
Hailes Mill
Mast
Mast
HAILES LOAN
Traprain
TRAPRAIN COTTS
Hailes Castle
Howkins Wood
Kippielaw Farmhouse
SUNNYSIDE COTTS
Old Hailes Burn
Sunnyside
Howkins
EH41
Hairy Craig
P
Luggate
Traprain Law
Cairndinnis
Luggate Burn
8
77
7
6
5
76
4
3
75
2
1
74
57
58
59
A
B
C
D
E
F

132
104

103
76

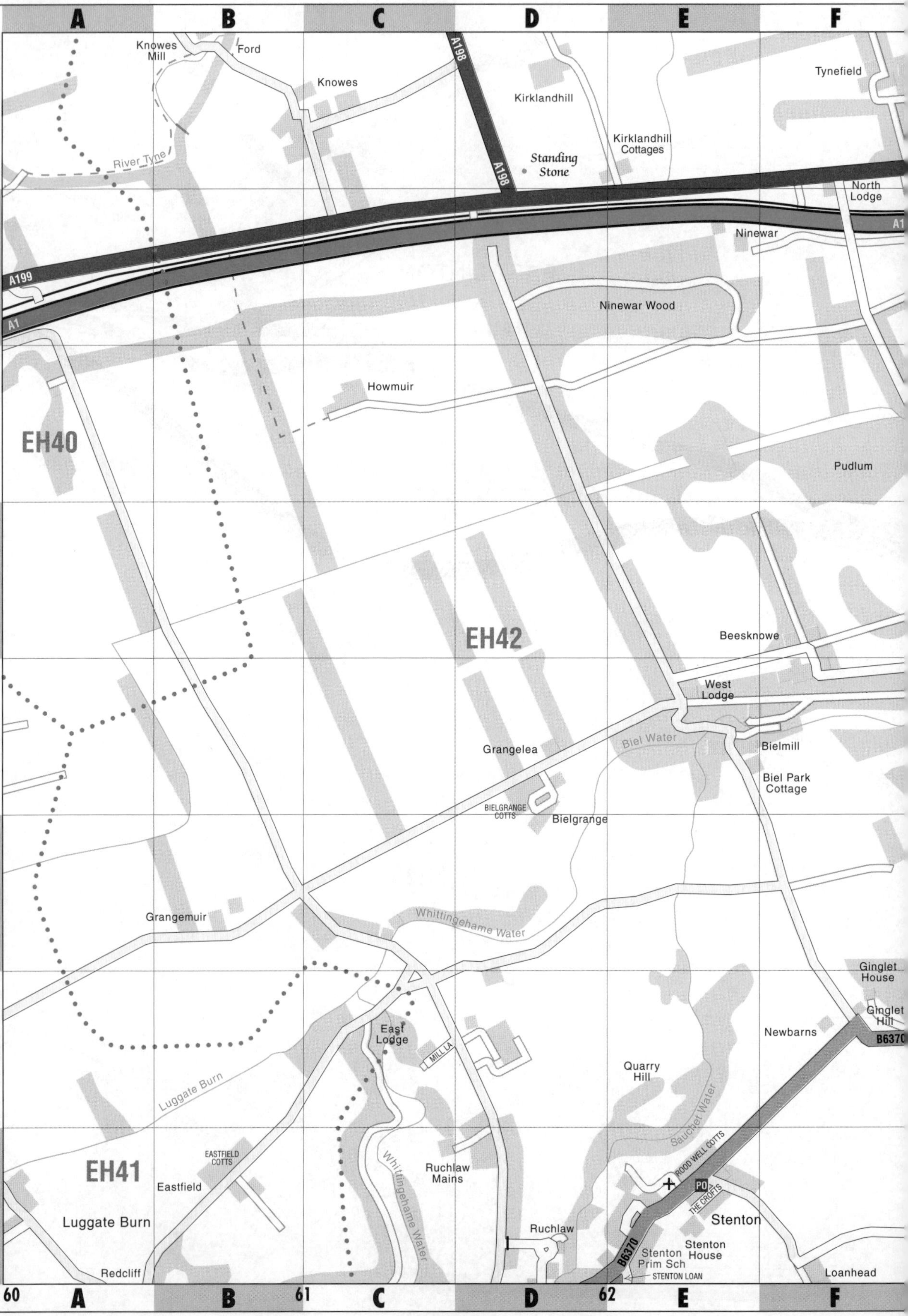
A
B
C
D
E
F
8
7
77
6
5
76
4
3
75
2
1
74
60
61
62
Knowes Mill
Ford
Knowes
A198
Kirklandhill
Kirklandhill Cottages
Standing Stone
Tynefield
North Lodge
River Tyne
A199
A1
Ninewar
Ninewar Wood
Howmuir
EH40
Pudlum
EH42
Beesknowe
West Lodge
Biel Water
Bielmill
Grangelea
Biel Park Cottage
BIELGRANGE COTTS
Bielgrange
Grangemuir
Whittingehame Water
Ginglet House
Ginglet Hill
B6370
East Lodge
MILL LA
Newbarns
Quarry Hill
Luggate Burn
Sauchet Water
ROOD WELL COTTS
EASTFIELD COTTS
EH41
Ruchlaw Mains
PO
THE CROFTS
Eastfield
Stenton
Luggate Burn
Ruchlaw
Stenton House
Stenton Prim Sch
STENTON LOAN
Redcliff
Loanhead

103
133

77
106

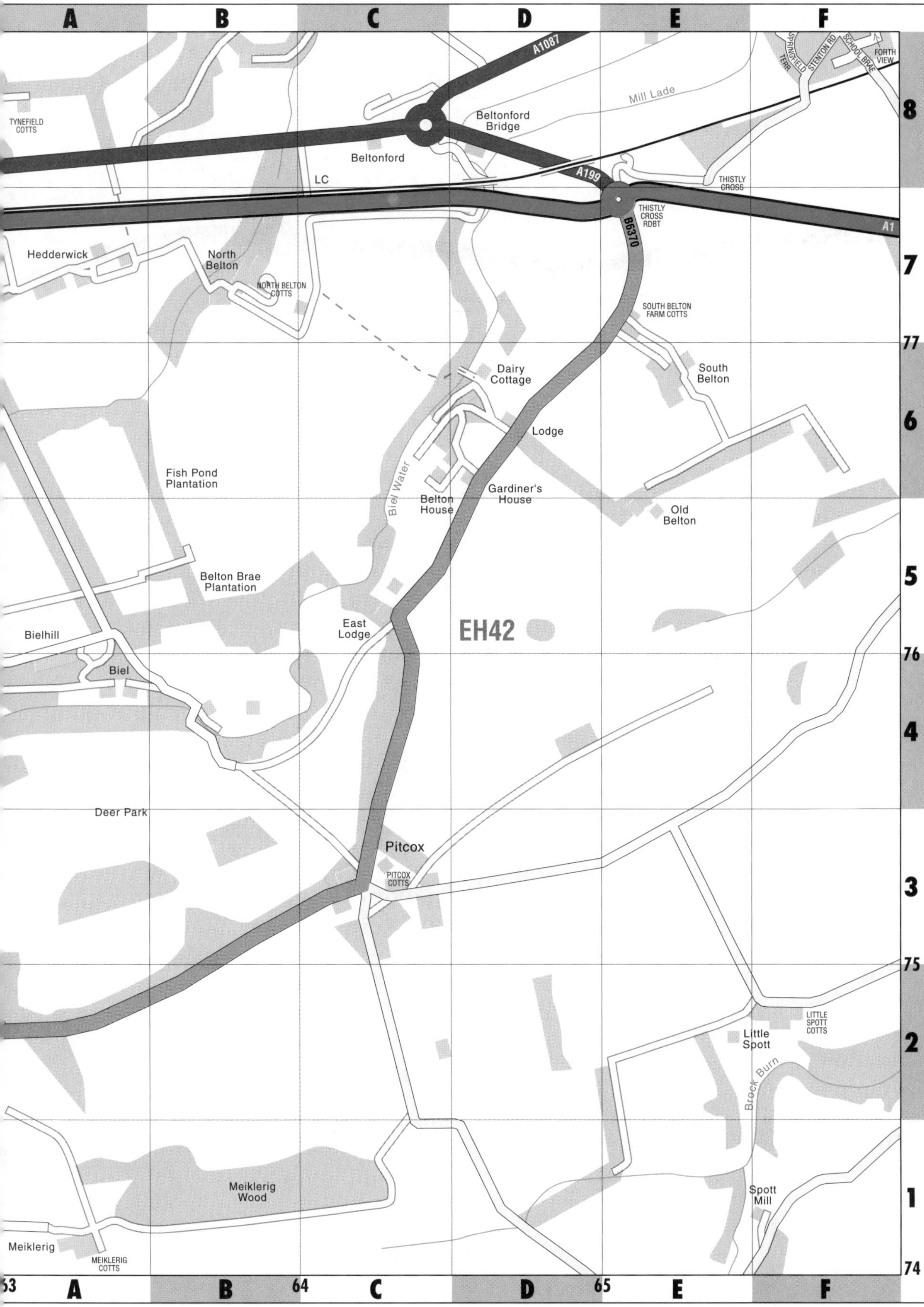
A
B
C
D
E
F
A1087
SPRINGFIELD TERR
STENTON RD
SCHOOL BRAE
FORTH VIEW
Mill Lade
8
TYNEFIELD COTTS
Beltonford Bridge
Beltonford
A199
LC
THISTLY CROSS
THISTLY CROSS RDBT
A1
B6370
Hedderwick
North Belton
NORTH BELTON COTTS
7
SOUTH BELTON FARM COTTS
77
Dairy Cottage
South Belton
6
Lodge
Fish Pond Plantation
Biel Water
Gardiner's House
Belton House
Old Belton
5
Belton Brae Plantation
East Lodge
EH42
Bielhill
Biel
76
4
Deer Park
Pitcox
PITCOX COTTS
3
75
LITTLE SPOTT COTTS
Little Spott
2
Brock Burn
Meiklerig Wood
Spott Mill
1
Meiklerig
MEIKLERIG COTTS
74
63
A
B
64
C
D
65
E
F

134
106

105
78

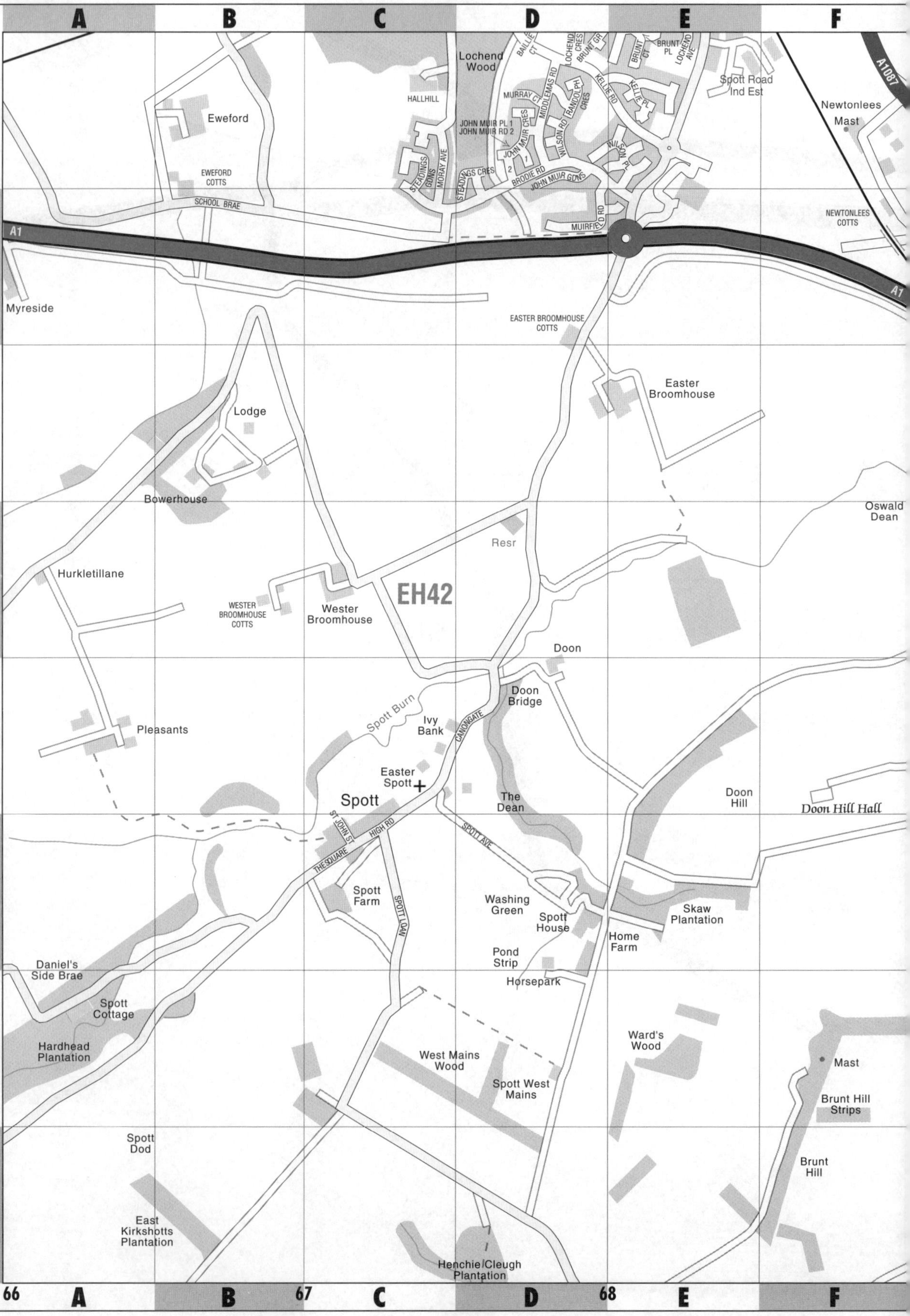
A
B
C
D
E
F
8
7
77
6
5
76
4
3
75
2
1
74
66
67
68
Lochend Wood
HALLHILL
BAILLIE CT
LOCHEND CRES
BRUNT GR
BRUNT CT
BRUNT PL
LOCHEND AVE
Spott Road Ind Est
A1087
Newtonlees Mast
Eweford
MURRAY CT
MIDDLEMAS RD
RANDOLPH CRES
KELLIE RD
KELLIE PL
JOHN MUIR PL 1
JOHN MUIR RD 2
JOHN MUIR CRES
WILSON RD
WILSON PL
STEADINGS GDNS
MORAY AVE
STEADINGS CRES
BRODIE RD
JOHN MUIR GDNS
EWEFORD COTTS
SCHOOL BRAE
MUIRFIELD RD
NEWTONLEES COTTS
A1
A1
Myreside
EASTER BROOMHOUSE COTTS
Easter Broomhouse
Lodge
Bowerhouse
Oswald Dean
Resr
Hurkletillane
EH42
WESTER BROOMHOUSE COTTS
Wester Broomhouse
Doon
Doon Bridge
Spott Burn
Ivy Bank
CANONGATE
Pleasants
Easter Spott
Spott
The Dean
Doon Hill
Doon Hill Hall
ST JOHN ST
HIGH RD
SPOTT AVE
THE SQUARE
Spott Farm
SPOTT LOAN
Washing Green
Spott House
Skaw Plantation
Home Farm
Pond Strip
Horsepark
Daniel's Side Brae
Spott Cottage
Hardhead Plantation
West Mains Wood
Ward's Wood
Spott West Mains
Mast
Brunt Hill Strips
Spott Dod
Brunt Hill
East Kirkshotts Plantation
Henchie Cleugh Plantation

105
135

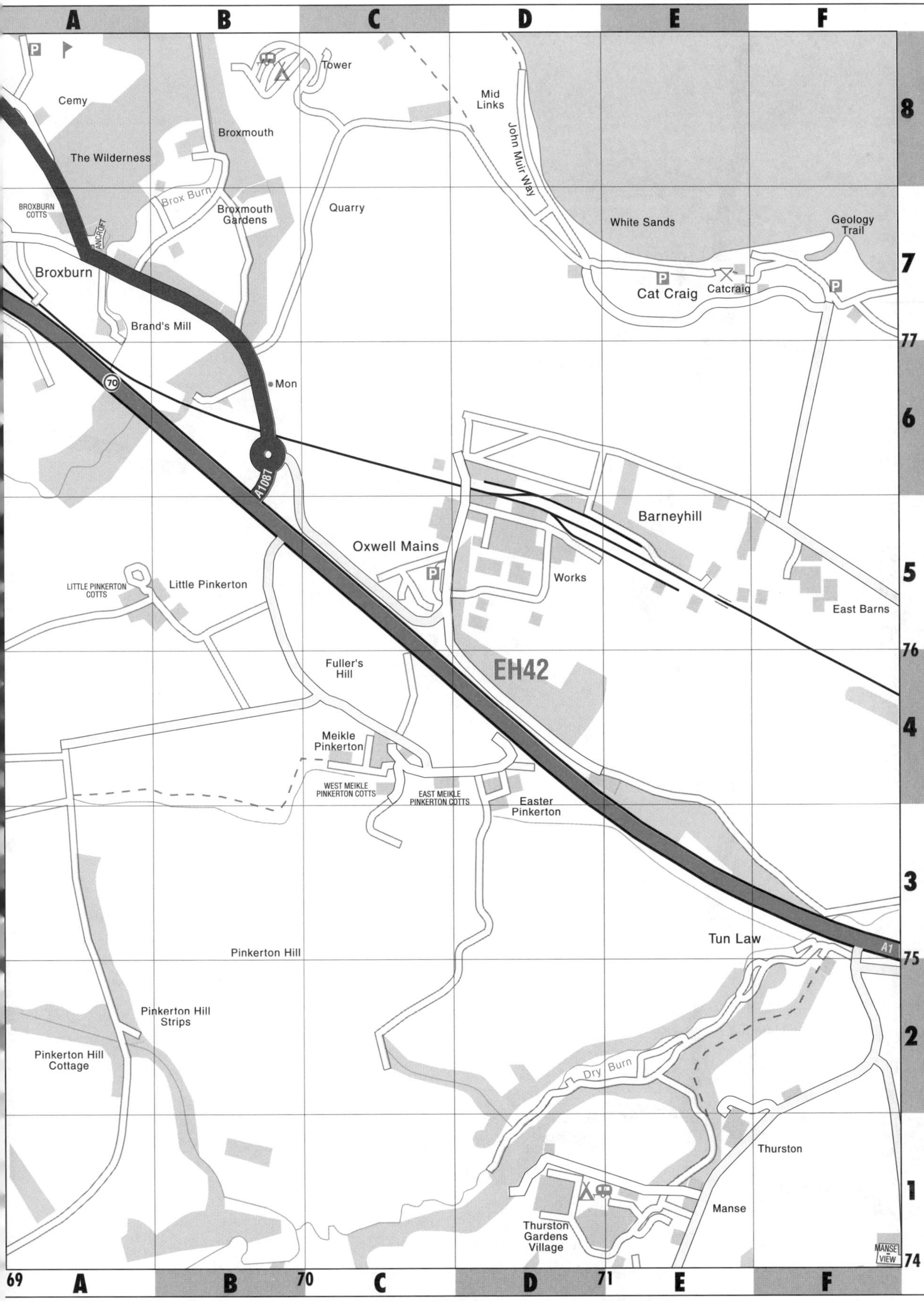
79
219
Tower
Mid
Links
John Muir Way
Cemy
Broxmouth
The Wilderness
BROXBURN
COTTS
Brox Burn
Broxmouth
Gardens
Quarry
White Sands
Geology
Trail
Broxburn
Cat Craig
Catcraig
Brand's Mill
Mon
70
A1087
Barneyhill
Oxwell Mains
Works
LITTLE PINKERTON
COTTS
Little Pinkerton
East Barns
Fuller's
Hill
EH42
Meikle
Pinkerton
WEST MEIKLE
PINKERTON COTTS
EAST MEIKLE
PINKERTON COTTS
Easter
Pinkerton
Tun Law
A1
Pinkerton Hill
Pinkerton Hill
Strips
Pinkerton Hill
Cottage
Dry Burn
Thurston
Manse
Thurston
Gardens
Village
MANSE
VIEW
A
B
C
D
E
F
8
7
77
6
5
76
4
3
75
2
1
74
69
70
71
136
218

80

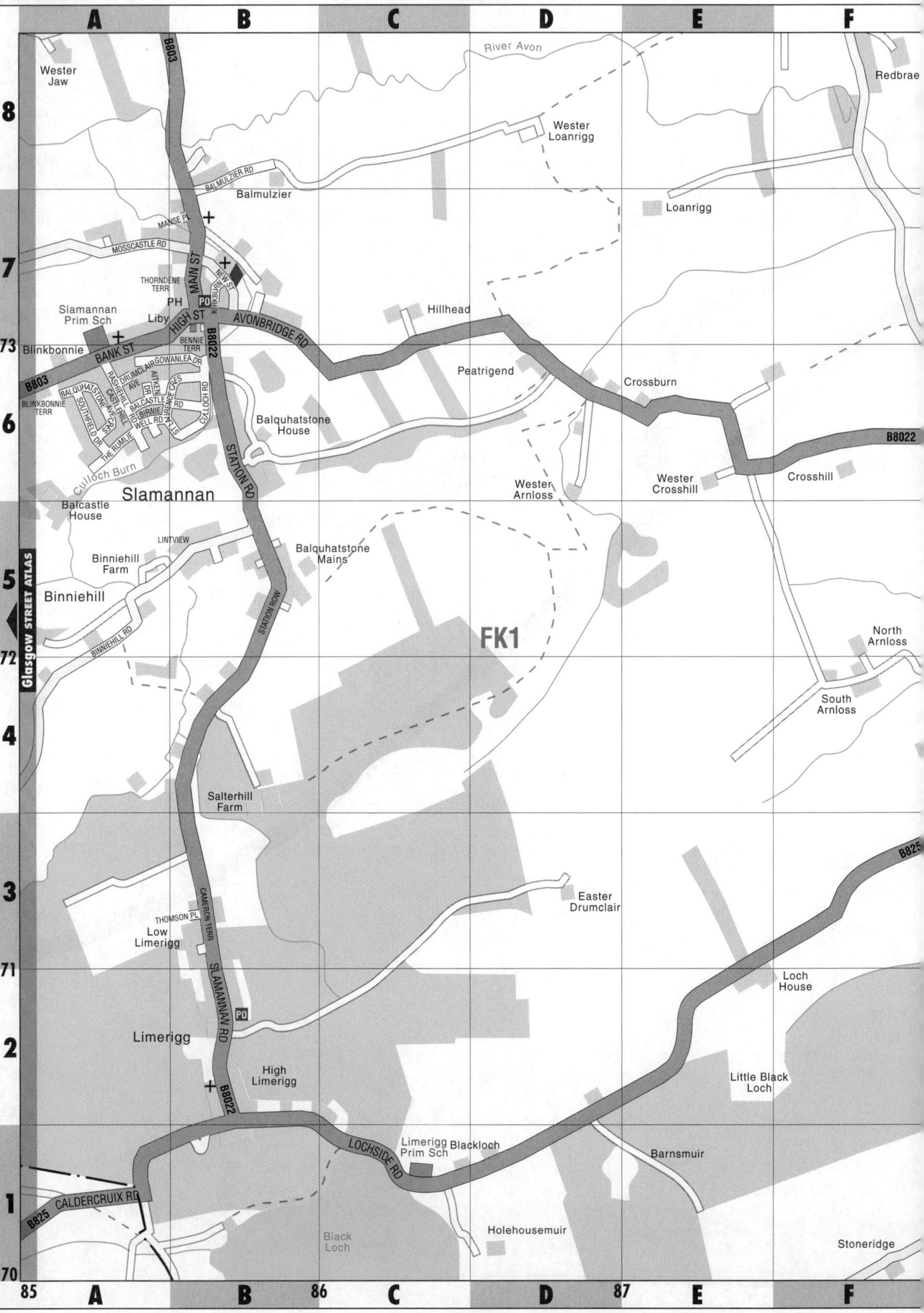
A
B
C
D
E
F
8
7
73
6
5
72
4
3
71
2
1
70
85
86
87
River Avon
Wester Jaw
Redbrae
B803
Wester Loanrigg
BALMULZIER RD
Balmulzier
Loanrigg
MANSE PL
MOSSCASTLE RD
MAIN ST
NEW ST
KIRKBURN
THORNDENE TERR
PH
PO
Slamannan Prim Sch
Liby
HIGH ST
AVONBRIDGE RD
Hillhead
Blinkbonnie
BANK ST
BENNIE TERR
B8022
GOWANLEA DR
DRUMCLAIR AVE
Peatrigend
Crossburn
AITKEN DR
BALCASTLE RD
BIRNIE
WELL RD
CULLOCH RD
BALQUHATSTONE CRES
SOUTHFIELD DR
BLINKBONNIE TERR
THE RUMLIE
Balquhatstone House
B8022
Culloch Burn
STATION RD
Wester Crosshill
Crosshill
Wester Arnloss
Slamannan
Balcastle House
LINTVIEW
Balquhatstone Mains
Binniehill Farm
Binniehill
STATION ROW
BINNIEHILL RD
FK1
North Arnloss
South Arnloss
Glasgow STREET ATLAS
Salterhill Farm
B825
Easter Drumclair
CAMERON TERR
THOMSON PL
Low Limerigg
SLAMANNAN RD
Loch House
PO
Limerigg
High Limerigg
Little Black Loch
B8022
LOCHSIDE RD
Limerigg Prim Sch
Blackloch
Barnsmuir
CALDERCRUIX RD
B825
Black Loch
Holehousemuir
Stoneridge

137

81
110

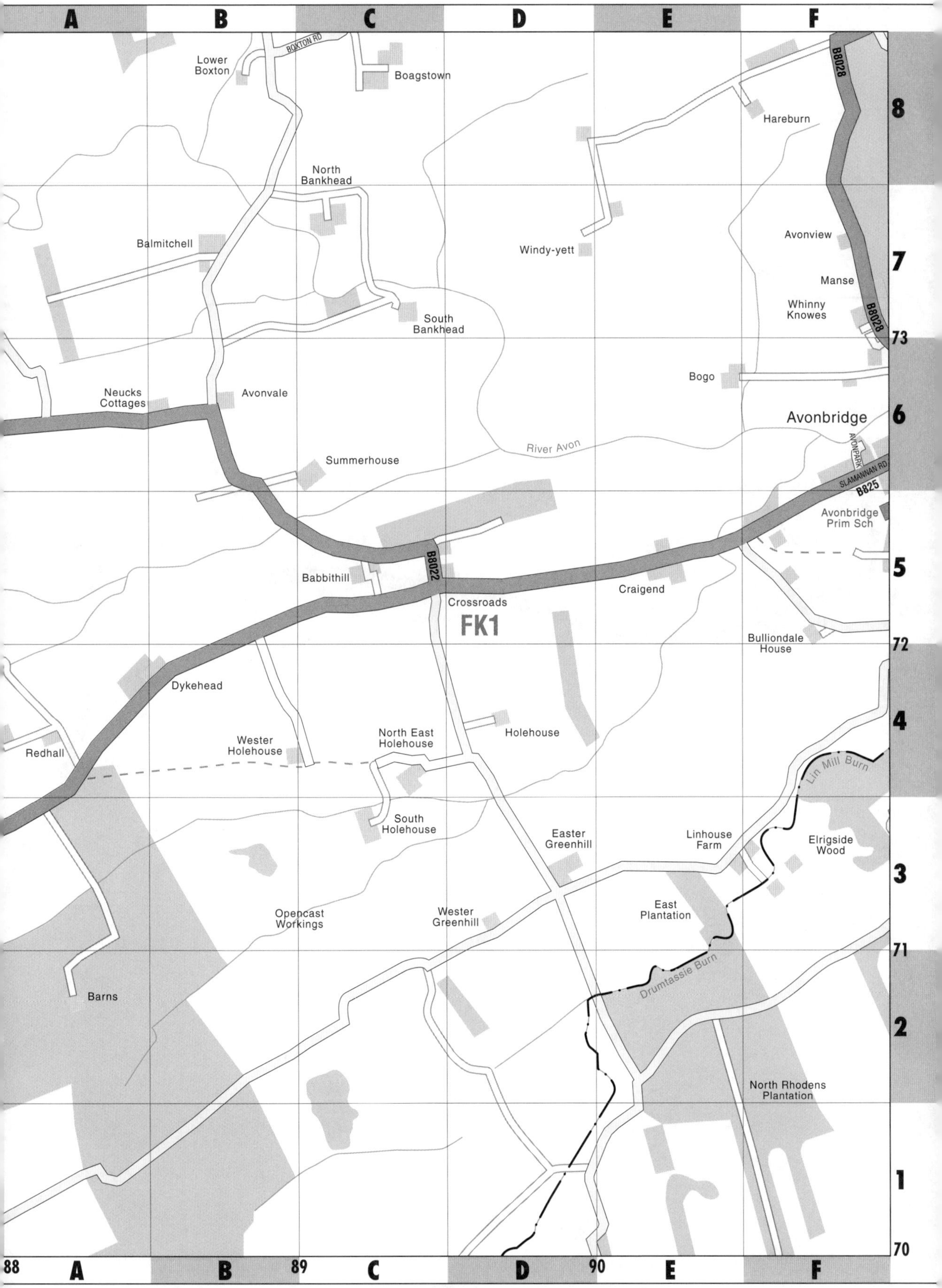

138
110

109
82

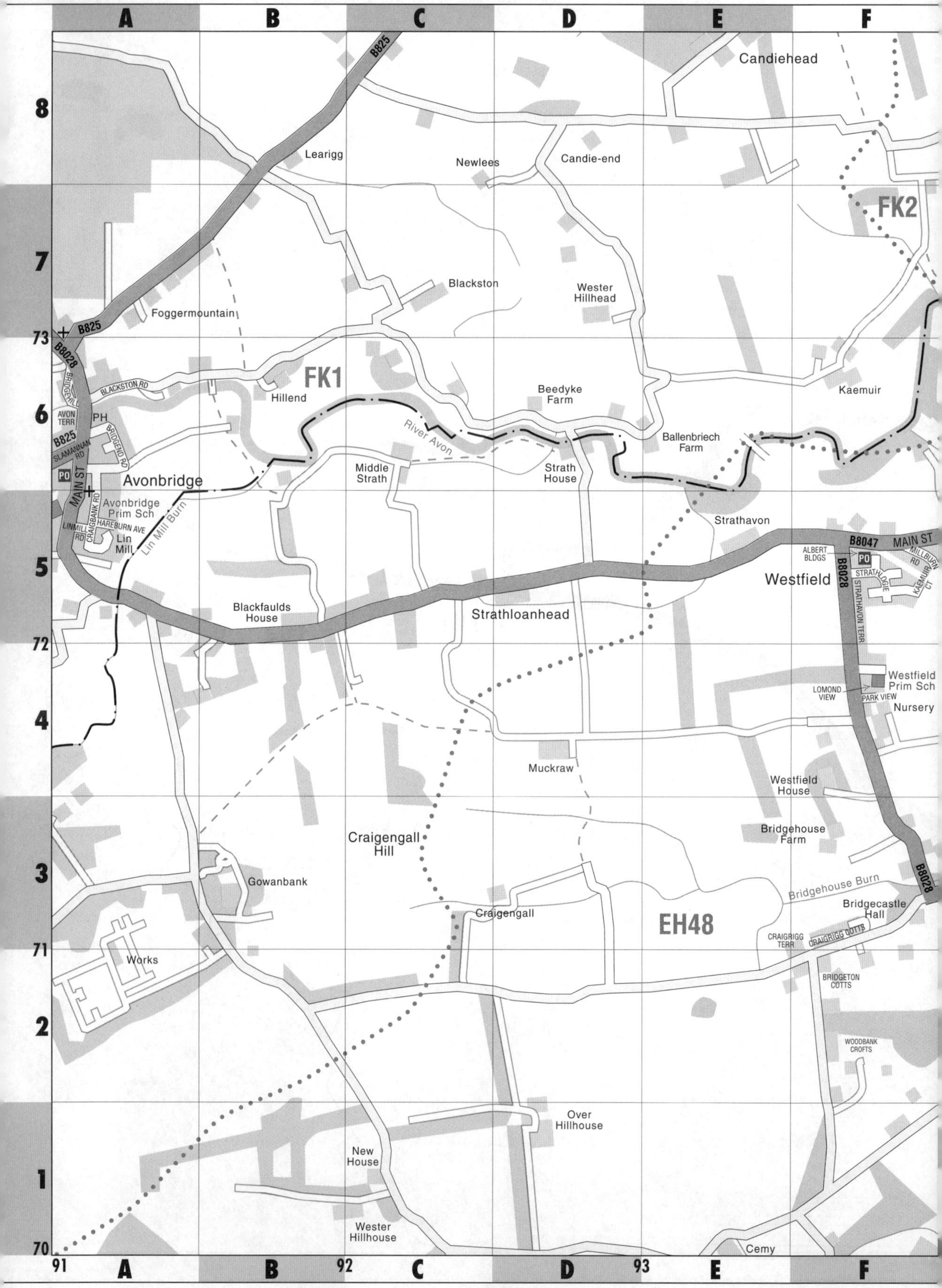
A
B
C
D
E
F
8
7
73
6
5
72
4
3
71
2
1
70
91
92
93
Candiehead
B825
Learigg
Newlees
Candie-end
FK2
Blackston
Wester Hillhead
Foggermountain
B825
B8028
BRIDGEMILL
BLACKSTON RD
FK1
Hillend
Beedyke Farm
Kaemuir
AVON TERR
PH
B825
SLAMANNAN RD
BRIDGEND RD
River Avon
Ballenbriech Farm
PO
MAIN ST
Avonbridge
Middle Strath
Strath House
Avonbridge Prim Sch
CRAIGBANK RD
LINMILL RD
HAREBURN AVE
Lin Mill
Lin Mill Burn
Strathavon
B8047
MAIN ST
ALBERT BLDGS
PO
MILLBURN RD
B8028
STRATHLOGIE
KAEMUIR CT
Westfield
Blackfaulds House
Strathloanhead
STRATHAVON TERR
Westfield Prim Sch
LOMOND VIEW
PARK VIEW
Nursery
Muckraw
Westfield House
Bridgehouse Farm
Craigengall Hill
B8028
Gowanbank
Bridgehouse Burn
Bridgecastle Hall
Craigengall
EH48
CRAIGRIGG TERR
CRAIGRIGG COTTS
Works
BRIDGETON COTTS
WOODBANK CROFTS
Over Hillhouse
New House
Wester Hillhouse
Cemy

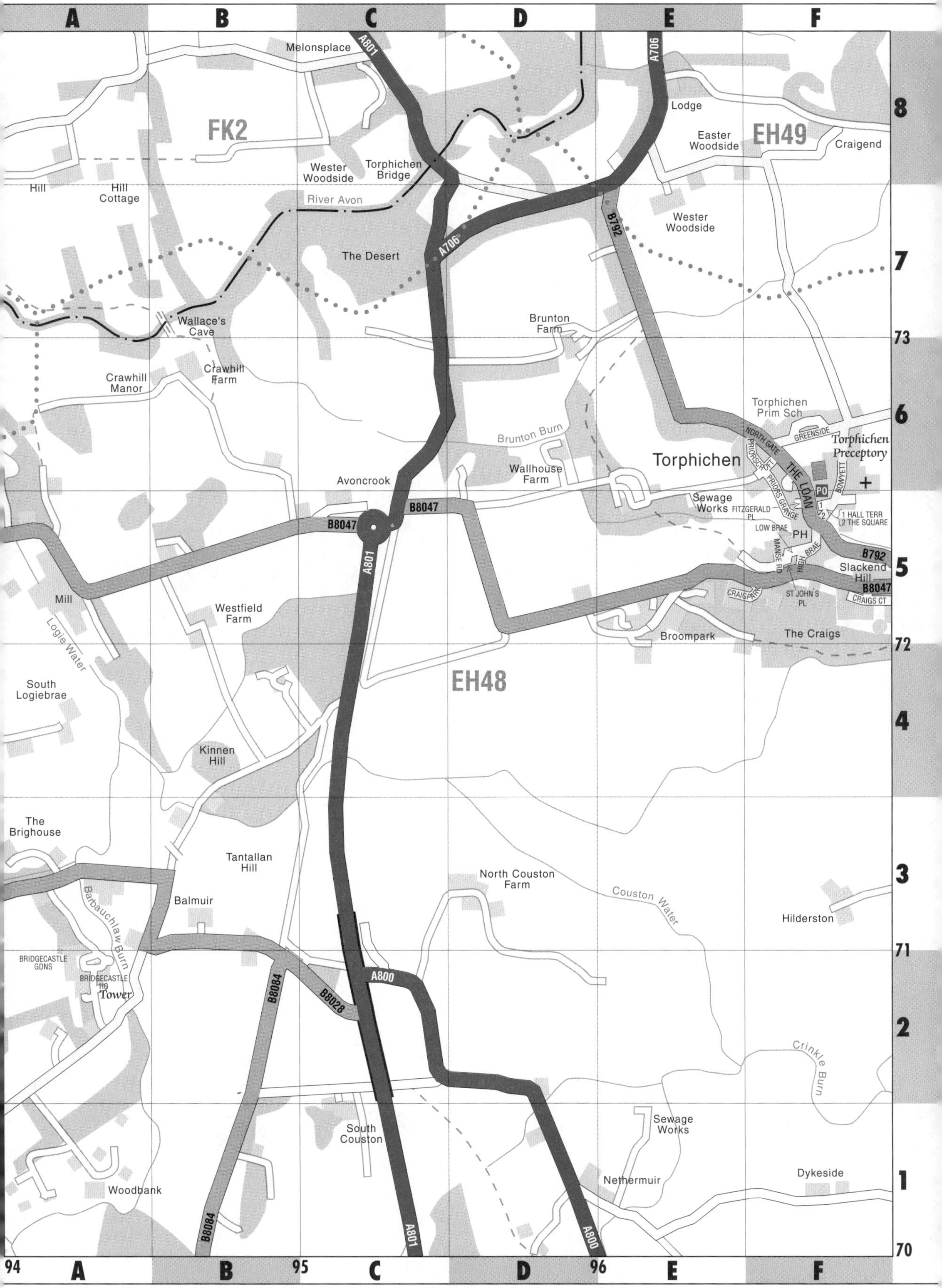
83
112
A
B
C
D
E
F
8
7
73
6
5
72
4
3
71
2
1
70
94
95
96
140
112
Melonsplace
A801
A706
FK2
EH49
EH48
Lodge
Easter Woodside
Craigend
Hill
Hill Cottage
Wester Woodside
Torphichen Bridge
River Avon
The Desert
Wester Woodside
B792
Wallace's Cave
Brunton Farm
Crawhill Manor
Crawhill Farm
Torphichen Prim Sch
Brunton Burn
GREENSIDE
Torphichen Preceptory
NORTH GATE
PRIORSCROFT
Torphichen
Wallhouse Farm
Avoncrook
THE LOAN
BOWYETT
PRIORS GRANGE
PO
Sewage Works
FITZGERALD PL
1 HALL TERR
2 THE SQUARE
B8047
LOW BRAE
PH
MANSE RD
HIGH BRAE
Slackend Hill
Mill
CRAIGSPARK
ST JOHN'S PL
CRAIGS CT
Westfield Farm
Logie Water
Broompark
The Craigs
South Logiebrae
Kinnen Hill
The Brighouse
Tantallan Hill
North Couston Farm
Couston Water
Balmuir
Barbauchlaw Burn
Hilderston
BRIDGECASTLE GDNS
BRIDGECASTLE HO
Tower
A800
B8084
B8028
Crinkle Burn
Sewage Works
South Couston
Nethermuir
Dykeside
Woodbank

111
84

A
B
C
D
E
F
8
7
73
6
5
72
4
3
71
2
1
70
97
98
99
Cow Hill
Tower
Lochcote Resr
Kipps
(remains of)
Kipps Farm
Kipps Hill
EH49
Beecraigs Wood
Beecraigs Country Park
Refuge Stone
Wairdlaw
Gormyre
Witch Craig Wood
Scottish Korean War Memorial
Hanging Rock Plantation
Gormyre Hill
Torpichen Hills
Stoney Manuel Plantation
Craigmailing
Cathlaw House
Slackend
B792
B8047
CRAIGS CT
MALLENS BRAE
CATHLAW LA
Cathlawhill
North Mine Plantation
Bishopbrae Strips
EH48
Cairnpapple Hill
Cairnpapple Henge & Cairn
Mast
P
The Glebe
Hilderston Hills
Knock
Bishopbrae
P
The Knock
Crinkle Burn
Resr
Crinkle Bridge
Ballencrieff Mains
Sheddon Braes
Raven Craig Wood
Bathgate Hills
Resr
Galabraes
Wester Drumcross
TORPHICHEN RD
B792
BALLENCRIEFF TOLL

111
141

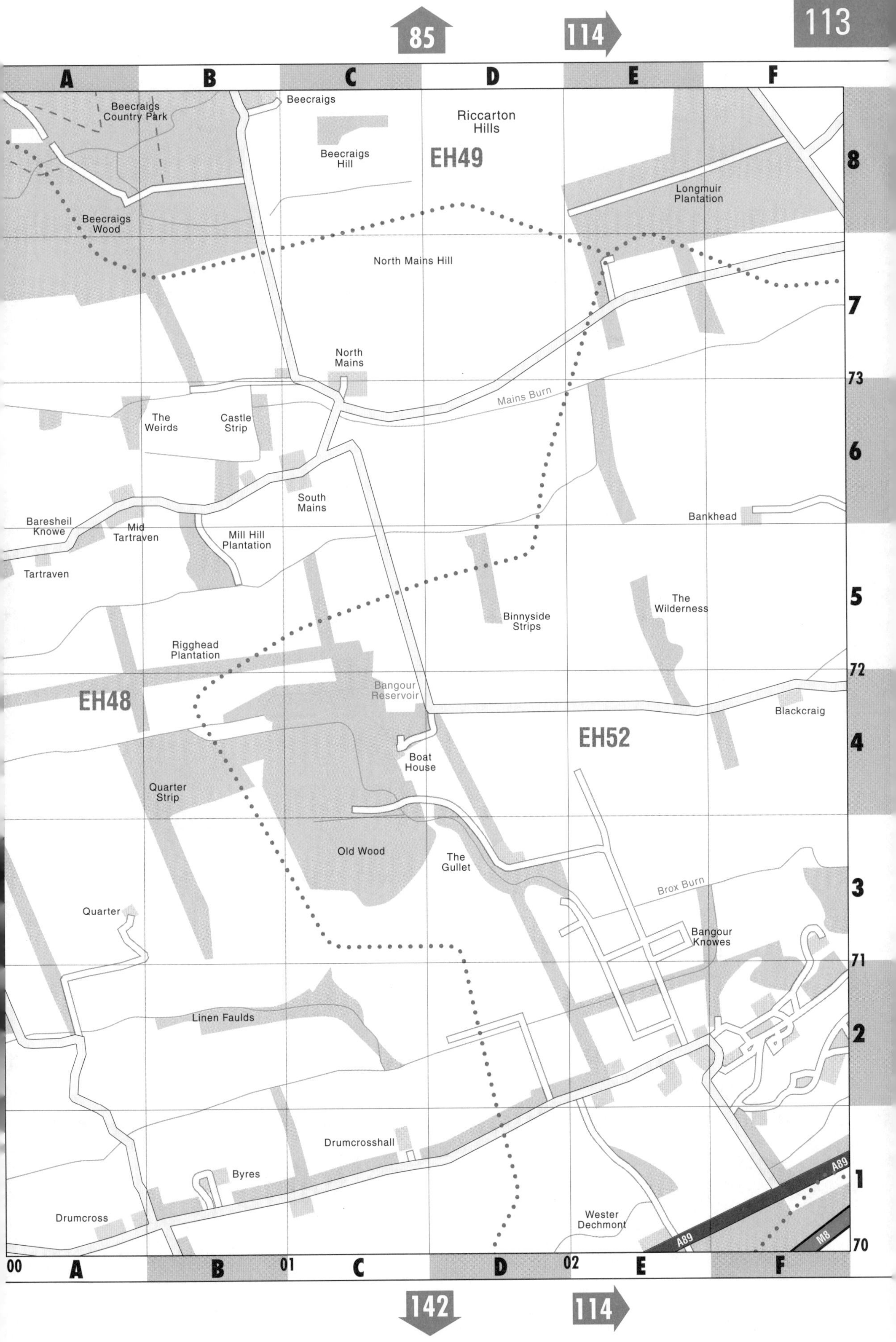
85
114
A
B
C
D
E
F
Beecraigs Country Park
Beecraigs
Riccarton Hills
Beecraigs Hill
EH49
Longmuir Plantation
Beecraigs Wood
North Mains Hill
8
7
73
North Mains
Mains Burn
The Weirds
Castle Strip
6
South Mains
Baresheil Knowe
Mid Tartraven
Mill Hill Plantation
Bankhead
Tartraven
5
The Wilderness
Binnyside Strips
Rigghead Plantation
72
Bangour Reservoir
EH48
Blackcraig
EH52
4
Boat House
Quarter Strip
Old Wood
The Gullet
3
Brox Burn
Quarter
Bangour Knowes
71
Linen Faulds
2
Drumcrosshall
Byres
1
A89
Drumcross
Wester Dechmont
A89
M8
70
00
01
02
A
B
C
D
E
F
142
114

113 86

A
B
C
D
E
F
8
7
73
6
5
72
4
3
71
2
1
70
03
04
05
Ochiltree Mill
Ecclesmachan Burn
EH49
Mains Burn
Hangingside
Binny Craig
Oatridge
Ecclesmachan Covert
B8046
WELLPARK
BYBURN
Oatridge Agriculture Coll
Mausoleum
Binny House
CH
Lodge
BINNY PK
Ecclesmachan
West Broadlaw
East Broadlaw
West Binny
Binny Burn
Upper Uphall
MANSE PK
EH52
Law
Law Wood
ECCLESMACHAN RD
FERNLEA
HOWIESON GN
Craigbeg
Craig Binning
East Bangour
ST ANDREW'S DR
THOMSON GR
THOMSON CT
BIRKDALE DR
MUIRFIELD DR
ROSEMOUNT DR
HAWTHORN PL
ROSE'S WLK
PO
Uphall
P
Forkneuk Farm
FORKNEUK STEADINGS
FORKNEUK RD
STRATHBROCK PL
WEST MAIN ST
A899
Rench
CH
SCHOOL PL
MACFARLANE PL
MILLBANK PL
JOHNSTON AVE
HOUSTOUN GDNS
FORREST WLK
MACLARDY CT
Burnhouse
Hotel
STANKARDS RD
Brox Burn
A89
BURNHOUSE RD
BURNHOUSE DR
GOODALL CRES
AFTON CT
BADGER WOOD
1 KNIGHTSRIDGE CT
2 CRAIGLAW PL
GOODALL PL
MAIN ST
KNIGHTSRIDGE RD
CRAIGLAW
BURNSIDE
PO
DEERHILL
DECHMONT RDBT
STATION RD
Dechmont
Dechmont Inf Sch
LIVINGSTON RD
Beugh Burn
B8046
Houston Mains Holdings
M8
A89
M8
3
Deer Hill
EH54
Hotel
LIVINGSTONE E RDBT
GALLACHER GN
EAGLES VW
DEER PARK DR
DEER PARK RD
Fairways Bsns Pk
Houstoun Ind Est
TODD SQ
NETTLEHILL RD
KINGSTHORNE PK
HUNTING PK
NETTLEHILL DR

113 143

87
116
A
B
C
D
E
F
Tar Hill
Hillend
Niddry Burn
Newbigging
North Greendykes
Wyndford
Newbigging Craig
NORTH GREENDYKES RD
GREENDYKES STEADINGS
Albyn Ind Est
Pyothall
Liggat Syke
EH52
ALBYN COTTS
GREENDYKES RD
YOUNGS RD
Greendykes Ind Est
Broxburn
Holygate
Kirkhill Prim Sch
Broxburn Acad
Buchan Park
Broxburn Prim Sch
Kirkhill
Uphall Prim Sch
EAST MAIN ST
WEST MAIN ST
A899
A89
Cemy
St Nicholas RC Prim Sch
Brox Burn
Ryal Burn
Union Canal
Ryal
Hawthorne Brae
Park House
Powflats
Holmes Cottages
Learielaw
Beugh Burn
Caw Burn
M8
STATION RD
Uphall
ROMAN CAMP COTTS
Lookaboutye
B8046
Uphall Station
EH54
EH53
PUMPHERSTON RD
Drumshoreland Muir
Poultry Farm
TA Ctr
8
7
73
6
5
72
4
3
71
2
1
70
06
07
08
144
116

115
88

A
B
C
D
E
F
8
7
73
6
5
72
4
3
71
2
1
70
09
10
11
Niddry
Union Canal
West Farm
West Wood
Newliston
Milrig
Home Farm
EH29
Palace Wood
M9
B800
A89
Peniel Place
Chesterlaw
BRIDGE ST
New Bridge
The Haugh
Brox Burn
RIVERSIDE
BROCKS WAY
CLIFTON VIEW
YOUNGS RD
SIMPSON RD
DUNNET WAY
DROVERS RD
FRESKYN PL
East Mains Ind Est
WESTERTON RD
TARTRAVEN PL
MAXWELL HO
Thistle Ind Est
LIGGET SYKE PL
KILPUNT RDBT
A899 EAST MAIN ST
KILPUNT GDNS
NEWHOUSES RD
HUNTER GDNS
KILPUNT VIEW
A89
EH52
Newbridge Ind Est
Almond Valley Viaduct
B7030
BURNVALE
Burnside
River Almond
Birdsmill Pig Farm
CLIFTONHALL RD
Clifton Trad Est
CLIFTONHALL YARDS
Kilpunt
Newhouses
Elm Cottage
Caw Burn
NEWHOUSE
PH
Birdsmill House
EH28
CLAYLANDS RD
Loup-o-Lees
M8
M8
Clifton Hall Sch
Muirend
Union Canal
Lin's Mill (dis)
CLIFTONHALL RD
Lin's Mill Aqueduct
P
CLIFTON RD
Clifton Mains
B7030
Illieston
EH53

115
145

89
118

A
B
C
D
E
F
8
7
73
6
5
72
4
3
71
2
1
70
12
13
14
Maitland Hog La
Maitland Bridge
Breastmill
B800 New Liston Rd
River Almond
Hallyards
Hallyards Rd
Hallyards Cotts
EH29
River Almond
Edinburgh Airport
EH12
Jubilee Rd
Almond Rd
Almond Ave
Ingliston Market
Hotel
PH
Fairview Rd
Lochend Rd
Sewage Works
Royal Highland Centre (Royal Highland Showground)
East Mains of Ingliston (Smallholdings)
Hallyards Rd
West Ingliston
Ingliston Rd
Lochend
A89
Edinburgh Rd
M9
A8
Glasgow Rd
M8
B7030
PH
Old Liston Rd
Bridge St
Riverside
PD
Parkside
Newbridge
Newbridge Rd
Newbridge Junc
Ratho Pk
Station Rd
Ratho Station
Queen Anne Dr
Lochend Ind Est
Harvest Dr
Hillwood Prim Sch
Hillwood Gdns
Hillwood Rd
Hillwood Cres
Hillwood Terr
Hillwood Ave
Hillwood Rise
Middle Norton
A8
Chariot Dr
Newbridge Ind Est
Queen Anne Pk
Harvest Rd
Cliftonhall Rd
Alexandra Bsns Pk
PH
Norton House
Norton Mains
Hillwood Cottage
EH28
Hillwood Quarry
Hillwood
M8
Ratho Byres
Freelands Cottage
Claylands Farm
Hillend
Works
Cemy
Freelands Rd
Freelands
Baird Rd
Ratho Hall
Manse
Edinburgh International Climbing Arena
Union Canal
Hallcroft Neuk
Hallcroft Cres
Hallcroft Gdns
Hallcroft Gn
Hallcroft Pk
Ratho Prim Sch
Liby
West Croft
East Croft
Ratho Pk Rd
Ratho Park Gardens
CH
Hallcroft Rise
Craigpark Ave
North St
PO
Main St
Lidgate Sh
Dalmahoy Rd
Wilkieston Rd
Hillview Cotts
Craig Park
Craigpark Cres
Lumsden Ct
Ratho
B7030 Cliftonhall Rd
Ransfield
Ratho Mains
Ransfield Cottages
Quarry

146
118

117 90

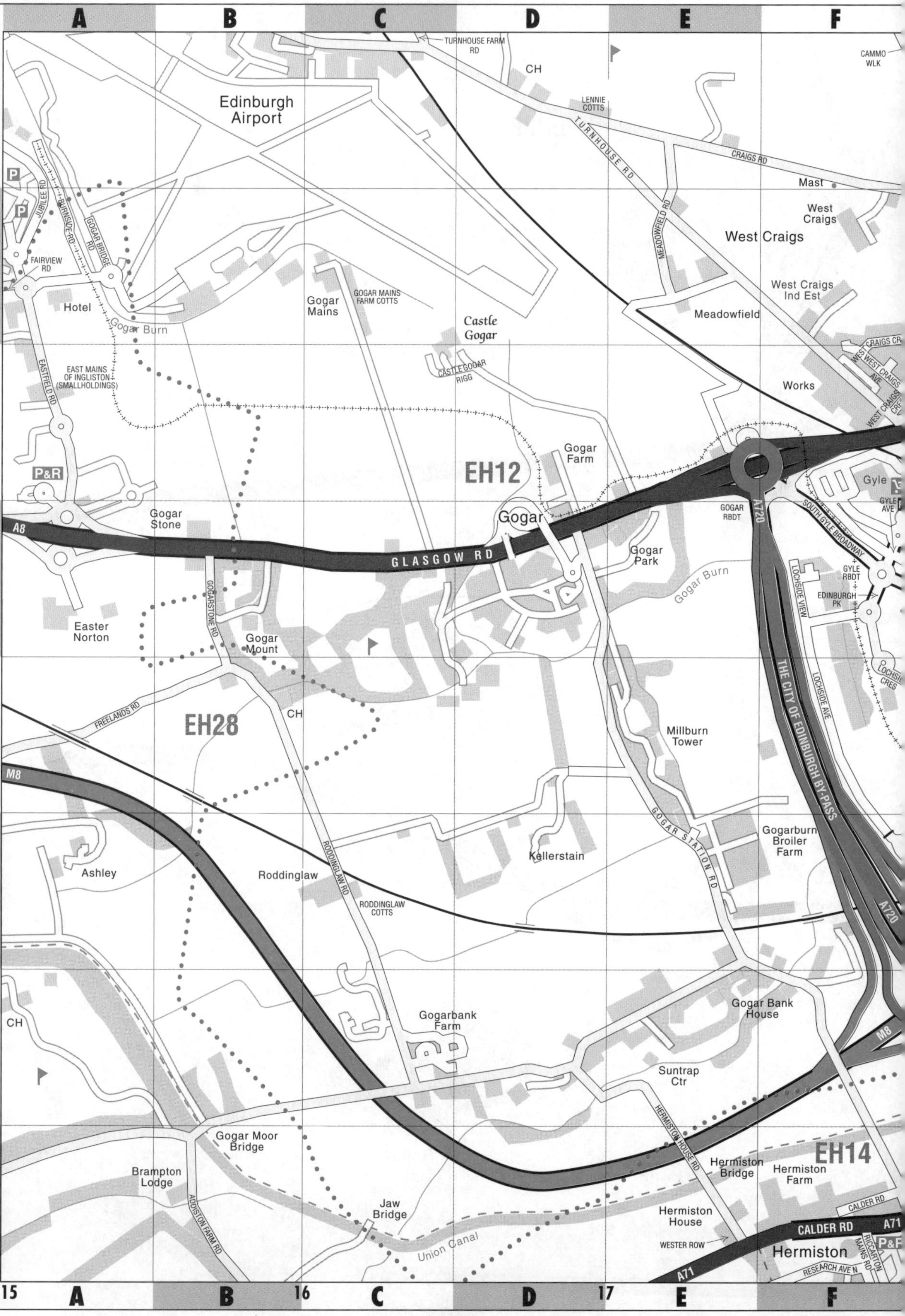
A B C D E F
8
7
73
6
5
72
4
3
71
2
1
70
15 A B 16 C D 17 E F
Edinburgh Airport
TURNHOUSE FARM RD
CH
LENNIE COTTS
TURNHOUSE RD
CRAIGS RD
CAMMO WLK
Mast
West Craigs
West Craigs
MEADOWFIELD RD
West Craigs Ind Est
Meadowfield
JUBILEE RD
BURNSIDE RD
GOGAR BRIDGE RD
FAIRVIEW RD
Hotel
Gogar Burn
Gogar Mains
GOGAR MAINS FARM COTTS
Castle Gogar
CASTLE GOGAR RIGG
EAST MAINS OF INGLISTON (SMALLHOLDINGS)
EASTFIELD RD
P&R
Works
Gogar Farm
EH12
Gogar
GOGAR RBDT
A720
Gyle
GYLE AVE
SOUTH GYLE BROADWAY
GYLE RBDT
EDINBURGH PK
LOCHSIDE VIEW
Gogar Stone
A8
GLASGOW RD
Gogar Park
Gogar Burn
Easter Norton
GOGARSTONE RD
Gogar Mount
LOCHSIDE CRES
LOCHSIDE AVE
FREELANDS RD
EH28
CH
THE CITY OF EDINBURGH BY-PASS
Millburn Tower
M8
GOGAR STATION RD
Gogarburn Broiler Farm
Kellerstain
Ashley
Roddinglaw
RODDINGLAW RD
RODDINGLAW COTTS
A720
CH
Gogarbank Farm
Gogar Bank House
M8
Suntrap Ctr
Gogar Moor Bridge
HERMISTON HOUSE RD
EH14
Brampton Lodge
Hermiston Bridge
Hermiston Farm
ADDISTON FARM RD
Jaw Bridge
Hermiston House
CALDER RD
CALDER RD
A71
Union Canal
WESTER ROW
Hermiston
RICCARTON MAINS RD
A71
RESEARCH AVE N

A7
1 KILCHURN CT
2 NEIDPATH CT
3 TOWARD CT
4 ROWALLAN CT

A8
1 AFFLECK CT
2 FINLAGGAN CT
3 BURNBRAE DR
4 BURNBRAE PL
5 BURNBRAE AVE
6 BURNBRAE GR

B7
1 CAERLAVEROCK CT
2 DUNOLLIE CT
3 KISIMUL CT

E6
1 CORSTORPHINE HOUSE AVE
2 CORSTORPHINE HOUSE TERR
3 SYCAMORE TERR

91
120

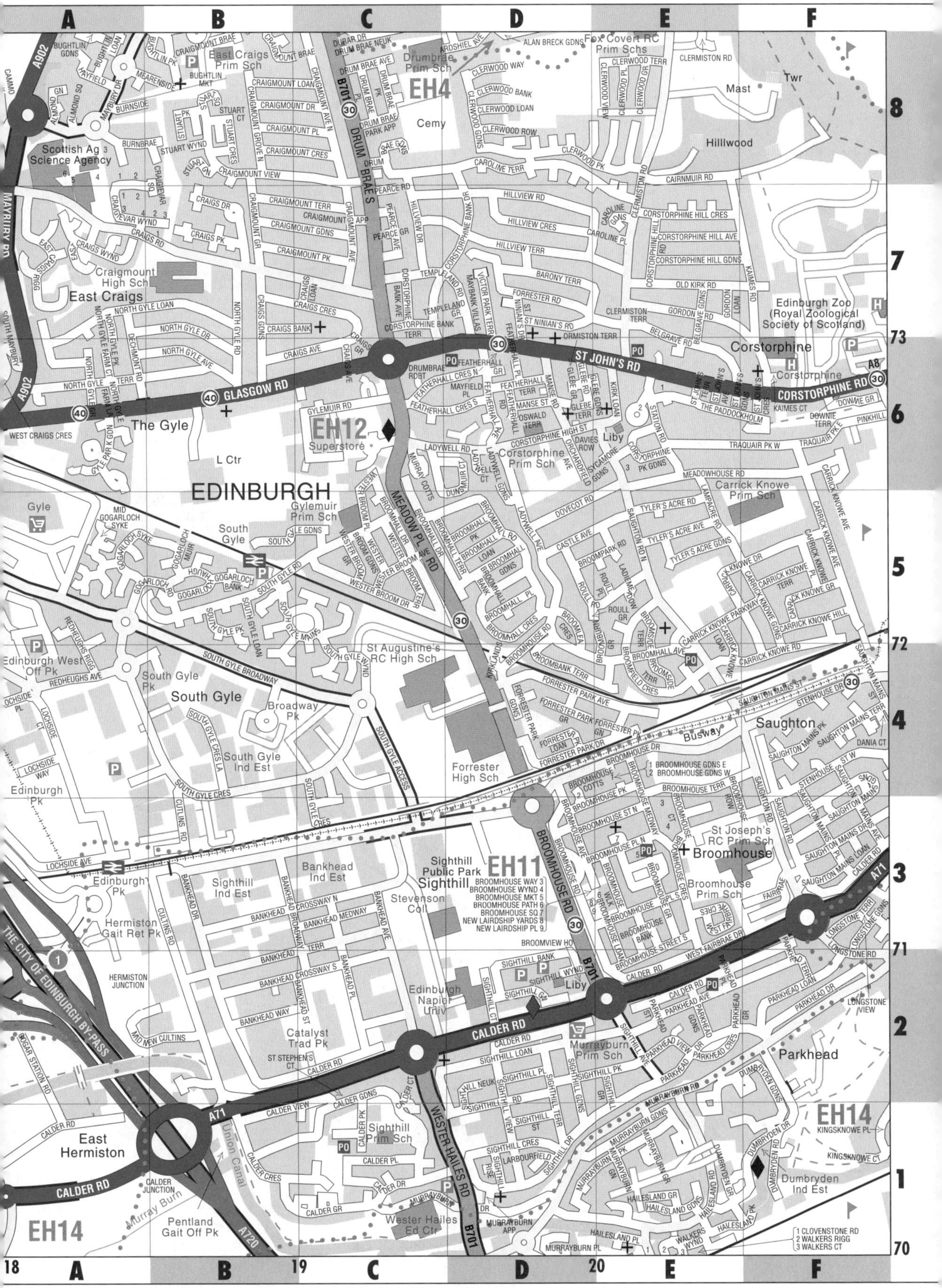

148
120

119
92

E7
1 COLTBRIDGE VALE
2 COLTBRIDGE MILLSIDE
3 KEW TERR
4 HAMPTON TERR
5 HAMPTON PL
6 WEST STANHOPE PL
7 PEMBROKE PL
8 CARBERRY PL

F6
1 EASTER DALRY RIGG
2 EASTER DALRY DR
3 WASHINGTON LA
4 EASTER DALRY PL
5 Dalry Prim Sch

F8
1 UPPER DAMSIDE
2 DAMSIDE
3 BELFORD MEWS
4 SUNBURY MEWS
5 DOUGLAS GDNS MEWS
6 ROTHESAY TERR
7 ROTHESAY PL
8 PALMERSTON PL

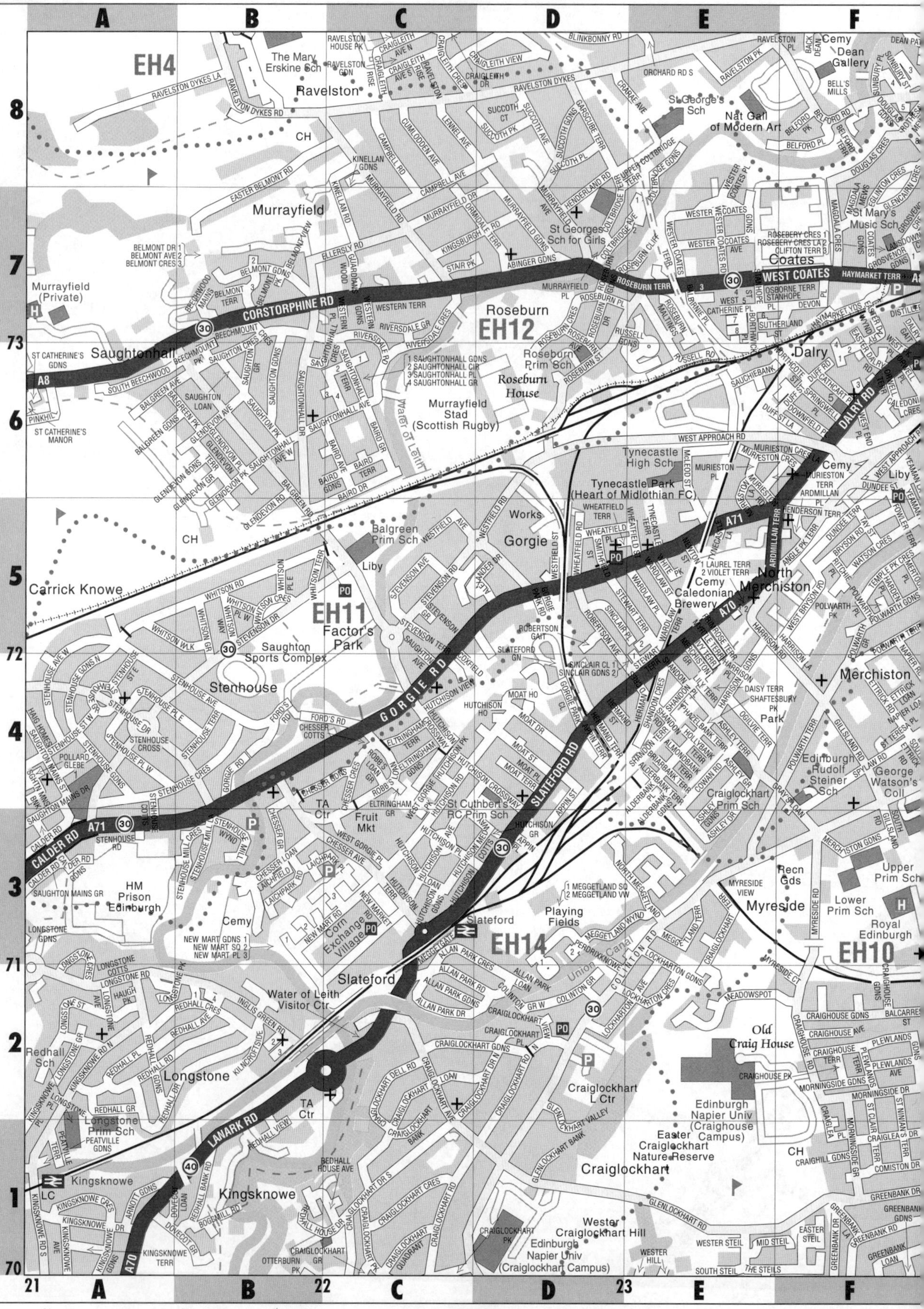

E5
1 SCIENNES PL
2 EAST SCIENNES ST
3 SCIENNES HOUSE PL
4 SCIENNES HILL PL
5 GRANGE CT
6 EAST PRESTON STREET LA
7 WEST NEWINGTON PL

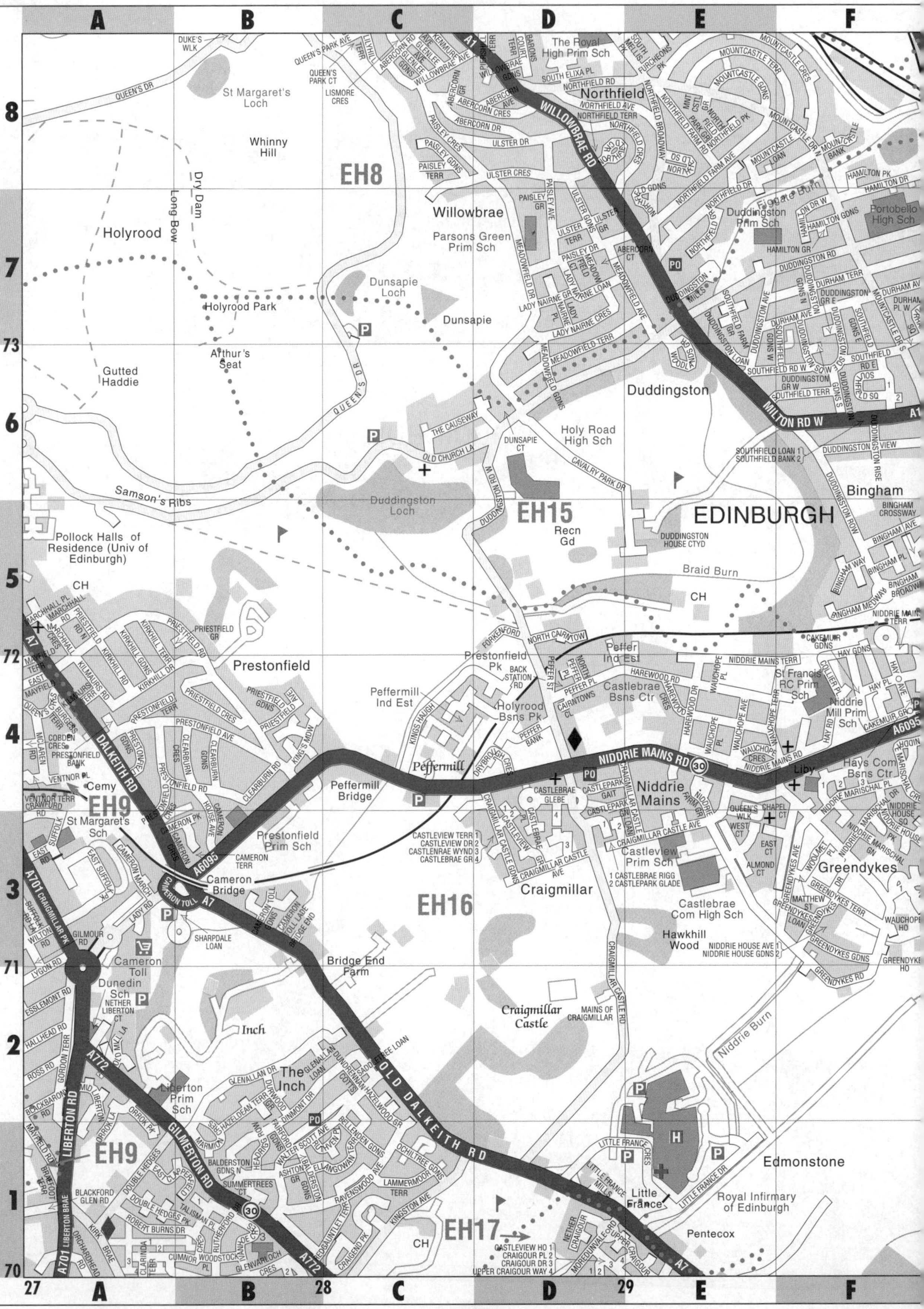

A1
1 JEAN ARMOUR AVE
2 SHANTER WAY
3 MOSSGIEL WLK
4 ALLOWAY LOAN

B1
1 TRESSILIAN GDNS
2 GREENMANTLE LOAN
3 St John Vianney RC Prim Sch

F4
1 NIDDRIE MARISCHAL GDNS
2 NIDDRIE MARISCHAL LOAN
3 NIDDRIE MARISCHAL ST

A8
1 ADELPHI GR
2 WILLIAMFIELD SQ
3 BEACH LA

95
124

152
124

A5
1 STONEYHILL WYND
2 CLAYKNOWES PL
3 STONEYHILL GDNS

123

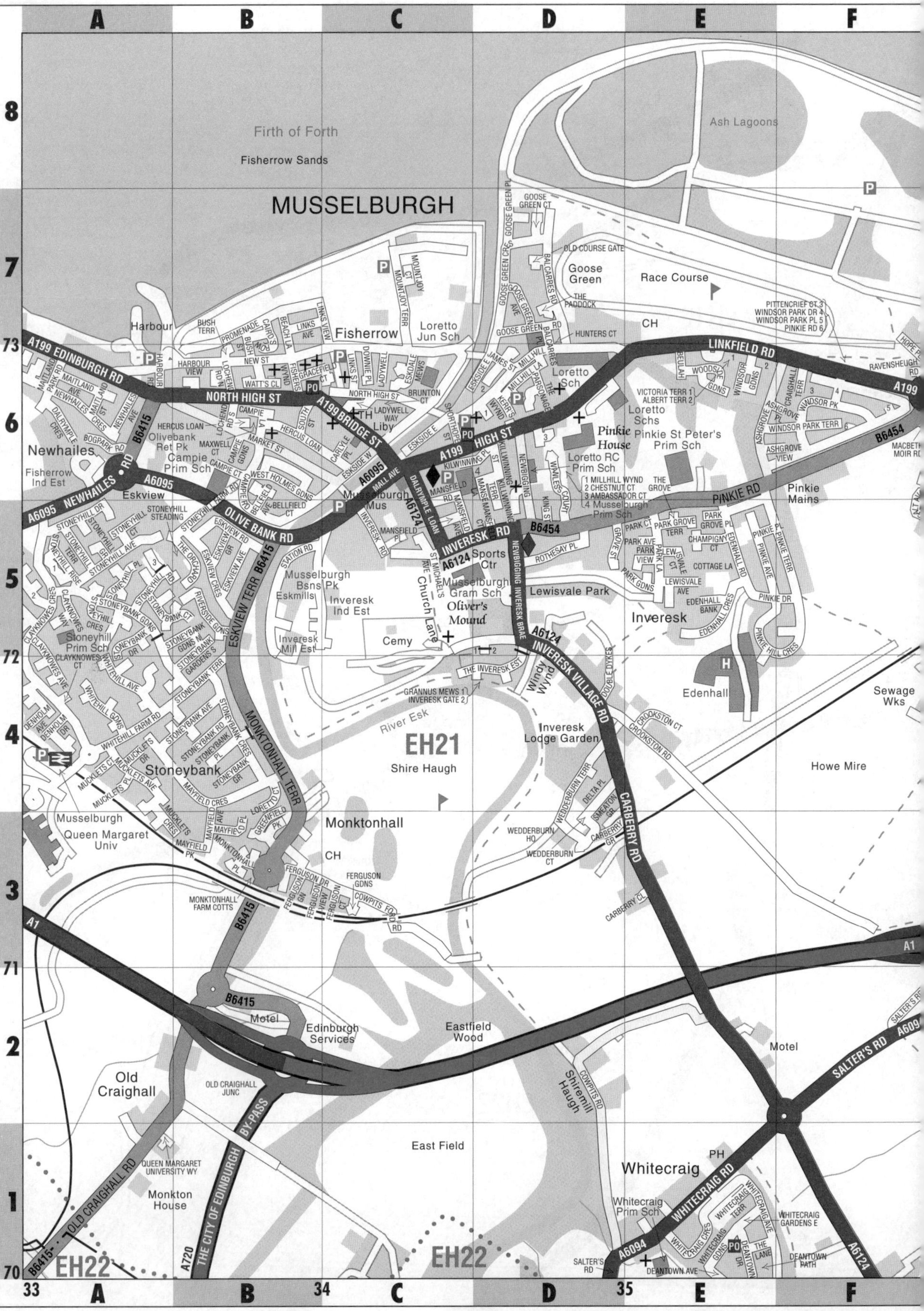
A
B
C
D
E
F
8
7
73
6
5
72
4
3
71
2
1
70
33
34
35
Firth of Forth
Fisherrow Sands
MUSSELBURGH
Ash Lagoons
Race Course
Goose Green
Harbour
Fisherrow
Loretto Jun Sch
Loretto Sch
Loretto Schs
Pinkie House
Pinkie St Peter's Prim Sch
Loretto RC Prim Sch
Pinkie Mains
Newhailes
Fisherrow Ind Est
Olivebank Ret Pk
Campie Prim Sch
Eskview
Musselburgh Mus
Musselburgh Bsns Pk
Eskmills
Inveresk Ind Est
Inveresk Mill Est
Cemy
Sports Ctr
Musselburgh Gram Sch
Oliver's Mound
Lewisvale Park
Inveresk
Edenhall
Sewage Wks
Stoneyhill Prim Sch
Stoneybank
Musselburgh Queen Margaret Univ
Monktonhall
River Esk
EH21
Shire Haugh
Inveresk Lodge Garden
Howe Mire
Motel
Edinburgh Services
Eastfield Wood
Old Craighall
Shiremill Haugh
East Field
Whitecraig
Whitecraig Prim Sch
Monkton House
EH22
A199 EDINBURGH RD
NORTH HIGH ST
A199 BRIDGE ST
A199 HIGH ST
LINKFIELD RD
A199
PINKIE RD
B6454
A6095 NEWHAILES RD
A6095
OLIVE BANK RD
ESKVIEW TERR B6415
MONKTONHALL TERR
B6415
A6124
INVERESK RD
INVERESK VILLAGE RD
CARBERRY RD
A1
SALTER'S RD
WHITECRAIG RD
A6094
OLD CRAIGHALL RD
THE CITY OF EDINBURGH BY-PASS
A720
OLD CRAIGHALL JUNC
QUEEN MARGARET UNIVERSITY WY
1 MILLHILL WYND
2 CHESTNUT CT
3 AMBASSADOR CT
4 Musselburgh Prim Sch
GRANNUS MEWS 1
INVERESK GATE 2
PITTENCRIEF CT 3
WINDSOR PARK DR 4
WINDSOR PARK PL 5
PINKIE RD 6
VICTORIA TERR 1
ALBERT TERR 2

123
153

96
126

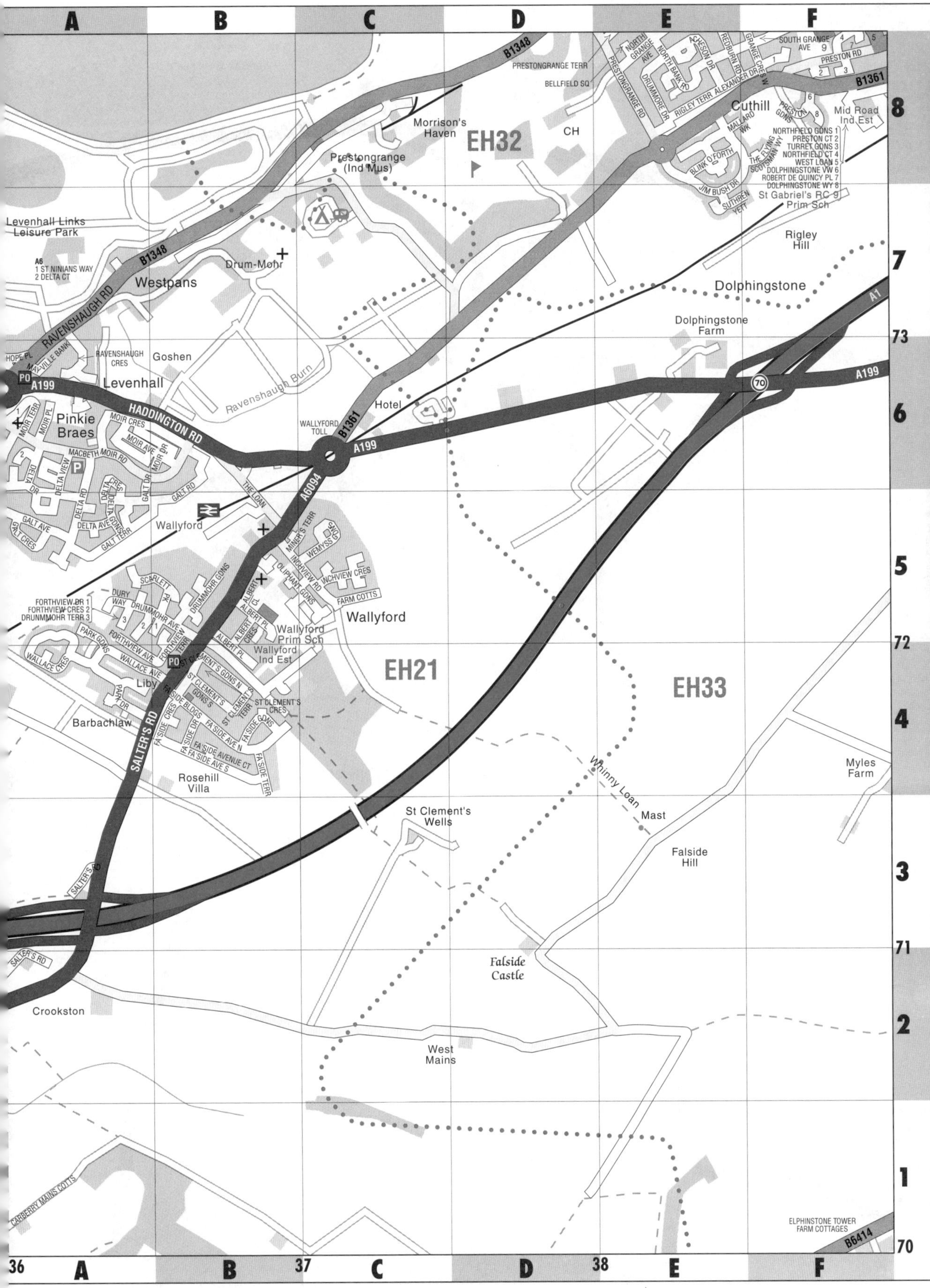
A
B
C
D
E
F
B1348
PRESTONGRANGE TERR
BELLFIELD SQ
PRESTONGRANGE RD
NORTH GRANGE AVE
NORTH BANK RD
DRUMMORE DR
ACHESON DR
REDBURN RD
GRANGE CRES W
SOUTH GRANGE AVE
PRESTON RD
B1361
RIGLEY TERR
ALEXANDER DR
Cuthill
Mid Road Ind Est
MALLARD WK
PRESTON GDNS
BLINK O'FORTH
THE FLYING SCOTSMAN WY
JIM BUSH DR
SUTHREN YETT
NORTHFIELD GDNS 1
PRESTON CT 2
TURRET GDNS 3
NORTHFIELD CT 4
WEST LOAN 5
DOLPHINGSTONE VW 6
ROBERT DE QUINCY PL 7
DOLPHINGSTONE WY 8
St Gabriel's RC Prim Sch
Morrison's Haven
EH32
CH
Prestongrange (Ind Mus)
Levenhall Links Leisure Park
A6
1 ST NINIANS WAY
2 DELTA CT
Drum-Mohr
Westpans
Rigley Hill
Dolphingstone
Dolphingstone Farm
RAVENSHAUGH RD
HOPE PL
MAVISVILLE BANK
RAVENSHAUGH CRES
Goshen
Levenhall
PO
A199
HADDINGTON RD
Ravenshaugh Burn
Hotel
A1
A199
Pinkie Braes
MOIR TERR
MOIR PL
MOIR CRES
MOIR AVE
MOIR DR
MACBETH MOIR RD
WALLYFORD TOLL
B1361
A199
DELTA DR
DELTA VIEW
DELTA RD
DELTA CRES
DELTA GDNS
DELTA AVE
GALT DR
GALT RD
GALT AVE
GALT CRES
GALT TERR
THE LOAN
A6094
Wallyford
MINER'S TERR
WEMYSS GDNS
INCHVIEW RD
INCHVIEW CRES
OLIPHANT GDNS
FARM COTTS
Wallyford
SCARLETT PK
DRUMMOHR GDNS
DRUMMOHR AVE
DURY WAY
FORTHVIEW DR 1
FORTHVIEW CRES 2
DRUMMOHR TERR 3
ALBERT CL
ALBERT PL
ALBERT CRES
Wallyford Prim Sch
Wallyford Ind Est
PARK GDNS
FORTHVIEW AVE
FORTHVIEW TERR
WALLACE CRES
WALLACE AVE
PO
ST CLEMENT'S GDNS N
ST CLEMENT'S GDNS S
ST CLEMENT'S TERR
ST CLEMENT'S CRES
Liby
PARK DR
Barbachlaw
EH21
EH33
SALTER'S RD
FA'SIDE CRES
FA'SIDE BLDGS
FA'SIDE DR
FA'SIDE AVE N
FA'SIDE GDNS
FA'SIDE AVENUE CT
FA'SIDE AVE S
FA'SIDE TERR
Rosehill Villa
Whinny Loan
Mast
Myles Farm
St Clement's Wells
Falside Hill
SALTER'S RD
SALTER'S RD
Falside Castle
Crookston
West Mains
CARBERRY MAINS COTTS
ELPHINSTONE TOWER FARM COTTAGES
B6414
8
7
73
6
5
72
4
3
71
2
1
70
36
37
38

154
126

125
C5
1 KERR WAY
2 MCNEILL WLK
3 MCNEILL WAY
4 GEORGE WLK
5 WILSON WLK
6 DEQUINCEY WLK
7 CAPONHALL CT
8 ELPHINSTONE WLK
9 SETON CT
10 PINKIE WLK
11 SOMERS PK
12 LAMMERVIEW

97
D5
1 KINGSLAW CT
2 FA'SIDE CRES
3 FA'SIDE AVE
4 CARLAVERROCK WLK
D6
1 CIVIC SQ
2 PLOUGH LA
3 CROWN CT
4 CADELL SQ
D7
1 SANDERSON'S WYND
2 SANDERSON'S GR
3 INCHKEITH GR
4 RIGGONHEAD CT
5 RIGGONHEAD GDNS
6 FORTHVIEW CT

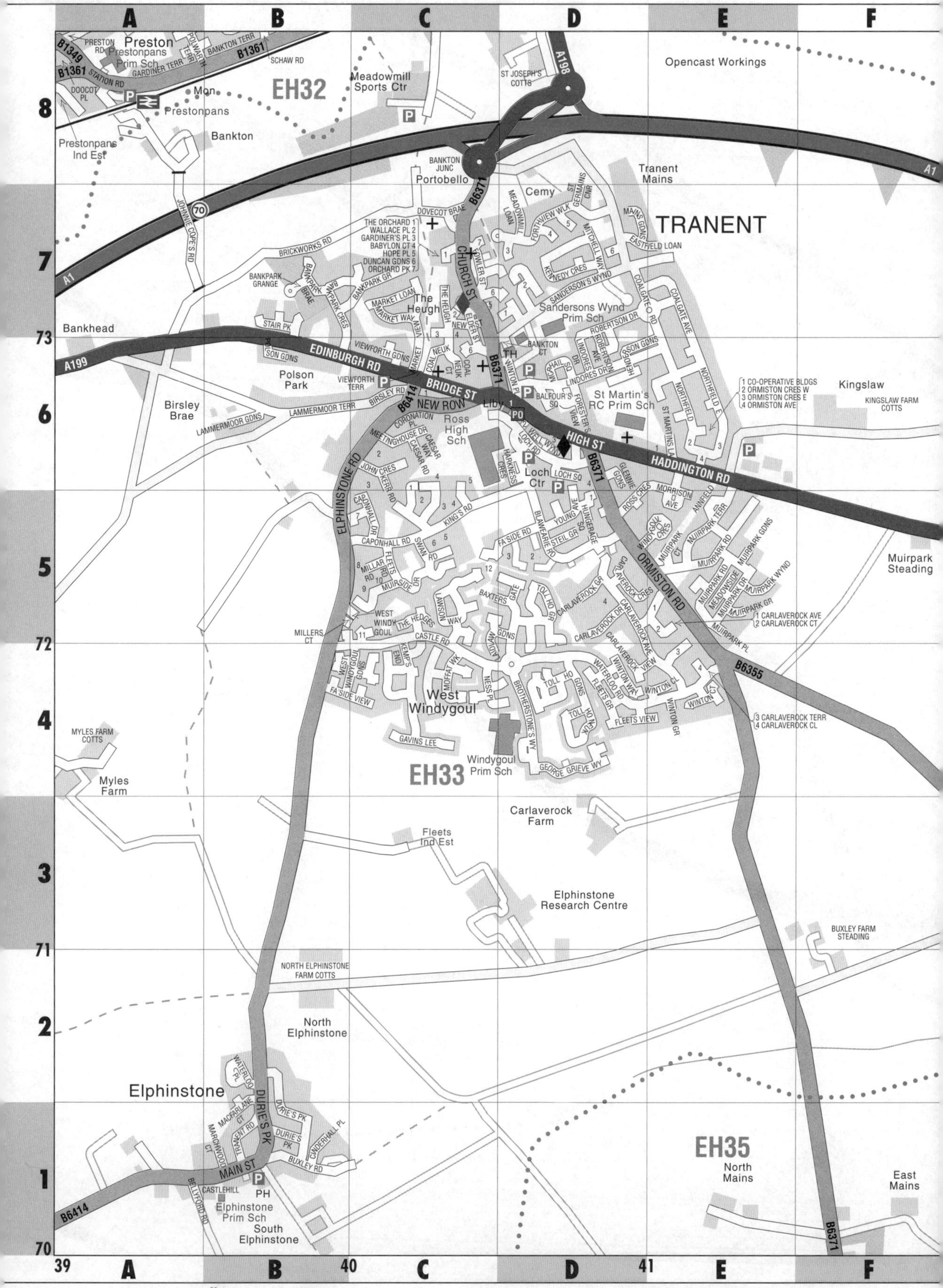
A
B
C
D
E
F
8
7
73
6
5
72
4
3
71
2
1
70
39
40
41
Preston
Prestonpans Prim Sch
Prestonpans
Prestonpans Ind Est
Bankton
Mon
EH32
Meadowmill Sports Ctr
Opencast Workings
ST JOSEPH'S COTTS
BANKTON JUNC
Portobello
Cemy
Tranent Mains
TRANENT
The Heugh
Sanderson Wynd Prim Sch
Bankhead
Polson Park
Birsley Brae
EDINBURGH RD
BRIDGE ST
NEW ROW
HIGH ST
HADDINGTON RD
Liby
PO
TH
Ross High Sch
Loch Ctr
St Martin's RC Prim Sch
Kingslaw
KINGSLAW FARM COTTS
1 CO-OPERATIVE BLDGS
2 ORMISTON CRES W
3 ORMISTON CRES E
4 ORMISTON AVE
ELPHINSTONE RD
ORMISTON RD
Muirpark Steading
1 CARLAVEROCK AVE
2 CARLAVEROCK CT
3 CARLAVEROCK TERR
4 CARLAVEROCK CL
MILLERS CT
West Windygoul
Windygoul Prim Sch
EH33
MYLES FARM COTTS
Myles Farm
Carlaverock Farm
Fleets Ind Est
Elphinstone Research Centre
BUXLEY FARM STEADING
NORTH ELPHINSTONE FARM COTTS
North Elphinstone
Elphinstone
DURIE'S PK
MAIN ST
BUXLEY RD
CASTLEHILL
PH
Elphinstone Prim Sch
South Elphinstone
EH35
North Mains
East Mains
A1
A199
A198
B1361
B1349
B6371
B6414
B6355

C6
1 INNES BLDGS
2 ELPHINSTONE CT
3 CAPONHALL WAY
4 MCNEILL PATH
5 GEORGE WLK
6 ELDER CT
125
155

98
128
A
B
C
D
E
F
8
7
6
5
4
3
2
1
73
72
71
70
42
43
44
EH32
Opencast Workings
Greendykes
GREENDYKES COTTS
Canty Burn
Hoprig Mains
B6363
A1
70
A199
West Adniston
WEST ADNISTON COTTS
Macmerry Bsns Pk
Macmerry Ind Est
GREENDYKES RD
McINTYRE LA
CHESTERHALL AVE
ST GERMAINS TERR
MOUNTFAIR GDNS
MOUNTFAIR PL
WINTON LOAN
Macmerry Prim Sch
STATION ROW
MAIN RD
WESTBANK GDNS
WESTBANK TERR
WESTBANK CT
WESTBANK
MERRYFIELD AVE
Macmerry
Penston
Penston Farm
PENSTON FARM COTTS
ROBINS NEUK
WESTBANK RD
PO
WHITELOCH CT
WHITELOCH RD
BRIERBUSH RD
Whiteloch Farm
ANNFIELD CT
BRIERBUSH CRES
EH33
By-ways of East Lothian
West Bank
The Mount
B6355
New Winton Wood
Whiteloch Bridge
New Winton
WINTON CT
WINTON TR
Whiteloch Covert
Puddle Burn
Walk Plantation
Winton Hill
EH34
Winton Smithy Cottage
WINTONHILL COTTS
Boggs Holdings
Winton Lea
EH35
Dean Burn
New Town
Wintonhill
B6355
156
128

127
99

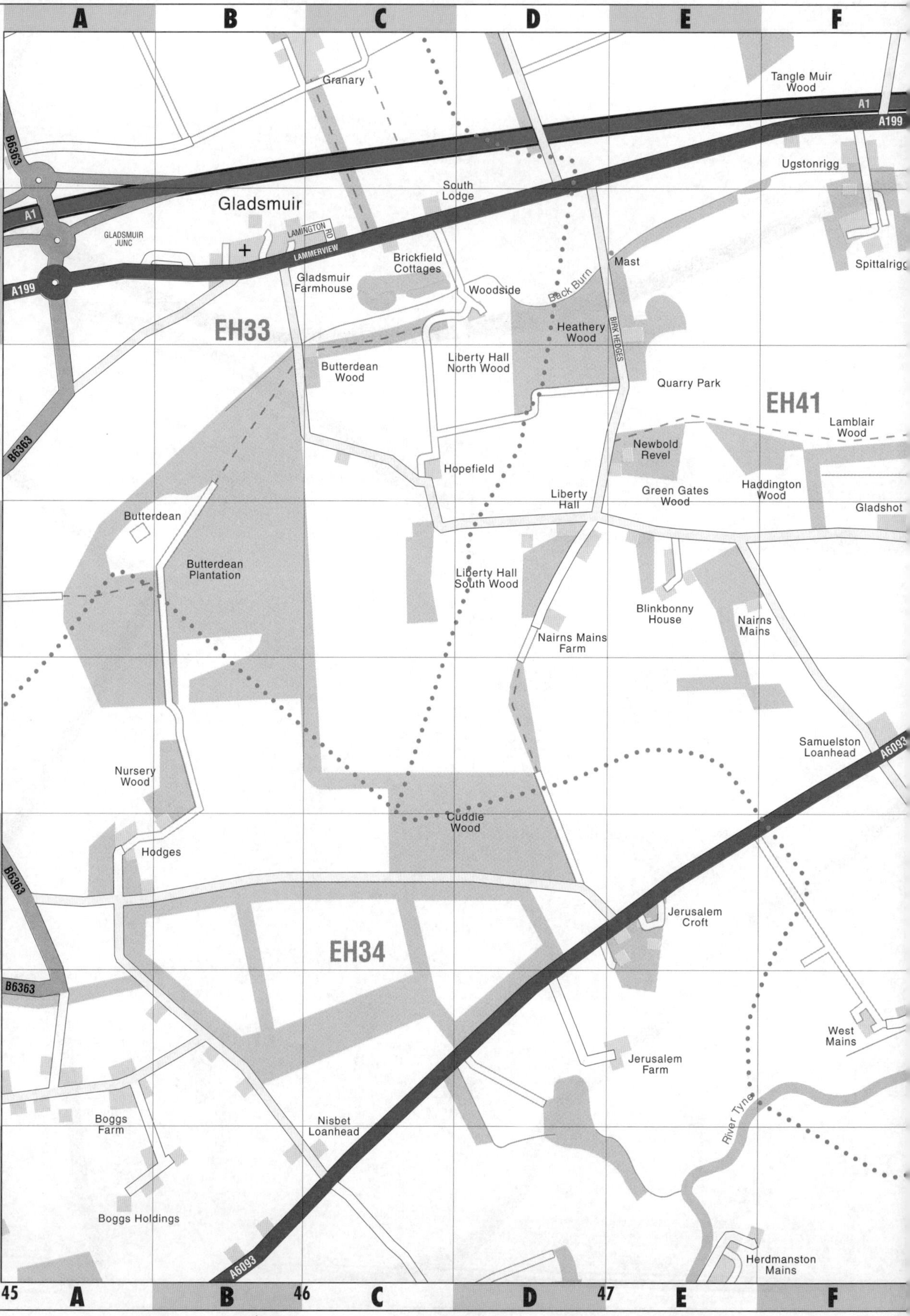
A
B
C
D
E
F
8
7
73
6
5
72
4
3
71
2
1
70
45
46
47
Granary
Tangle Muir Wood
A1
A199
B6363
Ugstonrigg
South Lodge
Gladsmuir
GLADSMUIR JUNC
LAMINGTON RD
LAMMERVIEW
Brickfield Cottages
Mast
Spittalrigg
Gladsmuir Farmhouse
Woodside
Back Burn
EH33
Heathery Wood
BIRK HEDGES
Butterdean Wood
Liberty Hall North Wood
Quarry Park
EH41
Lamblair Wood
Newbold Revel
Hopefield
Liberty Hall
Green Gates Wood
Haddington Wood
Gladshot
Butterdean
Butterdean Plantation
Liberty Hall South Wood
Blinkbonny House
Nairns Mains
Nairns Mains Farm
Samuelston Loanhead
A6093
Nursery Wood
Cuddie Wood
Hodges
Jerusalem Croft
EH34
West Mains
Jerusalem Farm
River Tyne
Boggs Farm
Nisbet Loanhead
Boggs Holdings
Herdmanston Mains

127
157

100
130

A
B
C
D
E
F
8
7
73
6
5
72
4
3
71
2
1
70
48
49
50
OAKTREE JUNC
70
A1
A199
B6471
GATESIDE AVE
GATESIDE RD
KNOWESLEY PK
ST LAURENCE
ALDERSTON RD
KNOWES RD
SOMNERFIELD GR
SOMNERFIELD AVE
SOMNERFIELD CRES
The Compass Sch
Ind Est
HOSPITAL RD
STATION RD
WEST RD
SOMNERFIELD CT 1
STATION CT 2
EDWARDS CT 3
BEECHWOOD RD 4
PEACHDALES 5
KENNEDY CT 6
LETHAM DR
ROSEHALL AVE
ROSEHALL CT
ROSEHALL A6093
ROSEHALL WLK
Gateside Commerce Pk
Knowesley
SOMNERFIELD PK
PARK LA
CLERKINGTON WLK
CLERKINGTON RD
BURNSIDE
FAIRWAY
ACREDALES WLK
ACREDALES
DOBSON'S VIEW
DOBSON'S PL
DOBSON'S WLK
WELLSIDE
CHALYBEATE
LONG CRAM
Knox Acad
Warehouses
Back Burn
Blackburn Wood
HADDINGTON
St Laurence House Burn
Letham House
Letham Burn
Dovecot
LETHAM MAINS SMALLHOLDINGS
Black House
Clerkington Mill
Letham Mains
Clerkington
Blackhouse Bridge
Heathery Hall Wood
Gladshot Cottage
Clerkington Kennels
Clerkington Mains
Black Wood
Heathery Hall
Sunny Netherside
B6368
Grants' Braes
Clerkington West Lodge
EH41
Barberfield
Grants' Braes Bridge
West Lodge
River Tyne
Westfield
WESTFIELD COTTS
Parkend
Mid Mains
East Mains
Samuelston Bridge
SAMUELSTON EAST MAINS COTTS
Samuelston
Begbie
Begbie Wood
EH34
Bolton
BOLTON STEADING
Colstoun Water

220
130

B8
1 MITCHELL'S CL
2 NEWTON PORT
3 JOHN BROWN CT
4 MARK LA
5 KILPAIR ST
6 BROWN ST
7 GOWL CL
8 TANNERY LA
9 WATERSIDE
10 ST ANNES PL
11 BREWERY CT
12 ROSS'S CL

129
101

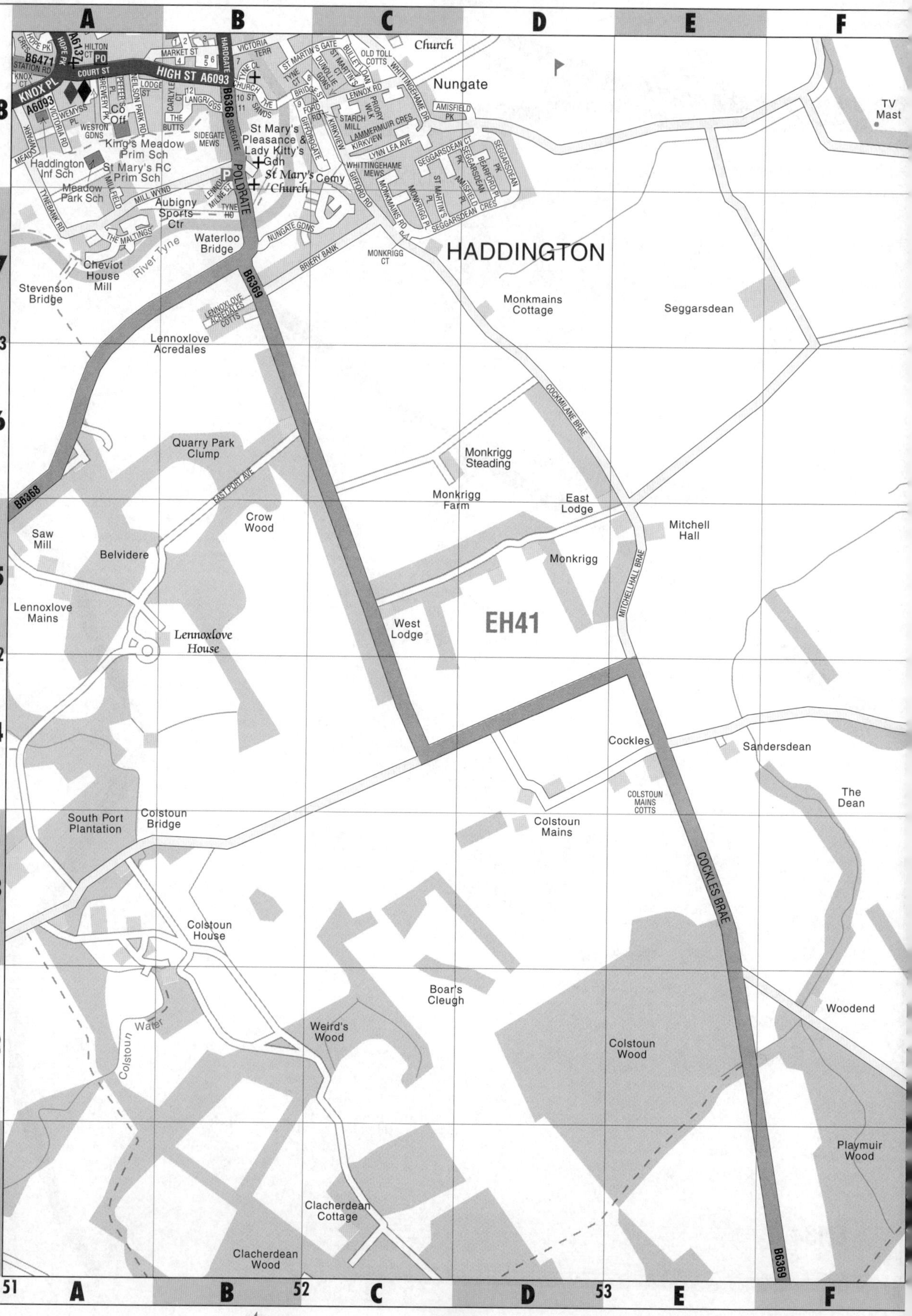

129
220

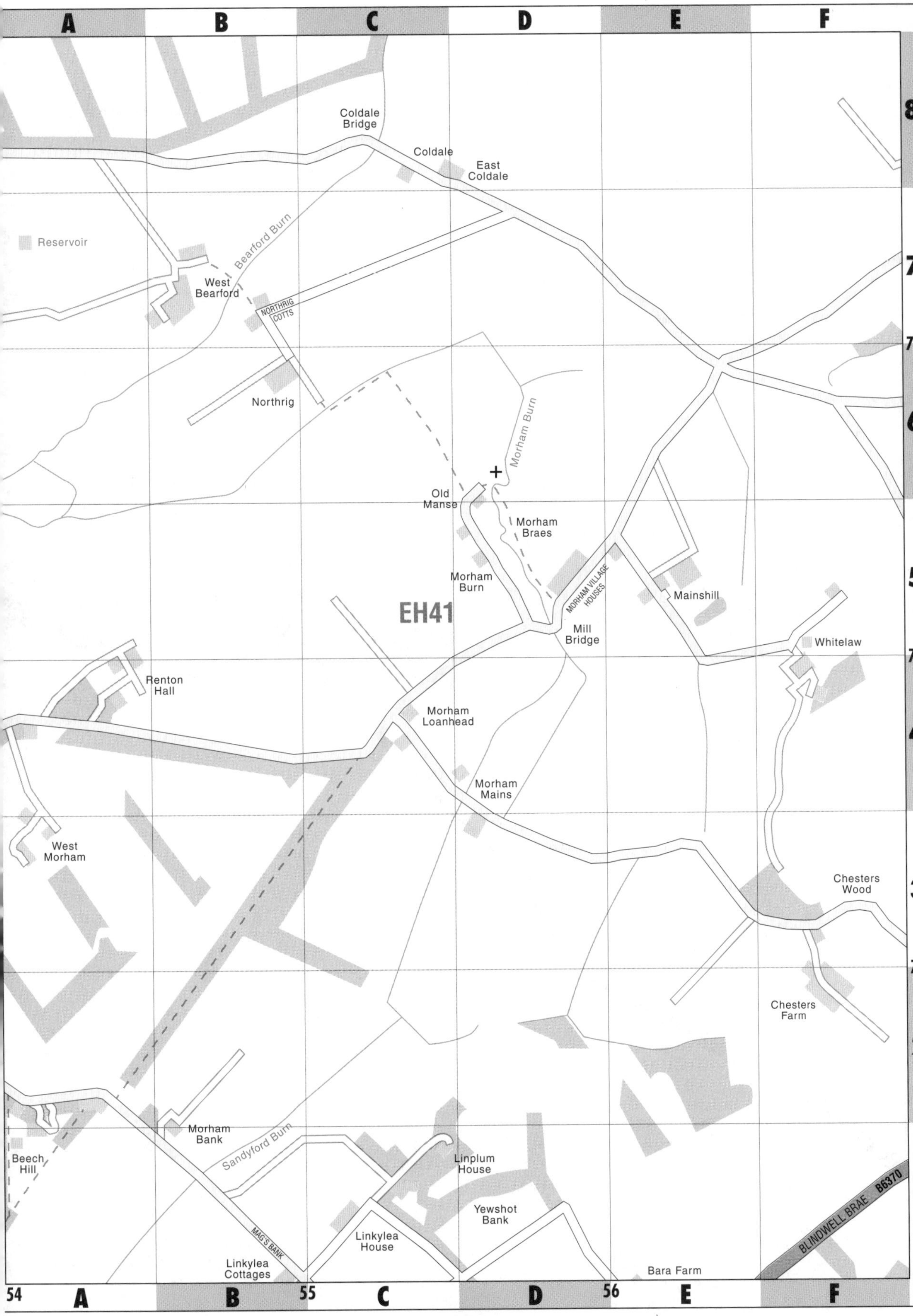
A B C D E F
8 7 73 6 5 72 4 3 71 2 1 70
54 55 56
Coldale Bridge
Coldale
East Coldale
Reservoir
Bearford Burn
West Bearford
NORTHRIG COTTS
Northrig
Morham Burn
Old Manse
Morham Braes
Morham Burn
EH41
MORHAM VILLAGE HOUSES
Mainshill
Mill Bridge
Whitelaw
Renton Hall
Morham Loanhead
Morham Mains
West Morham
Chesters Wood
Chesters Farm
Morham Bank
Sandyford Burn
Beech Hill
Linplum House
Yewshot Bank
Linkylea House
MAG'S BANK
Linkylea Cottages
Bara Farm
BLINDWELL BRAE
B6370

131
103

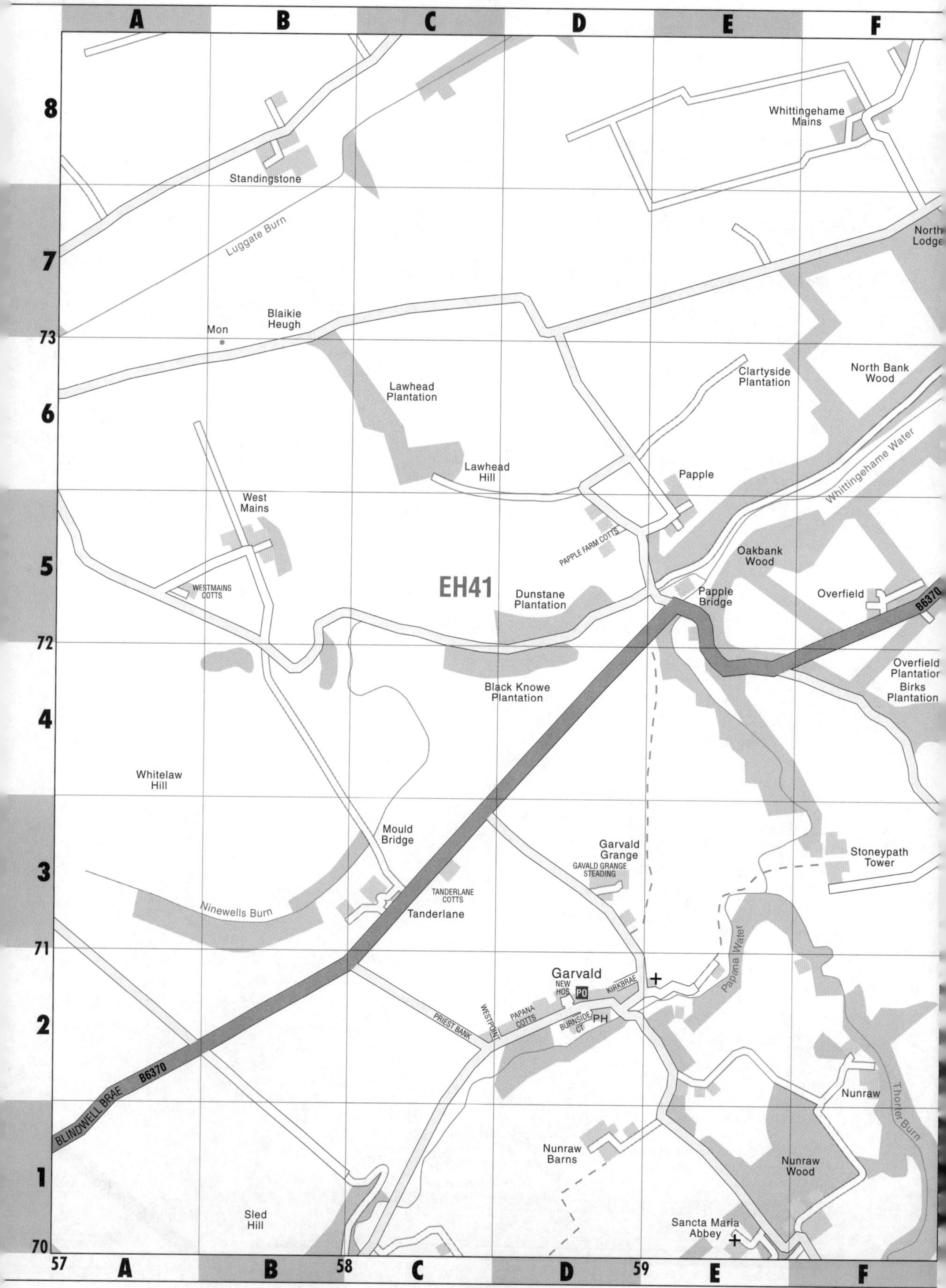
A
B
C
D
E
F
8
Standingstone
Whittingehame
Mains
Luggate Burn
7
North
Lodge
Mon
Blaikie
Heugh
73
Lawhead
Plantation
Clartyside
Plantation
North Bank
Wood
6
Lawhead
Hill
Papple
Whittingehame Water
West
Mains
PAPPLE FARM COTTS
Oakbank
Wood
5
WESTMAINS
COTTS
EH41
Dunstane
Plantation
Papple
Bridge
Overfield
B6370
72
Overfield
Plantation
Black Knowe
Plantation
Birks
Plantation
4
Whitelaw
Hill
Mould
Bridge
Garvald
Grange
GAVALD GRANGE
STEADING
Stoneypath
Tower
3
TANDERLANE
COTTS
Ninewells Burn
Tanderlane
71
Garvald
NEW
HOS
PO
KIRKBRAE
Papana Water
PRIEST BANK
WESTPOINT
PAPANA
COTTS
BURNSIDE
CT
PH
2
B6370
BLINDWELL BRAE
Nunraw
Thorter Burn
1
Nunraw
Barns
Nunraw
Wood
Sled
Hill
Sancta Maria
Abbey
70
57
58
59

131
221

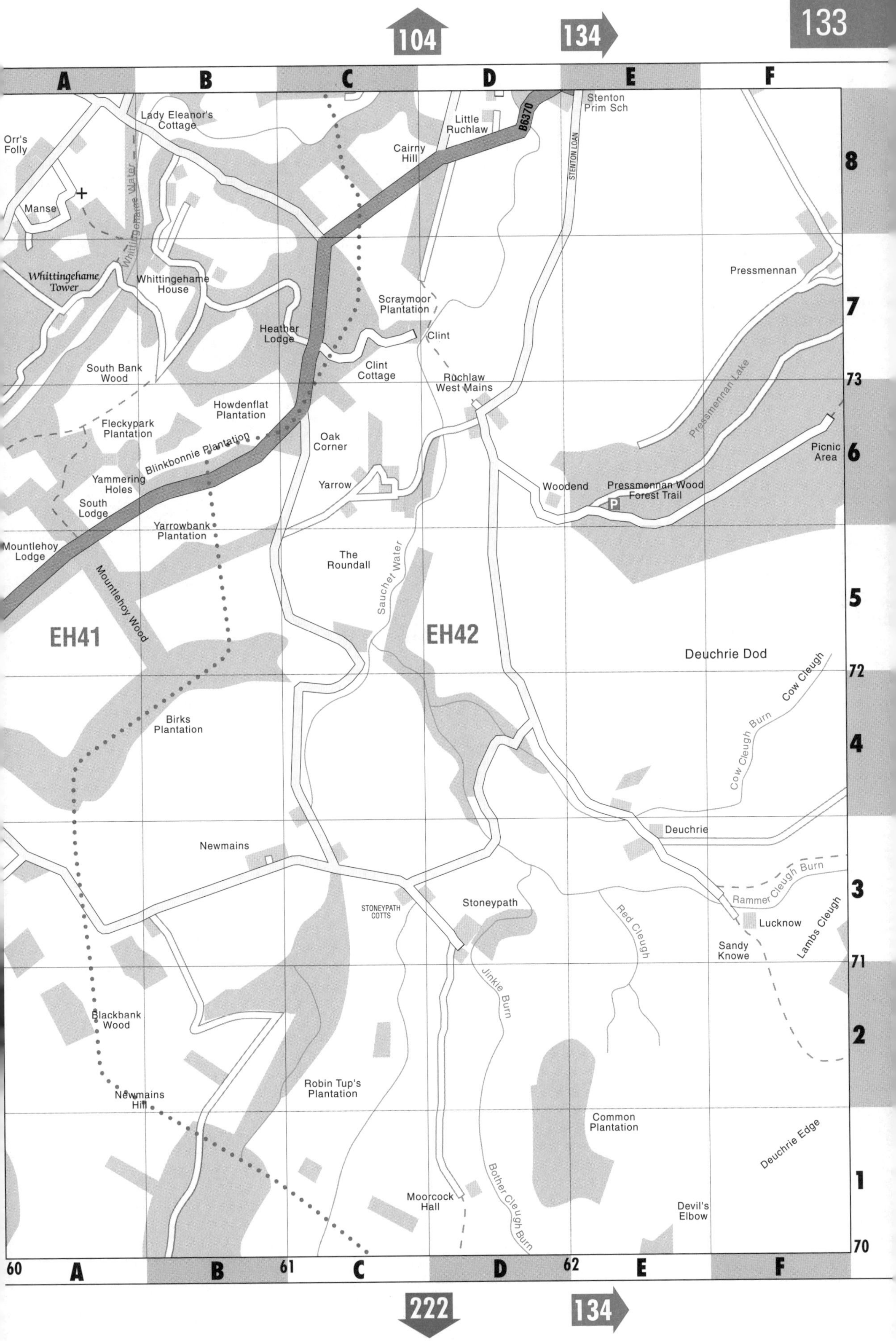
104
134
A
B
C
D
E
F
Orr's Folly
Lady Eleanor's Cottage
Little Ruchlaw
Cairny Hill
B6370
Stenton Prim Sch
STENTON LOAN
Manse
Whittingehame Water
Whittingehame Tower
Whittingehame House
Pressmennan
Scraymoor Plantation
Heather Lodge
Clint
South Bank Wood
Clint Cottage
Ruchlaw West Mains
Pressmennan Lake
Howdenflat Plantation
Fleckypark Plantation
Oak Corner
Picnic Area
Blinkbonnie Plantation
Yammering Holes
Yarrow
Woodend
Pressmennan Wood Forest Trail
South Lodge
Yarrowbank Plantation
Mountlehoy Lodge
The Roundall
Saucher Water
Mountlehoy Wood
EH41
EH42
Deuchrie Dod
Cow Cleugh
Cow Cleugh Burn
Birks Plantation
Newmains
Deuchrie
Rammer Cleugh Burn
STONEYPATH COTTS
Stoneypath
Red Cleugh
Lucknow
Lambs Cleugh
Sandy Knowe
Jinkie Burn
Blackbank Wood
Robin Tup's Plantation
Newmains Hill
Common Plantation
Deuchrie Edge
Bother Cleugh Burn
Moorcock Hall
Devil's Elbow
8
7
73
6
5
72
4
3
71
2
1
70
60
61
62
222
134

133
105

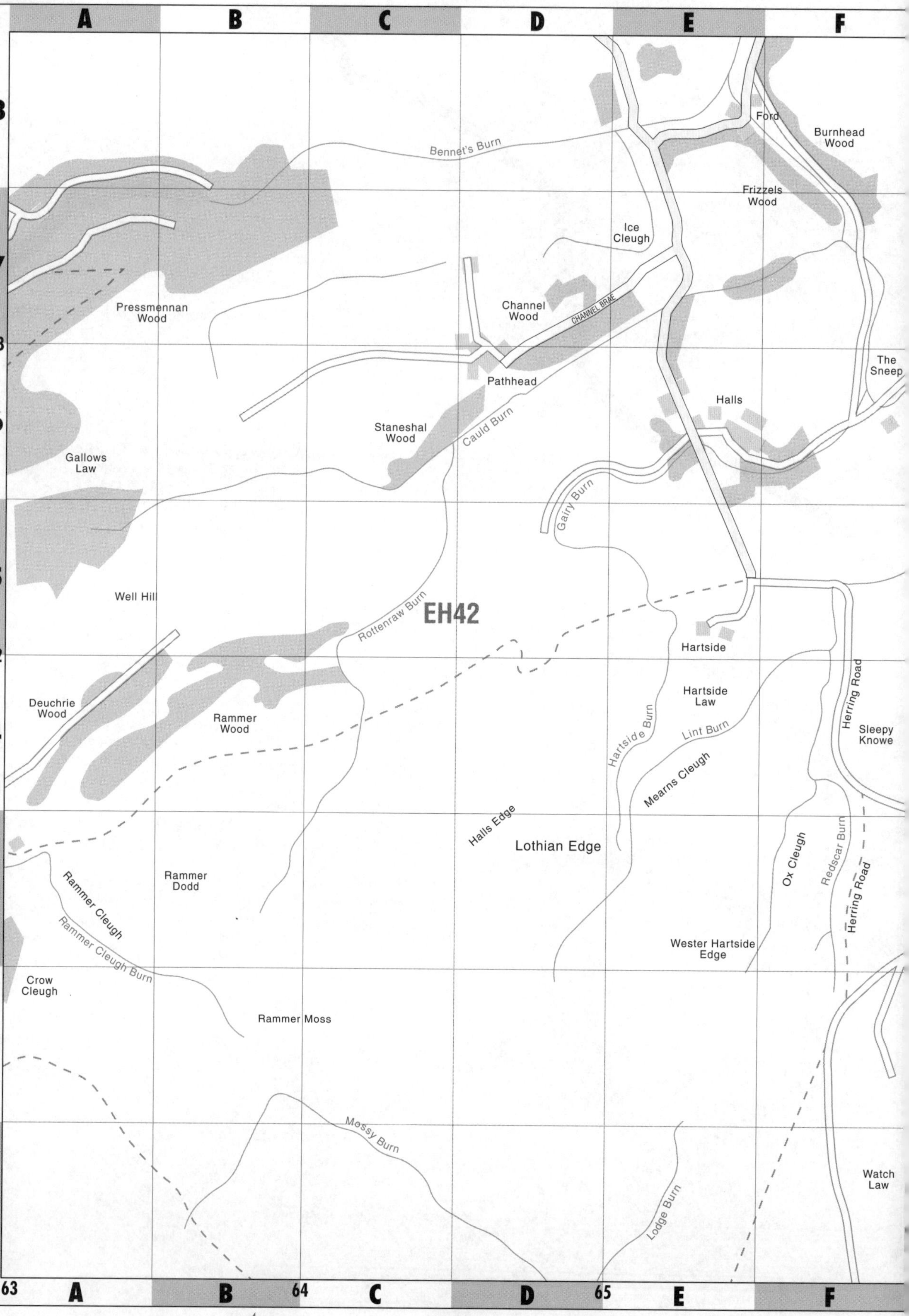
A
B
C
D
E
F
8
7
73
6
5
72
4
3
71
2
1
70
63
64
65
Ford
Burnhead Wood
Bennet's Burn
Frizzels Wood
Ice Cleugh
Pressmennan Wood
Channel Wood
CHANNEL BRAE
The Sneep
Pathhead
Halls
Staneshal Wood
Cauld Burn
Gallows Law
Gairy Burn
Well Hill
EH42
Rottenraw Burn
Hartside
Deuchrie Wood
Hartside Law
Herring Road
Rammer Wood
Hartside Burn
Lint Burn
Sleepy Knowe
Mearns Cleugh
Halls Edge
Lothian Edge
Rammer Cleugh
Rammer Dodd
Ox Cleugh
Redscar Burn
Herring Road
Rammer Cleugh Burn
Wester Hartside Edge
Crow Cleugh
Rammer Moss
Mossy Burn
Watch Law
Lodge Burn

133
222

106
136
A
B
C
D
E
F
The Chesters
Under Brunt
Hillend Plantation
The Brunt
Oak Wood
Highside Plantation
Highside Hill
Black Loch
8
7
73
6
Spruce Cleugh
How Burn
Woodhall Burn
Woodhall
Bradeley Hill
The Dod
WOODHALL COTTS
Meikle Hag Wood
Weatherly Burn
Dean Burn
Tinker's Leap
Priest's Pulpit
Oak Wood
5
Birkie Brae
Cross Burn
EH42
72
Weatherly
Croft Angry
4
Black Law
Dryden How
Boonslie Shank
Cockston Steel
High Wood
Steel Cleugh
Boonslie Burn
3
Easter Hartside Edge
Highwood Burn
71
2
Boonslie
1
Thorter Cleugh
Bransly Hill
70
66
67
68
223
136

135 107 218

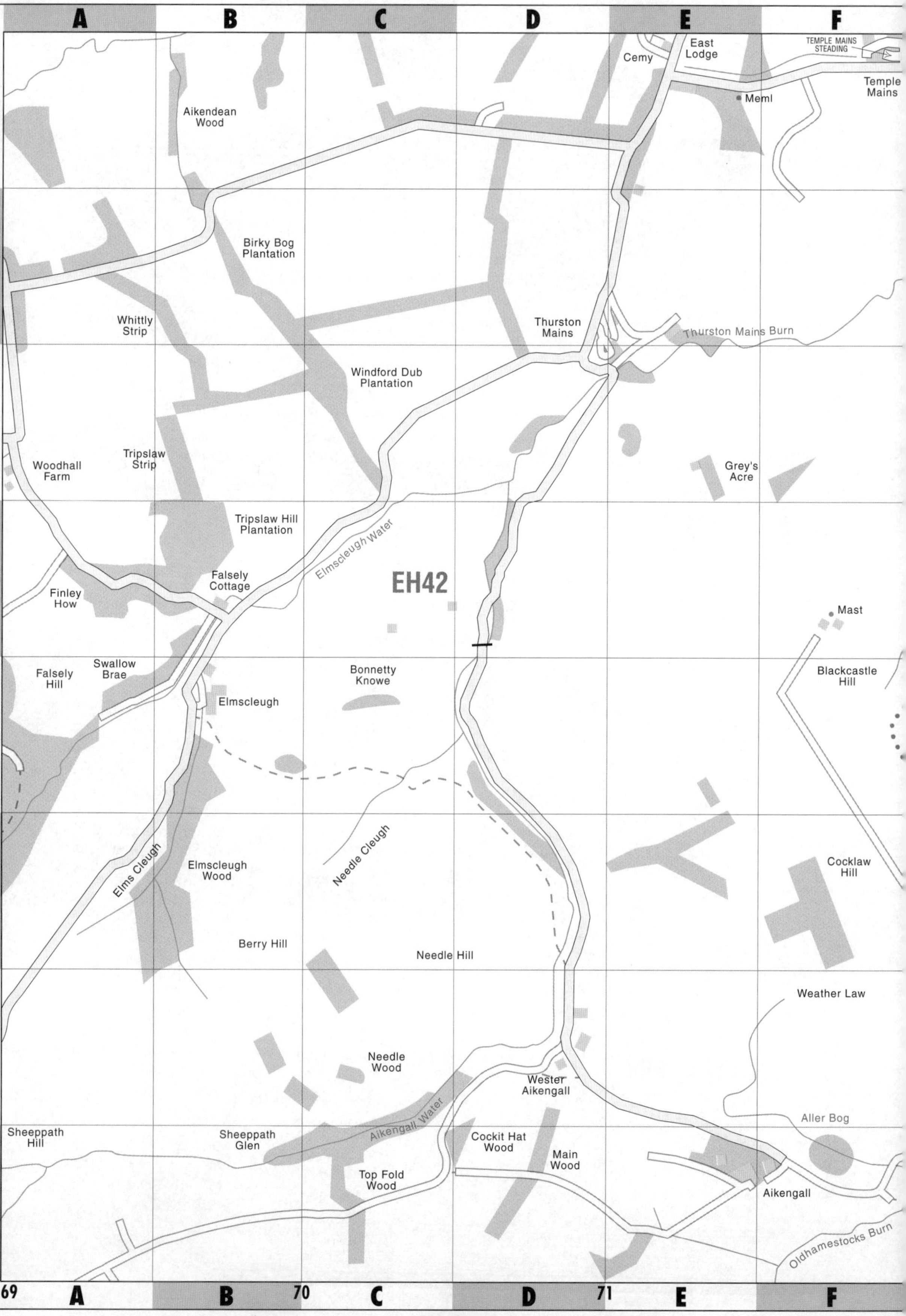
A
B
C
D
E
F
8
7
73
6
5
72
4
3
71
2
1
70
69
70
71
East Lodge
Cemy
TEMPLE MAINS STEADING
Temple Mains
Meml
Aikendean Wood
Birky Bog Plantation
Whittly Strip
Thurston Mains
Thurston Mains Burn
Windford Dub Plantation
Woodhall Farm
Tripslaw Strip
Grey's Acre
Tripslaw Hill Plantation
Elmscleugh Water
EH42
Falsely Cottage
Finley How
Mast
Falsely Hill
Swallow Brae
Bonnetty Knowe
Blackcastle Hill
Elmscleugh
Elms Cleugh
Elmscleugh Wood
Needle Cleugh
Cocklaw Hill
Berry Hill
Needle Hill
Weather Law
Needle Wood
Wester Aikengall
Aller Bog
Sheeppath Hill
Sheeppath Glen
Aikengall Water
Cockit Hat Wood
Main Wood
Top Fold Wood
Aikengall
Oldhamestocks Burn

135 223 218

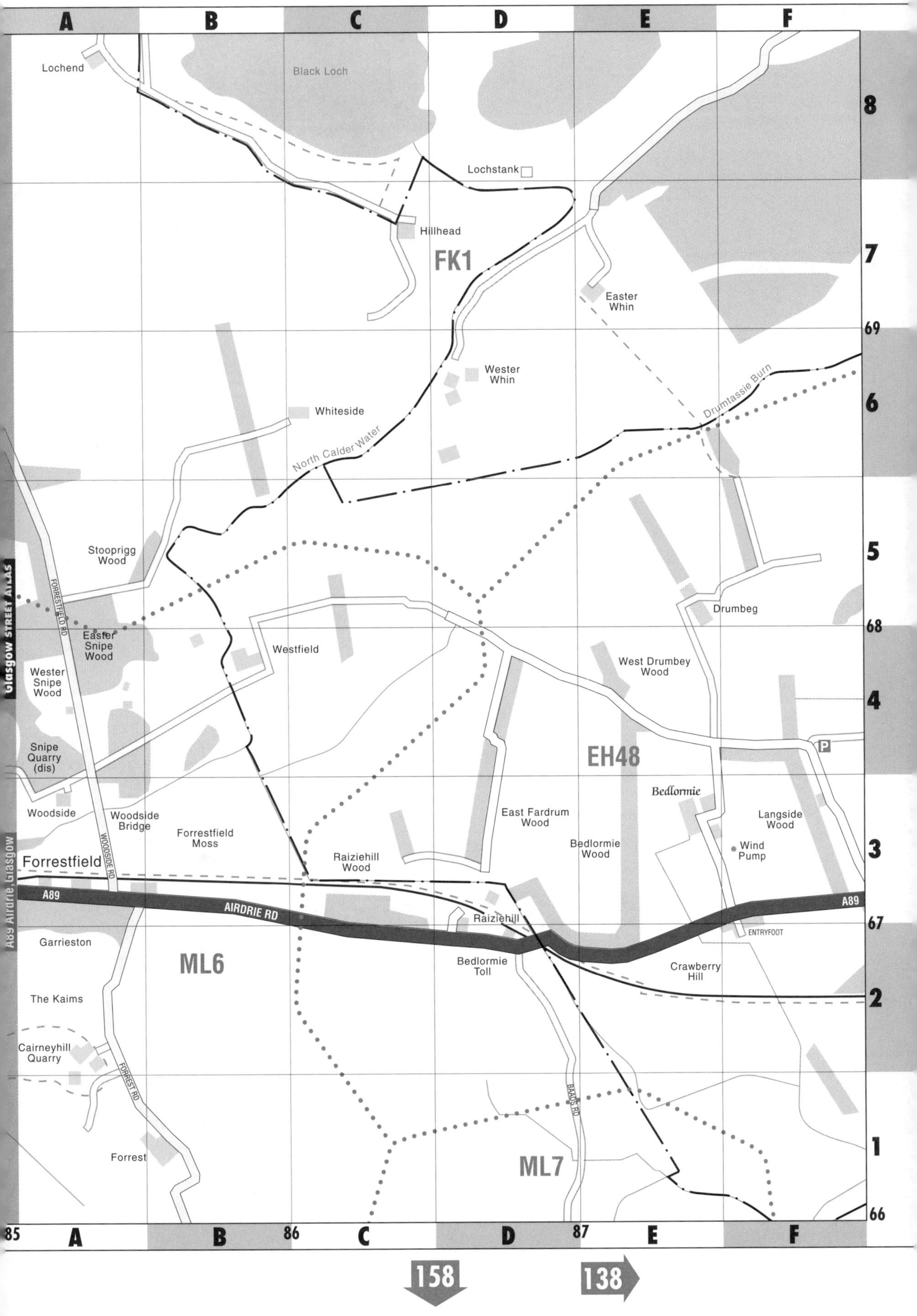
108
138
A
B
C
D
E
F
8
7
69
6
5
68
4
3
67
2
1
66
85
86
87
Lochend
Black Loch
Lochstank
Hillhead
FK1
Easter
Whin
Wester
Whin
Whiteside
North Calder Water
Drumtassie Burn
Stooprigg
Wood
FORRESTFIELD RD
Easter
Snipe
Wood
Wester
Snipe
Wood
Westfield
Drumbeg
West Drumbey
Wood
Snipe
Quarry
(dis)
EH48
Bedlormie
Woodside
Woodside
Bridge
Forrestfield
Moss
East Fardrum
Wood
Langside
Wood
Bedlormie
Wood
Wind
Pump
Forrestfield
WOODSIDE RD
Raiziehill
Wood
A89
AIRDRIE RD
Raiziehill
A89
ENTRYFOOT
Garrieston
ML6
Bedlormie
Toll
Crawberry
Hill
The Kaims
Cairneyhill
Quarry
FORREST RD
BAADS RD
Forrest
ML7
158
138
Glasgow STREET ATLAS
A89 Airdrie, Glasgow

137
109

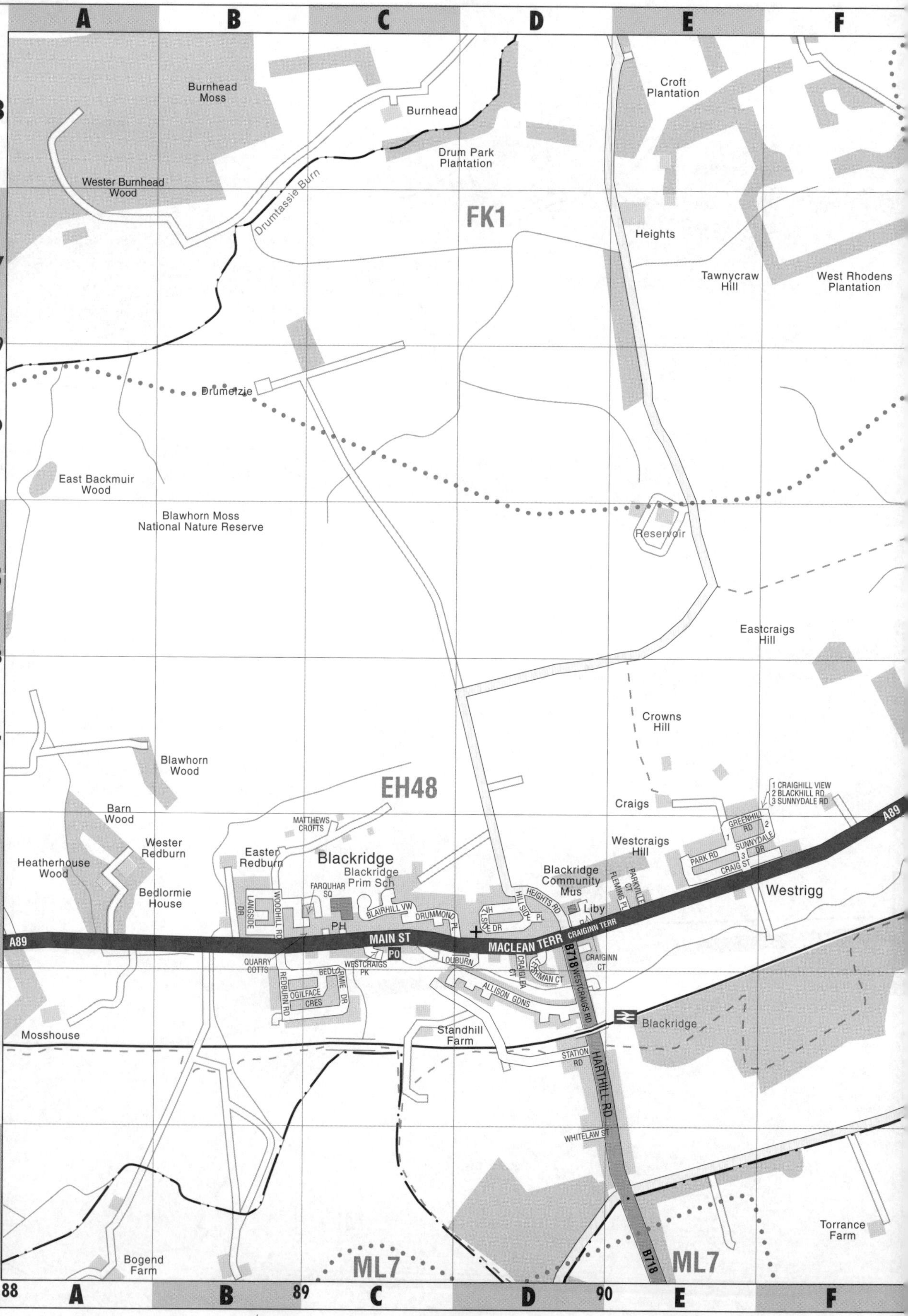
A
B
C
D
E
F
8
7
69
6
5
68
4
3
67
2
1
66
88
89
90
Burnhead Moss
Burnhead
Croft Plantation
Drum Park Plantation
Wester Burnhead Wood
Drumtassie Burn
FK1
Heights
Tawnycraw Hill
West Rhodens Plantation
Drumelzie
East Backmuir Wood
Blawhorn Moss National Nature Reserve
Reservoir
Eastcraigs Hill
Crowns Hill
Blawhorn Wood
EH48
Craigs
1 CRAIGHILL VIEW
2 BLACKHILL RD
3 SUNNYDALE RD
A89
Barn Wood
Wester Redburn
Heatherhouse Wood
Easter Redburn
Blackridge
Blackridge Prim Sch
MATTHEWS CROFTS
Westcraigs Hill
Blackridge Community Mus
Bedlormie House
FARQUHAR SQ
LANGSIDE DR
WOODHILL RD
BLAIRHILL VW
DRUMMOND PL
HEIGHTS RD
HILLSIDE
PL
DR
FLEMING PL
PARKVILLE CT
GREENHILL RD
SUNNYDALE DR
PARK RD
CRAIG ST
Westrigg
Liby
PH
MAIN ST
MACLEAN TERR
CRAIGINN TERR
PO
QUARRY COTTS
WESTCRAIGS PK
LOUBURN
CRAIGLEA CT
B718
WESTCRAIGS RD
CRAIGINN CT
BEDLORMIE DR
REDBURN RD
OGILFACE CRES
ALLISON GDNS
Standhill Farm
Blackridge
Mosshouse
STATION RD
HARTHILL RD
WHITELAW ST
Torrance Farm
Bogend Farm
ML7
ML7

137
159

110
140

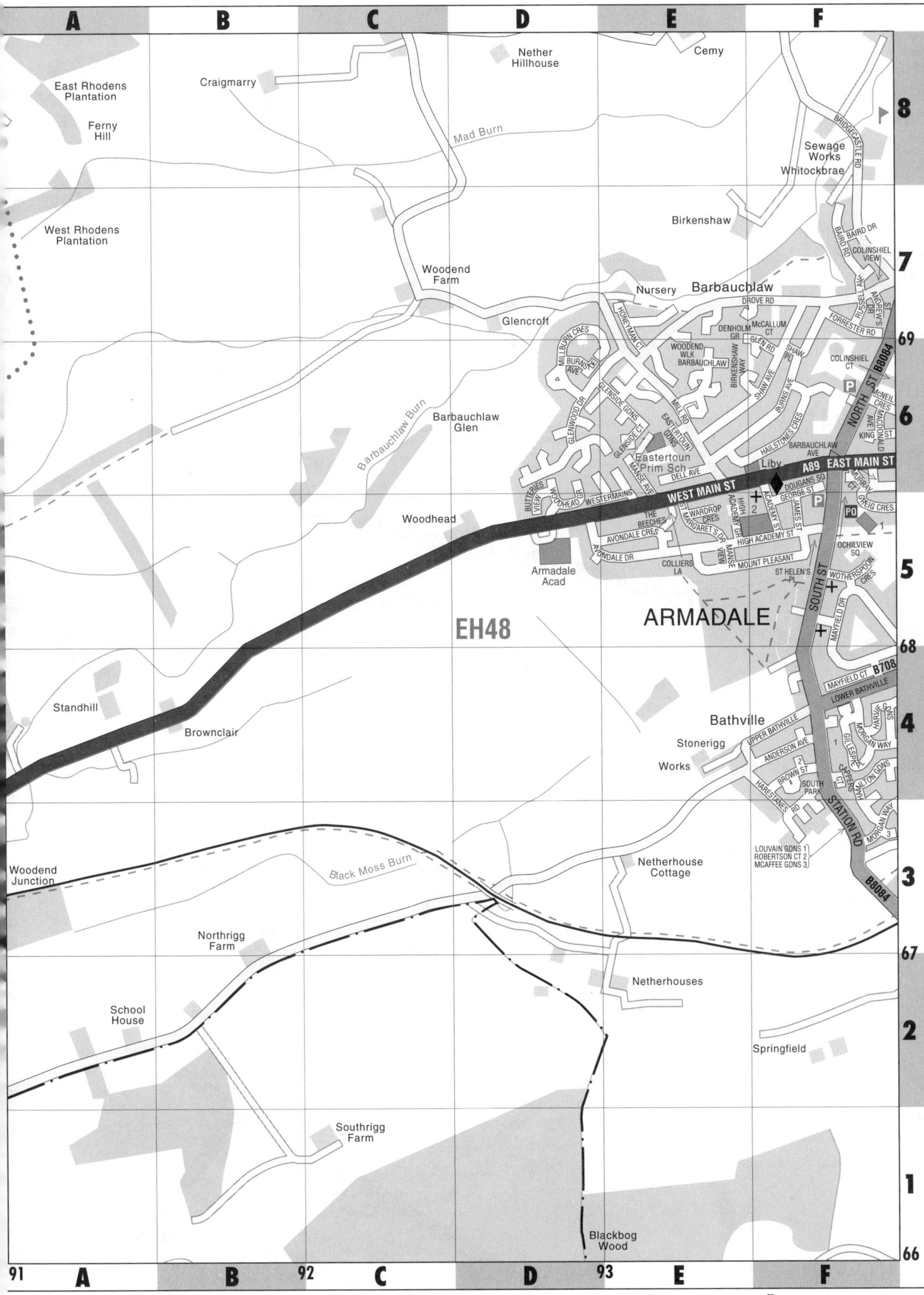

160
140

F5
1 St Anthony's RC Prim Sch
2 Armadale Prim Sch

139
111

A B C D E F
8
7
69
6
5
68
4
3
67
2
1
66
94 95 96
B8084
A801
A800
Belvedere Wood
Belvedere
BALLENCRIEFF MILL 1
BELVEDERE LA 2
BELVEDERE PL 3
BALLENCRIEFF RD 4
Bathgate Water
CHAPMAN'S BRAE
BALMUIR RD
JARDINE PL
Eastoun Farm
Works
CH
Colinshiel
NORTH ST
COLINSHIEL AVE 1
HAMILTON LA 2
EASTON RD
BURNSIDE RD
RACE RD
COLINSHIEL ST
HAMILTON RD
BUCHAN RD
MUIR RD
IRVINE CRES
MILLBURN RD
NEWLANDS CT
Middlerig
WOODHEAD PL
HOPE PARK GDNS
ASHBANK CT
MONKLAND RD
HAMILTON RD
HOPEPARK
A89
GLASGOW RD
BRIDGEND PL
BRIDGEND GDNS
BRIDGEND CT
MCNEIL CRES
KING ST
WATSON PL
BARLAW GDNS
BIRKDALE PK
Heatherfield
EAST MAIN ST
BATHGATE RD
ARMADALE
Armadale Stadium
Windyknowe Prim Sch
WINDYKNOWE CRES
DURHAM DR
HARDHILL DR
HARDHILL RD
B708
Windyknowe
WOOD TERR
GREIG CRES
FERRIER CRES
EWART AVE
MARCHES DR
THE MARCHES
CHURCH PL
ST PAUL'S DR
MALLACE AVE
Hardhill
SIBBALDS BRAE
HARDHILL TERR
BOGHEAD CRES
LANGFAULD GDNS
MEADOWPARK AVE
BRIDGEND PK
BARBAUCHLAW AVE
Mayfield
TEMPLE AVE
GRACIE'S WYND
HARDHILL PL
Garden Cottage
FALSIDE CRES
FALSIDE TERR
Cemy
DALLING AVE
MEADOWPARK RD
LOWER BATHVILLE
Kenbog
Hardhill Road Travelling Peoples Site
ROBERTSON AVE
MALCOLM CT
DALLING RD
YOUNG CRES
SYLVAN WAY
SIBBALD VW
DALYELL PL
CRICKETFIELD
WATT AVE
WOODLANDS COTTS
HEATHERVALE
WALK
WOODLANDS GR
MAYFIELD DR
CALDER CRES
GALLSWOOD GDNS
SOVEREIGN CT
ETNA CT
OLD GOLF COURSE RD
ATLAS CT
TARRAREOCH CT
Falside
B7002
EH48
Works
1 Armadale Ind Est
2 Bathville Bsns Ctr
HARVIE GDNS
WHITESIDE CT
WHITESIDE COTTS
FACTORY RD
Reyssie Law
Whiteside Ind Est
ROBERTSON GDNS
MORGAN WAY
FORREST PL
WHITESIDE FARM LA
Whiteside
BIRNIEHILL AVE
BIRNIEHILL CRES
BIRNIEHILL TERR
STANDHILL CT
Teepit Hill
Boghead Burn
Tarrareoch
WHITBURN RD
INCHCROSS
Armadale
Trees
West Mains
Inchcross Ind Est
STANDHILL RD
Standhill Farm
STATION RD
INCHCROSS DR
INCHCROSS PK
INCHCROSS STEADINGS
A7066
Hall Torbane Farm
Half Loaf Pond
Standhill Cottage
Inchmore
A706
STRAND DR
POTTISHAW RD
Mast
Tippethill
H

A6
1 CARRON CT
2 CAIRNPAPPLE HO
3 ENGINE PL
4 THE STEELYARD

A7
1 Waverley Street Ind Units
2 BELVEDERE RD
3 MANSEFIELD CT
4 HANOVER CL

B6
1 BLOOMFIELD PL
2 KEW GDNS
3 BALGROCHAN TERR
4 HELENSLEA COTTS
5 VIOLET BANK

B7
1 GLEN WAY
2 HATFIELD PL
3 GARDENERSWELL VILLAS
4 Balbardie Prim Sch

112
142

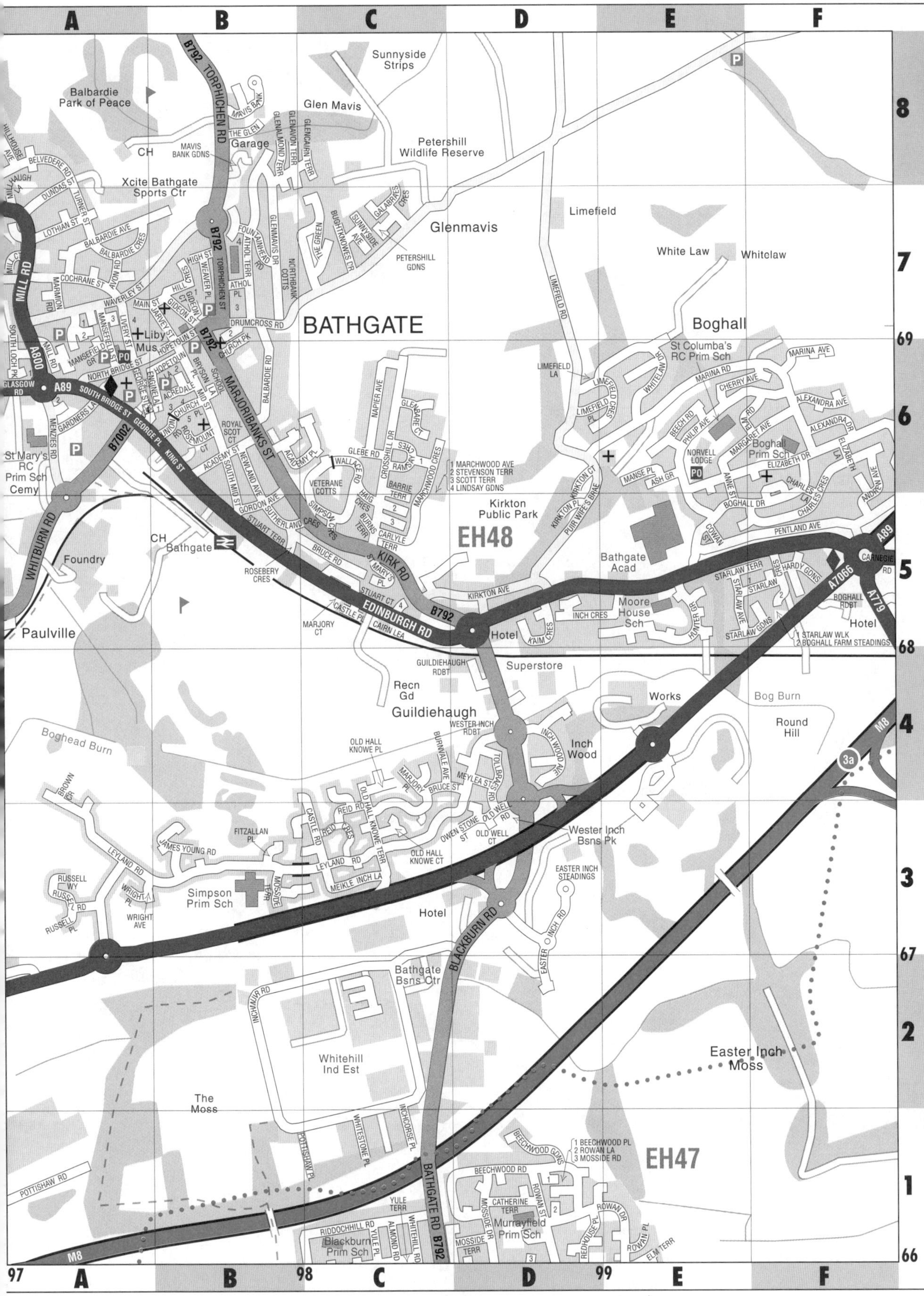

162
142

141
113

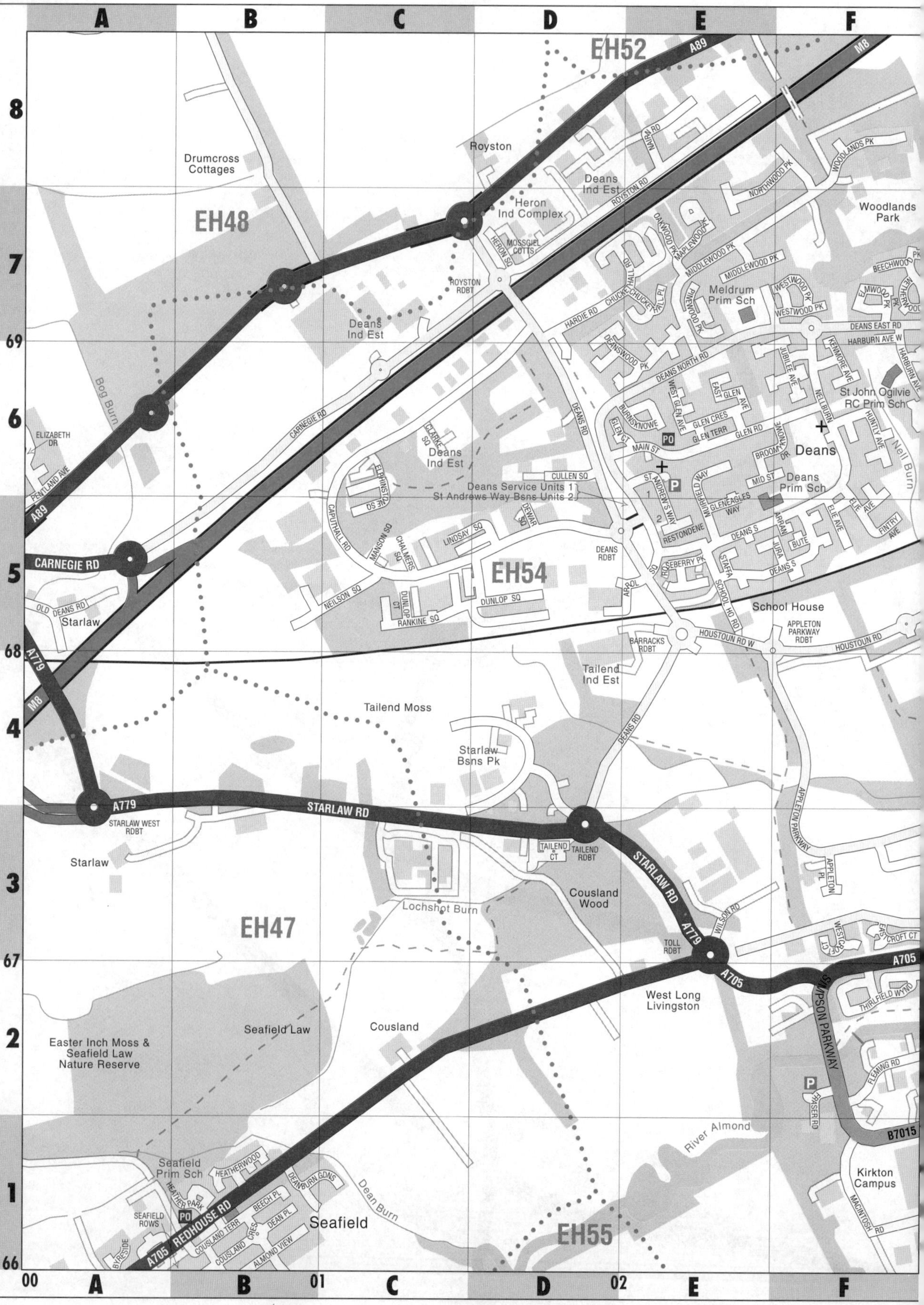
A
B
C
D
E
F
8
7
69
6
5
68
4
3
67
2
1
66
00
01
02
EH52
EH48
EH54
EH47
EH55
A89
M8
Royston
Drumcross Cottages
Deans Ind Est
Heron Ind Complex
ROYSTON RD
NAIRN RD
NORTHWOOD PK
WOODLANDS PK
Woodlands Park
HERON SQ
MOSSGIEL COTTS
ROYSTON RDBT
OAKWOOD PK
MAPLEWOOD PK
MIDDLEWOOD PK
Meldrum Prim Sch
WESTWOOD PK
BEECHWOOD
ELMWOOD PK
DEANS EAST RD
HARBURN AVE W
HARDIE RD
CHUCKETHALL RD
PINEWOOD PK
DEANSWOOD PK
DEANS NORTH RD
JUBILEE AVE
KENMORE AVE
St John Ogilvie RC Prim Sch
Bog Burn
ELIZABETH DR
PENTLAND AVE
CARNEGIE RD
CLARKE SQ
DEANS RD
WEST GLEN AVE
EAST GLEN AVE
BURNSKNOWE
GLEN CRES
GLEN TERR
GLEN RD
GLEN CT
MAIN ST
PO
NELLBURN
Deans
HUNTLY AVE
Nell Burn
BROOMY DR
CULLEN SQ
ELPHINSTONE SQ
Deans Service Units 1
St Andrews Way Bsns Units 2
ST ANDREW'S WAY
P
MUIRFIELD WAY
GLENEAGLES WAY
MID ST
Deans Prim Sch
ELLE AVE
FINTRY AVE
CAPUTHALL RD
DEWAR SQ
LINDSAY SQ
MANSON SQ
CHALMERS SQ
RESTONDENE
DEANS S
ARRAN
BUTE
STAFFA
IONA
DEANS RDBT
ROSEBERRY PK
ARROL SQ
CARNEGIE RD
OLD DEANS RD
Starlaw
NEILSON SQ
DUNLOP CT
DUNLOP SQ
RANKINE SQ
SCHOOL HO RD
School House
APPLETON PARKWAY RDBT
HOUSTOUN RD W
HOUSTOUN RD
BARRACKS RDBT
A779
Tailend Ind Est
Tailend Moss
Starlaw Bsns Pk
DEANS RD
STARLAW RD
STARLAW WEST RDBT
TAILEND CT
TAILEND RDBT
APPLETON PARKWAY
APPLETON PL
Starlaw
Cousland Wood
Lochshot Burn
WILSON RD
TOLL RDBT
WESTCROFT CT
EAST CROFT CT
A705
West Long Livingston
SIMPSON PARKWAY
THIRLFIELD WYND
Easter Inch Moss & Seafield Law Nature Reserve
Seafield Law
Cousland
FLEMING RD
FRASER RD
River Almond
B7015
Seafield Prim Sch
HEATHERWOOD
HEATHER PARK
DEANBURN GDNS
Dean Burn
Kirkton Campus
MACINTOSH RD
SEAFIELD ROWS
BYRESIDE
REDHOUSE RD
COUSLAND TERR
COUSLAND CRES
BEECH PL
DEAN PL
ALMOND VIEW
Seafield

141
163

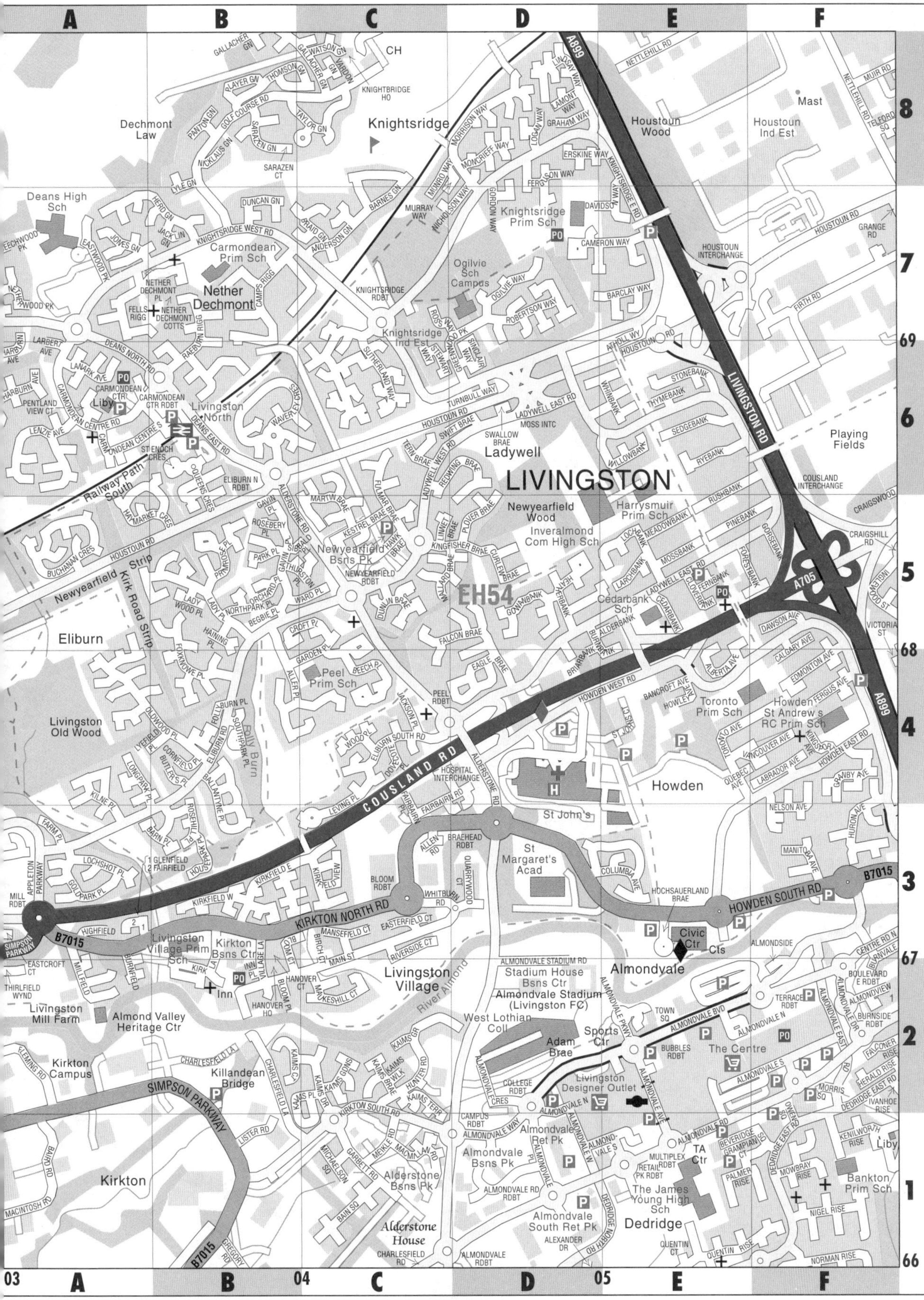
114
144
LIVINGSTON
Knightsridge
Dechmont Law
Deans High Sch
Nether Dechmont
Carmondean Prim Sch
Livingston North
Ladywell
Newyearfield Wood
Inveralmond Com High Sch
Harrysmuir Prim Sch
EH54
Houstoun Wood
Houstoun Ind Est
Playing Fields
Eliburn
Livingston Old Wood
Peel Prim Sch
Cedarbank Sch
Toronto Prim Sch
Howden St Andrew's RC Prim Sch
Howden
St John's
St Margaret's Acad
Almondvale
Livingston Village
Livingston Mill Farm
Almond Valley Heritage Ctr
Kirkton Campus
Killandean Bridge
Kirkton
Stadium House Bsns Ctr
Almondvale Stadium (Livingston FC)
West Lothian Coll
Adam Brae
Sports Ctr
The Centre
Livingston Designer Outlet
Almondvale Ret Pk
Almondvale Bsns Pk
Alderstone Bsns Pk
Alderstone House
Almondvale South Ret Pk
The James Young High Sch
Dedridge
Bankton Prim Sch
COUSLAND RD
LIVINGSTON RD
KIRKTON NORTH RD
HOWDEN SOUTH RD
SIMPSON PARKWAY
A899
A705
B7015
164
144

F2
1 Almondview Office Pk

143
115

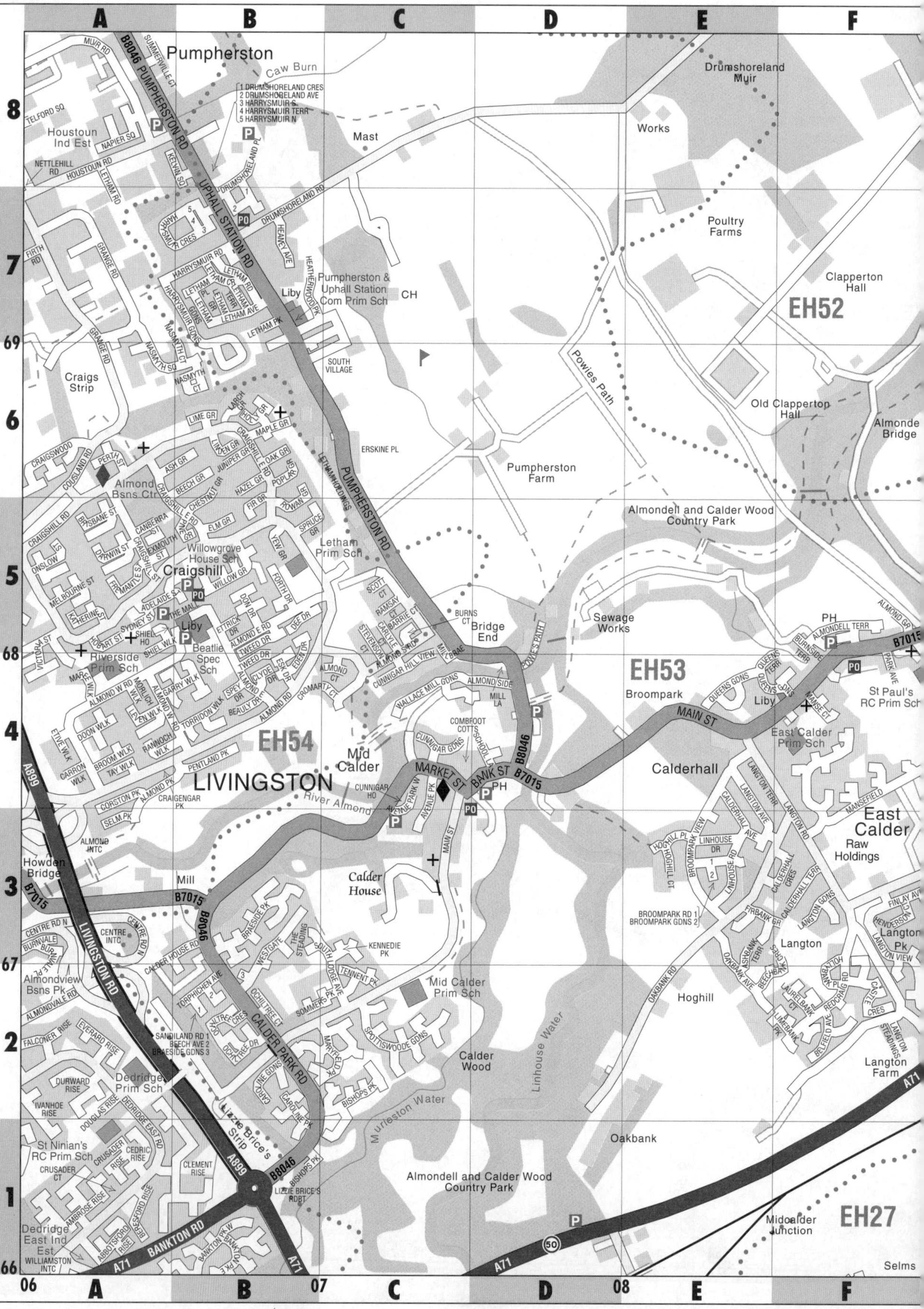
A
B
C
D
E
F
8
7
69
6
5
68
4
3
67
2
1
66
06
07
08
Pumpherston
Caw Burn
1 DRUMSHORELAND CRES
2 DRUMSHORELAND AVE
3 HARRYSMUIR S
4 HARRYSMUIR TERR
5 HARRYSMUIR N
Mast
Drumshoreland Muir
Works
Houstoun Ind Est
TELFORD SQ
MUIR RD
NAPIER SQ
NETTLEHILL RD
HOUSTOUN RD
LETHAM RD
KELVIN SQ
B8046 PUMPHERSTON RD
UPHALL STATION RD
DRUMSHORELAND RD
DRUMSHORELAND PL
HEANEY AVE
HEATHERWOOD PK
Poultry Farms
FIRTH RD
GRANGE RD
HARRYSMUIR RD
HARRYSMUIR CRES
HARRYSMUIR GDNS
LETHAM CL
LETHAM PL
LETHAM GR
LETHAM GDNS
LETHAM TERR
LETHAM DR
LETHAM AVE
LETHAM PK
NASMYTH CT
NASMYTH SQ
Pumpherston & Uphall Station Com Prim Sch
Liby
CH
Clapperton Hall
EH52
SOUTH VILLAGE
Craigs Strip
Powies Path
Old Clapperton Hall
Almond Bridge
LIME GR
LARCH GR
MAPLE GR
ERSKINE PL
CRAIGSWOOD
COUSLAND RD
PERTH ST
ASH GR
LINDEN GR
JUNIPER GR
OAK GR
POPLAR ST
Almond Bsns Ctr
BEECH GR
HAZEL GR
FIR GR
ROWAN GR
CHESTNUT GR
CRAIGSHILL E RD
CRAIGSHILL RD
BRISBANE ST
CANBERRA ST
EXMOUTH ST
ELM GR
YEW GR
SPRUCE GR
LETHAM ROCKINGS
PUMPHERSTON RD
Pumpherston Farm
Almondell and Calder Wood Country Park
ONSLOW
DARWIN ST
Willowgrove House Sch
Letham Prim Sch
Craigshill
FREMANTLE ST
MELBOURNE ST
WILLOW GR
FORTH DR
SCOTT CT
RAMSAY CT
BARRIE CT
BURNS CT
Bridge End
Sewage Works
KATHERINE ST
ADELAIDE ST
THE MALL
SYDNEY ST
HOBART ST
SHIEL HO
SHIEL WLK
Liby
Beatlie Spec Sch
ETTRICK DR
DON DR
DEE DR
ALMOND E RD
TWEED DR
EDEN DR
STEVENSON CT
CARLYLE CT
ALMOND S RD
CUNNIGAR HILL VIEW
MILL BRAE
POWIES PATH
PH
ALMOND GR
ALMONDELL TERR
BURNSIDE TERR
PARK AVE
B7015
VICTORIA ST
Riverside Prim Sch
MARIE WLK
ALMOND W RD
MORLICH WLK
GARRY WLK
SPEY DR
CLYDE DR
ESK DR
CROMARTY CT
ALMOND CT
ALMOND RD
WALLACE MILL GDNS
ALMOND SIDE
MILL LA
EH53
Broompark
QUEENS GDNS
QUEENS TERR
QUEENS GDNS
MANSE CT
Liby
St Paul's RC Prim Sch
ETIVE WLK
DOON WLK
LEVEN WLK
ALMOND W RD
TORRIDON WLK
BEAULY DR
EH54
COMBFOOT COTTS
SCHOOL LA
CUNNIGAR GDNS
B8046
MAIN ST
East Calder Prim Sch
RANNOCH WLK
CARRON WLK
BROOM WLK
TAY WLK
PENTLAND PK
Mid Calder
MARKET ST
BANK ST
B7015
Calderhall
LIVINGSTON
A899
CORSTON PK
ALMOND PK
CRAIGENGAR PK
SELM PK
CUNNIGAR HO
AVENUE PARK W
AVENUE PK
PH
River Almond
LANGTON TERR
LANGTON AVE
CALDERHALL AVE
LANGTON RD
MANSEFIELD
East Calder
ALMOND INTC
HOGHILL PL
BROOMPARK VIEW
LINHOUSE DR
Raw Holdings
Howden Bridge
B7015
Mill
Calder House
HOGHILL CT
LINHOUSE RD
CALDERHALL CRES
CALDERHALL TERR
FINLAY AVE
HENDERSON PL
B7015
BRAESIDE PK
WESTGATE
THE STEADING
BROOMPARK RD 1
BROOMPARK GDNS 2
FIRBANK GR
LANGTON GDNS
Langton Pk
CENTRE RD N
BURNVALE
CENTRE INTC
CENTRE RD N
LIVINGSTON RD
CALDER HOUSE RD
SOUTH LODGE AVE
KENNEDIE PK
ASHBANK TERR
Langton
LANGTON VIEW
Almondview Bsns Pk
ALMONDVALE RD
TORPHICHEN AVE
TENNENT PK
Mid Calder Prim Sch
OAKBANK RD
OAKBANK AVE
BEECHBANK
Hoghill
LAURELBANK CT
HOLLYBANK PK
REDCRAIG RD
CASTLE CRES
FALCONER RISE
EVERARD RISE
SANDILAND RD 1
BEECH AVE 2
BRAESIDE GDNS 3
OCHILTREE DR
OCHILTREE CT
CALDER PARK RD
SOMMERS PK
SPOTTISWOODE GDNS
MARYFIELD PK
LIMEBANK PK
BELFIELD AVE
LANGTON STEADINGS
Dedridge Prim Sch
DURWARD RISE
IVANHOE RISE
DOUGLAS RISE
DEDRIDGE EAST RD
CARLYLE GDNS
CAROLINE PK
BISHOPS PK
Calder Wood
Linhouse Water
Langton Farm
Lizzie Brice's Strip
Murieston Water
A71
St Ninian's RC Prim Sch
CRUSADER CT
CRUSADER RISE
CEDRIC RISE
CLEMENT RISE
B8046
BISHOPS PK
Oakbank
AMBROSE RISE
ABBOTSFORD RISE
BERESFORD RISE
LIZZIE BRICE'S RDBT
Almondell and Calder Wood Country Park
Dedridge East Ind Est
WILLIAMSTON INTC
BANKTON RD
A71
BANKTON PK W
BANKTON PK E
A71
A71
50
Midcalder Junction
EH27
Selms

143
165

116
146

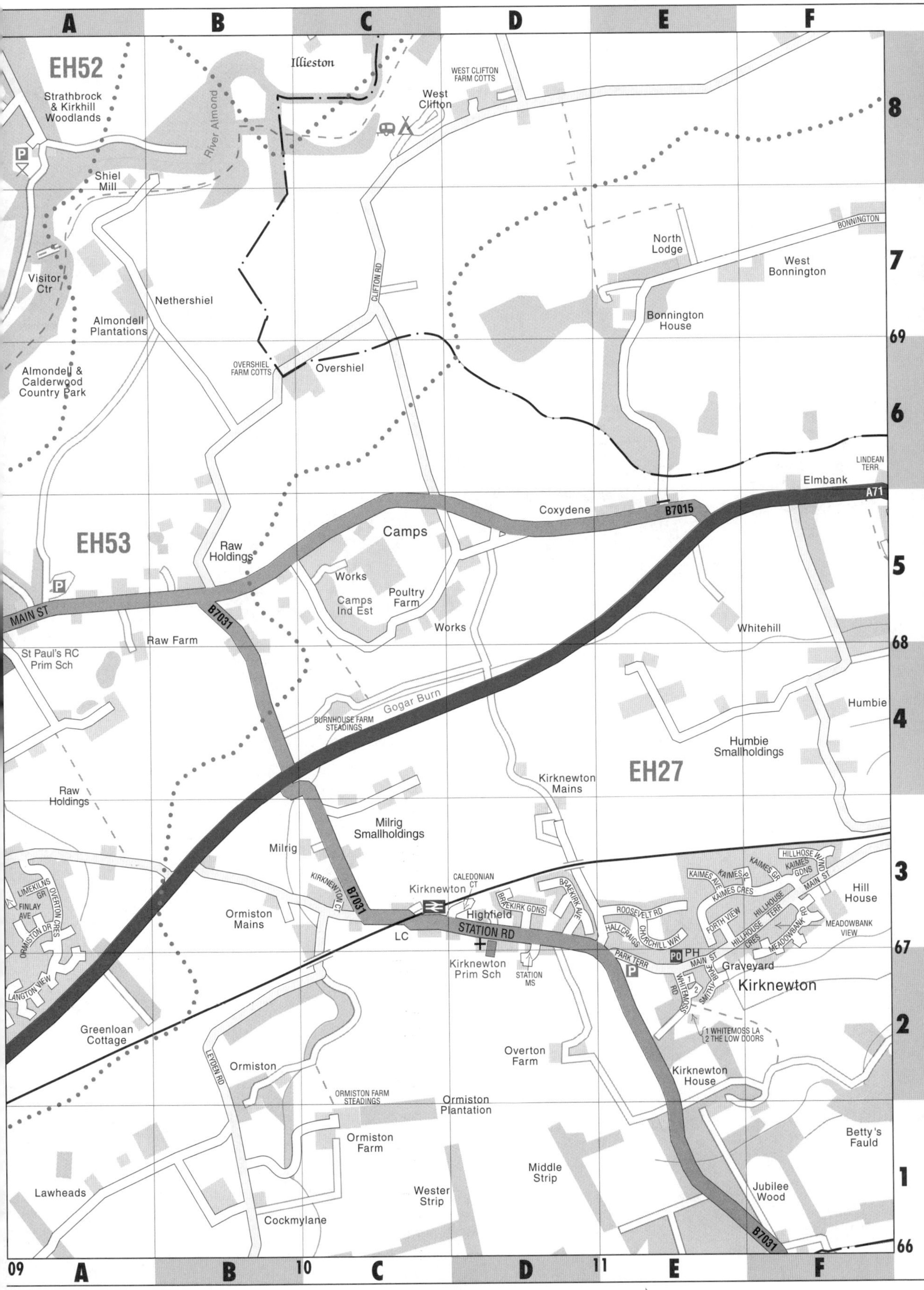
EH52
Strathbrock & Kirkhill Woodlands
Illieston
River Almond
West Clifton Farm Cotts
West Clifton
Shiel Mill
Visitor Ctr
Nethershiel
Almondell Plantations
Almondell & Calderwood Country Park
Clifton Rd
Overshiel Farm Cotts
Overshiel
North Lodge
Bonnington
West Bonnington
Bonnington House
Lindean Terr
Elmbank
A71
Coxydene
B7015
Camps
EH53
Raw Holdings
Works
Camps Ind Est
Poultry Farm
Works
Main St
B7031
Raw Farm
St Paul's RC Prim Sch
Whitehill
Humbie
Burnhouse Farm Steadings
Gogar Burn
Humbie Smallholdings
Raw Holdings
Kirknewton Mains
EH27
Milrig Smallholdings
Milrig
Kirknewton Ct
Caledonian Ct
Kirknewton
Highfield
Braekirk Gdns
Braekirk Ave
Hillhose Wynd
Kaimes Gr
Kaimes Pl
Kaimes Ave
Kaimes Gdns
Kaimes Cres
Main St
Hill House
Limekilns Gr
Overton Cres
Finlay Ave
Ormiston Dr
Ormiston Mains
Station Rd
Roosevelt Rd
Forth View
Hillhouse Terr
Hillhouse Cres
Meadowbank Rd
Meadowbank View
Hallcraigs
Churchill Way
LC
Kirknewton Prim Sch
Station Ms
Park Terr
PO
PH
Main St
Graveyard
Whitemoss Rd
Smithy Brae
Kirknewton
Langton View
1 Whitemoss La
2 The Low Doors
Greenloan Cottage
Leyden Rd
Ormiston
Overton Farm
Kirknewton House
Ormiston Farm Steadings
Ormiston Plantation
Betty's Fauld
Ormiston Farm
Middle Strip
Lawheads
Wester Strip
Jubilee Wood
Cockmylane
A B C D E F
8 7 69 6 5 68 4 3 67 2 1 66
09 10 11

166
146

145
117

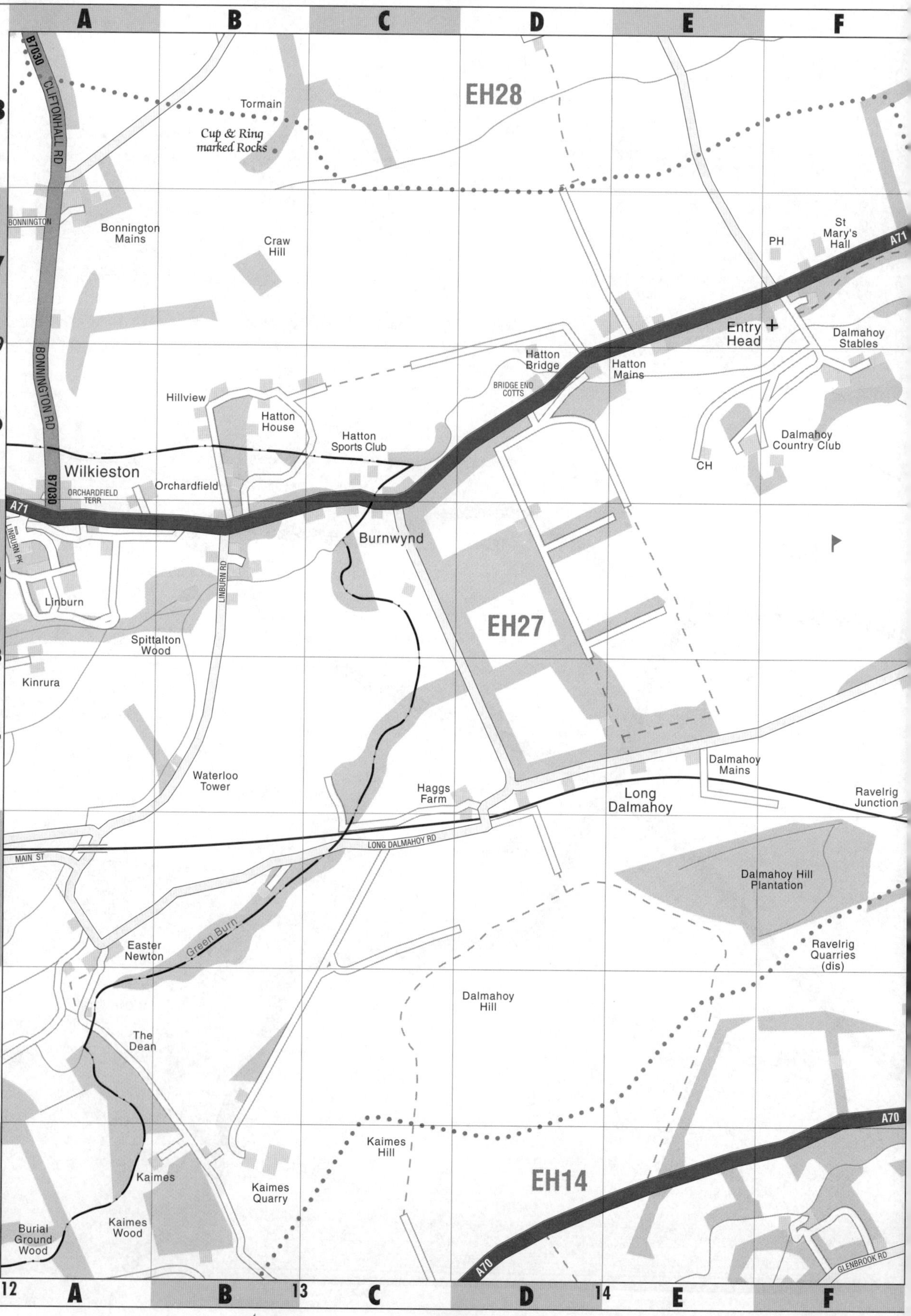
A
B
C
D
E
F
8
7
69
6
5
68
4
3
67
2
1
66
12
13
14
B7030
CLIFTONHALL RD
BONNINGTON RD
BONNINGTON
Tormain
Cup & Ring
marked Rocks
EH28
Bonnington
Mains
Craw
Hill
PH
St
Mary's
Hall
A71
Entry
Head
Dalmahoy
Stables
Hatton
Bridge
Hatton
Mains
BRIDGE END
COTTS
Hillview
Hatton
House
Hatton
Sports Club
Dalmahoy
Country Club
CH
Wilkieston
Orchardfield
ORCHARDFIELD
TERR
Burnwynd
LINBURN PK
LINBURN RD
Linburn
EH27
Spittalton
Wood
Kinrura
Waterloo
Tower
Haggs
Farm
Dalmahoy
Mains
Long
Dalmahoy
Ravelrig
Junction
MAIN ST
LONG DALMAHOY RD
Dalmahoy Hill
Plantation
Easter
Newton
Green Burn
Ravelrig
Quarries
(dis)
Dalmahoy
Hill
The
Dean
Kaimes
Hill
A70
Kaimes
Kaimes
Quarry
EH14
Kaimes
Wood
Burial
Ground
Wood
GLENBROOK RD

145
167

118
148

A
B
C
D
E
F
8
7
69
6
5
68
4
3
67
2
1
66
15
16
17
EH28
EH14
EH27
A71
A70
Addiston Mains
Addiston Bridge
Lodge
Crow Wood
Addistoun House
Gogar Burn
RESEARCH AVE N
RICCARTON MAINS RD
Heriot-Watt University
BOUNDARY RD E
RESEARCH AVE 1
RESEARCH AVE S
FIRST GAIT
SECOND GAIT
THIRD GAIT
FOURTH GAIT
BOUNDARY RD N
THE AVENUE
MEADOW RD
Riccarton
Liby
CAMERON SMAILL RD
Ellswood Cottage
Lover's Loan
WARRISTON FARM RD
Warriston
South Strip
Weaver's Knowe
Malcomstone
Muir o' Dean
LONG DALMAHOY RD
Cocklaw
Currichill
RICCARTON DR 1
RICCARTON AVE 2
FORTH VIEW CRES
Gowanhill
Murray Burn
GOWANHILL FARM RD
Currievale
Newhouse
NEWMILLS RD
LC
CURRIEVALE DR
CURRIEHILL RD
WEAVER'S KNOWE CRES
PALMER RD
PALMER PL
Currie Prim Sch
Currie Com High Sch
Woodlands Sch
FORTH VIEW AVE
FORTH VIEW RD
PENTLAND RD
PENTLAND VIEW PL
DOLPHIN GDNS W
DOLPHIN GDNS E
DOLPHIN AVE
DOLPHIN RD
PENTLAND AVE
CURRIEVALE PK
CURRIEVALE PARK GR
CURRIEHILL CASTLE DR
ROWANTREE AVE
ROWANTREE GR
STEWART GDNS
STEWART CRES
STEWART AVE
STEWART RD
CHERRY TREE AVE
CHERRY TREE LOAN
CHERRY TREE PK
CHERRY TREE GDNS
CHERRY TREE GR
CHERRY TREE CRES
NEWMILLS CRES
NEWMILLS GR
NEWMILLS AVE
OLD NEWMILLS RD
WILLOW TREE PL
Currie
WAULKMILL LOAN
1 CHERRY TREE VIEW
2 CHERRY TREE PL
3 STEWART PL
Lennox Tower
Duncan's Belt
Lymphoy
Water of Leith
Water of Leith Walkway
LANARK RD W
RAVELRIG RD
ADDISTON GR
ADDISTON PK
ADDISTON CRES
HORSBURGH BANK
HORSBURGH GR
HORSBURGH GDNS
DALMAHOY CRES
TURNER PK
TURNER AVE
STATION LOAN
Ravelrig Hill
PILMUIR GR
ASHLEY GRANGE
RAVELRIG WYND
RAVELRIG DR
RAVELRIG GAIT
RAVELRIG PK
RAVELRIG HILL
Ravelrig
Hannahfield
Balerno High Sch
BRIDGE RD
Malleny Garden
BAVELAW GN
Liby
Malleny House
LARCHFIELD
LADYCROFT
BURNSIDE PK
MAIN ST
BAVELAW GDNS
BAVELAW RD
DEANPARK BRAE
Sawpit Wood
Balerno
Black Wood
1 LARCHFIELD NEUK
2 QUARRY HOWE
3 SLAESIDE
4 DEANPARK CRES
5 MARCHBANK GDNS
6 DEANPARK SQ
7 DEANPARK GR
Larch Grove
JOHNSBURN RD
LOVEDALE RD
LOVEDALE GDNS
LOVEDALE AVE
LOVEDALE GR
LOVEDALE CRES
DEANPARK AVE
DEANPARK GDNS
MILLBANK
HARLAW RD
HARLAW GAIT
HARLAW BANK
Bankhead Farm
Bankhead House
GLENBROOK RD
JOHNSBURN GN
JOHNSBURN HAUGH
JOHNSBURN PK
CLAYHILLS PK
CLAYHILLS GR
DEANPARK CT
DEANPARK PLACE
DEANPARK BANK
MARCHBANK WAY
MANSFIELD RD
MALLENY AVE
PO
P

168
148

147
119

A
B
C
D
E
F
EH11
EH14
EH13
Murray Burn
RICCARTON MAINS RD
Riccarton Mains
QUARRYBANK END 1
QUARRYBANK CL 2
QUARRYBANK CT 3
MIDDLEKNOWE 4
MIDDLESHOT 5
MIDDLEPARK 6
QUARRYVIEW 7
MORVENSIDE CL 8
A720
QUARRY BANK
WESTBURN MIDDLEFIELD
MORVENSIDE
WESTBURN AVE
WESTBURN GR
WESTBURN PK
BABERTON MAINS
B701
Liby
MURRAYBURN JUNC
MURRAYBURN GATE
MURRAYBURN
PO
Westside Plaza
Wester Hailes
Wester Hailes
WALKERS RIGG
Canal View Prim Sch
HARVESTERS SQ
HARVESTERS PL
WESTER HAILES PK
DUMBEG PK
HARVESTERS WAY
GREENACRE
BARN PARK CRES
BARN PK
WESTER HAILES RD
CLOVENSTONE RD
CLOVENSTONE GDNS
Clovenstone Prim Sch
CLOVENSTONE PK
CLOVENSTONE DR
CLOVENSTONE RDBT
1 ALCORN SQ
2 ALCORN RIGG
THE CITY OF EDINBURGH BY-PASS
A70
HAILES GDNS
SPYLAW BANK RD
SPYLAW PK
PENTLAND AVE
GILLESPIE RD
B70
VIEWFIELD RD
MUIREND AVE
Baberton
BABERTON MAINS BRAE
BABERTON MAINS WAY
BABERTON MAINS HILL
BABERTON MAINS WOOD
BABERTON MAINS RISE
BABERTON MAINS LEA
BABERTON MAINS DELL
BABERTON MAINS GDNS
BABERTON MAINS GR
BABERTON MAINS TERR
BABERTON MAINS PK
BABERTON MAINS CRES
BABERTON MAINS AVE
BABERTON MAINS PL
BABERTON MAINS ROW
BABERTON MAINS VIEW
BABERTON MAINS CT
BABERTON MAINS LOAN
BABERTON MAINS GN
BABERTON MAINS DR
BABERTON MAINS BANK
BABERTON MAINS WYND
Baberton House
LC
Whitelaw
Wilderness Wood
Juniper Green Prim Sch
CH
BABERTON CRES
BABERTON CT
FOULIS CRES
MILLBRAE
WOODHALL TERR
WOODHALL AVE
WOODHALL DR
WOODHALL MILLBRAE
DORMER VIEW
LANARK RD
Woodall Mill
Campbell Park
WEST MILL RD
WOODFIELD AVE
WOODFIELD PK
CAMPBELL PARK CRES
CAMPBELL PARK DR
WOODHALL RD
WOODHALL GR
WOODHALL BANK
TORPHIN BANK
TORPHIN RD
A720
Corby Hill
Torphin
JUNIPER PARK RD
BELMONT RD
JUNIPER GR
JUNIPER TERR
JUNIPER AVE
JUNIPERLEE
JUNIPER PL
JUNIPER GDNS
JUNIPER LA 1
JUNIPER TERR 2
Juniper Green
BABERTON PK
BABERTON AVE
BABERTON LOAN
Water of Leith
Woodhall Mains
Corslet
NETHER CURRIE CRES
MUIR WOOD RD
MUIR WOOD CRES
MUIR WOOD PL
MUIR WOOD DR
MUIR WOOD GR
THOMSON DR
THOMSON GR
THOMSON RD
THOMSON CRES
Nether Currie Prim Sch
WEAVER'S KNOWE CRES
EASTER CURRIE PL
CORSLET RD
CORSLET PL
CORSLET CRES
BRYCE GDNS
BRYCE PL
BRYCE RD
BRYCE CRES
RICCARTON DR
RICCARTON AVE
RICCARTON GR
RICCARTON CRES
EASTER CURRIE CRES
EASTER CURRIE TERR
EASTER CURRIE CT
LANARK RD W
PROVOST HAUGH
Kinleith Ind Est
BLINKBONNY RD
Liby
CURRIEHILL RD
Moidart House
Blinkbonny
Currie
Cemy
BRAEBURN DR
1 PENTLAND VIEW
2 PENTLAND VIEW CT
3 Currie Prim Sch
Rosebank
KIRKGATE
Lennox Lea
Easter Kinleith
Middle Kinleith
Warklaw Hill
Mast
TORDUFF RD
Torduff Reservoir
Torduff Hill
Lodge
Blacklaws Burn
Wester Kinleith
HARLAW RD
Kinleith Burn
Clubbiedean Reservoir
Bonaly Country Park
Clubbiedean Burn
Bonaly Reservoir
8
7
69
6
5
68
4
3
67
2
1
66
18
19
20

147
169

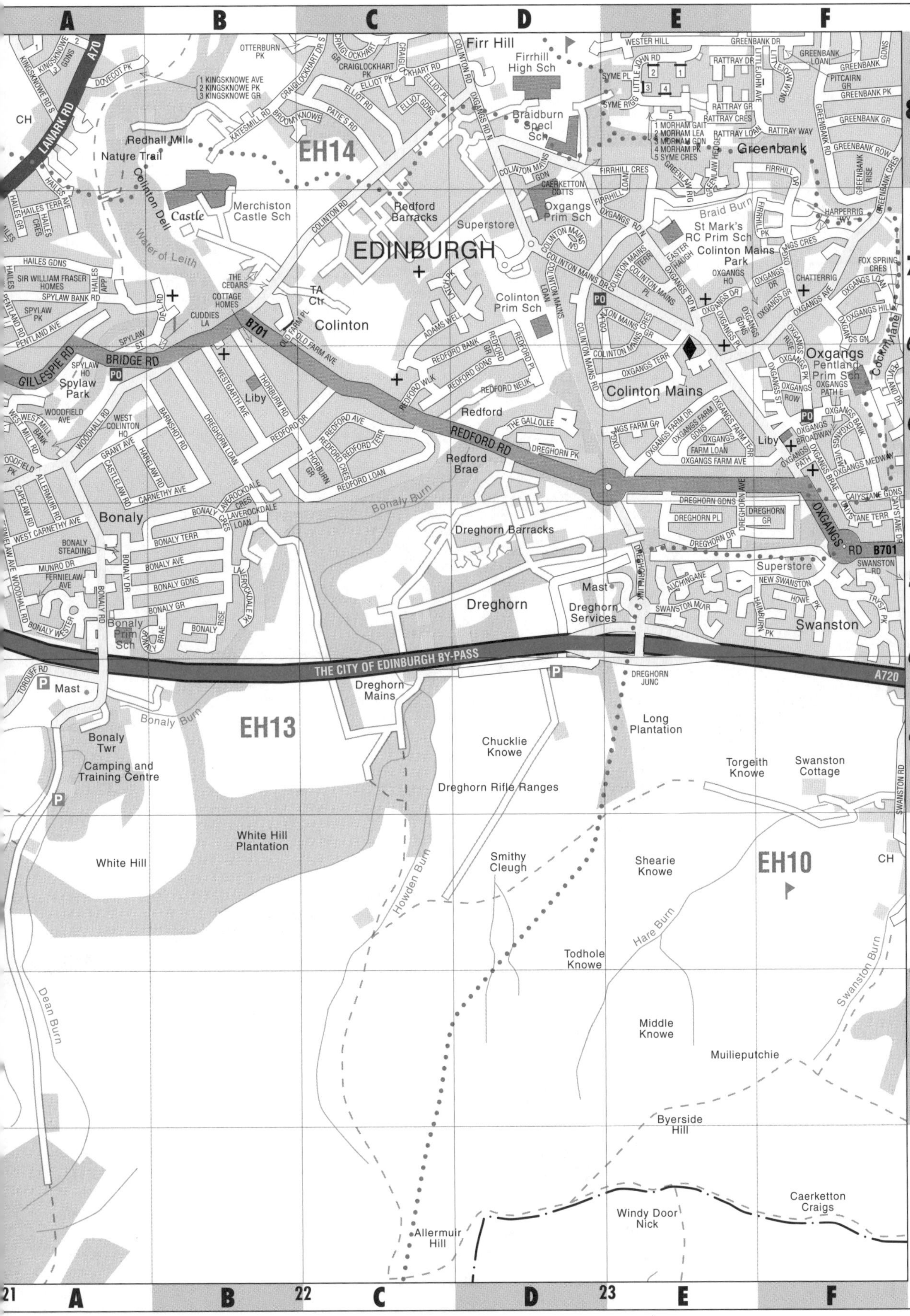
120
150
A
B
C
D
E
F
Firr Hill
Firrhill High Sch
Braidburn Specl Sch
Greenbank
EH14
Redhall Mill Nature Trail
Colinton Dell
Castle
Merchiston Castle Sch
Water of Leith
Redford Barracks
Superstore
EDINBURGH
Oxgangs Prim Sch
St Mark's RC Prim Sch
Colinton Mains Park
TA Ctr
Colinton
Colinton Prim Sch
Oxgangs
Pentland Prim Sch
Colinton Mains
Spylaw Park
Liby
Redford
Redford Brae
Bonaly
Bonaly Burn
Dreghorn Barracks
Superstore
Mast
Dreghorn
Dreghorn Services
Swanston
Bonaly Prim Sch
THE CITY OF EDINBURGH BY-PASS
A720
A70
LANARK RD
GILLESPIE RD
BRIDGE RD
REDFORD RD
B701
OXGANGS RD
DREGHORN JUNC
Dreghorn Mains
EH13
Bonaly Twr
Camping and Training Centre
Long Plantation
Chucklie Knowe
Torgeith Knowe
Swanston Cottage
Dreghorn Rifle Ranges
White Hill Plantation
White Hill
Smithy Cleugh
Shearie Knowe
EH10
CH
Howden Burn
Hare Burn
Todhole Knowe
Swanston Burn
Dean Burn
Middle Knowe
Muiliepuchie
Byerside Hill
Caerketton Craigs
Windy Door Nick
Allermuir Hill
8
7
6
5
4
3
2
1
69
68
67
66
21
22
23
170
150

149
121

A B C D E F
8 7 69 6 5 68 4 3 67 2 1 66
24 25 26
Braid Hills
The Braids
Masts
Buckstone Snab
Elf Loch
Liberton Tower Mains
Liberton Tower
Tower House
Liberton
Tower Farm
Riding School
Liberton House
EH16
Liberton Kennels
Meadowhead
Alnwickhill House
Alnwickhill
Comiston
Public Park
Braidburn Valley
Water Works
Buckstone Prim Sch
The Caiy Stane
Galachlaw
Fairmilehead
Mortonhall
Crem
Cemy
Morton House
EH10
EH17
Broomhills
Morton Mains
LOTHIANBURN JUNCTION
Swanston Burn
THE CITY OF EDINBURGH BY-PASS
Lothian Burn
Burdiehouse Burn
Masts
CH
PH
Buiselaw
Goldburn
White Hill
Hillend Public Park
Midlothian Snowsports Ctr
Country Park
Hillend
Hillend Hill
Boghall Plantation
Caerketton Hill
Pentland Burn
PENTLAND RD
DAMHEAD HOLDINGS SCHEME
Pentland Bridge
EH20
Works
Old Pentland
A702
A703
A720
A701
B701
COMISTON RD
BUCKSTONE TERR
BIGGAR RD
SEAFIELD MOOR RD
OXGANGS RD
FROGSTON RD W
FROGSTON BRAE
FROGSTON RD E
BRAID HILLS DR
LIBERTON DR
LIBERTON RD
STANEDYKEHEAD
MORTONHALL GATE
HOWDEN HALL CT
BUCKSTONE NEUK
HIGH BUCKSTONE
BUCKSTONE GR
BUCKSTONE CRES
SWANSTON RD
SWANSTON TERR
CAIYSIDE
WINTON LOAN
MOUNTHOOLY LOAN
KING MALCOLM CL
MARGARET ROSE LOAN 1
MARGARTE ROSE WAY 2
PENTLAND TERR
GREENBANK CRES
RISELAW RD
PENTLAND VIEW
FOX SPRING RISE
FOX SPRING CRES
SWAN SPRING AVE
CAIYSTANE GDNS
CAIYSTANE TERR
CAIYSTANE AVE
FAIRMILE AVE
SWANSTON PK
SWANSTON AVE
SWANSTON GR
SWANSTON DR
MORTONHALL PARK GR 1
MORTONHALL PARK LOAN 2
MORTONHALL PARK GN 3
CLACKMAE GR 1
LEADERVALE TERR 2
KEDSLIE PL 3
LEADERVALE RD
CLACKMAE RD
BROOMHILLS RD

149
171

A8
1 LEADERVALE RD
2 BEAUCHAMP GR
3 HAWKHEAD GR
4 CLARINDA TERR

B8
1 GLENVARLOCH CRES
2 RINGWOOD PL
3 INGLEWOOD PL
4 MONKBARNS GDNS
5 MANNERING PL
6 PLEYDELL PL

122

E6
1 The Faith Mission Coll

152

E7
1 MOREDUN PARK WLK
2 MOREDUN DELL

172

152

151
123

151
173

E1
1 CORTLEFERRY PK
2 CORTLEFERRY TERR
3 BROOMHILL PK
4 WESTFIELD CT
5 WESTFIELD DR
6 WESTFIELD BANK
7 MELVILLE TERR

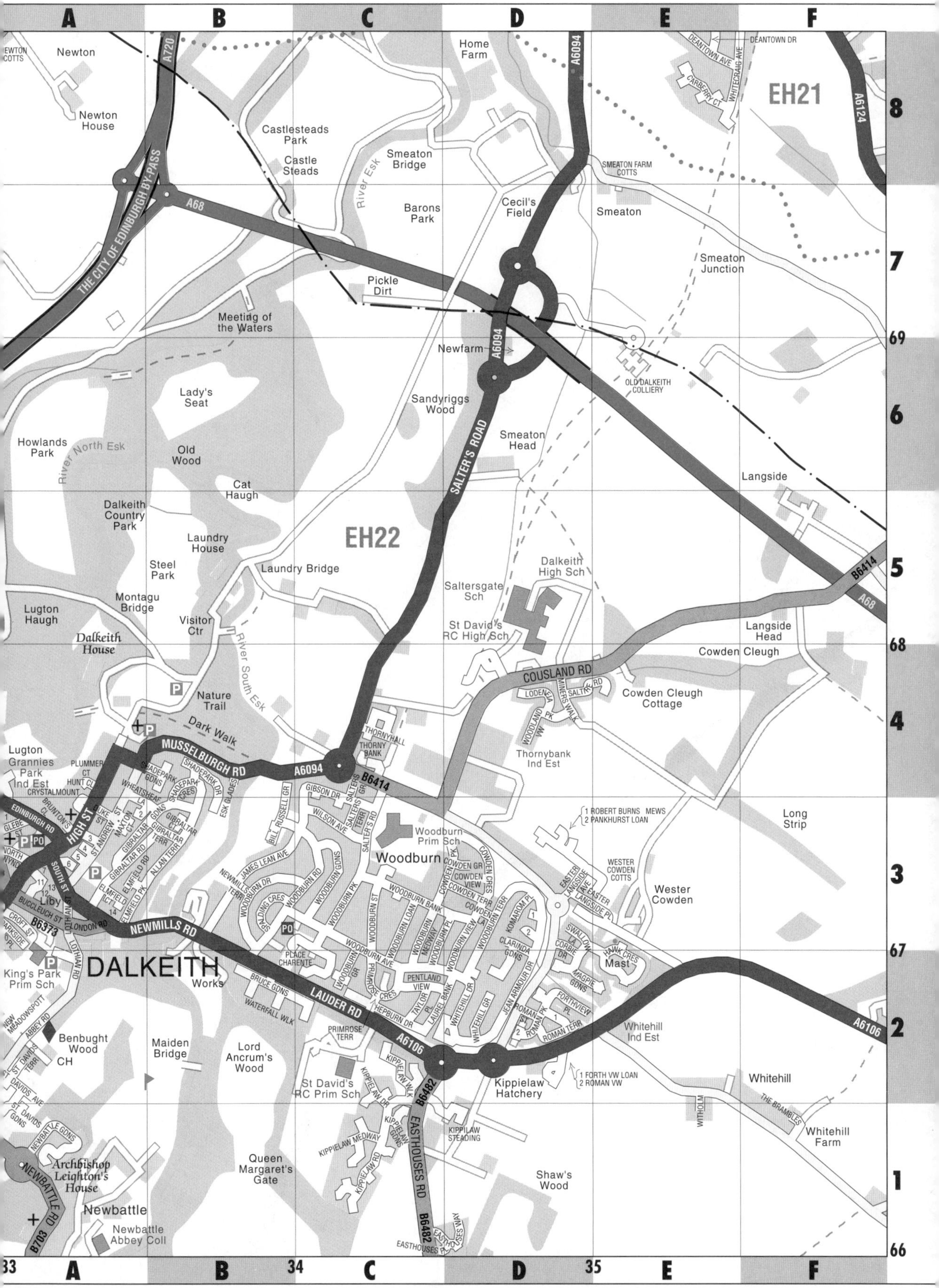

A3
1 BRIDGEND CT
2 LANSBURY CT
3 TAIT ST
4 ROBERTSON'S CL
5 WHITE'S CL
6 PETTIGREW'S CL
7 JARNAC CT
8 OLD EDINBURGH RD
9 ESBANK RD
10 PARKSIDE CT
11 ESKDAILL ST
12 WHITE HART ST
13 ESKDAILL CT
14 LAUDER LODGE

153
125

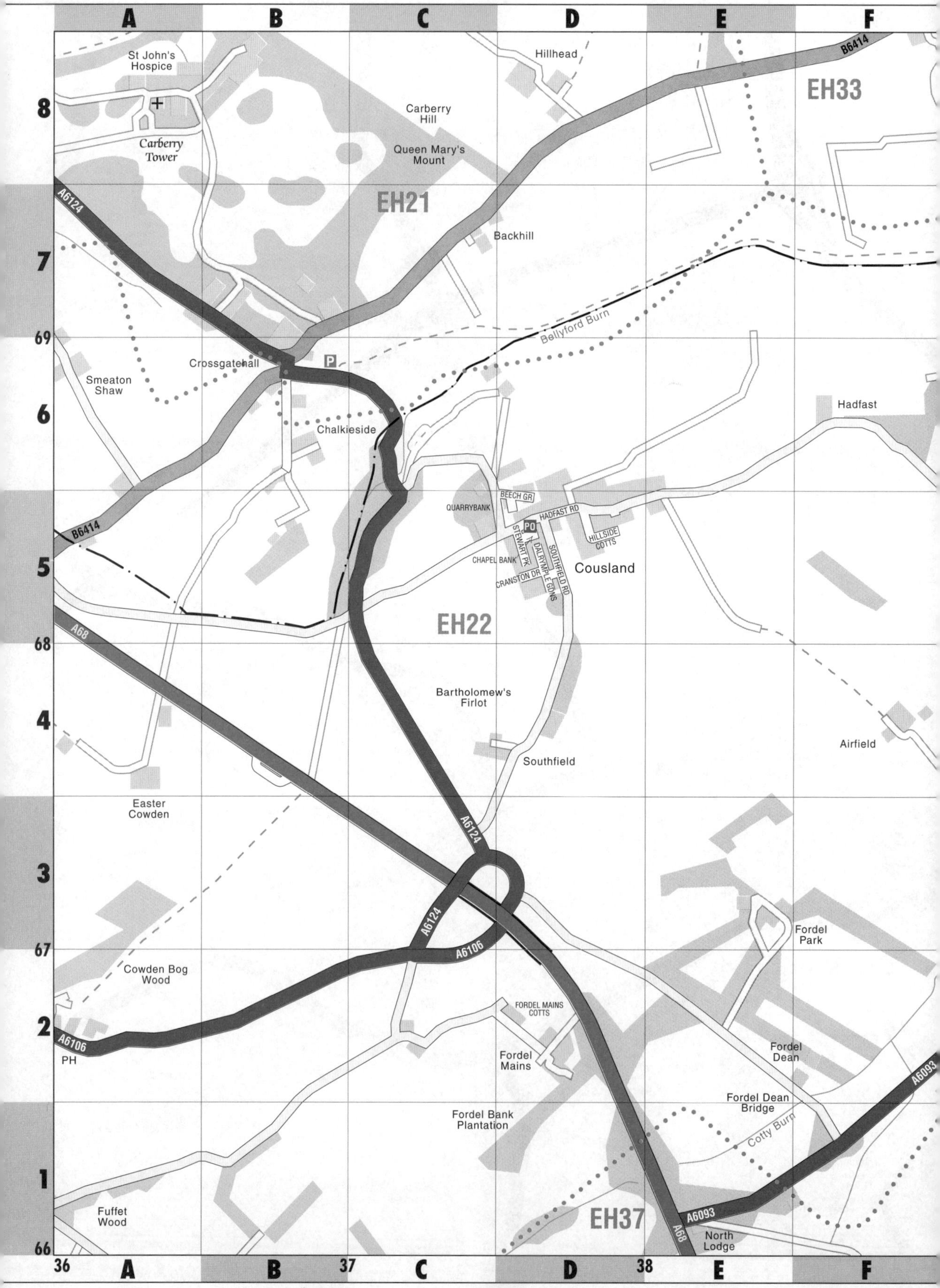
A
B
C
D
E
F
8
7
69
6
5
68
4
3
67
2
1
66
36
37
38
St John's Hospice
Hillhead
B6414
EH33
Carberry Hill
Carberry Tower
Queen Mary's Mount
EH21
A6124
Backhill
Bellyford Burn
Smeaton Shaw
Crossgatehall
P
Chalkieside
Hadfast
BEECH GR
QUARRYBANK
HADFAST RD
PO
HILLSIDE COTTS
STEWART PK
DALRYMPLE GDNS
SOUTHFIELD RD
CHAPEL BANK
CRANSTON DR
Cousland
B6414
EH22
A68
Bartholomew's Firlot
Airfield
Southfield
Easter Cowden
A6124
A6124
A6106
Fordel Park
Cowden Bog Wood
FORDEL MAINS COTTS
A6106
PH
Fordel Mains
Fordel Dean
Fordel Dean Bridge
A6093
Fordel Bank Plantation
Cotty Burn
Fuffet Wood
EH37
A6093
A68
North Lodge

153
175

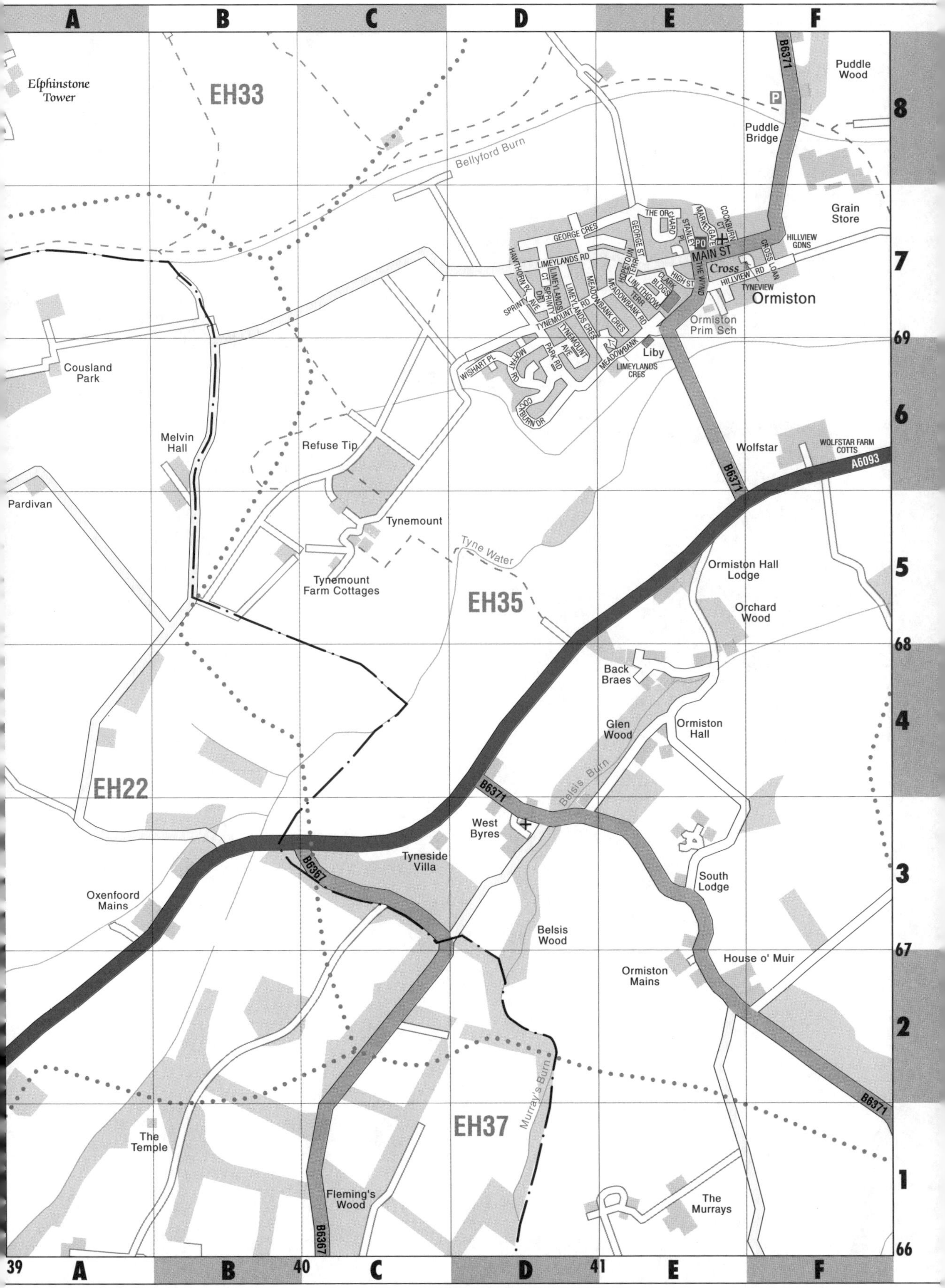
126
156
A
B
C
D
E
F
8
7
69
6
5
68
4
3
67
2
1
66
39
40
41
Elphinstone Tower
EH33
Puddle Wood
Puddle Bridge
Bellyford Burn
Grain Store
B6371
GEORGE CRES
THE ORCHARD
GEORGE ST
STANLEY PL
MARKET GATE
COCKBURN CT
MAIN ST
PO
HILLVIEW GDNS
CROSS LOAN
Cross
HILLVIEW RD
TYNEVIEW
Ormiston
HAWTHORN PL
LIMEYLANDS RD
SPRINTY AVE
SPRINTY DR
LIMEYLANDS CT
TYNEMOUNT RD
LIMEYLANDS CRES
MEADOWBANK CRES
MEADOWBANK RD
HOPETOUN TERR
LINLITHGOW TERR
CLARK BLDGS
HIGH ST
THE WYND
Ormiston Prim Sch
Liby
LIMEYLANDS CRES
MEADOWBANK
TYNEMOUNT AVE
PARK RD
MOFFAT RD
WISHART PL
COCKBURN DR
Cousland Park
Melvin Hall
Refuse Tip
Wolfstar
WOLFSTAR FARM COTTS
A6093
Pardivan
Tynemount
Tyne Water
Tynemount Farm Cottages
EH35
Ormiston Hall Lodge
Orchard Wood
Back Braes
Glen Wood
Ormiston Hall
Belsis Burn
EH22
B6371
West Byres
Tyneside Villa
B6367
South Lodge
Oxenfoord Mains
Belsis Wood
House o' Muir
Ormiston Mains
Murray's Burn
EH37
The Temple
Fleming's Wood
The Murrays
176
156

155
127

A
B
C
D
E
F
8
7
69
6
5
68
4
3
67
2
1
66
42
43
44
Mill
Winton West Mains
Walk Plantation
B6355
Dean Bridge (New)
B6363
BOGGS HOLDINGS
Dean Bridge (Old)
Winton Cottage
Winton House
Red Mains
EH35
Tyne Water
Puddle Burn
Pirnie Braes
A6093
Sewage Works
Rabbit Knowe
Pencaitland
PARK VIEW
B6355
PH
VINEFIELDS
DOVECOT WAY
PO
THE GLEBE
THE GREEN
BEECH TERR
DOVECOT PK
TYNEHOLM COTTS
Pencaitland Prim Sch
Easter Pencaitland
MILLWAY
Broomrigg
CASTLE VIEW
WOODHALL
THE CROSS
OLD FARM CT
LEMPOCKWELLS RD
Kiloran
Wester Pencaitland
WOODHALL RD
PL
QUEEN'S DR
TREVELYAN PL
A6093
Roselea
Tyneholm
P
TREVELYAN CRES
HUNTLAW RD
LAMBERTON CT
BRUCE GR
Blackford Burn
Black Wood
EH34
Woodhall
Big Wood
Burnt Wood
Fountainhall
Pencaitland Railway Walk
Huntlaw
LEMPOCKWELLS
EH35
Glenkinchie Distillery
P
GLENKINCHIE HOS
Kinchie Burn
Peastonbank
Temple Hall
B6371

155
177

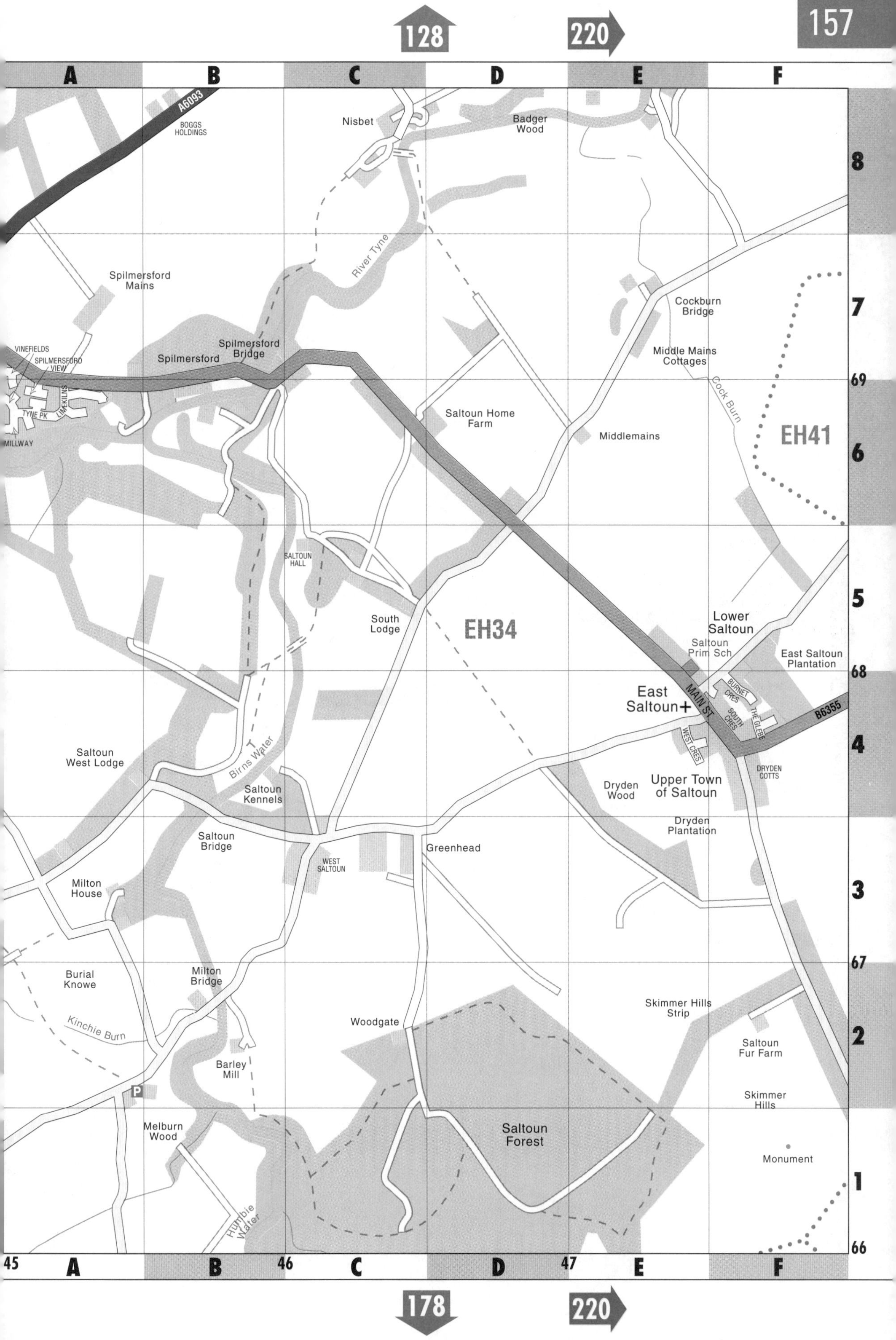
128
220
A
B
C
D
E
F
A6093
BOGGS HOLDINGS
Nisbet
Badger Wood
8
River Tyne
Spilmersford Mains
Cockburn Bridge
7
VINEFIELDS
SPILMERSFORD VIEW
Spilmersford
Spilmersford Bridge
Middle Mains Cottages
69
TYNE PK
LIMEKILNS
MILLWAY
Saltoun Home Farm
Middlemains
Cock Burn
EH41
6
SALTOUN HALL
5
South Lodge
EH34
Lower Saltoun
Saltoun Prim Sch
East Saltoun Plantation
68
East Saltoun
MAIN ST
BURNET CRES
SOUTH CRES
THE GLEBE
B6355
WEST CRES
4
Saltoun West Lodge
Birns Water
Saltoun Kennels
Dryden Wood
Upper Town of Saltoun
DRYDEN COTTS
Dryden Plantation
Saltoun Bridge
WEST SALTOUN
Greenhead
Milton House
3
Burial Knowe
Milton Bridge
67
Skimmer Hills Strip
Kinchie Burn
Woodgate
2
Saltoun Fur Farm
Barley Mill
P
Skimmer Hills
Melburn Wood
Saltoun Forest
Monument
1
Humbie Water
66
45
46
47
178
220

137

A B C D E F
8 7 65 6 5 64 4 3 63 2 1 62
85 86 87
ML6
EH48
Baads
BAADS RD
Forrestburn Water
Works
BLAIRMUCKHOLE AND FORRESTDYKE RD
Forrestburn
Bridgehill
Forrestburn Holding
Papperthill Craigs
Race Track
Works
FORREST RD
Forrestburn Water
Mast
Bentfoot
Forrestburn Reservoir
Blairmuckhole
Glasgow STREET ATLAS
Dewshills
ML7
Blairmains
M8
Mine (dis)
LLYNALLAN RD
5
B7057
South Blair
B7066
TV Station
DEWSHILL COTTS
Mast
M8
Welleslea
HOUSEO MUIR RD
North Hirst
SHOTTS RD
M8 Glasgow (A8)
Shotts Burn
HIRST RD
SOUTH HIRST RD
B7057
Mast
South Hirst
Resr
Easter Hassockrigg
SHOTTSBURN RD
B7066
Wester Hassockrigg
SHOTTS RD
River Almond
Opencast Workings
Cant Hills
B717
B7057
WEST BENHAR RD
NEWMILL AND CANTHILL RD
BENHAR RD
B717
Easter Baton

179

138
160
A
B
C
D
E
F
EH48
Blairhill Quarry
Loan Farm
Forestburn Water
Hill Farm
Blairmuckhill
Netherton Farm
Knowehead
Mast
M8
Harthill Service Area
Sewage Works
Greenrigg Prim Sch
WESTCRAIGS RD
B718
Treesbank Farm
Service Area
How Burn
BLAIRMUCKHOLE AND FORRESTDYKE RD
MOSSBURN AVE
Mossburn Ind Est
WEST MAIN ST
EAST MAIN ST
B7066
GREENRIGG COTTS
POLKEMMET LA
HOWBURN RD
HOWBURN CRES
PAXSTONE DR
PAXSTONE CRES
BANK RD
GIBBSHILL PL
LOAN PL
FORREST PL
PRIG WAY
MILLER ST
MOLLISON AVE
MILLER PL
HAWTHORN DR
DUNN TERR
DEER PATH
VIEWFIELD ST
VIEWFIELD PL
WHYTE ST
MURDOSTOUN CRES
MCLACHLAN VIEW
POLKEMMET RD
BURNBRAE RD
BURNS CRES
ALMOND TERR
OLD EASTFIELD ST
HEATHERBELL CT
B717
CHURCH ST
BERTRAM ST
BROOMHILL ST
BRESLIN TERR
PEDEN ST
BAIRD TERR
MINTHILL PL
ORR TERR
LIVINGSTONE QUADRANT
MUIRHEAD PL
COVENANTER RD
CUNNINGHAM DR
Alexander Peden Prim Sch
VICTORIA ST
VICTORIA RD
MILL RD
FLAX
ALBERT RD
BALBAKIE RD
SIDEHEAD RD
ARGYLL CT
BAILLIE AVE
Harthill
LLYNALLAN RD
HIRST RD
Tam's Loup Quarry
Eastfield
Paxtane
ML7
West Benhar
PH
River Almond
Works
WEST BENHAR RD
Active Workings
Spoil Heap
Mon
Brownhill Farm
8
7
65
6
5
64
4
3
63
2
1
62
88
89
90
180
160

159
139

A
B
C
D
E
F
EH48
Black Moss Burn
Balgornie
How Burn
Hare Moss Wood
4a
M8
Polkemmet Country Park
B7066
CH
Murraysgate Ind Est
B7069
WEST MAIN ST B7069
Greenrigg
Couch
River Almond
CULTSYKEFOOT
EAST MAIN ST B7066
GREENRIGG COTTS
St Josephs RC Prim Sch
Cult
Rigghouse
Burnhouse Ind Est
Burnhouse
ML7
EH47
Polkemmet Bsns Ctr
Polkemmet Colliery (dis)
Reveston House
Brow Plantation
Opencast Workings
Greenrigg
Cultrig Burn
Polkemmet Moor
Bickerton Burn
Crane Hillock
East Benhar
8
7
65
6
5
64
4
3
63
2
1
62
91
92
93

159
181

140
162

WHITBURN
EH48
EH47
East Whitburn
Blaeberryhill
Croftmalloch
Longridge
Tippethill
Torbanehill Mains
Strathalmond
Sewage Works
Drum
Pottishaw
River Almond
Whitburn Acad
Whitdale Prim Sch
Croftmalloch Prim Sch
Polkemmet Prim Sch
Burnhouse Sch
Longridge Prim Sch
Depot
Redmill Ind Est
West Foulshiels
Easter Blacklaws
Blacklaws
Bickerton Hall
Bickerton Burn
Foulshiels Burn
Cairnie
Kepscaith
Easter Longridge
South East Longridge
Back of Moss
Poultry Farm
Stonehead
Bents
Garden City
Latch Burn
White Burn
A706
A705
A801
M3
B8084
B7066
B7069
B7010
B7015
MAIN ST
A705 EAST MAIN ST
WEST MAIN ST
ARMADALE RD
MANSE RD
LONGRIDGE RD
BLAEBERRYHILL RD
1 WOODMUIR RD
2 PENTLAND WLK
1 DRUM PL
2 ALMOND CT
3 PENTLAND VIEW
LOCH AWE WAY 1
LOCH TROOL WAY 2
LOCH MAREE WAY 3
GARELOCH WAY 4
LOCH EARN WAY 5
LOCH FYNE WAY 6
Cemy
Liby
Hotel
Ind Est
Wks
PH
8
7
6
5
4
3
2
1
65
64
63
62
94
95
96
A
B
C
D
E
F

182
162

161
141

161
183

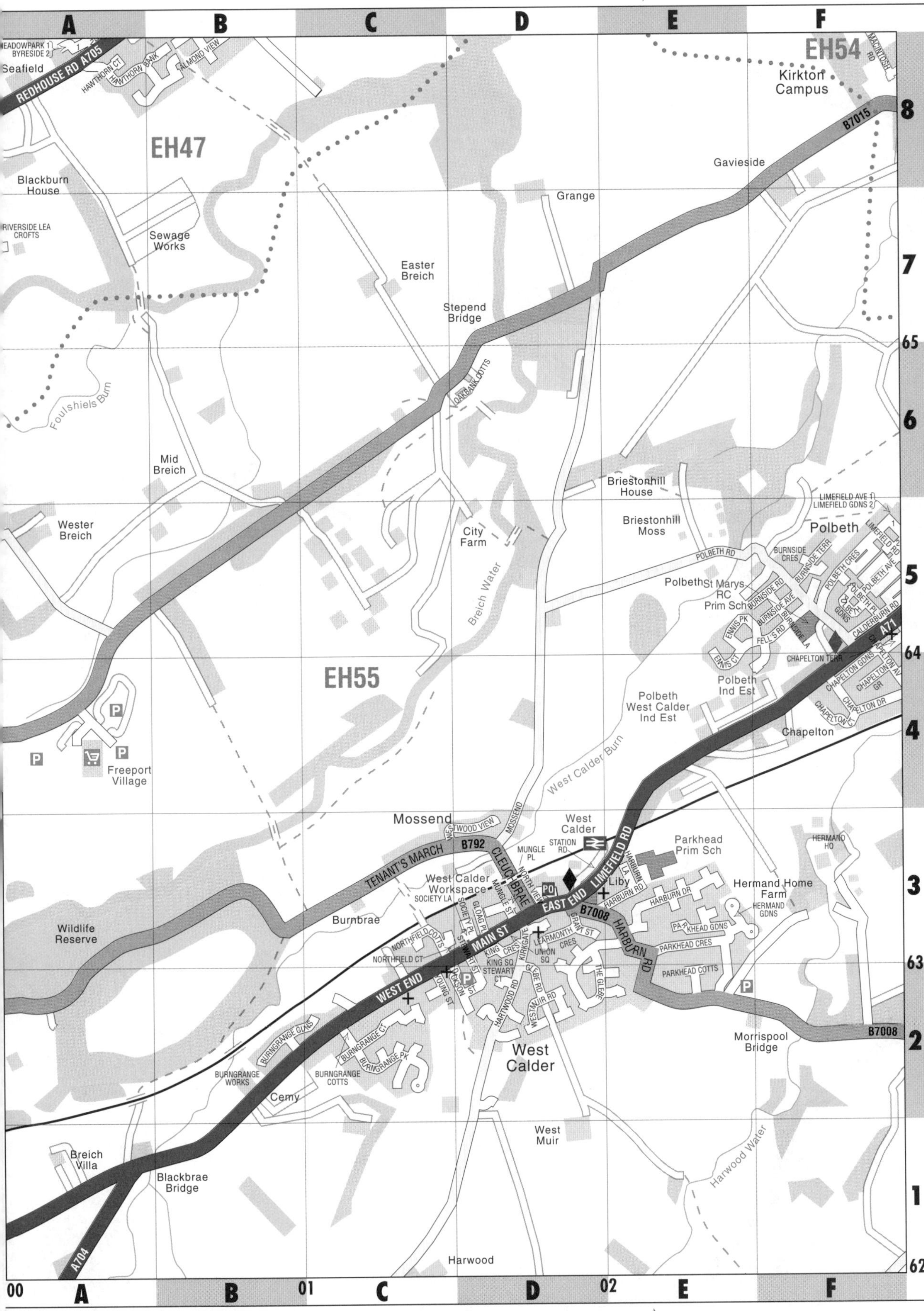
142
164
EH54
Kirkton Campus
EH47
Blackburn House
Sewage Works
Riverside Lea Crofts
Seafield
Redhouse Rd A705
Hawthorn Ct
Hawthorn Bank
Almond View
Gavieside
Grange
Easter Breich
Stepend Bridge
Oakbank Cotts
B7015
Foulshiels Burn
Mid Breich
Wester Breich
City Farm
Breich Water
Briestonhill House
Briestonhill Moss
Polbeth
Polbeth Rd
St Marys RC Prim Sch
Polbeth Ind Est
Polbeth West Calder Ind Est
Chapelton
A71
EH55
Freeport Village
West Calder Burn
Mossend
Tenant's March
B792
Cleuch Brae
Limefield Rd
Harburn Rd
East End
Main St
West End
West Calder Workspace
Society La
Burnbrae
West Calder
Station Rd
Liby
Parkhead Prim Sch
Hermand Home Farm
Parkhead Cres
Parkhead Cotts
B7008
Morrispool Bridge
Wildlife Reserve
Burngrange Works
Burngrange Cotts
Cemy
Breich Villa
Blackbrae Bridge
A704
West Muir
Harwood Water
Harwood
184
164

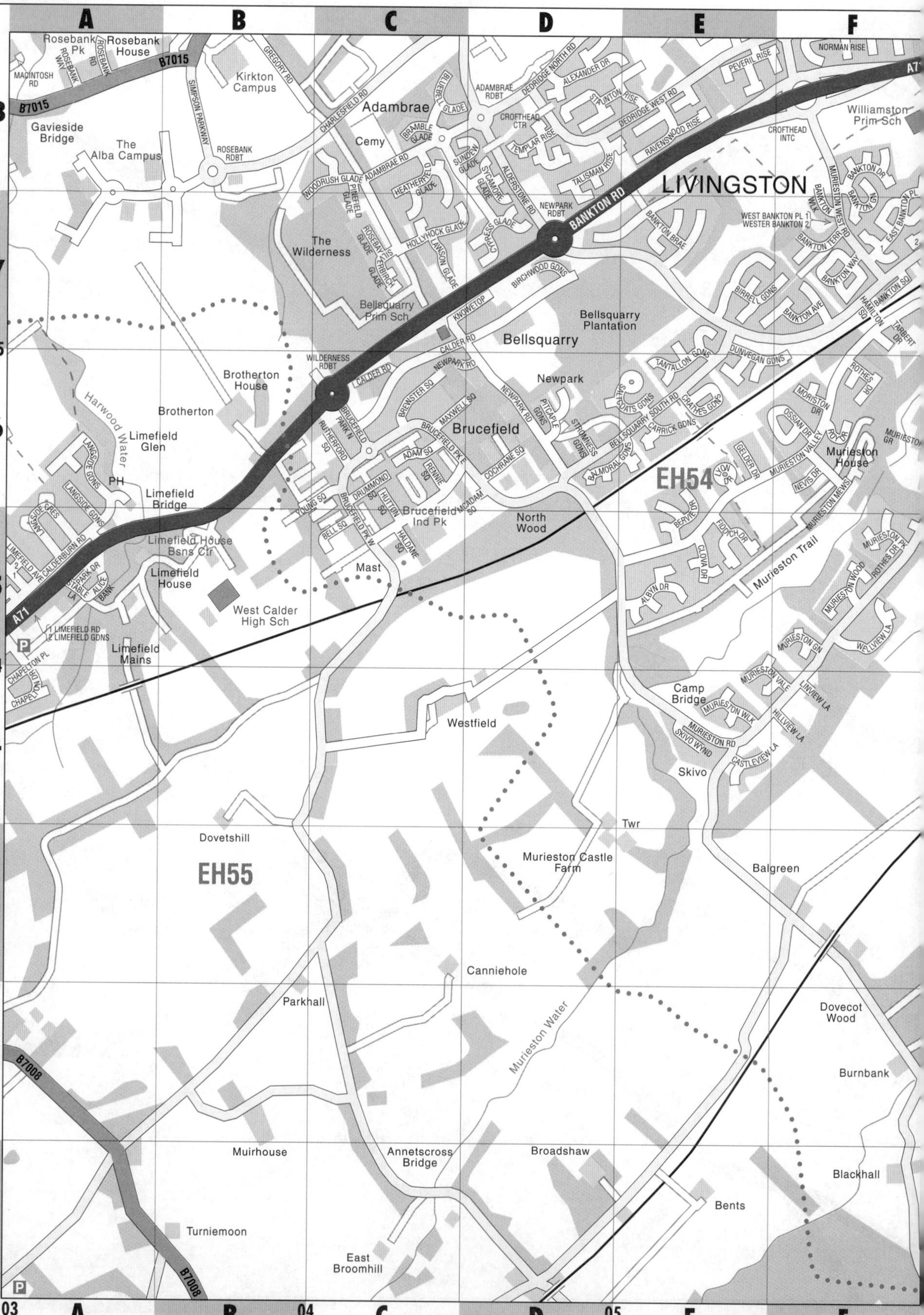
LIVINGSTON
Adambrae
Bellsquarry
Brucefield
Newpark
Bellsquarry Plantation
The Wilderness
Bellsquarry Prim Sch
Kirkton Campus
The Alba Campus
Gavieside Bridge
Rosebank Pk
Rosebank House
Brotherton House
Brotherton
Limefield Glen
Limefield Bridge
Limefield House Bsns Ctr
Limefield House
Limefield Mains
West Calder High Sch
Brucefield Ind Pk
North Wood
Mast
EH54
EH55
Williamston Prim Sch
Murieston House
Murieston Trail
Camp Bridge
Skivo
Westfield
Twr
Dovetshill
Murieston Castle Farm
Balgreen
Canniehole
Parkhall
Murieston Water
Dovecot Wood
Burnbank
Muirhouse
Annetscross Bridge
Broadshaw
Blackhall
Bents
Turniemoon
East Broomhill
Harwood Water
BANKTON RD
B7015
A71
B7008

144
166

A
B
C
D
E
F
BANKTON RD
BANKTON GDNS
BANKTON GR
BANKTON CT
EASTER BANKTON
BANKTON LA
BANKTON GLADE
BANKTON WOOD
1 BANKTON PK W
2 BANKTON PK E
Manse Covert
OAKBANK RDBT
A71
ASHWOOD CT
OAKBANK PARKWAY
Red Craig
Selms Tops
EH27
Williamston Bridge
MURIESTON EAST RD
Murieston Water
Oakbank Pk
OAKBANK PARK RD
OAKBANK PARK DR
Bankton House
3 EAST BANKTON PL
4 WESTER BANKTON
5 MURIESTON WEST RD
6 MURIESTON VALLEY
7 TEVIOT DR
Livingston South
Murieston Trail
Nether Williamston
MURIESTON WAY
MURIESTON GDNS
Blackraw
Selm Muir Reservoir (dis)
MURIESTON DR
MURIESTON RD
MURIESTON CT
EH54
Murieston
MURIESTON GR
Selm Muir Wood
EH53
Linhouse Water
Wellhead Farm
Corston
Morton Reservoir
Linn Caldron
Linnhouse Cottages
Morton
Mortonhill
Morton Burn
Linnhous
Linnhouse
Camilty Water
EH27
EH55
8
7
65
6
5
64
4
3
63
2
1
62
06
07
08

165
145

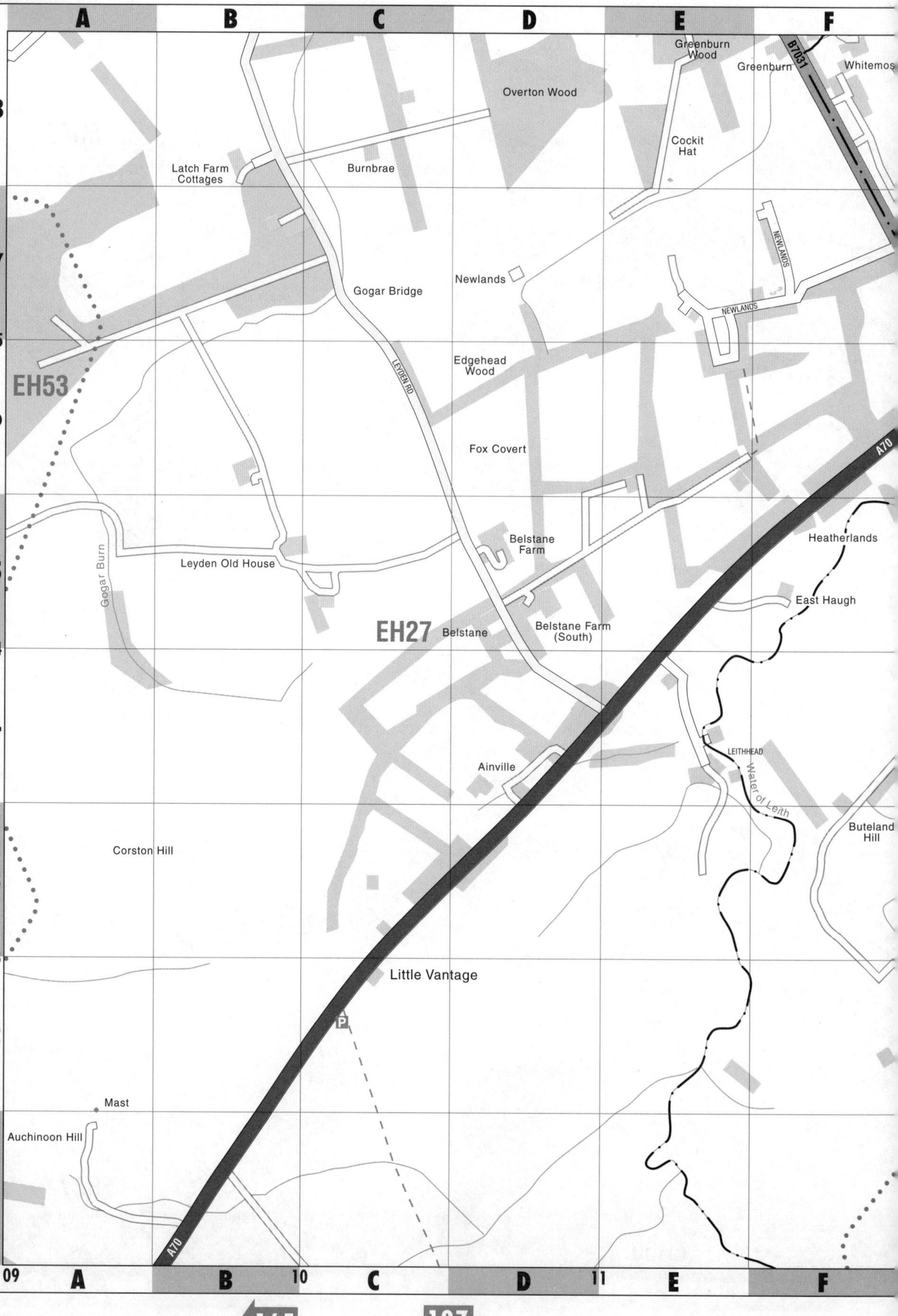
A
B
C
D
E
F
8
7
65
6
5
64
4
3
63
2
1
62
09
10
11
Greenburn Wood
Greenburn
Whitemos
B7031
Overton Wood
Cockit Hat
Latch Farm Cottages
Burnbrae
Newlands
Gogar Bridge
NEWLANDS
EH53
Edgehead Wood
LEYDEN RD
Fox Covert
A70
Heatherlands
Belstane Farm
Leyden Old House
Gogar Burn
East Haugh
EH27
Belstane
Belstane Farm (South)
Ainville
LEITHHEAD
Water of Leith
Buteland Hill
Corston Hill
Little Vantage
P
Mast
Auchinoon Hill

165
187

146
168
A
B
C
D
E
F
Boll-o-Bere
A70
Whelpside
Glenbrook House
GLENBROOK
Glenbrook
House of Cockburn
8
Airfield (dis)
Beechgrove Farm
7
Haughhead Farm
Cockburn
COCKBURNHILL RD
B7031
Inveroe
Ford
Water of Leith
65
House-o-Muir
Pirnie Hall
6
Buteland Farm
Cock Burn
EH27
Buteland House
Temple House
5
Cockburnhill
EH14
64
4
3
63
2
Bavelaw Burn
1
62
12
13
14
188
168

167
147

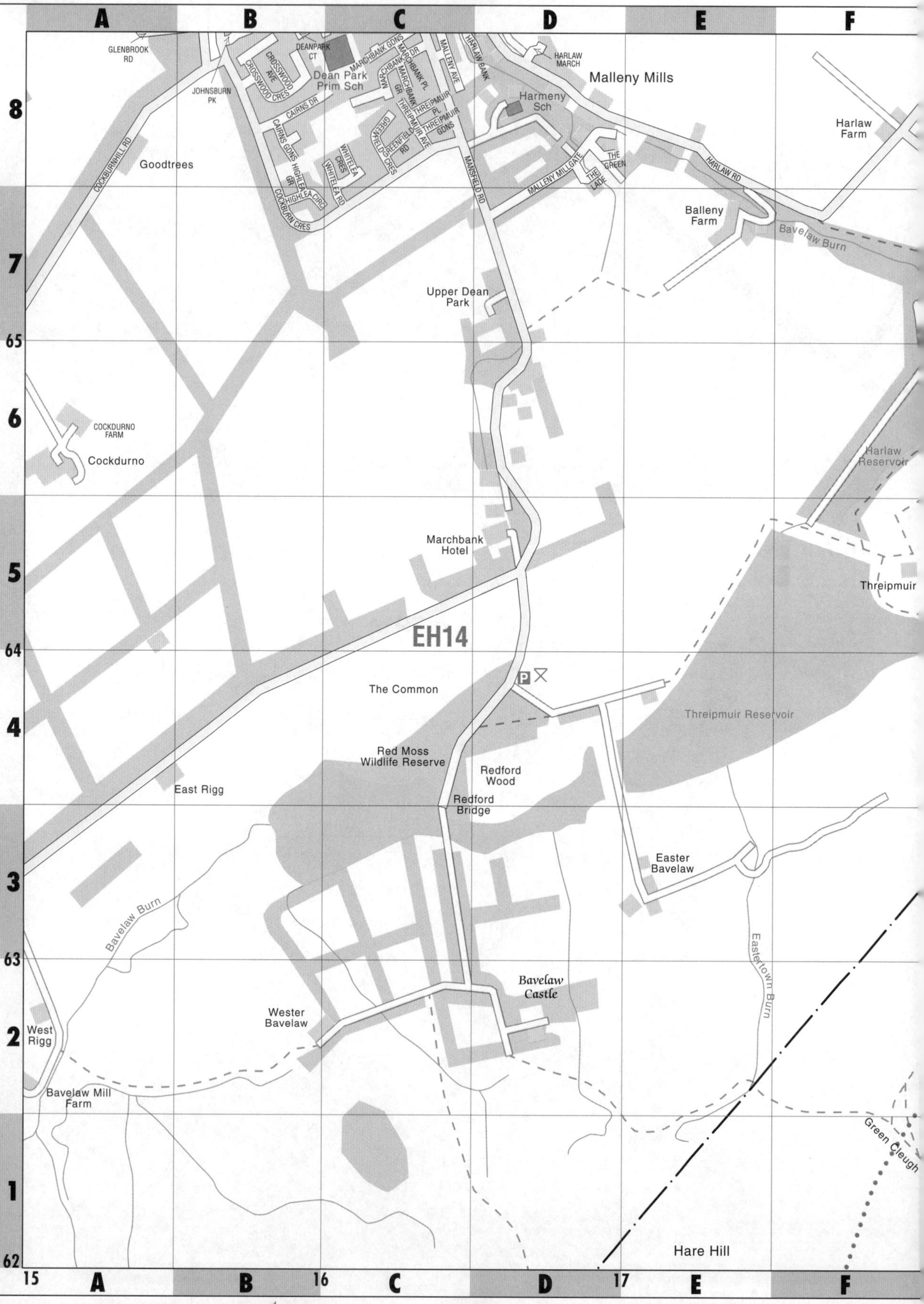
A
B
C
D
E
F
8
7
65
6
5
64
4
3
63
2
1
62
15
16
17
GLENBROOK RD
JOHNSBURN PK
DEANPARK CT
Dean Park Prim Sch
HARLAW MARCH
Malleny Mills
Harmeny Sch
Harlaw Farm
COCKBURNHILL RD
Goodtrees
MANSFIELD RD
MALLENY MILLGATE
HARLAW RD
Balleny Farm
Bavelaw Burn
Upper Dean Park
COCKDURNO FARM
Cockdurno
Harlaw Reservoir
Marchbank Hotel
Threipmuir
EH14
The Common
Threipmuir Reservoir
Red Moss Wildlife Reserve
Redford Wood
Redford Bridge
East Rigg
Easter Bavelaw
Bavelaw Burn
Eastertown Burn
Bavelaw Castle
Wester Bavelaw
West Rigg
Bavelaw Mill Farm
Green Cleugh
Hare Hill

167
189

148
170

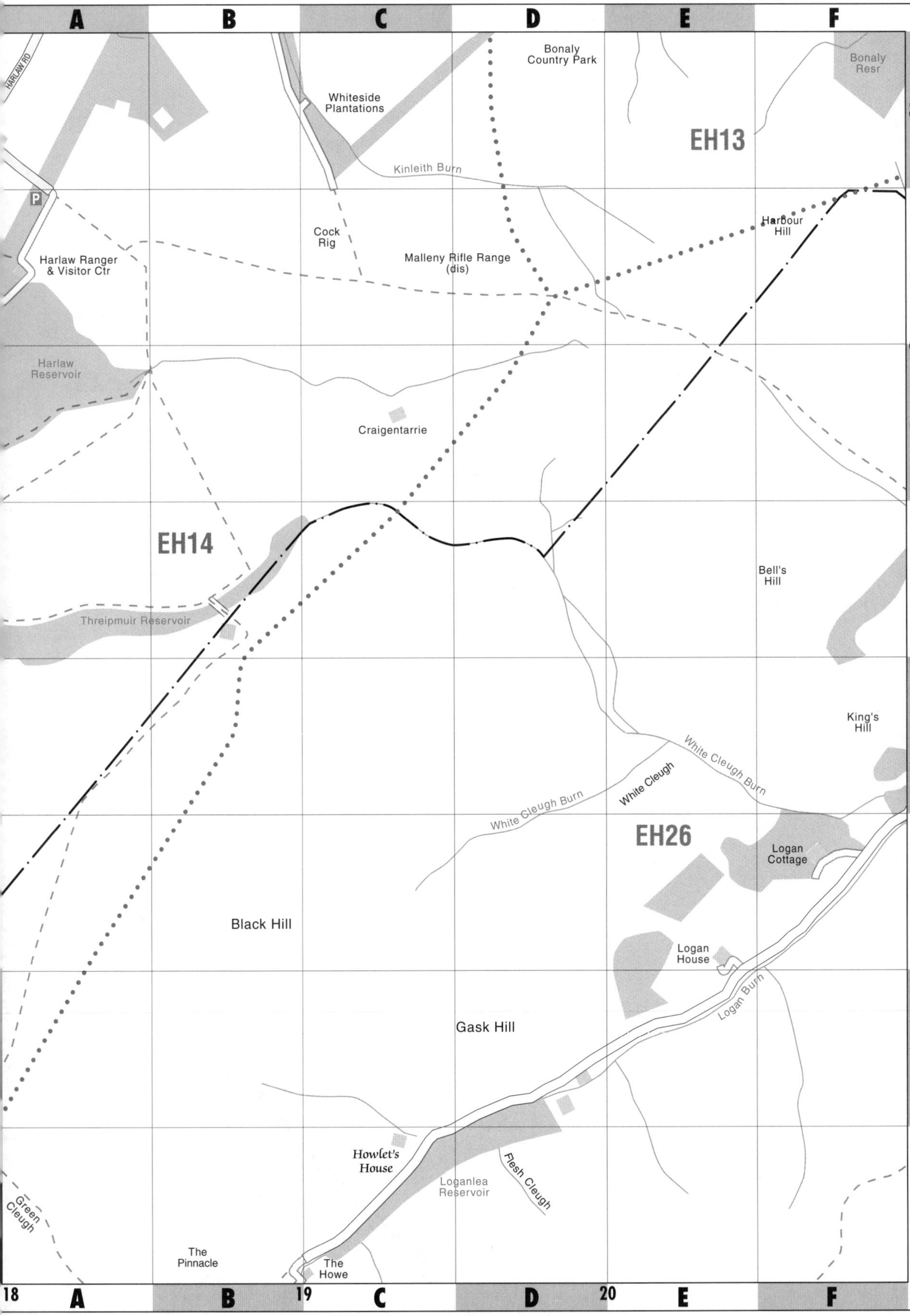
A
B
C
D
E
F
HARLAW RD
P
Bonaly
Country Park
Bonaly
Resr
Whiteside
Plantations
EH13
8
Kinleith Burn
Cock
Rig
Harbour
Hill
Harlaw Ranger
& Visitor Ctr
Malleny Rifle Range
(dis)
7
65
Harlaw
Reservoir
Craigentarrie
6
EH14
Bell's
Hill
5
Threipmuir Reservoir
64
King's
Hill
4
White Cleugh Burn
White Cleugh
White Cleugh Burn
EH26
Logan
Cottage
3
Black Hill
Logan
House
63
Logan Burn
Gask Hill
2
Howlet's
House
Loganlea
Reservoir
Flesh Cleugh
Green
Cleugh
1
The
Pinnacle
The
Howe
62
18
19
20

190
170

169
149

A
B
C
D
E
F
8
7
65
6
5
64
4
3
63
2
1
62
21
22
23
EH13
Capelaw Hill
Caerketton Hill
EH10
Boghall Burn
Fala Knowe
Kirk Burn
Woodhouselee Hill
Castlelaw Hill
Knightfield Rig
DANGER AREA
Woodhouselee
Castlelaw Firing Ranges
EH26
Kirk Bridge
Castle Knowe
Easter Howgate
Kirkton
Glencorse Reservoir
Castlelaw Fort & Earth House
P
Breakwater
Crosshouse
A702
Castlelaw
Glen Cottage
The Glen
Flotterstone Visitor Ctr
P
Crawley Cottages
Glencorse Burn
Flotterstone Bridge
PH
Turnhouse Hill
Turnhouse
HOUSE O' MUIR
Glencorse Mains
Rullion Green Cottage
White Craig Heads
MAURICEWOOD RD
BELWOOD RD
Belwood House
Mauricewood Mains
Nursery
Mast
A702

169
191

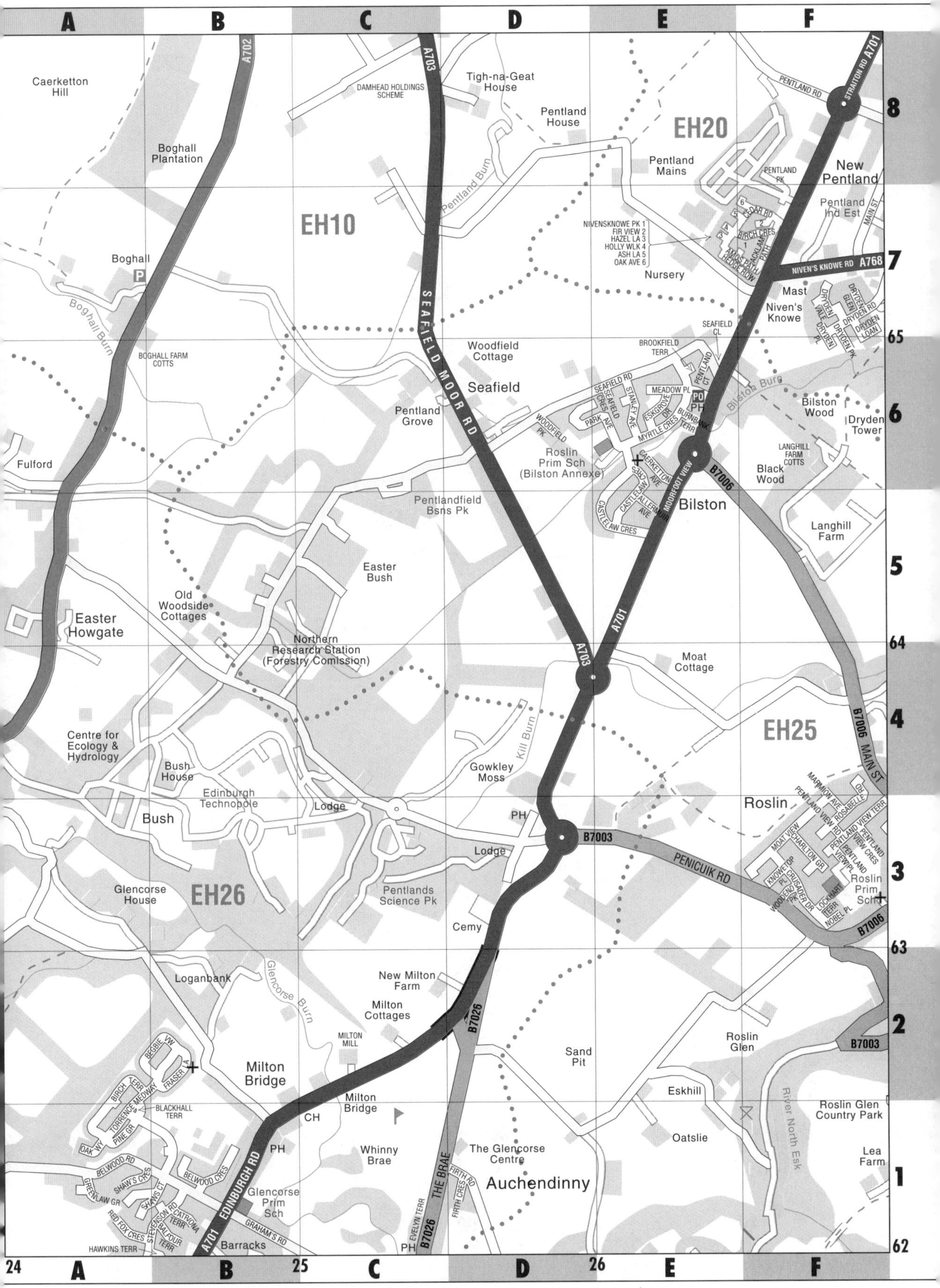
150
172
A B C D E F
Caerketton Hill
Boghall Plantation
Tigh-na-Geat House
Pentland House
EH20
Pentland Mains
New Pentland
Pentland Ind Est
EH10
Boghall
Boghall Burn
BOGHALL FARM COTTS
Woodfield Cottage
Seafield
Pentland Grove
SEAFIELD MOOR RD
Roslin Prim Sch (Bilston Annexe)
Bilston
Bilston Wood
Dryden Tower
Black Wood
Langhill Farm
Fulford
Pentlandfield Bsns Pk
Easter Bush
Old Woodside Cottages
Easter Howgate
Northern Research Station (Forestry Comission)
Moat Cottage
EH25
Centre for Ecology & Hydrology
Bush House
Edinburgh Technopole
Bush
Lodge
Gowkley Moss
Roslin
Glencorse House
EH26
Pentlands Science Pk
Cemy
PENICUIK RD
Roslin Prim Sch
Loganbank
New Milton Farm
Milton Cottages
Milton Bridge
Sand Pit
Roslin Glen
Eskhill
Oatslie
Roslin Glen Country Park
Whinny Brae
The Glencorse Centre
Auchendinny
Lea Farm
Glencorse Prim Sch
Barracks
EDINBURGH RD
THE BRAE
River North Esk
A702 A703 A701 A768 B7006 B7003 B7026
8 7 65 6 5 64 4 3 63 2 1 62
24 25 26
192
172

171
151

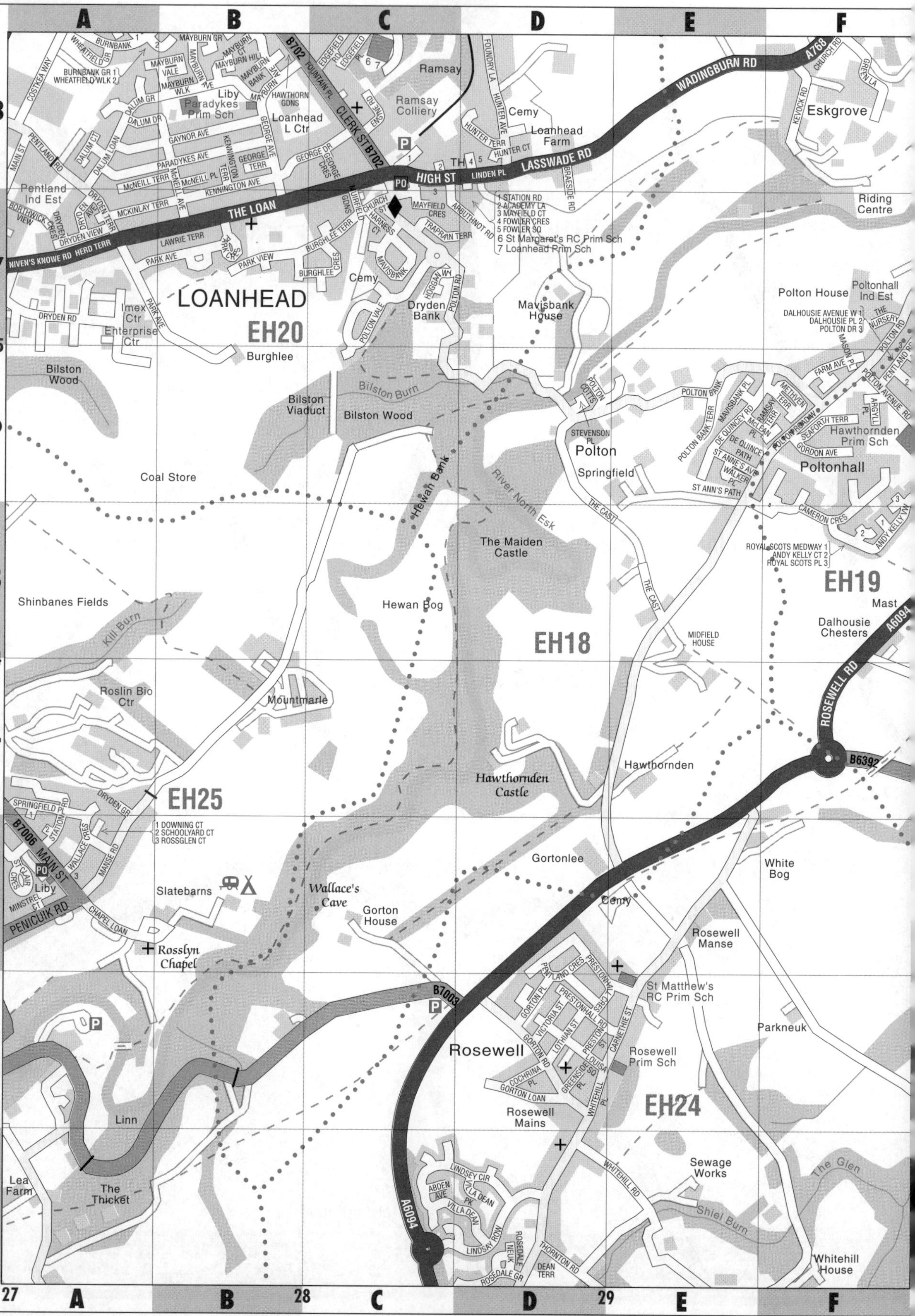
A
B
C
D
E
F
8
7
65
6
5
64
4
3
63
2
1
62
27
28
29
LOANHEAD
EH20
EH18
EH19
EH25
EH24
BURNBANK
WHEATFIELD
MAYBURN GR
MAYBURN CT
MAYBURN HILL
MAYBURN VALE
MAYBURN WLK
MAYBURN AVE
MAYBURN BANK
MAYBURN TERR
BURNBANK GR 1
WHEATFIELD WLK 2
COSTKEA WAY
Liby
Paradykes Prim Sch
HAWTHORN GDNS
Loanhead L Ctr
DALUM GR
DALUM DR
DALUM CT
DALUM LOAN
GAYNOR AVE
PARADYKES AVE
KENNINGTON TERR
GEORGE AVE
GEORGE TERR
GEORGE DR
GEORGE CRES
McNEILL TERR
McNEILL PL
McNEILL AVE
KENNINGTON AVE
MAIN ST
PENTLAND RD
Pentland Ind Est
BORTHWICK VIEW
DRYDEN CRES
DRYDEN AVE
DRYDEN TERR
DRYDEN VIEW
McKINLAY TERR
THE LOAN
NIVEN'S KNOWE RD
HERD TERR
LAWRIE TERR
PARK AVE
PARK VIEW
BURGHLEE TERR
BURGHLEE CRES
B702
FOUNTAIN PL
EDGEFIELD RD
EDGEFIELD
CLERK ST
ENGINE RD
Ramsay
Ramsay Colliery
FOUNDRY LA
HUNTER AVE
HUNTER TERR
HUNTER CT
Cemy
Loanhead Farm
TH
HIGH ST
LINDEN PL
LASSWADE RD
BRAESIDE RD
WADINGBURN RD
A768
CHURCH RD
GREEN LA
KEVOCK RD
Eskgrove
Riding Centre
MUIRFIELD GDNS
CHURCH ST
HARNESS CT
MAYFIELD CRES
TRAPRAIN TERR
ARBUTHNOT RD
1 STATION RD
2 ACADEMY LA
3 MAYFIELD CT
4 FOWLER CRES
5 FOWLER SQ
6 St Margaret's RC Prim Sch
7 Loanhead Prim Sch
MAVISBANK
Cemy
Dryden Bank
HOGGAN WAY
POLTON RD
POLTON VALE
DRYDEN RD
Imex Ctr
Enterprise Ctr
Burghlee
Mavisbank House
Polton House
Poltonhall Ind Est
DALHOUSIE AVENUE W 1
DALHOUSIE PL 2
POLTON DR 3
THE NURSERY
MASON PL
FARM AVE
PENTLAND RD
POLTON AVENUE RD
Bilston Wood
Bilston Burn
Bilston Viaduct
Bilston Wood
POLTON COTTS
POLTON BANK
STEVENSON PL
Polton
Springfield
MAVISBANK PL
POLTON BANK TERR
DE QUINCEY RD
DE QUINCEY PATH
McLEAN PL
RAMSAY TERR
METHVEN TERR
ST ANNE'S AVE
WALKER PL
ST ANN'S PATH
SEAFORTH TERR
ARGYLL PL
GORDON AVE
Hawthornden Prim Sch
Poltonhall
CAMERON CRES
ROYAL SCOTS MEDWAY 1
ANDY KELLY CT 2
ROYAL SCOTS PL 3
ANDY KELLY VW
Coal Store
Hewan Bank
River North Esk
THE CAST
The Maiden Castle
Shinbanes Fields
Hewan Bog
Mast
Dalhousie Chesters
A6094
Kill Burn
MIDFIELD HOUSE
Roslin Bio Ctr
Mountmarle
ROSEWELL RD
B6392
Hawthornden
Hawthornden Castle
SPRINGFIELD PL
DRYDEN GR
STATION RD
WALLACE CRES
MANSE RD
1 DOWNING CT
2 SCHOOLYARD CT
3 ROSSGLEN CT
B7006
MAIN ST
ST CLAIR CRES
Liby
MINSTREL CT
PENICUIK RD
Slatebarns
Wallace's Cave
Gortonlee
White Bog
Cemy
Gorton House
CHAPEL LOAN
Rosslyn Chapel
Rosewell Manse
B7003
PENTLAND CRES
PRESTONHALL CRES
GORTON PL
VICTORIA ST
PRESTONHALL RD
CARNETHIE ST
St Matthew's RC Prim Sch
Parkneuk
Rosewell
GORTON RD
LOTHIAN ST
PRESTON ST
LOUISA SQ
Rosewell Prim Sch
COCHRINA PL
GORTON LOAN
GREENSIDE PL
WHITEHILL PL
Rosewell Mains
Linn
Lea Farm
The Thicket
A6094
LINDSEY CIR
ABDEN AVE
VILLA DEAN PK
VILLA DEAN
LINDSAY ROW
NEUK
ROSEDALE GR
DEAN TERR
THORNTON RD
WHITEHILL RD
Sewage Works
Shiel Burn
The Glen
Whitehill House

171
193

152
174

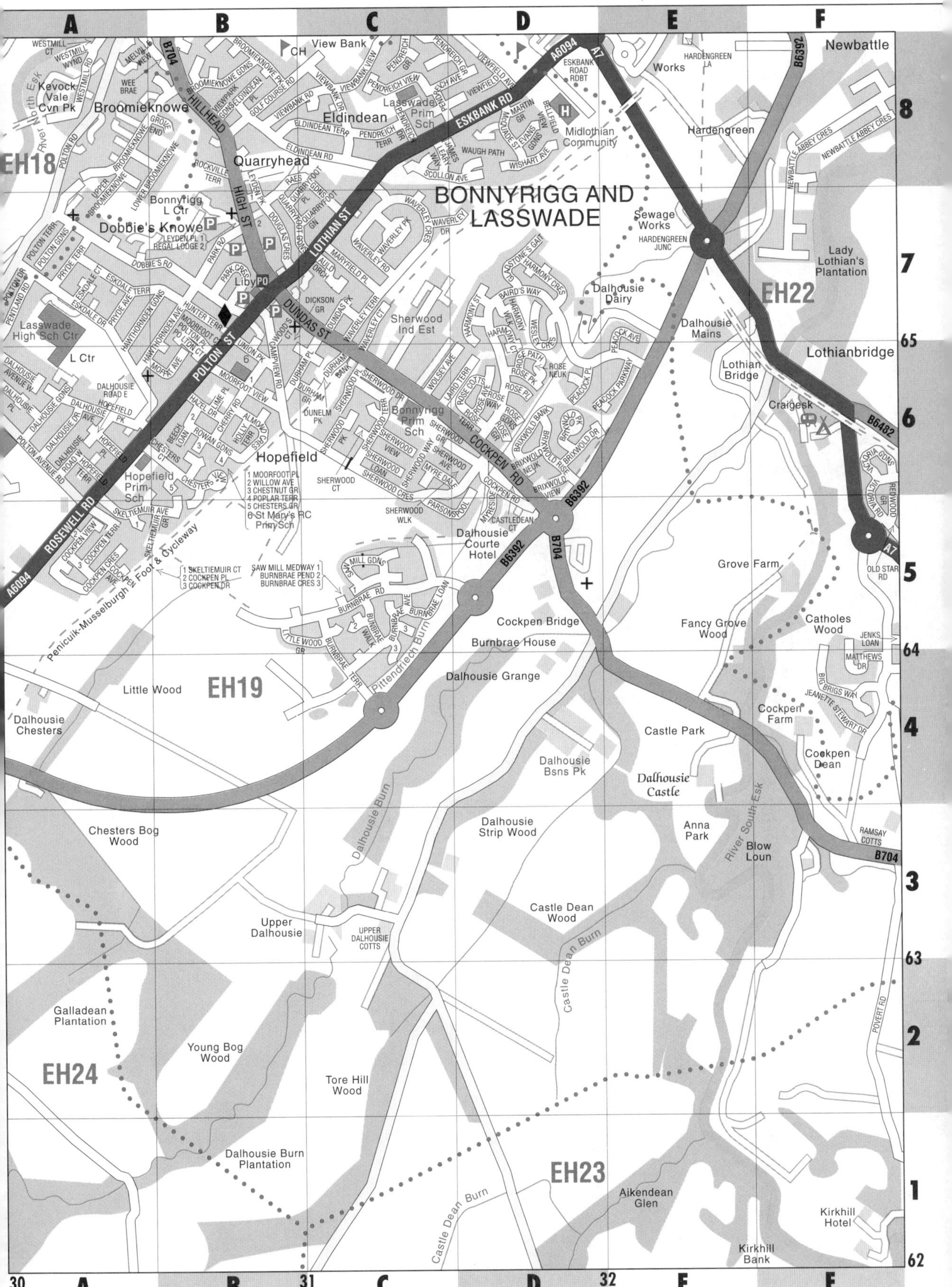

194
174

173
153

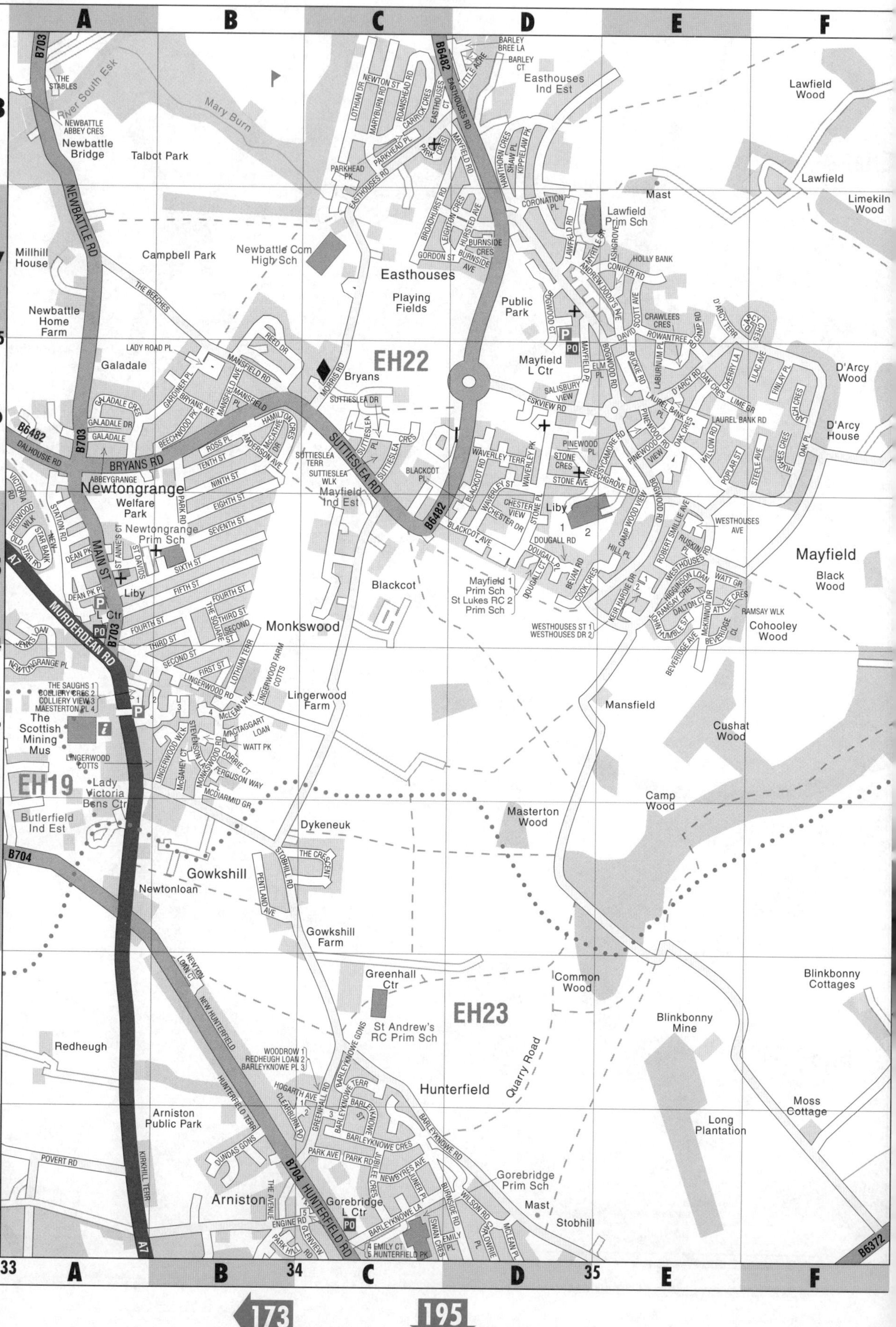
Newbattle Bridge
Talbot Park
Mary Burn
River South Esk
Millhill House
Campbell Park
Newbattle Com High Sch
Easthouses
Easthouses Ind Est
Playing Fields
Public Park
Lawfield Wood
Lawfield
Mast
Lawfield Prim Sch
Limekiln Wood
Newbattle Home Farm
Galadale
Bryans
EH22
Mayfield L Ctr
D'Arcy Wood
D'Arcy House
Newtongrange
Welfare Park
Newtongrange Prim Sch
Mayfield Ind Est
Liby
L Ctr
Blackcot
Mayfield 1 Prim Sch
St Lukes RC 2 Prim Sch
Mayfield
Black Wood
Monkswood
Cohooley Wood
Lingerwood Farm
Mansfield
The Scottish Mining Mus
Cushat Wood
EH19
Lady Victoria Bsns Ctr
Butlerfield Ind Est
Masterton Wood
Camp Wood
Dykeneuk
Gowkshill
Newtonloan
Gowkshill Farm
Greenhall Ctr
Common Wood
Blinkbonny Cottages
EH23
St Andrew's RC Prim Sch
Blinkbonny Mine
Redheugh
Hunterfield
Quarry Road
Arniston Public Park
Long Plantation
Moss Cottage
Arniston
Gorebridge L Ctr
Gorebridge Prim Sch
Mast
Stobhill
NEWBATTLE RD
BRYANS RD
MAIN ST
MURDERDEAN RD
SUTTIESLEA RD
EASTHOUSES RD
MAYFIELD RD
NEW HUNTERFIELD
HUNTERFIELD RD
KIRKHILL TERR
POVERT RD
BARLEYKNOWE RD
B703
B6482
A7
B704
B6372
33
34
35
62
63
64
65
A
B
C
D
E
F
1
2
3
4
5
6
7
8

173
195

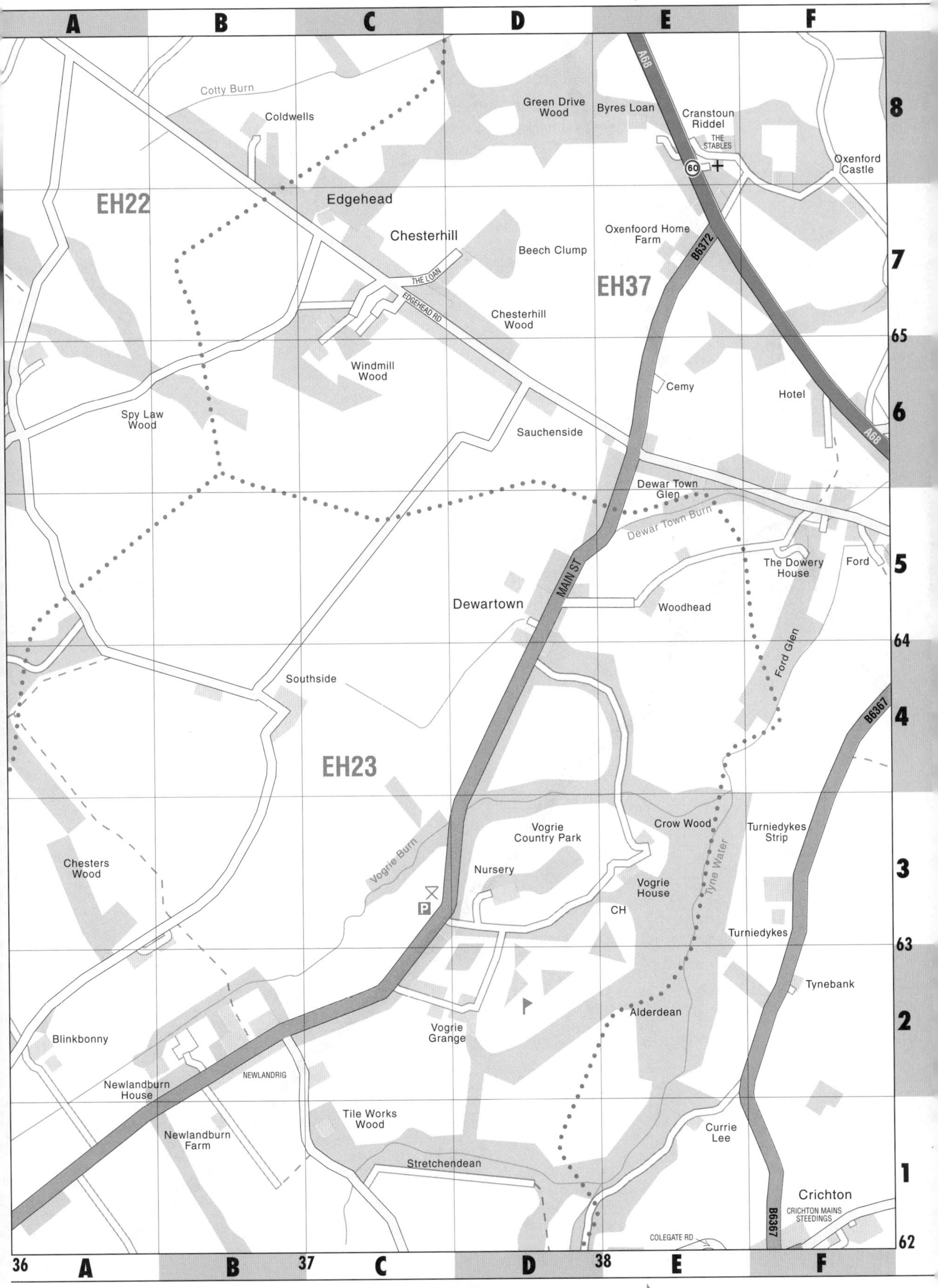
154
176
A
B
C
D
E
F
8
7
65
6
5
64
4
3
63
2
1
62
36
37
38
Cotty Burn
Coldwells
Green Drive Wood
Byres Loan
Cranstoun Riddel
THE STABLES
60
Oxenford Castle
A68
EH22
Edgehead
Chesterhill
THE LOAN
EDGEHEAD RD
Beech Clump
Oxenfoord Home Farm
B6372
EH37
Chesterhill Wood
Windmill Wood
Cemy
Hotel
Spy Law Wood
Sauchenside
Dewar Town Glen
Dewar Town Burn
The Dowery House
Ford
MAIN ST
Dewartown
Woodhead
Ford Glen
Southside
B6367
EH23
Crow Wood
Turniedykes Strip
Vogrie Country Park
Vogrie Burn
Chesters Wood
Nursery
Tyne Water
Vogrie House
P
CH
Turniedykes
Tynebank
Alderdean
Vogrie Grange
Blinkbonny
NEWLANDRIG
Newlandburn House
Tile Works Wood
Newlandburn Farm
Currie Lee
Stretchendean
Crichton
CRICHTON MAINS STEEDINGS
COLEGATE RD
196
176

175 155

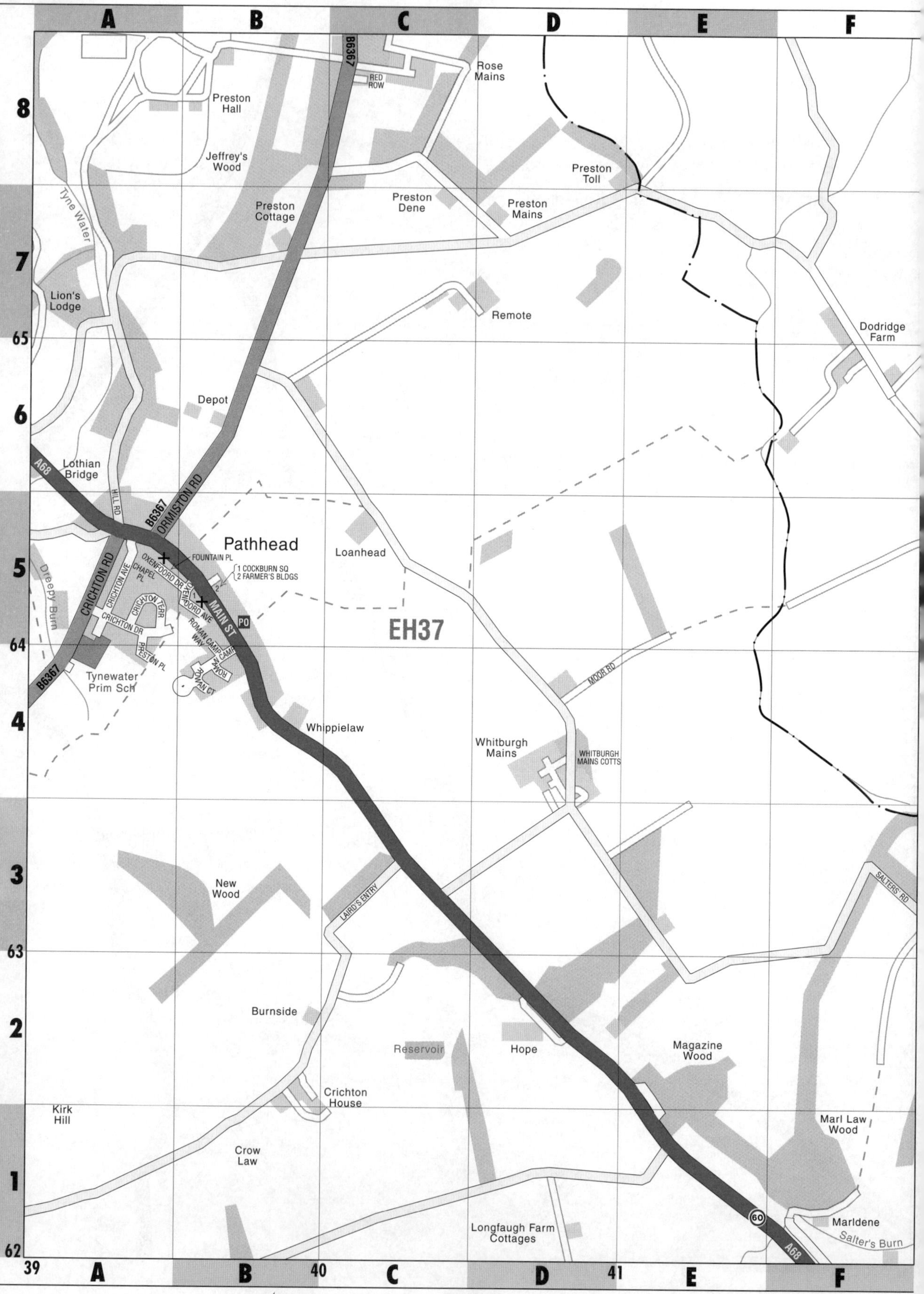
A B C D E F
8 7 65 6 5 64 4 3 63 2 1 62
39 40 41
B6367
RED ROW
Rose Mains
Preston Hall
Jeffrey's Wood
Preston Toll
Tyne Water
Preston Cottage
Preston Dene
Preston Mains
Lion's Lodge
Remote
Dodridge Farm
Depot
Lothian Bridge
A68
HILL RD
ORMISTON RD
Pathhead
FOUNTAIN PL
1 COCKBURN SQ
2 FARMER'S BLDGS
Loanhead
CRICHTON RD
CRICHTON AVE
CHAPEL PL
OXENFOORD DR
OXENFOORD AVE
MAIN ST
PO
Dreepy Burn
CRICHTON TERR
CRICHTON DR
ROMAN CAMP WAY
ROMAN CAMP
PRESTON PL
ROMAN CT
EH37
Tynewater Prim Sch
MOOR RD
Whippielaw
Whitburgh Mains
WHITBURGH MAINS COTTS
New Wood
LAIRD'S ENTRY
SALTERS' RD
Burnside
Reservoir
Hope
Magazine Wood
Crichton House
Kirk Hill
Marl Law Wood
Crow Law
60
Longfaugh Farm Cottages
Marldene
Salter's Burn

175 197

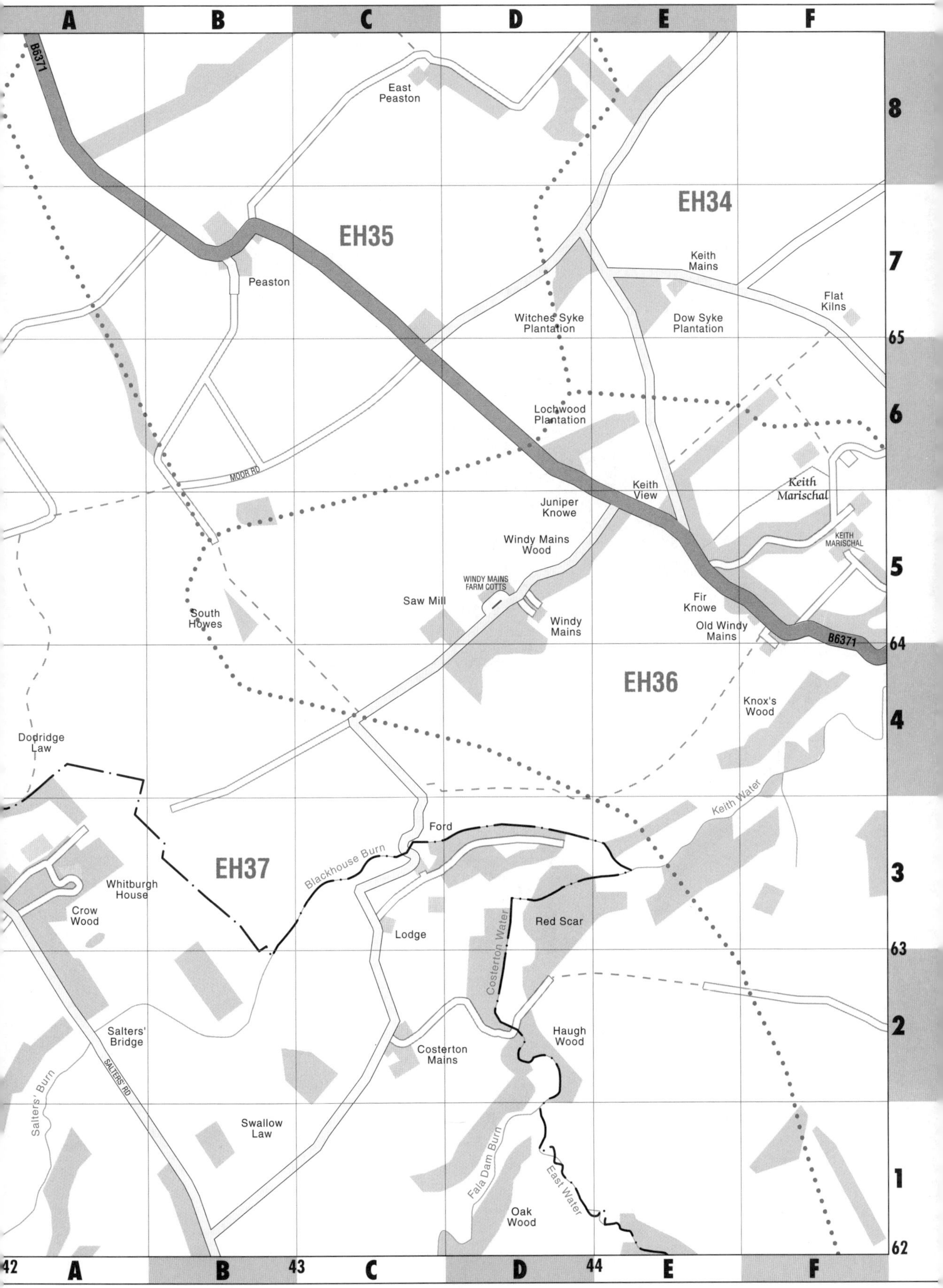
A
B
C
D
E
F
8
7
65
6
5
64
4
3
63
2
1
62
42
43
44
B6371
East Peaston
EH35
EH34
Peaston
Keith Mains
Flat Kilns
Witches Syke Plantation
Dow Syke Plantation
Lochwood Plantation
MOOR RD
Keith View
Keith Marischal
Juniper Knowe
Windy Mains Wood
KEITH MARISCHAL
WINDY MAINS FARM COTTS
Saw Mill
Windy Mains
Fir Knowe
Old Windy Mains
South Howes
EH36
Knox's Wood
Dodridge Law
Keith Water
Ford
Blackhouse Burn
EH37
Whitburgh House
Crow Wood
Red Scar
Lodge
Costerton Water
Haugh Wood
Salters' Bridge
Costerton Mains
SALTERS' RD
Salters' Burn
Swallow Law
Fala Dam Burn
East Water
Oak Wood

177 157 220

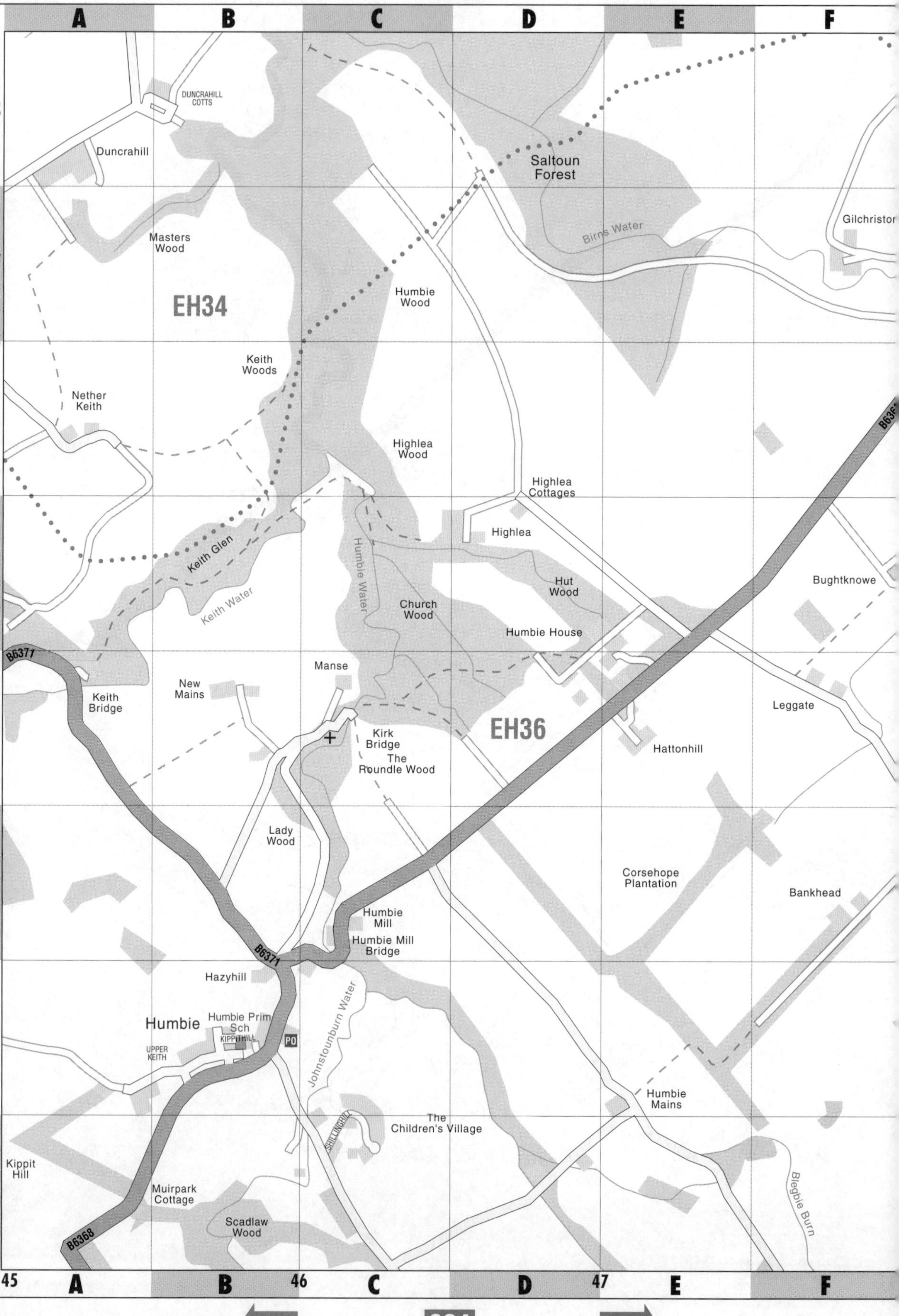

177 224 220

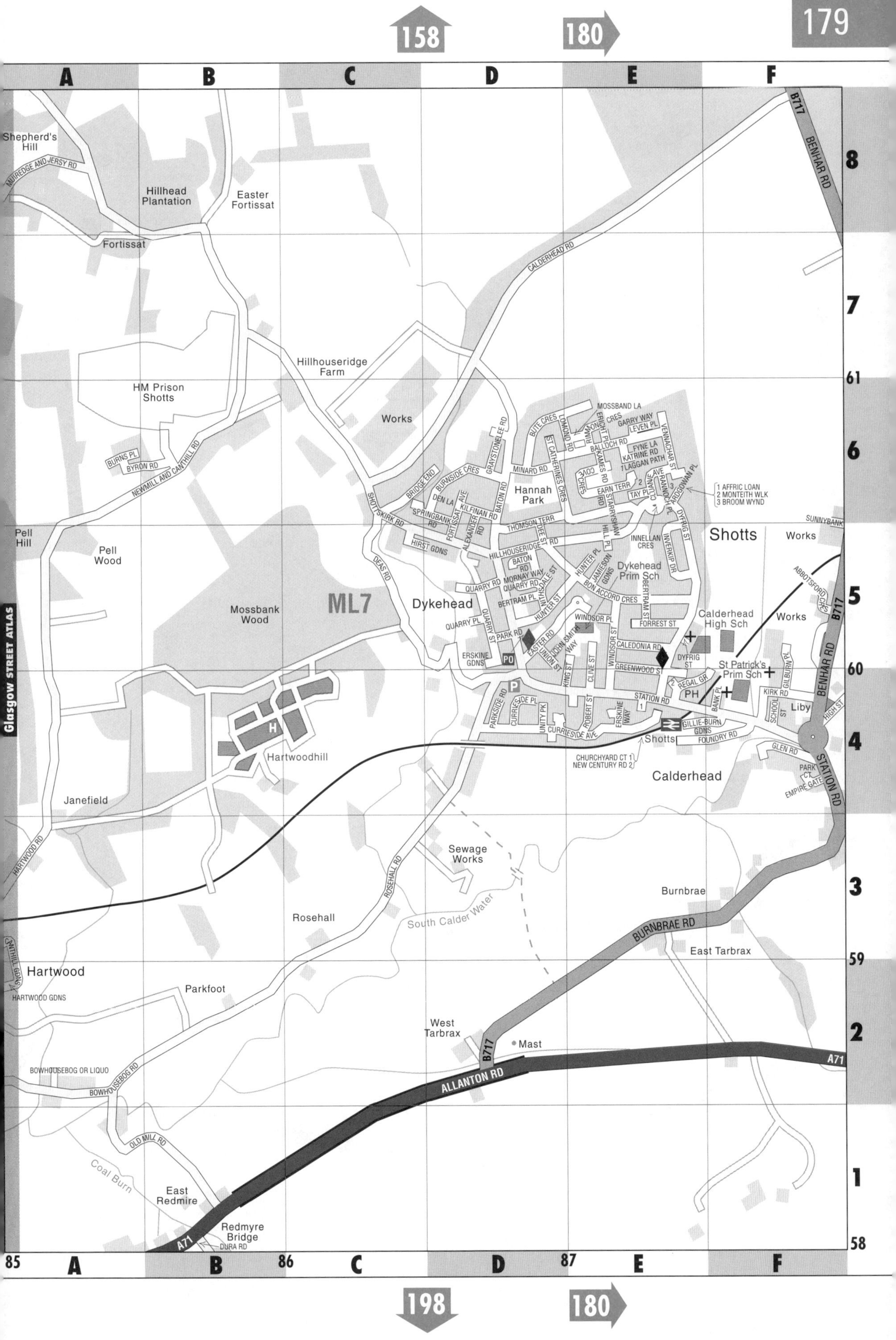
158
180
Shepherd's Hill
Hillhead Plantation
Easter Fortissat
Fortissat
MUIREDGE AND JERSY RD
CALDERHEAD RD
B717
BENHAR RD
Hillhouseridge Farm
HM Prison Shotts
Works
BURNS PL
BYRON RD
NEWMILL AND CANTHILL RD
Hannah Park
Pell Hill
Pell Wood
Mossbank Wood
ML7
Dykehead
Shotts
Works
Dykehead Prim Sch
Calderhead High Sch
St Patrick's Prim Sch
Works
Liby
1 AFFRIC LOAN
2 MONTEITH WLK
3 BROOM WYND
CHURCHYARD CT 1
NEW CENTURY RD 2
Hartwoodhill
Janefield
Calderhead
STATION RD
Sewage Works
Burnbrae
BURNBRAE RD
East Tarbrax
Rosehall
ROSEHALL RD
South Calder Water
Hartwood
HARTWOOD RD
HARTWOOD GDNS
Parkfoot
West Tarbrax
Mast
A71
ALLANTON RD
BOWHOUSEBOG OR LIQUO
BOWHOUSEBOG RD
OLD MILL RD
Coal Burn
East Redmire
Redmyre Bridge
DURA RD
Glasgow STREET ATLAS
198
180

179
159

A
B
C
D
E
F
8
7
61
6
5
60
4
3
59
2
1
58
88
89
90
B717
BENHAR RD
CH
Starryshaw Farm
South Calder Water
Spoil Heap
Stanebent
Cairneyhead
ML7
Stane
GRAY ST
HIGH ST
STABLE RD
CEDAR WYND
ROWAN CRES
HAZEL GR
CHARLES ST
TORBOTHIE RD
CLYDE DR
KELVIN DR
CALDER DR
HAWTHORN DR
HERBISON CRES
SOUTHFIELD AVE
SOUTHFIELD RD
SOUTHFIELD CRES
Stane Prim Sch
Torbothie
STANE GR
MANSE RD
CEMETERY RD
B7010
MAIN ST
CHARLOTTE ST
NEVIS PL
GARTEN DR
ELGOL PATH
Cemy
1 ETIVE WLK
2 UIG WAY
3 GAIR WYND
4 BOWMORE WLK
5 TORRIN LOAN
6 SPRINGHILL VIEW
7 DORNIE WYND
8 MORAR WAY
9 COIRE LOAN
10 SUNA PATH
11 SALEN LOAN
PO
SANDYHILL AVE
REDHAWS RD
SANDYVALE PL
LOCHABER CRES
TULLOCH RD
WYVIS PL
ONICH PL
APPIN TERR
SHIEL GDNS
NAVAR CT
MELFORD AVE
LAGGAN AVE
LANSDOWNE CRES
BRIDGE PL
KNOLL CROFT RD
HUNTLY TERR
Stane
BLINNY CT 1
TARBRAX PATH 2
SPRINGHILL RD
Springhill
B7010
EH47
BLACKHALL ST
BROWN ST
BELMONT DR
BERRYHILL PL
BEECHMOUNT CT
MULDRON TERR
ELMWOOD RD
LARCHFIELD PATH
NORTHFIELD AVE
Works
Springhill
STANE RD
SPRINGHILL AND LEADLOCH RD
HEADLESSCROSS RD B715
Knowton Farm
A71
Works
Lingore Linn
A71

179
199

160
182

ML7
Fauldhouse Moor
Moss
Tippet Knowe
Fauldhouse Hills
St John the Baptist RC Prim Sch
Liby
PO
Falla Hill Prim Sch
PH
Sports Ground
Greenburn
Benhar Junction
Warehouse
Fauldhouse Bsns Ctr
CH
Fauldhouse
Cemy
Leadloch
Braehead
Fauldhouse
Meadowfoot
SHOTTS RD
EH47
Wayside
Levenseat Ind Est
A71
Works
Meikle Eldrick
East Badallan
Breich Water
SPRINGHILL AND LEADLOCH RD
Wee Eldrick
West Badallan
Lingore Linn
Muldron Bridge
ML11
Shafts (dis)
Headlesscross
Risland Knowes
Muldron
Kitchen Linn
B715
B7010
B7015
LANRIGG RD
MAIN ST
SHEEPHOUSEHILL
MCKINNON RD
NORTH RD
LANRIGG AVE
SOUTH RD
PARK VIEW
EASTWOOD PK
LANRIGG CT
EASTFIELD VIEW
VICTORIA PK
VICTORIA RD
EASTFIELD RD
SCOTT PL
CROFTOOT DR
BARTON CT
BARTON TERR
KIRKHILL CT
BURNSIDE CRES
BELLONA TERR
OGILVY CRES
GREENWELL ST
QUARRY RD
EARLS PL
BURNSIDE TERR
BLACKFAULDS CT
WILLOW PK
WILLOW AVE
WILLOW GR
WILLOW VIEW
WILLOW BRAE
BURNBRAE
GOWANBRAE
GREENBURN RD
FALLA HILL PL
HARTHILL RD
CHURCH PL
GREENHILL CT
PARK PARADE
GLEBE CT
BADALLAN PL
ELDRICK LA
ELDRICK VIEW
ELDRICK CRES
ELDRICK AVE
THORNTON PL
FALLAS PL
WALKER RD
CALEDONIAN RD
PORTLAND PL
BRAESIDE CRES
CEMETERY RD
CALEDONIAN TERR
CADELL PL
BRIDGE ST
MEADOW CRES
BLACKFAULDS DR
A B C D E F
8 7 61 6 5 60 4 3 59 2 1 58
91 92 93

200
182

181
161

A
B
C
D
E
F
8
7
61
6
5
60
4
3
59
2
1
58
94
95
96
B7010
A706
B7015
Northfield
Burnhead
STONEHEAP CROFTS
Stoneheap
Blackhill
Nursery
Holehouseburn
Blackhill Bridge
Breich Water
Rashiehill
EH47
SHEEPHOUSEHILL
BREICHWATER PL
Breich Bridge
Glenburn
A71
RASHIEHILL TERR
RASHIEHILL CRES
Craighead
CROFTFOOT DR
Breich
BREICH TERR
WOODMUIR PL
WOODMUIR RD
Woodmuir Prim Sch
BLINKBONNY GDNS
Breich
East Handaxwood
Hotel
Croftfoot
Sewage Works
Woodmuir Burn
Woodmuir Farm
West Handaxwood
EH55
A704
Leven Seat
Works
Levenseat House
Linn Bridge
Longford Burn
Miller's Moss
Woodmuir Plantation
Rashiehill Muir
ML11
Quarry
A704
A706

162
184

A
B
C
D
E
F
EH47
ROSS CT
MOORELAND GDNS
Nether Longford
A71
WEST MAINS COTTS
A704
Newhouse
East White Sykes
Nether Longford Moss
Longford Burn
Longford
Spoil Heap
Longford Bridge
Rusha Farm
Poultry Farm
Longhill Burn
Pateshill Cottage
EH55
Works
Pate's Hill
Woodmuir Plantation
Harwood Water
8
7
61
6
5
60
4
3
59
2
1
58
97
98
99

202
184

183
163

A
B
C
D
E
F
8
7
61
6
5
60
4
3
59
2
1
58
00
01
02
A704
Cow
Hill
Cairnview
Mains
Little
Harwood
Hartwood
Hartwood
Bridge
West
Mains
Hartwood
Mains
Harwood Water
Mossend
Mid
Hartwood
WEST HARWOOD
CROFTS
West
Harwood
EH55
Baadsmill
Baad's Mill
Bridge
Bog Burn
Vein Syke
Adie's Syke
Coal Burn
Pearie
Law
Cobbinshaw
Reservoir
Benry
Bog
Benry
Bridge

183
203

164
186

A
B
C
D
E
F
B7008
West Broomhill
Tor Whitie
Torphin Bridge
HARBURN
Lodge
Coalheughead Farm
Bog Burn
CH
Bents Burn
Over Williamston
Whistle Lodge
Broadmeadow
East Torphin
Haymains
West Torphin
LC
Dog Bush Knowe
Harburn House
Black Burn
Harburnhead
EH55
Camilty Moss
Camp Wood
Camilty Plantation
Camilty Hill
EH27
Castle Greg
ROMAN FORTLET
Crosswood Burn
A70
P
Crosswood Bridge
Shear Bridge
Harburnhead Hill
B7008
Otter Burn
A70
8
7
61
6
5
60
4
3
59
2
1
58
03
04
05

204
186

185
165

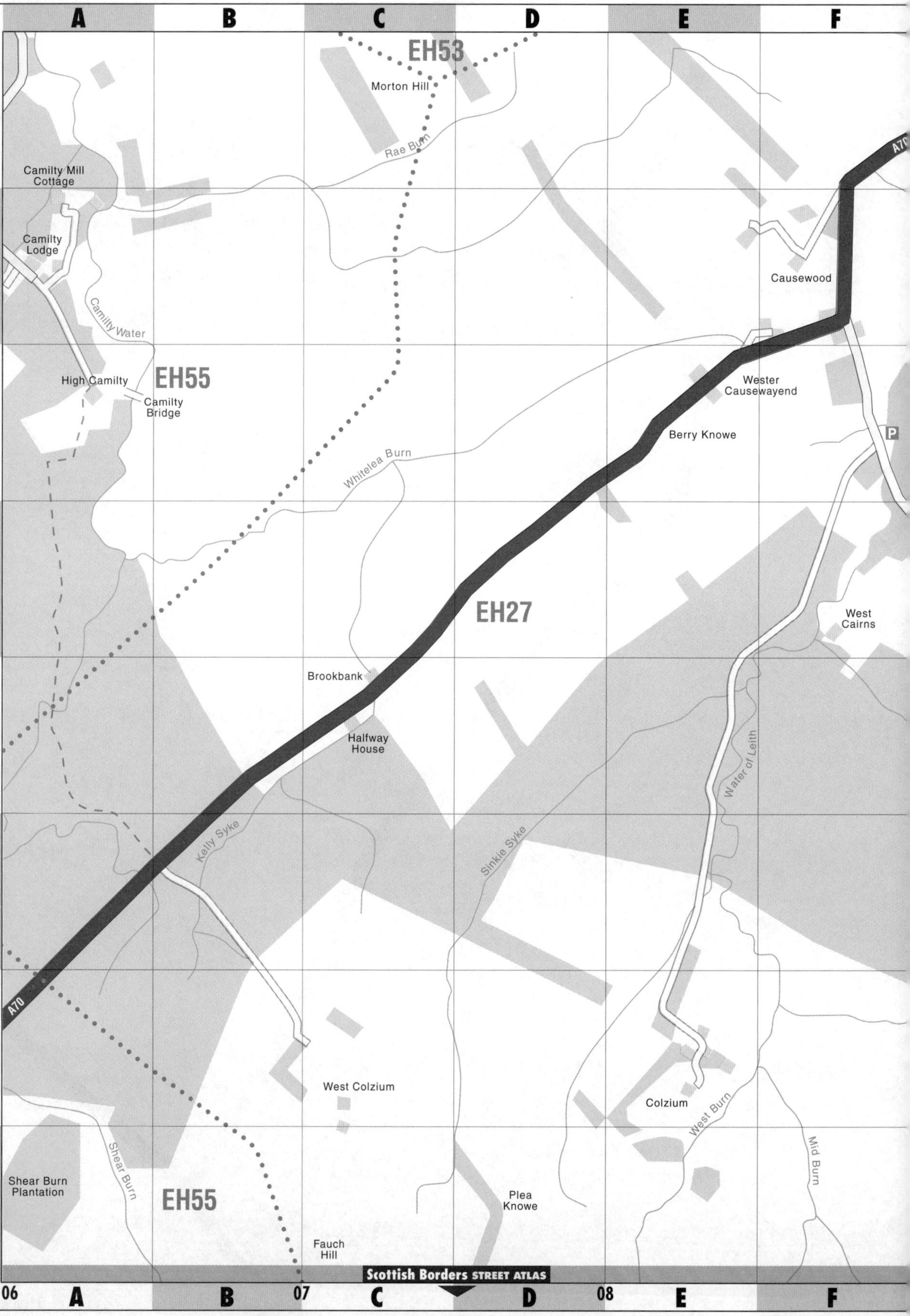
A
B
C
D
E
F
8
7
61
6
5
60
4
3
59
2
1
58
06
07
08
EH53
Morton Hill
Rae Burn
A70
Camilty Mill
Cottage
Camilty
Lodge
Causewood
Camilty Water
EH55
High Camilty
Camilty
Bridge
Wester
Causewayend
Berry Knowe
P
Whitelea Burn
EH27
West
Cairns
Brookbank
Halfway
House
Water of Leith
Kelly Syke
Sinkie Syke
A70
West Colzium
Colzium
West Burn
Shear Burn
Mid Burn
Shear Burn
Plantation
EH55
Plea
Knowe
Fauch
Hill
Scottish Borders STREET ATLAS

185

166
188
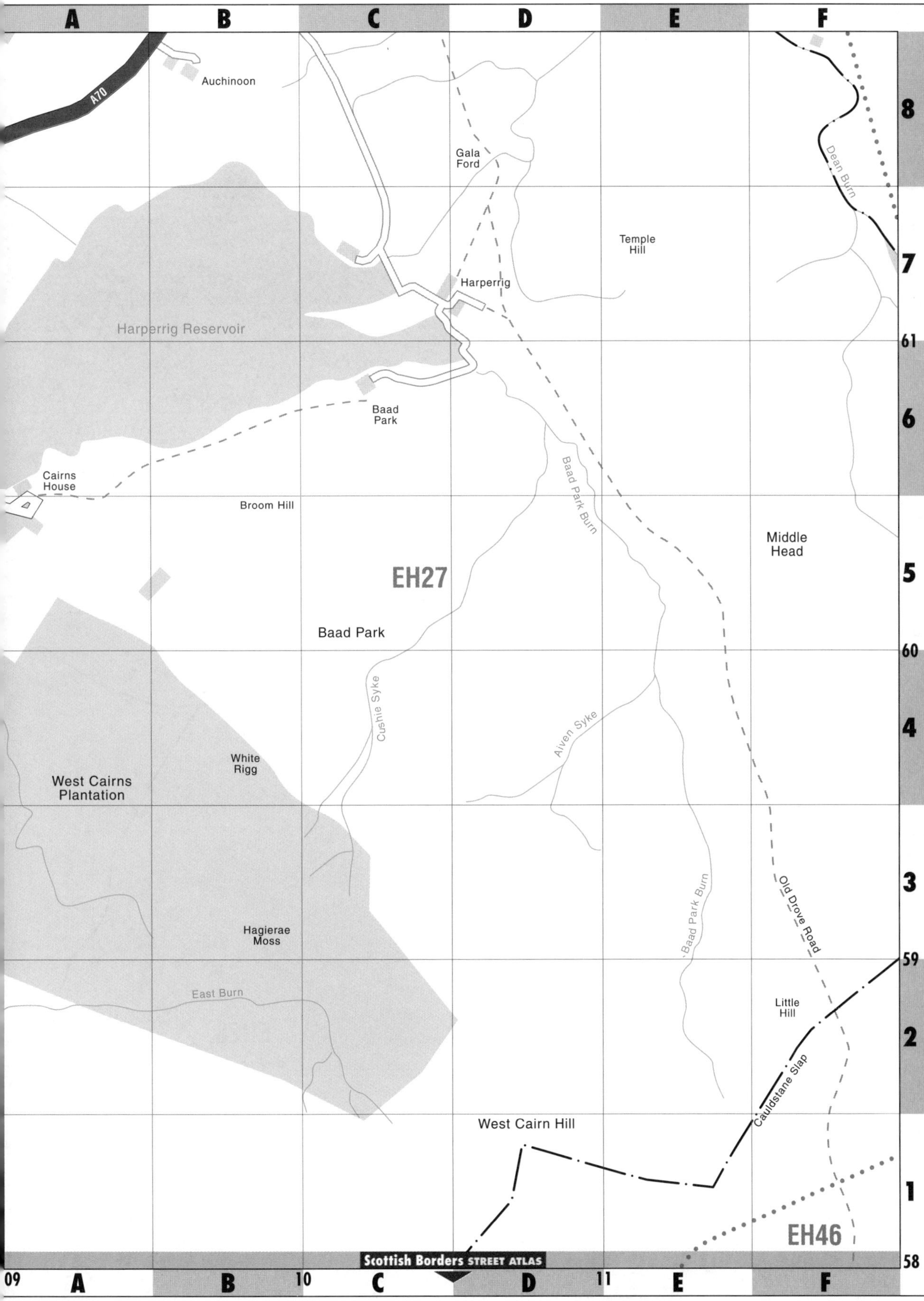
A
B
C
D
E
F
A70
Auchinoon
Gala
Ford
Dean Burn
8
Temple
Hill
7
Harperrig
Harperrig Reservoir
61
Baad
Park
6
Cairns
House
Broom Hill
Baad Park Burn
Middle
Head
EH27
5
Baad Park
60
Cushie Syke
Aiven Syke
4
White
Rigg
West Cairns
Plantation
3
Baad Park Burn
Old Drove Road
Hagierae
Moss
59
East Burn
Little
Hill
2
Cauldstane Slap
West Cairn Hill
1
EH46
58
09
10
11

188

187 167

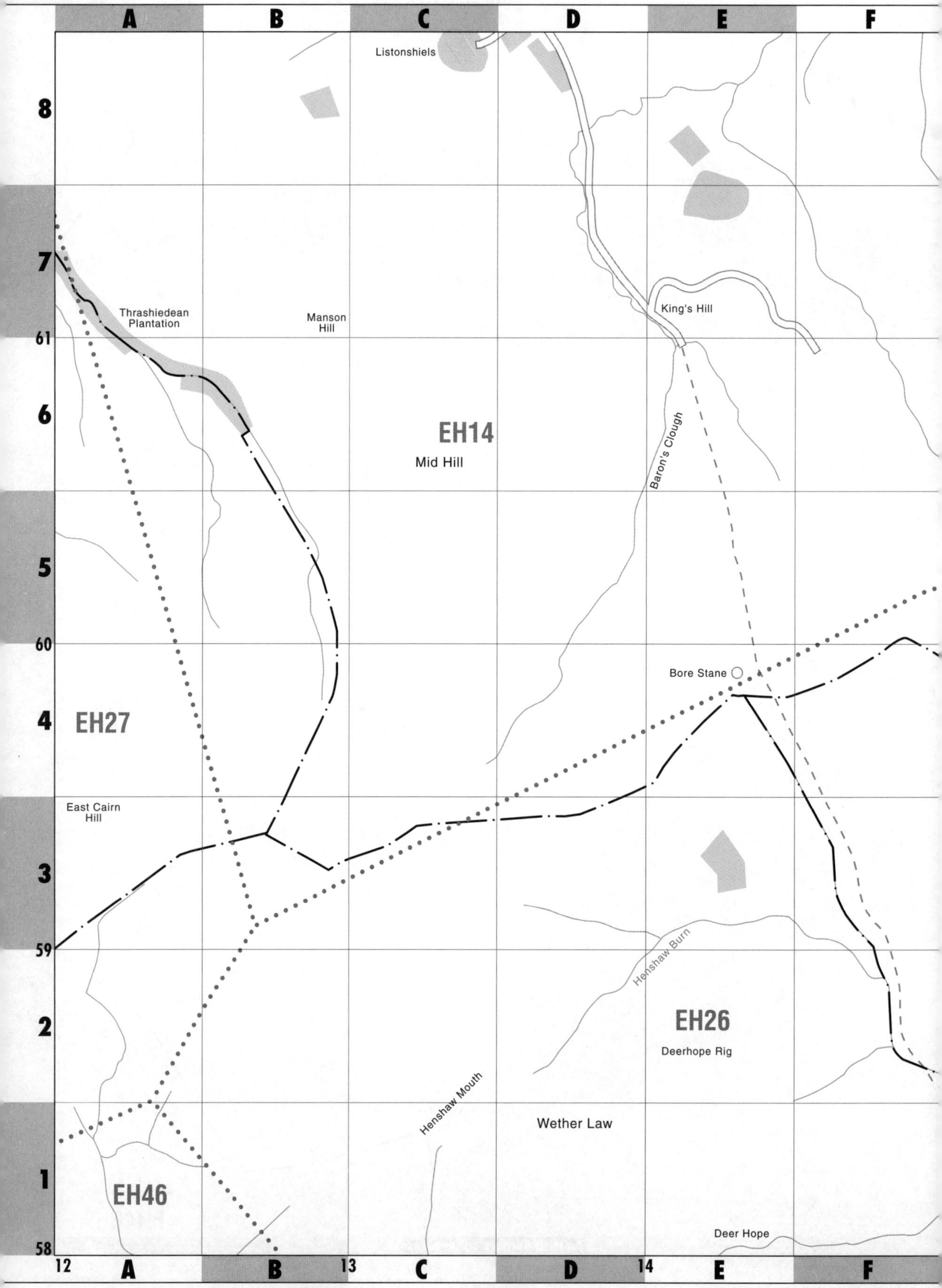
Listonshiels
Thrashiedean Plantation
Manson Hill
King's Hill
EH14
Mid Hill
Baron's Clough
Bore Stane
EH27
East Cairn Hill
EH26
Henshaw Burn
Deerhope Rig
Henshaw Mouth
Wether Law
EH46
Deer Hope

187 205

168
190

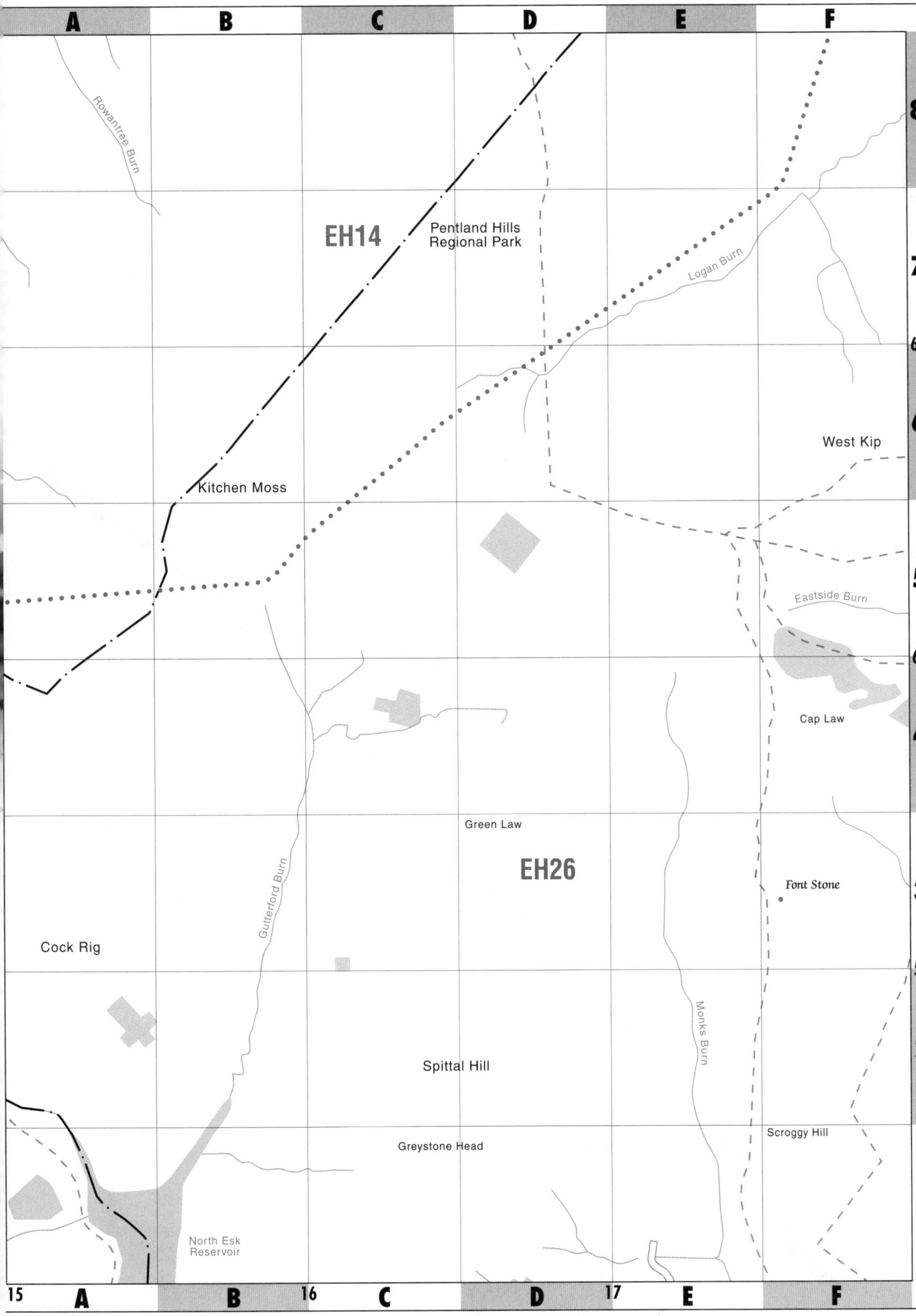
A
B
C
D
E
F
8
7
61
6
5
60
4
3
59
2
1
58
15
16
17
Rowantree Burn
EH14
Pentland Hills
Regional Park
Logan Burn
West Kip
Kitchen Moss
Eastside Burn
Cap Law
Green Law
EH26
Gutterford Burn
Font Stone
Cock Rig
Monks Burn
Spittal Hill
Scroggy Hill
Greystone Head
North Esk
Reservoir

206
190

189
169

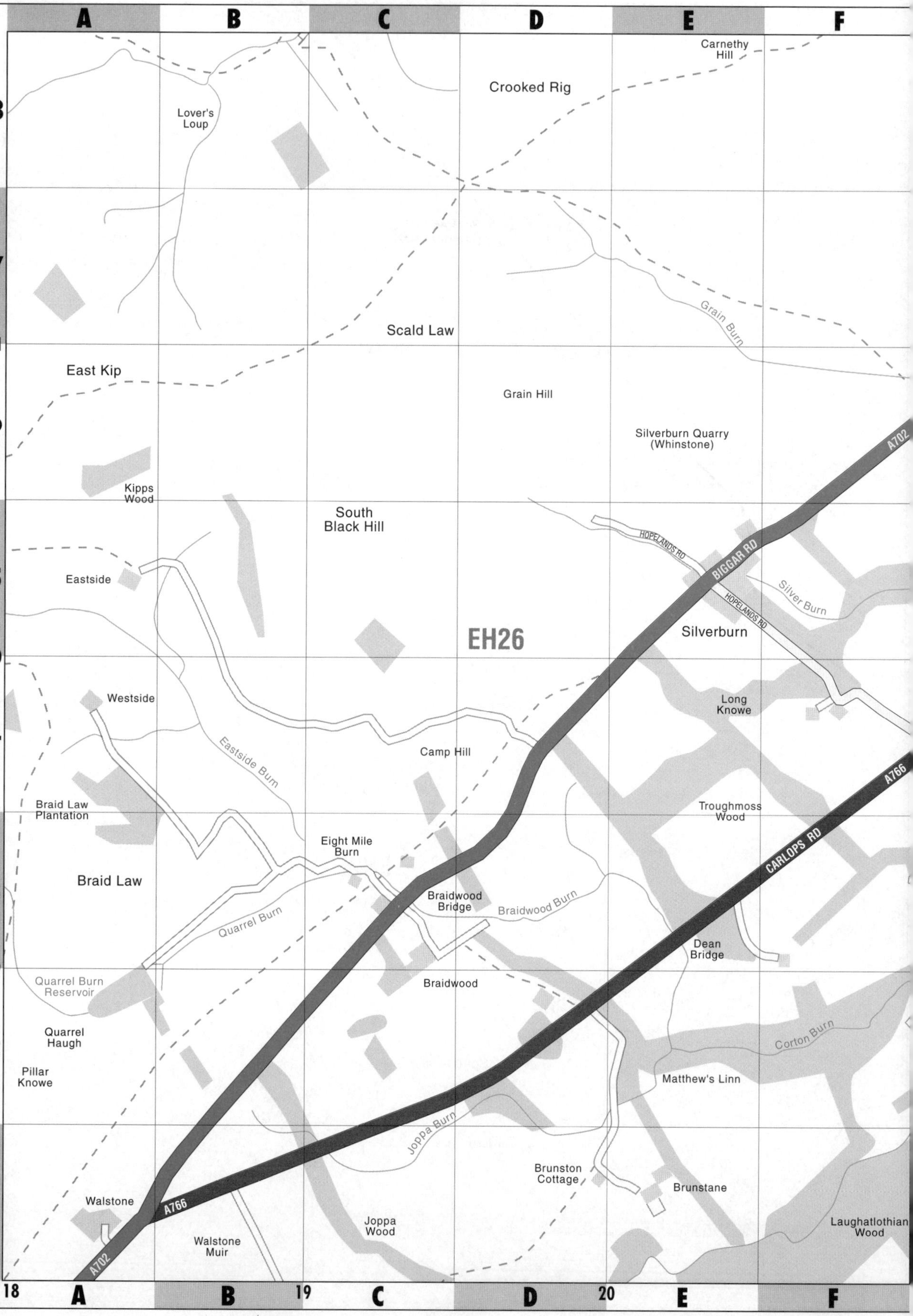
A
B
C
D
E
F
8
7
61
6
5
60
4
3
59
2
1
58
18
19
20
Carnethy Hill
Crooked Rig
Lover's Loup
Grain Burn
Scald Law
East Kip
Grain Hill
Silverburn Quarry (Whinstone)
A702
Kipps Wood
South Black Hill
HOPELANDS RD
BIGGAR RD
Eastside
Silver Burn
EH26
Silverburn
Westside
Long Knowe
Eastside Burn
Camp Hill
A766
Braid Law Plantation
Troughmoss Wood
Eight Mile Burn
CARLOPS RD
Braid Law
Braidwood Bridge
Braidwood Burn
Quarrel Burn
Dean Bridge
Quarrel Burn Reservoir
Braidwood
Quarrel Haugh
Corton Burn
Pillar Knowe
Matthew's Linn
Joppa Burn
Brunston Cottage
Brunstane
Walstone
Laughatlothian Wood
Joppa Wood
Walstone Muir

189
207

170
192

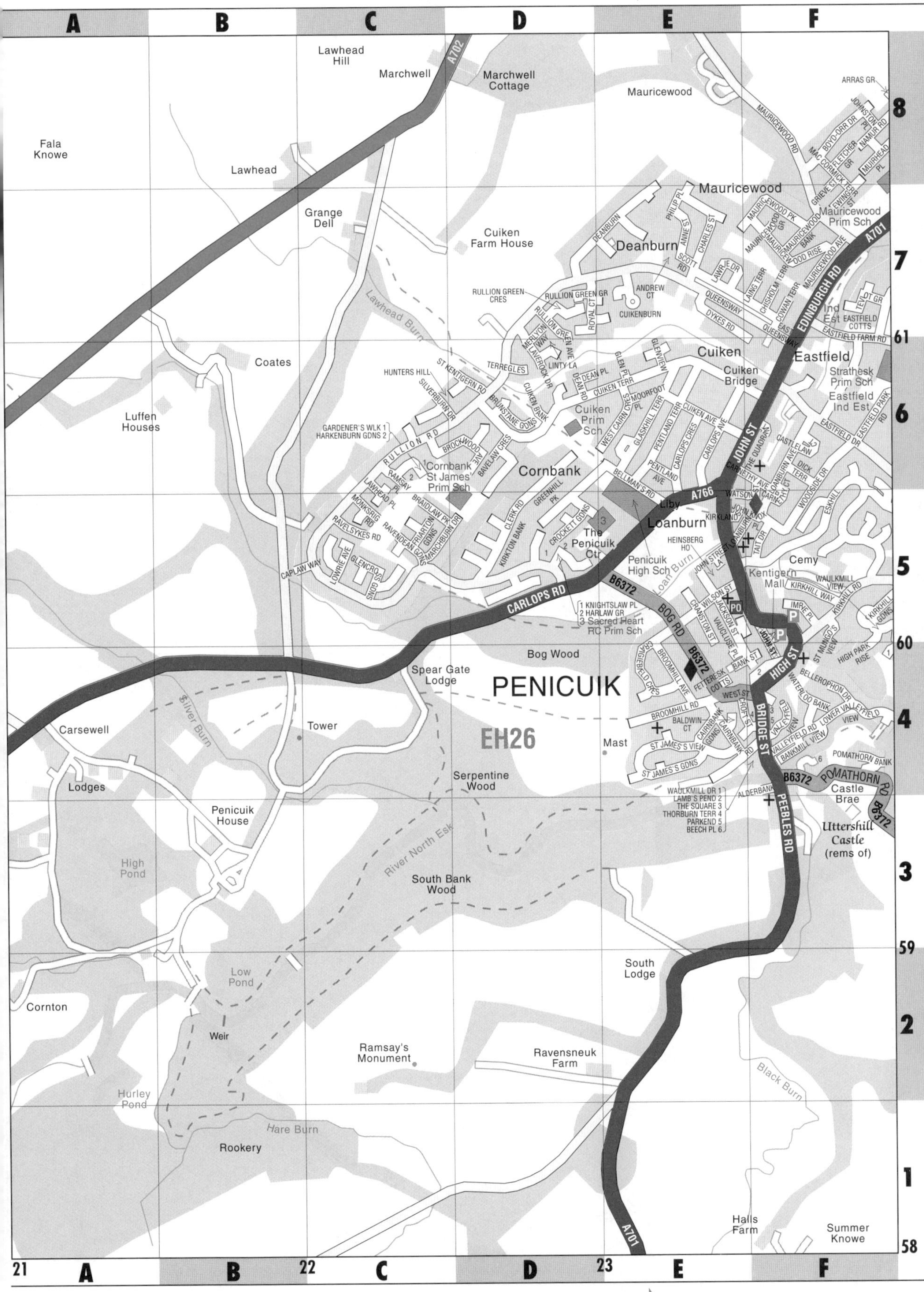
A
B
C
D
E
F
Lawhead Hill
Marchwell
Marchwell Cottage
Mauricewood
Fala Knowe
Lawhead
Grange Dell
Cuiken Farm House
Mauricewood
Deanburn
Mauricewood Prim Sch
Coates
Cuiken
Eastfield
Cuiken Bridge
Strathesk Prim Sch
Eastfield Ind Est
Luffen Houses
Cuiken Prim Sch
Cornbank
Cornbank St James' Prim Sch
Loanburn
The Penicuik Ctr
Penicuik High Sch
Cemy
Kentigern Mall
Bog Wood
Spear Gate Lodge
PENICUIK
EH26
Carsewell
Tower
Mast
Lodges
Serpentine Wood
Penicuik House
Castle Brae
Uttershill Castle (rems of)
High Pond
River North Esk
South Bank Wood
South Lodge
Low Pond
Cornton
Weir
Ramsay's Monument
Ravensneuk Farm
Hurley Pond
Hare Burn
Rookery
Black Burn
Halls Farm
Summer Knowe
Lawhead Burn
Silver Burn
Loan Burn
A702
A701
A766
B6372
CARLOPS RD
EDINBURGH RD
JOHN ST
HIGH ST
BRIDGE ST
PEEBLES RD
BOG RD
1 KNIGHTSLAW PL
2 HARLAW GR
3 Sacred Heart RC Prim Sch
WAULKMILL DR 1
LAMB'S PEND 2
THE SQUARE 3
THORBURN TERR 4
PARKEND 5
BEECH PL 6
GARDENER'S WLK 1
HARKENBURN GDNS 2
8
7
61
6
5
60
4
3
59
2
1
58
21
22
23

208
192

191 171

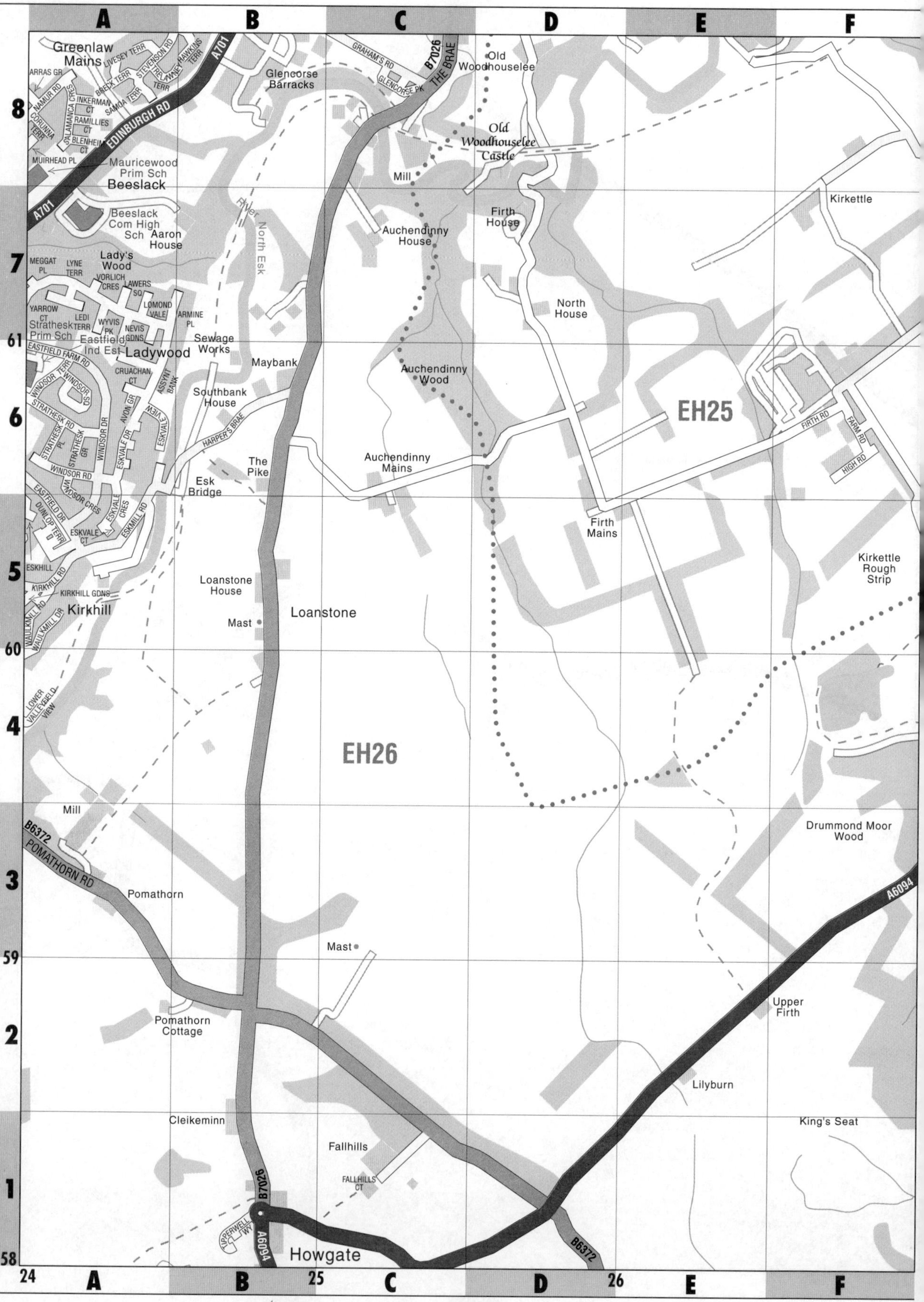

191 209

172
194

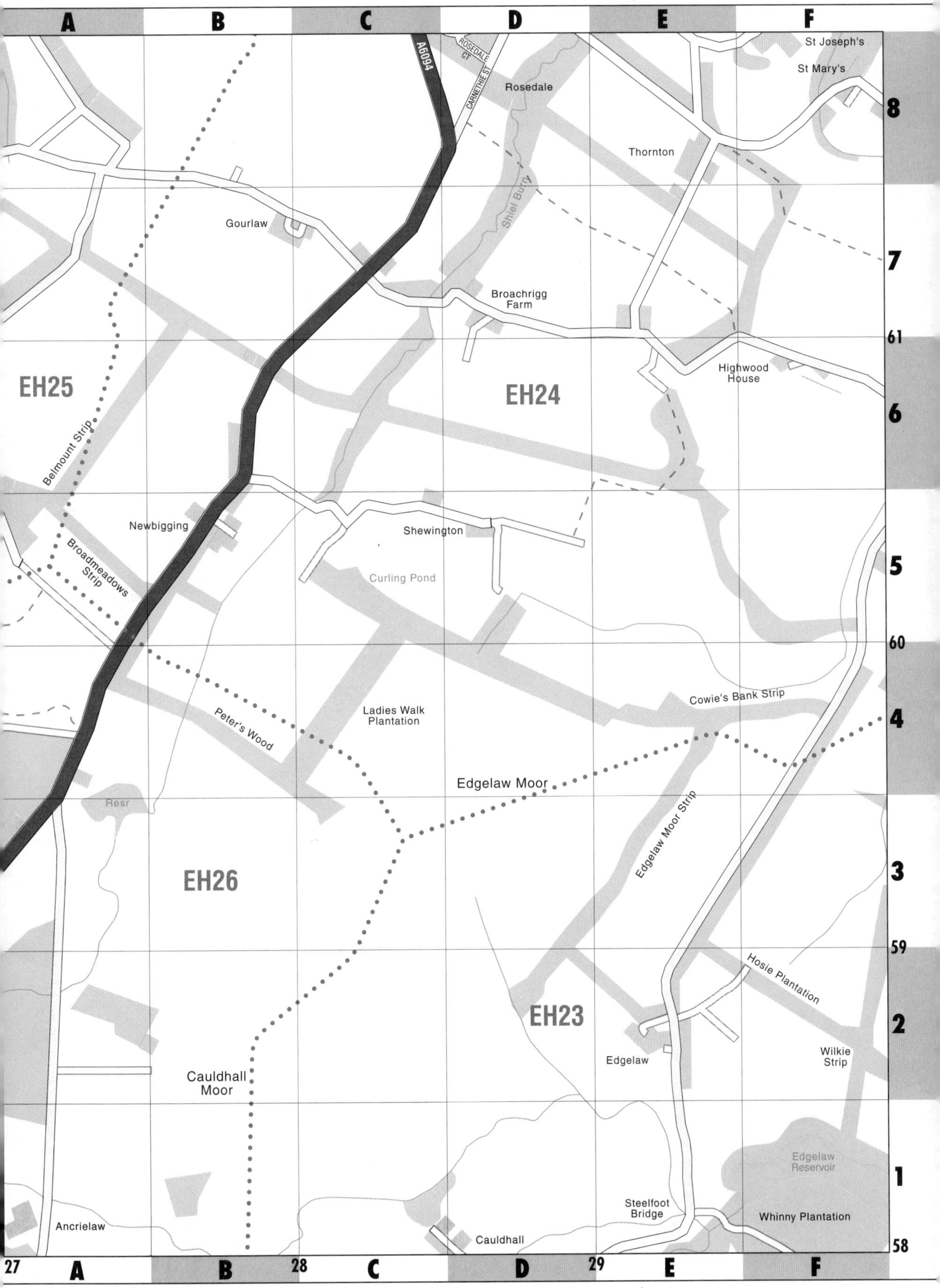
A
B
C
D
E
F
A6094
ROSEDALE CT
CARNETHIE ST
St Joseph's
St Mary's
Rosedale
8
Thornton
Gourlaw
Shiel Burn
7
Broachrigg Farm
61
Highwood House
EH25
EH24
6
Belmont Strip
Newbigging
Shewington
Broadmeadows Strip
Curling Pond
5
60
Cowie's Bank Strip
Ladies Walk Plantation
Peter's Wood
4
Edgelaw Moor
Resr
EH26
Edgelaw Moor Strip
3
59
Hosie Plantation
EH23
2
Edgelaw
Wilkie Strip
Cauldhall Moor
Edgelaw Reservoir
1
Steelfoot Bridge
Whinny Plantation
Ancrielaw
Cauldhall
58
27
A
B
28
C
D
29
E
F

210
194

193
173

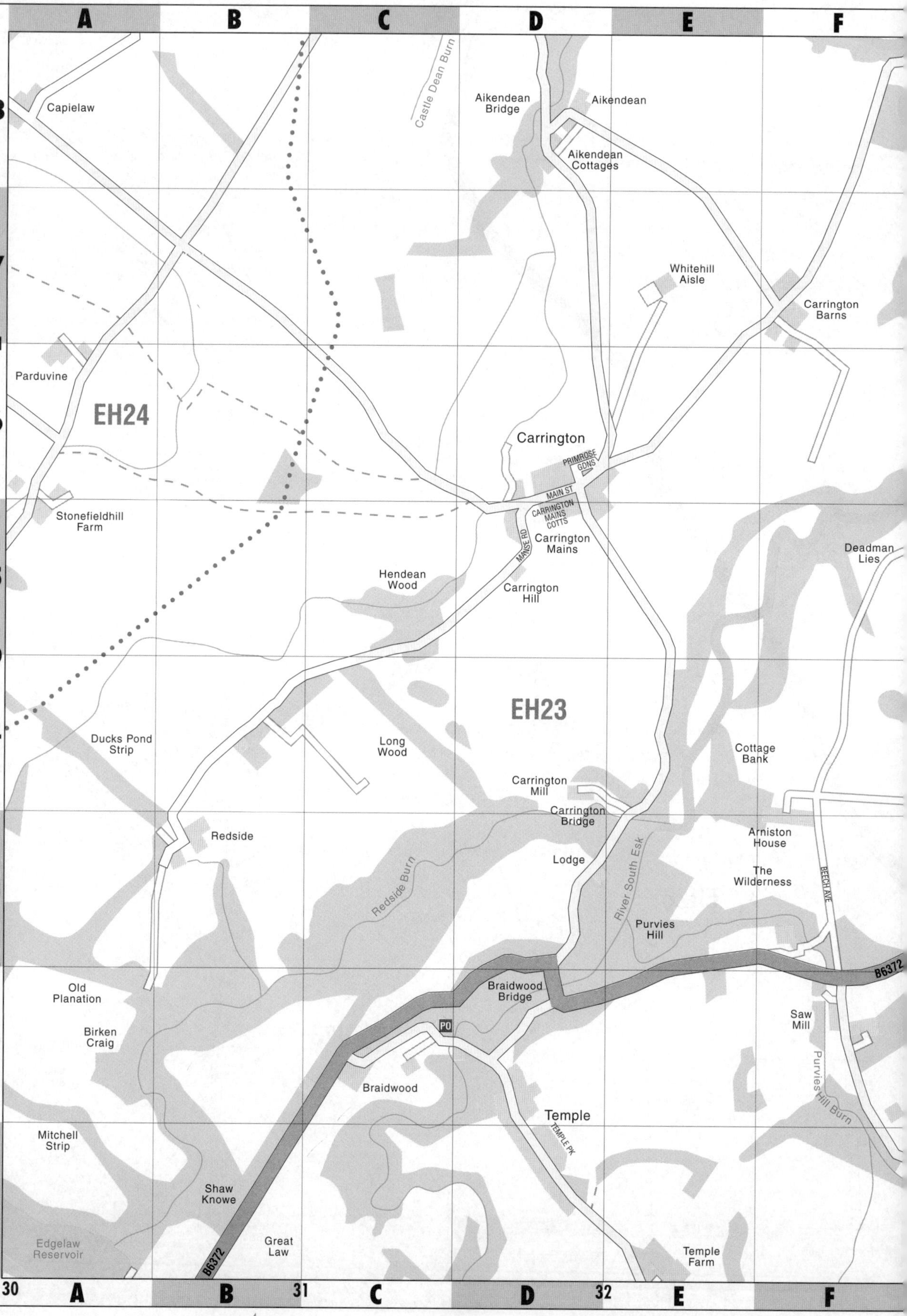
A
B
C
D
E
F
8
7
61
6
5
60
4
3
59
2
1
58
30
31
32
Capielaw
Castle Dean Burn
Aikendean Bridge
Aikendean
Aikendean Cottages
Whitehill Aisle
Carrington Barns
Parduvine
EH24
Carrington
PRIMROSE GDNS
MAIN ST
CARRINGTON MAINS COTTS
MANSE RD
Stonefieldhill Farm
Carrington Mains
Deadman Lies
Hendean Wood
Carrington Hill
EH23
Ducks Pond Strip
Long Wood
Cottage Bank
Carrington Mill
Carrington Bridge
Redside
Arniston House
Lodge
River South Esk
The Wilderness
BEECH AVE
Redside Burn
Purvies Hill
B6372
Old Planation
Braidwood Bridge
Saw Mill
PO
Birken Craig
Braidwood
Purvies Hill Burn
Temple
TEMPLE PK
Mitchell Strip
Shaw Knowe
Edgelaw Reservoir
Great Law
Temple Farm
B6372

193
211

174
196

A
B
C
D
E
F
Trotter's Bridge
Arniston Engine
Millbank House
Playing Fields
Gorebridge
Liby
HUNTERFIELD RD
B704
MAIN ST
STATION RD
Stobhill
Stobhill Prim Sch
Monteith Houses
Mossend
B6372
LADY BRAE
Shank Tongue
Saw Mill
Millstone Brow Cottages
Stobs
Shank Bridge
Shank
River South Esk
Sewage Wks
Stobs Mills
Ashbank
ROBERTSONS BANK
POWDERMILL BRAE
Robert Adams Wood
Harvieston Mains
Mount Cottage
Gore Water
Shank Avenue
Portland Clump
Baker's Avenue Wood
Bells Mains
Harvieston House
Arniston Mains
Harvieston Farm
Catcune Mill Cotts
Cemy
EH23
Catcune House
Haughhead
Catcune
Eastwood
Lodge
Carlisle Wood
Castle Law
Black Bog Wood
ARNISTON HOME FARM COTTS
Home Farm
Lodge
CARLISLE APPROACH
North Middleton
PO
PH
Middleton North Burn Bridge
Sheil Knowe
Crow Wood
Rylaw Knowe
William Wood
Guildie Howes
Castleton
Mast
Halkerston
Lime Works
Halk Law
Castleton Strip
Middleton North Burn
A7
8
7
61
6
5
60
4
3
59
2
1
58
33
34
35

212
196

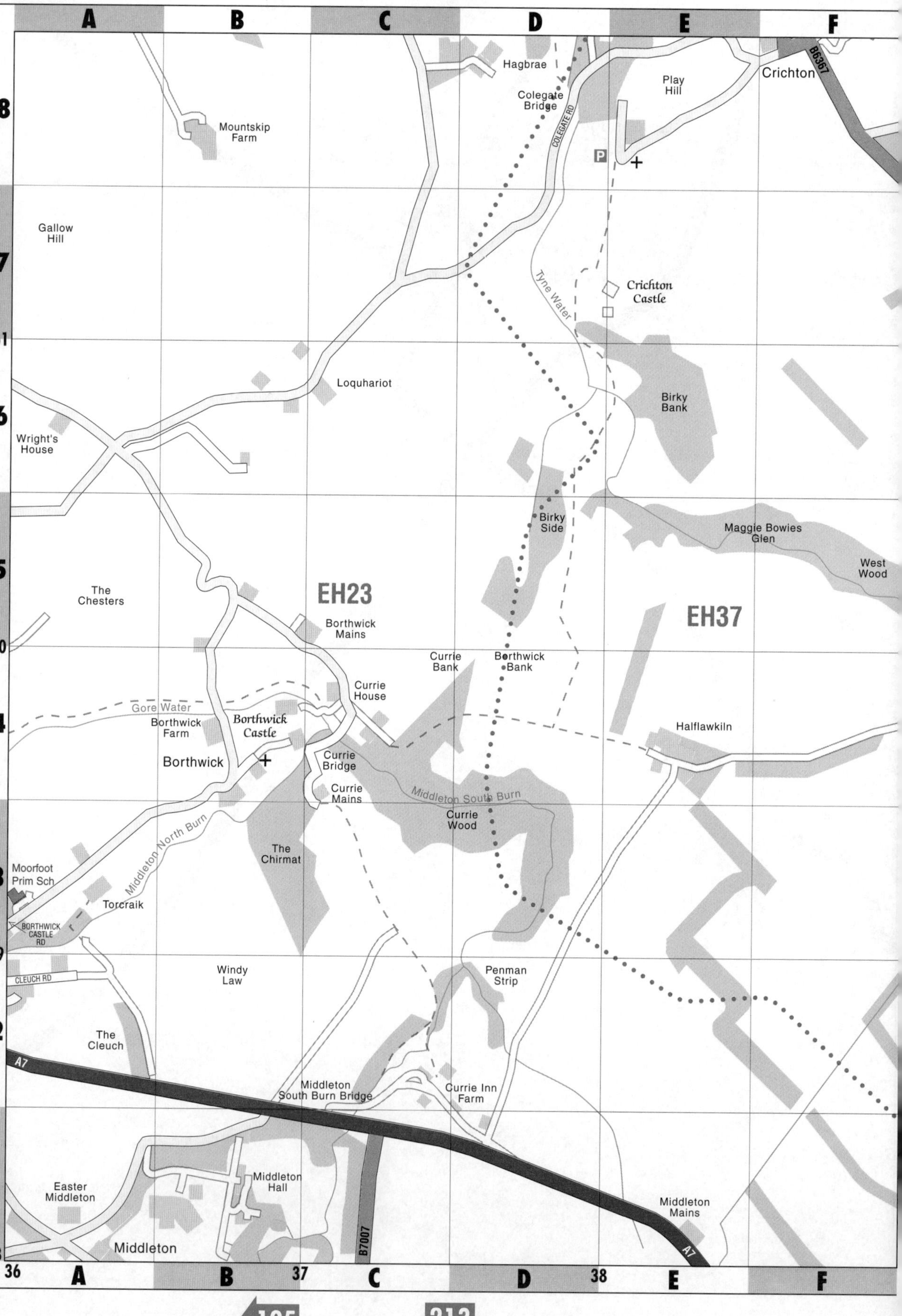
A
B
C
D
E
F
8
7
61
6
5
60
4
3
59
2
1
58
36
37
38
Hagbrae
Colegate Bridge
COLEGATE RD
Play Hill
Crichton
B6367
Mountskip Farm
P
Gallow Hill
Crichton Castle
Tyne Water
Loquhariot
Birky Bank
Wright's House
Birky Side
Maggie Bowies Glen
West Wood
The Chesters
EH23
Borthwick Mains
EH37
Currie Bank
Borthwick Bank
Currie House
Gore Water
Borthwick Farm
Borthwick Castle
Halflawkiln
Borthwick
Currie Bridge
Currie Mains
Middleton South Burn
Currie Wood
Middleton North Burn
The Chirmat
Moorfoot Prim Sch
Torcraik
BORTHWICK CASTLE RD
Windy Law
CLEUCH RD
Penman Strip
The Cleuch
A7
Middleton South Burn Bridge
Currie Inn Farm
Middleton Hall
Easter Middleton
B7007
Middleton Mains
Middleton

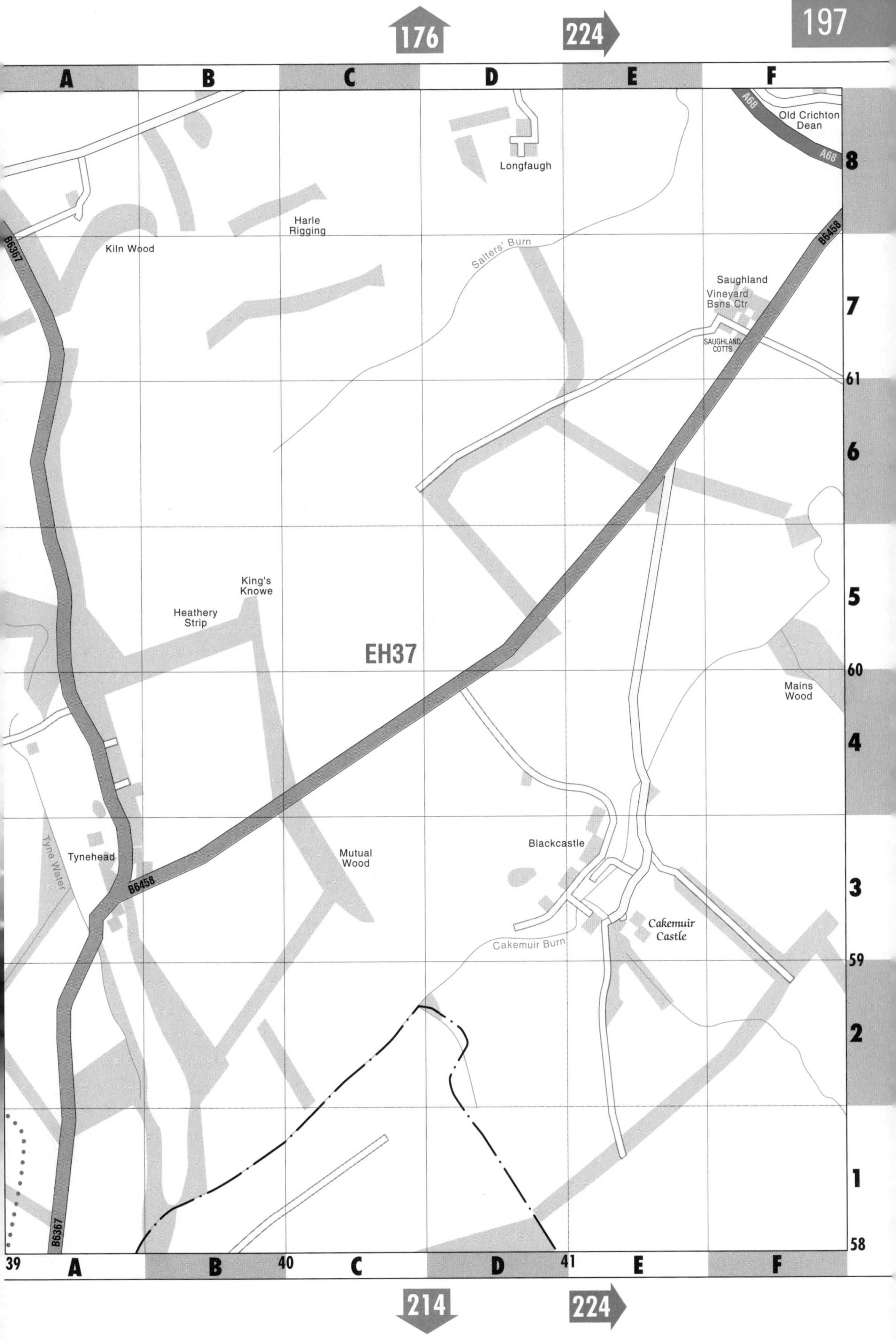
176
224
A
B
C
D
E
F
Old Crichton Dean
A68
Longfaugh
Harle Rigging
Kiln Wood
B6367
Salters' Burn
B6458
Saughland
Vineyard Bsns Ctr
SAUGHLAND COTTS
King's Knowe
Heathery Strip
EH37
Mains Wood
Tynehead
Tyne Water
Mutual Wood
Blackcastle
Cakemuir Castle
Cakemuir Burn
8
7
61
6
5
60
4
3
59
2
1
58
39
40
41
214
224

179

A
B
C
D
E
F
8
7
57
6
5
56
4
3
55
2
1
54
85
86
87
COLTNESS AVE
PO
ALLANTON RD A71
A71 Junc. 8 M74
Allanton
Prim Sch
PH
SCHOOL LA
REDMIRE CRES
DARMEID PL
MEID
HARTFIELD TERR
SPRINGHEAD RD
KINGSHILL RD
HOULDSWORTH CRES
WILSON RD
Allanton
HAWTHORN PL
Coal Burn
Opencast
Workings
ML7
Hartfield
Netherhall
Newark
Plantation
Upper
Daviesdykes
DURA RD
Glasgow STREET ATLAS
Kirkhall
Lower
Daviesdykes
Lodge
Hill
Winterhill
Dura
Brow
Farm
Mountpleasant
ML2
Sunnyside
Auchterhead
Summerside
Kingshill
Auchter Water
ML8

215

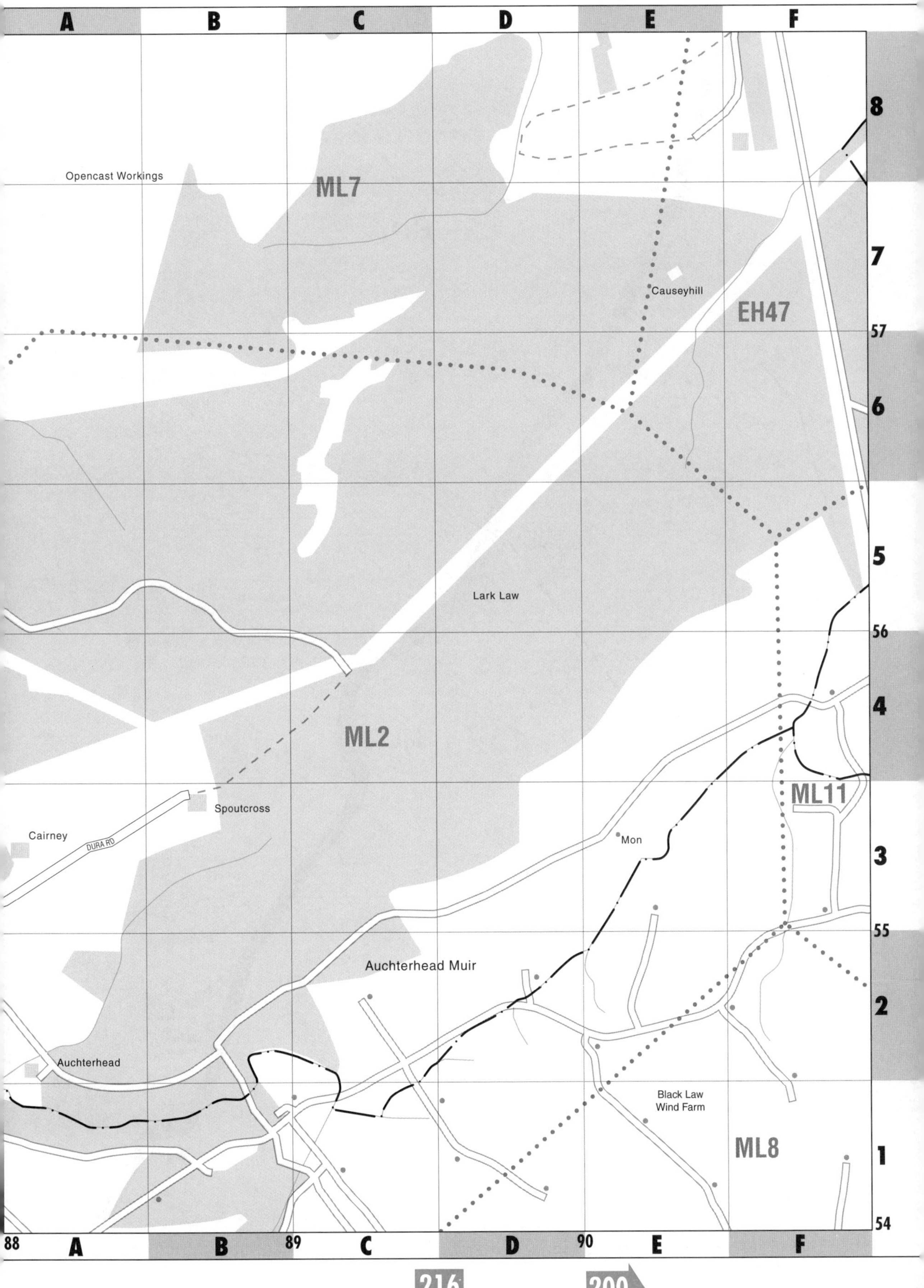
A
B
C
D
E
F
8
7
57
6
5
56
4
3
55
2
1
54
Opencast Workings
ML7
Causeyhill
EH47
Lark Law
ML2
Spoutcross
Cairney
DURA RD
ML11
Mon
Auchterhead Muir
Auchterhead
Black Law
Wind Farm
ML8
88
89
90

199
181

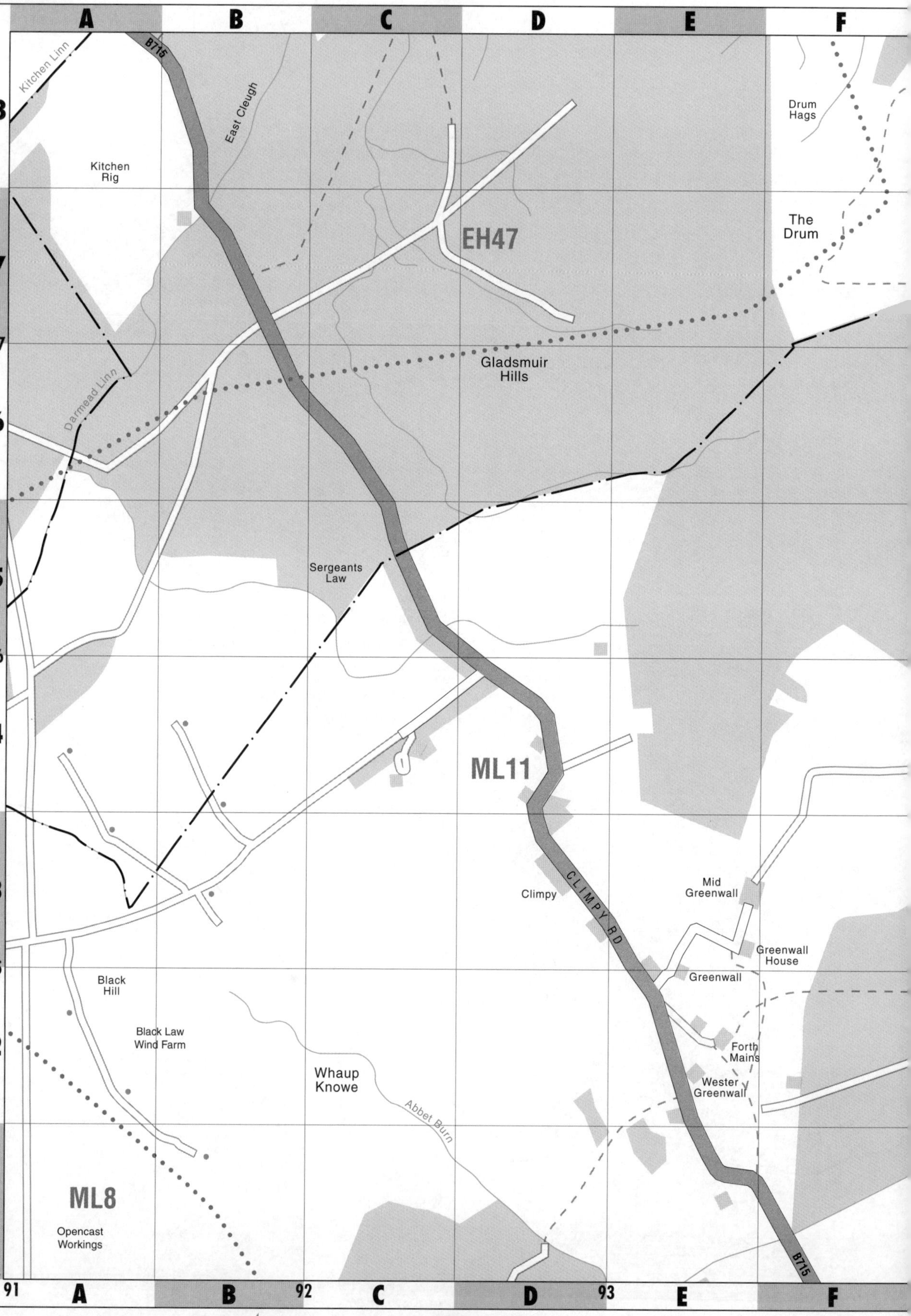

199
217

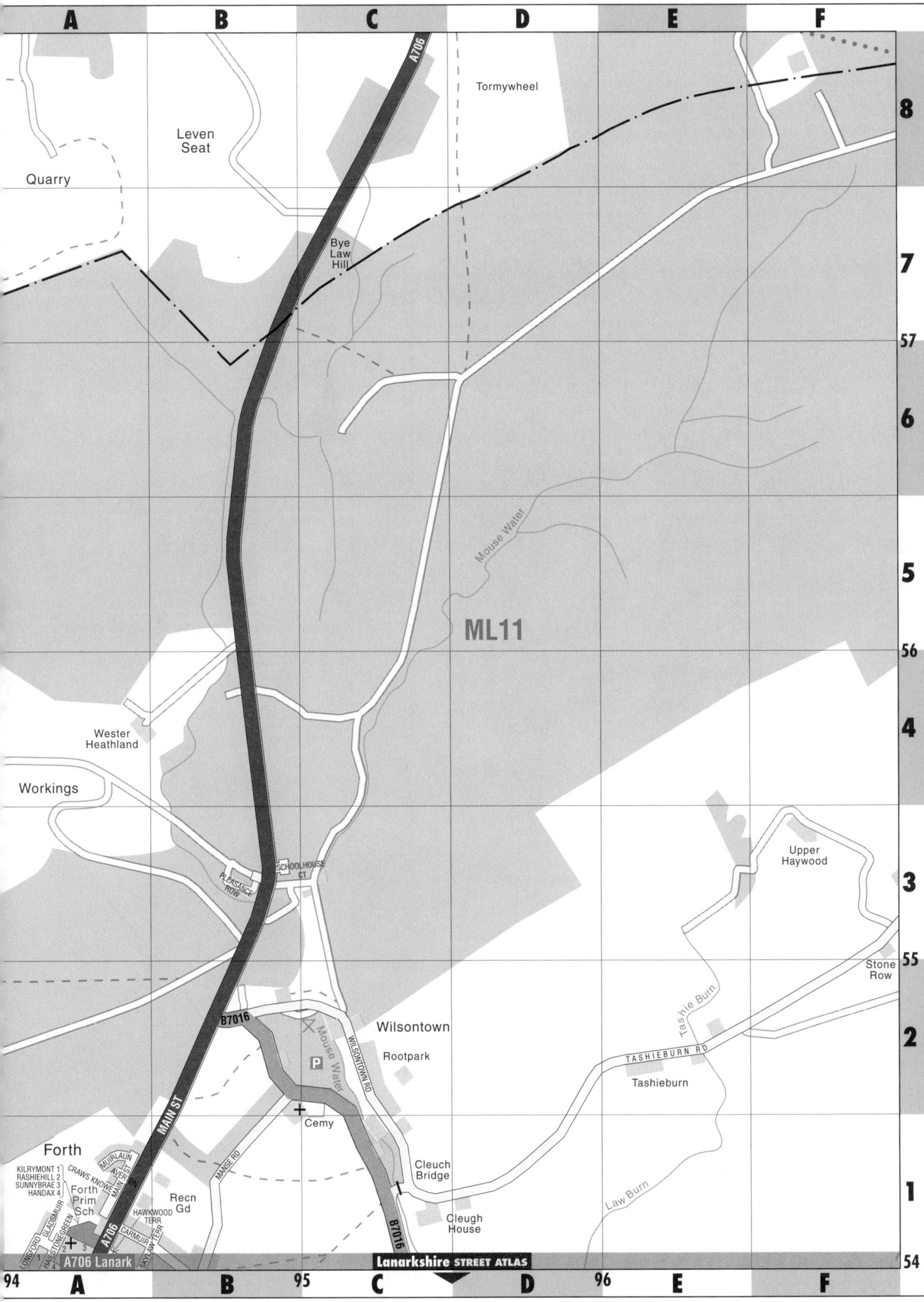
A
B
C
D
E
F
8
7
57
6
5
56
4
3
55
2
1
54
94
95
96
A706
Tormywheel
Leven
Seat
Quarry
Bye
Law
Hill
Mouse Water
ML11
Wester
Heathland
Workings
SCHOOLHOUSE
CT
PLEASANCE
ROW
Upper
Haywood
Stone
Row
Tashie Burn
TASHIEBURN RD
Tashieburn
Wilsontown
Rootpark
WILSONTOWN RD
B7016
P
Cemy
MAIN ST
MANSE RD
Cleuch
Bridge
Cleugh
House
Law Burn
Recn
Gd
Forth
Forth
Prim
Sch
KILRYMONT 1
RASHIEHILL 2
SUNNYBRAE 3
HANDAX 4
CRAWS KNOWE
MUIRLAUN
HAWKWOOD
TERR
CARMUIR
SKYLAW TERR
GLADSMUIR
HAILSTONEGREEN
LONGFORD
A706 Lanark

A
B
C
D
E
F
8
7
57
6
5
56
4
3
55
2
1
54
97
98
99
Hendry's Corse
Wormlaw Burn
Worm Law
Mosshat Burn
EH55
Mountainblaw Farm
Easter Mosshat
ML11
Wester Mosshat
MOSSHAT RD
Burnfoot Poultry Farm
Burnfoot
Bughtknowes
Old Manse
Dippool Water
TASHIEBURN RD
Crooklands
Lawhead View
Haywood
Pentland View
Memorial
Greenbank
Mid Auchengray
Hillhead of Auchengray
Auchengray
AUCHENGRAY RD

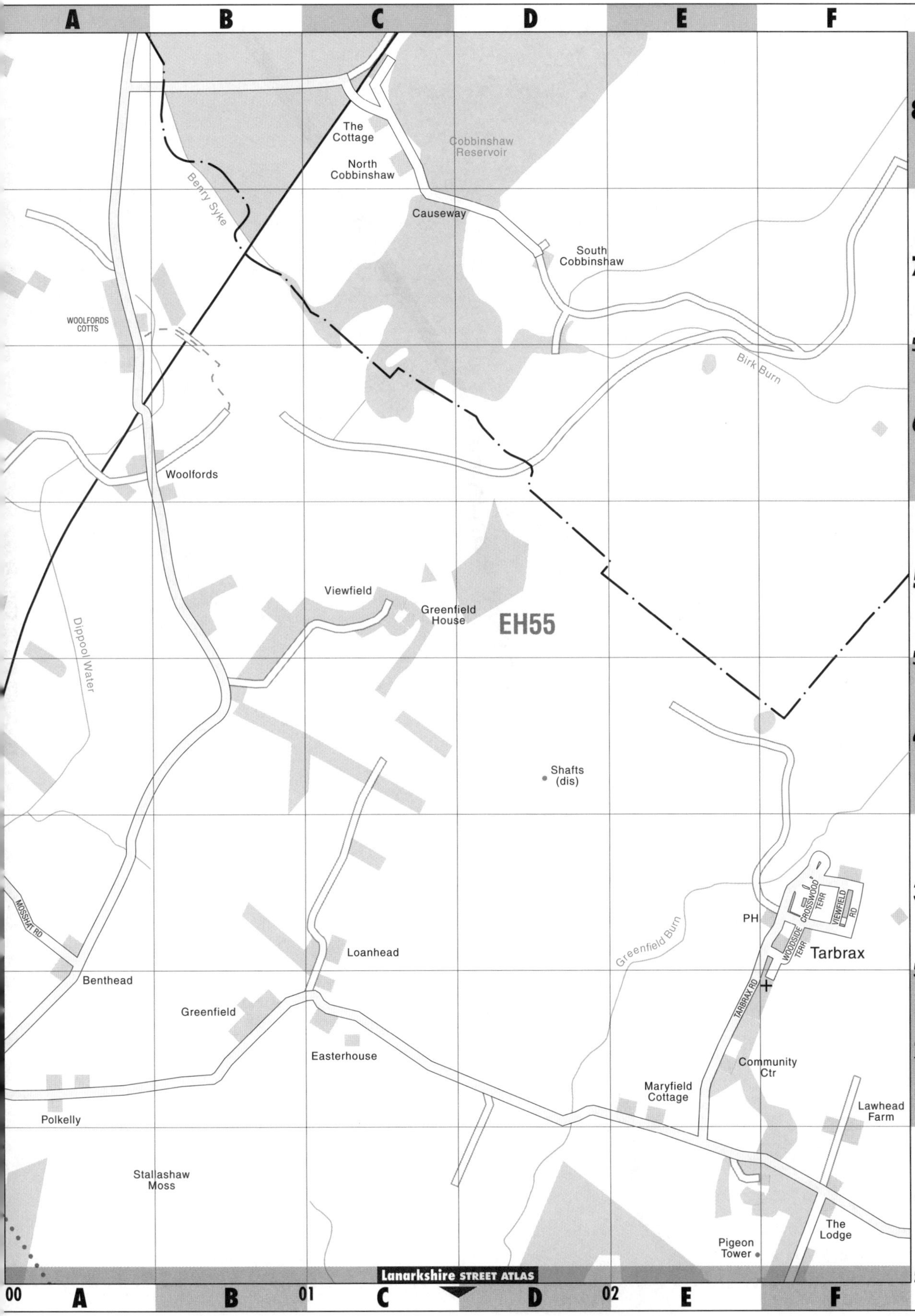
A
B
C
D
E
F
8
7
57
6
5
56
4
3
55
2
1
54
00
01
02
The Cottage
North Cobbinshaw
Cobbinshaw Reservoir
Causeway
South Cobbinshaw
Berry Syke
WOOLFORDS COTTS
Birk Burn
Woolfords
Viewfield
Greenfield House
EH55
Dippool Water
Shafts (dis)
PH
CROSSWOOD TERR
VIEWFIELD RD
WOODSIDE TERR
Tarbrax
Greenfield Burn
MOSSHAT RD
Loanhead
Benthead
TARBRAX RD
Greenfield
Easterhouse
Community Ctr
Maryfield Cottage
Lawhead Farm
Polkelly
Stallashaw Moss
The Lodge
Pigeon Tower

203 185

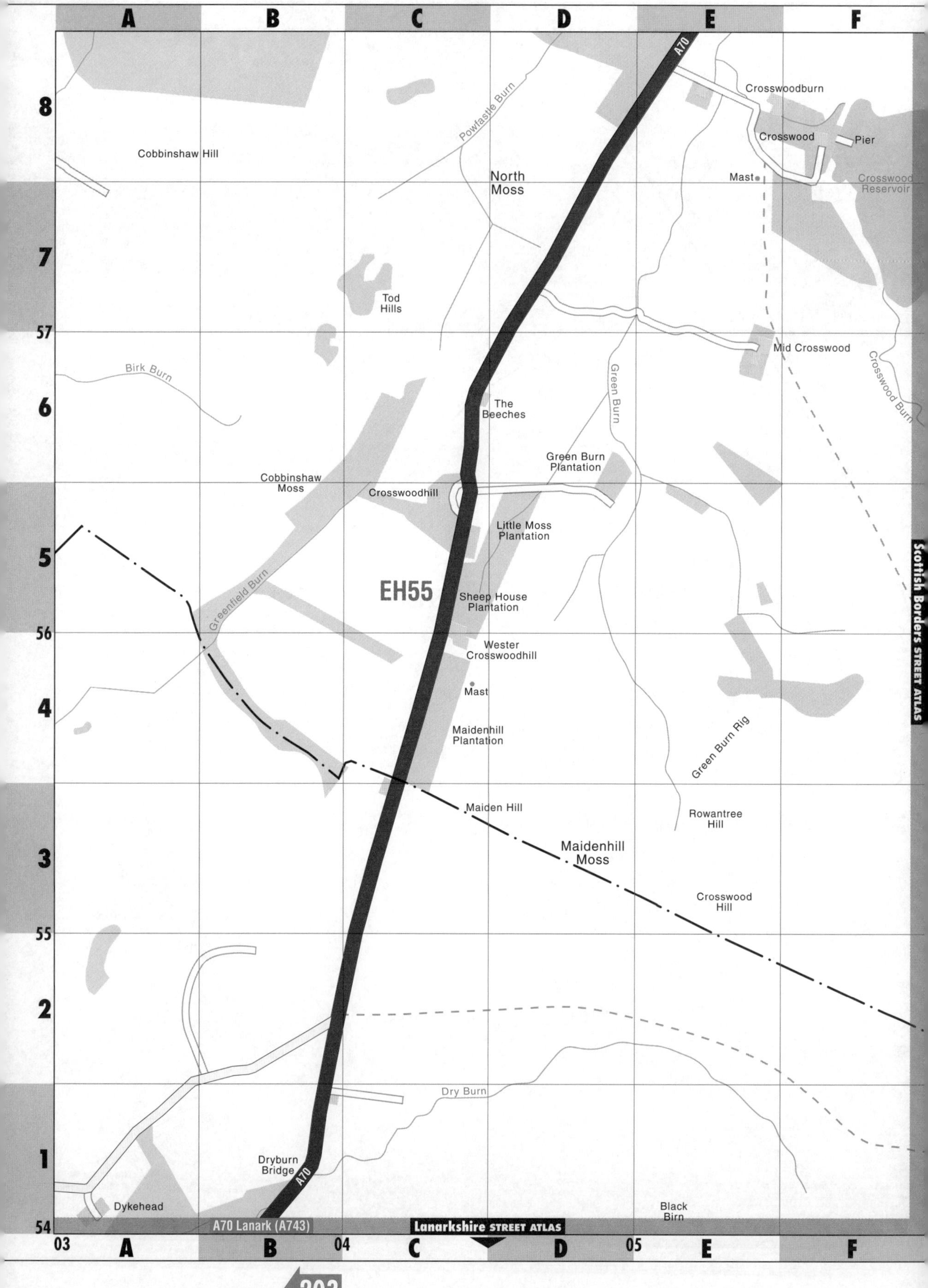
A B C D E F
8
7
57
6
5
56
4
3
55
2
1
54
03 04 05
A70
Crosswoodburn
Crosswood
Pier
Mast
Crosswood Reservoir
Powfastle Burn
Cobbinshaw Hill
North Moss
Tod Hills
Mid Crosswood
Crosswood Burn
Birk Burn
Green Burn
The Beeches
Green Burn Plantation
Cobbinshaw Moss
Crosswoodhill
Little Moss Plantation
EH55
Sheep House Plantation
Greenfield Burn
Wester Crosswoodhill
Mast
Maidenhill Plantation
Green Burn Rig
Maiden Hill
Rowantree Hill
Maidenhill Moss
Crosswood Hill
Dry Burn
Dryburn Bridge
A70
Dykehead
Black Birn
A70 Lanark (A743)
Lanarkshire STREET ATLAS
Scottish Borders STREET ATLAS

203

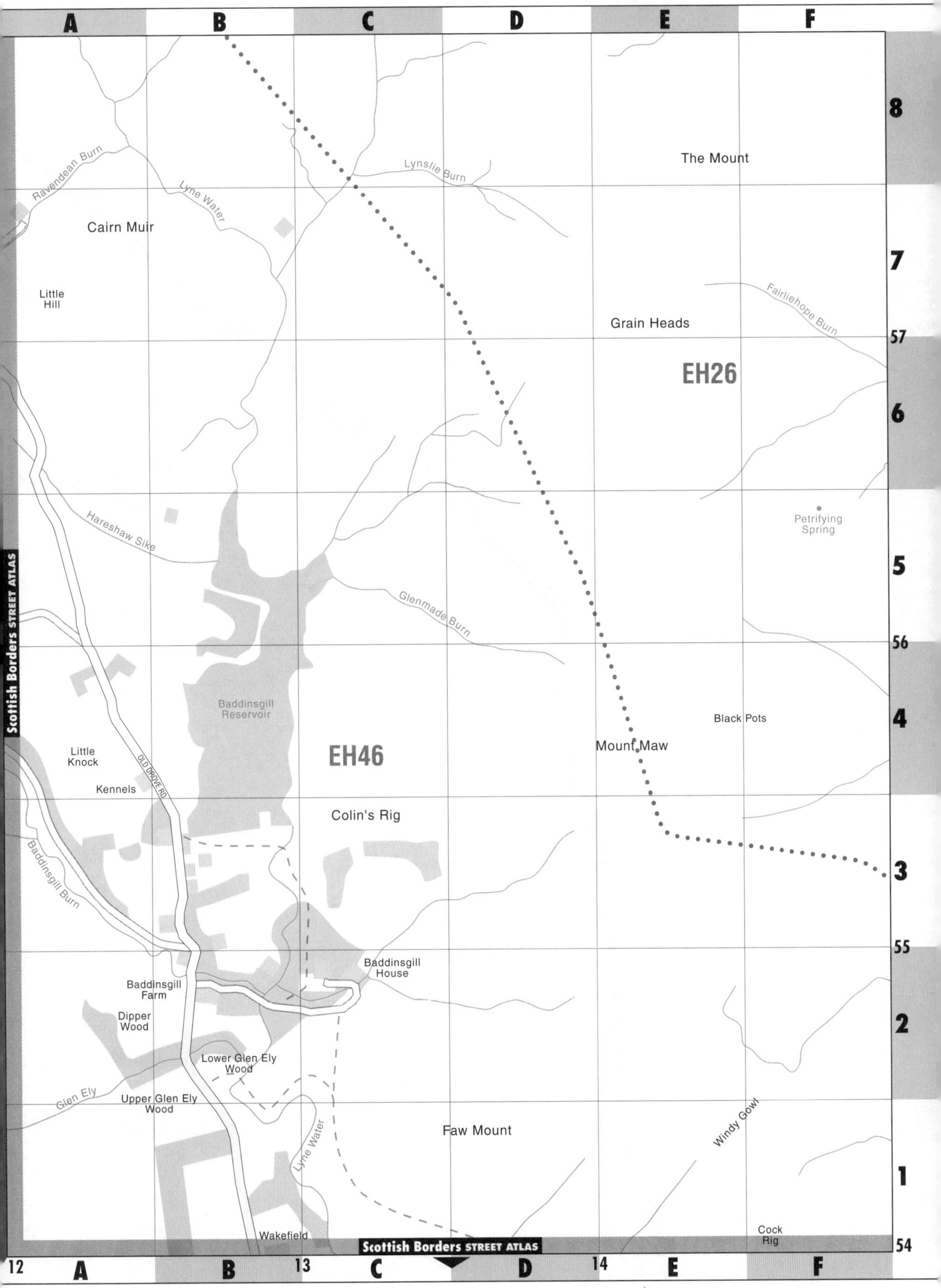
188
206
A
B
C
D
E
F
8
7
57
6
5
56
4
3
55
2
1
54
12
13
14
The Mount
Lynslie Burn
Ravendean Burn
Lyne Water
Cairn Muir
Little Hill
Grain Heads
Fairliehope Burn
EH26
Hareshaw Sike
Petrifying Spring
Glenmade Burn
Baddinsgill Reservoir
Black Pots
Mount Maw
Little Knock
OLD DROVE RD
EH46
Kennels
Colin's Rig
Baddinsgill Burn
Baddinsgill House
Baddinsgill Farm
Dipper Wood
Lower Glen Ely Wood
Glen Ely
Upper Glen Ely Wood
Faw Mount
Windy Gowl
Lyne Water
Wakefield
Cock Rig
Scottish Borders STREET ATLAS
206

205
189

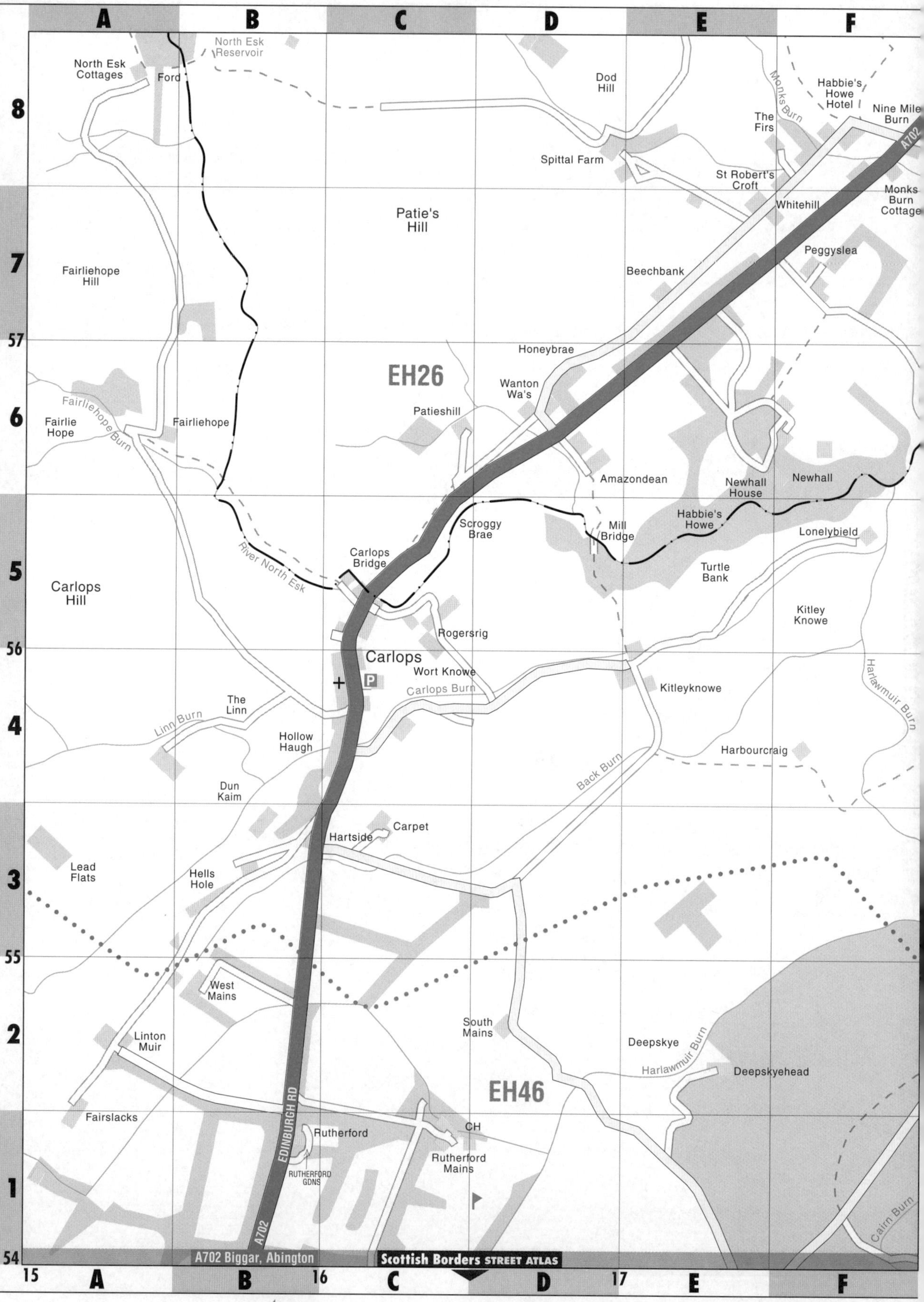
A
B
C
D
E
F
8
7
57
6
5
56
4
3
55
2
1
54
15
16
17
North Esk Reservoir
North Esk Cottages
Ford
Dod Hill
Habbie's Howe Hotel
Monks Burn
The Firs
Nine Mile Burn
A702
Spittal Farm
St Robert's Croft
Whitehill
Monks Burn Cottage
Patie's Hill
Peggyslea
Fairliehope Hill
Beechbank
Honeybrae
EH26
Wanton Wa's
Patieshill
Fairliehope Burn
Fairlie Hope
Fairliehope
Amazondean
Newhall House
Newhall
Scroggy Brae
Mill Bridge
Habbie's Howe
Lonelybield
Carlops Bridge
Turtle Bank
River North Esk
Carlops Hill
Kitley Knowe
Rogersrig
Carlops
Wort Knowe
Carlops Burn
Kitleyknowe
Harlawmuir Burn
The Linn
Linn Burn
Hollow Haugh
Harbourcraig
Back Burn
Dun Kaim
Carpet
Hartside
Lead Flats
Hells Hole
West Mains
South Mains
Linton Muir
Deepskye
Harlawmuir Burn
Deepskyehead
EH46
EDINBURGH RD
Fairslacks
Rutherford
CH
Rutherford Mains
RUTHERFORD GDNS
Cairn Burn
A702 Biggar, Abington

205

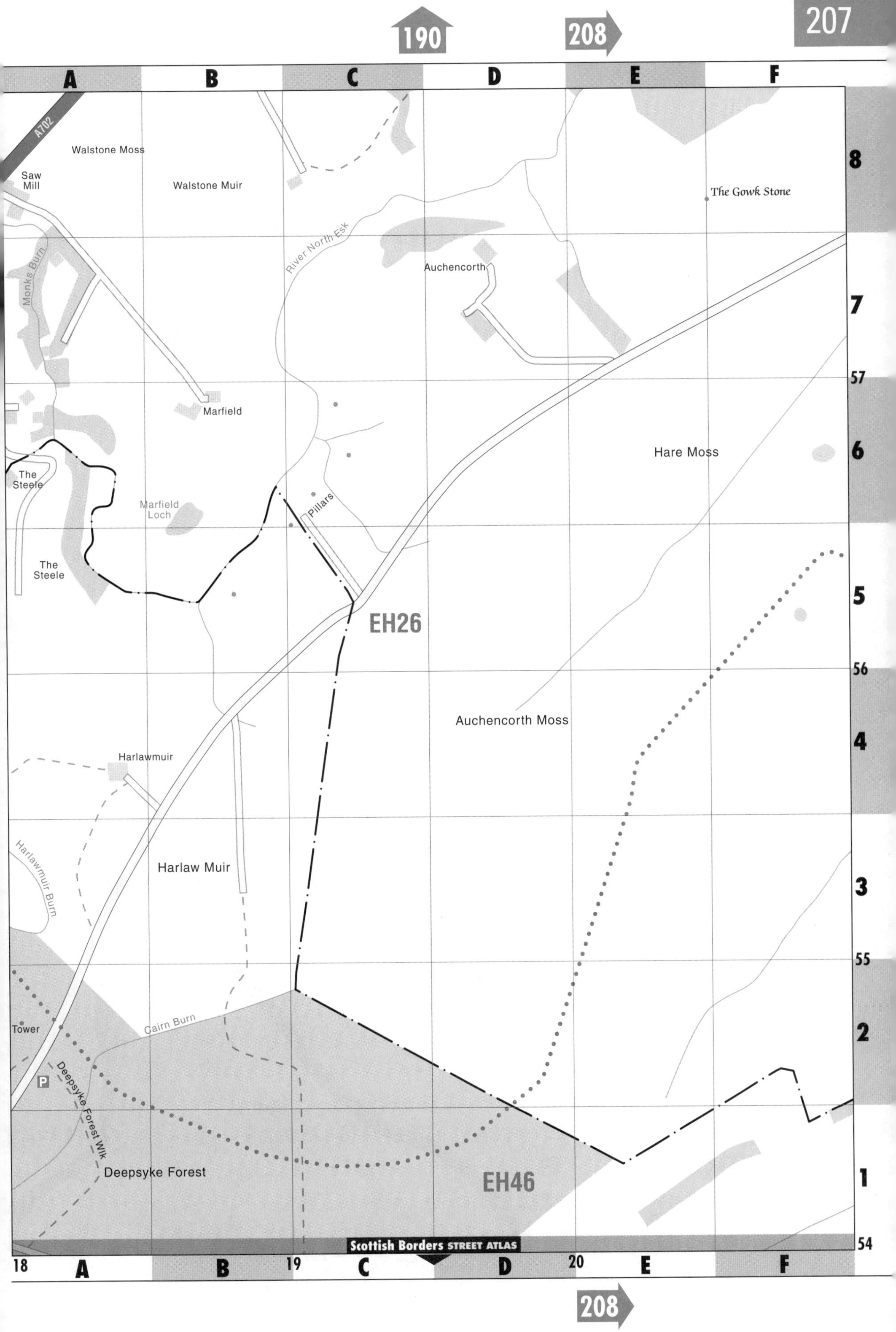
190
208
A
B
C
D
E
F
A702
Walstone Moss
Saw
Mill
Walstone Muir
The Gowk Stone
8
Monks Burn
River North Esk
Auchencorth
7
57
Marfield
Hare Moss
6
The
Steele
Marfield
Loch
Pillars
The
Steele
5
EH26
56
Auchencorth Moss
Harlawmuir
4
Harlawmuir Burn
Harlaw Muir
3
55
Cairn Burn
Tower
2
Deepsyke Forest Wlk
P
Deepsyke Forest
EH46
1
Scottish Borders STREET ATLAS
54
18
19
20
208

207
191

A
B
C
D
E
F
8
7
57
6
5
56
4
3
55
2
1
54
21
22
23
Dykeneuk
A701
Hare Burn
Nothorton
EH26
Braehead
Bowles
Black Burn
SPRINGFIELD RD
PEEBLES RD
Wellington Sch
Auchencorth Moss
Springfield
Rose View
A6094
Springfield Moss
Anne's Mill Bridge
Newstead
Woodend
Lead Burn
PH
Leadburn House
Leadburn
Leadburn Mains
A703
Rosemay
EH46
Rosehill
Baircochrane
Craigburn
Willow Burn
Mitchell Hill
Blairburn
Whim Park Cottage
Whim Pond
A701 Biggar (A702)
Scottish Borders STREET ATLAS

207

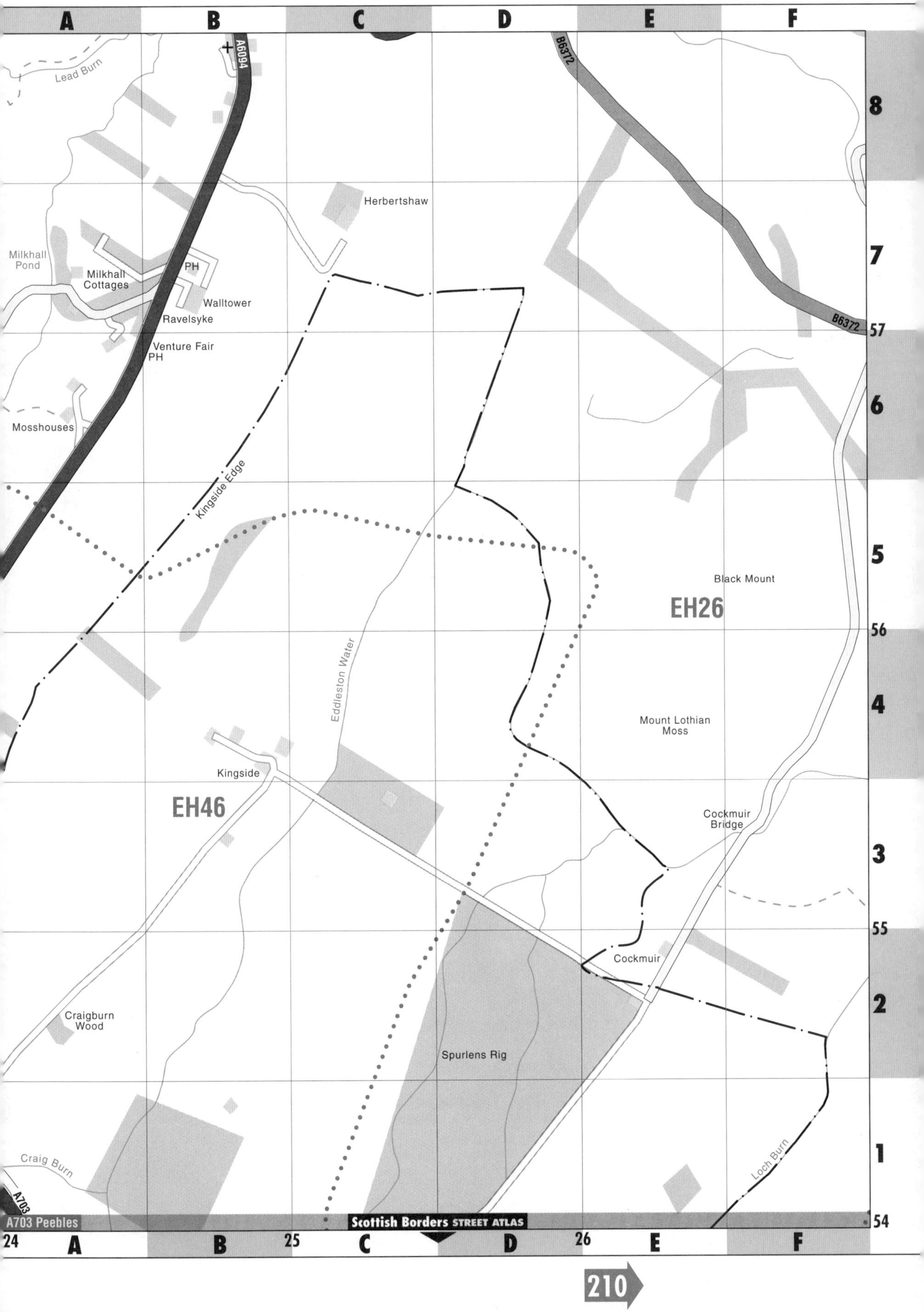
192
210
A
B
C
D
E
F
A6094
B6372
Lead Burn
Herbertshaw
Milkhall Pond
Milkhall Cottages
PH
Walltower
Ravelsyke
Venture Fair PH
Mosshouses
Kingside Edge
Black Mount
EH26
Eddleston Water
Mount Lothian Moss
Kingside
EH46
Cockmuir Bridge
Cockmuir
Craigburn Wood
Spurlens Rig
Craig Burn
A703
Loch Burn
8
7
57
6
5
56
4
3
55
2
1
54
24
25
26
A703 Peebles
210

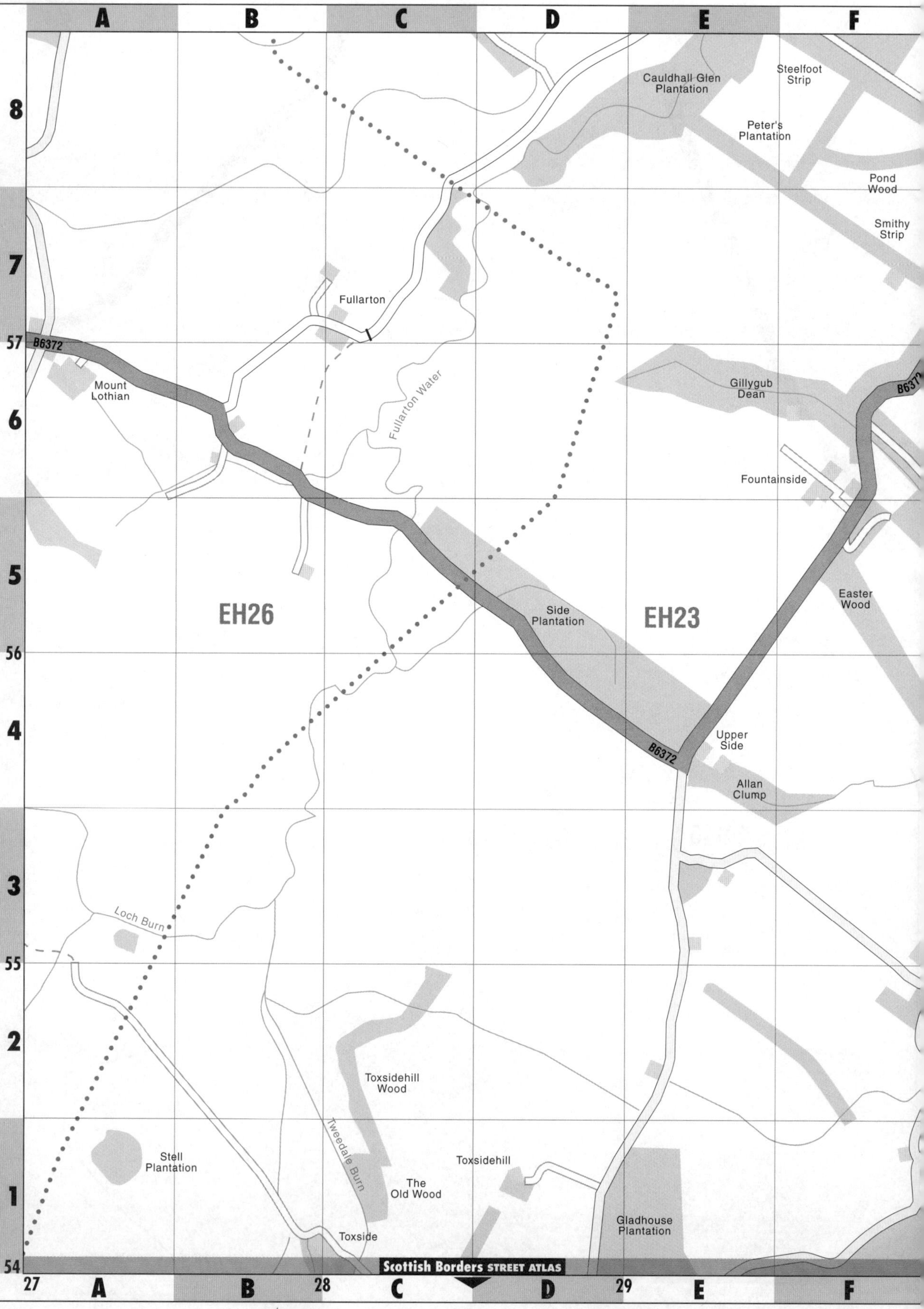
A
B
C
D
E
F
8
7
57
6
5
56
4
3
55
2
1
54
27
28
29
Cauldhall Glen Plantation
Steelfoot Strip
Peter's Plantation
Pond Wood
Smithy Strip
Fullarton
B6372
Mount Lothian
Fullarton Water
Gillygub Dean
B6372
Fountainside
EH26
Side Plantation
EH23
Easter Wood
B6372
Upper Side
Allan Clump
Loch Burn
Toxsidehill Wood
Tweedale Burn
Stell Plantation
Toxsidehill
The Old Wood
Toxside
Gladhouse Plantation

194
212
A
B
C
D
E
F
8
7
57
6
5
56
4
3
55
2
1
54
Rocks Wood
B6372
Saw Mill
Rosebery Farm
Rosebery
Walcot Burn
River South Esk
Mill Wood
Well Wood
Temple Farm
Pikeham Wood
Fountain Strip
Dove Wood
Millbank Cottage
Rosebery Filters
Broadhead Wood
Broadhead Cottage
Outerston
Yorkston
Rosebery Resr
EH23
River South Esk
Howburn
Gladhouse Mains
Cockmoor Wood
Blackburn Strip
Yorkston Moss
Gladhouse
P
P
Gladhouse Resr
Black Burn
30
31
32
A
B
C
D
E
F
212

211
195

A
B
C
D
E
F
8
7
57
6
5
56
4
3
55
2
1
54
33
34
35
Castleton Burn
Halkerston Glen
Common Hill
Hurcheon Hill
South Strip
Outerston
Esperston
Esperston Law
Rippy Bog
Allanshaw Wood
Middleton South Burn
Middleton North Burn
Chester Hill
EH23
Sowburnrig
Outerston Hill
Lass Law
Latch Burn
B7007
Wull Muir
EH38
Scottish Borders STREET ATLAS

211

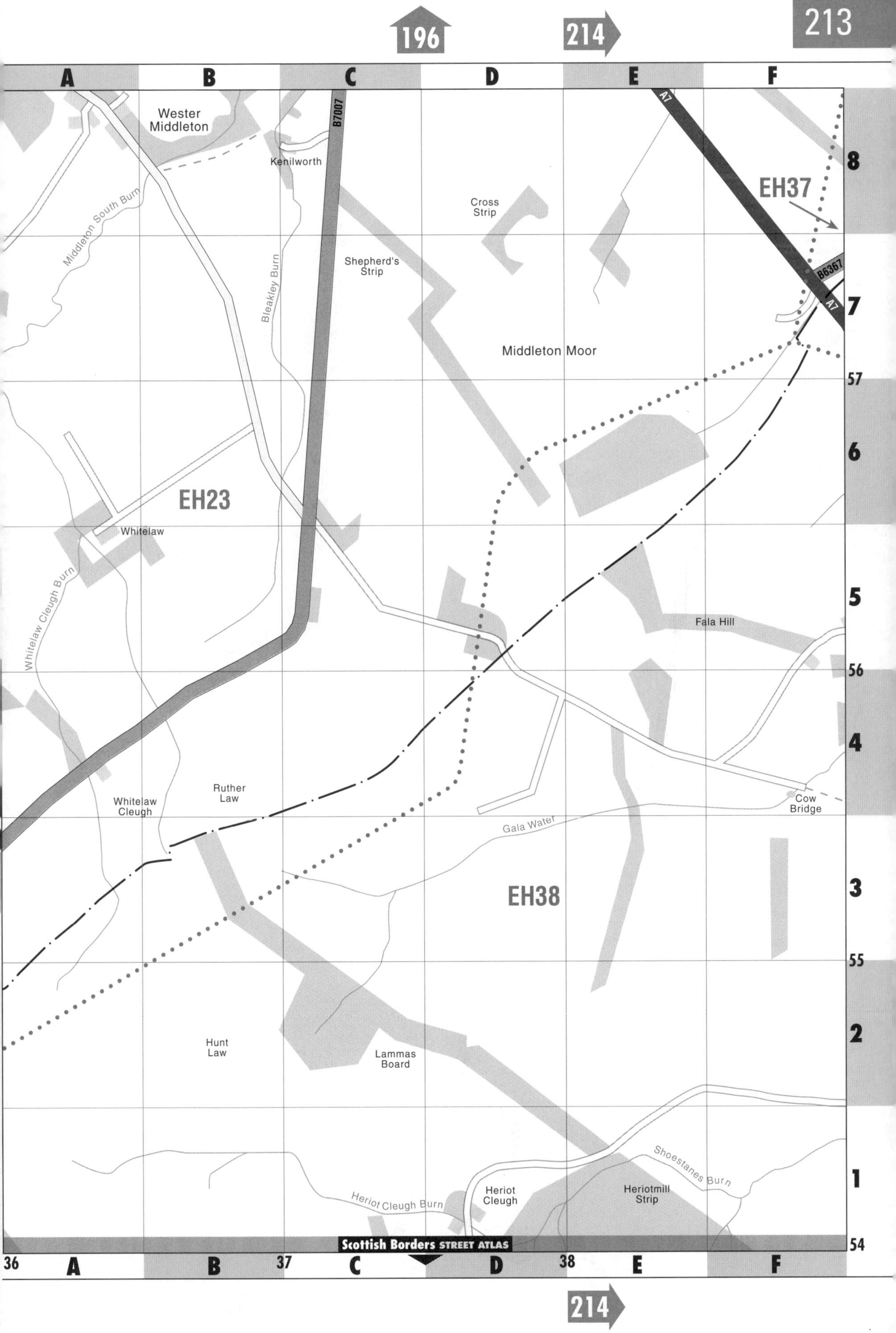
196
214
A
B
C
D
E
F
Wester Middleton
Kenilworth
B7007
A7
EH37
8
Middleton South Burn
Cross Strip
Shepherd's Strip
Bleakley Burn
B6367
A7
7
Middleton Moor
57
6
EH23
Whitelaw
Whitelaw Cleugh Burn
5
Fala Hill
56
4
Whitelaw Cleugh
Ruther Law
Cow Bridge
Gala Water
3
EH38
55
2
Hunt Law
Lammas Board
1
Shoestanes Burn
Heriot Cleugh
Heriotmill Strip
Heriot Cleugh Burn
54
36
A
B
37
C
D
38
E
F
214

213 197 224

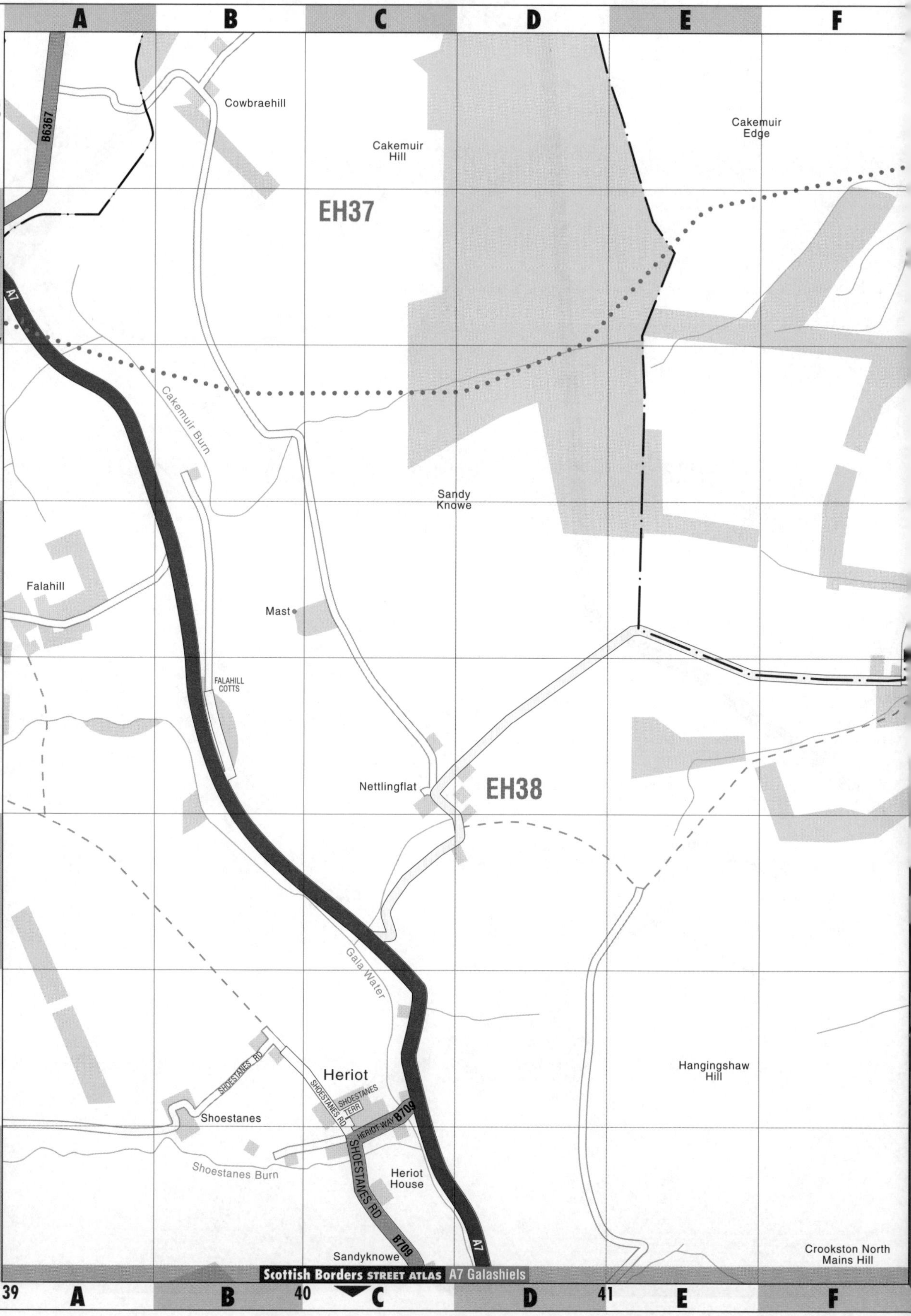
A B C D E F
8
7
57
6
5
56
4
3
55
2
1
54
39
40
41
B6367
Cowbraehill
Cakemuir Hill
Cakemuir Edge
EH37
A7
Cakemuir Burn
Sandy Knowe
Falahill
Mast
FALAHILL COTTS
Nettlingflat
EH38
Gala Water
Heriot
SHOESTANES RD
SHOESTANES TERR
Shoestanes
HERIOT WAY
B709
Shoestanes Burn
Heriot House
Sandyknowe
Hangingshaw Hill
Crookston North Mains Hill

213 224

198
216

A B C D E F
8 7 53 6 5 52 4 3 51 2 1 50
85 86 87
ML2
Kingshill Plantation
Black Law Wind Farm
King's Law
Gair Reservoirs
Bowridge Cottage
Bowridge Burn
Bowridge
Gair
Gair Farm
GAIR RD
Resr
ML8
Belstane Burn
Kingshaw Moss
Thorn
Under Thorn
Belstane Town Farm
Honeybank Bridge
Carluke Prim Sch
HONEYBANK CRES
BELSTANE GATE
GAIR CRES
Dyke
Fairyknowe View
Mast
STONEDYKE RD
DEESIDE DR
Albert Cottage
Moss-side
Moss-side Burn
Thornhome
West Highcross
THORN RD
Yieldshields Burn
B7056
Equestrian Centre
Carluke
MOORSIDE ST
HOPE ST
KING'S CRES
QUEEN'S CRES
WOODEND RD
ROSEMOUNT CT
CAIRNEYMOUNT RD
STANISTONE RD
MILLER ST
Carluke L Ctr
Carluke High Sch
Hillhead
Cauldron Gill
West Quarter
Yieldshields Farm
YIELDSHIELDS RD
Yieldshields
1 MANDORA CT
2 SRAEHOUSE WYND
3 MUIRLEE RD
4 CARLIN LA
5 CROSSEN LA
6 JOHNSTONE LA
7 DUNGAVEL LA
8 KELLY'S LA
9 DAVIDSON LA
10 CANDIMILNE CT
11 CARLOUK LA
Jock's Burn
A721
CARNWATH RD
KILNCADZOW RD
1 HIGH MDW
2 MEADOW CT
3 GOREMIRE RD
NORTHFLAT PL
Croftfoot
Coldstream Burn
Coldstream Bridge
B7056
BLENHEIM CT
MALPLAQUET CT
RAMILLIES CT
OUDENARDE CT
CORUNNA CT
GLENAFFOCH RD
PARKANDARROCH CRES
GLENMAVIS CRES
GLENMAVIS CT
MILLFOOT
RAMAGE RD
CANELUK AVE
CHARLES CRES
KELSO DR
WILTON RD
FOREST KIRK
BIRKFIELD PL
BIRKFIELD LOAN
ANGUS RD
1 EASTFIELD RD
2 TARBERT PL
GLENCOE RD
A721 Carnwath (A70)
A721 Carluke
Glasgow STREET ATLAS
Lanarkshire STREET ATLAS

216

215
199

A
B
C
D
E
F
8
7
53
6
5
52
4
3
51
2
1
50
88
89
90
ML2
Black Law
Black Law
Wind Farm
Birniehall
Netherton Burn
Thornmuir
ML8
Springfield
Reservoir
Hill of
Westerhouse
Middlehope
Farm
Easterseat
Springfield
Knowehead
Middlehouse
YIELDSHIELDS RD
B7056
Westerhouse
Netherton Burn
Damhead
East
Highcross
Coldstream Burn
Candymill Burn
ML11
Craigend
Mid
Coldstream

215

A
B
C
D
E
F
8
7
53
6
5
52
4
3
51
2
1
50
91
92
93
Abbey
Backshot
BIRNIEHALL 1
WHAUPHILL CRES 2
BANK TERR 3
TINTO VIEW 4
B715 CLIMPY RD
KINGSHILL VIEW
Forth
HIE DYKE
KNOWE
WHITTRET
THE NEUK
MERLINDALE
CLIMPY RD
WHAUPHILL
RAVENSWOOD
HARESIDE
WILSON CT
MERLINDALE
CLOGLANDS
WHITTRET KNOWE
LEA RIG
ABBEY PL
LONGDALES
A706 M8 Junc 4
Hare Hill
West Forth
A706
West Forth Croft
Whitecleugh
Upper Throughburn
ML8
Abbey Burn
Lower Throughburn
Haininghead
Throughburn Bridge
Lanarkshire STREET ATLAS
ML11
Covanhill
Through Burn
Mossplatt
Netherton Bridge
Browshott
Netherton Burn
Netherton
YIELDSHIELDS RD
Westertown
Brewshott
B7056
Mouse Water
Broadhouse Lea
A706
Newmains
Lewinside
A706 Lanark
Lanarkshire STREET ATLAS

107
136

Scale: 1¾ inches to 1mile
0 ¼ ½ mile
0 250m 500m 750m 1 km

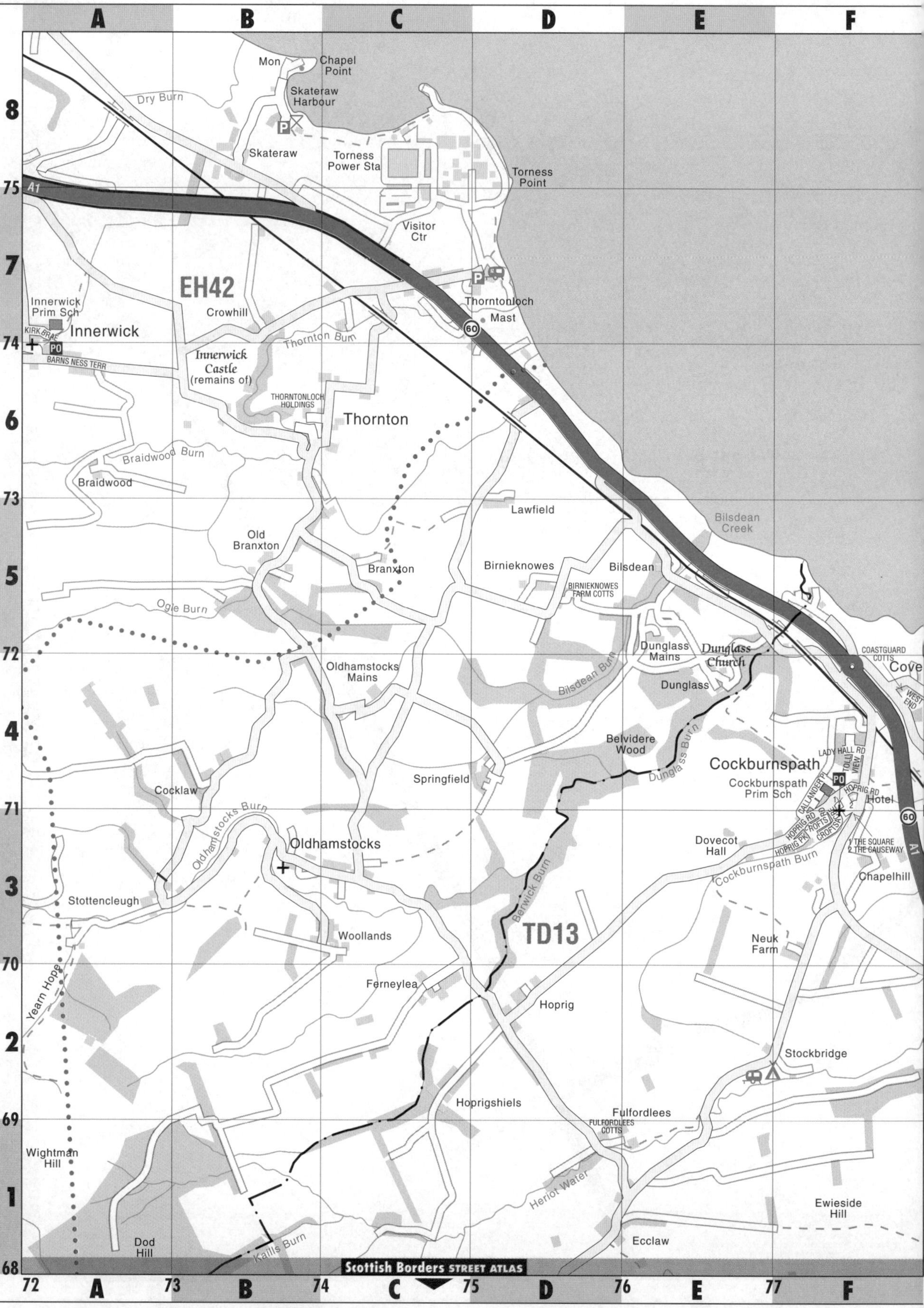

223

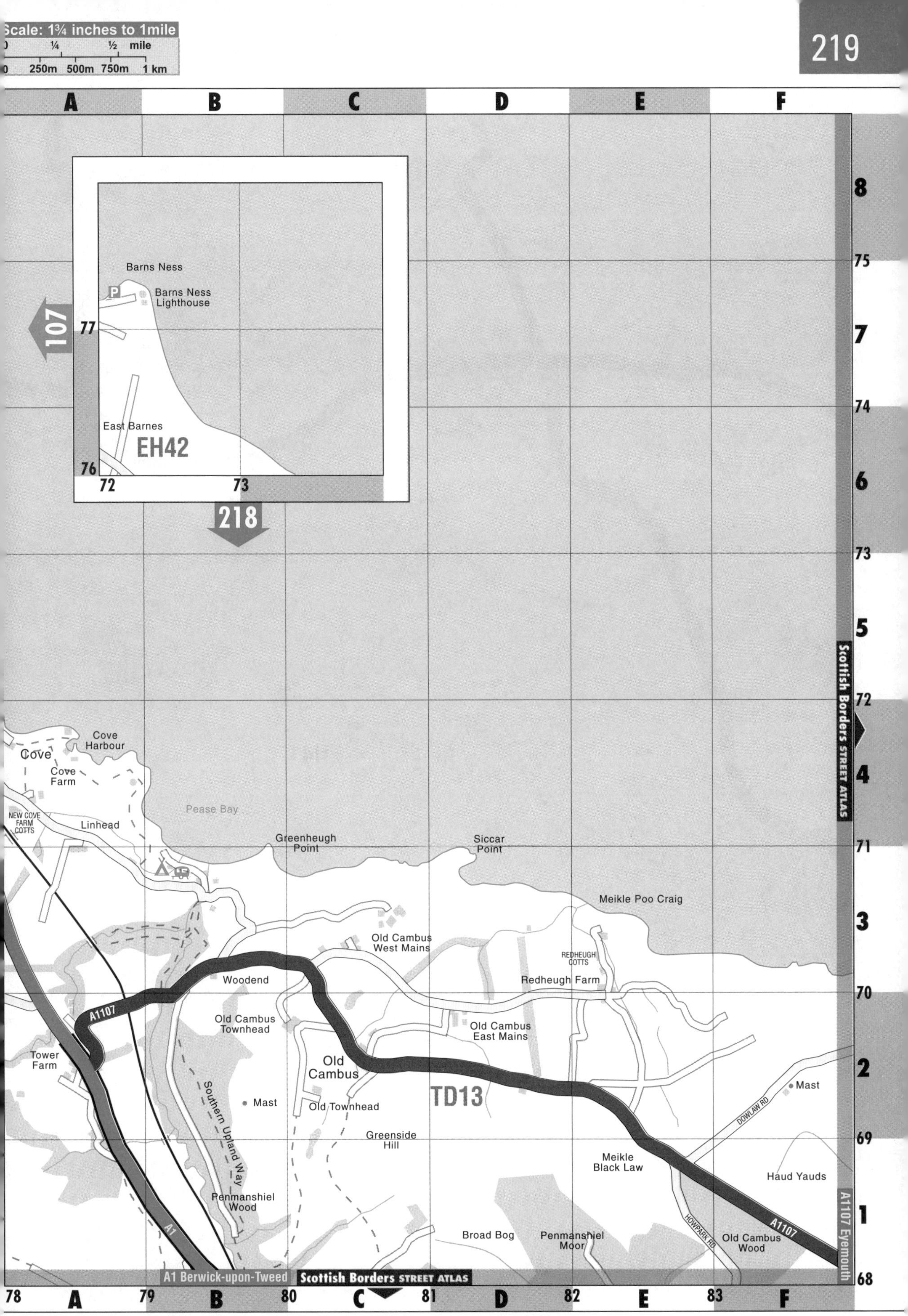
Scale: 1¾ inches to 1mile
¼
½ mile
250m 500m 750m 1 km
A
B
C
D
E
F
8
75
7
74
6
73
5
72
4
71
3
70
2
69
1
68
Barns Ness
Barns Ness Lighthouse
East Barnes
EH42
77
76
72
73
107
218
Cove
Cove Harbour
Cove Farm
NEW COVE FARM COTTS
Linhead
Pease Bay
Greenheugh Point
Siccar Point
Meikle Poo Craig
Old Cambus West Mains
REDHEUGH COTTS
Redheugh Farm
Woodend
A1107
Old Cambus Townhead
Old Cambus East Mains
Tower Farm
Old Cambus
Mast
Old Townhead
TD13
Southern Upland Way
Greenside Hill
DOWLAW RD
Meikle Black Law
Haud Yauds
Penmanshiel Wood
A1
Broad Bog
Penmanshiel Moor
HOWPARK RD
Old Cambus Wood
A1107 Eyemouth
Scottish Borders STREET ATLAS
A1 Berwick-upon-Tweed
78
79
80
81
82
83

157 129 130
Scale: 1¾ inches to 1mile
0 ¼ ½ mile
0 250m 500m 750m 1 km

178 225

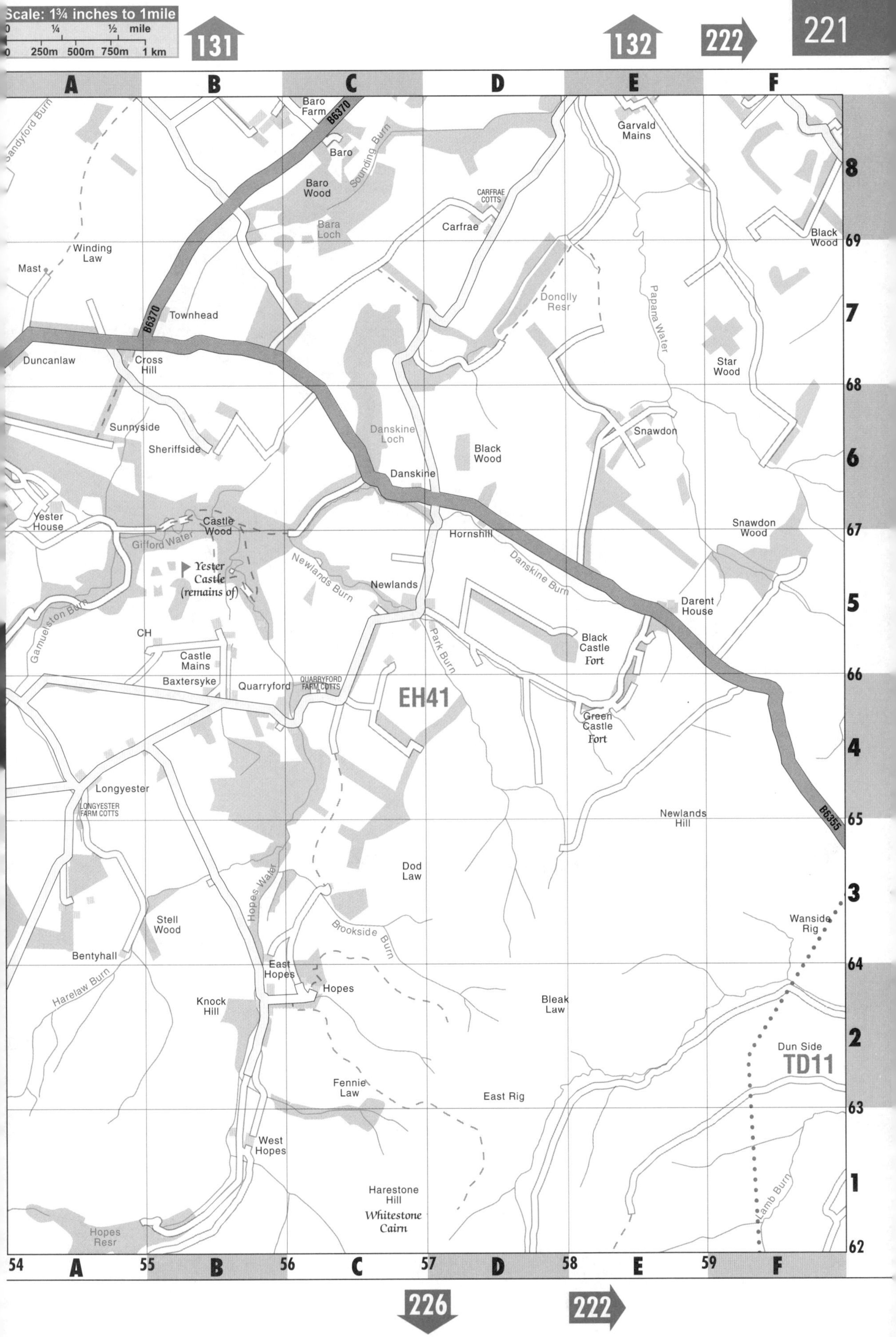
Scale: 1¾ inches to 1mile
0 ¼ ½ mile
0 250m 500m 750m 1 km
131
132
222
A B C D E F
8 69 7 68 6 67 5 66 4 65 3 64 2 63 1 62
54 55 56 57 58 59
Baro Farm
B6370
Baro
Sounding Burn
Baro Wood
Bara Loch
Garvald Mains
CARFRAE COTTS
Carfrae
Black Wood
Sandyford Burn
Winding Law
Mast
Donolly Resr
Papana Water
Townhead
Star Wood
Duncanlaw
Cross Hill
Sunnyside
Sheriffside
Danskine Loch
Snawdon
Black Wood
Danskine
Yester House
Castle Wood
Gifford Water
Hornshill
Snawdon Wood
Yester Castle (remains of)
Newlands Burn
Danskine Burn
Newlands
Darent House
Gamuelston Burn
CH
Park Burn
Black Castle Fort
Castle Mains
Baxtersyke
Quarryford
QUARRYFORD FARM COTTS
EH41
Green Castle Fort
Longyester
LONGYESTER FARM COTTS
Newlands Hill
B6355
Dod Law
Hopes Water
Stell Wood
Brookside Burn
Wanside Rig
Bentyhall
East Hopes
Harelaw Burn
Hopes
Knock Hill
Bleak Law
Dun Side
TD11
Fennie Law
East Rig
West Hopes
Harestone Hill
Whitestone Cairn
Lamb Burn
Hopes Resr
226
222

Scale: 1¾ inches to mile

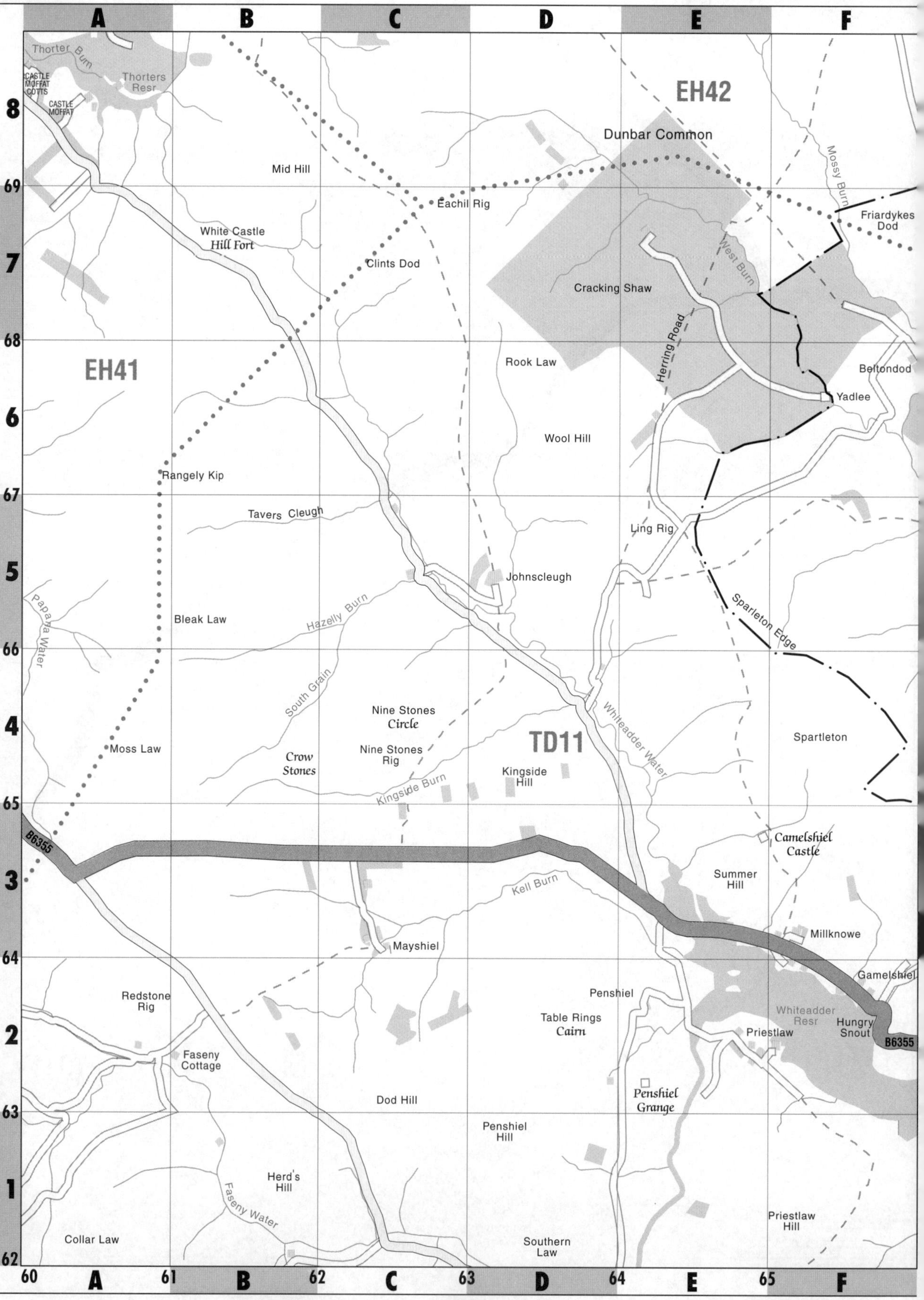

A B C D E F
Thorter Burn
CASTLE MOFFAT COTTS
Thorters Resr
CASTLE MOFFAT
EH42
Dunbar Common
Mid Hill
Eachil Rig
Mossy Burn
Friardykes Dod
White Castle
Hill Fort
Clints Dod
Cracking Shaw
West Burn
Herring Road
EH41
Rook Law
Beltondod
Yadlee
Wool Hill
Rangely Kip
Tavers Cleugh
Ling Rig
Johnscleugh
Papana Water
Bleak Law
Hazelly Burn
Sparleton Edge
South Grain
Nine Stones
Circle
Whiteadder Water
Spartleton
Moss Law
TD11
Crow Stones
Nine Stones Rig
Kingside Hill
Kingside Burn
B6355
Camelshiel Castle
Summer Hill
Kell Burn
Mayshiel
Millknowe
Gamelshiel
Redstone Rig
Penshiel
Table Rings
Cairn
Whiteadder Resr
Hungry Snout
Priestlaw
Faseny Cottage
Penshiel Grange
Dod Hill
Penshiel Hill
Herd's Hill
Faseny Water
Priestlaw Hill
Collar Law
Southern Law
8 69 7 68 6 67 5 66 4 65 3 64 2 63 1 62
60 61 62 63 64 65

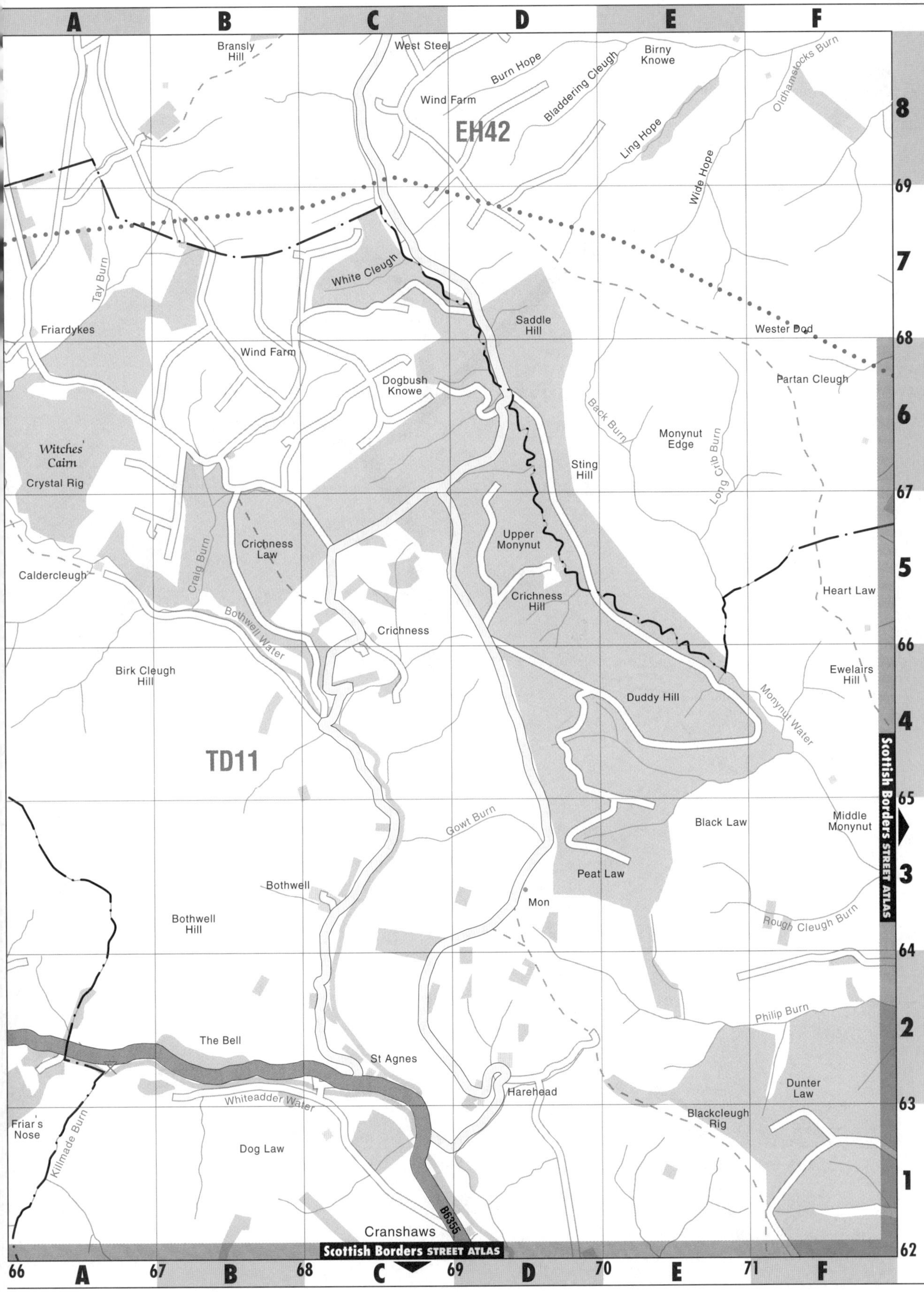
A B C D E F
West Steel
Bransly Hill
Burn Hope
Birny Knowe
Bladdering Cleugh
Oldhamstocks Burn
Wind Farm
EH42
Ling Hope
Wide Hope
White Cleugh
Tay Burn
Saddle Hill
Friardykes
Wind Farm
Wester Dod
Dogbush Knowe
Partan Cleugh
Back Burn
Monynut Edge
Witches' Cairn
Sting Hill
Crystal Rig
Long Crib Burn
Crichness Law
Upper Monynut
Craig Burn
Caldercleugh
Crichness Hill
Heart Law
Bothwell Water
Crichness
Birk Cleugh Hill
Ewelairs Hill
Duddy Hill
Monynut Water
TD11
Gowt Burn
Black Law
Middle Monynut
Peat Law
Bothwell
Mon
Bothwell Hill
Rough Cleugh Burn
Philip Burn
The Bell
St Agnes
Dunter Law
Harehead
Whiteadder Water
Blackcleugh Rig
Friar's Nose
Kilmade Burn
Dog Law
B6355
Cranshaws
8 69 7 68 6 67 5 66 4 65 3 64 2 63 1 62
66 67 68 69 70 71

197 177 178
Scale: 1¾ inches to 1mile

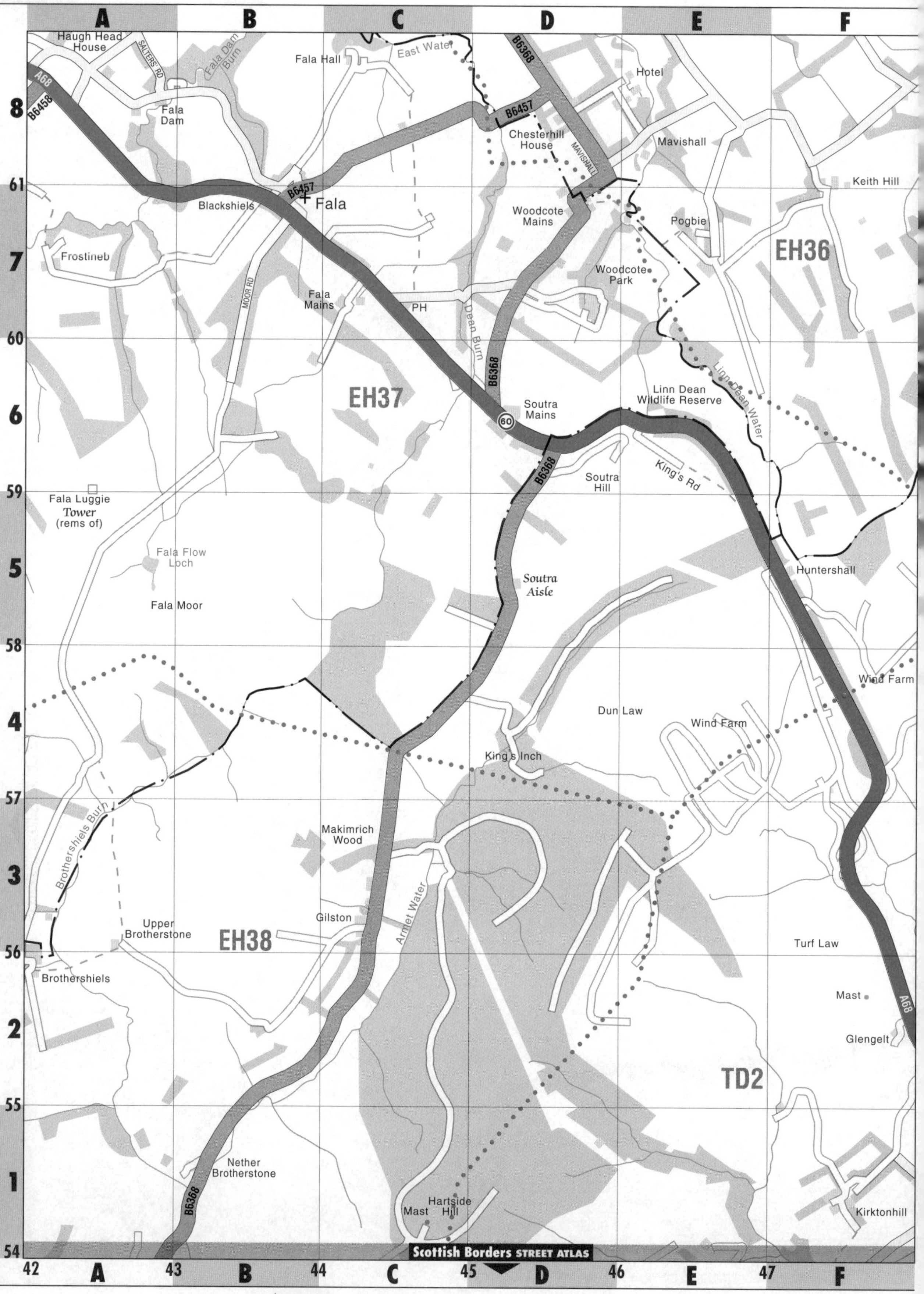

214

Scale: 1¾ inches to 1 mile

220
226

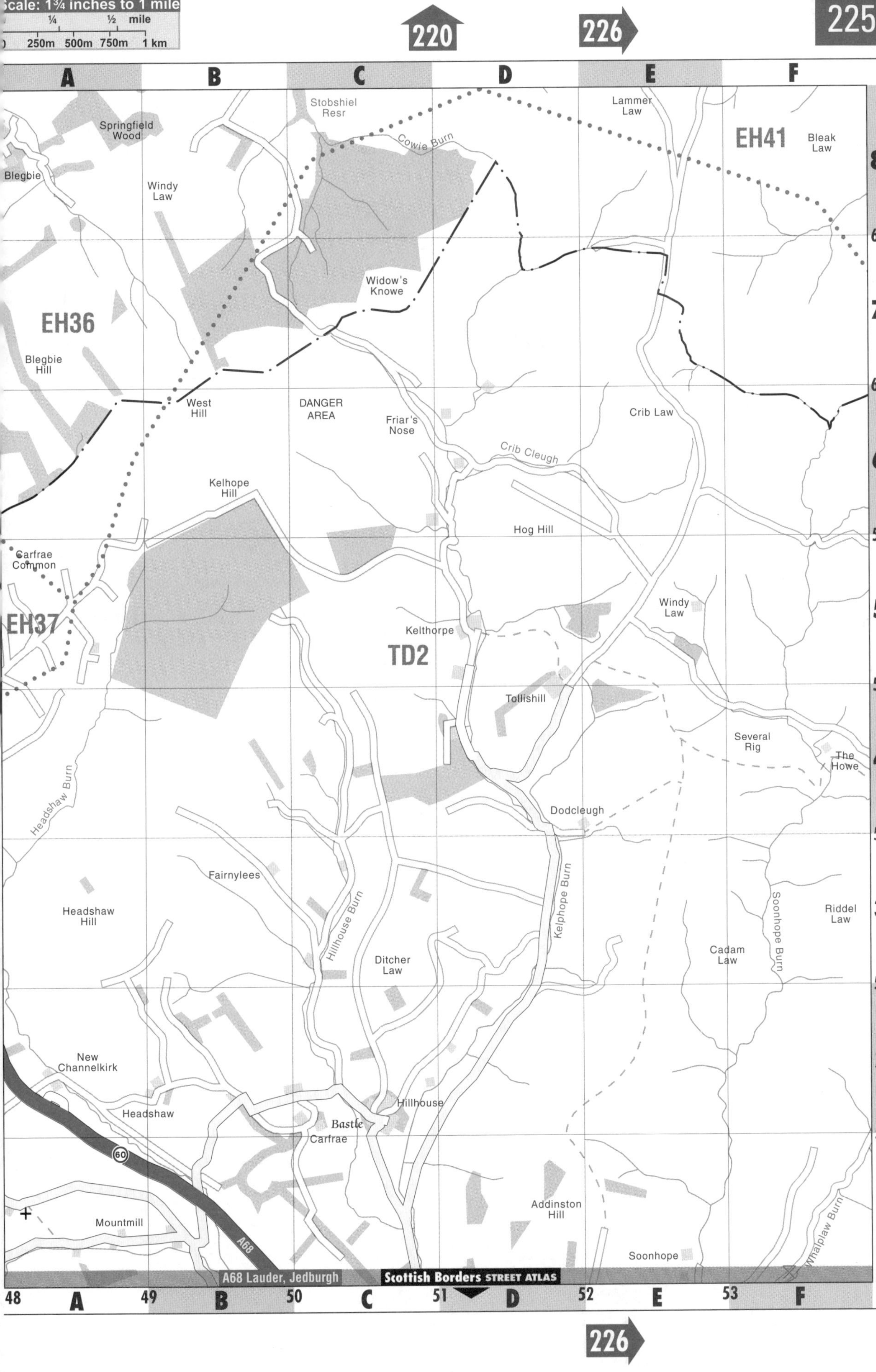
A
B
C
D
E
F
Stobshiel Resr
Lammer Law
EH41
Bleak Law
Springfield Wood
Cowie Burn
Blegbie
Windy Law
Widow's Knowe
EH36
Blegbie Hill
West Hill
DANGER AREA
Friar's Nose
Crib Law
Crib Cleugh
Kelhope Hill
Hog Hill
Carfrae Common
EH37
Windy Law
Kelthorpe
TD2
Tollishill
Several Rig
The Howe
Headshaw Burn
Dodcleugh
Fairnylees
Headshaw Hill
Hillhouse Burn
Kelphope Burn
Soonhope Burn
Riddel Law
Cadam Law
Ditcher Law
New Channelkirk
Hillhouse
Headshaw
Bastle
Carfrae
Addinston Hill
Mountmill
A68
Soonhope
Whalplaw Burn
A68 Lauder, Jedburgh
8
61
7
60
6
59
5
58
4
57
3
56
2
55
1
54
48
49
50
51
52
53

226

225
221

Scale: 1¾ inches to 1 mile
0 ¼ ½ mile
0 250m 500m 750m 1 km

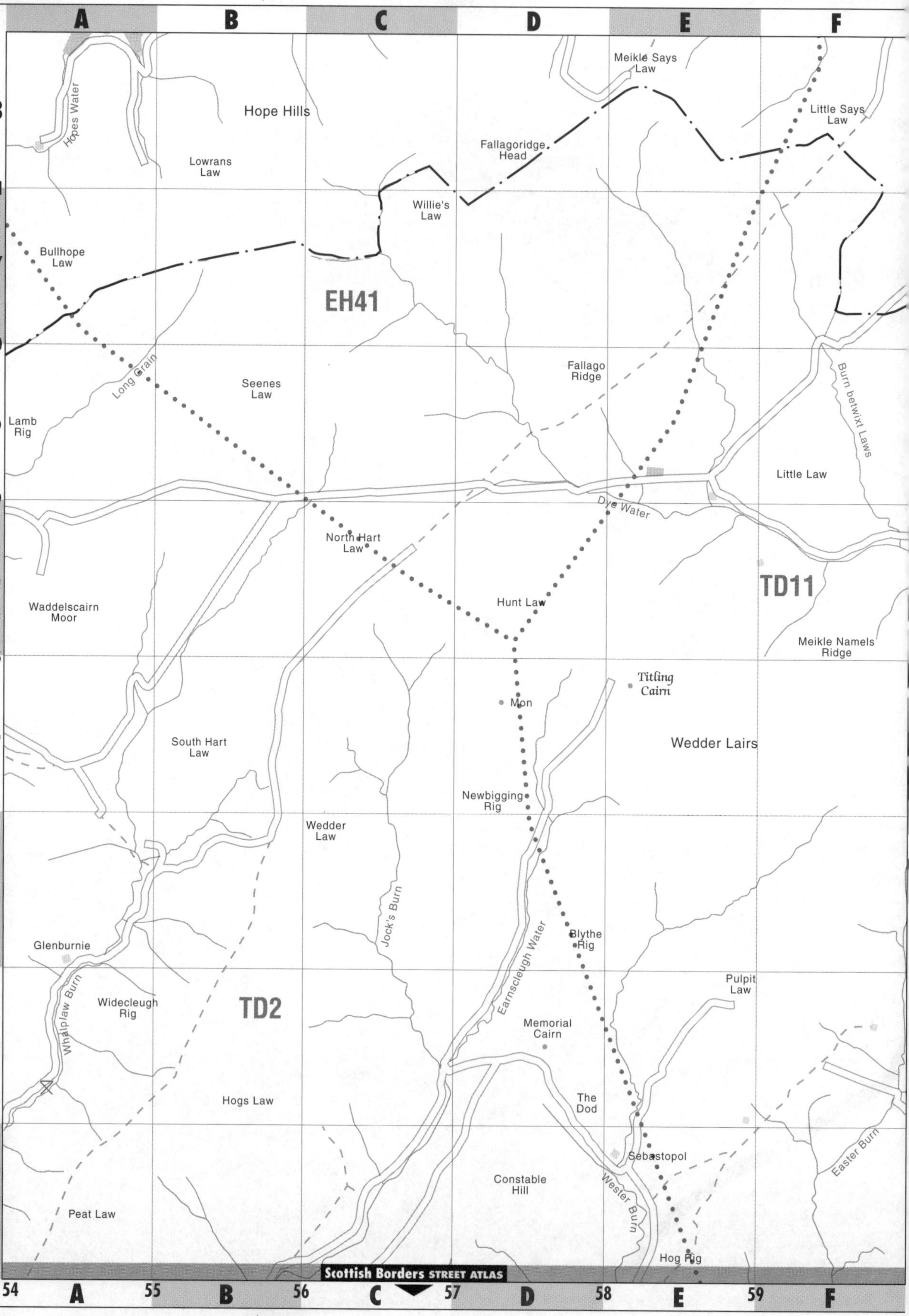
A B C D E F
8
61
7
60
6
59
5
58
4
57
3
56
2
55
1
54
Meikle Says Law
Little Says Law
Hope Hills
Hopes Water
Lowrans Law
Fallagoridge Head
Willie's Law
Bullhope Law
EH41
Long Grain
Seenes Law
Fallago Ridge
Burn betwixt Laws
Lamb Rig
Little Law
Dye Water
North Hart Law
TD11
Waddelscairn Moor
Hunt Law
Meikle Namels Ridge
Titling Cairn
Mon
South Hart Law
Wedder Lairs
Newbigging Rig
Wedder Law
Jock's Burn
Blythe Rig
Glenburnie
Earnscleugh Water
Pulpit Law
Whalplaw Burn
Widecleugh Rig
TD2
Memorial Cairn
The Dod
Hogs Law
Sebastopol
Easter Burn
Constable Hill
Wester Burn
Peat Law
Hog Rig
54 A 55 B 56 C 57 D 58 E 59 F

225

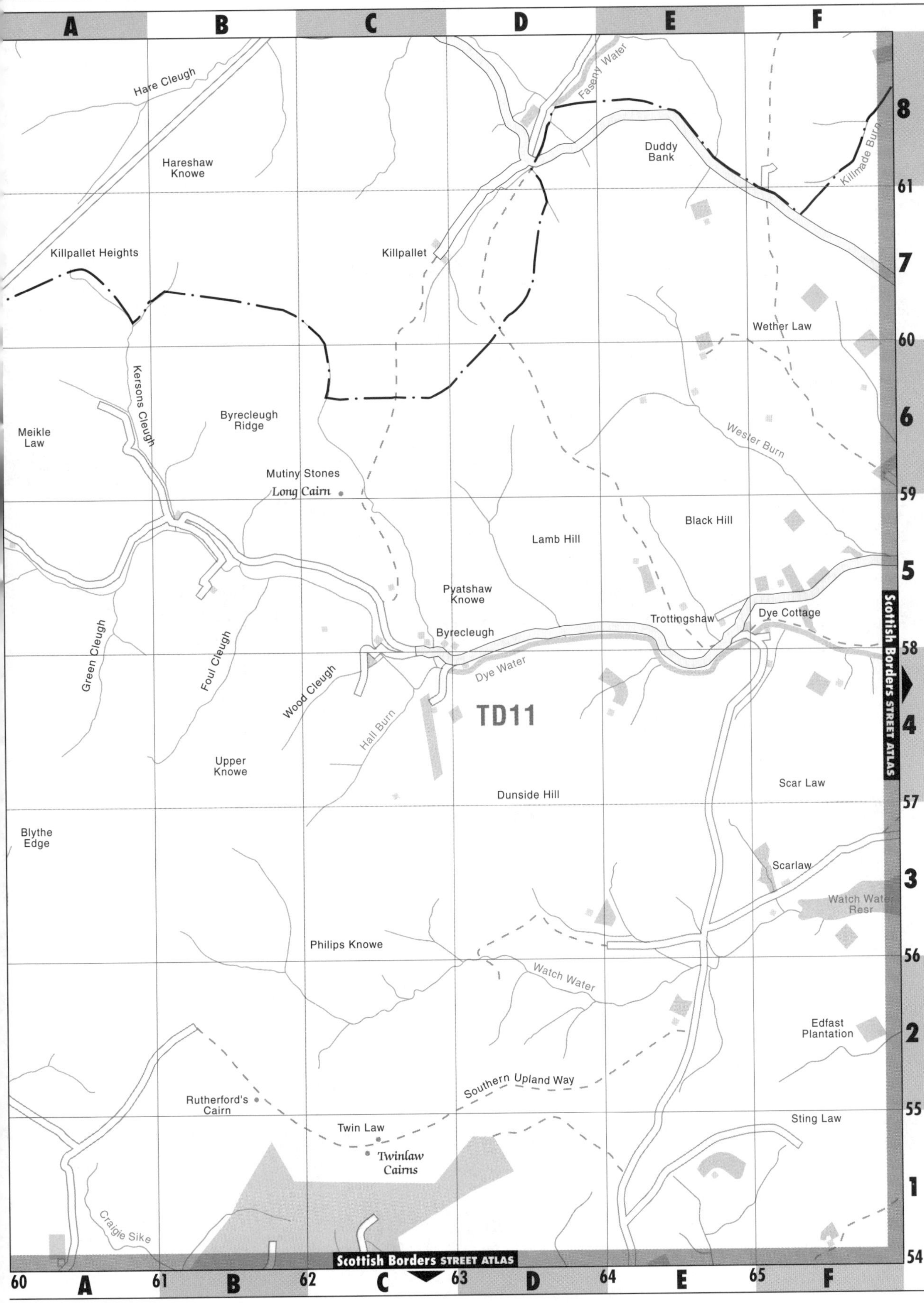
A
B
C
D
E
F
Hare Cleugh
Hareshaw Knowe
Faseny Water
Duddy Bank
Killmade Burn
Killpallet Heights
Killpallet
Wether Law
Meikle Law
Kersons Cleugh
Byrecleugh Ridge
Mutiny Stones
Long Cairn
Wester Burn
Black Hill
Lamb Hill
Pyatshaw Knowe
Trottingshaw
Dye Cottage
Byrecleugh
Green Cleugh
Foul Cleugh
Wood Cleugh
Dye Water
Hall Burn
TD11
Upper Knowe
Dunside Hill
Scar Law
Blythe Edge
Scarlaw
Watch Water Resr
Philips Knowe
Watch Water
Edfast Plantation
Southern Upland Way
Rutherford's Cairn
Twin Law
Twinlaw Cairns
Sting Law
Craigie Sike
8
61
7
60
6
59
5
58
4
57
3
56
2
55
1
54
60
61
62
63
64
65

92
93

Scale: 7 inches to 1 mile
0 110 yards 220 yards
0 125 m 250 m

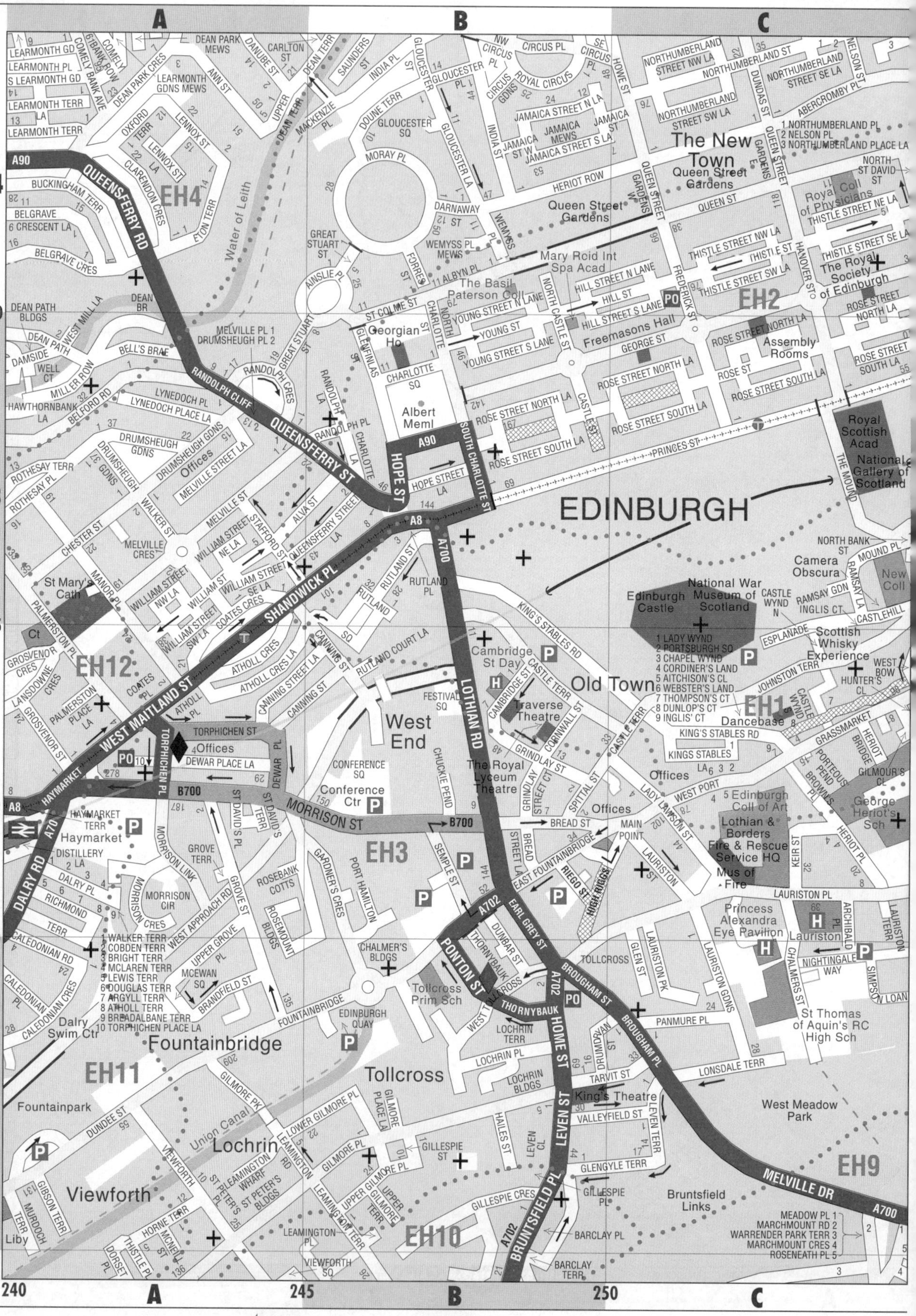
A B C
EDINBURGH
The New Town
Old Town
West End
Haymarket
Fountainbridge
Tollcross
Lochrin
Viewforth
Fountainpark
EH1
EH2
EH3
EH4
EH9
EH10
EH11
EH12
QUEENSFERRY RD
QUEENSFERRY ST
RANDOLPH CLIFF
HOPE ST
SHANDWICK PL
WEST MAITLAND ST
HAYMARKET
DALRY RD
LOTHIAN RD
MORRISON ST
EARL GREY ST
PONTON ST
HOME ST
LEVEN ST
BRUNTSFIELD PL
BROUGHAM ST
MELVILLE DR
PRINCES ST
QUEEN ST
GEORGE ST
HERIOT ROW
ROSE STREET NORTH LA
ROSE STREET SOUTH LA
THISTLE ST
HILL ST
YOUNG ST
CHARLOTTE SQ
MORAY PL
AINSLIE PL
ROYAL CIRCUS
CIRCUS PL
NORTHUMBERLAND ST
HOWE ST
DUNDAS ST
FREDERICK ST
HANOVER ST
CASTLE ST
NORTH CASTLE ST
MELVILLE ST
WALKER ST
MANOR PL
CHESTER ST
COATES CRES
ATHOLL CRES
TORPHICHEN ST
TORPHICHEN PL
DEWAR PL
GROVE ST
FOUNTAINBRIDGE
GILMORE PL
VIEWFORTH
GRASSMARKET
KING'S STABLES RD
JOHNSTON TERR
CASTLEHILL
THE MOUND
LAURISTON PL
LADY LAWSON ST
WEST PORT
TOLLCROSS
PANMURE PL
LONSDALE TERR
GLENGYLE TERR
BARCLAY PL
Queen Street Gardens
Georgian Ho
Albert Meml
Royal Scottish Acad
National Gallery of Scotland
Edinburgh Castle
National War Museum of Scotland
Camera Obscura
Scottish Whisky Experience
Royal Coll of Physicians
The Royal Society of Edinburgh
Assembly Rooms
Freemasons Hall
Mary Reid Int Spa Acad
The Basil Paterson Coll
St Mary's Cath
Traverse Theatre
The Royal Lyceum Theatre
Conference Ctr
Edinburgh Coll of Art
Lothian & Borders Fire & Rescue Service HQ
Mus of Fire
Princess Alexandra Eye Pavilion
Lauriston
George Heriot's Sch
St Thomas of Aquin's RC High Sch
Tollcross Prim Sch
King's Theatre
Dalry Swim Ctr
Bruntsfield Links
West Meadow Park
Union Canal
Water of Leith
Dancebase
Offices
Liby
1 LADY WYND
2 PORTSBURGH SQ
3 CHAPEL WYND
4 CORDINER'S LAND
5 AITCHISON'S CL
6 WEBSTER'S LAND
7 THOMPSON'S CT
8 DUNLOP'S CT
9 INGLIS' CT
1 WALKER TERR
2 COBDEN TERR
3 BRIGHT TERR
4 MCLAREN TERR
5 LEWIS TERR
6 DOUGLAS TERR
7 ARGYLL TERR
8 ATHOLL TERR
9 BREADALBANE TERR
10 TORPHICHEN PLACE LA
1 NORTHUMBERLAND PL
2 NELSON PL
3 NORTHUMBERLAND PLACE LA
MEADOW PL 1
MARCHMOUNT RD 2
WARRENDER PARK TERR 3
MARCHMOUNT CRES 4
ROSENEATH PL 5
A90
A8
A70
A700
A702
B700
4
740
3
735
2
730
1
725
240
245
250

120
121

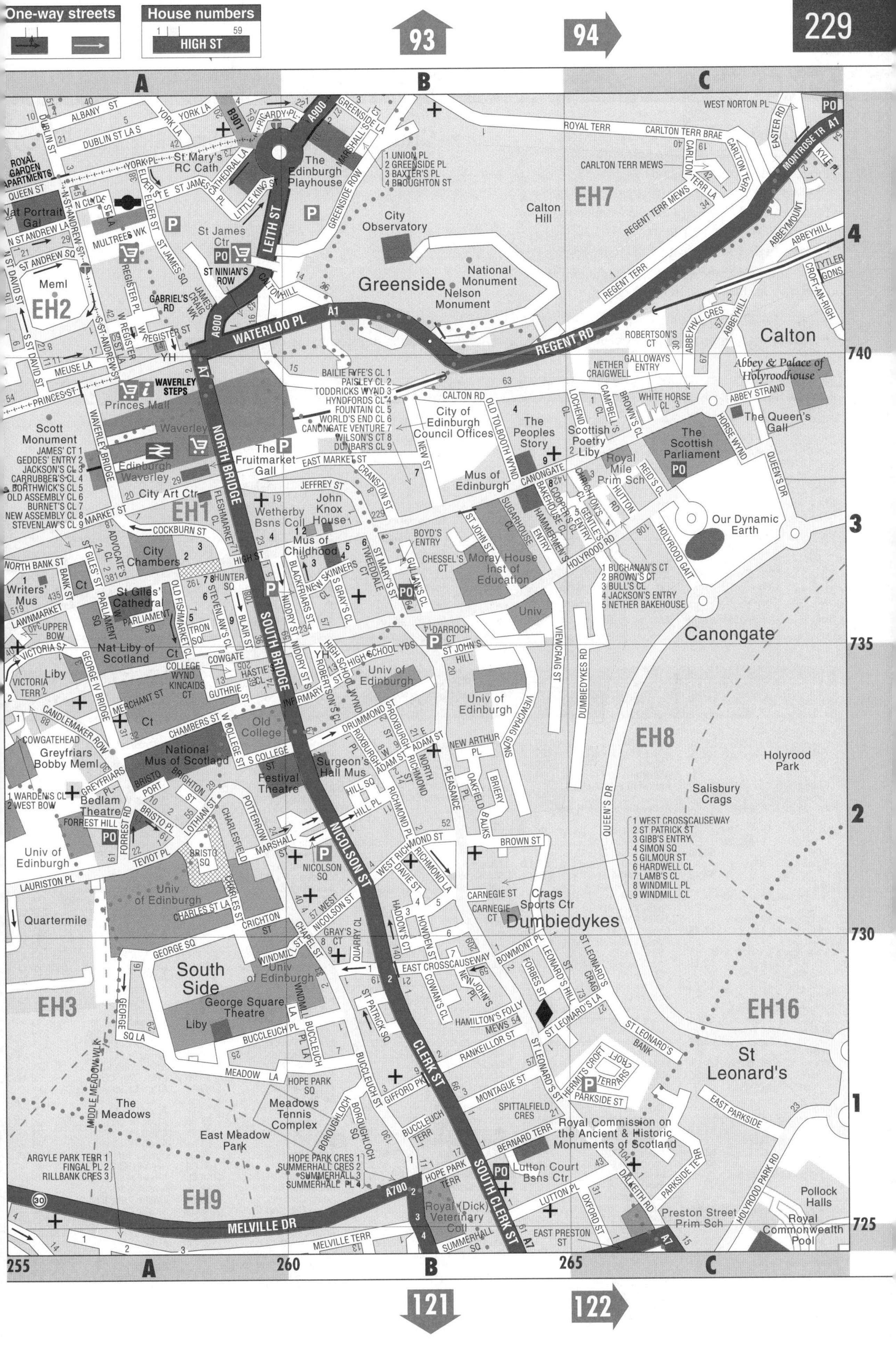
One-way streets
House numbers
HIGH ST
93
94
A
B
C
EH1
EH2
EH3
EH7
EH8
EH9
EH16
Greenside
Calton Hill
City Observatory
National Monument
Nelson Monument
Calton
Abbey & Palace of Holyroodhouse
The Queen's Gall
The Scottish Parliament
Our Dynamic Earth
Canongate
Holyrood Park
Salisbury Crags
Dumbiedykes
St Leonard's
South Side
The Meadows
East Meadow Park
Meadows Tennis Complex
Royal (Dick) Veterinary Coll
Royal Commonwealth Pool
Pollock Halls
Quartermile
Scott Monument
Princes Mall
Waverley
St Giles' Cathedral
Nat Liby of Scotland
National Mus of Scotland
Greyfriars Bobby Meml
Festival Theatre
Surgeon's Hall Mus
Old College
Univ of Edinburgh
George Square Theatre
Mus of Childhood
John Knox House
City of Edinburgh Council Offices
The Peoples Story
Mus of Edinburgh
Moray House Inst of Education
Crags Sports Ctr
Royal Commission on the Ancient & Historic Monuments of Scotland
Preston Street Prim Sch
NORTH BRIDGE
SOUTH BRIDGE
NICOLSON ST
CLERK ST
SOUTH CLERK ST
LEITH ST
WATERLOO PL
REGENT RD
MELVILLE DR
PRINCES ST
QUEEN'S DR
121
122
255
260
265
740
735
730
725

Index

Place name May be abbreviated on the map

Location number Present when a number indicates the place's position in a crowded area of mapping

Locality, town or village Shown when more than one place has the same name

Postcode district District for the indexed place

Page and grid square Page number and grid reference for the standard mapping

Church Rd **6** Beckenham BR2..........**53** C6

Cities, towns and villages are listed in CAPITAL LETTERS

Public and commercial buildings are highlighted in **magenta** **Places of interest** are highlighted in **blue** with a star*

Abbreviations used in the index

Acad	Academy	Comm	Common	Gd	Ground	L	Leisure	Prom	Promenade
App	Approach	Cott	Cottage	Gdn	Garden	La	Lane	Rd	Road
Arc	Arcade	Cres	Crescent	Gn	Green	Liby	Library	Recn	Recreation
Ave	Avenue	Cswy	Causeway	Gr	Grove	Mdw	Meadow	Ret	Retail
Bglw	Bungalow	Ct	Court	H	Hall	Meml	Memorial	Sh	Shopping
Bldg	Building	Ctr	Centre	Ho	House	Mkt	Market	Sq	Square
Bsns, Bus	Business	Ctry	Country	Hospl	Hospital	Mus	Museum	St	Street
Bvd	Boulevard	Cty	County	HQ	Headquarters	Orch	Orchard	Sta	Station
Cath	Cathedral	Dr	Drive	Hts	Heights	Pal	Palace	Terr	Terrace
Cir	Circus	Dro	Drove	Ind	Industrial	Par	Parade	TH	Town Hall
Cl	Close	Ed	Education	Inst	Institute	Pas	Passage	Univ	University
Cnr	Corner	Emb	Embankment	Int	International	Pk	Park	Wk, Wlk	Walk
Coll	College	Est	Estate	Intc	Interchange	Pl	Place	Wr	Water
Com	Community	Ex	Exhibition	Junc	Junction	Prec	Precinct	Yd	Yard

Index of towns, villages, streets, hospitals, industrial estates, railway stations, schools, shopping centres, universities and places of interest

1st–Air

1st St
Grangemouth, Chemical Works FK3 .... 62 D6
Grangemouth, Oil Refinery FK3 .... 62 A7
2nd St
Grangemouth, Chemical Works FK3 .... 62 D6
Grangemouth, Oil Refinery FK3 .... 62 A8
3rd St
Grangemouth, Chemical Works EH51 .... 62 D6
Grangemouth, Oil Refinery FK3 .... 62 A8
4th St
Grangemouth, Chemical Works EH51 .... 62 E6
Grangemouth, Oil Refinery FK3 .... 62 B8
5th St
Grangemouth, Chemical Works EH51 .... 62 E6
Grangemouth, Oil Refinery FK3 .... 62 B8
6th St
Grangemouth, Chemical Works EH51 .... 62 E6
Grangemouth, Oil Refinery FK3 .... 62 B8
7th St
Grangemouth, Chemical Works EH51 .... 62 E5
Grangemouth, Oil Refinery FK3 .... 62 C8
8th St FK3, EH51 .... 62 C8
92 Fettes Coll Prep Sch EH4 .... 92 F4

A

A1 Ind Pk EH15 .... 123 B7
Abbey Craig Ct FK9 .... 2 D3
Abbeycraig Pk FK9 .... 2 D4
Abbey Craig Rd FK10 .... 5 B1
Abbey Cres EH39 .... 54 B7
Abbey Ct EH39 .... 54 B7
Abbeyfield Ho EH4 .... 92 B2
Abbeygrange EH22 .... 174 A6
ABBEYHILL 94 A1
Abbeyhill EH8 .... 229 C4
Abbeyhill Cres EH8 .... 229 C4
Abbeyhill Ind Est EH8 .... 94 A1
Abbeyhill Prim Sch 9 EH7 .... 94 A1
Abbey Kings Park Hospl (private) FK7 .... 6 F5
Abbey La EH8 .... 94 A1
Abbey Mains EH41 .... 101 F4
Abbey Mews 3 EH39 .... 54 B7
Abbey Mill FK8 .... 7 C8
Abbeymount EH8 .... 229 C4
Abbey & Palace of Holyroodhouse* EH8 .... 229 C3
Abbey Park Pl KY12 .... 29 A3
ABBEY PARKS 29 B3
Abbey Pl ML11 .... 217 F7
Abbey Rd Dalkeith EH22 .... 153 A2
Dunbar EH42 .... 78 D2
North Berwick EH39 .... 54 B7
Stirling FK8 .... 2 C1
Abbey Road Pl FK8 .... 7 C8
Abbey St Edinburgh EH7 .... 94 A1
High Valleyfield KY12 .... 26 B2
Abbey Strand EH8 .... 229 C3
Abbeyview FK9 .... 2 D4
Abbey View Crossford KY12 .... 28 C1
Dunfermline KY11 .... 29 E2
Abbot Rd FK7 .... 7 D4
Abbots Cl EH39 .... 53 F7
Abbotsford Cres
Edinburgh EH10 .... 121 A4
Shotts ML7 .... 179 F5
Abbotsford Ct EH10 .... 121 A4
Abbotsford Dr
Grangemouth FK3 .... 61 F6
Laurieston FK2 .... 61 A4
Abbotsford Gdns FK2 .... 39 B1
Abbotsford Pk EH10 .... 121 A4
Abbotsford Pl FK8 .... 2 C1
Abbotsford Rd EH39 .... 53 E7
Abbotsford Rise EH54 .... 144 A1
Abbotsford St FK2 .... 60 B8
Abbotsgrange Rd FK3 .... 61 E7
Abbotshall Rd
Kirkcaldy KY1, KY2 .... 17 B3
Kirkcaldy, Linktown KY1, KY2 .... 17 A2
Abbotsinch Ct FK3 .... 61 F7
Abbotsinch Ind Est FK3 .... 61 F7
Abbotsinch Rd FK3 .... 61 F7
Abbots Mill KY2 .... 17 A3
Abbots Moss Dr FK1 .... 59 F1
Abbots Rd
Falkirk, Bankside FK2 .... 60 D8
Falkirk, Middlefield FK2 .... 60 D7
Grangemouth FK3 .... 61 D7
Abbots Road Rdbt FK2 .... 60 D8
Abbot St KY12 .... 29 A3
Abbots View FK2 .... 61 F3
Abbot's View
Burntisland KY3 .... 50 D8
Haddington EH41 .... 101 B2
Abbotsview Junc EH41 .... 101 B2
Abbots Wlk KY2 .... 16 F3
Abbott Ho Her Ctr* KY12 .... 29 A3
Abden Ave Kinghorn KY3 .... 35 A3
Rosewell EH24 .... 172 C1
Abden Ct KY3 .... 35 A3
Abden Pl KY3 .... 35 A3
Abel Pl KY11 .... 29 F4
Abercairney Cres FK2 .... 82 E6
Abercairney Pl FK3 .... 61 E7
ABERCORN 66 E2
Abercorn Ave EH8 .... 122 D8
Abercorn Cres EH8 .... 122 D8
Abercorn Ct
Edinburgh EH8 .... 122 D7
Winchburgh EH52 .... 88 A2
Abercorn Dr EH8 .... 122 D8
Abercorn Gdns EH8 .... 94 D1
Abercorn Gr EH8 .... 122 C8
Abercorn Pl EH52 .... 87 F2
Abercorn Rd EH8 .... 122 C8
Abercorn Terr EH15 .... 123 C8
Abercrombie Pl FK11 .... 3 F6
Abercrombie St FK1 .... 59 E6
Abercromby Dr FK9 .... 2 B8
Abercromby Pl
Edinburgh EH3 .... 228 C4
Stirling FK8 .... 7 A7
Tullibody FK10 .... 4 B2
Abercromby Prim Sch FK10 .... 4 B2
ABERDOUR 49 C7
Aberdour Castle* KY3 .... 49 C7
Aberdour Cres KY11 .... 29 D1
Aberdour Pl KY11 .... 29 D1
Aberdour Prim Sch KY3 .... 49 C8
Aberdour Rd
Burntisland KY3 .... 33 C1
Dunfermline KY11 .... 30 A1
Aberdour Sta KY3 .... 49 C7
ABERLADY 71 D4
Aberlady Bay Nature Reserve* EH32 .... 71 B7
Aberlady Mains Cotts EH32 .... 71 D4
Aberlady Prim Sch EH32 .... 71 C4
Aberlady Rd EH41 .... 100 F1
Aberlour St KY11 .... 46 E4
Abinger Gdns EH12 .... 120 D7
Abington Rd KY12 .... 28 F2
Aboyne Ave FK9 .... 2 C4
Aboyne Gdns KY2 .... 16 E8
Academy La EH20 .... 172 C8
Academy Pk EH6 .... 94 A4
Academy Pl
Bannockburn FK7 .... 7 E1
Bathgate EH48 .... 141 B6
Academy Rd Bo'ness EH51 .... 64 A7
Stirling FK8 .... 7 A8
Academy Sq KY11 .... 45 D3
Academy St Alloa FK10 .... 9 F8
Armadale EH48 .... 139 F5
Bathgate EH48 .... 141 B6
Edinburgh EH6 .... 94 A4
Acheson Dr EH32 .... 125 E8
Achray Ct FK10 .... 10 C5
Achray Dr Falkirk FK1 .... 60 A1
Stirling FK9 .... 2 A4
Acklam Path EH20 .... 171 F7
Acorn Cres FK5 .... 38 D1
Acorn Dr FK10 .... 4 A3
Acorn Rd KY4 .... 13 C6
Acredale EH48 .... 141 B6
Acredales
Haddington EH41 .... 129 F7
Linlithgow EH49 .... 85 A5
Acredales Wlk EH41 .... 129 F8
Acre Rd EH51 .... 64 D6
Acre View EH51 .... 64 C6
ADAMBRAE 164 C8
Adambrae Rd EH54 .... 164 C8
Adambrae Rdbt EH54 .... 164 D8
Adam Cres FK5 .... 38 F2
Adam Grossert Ct FK5 .... 38 D3
Adam Pl KY5 .... 14 A8
Adams Loan FK2 .... 39 A1
Adam Smith Cl KY1 .... 17 C4
Adam Smith Coll KY1 .... 17 B4
Adam Smith Coll (Priory Campus) KY1 .... 17 D5
Adam Smith Ct KY1 .... 17 C4
Adam Smith Theatre* KY2 .... 17 B4
Adamson Ave KY2 .... 17 B6
Adamson Cres KY12 .... 29 C5
Adamson Pl FK9 .... 2 B3
Adamson Rd KY5 .... 14 A8
Adam Sq EH54 .... 164 C6
Adam St FK2 .... 60 D6
Adams Well EH13 .... 149 C7
ADDIEBROWNHILL 162 E1
Addiebrownhill EH55 .... 162 D1
ADDIEWELL 162 E2
Addiewell Comb Prim Sch & St Thomas' RC Prim Sch EH55 .... 162 D1
Addiewell Sta EH55 .... 162 E1
Addiston Cres EH14 .... 147 C3
Addiston Farm Rd EH28 .... 118 B1
Addiston Gr EH14 .... 147 C3
Addiston Pk EH14 .... 147 C3
Adelaide St EH54 .... 144 A5
Adelphi Gr 1 EH15 .... 123 A8
Adelphi Pl EH15 .... 123 A8
Adia Rd KY12 .... 26 F1
Admiral Terr EH10 .... 121 B5
Admiralty Rd
Inverkeithing KY11 .... 47 B4
Rosyth KY11 .... 46 D4
Admiralty St EH6 .... 93 F6
Advocate's Cl EH1 .... 229 A3
Affleck Ct 3 EH12 .... 119 A8
Affric Dr FK2 .... 39 C1
Affric Loan ML7 .... 179 E6
Affric Way KY12 .... 28 B1
Afton Ct Dechmont EH52 .... 114 C2
Stirling FK7 .... 7 C5
Afton Dr FK6 .... 57 D7
Afton Gr KY11 .... 29 F5
Afton Pl EH5 .... 93 A5
Afton Terr EH5 .... 93 A5
Agnew Terr EH6 .... 93 D5
Ailsa Ct 3 FK2 .... 82 F7
Ailsa Gr KY2 .... 16 F8
Ainslie Gdns FK2 .... 61 F3
Ainslie Park L Ctr EH5 .... 92 E5
Ainslie Pl EH3 .... 228 B4
Airdrie Rd EH48, ML6 .... 137 B3
Airlie Dr FK2 .... 61 F2
Airlie Pl EH3 .... 93 C2
AIRTH 22 D3
Airth Dr FK7 .... 7 C4
Airth Prim Sch FK2 .... 22 E4
Airthrey Ave FK9 .... 2 B6
Airthrey Castle Yd FK9 .... 2 E6
Airthrey Dr FK5 .... 38 F4
Airthrey Rd FK9 .... 2 C5

Aitchison Dr FK5 38 B3
Aitchison Pl FK1 60 B3
Aitchison's Cl EH1 228 C2
Aitchison's Pl EH15 95 A1
Aitken Cres Falkirk FK2 61 A1
Stirling FK7 7 B2
Aitken Ct Dunbar EH42 78 D3
Kirkcaldy KY1 17 B2
Aitken Dr Slamannan FK1 108 A6
Whitburn EH47 161 B7
Aitken Gdns FK1 59 E6
Aitken Orr Dr EH52 115 F5
Aitken Rd FK1 59 D6
Aitken St KY1 17 E7
Aitken Terr FK1 59 D6
Akarit Rd FK5 38 E2
Alan Breck Gdns EH4 91 D1
Alba Campus The EH54 164 A8
Albany Bsns Ctr KY12 29 B4
Albany Ind Est KY12 29 B4
Albany St Dunfermline KY12 29 B4
Edinburgh EH1 229 A4
Albany Street La 7 EH3 93 D2
Alberta Ave EH54 143 E4
Albert Ave FK3 61 F8
Albert Bldgs EH48 110 F5
Albert Cl EH21 125 B5
Albert Cres EH21 125 B5
Albert Pl 5 Edinburgh EH7 93 E2
Stirling FK8 7 A7
Wallyford EH21 125 B5
Albert Rd Edinburgh EH6 94 B5
Falkirk FK1 60 A3
Harthill ML7 159 E5
Albert St Edinburgh EH7 93 F3
Rosyth KY11 46 E4
Albert Terr
Edinburgh EH10 121 A4
Musselburgh EH21 124 E6
Albion Bsns Ctr EH7 94 A2
Albion Gdns EH7 94 A2
Albion Pl EH7 94 A2
Albion Rd EH7 94 A2
Albion Terr EH7 94 A2
Albyn Cotts EH52 115 E6
Albyn Dr EH54 164 E5
Albyn Ind Est EH52 115 F7
Albyn Pl Broxburn EH52 115 E6
Edinburgh EH2 228 B4
Albyn Terr EH52 115 F5
Alcorn Rigg EH14 148 E7
Alcorn Sq EH14 148 E7
Alderbank Livingston EH54 143 E5
Penicuik EH26 191 F4
Alderbank Gdns EH11 120 E4
Alderbank Pl EH11 120 E4
Alderbank Terr EH11 120 E4
Alder Cres FK11 3 F5
Alder Gr Dunfermline KY11 29 D1
Westquarter FK2 61 B3
Alder Rd EH32 97 D3
ALDERSTON 100 E2
Alderston Ct KY12 29 D6
Alderston Dr KY12 29 D6
Alderstone Bsns Pk
EH54 143 C1
Alderstone Rd
Livingston, Adambrae
EH54 164 D7
Livingston, Howden EH54 143 D4
Alderston Gdns EH41 100 E1
Alderston Mdws EH41 100 E1
Alderston Pl EH41 100 E1
Alderston Rd EH41 129 E8
Aldhammer Ho EH32 96 F1
Alemoor Cres EH7 94 B3
Alemoor Pk EH7 94 B3
Alexander Ave Falkirk FK2 60 E5
Grangemouth FK3 61 C5
Alexander Ct
Clackmannan FK10 11 A5
Stirling FK9 2 F6
Alexander Dr
Bridge of Allan FK9 2 A8
Edinburgh EH11 120 D5
Livingston EH54 164 D8
Prestonpans EH32 125 F8
Alexander McLeod Pl FK7 8 E3
Alexander Peden Prim Sch
ML7 159 E5
Alexander Pk EH52 115 E4
Alexander Pl KY11 46 F3
Alexander Rd ML7 179 D5
Alexander St
Cowdenbeath KY4 13 D5
Dysart KY1 18 A8
Uphall EH52 115 A4
Alexander the Third St
KY3 34 F1
Alexander Way KY11 47 B8
Alexandra Ave EH48 141 F6
Alexandra Bsns Pk EH28 117 A5
Alexandra Dr Alloa FK10 9 F7
Bathgate EH48 141 F6
Alexandra Pl FK8 2 C1
Alexandra St
Dunfermline KY12 29 A5
Kirkcaldy KY1 17 C5
Alford Ave KY2 16 E7
Alford Gdns KY2 16 E7
Alford Way KY11 30 A4
Alfred Pl EH9 121 F4
Alhambra Theatre★ KY12 29 A3
Alice Bank EH55 164 A5
Alice Cox Wlk KY11 29 C1
Alice Gr KY4 30 E6
Aline Ct KY11 48 A2
Alison Gr KY12 28 B2
Alison St KY1 17 B2
Allanbank Rd FK5 38 C2
Allan Barr Ct FK1 60 B1
Allan Cres Denny FK6 36 D3
Dunfermline KY11 29 E2
Allan Ct Burntisland KY3 50 E8
Grangemouth FK3 40 E1
ALLANDALE 57 C2
Allandale Cotts FK4 57 C2
Allanfield EH7 93 F2
Allanfield Pl EH7 93 F2
Allan Lea Terr KY12 28 F5
Allan Park Cres EH14 120 C3
Allan Park Dr EH14 120 C2
Allan Park Gdns EH14 120 C2
Allan Park Ho 10 FK8 7 B7
Allan Park Loan EH14 120 D2
Allan Park Rd EH14 120 C2
Allan Pk Cowdenbeath KY4 13 A1
Kirkliston EH29 89 A2
Stirling FK8 7 A7
Allan Pl FK4 58 A4
Allan Rd EH47 160 E6
Allan's Prim Sch FK8 7 A7
Allan St EH4 93 A2
Allan Terr EH22 153 B3
ALLANTON 198 A8
Allanton Prim Sch ML7 198 B8
Allanton Rd ML7 179 D2
Allanvale Rd FK9 1 F7
Allanwater Apartments
FK9 2 A8
Allanwater Gdns FK9 2 A8
Allan Wlk FK9 1 F8
Allanwood Ct FK9 2 A8
Allardice Cres KY2 16 D5
Allen Gr KY12 26 E7
Allen Rd EH54 143 C3
Allermuir Ave EH25 171 E5
Allermuir Rd EH13 149 A6
Aller Pl EH54 143 B4
Allison Cres FK2 61 A1
Allison Gdns EH48 138 D2
Allison Pl EH29 89 B2
ALLOA 10 C5
Alloa Acad FK10 10 B5
Alloa Bsns Pk FK10 10 C7
Alloa Ind Est FK10 10 A6
ALLOA PARK 10 B5
Alloa Park Dr FK10 10 D5
Alloa Rd Clackmannan FK10 11 B4
Fishcross FK10 5 D3
Menstrie FK9 3 B3
Stenhousemuir FK5 38 F4
Stirling FK9 2 E3
Tullibody FK10 4 C3
Alloa Tower★ FK10 10 B6
Alloa Trad Ctr FK10 10 C7
Alloway FK2 61 A4
Alloway Cres FK4 57 F6
Alloway Dr Cowie FK7 20 D7
Kirkcaldy KY2 17 A7
Alloway Loan 4 EH16 122 A1
Alloway Wynd FK5 38 C4
Alma La FK2 60 B6
Alma St Falkirk FK2 60 B6
Inverkeithing KY11 47 C3
Alma Terr FK2 60 B6
Almond Ave EH12 117 F7
Almond Bank Cotts EH4 91 B5
Almondbank Terr EH11 120 E4
Almond Bsns Ctr EH54 144 A6
Almond Court E EH4 91 A3
Almond Court W EH4 91 A3
Almond Cres EH19 173 B6
Almond Ct
East Whitburn EH47 161 E7
Edinburgh EH16 122 E3
Falkirk FK2 60 E7
Livingston EH54 144 C4
Stirling FK7 7 C5
Almond E EH54 144 B4
Almond East Rd EH54 144 B5
Almondell & Calder Wood
Ctry Pk★ EH53 144 E5
Almondell Ct EH52 115 E5
Almondell Rd EH52 115 E5
Almondell Terr EH53 144 F5
Almond Gn EH12 119 A8
Almond Gr
East Calder EH53 144 F5
Queensferry EH30 89 C8
Almondhill Cotts EH29 89 C2
Almondhill Rd EH29 89 B2
Almondhill Steading EH29 89 B2
Almond Intc EH54 144 A3
Almond Pk EH54 144 A4
Almond Pl KY1 17 C7
Almond Rd
Blackburn EH47 141 C1
Dunfermline KY11 29 E2
Falkirk FK2 60 E7
Livingston EH54 144 B4
Ratho Station EH12, EH28 117 F7
Whitecross EH49 83 D5
Almondside Kirkliston EH29 89 B1
Livingston EH54 143 F2
Almond Side EH53 144 D4
Almond South Rd EH53 144 C4
Almond Sq
East Whitburn EH47 161 E7
Edinburgh EH12 119 A8
Almond St FK3 61 C6
Almond Terr Harthill ML7 159 C5
Whitecross EH49 83 F6
ALMONDVALE 143 E2
Almondvale Ave EH54 143 E2
Almondvale Bsns Pk
EH54 143 D1
Almondvale Bvd EH54 143 E2
Almondvale Cres EH54 143 D2
Almondvale Dr EH54 143 F2
Almondvale East Rd
EH54 143 F2
Almondvale Gdns EH47 162 D7
Almondvale N EH54 143 D2
Almondvale Parkway
EH54 143 E2
Almondvale Pl EH54 143 D1
Almondvale Rd EH54 143 E1
Almondvale Rdbt EH54 143 C1
Almondvale Ret Pk EH54 143 D1
Almondvale Road Rdbt
EH54 143 D1
Almondvale S EH54 143 D1
Almondvale South Ret Pk
EH54 143 D1
Almondvale Stadium
(Livingston FC)★ EH54 143 D2
Almondvale Stadium Rd
EH54 143 D2
Almondvale W EH54 143 D1
Almondvale Way EH54 143 D1
Almond Valley Heritage Ctr★
EH54 143 A2
Almondview EH54 143 F2
Almond View EH47 142 B1
Almondview Bsns Pk 1
EH54 143 F2
Almond West Rd EH54 144 A4
Alness Gr KY12 28 F2
ALNWICKHILL 150 E6
Alnwickhill Cres EH16 150 F6
Alnwickhill Ct EH16 150 F6
Alnwickhill Dr EH16 150 F6
Alnwickhill Gdns EH16 150 F6
Alnwickhill Gr EH16 150 F6
Alnwickhill Loan EH16 150 F6
Alnwickhill Pk EH16 151 A6
Alnwickhill Rd EH16 151 A7
Alnwickhill Terr EH16 150 F6
Alnwickhill View EH16 150 F6
Alpha St EH51 62 E5
ALVA 5 A6
Alva Acad FK12 5 B6
Alva Glen Nature Trail★
FK12 5 A8
Alva Ind Est FK12 5 C6
Alvanley Terr EH9 121 B5
Alva Pl EH7 94 A2
Alva Prim Sch FK12 5 A6
Alva St EH2 228 A3
Alyth Dr FK2 62 A1
Ambassador Ct EH21 124 D6
Amberley Path FK3 61 F6
Ambrose Rise EH54 144 A1
Amisfield Pk EH41 130 C8
Amisfield Pl
Haddington EH41 130 D7
Longniddry EH32 98 E5
Amos Path EH20 171 F7
Amulree Pl EH51 63 D7
Ancaster Pl FK1 60 A1
Anchorfield EH6 93 D6
Ancroft EH42 107 A7
Ancrum Bank EH22 152 F1
Ancrum Rd EH22 152 F1
Anderson Ave
Armadale EH48 139 F4
Crossford KY12 28 B2
2 Falkirk FK2 60 A8
Newtongrange EH22 174 B6
Anderson Cres FK1 81 E6
Anderson Dr
Cowdenbeath KY4 13 B2
Denny FK6 36 E1
Falkirk FK2 39 B2
Anderson Gdns FK2 82 E6
Anderson Gn EH54 143 C7
Anderson La
Kincardine FK10 23 E4
Rosyth KY11 46 D5
Anderson Park Rd FK6 36 F2
Anderson Pl Edinburgh EH6 93 E5
Stirling FK7 7 A4
Anderson St
Bonnybridge FK4 58 B5
Dysart KY1 18 A7
Kirkcaldy KY1 17 E6
Anderson Terr FK4 57 B3
Andrew Ave EH48 141 F6
Andrew Carnegie Birthplace
Mus★ 6 KY12 29 A3
Andrew Carnegie House★
KY12 28 F3
Andrew Cres FK5 38 D4
Andrew Ct EH26 191 E7
Andrew Dodd's Ave
EH22 174 E7
Andrew Hardie Dr FK10 10 A8
Andrew St KY5 14 A6
Andrew Stewart Hall FK9 2 D6
Andrew Wood Ct EH6 93 C6
Andy Kelly Ct EH19 172 F5
Andy Kelly View EH19 172 F5
Angle Park Terr EH11 120 F5
Angres Ct EH22 152 C7
Angus Rd Bo'ness EH51 63 D6
Carluke ML8 215 B1
Annabel Ct KY11 47 D2
Annan Ct FK1 60 C1
Annandale St EH7 93 E2
Annandale Street La EH7 93 E2
Anne Dr Bridge of Allan FK9 2 B6
Stenhousemuir FK5 38 E4
Anne St Alloa FK10 9 F8
Bathgate EH48 141 E6
Penicuik EH26 191 E7
Annet Rd FK6 57 D6
Annfield Edinburgh EH6 93 D6
Tranent EH33 126 E5
Annfield Ct EH33 127 C5
Annfield Dr FK7 7 C5
Annfield Farm Rd KY11 47 B7
Annfield Gdns FK8 7 B6
Annfield Gr FK8 7 B6
Annfield Pl 6 FK3 40 D1
Annfield St EH6 93 D6
Ann St EH4 228 A4
Anson Ave FK1 59 E4
Antigua St 2 EH1 93 E2
Antonine Ct EH51 63 D5
Antonine Gate FK4 57 A1
Antonine Gdns FK1 59 C5
Antonine Gr FK4 57 F3
Antonine Prim Sch FK4 58 A4
Antonine St FK1 59 C5
Antonine Wall★ FK4 58 D4
ANTONSHILL 38 E4
Antonshill Rdbt FK5 38 F5
Appin Cres
Dunfermline KY12 29 B4
Kirkcaldy KY2 16 E7
Appin Dr EH32 97 A2
Appin Gr FK2 61 F3
Appin Pl EH14 120 D3
Appin St EH14 120 D4
Appin Terr
Edinburgh EH14 120 D4
Shotts ML7 180 B3
Appleton Parkway EH54 142 F3
Appleton Parkway Rdbt
EH54 142 F5
Appleton Pl EH54 142 F3
Arboretum Ave EH3 93 A2
Arboretum Pl EH3 93 A3
Arboretum Rd EH3 93 A4
Arbroath Cres FK9 2 B4
Arbuthnot Rd EH20 172 C7
Arbuthnot St FK1 59 E6
Archers Ave FK7 7 C4
Archers Ct EH31 52 A2
Archibald Pl EH3 228 C2
Archibald Russell Ct FK2 61 E1
Ard Ct FK3 61 D5
Ardeer Pl KY11 29 C2
Arden St EH9 121 C5
Ardgay Cres FK4 58 A3
Ardgay Dr FK4 58 A3
Ardgay Rd FK4 58 A3
Ardgay Terr FK4 58 A3
Ardgowan Pl Cowie FK7 20 E8
Shotts ML7 179 E6
Ardmillan Pl EH11 120 F5
Ardmillan Terr EH11 120 E5
Ardmore Dr FK2 62 A1
Ardshiel Ave EH4 91 C1
Ardvreck Pl FK2 39 A3
Argyle Cres EH15 123 C7
Argyle Ct EH52 115 E5
Argyle Park Terr EH9 229 A1
Argyle Pl EH9 121 D5
Argyle St EH6 93 E6
Argyll Ave Falkirk FK2 60 C6
Stirling FK8 2 C1
Argyll Ct ML7 159 F5
Argyll Path FK6 57 D8
Argyll Pl Alloa FK10 10 C7
Bonnyrigg and Lasswade
EH19 172 F6
Argyll's Lodging★ FK8 7 A8
Argyll St FK10 10 C7
Argyll Terr EH11 228 A2
Arkaig Dr KY12 28 C1
Arkwright Ct EH39 54 A7
ARMADALE 139 E5
Armadale Acad EH48 139 D5
Armadale Ind Est EH48 140 A5
Armadale Prim Sch 2
EH48 139 F5
Armadale Rd EH47 161 B7
Armadale Sta EH48 140 A3
Armine Pl EH26 192 B7
Armour Ave FK7 20 D7
Armour Mews FK5 38 B4
Arneil Pl FK2 82 D7
ARNISTON 174 B1
Arniston Home Farm Cotts
EH23 195 A4
Arniston House★ EH23 194 F3
Arniston Rd KY11 30 A4
ARNOTHILL 60 A4
Arnothill FK1 60 A4
Arnothill Bank FK1 60 A4
Arnothill Ct FK1 59 F5
Arnothill Gdns FK1 60 A4
Arnothill La 1 FK1 59 F4
Arnothill Mews FK1 60 A4
Arnot St FK1 60 C4
Arnott Gdns EH14 120 A1
Arnprior Rd EH23 195 D8
Arns Gr FK10 9 E8
Arnswell FK10 5 C2
Arran EH54 142 F5
Arran Cres KY2 16 F7
Arran Ct Alloa FK10 10 B5
Grangemouth FK3 61 D6
Arran Pl EH15 123 C8
Arran Terr FK1 59 C4
Arras Gr EH26 192 A8
Arrol Cres FK10 10 C7
Arrol Pl EH30 89 C8
Arrol Sq EH54 142 E5
Arthur Ct KY4 13 D3
Arthur Pl KY4 13 D3
Arthur's Dr FK5 38 F2
Arthur St Cowdenbeath KY4 13 D3
Dunfermline KY12 29 B5
Edinburgh EH6 93 F3
Arthur Street La EH6 93 F3
Arthur View Cres EH22 152 B8
Arthur View Terr EH22 152 B8
Artillery Pk EH41 101 B1
Ashbank Ct EH48 140 E6
Ashbank Terr EH53 144 E3
Ashbrae Gdns FK7 7 B2
Ash Braes FK10 23 D4
Ashburnham Gdns EH30 68 D1
Ashburnham Loan EH30 68 D1
Ashburnham Rd EH30 89 D8
Ashcroft Ho FK5 38 B1
Ashfield Ct EH42 78 E1
Ashfield Pl EH42 78 E1
Ash Gr Alloa FK10 10 C6
Bathgate EH48 141 E6
Blackburn EH47 162 D8
Carnock KY12 27 C6
Cowdenbeath KY4 13 B4
Dunbar EH42 78 B1
Dunfermline KY11 46 D8
Livingston EH54 144 B6
Stenhousemuir FK5 38 F2
Westquarter FK2 61 B2
Ashgrove Mayfield EH22 174 E7
Musselburgh EH21 124 E6
Ashgrove Pl EH21 124 F6
Ashgrove View EH21 124 F6
Ash La EH20 171 F7
Ashley Ct EH49 84 E6
Ashley Dr EH12 120 E3
Ashley Gdns EH11 120 E4
Ashley Gr EH11 120 E4
Ashley Grange EH14 147 C2
Ashley Hall Gdns EH49 84 E6
Ashley Pl EH6 93 E4
Ashley Rd FK2 61 F3
Ashley St FK4 57 F6
Ashley Terr Alloa FK10 10 A8
Edinburgh EH11 120 E4
Ash Terr Blackburn EH47 162 D8
Stirling FK8 6 F5
Ashton Gr EH16 122 B1
Ashville Terr EH6 94 B3
Ashwood Ct EH53 165 C8
Asquith St KY1 17 B3
Assembly St EH6 94 A5
Assynt Bank EH26 192 A6
Astley Ainslie Hospl EH9 121 C3
Atheling Gr EH30 89 C7
ATHELSTANEFORD 101 E8
Athelstaneford Her Ctr★
EH39 101 E7
Athelstaneford Prim Sch
EH39 101 E7
Athol Cres FK2 61 A3
Atholl Cres EH3 228 A2
Atholl Crescent La EH3 228 A2
Atholl Pl Edinburgh EH3 228 A2
Falkirk FK2 60 C5
Stirling FK8 1 F2
Atholl Terr
Edinburgh EH11 228 A2
Kirkcaldy KY2 16 D7
Atholl View EH32 97 A2
Atholl Way EH54 143 E7
Athol Pl Bathgate EH48 141 B7
Dunfermline KY12 29 C4
Athol Terr EH48 141 B7
Atlas Ct EH48 140 B4
Atrium Way FK4 58 A3
Attlee Cres EH22 174 E5
Aubigny Sports Ctr EH41 130 A7
AUCHENBOWIE 19 B4
AUCHENDINNY 171 D1
AUCHENGRAY 202 E1
Auchengray Rd ML11 202 F1
Auchenhard Pl EH47 162 C2
Auchenhard Terr EH47 162 C2
Auchentyre Pl FK2 39 C3
Auchinbaird FK10 5 C2
Auchingane EH10 149 E5
Auchinleck Ct EH6 93 C6
Auchinleck's Brae EH6 93 D6
Auchterderran Rd KY5 14 B8
AUCHTERTOOL 15 A2
Auchtertool Prim Sch KY2 15 B2
Auction Mart 4 EH41 101 A1
Auld Brig Rd FK10 10 B6
Auldcathie Pl EH52 87 F3
Auldgate EH29 89 B1
Auldhame Cotts EH39 55 E5
Auldhill Ave EH49 86 C4
Auldhill Cotts EH49 86 C4
Auldhill Cres EH49 86 C3
Auldhill Ct EH49 86 C5
Auldhill Dr EH49 86 C4
Auldhill Entry EH49 86 C4
Auldhill Pl EH49 86 C4
Auldhill Rd EH49 86 C4
Auldhill Terr EH49 86 C4
Auldkirk Rd FK10 4 C3
Auld Orch EH19 173 C7
Auld School Wynd FK7 6 D5
Avalon Gdns EH49 84 D8
Ava St KY1 17 A2
Aven Dr FK2 60 F3
Avens Cl KY12 29 A5
Avenue Ind Est KY5 14 C7

Avenue Park W EH53.....144 C4
Avenue Pk
Bridge of Allan FK9.........1 F7
Mid Calder EH53.........144 C4
Avenue Rd Aberlady EH32 ..72 A5
Cockenzie & Port Seton
EH32.................97 C3
Dalkeith EH22...........152 E2
Avenue The
Bridge of Allan FK9.........2 A7
Falkirk FK2..............39 D2
Gifford EH41............220 F6
Gorebridge EH23..........174 B1
Inverkeithing KY11........47 E3
Lochgelly KY5............14 C7
Philpstoun EH49..........86 D7
Riccarton EH14..........147 F7
Whitburn EH47..........161 A6
Avenue Villas EH4........92 F2
Averton ML11............201 A1
Avonbank Ave FK3.........61 E6
Avonbank Gdns FK6.......36 D4
AVONBRIDGE............110 A6
Avonbridge Prim Sch
FK1....................110 A5
Avonbridge Rd FK1.......108 B7
Avon Ct FK1..............60 C2
Avondale Cres EH48.....139 E5
Avondale Dr EH48.......139 E5
Avondale Pl EH3..........93 B2
Avondale Rd FK2..........62 B3
Avondhu Gdns FK3.........61 F8
Avon Dr EH49.............84 D7
Avon Gr Edinburgh EH4.....91 A4
Penicuik EH26...........192 A6
Avonlea Dr FK2...........61 F3
Avonmill Rd EH49.........84 C8
Avonmill View EH49.......84 C7
Avonpark FK1............109 F6
Avon Pl Bo'ness EH51......63 F8
Edinburgh EH4...........91 A4
Linlithgow EH49..........85 A6
Avon Rd Bathgate EH48....141 A7
Edinburgh EH4...........91 A4
Grangemouth EH51........62 D7
Whitecross EH49..........83 F6
Avonside Dr FK6..........36 D5
Avon St Denny FK6........36 C4
Grangemouth FK3.........40 A1
Avon Terr FK1...........110 A6
Avontoun Pk EH49.........84 D6
Axwell Ho EH52..........116 B5
Ayres Wynd EH32..........96 F1
Aytoun Cres KY3..........33 E2
Aytoun Gr KY12...........28 E5

B

Baads Rd
Blackridge EH48, ML7.... 137 D1
Harthill ML7............158 E8
BABERTON...............148 C7
Baberton Ave EH14......148 D6
Baberton Cres EH14.....148 E6
Baberton Ct EH14........148 E6
Baberton Loan EH14.....148 D6
Baberton Mains EH14....148 C8
Baberton Mains Ave
EH14..................148 D7
Baberton Mains Bank
EH14..................148 D7
Baberton Mains Brae
EH14..................148 C7
Baberton Mains Cres
EH14..................148 D7
Baberton Mains Ct EH14 .148 D7
Baberton Mains Dell
EH14..................148 C7
Baberton Mains Dr EH14 .148 D7
Baberton Mains Gdns
EH14..................148 D7
Baberton Mains Gn
EH14..................148 D7
Baberton Mains Gr EH14 .148 D7
Baberton Mains Hill
EH14..................148 C7
Baberton Mains Lea
EH14..................148 C7
Baberton Mains Loan
EH14..................148 E7
Baberton Mains Pk EH14 148 D7
Baberton Mains Pl EH14 .148 D7
Baberton Mains Rise
EH14..................148 C7
Baberton Mains Row
EH14..................148 D7
Baberton Mains Terr
EH14..................148 D7
Baberton Mains View
EH14..................148 D7
Baberton Mains Way
EH14..................148 C7
Baberton Mains Wood
EH14..................148 C7
Baberton Mains Wynd
EH14..................148 D7
Baberton Pk EH14.......148 D6
Baberton Sq EH14.......148 D6
Bablins Wynd EH41......220 F6
Babylon Ct EH33.........126 C7
Back Cswy KY12...........42 D8
BACKDALE...............151 E2
Back Dean EH4..........120 F8
Backdean Rd EH22.......152 A8
Back La EH32.............71 D4
Backlee EH16...........151 A6
Backmarch Cres KY11.....46 E4
Backmarch Rd KY11......46 E4
BACKMUIR OF
PITFIRRANE..............28 A6
Back O' Hill Ind Est FK8....2 A2
Back O' Hill Rd FK8........1 F1
Back O'Yards KY11........47 B2
Back Rd Alva FK12..........4 E7
Dunbar EH42..............78 B2
Back St KY12..............42 D8
Back Station Rd
Edinburgh EH16.........122 D4
Linlithgow EH49..........85 B7
Backwell Ct KY12..........28 D5
Back Wlk 2 FK8.............7 B7
Backwood Ct FK10.........10 F5
Badallan Pl EH47........181 E6
Badger Brook EH52......115 D4
Badger Ct EH52..........115 C4
Badger Gr EH52..........115 D4
Badger La EH52..........115 C4
Badger Mdws EH52......115 D4
Badger Pk EH52.........115 C4
Badger Pl EH52.........115 D4
Badger Wlk EH52........115 D4
Badger Wood EH52.......114 C2
Baileyfield Cres EH15....123 A8
Baileyfield Est EH15....123 A8
Baileyfield Rd EH15.......94 F1
Bailie Fyfe's Cl EH1......229 B3
Bailie Gr EH15..........123 B6
Bailielands EH49..........85 D7
Bailie Path EH15........123 A6
Bailie Pl EH15..........123 B6
Bailie Terr EH15........123 B6
Baille Ct 2 FK10............5 C1
Baillie Ave ML7.........159 F5
Baillie St EH47.........161 A7
Baillie Waugh Rd FK7.......7 C3
Baingle Brae FK10..........4 B3
Baingle Cres FK10.........4 B3
BAINSFORD...............60 B8
Bainsford Prim Sch FK2 ..60 B8
Bain Sq EH54............143 C1
Bain St KY5...............14 B7
Baird Ave EH12..........120 C6
Baird Ct KY5..............14 A7
Baird Dr Armadale EH48...139 F7
Edinburgh EH12.........120 C6
Baird Gdns EH12........120 C6
Baird Gr EH12..........120 C6
Baird Rd Armadale EH48...139 F7
Livingston EH54.........143 A1
Ratho EH28.............117 D3
Baird St FK1..............59 D5
Baird's Way EH19........173 D7
Baird Terr
Edinburgh EH12.........120 C6
Haddington EH41........100 F1
Harthill ML7............159 C5
Bairns Ford Ave FK2......60 A7
Bairns Ford Ct FK2.......60 A7
Bairns Ford Dr FK2.......60 A7
Bakehouse Cl EH8........229 B3
Baker's Pl 8 EH3..........93 B2
Baker St Bo'ness EH51.....63 F6
Stirling FK8...............7 A8
Balbakie Rd ML7.........159 E5
Balbardie Ave EH48......141 A7
Balbardie Cres EH48.....141 A7
Balbardie Prim Sch 4
EH48..................141 B7
Balbardie Rd EH48.......141 B6
Balbirnie Pl EH12.......120 E7
Balcarres Ct EH10.......121 A2
Balcarres Pl EH21.......124 D7
Balcarres Rd EH21.......124 D7
Balcarres St EH10.......121 A2
Balcastle Rd FK1........108 A6
Balderstone's Wynd EH39 54 C7
Balderston Gardens N
EH16..................122 B1
Balderston Gdns EH16...122 B1
BALDRIDGEBURN..........28 D5
Baldridgeburn KY12......28 E5
Baldwin Cres KY2.........17 A5
Baldwin Ct EH26.........191 E4
BALERNO................147 D1
Balerno High Sch EH14..147 C2
Balfour Cres Plean FK7....20 D3
Stenhousemuir FK5.......38 C2
Balfour Ct
Dunfermline KY12........29 D5
Edinburgh EH12..........91 B1
Plean FK7...............20 D3
Balfour Pl EH6............93 F4
Balfour's Sq EH33.......126 D6
Balfour St Alloa FK10......10 C7
Bannockburn FK7..........7 C1
Bonnybridge FK4.........57 F6
Edinburgh EH6...........93 F3
Kirkcaldy KY2............17 B5
North Berwick EH39.......54 D7
Stirling FK8...............1 F2
Balfour Terr EH26.......171 B1
Balfron Loan EH4.........91 C1
Balgone Barns Cotts
EH39....................54 D2
Balgownie W KY12........42 C8
Balgreen Ave EH12......120 A6
Balgreen Gdns EH12.....120 A6
Balgreen Pk EH12........120 B6
Balgreen Prim Sch EH11 120 C5
Balgreen Rd EH11........120 B5
Balgrochan Terr 3 EH48 141 B6
Baliol St KY3.............34 F2
Ballantyne La EH6........93 F5
Ballantyne Pl EH54......143 B4
Ballantyne Rd EH6........93 F5
Ballast Bank KY11........47 C2
Ballater Dr FK9............2 C4
BALLENCRIEFF............72 B1
Ballencrieff Cotts EH32 ...72 A1
Ballencrieff Mains Farm
Cotts EH32..............71 F1
Ballencrieff Mill EH48....140 E8
Ballencrieff Rd EH48....140 E8
Ballencrieff Toll EH48....112 B1
Ballengeich Pass FK8......2 A1
Ballengeich Rd FK8.........1 F1
Ballingry La KY5..........14 B7
Ballingry St KY5..........14 A7
Balloch Rd ML7..........179 E6
Balmoral Dr Falkirk FK1....59 E3
Kirkcaldy KY2............16 D5
Balmoral Gdns
Grangemouth FK2.........82 D7
Livingston EH54.........164 D6
Balmoral Pl Edinburgh EH3 . 93 B2
Stenhousemuir FK5........38 E4
Stirling FK8...............7 A7
Balmoral Rd EH51.........62 E6
Balmoral St FK1...........59 E3
Balmuir Ave EH48........140 F8
Balmuir Rd EH48.........140 F7
Balmulzier Rd FK1.......108 B8
Balmwell Ave EH16......151 B5
Balmwell Gr EH16.......151 B5
Balmwell Pk EH16.......151 B5
Balmwell Terr EH16......151 A5
Balnacraig KY12..........28 B1
Balquharn Cotts FK12......4 D7
Balquhatstone Cres FK1..108 A6
Balquhidderock FK7........7 C4
Balquhidderock Wood
Nature Reserve★ FK7.....7 D3
Balsusney Rd KY2.........17 B5
Baltic Quay FK3...........40 D1
Baltic St EH6.............94 A5
Balure Cres FK7............8 D4
Balvaird Pl KY12..........29 C6
Balwearie Cres KY2.......17 A2
Balwearie Gdns KY2.......16 F1
Balwearie High Sch KY2..17 A1
Balwearie Rd KY2.........17 A2
Banchory Cotts KY2.......34 E5
Banchory Pl FK10..........4 C3
Banchory Prim Sch FK10...4 C3
Bancroft Ave EH54.......143 E4
Bandeath Ind Est FK7......9 A5
Bandeath Rd FK7...........8 D4
Bandon Ave KY1...........17 F8
Bangholm Ave EH5........93 B5
Bangholm Bower Ave EH5 93 B5
Bangholm Gr EH5..........93 C5
Bangholm Loan EH5.......93 C5
Bangholm Pk EH5..........93 B5
Bangholm Pl EH5..........93 B5
Bangholm Rd EH5..........93 B5
Bangholm Terr EH3........93 B4
Bangholm View EH5.......93 C5
Bangholm Villas EH5......93 C5
Bangly Brae EH41, EH32...100 A4
BANGLY HILL............100 B4
Bangor Rd EH6............93 F5
Bankfoot EH32............96 D1
BANKHEAD................57 E6
Bankhead Ave EH11......119 C3
Bankhead Broadway
EH11..................119 B3
Bankhead Cotts EH40......75 C6
Bankhead Cres FK4........57 D6
Bankhead Crossway N
EH11..................119 B3
Bankhead Crossway S
EH11..................119 C2
Bankhead Dr EH11.......119 B3
Bankhead Gr EH30........68 D1
Bankhead Ind Est EH11..119 C3
Bankhead Medway EH11 .119 C3
Bankhead Pl EH11.......119 B3
Bankhead Rd Fishcross FK10 5 D3
Queensferry EH30........89 E8
Bankhead St EH11.......119 C2
Bankhead Terr EH11.....119 B2
Bankhead Way EH11......119 B2
Bankhill Ct FK3...........61 D6
Bankmill View EH26......191 F4
Bankpark Brae EH33.....126 B7
Bankpark Cres EH33.....126 B7
Bankpark Gr EH33.......126 C7
Bank Pl ML7.............179 F4
Bank Rd East Linton EH40 ..103 E7
Harthill ML7............159 E5
BANKSIDE................60 C8
Bankside FK2.............60 C7
Bankside Ct FK6..........36 E2
Bankside Ind Est FK2.....60 D8
Bank St Alloa FK10........10 B6
Edinburgh EH1..........229 A3
Falkirk FK1..............60 B5
Grangemouth FK3.........40 A1
Inverkeithing KY11.......47 C2
Kincardine FK10..........23 D3
Kirkcaldy KY1............17 E7
Lochgelly KY5............14 B8
Mid Calder EH53........144 D4
North Berwick EH39.......54 B7
Penicuik EH26...........191 E4
Slamannan FK1..........108 A6
6 Stirling FK8.............7 A8
Whitburn EH47...........161 A7
Banks View FK2...........22 E4
Bank Terr ML11..........217 F8
Bankton Ave EH54.......164 F7
Bankton Brae EH54......164 E7
Bankton Ct
Livingston EH54.........165 B8
Tranent EH33...........126 D6
Bankton Dr EH54........164 F8
Bankton Gdns EH54......165 A8
Bankton Glade EH54.....165 A8
Bankton Gn EH54........164 F7
Bankton Gr EH54........165 A8
Bankton Junc EH33......126 C8
Bankton La EH54........165 A8
Bankton Park E EH54....144 B1
Bankton Park W EH54....144 B1
Bankton Prim Sch EH54..143 F1
Bankton Rd EH54........164 D8
Bankton Sq EH54........164 F7
Bankton Terr
Livingston EH54.........164 F7
Prestonpans EH32.........97 B1
Tranent EH32...........126 B8
Bankton Way EH54.......164 F7
Bankton Wlk EH54.......164 F7
Bankton Wood EH54.....165 A7
Bankview Terr FK4........57 E6
Bannerman Ave KY11......47 C3
Bannerman St KY12.......29 A5
Bannoch Brae KY12.......29 C3
BANNOCKBURN..............7 E2
Bannockburn Cross FK7....7 E1
Bannockburn Heritage Ctr★
FK7......................7 B2
Bannockburn High Sch
FK7......................7 D2
Bannockburn Hospl FK7..19 F7
Bannockburn Prim Sch
FK7......................7 E1
Bannockburn Rd
Cowie FK7...............20 C8
Stirling FK7...............7 C3
Bannockburn Station Rd
FK7......................8 A4
Bannock Rd FK7............8 C4
BANTASKIN...............59 F4
Bantaskine Dr FK1........59 F4
Bantaskine Gdns FK1.....59 E3
Bantaskine Prim Sch FK1 59 E4
Bantaskine Rd FK1........59 F4
Bantaskine St FK1........59 E3
Banton Pl FK4............58 A3
Baptie Pl EH51...........63 E5
Barassie Dr KY2...........17 A8
Barbara Stocks La KY12...42 D8
Barbauchlaw EH48.......139 E6
Barbauchlaw Ave EH48...139 F6
Barbour Ave FK7...........7 C3
Barbour Gr KY12..........28 E5
Barclay Pl EH10.........228 B1
Barclay Rd KY3............34 F3
Barclay St KY4............13 B3
Barclay Terr EH10.......228 B1
Barclay Way EH54.......143 E7
Barga Ct EH32............97 B4
Barham Rd KY11...........46 D1
Barkhill Rd EH49..........84 F6
Barkin Ct FK1.............60 B2
Barlaw Gdns EH48.......140 A6
Barley Bree La EH22.....174 D8
Barley Ct EH22..........174 D8
Barleyhill FK4............58 B5
Barleyhill Terr EH6.......94 B3
Barleyknowe Cres EH23..174 C1
Barleyknowe Gdns EH23 .174 C2
Barleyknowe La EH23....174 C1
Barleyknowe Pl EH23....174 C1
Barleyknowe Rd EH23....174 C1
Barleyknowe St EH23....174 C1
Barleyknowe Terr EH23..174 C2
Barnbougle Ride EH30.....90 C7
Barnego Rd FK6...........36 D3
Barnes Gn EH54.........143 C7
Barnet Cres KY1...........17 B1
Barnhill Dr FK10...........4 C2
Barnhill Pl KY11..........48 D4
Barnhill Rd KY11..........48 D4
Barn Park Cres EH14.....148 E8
Barn Pk EH14...........148 E7
Barn Pl EH54...........143 B3
Barn Rd FK8...............7 A8
Barns Ct EH47...........161 E7
Barnsdale Rd FK7..........7 A3
Barnshot Rd EH13........149 B6
Barns Ness Terr EH42....218 A6
Barns Pk KY11............48 A2
Barns The KY3............50 E8
BARNTON.................91 B3
Barnton Ave EH4..........91 D4
Barnton Avenue W EH4...91 B4
Barnton Brae EH4.........91 B4
Barnton Ct EH4...........91 B3
Barntongate Ave EH4.....91 B2
Barntongate Dr EH4......91 B2
Barntongate Terr EH4.....91 B2
Barnton Gdns EH4........91 E4
Barnton Gr EH4...........91 B3
Barnton Junc EH4.........91 B2
Barnton La FK1...........60 B4
Barnton Loan EH4.........91 E4
Barnton Park Ave EH4....91 D3
Barnton Park Cres EH4...91 C3
Barnton Park Dell EH4....91 D3
Barnton Park Dr EH4......91 C3
Barnton Park Gdns EH4...91 C3
Barnton Park Gr EH4......91 C3
Barnton Park Pl EH4......91 D3
Barnton Park View EH4...91 C3
Barnton Park Wood EH4 ..91 C2
Barnton Pk EH4...........91 E4
Barnton St FK8.............7 B8
Barnwell Rd FK9............2 C4
Baronscourt Rd EH8......94 D1
Baronscourt Terr EH8....122 D8
Barons Hill Ave EH49.....85 B7
Barons Hill Ct EH49.......85 B7
Barony Ct Bo'ness EH51....63 F5
Cambusbarron FK7........6 D6
Barony Pl 5 EH3...........93 D2
Barony St EH3............93 D2
Barony Terr EH12........119 D7
Barracks Rdbt EH54......142 E5
Barracks St EH32..........97 D4
Barra Pl FK5..............39 A4
Barrie Ct EH54..........144 C5
Barrie Pl
4 Dunfermline KY12......28 E5
Grangemouth FK3.........61 D5
Barrie Rd FK5.............38 F3
Barrie St KY12............28 E5
Barrie Terr EH48........141 C5
Barton Bldgs KY3..........35 A2
Barton Ct EH47..........181 E6
Barton Rd KY11...........46 B1
Barton Terr EH47........181 F6
Basil Paterson Coll The
EH2....................228 B4
Bass Rock View EH39.....55 B7
Bastion Wynd 7 FK8.......7 B7
Bathfield EH6.............93 E6
BATHGATE...............141 C7
Bathgate Acad EH48.....141 E5
Bathgate Bsns Ctr EH48..141 C2
Bathgate Rd
Armadale EH48.........140 B6
Blackburn EH47.........162 C8
East Whitburn EH48......161 E7
Bathgate Sta EH48......141 B5
Bath Pl EH15.............95 B1
Bath Rd EH6..............94 B5
Bath St EH15............123 B8
Bath Street La EH15.....123 B8
Bathville Bsns Ctr EH48..140 A5
Baton Rd ML7............179 D6
Batterflatts Gdns FK7.......6 F6
Batterflatts Ho FK7........6 F6
Battery Rd
Grangemouth FK3.........62 C8
North Queensferry KY11....68 C5
Battock Rd FK2............82 F7
Bavelaw Cres EH26......191 D6
Bavelaw Gdns EH14......147 C1
Bavelaw Gn EH14........147 C2
Bavelaw Rd EH14........147 C1
Baxter Cres FK6...........36 C1
Baxter Rd KY4.............30 F6
Baxters Gate EH33......126 D5
Baxter's Pl EH1..........229 B4
Baxter St FK7..............8 D4
Baxter's Wynd FK1........60 B4
Bayne Gdns EH49.........84 A6
Bayne St FK8...............2 A1
Bayswell Pk EH42.........78 D3
Bayswell Rd EH42.........78 D3
Bayview KY12.............26 E1
Bay View EH32............97 D4
Beach La Edinburgh EH15....95 B1
Musselburgh EH21.......124 B7
Beachmont Ct EH42.......78 E1
Beachmont Pl EH42.......78 F1
Beach Rd Grangemouth FK3 41 B1
North Berwick EH39.......54 B7
Beaconcroft FK9............2 C7
Beaconhurst Sch FK9.......2 C6
Beacon L Ctr KY3..........50 F8
BEANCROSS...............61 C4
Beancross Prim Sch FK3..61 C5
Beancross Rd FK3.........61 C5
Beancross Rdbt FK3.......61 B6
Bean Row FK1.............60 B4
Bearcroft Gdns FK3.......61 E7
Bearcroft Rd EH51........62 D8
Bearford Pl EH41........130 D8
Bearside Rd FK7............7 A3
Beath High Sch KY4.......13 B5
Beath View KY11..........29 E4
Beath View Rd KY4........13 A2
Beatlie Rd EH52...........88 A3
Beatlie Specl Sch EH54...144 B5
Beaton Ave FK7............7 C1
Beatty Ave FK8.............2 A2
Beatty Cres KY1...........17 D7
Beatty Ct KY1.............17 D7
Beatty Pl KY12............29 C5
Beauchamp Gr 2 EH16...151 A8
Beauchamp Rd EH16.....151 A8
Beauclerc St FK12..........5 A7
Beaufort Cres KY2.........16 D5
Beaufort Dr FK2...........39 A3
Beaufort Rd EH9.........121 D4
Beauly Cres KY11.........47 C8
Beauly Ct Falkirk FK1......60 C1
Grangemouth FK3.........61 D4
Beauly Dr EH54..........144 B4
Beauly Pl KY2.............16 F7
Beaumont Dr FK2.........39 B2
BEAVERBANK..............93 D4
Beaverbank Bsns Pk EH7 .93 C3
Beaverbank Pl EH7........93 D3
Beaverhall Rd EH7........93 D3
Beck Cres KY12...........29 C5
Beda Pl FK7...............8 C5
Bedford Ct Alloa FK10......10 A6
3 Edinburgh EH4.........93 A2
Bedford Pl FK10...........10 A6
Bedford St EH4...........93 A2
Bedford Terr EH15.......123 C8
Bedlam Theatre★ EH1...229 A2

Bedlormie Dr EH48 ......138 C2
Beech Ave
Carrington EH23 ....194 F3
Dalgety Bay KY3, KY11 .....48 F5
Mid Calder EH53 ....144 B2
Plean FK7 ....20 C3
Beechbank Cres EH53 ....144 E2
Beech Cres Denny FK6 .....36 C3
Larbert FK5 ....59 C8
Westquarter FK2..........61 B3
Beeches The
Armadale EH48 ....139 E5
Dalgety Bay KY11 ....48 C3
Gullane EH31.............52 B3
Lochgelly KY5 ....14 A8
Newtongrange EH22......174 A7
Beech Gdns FK7 ....6 F6
Beech Gr Cousland EH22 ..154 D5
Dunfermline KY11.........46 D8
Livingston EH54.........144 B6
Whitburn EH47 ....161 C6
Beech Grove Ave EH22...152 E1
Beechgrove Rd EH22.....174 E6
Beech La FK9..............2 B4
Beech Loan EH19.........173 B6
Beechmount Cres EH12..120 B7
Beechmount Ct ML7 .....180 B2
Beechmount Pk EH12....120 B6
Beech Pl Dunfermline KY12 .26 A1
Grangemouth FK3.........61 C6
Livingston EH54..........143 C4
Penicuik EH26...........191 F4
Seafield EH47 ....142 B1
Beech Rd EH48 ....141 E6
Beech St EH42............78 B1
Beech Terr EH34.........156 D6
Beech Tree Pk FK6 ....37 A2
Beech Tree The EH49 .....86 D4
Beech Way KY11...........48 A5
Beechwood Alloa FK10......5 E1
Crossford KY12...........28 B2
Linlithgow EH49 ....85 A5
Sauchie FK10..............5 D1
Beechwood Gdns
Blackburn EH47......... 141 D1
Stirling FK8 ....7 A5
Beechwood Gr EH54 .....115 A2
Beechwood Mains EH12..120 B7
Beechwood Pk
Livingston EH54..........142 F7
Newtongrange EH22......174 B6
Uphall Station EH54 .....115 A1
Beechwood Pl EH47 .....141 D1
Beechwood Rd
Blackburn EH47......... 141 D1
Haddington EH41 ....129 F8
Beechwood Terr EH6 ......94 B3
Beecraigs Ctry Pk★ EH49 .85 A1
BEESLACK...............192 A7
Beeslack Com High Sch
EH26..................192 A7
Begbie Pl EH54 ....143 B5
Begbie View EH26 ....171 B2
Begg Ave FK1 ....59 E4
Beldorney Pl KY12 ....29 D6
Belfield Ave EH53........144 F2
Belford Ave EH4..........92 E1
Belford Gdns EH4.........92 E1
Belford Mews 3 EH4 ....120 F8
Belford Pk EH4 ....120 F8
Belford Pl EH4...........120 F8
Belford Rd EH4 ....120 F8
Belford Terr EH4 ....120 F8
Belgrave Cres EH4.......228 A4
Belgrave Crescent La
EH4 ....228 A4
Belgrave Gdns EH12 .....119 E7
Belgrave Mews 8 EH4....92 F1
Belgrave Pl EH4 ....92 F1
Belgrave Rd EH12........119 E6
BELHAVEN 78 B1
Belhaven Bewery★ EH42..78 B1
Belhaven Hill Sch EH42...78 B2
Belhaven Hospl EH42.....78 B1
Belhaven Pl EH10........121 A2
Belhaven Rd EH42 ....78 C2
Belhaven Terr EH10......121 A2
Bellalmond Cres EH47 ...161 E7
Bell Ct Falkirk FK2 ....60 C7
Grangemouth FK3.........40 E1
Belleknowes Ind Est KY11 47 B4
Bellenden Gdns EH16....122 C1
Bellerophon Dr EH26 ....191 F4
Bellevue Edinburgh EH3 ....93 D2
Grangemouth FK2.........82 E7
Bellevue Ave EH42........78 E1
Bellevue Cres EH3 ....93 D2
Bellevue Gdns EH7........93 D3
Bellevue Gr EH7 ....93 D2
Bellevue Pk FK10 ....9 E6
Bellevue Pl EH7 ....93 D2
Bellevue Rd Alloa FK10 .....9 F6
Edinburgh EH7............93 D3
Bellevue St Edinburgh EH7..93 D2
Falkirk FK1 ....60 C4
Bellevue Terr Dunbar EH42 78 E1
Edinburgh EH7............93 D2
Bellfield Ave
Dalkeith EH22 ....152 E2
Musselburgh EH21 ....124 B5
Bellfield Cres KY1 ....18 A8
Bellfield Ct EH21.........124 B5
Bellfield La EH15 ....123 B8
Bellfield Rd
Bannockburn FK7 ....7 E1
Stirling FK8 ....7 B5
Bellfield Sq EH32 ....125 E8
Bellfield St EH15.........123 B8
Bellfield Terr EH15 ......123 B8
Bellfield View EH19......173 D8
Bellhouse Rd KY3.........49 B7
Bellman's Rd EH26.......191 E6
Bellman Way KY11.........48 B5
Bellona Terr EH47 ....181 F6
Bell Pl EH3 ....93 B2
Bell Rd KY11..............46 B2
Bell's Brae EH4..........228 A3
Bells Burn Ave EH49 ......85 C7
Bellsdyke Hospl FK5......38 D5
Bellsdyke Pl FK5..........38 A3
Bellsdyke Rd Falkirk FK2 ...39 C6
Stenhousemuir FK5........38 D4
Bellsdyke Rdbt FK5 ....38 B4
Bellsmains EH23.........195 D5
Bellsmeadow Rd FK1 .....60 C4
Bell's Mills EH4..........120 F8
Bell's Mill Terr EH52......87 F2
Bell Sq EH54.............164 C5
BELLSQUARRY 164 D7
Bellsquarry Prim Sch
EH54...................164 C7
Bellsquarry South Rd
EH54 ....164 E6
Bell Stane EH30 ....68 B1
Bell's Wynd FK1 ....60 B4
BELLYEOMAN.............29 D5
Bellyeoman La KY12 ......29 C5
Bellyeoman Prim Sch
KY12....................29 C5
Bellyeoman Rd KY12......29 C5
Bellyford Rd EH33 ....126 A1
Belmont Ave
Bonnybridge FK4..........57 D5
Edinburgh EH12..........120 B7
Shieldhill FK1.............81 E7
Belmont Cres EH12 ......120 B7
Belmont Dr
Edinburgh EH12..........120 B7
Shotts ML7 ....180 B2
Belmont Gdns EH12......120 B7
Belmont Pk EH12 ....120 B7
Belmont Rd EH14 ....148 D6
Belmont St FK1............60 C4
Belmont Terr EH12 ......120 B7
Belmont Twr FK1 ....60 C4
Belmont View EH12......120 B7
Belstane Gate ML8.......215 A3
Belstane Mews ML8......215 A3
Belstane Pk ML8.........215 A3
Belstane Rd ML8.........215 A3
Belsyde Ct EH49 ....84 D6
BELVEDERE 140 F8
Belvedere La EH48.......140 F8
Belvedere Pk EH6.........93 C6
Belvedere Pl EH48 ....140 F8
Belvedere Rd
Bathgate EH48 ....140 F8
2 Bathgate EH48........141 A7
Belwood Cres EH26......171 B1
Belwood Rd EH26........170 F1
Ben Alder Pl KY2 ....16 E5
Benarty St KY2 ....16 F5
Bendachin Dr KY12 ....29 E5
Bendameer Rd KY3 ....33 C1
Benhar Rd ML7 ....180 A6
Benjamin Dr EH51 ....63 E5
Ben Ledi Rd KY2...........16 F5
Ben Lomond Dr FK9 ....2 A4
Ben Lomond View KY12...27 A6
Bennachie Way KY11......30 B1
Bennet Wood Terr EH52...87 F3
Ben Nevis Pl KY2 ....16 F5
Bennie Mus★ EH48 ......141 A6
Bennie Terr FK1 ....108 B7
Bennochy Ave KY2.........17 A5
Bennochy Ct KY2 ....17 A5
Bennochy Gdns KY2 ......17 A5
Bennochy Gr KY2 ....17 A5
Bennochy Rd Kirkcaldy KY1 17 B4
Kirkcaldy, Templehall KY2 ...16 E6
Bennochy View KY2.......17 A5
Ben Sayers Pk EH39.......54 E6
Bentheads FK7 ....19 E8
BENTS 162 A2
Benview FK7 ....7 C2
Benview Terr FK10.........5 E4
Beresford Ave EH5........93 C5
Beresford Gdns EH5 ......93 C5
Beresford Pl EH5 ....93 B5
Beresford Rise EH54 .....144 A1
Beresford Terr EH5 ....93 C6
Bergen Ave KY11 ....30 A2
Berkeley St FK7 ....7 A4
Bernard Shaw St KY12 ....28 E5
Bernard's Smithy KY3.....32 D5
Bernard St EH6............94 A5
Bernard Terr EH8........229 B1
Berryhill FK7 ....20 E7
Berryhill Cres FK3 ....61 E6
Berryhill Pl ML7 ....180 B2
Berrylaw Pl KY12 ....28 E4
Berrylaw Rd KY12.........28 D4
Berry St KY5...............14 B7
Bertram Pl ML7..........179 D5
Bertram St Harthill ML7 ...159 C5
Shotts ML7 ....179 E5
Bervie Dr EH54 ....164 E5
Berwick Pl Dysart KY1 .....18 A8
Kirkcaldy KY1 ....17 C5
Beta Ctr FK9...............2 D5
Bethelfield Pl KY1 ....17 B2
Bethesda Gr FK2..........82 E6
Bethlehem Way EH7 ......94 B3
Beulah EH21.............124 E6
Bevan Dr FK12.............5 C7
Bevan Pl KY11 ....46 E3
Bevan Rd EH22 ....174 D5
Beveridge Ave EH22 .....174 E5
Beveridge Cl EH22 ....174 E5
Beveridge Pl 1 FK2 ....61 A1
Beveridge Rd KY1 ....17 B3
Beveridge Row EH42......78 A1
Beveridge Sq EH54 ......143 E1
Beveridge St KY11 ....29 C2
BEVERIDGEWELL..........28 F5
Bickerton Crofts EH47 ...161 E5
Bickerton Terr EH47 .....161 A5
Bickram Cres KY12 ....26 D7
Bielgrange Cotts EH42 ...104 D4
Bielside Gdns EH42 ....77 F1
Big Brigs Way EH22......173 F4
Biggar Rd Edinburgh EH10 .150 B3
Silverburn EH26 ....190 E5
Biggin Wa's KY1 ....17 F7
Bill Russel Gr EH22 ......153 B3
BILSTON 171 E5
BINGHAM 122 F6
Bingham Ave EH15.......123 A5
Bingham Broadway
EH15 ....123 A5
Bingham Cres EH15......123 A5
Bingham Crossway EH15 123 A5
Bingham Dr EH15........123 A5
Bingham Medway EH15..122 F5
Bingham Pl EH15 ....122 F5
Bingham Way EH15......122 F5
Binn Ave KY3 ....33 E2
Binney Wells KY1.........17 E6
BINNIEHILL..............108 A5
Binniehill Rd FK1 ....108 A5
Binnie Pl FK2.............39 F2
Binning Rd KY11...........47 B3
Binning Wood Rd EH42 ...75 F7
Binns The★ EH49 ....65 E1
Binny Pk EH52...........114 F7
Birch Ave FK8 ....6 F5
Birchbank KY4.............13 B2
Birch Cres EH20 ....171 F7
Birch Ct Edinburgh EH4.....91 B2
Livingston EH54..........143 C2
Birch Gr Dunfermline KY11 ..46 D8
Menstrie FK11..............3 F6
Birch Terr EH26 ....171 A2
Birchwood FK10 ....5 D2
Birchwood Gdns EH54 ...164 D7
Birdland Ave EH51........64 D7
Birkdale Dr EH52 ....114 F4
Birkdale Pk EH48 ....140 B6
Birkenshaw Way EH48 ...139 E6
Birkenside EH23 ....195 C6
Birkfield Loan ML8.......215 C1
Birkfield Pl ML8 ....215 C1
Birk Hedges EH41........128 E6
Birkhill Clay Mine★ EH49 .62 E2
Birkhill Cres EH51 ....63 F6
Birkhill Rd FK7 ....6 E6
Birkhill St EH51...........63 F6
Birkhill Sta★ EH49........62 F3
Birnam Gdns KY11........30 A4
Birnam Pl FK2 ....60 C5
Birnam Rd KY2 ....16 E8
Birnie Brae KY5............14 B7
Birniehall ML11..........217 F8
Birniehill Ave EH48 .....140 F4
Birniehill Cres EH48 .....140 F4
Birniehill Rd EH48 ......140 F4
Birniehill Terr EH48......140 F3
Birnieknowes Farm Cotts
TD13 ....218 D5
Birnie St KY5 ....14 B7
Birnie Well Rd FK1.......108 A6
Birrell Cl 5 KY1 ....17 D6
Birrell Dr KY11 ....29 D1
Birrell Gdns EH54........164 E7
Birrell's La KY1...........17 E7
Birrel's Wynd KY3 ....35 A3
Birsley Rd EH33..........126 C6
Bishops Gate EH52.......115 C5
Bishops Pk
Livingston EH53..........144 B1
Mid Calder EH53 ....144 C2
Bittern Ct KY11 ....30 A2
Blackadder Haven KY12...42 D8
Blackadder Pl EH5.........92 E6
Blackbarony Rd EH16 ....122 A2
Blackbraes Rd FK1.........81 F4
BLACKBURN..............162 D8
Blackburn Ave KY12 ......28 D6
Blackburn Crag EH17 ....151 D8
Blackburn Dr KY4..........13 A3
Blackburnhall EH47......162 D6
Blackburnhall Holdings
EH47 ....162 E6
Blackburn Prim Sch
EH47...................141 C1
Blackburn Rd
Addiewell EH55 .... 162 D3
Blackburn EH48......... 141 D3
Blackchapel Cl EH15 .....123 B4
Blackchapel Rd EH15 ....123 B4
Blackcot Ave EH22.......174 D5
Blackcot Dr EH22 ....174 D5
Blackcot Pl EH22 ....174 D5
Blackdykes Cotts EH39....55 C4
Blacket Ave EH9.........121 F5
Blacket Pl EH9...........121 F5
Blackfaulds Ct EH47 .....181 E6
Blackfaulds Dr EH47 .....181 E6
Blackfaulds Pl EH47 .....181 E6
Blackford Ave EH9.......121 D3
Blackford Bank EH9 .....121 E3
Blackford Brae Project Sch
EH9....................121 C3
Blackford Gate EH9......121 C3
Blackford Glen Cotts
EH16 ....121 F1
Blackford Glen Rd EH16..121 F1
Blackford Hill Gr EH9 ....121 D2
Blackford Hill Nature
Reserve★ EH16........ 121 D2
Blackford Hill Rise EH9 ..121 D2
Blackford Hill View EH9..121 D2
Blackford Rd EH9........121 C4
Blackfriars St EH1 ....229 B3
Blackgrange Rdbt FK9 .....3 D3
BLACKHALL 92 A2
Blackhall Prim Sch EH4...92 A1
Blackhall St ML7.........180 B3
Blackhall Terr EH26......171 A1
Blackhill Rd EH48........138 F3
Blackie Rd EH6 ....94 B4
Blacklaw Rd KY11.........29 D2
Blackmill Cres FK2........39 B3
Blackmount Terr FK2 .....82 E6
Blackmuir Pl FK10 ....4 D3
BLACKNESS 65 E4
Blackness Castle★ EH49 ..65 F5
Blackness Prim Sch EH49 65 C4
Blackness Rd EH49 ....85 B7
Blackraigs KY2 ....16 C7
BLACKRIDGE 138 C3
Blackridge Com Mus★
EH48................... 138 D3
Blackridge Prim Sch
EH48...................138 C3
Blackston Rd FK1........110 A6
Blackthorn Ct EH4 ....91 B2
Blackthorn Gr FK11........4 A5
Blackwood Cres EH9.....121 E5
Blackwood Ct KY11 ....46 F7
Blackwood Gdns KY11 ....46 F7
Blackwood Gn KY11.......46 F6
Blackwood Way KY11 .....46 F7
Blaeberry Gdns EH4 ......91 B2
BLAEBERRYHILL 161 C5
Blaeberryhill Rd EH47....161 C5
Blaefaulds Cres FK6 ......57 D8
Blair Ave EH51............63 E5
BLAIRBURN...............42 C8
Blairdenon Cres FK1......59 F3
Blairdenon Dr FK10........5 B2
Blairdenon Rd FK12........4 E6
Blair Dr Dunfermline KY12...29 B6
Kelty KY4 ....12 D8
Blairforkie Dr FK9 ....1 F8
Blair Gr KY12 ....26 A8
BLAIRHALL 26 A7
Blairhall Prim Sch KY12 ..26 A8
Blairhill View EH48 ......138 C3
Blairlodge Ave FK2 ....82 C8
BLAIRLOGIE 3 B6
Blairmore Rd KY2..........16 D8
Blairmuckhole & Forrestdyke
Rd ML7 ....158 E7
Blairmuir Terr EH52 .....115 F5
Blair Pl Falkirk FK2 ....59 F7
Kirkcaldy KY2 ....16 D5
Blair's Cotts FK2...........61 C1
Blair St Edinburgh EH1 ....229 A3
Kelty KY4.................12 D8
Blair Terr FK5 ....39 A4
Blairwood Terr KY12......26 E7
Blairwood Wlk KY12 .....26 E7
Blake St KY11 ....29 C1
Blamey Cres KY4 ....13 B2
Blandfield EH7............93 D3
Blantyre Terr EH10.......121 A4
Blawearie Rd EH33 ......126 D5
Blawhorn Moss National
Nature Reserve★ EH48 .138 B5
Bleachfield Edinburgh EH6..93 D4
Falkirk FK2 ....60 A5
Bleachfield Ct KY11.......29 E3
Blenheim Ct Carluke ML8..215 B1
Penicuik EH26 ....192 A8
Stirling FK9 ....2 C3
Blenheim Pl FK5..........38 E5
Blie Brae EH29............88 F2
Blindwell Brae EH41 .....131 F1
Blindwells FK12 ....4 F6
Blinkbonnie Terr FK1 ....108 A6
BLINKBONNY 148 B4
Blinkbonny Ave EH4 ......92 D1
Blinkbonny Cres EH4 .....92 C1
Blinkbonny Gdns
Edinburgh EH4............92 D1
West Calder EH55........182 E6
Blinkbonny Gr EH4........92 D1
Blinkbonny Grove W EH4..92 D1
Blinkbonny Rd
Currie EH14.............148 B4
Edinburgh EH4........... 120 D8
Falkirk FK1 ....59 E4
Blinkbonny Terr EH4......92 C1
Blink O'forth EH32.......125 E8
Blinny Ct ML7 ....180 A3
Bloom Ct EH54 ....143 B3
Bloomfield Pl 1 EH48 ...141 B6
Bloom Pl EH54...........143 B2
Bloom Rdbt EH54 ....143 C3
Bluebell Cl 15 FK1 ....60 B4
Bluebell Glade EH54 .....164 C8
Blyth Rd EH52 ....115 D4
Blyth St KY1 ....17 E8
Boat Gn EH3...............93 C3
Bobbin Wynd FK7..........6 D6
Bogend Rd
Bannockburn FK7 ....19 E8
Larbert FK2 ....38 B8
Torwood FK5 ....37 F8
Boggs Holdings EH34 ....128 A1
BOGHALL 141 E7
Boghall Dr EH48 ....141 E5
Boghall Farm Cotts
EH10 ....171 B6
Boghall Farm Steadings
EH48 ....141 F5
Boghall Prim Sch EH48 ..141 F6
Boghall Rdbt EH48.......141 F5
Boghead Cres EH48......140 E5
Bogies Wynd 9 KY1 ......17 D6
Boglily Cotts KY2 ....16 D3
Boglily Rd KY2............16 D3
Bogpark Rd EH21........124 A6
Bog Rd Laurieston FK2 .....60 F4
Penicuik EH26...........191 E5
Whitburn EH47 ....161 A7
Bog Rdbt FK2.............60 F4
Bog Road Ind Est FK2.....60 F4
Bogsmill Rd EH14........120 B1
Bog The EH51 ....64 A8
Bogwood Ct EH22.......174 D7
Bogwood Dr KY12 ....28 A2
Bogwood Rd EH22.......174 E6
Bohun Ct FK7..............7 D4
Bolam Dr KY3 ....33 F2
BOLTON.................129 F1
Bolton Council Hos
EH41 ....220 C8
Bolton Steading EH41....129 F1
Bo'mains Ind Est EH51....63 F5
Bo'mains Rd EH51 ....63 E6
Bomar Ave EH51..........64 A8
Bon Accord Cres ML7 ....179 E5
BONALY.................149 A5
Bonaly Ave EH13.........149 B5
Bonaly Brae EH13........149 B5
Bonaly Cres EH13........149 B5
Bonaly Ctry Pk★ EH13 ...148 F2
Bonaly Dr EH13..........149 A5
Bonaly Gdns EH13 ....149 B5
Bonaly Gr EH13..........149 B5
Bonaly Prim Sch EH13...149 A5
Bonaly Rd EH13..........149 A5
Bonaly Rise EH13 ....149 B5
Bonaly Steading EH13....149 A5
Bonaly Terr EH13 ....149 B5
Bonaly Wester EH13 .....149 A5
Bonar Pl EH6 ....93 D5
Bond St FK10 ....4 A3
BO'NESS 63 E8
Bo'ness Acad EH51 ....64 A6
Bo'ness Hospl EH51 ......63 E7
Bo'ness & Kinneil Rly★
EH51....................63 C7
Bo'ness Motor Mus★
EH51....................64 C8
Bo'ness Public Sch EH51 . 63 F7
Bo'ness Rd
Grangemouth FK3.........62 B6
Polmont FK2 ....61 F3
Queensferry EH30.........67 F1
Bo'ness Sta★ EH51 ....64 A8
Bonhard Ct EH51 ....64 B6
Bonhard Rd KY12 ....27 B7
Bonhard Way EH51 ....64 B5
Bonnar St KY12...........29 A4
BONNINGTON.............93 D4
Bonnington EH27........146 A7
Bonnington Ave EH6......93 D5
Bonnington Bsns Ctr EH6 . 93 F4
Bonnington Gait EH6 .....93 E4
Bonnington Gr EH6 ......93 D5
Bonnington Ind Est EH6 ..93 E4
Bonnington Mill Bsns Ctr
EH6.....................93 E5
Bonnington Rd
Edinburgh EH6............93 E4
Wilkieston EH27 ....146 A6
Bonnington Rd La EH6 ....93 E4
Bonnington Terr EH6 .....93 D5
Bonnybank Ct EH23 .....195 D8
Bonnybank Rd EH23 .....195 D8
BONNYBRIDGE............58 B5
Bonnybridge Hospl FK4...58 C6
Bonnybridge Ind Est FK4..58 A4
Bonnybridge Prim Sch
FK4.....................58 B6
Bonnybridge Rd FK4......57 E5
Bonnyfield Nature Reserve★
FK4.....................58 A5
Bonnyfield Rd FK4........57 F5
Bonnyhaugh EH6 ....93 D4
Bonnyhaugh La EH6 ......93 D4
Bonnyhill Rd
Bonnybridge FK4..........58 D3
Falkirk FK1 ....59 A4
Bonnymill Pl FK4 ....58 B5
Bonnymuir Cres FK4......57 F5
Bonnymuir Pl FK4 ....58 B5
BONNYRIGG AND
LASSWADE 173 D7
Bonnyrigg L Ctr EH19....173 B7
Bonnyrigg Prim Sch
EH19...................173 C6
Bonnyrigg Rd EH22 ......152 E1
Bonnyside Rd FK4 ....58 B5
Bonnyton Pl KY11.........29 D3
Bonnytoun Ave EH49......85 C8
Bonnytoun Terr EH49 .....85 C8
Bonnyvale Pl FK4 ....57 F5
Bonnyview Gdns FK4......58 B6
Bonnywood Ave FK4 ......58 B7
Boothacre La EH6 ....94 C4
Booth Ave KY11...........46 D5
Booth Pl FK1 ....60 B4
Boreland Pk KY11.........47 C3

Boreland Rd Dysart KY1 . . . . 18 A8
Inverkeithing KY11 . . . . 47 C3
BORESTONE 7 A2
Borestone Cres FK7 . . . . 7 A4
Borestone Ct FK7 . . . . 7 B2
Borestone Pl FK7 . . . . 7 A2
Borestone Prim Sch FK7 . . . 7 A2
Boroughdales EH42 . . . . 78 C2
Boroughloch EH8 . . . . 229 B1
Boroughloch Sq EH8 . . . . . 229 B1
Boroughmuir High Sch
EH10 . . . . 121 A5
Boroughmuir High Sch Annexe EH10 . . . . 121 A5
Borrowlea Rd FK7 . . . . 7 C7
Borrowmeadow Rd FK7 . . . . 7 E7
Borrows Gate FK9 . . . . 1 F3
BORROWSTOUN 63 F5
Borrowstoun Cres EH51 . . . 63 F5
BORROWSTOUN MAINS 63 E5
Borrowstoun Pl EH51 . . . . . 63 F5
Borrowstoun Rd EH51 . . . . . 64 A5
BORTHWICK 196 B4
Borthwick Castle Pl
EH23 . . . . 195 F3
Borthwick Castle Rd
EH23 . . . . 195 F2
Borthwick Castle Terr
EH23 . . . . 195 F3
Borthwick Pl EH12 . . . . 120 E7
Borthwick's Cl EH1 . . . . . . 229 A3
Borthwick View EH20 . . . . 172 A7
Boswall Ave EH5 . . . . 92 F5
Boswall Cres EH5 . . . . 92 F5
Boswall Dr EH5 . . . . 93 A5
Boswall Gdns EH5 . . . . 92 F5
Boswall Gn EH5 . . . . 93 A5
Boswall Gr EH5 . . . . 92 F5
Boswall Loan EH5 . . . . 92 F6
Boswall Parkway EH5 . . . . . 92 E6
Boswall Pl EH5 . . . . 92 F5
Boswall Quadrant EH5 . . . . 92 F5
Boswall Rd EH5 . . . . 93 A6
Boswall Sq EH5 . . . . 92 F5
Boswall Terr EH5 . . . . 92 F5
Boswell Dr Kinghorn KY3 . . . 35 A3
Oakley KY12 . . . . 26 F6
Boswell Rd KY5 . . . . 14 B8
Bothkennar Prim Sch FK2 39 F3
Bothkennar Rd FK2 . . . . 39 E3
Bothwell Ct KY11 . . . . 29 A2
Bothwell Gdns
Dunbar EH42 . . . . 78 D1
Dunfermline KY11, KY12 . . . . 29 A2
Bothwell Ho EH7 . . . . 94 A2
Bothwell St
Dunfermline KY11 . . . . 29 B2
Edinburgh EH7 . . . . 94 A2
Boulevard East Rdbt
EH54 . . . . 143 F2
Boundary Road E EH14 . . . 147 F8
Boundary Road N EH14 . . . 147 E7
Boundary St EH51 . . . . 64 B8
Bouprie Rise KY11 . . . . 48 B4
Bourtree Gr KY12 . . . . 26 D7
Bow Butts KY12 . . . . 29 A2
Bowhill Ct EH31 . . . . 52 B2
Bowhill Terr EH5 . . . . 93 B5
BOWHOUSE 61 E5
Bowhousebog or Liquo
ML7 . . . . 179 A2
Bowhousebog Rd ML7 . . . 179 A2
Bowhouse Dr KY1 . . . . 35 B8
Bowhouse Gdns
Alloa FK10 . . . . 10 B5
Kirkcaldy KY1 . . . . 35 B7
Bowhouse Prim Sch FK3 . . 61 E5
Bowhouse Rd Alloa FK10 . . . 10 B5
Grangemouth FK3 . . . . 61 D5
Bowhouse Sq FK3 . . . . 61 D5
Bowling Green Pl FK4 . . . . . 57 F5
Bowling Green Rd
Kirkliston EH29 . . . . 89 B1
Whitburn EH47 . . . . 161 A6
Bowling Green St KY4 . . . . . 13 C4
Bowling Green The EH6 . . . 93 F5
Bowling Green Wynd
KY12 . . . . 26 A7
Bowling La EH6 . . . . 93 F5
Bowmont Pl EH8 . . . . 229 B1
Bowmont Terr EH42 . . . . . . 78 E2
Bowmore Wlk ML7 . . . . . . 180 A3
Bow St FK8 . . . . 7 A8
Bowyett EH48 . . . . 111 F6
Boxton Rd California FK1 . . . 81 D1
Standburn FK1 . . . . 82 C3
Boyd La FK2 . . . . 60 B6
Boyd-Orr Dr EH26 . . . . 191 F8
Boyd Pl KY5 . . . . 14 A8
Boyd's Entry EH1 . . . . 229 B3
Boyd St Falkirk FK2 . . . . 60 B6
Laurieston FK2 . . . . 61 A3
Boyle Dr KY11 . . . . 46 E3
Bracken Ave FK1 . . . . 60 A2
Bracken La FK9 . . . . 2 B3
Brackenlees Rd FK2 . . . . . . 40 B5
Brackensbrae EH52 . . . . . . 115 B5
Bracklinn Brae KY12 . . . . . . 28 E5
Bracklinn Pl FK1 . . . . 59 F1
Bradbury St FK2 . . . . 39 B2
Braeburn Dr EH14 . . . . 148 B4
Braefoot Tyninghame EH42 . . 76 C3
Whitburn EH47 . . . . 161 B7
Braefoot Gr KY11 . . . . 48 B2
Braefoot Rd EH51 . . . . 64 A5
Braefoot Terr EH16 . . . . . . 122 A1
BRAEHEAD 7 C5
Braehead Alloa FK10 . . . . 4 D1
Alva FK10 . . . . 5 A7
Bo'ness EH51 . . . . 63 F7
Braehead Ave
Edinburgh EH4 . . . . 91 A3
Linlithgow EH49 . . . . 84 E5
Tullibody FK10 . . . . 4 C2
Braehead Bank EH4 . . . . 91 A3
Braehead Bsns Units
EH49 . . . . 84 E6
Braehead Cres EH4 . . . . 91 A3
Braehead Dr
Edinburgh EH4 . . . . 91 A3
Linlithgow EH49 . . . . 84 E5
Braehead Gr Bo'ness EH51 . 63 F7
Edinburgh EH4 . . . . 91 A3
Braehead Ho KY1 . . . . 17 D5
Braehead Loan EH4 . . . . 91 A3
Brae Head Lodge KY1 . . . . . 17 D5
Braehead Pk
Edinburgh EH4 . . . . 91 A3
Linlithgow EH49 . . . . 84 E5
Braehead Pl EH49 . . . . 84 E5
Braehead Prim Sch FK7 . . . 7 C4
Braehead Rd
Edinburgh EH4 . . . . 91 A3
Linlithgow EH49 . . . . 84 E6
Stirling FK7 . . . . 7 C3
Braehead Rdbt EH54 . . . . . 143 D3
Braehead Row EH4 . . . . 91 A3
Brae Heads Loan HE41 . . . 103 D5
Braehead Terr EH49 . . . . . . 84 E5
Braehead View EH4 . . . . 91 A3
Braekirk Ave EH27 . . . . . . 145 D3
Braekirk Gdns EH27 . . . . . 145 D3
Braemar Cres
Carluke ML8 . . . . 215 A3
Falkirk FK2 . . . . 60 C6
Braemar Dr Falkirk FK2 . . . . 60 C6
Halbeath KY11 . . . . 30 A4
Braemar Gdns Denny FK6 . . 36 D3
Grangemouth FK2 . . . . 82 D8
Halbeath KY11 . . . . 30 A4
Braemar Pl FK5 . . . . 39 A4
Braemount KY4 . . . . 13 A2
BRAEPARK 91 B3
Braepark Rd EH4 . . . . 91 A4
Brae Pk EH4 . . . . 91 A4
Brae Rd KY3, EH51 . . . . 62 D6
Braes High Sch FK2 . . . . . . 82 B8
Braeside Alloa FK10 . . . . 5 C1
Shieldhill FK1 . . . . 81 D6
Braeside Cres EH47 . . . . . . 181 D5
Braeside Gdns EH53 . . . . . 144 B2
Braeside Pk EH53 . . . . 144 B3
Braeside Pl
Grangemouth FK2 . . . . 82 B8
Laurieston FK2 . . . . 61 B4
Westquarter FK2 . . . . 61 B2
Braeside Rd
Gorebridge EH23 . . . . 195 D8
Loanhead EH20 . . . . 172 D8
Braeside Road N EH23 . . . 195 D8
Braeside Road S EH23 . . . 195 D7
Braes The Lochgelly KY5 . . . . 14 A8
Tullibody FK10 . . . . 4 D3
Braes View Denny FK6 . . . . . 57 D8
Shieldhill FK1 . . . . 81 E7
Brae The Bannockburn FK7 . . . 7 D1
Cambusbarron FK7 . . . . 6 D6
Penicuik EH26 . . . . 171 C1
Braeview East Linton EH40 103 D8
Laurieston FK2 . . . . 60 F3
Stenhousemuir FK5 . . . . 38 D2
Braewell Gdns EH49 . . . . . . 84 C7
Braid Ave EH10 . . . . 121 B2
Braidburn Cres EH10 . . . . . 121 A1
Braidburn Specl Sch
EH14 . . . . 149 D8
Braidburn Terr EH10 . . . . . 121 A1
Braid Cres EH10 . . . . 121 A1
Braid Farm Rd EH10 . . . . . 121 B1
Braid Gn EH54 . . . . 143 C7
Braid Hills App EH10 . . . . . 150 B8
Braid Hills Ave EH10 . . . . . 121 A1
Braid Hills Cres EH10 . . . . 150 A8
Braid Hills Dr EH10 . . . . . . 150 D8
Braid Hills Rd EH10 . . . . . . 150 B8
Braidlaw Pk EH26 . . . . 191 C5
Braid Mount EH10 . . . . 150 B8
Braid Mount Crest EH10 . . 150 B8
Braid Mount Rise EH10 . . . 150 B8
Braid Mount View EH10 . . 150 B8
Braid Rd EH10 . . . . 150 A8
Braigh Gdns KY12 . . . . 28 D6
Bramble Dr EH4 . . . . 91 B2
Bramble Glade EH54 . . . . . 164 C8
Brambles The EH22 . . . . . . 153 F1
Brambling Rd KY11 . . . . 30 A2
Bramdean Gr EH10 . . . . 150 B8
Bramdean Pl EH10 . . . . 150 B8
Bramdean Rise EH10 . . . . . 150 B8
Bramdean View EH10 . . . . 150 B8
Brand Dr EH15 . . . . 123 B7
Brandfield St EH3 . . . . 228 A1
Brand Gdns EH15 . . . . 123 C7
Brandon St EH3 . . . . 93 C2
Brandon Terr EH3 . . . . 93 C3
Brand Pl [2] EH7 . . . . 94 A1
Brands Row KY4 . . . . 30 F7
Brandyhill FK10 . . . . 5 E3
Brandy Riggs KY12 . . . . 27 D1
Brandy Wells KY12 . . . . 27 D1
Brankholm Brae KY11 . . . . . 46 C4
Brankholm Cres KY11 . . . . . 46 D5
Brankholm La KY11 . . . . 46 D2
Branning Ct [8] KY1 . . . . 17 D6
BRANSHILL 5 A1
Branshill Pk Alloa FK10 . . . . 10 B8
Sauchie FK10 . . . . 5 B1
Branshill Rd FK10 . . . . 10 B8
Branxton Wynd KY1 . . . . . . 35 B8
Bravo St EH51 . . . . 62 E5
Breadalbane Pl FK2 . . . . . . 62 A2
Breadalbane St EH6 . . . . . . 93 E4
Breadalbane Terr EH11 . . 228 A2
Bread St EH3 . . . . 228 B2
Bread Street La EH3 . . . . . 228 B2
Breakers Way KY11 . . . . 47 F2
Brechin Dr FK2 . . . . 62 A1
Breck Terr EH26 . . . . 192 A8
BREICH 182 F6
Breich Sta EH55 . . . . 182 D6
Breich Terr EH55 . . . . 182 E6
Breichwater Pl EH47 . . . . 182 A6
Brentham Ave FK8 . . . . 7 B5
Brentham Cres FK8 . . . . 7 B5
Brentwood Ct EH39 . . . . 54 B6
Breslin Terr ML7 . . . . 159 C5
Breton Ct FK1 . . . . 60 C3
Brewery Ct [11] EH41 . . . . 130 B8
Brewery La EH42 . . . . 78 B2
Brewery Pk EH41 . . . . 130 A8
Brewhouse Ct [5] FK10 . . . . 10 B6
Brewlands Ave EH51 . . . . . . 63 D5
Brewster Pl FK6 . . . . 36 C2
Brewster Sq EH54 . . . . 164 C6
Briarbank EH54 . . . . 143 D4
Briarbank Terr EH11 . . . . . 120 E4
Briar Brae FK2 . . . . 82 D8
Briarcliff St KY1 . . . . 17 F6
Briar Cotts EH47 . . . . 162 C2
Briardene FK2 . . . . 61 A3
Briarhill Ave KY11 . . . . 48 A3
Briar Pl KY11 . . . . 29 C3
Briar Rd FK10 . . . . 4 E2
Brickfield EH15 . . . . 95 A1
Brickworks Rd EH33 . . . . . 126 B7
Bridgecastle Gdns EH48 . . 111 A2
Bridgecastle Ho EH48 . . . . 111 A2
Bridgecastle Rd EH48 . . . . 139 F8
Bridge Cres FK6 . . . . 36 D2
Bridge End
East Whitburn EH47 . . . . . . 161 D7
Edinburgh EH16 . . . . 122 B3
Shotts ML7 . . . . 179 C6
Bridge End Cotts EH27 . . . 146 D6
Bridgehaugh Rd FK9 . . . . . . 2 B2
Bridgehill FK1 . . . . 110 A6
BRIDGEND 86 C4
Bridgend Ct
Bathgate EH48 . . . . 140 F6
[1] Dalkeith EH22 . . . . 153 A3
Bridgend Gdns EH48 . . . . . 140 F6
Bridgend Pk EH48 . . . . 140 F5
Bridgend Pl
Bathgate EH48 . . . . 140 F6
Whitburn EH47 . . . . 161 C7
Bridgend Prim Sch EH49 . . 86 C3
Bridgend Rd FK1 . . . . 110 A6
BRIDGENESS 64 C8
Bridgeness Cres EH51 . . . . 64 C7
Bridgeness La EH51 . . . . . . 64 C7
Bridgeness Rd EH51 . . . . . . 64 D7
BRIDGE OF ALLAN 2 A8
Bridge of Allan Prim Sch
FK9 . . . . 2 B6
Bridge of Allan Sta FK9 . . . . 1 E8
Bridge Pl Broxburn EH52 . . 115 E5
Denny FK6 . . . . 36 C2
Shotts ML7 . . . . 180 A3
Bridge Rd Balerno EH14 . . . 147 C2
Edinburgh EH13 . . . . 149 A6
Bridgeside Ave EH47 . . . . . 161 B5
Bridge St Bonnybridge FK4 . . 58 A5
Cowdenbeath KY4 . . . . 13 D3
Dunfermline KY12 . . . . 28 F3
East Linton EH40 . . . . 103 E7
Edinburgh EH15 . . . . 95 A1
Fauldhouse EH47 . . . . 181 E6
Haddington EH41 . . . . 130 B8
Kincardine FK10 . . . . 23 D4
Kirkcaldy KY1 . . . . 17 B1
Musselburgh EH21 . . . . 124 C6
Newbridge EH28 . . . . 117 A6
Penicuik EH26 . . . . 191 F4
Tranent EH33 . . . . 126 C6
Bridges The KY11 . . . . 48 A2
Bridge Street La EH15 . . . . 95 A1
Bridges View KY12 . . . . 29 F6
Bridge Terr [13] FK10 . . . . . 10 B6
Bridgeton Cotts EH48 . . . . 110 F2
Bridge View KY11 . . . . 68 C6
Brierbush Cres EH33 . . . . . 127 D5
Brierbush Rd EH33 . . . . . . 127 D5
Briery Bank EH41 . . . . 130 C7
Briery Bauks EH8 . . . . 229 B2
Brighouse Park Cl EH4 . . . . 91 C6
Brighouse Park Cres EH4 . 91 C6
Brighouse Park Ct EH4 . . . . 91 C6
Brighouse Park Gait EH4 . . 91 C6
Brighouse Park Gr EH4 . . . . 91 C6
Brighouse Park Rd EH4 . . . 91 C6
Brighouse Pk Gdns EH4 . . . 91 C6
Brighton Pl EH15 . . . . 123 A8
BRIGHTONS 82 C8
Brighton St EH1 . . . . 229 A2
Bright's Cres EH9 . . . . 121 F4
Bright Terr EH11 . . . . 228 A2
Brig-O-Doon Gr FK7 . . . . . . 20 E7
Brisbane St EH54 . . . . 144 A5
Bristo Pl EH1 . . . . 229 A2
Bristo Port EH1 . . . . 229 A2
Bristo Sq EH8 . . . . 229 A2
Britwell Cres EH7 . . . . 94 D2
Brixwold Bank EH19 . . . . . 173 D6
Brixwold Dr EH19 . . . . 173 D6
Brixwold Neuk EH19 . . . . . 173 D6
Brixwold Pk EH19 . . . . 173 D6
Brixwold Rise EH19 . . . . . . 173 D6
Brixwold View EH19 . . . . . 173 D6
Broadfaulds Cres EH47 . . . 161 A5
Broadgait EH31 . . . . 52 B3
Broadgait Ct EH31 . . . . 52 A3
Broadgait Gn EH31 . . . . 52 B3
Broadhaven EH42 . . . . 78 E2
Broadhurst Rd EH22 . . . . . 174 C7
Broadleys Ind Pk FK7 . . . . . 7 D5
Broadleys Rd FK7 . . . . 7 D7
Broadleys Rdbt FK7 . . . . 7 D6
Broadside Pl FK6 . . . . 36 D1
Broad St Alloa FK10 . . . . 10 B5
Cowdenbeath KY4 . . . . 13 C2
Denny FK6 . . . . 36 F2
Stirling FK8 . . . . 7 A8
Broad Wynd Edinburgh EH6 94 A5
[7] Kirkcaldy KY1 . . . . 17 D6
Brock Pl FK7 . . . . 7 B2
Brock St KY11 . . . . 68 B6
Brocks Way EH52 . . . . 116 A7
Brockwood Ave EH26 . . . . 191 D6
Brodick Gdns KY11 . . . . 30 A4
Brodick Pl FK1 . . . . 59 C4
Brodick Rd KY2 . . . . 16 E7
Brodie Ave EH39 . . . . 54 D6
Brodie Ct EH39 . . . . 54 D7
Brodie Rd EH42 . . . . 106 D8
Brodie St FK2 . . . . 60 B8
Brodie Wlk KY11 . . . . 30 A4
Broich The FK12 . . . . 4 E7
Bronte Pl FK5 . . . . 39 A3
Brookbank Terr ML8 . . . . . 215 A1
Brooke La FK3 . . . . 61 C5
Brooke St FK3 . . . . 61 C5
Brookfield Pl FK12 . . . . 5 A6
Brookfield Terr EH25 . . . . 171 E6
Brookside FK2 . . . . 61 E1
Brook St Alva FK12 . . . . 5 A6
Menstrie FK11 . . . . 3 F6
Broomage Ave FK5 . . . . 38 B3
Broomage Bank FK5 . . . . . . 38 C2
Broomage Cres FK5 . . . . . . 38 B3
Broomage Dr FK5 . . . . 38 B3
Broomage Pk FK5 . . . . 38 C1
Broombank Terr EH12 . . . 119 D4
Broomburn Gr EH12 . . . . . 119 E4
Broom Cres FK1 . . . . 60 A2
Broom Ct FK7 . . . . 7 C3
Broomfield Cres EH11 . . . 119 E3
Broomfield Dr KY12 . . . . . . 29 A5
Broomfield Rd KY4 . . . . 13 C5
Broom Gdns KY2 . . . . 16 C8
Broom Gr KY11 . . . . 46 F8
Broomhall Ave EH12 . . . . . 119 E4
Broomhall Bank EH12 . . . . 119 D5
Broomhall Cres EH12 . . . . 119 D5
Broomhall Dr EH12 . . . . . . 119 C5
Broomhall Gdns EH12 . . . . 119 D5
Broomhall Loan EH12 . . . . 119 D5
Broomhall Pk EH12 . . . . . . 119 D5
Broomhall Pl EH12 . . . . 119 D5
Broomhall Rd EH12 . . . . . . 119 D5
Broomhall Terr EH12 . . . . . 119 D5
Broomhead Dr KY12 . . . . . . 28 F5
Broomhead Ho KY12 . . . . . . 29 A5
Broomhead Pk KY12 . . . . . . 28 F5
Broomhill KY3 . . . . 50 E8
Broomhill Ave
Burntisland KY3 . . . . 33 E1
Larbert FK5 . . . . 59 C8
Penicuik EH26 . . . . 191 E4
Broomhill Ct FK9 . . . . 2 B3
Broomhill Dr EH22 . . . . 152 E1
Broomhill Pk [3] EH22 . . . . 152 E1
Broomhill Pl Denny FK6 . . . . 36 D4
Stirling FK7 . . . . 6 E6
Broomhill Rd
Bonnybridge FK4 . . . . 58 B4
Penicuik EH26 . . . . 191 E4
Broomhills Rd EH17 . . . . . . 150 F4
Broomhill St ML7 . . . . 159 C5
BROOMHOUSE 119 E3
Broomhouse Ave EH11 . . . 119 D3
Broomhouse Bank EH11 . . 119 E3
Broomhouse Cotts EH11 . . 119 E4
Broomhouse Cres EH11 . . . 119 E3
Broomhouse Ct EH11 . . . . . 119 E3
Broomhouse Dr EH11 . . . . 119 E4
Broomhouse Gardens E
EH11 . . . . 119 E4
Broomhouse Gardens W
EH11 . . . . 119 D4
Broomhouse Gr EH11 . . . . 119 E3
Broomhouse Loan EH11 . . 119 E3
Broomhouse Medway
EH11 . . . . 119 E4
Broomhouse Mkt EH11 . . . 119 E3
Broomhouse Path EH11 . . . 119 E3
Broomhouse Pk EH11 . . . . 119 E3
Broomhouse Place N
EH11 . . . . 119 E3
Broomhouse Place S
EH11 . . . . 119 E3
Broomhouse Prim Sch
EH11 . . . . 119 F3
Broomhouse Rd EH12 . . . . 119 D3
Broomhouse Row EH11 . . . 119 E3
Broomhouse Sq EH11 . . . . 119 E3
Broomhouse Street N
EH11 . . . . 119 E3
Broomhouse Street S
EH11 . . . . 119 E2
Broomhouse Terr EH11 . . . 119 E4
Broomhouse Way EH11 . . 119 E3
Broomhouse Wlk EH11 . . . 119 E3
Broomhouse Wynd EH11 119 E3
BROOMIEKNOWE 173 A8
Broomieknowe
Bonnyrigg and Lasswade
EH18 . . . . 173 A8
[1] Dunfermline KY11 . . . . . . 29 C3
Tullibody FK10 . . . . 4 D3
Broomieknowe Gdns
EH19 . . . . 173 B8
Broomieknowe Pk EH19 . . 173 B8
Broomknowe Dr FK10 . . . . . 23 D6
Broomlea Cres EH12 . . . . . 119 D5
Broompark E FK11 . . . . 4 A6
Broompark Gdns
Denny FK6 . . . . 36 E2
East Calder EH53 . . . . 144 E3
Broompark Rd
East Calder EH53 . . . . 144 E3
Edinburgh EH12 . . . . 119 E5
Broompark View EH53 . . . 144 E3
Broompark W FK11 . . . . 4 A6
Broom Pl KY2 . . . . 16 C8
Broom Rd Kirkcaldy KY2 . . . . 16 C7
Stirling FK7 . . . . 7 C4
BROOMRIDGE 7 D3
Broomridge Pl FK4 . . . . 57 D4
Broomridge Rd FK7 . . . . 7 B3
Broomside KY2 . . . . 16 C8
Broomside Pl FK5 . . . . 38 C1
Broomside Rd FK4 . . . . 58 B3
Broomside Terr EH12 . . . . 119 E5
Broomview Ho EH11 . . . . . 119 D2
Broom Wlk EH54 . . . . 144 A4
Broom Wynd ML7 . . . . 179 E6
Broomyhill Pl EH49 . . . . 84 D7
Broomyknowe EH14 . . . . . 149 B8
Broomyknowe Dr EH54 . . . 142 E6
Brora Pl KY12 . . . . 28 C1
Brosdale Ct FK1 . . . . 60 B2
Brotherstone's Way
EH33 . . . . 126 D4
Brougham Pl EH3 . . . . 228 C1
Brougham St EH3 . . . . 228 B1
BROUGHTON 93 D3
Broughton High Sch EH4 . 92 F2
Broughton Market EH3 . . . . 93 D2
Broughton Pl EH1 . . . . 93 D2
Broughton Place La EH1 . . 93 D2
Broughton Prim Sch EH7 . 93 D3
Broughton Rd EH7 . . . . 93 D3
Broughton St EH1 . . . . . . 229 A4
Brown Ave Alloa FK10 . . . . . . 4 F1
Stirling FK9 . . . . 2 B2
Brown Cres EH48 . . . . 141 A4
Brown Ct FK3 . . . . 61 D8
Brownieknowe Pl FK2 . . . . 59 F8
Brownrigg Farm Cotts
EH39 . . . . 74 C6
Brown's Cl EH8 . . . . 229 C3
Brown's Ct EH1 . . . . 229 C3
Brown's Pl
East Linton EH40 . . . . 103 D8
Edinburgh EH1 . . . . 228 C2
Brown St Armadale EH48 . . 139 F4
Edinburgh EH8 . . . . 229 B2
Falkirk FK1 . . . . 59 D5
[6] Haddington EH41 . . . . . 130 B8
Shotts ML7 . . . . 180 B3
Whitburn EH47 . . . . 161 A6
BROXBURN Broxburn 115 E6
Dunbar 107 A7
Broxburn Acad EH52 . . . . . 115 C5
Broxburn Cotts EH42 . . . . 107 A7
Broxburn Prim Sch EH52 115 E5
Bruart Ave FK5 . . . . 38 F3
Bruce Cres Falkirk FK2 . . . . . 39 B3
Plean FK7 . . . . 20 D3
Bruce Dr Fallin FK7 . . . . 8 C5
Stenhousemuir FK5 . . . . 38 F3
BRUCEFIELD Dunfermline . . . 29 C2
Murieston 164 D6
Brucefield Ave KY11 . . . . . . 29 B2
Brucefield Cres FK10 . . . . . 11 B4
Brucefield Dr EH47 . . . . . . 161 B6
Brucefield Feus KY11 . . . . . 29 C3
Brucefield Ho EH47 . . . . . . 161 D7
Brucefield Ind Pk EH54 . . 164 C5
Brucefield Park E EH54 . . 164 C6
Brucefield Park N EH54 . . 164 C6
Brucefield Park W EH54 . . 164 C5
Brucefield Terr KY4 . . . . . . 13 F6
Bruce Gate FK2 . . . . 22 D2
Bruce Gdns Dalkeith EH22 153 B2
Dunfermline KY11 . . . . 47 A8
[1] Grangemouth FK2 . . . . . . 82 D8
Bruce Gr EH34 . . . . 156 E5
Brucehaven Cres KY11 . . . . 45 E3
Brucehaven Rd KY11 . . . . . 45 D3
Bruce Pl FK3 . . . . 61 E8
Bruce Rd Bathgate EH48 . . . 141 C5
Grangemouth EH51 . . . . 62 E5
Bruce St Alloa FK10 . . . . 10 C7
Bannockburn FK7 . . . . 7 E1
Bathgate EH48 . . . . 141 C4
Clackmannan FK10 . . . . 11 A4
Dunfermline KY12 . . . . 28 F4
Edinburgh EH10 . . . . 121 A2
Falkirk FK2 . . . . 60 C6
Kinghorn KY3 . . . . 35 A3
Plean FK7 . . . . 20 D3
Stirling FK8 . . . . 2 B1
Bruce Terr
Cambusbarron FK7 . . . . 6 D5
Kinghorn KY3 . . . . 35 A3
Bruce View FK7 . . . . 7 B1
BRUNSTANE 123 D6

Brunstane Bank EH15 .... 123 D6
Brunstane Cres EH15 .... 123 D6
Brunstane Dr EH15 ...... 123 C6
Brunstane Gdns
Edinburgh EH15 .... 123 C7
Penicuik EH26 .... 191 D6
Brunstane Gdns Mews
EH15 .... 123 C7
Brunstane Mill Rd EH15 .. 123 F7
Brunstane Prim Sch
EH15 .... 123 C6
Brunstane Rd EH15 ...... 123 C7
Brunstane Road N EH15 .. 123 C8
Brunstane Road S EH15 .. 123 C6
Brunstane Sta EH15 ..... 123 C6
Brunswick Pl 7 EH7 ...... 93 E2
Brunswick Rd EH7 .... 93 F2
Brunswick St EH7 .... 93 E2
Brunswick Street La EH7 .. 93 E2
Brunswick Terr EH7 .... 93 F2
Brunt Ct EH42 .... 106 E8
Brunt Gr EH42 .... 106 D8
Brunt La EH42 .... 78 D1
Brunton Ct EH21 .... 124 C6
Brunton Pl 1 EH7 .... 93 F2
Brunton's Cl EH22 .... 153 A3
Brunton Terr EH7 .... 93 F2
Brunt Pl EH42 .... 106 E8
BRUNTSFIELD 121 B5
Bruntsfield Ave EH10 ... 121 B5
Bruntsfield Cres
Dunbar EH42 .... 78 D1
Edinburgh EH10 .... 121 B5
Bruntsfield Gdns EH10 .. 121 B5
Bruntsfield Pl EH10 ..... 121 B5
Bruntsfield Prim Sch
EH10 .... 121 A5
Bruntsfield Terr EH10 ... 121 B5
Bryans Ave EH22 .... 174 B6
Bryans Rd EH22 .... 174 A6
Bryce Ave Edinburgh EH7 ... 94 F2
Falkirk FK2 .... 39 B2
Bryce Cres EH14 .... 148 A5
Bryce Gdns EH14 .... 148 A5
Bryce Gr EH7 .... 94 F2
Bryce Pl EH14 .... 148 A5
Bryce Rd EH14 .... 148 A5
Bryden Ct FK3 .... 61 E8
Bryony The FK10 .... 4 B1
Bryson Pl Bathgate EH48 .. 141 B6
Stenhousemuir FK5 .... 38 C5
Bryson Rd EH11 .... 120 F5
Bryson St FK2 .... 60 B6
Bryson Street Ind Est FK2 60 B6
Bubbles Rdbt EH54 ...... 143 E2
Buccleuch Ct EH22 ...... 152 F4
Buccleuch Pl EH8 .... 229 A1
Buccleuch Place La EH3 . 229 B1
Buccleuch St
Dalkeith EH22 .... 153 A3
Edinburgh EH8 .... 229 B1
Buccleuch Terr EH8 ..... 229 B1
Buchanan Cres EH54 ..... 143 A5
Buchanan Ct Bo'ness EH51 . 63 E5
Falkirk FK2 .... 60 A8
Kirkcaldy KY1 .... 17 B2
Buchanan Dr FK9 .... 2 B3
Buchanan Gdns
Cairneyhill KY12 .... 27 D1
Polmont FK2 .... 61 D2
Buchanan's Ct EH1 ...... 229 C3
Buchanan St
Dunfermline KY12 .... 29 A3
Edinburgh EH6 .... 93 F3
Buchan Ave FK2 .... 39 B1
Buchan Ct EH52 .... 115 D5
Buchan La EH52 .... 115 E5
Buchan Pl FK3 .... 61 C5
Buchan Rd Bathgate EH48 . 140 F7
Broxburn EH52 .... 115 C5
Grangemouth FK3, EH51 ... 62 D6
Buckie Rd EH22 .... 174 E6
Buckingham Terr EH4 ... 228 A4
Buckstane Pk EH10 ...... 150 A7
Buckstone Ave EH10 ..... 150 B6
Buckstone Bank EH10 .... 150 B7
Buckstone Circ EH10 .... 150 C6
Buckstone Cl EH10 ...... 150 C6
Buckstone Cres EH10 ... 150 B7
Buckstone Crook EH10 .. 150 C5
Buckstone Ct EH10 ...... 150 B6
Buckstone Dell EH10 .... 150 B7
Buckstone Dr EH10 ...... 150 B7
Buckstone Gate EH10 ... 150 C6
Buckstone Gdns EH10 ... 150 B6
Buckstone Gn EH10 ...... 150 C6
Buckstone Gr EH10 ...... 150 B7
Buckstone Hill EH10 ..... 150 C7
Buckstone Howe EH10 ... 150 C6
Buckstone Lea EH10 ..... 150 C6
Buckstone Loan EH10 .... 150 C6
Buckstone Loan E EH10 . 150 C6
Buckstone Neuk EH10 ... 150 C7
Buckstone Pl EH10 ...... 150 B6
Buckstone Prim Sch
EH10 .... 150 C6
Buckstone Rd EH10 ...... 150 B6
Buckstone Rise EH10 .... 150 C6
Buckstone Row EH10 .... 150 C7
Buckstone Shaw EH10 ... 150 C5
Buckstone Terr EH10 .... 150 B6
Buckstone View EH10 ... 150 B7
Buckstone Way EH10 .... 150 B7
Buckstone Wood EH10 ... 150 B6
Buckstone Wynd EH10 ... 150 C6
Buckyburn Pl KY12 .... 29 E6
Buffies Brae KY12 .... 28 F4
Bughtknowes Dr EH48 ... 141 C7
BUGHTLIN 91 A1
Bughtlin Dr EH12 .... 91 A1
Bughtlin Gdns EH12 ..... 119 A8
Bughtlin Gn EH12 .... 91 A1
Bughtlin Loan EH12 ..... 119 A8
Bughtlin Mkt EH12 .... 119 B8
Bughtlin Pk EH12 .... 119 B8
Bughtlin Pl EH12 .... 91 A1
Buie Haugh EH29 .... 88 F1
Buie Rigg EH29 .... 88 F2
Builyeon Rd EH30 .... 89 A8
Buller St KY5 .... 14 B7
Bullet Loan EH41 .... 130 C8
Bulloch Cres FK6 .... 36 D1
Bull's Cl EH1 .... 229 C3
Bunbrae Wlk EH19 .... 173 C5
Bungalows The FK5 .... 38 B1
Buntine Cres FK7 .... 7 A3
Burder Pk FK2 .... 39 A2
BURDIEHOUSE 151 A4
Burdiehouse Ave EH17 ... 151 B4
Burdiehouse Burn Nature
Reserve★ EH17 .... 151 C4
Burdiehouse Cres EH17 .. 151 B4
Burdiehouse Crossway
EH17 .... 151 B4
Burdiehouse Dr EH17 .... 151 B4
Burdiehouse Loan EH17 .. 151 B4
Burdiehouse Medway
EH17 .... 151 B4
Burdiehouse Pl EH17 .... 151 B4
Burdiehouse Prim Sch
EH17 .... 151 B4
Burdiehouse Rd EH17 .... 151 A3
Burdiehouse Sq EH17 .... 151 A3
Burdiehouse St EH17 .... 151 B4
Burdiehouse Terr EH17 .. 151 B4
Burgess Hill EH49 .... 85 A6
Burgess Rd EH30 .... 68 C1
Burgess St EH6 .... 94 A5
Burgess Terr EH9 .... 122 A4
Burgh Ct KY5 .... 14 A7
Burghlee Cres EH20 ..... 172 C7
Burghlee Terr EH20 ...... 172 C7
Burgh Mews 1 FK10 .... 10 B6
Burgh Mills La EH49 ...... 84 C6
Burghmuir Ct EH49 .... 85 D8
Burghmuir Ind Est FK8 ..... 7 B6
Burghmuir Rd FK7 .... 7 B6
Burgh Rd KY4 .... 13 D4
Burghtoft EH17 .... 151 E5
Burleigh Cres KY11 .... 47 C3
Burleigh Way FK10 .... 10 C6
Burlington St EH6 .... 93 F5
Burnbank Cairneyhill KY12 .. 27 D1
Carnock KY12 .... 27 C7
Livingston EH54 .... 143 D5
Loanhead EH20 .... 172 A8
Burnbank Cres EH20 ..... 151 A1
Burnbank Gr EH20 .... 151 A1
Burnbank Rd Falkirk FK2 ... 60 B7
Grangemouth FK3 .... 61 D5
Burnbank Terr EH25 ..... 171 E6
Burnbrae Alloa FK10 .... 10 C8
Edinburgh EH12 .... 119 A8
Fauldhouse EH47 .... 181 F5
Sauchie FK10 .... 5 C1
Burnbrae Ave
Bonnyrigg EH19 .... 173 C5
5 Edinburgh EH12 .... 119 A8
Burnbrae Cres EH19 ..... 173 C4
Burnbrae Dr 3 EH12 ..... 119 A8
Burnbrae Gdns Alva FK12 .... 5 B6
Falkirk FK1 .... 60 A5
Burnbrae Gr 6 EH12 ..... 119 A8
Burnbrae Loan EH19 ..... 173 C5
Burnbrae Pend EH19 ..... 173 C5
Burn Brae Pk FK10 .... 23 F4
Burnbrae Pl 4 EH12 ..... 119 A8
Burnbrae Rd
Bonnyrigg EH19 .... 173 C4
Falkirk FK1 .... 60 A5
Harthill ML7 .... 160 A6
Shotts ML7 .... 179 E3
Stoneyburn EH47 .... 162 B1
Burnbrae Terr
Bonnyrigg and Lasswade
EH19 .... 173 C4
Whitburn EH47 .... 161 C6
Burndene Dr EH20 .... 151 A1
Burn Dr FK7 .... 7 C4
Burnee FK10 .... 5 E3
Burnet's Cl EH1 .... 229 A3
Burney Pl KY11 .... 46 E4
Burnfield EH54 .... 143 A2
Burnfield Pl FK2 .... 60 D7
Burnfoot Ct FK3 .... 61 D6
Burnfoot La 1 FK1 .... 60 B4
Burngrange Cotts EH55 .. 163 C2
Burngrange Ct EH55 ..... 163 C2
Burngrange Gdns EH55 .. 163 B2
Burngrange Pk EH55 .... 163 C2
Burngrange Works EH55 163 B2
Burnhead Cres EH16 .... 151 B6
Burnhead Gr EH16 .... 151 B6
Burnhead La FK1 .... 60 C4
Burnhead Loan EH16 .... 151 B6
Burnhead Path E EH16 .. 151 B6
Burnhead Path W EH16 .. 151 B6
Burnhead Rd FK5 .... 38 C3
Burnhouse Dr
Dechmont EH52 .... 114 C2
Whitburn EH47 .... 160 E5
Burnhouse Farm Steadings
EH27 .... 145 C4
Burnhouse Ind Est EH47 . 160 F5
Burnhouse Rd EH52 ..... 114 C3
Burnhouse Sch EH47 .... 161 A5
Burnlea Dr EH47 .... 162 A1
Burnlea Pl EH47 .... 162 A1
Burns Ave Armadale EH48 . 139 F6
Grangemouth FK3 .... 61 D5
Stenhousemuir FK5 .... 38 C5
Burns Cres Harthill ML7 ... 159 F6
Laurieston FK2 .... 60 F4
Whitburn EH47 .... 161 A6
Burns Ct EH54 .... 144 C5
BURNSIDE 5 C7
Burnside Dechmont EH52 .. 114 B2
Edinburgh EH12 .... 119 A8
Haddington EH41 .... 129 E8
Prestonpans EH32 .... 96 E1
Burnside Ave
Armadale EH48 .... 139 D6
Easthouses EH22 .... 174 D7
Kinghorn KY3 .... 34 F3
Polbeth EH55 .... 163 F5
Burnside Bsns Ct KY11 .... 47 C4
Burnside Cotts EH49 ...... 86 E4
Burnside Cres
Clackmannan FK10 .... 11 B5
Easthouses EH22 .... 174 D7
Fauldhouse EH47 .... 181 E6
Plean FK7 .... 20 C4
Polbeth EH55 .... 163 F5
Rosyth KY11 .... 47 A5
Shotts ML7 .... 179 D6
Burnside Ct Alva FK12 ...... 5 A7
Falkirk, Camelon FK1 ...... 59 E5
Garvald EH41 .... 132 D2
Burnside Gdns
1 Burntisland KY3 .... 33 D1
Whitecross EH49 .... 83 F6
Burnside La EH55 .... 163 F5
Burnside Pk EH14 .... 147 C2
Burnside Pl Falkirk FK2 .... 39 B3
Rosyth KY11 .... 47 A4
Burnside Rd
Bathgate EH48 .... 140 F7
Gorebridge EH23 .... 174 D1
Menstrie FK11 .... 3 F6
Polbeth EH55 .... 163 F5
Ratho Station EH12 ..... 118 A7
Uphall EH52 .... 115 A4
Burnside Rdbt EH54 ..... 143 F2
Burnside St Alloa FK10 ..... 5 D1
Rosyth KY11 .... 47 A5
Stirling FK7 .... 7 C6
Burnside Terr
Addiewell EH55 .... 162 D1
Cowdenbeath KY4 .... 13 A2
East Calder EH53 .... 144 F5
Falkirk FK1 .... 59 E5
Fauldhouse EH47 .... 181 E6
Oakley KY12 .... 27 A7
Polbeth EH55 .... 163 F5
Redding FK2 .... 61 B1
Burnside View EH55 ..... 162 D1
Burnsknowe EH54 .... 142 E6
Burns Pl ML7 .... 179 A6
Burns St Dunfermline KY12 .. 28 E5
Edinburgh EH6 .... 94 A4
High Valleyfield KY12 ..... 26 A2
Kelty/Cowdenbeath KY4 .... 30 F6
Stirling FK8 .... 2 A2
Burns Terr Bathgate EH48 . 141 C5
Cowie FK7 .... 20 D7
BURNTISLAND 33 E2
Burntisland Prim Sch KY3 33 F1
Burntisland Rd KY3 .... 34 F2
Burntisland Sta KY3 .... 50 E8
Burnvale Broxburn EH52 .. 116 A4
Livingston EH54 .... 143 F3
Burnvale Ave EH48 ...... 141 C4
Burnvale Pl EH54 .... 144 A3
BURNWYND 146 C5
Burt Ave KY3 .... 34 F3
Burt Gr KY11 .... 29 E1
Burt St KY12 .... 29 A6
BUSH 171 B3
Bush St EH21 .... 124 B6
Bush Terr EH21 .... 124 B6
Bute EH54 .... 142 F5
Bute Cres Dunfermline KY11 29 E3
Shotts ML7 .... 179 D6
Bute Pl FK3 .... 61 D6
Bute St FK2 .... 60 B6
Bute Wynd KY1 .... 17 B2
Butlerfield Ind Est EH22 . 174 A3
Butler's Pl EH54 .... 143 B4
Butterdean Wood★
EH33 .... 128 C6
Butteries View EH48 .... 139 D5
Butts The EH41 .... 130 B8
Buxley Farm Steading
EH33 .... 126 F3
Buxley Rd EH33 .... 126 B1
Byburn EH52 .... 114 F8
By-Pass Rd FK4 .... 57 E5
Byrehope Rd EH52 ...... 115 B4
Byreside EH47 .... 142 A1
Byres The KY11 .... 46 C5
Byron Rd ML7 .... 179 B6

C

Cables Wynd EH6 .... 93 F5
Cables Wynd Ho EH6 ...... 93 F5
Caddell's Row Cotts EH4 .. 91 B5
Cadell Dr FK2 .... 39 A5
Cadell Pl
Cockenzie & Port Seton
EH32 .... 97 C4
Fauldhouse EH47 .... 181 E5
Cadell Reach KY11 .... 47 A7
Cadell Sq 4 EH33 .... 126 D6
Cadgers Loan FK7 .... 20 B2
Cadiz St EH6 .... 94 A5
Cadogan Rd EH16 .... 151 A7
Cadzow Ave EH51 .... 63 F6
Cadzow Cres EH51 .... 63 F7
Cadzow La EH51 .... 63 F7
Cadzow Pl EH7 .... 94 A1
Caerketton Ave EH25 .... 171 E6
Caerketton Cotts EH13 .. 149 D8
Caerlaverock Ct 1 EH12 . 119 B7
Caesar Rd EH33 .... 126 C6
Caesar Way EH33 .... 126 C6
Caird's Row EH21 .... 124 B7
Cairnbank Gdns EH26 ... 191 E4
Cairnbank Rd EH26 ..... 191 E4
Cairncubie Rd KY12 ...... 29 C8
CAIRNEYHILL 27 C2
Cairneyhill Prim Sch
KY12 .... 27 D2
Cairneyhill Rd KY12 ...... 28 B2
Cairneymount Ave FK2 .... 83 A6
Cairneymount Rd ML8 ... 215 A2
Cairngorm Cres KY2 ...... 16 F5
Cairngorm Rd FK3 .... 61 E5
Cairn Gr KY12 .... 28 C2
Cairnhill Ct ML8 .... 215 A2
Cairnie Pl EH47 .... 161 A5
Cairn Lea EH48 .... 141 C5
Cairnmuir Rd EH12 ..... 119 E8
Cairnoch Way FK7 .... 7 F1
Cairnoch Wlk FK6 .... 36 D1
Cairnpapple Henge & Cairn★
EH48 .... 112 D4
Cairnpapple Ho 2 EH48 . 141 A6
Cairns Dr EH14 .... 168 B8
Cairns Gdns EH14 .... 168 B8
Cairn's La EH51 .... 64 B7
Cairns Street E KY1 .... 17 E7
Cairns Street W KY1 ...... 17 D7
Cairns The
Charlestown KY11 .... 45 A4
Menstrie FK11 .... 4 A6
Cairntows Cl EH16 ...... 122 D4
Cairnwell Pl
Cairneyhill KY12 .... 27 D1
Kirkcaldy KY2 .... 16 F7
Caithness Ct KY1 .... 17 E7
Caithness Dr KY11 .... 30 C1
Caithness Pl Edinburgh EH5 93 B5
Kirkcaldy KY1 .... 17 E7
Caiyside EH10 .... 150 A4
Caiystane Ave EH10 ..... 150 A5
Caiystane Cres EH10 .... 150 A6
Caiystane Dr EH10 ...... 149 F5
Caiystane Gdns EH10 ... 150 A6
Caiystane Hill EH10 ..... 150 A6
Caiystane Terr EH10 .... 150 A5
Caiystane View EH10 .... 150 A5
Cakemuir Gdns EH16 .... 122 F4
Cakemuir Gr EH16 .... 122 F4
Calaisburn Pl KY11 .... 29 E1
Calais View KY11 .... 29 F1
Calaiswood Sch KY11 ..... 30 B1
Calderburn Rd EH55 .... 164 A5
Calder Cres
Armadale EH48 .... 140 A5
Edinburgh EH11 .... 119 B1
Caldercruix Rd FK1 ..... 108 A1
Calder Ct Edinburgh EH11 .. 119 C2
Stirling FK7 .... 7 C5
Calder Dr Edinburgh EH11 . 119 C1
Shotts ML7 .... 180 B4
Calder Gdns EH11 .... 119 C2
Calder Gr EH11 .... 119 C1
CALDERHALL 144 E4
Calderhall Ave EH53 ..... 144 E3
Calderhall Cres EH53 .... 144 F3
Calderhall Terr EH53 .... 144 F3
CALDERHEAD 179 E4
Calderhead High Sch
ML7 .... 179 F5
Calderhead Rd ML7 ..... 179 D7
Calder House Rd EH53 ... 144 B3
Calder Junc EH11 .... 119 B1
Calder Park Rd EH53 .... 144 B2
Calder Pk EH11 .... 119 C1
Calder Pl Dalgety Bay KY11 . 48 A3
Edinburgh EH11 .... 119 C1
Falkirk FK1 .... 60 D1
Calder Rd
Edinburgh, Sighthill
EH11 .... 119 D2
Edinburgh, Stenhouse
EH11 .... 120 A3
Hermiston EH14 .... 118 F1
Livingston EH54 .... 164 C7
Calder Rd Gdns EH11 ... 120 A3
Calder's Lawn EH41 ..... 101 A1
Calder View EH11 .... 119 B1
Caledon Gn FK3 .... 61 B7
Caledonia Ct KY11 .... 46 D5
Caledonia Hts KY11 .... 46 C3
Caledonian Brewery★
EH11 .... 120 E5
Caledonian Cres EH11 ... 228 A1
Caledonian Ct Falkirk FK2 .. 60 C7
Kirknewton EH27 .... 145 D3
Caledonian Pl EH11 ..... 228 A1
Caledonian Rd Alloa FK10 ... 9 F6
Edinburgh EH11 .... 228 A1
Fauldhouse EH47 .... 181 D5
Caledonian Terr EH47 ... 181 D5
Caledonia Rd Kirkcaldy KY2 17 A4
Rosyth KY11 .... 46 A1
Shotts ML7 .... 179 E5
Caledonia Terr FK4 .... 57 F5
Caledonia Way KY11 ...... 46 A3
Calender Ave KY1 .... 17 C7
Calgary Ave EH54 .... 143 F4
CALIFORNIA 81 E5
California Prim Sch FK1 .. 81 F5
California Rd
Maddiston FK2 .... 82 F6
Shieldhill FK1 .... 81 E6
California Terr FK1 .... 81 F5
Callander Dr FK5 .... 59 C8
Callander Pl TD13 .... 218 F4
Callander Terr KY11 .... 30 A4
Callendar Ave FK1 .... 60 B1
Callendar Bsns Pk FK1 .... 60 E3
Callendar Bvd FK1 .... 60 E3
Callendar House★ FK1 .... 60 D3
Callendar Park Dr FK1 .... 60 D4
Callendar Park Terr FK1 .. 60 D4
Callendar Park View FK1 .. 60 D4
Callendar Park Wlk FK1 ... 60 D4
Callendar Rd FK1 .... 60 D4
Callendar Riggs FK1 .... 60 C4
Callendar Square Sh Ctr 5
FK1 .... 60 B4
Calliope Rd KY11 .... 46 B1
CALTON 229 C4
Calton Cres FK7 .... 7 B4
Caltonhill EH1 .... 229 B4
Calton Hill★ EH7 .... 229 B4
Calton Rd EH8 .... 229 B3
Caltrop Pl FK7 .... 7 E3
Calum Macdonald Ct
KY11 .... 46 E3
Cambridge Ave EH6 .... 93 F3
Cambridge Gdns EH6 ..... 93 E3
Cambridge St Day Hospl
EH1 .... 228 B2
Cambridge St EH1 .... 228 B2
CAMBUS 9 B8
CAMBUSBARRON 6 C6
Cambusbarron Prim Sch
FK7 .... 6 D5
CAMBUSKENNETH 2 D1
Cambuskenneth Abbey★
FK9 .... 7 D8
Cambusnethan St 1 EH7 .. 94 B1
Cambus Pools Wildlife
Reserve★ FK10 .... 8 F8
Camdean Cres KY11 .... 46 D5
Camdean La KY11 .... 46 D5
Camdean Prim Sch KY11 .. 46 D4
CAMELON 59 C5
Camelon Ed Ctr 1 FK1 .... 59 E5
Camelon Rd FK1 .... 59 F5
Camelon Rdbt FK1 .... 59 D6
Camelon Sta FK1 .... 59 D6
Camera Obscura★ EH1 .. 228 C2
Cameron Cres
Bonnyrigg and Lasswade
EH19 .... 172 F5
Edinburgh EH16 .... 122 B3
Cameron Dr KY1 .... 18 A8
Cameron Gr KY11 .... 47 B3
Cameron House Ave
EH16 .... 122 B3
Cameronian Dr ML8 ..... 215 B1
Cameronian St 9 FK8 ...... 7 B7
Cameron Knowe EH49 .... 86 D6
Cameron March EH16 ... 122 A3
Cameron Pk EH16 .... 122 B3
Cameron Pl FK2 .... 39 B2
Cameron Smaill Rd
EH14 .... 147 E7
Cameron St KY12 .... 28 E4
Cameron Terr
Edinburgh EH16 .... 122 B3
Limerigg FK1 .... 108 B3
Cameron Toll EH16 ..... 122 B3
Cameron Toll Gdns EH16 122 B3
Cameron Toll Lade EH16 122 B3
Cameron Toll Sh Ctr
EH16 .... 122 A3
Cameron Way
Livingston EH54 .... 143 E7
Prestonpans EH32 .... 97 A2
Camilla Gr KY2 .... 15 C2
Camilla Rd KY2 .... 15 B2
CAMMO 90 F2
Cammo Bank EH4 .... 91 A2
Cammo Brae EH4 .... 91 A2
Cammo Cres EH4 .... 91 A2
Cammo Gdns EH4 .... 91 A2
Cammo Gr EH4 .... 90 F2
Cammo Hill EH4 .... 90 F2
Cammo Parkway EH4 ...... 91 A2
Cammo Pl EH4 .... 91 A2
Cammo Rd EH4, EH12 ...... 90 E2
Cammo Wlk EH4, EH12 .... 90 F1
Campbell Ave EH12 ...... 120 C8
Campbell Cres
Laurieston FK2 .... 60 F3
Lochgelly KY5 .... 14 B8
Campbell Ct
Longniddry EH32 .... 98 D5
Stirling FK7 .... 6 F4
Campbell Dr FK5 .... 38 B2
Campbell Park Cres
EH13 .... 148 F6
Campbell Park Dr EH13 .. 148 F6
Campbell Pl FK2 .... 59 F7
Campbell Rd
Edinburgh EH12 .... 120 C8
Longniddry EH32 .... 98 D5
Campbell's Cl EH8 .... 229 C3
Campbell St KY12 .... 29 A4
Campend Cotts EH22 .... 152 D5

Camperdown Rd
Inverkeithing/Dunfermline
KY11 46 D1
Rosyth KY11 46 C1
Campfield St FK2 60 B6
Campie Ct EH21 124 B6
Campie Gdns EH21 124 B6
Campie La EH21 124 B6
Campie Prim Sch EH21 124 B6
Campie Rd EH21 124 B6
Campie Terr FK2 39 F2
Camp Rd Crombie KY12 44 D5
Mayfield EH22 174 E7
Campsie Cres KY2 16 F7
Campsie Rd FK3 61 E5
Camps Ind Est EH27 145 C5
Camps Rd KY12 27 C6
Camps Rigg EH54 143 B7
CAMPTOUN 100 F8
Campus Rdbt EH54 143 C1
Campview EH22 152 B7
Campview Ave EH22 152 B7
Campview Cres EH22 152 C7
Campview Gdns EH22 152 B7
Campview Gr EH22 152 C7
Campview Rd EH19 173 B6
Campview Terr EH22 152 B7
Camp Wood View EH22 174 E5
Camus Ave EH10 150 A6
Camus Pk EH10 150 A6
Canaan La EH10 121 B3
Canal Bank Ind Est FK4 58 A4
Canal Ct EH49 86 F4
Canal Side Dr FK2 61 A1
Canal St
Falkirk, Camelon FK1 59 D5
Falkirk FK2 60 B7
Canal Terr EH49 85 A6
Canal View Prim Sch
EH14 148 E8
Canal Wlk FK2 61 C1
Canalyard Ind Est FK1 60 B1
Canavan Ct Falkirk FK2 60 C7
Stirling FK7 7 C3
Canavan Pk FK2 60 C7
Canberra St EH54 144 A5
Candie Cres FK3 61 E6
Candie Rd FK3 62 A8
Candimilne Ct ML8 215 B1
Candlemaker Row EH1 229 A2
Candlemaker's Cres
EH17 151 F6
Candlemaker's Pk EH17 151 F6
Candleriggs FK10 10 B6
Candleriggs Ct 7 FK10 10 B6
Caneluk Ave ML8 215 B1
Canmore Dr FK5 38 E4
Canmore Gr KY12 29 B5
Canmore Prim Sch KY11 29 E1
Canmore St
Dunfermline KY12 29 A3
Kinghorn KY3 34 F1
Queensferry EH30 89 B8
Canmore Terr KY12 29 A7
Canning St EH3 228 B2
Canning Street La EH3 228 A2
Cannonmills Br EH3 93 C3
Cannons Way FK2 39 A1
Cannon Wynd EH6 93 E6
Cannop Cres EH47 161 F1
Canon Byrne Glebe KY1 17 C5
CANONGATE 229 C3
Canongate Edinburgh EH8 229 B3
Spott EH42 106 D4
Canongate Venture EH1 229 B3
Canon La EH3 93 C2
Canon Lynch Ct KY12 28 F4
CANONMILLS 93 C2
Canonmills EH3 93 C3
Canon St EH3 93 C2
Canthill Gdns ML7 179 A3
Cantlie Pl KY11 46 E3
Cantsdam Rd KY4 12 F7
Canty Gr EH32 98 C3
Capelaw Rd EH13 149 A5
Caplaw Way EH26 191 C5
Caponflat Cres EH41 100 F1
Caponhall Ct 7 EH33 126 C5
Caponhall Dr EH33 126 C5
Caponhall Rd EH33 126 C5
Caponhall Way 3 EH33 126 C6
Cappers Ct EH48 139 F4
Captain's Dr EH16 151 B5
Captain's Loan EH16 151 B6
Captain's Rd EH16, EH17 151 B5
Captain's Row EH16 151 B6
Caputhall Rd EH54 142 C5
Carberry Cl EH21 124 E3
Carberry Ct EH21 153 E8
Carberry Gr EH21 124 D3
Carberry Mains Cotts
EH21 125 A1
Carberry Pl 8 EH12 120 E7
Carberry Rd EH21 124 E3
Carbrook Dr FK7 20 C3
Carbrook Pl FK3 61 E6
Carcraig Pl KY11 48 B3
Cardross Ave EH52 115 B5
Cardross Cres EH52 115 C5
Cardross Rd EH52 115 C5
Cardrowan Rd FK7 20 D1
Carey Ct FK7 20 C4
Carfrae Cotts EH41 221 D8
Carfrae Gdns EH4 92 A2
Carfrae Gr EH4 92 A2
Carfrae Pk EH4 92 A2
Carfrae Rd EH4 92 A2
Cargilfield Sch EH4 91 B4
Cargilfield View EH4 91 B4
Cargil Terr EH5 93 B5
Carhowden Rd FK2 61 B3
Carlaverock Ave EH33 126 D5
Carlaverock Cl EH33 126 E4
Carlaverock Cres EH33 126 D5
Carlaverock Ct EH33 126 E5
Carlaverock Dr EH33 126 D5
Carlaverock Gr EH33 126 D5
Carlaverock Terr EH33 126 E4
Carlaverock View EH33 126 D4
Carlaverock Wlk 4
EH33 126 D5
Carledubs Ave EH52 115 A5
Carledubs Cres EH52 115 A6
Carlekemp EH39 53 F8
Carlie Ave FK9 2 A6
Carlin Craig KY3 34 F1
Carlin Cres KY3 34 F1
Carlingnose Ct KY11 68 C6
Carlingnose Pk KY11 68 C6
Carlingnose Point KY11 68 C6
Carlingnose View KY11 68 C6
Carlingnose Way KY11 68 C6
Carlin La ML8 215 B1
Carlisle App EH23 195 C3
CARLOPS 206 C4
Carlops Ave EH26 191 E6
Carlops Cres EH26 191 E6
Carlops Rd EH26 191 D5
Carlouk La ML8 215 B1
Carlowrie Ave EH30 89 E7
Carlowrie Cres EH30 89 E7
Carlowrie Farm Cotts
EH29 89 F4
Carlowrie Pl EH23 174 D1
Carlton Terr EH7 229 C4
Carlton Terrace Brae
EH7 229 C4
Carlton Terrace La EH7 229 C4
Carlton Terrace Mews
EH7 229 C4
CARLUKE 215 A2
Carluke High Sch ML8 215 A2
Carluke L Ctr ML8 215 B2
Carluke Prim Sch ML8 215 A3
Carlyle Ct
Haddington EH41 130 B8
Livingston EH54 144 C5
Carlyle Gdns EH41 101 A1
Carlyle La 1 KY12 28 E5
Carlyle Pl Edinburgh EH7 94 A2
Musselburgh EH21 124 C6
Carlyle Rd KY1 17 B4
Carlyle St KY12 26 B2
Carlyle Terr EH48 141 C5
Carmel Ave EH29 89 A2
Carmelaws EH49 85 A5
Carmelite Rd EH30 89 B8
Carmel Rd EH29 89 A1
Carmichael Ct FK9 2 A7
Carmichael Pl EH6 93 E4
Carmondean Centre Rd
EH54 143 A6
Carmondean Centre Rdbt
EH54 143 B6
Carmondean Centre S
EH54 143 A6
Carmondean Ctr EH54 143 A6
Carmondean Prim Sch
EH54 143 B7
Carmuir ML11 201 A1
CARMUIRS 59 B5
Carmuirs Ave FK1 59 C5
Carmuirs Dr FK1 59 B6
Carmuirs Prim Sch FK1 59 D5
Carmuirs St FK1 59 D5
Carnach FK10 10 D6
Carnaughton Pl FK12 4 F6
Carnbee Ave EH16 151 C6
Carnbee Cres EH16 151 C6
Carnbee Dell EH16 151 C6
Carnbee End EH16 151 C6
Carnbee Pk EH16 151 C6
Carnbee Pl KY12 29 C4
Carnegie Ave KY11 46 E7
Carnegie Campus (Bsns Pk)
KY11 46 E7
Carnegie Coll KY11 30 A5
Carnegie Ct
Dunfermline KY12 29 A4
Edinburgh EH8 229 B2
Carnegie Dr
Dunfermline KY12 29 A4
Falkirk FK1 59 D6
Carnegie Drive Ret Pk
KY12 29 A4
Carnegie L Ctr KY12 29 A4
Carnegie Prim Sch KY11 47 D3
Carnegie Rd EH54 142 B6
Carnegie St EH8 229 B2
Carneil Rd KY12 27 C7
Carneil Terr KY12 27 C6
Carnethie St EH24 172 E2
Carnethy Ave
Edinburgh EH13 149 B6
Penicuik EH26 191 F6
Carnethy Cres KY2 16 F7
Carnethy Ct EH26 191 F5
CARNOCK 27 D6
Carnock Mill KY12 27 C7
Carnock Prim Sch KY12 27 C7
Carnock Rd
Dunfermline KY12 26 F7
Gowkhall KY12 27 E7
Carnock St FK7 20 E8
Carnwaith La ML8 215 B1
Carnwath Rd ML8 215 A1
Caroline Cres FK12 4 F6
Caroline Gdns
Edinburgh EH12 119 E7
Mid Calder EH53 144 B2
Caroline Park Ave EH5 92 D7
Caroline Pk EH53 144 B2
Caroline Pl EH12 119 E7
Caroline Terr EH12 119 D8
Carpenters Wynd FK10 9 F6
Carperstane EH39 54 D1
Carpet La EH6 94 A5
Carradale Ave FK1 59 C4
Carribber Ave EH49 84 A6
Carrick Cres EH22 174 C8
Carrick Ct FK7 7 C5
Carrick Dr KY11 48 A3
Carrick Gdns EH54 164 E6
Carrick Gr KY11 48 A3
Carrick Knowe Ave EH12 119 F5
Carrick Knowe Dr EH12 119 E5
Carrick Knowe Gdns
EH12 119 F5
Carrick Knowe Gr EH12 119 F5
Carrick Knowe Hill EH12 119 F5
Carrick Knowe Loan
EH12 119 E5
Carrick Knowe Parkway
EH12 119 E5
Carrick Knowe Pl EH12 119 F5
Carrick Knowe Prim Sch
EH12 119 F5
Carrick Knowe Rd EH12 119 F4
Carrick Knowe Terr
EH12 119 F5
Carrick Pl Falkirk FK2 39 A3
Falkirk, Tamfourhill FK1 59 C4
CARRIDEN 64 C7
Carriden Brae EH51 64 D6
Carriden Glade EH51 64 D7
Carriden Ind Est EH51 64 E7
Carriden Pl EH51 64 C6
Carriden View EH51 64 C6
CARRINGTON 194 D6
Carrington Cres EH4 92 E3
Carrington Mains Cotts
EH23 194 D5
Carrington Rd EH4 92 F2
CARRON 39 A2
Carronbank Ave FK2 39 B2
Carronbank Cres FK6 36 E3
Carronbank Ct FK2 39 B2
Carron Ct 1 EH48 141 A6
Carronflats Rd FK3 61 E8
Carron Gr KY11 29 F4
Carrongrange Ave FK5 38 E2
Carrongrange Gdns FK5 38 E1
Carrongrange Gr FK5 38 E1
Carrongrange Rd FK5 38 E2
Carrongrange Sch FK5 38 E2
Carrongrove Ave FK2 39 A2
Carrongrove Bsns Pk FK2 39 A2
Carrongrove Rd FK2 39 A2
Carronhall Ave FK2 39 C4
Carron La KY11 29 F4
Carronlea Dr FK2 39 A2
Carron Pl Edinburgh EH6 94 B5
Grangemouth FK3 61 D4
Kirkcaldy KY2 16 D8
Stirling FK7 7 B2
Carron Prim Sch FK2 39 A2
Carron Rd FK2 39 A1
Carron Rdbt FK2 39 A2
CARRONSHORE 39 C3
Carronshore Prim Sch
FK2 39 C4
Carronshore Rd FK2 39 B2
Carronside Pl FK6 36 E3
Carronside St FK2 60 B8
Carron Terr FK2 82 E7
Carronvale Ave FK5 38 D1
Carronvale Rd Larbert FK5 59 D8
Stenhousemuir FK5 38 C1
Carronview FK5 38 D2
Carron View FK2 82 E7
Carron Wlk EH54 144 A4
Carrubber's Cl EH1 229 A3
Carsaig Ct FK9 2 A5
Carsebridge Ct FK10 10 C8
Carsebridge Rd FK10 10 D8
Carsebridge Row FK10 10 D8
Carse Cres FK2 61 A4
Carse Knowe EH49 85 D7
Carse Terr FK10 9 F8
Carseview Bannockburn FK7 7 E2
Tullibody FK10 4 A3
Carse View Airth FK2 22 E4
Bo'ness EH51 63 D5
Carson Pl KY11 46 C5
Carswell Pl KY12 28 F6
Cartmore Rd KY5 14 A8
Cask Cres FK9 7 C8
Casselbank St EH6 93 F4
Cassel's La EH6 93 F4
Castellau Cotts EH42 78 D2
Castings Ave FK2 60 B7
Castings Ct Falkirk FK2 60 B7
Falkirk, Middlefield FK2 60 E6
Castings Dr FK2 60 B6
Castings Ho FK2 60 B7
Castings Rd FK2 60 E6
Castings The KY12 28 D6
Castlandhill Farm Steadings
KY11 46 F2
Castlandhill Rd KY11 47 A2
Castle Ave Airth FK2 22 E3
Castle Ave *continued*
Cockenzie & Port Seton
EH32 97 E4
Edinburgh EH12 119 D5
Falkirk FK2 39 C3
Gorebridge EH23 195 C8
Castleblair 2 KY12 28 F4
Castleblair La 2 KY12 28 F5
Castleblair Mews 3 KY12 28 F5
CASTLEBLAIR PARK 28 F4
Castleblair Pk KY12 28 F5
Castle Brae KY11 46 F6
Castlebrae Bsns Ctr
EH16 122 E4
Castlebrae Com High Sch
EH16 122 E3
Castlebrae Glebe EH16 122 D4
Castlebrae Gr EH16 122 D3
Castlebrae Pl EH16 122 D3
Castlebrae Rigg EH16 122 D3
Castlebrae Wynd EH16 122 D3
Castle Bsns Pk The FK9 1 E2
Castle Cres Denny FK6 36 D2
East Calder EH53 144 F2
Falkirk FK2 60 D7
Torwood FK5 37 E7
Castle Ct Dunfermline KY11 46 F6
Falkirk FK2 60 C7
Menstrie FK11 3 F6
Stirling FK8 7 A8
Castledean Ct EH19 173 D6
Castle Dr Airth FK2 22 E3
Dunfermline KY11 46 E6
Falkirk FK2 60 C8
Stenhousemuir FK5 38 F2
Castlegait 6 FK8 7 B7
Castle Gate Dunbar EH42 78 D3
Rosyth KY11 46 E3
Castle Gogar★ EH12 118 D7
Castle Gogar Rigg EH12 118 C6
Castlehill Bo'ness EH51 63 D6
Edinburgh EH1 228 C3
Elphinstone EH33 126 B1
Castlehill Ave FK1 108 A6
Castlelaurie Ind Est FK2 60 C7
Castlelaurie St FK2 60 C7
Castlelaw Cres EH25 171 E5
Castlelaw Ct EH26 191 F6
**Castlelaw Fort & Earth
House**★ EH26 170 D4
Castlelaw Rd EH13 149 A6
CASTLELOAN 63 D7
Castle Mains EH39 53 B5
Castlemains Pl EH39 53 C5
Castle Mains Pl EH39 53 B5
Castle Moffat EH14 222 A8
Castle Moffat Cotts
EH14 222 A8
Castlemount Terr KY2 16 C8
Castlepark Gait EH16 122 D4
Castlepark Glade EH16 122 D3
Castlepark Gn EH16 122 D4
Castle Pk Dirleton EH39 53 A4
Kincardine FK10 23 D6
Castle Pl Bathgate EH48 141 C5
Dunbar EH42 78 D3
Falkirk FK2 60 D7
Gorebridge EH23 195 C8
Castlerankine Rd FK6 36 C2
Castle Rd Bathgate EH48 141 C3
Cockenzie & Port Seton
EH32 97 E4
Falkirk FK2 60 C8
Menstrie FK11 3 F6
Rosyth KY11 46 E2
Stirling FK9 2 C3
Tranent EH33 126 B4
Winchburgh EH52 88 A2
Castlerig KY3 34 F2
Castle Row KY12 28 C6
Castle St Alloa FK10 10 A5
Clackmannan FK10 11 A4
Dunbar EH42 78 D3
Edinburgh EH2 228 B3
Castle Terr
Clackmannan FK10 11 A4
Cockenzie & Port Seton
EH32 97 E4
Denny FK6 36 C2
Edinburgh EH2 228 B2
Winchburgh EH52 88 A2
Castleton Cotts EH39 55 E7
Castleton Cres FK3 61 D6
Castle Vale FK9 2 A4
Castle View Aberdour KY3 49 C8
Airth FK2 22 D2
Cockenzie & Port Seton
EH32 97 E4
Dunfermline KY11 46 F6
Fallin FK7 8 D4
Gorebridge EH23 195 C7
Pencaitland EH34 156 D6
Castleview Dr
Bridge of Allan FK9 2 A7
Edinburgh EH16 122 D3
Castleview Gr EH16 122 D3
Castleview Ho EH17 122 D1
Castleview La EH54 164 E4
Castleview Prim Sch
EH16 122 E3
Castleview Sch 2 FK8 1 F2
Castleview Terr
Edinburgh EH16 122 D4
Longcroft FK4 57 A3
Castle Wlk EH32 97 E4
Castle Wynd Kinghorn KY3 34 F2
4 Stirling FK8 7 A8
Castle Wynd N EH1 228 C2
Castle Wynd S EH1 228 C2
Cast The EH18 172 D5
Catalyst Trad Pk EH11 119 C2
CAT CRAIG 107 E7
Cathcart Pl EH11 120 F6
Cathedral La EH1 229 A4
Catherine St FK7 7 C1
Catherines Wynd KY12 25 F2
Catherine Terr EH47 141 D1
Cathlaw La EH48 112 A5
Cathrine Gr EH51 64 A5
Catriona Terr EH26 171 B1
Cattle Market FK10 11 A4
Cauldcoats Holdings
EH49 65 B2
Cauldhame Cres FK7 6 C5
Cauldhame Farm Rd FK2 59 F7
Cauldhame St FK2 59 F8
CAUSEWAYHEAD 2 B4
Causewayhead Rd FK9 2 C3
Causeway La KY12 26 E1
Causewayside EH9 121 E5
Causeway The
Bridge of Allan FK9 2 D5
Cockburnspath TD13 218 F4
Edinburgh EH15 122 C6
Cavalry Park Dr EH15 122 D6
Cawder Gdns FK9 1 F8
Cawder Rd FK9 1 F7
Cawdor Cres KY2 16 E6
Cecil St FK7 7 B6
Cedar Ave Kirkcaldy KY1 17 C8
Stirling FK8 6 F5
Cedarbank EH54 143 E5
Cedarbank Sch EH54 143 E5
Cedar Cres
Cowdenbeath KY4 13 D6
Westquarter FK2 61 A2
Whitburn EH47 161 C6
Cedar Dr EH32 97 C3
Cedar Gr Dunfermline KY11 46 D8
Menstrie FK11 3 F5
Stenhousemuir FK5 38 D1
Cedar Rd EH20 171 F7
Cedar St Dunbar EH42 78 B2
Grangemouth FK3 61 D7
Cedars The
Edinburgh EH13 149 B7
Tullibody FK10 4 B2
Cedar Wynd ML7 180 B4
Cedric Rise EH54 144 A1
Cemetery Rd
Dalkeith EH22 152 F2
Fauldhouse EH47 181 D5
Prestonpans EH32 96 F2
Shotts ML7 180 B4
Central Ave FK3 61 C5
Central Bvd FK5 38 B4
Central Dock Rd FK3 40 E2
Central Dr FK5 38 F3
Central Park Ave FK5 38 B4
Central Park Bsns Pk FK5 38 B4
**Central Pk (Cowdenbeath
FC)** KY4 13 C4
Central Rd KY12 44 D7
Central Ret Pk FK1 60 C5
Central Way KY11 48 C5
Centre Intc EH54 144 A3
Centre Road N EH53,
EH54 144 A3
Centre The EH54 143 E2
Centurion Way FK2 59 D6
Chacefield St FK4 58 A6
Chacefield Wood FK6 57 E7
Chalmers Bldg EH49 84 D7
Chalmer's Bldgs EH3 228 B1
Chalmers Cres EH9 121 D5
Chalmers Ho KY12 28 F3
Chalmers Sq EH54 142 C5
Chalmers St
Dunfermline KY12 28 F4
Edinburgh EH3 228 C1
Chalmerston Rd FK9 1 B2
Chalton Ct FK9 2 B7
Chalton Rd FK9 2 B7
Chalybeate EH41 129 F7
Chamberfield Rd KY12 29 C6
Chamberlain Rd EH10 121 B4
Chambers Dr FK2 39 B2
Chambers St EH1 229 A2
Chamfron Gdns FK7 7 E3
Champany Holdings EH49 65 A2
Champfleurie Cotts EH49 86 A5
Champfleurie Mews EH49 86 C5
Champfleurie Stables
EH49 86 B6
Champigny Ct EH21 124 E5
Chancelot Cres EH6 93 C5
Chancelot Gr EH5 93 C5
Chancelot Terr EH6 93 C5
Chandlers Rise KY11 47 F4
Chandler's Rise KY11 47 F4
Chandlers Wlk KY11 47 F4
Channel Brae EH42 134 D7
CHAPEL 16 C8
Chapel Bank EH22 154 D5
Chapel Cres FK2 39 B3
Chapelcroft FK7 6 D6
Chapel Ct EH16 122 F3
Chapel Dr FK5 38 E3
Chapelfauld Gn KY11 29 F3
Chapel Gr KY2 16 C8
Chapelhill
Clackmannan FK10 11 A3
Dirleton EH39 53 A4
Kirkcaldy KY2 16 D8
Chapelhill St FK10 23 D5
Chapel La Edinburgh EH6 94 A5

Chapel La *continued*
Falkirk FK1 60 B5
Chapel Level KY2 16 F8
Chapel Loan EH25 172 A3
Chapel Pl
High Valleyfield KY12 26 B2
Inverkeithing KY11 47 C3
Kirkcaldy KY2 16 C8
North Queensferry KY11 68 C5
Pathhead EH37 176 A5
Chapel Rd KY2 16 C8
Chapel St Cowdenbeath KY4 13 C3
7 Dunfermline KY12 28 F4
Edinburgh EH8 229 B1
High Valleyfield KY12 26 B2
Kincardine FK10 23 E3
Lochgelly KY5 14 B8
Chapelton Ave EH55 163 F4
Chapelton Ct EH55 163 F4
Chapelton Dr EH55 164 A4
Chapelton Gdns EH55 163 F4
Chapelton Gr EH55 163 F4
Chapelton Pl EH55 164 A4
Chapelton Terr EH55 163 F5
Chapel Villas KY11 48 B2
Chapelwell Pl KY11 29 F3
Chapel Wynd EH1 228 C2
Chapman's Brae EH48 140 F8
Charing Cross 1 FK3 40 D1
Chariot Dr EH28 117 A5
Charles Ave FK9 2 B6
Charles Cres
Bathgate EH48 141 F5
Carluke ML8 215 B1
Charles Ct KY11 45 F3
Charles Dr FK5 59 C8
Charlesfield EH8 229 A2
Charlesfield La EH54 143 B2
Charlesfield Rd EH54 164 C8
Charles La EH48 141 F6
Charles Logan Pl KY11 46 F4
Charles Rodger Pl FK9 2 A6
Charles St Alloa FK10 9 F8
Dunfermline KY11 29 B2
Edinburgh EH8 229 A2
Penicuik EH26 191 E7
Shotts ML7 180 B4
Stirling FK8 7 A5
Charles Street La EH8 229 A2
CHARLESTOWN 45 B4
Charles Way KY11 45 E3
Charles Way S KY11 45 E3
Charlotte Dundas Ct FK3 61 E6
Charlotte Hill Ct FK5 38 B3
Charlotte La EH2 228 B3
Charlotte Sq EH2 228 B3
Charlotte St
Grangemouth FK2 82 D8
Kirkcaldy KY1 17 B3
Shotts ML7 180 A3
Charlton Gr EH25 171 F3
Charrier The FK11 3 F6
Charterhall Gr EH9 121 D3
Charterhall Rd EH9 121 D2
Charteris Ct EH32 98 D5
Charteris Pk EH32 98 D5
Charteris Rd EH32 98 D5
CHARTERSHALL 7 A1
Chartershall Rd
Bannockburn FK7 19 A6
Stirling FK7 7 A1
Charter St FK7 7 A3
Chattan Ave FK9 2 B4
Chattan Ind Est FK4 58 C4
Chatterrig EH13 149 F7
Checkbar Rdbt FK5 58 C7
Cherry Ave EH48 141 E6
Cherrybank KY12 29 D5
Cherry La EH22 174 E6
Cherry Pl KY4 13 C3
Cherry Rd EH19 173 B6
Cherryton Dr FK10 11 A5
Cherry Tree Ave EH14 147 E3
Cherry Tree Cres EH14 147 E3
Cherry Tree Gdns EH14 147 D3
Cherry Tree Gr EH14 147 D3
Cherry Tree Loan EH14 147 E3
Cherry Tree Pk EH14 147 D3
Cherry Tree Pl EH14 147 E3
Cherry Tree View EH14 147 E3
Chessel's Ct EH8 229 B3
Chesser Ave EH14 120 C3
Chesser Cotts EH11 120 C4
Chesser Cres EH14 120 C4
Chesser Gdns EH11 120 B4
Chesser Gr EH14 120 B3
Chesser Loan EH14 120 B3
Chester Dr EH22 174 D5
Chesterhall Ave EH33 127 D6
CHESTERHILL 175 C7
Chesters Ct EH19 173 B6
Chesters Gr EH19 173 B6
Chester St EH3 228 A3
Chesters The EH39 72 F4
Chesters View EH19 173 B6
Chester View EH22 174 D5
Chestnut Ave Kirkcaldy KY1 17 C7
Whitburn EH47 161 C6
Chestnut Cres FK6 36 C3
Chestnut Ct EH21 124 D6
Chestnut Gr Bo'ness EH51 63 C5
Bonnyrigg and Lasswade
EH19 173 B6
Cockenzie & Port Seton
EH32 97 D3
Dunfermline KY11 46 E8
Livingston EH54 144 B5
Stenhousemuir FK5 38 F3

Chestnut Gr *continued*
Winchburgh EH52 87 F2
Chestnut La FK10 4 A3
Chestnut St EH5 92 E7
Cheviot Pl FK3 61 E5
Cheviot Rd KY2 16 F7
Cheyne St EH4 93 A2
Chief's Cl 6 KY1 17 D6
Chisholm Ave FK9 2 B4
Chisholm Cres KY5 14 A7
Chisholm Pl FK3 61 B6
Chisholm St KY12 29 D8
Chisholm Terr EH26 191 F7
Chrichton's Cl EH8 229 C3
Chrisella Terr FK2 83 A6
Christian Cres EH15 123 C7
Christian Gr EH15 123 B7
Christiemiller Ave EH7 94 E2
Christiemiller Gr EH7 94 E1
Christiemiller Pl EH7 94 E2
Christie Pl KY1 17 D7
Christie St KY12 29 B5
Christie Terr FK5 38 E3
Chuckethall Pl EH54 142 E7
Chuckethall Rd EH54 142 E7
Chuckie Pend EH3 228 B2
Church Ct Alloa FK10 10 A6
Kirkcaldy KY1 17 C4
Philpstoun EH49 86 D6
Church Gdns
Longniddry EH32 98 E5
Stoneyburn EH47 162 B1
Church Gr Alloa FK10 5 C1
Burntisland KY3 33 D1
Church Hill EH10 121 B4
Churchhill Dr EH10 121 B4
Church Hill Pl EH10 121 B4
CHURCHILL 121 B4
Churchill Dr FK9 2 A6
Churchill Pl Falkirk FK2 60 C7
Rosyth KY11 46 F3
Churchill St FK10 9 F8
Churchill Way EH27 145 E3
Church La Denny FK6 36 D3
Kirkcaldy KY1 17 C4
Limekilns KY11 45 D3
Plean FK7 20 D2
Church Pk EH48 141 B6
Church Pl Armadale EH48 140 A5
Bathgate EH48 141 B6
Crossgates KY4 30 F7
Falkirk FK2 60 B6
Fauldhouse EH47 181 E6
Inverkeithing/Dunfermline
KY11 45 D3
Longridge EH47 161 C1
Church Rd Bo'ness EH51 63 E7
Bonnyrigg and Lasswade
EH18 151 F1
California FK1 81 F5
North Berwick EH39 54 C7
Church St Addiewell EH55 162 D1
Alloa FK10 10 A6
Bonnybridge FK4 58 C3
Broxburn EH52 115 E5
Burntisland KY3 33 D1
Cowdenbeath KY4 13 D3
Dunbar EH42 78 E2
Falkirk FK2 39 C2
Haddington EH41 130 B8
Harthill ML7 159 C5
Inverkeithing KY11 47 C3
Kingseat KY12 12 B1
Kirkcaldy KY1 17 E6
Limekilns KY11 45 D3
Loanhead EH20 172 D7
Lochgelly KY5 14 B7
Stenhousemuir FK5 38 E3
Tranent EH33 126 C7
Churchway EH32 98 E5
Church Wlk Denny FK6 36 E2
Kinghorn KY3 35 A3
Church Wynd EH51 63 F7
Churchyard Ct ML7 179 E4
Cinderhall Pl EH33 126 B1
Circle The EH22 152 B8
Circus Gdns EH3 228 B4
Circus La EH3 93 B2
Circus Pl EH3 228 B4
Citadel Pl EH6 93 F6
Citadel St EH6 93 F6
Citron Glebe 4 KY1 17 D6
City Art Ctr★ EH1 229 A3
City Obsy★ EH7 229 B4
City of Edinburgh By-Pass
The
Dalkeith EH18, EH22 152 C4
Edinburgh, Dreghorn EH10,
EH13 149 C4
Edinburgh, East Hermiston EH11,
EH12, EH14 119 A2
Edinburgh, Fairmilehead EH10,
EH20 150 C3
Civic Sq 1 EH33 126 D6
Clackmae Gr EH16 150 F8
Clackmae Rd EH16 150 F8
CLACKMANNAN 11 B3
Clackmannan Prim Sch
FK10 11 A4
Clackmannan Rd FK10 10 D6
Clackmannanshire Com
Healthcare Ctr FK10 10 C8
Clackmannan Tower★
FK10 10 F4
Clanranald Ave EH32 97 B2
Clanranald Pl FK1 59 F1
Clarebank Cres EH6 94 B4
Clare Ct EH39 54 B7

Claremont FK10 9 F8
Claremont Bank EH7 93 D3
Claremont Bsns Ctr FK10 10 A6
Claremont Cres EH7 93 D3
Claremont Ct EH7 93 D3
Claremont Dr FK9 2 C7
Claremont Gdns EH6 94 B4
Claremont Gr EH7 93 D3
CLAREMONT PARK 94 C4
Claremont Pk EH6 94 B4
Claremont Prim Sch FK10 9 E8
Claremont Rd EH6 94 B4
Claremont St FK4 57 F6
Clarence St EH3 93 B2
Clarendon Cres
Edinburgh EH4 228 A4
Linlithgow EH49 85 B6
Clarendon Pl FK8 7 A7
Clarendon Rd
Linlithgow EH49 85 B6
Stirling FK8 7 A7
Claret Rd
Grangemouth, Bowhouse
FK3 61 E6
Grangemouth, Oil Refinery
FK3 62 C7
Clarinda Ave FK1 59 B5
Clarinda Gdns EH22 153 D3
Clarinda Pl FK5 38 C4
Clarinda Terr EH16 122 A1
Clark Ave Edinburgh EH5 93 C5
Linlithgow EH49 84 E8
Clark Bldgs EH35 155 E7
Clarke Sq EH54 142 C6
Clark Pl Edinburgh EH5 93 B5
Kirkcaldy KY2 17 A5
Clark Rd Edinburgh EH5 93 B5
Inverkeithing KY11 47 B2
Clarkson Rd EH52 115 D5
Clark St FK7 7 B2
Claverhouse Dr EH16 151 B8
Clay Acres Ct 3 KY12 28 F4
Claycrofts Pl FK7 7 B6
Clayhills Dr FK7 6 E5
Clayhills Gr EH14 147 B1
Clayhills Pk EH14 147 B1
Clayknowes Ave EH21 124 A4
Clayknowes Cres EH21 124 A5
Clayknowes Ct EH21 124 A4
Clayknowes Dr EH21 123 F5
Clayknowes Pl 2 EH21 124 A5
Clayknowes Way EH21 124 A5
Claylands Rd EH28 116 F3
Claymore Dr FK7 7 D3
Clearburn Cres EH16 122 B4
Clearburn Gdns EH16 122 B4
Clearburn Rd
Edinburgh EH16 122 B4
Gorebridge EH23 174 B1
Cleaves The FK10 4 B1
Cleekim Dr EH15 123 B4
Cleekim Rd EH15 123 B4
Cleghorn Dr EH52 115 B5
CLEIKIMIN 123 B5
Cleikiminfield EH15 123 B4
Cleikiminrig EH15 123 B4
Cleish Gdns KY2 16 F6
Cleish Pl KY11 29 F2
Cleish Rd KY11 29 F2
Cleland St EH47 161 B7
Clement Rise EH54 144 B1
Clerics Hill EH29 89 A1
Clerk Gr KY11 29 F1
Clerkington Rd EH41 129 E8
Clerkington Wlk EH41 129 E8
Clerk Rd EH26 191 D5
Clerk St Edinburgh EH8 229 B1
Loanhead EH20 172 C8
CLERMISTON 91 D1
Clermiston Ave EH4 91 D2
Clermiston Cres EH4 91 E2
Clermiston Dr EH4 91 D2
Clermiston Gdns EH4 91 D2
Clermiston Gn EH4 91 D2
Clermiston Gr EH4 91 D2
Clermiston Hill EH4 91 E2
Clermiston Loan EH4 91 D2
Clermiston Medway EH4 91 D2
Clermiston Pk EH4 91 D2
Clermiston Pl EH4 91 D2
Clermiston Prim Sch EH4 91 C2
Clermiston Rd EH12 119 E7
Clermiston Road N EH4 91 E2
Clermiston Terr EH12 119 E7
Clermiston View EH4 91 E2
Clerwood Bank EH12 119 D8
Clerwood Gdns EH12 119 D8
Clerwood Gr EH12 119 E8
Clerwood Loan EH12 119 D8
Clerwood Pk EH12 119 D8
Clerwood Pl EH12 119 E8
Clerwood Row EH12 119 D8
Clerwood Terr EH12 119 E8
Clerwood View EH12 119 E8
Clerwood Way EH12 119 D8
Cleuch Ave
North Middleton EH23 195 F2
Tullibody FK10 4 B2
Cleuchbrae EH55 163 D3
Cleuch Dr FK12 4 E7
Cleuch Pl FK2 82 F7
Cleuch Rd
North Middleton EH23 195 F2
Stirling FK9 2 C3
Cleveland Dr KY11 47 B2
Clifford Pk FK11 4 A7
Clifford Rd
North Berwick EH39 54 C6

Clifford Rd *continued*
Stirling FK8 7 B5
Cliftonhall Rd EH28 116 F4
Clifton Hall Sch EH28 116 D2
Cliftonhall Yards EH28 116 F4
Clifton Rd Livingston EH53 145 C7
Newbridge EH28 116 E2
Clifton Terr 3 EH12 120 F7
Clifton Trad Est EH28 116 F4
Clifton View EH52 116 A6
Climpy Rd ML11 200 D3
Clinkum Bank KY12 26 C3
Clinton Rd EH9 121 B4
Clive St ML7 179 E4
Cloanden Pl KY2 17 A3
Clockluine Rd KY11 47 E6
Clockmill La EH7, EH8 94 B1
Cloglands ML11 217 F7
Close The KY11 46 D1
Clova Dr EH54 164 E5
Clovenstone Dr EH14 148 E7
Clovenstone Gdns EH14 148 F8
Clovenstone Pk EH14 148 E7
Clovenstone Prim Sch
EH14 148 E7
Clovenstone Rd EH14 148 E8
Clovenstone Rdbt EH14 148 E7
Cloverbank EH54 143 E5
Cloverfoot Cotts EH16 123 B2
Clover Pl EH51 63 E5
Clover Way KY12 26 A8
Cloves The FK11 4 A5
Cluanie Ave ML7 179 E6
Clufflat EH30 67 F2
Clufflat Brae EH30 67 F2
Clune Rd KY12 27 E7
Clunie Rd KY11 29 E3
Clunivar St KY12 28 D5
Cluny Ave EH10 121 B2
Cluny Dr Edinburgh EH10 121 B2
Stenhousemuir FK5 38 F4
Cluny Gdns EH10 121 C2
Cluny Pl EH10 121 C3
Cluny Terr EH10 121 B2
Clyde Cres
Dunfermline KY11 29 F2
Larbert FK5 38 B3
Clyde Dr Livingston EH54 144 B4
Shotts ML7 180 B4
Clydesdale St EH51 63 F6
Clyde St Falkirk FK1 59 E5
Grangemouth FK3 40 B1
Clydevale Pl EH54 115 A2
Clydevale Terr EH54 115 A1
Coalgate FK10 10 B6
Coalgate Ave EH33 126 E7
Coalgate Rd EH33 126 D7
Coalhill EH6 93 F5
Coal Neuk EH33 126 C6
Coal Neuk Ct EH33 126 C6
Coalpots Way FK10 5 E3
Coal Rd KY12 28 F3
Coal Wynd Bannockburn FK7 7 D1
Kirkcaldy KY1 17 C4
Coal Wynd Ind Est KY1 17 C4
Coastguard Cotts TD13 218 F4
COATES 120 F7
Coates Cotts EH32 99 F4
Coates Cres EH3 228 A3
Coates Gdns EH12 120 F7
Coates Pl EH3 228 A2
Coatfield La EH6 94 A5
Coats Cres FK10 4 E1
Cobblebrae Cres FK2 39 B1
Cobden Cres EH9 121 F4
Cobden Ct KY4 30 F6
Cobden Rd EH9 121 F4
Cobden St FK12 5 A6
Cobden Terr EH11 228 A2
Coblecrook Gdns FK12 4 F6
Coblecrook La FK12 4 F6
Coblecrook Pl FK12 4 F6
Coburg St EH6 93 F5
Cochrane Ave Falkirk FK1 60 B4
Inverkeithing KY11 47 D2
Cochrane Cres FK12 4 E7
Cochrane Pl EH6 94 A4
Cochrane Rd KY11 46 B1
Cochrane Sq EH54 164 D6
Cochrane St
Bathgate EH48 141 A7
Falkirk FK1 60 B4
Cochranes The FK12 5 B7
Cochrane Way KY11 48 A5
Cochrane Wlk KY11 29 F4
Cochrie Pl FK10 4 C2
Cochrina Pl EH24 172 D2
Cockburn Cres
Balerno EH14 168 B7
Whitecross EH49 84 A6
Cockburn Ct EH35 155 E7
Cockburn Dr EH35 155 D6
Cockburnhill Rd EH14 168 A8
COCKBURNSPATH 218 E4
Cockburnspath Prim Sch
TD13 218 F4
Cockburn Sq EH37 176 B5
Cockburn St
Edinburgh EH1 229 A3
Falkirk FK1 60 B4
Cockdurno Farm EH14 168 A6
COCKENZIE & PORT
SETON 97 B5
Cockenzie Prim Sch EH32 97 C3
Cocklaw St KY4 12 D8
Cockles Brae EH41 130 E3
Cockmilane Brae EH41 130 D6
Cockpen Ave EH19 173 A5

Cockpen Cres EH19 173 A5
Cockpen Dr EH19 173 A5
Cockpen Pl EH19 173 A5
Cockpen Rd EH19 173 D6
Cockpen Terr EH19 173 A5
Cockpen View EH19 173 A5
Coillesdene Ave EH15 123 D7
Coillesdene Cres EH15 123 D7
Coillesdene Dr EH15 123 D7
Coillesdene Gdns EH15 123 D7
Coillesdene Gr EH15 123 D7
Coillesdene Ho EH15 123 D7
Coillesdene Loan EH15 123 E7
Coillesdene Terr EH15 123 D7
Coire Loan ML7 180 B3
Coldingham Pl KY12 29 D4
Colegate Rd EH23, EH37 196 D8
Coles Pl KY4 31 A6
Colinshiel Ave EH48 140 E7
Colinshiel Ct EH48 139 F6
Colinshiel St EH48 140 E7
Colinshiel View EH48 139 F7
Colinswell Rd KY3 33 D1
COLINTON 149 C7
Colinton Gr EH14 120 D2
Colinton Grove W EH14 120 D2
COLINTON MAINS 149 E6
Colinton Mains Cres
EH13 149 E6
Colinton Mains Dr EH13 149 D7
Colinton Mains Gdn
EH13 149 D8
Colinton Mains Gn EH13 149 D7
Colinton Mains Gr EH13 149 E7
Colinton Mains Loan
EH13 149 D7
Colinton Mains Pl EH13 149 E7
Colinton Mains Rd EH13 149 D6
Colinton Mains Terr
EH13 149 E7
Colinton Prim Sch EH13 149 D7
Colinton Rd
Edinburgh EH10, EH14 120 E3
Edinburgh, Firr Hill EH13,
EH14 149 D8
College Cres FK2 60 D7
College Rdbt EH54 143 D2
College Wynd EH1 229 A2
Collier Pl EH16 122 F4
Colliers La EH48 139 E5
Colliers Rd FK7 8 D4
Colliers Way FK7 7 C1
Colliery Cres EH22 174 A4
Colliery View EH22 174 B4
Collingwood Ct FK1 59 E5
Collins Cres KY11 47 F2
Collins Pl EH3 93 B2
Collinswell Dr KY3 33 D1
Colliston Rd KY12 29 D6
Coll Pl FK3 61 D6
Collyland Rd FK10 5 D3
Colmestone Gate EH10 150 A6
Colonsay Ave FK2 61 D2
Colonsay Terr FK1 60 B2
Colonsay Way EH5 92 C6
Colquhoun St FK7 7 C6
Colquhoun Terr FK7 7 C6
Colsnaur FK11 4 A6
Colstoun Mains Cotts
EH41 130 E4
Coltbridge Ave EH12 120 D7
Coltbridge Gdns EH12 120 E8
Coltbridge Millside 2
EH12 120 E7
Coltbridge Terr EH12 120 D7
Coltbridge Vale 1 EH12 120 E7
Coltness Ave ML7 198 A8
Colton Ct KY12 28 E4
Columba Ave EH4 92 B2
Columba Rd EH4 92 B2
Columbia Ave EH54 143 E3
Colville Gdns FK10 10 A6
Colville Pl EH3 93 B2
Colvin St EH42 78 E3
Combfoot Cotts EH53 144 C4
COMELY BANK 92 F2
Comely Bank Ave EH4 93 A2
Comely Bank Gr EH4 92 F2
Comely Bank Pl EH4 93 A2
Comely Bank Place Mews 2
EH4 93 A2
Comely Bank Rd EH4 92 F1
Comely Bank Row EH4 93 A2
Comely Bank St EH4 92 F2
Comely Bank Terr 1 EH4 93 A2
Comely Green Cres 6
EH7 94 A1
Comely Green Pl 5 EH7 94 A1
Comely Park Gdns 17 FK1 60 B4
Comely Park La KY12 29 A3
Comely Park Prim Sch
FK1 60 B4
Comely Park Terr 14 FK1 60 B4
Comely Pk
Dunfermline KY12 29 B3
Grangemouth FK2 82 E7
Comely Pl FK1 60 B4
Comely Terr FK2 82 E7
COMISTON 150 A6
Comiston Dr EH10 121 A1
Comiston Gdns EH10 121 A2
Comiston Gr EH10 150 A7
Comiston Pl EH10 121 B2
Comiston Rd EH10 150 A7
Comiston Rise EH10 150 A7

Comiston Springs Ave EH10 150 A7
Comiston Terr EH10 121 A2
Comiston View EH10 150 A7
Commando Access Way KY11 46 C1
Commercial Prim Sch KY11 29 C3
Commercial Rd KY11 47 C2
Commercial School La [4] KY12 29 A3
Commercial St
  Edinburgh EH6 93 F6
  Kirkcaldy KY1 17 D6
Commercial Wharf EH6 94 A6
Commissioner St EH51 64 A8
Commodores Wlk KY11 46 C1
Compass Sch The EH41 129 F8
Compressor House Rd FK3 62 C5
Compton Rd FK3 61 C5
COMRIE 26 D7
Comrie Terr EH51 63 F6
Comyn Dr FK2 82 C7
Concorde Way KY11 47 D3
Coneyhill Rd FK9 2 B7
Coneypark FK7 6 E6
Conference Sq EH3 228 B2
Congalton Mains Cotts EH39 74 A6
Conifer Rd EH22 174 E7
Coningsby Pl FK10 10 A6
Connaught Pl EH6 93 D5
Connelly Ct KY12 26 F7
Conner Ave FK2 60 A8
Connolly Dr FK6 36 C4
Connolly Pl FK6 36 F1
Conroy Ct [1] FK6 36 E1
Considine Gdns [4] EH8 94 C1
Considine Terr [3] EH8 94 C1
Constable Rd FK7 7 B6
Constitution Pl EH6 94 A6
Constitution St EH6 94 A5
Conwaine St [2] FK8 7 B8
Conway Ct FK1 59 F4
Cook Cres EH22 174 D5
Cookies Wynd EH32 96 E1
Cook Pl KY1 18 A8
Cook Sq KY5 14 B8
Cook St KY1 18 A8
Cooperage Quay FK8 7 C8
Cooperage Way FK10 10 D8
Co-operative Bldgs EH33 126 E6
Cooper Bsns Pk EH52 115 E5
Cooper's Cl EH8 229 B3
Cooper's La FK10 23 E4
Cope La EH32 97 C4
Copeland Cres KY4 13 B2
Copland Pl FK12 4 F7
Copper Beech Wynd KY12 27 D1
Corbett Pl KY11 29 F1
Corbie Dr EH22 153 D2
Corbiehall EH51 63 E7
Corbiehill Ave EH4 92 A3
Corbiehill Cres EH4 91 F3
Corbiehill Gdns EH4 92 A3
Corbiehill Gr EH4 92 A3
Corbiehill Pk EH4 92 A3
Corbiehill Pl EH4 91 F3
Corbiehill Rd EH4 92 A3
Corbiehill Terr EH4 91 F3
Corbieshot EH15 123 B5
Corbiewood Dr FK7 19 E8
Corbiewynd EH15 123 B5
Cordiner Cl FK8 1 F2
Cordiner's Land EH1 228 C2
Corentin Ct FK1 60 C3
Cormailin Pl KY12 26 B2
CORNBANK 191 D6
Cornbank St James' Prim Sch EH26 191 D5
Corn Exchange Rd [1] FK8 7 B7
Corn Exchange Village EH14 120 C3
Cornfield Pl EH54 143 B4
Cornhill Cres FK7 7 B3
Cornhill Terr EH6 94 B4
CORNTON 2 B3
Cornton Bsns Pk FK9 2 B2
Cornton Cres FK9 2 A5
Cornton Prim Sch FK9 2 A4
Cornton Rd FK9 2 A4
Cornton Vale Cotts FK9 2 A4
Cornwallis Pl EH3 93 D2
Cornwall St EH1 228 B2
Corona Cres FK4 57 F5
Coronation Pl
  Easthouses EH22 174 D7
  Skinflats FK2 39 F3
  Tranent EH33 126 C6
Corpach Dr KY12 28 F2
Corporation St FK1 60 C4
Corrennie Dr EH10 121 B2
Corrennie Gdns EH10 121 B1
Corrie Ave FK5 38 F4
Corrie Ct EH22 174 B4
Corrie Pl FK1 59 C4
CORSLET 148 A6
Corslet Cres EH14 148 B5
Corslet Pl EH14 148 A5
Corslet Rd EH14 148 A5
Corston Pk EH54 144 A4
CORSTORPHINE 119 F6
Corstorphine Bank Ave EH12 119 C7
Corstorphine Bank Dr EH12 119 D7
Corstorphine Bank Terr EH12 119 C7
Corstorphine High St EH12 119 D6
Corstorphine Hill Ave EH12 119 E7
Corstorphine Hill Cres EH12 119 E7
Corstorphine Hill Gdns EH12 119 E7
Corstorphine Hill Nature Reserve★ EH4 91 E2
Corstorphine Hill Rd EH12 119 E7
Corstorphine Hospl EH12 119 F6
Corstorphine House Ave [1] EH12 119 E6
Corstorphine House Terr [2] EH12 119 E6
Corstorphine Park Gdns EH12 119 E6
Corstorphine Prim Sch EH12 119 D6
Corstorphine Rd EH12 120 B7
Cortachy Ave FK2 39 A3
Cortleferry Dr EH22 152 E1
Cortleferry Gr EH22 152 E1
Cortleferry Pk [1] EH22 152 E1
Cortleferry Terr [2] EH22 152 E1
Corunna Ct ML8 215 B1
Corunna Pl EH6 93 F5
Corunna Terr EH26 192 A8
Cossars Wynd EH42 78 D2
Costkea Way EH20 172 A8
Cotburn Cres KY3 33 F2
Cotland Dr FK2 59 F8
Cotlands Ave EH32 98 D4
Cotlands Pk EH32 98 D4
Cotlaws EH29 89 A1
Cottage Cres FK1 59 E5
Cottage Gn EH4 91 B4
Cottage Homes EH13 149 B7
Cottage La EH21 124 E5
Cottage Pk EH4 92 A1
Cottages The EH42 77 F1
Cotton La FK2 61 A3
Cotts The EH49 86 F3
Coulport Pl KY12 28 F2
Council Hos EH39 101 E7
Countess Ave EH42 78 D2
Countess Cres EH42 78 D2
Countess of Moray Hospl KY3 49 B7
Countess Rd EH42 78 D2
County Houses KY4 31 A6
County Rd EH32 96 E1
County Sq EH32 96 E1
Couper Ave EH39 54 C6
Couperfield EH6 93 F6
Couper Gr KY11 29 F1
Couper St EH6 93 F6
Courthill FK12 5 A7
Court St EH41 130 A8
Courtyard The Falkirk FK1 60 E3
  Oakley KY12 26 F5
COUSLAND 154 D5
Cousland Cres EH47 142 B1
Cousland Intc EH54 143 F5
Cousland Rd
  Dalkeith EH22 153 D4
  Livingston, Craigshill EH54 144 A6
  Livingston, Livingston Village EH54 143 C4
Cousland Terr EH47 142 B1
Couston Dr KY11 48 B4
Couston Pl KY11 48 B4
Couston Rd KY11 48 B4
Couston St KY12 29 B4
COVE 219 A4
Cove Cres ML7 179 E6
Covenanter Rd ML7 159 D4
Covenanters La EH30 68 B1
Covenanters Rise KY11 46 E6
Cowal Pl KY11 30 C1
Cowane St FK8 2 B1
Cowan Rd EH11 120 E4
Cowan's Cl EH8 229 B1
Cowan St Bathgate EH48 141 E5
  Bonnybridge FK4 58 A6
Cowan Terr EH26 191 F7
COWDENBEATH 13 E4
Cowdenbeath Bsns Ctr KY4 13 D3
Cowdenbeath L Ctr KY4 13 C4
Cowdenbeath Prim Sch KY4 13 D3
Cowdenbeath Rd KY3 33 E2
Cowdenbeath Sta KY4 13 D4
Cowden Cres EH22 153 D3
Cowden Gr EH22 153 D3
Cowden Hill Gdns FK4 58 B6
Cowdenhill Rd EH51 64 B7
Cowden La EH22 153 D3
Cowden Pk EH22 153 D3
Cowden Terr EH22 153 D3
Cowden View EH22 153 D3
Cowgate EH1 229 A2
Cowgatehead EH1 229 A2
COWIE 20 D7
Cowiehall Rd FK7 20 D8
Cowie Prim Sch FK7 20 D7
Cowie Rd Bannockburn FK7 7 E1
  Cowie FK7 20 A8
Cowpits Ford Rd EH21 124 C3
Cowpits Rd EH21 124 D2
Cow Wynd FK1 60 B4
COXET HILL 6 F4
Coxfield EH11 120 C4
Coxithill Rd FK7 7 A3
Cragganmore FK10 4 A2
Crags Sp Ctr EH3 229 B2
Craigallan Pk EH51 64 B7
Craig Ave
  Haddington EH41 101 B1
  Whitburn EH47 160 F6
Craigbank Alloa FK10 5 C1
  Crossford KY12 28 C2
Craigbank Prim Sch FK10 5 C1
Craigbank Rd FK1 110 A5
Craigbeath Ct KY4 13 B5
Craigburn Ct [4] FK1 59 F2
Craig Cres FK9 2 D3
Craigcrook Ave EH4 92 A2
Craigcrook Gdns EH4 92 B1
Craigcrook Gr EH4 92 A1
Craigcrook Pk EH4 92 A1
Craigcrook Pl [6] EH4 92 C2
Craigcrook Rd EH4 91 F3
Craigcrook Sq EH4 92 A2
Craigcrook Terr [5] EH4 92 C2
Craig Ct Bridge of Allan FK9 2 A5
  Burntisland KY3 33 D2
Craigdimas Gr KY11 48 A2
Craigearn Ave KY2 16 B7
Craigearn Pl KY2 16 C7
Craigend Dr FK2 83 A6
Craigend Pk EH16 122 C1
Craigend Rd FK7 7 A3
Craigengar Ave EH52 115 A4
Craigengar Pk EH54 144 A4
CRAIGENTINNY 94 E2
Craigentinny Ave EH7 94 E2
Craigentinny Avenue N EH6 94 D4
Craigentinny Cres EH7 94 E2
Craigentinny Gr EH7 94 E1
Craigentinny Pl EH7 94 E1
Craigentinny Prim Sch EH7 94 D2
Craigentinny Rd EH7 94 D2
Craigflower Ct KY12 26 E1
Craigflower Gdns KY12 26 E1
Craigflower Ho KY12 26 E1
Craigflower View KY12 43 E8
Craigfoot Ct KY1 35 B6
Craigfoot Pl KY1 35 B7
Craigfoot Wlk KY1 35 B7
Craigford Dr FK7 7 D1
Craigforth Cres FK8 1 F1
Craighall Ave EH6 93 C6
Craighall Bank EH6 93 C6
Craighall Cres EH6 93 C6
Craighall Gdns EH6 93 C5
Craighall Rd EH6 93 C6
Craighall St FK8 1 E1
Craighall Terr
  Edinburgh EH6 93 C5
  Musselburgh EH21 124 F6
Craighill Gdns EH10 120 F1
Craighill View EH48 138 E3
Craigholm La KY3 33 F1
Craighorn FK11 4 A5
Craighorn Dr FK1 59 E2
Craighorn Rd FK12 4 E6
Craighouse Ave EH10 120 F2
Craighouse Gdns EH10 120 F2
Craighouse Pk EH10 120 F2
Craighouse Rd EH10 120 F2
Craighouse Terr EH10 120 F2
Craigiebield Cres EH26 191 E4
Craigie Ct FK5 38 B2
CRAIGIELAW 71 A4
Craigielaw Farm Cotts EH32 71 B4
Craigielaw Pk EH32 71 A4
Craigievar Ave FK2 39 A3
Craigievar Cl KY12 29 E5
Craigievar Gdns KY2 16 E5
Craigievar Sq EH12 119 B7
Craigievar Wynd EH12 119 A7
Craiginn Ct EH48 138 D3
Craiginn Terr EH48 138 D3
Craigkennochie Terr KY3 33 F1
Craiglaw EH52 114 C2
Craiglaw Pl EH52 114 C2
Craiglaw Terr [3] FK2 82 D8
Craiglea FK9 2 C3
Craiglea Ct EH48 138 D3
Craiglea Dr EH10 121 A2
Craiglea Pl EH10 120 F1
CRAIGLEITH 92 D2
Craigleith FK10 5 E3
Craigleith Ave Falkirk FK1 59 E2
  North Berwick EH39 54 D6
Craigleith Avenue N EH4 120 C8
Craigleith Avenue S EH4 120 C8
Craigleith Bank EH4 92 C1
Craigleith Cres EH4 92 C1
Craigleith Dr EH4 92 D1
Craigleith Gdns EH4 92 C1
Craigleith Gr EH4 92 C1
Craigleith Hill EH4 92 D1
Craigleith Hill Ave EH4 92 D2
Craigleith Hill Cres EH4 92 D2
Craigleith Hill Gdns EH4 92 E2
Craigleith Hill Gn EH4 92 D2
Craigleith Hill Gr EH4 92 D2
Craigleith Hill Loan EH4 92 D2
Craigleith Hill Pk EH4 92 D2
Craigleith Hill Row EH4 92 D2
Craigleith Rd
  Edinburgh EH4 92 E1
  Grangemouth FK3 61 D6
Craig Leith Rd FK7 7 D6
Craigleith Ret Pk EH4 92 D2
Craigleith Rise EH4 120 C8
Craigleith Terr FK12 5 A7
Craigleith View
  Edinburgh EH4 120 D8
  [1] North Berwick EH39 54 B7
  Tullibody FK10 4 D3
CRAIGLOCKHART 120 D1
Craiglockhart Ave EH14 120 C2
Craiglockhart Bank EH14 120 C1
Craiglockhart Cres EH14 120 C1
Craiglockhart Dell Rd EH14 120 C2
Craiglockhart Drive N EH14 120 D2
Craiglockhart Drive S EH14 120 C1
Craiglockhart Gdns EH14 120 C2
Craiglockhart Gr EH14 149 C8
Craiglockhart L Ctr EH14 120 D2
Craiglockhart Loan EH14 120 C2
Craiglockhart Pk EH14 120 C1
Craiglockhart Pl EH14 120 D2
Craiglockhart Prim Sch EH11 120 E4
Craiglockhart Quadrant EH14 120 C1
Craiglockhart Rd EH14 120 C1
Craiglockhart Road N EH14 120 D2
Craiglockhart Terr EH14 120 E3
Craiglockhart View EH14 120 D2
Craigluscar Ct KY12 28 B7
Craigluscar La KY12 28 A6
Craigluscar Rd KY12 28 B7
CRAIGMILLAR 122 D3
Craigmillar Castle★ EH16 122 D2
Craigmillar Castle Ave
  Edinburgh, Craigmillar EH16 122 D3
  Edinburgh, Niddrie Mains EH16 122 E3
Craigmillar Castle Gdns EH16 122 D3
Craigmillar Castle Loan EH16 122 E4
Craigmillar Castle Rd EH16 122 D2
Craigmillar Pk EH16 122 A3
Craigmillar Pl FK5 38 F4
Craigmore Gdns KY12 26 E1
Craigmount KY2 16 D7
Craigmount App EH12 119 C7
Craigmount Ave EH12 119 C7
Craigmount Avenue N EH4 91 B1
Craigmount Bank EH4 91 B1
Craigmount Bank W EH4 91 B1
Craigmount Brae EH12 91 B1
Craigmount Cres EH12 119 C8
Craigmount Ct EH4 91 B2
Craigmount Dr EH12 119 B8
Craigmount Gdns EH12 119 C7
Craigmount Gr EH12 119 B7
Craigmount Grove N EH12 119 B8
Craigmount High Sch EH12 119 B7
Craigmount Hill EH4 91 B1
Craigmount Loan EH12 119 B8
Craigmount Pk EH12 119 C7
Craigmount Pl EH12 119 C8
Craigmount Terr EH12 119 C7
Craigmount View EH12 119 B8
Craigmount Way EH12 91 C1
Craigmuir Pl EH4 92 C5
Craigmyle St KY12 29 C5
Craigomus Cres FK11 3 F6
Craigour Ave EH17 151 D8
Craigour Cres EH17 151 E8
Craigour Dr EH17 151 E8
Craigour Gdns EH17 151 E8
Craigour Gn EH17 151 D8
Craigour Gr EH17 151 E8
Craigour Loan EH17 151 E8
Craigour Park Prim Sch EH17 151 E7
Craigour Pl EH17 122 D1
Craigour Terr EH17 151 E8
Craigpark EH48 111 F5
Craigpark Ave EH28 117 C2
Craigpark Cres EH28 117 C2
Craigridge Pl KY11 48 C5
Craigrie Rd FK10 10 F4
Craigrie Terr FK10 11 A4
Craigrigg Cotts EH48 110 F3
Craigrigg Terr EH48 110 E3
Craigroyston Gr EH4 92 A4
Craigroyston High Sch EH4 92 B4
Craigroyston Pl EH4 92 A5
Craigroyston Prim Sch EH4 92 B4
Craigs Ave EH12 119 C6
Craigs Bank EH12 119 B7
Craigs Chalet Pk EH49 84 B4
Craigs Cres
  Edinburgh EH12 119 C7
Craigs Cres *continued*
  Grangemouth FK2 82 F7
Craigs Ct EH48 111 F5
Craigs Dr EH12 119 B7
Craigseaton EH52 115 B6
Craigs Gdns EH12 119 B7
Craigs Gr EH12 119 C6
CRAIGSHILL 144 B5
Craigshill East Rd EH54 144 A5
Craigshill Rd EH54 144 A5
Craigshill St EH54 144 A5
Craigs Loan EH12 119 C7
Craigs Pk EH12 119 B7
Craigs Rd Edinburgh EH12 119 B7
  West Craigs EH12 118 E8
Craigs Rdbt FK7 7 B7
Craig St Blackridge EH48 138 E3
  Rosyth KY11 47 A4
Craigs Terr FK2 82 E7
Craigston Dr KY12 29 D5
Craigston Pk KY12 29 D5
Craigs Way FK2 82 F7
Craigswood EH54 144 A6
Craig The KY11 46 D3
Craigton Cres FK12 4 F6
Craigton Ct EH52 87 F2
Craigton Pl
  Cowdenbeath KY4 13 C2
  Winchburgh EH52 87 F2
Craigview Alloa FK10 5 D2
  Bo'ness EH51 64 C7
Craigward FK10 10 A6
Craigwell Path KY12 44 D7
Crame Terr EH22 152 E2
CRAMOND 91 C5
Cramond Ave EH4 91 C5
Cramond Bank EH4 91 B5
CRAMOND BRIDGE 90 F3
Cramond Bridge Cotts EH4 90 F3
Cramond Brig Toll EH4 90 F4
Cramond Cres EH4 91 B5
Cramond Ct FK1 60 B2
Cramond Gdns
  Edinburgh EH4 91 B5
  Kirkcaldy KY2 16 F7
Cramond Glebe Gdns EH4 91 C6
Cramond Glebe Rd EH4 91 B6
Cramond Glebe Terr EH4 91 B6
Cramond Gn EH4 91 B6
Cramond Gr EH4 91 B5
Cramond Pk EH4 91 B5
Cramond Pl
  Dalgety Bay KY11 48 C4
  Edinburgh EH4 91 C5
Cramond Prim Sch EH4 91 B5
Cramond Regis EH4 91 B4
Cramond Road N EH4 91 C5
Cramond Road S EH4 91 E4
Cramond Roman Fort★ EH4 91 C6
Cramond Terr EH4 91 B5
Cramond Vale EH4 91 A5
Cramond Village EH4 91 B7
CRANSHAWS 223 C1
Cranshaws Dr FK2 61 C2
Cranston Dr EH22 154 D5
Cranston St
  Edinburgh EH8 229 B3
  Penicuik EH26 191 E5
Crarae Ave EH12 120 D8
Crathes Ave FK5 39 A4
Crathes Gdns EH54 164 E6
Crathie Dr FK6 36 D3
Crathie Way KY11 30 A4
Craufurdland EH4 91 A3
Crawfield Ave EH51 63 D6
Crawfield La EH51 63 F5
Crawfield Rd EH51 63 E4
Crawford Dr FK2 82 B7
Crawford Pl KY12 29 C7
Crawford Sq FK2 22 D4
Crawfurd Rd EH16 122 A3
Crawhall Pl [2] FK5 38 B2
Crawlees Cres EH22 174 E6
Craws Knowe ML11 201 A1
Creel Ct EH39 54 C7
Creran Dr FK6 57 D6
Crescent The
  Edinburgh EH10 121 A2
  Gorebridge EH23 174 C3
  Rosyth KY11 46 B1
Crest Bsns Ctr FK7 7 D5
Creteil Ct FK1 60 C3
Creteil Pl FK3 61 D8
Crewe Bank EH5 92 E5
Crewe Cres EH5 92 E5
Crewe Gr EH5 92 E5
Crewe Loan EH5 92 D5
Crewe Pl EH5 92 D5
Crewe Road Gdns EH5 92 D5
Crewe Road N EH5 92 D5
Crewe Road S EH4 92 E3
Crewe Road W EH5 92 D5
Crewe Terr EH5 92 E5
Crewe Toll EH4 92 D4
CRICHTON 196 F8
Crichton Ave EH37 176 A5
Crichton Castle★ EH37 196 E7
Crichton Dr
  Grangemouth FK3 61 E8
  Pathhead EH37 176 A5
Crichton Mains Steedings EH37 175 F1
Crichton Rd EH37 176 A5
Crichton St EH8 229 A2
Crichton Terr EH37 176 A5
Cricketfield Pl EH48 140 A5

Cricket Pl FK2 61 C1
Crighton Pl 2 EH6 93 F3
Crimond Pl FK1 81 E7
Crinan Pl KY11 30 A4
Cringate Gdns FK7 7 F1
Croall St 6 EH7 93 E2
Crockers Hedges EH41 102 C4
Crockett Gdns EH26 191 D5
Crockett Pl FK2 60 B8
Croft-An-Righ EH8 229 C4
Croft An Righ KY3 35 A4
Croften Righ KY11 47 C3
Crofters Gate EH47 161 E6
Crofters Way EH47 161 E6
Croft Est FK4 57 B3
Croftfoot Dr EH47 182 A6
Croftfoot Pl FK6 36 D4
Croft Gdns KY12 27 C7
Crofthead Ct FK8 2 A1
Crofthead Ctr EH54 164 D8
Crofthead Intc EH54 164 F8
Crofthead Rd Stirling FK8 2 A1
Stoneyburn EH47 162 A1
Crofthead St FK2 59 F8
CROFTMALLOCH 161 B5
Croftmalloch Prim Sch
EH47 161 B5
Croftmalloch Rd EH47 161 B5
Croft Pl EH54 143 C5
Croftsacre TD13 218 F3
Croftshaw Rd FK12 5 A7
Croftside Ct FK3 61 E6
Crofts Rd TD13 218 F3
Croft's Rd FK10 4 B3
Croft St Dalkeith EH22 153 A3
Penicuik EH26 191 E4
Crofts The EH42 104 E1
Cromar Dr KY11 47 C8
Cromarty Campus KY11 46 C1
Cromarty Ct EH54 144 C4
Cromarty Pl KY1 17 E7
CROMBIE 44 D7
Crombie Prim Sch KY12 44 D7
Cromwell Anchorage
EH42 78 E3
Cromwell Ct EH42 78 E3
Cromwell Dr FK1 60 D4
Cromwell Pl EH6 93 E6
Cromwell Quay EH42 78 E3
Cromwell Rd
Burntisland KY3 33 F1
Falkirk FK1 60 D4
North Berwick EH39 54 A7
Rosyth KY11 46 F5
Cromwell Road W FK1 60 D4
Crookston Ct EH21 124 E4
Crookston Rd EH21 124 E4
Crophill FK10 5 C2
Crosbies Ct FK8 7 B7
Cross Brae FK1 81 D6
CROSSBURN 108 E6
Cross Cotts EH32 97 A1
Crossen La ML8 215 B1
CROSSFORD 28 B1
Crossford Prim Sch KY12 28 A2
Crossgatehead Rd FK2 82 D8
CROSSGATES 30 F6
Crossgates Prim Sch KY4 30 E6
Crossgreen Dr EH52 115 A5
Crossgreen Pl EH52 115 A5
Crosshall Pl FK1 81 D6
Crosshill Dr
Bathgate EH48 141 C6
Bo'ness EH51 63 F5
Cross Loan EH35 155 F7
Crossroads KY11 30 B5
Crossroads Pl KY11 46 F4
Cross Row KY11 45 B4
Cross St Dysart KY1 18 A7
Falkirk FK2 39 B1
Cross The 8 Alloa FK10 10 B6
Linlithgow EH49 85 A7
Lochgelly KY5 14 B7
Pencaitland EH34 156 E6
Cross Way KY11 48 C5
Crosswood Ave EH14 168 B8
Crosswood Cres EH14 168 B8
Crosswood Terr EH55 203 F3
Cross Wynd KY12 29 A4
Crowhill Rd KY11 48 D4
Crown Ct 3 EH33 126 D6
Crownest Loan FK5 38 E2
Crown Gdns FK10 9 F8
Crown Pl EH6 93 F4
Crown St EH6 93 F4
Crozier Cres FK5 38 B2
Cruachan Ave FK9 2 B3
Cruachan Ct Falkirk FK1 60 C2
Penicuik EH26 192 A6
Cruachan Pl FK3 61 F5
Cruckburn Wynd FK7 6 F4
Cruden Rd EH51 62 D5
Cruickness Rd KY11 68 C8
Cruickshank Dr FK1 81 D6
Cruikshank's Ct 3 FK6 36 E1
Crum Cres FK7 7 C2
Crusader Ct EH54 144 A1
Crusader Dr EH25 171 F3
Crusader Rise EH54 144 A1
Crystalmount EH22 153 A4
Cuddies La EH13 149 B7
Cuddyhouse Rd KY4, KY12 12 D3
Cuddy La EH10 121 A3
Cuffabouts EH51 64 D7
Cuguen Pl EH18 152 B1
CUIKEN 191 E6
Cuiken Ave EH26 191 E6
Cuiken Bank EH26 191 D6
Cuikenburn EH26 191 E7
Cuiken Prim Sch EH26 191 D6
Cuiken Terr EH26 191 E6
Cuil Gr KY12 28 D5
Cuillin Ct FK1 60 C1
Cuillin Pl FK3 61 E5
Culduie Circ FK2 62 A1
Cullalo Cres KY3 49 C8
Cullaloe Ct KY11 48 C4
Cullaloe Nature Reserve★
KY3 32 B4
Cullaloe View KY4 13 C2
Cullen Cres KY2 16 E7
Cullen Sq EH54 142 D6
Culloch Rd FK1 108 B6
Culmore Pl FK1 60 E1
CULROSS 42 C8
Culross Abbey★ KY12 25 D1
Culross Palace★ KY12 42 C8
Culross Prim Sch KY12 42 D8
Cultenhove Cres
Grangemouth FK3 61 E6
Stirling FK7 7 A3
Cultenhove Pl FK7 7 A3
Cultenhove Rd
Stirling, Coxet Hill FK7 7 A3
Stirling FK7 7 A4
Cultins Rd EH11 119 B3
Cult Ness KY11 46 D3
Cultrig Dr EH47 161 A5
Culvain Pl FK1 60 C2
Culzean Cres KY2 16 C7
Culzean Pl FK5 38 F4
Cumberland St EH3 93 C2
Cumbernauld Rd FK4 57 A3
Cumbrae Ct KY2 17 A8
Cumbrae Dr FK1 59 C4
Cumbrae Terr KY2 17 A8
Cumin Pl EH9 121 E4
Cumlodden Ave EH12 120 C8
Cumnor Cres EH16 122 B1
Cunnigar Gdns EH53 144 C4
Cunnigar Hill View EH53 144 C4
Cunnigar Ho EH53 144 C4
Cunningham Cres EH52 115 D6
Cunningham Ct
Longniddry EH32 98 D4
North Berwick EH39 54 A6
Cunningham Dr ML7 159 D5
Cunningham Gdns FK2 60 F5
Cunningham Rd
Rosyth KY11 46 D2
Stenhousemuir FK5 39 A3
Stirling FK7 7 D7
Cunningham St FK3 61 C6
Curlew Brae EH54 143 D5
Curlew Gdns KY11 30 A2
Curling Knowe KY4 30 F6
Curling Pk KY4 30 F6
Curling Pond La EH47 161 B1
Curran Cres EH52 115 F5
CURRIE 147 F3
Currie High Sch EH14 147 F4
Curriehill Castle Dr
EH14 147 D4
Curriehill Rd EH14 147 F5
Curriehill Sta EH14 147 F5
Currie Prim Sch EH14 147 F4
Currieside Ave ML7 179 E4
Currieside Pl ML7 179 D4
Currievale Dr EH14 147 E4
Currievale Farm EH14 147 E5
Currievale Park Gr EH14 147 E4
Currievale Pk EH14 147 E4
Cursiter Ct FK5 38 B2
Cushenquarter Dr FK7 20 D3
Custom House Sq EH42 78 E3
Customs Rdbt FK8 2 B1
Customs Wharf EH6 94 A6
Custonhall Pl FK6 36 D2
CUTHILL 96 E1
Cuthill Brae EH55 162 E3
Cuthill Cres EH47 162 C2
Cuthill Terr EH47 162 C2
Cuttyfield Pl FK2 39 C3
Cypress Glade EH54 164 D7
Cypress Gr KY11 46 C8

D

Daiches Braes EH15 123 D6
Daintree Terr FK1 59 E5
Dairy Cotts EH39 53 A1
Daisyhill Ct EH47 162 D7
Daisyhill Rd EH47 162 D7
Daisy Terr EH11 120 E4
Dalbeath Cres KY4 13 A2
Dalbeath Gdns KY4 12 F1
Dalbeath Marsh Nature
Reserve★ KY4 12 F4
Dalcross Way KY12 29 E5
Dalderse Ave FK2 60 B6
Dalgety Ave EH7 94 B2
DALGETY BAY 48 C3
Dalgety Bay Prim Sch
KY11 48 B4
Dalgety Bay Sports & L Ctr
KY11 48 A4
Dalgety Bay Sta KY11 47 F5
Dalgety Gdns KY11 48 D5
Dalgety House View KY11 48 D4
Dalgety Rd EH7 94 B2
Dalgety St EH7 94 B1
Dalgleish Ct FK8 7 B8
Dalgrain Ind Est FK3 40 C1
Dalgrain Rd FK3 40 B1
Dalhousie Ave EH19 173 A6
Dalhousie Avenue W
EH19 173 A6
Dalhousie Bank EH22 152 F2
Dalhousie Bsns Pk EH19 173 D4
Dalhousie Cres EH22 152 F1
Dalhousie Dr EH19 173 A6
Dalhousie Gdns EH19 173 A6
Dalhousie Pl EH19 173 A6
Dalhousie Rd EH22 152 E1
Dalhousie Road E EH19 173 A6
Dalhousie Road W EH19 173 A6
Dalhousie Terr EH10 121 A2
DALKEITH 153 A2
Dalkeith Ctry Pk★ EH22 153 A5
Dalkeith High Sch EH22 153 D5
Dalkeith Rd
Edinburgh, Prestonfield
EH16 122 A4
Edinburgh, St Leonard's
EH16 229 C1
Dalkeith St EH15 123 C7
Dallas Ave KY3 33 F1
Dallas Dr KY2 16 E7
Dalling Ave EH48 140 F5
Dalling Rd EH48 140 F5
Dalmahoy Cres EH14 147 C3
Dalmahoy Rd EH28 117 D2
DALMENY 89 F7
Dalmeny House★ EH30 69 D1
Dalmeny Prim Sch EH30 89 E7
Dalmeny Rd EH6 93 D5
Dalmeny St EH6 93 F3
Dalmeny Sta EH30 89 D8
Dalmeny View KY11 48 C4
Dalmore Dr FK12 4 E6
Dalmorglen Pk FK7 6 F6
Dalratho Rd FK3 61 E8
DALRY 120 F6
Dalry Gait EH12 120 F7
Dalrymple Cres
Edinburgh EH9 121 E4
Musselburgh EH21 124 A6
Dalrymple Gdns EH22 154 D5
Dalrymple Loan EH21 124 C5
Dalry Pl EH11 228 A2
Dalry Prim Sch 5 EH11 120 F6
Dalry Swim Ctr EH11 228 A1
Dalton Ct EH22 174 E5
Dalum Ct EH20 172 A8
Dalum Dr EH20 172 A8
Dalum Gr EH20 172 A8
Dalum Loan EH20 172 A8
Dalyell Pl EH48 140 A5
Daly Gdns KY12 25 F2
Dalziel Ct EH47 162 C2
Dalziel Pl EH7 94 B1
Damhead Holdings Scheme
Bilston EH10 171 C8
Edinburgh EH10 150 D1
Damside EH4 228 A3
Dancebase★ EH3 228 C2
DANDERHALL 152 C7
Danderhall Cres EH22 152 B7
Danderhall Prim Sch
EH22 152 B8
Dania Ct EH11 119 F4
Daniel Pl KY11 46 C5
Danube St EH4 228 A4
D'arcy Cres EH22 174 F7
D'arcy Rd EH22 174 E6
D'arcy Terr EH22 174 E7
Dargai Pl EH52 115 A5
Darian La EH51 63 F7
Darmeid Pl ML7 198 B8
Darnaway St EH3 228 B4
Darnell Rd EH5 93 B5
Darney Terr KY3 34 F2
Darnley St FK8 7 A8
Darrach Dr FK6 36 A2
Darroch Ct EH8 229 B3
Darwin St EH54 144 A5
Davaar Dr KY2 16 E8
Davaar Pl FK1 59 C4
Davenport Pl KY11 46 F3
David Ave FK8 7 A5
David Cres KY11 47 A8
David Henderson Ct KY12 29 A4
David Lloyd Edinburgh
Newhaven Harbour Ctr
EH6 93 D7
David Millar Pl 5 KY12 28 E5
David Scott Ave EH22 174 E7
David's Loan FK2 39 D1
Davidson Gdns EH4 92 A3
Davidson La ML8 215 B1
Davidson Pk EH4 92 E3
Davidson Pl EH41 100 F1
Davidson Rd EH4 92 E3
DAVIDSONS MAINS 91 E3
Davidson's Mains Prim Sch
EH4 91 F3
Davidson St FK7 7 C1
Davidson Terr EH41 100 F1
Davidson Way EH54 143 E7
David St Dunfermline KY12 29 A5
Kirkcaldy KY1 17 B3
Lochgelly KY5 14 B8
David The First St KY3 34 F2
Davies Row EH12 119 D6
Davie St EH8 229 B2
Daviot Rd KY12 29 E5
Dawson Ave Alloa FK10 9 F8
Livingston EH54 143 F5
Dawson Pl EH51 63 E5
Dawson St FK2 60 B8
Deacons Ct EH49 85 A5
DEAN 92 F1
Dean Acres KY12 26 D7
Dean Bank La EH3 93 B2
Deanbank Pl EH23 195 D7
Dean Br EH4 228 A4
DEANBURN 191 E7
Deanburn EH26 191 E7
Deanburn Gdns EH47 142 B1
Deanburn Gr EH51 63 D6
Deanburn Pk EH49 84 F5
Deanburn Prim Sch EH51 63 D5
Deanburn Rd EH49 84 F5
Deanburn Wlk EH51 63 D6
Dean Cres FK8 2 C1
Dean Ct EH32 98 C4
Dean Dr KY12 28 A2
Deanery Cl EH7 94 C1
DEANFIELD 63 D7
Deanfield Cres EH51 63 E7
Deanfield Dr EH51 63 E6
Deanfield Pl EH51 63 E7
Deanfield Rd EH51 63 E7
Deanfield Terr EH51 63 E6
Dean Gallery★ EH4 120 F8
Deangate Gdns EH51 63 D6
Dean Gr KY12 28 B2
Deanhaugh St EH3 93 B2
Deanpark Ave EH14 147 C1
Deanpark Bank EH14 147 C1
Deanpark Brae EH14 147 C1
Deanpark Cres EH14 147 C1
Dean Park Cres EH4 228 A4
Deanpark Ct EH14 147 B1
Deanpark Gdns EH14 147 C1
Deanpark Gr EH14 147 C1
Dean Park Mews EH4 93 A2
Deanpark Pl EH14 147 C1
Dean Park Pl EH22 174 A5
Dean Park Prim Sch
EH14 168 C8
Deanpark Sq EH14 147 C1
Dean Path EH4 92 F1
Dean Path Bldgs EH4 228 A3
Dean Pk Gowkhall KY12 27 E7
Longniddry EH32 98 C4
Newtongrange EH22 174 A5
Dean Pl Penicuik EH26 191 D6
Seafield EH47 142 B1
Dean Rd Bo'ness EH51 63 E6
Kirkcaldy KY2 17 A4
Longniddry EH32 98 C4
Penicuik EH26 191 D6
Dean Ridge KY12 27 E7
DEANS 142 F6
Deans East Rd
Livingston, Deans EH54 142 F7
Livingston, Nether Dechmont
EH54 143 B6
Deans High Sch EH54 143 A7
Deans Ind Est EH54 142 C6
Deans North Rd
Livingston, Deans EH54 142 E6
Livingston, Nether Dechmont
EH54 143 A6
Deans Prim Sch EH54 142 E5
Deans Rd EH54 142 D6
Deans Rdbt EH54 142 D5
Deans S EH54 142 E5
Deans Service Units
EH54 142 E6
Dean St Edinburgh EH4 93 A2
Whitburn EH47 161 A6
Deanswood Pk EH54 142 E6
Dean Terr Edinburgh EH4 228 A4
Rosewell EH24 172 D1
Dean The EH40 75 E1
Deantown Ave EH21 153 E8
Deantown Dr EH21 124 E1
Deantown Path EH21 124 E1
Deas Rd Inverkeithing KY11 47 B2
Shotts ML7 179 C5
Deas Wharf KY1 17 C4
DECHMONT 114 C2
Dechmont Inf Sch EH52 114 B2
Dechmont Rd EH12 119 A6
Dechmont Rdbt EH52 114 D2
DEDRIDGE 143 E1
Dedridge East Ind Est
EH54 144 A1
Dedridge East Rd EH54 144 A1
Dedridge North Rd EH54 164 D8
Dedridge Prim Sch EH54 144 A2
Dedridge West Rd EH54 164 E8
Dee Dr EH54 144 B5
Dee Pl KY11 29 F2
Deep Sea World (Scotland's
National Aquarium)★
KY11 68 C5
Deerhill EH52 114 C2
Deerpark FK10 5 E1
Deer Park Dr EH54 114 D1
Deerpark Prim Sch FK10 5 F1
Deer Park Rd
Abercorn EH30 66 F2
Dechmont EH54 114 D1
Deer Path ML7 159 E5
Deeside Dr ML8 215 A3
Deeside Pl KY11 30 C1
Dee St ML7 179 D5
Delaney Ct FK10 10 A6
Delisle St EH42 78 D2
Dell Ave EH48 139 E6
Dell Rd EH13 149 B7
Delph Rd FK10 4 C2
Delphwood Cres FK10 4 D2
Delph Wynd FK10 4 C2
Delta Ave EH21 125 A5
Delta Cres EH21 125 A6
Delta Ct 2 EH21 125 A6
Delta Dr EH21 125 A6
Delta Gdns EH21 125 A5
Delta Pl EH21 124 D4
Delta Rd EH21 125 A5
Delta View EH21 125 A6
De Moray Ct FK9 2 A4
Demoreham Ave FK6 36 F1
Dempster Pl KY12 28 F5
Denbecan FK10 10 D5
Denburn Pl KY2 17 C6
Denburn Rd KY1 17 D7
Denend Cres KY2 17 B6
Denham Green Ave EH5 93 B5
Denham Green Pl EH5 93 B5
Denham Green Terr EH5 93 B5
Denholm Ave EH21 123 F4
Denholm Dr EH21 124 A4
Denholm Gr EH48 139 E7
Denholm Rd EH21 123 F5
Denholm Way EH21 123 F4
Den La ML7 179 D6
DENNY 36 F1
Denny High Sch FK6 57 E8
DENNYLOANHEAD 57 D5
Denny Prim Sch FK6 36 D2
Denny Rd Denny FK4 57 E6
Larbert FK5 38 A1
Denovan Rd FK6 36 E4
Den Rd KY2, KY1 17 C6
De Quincey Path EH18 172 E6
De Quincey Rd EH18 172 E6
Dequincey Wlk 6 EH33 126 C5
Derby St EH6 93 D6
Deroran Pl FK8 6 F5
Derwent Ave FK1 59 F4
Devlin Ct FK7 7 B2
Devonbank FK10 5 E3
Devon Ct FK10 4 B2
Devon Dr FK10 4 E4
Devon Pl Cambus FK10 4 A1
Edinburgh EH12 120 F7
Devon Rd FK10 10 C6
Devon St FK3 40 A1
Devon Terr KY11 29 E2
Devon Valley Dr FK10 5 D2
Devon Village FK10 5 E4
Devonway FK10 10 F5
Dewar Ave FK10 23 E4
Dewar Pl EH3 228 A2
Dewar Place La EH3 228 A2
Dewar Sq EH54 142 D5
Dewar St Dunfermline KY12 28 F4
Lochgelly KY5 14 A7
DEWARTOWN 175 D5
Dewshill Cotts ML7 158 B4
Dew Way KY11 46 D1
Dickburn Cres FK4 57 F5
Dick Cres KY3 33 E1
Dick Gdns EH47 160 F6
Dickies Wells FK12 5 C7
Dick Pl Edinburgh EH9 121 D4
Rosyth KY11 46 E5
Stoneyburn EH47 162 C2
Dickson Ct
Dunfermline KY12 29 A2
Lochgelly KY5 14 A7
Dicksonfield EH7 93 E2
Dickson Gr EH19 173 B7
Dickson St
Dunfermline KY12 29 A1
Edinburgh EH6 93 F3
West Calder EH55 163 D2
Dick St KY12 29 C5
Dick Terr EH26 191 F6
Dinmont Dr EH16 122 B2
DIRLETON 53 B4
Dirleton Ave EH39 54 A7
Dirleton Castle★ EH39 53 B4
Dirleton Ct EH39 53 F7
Dirleton Gdns FK10 9 F7
Dirleton La FK10 9 F6
Dirleton Prim Sch EH39 53 A4
Dirleton Rd Dirleton EH39 53 B5
North Berwick EH39 53 E6
Distillery La EH11 120 F7
Distillery Wynd EH40 103 E7
Diverswell FK10 5 D2
Dixon Ct EH47 160 F5
Dixon Terr EH47 161 A5
Dobbie Ave Larbert FK5 59 C8
Stenhousemuir FK5 38 C1
DOBBIE'S KNOWE 173 A7
Dobbie's Rd EH18 173 A7
Dobson's Pl EH41 129 F8
Dobson's View EH41 129 F8
Dobson's Wlk EH41 129 F7
Dochart Cres FK2 61 F2
Dochart Dr EH4 91 C1
Dochart Path FK3 61 D5
Dochart Pl FK1 60 D2
Dock Pl EH6 93 F6
Dock Rd FK3 40 D1
Dock St Bo'ness EH51 64 A8
Edinburgh EH6 93 F6
Falkirk FK2 39 C2
Doctor's Pk FK10 23 E3
Dog Well Wynd EH49 85 A7
Dollar Ave FK2 60 A7
Dollar Cres KY2 16 D7
Dollar Ct 2 KY12 28 E5
Dollar Gdns FK2 60 A7
Dollar Gr KY3 33 E1
Dollar Ind Est FK1, FK2 60 A5
Dollar Rd KY3 33 E1
Dolphin Ave EH14 147 F4
Dolphin Gardens E EH14 147 F4

Dolphin Gardens W EH14 147 E4
DOLPHINGSTONE 125 F7
Dolphingstone View EH32 125 F8
Dolphingstone Way EH32 125 F8
Dolphin Rd EH14 147 F4
Donaldson Ave FK10 4 E1
Donaldson Ct FK10 23 E3
Donaldson Pl FK7 6 D6
Donaldson Rd FK2 61 A1
Donaldson's EH49 84 F5
Donald St KY12 29 C6
Don Dr EH54 144 B5
Donibristle Gdns KY11 48 B2
Donibristle Ho KY11 48 B2
Donibristle Ind Est KY11 48 B5
Donibristle Ind Pk KY11 48 A4
Donibristle Prim Sch KY11 48 B2
Donnelly Ho FK9 2 D6
Don Rd KY11 29 F1
Don St FK3 40 A1
Doocot Brae EH51 64 B7
Doo'cot Brae FK10 10 A8
Doo'cot Hill FK10 5 D2
Doocot Pl EH32 126 A8
Doo Dells La KY3 34 F2
Doon Ave EH42 78 C2
Doon Hill Hall★ EH42 106 F4
Doon Wlk EH54 144 A4
Dora Ct KY4 13 D6
Dornie Wynd ML7 180 B3
Dornoch Pl KY11 47 C8
Dorrator Ct FK1 59 E5
Dorrator Rd FK1 59 E6
Dorset Pl EH10 121 A5
Double Dykes EH21 124 D4
Double Hedges Pk EH16 122 A1
Double Hedges Rd EH16 122 A1
Double Row KY11 45 B4
Dougall Ct EH22 174 D5
Dougall Pl EH22 174 D5
Dougall Rd EH22 174 D5
Dougans Sq EH48 139 F6
Douglas Ave Airth FK2 22 D3
Grangemouth, Bowhouse FK3 61 E6
Grangemouth, Brightons FK2 82 D8
Linlithgow EH49 84 E6
Douglas Cres
Bonnyrigg and Lasswade EH19 173 B7
Edinburgh EH12 120 F8
Longniddry EH32 98 E6
Douglas Dr Bo'ness EH51 63 E6
Crossford KY12 28 A2
Dunfermline KY12 28 E5
Stirling FK7 7 C4
Douglas Gardens Mews 5 EH4 120 F8
Douglas Gdns EH4 120 F8
Douglas Pk KY12 28 E6
Douglas Pl Bo'ness EH51 63 F6
Linlithgow EH49 84 E6
Stenhousemuir FK5 38 F4
Douglas Rd Bo'ness EH51 63 F6
Longniddry EH32 98 E6
Rosyth KY11 46 C2
Douglas Rise EH54 144 A2
Douglas St Bannockburn FK7 7 E1
Dunfermline KY12 29 A4
Kirkcaldy KY1 17 B3
Stirling FK8 2 B1
Douglas Terr Bo'ness EH51 63 F6
Edinburgh EH11 228 A2
Stirling FK7 6 E6
Douglas Wynd EH52 115 B6
Doune Cres FK5 39 A4
Doune Pk KY11 48 C4
Doune Terr EH3 228 B4
Dovecot Brae EH33 126 C7
Dovecot Cres KY1 18 B8
Dovecote Pl EH54 143 C4
Dovecot Gr EH14 120 B1
Dovecot Loan EH14 120 A1
Dovecot Pk Aberdour KY3 49 B6
Edinburgh EH14 149 A8
Linlithgow EH49 85 D8
Pencaitland EH34 156 E6
Dovecot Pl
Dunfermline KY11 47 A7
Tullibody FK10 4 B3
Dovecot Rd
Edinburgh EH12 119 D5
Tullibody FK10 4 B3
Westquarter FK2 61 A2
Dovecot Way
Dunfermline KY11 47 A7
Pencaitland EH34 156 E7
Dovecot Wynd KY11 46 F7
Dovehill FK10 10 B8
Dover Dr KY11 47 A8
Dover Hts KY11 47 A8
Dover Pk KY11 47 A8
Dover Way KY11 47 A8
Dowan Pl FK7 6 E6
Dower Cres EH51 64 B8
Dower Pl FK2 22 D4
Dowie's Mill Cotts EH4 90 F4
Dowie's Mill La EH4 90 F4
Dowlaw Rd TD13, TD14 219 F2
Downfield KY4 13 C6
Downfield Pl EH11 120 F6
Downie Gr EH12 119 F6
Downie Pl EH21 124 C6
Downie Terr EH12 119 F6
Downing Ct EH25 172 A4
Downing Point KY11 48 B2
Downs Cres FK10 9 F6
Dr Campbell Ave FK7 20 D8
DREGHORN 149 D5
Dreghorn Ave EH13 149 E5
Dreghorn Dr EH13 149 E5
Dreghorn Gdns EH13 149 E6
Dreghorn Gr EH13 149 F5
Dreghorn Junc EH10, EH13 149 E5
Dreghorn Link EH13 149 E5
Dreghorn Loan EH13 149 B6
Dreghorn Pk EH13 149 D6
Dreghorn Pl EH13 149 E5
DREM 73 A4
Drem Farm Cotts EH39 73 A4
Drem Sta EH39 73 A3
Drip Rd FK9 1 F2
Dronachy Rd KY2 16 F4
Drossie Rd FK1 60 A3
Drove Loan FK6 57 F6
Drove Loan Cres FK6 57 E7
Drove Rd EH48 139 F7
Droverhall Ave KY4 31 A6
Droverhall Pl KY4 31 A6
Drover Pl FK5 38 C4
Drover Round FK5 38 C4
Drovers Rd EH52 116 A6
Dr Porter Gdns FK7 8 D4
DRUM 94 A2
Drumacre Rd EH51 64 B6
Drum Ave EH17 151 E6
Drumbowie Prim Sch FK1 82 D2
DRUMBRAE 91 C2
Drum Brae Ave EH12 119 C8
Drum Brae Cres EH4 91 C2
Drum Brae Dr EH4 91 D1
Drum Brae Gdns EH12 119 C8
Drum Brae Gr EH4 91 C1
Drumbrae L Ctr EH4 91 C1
Drum Brae N EH4 91 B2
Drum Brae Neuk EH12 119 C8
Drum Brae Park App EH12 119 C8
Drum Brae Pk EH12 119 C8
Drum Brae Pl EH12 119 C8
Drumbrae Prim Sch EH4 119 C8
Drumbrae Rdbt EH12 119 C6
Drum Brae S EH12 119 C8
Drum Brae Terr EH4 91 C1
Drum Brae Wlk EH4 91 B1
Drumclair Ave FK1 108 A6
Drum Cotts Bo'ness EH51 64 C6
Edinburgh EH17 151 F5
Drum Cres EH17 151 F6
Drumcross Rd EH48 141 B7
Drumdryan St EH3 228 B1
Drum Farm La EH51 64 C6
Drumlanrig Pl FK5 38 F4
Drummohr Ave EH21 125 B5
Drummohr Gdns EH21 125 B5
Drummond Com High Sch 10 EH7 93 D2
Drummond La FK8 7 A6
Drummond Pk FK3 61 E6
Drummond Pl
Blackridge EH48 138 C3
Bonnybridge FK4 58 A7
Dunfermline KY12 29 D5
Edinburgh EH3 93 D2
Falkirk FK1 59 F2
Grangemouth FK3 61 E8
Stirling FK8 7 A6
Drummond Place La FK8 7 A6
Drummond Sq
Livingston EH54 164 C6
Lochgelly KY5 14 B8
Drummond St EH8 229 B2
Drummore Dr EH32 125 E8
Drummormie Rd KY12 27 C1
Drumpark Ave EH51 64 B6
Drumpark St FK7 7 B3
Drum Pl
East Whitburn EH47 161 E7
Edinburgh EH17 151 F6
Drum Rd Bo'ness EH51 64 C6
Dunfermline KY11 29 F2
Drumsheugh Gdns EH3 228 A3
Drumsheugh Pl EH3 228 A2
Drumshoreland Ave EH53 144 B7
Drumshoreland Cres EH53 144 B7
Drumshoreland Pl EH53 144 B8
Drumshoreland Rd EH53 144 B7
Drumside Terr EH51 64 C7
Drum St EH17 151 F5
Drum Terr EH7 94 A2
Drum View Ave EH22 152 B8
Drumview Gdns EH51 64 A5
Drummohr Terr EH21 125 A5
Drybrough Cres EH16 122 D4
Dryburgh Ave FK6 36 D2
Dryburgh Way FK3 61 F6
Dryden Ave EH20 172 A7
Dryden Cotts EH34 157 F4
Dryden Cres EH20 172 A7
Dryden Gait EH7 93 E3
Dryden Gdns EH7 93 E3
Dryden Glen EH20 171 F7
Dryden Gr EH25 172 A4
Dryden Loan EH20 171 F7
Dryden Pk EH20 171 F7
Dryden Pl Edinburgh EH9 121 F5
Loanhead EH20 171 F7
Dryden Rd EH20 171 F7
Dryden St EH7 93 E3
Dryden Terr Edinburgh EH7 93 E3
Loanhead EH20 172 A7
Dryden Vale EH20 171 F7
Dryden View EH20 172 A7
DRYLAW 92 C3
Drylaw Ave EH4 92 C2
Drylaw Cres EH4 92 B3
Drylaw Gdns
East Linton EH40 103 D8
Edinburgh EH4 92 B3
Drylaw Gn EH4 92 B2
Drylaw Gr EH4 92 B2
Drylawhill EH40 75 D1
Drylaw House Gdns EH4 92 B3
Drylaw House Paddock EH4 92 B3
Drylaw Terr EH40 103 D8
Drylie Ct KY4 13 B4
Drylie St KY4 13 B4
Drysdale Ave EH47 161 B7
Drysdale St FK10 10 B6
Duart Cres EH4 91 C1
Dublin Meuse EH3 93 C1
Dublin St EH1 229 A4
Dublin Street Lane N 2 EH3 93 D2
Dublin Street Lane S EH1 229 A4
Duchess Anne Cotts EH51 63 C6
DUDDINGSTON 122 E6
Duddingston Ave EH15 122 E7
Duddingston Cres
Edinburgh EH15 123 B6
Newton EH52 88 A8
Duddingstone Terr EH52 88 A8
Duddingston Gardens N EH15 122 F7
Duddingston Gardens S EH15 122 F6
Duddingston Grove E EH15 122 F7
Duddingston Grove W EH15 122 F6
Duddingston House Ctyd EH15 122 E5
Duddingston Loan EH15 122 E6
Duddingston Mains Cotts EH15 123 B6
Duddingston Mills EH8 122 E7
Duddingston Park S EH15 123 A5
Duddingston Pk EH15 123 A7
Duddingston Prim Sch EH15 122 E7
Duddingston Rd EH15 122 F7
Duddingston Rise EH15 122 F6
Duddingston Road W EH16 122 D5
Duddingston Row EH15 122 F5
Duddingston Square E EH15 122 F7
Duddingston Square W EH15 122 F6
Duddingston View EH15 122 F6
Duddingston Yds EH15 123 A5
Dudgeon Pl EH29 89 B2
Dudley Ave EH6 93 D6
Dudley Avenue S EH6 93 E5
Dudley Bank EH6 93 D6
Dudley Cres EH6 93 D6
Dudley Gdns EH6 93 D6
Dudley Gr EH6 93 D6
Dudley Terr EH6 93 D6
Duff Cres FK8 1 F1
Duff Ct EH39 54 A7
Duff Rd EH11 120 F6
Duff St EH11 120 F6
Duff Street La EH11 120 F6
Duffy Pl KY11 46 E3
Dugald Stewart Ave EH51 64 A7
Duke Pl EH6 94 A4
Duke St Alva FK12 5 A7
Bannockburn FK7 7 C1
Clackmannan FK10 11 B4
Dalkeith EH22 153 A3
Denny FK6 36 C2
Dunbar EH42 78 A2
Edinburgh EH6 94 A4
Grangemouth FK3 61 F8
Rosewell EH24 172 D1
West Barns EH42 77 F1
Duke's Wlk EH8 94 B1
Duloch Park Prim Sch KY11 30 B1
Dumbarton Rd
Cambusbarron FK8 6 E8
Stirling FK8 7 B7
Dumbeg Pk EH14 148 D8
DUMBIEDYKES 229 B2
Dumbiedykes Rd EH8 229 C2
Dumbryden Dr EH14 119 F1
Dumbryden Gdns EH14 119 F2
Dumbryden Gr EH14 119 E1
Dumbryden Ind Est EH14 119 F1
Dumbryden Rd EH14 119 F1
Dumyat Ave FK10 4 B2
Dumyat Dr FK1 59 E3
Dumyat L Ctr FK11 4 A7
Dumyat Rd Alva FK12 4 F6
Menstrie FK11 3 F6
Stirling FK9 2 C3
Dumyat Rise FK5 38 C5
Dumyat St FK10 4 F1
Dunard Gdn EH9 121 D3
Dunavon Gdns FK6 36 D4
DUNBAR 78 D1
Dunbar Ave FK5 38 F4
Dunbar Gate FK6 36 E3
Dunbar Gram Sch EH42 78 C3
Dunbar L Pool EH42 78 D3
Dunbar Pl KY2 16 E5
Dunbar Prim Sch EH42 78 C2
Dunbar Rd
Haddington EH41 101 B1
North Berwick EH39 54 E6
Dunbar's Cl EH1 229 B3
Dunbar St EH3 228 B1
Dunbar Sta EH42 78 E1
Dunbar Town House Mus★ EH42 78 D2
Duncairn Ave FK4 57 F6
Duncan Ave FK2 39 B3
Duncan Buchanan Ct FK8 2 A2
Duncan Cres KY11 29 E2
Duncan Ct EH39 54 A6
Duncan Gdns EH33 126 C7
Duncan Gn EH54 143 B7
Duncan Pl EH6 94 A4
Duncanson Ave FK10 10 A8
Duncanson Dr KY3 34 A1
Duncan St Bonnybridge FK4 57 F5
Edinburgh EH9 121 F4
Kirkcaldy KY2 17 A4
Duncarron Ind Est FK6 36 F1
Duncarron Pl FK6 36 E2
Duncrahill Cotts EH34 178 B8
Duncur Rd EH31 52 C3
Dundaff Ct FK6 36 D1
Dundarroch St FK5 38 B1
Dundas Ave
North Berwick EH39 54 C6
Queensferry EH30 89 C8
Dundas Cotts FK4 57 A2
Dundas Cres
Clackmannan FK10 11 A4
Dalkeith EH22 152 E2
Laurieston FK2 61 A3
Dundas Gdns EH23 174 B1
Dundas Gr EH22 152 E2
Dundas Pk EH19 173 C7
Dundas Pl EH29 89 B2
Dundas Rd Dalkeith EH22 152 E2
Laurieston FK2 61 A4
North Berwick EH39 54 D6
Rosyth KY11 67 D8
Stirling FK9 2 A3
Dundas St Bathgate EH48 141 A8
Bo'ness EH51 63 F7
Bonnyrigg and Lasswade EH19 173 C7
Edinburgh EH3 228 C4
Grangemouth FK3 61 C8
Lochgelly KY5 14 B7
Townhill KY12 29 C7
Dundee Ct 5 FK2 60 A8
Dundee Pl FK2 60 A8
Dundee St EH11 228 A1
Dundee Terr EH11 120 F5
Dundonald Rd KY11 46 C3
Dundonald St EH3 93 C2
Dundonnell Way KY11 30 A1
Dundrennan Cotts EH16 122 C2
Dunearn Bank KY3 33 D1
Dunearn Dr KY2 16 F6
Dunearn Prim Sch KY2 16 E7
Dunedin Sch EH16 122 A2
Dunedin St EH7 93 D3
Dunelm Pk EH19 173 C6
DUNFERMLINE 29 C5
Dunfermline Abbey★ KY12 28 F3
Dunfermline Bsns Ctr KY11 29 B1
Dunfermline Bsns Pk KY11 46 D5
Dunfermline High Sch KY11 29 B1
Dunfermline Mus★ KY12 29 B3
Dunfermline Queen Margaret Sta KY12 29 F5
Dunfermline Rd
Crossgates KY4 30 E6
Limekilns KY11 45 E4
Dunfermline Support Ctr 5 KY12 29 A3
Dunfermline Town Sta KY12 29 B3
Dunfermline Wynd KY11 47 A2
Dungavel La ML8 215 B1
Dunglass Church★ TD13 218 E4
Dunimarle St KY12 26 A2
DUNIPACE 36 D4
Dunipace Cres KY12 29 E5
Dunipace Prim Sch FK6 36 D3
Dunkeld Pl FK2 39 C1
Dunlaw Wynd EH16 151 B6
Dunlin Brae EH54 143 C5
Dunlin Dr KY11 30 B4
Dunlop Ct EH54 142 C5
Dunlop's Ct EH1 228 C2
Dunlop Sq EH54 142 D5
Dunlop Terr EH26 192 A5
Dunmar Cres FK10 4 E1
Dunmar Dr FK10 4 E1
DUNMORE 22 C7
Dunn Cres KY11 29 E3
Dunnet Way EH52 116 A6
Dunnikier Prim Sch KY2 17 B5
Dunnikier Rd KY1 17 C5
Dunnikier Way KY1 17 B8
Dunning Pl FK2 39 C1
Dunnottar Dr FK5 38 F4
Dunnottar Pl KY2 16 E4
Dunn Pl EH52 87 E2
Dunn St EH52 115 B5
Dunn Terr ML7 159 F6
Dunollie Ct 2 EH12 119 B7
Dunollie Gdns EH41 130 C8
Dunpender Dr EH41 100 F1
Dunpender Rd EH40 103 C8
Dunrobin Ave FK5 38 F5
Dunrobin Pl EH3 93 B2
Dunrobin Rd KY2 16 E4
Dunsapie Ct EH15 122 D6
Dunsire St KY1 17 E8
Dunsmuir Ct EH12 119 D6
Duns Rd EH41 220 F7
Dunster Rd FK9 2 C3
Dunure Cres FK4 58 A5
Dunure Pl KY2 16 E4
Dunure St FK4 58 A5
Dunvegan Ave
Kirkcaldy KY2 16 D5
Stenhousemuir FK5 38 F4
Dunvegan Ct Alloa FK10 10 B6
Crossford KY12 28 B1
Edinburgh EH4 91 B4
Dunvegan Dr Falkirk FK2 39 C1
Stirling FK9 2 B3
Dunvegan Gdns EH54 164 E6
Dunvegan Pl
Bonnybridge FK4 57 F6
Polmont FK2 62 A1
Dura Rd ML2, ML7 198 C5
Durar Dr EH4 91 C1
Durham Ave
Bathgate EH48 140 E6
Edinburgh EH15 122 F7
Durham Bank EH19 173 C6
Durham Dr Bathgate EH48 140 E6
Edinburgh EH15 123 A6
Durham Gardens N EH15 123 A7
Durham Gardens S EH15 123 A6
Durham Gr
Bonnyrigg and Lasswade EH19 173 C6
Edinburgh EH15 123 A7
Durham Pl EH19 173 C6
Durham Place E EH15 123 A7
Durham Place La EH15 123 A7
Durham Place W EH15 122 F7
Durham Rd EH15 123 A7
Durham Road S EH15 123 A6
Durham Sq EH15 123 A7
Durham Terr
Edinburgh EH15 122 F7
Newmills KY12 26 C1
Durie Pk KY3 50 D8
Durie Pl KY11 29 F4
Durie's Pk EH33 126 B1
Durwood Gr EH16 122 B2
Dury Way EH21 125 A5
Dyfrig St ML7 179 E5
Dyke Brow ML7 160 A6
Dyke Ct ML7 160 A6
DYKEHEAD 179 D5
Dykehead Prim Sch ML7 179 E5
Dyke Rd ML7 160 A6
Dykeside Rd EH48 140 F8
Dykes Rd EH26 191 E7
Dymond Gr KY11 46 F8
DYSART 18 B7
Dysart Prim Sch KY1 18 A7
Dysart Rd KY1 17 F6
Dysart View KY1 18 B8

E

Eagle Brae EH54 143 D4
Eagle Rock★ EH4 91 A7
Eagles View EH54 114 C1
Eardley Cres KY11 47 A7
Eardley Pl 1 FK5 38 B2
Earl Grey St EH3 228 B2
Earl Haig Gdns EH5 93 B5
Earl of Mar Ct FK10 10 B6
Earlsburn Ave FK7 7 A3
Earls Ct FK10 10 B5
Earl's Gate Rdbt FK3 61 A7
Earlshill Dr FK7 7 F1
Earls Pl EH47 181 E6
Earl's Rd FK3 61 B8
Earlston Pl 3 EH7 94 A1
Earn Ct Alloa FK10 10 C6
Grangemouth FK3 61 D5
Earn Gr KY11 29 F4
Earn Pl FK6 57 D6
Earn Rd KY1 17 D8
Earn Terr ML7 179 E6
Earthship Fife & Ecology Ctr★ KY3 34 D4
East Adam St EH8 229 B2
East Albert Rd KY1 17 C5
East Ave KY12 26 A7
East Baldridge Dr KY12 28 E5
East Bankton Pl EH54 164 F7
East Barnton Ave EH4 91 E3
East Barnton Gdns EH4 91 E3
East Bay KY11 68 C5
East Boreland Pl FK6 36 D3
East Bridge St FK1 60 C4
East Brighton Cres EH15 123 A8
East Broomhill Rd KY3 50 E8
East Broughton Pl 8 EH3 93 D2
East Burn Ct KY1 17 D7
Eastburn Dr FK1 60 C4
Eastburn Twr FK1 60 C4
East Caiystane Pl EH10 150 A5
East Caiystane Rd EH10 150 B5

EAST CALDER 144 F3
East Calder Prim Sch EH53 144 F4
East Campbell Ct EH32 98 D5
East Camus Pl EH10 150 A6
East Camus Rd EH10 150 A6
East Castle Rd EH10 121 A5
East Castle St FK10 10 B5
East Champanyie EH9 121 E3
East Clapperfield EH16 122 A1
East Claremont St EH7 93 D3
East Comiston EH10 150 A6
EAST CRAIGS 119 A7
East Craigs Prim Sch EH12 119 B8
East Craigs Rigg EH12 119 A7
East Craigs Wynd EH12 119 A7
East Croft EH28 117 E2
Eastcroft Ct EH54 142 F3
Eastcroft Dr FK2 62 A2
East Croft St FK5 38 B1
East Cromwell St EH6 93 F6
East Crosscauseway EH8 229 B1
East Ct
  Edinburgh, Greendykes EH16 122 E3
  [1] Edinburgh, Ravelston EH4 92 C1
East Dr Dunfermline KY12 29 B3
  Stenhousemuir FK5 38 C1
East End EH55 163 D3
East End Park (Dunfermline Athletic FC) KY12 29 C4
EASTER ABERDOUR 49 C8
Easter Bankton EH54 165 A8
Easter Belmont Rd EH12 120 B8
Easter Broomhouse Cotts EH42 106 D7
Easter Carmuirs Prim Sch FK1 59 B6
Easter Cornton Rd FK9 2 B4
Easter Craiglockhart Hill Nature Reserve★ EH10 120 E1
Easter Currie Cres EH14 148 A5
Easter Currie Ct EH14 148 A4
Easter Currie Pl EH14 148 A5
Easter Currie Terr EH14 148 A4
Easter Dalry Dr [2] EH11 120 F6
Easter Dalry Pl [4] EH11 120 F6
Easter Dalry Rd EH11 120 F6
Easter Dalry Rigg [1] EH11 120 F6
Easter Dalry Wynd EH11 120 F7
Easter Drylaw Ave EH4 92 C3
Easter Drylaw Bank EH4 92 C3
Easter Drylaw Dr EH4 92 D3
Easter Drylaw Gdns EH4 92 C3
Easter Drylaw Gr EH4 92 C3
Easter Drylaw Loan EH4 92 C3
Easter Drylaw Pl EH4 92 C4
Easter Drylaw View EH4 92 D4
Easter Drylaw Way EH4 92 C3
Easter Ferrygate Pk EH39 53 E7
Easterfield Ct EH54 143 C3
Easter Haugh EH13 149 E7
Easter Hermitage EH6 94 B3
EASTER HOWGATE 171 A5
Easter Inch Moss & Seafield Law Nature Reserve★ EH47 142 A2
Easter Inch Rd EH48 141 D2
Easter Inch Steadings EH48 141 D3
Easter Langside Ave EH22 153 D3
Easter Langside Pl EH22 153 D3
Easter Livilands FK7 7 C4
EASTER MILLERHILL 152 E8
Eastern Ind Est EH15 123 C4
Easter Park Dr EH4 91 E4
EASTER PENCAITLAND 156 F6
Easter Rd Broxburn EH52 115 F5
  Edinburgh, Hillside EH7 93 F2
  Edinburgh, South Leith EH7 94 A4
  Shotts ML7 179 D5
Easter Road Stadium (Hibernian FC) EH7 94 A2
Easter Steil EH10 120 F1
Easterton Cres FK7 20 E7
Easterton Dr FK7 20 E7
Easterton Gr FK7 20 E7
Eastertoun Gdns EH48 139 E6
Eastertoun Prim Sch EH48 139 E6
Easter Warriston EH7 93 C4
East Farm of Gilmerton EH17 151 E6
East Fenton Farm Cotts EH39 73 C8
East Fergus Pl KY1 17 B3
East Fettes Ave EH4 92 F3
EASTFIELD Harthill 159 C4
  Penicuik 191 F6
Eastfield EH15 123 F7
Eastfield Cotts
  Penicuik EH26 191 F7
  Stenton EH41 104 B1
Eastfield Dr EH26 191 F6
Eastfield Farm Rd EH26 191 F7
Eastfield Gdns EH15 123 E7
Eastfield Ind Est EH26 191 F6
Eastfield Loan EH33 126 D7
Eastfield Park Rd EH26 191 F6
Eastfield Pl EH15 123 F7
Eastfield Rd Carluke ML8 215 A1
  Fauldhouse EH47 181 F7
  North Berwick EH39 54 D6
  Ratho Station EH28 118 A6
Eastfield View EH47 181 F7
EAST FORTUNE 74 B3
East Fountainbridge EH3 228 B2
East Garleton Cotts EH39 100 F6
Eastgate KY3 34 F3
East Glen Ave EH54 142 E6
East Harbour Rd KY11 45 B3
EAST HERMISTON 119 A1
East Hermitage Pl EH6 94 A4
EASTHOUSES 174 C7
Easthouses Ct EH22 174 C8
Easthouses Ind Est EH22 174 D8
Easthouses Pl EH22 153 C1
Easthouses Rd
  Dalkeith EH22 153 C1
  Easthouses EH22 174 C7
Easthouses Way EH22 153 C1
East Kilngate Pl EH17 151 D5
East Kilngate Rigg EH17 151 D5
East Kilngate Wynd EH17 151 D5
East Leven St KY3 50 E8
East Lillypot EH5 93 B5
East Link Rd FK9 2 D5
East Links Family Pk★ EH42 77 D2
East Links Rd Dunbar EH42 78 E2
  Gullane EH31 52 A2
EAST LINTON 103 C7
East Linton Prim Sch EH40 103 D7
East Linton Station Ind Site EH40 103 D7
East Loan EH32 97 A1
East London St EH7 93 D2
East Lorimer Pl EH32 97 C4
East Mains FK11 4 A6
East Mains Ind Est EH52 116 B6
East Mains of Ingliston EH28 118 A6
East Main St
  Armadale EH48 140 A6
  Blackburn EH47 162 D7
  Broxburn EH52 115 F5
  Harthill ML7 159 F5
  Uphall EH52 115 A4
  Whitburn EH47 161 B7
East March St KY1 17 E7
East Market St EH8 229 B3
East Mayfield EH9 121 F4
East Meikle Pinkerton Cotts EH42 107 C4
East Mill Rd EH49 84 D7
East Montgomery Pl [3] EH7 93 F2
East Murrayfield FK7 7 E1
East Newington Pl EH9 121 F5
East Norton Pl EH7 93 F1
Easton Ct FK8 2 B2
Easton Dr FK1 81 D7
Easton Rd EH48 140 F7
East Parkside EH16 229 C1
East Pier St EH51 63 F8
East Pilton Farm Ave EH5 92 E5
East Pilton Farm Rigg EH5 92 E5
East Pilton Farm Wynd EH5 92 F5
East Plean Prim Sch FK7 20 C3
East Port KY12 29 A4
East Port Ave EH41 130 B6
East Preston St EH8 121 F5
East Preston Street La [6] EH8 121 E5
East Quality St KY1 18 A7
East Queensway EH26 191 F7
East Rd Grangemouth FK3 62 C5
  North Berwick EH39 54 D7
East Restalrig Terr EH6 94 B4
EAST SALTOUN 157 E4
East Savile Rd EH16 121 F3
East Sciennes St [2] EH9 121 E5
East Scotland Street La [1] EH3 93 D2
East Seaside EH32 96 F2
East Stirling St FK12 5 B7
East Suffolk Rd EH16 122 A3
East Telferton EH7 94 F1
East Terr EH30 68 C1
East Toll KY3 33 E1
East Trinity Rd EH5 93 C6
East Vennel FK10 10 B6
East Vows Wlk KY1 35 B7
East Way KY11 48 C5
East Werberside EH4 92 E4
East Werberside Pl EH4 92 E4
EAST WHITBURN 161 E7
East Whitefield KY12 29 F6
Eastwood Pk
  Fauldhouse EH47 181 F7
  Livingston EH54 143 A7
Ebenezer Pl FK1 81 F5
Eccles Ct FK7 7 A4
ECCLESMACHAN 114 F7
Ecclesmachan Rd EH52 114 F5
Eccles Pl FK2 83 A5
Echline EH30 88 F8
Echline Ave EH30 89 A8
Echline Dr EH30 67 F1
Echline Gdns EH30 67 F1
Echline Gn EH30 67 F1
Echline Gr EH30 68 A1
Echline Pk EH30 88 F8
Echline Pl EH30 88 F8
Echline Prim Sch [1] EH30 68 A1
Echline Rigg EH30 68 A1
Echline Terr EH30 89 A8
Echline View EH30 89 A8
Echobank KY11 47 B2
Eden Dr EH54 144 B4
Edenhall Bank EH21 124 E5
Edenhall Cres EH21 124 E5
Edenhall Hospl EH21 124 E4
Edenhall Rd EH21 124 E5
Eden La EH10 121 B3
Eden Rd Alloa FK10 9 F8
  Dunfermline KY11 29 E2
Edgar St KY12 29 A3
Edgefield Pl EH20 172 C8
Edgefield Rd EH20 151 C1
Edgefield Road Ind Est EH20 151 C1
EDGEHEAD 175 C7
Edgehead Rd EH37 175 C7
Edina Pl EH7 94 A2
Edina St EH7 93 F2
EDINBURGH 228 C3
Edinburgh Acad (Prep Sch) The EH3 93 A4
Edinburgh Acad The EH3 93 B2
Edinburgh Airport EH12 118 B8
Edinburgh Butterfly & Insect World★ EH18 152 C3
Edinburgh Castle★ EH1 228 C3
Edinburgh Coll of Art EH3 228 C2
Edinburgh Int Climbing Arena EH28 117 B2
Edinburgh Napier Univ EH11 119 D2
Edinburgh Napier Univ (Comely Bank Campus) EH4 92 E2
Edinburgh Napier Univ (Craighouse Campus) EH11 120 E2
Edinburgh Napier Univ (Craiglockhart Campus) EH14 120 D1
Edinburgh Napier Univ (Marchmont Campus) EH9 121 D5
Edinburgh Napier Univ (Merchiston Campus) EH10 121 A4
Edinburgh Park Sta EH11 119 A3
Edinburgh Pk EH12 118 F5
Edinburgh Pk EH12 119 A4
Edinburgh Playhouse The★ EH1 229 B4
Edinburgh Quay EH3 228 B1
Edinburgh Rd
  Bathgate EH48 141 C5
  Carlops EH46 206 B1
  Cockenzie & Port Seton EH32 97 B3
  Dalkeith EH22 153 A3
  Harthill ML7 159 C5
  Linlithgow EH49 85 B7
  Musselburgh EH21 124 A6
  Newbridge EH28 117 A6
  Penicuik EH26 192 A8
  South Queensferry EH30 68 C1
  Tranent EH33 126 B6
  West Barns EH42 77 F1
Edinburgh Rudolf Steiner Sch EH10 120 F4
Edinburgh Sch of Agriculture EH16 121 F1
Edinburgh's Telford Coll EH5 92 C6
Edinburgh Technopole EH26 171 B4
Edinburgh Waverley Sta EH1 229 A3
Edinburgh West Off Pk EH12 119 A4
Edinburgh Zoo (Royal Zoological Society of Scotland)★ EH12 119 F7
Edington Cottage Hospl EH39 54 C7
Edington Pl KY1 18 B8
EDMONSTONE 152 A8
Edmonstone Ave EH22 152 B8
Edmonstone Dr EH22 152 B8
Edmonstone Rd EH22 152 B8
Edmonstone Terr EH22 152 B8
Edmonton Ave EH54 143 F4
Edward Ave
  Stenhousemuir FK5 38 E4
  Stirling FK8 2 C1
Edward Pl FK2 39 F3
Edward Rd FK8 2 B1
Edwards Ct EH41 129 F8
Edward St
  Dunfermline KY12 29 B5
  Kirkcaldy KY2 17 B7
Edzell Way KY11 30 A1
Eglingtoun Dr KY12 28 F6
Eglinton Cres EH12 120 F7
Eglinton Pl KY11 47 D2
Egypt Mews EH10 121 C3
Eighth St EH22 174 B5
Eildon St EH3 93 C3
Eildon Terr EH3 93 C4
Elam Terr EH51 63 E7
Elbe St EH6 94 A5
Elcho Ct EH32 98 E5
Elcho Pl EH32 97 C4
Elcho Rd EH32 98 E5
Elcho Terr Aberlady EH32 71 C4
  Edinburgh EH15 123 C8
Elcho Terr *continued*
  Longniddry EH32 98 E5
Elder Ct [6] EH33 126 C6
Elder Pl KY11 46 E5
Elderslie Dr FK2 82 B7
Elder St Dunbar EH42 78 B1
  Edinburgh EH1 229 A4
  Tranent EH33 126 C7
Elder Street E EH1 229 A4
ELDINDEAN 173 C8
Eldindean Ct KY12 28 D6
Eldindean Pl EH19 173 B8
Eldindean Rd EH19 173 C8
Eldindean Terr EH19 173 C8
Eldin Ind Est EH20 151 C2
Eldin Pl EH18 152 A1
Eldrick Ave EH47 181 E5
Eldrick Cres EH47 181 D5
Eldrick La EH47 181 D6
Eldrick View EH47 181 E5
Electra Pl EH15 95 A1
Elgin Ct KY12 29 A2
Elgin Dr FK7 7 C3
Elgin Pl FK1 60 C4
Elgin Rd KY4 13 D4
Elgin St Dunfermline KY12 29 A2
  Edinburgh EH7 93 F2
  Kirkcaldy KY2 17 B6
Elgin Street N EH7 93 F2
Elgin Terr EH7 93 F2
Elgol Path ML7 180 B3
ELIBURN 143 A5
Eliburn North Rdbt EH54 143 B6
Eliburn Rd EH54 143 B4
Eliburn South Rd EH54 143 C4
Elie Ave EH54 142 F5
Elim Dr FK1 81 C6
Elizabeth Ave
  Grangemouth FK3 61 E8
  Stenhousemuir FK5 38 C2
Elizabeth Cres FK1 59 B6
Elizabeth Dr EH48 141 F6
Elizabeth Gdns EH47 162 B2
Elizabeth La EH48 141 F6
Elizabeth St
  Dunfermline KY11 29 D2
  Stirling FK8 7 A5
Elizafield EH6 93 E4
Ellaleen Gr KY12 28 B1
Ellangowan Terr EH16 122 C1
Ellen's Glen Loan EH17 151 C7
Ellen's Glen Rd EH17 151 C7
Ellen St EH47 161 B7
Ellersly Rd EH12 120 C7
Elliot Gdns EH14 149 C8
Elliothill St KY11 29 B2
Elliot Pk EH14 149 C8
Elliot Pl Edinburgh EH14 149 C8
  [5] Larbert FK5 38 B2
Elliot Rd EH14 149 C8
Elliot St Dunfermline KY11 29 B2
  Edinburgh EH7 93 F2
Elliot Terr FK2 60 A8
Ellisland Ave KY2 17 A7
Ellis Pl EH52 115 B5
Ellon Pl KY12 29 D6
Ellon Rd KY2 16 C7
Elmbank FK11 4 A6
Elmbank Cres FK4 57 D6
Elmbank Rd FK7 7 A3
Elmbank St FK3 61 C6
Elm Ct EH47 162 E8
Elm Dr FK2 61 A2
Elmfield Ct EH22 153 A3
Elmfield Pk EH22 153 A3
Elmfield Rd EH22 153 A3
Elm Gr Blackburn EH47 162 E8
  Dunfermline KY11 46 C8
  Livingston EH54 144 B5
  Stenhousemuir FK5 38 D1
Elm Pk EH47 162 E8
Elm Pl Edinburgh EH6 94 B4
  Kirkcaldy KY2 16 F5
  Mayfield EH22 174 D6
Elm Rd EH48 141 E6
Elm Row
  Bonnyrigg and Lasswade EH18 152 B1
  Edinburgh EH7 93 E2
Elm Sq EH47 161 C6
Elm St Dunbar EH42 78 B1
  Stirling FK8 1 E1
Elm Terr EH47 162 E8
Elmwood Pk EH54 142 F7
Elmwood Rd ML7 180 B2
Elmwood Terr EH6 94 B3
ELPHINSTONE 126 A1
Elphinstone Cres FK2 22 E4
Elphinstone Ct [2] EH33 126 C6
Elphinstone Prim Sch EH33 126 B1
Elphinstone Rd EH33 126 B5
Elphinstone Sq EH54 142 C6
Elphinstone St FK10 23 E4
Elphinstone Tower Farm Cotts HE33 125 F1
Elphinstone Wlk [8] EH33 126 C5
Elpin FK10 10 D5
Eltringham Gdns EH14 120 C4
Eltringham Gr EH14 120 C4
Eltringham Terr EH14 120 C4
Emily Ct EH23 174 C1
Emily Pl EH23 174 D1
Emma's Way FK4 57 F5
Empire Gate ML7 179 F4
Empire St EH47 161 A7
Endrick Ct FK5 38 C5
Endrick Dr FK6 57 E6
Endrick Pl FK7 7 A4
Engelen Dr FK10 10 B5
Engine Gn The FK10 5 D3
Engine La EH48 141 B6
Engine Pl [3] EH48 141 A6
Engine Rd
  Gorebridge EH23 174 B1
  Loanhead EH20 172 C8
Ennis Ct EH55 163 E4
Ennis Pk EH55 163 E5
Enterprise Ctr EH20 172 A7
Enterprise Way KY11 46 E6
Entryfoot EH48 137 F2
ENTRY HEAD 146 E7
Eppiestane Rd EH47 161 C6
Epworth Gdns FK2 82 B8
Erbach Ave FK2 61 B4
Ercall Rd FK2 82 E8
Erica Gr KY11 46 E8
Ericht Pl ML7 179 E6
Eriskay Ct FK1 60 C2
Erngath Rd EH51 64 A7
Erskine Beveridge Ct KY11 29 B2
Erskine Brae KY12 25 D1
Erskine Gdns ML7 179 D5
Erskine Hill FK2 61 E1
Erskine La [4] FK5 38 B2
Erskine Loan EH31 52 A3
Erskine Pl
  Clackmannan FK10 10 F5
  Mid Calder EH53 144 C6
Erskine Rd Broxburn EH52 115 C6
  Gullane EH31 52 A3
Erskine Sq KY11 29 C2
Erskine St Alloa FK10 10 B7
  Alva FK12 5 A7
  Lochgelly KY5 14 A6
Erskine Way
  Livingston EH54 143 D8
  Shotts ML7 179 E4
Erskine Wynd KY12 27 A7
Esdaile Bank EH9 121 D4
Esdaile Pk EH9 121 D4
ESKBANK 152 F2
Eskbank Ct EH22 152 E2
Eskbank Rd
  Bonnyrigg and Lasswade EH22 173 D8
  Dalkeith EH22 152 F2
Eskbank Road Rdbt EH22 152 D1
Eskbank Terr EH22 152 F2
Eskdaill Ct [13] EH22 153 A3
Eskdaill St [11] EH22 153 A3
Eskdale Ct EH19 173 A7
Eskdale Dr EH19 173 A7
Eskdale Mews EH21 124 C6
Eskdale Terr EH19 173 A7
Esk Dr EH54 144 B4
Eskfield Gr EH22 152 D2
Esk Glades EH22 153 B4
ESKGROVE 172 F8
Eskgrove Dr EH25 171 E6
Eskhill EH26 191 F5
Eskmill Rd EH26 192 A5
Eskmills EH21 124 B5
Esk Pl EH22 152 F3
Eskside Ct EH22 152 F4
Eskside E EH21 124 C6
Eskside W EH21 124 C6
Eskvale Cres EH26 192 A5
Eskvale Ct EH26 192 A5
Eskvale Dr EH26 192 A6
Eskvale View EH26 192 A6
Eskview Ave EH21 124 B5
Eskview Cres EH21 124 B5
Eskview Gr Dalkeith EH22 152 F3
  Musselburgh EH21 124 B5
Eskview Rd Mayfield EH22 174 D6
  Musselburgh EH21 124 B5
Eskview Terr EH21 124 B5
Eskview Villas EH22 152 F2
Esmonde Ct KY11 46 E2
Esplanade Edinburgh EH1 228 C3
  Kirkcaldy KY1 17 C2
  [1] Stirling FK8 7 A8
Esplanade Terr EH15 123 D8
Essendean Pl EH4 91 D1
Essendean Terr EH4 91 D1
Essex Brae EH4 91 A4
Essex Pk EH4 91 A4
Essex Rd EH4 91 A4
Esslemont Rd EH16 122 A2
Estate Ave FK1 60 C4
Ethel Terr EH10 121 A2
Etive Pl Dalgety Bay KY11 48 A2
  Stirling FK9 2 B3
Etive Way FK2 62 A2
Etive Wlk Livingston EH54 144 A4
  Shotts ML7 180 B3
Etna Ct EH48 140 B5
Etna Ct FK2 60 D7
Etna Rd FK2 60 D7
Etna Road Rdbt FK2 60 E7
Eton Terr EH4 228 A4
Ettrick Cres KY11 48 A4
Ettrick Ct Falkirk FK1 60 D1
  Grangemouth FK3 61 F6
Ettrickdale Pl EH3 93 B3
Ettrick Dr EH54 144 B5
Ettrick Gr EH10 121 A5
Ettrick Loan EH10 120 F4
Ettrick Rd EH10 120 F4

Evans Gdns EH19 173 D8
Evans St FK5 38 C3
Eva Pl EH9 121 E2
Evelyn Terr EH26 171 C1
Everard Rise EH54 144 A2
Evergreen Trailer Ct FK6 37 A2
Evershed Ct KY11 29 E1
Evershed Dr KY11 29 E1
Ewart Ave EH48 140 A5
Ewart Gr EH51 63 F5
Eweford Cotts EH42 106 B8
Ewerland EH4 91 A4
Ewing Ave FK2 60 B7
Ewing Ct FK7 7 C3
Ewing Dr FK2 60 B7
Ewing Pl FK2 60 B7
Ewing St Cowdenbeath KY4 13 B2
Lochgelly KY5 14 A6
Penicuik EH26 191 F7
Ewingston Mill Steading
EH36 220 B3
Ewington Pl EH47 162 B2
Excise La FK10 23 E3
Excise St FK10 23 F4
Exmouth St EH54 144 A5
Eyre Cres EH3 93 C2
Eyre Pl EH3 93 C2
Eyre Place La EH3 93 C2
Eyre Terr EH3 93 C2

F

FACTOR'S PARK 120 C5
Factory Rd Bathgate EH48 140 F4
Cowdenbeath KY4 13 D4
Kirkcaldy KY1 17 D6
Fair-A-Far EH4 91 B5
Fair-A-Far Cotts EH4 91 B5
Fair-A-Far Shot EH4 91 B5
Fairbairn Pl EH54 143 C3
Fairbairn Rd EH54 143 C3
Fairbrae EH11 119 F3
Fairfax Ct KY3 33 E1
FAIRFIELD 5 B2
Fairfield Alloa FK10 5 C1
Livingston EH54 143 A3
Fairfield Ave FK4 58 A6
Fairfield Pl FK2 60 C5
Fairfields FK2 21 E5
Fairfield Sch FK10 5 B1
Fairford Gdns EH16 122 B1
Fairgreen Pl FK7 19 E8
Fairhaven Terr FK2 82 A8
Fairhill Rd FK7 7 B1
Fairinsfell EH52 115 B5
Fair Isle Prim Sch KY2 16 E8
Fair Isle Rd KY2 16 E8
Fairley Ct KY12 27 D1
Fairley Dr FK5 38 A3
Fairlie Dr FK1 59 D5
Fairlie Gdns FK1 59 D5
Fairlie St FK1 59 C5
Fairmile Ave EH10 150 B5
FAIRMILEHEAD 150 B5
Fairmont Pk EH47 160 F6
Fairmount Dr FK10 5 B2
Fair Pl KY11 47 B3
Fairspark Terr EH51 63 D5
Fairview Rd EH12, EH28 117 F7
Fairway EH41 129 E8
Fairways KY12 29 B6
Fairways Ave FK2 82 F6
Fairways Bsns Pk EH54 114 D1
Fairways Pl FK4 58 B7
Fairway The KY1 17 F8
Fairyburn Rd FK10 9 F8
Fairy Fa' Cres KY4 30 F6
Fairykirk Rd KY11 47 A3
Faith Mission Coll The 1
EH17 151 E6
FALA 224 C7
Falahill Cotts EH38 214 B4
Falcon Ave EH10 121 B3
Falcon Brae EH54 143 D5
Falcon Ct EH10 121 B3
Falcon Dr FK5 38 B3
Falconer Ct FK7 7 C3
Falconer Rise EH54 144 A2
Falcon Gdns EH10 121 B3
Falcon Rd EH10 121 B3
Falcon Road W EH10 121 B3
Falcons The EH31 52 B3
FALKIRK 60 D6
Falkirk & District Royal Infmy
FK1 60 A4
Falkirk Grahamston Sta
FK1 60 B5
Falkirk High Sch FK1 59 E4
Falkirk High Sta FK1 60 A3
Falkirk Rd Bannockburn FK7 19 F8
Bonnybridge FK4 58 C6
Cowie FK7 20 A6
Falkirk FK2, FK3 60 F6
Falkirk, Glen Village FK1 60 B1
Larbert FK5 38 B1
Linlithgow EH49 84 E7
Falkirk Stadium The (Falkirk
FC) FK2 60 F6
Falkirk Wheel The★ FK1 59 A5
Falkland Gdns EH12 91 E1
Falkland Pl FK5 38 E4
Falla Hill Pl EH47 181 D6
Falla Hill Prim Sch EH47 181 D6
Fallas Pl EH47 181 D5
Fallhills Ct EH26 192 C1
FALLIN 8 C4
Fallin Prim Sch FK7 8 D5
Fallodon Cres KY2 17 A3
FALSIDE 140 E5
Falside Cres EH48 140 E5
Falside Dr EH48 140 E5
Falside Terr EH48 140 E5
Faraday Pl EH55 162 E2
Farm Ave EH18 172 F6
Farm Cotts EH21 125 C5
Farmer's Bldgs EH37 176 B5
Farm Pl EH54 143 A3
Farm Rd Cowdenbeath KY4 13 B3
Cowie FK7 20 D8
Crombie KY12 44 D6
Fallin FK7 8 D4
Roslin EH25 192 F6
Farm Row KY12 30 B6
Farm St FK2 39 A1
Farmstead Rd KY11 47 F4
Farmstead Way EH51 64 C6
Farne Ct KY2 16 F8
Farnell Way KY12 29 D6
Farquharson Way FK1 59 F1
Farquhar Sq EH48 138 C3
Farquhar Terr EH30 68 A1
Farrer Gr EH7 94 E1
Farrer Terr EH7 94 F1
Farrier Ct EH47 162 D7
Fa'side Ave 3 EH33 126 D5
Fa'side Avenue Ct EH21 125 B4
Fa'side Avenue N EH21 125 B4
Fa'side Avenue S EH21 125 B4
Fa'side Bldgs EH21 125 B4
Fa'side Cres
2 Tranent EH33 126 D5
Wallyford EH21 125 B4
Fa'side Dr EH21 125 B4
Fa'side Gdns EH21 125 B4
Fa'side Rd EH33 126 D5
Fa'side Terr EH21 125 B4
Fa'side View EH33 126 B4
FAUCHELDEAN 87 F1
Fauldburn EH12 91 B1
Fauldburn Pk EH12 91 B1
FAULDHOUSE 181 E5
Fauldhouse Bsns Ctr
EH47 181 E6
Fauldhouse Rd EH47 161 B2
Fauldhouse Sta EH47 181 C5
Featherhall Ave EH12 119 D6
Featherhall Crescent N
EH12 119 D6
Featherhall Crescent S
EH12 119 D6
Featherhall Gr EH12 119 D6
Featherhall Pl EH12 119 D6
Featherhall Rd EH12 119 D6
Featherhall Terr EH12 119 D6
Fell's Rd EH55 163 F5
Fells Rigg EH54 143 A7
Fendoch Rd FK3 61 F7
FENTON BARNS 73 B8
Fenton Barns Farm Cotts
EH39 73 A8
Fenton Barns Ret Village
EH39 53 A1
Fenton St FK10 10 A7
Fentoun Gait EH31 52 C2
Feregait FK10 23 E4
Fergus Ave EH54 143 F4
Ferguson Ct EH21 124 C3
Ferguson Dr Denny FK6 36 D1
Falkirk FK2 39 A5
Musselburgh EH21 124 B3
Ferguson Gdns EH21 124 C3
Ferguson Gn EH21 124 B3
Ferguson Gr FK4 58 B6
Ferguson Pl KY3 33 F1
Ferguson Rd KY11 47 A7
Ferguson St FK8 1 F2
Ferguson View EH21 124 B3
Ferguson Way
Livingston EH54 143 D8
Newtongrange EH22 174 B4
Fergus Pl KY11 29 D1
Fergusson Rd EH52 115 E5
Fergus Wynd KY1 17 B1
Fernbank Cornton FK9 2 B3
Livingston EH54 143 E5
FERNIEHILL 151 E7
Ferniehill Ave EH17 151 E6
Ferniehill Dr EH17 151 F6
Ferniehill Gdns EH17 151 F7
Ferniehill Gr EH17 151 E6
Ferniehill Pl EH17 151 E6
Ferniehill Rd EH17 151 E7
Ferniehill Sq EH17 151 E6
Ferniehill St EH17 151 E7
Ferniehill Terr EH17 151 E6
Ferniehill Way EH17 151 F7
Fernielaw Ave EH13 149 A5
Fernie Pl KY12 28 E5
Fernieside Ave EH17 151 E8
Fernieside Cres EH17 151 E7
Fernieside Dr EH17 151 E8
Fernieside Gdns EH17 151 E7
Fernieside Gr EH17 151 F7
Fernieside Pl EH17 151 E7
Fernlea EH52 114 F5
Fern Lea Gr FK2 39 C3
Ferrard Rd KY2 17 A4
Ferrier Cres EH48 140 A6
Ferris Way KY11 48 B4
Ferrybarns Ct KY11 68 B6
Ferryburn Gn EH30 89 C8
Ferry Ct FK9 2 A3
Ferryfield EH5 93 A4
Ferry Gait Cres EH4 92 A4
Ferry Gait Dr EH4 92 A4
Ferry Gait Gdns 2 EH4 92 A4
Ferry Gait Pl 3 EH4 92 A4
Ferry Gait Wlk 1 EH4 92 A4
Ferrygate Cottages EH39 53 C6
Ferryhill Prim Sch EH4 92 C3
Ferryhill Rd
Inverkeithing KY11 47 B1
North Queensferry KY11 68 B7
Ferry La KY11 68 B6
Ferry Muir EH30 89 B7
Ferrymuir Gait EH30 89 B8
Ferrymuir La EH30 89 B8
Ferrymuir Rd EH30 89 B8
Ferry Orch FK9 2 D1
Ferry Rd
Edinburgh, Drylaw EH4,
EH5 92 D4
Edinburgh, Trinity EH5 93 C5
North Queensferry KY11 68 B6
South Alloa FK7 9 F4
Stirling FK9 2 D1
Ferry Road Ave EH4 92 C4
Ferry Road Dr EH4 92 D5
Ferry Road Gdns EH4 92 C4
Ferry Road Gr EH4 92 C4
Ferry Road Pl EH4 92 C4
Ferry Toll Pl KY11 46 E1
Ferry Toll Rd KY11 46 E1
Festival Sq EH3 228 B2
Festival Theatre★ EH8 229 A2
Fetteresk Cotts EH26 191 E4
Fettes Ave EH4 92 F2
Fettes Coll EH4 92 F3
Fettes Ct EH4 92 E2
Fettes Rise EH4 92 F4
Fettes Row EH3 93 C2
Fiddich Dr EH54 164 E5
Fidra Ave Burntisland KY3 33 D1
Dirleton EH39 53 B5
Fidra Ct EH39 53 F7
Fidra Rd EH39 54 A7
Fieldfare View KY11 30 A3
Fife Coll (Priory Campus)
KY1 17 C5
Fife Leisure Pk KY11 30 C5
Fife Pl KY11 46 B2
Fifth St EH22 174 B5
Figgate Bank EH15 95 B1
Figgate La EH15 95 B1
Figgate St EH15 95 A1
Fillyside Ave EH7 94 E2
Fillyside Rd EH7, EH15 94 E3
Fillyside Terr EH7 94 E3
Fincastle Pl FK7 20 D8
Finches The EH31 52 B3
Findhorn Pl
Edinburgh EH9 121 E4
Falkirk FK1 60 D2
Kirkcaldy KY2 16 E8
Findlay Ave EH7 94 C3
Findlay Cotts EH7 94 C3
Findlay Cres KY11 46 E4
Findlay Gdns EH7 94 C3
Findlay Gr EH7 94 C3
Findlay Medway EH7 94 C3
Findlay St KY11 46 E4
Fingal Pl EH9 229 A1
Finglen Cres FK10 4 C4
Fingzies Pl EH6 94 B4
Finistere Ave FK1 60 B3
Finlaggan Ct 2 EH12 119 A8
Finlarig Ct FK5 38 F4
Finlay Ave EH53 144 F3
Finlay Pl EH22 174 F6
Finlayson Pl FK5 38 C5
Fintry Ave EH54 142 F5
Fintry Rd FK3 61 E5
Firbank Gr EH53 144 E3
Fire Mus★ EH3 228 C2
Fir Gr Dunfermline KY11 46 E8
Livingston EH54 144 B5
Westquarter FK2 61 B2
Fir La FK5 38 D1
Firpark Terr FK7 6 C5
FIRR HILL 149 D8
Firrhill Cres EH13 149 E8
Firrhill Dr EH13 149 E7
Firrhill High Sch EH14 149 D8
Firrhill Loan EH13 149 E7
Firrhill Pk EH13 149 F7
Firs Cres FK7 7 D2
Firs Entry FK7 7 D2
Firs Rd FK10 4 D2
Firs St FK2 60 C6
First Gait EH14 147 E8
Firs The Bannockburn FK7 7 D2
Dalgety Bay KY11 48 B2
First St EH22 174 B4
Firth Cres EH26 171 D1
Firth Rd Livingston EH54 143 F7
Penicuik EH26 171 D1
Roslin EH25 192 F6
Fir View EH20 171 F7
Firwood Dr EH51 63 D5
FISHCROSS 5 E3
Fishcross Prim Sch FK10 5 D3
Fishergate Rd EH32 97 E3
Fishermans Wlk FK9 2 A3
FISHERROW 124 C7
Fisherrow Ind Est EH21 124 A6
Fishers Rd EH32 97 D4
Fishers' Rd EH49 63 D3
Fishers Wynd EH21 124 B6
Fishmarket Sq EH6 93 D7
Fishwives' Cswy EH15 95 A1
Fitzallan Pl EH48 141 B3
Fitzgerald Pl EH48 111 F5
Fitzroy Sq KY1 18 A7
Fitzroy St KY1 18 A7
Five Gates EH42 76 B5
Fivestanks Ct EH52 115 A5
Fivestanks Pl EH52 115 B5
Flare Rd FK3 62 B5
Flax Mill Rd ML7 159 F5
Fleets Gr EH33 126 D4
Fleets Ind Est EH33 126 C3
Fleets Rd EH33 126 C5
Fleets View EH33 126 D4
Fleming Ct FK6 57 D8
Fleming Dr FK5 39 A3
Fleming Gdns FK1 59 E6
Fleming Pl EH48 138 E3
Fleming Rd EH54 142 F2
Fleming St FK6 36 E1
Flemington Gdns EH47 160 F6
Fleming Way KY3 33 E2
Fleshmarket Cl EH1 229 A3
Flesh Wynd 11 KY1 17 D6
Fletcher Gr EH26 191 F8
Fleurs Pk FK9 1 F3
Flint Cres FK7 20 D8
Floors Pl KY2 16 D5
Floors Terr EH42 78 C2
Florabank Rd EH41 101 A1
Flora Stevenson Prim Sch 4
EH4 92 F2
Flotterstone Visitor Ctr★
EH26 170 E3
Flower Pl KY4 12 F8
Flying Scotsman Way The
EH32 125 F8
Fodbank View KY11 29 E4
Fod St KY11 30 B5
Follyburn Pl EH54 143 B4
Foote St KY5 14 A6
Foot Pl KY11 46 E3
Forbes Cres FK5 38 D1
Forbes Ct FK2 60 E6
Forbeslea Gdns KY12 27 E7
Forbes Rd Edinburgh EH10 121 B5
Falkirk FK1 60 D4
Rosyth KY11 46 C2
Forbes St Alloa FK10 9 F6
Edinburgh EH8 229 B1
Forbes Terr KY2 17 B5
FORDELL 31 B6
Fordell Bank KY11 48 C4
Fordell Gdns
Dalgety Bay KY11 47 E7
Kirkcaldy KY2 16 D5
Fordell Ind Est KY4 13 B1
Fordell Way KY11 47 D2
Fordel Mains Cotts EH22 154 D2
Ford Rd Bonnybridge FK4 58 A5
Haddington EH41 130 C8
Ford's Rd EH11 120 B4
Ford View KY12 27 C1
Fordyce Gdns FK1 59 E4
Forebraes FK10 10 B7
Foredale Terr EH51 64 D7
Foreshore Way EH51 64 D7
Foreshot Terr EH39 53 B5
Forestbank EH54 143 E5
Forester Gr FK10 4 F1
Forester's Lea Cres KY12 29 E4
Forester's View EH33 126 D6
Forest Kirk ML8 215 B1
Forest Pl KY12 29 D7
Forest Rd KY12 29 D7
Forest View FK2 61 F1
Forfar Pl FK2 62 A1
Forge The KY12 28 C6
Forgie Cres FK2 83 A5
Forglen Cres FK9 2 A6
Forglen Rd FK9 2 B6
Forkenford EH16 122 D5
Forker Ave KY11 46 D4
Forkneuk Rd EH52 114 E4
Forkneuk Steadings
EH52 114 E4
Forman Gr KY11 29 E1
Forres Dr KY2 16 C7
Forres St EH3 228 B4
Forrester Ct KY5 14 B7
Forrester Gait FK5 37 E6
Forrester High Sch EH12 119 D4
Forrester Park Ave EH12 119 D4
Forrester Park Dr EH12 119 D4
Forrester Park Gdns
EH12 119 D4
Forrester Park Gn EH11 119 E4
Forrester Park Gr EH12 119 D4
Forrester Park Loan
EH12 119 D4
Forrester Pl FK2 22 D3
Forrester Rd
Armadale EH48 139 F7
Edinburgh EH12 119 D7
Forrester St FK2 61 A1
FORRESTFIELD 137 A3
Forrestfield Rd ML6 137 A5
Forrest Hill EH1 229 A2
Forrest Pl Armadale EH48 140 A4
Harthill ML7 159 E5
Forrest Rd Edinburgh EH1 229 A2
Forrestfield ML6 137 A1
Harthill ML6, ML7 158 B6
Stirling FK8 2 B1
Forrest St ML7 179 E5
Forrest Wlk EH52 114 F3
Forsyth La FK7 7 C1
Forteviot Ho EH17 151 D8
FORTH 201 A1
Forth Ave Kirkcaldy KY2 17 A4
Larbert FK5 38 B3
Forth Ave Ind Est KY2 17 A3
Forthbank Ind Est FK10 10 B4
Forthbank Pl KY12 25 F1
Forthbank Stadium (Stirling
Albion FC) FK7 7 E7
Forth Bridge Visitor Ctr★
KY11 68 A6
Forthclyde Way FK3 40 B1
Forth Cres Alloa FK10 10 C5
Dalgety Bay KY11 48 B4
High Valleyfield KY12 26 B2
Stirling FK8 7 B8
Forth Ct
Cockenzie & Port Seton
EH32 97 E4
Dalgety Bay KY11 48 B4
Dunfermline KY12 29 A2
Stirling FK8 2 B1
Forth Dr EH54 144 B5
Forth Gdns
Cockenzie & Port Seton
EH32 97 E4
Oakley KY12 26 E7
Forth Gr EH32 97 E4
Forth Ind Est EH5 92 E7
Fort Ho EH6 93 E6
Forth Park Dr KY2 17 A5
Forth Park Gdns KY2 17 A5
Forth Park Maternity Hospl
KY2 17 A5
Forth Pk Bridge of Allan FK9 2 A5
Queensferry EH30 89 E8
Stirling FK9 1 F5
Forth Pl Burntisland KY3 50 E8
Queensferry EH30 67 F1
Stirling FK8 7 B8
Forth Prim Sch ML11 201 A1
Forth Rd KY11 46 B2
Forth Reach KY11 47 F2
Forthside Terr KY11 68 C5
Forthside Way FK7 7 B8
Forth St Cambus FK10 9 A8
Dunfermline KY12 29 A2
Edinburgh EH1 93 D2
Fallin FK7 8 C4
Grangemouth FK3 61 D8
Kincardine FK10 23 D3
North Berwick EH39 54 C7
Stirling FK8 2 B1
Forth Street La EH39 54 C7
Forth Terr
Grangemouth FK3 61 D8
Queensferry EH30 89 D8
Forthvale FK11 4 A6
Forthvale Ct FK9 2 B2
Forth Valley Coll FK8 2 A2
Forth Valley Coll
Clackmannan FK10 10 B8
Forth Valley Coll Falkirk
FK2 60 E6
Forth Valley Coll Raploch
Campus FK8 2 A2
Forth Valley Coll Stirling
FK7 7 C6
Forth Valley Royal Hospl
FK5 37 F3
Forthview FK7 7 E1
Forth View
Dalgety Bay KY11 48 B4
Inverkeithing KY11 47 B2
Kincardine FK10 23 F3
Kirknewton EH27 145 E3
Stirling FK8 2 B1
West Barns EH42 77 F1
Forthview Ave EH21 125 A4
Forth View Ave EH14 147 F4
Forth View Cotts KY12 26 A1
Forthview Cres
Bo'ness EH51 63 D6
Musselburgh EH21 125 A5
Forth View Cres
Currie EH14 147 F4
Danderhall EH22 152 B7
Edinburgh EH14 147 F5
Forthview Ct 5 Falkirk FK1 59 F2
6 Tranent EH33 126 D7
Forthview Dr EH21 125 B5
Forthview Gdns FK2 82 C8
Forth View Ind Est KY12 26 B1
Forth View Loan EH22 153 D2
Forthview Pl EH22 153 D2
Forthview Prim Sch EH4 92 D4
Forthview Rd
Edinburgh EH4 92 C2
Longniddry EH32 98 E6
Forth View Rd EH14 147 F4
Forthview Terr
Edinburgh EH4 92 B2
Falkirk FK1 60 C4
Grangemouth FK2 82 B8
Newmills KY12 26 D1
Wallyford EH21 125 B4
Forthview Wlk EH33 126 D7
Forth Wynd EH32 97 E4
Forties Campus KY11 46 D1
Forties Rd FK3, EH51 62 D5
Fortingall Cres FK2 62 A2
Fortissat Ave ML7 179 D6
Fort Kinnaird Sh Ctr
EH15 123 C4
Fort Prim Sch
Edinburgh EH6 93 E6
Edinburgh EH6 93 E6
Fortuna Ct FK1 60 C4
Fortune Ave EH41 101 A1
Foulden Pl KY12 29 D3

Foulford Pl KY4 13 B4
Foulford Prim Sch KY4 13 B5
Foulford Rd KY4 13 B4
Foulford St KY4 13 C4
Foulis Cres EH14 148 E6
Foulshiels Rd EH47 162 C2
Foundry La EH20 151 D1
Foundry Loan FK5 38 B2
Foundry Rd
Bonnybridge FK4 58 B5
Shotts ML7 179 F4
Foundry St
Dunfermline KY12 29 A4
Falkirk FK2 60 A8
FOUNTAINBRIDGE 228 A1
Fountainbridge EH3 228 A1
Fountain Cl EH1 229 B3
Fountainhall Rd EH9 121 E4
Fountainhead Rd EH48 141 B7
Fountainpark EH11 229 A1
Fountainpark Cres EH51 64 C7
Fountain Pl
Cowdenbeath KY4 13 D3
Loanhead EH20 172 C8
Pathhead EH37 176 A5
Fountain Rd FK9 2 A7
Fourth Gait EH14 147 E7
Fourth St EH22 174 B5
Fowler Cres Denny FK6 36 E1
Loanhead EH20 172 D8
Maddiston FK2 83 A5
Fowler Pl FK2 61 E3
Fowlers Ct EH32 96 F2
Fowler Sq EH20 172 D8
Fowler St EH33 126 C7
Fowler Terr EH11 120 F5
Fox Covert Ave EH12 91 E1
Fox Covert Gr EH12 91 E1
Fox Covert RC Prim Schs
EH12 91 E1
Foxdale Ave FK4 58 A3
Foxdale Ct FK4 58 A3
Foxdale Dr FK4 58 A3
Foxdale Pl FK4 58 A3
Foxglove Neuk KY12 29 A5
Foxknowe Pl EH54 143 B4
Fox Spring Cres EH10 150 A7
Fox Spring Rise EH10 150 A7
Fox St EH6 94 B5
Frances Ind Pk KY1 18 B8
Frances View KY1 18 A8
Franchi Dr FK5 38 F5
Francis Ct KY12 28 D5
Francis St KY5 14 B7
FRANKERTON 36 A2
Frankfield Cres KY11 48 D4
Frankfield Pl KY11 48 C4
Frankfield Rd KY11 48 D4
Fraser Ave Edinburgh EH5 93 A5
Inverkeithing KY11 47 D2
Fraser Cres EH5 93 A5
Fraser Dr KY5 14 B7
Fraser Gdns EH5 93 A5
Fraser Gr EH5 93 A5
Fraser La EH26 171 B2
Fraser of Allander Ho FK9 2 D6
Fraser Pl Dysart KY1 18 A8
Grangemouth FK3 61 D6
Stirling FK9 2 B4
Fraser Rd EH54 142 F2
Frederick Cres KY11 29 B2
Frederick St EH2 228 C4
Frederick Wilson Pk KY2 17 A7
Freeland Ave EH52 115 B5
Freelands Rd EH28 117 E3
Freeland Terr EH52 115 B5
Freeport Village EH55 163 A4
Fremantle St EH54 144 A5
Freskyn Pl EH52 116 A6
Frew Ct KY11 29 C1
Frew Pl KY12 12 A1
Friar's Bank Terr EH42 78 D2
Friars Brae EH49 85 A6
Friar's Croft EH42 78 D2
Friars Loan EH49 85 A6
Friars St FK8 7 B8
Friars Way EH49 85 A5
Friarton Gdns EH26 191 C5
Friary Ct KY11 47 C2
Friendship Gdns FK2 39 C3
Frobisher Ave FK1 59 F4
Frogston Ave EH10 150 B5
Frogston Brae EH17 150 E4
Frogston Gdns EH10 150 C5
Frogston Gr EH10 150 C5
Frogston Road E EH17 150 F5
Frogston Road W EH10 150 C4
Frogston Terr EH10 150 C5
Fruitmarket Gall The★
EH3 229 A3
Fulfordlees Cotts TD13 218 D1
Fullerton Dr FK2 61 E3
Fulmar Brae EH54 143 C5
Fulmar Cres FK5 38 C5
Fulmar Dr KY11 30 A2
Fulmar Way KY11 48 B4
Furcheons Pk EH8 122 E8
Furnace Pl KY4 13 E6
Furniss Ave KY11 46 D5
Fyne La ML7 179 E6

G

Gaberston Ave FK10 10 C7
Gabriel's Rd EH2 229 A4
Gagarin Way KY4 13 E6
Gair Cres ML8 215 A3
Gairdoch Dr FK2 39 C3
Gairdoch St FK2 60 B8
Gairloch Cres FK2 61 C2
Gair Rd ML8 215 B5
Gair Wynd ML7 180 B3
Galabraes Cres EH48 141 C7
Galachlawshot EH10 150 C6
Galachlawside EH10 150 C5
Galadale EH22 174 A6
Galadale Cres EH22 174 A6
Galadale Dr EH22 174 A6
Gala Gn EH42 78 B2
Galbraith Cres FK5 38 C4
Gallacher Gn EH54 143 C8
Gallacher Pl KY4 13 E6
Gallamuir Dr FK7 20 D3
Gallamuir Rd FK7 20 D5
GALLATOWN 17 E8
Gallolee The EH13 149 D6
Galloway Cres EH52 115 C6
Galloway Ct FK1, FK2 60 B6
Galloways Entry EH8 229 C3
Galloway St FK1 60 B6
Gallowsknowe EH49 84 D7
Gallows Loan KY12 25 D2
Gallow View EH52 88 A8
Gallswood Gdns EH48 140 B5
Galmeilen EH52 115 C5
Galt Ave EH21 125 A5
Galt Cres EH21 125 A5
Galt Dr EH21 125 A6
Galt Rd EH21 125 B5
Galt Terr EH21 125 A5
Gambeson Cres FK7 7 D3
Gamekeeper's Loan EH4 91 B5
Gamekeeper's Pk EH4 91 B5
Gamekeeper's Rd EH4 91 B5
Gannel Hill View FK10 5 E4
Garbett Pl FK2 60 A7
Garbett Rd EH54 143 C1
Garden City EH47 162 A2
Garden Ct KY12 29 D7
Gardeners Ct KY12 29 B4
GARDENERS' LAND 29 B4
Gardeners' St KY12 29 B4
Gardener St EH42 78 C3
Gardenerswell Villas [3]
EH48 141 B7
Gardener's Wlk EH26 191 C6
Gardenhead FK2 61 F2
Garden Pl Cairneyhill KY12 27 C1
Clackmannan FK10 11 A4
Livingston EH54 143 C4
Townhill KY12 29 D7
Garden St FK1 60 C5
Gardens The
Aberlady EH32 71 D5
Dirleton EH39 53 B5
Garden Terr
Clackmannan FK10 11 A4
Edinburgh EH4 91 E4
Falkirk FK1 60 C5
Westquarter FK2 61 A2
Gardiner Cres EH32 97 B1
Gardiner Gr EH4 92 B2
Gardiner Pl
Cowdenbeath KY4 13 B2
Newtongrange EH22 174 B6
Gardiner Rd
Cowdenbeath KY4 13 C2
Edinburgh EH4 92 B2
Prestonpans EH32 97 A1
Gardiner's Cl EH32 97 C4
Gardiner's Pl EH33 126 C7
Gardiner St KY5 14 B7
Gardiner Terr
Edinburgh EH4 92 B2
Prestonpans EH32 126 A8
Gardner Cres EH47 160 F6
Gardner's Cres EH3 228 B2
Gardners La EH48 141 A6
Gardner Terr EH47 162 A1
Gardrum Gdns FK1 81 D7
Gardrum Pl FK2 82 F7
Gardrum Terr FK1 81 F5
Gareloch Way EH47 161 D7
Garleton Ct EH31 52 B2
Garleton Dr EH41 100 F1
GARLETON HILLS 101 A5
Garleton Pk EH32 71 C4
Garngrew Rd FK4 57 A3
Garrison Pl FK1 60 B5
Garry Pl Falkirk FK1 60 D2
Grangemouth FK3 61 E5
Garry St KY5 14 B8
Garry Way ML7 179 E6
Garry Wlk EH54 144 B4
Garscube Terr EH12 120 D8
Gartclush Gdns FK7 19 E8
Gartcows Ave FK1 60 A4
Gartcows Cres FK1 60 A3
Gartcows Dr FK1 60 A4
Gartcows Gdns [5] FK1 59 F4
Gartcows Pl FK1 60 A3
Gartcows Rd FK1 60 A3
Garten Dr ML7 180 B3
Garthill Gdns FK1 60 A4
Garthill La FK1 60 A4
Gartmorn Dam Ctry Pk★
FK10 11 B8
Gartmorn Rd FK10 5 D1
GARVALD 132 D2
Garvald La FK6 36 C1
Garvald Rd FK6 57 D7
Garvally Cres FK10 10 A8
Garvock Bank KY11 29 F4
GARVOCK HILL 29 C4
Garvock Hill KY12 29 D4
Garvock Terr KY12 29 D4
Gascoigne Ct [8] FK2 60 A8
Gasworks La
North Berwick EH39 53 F6
Whitburn EH47 161 B7
Gas Wynd KY1 17 B2
Gateside Ave
Bonnybridge FK4 58 C6
Haddington EH41 100 D1
Gateside Commerce Pk
EH41 129 D8
Gateside Ct KY4 13 A3
Gateside Ind Est KY4 13 A3
Gateside Rd
Haddington EH41 129 D8
Kirkliston EH29 89 A1
Stirling FK7 7 A3
Whitburn EH47 160 F6
Gateway Bsns Pk FK3 61 C5
Gauger's Bush EH42 76 B7
Gauze Ct EH51 64 A6
Gauze Pl EH51 64 A6
Gauze Rd EH51 64 A6
Gavald Grange Steading
EH41 132 D3
Gavin Pl EH54 143 B5
Gavins Lee EH33 126 C4
Gavins Rd FK10 4 F1
GAYFIELD 93 E3
Gayfield Cl [4] EH1 93 E2
Gayfield Pl [8] EH7 93 E2
Gayfield Place La EH1 93 E2
Gayfield Sq EH1 93 E2
Gayfield St EH1 93 E2
Gayfield Street La [6] EH1 93 D2
Gaynor Ave EH20 172 B8
Gean Rd FK10 9 F8
Geatons Rd KY5 14 C8
Geddes' Entry EH1 229 A3
Gelder Dr EH54 164 E6
Gellatly Rd KY11 29 D2
Gentle's Entry EH8 229 C3
George Ave EH20 172 B8
George Burn Wynd KY1 17 C3
George Cres
Loanhead EH20 172 C8
Ormiston EH35 155 D7
George Dr EH20 172 C8
George Grieve Way
EH33 126 D4
George Heriot's Sch EH3 228 C2
George IV Bridge EH1 229 A2
George Laing Ct FK5 38 E2
George Pl EH48 141 A6
George Sq EH8 229 A1
George Square La EH8 229 A1
George Square Theatre★
EH8 229 A1
George St Alva FK12 5 A6
Armadale EH48 139 F6
Bathgate EH48 141 A6
Bo'ness EH51 63 F6
Cowdenbeath KY4 13 B4
Dunfermline KY11 29 B2
Edinburgh EH2 228 B3
Falkirk FK2 60 B5
Grangemouth FK3 61 F8
Kincardine FK10 23 E3
Kirkcaldy KY1 17 B3
Laurieston FK2 60 F3
Ormiston EH35 155 E7
Stenhousemuir FK5 38 C3
George Terr EH20 172 B8
George Watson's Coll
EH10 120 F3
George Watson's Coll Lower
Prim Sch EH10 120 F3
George Watson's Coll Upper
Prim Sch EH10 120 F3
George Way [5] EH33 126 C6
George Wlk [4] EH33 126 C5
Georgian House★ EH2 228 B3
Gerald Terr FK5 38 E3
Gibbdun Pl FK5 57 E7
Gibb's Entry EH8 229 B2
Gibbshill Pl ML7 159 D5
Gib Gr KY11 29 E1
Gibraltar Ct EH22 153 B3
Gibraltar Gdns EH22 153 B3
Gibraltar Rd EH22 153 A3
Gibraltar Terr EH22 153 B3
Gibson Dr EH22 153 C4
Gibsongray St FK2 60 A7
Gibson St Denny FK6 36 E1
Edinburgh EH7 93 E4
Gibson Terr EH11 228 A1
Gideon Ct EH48 141 B7
Gideon St EH48 141 B7
GIFFORD 220 F6
Giffordgate EH41 130 B8
Gifford Pk EH8 229 B1
Gifford Rd EH41 130 C7
Gilberstoun EH15 123 D5
Gilberstoun Brig EH15 123 D5
Gilberstoun Loan EH15 123 D5
Gilberstoun Pl EH15 123 D6
Gilberstoun Wynd EH15 123 D5
Gilbert Ave EH39 54 C6
Gilburn Pl Bo'ness EH51 63 D6
Shotts ML7 179 F4
Gilchrist Cres EH47 161 B6
Gilchrist Dr FK1 59 E4
GILCHRISTON 220 A4
Giles St EH6 93 F5
Gilfillan Pl FK2 39 C2
Gilfillan Rd KY11 29 E4
Gillespie Cres EH10 228 B1
Gillespie Gr KY12 26 E7
Gillespie Pl
Armadale EH48 139 F4
Edinburgh EH11 228 B1
Stirling FK7 7 B1
Gillespie Rd EH13 148 F6
Gillespie St EH3 228 B1
Gillespie Terr FK7 20 D2
Gillie-burn Gdns ML7 179 E4
Gillie Ct KY11 29 C2
Gillies Dr FK7 7 C4
Gillies Hill FK7 6 D5
Gill Pk FK6 36 E2
Gillsland Rd EH10 120 F4
Gill Way KY11 46 C5
GILMERTON 151 F6
Gilmerton Dykes Ave
EH17 151 D5
Gilmerton Dykes Cres
EH17 151 C6
Gilmerton Dykes Dr
EH17 151 D5
Gilmerton Dykes Gdns
EH17 151 C6
Gilmerton Dykes Gr
EH17 151 C6
Gilmerton Dykes Loan
EH17 151 D5
Gilmerton Dykes Pl
EH17 151 C6
Gilmerton Dykes Rd
EH17 151 D5
Gilmerton Dykes St
EH17 151 D5
Gilmerton Dykes Terr
EH17 151 D5
Gilmerton Dykes View
EH17 151 D5
Gilmerton Pl EH17 151 D5
Gilmerton Prim Sch
EH17 151 D6
Gilmerton Rd
Bonnyrigg and Lasswade
EH18 152 C4
Dalkeith EH22 152 E3
Edinburgh EH17 151 D7
Gilmerton Road Rdbt
EH22 152 D3
Gilmerton Station Rd
EH17 151 E4
Gilmore Pk EH11 228 A1
Gilmore Place La EH3 228 B1
Gilmour Rd EH16 121 F3
Gilmour St
Cowdenbeath KY4 13 D6
Edinburgh EH8 229 B2
Gilsay Ct FK1 60 C2
Gilston Cres FK2 62 A1
Gipsy La KY11 29 F3
Gladney Sq KY1 17 B2
GLADSMUIR 128 B7
Gladsmuir ML11 201 A1
Gladsmuir Junc EH33 128 A7
Gladstone Pl
Dunfermline KY12 29 A5
Edinburgh EH6 94 B4
Stirling FK8 7 A6
Gladstone Rd FK5 38 D3
Gladstone's Gait EH19 173 D7
Gladstone Terr EH9 121 E5
Glaive Ave FK7 7 D3
Glamaig Way KY11 30 B1
Glamis Gdns
Dalgety Bay KY11 48 B3
Polmont FK2 61 F1
Glamis Pl KY11 48 B3
Glamis Rd KY2 16 D7
Glamis Terr KY3 34 F3
Glanville Pl [7] EH3 93 B2
Glasclune Ct EH39 54 D7
Glasclune Gdns EH39 54 D7
Glasgow Rd
Bathgate EH48 140 F6
Denny FK6 36 E1
Edinburgh EH12 119 B6
Falkirk FK1 59 C6
Gogar EH12 118 C5
Longcroft FK4 57 C4
Stirling FK7 7 B2
Glaskhill Terr EH26 191 E6
Glass Cres EH52 87 F2
Glassel Park Rd EH32 98 D4
Glasshouse Loan FK10 10 A6
Glass Pl EH52 87 F2
Glass Rd EH52 87 F1
Glasswork St KY1 17 B3
Glebe Ave Stirling FK8 7 A7
Uphall EH52 115 A4
Glebe Cres Alva FK12 5 B7
Athelstaneford EH39 101 F7
Stirling FK8 7 A7
Glebe Ct EH47 181 D6
Glebe Gdns
Edinburgh EH12 119 E6
[3] Prestonpans EH32 96 F1
Glebe Gr EH12 119 D6
Glebe Pk Inverkeithing KY11 47 B1
Kirkcaldy KY1 17 C5
Glebe Pl
Bonnyrigg and Lasswade
EH18 151 F1
Burntisland KY3 33 E1
Kinghorn KY3 34 F3
Uphall EH52 115 A4
Glebe Rd Bathgate EH48 141 C6
Edinburgh EH12 119 D6
Kincardine FK10 23 E5
Uphall EH52 115 A4
West Calder EH55 163 D2
Glebe Rd *continued*
Whitburn EH47 161 A6
Glebe St Dalkeith EH22 153 A3
Denny FK6 36 E2
Falkirk FK1 60 B5
Glebe Terr Alloa FK10 10 A6
Edinburgh EH12 119 D6
Haddington EH41 101 A1
Inverkeithing KY11 47 B1
Uphall EH52 115 A5
Glebe The Aberdour KY3 49 C8
Alva FK12 5 B7
Clackmannan FK10 11 A4
Dalmeny EH30 89 E7
East Linton EH40 103 E8
East Saltoun EH34 157 F4
Edinburgh EH4 91 B6
Kirkliston EH29 89 A1
Linlithgow EH49 85 A5
North Berwick EH39 53 A5
Pencaitland EH34 156 F7
West Calder EH55 163 D2
Gledhill Ave EH51 64 D5
Glenafeoch Rd ML8 215 A1
Glen Albyn Dr KY2 16 B8
Glenallan Dr EH16 122 B2
Glenallan Loan EH16 122 B2
Glenalmond EH47 161 C5
Glenalmond Ct
Broxburn EH52 115 B5
Whitburn EH47 161 C5
Glenalmond Terr EH48 141 B8
Glenard View EH51 64 D6
Glen Artney Gr KY11 29 D1
Glenavon Dr KY12 27 C1
Glen Avon Pl FK2 82 F7
Glenavon Terr EH48 141 B8
Glenbank FK1 60 B1
Glenbare Ct EH48 141 C6
Glen Beasdale Ct KY11 29 D1
Glenbervie FK5 38 A4
Glenbervie Ave FK5 38 A3
Glenbervie Bsns Pk FK5 38 A4
Glenbervie Cres FK5 38 B3
Glenbervie Dr FK5 38 A3
Glenbervie Gr KY11 29 D1
Glenbervie Rd FK3 61 F6
Glenbo Dr FK6 57 E7
Glen Brae FK1 60 A3
Glenbrae Ct FK1 60 B3
Glen Bridge KY12 28 F4
Glenbridge Ct KY12 28 F4
Glenbrook EH14 167 E8
Glenbrook Rd EH14 147 A1
Glen Bruar Pl KY2 16 B8
Glenburn Gdns EH47 161 D6
Glenburn Gr KY12 26 E7
Glenburn Rd Falkirk FK1 60 D1
North Berwick EH39 54 D6
Glenburn Way EH51 63 D5
Glencairn Cres EH12 120 F7
Glencairn St Falkirk FK1 59 B5
Stirling FK7 7 B3
Glencairn Terr EH48 141 C8
Glen Clova Cres KY12 27 C1
Glencoe EH47 161 D6
Glencoe Path EH32 97 A2
Glencoe Rd Carluke ML8 215 A1
Stirling FK8 2 A1
Glencorse Pk EH26 192 C8
Glencorse Prim Sch
EH26 171 B1
Glencoul Ave KY11 48 A3
Glen Cres Falkirk FK1 60 B1
Livingston EH54 142 E6
Glencross Gdns EH26 191 C5
Glen Ct EH54 142 D6
Glendevon Ave EH12 120 B6
Glendevon Cotts EH52 87 D2
Glendevon Ct EH52 87 F2
Glendevon Dr Falkirk FK2 82 F7
Stirling FK8 1 F2
Glendevon Gdns EH12 120 B6
Glendevon Gr EH12 120 B6
Glendevon Pk
Edinburgh EH12 120 B6
Winchburgh EH52 87 E2
Glendevon Pl EH12 120 B6
Glendevon Rd EH12 120 B5
Glendevon Terr EH12 120 B6
Glendinning Cres EH16 151 B8
Glendinning Dr EH29 88 F2
Glendinning Pl EH29 88 F2
Glendinning Rd EH29 88 F2
Glendinning Way EH29 89 A2
Gleneagles Ct EH47 161 C5
Gleneagles Way EH54 142 E5
Glenesk Cres EH22 152 F2
Glenfarg Cres KY4 13 D5
Glenfield Carnock KY12 27 C6
Livingston EH54 143 A3
Glenfield Ave KY4 13 C6
Glenfield Cres KY4 13 C5
Glenfield Ct KY4 13 C5
Glenfield Gdns KY4 13 C5
Glenfield Ind Est KY4 13 C6
Glenfield Rd KY4 13 C5
Glenfinlas St EH3 228 B3
Glen Fruin Gr KY11 29 D1
Glenfuir Ct FK1 59 D4
Glenfuir Rd FK1 59 E5
Glenfuir St FK1 59 C5
Glengairn Wlk KY11 29 D1
Glengarry Cres FK1 59 F2
Glengarry Terr EH32 97 A2

Glen Gdns FK1 60 A3
Glengyle Terr EH3 228 C1
Glenisla Ct EH47 161 D5
Glenisla Gardens La EH9 121 D3
Glenisla Gdns EH9 121 D3
Glenisla Gr KY11 29 D1
Glen Isla Rd KY2 16 C8
Glen Kinchie FK10 4 A2
Glenkinchie Distillery★ EH34 156 E2
Glenkinchie Hos EH34 156 E2
Glenlee Ave EH8 122 C8
Glenlee Gdns EH8 122 C8
Glenlockhart Bank EH14 120 D1
Glenlockhart Rd EH11 120 E1
Glenlockhart Valley EH14 120 D2
Glen Lyon Ct FK2 62 A2
GLENMAVIS 141 D7
Glenmavis Cres ML8 215 A1
Glenmavis Ct ML8 215 A1
Glenmavis Dr EH48 141 B7
Glenmore EH47 161 C6
Glenmore Dr FK4 57 F6
Glen More Gdns KY2 16 B8
Glen Moriston Dr KY12 27 C1
Glen Nevis Dr KY11 29 D1
Glennie Gdns EH33 126 D6
Glenochil Pk FK10 4 E4
Glenochil Rd FK1 60 A3
Glenochil Terr FK10 4 E4
Glenogle Ct EH3 93 B2
Glen Ogle Ct FK2 62 A2
Glenogle Ho 3 EH3 93 B2
Glenogle Pl 4 EH3 93 B2
Glenogle Rd EH3 93 B2
Glenogle Swim Ctr EH3 93 B2
Glenogle Terr EH3 93 B2
Glenorchy Rd EH39 54 B6
Glenorchy Terr EH9 121 F4
Glenpeffer Ave EH32 71 D4
Glen Pl EH26 191 E6
Glen Rd Armadale EH48 139 F6
Livingston EH54 142 E6
Plean FK5, FK7 37 D8
Shotts ML7 179 F4
Torwood FK5 37 D7
GLENSBURGH 40 A1
Glensburgh Rd FK3 61 A8
Glenshee EH47 161 C5
Glenshiel Gr KY11 29 D1
Glenside Ct
Armadale EH48 139 E6
Grangemouth FK3 61 E6
Glenside Gdns EH48 139 E6
Glen St EH3 228 C1
Glen Terr Denny FK6 36 D1
Livingston EH54 142 E6
Glen The Bathgate EH48 141 B8
Tullibody FK10 4 C3
Glentye Dr FK10 4 D4
Glentye Gdns FK1 59 E2
Glen Tye Rd FK7 7 D5
Glenure Loan EH4 91 D1
Glenvarloch Cres 1 EH16 151 B8
Glenview Frankerton FK6 36 A3
Menstrie FK11 4 A6
Penicuik EH26 191 E6
Glen View Bo'ness EH51 63 D4
Bonnybridge FK4 57 D5
Glenview Cres EH47 162 B2
Glen View Cres EH23 195 C8
Glen View Ct EH23 195 C8
Glenview Dr FK1 59 F2
Glen View Pl EH23 195 C7
Glenview Rd EH47 162 B1
Glen View Rd EH23 174 C1
Glen View Wlk EH23 195 D7
GLEN VILLAGE 60 B1
Glen Way 1 EH48 141 B7
Glenwinnel Rd FK12 4 E7
Glenwood Dr EH48 139 D6
Glenyards Rd FK4 57 F2
Gloag Pl EH55 163 D3
Globe Pk EH52 115 C5
Globe Rd KY11 46 D2
Glomach Gr KY12 28 E5
Gloucester La EH3 228 B4
Gloucester Pl EH3 228 B4
Gloucester Sq EH3 228 B4
Gloucester St EH3 228 B4
Glover's Ct KY3 35 A3
Glowrorum Dr FK6 57 E7
Glynwed Ct FK2 60 C7
Godfrey Ave FK6 36 D1
Godfrey Cres FK5 38 C1
Goff Ave EH7 94 F1
GOGAR 118 D5
Gogarbank Farm EH12 118 C2
Gogar Bridge Rd EH12 118 A7
Gogar Loan FK9 3 D5
Gogarloch Bank EH12 119 B5
Gogarloch Haugh EH12 119 B5
Gogarloch Muir EH12 119 B5
Gogarloch Rd EH12 119 B5
Gogarloch Syke EH12 119 A5
Gogar Mains Farm Cotts EH12 118 C7
Gogar Pl FK7 7 C2
Gogar Rbdt HE12 118 E5
Gogar Sta Rd EH14 119 A2
Gogar Station Rd EH12 118 E3
Gogarstone Rd EH12, EH28 118 B5
GOLDENACRE 93 B4
Goldenacre Terr EH3 93 B4
Goldenstones Ave EH42 78 E1
Goldpark Pl EH54 143 A3
Golf Course Rd
Bonnyrigg and Lasswade EH19 173 B8
Cowdenbeath KY4 13 C6
Linlithgow EH49 84 E5
Livingston EH54 143 B8
Golf Ct EH32 71 C4
Golf Dr EH32 97 E4
Golfdrum St KY12 28 E4
Golf House Rd EH42 78 F1
Gollet Way KY12 43 F8
Goodall Cres EH52 114 B2
Goodall Pl EH52 114 B2
Goodman Pl FK2 82 E7
Goodtrees Gdns EH17 151 D8
Goodtrees Terr EH17 151 D8
Goosecroft Rd FK8 7 B8
Goosedubs Pl FK2 59 F8
Goose Gn Ct EH21 124 D7
Goose Green Ave EH21 124 D7
Goose Green Cres EH21 124 D7
Goose Green Pl EH21 124 D7
Goose Green Rd
Gullane EH31 52 A2
Musselburgh EH21 124 D7
Gordon Ave
Bathgate EH48 141 B5
Bonnyrigg and Lasswade EH19 172 F6
Gordon Cres FK9 2 A8
Gordon Ct Broxburn EH52 115 F5
Edinburgh EH6 94 A4
Gordon Dr FK10 10 C7
Gordon Loan EH12 119 E7
Gordon Pl FK1 59 E5
Gordon Rd
Edinburgh EH12 119 E7
Rosyth KY11 46 B2
Gordon St
Cowdenbeath KY4 13 D6
Easthouses EH22 174 C7
Edinburgh EH6 94 A4
Lochgelly KY5 14 A8
Gordon Terr
Dunfermline KY11 29 B1
Edinburgh EH16 122 A2
Gordon Way EH54 143 D7
Gore Ave EH23 195 D8
GOREBRIDGE 195 B8
Gorebridge L Ctr EH23 174 C1
Gorebridge Prim Sch EH23 174 C1
Goremire Rd ML8 215 C1
GORGIE 120 D5
Gorgie Mills Sch EH11 120 D5
Gorgie Park Cl EH14 120 D4
Gorgie Park Rd EH14 120 D4
Gorgie Pk Cl EH14 120 D4
Gorgie Rd EH14 120 C4
Gorrie St Denny FK6 36 D2
Dunfermline KY11 29 C2
Gorsebank EH54 143 F5
Gorton Loan EH24 172 D2
Gorton Pl EH24 172 D2
Gorton Rd EH24 172 D2
Gort Pl FK3 61 C5
Goschen Pl EH52 115 B5
Goschen Terr EH52 115 B5
Gosford House★ EH32 71 A2
Gosford Pl EH6 93 D5
Gosford Rd
Cockenzie & Port Seton EH32 97 C4
Kirkcaldy KY2 16 C7
Longniddry EH32 98 E6
Gosford Wlk EH32 97 C4
Goshen Pl FK5 38 E2
Gote La EH30 68 B1
Goulden Pl KY12 28 D6
Gourlaybank EH41 101 A1
Gourlay St KY2 17 A4
Gowan Ave FK2 60 B6
Gowanbank EH54 143 D5
Gowanbrae EH47 181 E5
Gowanbrae Dr KY12 29 D4
Gowanbrae Pl KY12 29 D4
Gowanbrae Terr KY12 29 D4
Gowanhill Farm Rd EH14 147 C5
Gowanhill Gdns FK8 1 F1
Gowan La FK2 60 B6
Gowanlea Dr FK1 108 B6
Gow Cres KY1 17 B4
GOWKHALL 27 F7
GOWKSHILL 174 B3
Gowl Cl 7 EH41 130 B8
Gracefield Ct EH21 124 B6
GRACEMOUNT 151 B5
Gracemount Ave EH16 151 B7
Gracemount Bsns Pav EH16 151 C5
Gracemount Dr EH16 151 B6
Gracemount High Sch EH16 151 C6
Gracemount House Dr EH16 151 B6
Gracemount L Ctr EH16 151 B5
Gracemount Pl EH16 151 B6
Gracemount Prim Sch EH16 151 B6
Gracemount Rd EH16 151 A5
Gracemount Sq EH16 151 B6
Grace St KY5 14 C8
Gracie Cres FK7 8 D4
Gracie's Wynd EH48 140 B5
Gradlon Pl FK1 60 B3
Graeme High Sch FK1 60 E4
Graeme Pl FK1 59 E1
Graham Ave Larbert FK5 38 B3
Stirling FK9 2 C4
Graham Cres EH51 64 B7
Graham Ct EH47 162 E8
Grahamsdyke Ave EH51 64 B7
Grahamsdyke Cres FK4 58 A3
Grahamsdyke La EH51 64 B7
Grahamsdyke Pl EH51 64 B6
Grahamsdyke Rd
Bo'ness EH51 64 C6
Bonnybridge FK4 58 A4
Grahamsdyke St FK2 60 F4
Grahamsdyke Terr EH51 64 B7
Grahams Rd FK1 60 B6
Graham's Rd EH26 171 B1
Grahams Road Rdbt FK1 60 B5
Graham St
Bridge of Allan FK9 2 B7
Edinburgh EH6 93 E5
GRAHAMSTON 60 A6
Graham Terr FK2 22 D4
Graham Way EH54 143 D8
Grainger St KY5 14 B8
Grampian Cres FK3 61 E5
Grampian Ct KY11 46 E2
Grampian Gdns KY2 16 F5
Grampian Pl KY11 46 E1
Grampian Rd Rosyth KY11 46 E2
Stirling FK7 6 E6
Grampion Ct EH54 143 E1
Granary Rd FK2 60 A8
Granary Sq FK2 60 B7
Granary The EH42 78 E3
Granby Ave EH54 143 F4
Granby Rd EH16 121 F3
Grandfield EH6 93 C5
Grandville EH6 93 C6
Grange Ave FK2 60 D6
Grangeburn Rd FK3 40 E1
Grange Cotts KY2 34 F5
Grange Cres EH9 121 D4
Grange Crescent E EH32 96 F1
Grange Crescent W EH32 125 F8
Grange Ct
5 Edinburgh EH9 121 E5
North Berwick EH39 54 C6
Grange Dr
Dunfermline KY11 46 C8
Falkirk FK2 60 D6
Grange Gdns FK9 2 C7
Grange Gr EH32 96 F1
Grange Knowe EH49 85 D8
Grange La FK3 40 C1
Grangelea Ct FK3 61 E8
Grange Loan Bo'ness EH51 64 B7
Edinburgh EH9 121 D4
Grange Loan Gdns EH9 121 D4
GRANGEMOUTH 61 B7
Grangemouth Ent Ctr FK3 61 A7
Grangemouth High Sch FK3 61 E5
Grangemouth Mus★ FK3 40 D1
Grangemouth Rd
Bo'ness EH51 63 B6
Falkirk FK2 60 E5
Grangemouth EH51 62 D5
GRANGEPANS 64 A7
Grangepans EH51 64 B8
Grangepans Ind Est EH51 64 B8
Grange Pk KY11 29 C1
Grange Pl
Grangemouth FK3 61 D8
Redding FK2 61 C1
Grange Prim Sch EH51 64 B7
Grange Rd Alloa FK10 9 F6
Bridge of Allan FK9 2 C6
Broxburn EH52 115 F4
Burntisland KY3 33 D1
Dunfermline KY11 46 C6
Edinburgh EH9 121 D5
Livingston EH54 144 A7
North Berwick EH39 54 B6
Polmont FK3 61 F4
Prestonpans EH32 96 F1
Grange Terr Bo'ness EH51 64 B7
Edinburgh EH9 121 D3
Grange The FK2 82 E8
Grange View
Linlithgow EH49 85 C8
Stenhousemuir FK5 38 E1
Grange Wynd KY11 46 C8
Grannies Park Ind Est EH22 153 A4
Grannus Mews EH21 124 D5
Grant Ave EH13 149 A6
GRANTON 92 E7
Granton Cres EH5 92 F6
Granton Gdns EH5 92 F6
Granton Gr EH5 92 F6
Granton Harbour★ EH5 92 F8
Granton Mains Ave EH4 92 C6
Granton Mains Bank EH4 92 C6
Granton Mains Brae EH4 92 D6
Granton Mains Ct EH4 92 C6
Granton Mains E EH4 92 D6
Granton Mains Gait EH4 92 C6
Granton Mains Vale EH4 92 C6
Granton Mains Wynd EH4 92 C6
Granton Medway EH5 92 E6
Granton Mill Cres EH4 92 C6
Granton Mill Dr EH4 92 C6
Granton Mill March EH4 92 B5
Granton Mill Pk EH4 92 B5
Granton Mill Pl EH4 92 C6
Granton Mill Rd EH4 92 B5
Granton Mill W EH4 92 B5
Granton Park Ave EH5 92 E7
Granton Pl EH5 92 F6
Granton Prim Sch EH5 92 F6
Granton Rd EH5 93 A6
Granton Sq EH5 92 F7
Granton Terr EH5 92 F6
Granton View
Dalgety Bay KY11 47 F2
Edinburgh EH5 92 F6
Grant Pl FK9 2 B4
Grant Rd EH32 97 A2
Grants Bank KY12 29 A4
Grant St Alloa FK10 9 F6
West Calder EH55 163 D3
Grantully Pl EH9 121 F4
Granville Terr EH10 121 A5
Granville Way KY11 46 E3
Grassmarket EH1 228 C2
Gray Buchanan Ct FK2 61 D2
Gray Pk KY4 13 C6
Gray Pl KY11 47 C3
Gray's Ct EH8 229 B2
Graysknowe 4 EH14 120 B2
Gray's Loan EH10 120 F4
Gray St ML7 180 A4
Graystale Rd FK7 7 A3
Graystonelee Rd ML7 179 D6
Great Cannon Bank EH15 95 A1
Great Carleton Pl EH16 123 A3
Great Carleton Sq EH16 123 A3
Great Junction St EH6 93 F5
Great King St EH3 93 C2
Great Michael Cl EH6 93 C7
Great Michael Rd KY11 46 B1
Great Michael Rise EH6 93 D6
Great Michael Sq EH6 93 D7
Great Stuart St EH3 228 A3
Grebe Gdns KY11 30 A1
Greenacre EH14 148 E7
Greenacre Ct FK7 7 E1
Greenacre Dr FK4 58 A3
Greenacre Pl
Bannockburn FK7 7 E1
Bonnybridge FK4 58 A3
Greenacre Rd FK4 58 A3
Greenacres KY12 12 B1
Green Apron Pk EH39 54 B6
GREENBANK Edinburgh 149 F8
Falkirk 59 C3
Greenbank Ave EH10 121 A1
Greenbank Cres EH10 150 A8
Greenbank Ct FK1 59 D4
Greenbank Dr
Cowdenbeath KY4 13 A2
Edinburgh EH10 120 F1
Greenbank Gdns EH10 149 F8
Greenbank Gr EH10 149 F8
Greenbank La EH10 120 F1
Greenbank Loan EH10 120 F1
Greenbank Pk EH10 149 F8
Greenbank Pl
Edinburgh EH10 121 A1
Falkirk FK1 59 D4
Greenbank Rd
Edinburgh EH10 120 F1
Falkirk, Greenbank FK1 59 D3
Falkirk, Summerford FK2 59 D4
Greenbank Rise EH10 149 F8
Greenbank Row EH10 149 F8
Greenbank Terr EH10 121 A1
GREENBURN 181 F6
Greenburn Rd EH47 181 E5
Greencornhills Rdbt FK7 19 F8
Greencraig Ave FK1 61 B4
Greendale Pk EH4 92 A4
GREENDYKES 122 F3
Greendykes Ave EH16 122 F3
Greendykes Cotts EH33 127 C8
Greendykes Dr EH16 122 F3
Greendykes Gdns EH16 122 F3
Greendykes Ho EH16 122 F3
Greendykes Ind Est EH52 115 D6
Greendykes Loan EH16 122 F3
Greendykes Rd
Broxburn EH52 115 E6
Edinburgh EH16 122 F2
Tranent EH33 127 D6
Greendykes Steadings EH52 115 E7
Greendykes Terr EH16 122 F3
Greenend Dr EH17 151 C8
Greenend Gdns EH17 151 C7
Greenend Gr EH17 151 C8
Greenfield Cres EH14 168 C8
Greenfield Pk EH21 124 B3
Greenfield Rd EH14 168 C8
Greenfield St Alloa FK10 10 B7
Bonnybridge FK4 58 B6
Greenhall Rd EH23 174 C1
Greenhead FK12 5 B6
Greenheads Rd EH39 54 E6
GREENHILL 58 A2
Greenhill Ct
Edinburgh EH10 121 B5
Fauldhouse EH47 181 E6
Greenhill Gdns EH10 121 B4
Greenhill Pk
Edinburgh EH10 121 B4
Penicuik EH26 191 D5
Greenhill Pl EH10 121 B4
Greenhill Rd
Blackridge EH48 138 E3
Bonnybridge FK4 58 A3
Greenhill Terr EH10 121 B5
Greenhithe Terr FK2 82 E7
Greenhorn's Well Ave 3 FK1 59 F3
Greenhorn's Well Cres 1 FK1 59 F3
Greenhorn's Well Dr 2 FK1 59 F3
Green La
Bonnyrigg and Lasswade EH18 172 F8
Grangemouth FK3 61 E8
Greenlaw Gr EH26 171 A1
Greenlaw Hedge EH13 149 E8
GREENLAW MAINS 192 A8
Greenlaw Rig EH13 149 E8
Greenloanings KY2 16 D8
Greenmantle Loan 2 EH16 122 B1
Greenmount KY4 13 A2
Greenmount Dr
Burntisland KY3 33 F1
Shieldhill FK1 81 C6
Greenmount Road N KY3 33 F2
Greenmount Road S KY3 34 A1
Greenpark EH17 151 C8
Greenpark Dr FK2 61 E2
Greenrigg Cotts ML7 159 F5
Greenrigg Prim Sch ML7 159 F6
Greenshank Dr KY11 30 A2
GREENSIDE 229 B4
Greenside EH48 111 F6
Greenside La EH1 229 B4
Greenside Pl
Edinburgh EH1 229 B4
Rosewell EH24 172 D2
Greenside Row EH1 229 B4
Greenside St FK10 10 B6
Green St Edinburgh EH7 93 D2
Townhill KY12 29 C8
Greens The FK2 82 E6
Green The Alva FK12 5 A7
Balerno EH14 168 D8
Bathgate EH48 141 C7
Edinburgh EH4 91 F4
Loanhead EH20 151 C1
Pencaitland EH34 156 F6
West Barns EH42 77 F1
Green Tree La EH51 63 D5
Greenvale Dr FK2 82 E8
Greenwells Dr FK2 82 F8
Greenwell St EH47 181 F6
Greenwell Terr FK2 82 E7
Greenwood Ave FK8 7 A8
Greenwood Pk EH54 143 D6
Greenwood St ML7 179 E5
Gregory Rd EH54 164 B8
Greig Cres EH48 140 A5
Greig Ct KY11 47 B2
Greig Pl KY5 14 A7
Greig Rd KY11 46 B2
Grendon Ct FK8 7 A6
Grendon Gdns FK8 7 A6
Grenville Ct FK1 59 F4
Grey Craigs KY12 27 D2
Greyfriars EH1 229 A2
Greyfriars Bobby Meml★ EH1 229 A2
Greyfriar's Wlk KY11 47 C3
Greygoran FK10 5 C2
Grey School Cnr EH32 96 F1
Grierson Ave EH5 93 A6
Grierson Cres
Cambusbarron FK7 6 D6
Edinburgh EH5 93 A6
Grierson Gdns EH5 93 A6
Grierson Rd EH5 92 F6
Grierson Sq EH5 93 A6
Grierson Villas EH5 93 A6
Grieve Ct EH26 191 F8
Grieve St Dunfermline KY12 28 E4
Kirkcaldy KY2 17 A6
Griffith Dr EH47 161 A6
Griffiths St FK1 60 B4
Grigor Ave EH4 92 D3
Grigor Dr EH4 92 D3
Grigor Gdns EH4 92 E3
Grigor Terr EH4 92 D3
Grindlay St EH3 228 B2
Grindlay Street Ct EH3 228 B2
Groathill Ave EH4 92 C2
Groathill Gardens E 2 EH4 92 C2
Groathill Gardens W 1 EH4 92 C2
Groathill Loan EH4 92 C3
Groathill Road N EH4 92 C3
Groathill Road S EH4 92 C2
Grodwell Dr FK12 4 E7
Grosvenor Cres EH12 120 F7
Grosvenor Gdns EH12 120 F7
Grosvenor St EH12 228 A2
Grove Cres FK2 39 A2
Grove End EH18 173 B8
Grove St Denny FK6 36 C2
Edinburgh EH3 228 A2
Musselburgh EH21 124 D5
Grove Terr EH3 228 A2
Grove The EH21 124 E5
Grundie's Well Rd EH17 151 E6
Guardians Wood EH12 120 C7
Guardwell Cres EH17 151 C7
Guardwell Glen EH17 151 D7
Guildhall St KY12 29 A3
GUILDIEHAUGH 141 C4
Guildiehaugh Rdbt EH48 141 D5
Guildie Howes Rd EH23 195 F2
Guildry Gr KY12 29 E4
Guildry The EH49 65 E5

GULLANE 52 A1
GULLANE HILL 51 E2
Gullane Prim Sch EH31 52 B2
Gullan's Cl EH1 229 B3
Gunner Rd FK3, EH51 62 C8
Gunn Rd FK3 61 C5
Guthrie Cres FK5 38 B2
Guthrie St EH1 229 A2
Guttergates Rd KY11 30 B5
Gyle Ave EH12 118 F5
Gylemuir Prim Sch EH12 119 C5
Gylemuir Rd EH12 119 C6
Gyle Park Gdns EH12 119 A6
Gyle Rbdt EH12 118 F5
Gylers Rd EH39 53 A4
Gyle Sh Ctr EH12 119 A5

H

HADDINGTON 130 D7
Haddington Inf Sch EH41 130 A8
Haddington Pl
Aberlady EH32 71 D4
Edinburgh EH7 93 E2
Haddington Rd
East Linton EH40 103 D7
Musselburgh EH21 125 B6
North Berwick EH39 54 C5
Tranent EH33 126 E6
Haddington Station Ind Est EH41 129 F8
Haddon's Ct EH8 229 B2
Haddow Gr KY3 50 D8
Hadfast Rd EH22 154 D5
Hadrian Way EH51 64 B6
HAGGS 57 A3
Haig Ave Kirkcaldy KY1 17 D7
Stirling FK8 2 A2
Haig Cres Bathgate EH48 141 C5
Dunfermline KY12 29 C5
Haig Homes EH11 120 A4
Haig St FK3 61 C6
Hailes App EH13 149 A7
Hailes Ave EH13 149 A7
Hailes Bank EH13 149 A7
Hailes Castle* EH41 103 A4
Hailes Cres EH13 149 A7
Hailes Gdns EH13 149 A7
Hailes Gr EH13 149 A7
Hailesland Gdns EH14 119 E1
Hailesland Gr EH14 119 E1
Hailesland Pk EH14 119 F1
Hailesland Pl EH14 119 E1
Hailesland Rd EH14 119 E1
Hailes Loan HE41 103 B4
Hailes Pk EH13 148 F7
Hailes Pl Dunfermline KY12 29 D4
2 Inverkeithing/Dunfermline KY11 29 C3
Hailes St EH3 228 B1
Hailes Terr EH13 149 A7
Hailstonegreen ML11 201 A1
Hailstones Cres EH48 139 F6
Hainburn Pk EH10 149 F5
Haining Gr FK2 83 B5
Haining Pl
Grangemouth FK3 61 F8
Livingston EH54 143 B5
Haining Rd EH49 83 F6
Haining Terr EH49 83 F6
Haining Valley Steadings EH49 83 E6
HALBEATH 30 A5
Halbeath Dr KY11 29 F5
Halbeath Intc Bsns Pk KY11 30 B6
Halbeath Pl KY11 29 E5
Halbeath Rd
Dunfermline KY11 29 D5
Halbeath KY11 30 A5
Halbeath Ret Pk KY11 30 A6
Halberts Cres FK7 7 B2
Haldane Ave
Bridge of Allan FK9 2 A6
Haddington EH41 100 E1
Haldane Gr KY12 26 D7
Haldane Sq EH54 164 C5
Halket Cres FK2 39 C2
Halkettshall KY11 45 C4
Halkett Cres KY11 29 D2
Hallam Rd FK5 38 D2
Hallcraigs EH27 145 E3
Hall Cres EH31 52 A2
Hallcroft Cl EH28 117 C2
Hallcroft Cres EH28 117 C2
Hallcroft Gdns EH28 117 C2
Hallcroft Gn EH28 117 C2
Hallcroft Neuk EH28 117 C2
Hallcroft Pk EH28 117 C2
Hallcroft Rise EH28 117 C2
Halley's Ct KY1 17 B2
HALLGLEN 60 D1
Hallglen Prim Sch FK1 60 B1
Hallglen Rd FK1 60 B1
Hallglen Sh Ctr FK1 60 C1
Hallglen Terr FK1 60 B1
Hallhead Rd EH16 122 A2
Hallhill EH42 106 C8
Halliburton Terr EH39 53 A4
Hallows The KY1 17 F8
Hallpark FK10 10 C8
Hall Rd EH52 115 E5
Hall Row KY11 45 B4
Hall St Cowdenbeath KY4 13 C4
Lochgelly KY5 14 B8
Hall Terr EH48 111 F5
Hallyards Cotts EH29 117 B8
Hallyards Rd
Newbridge EH29 117 B8
Ratho Station EH28 117 D6
Halmyre St EH6 93 F4
Halyard Rise KY11 47 F2
Halyard Terr KY2 15 B2
Hamburgh Pl EH6 93 E6
Hamilton Ave
Linlithgow EH49 84 E6
Stenhousemuir FK5 38 E4
Hamilton Cres
Grangemouth FK2 82 E6
Gullane EH31 52 A2
Newtongrange EH22 174 B6
Hamilton Ct EH39 54 A7
Hamilton Dr
Edinburgh EH15 122 F8
Falkirk FK1 60 A4
Stirling FK9 2 C4
Hamilton Drive W EH15 122 F7
Hamilton Gdns
Armadale EH48 139 F4
Edinburgh EH15 122 F7
Hamilton Gr EH15 122 F7
Hamilton La
Bathgate EH48 140 E7
Bo'ness EH51 63 F8
Hamilton Pk
Edinburgh EH15 122 F8
Linlithgow EH49 84 F6
Hamilton Pl Edinburgh EH3 93 B2
Linlithgow EH49 84 E6
Rosyth KY11 46 E4
Hamilton Rd
Bathgate EH48 140 F7
Grangemouth FK3 61 E6
Gullane EH31 52 B2
North Berwick EH39 54 A7
Stenhousemuir FK5 38 D6
Hamiltons Cl EH30 68 C1
Hamilton's Folly Mews EH8 229 B1
Hamilton Sq Bo'ness EH51 63 D5
Livingston EH54 164 F7
Hamilton St Falkirk FK1 59 D6
Lochgelly KY5 14 B6
Hamilton Terr
Edinburgh EH15 123 A7
High Valleyfield KY12 26 B2
Inverkeithing KY11 47 C2
Hamilton Way EH47 161 E6
Hamilton Wynd EH6 93 E6
Hammermen's Entry EH8 229 B3
Hampton Pl 5 EH12 120 E7
Hampton Terr 4 EH12 120 E7
Handax ML11 201 A1
Haney's Way EH51 64 B8
Hanlon Gdns FK2 82 E7
Hannah Pk (Shotts Bon Accord FC) ML7 179 D6
Hanover Cl 4 EH48 141 A7
Hanover Ct
Broxburn EH52 115 E5
Livingston EH54 143 B2
Stirling FK9 2 D4
Hanover Grange FK3 61 D8
Hanover Ho EH54 143 B2
Hanover St EH2 228 C4
Happy Valley Rd EH47 162 E7
Harbour Ct EH42 78 D3
Harbour Dr KY11 47 F3
Harbour La EH30 68 B1
Harbour Pl Burntisland KY3 50 E8
Dalgety Bay KY11 47 F2
Edinburgh EH15 95 A1
Inverkeithing KY11 47 C2
Harbour Rd Bo'ness EH51 64 C7
Kinghorn KY3 35 A2
Musselburgh EH21 124 A6
Harbour View EH21 124 B6
Harbour Way KY11 48 A4
HARBURN 185 C8
Harburn EH55 185 C8
Harburn Ave EH54 142 F6
Harburn Avenue W EH54 142 F6
Harburn Dr EH55 163 E3
Harburn La EH55 163 E3
Harburn Rd EH55 163 E3
Harcourt Rd KY2 17 B5
Hardengreen Bsns Ctr EH22 152 E1
Hardengreen Ind Est EH22 152 E1
Hardengreen Junc EH22 173 E7
Hardengreen La EH22 152 E1
Harden Pl EH11 120 F5
Hardgate EH41 101 B1
Hardgate Ct EH41 101 B1
Hardhill Dr EH48 140 E6
Hardhill Pl EH48 140 B5
Hardhill Rd EH48 140 E6
Hardhill Road Travelling Peoples Site EH48 140 C5
Hardhill Terr EH48 140 E5
Hardie Cres FK7 8 C4
Hardie Ct FK7 7 C3
Hardie Rd EH54 142 D7
Hardie Terr EH40 103 D8
Hardwell Cl EH8 229 B2
Hardy Gdns EH48 141 F5
Hareburn Ave FK1 110 A5
Harelaw EH22 152 D8
Harelaw Rd EH13 149 B6
Hares Cl EH32 97 C4
Hareside ML11 217 F8
Harestanes Rd EH48 139 F3
Harewood Cres EH16 122 E4
Harewood Dr EH16 122 E4
Harewood Rd EH16 122 E4
Harkenburn Gdns EH26 191 C6
Harkness Cres EH33 126 D6
Harlands The FK10 9 E7
Harlaw Bank EH14 168 C8
Harlaw Gait EH14 147 D1
Harlaw Gr EH26 191 D5
Harlaw Hill EH32 96 F2
Harlawhill Gdns EH32 97 A2
Harlaw March EH14 168 D8
Harlaw Ranger & Visitor Ctr* EH14 169 A7
Harlaw Rd Balerno EH14 168 E8
Currie EH14 148 A2
Harley Ct FK2 60 B8
Harley Gdns FK4 58 B5
Harley St KY11 47 A4
Harlington Pl FK2 82 E7
Harlow Ave FK2 61 D1
Harmeny Sch EH14 168 D8
Harmony Cres EH19 173 D7
Harmony Ct EH19 173 D7
Harmony St EH19 173 D7
Harmony Wlk EH19 173 D7
Harness Ct EH20 172 C7
Harpenside Cres EH39 53 C5
Harperdean Cotts EH41 101 A3
Harperdean Terr EH41 100 F1
Harperrig Way EH13 149 F7
Harper's Brae EH26 192 B6
Harriebrae Pk KY12 28 F4
Harrier Ct KY11 30 A2
Harriet St KY1 17 E6
Harris Ct FK10 10 B5
Harris Dr KY2 16 F8
Harrismith Pl EH7 94 A2
Harrison Gdns EH11 120 E4
Harrison La EH11 120 F5
Harrison Pl
Edinburgh EH11 120 E4
Falkirk FK1 59 F5
Harrison Rd EH11 120 E5
Harris Pl Dunfermline KY11 29 C1
Grangemouth FK3 61 C5
Harrysmuir Cres EH53 144 A7
Harrysmuir Gdns EH53 144 B7
Harrysmuir N EH53 144 B7
Harrysmuir Prim Sch EH54 143 E5
Harrysmuir Rd EH53 144 B7
Harrysmuir S EH53 144 B7
Harrysmuir Terr EH53 144 B7
Hartfield Terr ML7 198 B8
HARTHILL 159 F5
Harthill Rd
Blackridge EH48 138 D2
Fauldhouse EH47 181 D6
Hartington Gdns EH10 121 A5
Hartington Pl EH10 121 A5
Hartley Pl FK3 61 B6
Hart St EH1 93 D2
Hart Street La EH1 93 D2
HARTWOOD 179 A3
Hartwood Gdns ML7 179 A2
Hartwoodhill Hospl ML7 179 C4
Hartwood Rd Shotts ML7 179 A3
West Calder EH55 163 D2
Hart Wynd FK7 7 F1
Harvest Dr EH28 117 B5
Harvesters Pl EH14 148 E8
Harvesters Sq EH14 148 E8
Harvesters Way EH14 148 D8
Harvest Rd EH28 117 B5
Harvest St FK9 2 A4
Harvey Ave FK2 61 F2
Harvey Wynd FK8 2 A1
Harvie Gdns EH48 139 F4
Harvieston Villas EH23 195 D7
Hastie's Cl EH1 229 A2
Hatfield Pl 2 EH48 141 B7
Hatton Pl EH9 121 D5
Haugh Gdns FK2 39 B1
Haugh Park EH14 120 A2
Haugh Rd Burntisland KY3 50 D8
North Berwick EH39 54 F7
Stirling FK9 2 B2
Haugh St Edinburgh EH3 93 B2
Falkirk FK2 39 B1
Haughs Way FK6 36 F2
Haven's Edge KY11 45 E3
Haven The
Dalgety Bay KY11 47 F2
South Alloa FK7 9 F3
Hawes Brae EH30 68 D1
Hawk Brae EH54 143 C5
Hawkcraig Rd KY3 49 D7
Hawk Cres EH22 153 E2
Hawkhead Cres EH16 151 A8
Hawkhead Gr 3 EH16 151 A8
Hawkhill EH7 94 B3
Hawkhill Ave EH7 94 A3
Hawkhill Rd Alloa FK10 10 C6
Kincardine FK10 23 D5
Hawkill Cl EH7 94 A3
Hawkins Terr EH26 192 B8
Hawksmuir 3 KY1 17 D6
Hawkwood Terr ML11 201 A1
Hawley Rd FK1 60 D4
Hawthorn Bank
Carnock KY12 27 C6
Cockenzie & Port Seton EH32 97 B4
Seafield EH47 163 A8
South Queensferry EH30 68 B1
Hawthornbank La EH4 228 A3
Hawthornbank Pl EH6 93 C5
Hawthornbank Rd EH41 100 F1
Hawthornbank Terr EH6 93 E6
Hawthorn Cres
Cowdenbeath KY4 12 F1
Easthouses EH22 174 D8
Fallin FK7 8 D4
Stirling FK8 1 F2
Hawthorn Ct EH47 163 A8
Hawthornden Ave EH19 173 B7
Hawthornden Gdns EH19 173 A7
Hawthornden Pl EH7 93 E3
Hawthornden Prim Sch EH19 172 F6
Hawthorn Dr Denny FK6 36 D3
Falkirk FK1 59 E4
Fallin FK7 8 C4
Harthill ML7 159 E6
Shotts ML7 180 C4
Hawthornebank Pl EH6 93 D6
Hawthornebank Terr EH6 93 E6
Hawthorne Pl FK5 38 D1
Hawthorn Gdns EH20 151 B1
Hawthorn Pl Allanton ML7 198 A8
Edinburgh EH17 151 E5
Ormiston EH35 155 D7
Uphall EH52 114 F4
Hawthorn Rd EH32 97 B1
Hawthorn St FK3 61 C6
Hawthorns The EH31 52 B3
Hawthorn Terr EH32 97 B3
Hawthornvale EH6 93 D6
Hay Ave EH16 122 F4
Hay Dr EH16 123 A4
HAYFIELD 17 B6
Hayfield Edinburgh EH12 119 A8
Falkirk FK2 60 C7
Hayfield Ind Est KY2 17 A7
Hayfield Pl KY2 17 A7
Hayfield Rd Falkirk FK2 60 C7
Kirkcaldy KY1, KY2 17 C7
Hayfield Terr FK6 57 E7
Hayford Mills FK7 6 D6
Hayford Pl FK7 6 D6
Haygate Ave FK2 82 E8
Hay Gdns EH16 122 F5
Hay Gr KY11 29 F1
Haymarket EH12 228 A2
Haymarket Cres EH54 143 A5
Haymarket Sta EH12 228 A2
Haymarket Terr EH12 120 F7
Haymarket Yds EH12 120 F7
Haypark Bsns Ctr FK2 61 E2
Haypark Rd FK6 57 D6
Hay Pl EH16 122 F4
Hay Rd EH16 122 F4
Hays Com Bsns Ctr EH16 122 F4
HAYWOOD 202 A2
Hayworth Ave FK2 61 B4
Hazel Ave Kirkcaldy KY2 17 B6
Menstrie FK11 3 F6
Hazelbank Gdns FK8 2 A2
Hazelbank Terr EH11 120 E4
Hazel Cres FK6 36 D3
Hazel Ct EH42 78 B1
Hazeldean Ave EH51 63 D5
Hazeldean Terr EH16 122 B2
Hazel Dr EH19 173 B6
Hazel Gr Dunfermline KY11 46 E8
Falkirk FK2 60 D7
Livingston EH54 144 B6
Shotts ML7 180 B4
Hazelhurst FK2 82 E8
Hazel La EH20 171 E7
Hazel Rd FK3 61 C6
Hazelwood Gr EH16 122 C2
Headlesscross Rd EH47 180 F2
HEAD OF MUIR 57 E6
Head of Muir Prim Sch FK6 57 D6
Headrigg Row EH16 122 B1
Headrig Rd EH30 88 D8
HEADWELL 29 B5
Headwell Ave KY12 29 B5
Headwell Ct KY12 29 B5
Headwell Rd KY12 29 A5
Headwell Sch KY12 29 B5
Heaney Ave EH53 144 B7
Heather Ave FK1 81 C6
Heatherbank EH54 143 D5
Heatherbell Ct ML7 159 D5
Heatherdale Gdns FK6 57 E7
Heatherfield Glade EH54 164 C8
Heather Gr
Dunfermline KY11 46 F8
Maddiston FK2 83 A5
Heather Pk EH47 142 B1
Heathervale Wlk EH48 140 B5
Heatherwood EH47 142 B1
Heatherwood Pk EH53 144 B7
Heathery The KY11 46 F7
Heath Rd KY11 46 F3
Hedge Row EH20 171 E7
Hedges Loan FK7 7 E1
Hedges The Falkirk FK1 59 E5
Tranent EH33 126 C5
Heggie's Wynd KY1 17 B1
Heights Rd EH48 138 D3
Heinsberg Ho EH26 191 E5
Helen La KY11 68 C6
HELENSFIELD 11 A5
Helenslea Cotts 4 EH48 141 B6
Helmsdale Pk KY12 28 F2
Henderland Rd EH12 120 D7
Henderson Ave FK10 10 A8
Henderson Cres EH52 115 B5
Henderson Ct EH53 144 F3
Henderson Gdns
Edinburgh EH6 93 F5
Henderson Gdns *continued*
Tranent EH33 126 D6
Henderson Pl Alva FK12 5 A7
Broxburn EH52 115 B5
Edinburgh EH3 93 C2
Stirling FK7 20 C4
Henderson Place La EH3 93 B2
Henderson Row EH3 93 B2
Henderson St
Bridge of Allan FK9 2 B7
Edinburgh EH6 93 F5
Kingseat KY12 12 B1
Lochgelly KY5 14 A8
Henderson Terr EH11 120 F5
Hendry Cres KY2 17 A6
Hendry Rd KY2 17 A6
Hendry St FK2 60 B7
Hendry's Wynd KY1 17 B2
Hennings The FK10 5 C1
Henry Ross Pl EH30 68 B1
Henryson Cres FK5 38 B2
Henryson Rd KY11 29 E4
Henry St Alva FK12 5 A6
Bo'ness EH51 64 A5
Grangemouth FK3 61 E8
Hens Nest Rd EH47 161 E6
Hepburn Dr EH22 153 C2
Hepburn Rd 3 EH41 101 A1
Herald Rise EH54 143 F2
Herbertshire St FK6 36 E2
Herbison Cres ML7 180 A4
Hercus Loan EH21 124 B6
Herd Gn EH54 143 B7
Herdmanflatt EH41 101 A1
Herdmanflatt Hospl EH41 101 A1
Herdshill Ave FK1 81 C6
Herd Terr EH20 172 A7
HERIOT 214 C2
Heriot Bridge EH1 228 C2
Heriot Gdns Brightons FK2 61 D1
Burntisland KY3 33 F1
Heriothill Terr EH7 93 C3
Heriot Pl EH3 228 C2
Heriot Row EH3 228 B4
Heriot St KY11 47 C2
Heriot-Watt Univ EH14 147 E8
Heriot Way EH38 214 C1
Heritage Dr FK2 39 A3
Hermand Cres EH11 120 E4
Hermand Gdns EH55 163 E3
Hermand Ho EH55 163 F3
Hermand St EH11 120 D4
Hermand Terr EH14 120 D4
HERMISTON 118 F1
Hermiston Gait Ret Pk EH11 119 A3
Hermiston House Rd EH12, EH14 118 E1
Hermiston Junc EH11, EH12 119 A2
HERMITAGE 94 B3
Hermitage Dr EH10 121 B1
Hermitage Gdns EH10 121 B2
Hermitage of Braid Nature Reserve* EH10 121 C1
Hermitage Park Gr EH6 94 B3
Hermitage Park Lea EH6 94 B3
Hermitage Park Prim Sch EH6 94 B3
Hermitage Park S EH6 94 B3
Hermitage Pk EH6 94 B3
Hermitage Pl EH6 94 A4
Hermitage Rd FK9 2 E6
Hermitage Terr EH10 121 B2
Hermits Croft EH8 229 C1
Heron Ind Complex EH54 142 D7
Heron Pl EH5 92 F7
Heron Sq EH54 142 D7
Hervey St FK10 10 A8
Hesperus Crossway EH5 92 F7
Hetherington Dr FK10 11 B4
HEUGH 54 F5
Heugh Brae EH39 54 E5
Heugh Rd EH39 54 E6
Heugh St FK1 60 A3
Heugh Study EH39 54 E5
Heugh The
North Berwick EH39 54 E5
Tranent EH33 126 C7
Hewitt Pl KY3 49 C7
Hie Dyke ML11 217 E8
Higginson Loan EH22 174 E5
High Academy Gr EH48 139 E5
High Academy St EH48 139 E5
High Beveridgewell KY12 28 F5
HIGH BONNYBRIDGE 58 C3
High Brae EH48 111 F5
High Buckstone EH10 150 C6
Highfield Livingston EH54 143 A3
North Berwick EH39 54 B3
Highfield Ave EH49 84 E7
Highfield Cres EH49 84 E7
Highfield Rd EH39 54 A6
Highland Dr FK5 38 C3
Highland Dykes Cres FK4 58 A6
Highland Dykes Dr FK4 58 B6
Highlander Way FK10 4 D2
Highlea Circ EH14 168 B7
Highlea Gr EH14 168 B8
High Mdw ML8 215 C1
High Mill Rd ML8 215 A2
High Park Rise EH26 191 F4
High Port EH49 85 B7

High Rd Maddiston FK2 ..... 83 A5
Roslin EH25 ..... 192 F6
Spott EH42 ..... 106 C3
High Riggs EH3 ..... 228 B2
High School Wynd EH1 ..... 229 B2
High School Yds EH1 ..... 229 B2
High St Aberdour KY3 ..... 49 B7
Aberlady EH32 ..... 71 C4
Airth FK2 ..... 22 D3
Alloa FK10 ..... 10 B6
Bathgate EH48 ..... 141 B7
Bonnybridge FK4 ..... 58 A5
Bonnyrigg and Lasswade, Broomieknowe EH19 ..... 173 B7
Bonnyrigg and Lasswade EH18 ..... 152 A1
Burntisland KY3 ..... 50 E8
Clackmannan FK10 ..... 10 F4
Cockenzie & Port Seton EH32 ..... 97 C4
Cowdenbeath KY4 ..... 13 D4
Dalkeith EH22 ..... 153 A3
Dunbar, Belhaven EH42 ..... 78 A2
Dunbar EH42 ..... 78 D2
Dunfermline KY12 ..... 29 A3
Dysart KY1 ..... 18 A7
East Linton EH40 ..... 103 D8
Edinburgh EH1 ..... 229 A3
Falkirk FK1 ..... 60 B4
Gifford EH41 ..... 220 F6
Haddington EH41 ..... 130 B8
Inverkeithing KY11 ..... 47 B2
Kincardine FK10 ..... 23 E4
Kinghorn KY3 ..... 34 F2
Kirkcaldy KY1 ..... 17 C3
Kirkliston EH29 ..... 89 B1
Linlithgow EH49 ..... 85 A7
Loanhead EH20 ..... 172 C8
Lochgelly KY5 ..... 14 B7
Musselburgh EH21 ..... 124 D6
North Berwick EH39 ..... 54 C7
Ormiston EH35 ..... 155 E7
Penicuik EH26 ..... 191 F4
Prestonpans EH32 ..... 96 E1
Shotts ML7 ..... 179 F4
Slamannan FK1 ..... 108 B7
South Queensferry EH30 ..... 68 C1
Tranent EH33 ..... 126 D6
High Station Ct FK1 ..... 60 A3
High Station Rd FK1 ..... 60 A3
HIGH VALLEYFIELD 26 A2
High View Gr FK1 ..... 81 D6
Hillary Rd FK5 ..... 38 E1
Hillbank KY11 ..... 47 B3
Hillcoat Loan EH15 ..... 95 A1
Hillcoat Pl EH15 ..... 95 A1
Hill Cres EH48 ..... 141 B7
Hillcrest Bo'ness EH51 ..... 63 F5
Cowdenbeath KY4 ..... 13 B3
Hillcrest Ave KY2 ..... 16 E6
Hillcrest Dr FK10 ..... 10 C6
Hillcrest Pl FK6 ..... 57 D7
Hillcrest Rd 1 FK1 ..... 59 F2
Hillcrest Sq FK2 ..... 81 F7
Hill Ct Dunfermline KY12 ..... 29 D5
South Queensferry EH30 ..... 68 B1
HILLEND 47 E4
Hillend Ind Pk KY11 ..... 48 C5
Hillend Rd KY11 ..... 47 D3
Hillfield Cres KY11 ..... 47 B3
Hillfield Rd KY11 ..... 47 B2
Hillfoots Rd Menstrie FK9 ..... 3 C6
Stirling FK9 ..... 2 E4
Hillfoot Terr ML8 ..... 215 A1
Hill Gr KY12 ..... 26 D7
Hillhead EH19 ..... 173 B8
Hillhead Ave ML8 ..... 215 A2
Hillhead Dr FK1 ..... 59 F2
Hillhose Wynd EH27 ..... 145 F3
Hillhouse Ave EH48 ..... 140 F8
Hillhouse Cres EH27 ..... 145 F3
Hillhouse Farm Steadings EH49 ..... 85 B3
Hillhouse Rd Denny FK6 ..... 57 E7
Edinburgh EH4 ..... 92 B2
Hillhouseridge Rd ML7 ..... 179 D5
Hillhouse Terr EH27 ..... 145 F3
Hillock Ave FK2 ..... 61 C2
HILL OF BEATH 13 A1
Hill of Beath Prim Sch KY4 ..... 12 F1
Hill of Kinnaird FK2 ..... 38 E7
Hill of St Margaret KY12 ..... 29 F5
Hillpark Ave EH4 ..... 91 F3
Hillpark Brae EH4 ..... 91 F1
Hillpark Cres
Bannockburn FK7 ..... 7 C2
Edinburgh EH4 ..... 91 F2
Hillpark Ct EH4 ..... 91 F3
Hillpark Dr Bannockburn FK7 ..... 7 D2
Edinburgh EH4 ..... 91 F3
Hillpark Gdns EH4 ..... 91 F2
Hillpark Gn EH4 ..... 91 F2
Hillpark Gr EH4 ..... 91 F2
Hillpark Loan EH4 ..... 92 A2
Hillpark Rd EH4 ..... 91 F2
Hillpark Terr EH4 ..... 91 F2
Hillpark Way EH4 ..... 92 A2
Hillpark Wood EH4 ..... 92 A2
Hill Pk FK10 ..... 10 B7
Hill Pl Alloa FK10 ..... 10 A8
Edinburgh EH8 ..... 229 B2
Kirkcaldy KY1 ..... 17 C4
Mayfield EH22 ..... 174 E5
Shotts ML7 ..... 179 E5
Hill Rd Gullane EH31 ..... 51 F2
Harthill ML7 ..... 159 D5
Pathhead EH37 ..... 176 A5
HILLSIDE 93 F2
Hillside FK10 ..... 5 C2
Hillside Ave KY11 ..... 48 A3
Hillside Camp Rd KY11 ..... 46 E1
Hillside Cotts
Cousland EH22 ..... 154 D5
Linlithgow EH49 ..... 85 C7
Hillside Cres EH7 ..... 93 F2
Hillside Crescent N EH23 ..... 195 D8
Hillside Crescent S EH23 ..... 195 D8
Hillside Dr EH48 ..... 138 D3
Hillside Gr EH51 ..... 64 C6
Hillside Pl
Blackridge EH48 ..... 138 D3
Longridge EH47 ..... 161 C1
Hillside Rd EH30 ..... 90 D4
Hillside Sch KY3 ..... 49 C8
Hillside St EH7 ..... 93 F2
Hillside Terr Alloa FK10 ..... 10 B7
Edinburgh EH30 ..... 90 D5
Westquarter FK2 ..... 61 B3
Hill Sq EH8 ..... 229 B2
Hill St Alloa FK10 ..... 10 B7
Cowdenbeath KY4 ..... 13 C4
Dunfermline KY12 ..... 29 A4
Dysart KY1 ..... 18 A7
Edinburgh EH2 ..... 228 C4
Inverkeithing KY11 ..... 47 B2
Kirkcaldy KY1 ..... 17 B3
Stirling FK7 ..... 7 B3
Hill Street North La EH2 ..... 228 C4
Hill Street South La EH2 ..... 228 C4
Hilltop EH49 ..... 84 D7
Hilltown Terr EH22 ..... 123 C1
Hillview Cowdenbeath KY4 ..... 13 B3
Edinburgh EH4 ..... 92 B2
Oakley KY12 ..... 26 E7
Hillview Ave EH52 ..... 115 F6
Hillview Cotts EH28 ..... 117 D2
Hillview Cres
Crossgates KY4 ..... 30 E6
Edinburgh EH12 ..... 119 D7
Hillview Ct KY12 ..... 30 A6
Hillview Dr
Bridge of Allan FK9 ..... 2 A6
Edinburgh EH12 ..... 119 C7
Hillview Gdns EH35 ..... 155 F7
Hillview La EH54 ..... 164 F4
Hillview Pl Broxburn EH52 ..... 115 F5
Crossgates KY4 ..... 30 E6
Fallin FK7 ..... 8 C4
Hillview Rd
Bonnybridge FK4 ..... 58 C3
Edinburgh EH12 ..... 119 D7
5 Grangemouth FK2 ..... 82 D8
Ormiston EH35 ..... 155 E7
Stenhousemuir FK5 ..... 38 C3
Hillview Terr Alloa FK10 ..... 10 C6
Edinburgh EH12 ..... 119 D7
Hillwood Ave EH28 ..... 117 C5
Hillwood Cres EH28 ..... 117 C5
Hillwood Gdns EH28 ..... 117 C6
Hillwood Pl EH30 ..... 68 B1
Hillwood Prim Sch EH28 ..... 117 C5
Hillwood Rd EH28 ..... 117 C5
Hillwood Rise EH28 ..... 117 C5
Hillwood Terr
Ratho Station EH28 ..... 117 C5
Rosyth KY11 ..... 47 A3
Hilton FK7 ..... 20 E8
Hilton Cres FK10 ..... 10 D7
Hilton Ct EH41 ..... 130 A8
Hilton Farm Steadings KY11 ..... 46 B3
Hilton Rd Alloa FK10 ..... 10 D7
Cairneyhill KY12 ..... 27 E1
Rosyth KY11 ..... 46 C2
Hilton Terr FK7 ..... 8 C4
Hilton View KY4 ..... 13 E6
Hirst Cres FK7 ..... 8 D4
Hirst Ct FK7 ..... 8 D4
Hirst Gdns ML7 ..... 179 C5
Hirst Rd ML7 ..... 158 D3
Hoban Sq EH52 ..... 115 F6
Hobart St EH54 ..... 144 A5
Hochsauerland Brea EH54 ..... 143 E3
Hodge St FK1 ..... 60 B4
Hogan Pl FK4 ..... 57 E5
Hogarth Ave EH23 ..... 174 C2
Hoggan Cres KY11 ..... 29 C2
Hoggan Way Alva FK12 ..... 4 F6
Loanhead EH20 ..... 172 C7
Hoghill Ct EH53 ..... 144 E3
Hoghill Pl EH53 ..... 144 E3
Holborn Pl KY11 ..... 46 F5
Holbourne Pl FK11 ..... 4 A7
Holden Way KY11 ..... 48 B5
Holly Ave FK5 ..... 38 F3
Holly Bank EH22 ..... 174 E7
Hollybank Pl EH53 ..... 144 F2
Hollybank Terr EH11 ..... 120 E4
Holly Cres KY11 ..... 46 E8
Holly Gr Livingston EH54 ..... 144 B6
Menstrie FK11 ..... 3 F6
Hollyhock Glade EH54 ..... 164 C7
Holly Pl KY1 ..... 17 C7
Holly Terr EH19 ..... 173 B6
Holly Wlk EH20 ..... 171 E7
Holmes Ct EH52 ..... 115 B4
Holmes Farm La EH52 ..... 115 B5
Holmes Gdns EH52 ..... 115 C4
Holmes Holdings EH52 ..... 115 C4
Holmes Rd EH52 ..... 115 B4
Holmlea Ave 2 FK2 ..... 82 D8
Holton Cotts FK10 ..... 5 C1
Holton Cres FK10 ..... 5 C1
Holton Ct 1 FK10 ..... 5 C1
Holton Sq FK10 ..... 5 C1
Holy Cross RC Prim Sch EH6 ..... 93 C5
Holy Family RC Prim Sch EH52 ..... 87 E2
HOLYGATE 115 D6
Holygate Pl EH52 ..... 115 D5
Holy Name RC Prim Sch KY12 ..... 26 E7
HOLYROOD 122 A7
Holyrood Bsns Pk EH16 ..... 122 D4
Holyrood Gait EH8 ..... 229 C3
Holy Rood High Sch EH15 ..... 122 D6
Holyrood Park Rd EH16 ..... 229 C1
Holyrood Pk* EH8, EH15, EH16 ..... 122 B7
Holyrood Pl
Dunfermline KY12 ..... 29 B4
Stenhousemuir FK5 ..... 38 E4
Holyrood Rd EH8 ..... 229 C3
Home Farm Cotts
Bonnybridge FK6 ..... 57 F6
Edinburgh EH30 ..... 90 E7
Home Farm Rd FK7 ..... 6 E5
Home Pk KY3 ..... 49 C7
Home St EH3 ..... 228 B1
Homesteads The FK8 ..... 6 D7
Honeybank Cres ML8 ..... 215 A3
Honeyman Ct EH48 ..... 139 E7
Hood Pl KY11 ..... 46 E2
Hookney Terr FK6 ..... 36 C2
Hope Cotts EH51 ..... 64 D5
HOPEFIELD 173 B6
Hopefield Dr EH47 ..... 162 C8
Hopefield Pk EH19 ..... 173 A6
Hopefield Pl
Blackburn EH47 ..... 162 C8
Bonnyrigg and Lasswade EH19 ..... 173 A6
Hopefield Prim Sch EH19 ..... 173 A6
Hopefield Rd EH47 ..... 162 C8
Hopefield Terr
Bonnyrigg and Lasswade EH19 ..... 173 A6
Edinburgh EH6 ..... 93 E6
Hope La EH15 ..... 123 B7
Hopelands Rd EH26 ..... 190 E5
Hope Lane N EH15 ..... 123 B8
Hopepark EH48 ..... 140 E6
Hope Park Cres
Edinburgh EH8 ..... 229 B1
2 Haddington EH41 ..... 101 A1
Hope Park Gdns EH48 ..... 140 E6
Hope Park Sq EH8 ..... 229 B1
Hopepark Terr FK4 ..... 57 F6
Hope Park Terr EH8 ..... 229 B1
Hope Pk EH41 ..... 101 A1
Hope Pl Musselburgh EH21 ..... 124 F6
Tranent EH33 ..... 126 C7
Hope St Bo'ness EH51 ..... 63 F8
Carluke ML8 ..... 215 A2
Cowdenbeath KY4 ..... 13 E6
Edinburgh EH2 ..... 228 B3
Falkirk FK1 ..... 60 B5
Inverkeithing KY11 ..... 47 B1
Queensferry EH30 ..... 89 B8
Stirling FK8 ..... 1 F1
Hope Street La EH2 ..... 228 B3
Hope Terr EH9 ..... 121 C4
Hopetoun Cres EH7 ..... 93 E2
Hopetoun Dr
Bridge of Allan FK9 ..... 2 A8
Haddington EH41 ..... 101 A1
Hopetoun Fishery* EH52 ..... 88 B5
Hopetoun House* EH30 ..... 66 F2
Hopetoun La EH48 ..... 141 B6
Hopetoun Mews 1 EH41 ..... 101 A1
Hopetoun Mon* EH39 ..... 100 E5
Hopetoun Pk EH31 ..... 52 A3
Hopetoun Pl KY2 ..... 16 C6
Hopetoun Rd EH30 ..... 68 A1
Hopetoun St
Bathgate EH48 ..... 141 B6
Edinburgh EH7 ..... 93 E3
Hopetoun Terr
Gullane EH31 ..... 52 A3
Ormiston EH35 ..... 155 E7
Hopetoun View KY11 ..... 48 C4
Hopeward Ct KY11 ..... 48 C3
Hopeward Mews KY11 ..... 48 C2
Hoprig EH33 ..... 99 A1
Hoprig Pk TD13 ..... 218 F3
Hoprig Rd TD13 ..... 218 F3
Hornbeam Cres FK2 ..... 61 A3
Hornel Pl FK5 ..... 38 D2
Horne Terr EH11 ..... 228 A1
Horsburgh Bank EH14 ..... 147 C3
Horsburgh Gdns EH14 ..... 147 C3
Horsburgh Gr EH14 ..... 147 C3
Horse Wynd EH8 ..... 229 C3
Hoseason Gdns EH4 ..... 91 D1
Hosie Rigg EH15 ..... 123 B5
Hospital Cross Head KY11 ..... 29 C1
Hospital Hill KY11 ..... 29 B1
Hospital Intc EH54 ..... 143 D4
Hospital Rd EH41 ..... 100 F1
Hot Pot Wynd KY1 ..... 18 A6
Houldsworth Cres ML7 ..... 198 A8
Houldsworth St KY12 ..... 26 A7
Houliston Ave KY11 ..... 47 B3
House O'Hill Ave EH4 ..... 92 A3
House O'Hill Brae EH4 ..... 92 A3
House O'Hill Cres EH4 ..... 92 A3
House O'Hill Gdns EH4 ..... 92 B3
House O'Hill Gn EH4 ..... 92 A3
House O'Hill Gr EH4 ..... 92 A3
House O'Hill Pl EH4 ..... 92 A3
House O'Hill Rd EH4 ..... 92 B3
House O'Hill Row EH4 ..... 92 B3
House O'Hill Terr EH4 ..... 92 B2
House O' Muir EH26 ..... 170 E2
House O' Muir Rd ML7 ..... 158 B3
Housepark Pl EH54 ..... 143 B3
Houston Ct 1 KY12 ..... 28 F4
Houston Ind Est EH54 ..... 144 A8
Houston Rd EH54 ..... 115 A1
Houston Terr EH54 ..... 115 A1
Houstoun Gdns EH52 ..... 114 F3
Houstoun Ind Est
Dechmont EH54 ..... 114 E1
Livingston EH54 ..... 143 F8
Houstoun Intc EH54 ..... 143 E7
Houstoun Mains Holdings EH52 ..... 114 E2
Houstoun Rd
Livingston, Eliburn EH54 ..... 143 B5
Livingston, Ladywell EH54 ..... 143 D6
Houstoun Road W EH54 ..... 142 E5
Howard Cres KY11 ..... 29 C2
Howard Pl Dysart KY1 ..... 18 A7
Edinburgh EH3 ..... 93 C3
Howard St Edinburgh EH3 ..... 93 C3
Falkirk FK1 ..... 59 F4
Howburn Cres ML7 ..... 159 E6
Howburn Rd ML7 ..... 159 D6
HOWDEN 143 E4
Howden East Rd EH54 ..... 143 F4
Howden Hall Cres EH16 ..... 150 F6
Howden Hall Ct EH16 ..... 150 F6
Howden Hall Dr EH16 ..... 150 F5
Howden Hall Gdns EH16 ..... 151 A6
Howden Hall Loan EH16 ..... 150 F6
Howden Hall Pk EH16 ..... 150 F5
Howden Hall Rd EH16 ..... 151 A5
Howden Hall Way EH16 ..... 151 A5
Howden St Andrew's RC Prim Sch EH54 ..... 143 F4
Howden South Rd EH54 ..... 143 E3
Howden St EH8 ..... 229 B1
Howden West Rd EH54 ..... 143 D4
Howe Ness KY11 ..... 46 D3
Howe Pk EH10 ..... 149 F5
Howe St EH3 ..... 228 C4
Howetown FK10 ..... 5 D4
HOWGATE 192 B1
Howieson Ave EH51 ..... 63 F5
Howieson Gn EH52 ..... 114 F4
Howie's Pl FK1 ..... 59 B4
Howlands Rd FK7 ..... 7 A3
Howley Ave EH54 ..... 143 E4
Howpark Rd TD13, TD14 ..... 219 E1
Hudson Rd KY11 ..... 46 F3
Hugh Ave KY5 ..... 14 B8
Hughes Cres EH22 ..... 174 F6
Hugh Miller Pl EH3 ..... 93 B2
Hugh Pl KY5 ..... 14 B8
Hugh Russell Pl EH30 ..... 89 B8
Huly Hill Rd EH28 ..... 117 A5
HUMBIE 178 B2
Humbie Cotts EH29 ..... 88 F4
Humbie Prim Sch EH36 ..... 178 B2
Humbie Rd EH29 ..... 89 A2
Humbie Smallholdings EH27 ..... 145 F4
Humbie Terr KY3 ..... 49 C8
Hume Cres FK9 ..... 2 A6
Hume Ct FK9 ..... 2 A6
Hummel Rd EH31 ..... 51 F2
Hungerage Sq EH33 ..... 126 D5
Huntburn Ave EH49 ..... 85 C7
Hunt Cl EH22 ..... 153 A4
Hunter Ave EH20 ..... 172 D8
Hunter Ct EH20 ..... 172 D8
HUNTERFIELD 174 D2
Hunterfield Ct EH23 ..... 195 C8
Hunterfield Pk EH23 ..... 174 C1
Hunterfield Rd EH23 ..... 195 C8
Hunterfield Terr EH23 ..... 174 B1
Hunter Gdns
Bonnybridge FK4 ..... 58 A5
Broxburn EH52 ..... 116 A5
Denny FK6 ..... 36 D2
Hunter Gr Bathgate EH48 ..... 141 E5
Whitburn EH47 ..... 160 F5
Hunter Pl Dunfermline KY12 ..... 28 E5
Falkirk FK2 ..... 39 A4
Kirkcaldy KY1 ..... 17 B3
Shotts ML7 ..... 179 E5
Hunter Rd EH54 ..... 143 C2
Hunter's Cl EH1 ..... 228 C2
Hunters Ct EH21 ..... 124 D7
Hunters Hill EH26 ..... 191 C6
Hunter's La EH47 ..... 161 A6
Hunter Sq Edinburgh EH1 ..... 229 A3
Gorebridge EH23 ..... 195 D8
Hunter St Kirkcaldy KY1 ..... 17 B4
Shotts ML7 ..... 179 D5
Hunter Terr
Bonnyrigg and Lasswade EH19 ..... 173 B7
Loanhead EH20 ..... 172 D8
Huntingdon Pl EH7 ..... 93 E2
Hunting Pk EH54 ..... 114 F1
HUNTINGTON 100 B1
Huntlaw Rd EH34 ..... 156 E6
Huntly Ave EH54 ..... 142 F6
Huntly Cres Kirkcaldy KY2 ..... 16 C8
Stirling FK8 ..... 1 F2
Huntly St EH3 ..... 93 C3
Huntly Terr ML7 ..... 180 B3
Hunt Pl KY12 ..... 28 B1
Huron Ave EH54 ..... 143 F3
Hursted Ave EH22 ..... 174 D7
Hurworth St FK1 ..... 59 F3
Husband Pl KY11 ..... 29 F1
Hutchison Ave EH14 ..... 120 C3
Hutchison Cotts EH14 ..... 120 C3
Hutchison Crossway EH14 ..... 120 C4
Hutchison Gdns EH14 ..... 120 C3
Hutchison Gn KY11 ..... 29 B1
Hutchison Gr EH14 ..... 120 D3
Hutchison Ho EH14 ..... 120 D4
Hutchison Loan EH14 ..... 120 C3
Hutchison Medway EH14 ..... 120 D3
Hutchison Pk EH14 ..... 120 C4
Hutchison Pl EH14 ..... 120 C3
Hutchison Rd EH14 ..... 120 C4
Hutchison Terr EH14 ..... 120 C3
Hutchison View EH14 ..... 120 C4
Hutton Pk FK10 ..... 10 C7
Hutton Rd EH8 ..... 229 C3
Hutton Sq EH54 ..... 164 C6
Hyndford Ho EH39 ..... 54 A7
Hyndfords Cl EH1 ..... 229 B3
Hyvot Ave EH17 ..... 151 D6
Hyvot Bank Ave EH17 ..... 151 E6
Hyvot Ct EH17 ..... 151 D5
Hyvot Gdns EH17 ..... 151 D6
Hyvot Gn EH17 ..... 151 D5
Hyvot Gr EH17 ..... 151 D6
Hyvot Loan EH17 ..... 151 D6
Hyvot Mill Dr EH17 ..... 151 D6
Hyvot Pk EH17 ..... 151 D5
Hyvot Rd EH17 ..... 151 D6
Hyvot Terr EH17 ..... 151 D6
Hyvot View EH17 ..... 151 D5

I

Ibris Pl EH39 ..... 54 A7
Icehouse Brae N FK2 ..... 61 B4
Icehouse Brae S FK2 ..... 61 B4
Imex Ctr EH20 ..... 172 A7
Implement Rd EH42 ..... 77 E1
Imrie Pl EH26 ..... 191 F5
Inch Ave KY3 ..... 49 B6
Inch Colm Ave FK5 ..... 38 C4
Inchcolm Dr KY11 ..... 68 B6
Inchcolm Rd KY11 ..... 29 E3
Inchcolm Terr EH30 ..... 89 B8
Inchcorse Pl EH48 ..... 141 C1
Inch Cres EH48 ..... 141 D5
Inchcross EH48 ..... 140 F3
Inchcross Dr EH48 ..... 140 F2
Inchcross Ind Est EH48 ..... 140 E3
Inchcross Pk EH48 ..... 140 F2
Inchcross Steadings EH48 ..... 140 F2
Inches Rdbt FK5 ..... 38 C4
Inches The
Dalgety Bay KY11 ..... 48 B2
Grangemouth FK3 ..... 61 E8
Inchgarvie Ave KY3 ..... 33 D1
Inchgarvie Cres KY11 ..... 29 E3
Inchgarvie Pk EH30 ..... 68 A1
Inchgarvie Rd KY2 ..... 16 F8
Inch Garvie Terr FK5 ..... 38 C4
Inchkeith Ave EH30 ..... 89 C8
Inchkeith Cres KY1 ..... 35 B6
Inchkeith Ct KY11 ..... 29 F3
Inchkeith Dr KY11 ..... 29 F3
Inchkeith Gr 3 EH33 ..... 126 D7
Inchkeith Pl FK1 ..... 60 B2
Inchmickery Ave KY11 ..... 48 D5
Inchmickery Rd KY11 ..... 48 C5
Inchmuir Rd EH48 ..... 141 B2
Inchna FK11 ..... 4 A6
INCH THE 122 B2
Inchview EH32 ..... 96 E1
Inch View Kinghorn KY3 ..... 34 F1
Kirkcaldy KY1 ..... 35 B7
Inchview Cres EH21 ..... 125 C5
Inchview Gdns KY11 ..... 48 B3
Inchview N EH32 ..... 96 E1
Inchview Rd EH21 ..... 125 C5
Inchview Terr EH7 ..... 94 F1
Inch Wood Ave EH48 ..... 141 D4
Inchyra Pl FK3 ..... 61 F6
Inchyra Rd FK3 ..... 61 E5
India Pl EH3 ..... 228 B4
India St EH3 ..... 228 B4
Industrial Rd EH6 ..... 94 B4
Industry Homes EH6 ..... 93 E5
Industry La EH6 ..... 93 E5
Infirmary St EH1 ..... 229 B2
Ingleston Ave FK6 ..... 36 D4
Inglewood Gdns FK10 ..... 10 A8
Inglewood Ho FK10 ..... 4 F1
Inglewood Pl 3 EH16 ..... 151 B8
Inglewood Rd FK10 ..... 9 F8
Inglewood St EH54 ..... 143 F5
Inglis Ave EH32 ..... 97 C4
Inglis Cres KY3 ..... 34 F3
Inglis' Ct EH1 ..... 228 C2
Inglis Dr FK2 ..... 39 C2
Inglis Farm EH32 ..... 97 C3
Inglis Green Gait 3 EH14 ..... 120 B2
Inglis Green Rd EH14 ..... 120 B2
Inglis Green Rigg 2 EH14 ..... 120 B2
Inglis La KY12 ..... 28 F5
Inglis Pl FK2 ..... 82 E8
Inglis St KY12 ..... 29 A4
Ingliston Rd EH28 ..... 117 F6
Ingram Pl FK2 ..... 82 E6

Inkerman Ct EH26 ....192 A8
Innellan Cres ML7 ....179 E6
Innerpeffray Dr FK2.......39 A3
INNERWICK..............218 A7
Innerwick Prim Sch
EH42...................218 A7
Innes Bldgs 1 EH33 .....126 C6
Innova Way KY11 ....46 D1
Inn Pl EH54..............143 B2
Institution St KY1.........17 E7
Inverallan Ct FK9 ....1 F8
Inverallan Dr FK9 ....1 F7
Inverallan Rd FK9...........1 F7
Inveralmond Com High Sch
EH54.................. 143 D5
Inveralmond Dr EH4 ......91 A5
Inveralmond Gdns EH4....91 A5
Inveralmond Gr EH4 ......91 A5
Inverary Dr FK5...........38 F5
Inveravon Rd EH20........151 B1
Inveravon Rdbt EH51......62 D5
INVERESK...............124 E5
Inveresk Brae EH21......124 D5
Inveresk Est The EH21 ...124 D4
Inveresk Gate EH21......124 D5
Inveresk Ind Est EH21....124 C5
Inveresk Lodge Gdn*
EH21.................. 124 D4
Inveresk Mill Est EH21...124 B5
Inveresk Rd EH21........124 C5
Inveresk Village Rd
EH21..................124 D4
Inverewe Pl KY11.........30 A1
INVERKEITHING...........47 B1
Inverkeithing Her Ctr*
KY11...................47 B2
Inverkeithing High Sch
KY11...................47 D3
Inverkeithing Prim Sch
KY11...................47 D3
Inverkeithing Rd
Aberdour KY3 ....49 B7
Crossgates KY4...........30 E6
Inverkeithing Sta KY11....47 C3
Inverkip Dr ML7 ....179 E5
INVERLEITH 93 A4
Inverleith Ave EH3........93 B4
Inverleith Avenue S EH3 ..93 B4
Inverleith Gdns EH3.......93 A4
Inverleith Gr EH3 ....92 F3
Inverleith Pl EH3..........93 A4
Inverleith Place La EH3 ...93 B4
Inverleith Row EH3 ....93 B4
Inverleith Terr EH3 ....93 B3
Inverleith Terrace La EH3 .93 C3
Invertiel Bank KY1........17 B1
Invertiel Rd KY1 ....35 A8
Invertiel Terr KY1.........17 B1
Inzievar Ho KY12..........26 F4
Inzievar Prim Sch KY12....26 E7
Inzievar Terr KY12 ....27 A6
Iona Pl FK1...............60 B2
Iona Rd KY11 ....29 E3
Iona St EH6...............93 F3
Iona Street La EH6........93 F3
Ireland Ave EH47 ....160 F6
Irene Terr FK1............82 E2
Ironmills Rd EH22........152 F3
Irvine Cres EH48.........140 F6
Irvine Pl FK8 ....7 A8
Irving Ct FK1 ....59 E5
Islands Cres FK1..........60 B2
Islay Ct FK3 ....61 D5
Islay Rd KY11 ....29 E2
Ivanhoe Cres EH16.......122 B1
Ivanhoe Pl FK8 ....2 A2
Ivanhoe Rise EH54 ....144 A2
Ivybank Ct FK2 ....61 E2
Ivy Gr KY11...............46 E8
Ivy La KY1................18 A7
Ivy Terr EH11 ....120 E5
Izatt Ave KY11 ....29 B1
Izatt Terr FK10............11 A4

J

Jack Kane Sports Ctr
EH15...................123 A4
Jacklin Gn EH54 ....143 B7
Jackson Ave FK3 ....61 D7
Jackson Pl EH54..........143 C4
Jackson's Cl EH1 ....229 A3
Jackson's Entry EH8 .....229 C3
Jackson St EH26.........191 E5
Jacobite Way EH32 ....97 B1
Jacob Pl FK1 ....60 B3
Jacobs Way EH23........195 C8
Jamaica Mews EH3.......228 B4
Jamaica St EH3..........228 B4
Jamaica Street North La
EH3....................228 B4
Jamaica Street South La
EH3....................228 B4
Jamaica Street W EH3 ...228 B4
James Bank KY12.........29 A4
James Cornwall Ct FK3 ...61 F6
James Craig Wk EH2.....229 A4
James Croft Dr FK1.......59 F1
James Ct KY4.............13 C2
James' Ct EH1...........229 A3
James Gillespie's High Sch
EH9....................121 C5
James Gillespie's Prim Sch
EH9....................121 C5
James Gr KY1 ....17 B2
James Hog Cres KY12.....26 F6
James Lean Ave EH22....153 B3
James Leary Way EH19...173 C8
James Miller Rd KY11.....46 E2
Jameson Pl EH6..........93 F3
James' Park La KY3.......33 F1
James' Pk KY3............33 F1
James Short Pk FK1 ......60 B3
James Smith Ave FK2.....82 E6
James St Alva FK12.........5 A6
Armadale EH48..........139 F5
Bannockburn FK7 ....7 C1
Cowdenbeath KY4.........13 C2
Dunfermline KY12.........29 A4
Edinburgh EH15..........123 C8
Falkirk FK2 ....60 B6
Laurieston FK2 ....61 A3
Longcroft FK4 ....57 A3
Musselburgh EH21 .... 124 D6
Stenhousemuir FK5........38 D2
Stirling FK8 ....2 B1
James Street La EH15....123 C8
James Watt Ave EH51.....64 A7
James Wilson Dr FK2 .....83 A5
James Wylie Pl FK10......23 F4
James Young High Sch The
EH54...................143 E1
James Young Rd EH48 ...141 B3
Jamieson Ave
Bo'ness EH51 ....63 E6
Stenhousemuir FK5........38 E3
Jamieson Gdns ML7 .....179 E5
Janefield EH17 ....151 A4
Jane St EH6 ....93 F4
Jardine Pl EH48 ....140 E7
Jarnac Ct 7 EH22 ....153 A3
Jarvey St EH48 ....141 B7
Jarvie Pl 6 FK2 ....60 A8
Jarvie Rd FK2 ....61 A1
Jasper Ave FK2...........61 A4
Jawbanes Rd KY2.........35 A8
Jean Armour Ave 1
EH16 ....122 A1
Jean Armour Dr EH22....153 D2
Jean Armour Gdns KY2 ...17 A7
Jeanette Stewart Dr
EH22 ....173 F4
Jeffrey Ave EH4 ....92 B1
Jeffrey Bank EH51 ....63 F7
Jeffrey St EH1...........229 B3
Jeffrey Terr FK2..........61 F2
Jellyholm Rd FK10........10 E8
Jenks Loan EH22 ....174 A5
Jennie Rennie's Rd KY11..29 B1
Jessfield Pl EH51 ....63 F5
Jessfield Terr EH6........93 D6
Jewel & Esk Coll
Dalkeith EH22 ....152 F1
Edinburgh EH15......... 123 D6
Jewel The EH15 ....123 B5
Jim Bush Dr EH32 ....125 E7
Jock's Hill Cres EH49 .....84 E7
JOCK'S LODGE............94 D1
Jock's Lodge 8 EH8......94 C1
John Bernard Way EH23 .195 C6
John Brown Ct EH41 .....101 B1
John Connelly Ct 3 KY12 .28 E5
John Cotton Bsns Ctr EH7 94 A2
John Cowane Row FK9.....2 A4
John Cres EH33..........126 C6
John Davidson Dr FK6 ....36 C4
John Humble St EH22....174 E5
John Hunter Ct KY1........17 B4
John Knox Ho* EH1.....229 B3
John Knox Pl EH26.......191 F5
John Knox Rd EH32 ....98 E5
John McDouall Stuart Mus*
KY1....................18 A7
John Mason Ct EH30.......89 C8
John Muir Birthplace*
EH42...................78 D2
John Muir Cres EH42 ....106 D8
John Muir Ctry Pk* EH42 77 D4
John Muir Gdns EH42....106 D8
John Muir Pl EH42.......106 D8
John Muir Rd EH42 ......106 D8
John Murray Dr FK9 ....2 A8
Johnnie Cope's Rd EH33 .126 A7
Johnny Moat Pl EH32 .....96 F1
John O'Hara Ct FK1.......59 D5
John Row Pl KY12 ....27 A7
John Rushforth Pl FK8.....1 F3
Johnsburn Gn EH14......147 B1
Johnsburn Haugh EH14 ..147 B1
Johnsburn Pk EH14......168 B8
Johnsburn Rd EH14.......147 B1
John's La EH6.............94 A5
John Smith Way ML7 ....179 D5
John's Pl EH6 ....94 A5
John St Dunfermline KY11...29 B2
Edinburgh EH15.........123 C8
Falkirk FK2 ....60 B7
Kincardine FK10 ....23 D3
Kirkcaldy KY2 ....17 B5
Longcroft FK4 ....57 A3
Penicuik EH26...........191 F6
Johnston Ave
Stenhousemuir FK5........38 F3
Stirling FK9 ....2 B3
Uphall EH52.............114 F3
Johnston Cres
Dunfermline KY11.........29 B1
Lochgelly KY5 ....14 B7
Johnston Ct 7 Falkirk FK2 .60 A8
Uphall EH52.............114 F4
Johnstone Ct FK12.........5 A6
Johnstone La ML8 ....215 B1
Johnstone St Alva FK12.....5 A6
Menstrie FK11.............3 F6
Johnston Pk
Cowdenbeath KY4.........13 C5
Inverkeithing KY11 ....47 B2
Johnston Pl Denny FK6 ....36 C1
Penicuik EH26...........191 F8
Johnston St FK7 ....7 C1
Johnston Terr
Cockenzie & Port Seton
EH32...................97 D4
Edinburgh EH1...........228 C2
John Street La
Edinburgh EH15..........123 C8
Penicuik EH26...........191 E5
John Street Lane E EH15 123 C8
John Street Lane W
EH15 ....123 C8
John Stuart Gait KY12.....26 F6
John Wood Pl KY4.........30 F7
Jones Ave FK5............59 C8
Jones Gn EH54 ....143 A7
Jones St KY12 ....12 A1
JOPPA..................123 D7
Joppa Gdns EH15........123 C7
Joppa Gr EH15...........123 C7
Joppa Pk EH15 ....123 D7
Joppa Rd EH15 ....123 D7
Joppa Station Pl EH15 ...123 C7
Joppa Terr EH15.........123 C7
Jordan La EH10..........121 B3
Joseph Cumming Gdns
EH52 ....115 B4
Joseph Scott Gdns EH52 .115 E4
Jubilee Ave EH54 ....142 F6
Jubilee Cres EH23 ....174 C1
Jubilee Ct KY12...........29 A3
Jubilee Dr KY11 ....46 B1
Jubilee Rd Denny FK6......36 E3
Ratho Station EH12.......118 A7
Whitburn EH47 ....161 A6
Jubilee Way FK4..........57 F5
Junction Pl 12 Alloa FK10 ..10 B6
Edinburgh EH6............93 F5
Junction Rd KY1...........17 D7
Juner Pl EH23 ....174 C1
Juniper Ave EH14........148 C5
Juniper Gdns EH14 ......148 C6
Juniper Gr
Dunfermline KY11.........46 D8
Edinburgh EH14..........148 C6
Livingston EH54..........144 B6
JUNIPER GREEN 148 C6
Juniper Green Prim Sch
EH14.................. 148 D6
Juniper La EH14 ....148 C6
Juniperlee EH14 ....148 D5
Juniper Park Rd EH14....148 D6
Juniper Pl EH14 ....148 C5
Juniper Terr EH14 ....148 D6
Jura EH54 ....142 F5
Jura Pl FK3...............61 D5
Justinhaugh Dr EH49 .....84 D7
Jute Pl KY1...............17 C7
Jutland St KY11...........46 D6

K

Kaemuir Ct EH48 ....110 F5
Kaim Cres EH48 ....141 D5
KAIMES 151 A5
Kaimes Ave EH27 ....145 E3
Kaimes Cres EH27 ....145 E3
Kaimes Ct EH12..........119 F6
Kaimes Gdns EH27.......145 F3
Kaimes Gr EH27 ....145 F3
Kaimes Pl EH27..........145 E3
Kaimes Rd EH12 ....119 F7
Kaimes Specl Sch EH16..151 C6
Kaimes View EH22.......152 B7
Kaims Brae EH54 ....143 C2
Kaims Ct EH54...........143 B2
Kaims Dr EH54...........143 C2
Kaims Gdns EH54........143 C2
Kaims Gr EH54...........143 C2
Kaims Pl EH54...........143 B2
Kaims Terr EH54.........143 C2
Kaims Wlk EH54 ....143 C2
Kames Pl KY12 ....29 D5
Kames Rd ML7...........179 E6
Karries Ct FK6............57 B8
Katesmill Rd EH14 ......149 B8
Katherine St Kirkcaldy KY2 .17 B6
Livingston EH54..........144 A5
Katrine Cres KY2 ....16 E8
Katrine Ct FK10...........10 C5
Katrine Dr KY12 ....28 B1
Katrine Pl FK6............57 D6
Katrine Rd Shotts ML7 ...179 E6
Whitburn EH47 .... 161 D7
Kay Gdns EH32 ....97 C4
Kay Rd KY12..............43 F8
Keavil Farm Steadings
KY12 ....45 B8
Keavil Pl KY12............28 B1
Kedslie Pl EH16.........150 F7
Kedslie Rd EH16 ....150 F8
KEILARSBRAE.............10 D8
Keilarsbrae FK10 ....10 C8
Keir Ave FK8 ....2 A2
Keir Ct FK9 ....2 A7
Keirfold Ave FK10.........4 D3
Keir Gdns FK9 ....2 A7
Keir Hardie Ave FK2 ......61 A3
Keir Hardie Dr EH22 .....174 E5
Keir Hardie Rd FK12 ....5 C7
Keir Hardie Terr KY11.....29 B1
Keirsbeath Ct KY12 ....12 B2
Keirsbeath Rise KY12 .....12 B1
Keir St Bridge of Allan FK9....2 A7
Cowdenbeath KY4.........13 B4
Edinburgh EH3...........228 C2
Keith Ave FK7 ....7 C4
Keith Cres EH4 ....92 B1
Keith Gdns EH52.........115 C6
Keith Marischal EH36 ....177 F5
Keith Pl Dunfermline KY12 ..29 D4
Inverkeithing KY11 ....47 C3
Keith Rd KY11 ....46 C1
Keith Row EH4 ....92 C1
Keith St FK10.............23 D3
Keith Terr EH4............92 B1
Kekewich Ave EH7........94 F2
Kelliebank FK10 ....9 E6
Kelliebank Ind Est FK10....9 F5
Kellie Pl Alloa FK10........10 A7
Dunbar EH42............106 E8
Kellie Rd EH42...........106 D8
Kelly Ct FK8 ....7 A8
Kelly Dr FK6..............36 E3
Kelly's La ML8...........215 B1
Kellywood Cres FK10 .....23 F3
Kelso Dr ML8............215 C1
Kelso Pl KY2..............17 B6
Kelso St EH52 ....115 B5
Kelt Rd FK6..............57 A6
KELTY 12 D8
Kelty Ave EH51 ....64 A7
Kelvin Dr ML7 ....180 B4
Kelvin Sq EH54 ....144 B8
Kelvin St FK3 ....40 A1
Kemper Ave FK1..........60 C3
Kemp Pl EH3 ....93 B2
Kemp's Cnr EH7 ....94 C2
Kemp's End EH33........126 C4
Kempston Pl EH30........89 C8
Kendieshill Ave FK2.......83 A5
Kenilworth Ct FK9 ....2 B7
Kenilworth Dr
Edinburgh EH16..........151 B8
Laurieston FK2 ....60 F4
Kenilworth Gate FK9.......2 C7
Kenilworth La FK3 ....61 C5
Kenilworth Rd FK9.........2 B7
Kenilworth Rise EH54....143 F1
Kenilworth St FK3 ....61 D5
Kenmore Ave
Livingston EH54..........142 F6
Polmont FK2 ....62 A2
Kenmore Terr KY2.........16 E7
Kenmuir St FK1...........59 A5
Kenmure Ave EH8 ....122 C8
Kenmure Pl
Dunfermline KY12.........29 C5
Stenhousemuir FK5........38 F4
Kennard Rd FK2 ....82 C8
Kennard St Falkirk FK2.....60 C6
Lochgelly KY5 ....14 B8
Kennedie Pk EH53 ....144 C3
Kennedy Cres
Dunfermline KY12.........29 B5
Kirkcaldy KY2 ....17 B6
Tranent EH33........... 126 D7
Kennedy Ct EH41 ....129 F8
Kennedy Way FK2 ....22 E3
Kenneil Mus & Roman
Fortlet* EH51...........63 C6
KENNET..................11 C2
Kennet Village FK10 ......11 D3
Kenningknowes Rd FK7 ....6 E5
Kennington Ave EH20....172 B8
Kennington Terr EH20 ...172 B8
Kentigern Mall EH26.....191 F5
Kent Rd Alloa FK10 ....9 F8
Stirling FK7 ....7 B5
Kent St KY12 ....29 C6
Keppel Rd EH39 ....54 A6
Keppock Cres EH32.......97 B2
Keppock Pl FK1...........59 F1
Kepscaith Cres EH47.....161 B5
Kepscaith Gr EH47.......161 B5
Kepscaith Rd EH47.......161 B5
Kerr Ave EH22 ....152 E2
Kerr Cres FK4 ....57 A3
Kerr Ct KY3...............33 E1
Kerrisk Dr KY11...........29 F1
Kerr Pl Denny FK6 ....36 D2
Dunfermline KY11.........29 F1
Kerr Rd EH33 ....126 C6
Kerr St EH3...............93 B2
Kerr's Wynd EH21 ....124 D6
Kerr Way 1 EH33........126 C5
Kersebonny Rd FK7 ....6 C7
Kerse Gdns FK2...........60 E5
Kersegreen Rd FK10 ......10 F5
Kersehill Circ FK2 ....60 C7
Kersehill Cres FK2 ....60 C7
Kerse La FK1 ....60 C4
Kerse Pl FK1 ....60 C5
Kerse Rd Grangemouth FK3 .61 D8
Stirling, Loanhead FK7 .....7 E5
Kersiebank Ave FK3 ......61 E6
Kersie Rd FK7 ....9 A3
Kersie Terr FK7............9 E3
Kestrel Ave KY11 ....30 B3
Kestrel Brae EH54 ....143 C5
Kestrel Dr FK2............82 E7
Kestrel Way KY11.........30 A2
Kettil'stoun Cres EH49 ....84 D5
Kettil'stoun Ct EH49 ......84 D5
Kettil'stoun Gr EH49 ......84 D5
Kettil'stoun Mains EH49...84 D5
Kettilstoun Rd EH49.......84 D7
Keverkae FK10.............9 F6
Kevock Rd EH18 ....172 F8
Kew Gdns 2 EH48........141 B6
Kew Terr 3 EH12........120 E7
Kidd St KY1 ....17 D7
Kidlaw Cres FK10..........4 D3
Kier Ct FK9 ....2 B7
KILBAGIE.................11 D1
Kilbagie St FK10..........23 D4
Kilbean Dr FK1 ....59 E2
Kilbirnie Terr FK6 ....36 D3
Kilbrennan Dr FK1 ....59 B4
Kilburn Rd KY12 ....28 A2
Kilchurn Ct 1 EH12......119 A7
Kilcruik Rd KY3...........34 F3
Kildean Hospl FK8 ....1 F2
Kildimmery EH49 ....85 E6
Kildonan Pk KY12.........28 F2
Kildrummy Ave FK5.......38 F4
KILDUFF 101 C8
Kilduthie Pl FK10 ....23 D6
Kilfinan Rd ML7 ....179 D6
Kilgour Ave KY1 ....17 D7
Kilgraston Rd EH9 ....121 D4
Killin Ct KY12.............28 F2
Killin Dr FK2..............62 A2
Killochan Way KY12.......29 D5
Kilmartin Way KY12.......29 C5
Kilmaurs Rd EH16........122 A4
Kilmaurs Terr EH16 ......122 A4
Kilmory Ct FK1 ....59 C4
Kilmory Gdns ML8 ....215 A3
Kilmundy Dr KY3 ....33 D1
Kilmun Rd KY2 ....16 D7
Kilncadzow Rd ML8......215 C1
Kilncraigs Ct FK10 ....10 C5
Kilncraigs Rd FK10........10 C6
Kilncroftside EH14.......120 B2
Kilne Pl EH54............143 A4
Kilngate Brae EH17 ......151 D5
Kilns Pl FK2 ....59 F6
Kilns Rd FK1..............60 A5
Kilpair St 5 EH41.......130 B8
Kilpunt Gdns EH52.......116 A5
Kilpunt Rdbt EH52 ....116 A5
Kilpunt View EH52 ....116 A5
Kilrie Cotts KY2...........33 F7
Kilrymont ML11..........201 A1
Kilsland Terr EH51........63 D7
Kilspindie Ct EH32........71 D4
Kilsyth Rd FK4............57 A3
Kilwinning Pl EH21 ......124 C6
Kilwinning St EH21 ......124 D6
Kilwinning Terr EH21 ....124 D6
Kimmerghame Dr EH4 ....92 E4
Kimmerghame Loan EH4..92 E4
Kimmerghame Pl EH4 ....92 E4
Kimmerghame View EH4..92 E3
Kinacres Gr EH51 ....64 D7
Kincaids Ct EH3 ....229 A2
Kincairne Ct FK10.........23 E4
KINCARDINE..............23 F4
Kincardine Rd FK2........39 C3
Kincraig Pl KY12..........28 F2
Kinellan Gdns EH12......120 C8
Kinellan Rd EH12 ....120 C7
King Cres EH55 ....163 D3
King Edwards Way EH29 ..89 A1
Kingfisher Brae EH54 ....143 C5
Kingfisher Pl KY11.........30 A3
KINGHORN 35 A2
Kinghorn Pl EH6...........93 D5
Kinghorn Prim Sch KY3...34 F2
Kinghorn Rd
Burntisland KY3...........34 A1
Kirkcaldy KY1, KY2 ....35 B7
Kinghorn Sta KY3.........34 F2
King James Dr FK10 ....4 C2
King James IV Rd KY11....46 C1
Kinglass Ave EH51 ....64 A7
Kinglass Ct EH51..........64 A6
Kinglass Dr EH51 ....64 A6
Kinglass Pk EH51..........64 A5
King Malcolm Cl EH10 ...150 D5
King O' Muirs Ave FK10 ....4 E4
King O' Muirs Dr FK10 .....4 D4
King O' Muirs Farm Steading
FK10 ....4 F4
King O' Muirs Rd FK10 .....4 E4
King Robert Ct FK8 ....1 E1
King's Ave EH32 ....98 D4
Kingsburgh Cres EH5 .....92 E7
Kingsburgh Ct EH40 .....103 D8
Kingsburgh Gdns EH40...103 D8
Kingsburgh Rd EH12.....120 C7
King's Cramond EH4.......91 B4
King's Cres Carluke ML8 ..215 A2
Rosyth KY11 ....46 E4
Kings Ct 7 Falkirk FK1.....60 B4
Stenhousemuir FK5........38 D2
King's Ct Alloa FK10 ....10 A7
Longniddry EH32..........98 D4
Kings Dr KY11 ....47 A8
King's Dr KY3.............34 F3
KINGSEAT 12 B1
Kingseat Ave FK3 ....61 D6
KINGSEATHILL............29 C6
Kingseat Pl FK1...........59 F3
Kingseat Rd
Dunfermline KY12.........29 D6
Halbeath KY11, KY12 ......30 B6
Kingsfield EH49...........85 D8
Kingsgate Sh Ctr KY12....29 A4
Kings Gn EH11...........120 E5
King's Gr EH32 ....98 C4
Kings Haugh EH16 ....122 C4
Kingshill Rd ML7.........198 A8
Kingshill View ML11 .....217 F8
King's Knoll EH39.........54 B7

King's Knoll Gdns EH39 . . . 54 C7
King's Knot★ FK8 . . . . 6 F8
KINGSKNOWE 120 B1
Kingsknowe Ave EH14 . . . 120 A1
Kingsknowe Cres EH14. . . 120 A1
Kingsknowe Ct EH14. . . . . 119 F1
Kingsknowe Dr EH14. . . . . 120 A1
Kingsknowe Gdns EH14 . . 120 A1
Kingsknowe Gr EH14. . . . . 149 A8
Kingsknowe Pk EH14 . . . . 149 A8
Kingsknowe Pl EH14 . . . . . 119 F1
Kingsknowe Road N
EH14 . . . . 120 A2
Kingsknowe Road S
EH14 . . . . 120 A1
Kingsknowe Sta EH14. . . . 120 A1
Kingsknowe Terr EH14. . . 120 A1
Kingslaw Ct 1 EH33 . . . . . 126 D5
Kingslaw Farm Cotts
EH33 . . . . 126 F6
Kingsley Ave FK5 . . . . 38 F3
King's Mdw EH16 . . . . 122 B4
King's Meadow Prim Sch
EH41. . . . . 130 A8
King's Park Prim Sch
EH22. . . . . 153 A2
King's Park Rd FK8 . . . . 7 A7
King's Pk EH32 . . . . 98 D5
King's Pl KY11. . . . . 46 E4
Kingsport Ave EH54. . . . . . 143 F4
King Sq EH55. . . . . 163 D3
Kings Rd FK3. . . . . 61 F8
King's Rd Edinburgh EH15 . . 95 A1
Longniddry EH32. . . . . 98 D5
Rosyth KY11 . . . . 46 E5
Tranent EH33. . . . . 126 C5
Whitburn EH47 . . . . 161 A6
King's Road Prim Sch
KY11. . . . . 46 E4
King's Stables La EH1. . . . 228 C2
King's Stables Rd EH1 . . . 228 C2
King St Alloa FK10. . . . . 10 B7
Armadale EH48. . . . . 140 A6
Bathgate EH48 . . . . 141 B6
Cowdenbeath KY4 . . . . 13 B4
Edinburgh EH6. . . . . 93 F5
Falkirk FK2 . . . . 60 C6
Fallin FK7. . . . . 8 C4
Inverkeithing KY11 . . . . 47 C2
Kirkcaldy KY2 . . . . 17 B6
Musselburgh EH21 . . . . . . 124 D5
Shotts ML7 . . . . 179 E4
Stenhousemuir, Antonshill
FK5. . . . . 38 F3
Stirling FK8 . . . . 7 B7
Kingstables La 3 FK8. . . . . . 7 A8
King's Terr EH15. . . . . 94 F1
King's Theatre★ EH3. . . . . 228 B1
Kingsthorne Pk EH54 . . . . 114 F1
KINGSTON. 54 A1
Kingston Ave EH16. . . . . . . 122 C1
Kingston Cotts EH39 . . . . . . 53 E1
Kingswell Pk FK10. . . . . 10 C7
Kinleith Ind Est EH14 . . . . 148 B4
Kinloch Pl FK3. . . . . 61 E5
Kinloss Ct KY12. . . . . 26 A2
Kinnaird Ave FK2 . . . . 39 B3
Kinnaird Dr FK5 . . . . 38 E3
Kinnaird Pl
Dunfermline KY12. . . . . 29 D6
Kirkcaldy KY2 . . . . 16 D4
Kinnaird Prim Sch FK5 . . . 38 D5
Kinnear Rd EH3. . . . . 93 A4
KINNEIL. 63 D5
Kinneil Dr EH51. . . . . 63 D6
Kinneil Prim Sch EH51. . . . 63 F6
Kinneil Rd EH51 . . . . 63 D7
Kinneil Sta★ EH51. . . . . 63 D7
Kinnell Rd KY11 . . . . 47 B2
Kinninmonth St KY1 . . . . . . 17 B2
Kinnis Ct KY11. . . . . 29 F1
Kinnonmonth Ave 5 KY3 . 33 D1
Kintail Pl KY11. . . . . 30 A4
Kintyre Pl FK1. . . . . 59 C4
Kippielaw Dr EH22. . . . . . . 153 C2
Kippielaw Gdns EH22 . . . . 153 C1
Kippielaw Medway EH22 . 153 C1
Kippielaw Pk EH22. . . . . . . 174 D8
Kippielaw Rd EH22. . . . . . . 153 C1
Kippielaw Wlk EH22 . . . . . 153 C2
Kippilaw Steading EH22. . 153 D1
Kippithill EH36 . . . . 178 B2
Kirk Ave FK5 . . . . 38 E2
Kirkbank Rd KY3. . . . . 33 F1
Kirkbrae Clackmannan FK10. 10 F4
Garvald EH41 . . . . 132 D2
Kirk Brae Edinburgh EH16. . 151 A8
Innerwick EH42. . . . . 218 A7
Kincardine FK10 . . . . 23 E5
Longridge EH47. . . . . 161 C1
Kirkbride Terr FK7. . . . . 20 C3
Kirkburn FK1 . . . . 108 B7
KIRKCALDY. 17 C3
Kirkcaldy High Sch KY1. . . 17 B8
Kirkcaldy Mus & Art Gallery★
KY1. 17 B4
Kirkcaldy North Prim Sch
KY2. 17 B6
Kirkcaldy Rd
Burntisland KY3. . . . . 33 F2
Crossgates KY4. . . . . 31 A6
Kinghorn KY3. . . . . 35 A4
Kirkcaldy Sta KY1 . . . . 17 A4
Kirkcaldy West Prim Sch
KY1. 17 B2
Kirk Cramond EH4. . . . . 91 C6
Kirkfield E EH54 . . . . 143 B3
Kirkfield View EH54. . . . . . 143 C3
Kirkfield W EH54 . . . . 143 B3
Kirkflat EH52 . . . . 115 A5
Kirkford Ct KY4. . . . . 13 A4
Kirkgate Alloa FK10. . . . . 10 B6
Burntisland KY3. . . . . 50 E8
Currie EH14. . . . . 148 A3
Dunfermline KY12. . . . . 28 F3
Edinburgh EH16. . . . . 151 A7
Inverkeithing KY11 . . . . 47 B4
Linlithgow EH49 . . . . 85 A7
West Calder EH55. . . . . 163 D3
Kirkgate Ho EH6. . . . . 94 A4
Kirkhall Pl FK6 . . . . 36 E2
KIRKHILL 192 A5
Broxburn 115 C5
Kirkhill Ct Broxburn EH52. . 115 C5
Fauldhouse EH47 . . . . 181 E6
Gorebridge EH23. . . . . 195 C8
Kirkhill Dr EH16 . . . . 122 A4
Kirkhill Gdns
Edinburgh EH16. . . . . 122 A5
Penicuik EH26 . . . . 191 F5
Kirkhill Pk EH52 . . . . 115 C5
Kirkhill Pl EH52. . . . . 115 D5
Kirkhill Prim Sch EH52 . . 115 B6
Kirkhill Rd Broxburn EH52 . 115 D5
Edinburgh EH16. . . . . 122 A4
Penicuik EH26 . . . . 191 F5
Kirkhill Terr
Broxburn EH52 . . . . 115 C5
Edinburgh EH16. . . . . 122 A5
Gorebridge EH23. . . . . 174 A1
Kirkhill Way EH26. . . . . 191 F5
Kirk La EH54. . . . . 143 B2
Kirkland Dr FK6 . . . . 36 B2
Kirklands Dunfermline KY12 29 A2
Edinburgh EH12. . . . . 119 D4
Penicuik EH26 . . . . 191 E5
Kirklands Park Cres EH29 . 88 F2
Kirklands Park Gdns EH29. 88 F2
Kirklands Park Gr EH29 . . . 88 F2
Kirklands Park Rigg EH29 . 88 F2
Kirklands Park St EH29. . . . 88 F2
Kirklands The FK7 . . . . 6 F3
KIRKLISTON. 89 B1
Kirkliston L Ctr EH29 . . . . . 88 F2
Kirkliston Prim Sch EH29 . 89 A2
Kirkliston Rd EH30. . . . . 89 B8
Kirk Loan EH12 . . . . 119 E6
KIRKNEWTON. 145 F2
Kirknewton Ct EH27 . . . . . 145 C3
Kirknewton Prim Sch
EH27. . . . . 145 D2
Kirknewton Sta EH27 . . . . 145 C3
Kirk Pk Dunbar EH42. . . . . . . 78 B2
Edinburgh EH16. . . . . 151 B8
Kirk Pl EH51. . . . . 64 D7
Kirk Ports EH39. . . . . 54 C7
Kirk Rd Aberlady EH32. . . . . . 71 C4
Bathgate EH48 . . . . 141 C5
Shotts ML7 . . . . 179 F4
Kirkside Cres FK7. . . . . 7 B5
Kirkslap FK6. . . . . 36 E2
Kirk St Culross KY12 . . . . 25 D1
Edinburgh EH6. . . . . 93 F4
Kincardine FK10 . . . . 23 E4
Prestonpans EH32. . . . . 96 F2
Kirkstyle Gdns EH29 . . . . . . 89 B1
KIRKTON Burntisland 33 D1
Livingston 143 A1
Kirkton Ave EH48 . . . . 141 D5
Kirkton Bank EH26. . . . . 191 D5
Kirkton Bsns Ctr EH54 . . . 143 B3
KIRKTON CAMPUS 163 F8
Kirkton Campus EH54. . . . . 164 B8
Kirkton Ct EH48. . . . . 141 D6
Kirkton Dr KY3 . . . . 33 D1
Kirkton North Rd EH54 . . . 143 C3
Kirkton Pl Bathgate EH48 . . 141 D5
Cowdenbeath KY4. . . . . 13 B5
Falkirk FK2 . . . . 39 C3
Kirkton Rd KY3 . . . . 33 E1
Kirkton South Rd EH54. . . 143 C2
Kirkview EH41 . . . . 130 C8
Kirkway FK2. . . . . 22 D4
Kirkwood Ave FK2 . . . . 61 C2
Kirkwood Cres KY12 . . . . 28 B2
Kirk Wynd
Clackmannan FK10 . . . . 11 A5
2 Falkirk FK1. . . . . 60 B4
Kirkcaldy KY1 . . . . 17 C4
Stirling FK7 . . . . 7 B4
Kisimul Ct 3 EH12. . . . . 119 B7
Kitchener Cres EH32. . . . . . . 98 E5
Kittle Yds EH9 . . . . 121 E4
Klondyke St EH21. . . . . 123 E4
Knapphill KY11 . . . . 46 F7
Knightsbridge Ho EH54 . . 143 C8
Knightslaw Pl EH26 . . . . 191 D5
KNIGHTSRIDGE 143 C8
Knightsridge Ct EH52 . . . . 114 C2
Knightsridge East Rd
EH54 . . . . 143 D8
Knightsridge Ind Est
EH54. . . . . 143 C7
Knightsridge Prim Sch
EH54. . . . . 143 D7
Knightsridge Rd EH52. . . . 114 C2
Knightsridge Rdbt EH54. . 143 C7
Knightsridge West Rd
EH54 . . . . 143 B7
Knights Way FK6 . . . . 36 C2
Knockenhair Rd EH42. . . . . . 78 B2
Knockhill Cl KY5. . . . . 14 B7
Knockhouse Farm Cotts
KY12 . . . . 28 B4
Knockhouse Gdns KY12 . . . 28 B2
Knockhouse Rd KY12 . . . . . . 28 B2
Knockhouse Terr KY12. . . . 28 B2
Knoll Croft Rd ML7 . . . . . . 180 A3
Knowehead Rd
Crossford KY12. . . . . 28 A2
Redding FK2 . . . . 61 C2
Knowepark Ct EH47. . . . . . 162 A2
Knowepark Rd EH47 . . . . . 162 A1
Knowesley Pk EH41 . . . . . . 129 D8
Knowes Rd EH41. . . . . 129 E8
Knowe The Alloa FK10 . . . . . . 5 C2
Dalgety Bay KY11 . . . . 48 C3
Knowetop EH54. . . . . 164 C7
Knowetop Pl EH25 . . . . 171 F3
Knowfaulds Rd FK10 . . . . 4 B3
Knox Acad EH41 . . . . 129 F8
Knox Ct EH41 . . . . 130 A8
Knox Pl EH41 . . . . 130 A8
Komarom Pl EH22 . . . . 153 D3
Kyle Ave FK7 . . . . 20 E7
Kyle Cres KY11 . . . . 30 C1
Kyle Pl EH7. . . . . 229 C4
Kyles The KY1 . . . . 17 E6

L

Labrador Ave EH54 . . . . . . 143 F4
Laburnum Arch Ct 4
EH32 . . . . 96 F1
Laburnum Ave EH32 . . . . . . 97 E3
Laburnum Dr KY1. . . . . 17 C8
Laburnum Gr
Burntisland KY3. . . . . 33 F2
Stirling FK8 . . . . 6 F5
Laburnum Pl EH22. . . . . 174 E6
Laburnum Rd
Dunfermline KY11. . . . . 29 C1
Whitburn EH47 . . . . 161 C6
Lade Braes KY11. . . . . 48 B3
Lade Ct EH49 . . . . 84 E7
Lade Dr FK5 . . . . 59 C8
Lade Gn KY11. . . . . 48 B3
Ladehead EH6. . . . . 93 D4
Lade Mill FK7. . . . . 7 C1
Lade Rd FK4. . . . . 58 A5
Ladeside Ave EH47. . . . . . . 162 C8
Ladeside Cres FK5. . . . . 38 E1
Ladeside Dr EH47. . . . . 162 C8
Ladeside Gdns EH47 . . . . . 162 B8
Ladeside Prim Sch FK5 . . . 59 C8
Ladeside Rd EH47. . . . . 162 C8
Lade The EH14. . . . . 168 D8
Ladiemeadow EH12. . . . . . 119 E5
Lady Anne Ct KY4. . . . . 30 E6
Lady Brae EH23. . . . . 195 D7
Lady Brae Pl EH23 . . . . 195 E8
Ladyburn Pl KY3. . . . . 35 A3
Lady Campbell's Wlk
KY12 . . . . 29 A4
Ladycroft EH14 . . . . 147 C2
Lady Ct EH47 . . . . 161 E7
Lady Emily Way EH23 . . . . 195 C8
Lady Hall Rd TD13 . . . . 218 F4
Lady Helen Cotts KY5 . . . . . 15 B8
Lady Helen St KY1 . . . . 17 B2
Lady Jane Gdns EH39 . . . . . 54 D6
Lady Jane Rd EH39 . . . . 54 D6
Lady Lawson St EH3 . . . . . 228 C2
Lady Menzies Pl 3 EH7. . . 94 A2
Lady Nairn Ave KY1 . . . . 17 F6
Lady Nairne Cres EH8 . . . . 122 D7
Lady Nairne Gr EH8. . . . . . 122 D7
Lady Nairne Loan EH8 . . . 122 D7
Lady Nairne Pl EH8 . . . . . . 122 D7
Lady Nairne Rd KY12. . . . . . 28 E6
Lady Pl EH54 . . . . 143 B5
Lady Rd EH16. . . . . 122 A3
Lady Road Pl EH22. . . . . . . 174 B6
Ladysgate Ct FK2 . . . . 39 B3
Ladysmill FK2 . . . . 60 D5
Ladysmill Ct KY12. . . . . 29 A1
Ladysmill Ind Est FK1. . . . . 60 C5
Ladysmith Rd EH9 . . . . 121 E2
Ladysneuk Rd FK9 . . . . 2 D2
Lady Victoria Bsns Ctr
EH22. . . . . 174 A4
LADYWELL 143 D6
Ladywell EH21. . . . . 124 C6
Ladywell Ave EH12. . . . . . . 119 D5
Ladywell Ct
Edinburgh EH12. . . . . 119 D6
Larbert FK5 . . . . 38 A3
Ladywell Dr FK10 . . . . 4 B3
Ladywell East Rd EH54 . . . 143 D6
Ladywell Gdns EH12 . . . . . 119 D5
Ladywell Gr FK10 . . . . 11 A4
Ladywell Pl FK10 . . . . 4 B3
Ladywell Rd EH12. . . . . 119 D6
Ladywell View EH51. . . . . . . 63 D5
Ladywell Way EH21 . . . . . . 124 C6
Ladywell West Rd EH54 . . 143 C6
LADYWOOD 192 A6
Ladywood FK10. . . . . 11 C4
Ladywood Pl EH54. . . . . 143 B5
Lady Wynd EH1. . . . . 228 C2
Lafferty Pl FK6 . . . . 36 F1
Lagan Rd ML8. . . . . 215 A1
Laggan Ave ML7. . . . . 180 B3
Laggan Path ML7 . . . . 179 E6
Laichfield EH14. . . . . 120 B3
Laichpark Pl EH14 . . . . 120 B3
Laichpark Rd EH14. . . . . 120 B3
Laidlaw Gdns EH33 . . . . . . 126 C4
Laing Gdns EH52. . . . . 115 C6
Laing Terr
Edinburgh EH15. . . . . 123 C8
Penicuik EH26 . . . . 191 F7
Laird's Dr FK10 . . . . 11 B3
Laird's Entry EH37 . . . . 176 C3
Laird Terr EH19. . . . . 173 D6
Lairox Terr FK6. . . . . 36 D3
Lakeside Rd KY2. . . . . 16 F4
Lamb Ct EH39 . . . . 54 A7
Lambert Dr KY12 . . . . 29 D4
Lamberton Ave FK7. . . . . 7 C3
Lamberton Ct EH34 . . . . . . 156 E6
Lambert Terr FK10. . . . . 10 C7
Lambie St EH47. . . . . 161 B7
Lamb's Cl EH8 . . . . 229 B1
Lambs Ct EH6 . . . . 93 C7
Lamb's Pend EH26. . . . . 191 F4
Lamer Ct EH42. . . . . 78 E3
Lamer St EH42. . . . . 78 E3
Lamington Rd EH33. . . . . . . 128 C7
Lammerlaws Rd KY3 . . . . 50 F8
Lammermoor Gdns EH33 126 B6
Lammermoor Terr
Edinburgh EH16. . . . . 122 C1
Tranent EH33. . . . . 126 B6
Lammermuir Cres
Dunbar EH42. . . . . 78 C2
Haddington EH41 . . . . 130 C8
Lammermuir Ct EH31 . . . . . 52 B2
Lammermuir Pl KY2 . . . . 16 F5
Lammerview
Gladsmuir EH33 . . . . 128 C7
12 Tranent EH33. . . . . 126 C5
Lammerview Terr EH31 . . . 52 A2
Lamond View FK5 . . . . 38 D1
Lamont Cres FK7 . . . . 8 D5
Lamont Way EH54 . . . . 143 D8
Lampacre Rd EH12. . . . . 119 E5
Lanark Ave EH54. . . . . 143 A6
Lanark Rd
Edinburgh, Kingsknowe
EH14. . . . . 120 B1
Edinburgh, Wester Hailes
EH14. . . . . 148 E6
Lanark Road W EH14. . . . . 147 D3
Landale Gdns KY3 . . . . 33 E2
Landale Pl KY3 . . . . 33 E2
Landale St KY5 . . . . 14 B8
Lane The EH21. . . . . 124 E1
Langfauld Gdns EH48 . . . . 140 E5
Langhill Farm Cotts
EH25 . . . . 171 F6
Langhill Pl FK6 . . . . 36 C1
Langlaw Rd EH22 . . . . 174 D8
LANGLEES. 39 D1
Langlees Prim Sch FK2 . . . 60 B8
Langlees St FK2 . . . . 39 C1
Lang Loan
Edinburgh EH17, EH20 . . . . 151 C3
Loanhead EH20. . . . . 151 B2
Lang Rigg EH30. . . . . 68 A1
Langriggs EH41. . . . . 130 B8
Langside EH40. . . . . 103 D8
Langside Cres EH55. . . . . . . 164 A5
Langside Dr EH48. . . . . 138 B3
Langside Gdns EH55 . . . . . 164 A6
LANGTON 144 F3
Langton Ave EH53 . . . . 144 E4
Langton Gdns EH53 . . . . . . 144 F3
LANGTON PK 144 F3
Langton Rd
East Calder EH53 . . . . 144 F3
Edinburgh EH9. . . . . 121 E3
Westquarter FK2. . . . . 61 A3
Langton Steadings EH53 . 144 F2
Langton Terr EH53. . . . . 144 E4
Langton View EH53 . . . . . . 144 F3
Lanrigg Ave EH47. . . . . 181 E7
Lanrigg Ct EH47 . . . . 181 F7
Lanrigg Rd EH47. . . . . 181 F7
Lansbury Ct 2 EH22 . . . . . 153 A3
Lansbury St KY1 . . . . 17 E7
Lansdowne Cres
Edinburgh EH12. . . . . 228 A2
Kincardine FK10 . . . . 23 E4
Shotts ML7 . . . . 180 B3
Lapicide Pl EH6. . . . . 93 E5
La Porte Prec 5 FK3. . . . . . . 40 D1
Lapwing Dr KY11 . . . . 47 B7
Larach Ct KY2 . . . . 16 C8
LARBERT. 38 B2
Larbert Ave EH54 . . . . 143 A6
Larbert High Sch FK5. . . . . 38 E1
Larbert Rd FK4 . . . . 58 B6
Larbert Sta FK5 . . . . 38 C2
Larbert Village Prim Sch
FK5. . . . . 38 B1
Larbourfield EH11 . . . . 119 D1
Larchbank EH54. . . . . 143 E5
Larch Cres EH22. . . . . 174 F6
Larch Dr EH47. . . . . 161 C6
Larchfield EH14. . . . . 147 C2
Larchfield Neuk EH14 . . . . 147 C2
Larchfield Path ML7 . . . . . 180 B2
Larch Gr Dunfermline KY11. . 46 D8
Livingston EH54. . . . . 144 B6
Stenhousemuir FK5. . . . . 38 F3
Larch St FK3. . . . . 61 C6
Largo Pl EH6 . . . . 93 E6
Larkfield Dr EH22. . . . . 152 E1
Larkfield Rd EH22. . . . . 152 E2
Lasswade Bank EH17. . . . . 151 C5
Lasswade Ct EH18 . . . . 152 A1
Lasswade Gr EH17 . . . . 151 C5
Lasswade High Sch Ctr
EH19. . . . . 173 A7
Lasswade Prim Sch
EH19. . . . . 173 C8
Lasswade Rd
Bonnyrigg and Lasswade EH17,
EH20. . . . . 151 F2
Dalkeith EH22 . . . . 152 E2
Edinburgh EH16, EH17 . . . 151 C6
Loanhead EH20. . . . . 172 D8
Latchburn View EH47 . . . . 162 C7
Latch Pk EH13. . . . . 149 C7
Latch Rd EH42. . . . . 78 E1
Latch The KY12 . . . . 27 C1
Lathallan Dr FK2. . . . . 61 E2
Lauderdale Cres EH42 . . . . 78 C2
Lauderdale St EH9. . . . . 121 C5
Lauder Loan EH9 . . . . 121 E4
Lauder Lodge 14 EH22 . . . 153 A3
Lauder Pl EH40 . . . . 103 E6
Lauder Rd Dalkeith EH22 . . 153 C2
Edinburgh EH9. . . . . 121 D4
Kirkcaldy KY2 . . . . 17 C6
Lauder St KY12 . . . . 29 C6
Laura Fergusson Ct EH12 . 91 B1
Laurel Bank EH22. . . . . 153 C2
Laurelbank Ave FK4. . . . . . . 58 A3
Laurelbank Ct EH53 . . . . . . 144 F2
Laurel Bank Pl EH22 . . . . . 174 E6
Laurel Bank Rd EH22. . . . . 174 E6
Laurel Cres KY2 . . . . 17 B7
Laurel Ct Denny FK6 . . . . 36 D3
Falkirk FK1 . . . . 59 C6
Laurel Gdns KY12. . . . . 27 F6
Laurel Gr Bonnybridge FK4. . 57 F3
Westquarter FK2. . . . . 61 A2
Laurelhill Bsns Pk FK7. . . . . 6 F6
Laurelhill Gdns FK8. . . . . 6 F5
Laurelhill Pl FK8. . . . . 7 A5
Laurel Pl FK4 . . . . 57 F3
Laurel Rd KY11 . . . . 46 C2
Laurels The FK10 . . . . 4 B1
Laurel Terr EH11. . . . . 120 E5
Laurencecroft Rd FK8. . . . . . 2 B2
Laurie Gdns FK2 . . . . 82 B8
Laurie St EH6. . . . . 94 A4
LAURIESTON 61 B4
Laurieston Ind Est FK2. . . . 60 F3
Laurieston Prim Sch FK2 . 61 A3
Laurieston Rd FK3 . . . . 61 A6
Lauriston Building EH3 . . 228 C2
Lauriston Castle★ EH4. . . . 91 E5
Lauriston Dr KY12 . . . . 29 D5
Lauriston Farm Rd EH4 . . . 91 F4
Lauriston Gdns EH3. . . . . . 228 C1
Lauriston Pk EH3 . . . . 228 C1
Lauriston Pl EH3. . . . . 228 C2
Lauriston St EH3. . . . . 228 C2
Lauriston Terr EH3 . . . . . . 228 C2
Laurmont Ct FK2 . . . . 61 A3
Laverockbank Ave EH5. . . . 93 C6
Laverockbank Cres EH5. . . 93 C6
Laverockbank Gdns EH5 . . 93 C6
Laverockbank Gr EH5. . . . . 93 C6
Laverockbank Rd EH5. . . . . 93 C6
Laverockbank Terr EH5 . . . 93 C6
Laverockdale Cres EH13 . 149 B6
Laverockdale Loan EH13 . 149 B5
Laverockdale Pk EH13 . . . 149 B5
Laverock Dr EH26. . . . . 191 D6
Laverock Pk EH49. . . . . 85 A5
Lavery Ave FK5 . . . . 38 B1
Lawers Cres FK2. . . . . 62 A1
Lawers Pl FK3 . . . . 61 E5
Lawers Sq EH26 . . . . 192 A7
Lawfield Prim Sch EH22 174 D7
Lawfield Rd EH22. . . . . 174 D7
Lawhead Cotts EH40 . . . . . . 75 F3
Lawhead Pl EH26 . . . . 191 C6
Lawhouse Toll EH15 . . . . . 123 B4
Lawnmarket EH1 . . . . 229 A3
Law Pl Denny FK6. . . . . 36 E1
Edinburgh EH15. . . . . 95 A1
Law Prim Sch EH39. . . . . 54 C6
Law Rd Dunfermline KY11. . . 29 F4
North Berwick EH39 . . . . 54 C7
Lawrence Ct FK5 . . . . 38 B5
Lawrie Dr EH26. . . . . 191 E7
Lawrie Terr EH20 . . . . 172 B7
Lawson Cres EH30 . . . . 89 C8
Lawson Ct EH42 . . . . 78 D2
Lawson Gdns KY1. . . . . 17 E8
Lawson Glade EH54. . . . . . . 164 C7
Lawson Pl Dunbar EH42 . . . . 78 D2
Maddiston FK2 . . . . 83 A5
Lawson St KY1. . . . . 17 E8
Lawson Way EH33 . . . . 126 C5
Lawswell FK10. . . . . 5 E3
Laxdale Dr FK6 . . . . 57 D7
Laxford Cres KY11 . . . . 48 A3
LEADBURN 208 F3
Leadburn Ave KY12 . . . . 29 A7
Leadervale Rd EH16. . . . . . . 150 F8
Leadervale Terr EH16 . . . . 150 F8
Leadside Cres KY12. . . . . 29 A7
Leamington Pl EH10 . . . . . 228 B1
Leamington Rd EH3. . . . . . . 228 A1
Leamington Terr EH10 . . . 121 B5
Leamington Wharf EH3 . . 228 A1
Leapark Dr FK4 . . . . 57 F3
Lea Rig ML11. . . . . 217 F7
Learmonth Ave EH4. . . . . 92 F2
Learmonth Cres
Edinburgh EH4. . . . . 92 F2
West Calder EH55. . . . . 163 D3
Learmonth Ct EH4 . . . . 92 F1
Learmonth Gardens La 1
EH4 . . . . 92 F1
Learmonth Gdns EH4 . . . . . 92 F1
Learmonth Gr EH4. . . . . 92 F2
Learmonth Pk 2 EH4. . . . . . 92 F2
Learmonth Pl EH4 . . . . 228 A4

Learmonth St FK1 60 B4
Learmonth Terr EH4 228 A4
Learmonth Terrace La
EH4 228 A4
Learmouth Garden Mews 4
EH4 93 A2
Leaston Farm Cotts
EH36 220 A2
Lec Ct FK2 60 F4
Ledi Ave FK10 4 B2
Ledi Pl FK1 81 E7
Ledi Terr EH26 192 A7
Ledi View FK9 2 B3
Ledmore Pl FK1 60 E1
Lee Cres EH15 123 B8
Legion Ct KY2 17 A5
Leighton Cres EH22 174 D7
Leighton St KY12 26 B2
Leishman Ct EH48 138 D2
Leishman Dr KY11 29 D1
Leishman Twr FK1 60 C4
Leisure Bowl The FK10 10 B7
LEITH 94 C6
Leith Acad EH6 94 A3
Leith Ave KY3 33 F2
Leithhead EH27 166 E4
Leith Pl FK6 57 D7
Leith Prim Sch EH6 94 A4
Leith St EH1 229 A4
Leith Victoria Swim Ctr
EH6 93 F5
Leith Walk Prim Sch EH7 93 E2
Leith Waterworld EH6 94 A4
Leith Wlk EH7 93 F3
Lempockwells EH34 156 F4
Lempockwells Rd EH34 156 E6
Lendrick Ave FK1 59 F2
Lennel Ave EH12 120 C8
Lennie Cotts EH12 118 D8
Lennox Ave FK7 7 A4
Lennox Gdns EH49 84 D7
Lennoxlove Acredales Cotts
EH41 130 B7
Lennoxlove House
EH41 130 B5
Lennox Milne Ct EH41 130 B8
Lennox Rd EH41 130 C8
Lennox Row EH5 93 B6
Lennox St EH4 228 A4
Lennox Street La EH4 228 A4
Lennox Terr FK3 61 F5
Lennymuir EH12 90 B1
Leny Cres FK1 60 A1
Leny Pl KY12 29 B5
Lenzie Ave EH54 143 A6
Leopold Pl 1 EH7 93 E2
Leslie Pl EH3 93 B2
Leslie Rd KY11 46 F5
Leslie St KY1 35 B8
Leslie Way EH42 78 D1
Lesslie's Bldgs KY3 33 E1
Lestrange Ave FK12 5 B7
LETHAM 39 C8
Letham Ave EH53 144 B7
Letham Cotts FK2 39 D8
Letham Cres EH53 144 B7
Letham Dr EH41 129 F8
Letham Gait KY11 47 F3
Letham Gdns Dunbar EH42 78 D2
Pumpherston EH53 144 B7
Letham Gr EH53 144 B7
Letham Hill Ave KY11 47 E4
Letham Holdings EH53 144 C6
Letham Mains Smallholdings
EH41 129 C7
Letham Pk Dunbar EH42 78 D2
Pumpherston EH53 144 B7
Letham Pl Dunbar EH42 78 C3
Pumpherston EH53 144 B7
Letham Prim Sch EH54 144 B5
Letham Rd Dunbar EH42 78 C2
Pumpherston EH54 144 A8
Letham Rise KY11 47 F3
Letham Terr EH53 144 B7
Letham Terrs FK2 22 C1
Letham Way KY11 47 F3
Lethen View FK10 4 C3
Leuchatsbeath Dr KY4 13 B5
Leven Cl EH3 228 B1
Leven Ct FK10 10 C5
LEVENHALL 125 A6
Leven Pl ML7 179 E6
LEVEN SEAT 182 A4
Levenseat Ind Est EH47 181 B4
Leven St Edinburgh EH3 228 B1
Falkirk FK2 60 B8
Leven Terr EH3 228 C1
Leven Wlk EH54 144 A4
Leving Pl EH54 143 C3
Lewis Ct Alloa FK10 10 B5
Falkirk FK1 60 B2
Lewis Rd FK2 61 F1
Lewis Terr EH11 228 A2
Lewisvale Ave EH21 124 E5
Lewisvale Ct EH21 124 E5
Leyden Pk EH19 173 B8
Leyden Pl EH19 173 B7
Leyden Rd EH27 166 C6
Leyland Rd EH48 141 C3
Leys Park Rd KY12 29 B4
LIBERTON 150 F7
Liberton Brae EH16 151 A8
Liberton Dr EH16 150 E7
Liberton Gdns EH16 151 A6
Liberton High Sch EH17 151 C8
Liberton Hospl EH16 151 B7
Liberton Pl EH16 151 B7
Liberton Prim Sch EH16 122 A2
Liberton Rd EH16 122 A1
Library La 7 FK3 40 D1
Liddesdale Pl EH3 93 B2
Liddle Dr EH51 63 E5
Lidgate Shot EH28 117 E2
Liggar's Pl KY12 28 F1
Liggat Pl EH52 115 F5
Liggat Syke EH52 115 B5
Ligget Syke Pl EH52 116 A5
Lighton Terr EH47 162 B1
Lilac Ave EH22 174 F6
Lilac Cres KY1 17 C8
Lilac Gr KY11 46 D8
Lillies La EH41 220 F7
Lilly's La KY11 29 B1
Lilybank Ct FK10 5 D1
Lilyhill Terr EH8 94 C1
Lily Terr EH11 120 E4
Lime Ave EH30 66 F2
Limebank Pk EH53 144 F2
Limefield EH17 151 E5
Limefield Ave EH55 164 A5
Limefield Cres EH48 141 E6
Limefield Gdns EH55 164 A5
Limefield House Bsns Ctr
EH55 164 B5
Limefield La EH48 141 D6
Limefield Pl EH48 141 D6
Limefield Rd
Bathgate EH48 141 D7
Polbeth EH55 164 A5
West Calder EH55 163 E3
Lime Gr Dunfermline KY11 29 E1
Livingston EH54 144 B6
Mayfield EH22 174 D8
North Berwick EH39 54 F6
Polmont FK2 61 E2
Stenhousemuir FK5 38 D1
LIMEKILNS 45 E3
Limekilns EH34 157 A6
Limekilns Gr EH53 145 A3
Limekilns Prim Sch KY11 45 E3
Limekilns Rd KY12 28 F1
Lime Pl EH19 173 B6
Lime Rd FK1 59 B4
LIMERIGG 108 B2
Limerigg Prim Sch FK1 108 C1
Lime St FK3 61 C6
Limes The EH10 121 A4
Limetree Wlk EH42 76 D5
Lime Tree Wlk FK10 10 A5
Limeylands Cres EH35 155 E6
Limeylands Ct EH35 155 D7
Limeylands Rd EH35 155 D7
Limpet Ness KY11 46 D3
Lina St KY2 17 B5
Linburn Gr KY11 29 F4
Linburn Pk EH27 146 A5
Linburn Pl KY11 29 F3
Linburn Rd
Dunfermline KY11 29 F3
Wilkieston EH27 146 B5
Lindean Pl EH6 94 B4
Lindean Terr EH27 145 F6
Linden Ave Denny FK6 36 C3
Stirling FK7 7 C6
Linden Gr EH54 144 B6
Linden Pl EH20 172 D8
Lindores Dr Kirkcaldy KY2 16 E8
Tranent EH33 126 D6
Lind Pl FK4 57 C4
Lindsay Dr FK9 2 B4
Lindsay Gdns EH48 141 C5
Lindsay Pl Edinburgh EH6 93 E5
Lochgelly KY5 14 A8
Lindsay Rd EH6 93 E6
Lindsay Row EH24 172 D1
Lindsay Sq EH54 142 D5
Lindsay St EH6 93 E6
Lindsay's Wynd KY12 26 F6
Lindsay Way EH54 143 D8
Lindsey Cir EH24 172 D1
Lingerwood Farm Cotts
EH22 174 A4
Lingerwood Rd EH22 174 B4
Lingerwood Wlk EH22 174 B4
Linhouse Dr EH53 144 E3
Linhouse Rd EH53 144 E3
Linkfield Rd EH21 124 E6
Link Rd Crombie KY12 44 D6
Dalgety Bay KY11 47 F3
Oakley KY12 26 F7
Links Ave EH21 124 B7
Links Ct Bo'ness EH51 64 A8
Cockenzie & Port Seton
EH32 97 D4
Links Dr KY12 28 A2
Links Gardens La EH6 94 B5
Links Gdns EH6 94 B4
Links Pl Bo'ness EH51 64 B7
Burntisland KY3 50 E8
Cockenzie & Port Seton
EH32 97 E4
Edinburgh EH6 94 A5
Links Rd Bo'ness EH51 64 A8
Cockenzie & Port Seton
EH32 97 E4
Longniddry EH32 98 E5
North Berwick EH39 54 B7
Links St Kirkcaldy KY1 17 B2
Musselburgh EH21 124 C6
Links View
Cockenzie & Port Seton
EH32 97 E4
Musselburgh EH21 124 C7
Links Wlk EH32 97 E4
LINKTOWN 17 B2
LINLITHGOW 85 C6
Linlithgow Acad EH49 84 E5
LINLITHGOW BRIDGE 84 D8
Linlithgow Bridge Prim Sch
EH49 84 D7
Linlithgow Canal Ctr
EH49 85 A6
Linlithgow L Ctr EH49 84 D5
Linlithgow Palace EH49 85 A7
Linlithgow Pl FK5 38 E4
Linlithgow Prim Sch EH49 84 F6
Linlithgow Rd EH51 63 F6
Linlithgow Sta EH49 85 B7
Linlithgow Story Mus The
EH49 85 A7
Linlithgow Terr EH35 155 E7
Linmill Rd FK1 110 A5
Linn Dean Wildlife Reserve
EH36 224 E6
Linnet Brae EH54 143 C5
Linnet Way KY11 30 A2
Linn Mill Clackmannan FK10 11 D6
Queensferry EH30 67 E2
Linn Pl Airth FK2 22 E3
Broxburn EH52 115 E4
Linsay Macdonald Ct
KY12 29 D3
Linties Nest KY3 34 F2
Linton Ct KY3 35 A4
Linton La KY2 16 E6
Linton Pl KY11 46 E3
Lint Riggs FK1 60 B5
Lintview FK1 108 B5
Linty La EH26 191 D6
Linum Gr KY1 17 C7
Linview La EH54 164 F4
Linwell Ct KY3 34 B1
Lionthorn Rd FK1 59 F1
Lion Well Wynd EH49 84 F7
Lipney FK11 4 A6
Lismore Ave
5 Edinburgh EH8 94 C1
Kirkcaldy KY2 16 F8
Lismore Cres EH8 94 C1
Lismore Ct FK1 60 B2
Lismore Pl KY2 16 F7
Lister Ct FK9 2 A6
Lister Rd EH54 143 B1
Listloaning Pl EH49 84 D7
Listloaning Rd EH49 84 D7
Liston Dr EH29 89 A2
Liston Pl EH29 89 A2
Liston Rd EH29 89 A1
Lithgow Pl FK6 57 C8
Little Acre EH22 174 D8
Little Carriden EH51 64 D5
Little Craigs View 3 KY3 33 D1
Little Denny Rd FK6 36 D1
Little Foothorn KY12 44 E6
Little France Cres EH16 122 E1
Little France Dr EH16 122 E1
Little France Ho EH17 151 D8
Little France Mills EH16 122 D1
Littlejohn Ave EH10 149 F8
Littlejohn Rd EH10 149 E8
Littlejohn Wynd EH10 149 F8
Little King St EH1 229 A4
Little Mill Bsns Pk EH49 84 C8
Little Pinkerton Cotts
EH42 107 A5
Little Rd EH16 151 B7
Little Sales Ave KY11 47 F3
Little Sandhaven KY12 42 D8
Little Spott Cotts EH42 105 F2
Little Wood Gr EH19 173 B5
Livery St EH48 141 A7
Livesay Rd KY11 46 D1
Livesey Terr EH26 192 A8
Livilands Ct FK8 7 B5
Livilands Gate FK8 7 B5
Livilands La FK8 7 B5
LIVINGSTON 143 D6
Livingston Designer Outlet
EH54 143 D2
Livingstone Cres FK2 60 E5
Livingstone Dr
Bo'ness EH51 63 D6
Burntisland KY3 33 F2
Laurieston FK2 60 F2
Livingstone E Rdbt EH54 114 D1
Livingstone Pl EH9 121 D5
Livingstone Quadrant
ML7 159 D4
Livingstone St EH55 162 E2
Livingstone Terr FK2 61 B1
Livingstone Way FK10 11 A5
Livingston La KY3 49 C7
Livingston Mill Farm
EH54 143 A2
Livingston North Sta
EH54 143 B6
Livingston Rd
Dechmont EH52, EH54 114 D1
Livingston EH54 143 E6
Livingston South Sta
EH54 165 A7
LIVINGSTON VILLAGE 143 C2
Livingston Village Prim Sch
EH54 143 B3
Lixmount Ave EH5 93 C6
Lixmount Gdns EH5 93 C6
Lizzie Brice's Rdbt EH54 144 B1
Llynallan Rd ML7 158 F4
LOAN 83 C4
LOANBURN 191 E5
Loanburn EH26 191 E5
Loanburn Ave EH26 191 F6
Loanfoot Cres EH52 115 A5
Loanfoot Gdns FK7 20 C4
Loanfoot Rd EH52 115 A4
LOANHEAD Roslin 172 B7
Stirling 7 E6
Loanhead Ave Denny FK4 57 D6
Grangemouth FK3 61 E6
Loanhead Cotts EH29 89 B2
Loanhead L Ctr EH20 172 B8
Loanhead Pl KY2 17 A5
Loanhead Prim Sch
EH20 172 C8
Loanhead Rd EH20 151 A2
Loaning Cres EH7 94 D2
Loaninghill Pk EH52 115 B4
Loaninghill Rd EH52 115 B4
Loaning Rd EH7 94 D2
Loan Pl ML7 159 E6
LOANSTONE 192 B5
Loan The Bo'ness EH51 63 D6
Loanhead EH20 172 B7
Pathhead EH37 175 C7
South Queensferry EH30 68 B1
Torphichen EH48 111 F6
Wallyford EH21 125 B6
Lochaber KY11 45 B4
Lochaber Cres ML7 180 B3
Lochaber Dr FK5 38 E3
Loch Awe Way EH47 161 B7
Lochbank EH54 143 E5
Lochbrae FK10 5 D2
Lochbridge Rd EH39 54 D6
Loch Ctr EH33 126 D6
Loch Earn Way EH47 161 C7
LOCHEND 94 B2
Lochend Ave Dunbar EH42 78 E1
Edinburgh EH7 94 B3
Lochend Castle Barns
EH7 94 B2
Lochend Cl EH8 229 C3
Lochend Cres
Dunbar EH42 78 D1
Edinburgh EH7 94 C2
Lochend Dr EH7 94 C2
Lochend Gdns
Dunbar EH42 78 D1
Edinburgh EH7 94 B2
Lochend Gr EH7 94 C2
Lochend Ho EH7 94 C2
Lochend Ind Est EH28 117 B5
Lochend Pk EH7 94 B3
Lochend Quadrant EH7 94 C2
Lochend Rd Dunbar EH42 78 E1
Edinburgh EH7 94 B3
Ratho Station EH28, EH29 117 A7
Lochend Road N EH21 124 B6
Lochend Road S
Edinburgh EH7 94 B2
Musselburgh EH21 124 B6
Lochend Sq EH7 94 B2
Loch Fyne Way EH47 161 C7
LOCHGELLY 14 C7
Lochgelly Ind Pk KY5 14 D7
Lochgelly North Specl Sch
KY5 14 B8
Lochgelly Rd KY4 13 D5
Lochgelly South Prim Sch
KY5 14 B7
Lochgelly West Prim Sch
KY5 14 A7
Lochgreen Rd FK1 59 E2
Lochgreen Rdbt FK1 59 F2
Lochhead Ave FK6 36 E1
Lochhead Ct KY12 29 A6
Lochhill Cotts EH32 99 E7
Lochies Rd Burntisland KY3 34 A1
Clackmannan FK10 11 A4
Lochies Sch FK10 5 F1
Lochinvar Pl FK4 58 C3
Lochinvar Rd KY11 46 C1
Lochlands Ave FK5 59 B8
Lochlands Bsns Pk FK5 59 B8
Lochlands Ind Est FK5 59 A8
Lochlands Loan FK5 59 B7
Lochlea Gr KY2 17 A7
Lochlea Terr KY2 17 A7
Loch Linnhe Ct EH47 161 C7
Lochmaben Dr FK5 38 F4
Loch Maree Way EH47 161 B7
Lochpark Pl FK6 36 E2
Loch Pl EH30 68 B1
Loch Rd Edinburgh EH4 92 A2
South Queensferry EH30 68 B1
Tranent EH33 126 D6
Lochridge Pl FK6 36 D1
LOCHRIN 228 A1
Lochrin Bldgs EH3 228 B1
Lochrin Pl EH3 228 B1
Lochrin Terr EH3 228 B1
Lochshot Pl EH54 143 A3
Lochside Ave EH12 118 F4
Lochside Cotts FK2 61 B2
Lochside Cres
Edinburgh EH12 118 F4
Redding FK2 61 B2
Lochside Ct EH12 119 A4
Lochside Pl EH12 119 A4
Lochside Rd FK1 108 C1
Lochside View EH12 118 F5
Lochside Way EH12 119 A4
Loch Sq EH33 126 D6
Loch St KY12 29 C7
Loch Trool Way EH47 161 B7
Lochwood Pk KY12 12 B1
Lockerby Cotts EH16 151 C6
Lockerby Cres EH16 151 C6
Lockerby Gr EH16 151 C6
Lockharton Ave EH11 120 E2
Lockharton Cres EH11 120 E2
Lockharton Gdns EH14 120 E3
Lockhart Terr EH25 171 F3
Lock Rd KY11 67 B8
Lock Sixteen FK1 59 D5
Lodeneia Pk EH22 153 D4
Lodge Dr FK5 38 F2
Lodge St EH41 130 A8
LOGANLEA 162 C1
Loganlea Ave EH7 94 D1
Loganlea Cres EH55 162 C1
Loganlea Dr EH7 94 D2
Loganlea Gdns EH7 94 C2
Loganlea Loan EH7 94 D1
Loganlea Pl
Addiewell EH55 162 D1
Edinburgh EH7 94 D1
Loganlea Rd
Addiewell EH55 162 C1
Edinburgh EH7 94 D2
Loganlea Terr
Addiewell EH55 162 C1
Edinburgh EH7 94 D2
Logan Rd KY12 43 F8
Logan St EH3 93 C2
Logan Way EH54 143 D8
Logie Dr FK5 38 A3
Logie Green Gdns EH7 93 C3
Logie Green Loan EH7 93 C3
Logie Green Rd EH7 93 C3
Logie La Bridge of Allan FK9 2 C7
Stirling FK9 2 D4
Logie Mill EH7 93 D3
Logie Pl KY12 28 D5
Logie Rd FK9 2 D4
Lomond Cres
Dunfermline KY11 29 F2
Stenhousemuir FK5 38 F3
Stirling FK9 2 B4
Whitburn EH47 161 A6
Lomond Ct FK10 10 C5
Lomond Dr Bannockburn FK7 7 E1
Falkirk FK2 39 C1
Lomond Gdns KY2 16 F5
Lomond Rd Edinburgh EH5 93 B6
Grangemouth FK3 61 E5
Shotts ML7 179 E6
Lomond St FK10 4 E1
Lomond Vale EH26 192 A7
Lomond View EH48 110 F4
Lomond Way FK6 57 D6
Lomond Wlk EH20 151 A1
London Rd Dalkeith EH22 153 A3
Edinburgh EH7, EH8 94 B1
London St EH3 93 D2
Loney Cres FK6 57 E8
Longannet Cotts FK10 24 B1
Longannet Power Sta
FK10 41 D7
Longannet Rdbt FK10 24 A2
Longbraes Gdns KY2 16 D6
Long Byres EH52 115 E5
Long Craig Rigg EH5 92 C7
Long Craigs EH32 97 E4
Long Craigs Terr KY3 35 A3
Long Craig Wlk KY1 35 B8
Long Cram EH41 129 F7
LONGCROFT 57 B3
Longcroft Gdns EH49 84 E7
Longcroft Holdings FK4 57 B3
Long Crook EH30 89 A8
Longdales ML11 217 F7
Longdales Ave FK2 60 A8
Longdales Ct FK2 60 A8
Longdales Pl FK2 60 A8
Longdales Rd FK2 60 A8
LONG DALMAHOY 146 E4
Long Dalmahoy Rd
Currie EH14 147 C5
Ratho EH27 146 C3
Longdyke Pl FK2 39 C4
Longdykes Rd EH32 97 B2
Longford ML11 201 A1
Longformacus Rd EH16 151 B7
Longhill Gdns KY11 48 B3
Longnewton Cotts EH41 220 D3
LONGNIDDRY 98 F5
Longniddry Farm Cotts
EH32 98 E5
Longniddry Prim Sch
EH32 98 E5
Longniddry Sta EH32 98 F5
Longpark Pl EH54 143 A4
LONGRIDGE 161 C1
Longridge Prim Sch
EH47 161 C2
Longridge Rd EH47 161 A5
Long Row Halbeath KY12 30 A7
Menstrie FK11 4 A7
Tyninghame EH42 76 C3
LONGSTONE 120 B2
Longstone Ave
East Linton EH40 103 D7
Edinburgh EH14 120 A2
Longstone Cotts EH14 120 A2
Longstone Cres EH14 120 A3
Longstone Gdns EH11 119 F3
Longstone Gr EH14 120 A2
Longstone Pk EH14 120 A2
Longstone Pl EH14 120 A2
Longstone Prim Sch
EH14 120 A1
Longstone Rd EH14 120 A2
Longstone St EH14 120 A2
Longstone Terr EH11 119 F3
Longstone View EH11 119 F3

Longyester Farm Cotts
EH41 221 A4
Lonsdale Cres KY3 33 E1
Lonsdale Terr EH3 228 C1
Lookaboutye Brae FK10 11 A3
Loom Rd KY2 17 B6
Lord Gambier Wharf KY1 17 D5
Lord President Rd EH39 54 A7
Loretto Ct EH21 124 B4
Loretto Jun Sch EH21 124 C6
Loretto RC Prim Sch
EH21 124 D6
Loretto Schs EH21 124 D6
Lorimar Pl FK2 39 B2
Lorimer Gdns KY12 29 D6
Lorimer View EH14 148 E6
Lorne Gdns FK2 60 F3
Lorne Gr EH20 151 A1
Lorne Ho KY12 29 A4
Lorne La EH39 54 C7
Lorne Pl EH6 93 F3
Lorne Prim Sch EH6 93 F3
Lorne Rd FK5 38 C2
Lorne Sq EH6 93 F3
Lorne St Edinburgh EH6 93 F3
Kirkcaldy KY1 17 E7
Lorn Pl KY11 30 C1
Lornshill Acad FK10 4 E2
Lornshill Cres FK10 9 F8
Losshill FK11 4 A6
Lothian Bank EH22 152 F1
LOTHIANBRIDGE 173 F6
Lothianburn Junc EH10 150 B4
Lothian Cres Bo'ness EH51 64 A6
Stirling FK9 2 C3
Lothian Ct KY11 47 D2
Lothian Dr EH22 174 C8
Lothian Rd Dalkeith EH22 153 A2
Edinburgh EH1 228 B2
Lothian St Bathgate EH48 141 A7
Bo'ness EH51 64 A6
Bonnyrigg and Lasswade
EH19 173 C7
Burntisland KY3 50 E8
Dalkeith EH22 153 A3
Edinburgh EH1 229 A2
Rosewell EH24 172 D2
Lothians View KY11 47 A2
Lothian Terr Kirkcaldy KY2 17 A7
Newtongrange EH22 174 B4
Louburn EH48 138 D3
Loudens Wlk FK6 36 D5
Loughborough Rd KY1 17 F7
Loughrigg KY11 47 A7
Louisa Sq EH24 172 D2
Louise St KY11 29 D2
Louvain Gdns EH48 139 F4
Lovedale Ave EH14 147 B1
Lovedale Cres EH14 147 B1
Lovedale Gdns EH14 147 C1
Lovedale Gr EH14 147 B1
Lovedale Rd EH14 147 C1
Lovells Glen EH49 84 C8
Lovers La EH30 89 C8
Lovers Loan Alva FK12 5 B7
Dunfermline KY12 28 F2
Lovers Wlk FK8 2 B1
Low Brae EH48 111 F5
Low Causewayside
Culross KY12 42 D8
Newmills KY12 26 C1
Low Cswy Culross KY12 25 E1
Torryburn KY12 26 E1
Low Doors The EH27 145 E2
Lower Alderston Rd
EH41 100 E1
Lower Bathville EH48 140 A5
Lower Bridge St FK8 2 A1
Lower Broomieknowe
EH18 173 A8
Lower Castlehill FK8 2 A1
Lower Gilmore Pl EH3 228 B1
Lower Glebe KY3 49 C8
Lower Granton Rd EH5 93 A7
Lower Joppa EH15 123 C8
Lower London Rd EH7 94 A1
Lower Ridge Ct EH47 161 B2
LOWER SALTOUN 157 F5
Lower Valleyfield View
EH26 191 F4
Low Port Prim Sch EH49 85 A7
Lowrie Ave EH26 191 C5
Lowry Pl KY11 46 F4
LOW TORRY 26 D1
LOW VALLEYFIELD 26 A1
Ludgate FK10 10 A6
Luffness Ct EH32 71 D4
Luffness Gdns EH32 71 D4
Luffness Mains Cotts
EH32 72 B4
Lufra Bank EH5 93 A6
Lugton Brae EH22 152 F4
Lulach Ct KY11 47 A8
Lumley Ct FK3 61 D8
Lumley Pl FK3 61 D8
Lumley St FK3 61 D8
LUMPHINNANS 13 E6
Lumphinnans Prim Com Sch
KY4 13 D5
Lumphinnans Rd KY5 14 A7
Lumsdaine Dr KY11 48 A1
Lumsden Ct
Broxburn EH52 115 C5
Ratho EH28 117 D2
Lundin Rd KY12 28 A4
Lussielaw Rd EH9 121 F3
Lutton Court Bsns Ctr
EH8 229 B1
Lutton Pl EH8 229 B1
Lyall Cres FK2 61 E2
Lyars Rd EH32 98 E6
Lyarthall EH52 115 C5
Lychgate La EH52 115 D5
Lychgate Rd FK10 4 B2
Lydgait EH41 101 A1
Lydgait Gdns EH41 101 A1
Lyefield Pl EH54 143 B4
Lygon Rd EH16 121 F2
Lyle Gn EH54 143 B8
Lynburn Prim Sch KY11 29 F2
Lynebank Hospl KY11 30 A5
Lyneburn Cres KY11 30 B5
Lynedoch Pl EH3 228 A3
Lynedoch Place La EH3 228 A3
Lyne Gr KY12 28 C2
Lyness Ct FK2 61 E2
Lyne St EH7 94 A1
Lyne Terr EH26 192 A7
Lynn Lea Ave EH41 130 C8
Lyon Cres FK9 2 A6
Lyoncross FK4 57 D4
Lyon Ct EH51 63 D6
Lyon Dr EH54 164 E6

M

MacAdam Pl FK1 59 D6
McAdam Sq EH54 164 D6
McAffee Gdns EH48 139 F3
McAllister Ct FK7 7 D1
MacAlpine Ct FK10 4 D3
MacArthur Cres FK2 82 E6
McAulay Brae FK7 20 C3
Macbeth Moir Rd EH21 125 A6
Macbeth Rd KY11 29 E3
Mccafferty Way FK3 40 C1
McCall Gdns EH40 103 D7
McCallum Ct EH48 139 F7
McCambridge Pl FK5 38 C5
McCann Ave EH52 115 B5
McCann Ct FK7 20 C4
Mccartney Rd FK5 38 C4
McCathie Dr EH22 174 B6
McClelland Cres KY11 29 B1
McCormack Pl FK5 38 D4
Mac Cormick Terr EH26 191 F8
Mccraken Ct FK1 81 F5
McDiarmid Gr EH22 174 B4
MacDonald Ave EH48 139 F6
McDonald Cres FK2 60 C7
McDonald Ct KY12 27 D1
MacDonald Ct FK5 38 B5
MacDonald Dr FK7 7 A4
MacDonald Gdns EH47 162 E8
McDonald Pl EH7 93 E3
MacDonald Pl KY3 34 A2
McDonald Rd EH7 93 E3
MacDonald Sq KY11 30 B5
McDonald St
Edinburgh EH7 93 E3
Inverkeithing/Dunfermline
KY11 47 B7
McDouall Stuart Pl KY1 18 A7
MacDowall Rd EH9 121 F3
Macduff Cres KY3 34 F2
Mace Ct FK7 7 D3
McEwan Sq EH3 228 A1
Macfarlane Cres FK1 60 B5
Macfarlane Ct EH33 126 B1
Macfarlane Pl EH52 114 F3
McGahey Ct EH22 174 B4
McGhee Pl FK1 59 F2
McGinley Way EH49 84 D5
McGowan Rd FK2 60 C7
McGregor Ave KY5 14 A8
McGregor Pend EH32 97 B2
McGrigor Rd Rosyth KY11 46 D2
Stirling FK7 7 A4
Machrie Ct FK1 59 C4
Mcinally Cres FK2 59 F8
Macindoe Cres KY1 17 D7
McIntosh Ct EH52 115 C5
Macintosh Pl FK1 60 A1
Macintosh Rd
Livingston EH54 142 F1
Livingston EH54 163 F8
McIntyre La EH33 127 D6
McKane Pl KY12 28 F1
McKay Dr KY11 29 F1
McKell Ct FK1 60 A3
McKenzie Cres KY5 14 C7
McKenzie Pl 7 FK1 59 F2
Mackenzie Pl EH3 228 B4
McKenzie St KY1 17 E7
Mackenzie Terr FK3 61 C6
Mackie Pl KY11 29 F2
McKinlay Cres FK10 10 C7
McKinlay Terr EH20 172 A7
McKinnon Dr EH22 174 E5
McKinnon Rd EH47 181 F7
McLachlan Ave FK7 7 B2
MacLachlan Ave FK6 36 C1
McLachlan Gdns EH32 97 B2
McLachlan St FK5 38 C2
MacLardy Ct EH52 114 F3
McLaren Ave EH49 84 A6
McLaren Ct FK5 38 D2
McLaren Rd EH9 122 A4
McLaren Terr
Edinburgh EH11 228 A2
Stirling FK7 7 B3
MacLaren Terr FK2 39 A2
McLauchlan Rise KY3 49 B7
McLauchlan View ML7 159 F6
Maclean Cres FK12 5 C7
Maclean Ct FK7 7 C3
Maclean Gate KY11 46 F7
Maclean Gdns KY11 46 E7
McLean Pl
Bonnyrigg and Lasswade
EH18 172 E6
Gorebridge EH23 174 D1
Maclean Pl KY11 46 E7
McLean Prim Sch KY12 28 E5
Maclean Terr EH48 138 C3
Maclean Way KY11 46 E7
McLean Wlk EH22 174 B4
Maclean Wlk KY11 46 E7
McLeod Cres EH32 96 F1
McLeod St Broxburn EH52 115 E6
Edinburgh EH11 120 E6
McMartin Ct EH47 161 D7
MACMERRY 127 D5
Macmerry Bsns Pk EH33 127 D6
Macmerry Ind Est EH33 127 E6
Macmerry Prim Sch
EH33 127 D6
Macmillan Rd EH54 143 C1
McNab Gdns FK1 59 F2
Macnair Ave EH39 54 C6
McNeil Cres EH48 140 A6
McNeill Ave EH20 172 B8
McNeill Path 4 EH33 126 C6
McNeill Pl EH20 172 B8
McNeill St EH11 228 A1
McNeill Terr EH20 172 A8
McNeill Way 3 EH33 126 C5
McNeill Wlk 2 EH33 126 C5
McPhail Sq EH33 126 D6
Macpherson Dr FK8 2 A2
Macpherson Pl 6 FK1 59 F2
McQuade St EH19 173 D8
McRae Cres KY3 33 F2
McRobert Ctr FK9 2 D5
McTaggart Ave FK6 36 E2
MacTaggart Loan EH22 174 B4
McVean Pl FK4 57 B4
Madderfield Mews EH49 85 B7
MADDISTON 82 D7
Maddiston Prim Sch FK2 82 F7
Maddiston Rd FK2 82 E8
Madeira Pl EH6 93 E5
Madeira St EH6 93 E6
Madelvic Sq EH5 92 E7
Madill Pl FK5 38 F3
Madison Pl FK3 61 D8
Maesterton Pl EH22 174 B4
Magdala Cres EH12 120 F7
Magdala Mews EH12 120 F7
MAGDALENE 123 B6
Magdalene Ave EH15 123 B6
Magdalene Ct EH15 123 B6
Magdalene Dr EH15 123 B6
Magdalene Gdns EH15 123 B6
Magdalene Loan EH15 123 B6
Magdalene Medway
EH15 123 B6
Magdalene Pl EH15 123 B6
Maggie Wood's Loan FK1 59 F4
Magnus Rd EH51 62 D5
Magpie Gdns EH22 153 D2
Mag's Bank EH41 131 B1
Maidencraig Cres EH4 92 C2
Maidencraig Gr EH4 92 C2
MAIDENPARK 63 E6
Maidenpark Pl EH51 63 E6
Maidlands EH49 85 C7
Maid of the Forth EH30 68 D1
Main Point EH3 228 C2
Main Rd Charlestown KY11 45 B4
Crombie KY12 44 E7
Grangemouth FK3 62 B8
Macmerry EH33 127 C5
North Queensferry KY11 68 B6
Mains Farm Pl EH47 161 E6
Mains Gdns EH33 126 D7
Mains of Craigmillar
EH16 122 D2
Mains Rd Harthill ML7 159 E5
Linlithgow EH49 84 E6
Main St Aberdour KY3 49 C8
Airth FK2 22 D4
Alloa FK10 5 D1
Auchtertool KY2 15 B2
Avonbridge FK1 110 A6
Balerno EH14 147 C1
Bannockburn FK7 7 D1
Bathgate EH48 141 A7
Blackridge EH48 138 C3
Bo'ness EH51 64 A8
Bonnybridge FK4 58 B5
Cairneyhill KY12 27 D1
California FK1 81 F5
Cambusbarron FK7 6 D5
Cambus FK10 9 B8
Carnock KY12 27 C7
Carrington EH23 194 D6
Clackmannan FK10 11 A4
Comrie KY12 26 D7
Cowdenbeath, Hill of Beath
KY4 13 A1
Cowdenbeath, Lumphinnans
KY4 13 E6
Cowie FK7 20 D7
Crossford KY12 28 C2
Crossgates KY4 30 F6
Dalgety Bay KY11 47 F4
Dalmeny EH30 89 E7
Dechmont EH52 114 C2
East Calder EH53 144 E4
Main St *continued*
East Saltoun EH34 157 E4
East Whitburn EH47 161 D7
Edinburgh EH4 91 F3
Elphinstone EH33 126 B1
Falkirk, Bainsford FK2 60 B7
Falkirk, Camelon FK1 59 E5
Falkirk, Carronshore FK2 39 C3
Fallin FK7 8 E3
Fauldhouse EH47 181 D6
Forth ML11 201 B1
Gifford EH41 220 F7
Gorebridge EH23 195 C7
Grangemouth, Brightons
FK2 82 D8
Grangemouth, Rumford FK2 82 F7
Gullane EH31 52 B2
Halbeath KY11 30 B5
High Valleyfield KY12 25 F1
Hill of Beath KY4 30 F8
Kingseat KY12 12 B1
Kirkliston EH29 89 A2
Kirknewton EH27 145 E2
Limekilns KY11 45 D3
Linlithgow EH49 84 D7
Livingston, Deans EH54 142 E6
Livingston, Livingston Village
EH54 143 C2
Loanhead EH20 171 F7
Lochgelly KY5 14 B7
Longniddry EH32 98 E5
Longridge EH47 161 C1
Mid Calder EH53 144 C3
Newton EH52 88 A8
Newtongrange EH22 174 A5
North Queensferry KY11 68 C5
Ormiston EH35 155 E7
Pathhead, Dewartown
EH23 175 D5
Pathhead EH37 176 B5
Philpstoun EH49 86 D7
Plean FK7 20 D3
Polmont FK2 61 E2
Ratho EH28 117 D2
Redding FK2 61 C2
Roslin EH25 172 A3
Shieldhill FK1 81 D6
Shotts ML7 180 A3
Slamannan FK1 108 B7
Stenhousemuir FK5 38 E2
Stenhousemuir, Larbert FK5 38 C2
Stirling FK7 7 B4
Stoneyburn, Bents EH47 162 A1
Stoneyburn EH47 162 B2
Torryburn KY12 26 D1
Townhill KY12 29 D8
Tullibody FK10 4 B2
Tyninghame EH42 76 C3
West Calder EH55 163 D3
Westfield EH48 110 F5
Winchburgh EH52 88 A3
Main Street E FK11 4 A6
Main Street W
Dalgety Bay KY11 47 E4
Menstrie FK11 3 F6
Mair End EH32 71 C4
Maitland Ave
Bannockburn FK7 7 D1
Musselburgh EH21 124 A6
Maitland Cres FK7 7 B3
Maitland Hog La EH29 89 A1
Maitland Park Rd EH21 124 A6
Maitland Rd
Kirkliston EH29 89 A2
Rosyth KY11 67 B8
Maitland St
Dunfermline KY12 28 F4
Musselburgh EH21 124 A6
Majors Loan FK1 60 A4
Majors Pl FK1 60 A3
Malbet Pk EH16 151 B7
Malbet Wynd EH16 151 C7
Malcolm Ct
Bathgate EH48 140 F5
Dunfermline KY11 29 B1
Malcolm Dr FK5 38 E4
Malcolm St
Dunfermline KY11 29 B2
Dunfermline KY11 29 C2
Malcolm's Wynd KY1 17 C5
Mallace Ave EH48 140 B5
Mallard Brae EH54 143 C5
Mallard Gr KY11 30 A1
Mallard Wlk EH32 125 E8
Mall Ave EH21 124 C6
Mallens Brae EH48 112 A5
Malleny Ave EH14 147 C1
Malleny Gdn EH14 147 D2
Malleny Millgate EH14 168 D8
Mall Sh Ctr The 6 FK1 60 B4
Mall The EH54 144 B5
Malplaquet Ct ML8 215 B1
Malta Gn EH3 93 B2
Malta Terr EH3 93 B2
Maltings Rd KY1 17 D7
Maltings The
Auchtertool KY2 15 B2
Falkirk FK1 59 F5
Haddington EH41 130 A7
Linlithgow EH49 84 D6
North Berwick EH39 101 F8
Mamre Dr FK1 81 F5
Mandela Ave FK2 60 C7
Manderston St EH6 93 F4
Mandora Ct ML8 215 B1
Manitoba Ave EH54 143 F3
Mannafields Christian Sch 5
EH7 93 F2
Mannan Dr FK10 11 B4
Mannering Pl 5 EH16 151 B8
Mannerston Holdings
EH49 65 D3
Mannfield Ave FK4 57 F4
Manor Cres FK10 4 B2
Manor Gdns Dunbar EH42 78 A2
Inverkeithing/Dunfermline
KY11 30 A2
Manor Loan FK9 3 B5
Manor Pl EH3 228 A3
MANOR POWIS 3 B3
Manor Powis Cotts FK9 3 B3
Manor St FK1 60 B4
Manor Steps FK9 3 C3
Manor Wynd FK2 83 A5
Man O' War Way EH51 64 B8
Manse Ave
Armadale EH48 139 E6
Whitburn EH47 161 A6
Manse Cres FK7 7 B4
Manse Ct EH53 144 F4
Mansefield
Athelstaneford EH39 101 F7
East Calder EH53 144 F4
Mansefield Ct
3 Bathgate EH48 141 A7
Livingston EH54 143 C3
Mansefield Gr EH48 141 A6
Mansefield St EH48 141 A7
Manse Gr EH47 162 C2
Manse La Burntisland KY3 33 E1
Cockenzie & Port Seton
EH32 97 C4
Musselburgh EH21 124 D6
Manse Pk EH52 114 F5
Manse Pl Aberdour KY3 49 B7
Bannockburn FK7 7 E1
Bathgate EH48 141 E6
Falkirk FK1 60 B4
Inverkeithing KY11 47 B2
Slamannan FK1 108 B7
Manse Rd
Carrington EH23 194 D5
Crossgates KY4 30 E7
Dirleton EH39 53 A5
Edinburgh EH12 119 D6
Forth ML11 201 B1
Inverkeithing KY11 47 B2
Kincardine FK10 23 E5
Kinghorn KY3 34 F3
Kirkliston EH29 89 A1
Linlithgow EH49 85 A6
Roslin EH25 172 A3
Shotts ML7 180 A3
Torphichen EH48 111 F5
Whitburn EH47 161 B6
Manse St Aberdour KY3 49 C7
Edinburgh EH12 119 D6
Manse Terr FK10 11 A4
Manse View
Armadale EH48 139 E5
Innerwick EH42 107 F1
Philpstoun EH49 86 D7
Mansewood Cres EH47 161 B6
Mansfield Ave Alloa FK10 5 D1
Musselburgh EH21 124 C5
Newtongrange EH22 174 B6
Mansfield Ct EH21 124 D5
Mansfield Pl
Edinburgh EH3 93 D2
Musselburgh EH21 124 C5
Newtongrange EH22 174 B6
Mansfield Rd
Balerno EH14 168 C8
Musselburgh EH21 124 C6
Newtongrange EH22 174 B6
Mansionhouse Rd
Edinburgh EH9 121 D5
Falkirk FK1 59 D5
Manson Sq EH54 142 C5
Manuel Rigg FK2 82 E6
Manuel Sta EH49 84 A7
Manuel Terr EH49 83 F6
Maple Ave FK5 38 F3
Maple Ct 10 FK10 10 B6
Maple Gr EH54 144 B6
Maple Pl FK6 36 C3
Maple St KY2 17 B7
Maplewood Pk EH54 142 E7
Maranatha Cres FK2 82 C8
Marchbank Dr EH14 168 C8
Marchbank Gdns EH14 168 C8
Marchbank Gr EH14 168 C8
Marchbank Pl EH14 168 C8
Marchbank Way EH14 147 C1
Marchburn Dr EH26 191 C5
Marches Dr EH48 140 A5
Marches The
Armadale EH48 140 A5
8 Stirling FK8 7 B7
Marchfield Gr EH4 92 A3
Marchfield Park La EH4 91 F3
Marchfield Pk EH4 91 F3
Marchfield Terr EH4 92 A3
March Gait EH4 91 F2
Marchglen FK13 5 F5
March Gr EH4 92 A2
Marchhall Cres EH16 122 A5
Marchhall Pl EH16 122 A5
Marchhall Rd EH16 122 A5
Marchlands Ave EH51 64 A7
Marchlands La EH51 64 A7
Marchlands Terr EH51 63 F7
MARCHMONT 121 C5
Marchmont Ave FK2 61 E2
Marchmont Cres EH9 121 D5
Marchmont Ct FK2 61 F2

Marchmont Mews FK2 ... 61 F2
Marchmont Rd EH9 ... 121 C5
Marchmont St EH9 ... 121 C5
March Pines EH4 ... 91 F2
March Rd EH4 ... 92 A2
Marchside Ct FK10 ... 5 C1
Marchwood Ave EH48 ... 141 C6
Marchwood Cres EH48 ... 141 C6
Marchwood Ct EH33 ... 126 B1
Mardale Cres EH10 ... 121 A4
Maree Ct FK10 ... 10 C6
Maree Pl Crossford KY12 ... 28 B1
Kirkcaldy KY2 ... 16 E8
Maree Wlk EH54 ... 144 A4
Margaret Ave
Bathgate EH48 ... 141 F6
Longcroft FK4 ... 57 A3
Margaret Ct FK6 ... 36 E1
Margaret Dr FK4 ... 58 A6
Margaret Rd FK7 ... 7 C2
Margaret Rose Ave EH10 150 C5
Margaret Rose Cres
EH10 ... 150 C5
Margaret Rose Dr EH10 .. 150 C5
Margaret Rose Loan
EH10 ... 150 C5
Margaret Rose Way
EH10 ... 150 C5
Margaret Rose Wlk
EH10 ... 150 C5
Margaret Terr FK5 ... 38 E4
Maria St KY1 ... 17 C5
Marina Ave EH48 ... 141 F6
Marina Rd EH48 ... 141 E6
Marine Dr EH4 ... 92 A6
Marine Espl EH6 ... 94 C5
Marine Par EH39 ... 54 D7
Mariner Ave FK1 ... 59 B5
Marine Rd Dunbar EH42 ... 78 C3
Gullane EH31 ... 52 A3
Mariner Dr FK1 ... 59 B5
Mariner Gdns FK1 ... 59 C6
Mariner Rd FK1 ... 59 C5
Mariners St KY2 ... 17 B6
Mariner St FK1 ... 59 B5
Mariners Wlk KY11 ... 47 F3
Marine Terr EH31 ... 52 A3
Marion St KY1 ... 17 B2
Marionville Ave EH7 ... 94 C1
Marionville Cres EH7 ... 94 C2
Marionville Dr EH7 ... 94 C2
Marionville Gr EH7 ... 94 C2
Marionville Meadway EH7 94 C2
Marionville Pk EH7 ... 94 B1
Marionville Rd EH7 ... 94 B2
Marion Wilson View FK5 .. 38 C3
Marischal Pl 7 EH4 ... 92 C2
Maritime La EH6 ... 94 A5
Maritime St EH6 ... 94 A5
Marjoribanks St EH48 ... 141 B6
Marjory Ct EH48 ... 141 C5
Marjory Pl EH48 ... 141 C4
Market Ct 5 EH41 ... 101 A1
Marketgate EH35 ... 155 E7
Market La EH49 ... 85 A7
Market Loan EH33 ... 126 C7
Market Pl
North Berwick EH39 ... 54 C7
Whitburn EH47 ... 161 A7
Market St Bo'ness EH51 ... 63 F8
Dunfermline KY12 ... 29 A4
Edinburgh EH1 ... 229 A3
Haddington EH41 ... 130 B8
Mid Calder EH53 ... 144 C4
Musselburgh EH21 ... 124 B6
Market View EH33 ... 126 C7
Market Way EH33 ... 126 C7
Markfield Rd KY11 ... 48 C4
Mark La 4 EH41 ... 130 B8
Markle Steading EH40 ... 103 A8
Marlborough Dr FK9 ... 2 C3
Marlborough St EH15 ... 123 B8
Marly Gn EH39 ... 54 B6
Marly Rise EH39 ... 54 B6
Marmion Ave EH25 ... 171 F3
Marmion Cres
Edinburgh EH16 ... 122 B1
North Berwick EH39 ... 54 B7
Marmion Ct 4 EH39 ... 54 B7
Marmion Rd
Bathgate EH48 ... 141 A7
Grangemouth FK3 ... 61 D5
North Berwick EH39 ... 54 C7
Marmion St FK2 ... 60 B8
Mar Pl Alloa FK10 ... 10 A7
Alloa, Sauchie FK10 ... 5 C1
Stirling FK8 ... 7 A8
Marquis Dr FK10 ... 11 B4
Marrfield Rd EH54 ... 115 A1
Marrfield Terr EH54 ... 115 A1
Marschal Ct FK7 ... 7 D3
Marsden Ct FK9 ... 2 D4
Marshal Dr FK1 ... 81 F5
Marshall Pl KY11 ... 29 B1
Marshall Rd EH29 ... 89 A1
Marshall's Ct EH1 ... 229 B4
Marshall St
Cockenzie & Port Seton
EH32 ... 97 B4
Cowdenbeath KY4 ... 13 D3
Edinburgh EH8 ... 229 A2
Grangemouth FK3 ... 61 D8
Marshall Terr FK3 ... 61 D8
Marshall Twr FK1 ... 60 D4
Marshall Way FK10 ... 4 C4
Marshill FK10 ... 10 A6
Mar St FK10 ... 10 B6
Mar Terr FK10 ... 11 A4
Martin Brae EH54 ... 143 C5
Martin Gr EH19 ... 173 D8
Martin Pl EH22 ... 152 E2
Maryburn Rd EH22 ... 174 C8
Mary Erskine Sch The
EH4 ... 92 B1
Mary Erskine & Stewart's
Melville Jun Sch The 1
EH4 ... 92 E1
Maryfield
2 Edinburgh, Drum EH7 ... 93 F2
Edinburgh, Portobello EH15 . 95 B1
Maryfield Dr EH51 ... 64 D6
Maryfield Pk EH53 ... 144 C2
Maryfield Pl
Bonnyrigg and Lasswade
EH19 ... 173 C7
2 Edinburgh EH7 ... 94 A2
Falkirk FK1 ... 59 B4
Maryflats Pl FK3 ... 61 E7
Maryhall St KY1 ... 17 C5
Mary Pl Clackmannan FK10 .. 11 A5
Dunfermline KY11 ... 29 B2
Mary Reid Int Spa Acad
EH3 ... 228 B4
Mary's Pl EH4 ... 93 A2
Mary Sq FK2 ... 61 A4
Mary St FK2 ... 60 F4
Mary Stevenson Dr FK10 .. 10 A8
Mary Street Rdbt FK2 ... 60 F3
Marytree Ho EH17 ... 151 D8
Marywell KY1 ... 17 C5
Masefield Way EH12 ... 90 B1
Mason Pl EH18 ... 172 F6
Massereene Rd KY2 ... 16 F5
Masterton Prim Sch KY11 47 B8
Masterton Rd KY11 ... 47 A7
Mathers Ave EH47 ... 160 F6
Mather Terr FK2 ... 60 F4
Mathew Ct FK3 ... 61 D8
Mathieson Pl KY11 ... 29 F1
Matthews Crofts EH48 ... 138 C3
Matthews Dr EH22 ... 173 F4
Matthew St
Edinburgh EH16 ... 122 F3
Kirkcaldy KY2 ... 17 B6
Mauchline Gr KY2 ... 17 A8
Maukeshill Ct EH54 ... 143 C2
Mauldeth Rd EH52 ... 115 C5
Maule Terr EH31 ... 52 A2
Maulsford Ave EH22 ... 152 B7
Maurice Ave FK7 ... 7 D4
Maurice Pl EH9 ... 121 D2
MAURICEWOOD ... 191 E7
Mauricewood Ave EH26 .. 191 F7
Mauricewood Bank EH26 191 F7
Mauricewood Gr EH26 .. 191 F7
Mauricewood Pk EH26 ... 191 F7
Mauricewood Prim Sch
EH26 ... 192 A8
Mauricewood Rd EH26 .. 191 F8
Mauricewood Rise EH26 . 191 F7
Mavisbank EH20 ... 172 C7
Mavis Bank EH48 ... 141 B8
Mavisbank Ave FK1 ... 81 C6
Mavisbank Gdns EH48 ... 141 B8
Mavisbank Pl EH18 ... 172 E6
Mavishall EH37 ... 224 D8
Maxton Cres FK12 ... 5 C7
Maxton Ct EH22 ... 153 A3
Maxton Pl KY11 ... 46 E3
Maxwell Cres KY4 ... 13 A2
Maxwell Ct EH21 ... 124 B6
Maxwell Pl 6 FK8 ... 7 B8
Maxwell Rd EH39 ... 53 A4
Maxwell Sq EH54 ... 164 C6
Maxwell St EH10 ... 121 A3
Maxwell Twr FK1 ... 60 D3
Maybank Villas EH12 ... 119 D7
Mayburn Ave EH20 ... 151 B1
Mayburn Bank EH20 ... 172 B8
Mayburn Cres EH20 ... 151 B1
Mayburn Ct EH20 ... 172 B8
Mayburn Dr EH20 ... 151 B1
Mayburn Gr EH20 ... 172 B8
Mayburn Hill EH20 ... 172 B8
Mayburn Loan EH20 ... 151 B1
Mayburn Terr EH20 ... 151 B1
Mayburn Vale EH20 ... 172 B8
Mayburn Wlk EH20 ... 172 B8
Maybury Dr EH12 ... 119 A8
Maybury Rd
Edinburgh, Bughtlin EH4,
EH12 ... 91 A1
Edinburgh, East Craigs
EH12 ... 119 A7
MAYFIELD Armadale ... 140 A5
Dalkeith ... 174 F5
Edinburgh ... 121 F4
Mayfield Ave EH21 ... 124 B3
Mayfield Cres
Clackmannan FK10 ... 11 A5
Loanhead EH20 ... 172 C7
Musselburgh EH21 ... 124 B4
Mayfield Ct
Armadale EH48 ... 139 F4
Loanhead EH20 ... 172 C8
Stirling FK7 ... 7 B3
Mayfield Dr
Armadale EH48 ... 139 F5
Longcroft FK4 ... 57 B3
Mayfield Gardens La
EH9 ... 121 F4
Mayfield Gdns EH9 ... 121 F4
Mayfield Gdns La EH9 ... 121 F4
Mayfield Ind Est EH22 ... 174 C5
Mayfield L Ctr EH22 ... 174 D6
Mayfield Mews 2 FK1 ... 59 F4
Mayfield Pk EH21 ... 124 B3
Mayfield Pl
Edinburgh EH12 ... 119 D6
Mayfield EH22 ... 174 D6
Musselburgh EH21 ... 124 B3
Mayfield Prim Sch EH22 174 D5
Mayfield Rd
Easthouses EH22 ... 174 D8
Edinburgh EH9 ... 121 F3
Redding FK2 ... 61 C2
Mayfield St FK7 ... 7 B4
Mayfield Terr EH9 ... 121 F4
Mayflower St KY12 ... 29 C7
Maygate 3 KY12 ... 29 A3
Mayne Ave FK9 ... 2 B6
Mayshade Rd EH20 ... 151 B1
May Terr EH39 ... 54 A7
Mayville Bank EH21 ... 125 A6
Mayville Gardens E EH5 ... 93 C6
Mayville Gdns EH5 ... 93 C6
Mayville Pk EH42 ... 78 C3
MEADOWBANK ... 94 B2
Meadowbank
Edinburgh EH8 ... 94 B1
Livingston EH54 ... 143 E5
Ormiston EH35 ... 155 E6
Meadowbank Ave 6 EH8 . 94 B1
Meadowbank Cres
Edinburgh EH8 ... 94 B1
Ormiston EH35 ... 155 D7
Meadowbank Pl 1 EH8 ... 94 C1
Meadowbank Rd
Kirknewton EH27 ... 145 F3
Ormiston EH35 ... 155 E7
Meadowbank Sh Pk EH8 .. 94 A2
Meadowbank Sports Ctr
EH7 ... 94 B1
Meadowbank St FK2 ... 61 C1
Meadowbank Terr 5 EH8 94 B1
Meadowbank View EH27 . 145 F3
Meadow Cres EH47 ... 181 E5
Meadow Ct Burntisland KY3 33 E1
Carluke ML8 ... 215 C1
Denny FK6 ... 36 D4
Meadow Dr EH47 ... 162 A1
Meadowend KY12 ... 28 C2
Meadowfield
Burntisland KY3 ... 33 E2
Cowdenbeath KY4 ... 13 C6
Dalgety Bay KY11 ... 48 B4
Meadowfield Ave EH8 ... 122 E7
Meadowfield Ct EH8 ... 122 D7
Meadowfield Dr EH8 ... 122 D7
Meadowfield Gdns EH8 .. 122 D6
Meadowfield Ind Est KY3 . 33 E1
Meadowfield Rd EH12 ... 118 E7
Meadowfield Terr EH8 ... 122 D6
Meadowforth Rd FK7 ... 7 C7
Meadow Gn FK10 ... 5 B1
Meadow Gr FK10 ... 11 D3
Meadowhead Ave EH55 .. 162 E1
Meadowhead Cres EH55 . 162 E1
Meadowhead Gdns EH55 162 E1
Meadowhead Gr EH55 ... 162 E1
Meadowhead Loan EH55 . 162 E1
Meadowhead Pl EH55 ... 162 D1
Meadowhead Terr EH55 . 162 D1
Meadowhouse Rd EH12 .. 119 E6
Meadow La EH8 ... 229 A1
Meadowland Rd FK9 ... 2 A6
Meadowmill Loan EH33 .. 126 D7
Meadowmill Sports Ctr
EH33 ... 126 C8
Meadowpark
Haddington EH41 ... 130 A8
Seafield EH47 ... 163 A8
Meadowpark Ave EH48 .. 140 F5
Meadowpark Cres EH48 .. 140 F5
Meadowpark Rd EH48 ... 140 F5
Meadow Park Sch EH41 .. 130 A8
Meadow Pk FK12 ... 5 A6
Meadow Pl Bilston EH25 .. 171 E6
Dunfermline KY11 ... 29 F3
Edinburgh EH9 ... 228 C1
Stirling FK8 ... 2 C1
Stoneyburn EH47 ... 162 A1
Meadow Place La EH9 ... 121 D5
Meadow Place Rd EH12 .. 119 C5
Meadow Rd
Riccarton EH14 ... 147 F7
Stoneyburn EH47 ... 162 A1
Meadowside EH33 ... 126 E5
Meadowspot EH11 ... 120 E2
Meadow St FK1 ... 60 C4
Meadows Tennis Complex
EH8 ... 229 A1
Meadows The
Falkirk, Carronshore FK2 ... 39 B2
Falkirk FK1 ... 60 C4
Stirling FK9 ... 2 B3
Meadows Yard Nature
Reserve* EH7 ... 94 E3
Meadow View
Crossford KY12 ... 28 B2
Halbeath KY12 ... 30 B6
Mearenside EH12 ... 119 A8
Medwyn Pl FK10 ... 9 F6
Meeks Rd FK2 ... 60 B5
Meetinghouse Dr EH33 .. 126 C6
Meggat Pl EH26 ... 192 A7
Meggetgate EH14 ... 120 C3
Meggetland Sq EH14 ... 120 D3
Meggetland Terr EH14 .. 120 E3
Meggetland View EH14 .. 120 D3
Meggetland Wynd EH14 .. 120 D3
Meikle Inch La EH48 ... 141 C3
Meikle Rd EH54 ... 143 C1
Meiklerig Cotts EH42 ... 105 A1
Meikle Sq KY1 ... 18 A7
Melbourne Pl EH39 ... 54 D7
Melbourne Rd
Broxburn EH52 ... 115 F5
North Berwick EH39 ... 54 D7
Melbourne St EH54 ... 144 A5
Meldrum Cres KY3 ... 33 D1
Meldrum Ct KY11 ... 29 F1
Meldrum Prim Sch EH54 142 E7
Meldrum Rd KY2 ... 17 B5
Melford Ave ML7 ... 180 B3
Melfort Dr FK7 ... 7 C4
Melgund Pl KY5 ... 14 B8
Melgund Terr EH7 ... 93 D2
Mellerstain Rd KY2 ... 16 C6
Mellock Gdns FK1 ... 59 E2
Mellor Ct KY11 ... 46 E4
Melrose Cres KY2 ... 17 C6
Melrose Dr FK3 ... 61 F6
Melrose Pl 9 FK1 ... 60 B4
Melville Cotts EH18 ... 152 C4
Melville Cres EH3 ... 228 A3
Melville Dr EH9 ... 229 A1
Melville Dykes Rd EH18 .. 152 C1
Melville Dykes Road Rdbt
EH22 ... 152 D2
Melville Gate EH22 ... 152 D3
Melville Gate Rd EH22 ... 152 E4
Melville Gdns KY3 ... 50 D8
Melville Grange Cotts
EH18 ... 152 B4
Melville La 3 FK1 ... 60 B5
Melville Pl
Bridge of Allan FK9 ... 2 A7
Dunfermline KY12 ... 29 B4
Edinburgh EH3 ... 228 A2
Kirkcaldy KY2 ... 16 D5
Melville Rd EH22 ... 152 E2
Melville St Edinburgh EH3 . 228 A3
2 Falkirk FK1 ... 60 B5
Lochgelly KY5 ... 14 B8
Melville Street La EH3 ... 228 A3
Melville Terr
7 Dalkeith EH22 ... 152 E1
Edinburgh EH9 ... 229 B1
Stirling FK8 ... 7 B6
Melville View EH18 ... 173 A8
MENSTRIE ... 3 E6
Menstrie Bsns Ctr FK11 ... 3 F6
Menstrie Castle* FK11 ... 3 F6
Menstrie Pl FK10 ... 4 A6
Menstrie Prim Sch FK11 ... 4 A6
Menstrie Rd FK10 ... 4 C3
Menteith Ct FK10 ... 10 C6
Menteith Dr KY11 ... 29 F1
Menteith Rd FK9 ... 2 A3
Mentone Ave EH15 ... 95 B1
Mentone Gdns EH9 ... 121 F4
Mentone Terr EH9 ... 121 F4
Menzies Cres KY2 ... 16 F5
Menzies Dr FK8 ... 2 A2
Menzies Rd EH48 ... 141 A6
Mercat Gait Ctr EH32 ... 97 A1
Mercat Pl FK10 ... 11 B4
Mercat Sh Ctr KY1 ... 17 C3
Mercat Wynd 2 FK10 ... 10 B6
Mercer Pl KY11 ... 29 E4
Mercer St FK10 ... 23 E3
Merchant St EH1 ... 229 A2
Merchants Way KY11 ... 47 C2
MERCHISTON ... 120 F4
Merchiston Ave
Edinburgh EH10 ... 121 A5
Falkirk FK2 ... 60 A7
Merchiston Bank Ave
EH10 ... 121 A4
Merchiston Bank Gdns
EH10 ... 121 A4
Merchiston Castle Sch
EH14 ... 149 B7
Merchiston Cres EH10 ... 121 A4
Merchiston Gdns
Edinburgh EH10 ... 120 F3
Falkirk FK2 ... 60 A6
Merchiston Gr EH11 ... 120 E4
Merchiston Ind Est FK2 ... 60 C8
Merchiston Mews EH10 .. 121 A5
Merchiston Pk EH10 ... 121 A5
Merchiston Pl EH10 ... 121 A5
Merchiston Rd FK2 ... 60 A6
Merchiston Rdbt FK2 ... 60 A6
Merchiston Terr FK2 ... 60 A7
Meredith Dr FK5 ... 38 F3
Merker Terr EH49 ... 84 E6
Merkland Cres KY11 ... 48 A3
Merkland Dr FK1 ... 60 E1
Merlindale ML11 ... 217 F8
Merlin Dr KY11 ... 47 A7
Merlin Way KY11 ... 48 C5
Merlyon Way EH26 ... 191 D7
Merrick Rd FK3 ... 61 F5
Merrick Way FK3 ... 61 F5
Merryfield Ave EH33 ... 127 D5
Merrylees EH49 ... 65 D1
Mertoun Pl EH11 ... 120 F5
Merville Cres FK1 ... 81 F5
Merville Terr FK1 ... 81 F5
Methven Dr KY12 ... 29 B5
Methven Pl KY1 ... 17 B2
Methven Rd KY1 ... 17 B2
Methven Terr EH18 ... 172 F6
Meuse La EH2 ... 229 A3
Meylea St EH48 ... 141 D4
Michaelson Sq EH54 ... 143 C1
Mid Beveridgewell KY12 .. 28 F5
Mid Brae 1 KY12 ... 28 F5
MID CALDER ... 144 C4
Mid Calder Prim Sch
EH53 ... 144 C2
Mid Cswy KY12 ... 42 D8
Middlebank Ave 1 KY11 .. 47 C8
Middlebank Cres 2 KY11 . 47 C8
Middlebank Holdings
KY11 ... 47 B6
Middlebank Rise KY11 ... 47 C8
Middlebank St KY11 ... 47 A4
Middlebank Wildlife Ctr
(SSPCA)* KY11 ... 47 B6
Middleby Ct EH9 ... 121 F4
Middleby St EH9 ... 121 F4
MIDDLEFIELD ... 60 D6
Middlefield EH7 ... 93 E3
Middlefield Ind Est FK2 ... 60 E7
Middlefield Rd FK2 ... 60 D6
Middle Jetty Rd KY11 ... 67 B8
Middleknowe EH14 ... 148 C8
Middlemas Rd EH42 ... 106 D8
Middlemass Ct FK2 ... 60 B6
Middle Meadow Wlk
EH8 ... 229 A1
Middlemuir Rd FK7 ... 7 C6
Middle Norton EH28 ... 117 F5
Middlepark EH14 ... 148 C8
Middleshot EH14 ... 148 C8
Middleshot Rd EH31 ... 52 A3
Middleshot Sq EH32 ... 97 B2
Middle Street La FK3 ... 40 C1
MIDDLETON ... 196 A1
Middleton FK11 ... 4 A5
Middleton Ave EH52 ... 115 A4
Middleton Rd EH52 ... 115 A4
Middle Wlk KY12 ... 29 B3
Middlewood Pk EH54 ... 142 E7
Midfield Ho EH18 ... 172 E5
Mid Gogarloch Syke
EH12 ... 119 A5
Midhope Pl EH52 ... 87 F2
Mid Liberton EH16 ... 122 A2
Midlothian Community Hospl
EH19 ... 173 D8
Midlothian Snowsports Ctr*
EH10 ... 150 A2
Midmar Ave EH10 ... 121 C2
Midmar Dr EH10 ... 121 C2
Midmar Gdns EH10 ... 121 B2
Mid New Cultins EH11 ... 119 B2
Mid Rd KY3 ... 34 F3
Mid Road Ind Est EH32 ... 125 F8
Mid St Bathgate EH48 ... 141 B6
Kirkcaldy KY1 ... 17 D6
Livingston EH54 ... 142 E6
Lochgelly KY5 ... 14 B7
Mid Steil EH11 ... 120 E1
Midthorn Cres FK2 ... 60 E5
Midtown FK11 ... 3 F6
MILESMARK ... 28 D6
Milesmark Ct KY12 ... 28 C6
Milesmark Prim Sch KY12 28 D5
Millar Cres EH10 ... 121 A3
Millar Pl Bonnybridge FK4 ... 58 B3
Edinburgh EH10 ... 121 A3
Falkirk FK2 ... 39 A5
Stirling FK8 ... 2 C1
Millar Place La EH10 ... 121 A3
Millar Rd EH33 ... 126 C5
Millars Wynd FK10 ... 5 C2
Millbank EH14 ... 147 C1
Millbank Cres FK10 ... 11 A5
Millbank Gr EH23 ... 195 C7
Millbank Pl EH52 ... 114 F4
Millbank Sq EH47 ... 161 B7
Millbank Terr 4 FK2 ... 82 F7
Millbrae EH53 ... 144 C5
Millbrae Wynd 1 EH14 .. 120 B2
Millbrook Pl FK11 ... 3 F6
Millburn Cres EH48 ... 139 D6
Millburn Rd
Bathgate EH48 ... 140 F6
Westfield EH48 ... 110 F5
Millburn St FK2 ... 60 D5
Mill Ct Bathgate EH48 ... 141 A7
Falkirk FK2 ... 39 B3
Milldean Gr KY12 ... 29 D5
Milledge ML8 ... 215 A2
Millenium Ave KY11 ... 46 C1
Millennium Wheel Dr FK1 59 A5
Miller Ave KY12 ... 28 B2
Miller Cres EH51 ... 64 D5
Millerfield EH49 ... 84 D7
Millerfield Pl EH9 ... 121 D5
Millerhill Rd EH22 ... 152 D7
Miller Pk FK2 ... 61 F1
Miller Pl Airth FK2 ... 22 E4
Harthill ML7 ... 159 F6
Miller Rd Dunfermline KY12 . 28 E5
Grangemouth EH51 ... 62 E5
Miller Row EH4 ... 228 A3
Millers Ct EH33 ... 126 B5
Miller St Carluke ML8 ... 215 A2
Harthill ML7 ... 159 E6
Kirkcaldy KY1 ... 17 F8
Mill Farm Rd KY3 ... 49 B7
Millfield Haddington EH41 . 130 A7
Livingston EH54 ... 143 A2
Millfield Dr FK2 ... 61 E2
Millflats St FK2 ... 39 A1
Millgate EH52 ... 87 F2
Millhall Gdns FK2 ... 61 F3
Millhall Rd FK7 ... 7 D5
Millhaugh La EH48 ... 141 A7
Millhill EH21 ... 124 D6
Mill Hill FK7 ... 6 D6

Millhill La EH21 . . . . . 124 D6
Millhill St KY11 . . . . . 29 B2
Millhill Wynd EH21 . . . . . 124 D6
Millhouse 9 EH3 . . . . . 93 B2
Millie St KY1 . . . . . 17 D6
Mill La Edinburgh EH6 . . . . . 93 F5
Kincardine FK10 . . . . . 23 E3
Stenton EH42 . . . . . 104 C2
Mill Lade EH49 . . . . . 84 E7
Mill of Airthrey Ct FK9 . . . . . 1 F8
Mill Pl EH49 . . . . . 84 C8
Mill Rd Alloa FK10 . . . . . 10 B6
Armadale EH48 . . . . . 139 E6
Bathgate EH48 . . . . . 141 A7
Blackburn EH47 . . . . . 162 C7
Cambusbarron FK7 . . . . . 6 D6
Clackmannan FK10 . . . . . 11 A5
Dunfermline KY11 . . . . . 29 B2
Falkirk FK2 . . . . . 39 B3
Harthill ML7 . . . . . 159 F5
Linlithgow EH49 . . . . . 84 C7
Mill Rdbt EH54 . . . . . 143 A3
Mill Road Ind Est EH49 . . . . . 84 D8
Millside EH12 . . . . . 120 D7
Mill St Alloa FK10 . . . . . 10 B6
Dunfermline KY12 . . . . . 28 F4
Kirkcaldy KY1 . . . . . 17 B1
Mill Walk Bsns Pk EH39 . . . . . 54 E6
Millway EH34 . . . . . 157 A6
Mill Wynd
East Linton EH40 . . . . . 103 E7
Haddington EH41 . . . . . 130 A7
Prestonpans EH32 . . . . . 96 F2
Miln-Acre EH6 . . . . . 93 D4
Milne Cres KY4 . . . . . 13 C3
Milne Park Rd FK7 . . . . . 19 E8
Milne Rd Dunfermline KY11 . 47 A7
Rosyth KY11 . . . . . 46 E1
Milnquarter Rd FK4 . . . . . 58 A3
Milrig Smallholdings
EH27 . . . . . 145 C3
Milsey Ct EH39 . . . . . 54 D7
Milton FK7 . . . . . 7 C1
Milton Brae FK7 . . . . . 7 B2
MILTON BRIDGE 171 B2
Milton Cl FK6 . . . . . 36 D3
Milton Cres
Bannockburn FK7 . . . . . 7 C1
Edinburgh EH15 . . . . . 123 A6
Milton Dr EH15 . . . . . 123 D7
Milton Gardens N EH15 . . 123 A6
Milton Gardens S EH15 . . 123 A6
Milton Gdns FK7 . . . . . 7 B1
Milton Glen EH15 . . . . . 123 E7
Milton Gn KY12 . . . . . 29 A2
Milton Gr Bannockburn FK7 . . 7 C1
Edinburgh EH15 . . . . . 123 E7
Milton Link EH15 . . . . . 123 C6
Milton Mill EH26 . . . . . 171 C2
Milton Pk KY2 . . . . . 15 B2
Milton Pl FK6 . . . . . 36 D3
Milton Rd Bannockburn FK7 . . 7 C1
Edinburgh EH15 . . . . . 123 B6
Kirkcaldy KY1 . . . . . 17 B2
Milton Road E EH15 . . . . . 123 D7
Milton Road W EH15 . . . . . 122 F6
Milton Row FK6 . . . . . 36 E3
Milton St EH8 . . . . . 94 A1
Milton Terr
Edinburgh EH15 . . . . . 123 E7
Stirling FK7 . . . . . 7 B1
Minard Rd ML7 . . . . . 179 D6
Mine Rd FK9 . . . . . 2 A8
Miner's Terr EH21 . . . . . 125 B5
Miners Wlk EH22 . . . . . 153 D4
MINGLE 64 A6
Mingle Pl EH51 . . . . . 64 A6
Minstrel Ct EH25 . . . . . 172 A3
Minthill Pl ML7 . . . . . 159 D5
Minto Ct FK12 . . . . . 5 B6
Minto Gdns FK12 . . . . . 5 B6
Minto Pl KY2 . . . . . 16 F4
Minto St Edinburgh EH9 . . . 121 F4
Lochgelly KY5 . . . . . 14 B8
Mission La 8 FK1 . . . . . 60 B4
Mitchell Cres Alloa FK10 . . . . . 9 F7
Cowdenbeath KY4 . . . . . 13 A1
Mitchellhall Brae EH41 . . . 130 E5
Mitchell Pl Falkirk FK1 . . . . . 59 E1
2 Kirkcaldy KY1 . . . . . 17 D6
Mitchell Rd KY11 . . . . . 46 C1
Mitchell's Cl 1 EH41 . . . . . 130 B8
Mitchell St Dalkeith EH22 . . 152 F3
Edinburgh EH6 . . . . . 94 A5
Kirkcaldy KY1 . . . . . 17 C4
Mitchell Way EH33 . . . . . 126 D7
Mitchell Wlk KY11 . . . . . 46 F3
Moat Dr EH14 . . . . . 120 D4
Moat Ho EH14 . . . . . 120 D4
Moat Pl EH14 . . . . . 120 D4
Moat St EH14 . . . . . 120 D4
Moat Terr EH14 . . . . . 120 D4
Moat View EH25 . . . . . 171 F3
Mochray Ct FK4 . . . . . 57 E5
Mochrum Dr KY12 . . . . . 45 B8
Modan Rd FK7 . . . . . 7 A3
Moffat Ave
Bonnyrigg and Lasswade
EH19 . . . . . 173 B6
Falkirk FK2 . . . . . 39 C3
Moffat Cres KY5 . . . . . 14 A7
Moffat Pl FK4 . . . . . 58 A4
Moffat Rd EH35 . . . . . 155 D6
Moffat Wlk EH33 . . . . . 126 C4
Moidart Rd EH47 . . . . . 161 D7
Moira Pk EH7 . . . . . 94 E1
Moira Terr EH7 . . . . . 94 E1
Moira Terrace La EH7 . . . . . 94 E1
Moir Ave EH21 . . . . . 125 A6
Moir Cres EH21 . . . . . 125 A6
Moir Ct KY4 . . . . . 12 E8
Moir Dr EH21 . . . . . 125 B6
Moir Pl EH21 . . . . . 125 A6
Moir St FK10 . . . . . 10 A8
Moir Terr EH21 . . . . . 125 A6
Mollison Ave ML7 . . . . . 159 E6
Monar Ct KY11 . . . . . 48 A3
Monastery St KY12 . . . . . 29 A3
Moncks Rd FK1 . . . . . 60 D4
Moncrieffe Ho EH17 . . . . . 151 D8
Moncrieff Terr EH9 . . . . . 121 E5
Moncrieff Way EH54 . . . . . 143 D8
Moncur St KY12 . . . . . 29 C7
Monkbarns Gdns 4
EH16 . . . . . 151 B8
Monkland Rd EH48 . . . . . 140 F6
Monkmains Rd EH41 . . . . . 130 C7
Monkrigg Ct EH41 . . . . . 130 C7
Monkrigg Pl EH41 . . . . . 130 C7
Monkrigg Steading
EH41 . . . . . 130 D6
Monksrig Rd EH26 . . . . . 191 C5
MONKSWOOD 174 B5
Monkswood Rd EH22 . . . . . 174 B4
MONKTONHALL 124 C3
Monktonhall Farm Cotts
EH21 . . . . . 124 B3
Monktonhall Pl EH21 . . . . . 124 B3
Monktonhall Terr EH21 . . 124 B4
Monkwood Ct EH9 . . . . . 121 D4
Monmouth Terr EH3 . . . . . 93 B4
Montague St EH8 . . . . . 229 B1
Montagu Terr EH3 . . . . . 93 B4
Monteith Wlk ML7 . . . . . 179 E6
Montfort Pl FK1 . . . . . 60 B3
Montgomery Cres FK2 . . . . . 39 B2
Montgomery Dr FK2 . . . . . 39 B2
Montgomery Pl FK2 . . . . . 39 B2
Montgomery St
Edinburgh EH7 . . . . . 93 F2
Falkirk FK2 . . . . . 60 E5
Grangemouth FK3 . . . . . 61 C6
Kirkcaldy KY2 . . . . . 17 B5
Montgomery Street La
EH7 . . . . . 93 E2
Montgomery Way FK9 . . . . . 2 B3
Montgomery Well FK2 . . . . . 39 B2
Montpelier EH10 . . . . . 121 B5
Montpelier Pk EH10 . . . . . 121 A5
Montpelier Terr EH10 . . . . . 121 A5
Montrose Rd Polmont FK2 . . 62 A1
Stirling FK9 . . . . . 2 C4
Montrose Terr EH7 . . . . . 229 C4
Montrose Way FK4 . . . . . 57 D5
Monument View FK8 . . . . . 2 B2
Moodie St KY12 . . . . . 29 A3
Moore Cotts EH52 . . . . . 115 D5
Moore House Sch EH48 . . 141 E5
Mooreland Gdns EH55 . . . 162 C1
Moorelands EH55 . . . . . 162 C1
Moorelands Pl EH55 . . . . . 162 D1
Moorfield Cotts EH22 . . . . . 152 C8
Moorfoot Ct EH19 . . . . . 173 B7
Moorfoot Pl
Bonnyrigg and Lasswade
EH19 . . . . . 173 B6
Penicuik EH26 . . . . . 191 E6
Moorfoot Prim Sch
EH23 . . . . . 196 A3
Moorfoot View
Bilston EH25 . . . . . 171 E5
Bonnyrigg and Lasswade
EH19 . . . . . 173 B6
Gorebridge EH23 . . . . . 195 C7
Moorings The KY11 . . . . . 47 F2
Moor Rd Fala EH37 . . . . . 224 B7
Pathhead EH37 . . . . . 176 D4
Pencaitland EH35, EH37 . . . 177 B6
Moorside St ML8 . . . . . 215 A2
Morar Ct FK3 . . . . . 61 D5
Morar Dr FK2 . . . . . 39 C1
Morar Pl FK3 . . . . . 61 D5
Morar Rd KY12 . . . . . 28 B1
Morar Way ML7 . . . . . 180 B3
Moray Ave EH42 . . . . . 106 C8
Moray Ct Auchtertool KY2 . . . 15 B2
Dalgety Bay KY11 . . . . . 48 A3
Moray Dr EH49 . . . . . 84 E6
Moray House Inst of Ed
EH8 . . . . . 229 B3
Moray Park Terr EH7 . . . . . 94 A2
Moray Pk KY11 . . . . . 48 A4
Moray Pl Edinburgh EH3 . . . 228 B4
Grangemouth FK3 . . . . . 61 E7
Linlithgow EH49 . . . . . 84 E6
Moray Prim Sch FK3 . . . . . 61 E7
Morayvale KY3 . . . . . 49 C8
Moray Way N KY11 . . . . . 48 C4
Moray Way S KY11 . . . . . 48 B2
MOREDUN 151 D8
Moredun Dell 2 EH17 . . . 151 E7
Moredun Dykes Rd EH17 151 D6
Moredun Ho EH17 . . . . . 151 D8
Moredun Park Ct EH17 . . . 151 D7
Moredun Park Dr EH17 . . . 151 D7
Moredun Park Gdns
EH17 . . . . . 151 D7
Moredun Park Gn EH17 . . . 151 E7
Moredun Park Gr EH17 . . . 151 E7
Moredun Park Loan
EH17 . . . . . 151 D7
Moredun Park Rd EH17 . . . 151 E8
Moredun Park St EH17 . . . 151 E7
Moredun Park View
EH17 . . . . . 151 E7
Moredun Park Way
EH17 . . . . . 151 D7
Moredun Park Wlk 1
EH17 . . . . . 151 E7
Moredunvale Bank EH17 . 151 D8
Moredunvale Gn EH17 . . . 151 D8
Moredunvale Gr EH17 . . . 151 D8
Moredunvale Loan EH17 . 151 D8
Moredunvale Pk EH17 . . . 151 D8
Moredunvale Pl EH17 . . . 151 D8
Moredunvale Rd EH17 . . . 151 D8
Moredunvale Way EH17 . . 151 D8
Morgan Ct FK7 . . . . . 7 C3
Morgan Way EH48 . . . . . 140 A4
Morham Gait EH10 . . . . . 149 E8
Morham Gdn EH10 . . . . . 149 E8
Morham Lea EH10 . . . . . 149 E8
Morham Pk EH10 . . . . . 149 E8
Morham Village Houses
EH41 . . . . . 131 D5
Morison Gdns EH30 . . . . . 68 B1
Moriston Ct FK3 . . . . . 61 E4
Moriston Dr EH54 . . . . . 164 F6
Morley Cres FK7 . . . . . 7 A3
Morlich Cres KY11 . . . . . 48 A2
Morlich Ct KY11 . . . . . 48 A2
Morlich Gr KY11 . . . . . 48 A2
Morlich Pk KY11 . . . . . 48 A2
Morlich Pl KY11 . . . . . 48 A2
Morlich Rd KY11 . . . . . 48 A2
Morlich Wlk EH54 . . . . . 144 A4
Mornay Way ML7 . . . . . 179 D5
MORNINGSIDE 121 A2
Morningside Ct EH10 . . . 121 A2
Morningside Dr EH10 . . . 121 A2
Morningside Gdns EH10 . . 120 F2
Morningside Gr EH10 . . . 120 F1
Morningside Pk EH10 . . . 121 A3
Morningside Pl EH10 . . . 121 A3
Morningside Rd EH10 . . . 121 B3
Morningside Terr EH10 . . 121 A3
Morris Ct KY11 . . . . . 47 C2
Morrison Ave
Bonnybridge FK4 . . . . . 57 F6
Tranent EH33 . . . . . 126 E5
Morrison Cir EH3 . . . . . 228 A2
Morrison Cres EH3 . . . . . 228 A2
Morrison Dr
Bannockburn FK7 . . . . . 7 C2
Dunfermline KY11 . . . . . 46 F8
Morrison Link EH3 . . . . . 228 A2
Morrison St EH3 . . . . . 228 A2
Morrison Way EH54 . . . . . 143 D8
Morris Rd EH22 . . . . . 174 C6
Morris Sq EH54 . . . . . 143 F2
Morris Terr FK8 . . . . . 7 A8
Mortimer Ct KY11 . . . . . 48 B2
MORTONHALL 150 E5
Mortonhall Gate EH16 . . . 150 E5
Mortonhall Park Ave
EH17 . . . . . 150 F5
Mortonhall Park Bank
EH17 . . . . . 151 A5
Mortonhall Park Cres
EH17 . . . . . 151 A5
Mortonhall Park Dr
EH17 . . . . . 151 A5
Mortonhall Park Gdns
EH17 . . . . . 150 F5
Mortonhall Park Gr EH17 150 F5
Mortonhall Park Loan
EH17 . . . . . 150 F5
Mortonhall Park Pl EH17 151 A5
Mortonhall Park Terr
EH17 . . . . . 151 A5
Mortonhall Park Way
EH17 . . . . . 150 F5
Mortonhall Rd EH9 . . . . . 121 D3
Morton St EH15 . . . . . 123 C7
Morven Ct FK1 . . . . . 60 C2
Morven Dr FK2 . . . . . 61 D2
Morven Gr KY2 . . . . . 16 F7
Morven Pl KY11 . . . . . 48 A3
Morvenside EH14 . . . . . 148 C8
Morvenside Cl EH14 . . . . . 148 C8
Morven St EH4 . . . . . 91 C1
Mossband La ML7 . . . . . 179 E6
Mossbank
Cowdenbeath KY4 . . . . . 13 B2
Livingston EH54 . . . . . 143 E5
Rosyth KY11 . . . . . 46 F5
Mossburn Ave ML7 . . . . . 159 D5
Mossburn Ind Est ML7 . . 159 D5
Mosscastle Rd FK1 . . . . . 108 A7
MOSSEND 163 C3
Mossend EH55 . . . . . 163 D3
Mossend Terr KY4 . . . . . 13 B2
Mossgiel Ave Cowie FK7 . . . 20 D7
Stirling FK8 . . . . . 2 A2
Mossgiel Cotts EH54 . . . . . 142 D7
Mossgiel St FK1 . . . . . 59 B5
Mossgiel Terr FK2 . . . . . 61 A3
Mossgiel Wlk 3 EH16 . . . 122 A1
MOSSGREEN 31 A6
Mosshall Ind Est EH47 . . 162 B7
Mosshat Rd EH55 . . . . . 202 F3
Mosshouse FK7 . . . . . 6 F4
Mosside Ct EH47 . . . . . 162 D8
Mosside Dr EH47 . . . . . 141 D1
Mosside Rd EH47 . . . . . 162 D8
Mosside Terr
Bathgate EH48 . . . . . 141 B3
Blackburn EH47 . . . . . 141 D1
Moss Intc EH54 . . . . . 143 D6
Moss Rd Airth FK2 . . . . . 21 E7
Fallin FK7 . . . . . 8 C4
Moss-Side Rd KY4 . . . . . 13 B3
Moss Way KY11 . . . . . 48 B5
Moston Terr EH9 . . . . . 121 F4
Motion St KY5 . . . . . 14 A7
Moubray Gdns FK10 . . . . . 4 B1
Moubray Gr EH30 . . . . . 89 C8
Moubray Rd KY11 . . . . . 48 C5
Moulin Way KY12 . . . . . 29 E5
Mound Pl EH1 . . . . . 228 C3
Mound The EH2 . . . . . 228 C3
Mount Alvernia EH16 . . . . . 151 B7
Mount Bartholomew FK4 . . 58 A5
Mountbatten Pl KY11 . . . . . 46 E3
Mountbatten St FK3 . . . . . 61 C5
Mountcastle Bank EH8 . . . 122 F8
Mountcastle Cres EH8 . . . 122 F8
Mountcastle Drive N
EH8 . . . . . 122 F8
Mountcastle Drive S
EH15 . . . . . 123 A6
Mountcastle Gdns EH8 . . . 122 E8
Mountcastle Gn 1 EH8 . . . 94 E1
Mountcastle Gr EH8 . . . . . 122 E8
Mountcastle Loan EH8 . . . 122 E8
Mountcastle Pk 3 EH8 . . . 94 E1
Mountcastle Pl 2 EH8 . . . 94 E1
Mountcastle Terr EH8 . . . 122 E8
Mountfair Gdns EH33 . . . . . 127 C5
Mountfair Pl EH33 . . . . . 127 C5
Mount Grange EH9 . . . . . 121 C4
Mount Hooly Cres KY11 . . . 68 C6
Mounthooly Loan EH10 . . 150 D5
Mount Hope FK9 . . . . . 2 B7
Mountjoy Ct EH21 . . . . . 124 C7
Mountjoy Terr EH21 . . . . . 124 C7
Mount Lodge Pl EH15 . . . . . 123 B8
Mount Oliphant FK7 . . . . . 20 D7
Mount Pleasant EH48 . . . . . 139 F5
Mount Vernon Rd EH16 . . 151 B8
Mount William FK10 . . . . . 5 E1
Mowbray Gdns KY4 . . . . . 30 E6
Mowbray Rise EH54 . . . . . 143 F1
Mowbrey Ct FK7 . . . . . 7 D4
Moy Ct FK3 . . . . . 61 D5
Mucklehill Pk KY11 . . . . . 47 A2
Mucklets Ave EH21 . . . . . 124 A4
Mucklets Cres EH21 . . . . . 124 A3
Mucklets Ct EH21 . . . . . 124 A4
Mucklets Dr EH21 . . . . . 124 A4
Mucklets Pl EH21 . . . . . 124 A4
Mudale Ct FK1 . . . . . 60 D1
MUIRALEHOUSE 19 E8
Muiralehouse Rd FK7 . . . . . 19 E8
Muiravonside Ctry Pk*
EH49 . . . . . 83 E4
Muir Ct KY4 . . . . . 30 E6
Muirdale Terr EH4 . . . . . 92 B2
Muirdyke Ave FK2 . . . . . 39 C3
Muiredge and Jersy Rd
ML7 . . . . . 179 A8
Muirend Ave EH14 . . . . . 148 E7
Muirend Ct EH51 . . . . . 64 B6
Muirend Rd FK7 . . . . . 7 B5
Muirepark Ct EH51 . . . . . 64 A6
MUIRFIELD 52 C3
Muirfield Apartments
EH31 . . . . . 52 B2
Muirfield Cres EH31 . . . . . 52 B2
Muirfield Ct EH40 . . . . . 103 E7
Muirfield Dr Gullane EH31 . . 52 B2
Uphall EH52 . . . . . 114 E4
Muirfield Gdns
Gullane EH31 . . . . . 52 B2
Loanhead EH20 . . . . . 172 C7
Muirfield Gr EH31 . . . . . 52 C2
Muirfield Ho EH31 . . . . . 52 B3
Muirfield Pk EH31 . . . . . 52 B3
Muirfield Rd
Dunbar EH42 . . . . . 106 D7
Stenhousemuir FK5 . . . . . 38 E2
Muirfield Station EH31 . . . 52 B2
Muirfield Steading EH31 . . 52 C3
Muirfield Terr EH31 . . . . . 52 B2
Muirfield Way EH54 . . . . . 142 E6
Muirhall Pl FK5 . . . . . 38 C3
Muirhall Rd FK5 . . . . . 38 C3
Muirhead Ave FK2 . . . . . 60 A8
Muirhead Pl Falkirk FK2 . . . 82 A8
Harthill ML7 . . . . . 159 D4
Penicuik EH26 . . . . . 191 F8
Muirhead Rd FK5 . . . . . 38 E4
MUIRHOUSE 92 B6
Muirhouse Ave EH4 . . . . . 92 B4
Muirhouse Avenue N EH4 . 92 B4
Muirhouse Bank EH4 . . . . . 92 B4
Muirhouse Cl EH4 . . . . . 92 A4
Muirhouse Cres EH4 . . . . . 92 B5
Muirhouse Ct EH4 . . . . . 92 A5
Muirhouse Dr EH4 . . . . . 92 A5
Muirhouse Gdns EH4 . . . . . 92 A5
Muirhouse Gn EH4 . . . . . 92 B4
Muirhouse Gr EH4 . . . . . 92 A5
Muirhouse Loan EH4 . . . . . 92 B5
Muirhouse Medway EH4 . . 92 A5
Muirhouse Parkway EH4 . . 92 A5
Muirhouse Pk EH4 . . . . . 92 A4
Muirhouse Place E EH4 . . . 92 B4
Muirhouse Place W EH4 . . 92 B4
MUIRHOUSES 64 D5
Muirhouses Ave EH51 . . . . . 64 C6
Muirhouses Cres EH51 . . . 64 C6
Muirhouses Sq EH51 . . . . . 64 C7
Muirhouse Terr EH4 . . . . . 92 A4
Muirhouse View EH4 . . . . . 92 A5
Muirhouse Way EH4 . . . . . 92 B4
Muirlaun ML11 . . . . . 201 A1
Muirlee Rd ML8 . . . . . 215 B1
Muirpark EH22 . . . . . 152 E1
Muirpark Ct EH33 . . . . . 126 E5
Muirpark Dr Shieldhill FK1 . . 81 D6
Tranent EH33 . . . . . 126 E5
Muirpark Gdns
Tranent EH33 . . . . . 126 E5
Tullibody FK10 . . . . . 4 E4
Muirpark Gr EH33 . . . . . 126 E5
Muirpark Pl EH33 . . . . . 126 E5
Muirpark Rd EH33 . . . . . 126 E5
Muirpark Terr EH33 . . . . . 126 E5
Muirpark Wynd EH33 . . . . . 126 E5
Muir Pl Dunfermline KY12 . . . 29 D7
Lochgelly KY5 . . . . . 14 C8
Muir Rd Bathgate EH48 . . . . . 140 F7
Lochgelly KY5 . . . . . 14 C8
Pumpherston EH54 . . . . . 144 A8
Townhill KY12 . . . . . 29 D7
Muir's Ct EH52 . . . . . 114 F4
Muirside Ave FK10 . . . . . 4 C3
Muirside Ct KY12 . . . . . 27 C1
Muirside Dr EH33 . . . . . 126 C5
Muirside Gr KY12 . . . . . 27 C1
Muirside La KY12 . . . . . 44 C8
Muirside Rd
Cairneyhill KY12 . . . . . 27 C1
Tullibody FK10 . . . . . 4 C3
Muir St FK5 . . . . . 38 D2
Muirs The FK10 . . . . . 4 C4
MUIRTON 7 E6
Muirton Rd FK7 . . . . . 7 E6
Muirton Rdbt FK7 . . . . . 7 F7
Muirton Way KY11 . . . . . 48 B5
Muir Wood Cres EH14 . . . 148 B5
Muir Wood Dr EH14 . . . . . 148 B5
Muir Wood Gr EH14 . . . . . 148 B5
Muir Wood Pl EH14 . . . . . 148 B5
Muir Wood Rd EH14 . . . . . 148 B6
Mulberry Dr KY11 . . . . . 29 E1
Mulberry Pl EH6 . . . . . 93 D5
Muldron Terr ML7 . . . . . 180 B2
Mull Ct Alloa FK10 . . . . . 10 B5
Grangemouth FK3 . . . . . 61 D6
Mulloch Ave 1 FK2 . . . . . 60 A8
Multiplex Rdbt EH54 . . . . . 143 E1
Multrees Wk EH1 . . . . . 229 A4
Multrees Wlk Sh EH2 . . . 229 A4
Mumrills Rd FK2 . . . . . 61 C4
MUNGAL 60 A8
Mungalend FK2 . . . . . 60 B7
Mungalend Ct FK2 . . . . . 60 B7
Mungalend Rdbt FK2 . . . . . 60 B8
Mungalhead Rd FK2 . . . . . 60 A7
Mungal Mill Ct FK2 . . . . . 59 F8
Mungal Pl FK2 . . . . . 60 B8
Mungle Pl EH55 . . . . . 163 D3
Mungle St EH55 . . . . . 163 D3
Mungoswells Cotts EH39 . . 72 D2
Munnoch Way FK7 . . . . . 20 C4
Munro Ave FK9 . . . . . 2 B4
Munro Dr EH13 . . . . . 149 A5
Munro Gate FK9 . . . . . 2 A5
Munro Gdns FK2 . . . . . 60 F3
Munro Pl FK10 . . . . . 9 F6
Munro Rd FK7 . . . . . 7 E6
Munro St Kirkcaldy KY1 . . . . . 17 B2
Stenhousemuir FK5 . . . . . 38 E3
Munro Way EH54 . . . . . 143 C8
Murano Pl EH7 . . . . . 93 F2
Murderdean Rd EH22 . . . . . 174 A5
Murdoch Terr EH11 . . . . . 228 A1
Murdostoun Cres ML7 . . . . . 159 F6
Murieston Cres EH11 . . . . . 120 E6
Murieston Crescent La
EH11 . . . . . 120 F6
Murieston Ct EH54 . . . . . 165 A6
Murieston Dr EH54 . . . . . 165 A6
Murieston East Rd EH54 . . 165 B8
Murieston Gdns EH54 . . . . . 165 A7
Murieston Gn EH54 . . . . . 164 F5
Murieston Gr EH54 . . . . . 165 A6
Murieston La EH11 . . . . . 120 E6
Murieston Mews EH54 . . . 164 F6
Murieston Pk EH54 . . . . . 164 F5
Murieston Pl EH11 . . . . . 120 E6
Murieston Rd
Edinburgh EH11 . . . . . 120 E6
Livingston EH54 . . . . . 164 E4
Murieston Terr EH11 . . . . . 120 E6
Murieston Vale EH54 . . . . . 164 E4
Murieston Valley EH54 . . . 164 F6
Murieston Way EH54 . . . . . 165 A7
Murieston West Rd EH54 164 F7
Murieston Wlk EH54 . . . . . 164 E4
Murieston Wood EH54 . . . 164 F5
Murnin Ct FK7 . . . . . 7 C3
Murnin Rd FK4 . . . . . 58 A4
Murnin Road Ind Est FK4 . 58 A4
Murrayburn App EH11 . . . 119 D1
Murrayburn Dr EH14 . . . . . 119 D1
Murrayburn Gate EH14 . . . 148 D8
Murrayburn Gdns EH14 . . 119 E1
Murrayburn Gn EH14 . . . . . 119 E1
Murrayburn Gr EH14 . . . . . 119 E1
Murrayburn Junc EH14 . . . 148 D8
Murrayburn Pk EH14 . . . . . 119 E1
Murrayburn Pl EH14 . . . . . 119 D1
Murrayburn Prim Sch
EH11 . . . . . 119 E2
Murrayburn Rd EH14 . . . . . 119 E2
Murray Cotts EH12 . . . . . 119 C6
Murray Cres FK2 . . . . . 83 A6
Murray Ct Armadale EH48 . . 139 F6
Dunbar EH42 . . . . . 106 D8
MURRAYFIELD 120 B7
Murrayfield Ave EH12 . . . . . 120 D7
Murrayfield Dr
Blackburn EH47 . . . . . 162 D8
Edinburgh EH12 . . . . . 120 C7

Murrayfield Gdns EH12 120 D7
Murrayfield Hospl (Private) EH12 120 A7
Murrayfield Pl
Bannockburn FK7 7 D1
Edinburgh EH12 120 D7
Murrayfield Prim Sch EH47 141 D1
Murrayfield Rd EH12 120 C7
Murrayfield Stadium (Scottish Rugby) EH12 120 C6
Murrayfield Terr
Bannockburn FK7 7 D1
Blackburn EH47 162 D8
Murray Pl Aberdour KY3 49 C8
Cambusbarron FK7 6 D5
Stirling FK8 7 B7
Murrays Brae The EH17 151 C4
Murraysgate Cres EH47 160 F6
Murraysgate Ind Est EH47 160 F6
Murrayshall Rd FK7 7 B3
Murrays The EH17 151 C4
Murray Terr KY2 17 B5
Murray Way EH54 143 D8
Murray Wlk KY11 29 E4
Murrell Rd KY3 49 C8
Murrel Terr KY3 49 C8
Museum of Childhood* EH1 229 B3
Museum of Communication* KY3 50 E8
Museum of Edinburgh* EH8 229 B3
Museum of Fire* EH3 228 C2
Music Hall La 2 KY12 29 A3
MUSSELBURGH 124 C7
Musselburgh Bsns Pk EH21 124 B5
Musselburgh Grammar Sch EH21 124 C5
Musselburgh Gram Sch EH21 124 C5
Musselburgh Mus* EH21 124 C6
Musselburgh Prim Sch EH21 124 C6
Musselburgh Rd
Dalkeith EH22 153 B4
Edinburgh EH15 123 E7
Musselburgh Sports Ctr EH21 124 D5
Musselburgh Sta EH21 124 A4
Myers Ct KY12 29 D5
Myles Farm Cotts EH33 126 A4
Myles Ho FK8 7 A8
Mylneburn Gdns KY11 45 D3
Mylne Pl FK2 39 B2
Myothill Rd FK6 57 D7
Myot View FK6 36 A3
Myre Cres KY3 35 A3
Myre Dale EH19 173 C6
MYRESIDE 120 E3
Myreside EH19 173 D5
Myreside Ct EH10 120 F2
Myreside Rd EH10 120 F3
Myreside View EH14 120 E3
Myreton FK11 4 A6
Myreton Dr FK7 19 E8
Myreton Motor Mus* EH32 72 B3
Myreton Rd FK3 61 D6
Myreton Way FK1 59 F3
Myretongate FK12 4 E6
Myrtle Cres Bilston EH25 171 E6
Kirkcaldy KY2 17 B7
Myrtle Gr EH22 174 D7
Myrtle Terr EH11 120 E5
Myrtle Wynd KY12 28 F5

N

Nagle Rd KY12 12 A1
Nailer Rd Falkirk FK1 59 E6
Stirling FK7 7 B2
Nairn Ct FK1 60 D1
Nairn Rd EH54 142 E8
Nairn St KY1 17 D6
Naismith Ct FK3 40 E1
Namayo Ave FK2 61 A4
Namur Rd EH26 192 A8
Nantwich Dr EH7 94 E3
Napier Ave EH48 141 C6
Napier Cres FK2 60 A7
Napier Loan EH10 120 F4
Napier Pl FK2 60 A7
Napier Rd EH10 121 A4
Napier Sq EH54 144 A8
Napier St KY1 17 E8
Nasmyth Ct EH54 144 B6
Nasmyth Rd KY11 46 B2
Nasmyth Sq EH54 144 A6
Natal Pl KY4 13 D3
National Gallery of Scotland* EH2 228 C3
National Liby of Scotland* EH1 229 A2
National Monument* EH7 229 B4
National Museum of Flight* EH39 74 C1
National Museum of Scotland* EH1 229 A2
National Museums Collection Ctr* EH5 92 D6
National Portrait Gall* EH2 229 A4
National War Museum of Scotland* EH1 228 C3
Navar Ct ML7 180 A3
Nebit The FK12 4 E6
Neidpath Ct
2 Edinburgh EH12 119 A7
Longniddry EH32 98 E5
Neidpath Dr FK5 39 A4
Neidpath Pl KY12 29 D6
Neilson Ct EH47 162 B8
Neilson Gr KY3 33 E1
Neilson Park Rd EH41 130 A8
Neilson Sq EH54 142 C5
Neilson St FK1 60 B4
Nellburn EH54 142 F6
Nellfield EH16 151 B8
Nelson Ave EH54 143 F3
Nelson Gdns FK3 40 E1
Nelson Monument* EH7 229 B4
Nelson Pl FK7 7 C6
Nelson Rd EH51 62 E6
Nelson St Edinburgh EH3 228 C4
Grangemouth FK3 61 E8
Kirkcaldy KY2 17 B6
Rosyth KY11 46 E5
Ness Pl EH33 126 C4
Ness The KY12 26 E1
Nether Bakehouse EH8 229 C3
Netherbank EH16 150 F6
Netherbank View EH16 150 F6
Netherbeath Rd KY4 30 F8
Netherby Rd Airth FK2 22 D4
Edinburgh EH5 93 A6
Nether Craigour EH17 122 D1
Nether Craigwell EH8 229 C3
Nether Currie Cres EH14 148 B5
Nether Currie Pl EH14 148 B5
Nether Currie Prim Sch EH14 148 B5
Nether Currie Rd EH14 148 B5
NETHER DECHMONT 143 B7
Nether Dechmont Cotts EH54 143 B7
Nether Dechmont Pl EH54 143 B7
Netherfaulds Dr FK6 36 D1
Netherfield Rd FK2 61 D1
Nethergate KY3 35 A2
Nethergate The FK12 4 E6
Netherlaw EH39 54 B6
NETHER LIBERTON 121 F3
Nether Liberton Ct EH16 122 A2
Nethermains Prim Sch FK6 36 D1
Nethermains Rd FK6 36 C2
Nethershot Rd EH32 97 A2
Nether St Dysart KY1 18 B7
Kirkcaldy KY1 17 D6
Netherton Gr EH47 161 B4
Netherton Pl EH47 161 B4
Netherton Rd KY4 13 C6
Netherton St ML7 159 D5
Nethertown Broad St KY12 29 A2
Netherwood Pk EH54 143 A7
Nettlehill Dr EH54 115 A1
Nettlehill Rd
Livingston EH54 143 F8
Uphall Station EH54 115 A1
Neuk The ML11 217 F8
Nevis Cres FK10 10 B8
Nevis Dr EH54 164 F6
Nevis Gdns EH26 192 A7
Nevis Pl Falkirk FK1 60 C2
Grangemouth FK3 61 E5
Shotts ML7 180 B3
New Arthur Pl EH8 229 B2
New Assembly Cl EH1 229 A3
NEWBATTLE 153 A1
Newbattle Abbey Coll EH22 153 A1
Newbattle Abbey Cres EH22 173 F8
Newbattle Com High Sch EH22 174 C7
Newbattle Gdns EH22 153 A1
Newbattle Rd
Dalkeith EH22 152 F2
Newtongrange EH22 174 A7
Newbattle Terr EH10 121 B4
New Bell's Ct EH6 94 A5
Newbiggin Cres FK10 4 C2
NEWBIGGING 15 C2
Newbigging
Auchtertool KY2 15 C2
Musselburgh EH21 124 D5
Newbigging Rd KY12 27 C7
Newbigging Terr KY2 15 C2
Newbiggin Rd FK3 61 E6
NEWBRIDGE 117 A6
Newbridge Ind Est EH28 116 F5
Newbridge Junc EH28 117 B6
Newbridge Rd EH28 117 A5
New Broompark EH5 92 E7
New Broughton 4 EH3 93 D2
Newburn Pl KY12 29 D3
Newbyres Ave EH23 174 C1
Newbyres Cres EH23 195 C8
Newbyres Gdns EH23 195 C8
Newbyth Stables EH40 75 D5
Newbyth Steading EH40 75 D5
Newcarron Ct 3 FK2 60 A8
New Carron Rd FK2, FK5 39 A3
New Century Rd ML7 179 E4
New Coll EH1 228 C3
New Cove Farm Cotts TD13 219 A4
NEWCRAIGHALL 123 E4
Newcraighall Bsns Pk EH15 123 B4
Newcraighall Dr EH21 123 D4
Newcraighall Prim Sch EH21 123 E4
Newcraighall Rd EH15 123 C4
Newcraighall Sta EH21 123 D4
New Cut Rigg EH6 93 D5
NEWHAILES 124 A6
Newhailes Ave EH21 124 A6
Newhailes Cres EH21 124 A6
Newhailes Ind Est EH21 123 F5
Newhailes Rd EH21 123 F5
Newhall (Gdn)* EH26 206 F6
New Hallglen Rd FK1 60 D2
Newhalls Rd EH30 68 C1
NEWHAVEN 93 D6
Newhaven Main St EH6 93 D7
Newhaven Pl EH6 93 D7
Newhaven Rd EH6 93 D5
New Holygate EH52 115 D5
New Hos Drem EH39 73 A4
East Fortune EH39 74 D3
Garvald EH41 132 D2
Newhouse FK8 7 A5
Newhouse Ave EH42 78 E1
Newhouse Bsns Pk FK3 61 C7
Newhouse Dr FK1 59 E2
Newhouse Pl EH42 78 F1
Newhouse Rd FK3 61 D7
Newhouses Rd EH52 116 A4
Newhouse Terr EH42 78 E1
New Hunterfield EH23 174 B2
NEWINGTON 121 E4
Newington La FK5 37 D6
Newington Rd EH9 121 E5
New John's Pl EH8 229 B1
New La EH6 93 D6
New Lairdship Pl EH11 119 D3
New Lairdship Yards EH11 119 D3
Newland Ave EH48 141 B6
Newlandrig EH23 175 B2
Newlands EH27 166 F7
Newlands Ct
Bathgate EH48 140 F6
Stirling FK7 20 D2
Newlands Pk
Dunfermline KY12 29 B5
Edinburgh EH9 121 F4
Newlands Pl FK10 4 C3
Newlands Rd
Bannockburn FK7 19 D8
Grangemouth FK3 61 C6
Polmont FK2 82 C8
Newlands Road Rdbt 5 FK2 82 C8
New Line Rd FK7 19 A7
NEWLISTON 16 C6
Newliston Dr KY2 16 C7
New Liston Rd EH29 89 A1
Newmains Rd EH29 89 A2
Newmarket FK7 7 E1
New Market Rd EH14 120 C3
Newmarket St 7 FK1 60 B5
New Mart Gdns EH14 120 B3
New Mart Pl EH14 120 C3
New Mart Rd EH14 120 B3
New Mart Sq EH14 120 B3
New Meadowspott EH22 153 A2
Newmill and Canthill Rd ML7 179 B6
NEWMILLS 26 D1
Newmills FK10 4 B3
Newmills Ave EH14 147 D3
Newmills Cres EH14 147 D3
Newmills Gr EH14 147 D3
Newmills Rd Currie EH14 147 C4
Dalkeith EH22 153 B3
Newmills Terr EH22 153 B3
New Orchardfield EH6 93 F4
Newpark Cres FK7 7 A2
Newpark Rd
Livingston EH54 164 D6
Stirling FK7 7 B2
Newpark Rdbt EH54 164 D7
NEW PENTLAND 171 F7
New Rd FK7 7 D2
New Row Dunfermline KY12 29 A3
East Fortune EH39 74 B3
Kincardine FK10 24 A3
Tranent EH33 126 C6
New Skinners Cl EH1 229 B3
New St Bridge of Allan FK9 1 F8
Cockenzie & Port Seton EH32 97 C4
Edinburgh EH8 229 B3
Musselburgh EH21 124 B6
Prestonpans EH32 96 F1
Slamannan FK1 108 B7
Tranent EH33 126 C7
New Star Bank EH22 174 A5
New Struan Sch FK10 9 F7
New Swanston EH10 149 F5
Newtoft St EH17 151 E6
NEWTON 88 A8
Newton Ave FK2 40 A3
Newton Church Rd EH22 152 C7
Newton Cotts EH22 153 A8
Newton Cres KY11 47 A4
NEWTONGRANGE 174 A6
Newtongrange L Ctr EH19 174 A5
Newtongrange Pl EH22 174 A4
Newtongrange Prim Sch EH22 174 B5
Newtonlees Cotts EH42 106 F7
Newton Loan Ct EH23 174 B2
Newtonmore Dr KY2 16 F8
Newton Pl KY11 46 F4
Newton Port EH41 101 B1
Newton Rd FK2 40 A2
Newtonshaw FK10 5 C1
Newton St
Easthouses EH22 174 C8
Edinburgh EH11 120 E5
NEWTON VILLAGE 152 D7
New Tower Pl EH15 95 B1
NEWTOWN 63 F6
NEW TOWN 127 E1
Newtown EH51 63 F6
Newtown Cotts EH51 63 F6
Newtown St EH51 63 F6
New Well Wynd EH49 84 F6
NEW WINTON 127 B3
Newyearfield Bsns Pk EH54 143 C5
Newyearfield Rdbt EH54 143 C5
Ney Ct KY11 30 A1
Nichollfield EH6 93 D6
Nicholson Pl FK1 59 F2
Nicholson Way EH54 143 D7
Nicklaus Gn EH54 143 B8
Nicol Dr KY3 34 A2
Nicol Pl EH52 115 D5
Nicol Rd EH52 115 D6
Nicolson Sq EH8 229 B2
Nicolson St EH8 229 B2
Nicol St KY1 17 B3
Nicolton Ave FK2 82 E7
Nicolton Ct 2 FK2 82 F7
Nicolton Rd FK2 83 B8
NIDDRIE 123 A3
Niddrie Cotts EH15 123 C4
Niddrie Farm Gr EH16 122 E4
Niddrie House Ave EH16 122 F3
Niddrie House Dr EH16 123 A3
Niddrie House Gdns EH16 122 F3
Niddrie House Pk EH16 122 F3
Niddrie House Sq EH16 122 F3
NIDDRIE MAINS 122 E4
Niddrie Mains Ct EH16 123 A4
Niddrie Mains Dr EH16 123 A4
Niddrie Mains Rd EH16 122 D4
Niddrie Mains Terr EH16 122 E4
NIDDRIE MARISCHAL 123 A3
Niddrie Marischal Cres EH16 122 F4
Niddrie Marischal Dr EH16 122 F3
Niddrie Marischal Gdns 1 EH16 122 F4
Niddrie Marischal Gn EH16 122 F3
Niddrie Marischal Gr EH16 123 A4
Niddrie Marischal Loan 2 EH16 122 F4
Niddrie Marischal Pl EH16 122 F4
Niddrie Marischal Rd EH16 123 A4
Niddrie Marischal St 3 EH16 122 F4
NIDDRIE MILL 123 A4
Niddrie Mill Ave EH15 123 A4
Niddrie Mill Cres EH15 123 A5
Niddrie Mill Dr EH15 123 A4
Niddrie Mill Gr EH15 123 A4
Niddrie Mill Pl EH15 123 A4
Niddrie Mill Prim Sch EH16 122 F4
Niddrie Mill Terr EH15 123 A4
Niddry EH52 87 F1
Niddry Rd EH52 87 F2
Niddry St EH1 229 A3
Niddry Street S EH1 229 B2
Niddry View EH52 87 F2
Nigel Loan EH16 151 B8
Nigel Rise EH54 143 F1
Nightingale Way EH3 228 C2
Nile Gr EH10 121 B3
Nile St KY2 17 B6
Nimmo Ave EH32 97 A1
Ninian Rd EH51 62 E6
Ninth St EH22 174 B6
Nisbet Dr FK6 36 D2
Nisbet Rd EH31 51 F2
Nithsdale Pl KY11 30 C1
Nithsdale St ML7 179 D5
Nith St KY11 29 F2
Niven Rd KY11 47 C3
Nivensknowe Pk EH20 171 F7
Niven's Knowe Rd EH20 171 F7
No 1 Dock Road E KY11 46 B1
No 1 Dock Road W KY11 46 B1
No 2 Dock Road E KY11 46 B1
No 2 Dock Road W KY11 46 B1
No 3 Dock Road W KY11 46 B1
No 7 Pit Rd KY4 13 C4
Nobel Pl EH25 171 F3
Nobel View FK2 82 A8
Noble Pl EH6 94 B4
Normand Brae KY1 18 A7
Normand Rd KY1 18 A8
Normandy Pl KY11 46 E2
Norman Rise EH54 143 F1
North Approach Rd FK10 23 E3
North Ave FK2 83 B7
Northbank Cotts EH48 141 B7
Northbank Ct EH51 64 A5
Northbank Dr EH51 64 A5
Northbank Pk EH51 63 F5
Northbank Rd KY12 27 D1
North Bank Rd EH32 96 E1
North Bank St EH1 229 A3
North Belton Cotts EH42 105 B7
NORTH BERWICK 54 D8
North Berwick High Sch EH39 54 C6
North Berwick Sports Ctr EH39 54 C6
North Berwick Sta EH39 54 B7
North Bridge EH1 229 A3
North Bridge St
Bathgate EH48 141 A6
Grangemouth FK3 40 C1
NORTH BROOMAGE 38 A4
North Broomage Rdbt FK5 38 A3
North Bughtlin Bank EH12 91 B1
North Bughtlin Brae EH12 91 B1
North Bughtlinfield EH12 91 A1
North Bughtlin Gate EH12 91 B1
North Bughtlin Neuk EH12 91 B1
North Bughtlin Pl EH12 91 B1
North Bughtlin Rd EH12 91 B1
North Bughtlinrig EH12 91 A1
North Bughtlinside EH12 91 A1
North Cairntow EH16 122 D5
North Castle St Alloa FK10 10 A5
Edinburgh EH2 228 B4
North Charlotte St EH2 228 B3
Northcliff KY11 68 B6
North Clyde Street La EH1 229 A4
Northcote St EH11 120 F6
North Cres EH32 97 A1
North East Circus Pl 6 EH3 93 B2
North East Cumberland Street La EH3 93 C2
North Elphinstone Farm Cotts EH33 126 B2
North End FK7 6 D6
Northern Research Station (Forestry Commission) EH25 171 B4
North Esk Rd KY11 46 C2
NORTHFIELD 122 D8
Northfield
Cowdenbeath KY4 13 C6
Tranent EH33 126 E6
Northfield Ave
Edinburgh EH8 122 D8
Shotts ML7 180 B2
Northfield Broadway EH8 122 E8
Northfield Cir EH8 122 D8
Northfield Cotts EH55 163 C3
Northfield Cres
Edinburgh EH8 122 E8
Longridge EH47 161 C1
Northfield Ct
Prestonpans EH32 125 F8
West Calder EH55 163 C3
Northfield Dr EH8 122 E7
Northfield E EH33 126 E6
Northfield Farm Ave EH8 122 E8
Northfield Farm Rd EH8 122 E8
Northfield Gdns
Clackmannan FK10 11 B4
Edinburgh EH8 122 E7
Prestonpans EH32 125 F8
Northfield Gr EH8 122 E7
Northfield Mdws EH47 161 B1
Northfield Park Gr EH8 122 E8
Northfield Pk EH8 122 E8
Northfield Rd Denny FK6 36 C4
Edinburgh EH8 122 D8
Northfield Sq EH8 122 E8
Northfield Terr
Edinburgh EH8 122 D8
Longridge EH47 161 C1
Northflat Pl ML8 215 C1
North Fort St EH6 93 E6
North Gate EH48 111 F6
North Grange Ave EH32 96 E1
North Grange Gr EH32 96 F1
North Grange Rd EH32 96 F1
North Green Dr FK2 22 D4
North Greendykes Rd EH52 115 E7
North Greens EH15 123 B5
North Gyle Ave EH12 119 B6
North Gyle Dr EH12 119 B7
North Gyle Farm Ct EH12 119 A6
North Gyle Farm La EH12 119 A6
North Gyle Gr EH12 119 A6
North Gyle Loan EH12 119 A7
North Gyle Pk EH12 119 A7
North Gyle Rd EH12 119 B7
North Gyle Terr EH12 119 A6
North High St EH21 124 B6
North Hillhousefield EH6 93 E6
North Junction St EH6 93 E6
North Larches KY11 29 F4
Northlawn Ct EH4 91 E4
Northlawn Terr EH4 91 E4
NORTH LEITH 93 E7
North Leith Mall EH6 93 E6
North Leith Mill EH6 93 F6
North Leith Sands EH6 93 E6
North Loanhead KY11 45 E3
North Lorimer Pl EH32 97 B4
North Main St FK2 39 C3

North Meggetland EH14 ... 120 E3
NORTH MERCHISTON ... 120 E5
NORTH MIDDLETON ... 195 F3
North Muir Ave FK2 ... 82 A8
North Overgate KY3 ... 34 F3
Northpark Pl EH54 ... 143 B5
North Park Terr EH4 ... 93 A2
North Peffer Pl EH16 ... 122 D4
North Pilrig Hts EH7 ... 93 D4
NORTH QUEENSFERRY ... 68 D6
North Queensferry Prim Sch KY11 ... 68 C6
North Queensferry Sta KY11 ... 68 C6
North Rd Dunbar EH42 ... 78 C3
Fauldhouse EH47 ... 181 E7
Inverkeithing KY11 ... 47 C4
North Reeves Pl EH47 ... 161 B5
North Richmond St EH8 ... 229 B2
Northrig Cotts EH41 ... 131 B7
North Roundall KY11 ... 45 E3
North Row KY11 ... 45 B4
North St Andrew La EH2 ... 229 A4
North St Andrew St EH2 ... 229 A4
North St David St EH2 ... 229 A4
North Seton Pk EH32 ... 97 D4
North Shore Rd FK3 ... 40 E2
North St Alloa FK10 ... 10 A7
Armadale EH48 ... 139 F6
Bo'ness EH51 ... 63 F8
Clackmannan FK10 ... 11 A4
Dunbar EH42 ... 78 A2
Falkirk FK2 ... 60 B8
Lochgelly KY5 ... 14 A7
Ratho EH28 ... 117 D2
Stirling FK9 ... 2 D1
Northumberland Place La EH3 ... 228 C4
Northumberland St EH3 ... 228 C4
Northumberland Street NW La EH3 ... 228 C4
Northumberland Street SE La EH3 ... 228 C4
Northumberland Street SW La EH3 ... 228 C4
North View Burntisland KY3 ... 50 F8
West Calder EH55 ... 163 D3
North View Cotts KY4 ... 31 A8
North Way KY11 ... 48 C5
North Werber Pk EH4 ... 92 E3
North Werber Pl EH4 ... 92 E4
North West Cumberland Street La EH3 ... 93 C2
Northwood Pk EH54 ... 142 E7
Northwood Rd FK10 ... 4 D2
North Wynd EH22 ... 153 A3
Norton Pk EH7 ... 94 A2
Norton Pl KY11 ... 29 E1
Norton St FK12 ... 5 B7
Norval Pl KY11 ... 46 F4
Norvell Lodge EH48 ... 141 E6
Norway Gdns KY11 ... 30 A2
Norwood Ave Alloa FK10 ... 9 F7
Bonnybridge FK4 ... 58 B7
Whitburn EH47 ... 161 B5
Norwood Cres FK10 ... 9 F7
Norwood Ct
Bonnybridge FK4 ... 58 B7
Whitburn EH47 ... 161 A5
Norwood Gr FK10 ... 9 F7
Norwood Ind Est EH47 ... 161 A5
Norwood Pl FK4 ... 58 B7
Nosirrom Terr EH49 ... 65 E5
Novar Cres KY1 ... 17 B2
NUNGATE ... 130 C8
Nungate Gdns EH41 ... 130 C7
Nungate Rd EH39 ... 54 B7
Nursery Rd FK1 ... 59 E4
Nursery The EH18 ... 172 F7

O

Oak Ave EH20 ... 171 F7
Oakbank FK2 ... 61 A2
Oakbank Ave EH53 ... 144 E2
Oakbank Cotts EH55 ... 163 D6
Oakbank Park Dr EH53 ... 165 C7
Oakbank Park Rd EH53 ... 165 C8
Oakbank Parkway EH53 ... 165 C8
Oakbank Park Way EH53 ... 165 C8
Oakbank Pk EH54 ... 165 B8
Oakbank Pl EH52 ... 88 A2
Oakbank Rd EH53 ... 144 E2
Oakbank Rdbt EH53 ... 165 C8
Oak Cres Mayfield EH22 ... 174 E6
Plean FK7 ... 20 C3
Oak Dr Fallin FK7 ... 8 D4
Stenhousemuir FK5 ... 38 D1
Oakfield Pl EH8 ... 229 B2
Oakfield St KY4 ... 12 F8
Oak Gr Dunfermline KY11 ... 46 E8
Livingston EH54 ... 144 B6
Oakhill View FK2 ... 83 B6
Oak La EH12 ... 91 E1
Oaklands Sch EH4 ... 92 B4
OAKLEY ... 26 F7
Oakley Ind Est KY12 ... 26 F7
Oak Pl EH22 ... 174 F6
Oak St FK8 ... 1 F1
Oaktree Ct KY1 ... 17 C8
Oaktree Junc EH41 ... 129 B8
Oaktree Sq KY1 ... 17 C8
Oakum Bay KY12 ... 26 C1
Oakville Terr EH6 ... 94 B3
Oak Way EH26 ... 171 A1
Oakwood Pk EH54 ... 142 E7
Oakwood Sch FK2 ... 60 F4
Oatlands Pk EH49 ... 85 B5
Oatridge Agricultural Coll EH52 ... 114 F8
Oberon FK10 ... 9 F8
Observatory Gn EH9 ... 121 E2
Observatory Rd EH9 ... 121 E2
Ocean Dr EH6 ... 93 E7
Ocean Terminal Sh Ctr EH6 ... 93 F7
Ocean Way EH6 ... 94 A6
Ochil Ave KY2 ... 16 F5
Ochil Cres FK8 ... 2 B2
Ochil Ct Queensferry EH30 ... 89 C8
Tullibody FK10 ... 4 C3
Ochil Dr Maddiston FK2 ... 83 A5
Stenhousemuir FK5 ... 38 E3
Ochil Gdns FK4 ... 57 F2
Ochil Hills Woodland Pk★ FK12 ... 5 E8
Ochil La EH47 ... 160 F6
Ochilmount FK7 ... 7 F1
Ochil Rd Alva FK12 ... 5 B7
Menstrie FK11 ... 4 A7
Stirling FK9 ... 2 C4
Ochil St Alloa FK10 ... 10 A7
Fallin FK7 ... 8 C4
Grangemouth FK3 ... 61 D7
Tullibody FK10 ... 4 B3
Ochil Terr
Dunfermline KY11 ... 29 E2
Falkirk FK2 ... 39 A2
Ochiltree Cres EH53 ... 144 B2
Ochiltree Ct EH53 ... 144 B2
Ochiltree Dr EH53 ... 144 B2
Ochiltree Gdns EH16 ... 122 C1
Ochiltree Terr FK1 ... 59 B5
Ochilvale Terr FK10 ... 5 D3
Ochilview Alva FK12 ... 5 A7
Cowie FK7 ... 20 E6
Ochil View
Cowdenbeath KY4 ... 13 E6
Denny FK6 ... 57 D8
Kincardine FK10 ... 23 D4
Shieldhill FK1 ... 81 D7
Ochil View Ct FK5 ... 38 C5
Ochilview Dr KY12 ... 26 B2
Ochilview Pk (Stenhousemuir FC & E Stirlingshire FC) FK5 ... 38 D3
Ochilview Pl EH51 ... 63 E6
Ochilview Rd EH51 ... 63 E6
Ochilview Sq EH48 ... 139 F5
Ochilview Terr EH51 ... 63 E6
Ochre Cres FK7 ... 20 C8
Octavia St KY2 ... 17 B5
Ogilface Cres EH48 ... 138 C2
Ogilvie Pl FK9 ... 2 A6
Ogilvie Rd FK8 ... 7 A5
Ogilvie Sch Campus EH54 ... 143 D7
Ogilvie Terr EH11 ... 120 E4
Ogilvie Way EH54 ... 143 D7
Ogilvy Cres EH47 ... 181 F6
O'Hanlon Way FK8 ... 1 F2
Old Abbey Rd EH39 ... 54 B7
Old Assembly Cl EH1 ... 229 A3
Old Bellsdyke Rd FK5 ... 38 A3
Old Brewery La FK10 ... 10 B7
Old Bridge St 11 FK10 ... 10 B6
Old Bridge Wynd FK9 ... 2 A4
Old Broughton 3 EH3 ... 93 D2
Old Burdiehouse Rd EH17 ... 151 A3
OLD CAMBUS ... 219 C2
Old Church La EH15 ... 122 C6
Old College EH1 ... 229 A2
Old Course Gate EH21 ... 124 D7
OLD CRAIGHALL ... 124 A2
Old Craighall Junc EH21 ... 124 B2
Old Craighall Rd EH22 ... 152 F8
Old Dalkeith Colliery EH22 ... 153 E6
Old Dalkeith Rd
Danderhall EH16 ... 152 C6
Edinburgh EH16 ... 122 C2
Old Dean Rd EH32 ... 98 D4
Old Deans Rd EH48 ... 142 A5
Old Denny Rd FK5 ... 38 A3
Old Drove Rd
Cambusbarron FK7 ... 6 C5
Carlops EH46 ... 205 B4
Old Eastfield St ML7 ... 159 D5
Old Edinburgh Rd EH22 ... 152 F3
Old Farm Ave EH13 ... 149 C7
Old Farm Ct EH34 ... 156 E6
Old Farm Pl EH13 ... 149 B7
Old Fishmarket Cl EH1 ... 229 A3
Old Forge Gr KY12 ... 26 E7
Old Glendevon Farm Cotts EH52 ... 87 D1
Old Golf Course Rd EH48 ... 140 B4
Old Granary EH39 ... 54 C8
Old Hall Knowe Pl EH48 ... 141 C4
Old Hall Knowe Terr EH48 ... 141 C4
OLDHAMSTOCKS ... 218 C3
Old Hillview Pl KY4 ... 30 E6
Old Kirk Pl KY12 ... 29 D4
Old Kirk Rd
Dunfermline KY12 ... 29 D4
Edinburgh EH12 ... 119 E7
North Queensferry KY11 ... 68 C6
Old Linburn Rd KY11 ... 29 F4
Old Liston Rd EH28 ... 117 A6
Old Mill Ct
Dunfermline KY11 ... 29 B2
East Whitburn EH47 ... 161 F7
Old Mill Gr EH47 ... 161 F7
Old Mill La
Edinburgh EH16 ... 122 A2
Gifford EH41 ... 220 F7
Oakley KY12 ... 26 E6
Old Mill Rd
Broxburn EH52 ... 115 F5
Hartwood ML7 ... 179 B1
Old Mill Way FK6 ... 36 B2
Old Newmills Rd EH14 ... 147 D3
Old Orch The KY11 ... 45 D3
OLD PENTLAND ... 150 F1
Old Perth Rd KY4 ... 13 A4
OLD PHILPSTOUN ... 86 F7
Old Redding Rd FK2 ... 60 F3
Old Refinery Rd FK3 ... 62 A8
Old St Mary's La EH51 ... 64 A8
Old Sch Ct 1 EH49 ... 84 E6
Old School Ct FK10 ... 4 B2
Old Schoolhouse The KY4 ... 31 A6
Old Sheriffmuir Rd FK9 ... 2 C6
Old Star Rd EH22 ... 174 A5
Old Tolbooth Wynd EH8 ... 229 B3
Old Toll Cottages EH41 ... 130 C8
OLD TOWN ... 228 B2
Old Town Bannockburn FK7 ... 7 D1
Broxburn EH52 ... 115 F5
Old Town Jail Mus★ 7 FK8 ... 7 A8
Oldwalls Pl FK3 ... 61 E7
Oldwalls Rd FK3, EH51 ... 62 C8
Old Well Ct EH48 ... 141 D3
Old Well Rd EH48 ... 141 D3
Oldwood Pl EH54 ... 143 B4
Oliphant Ct FK8 ... 2 B1
Oliphant Gdns EH21 ... 125 C5
Olive Bank Rd EH21 ... 124 B5
Olivebank Ret Pk EH21 ... 124 A6
Oliver Rd FK1 ... 60 D4
Ollerton Ct KY1 ... 17 B5
Olympia Arc KY1 ... 17 B3
Onich Pl ML7 ... 180 B3
Onslow St EH54 ... 144 A5
Orchard Bank EH4 ... 92 E1
ORCHARD BRAE ... 92 E1
Orchard Brae EH4 ... 92 F1
Orchard Brae Ave EH4 ... 92 E1
Orchard Brae Gardens W EH4 ... 92 E1
Orchard Brae Gdns EH4 ... 92 F1
Orchard Brae W 1 EH4 ... 92 F2
Orchard Cres
Edinburgh EH4 ... 92 D1
Prestonpans EH32 ... 96 F1
Orchardcroft 5 FK8 ... 7 B7
Orchard Ct
East Linton EH40 ... 103 E6
Kinghorn KY3 ... 35 A4
Longniddry EH32 ... 98 D4
Orchard Dr EH4 ... 92 D1
Orchardfield EH40 ... 103 D7
Orchardfield Ave EH12 ... 119 D6
Orchardfield Terr EH27 ... 146 A6
Orchard Gdns KY3 ... 35 A4
Orchard Gr Crombie KY12 ... 44 D6
Edinburgh EH4 ... 92 F2
Falkirk FK2 ... 83 B5
Haddington EH41 ... 101 A1
Kincardine FK10 ... 23 E3
Polmont FK2 ... 61 F2
Orchardhead Loan EH16 ... 151 A8
Orchardhead Rd EH16 ... 151 A8
Orchardhead Way KY11 ... 46 D2
Orchard House Day Hospl FK8 ... 2 A1
Orchard La
Dunfermline KY11 ... 29 D1
Dysart KY1 ... 18 A7
Orchard Pk EH33 ... 126 C7
Orchard Pl Dysart KY1 ... 18 A7
Edinburgh EH4 ... 92 E1
Livingston EH54 ... 143 B5
Orchard Rd
Bridge of Allan FK9 ... 2 A6
Edinburgh EH4 ... 92 E1
Grangemouth FK3 ... 62 C8
Kinghorn KY3 ... 34 F3
Orchard Road S EH4 ... 92 D1
Orchardson Rd FK5 ... 38 B2
Orchard Sq KY11 ... 45 D3
Orchard St Falkirk FK1 ... 60 B5
Grangemouth FK3 ... 61 D7
Orchard Terr
Edinburgh EH4 ... 92 E1
Kinghorn KY3 ... 34 F4
Torryburn KY12 ... 26 F1
Orchard The
Crossford KY12 ... 28 B2
Grangemouth FK2 ... 82 D8
Musselburgh EH21 ... 124 B5
Ormiston EH35 ... 155 E7
Tranent EH33 ... 126 C7
Tullibody FK10 ... 4 B2
Orchard Toll EH4 ... 92 E1
Orchard View EH22 ... 152 E2
Ordnance Rd KY12 ... 44 D6
Oriel Cres KY2 ... 17 A4
Oriel Rd KY2 ... 16 E5
Orkney Ct FK10 ... 10 B5
Orkney Pl Falkirk FK1 ... 60 B2
Kirkcaldy KY1 ... 17 E7
Orlit Cotts EH39 ... 74 D3
Ormelie Terr EH15 ... 123 C8
Ormidale Terr EH12 ... 120 D7
ORMISTON ... 155 F7
Ormiston Ave EH33 ... 126 E6
Ormiston Crescent E EH33 ... 126 E6
Ormiston Crescent W EH33 ... 126 E6
Ormiston Cross★ EH35 ... 155 E7
Ormiston Dr Alloa FK10 ... 4 E2
East Calder EH53 ... 145 A3
Ormiston Farm Steadings EH27 ... 145 C2
Ormiston Pk KY12 ... 29 C6
Ormiston Pl EH32 ... 96 E1
Ormiston Prim Sch EH35 ... 155 E7
Ormiston Rd
Pathhead EH37 ... 176 A5
Tranent EH33 ... 126 E5
Ormiston Terr EH12 ... 119 D6
Ormond Ct FK5 ... 38 A3
Oronsay Ave FK2 ... 83 A6
Orrin Gr KY11 ... 48 A3
Orrock Dr KY3 ... 33 E2
Orrok La EH16 ... 122 A1
Orrok Pk EH16 ... 122 A2
Orr Terr ML7 ... 159 C4
Orwell Pl Dunfermline KY12 ... 29 C4
Edinburgh EH11 ... 120 F6
Orwell Terr EH11 ... 120 F6
Osborne Ct EH32 ... 97 C4
Osborne Dr FK10 ... 23 F4
Osborne Gdns FK1 ... 59 F3
Osborne House Sch KY1 ... 18 A7
Osborne St FK1 ... 59 F3
Osborne Terr
Cockenzie & Port Seton EH32 ... 97 C4
Edinburgh EH12 ... 120 E7
Osprey Cres KY11 ... 30 A3
Ossian Dr EH54 ... 164 F6
Ostlere Rd KY2 ... 17 A4
Oswald Ave FK3 ... 61 F8
Oswald Ct EH9 ... 121 D3
Oswald Rd EH9 ... 121 D3
Oswald St FK1 ... 60 B4
Oswalds Wynd KY1 ... 17 C4
Oswald Terr EH12 ... 119 D6
Otterburn Pk EH14 ... 149 B8
Otterston Gr KY11 ... 48 B4
Otterston Pl KY2 ... 16 E8
Oudenarde Ct ML8 ... 215 B1
Our Dynamic Earth★ EH8 ... 229 C3
Our Lady of Lourdes RC Prim Sch EH47 ... 162 C8
Our Lady's Prim Sch 1 FK8 ... 1 F2
Our Lady's RC Prim Sch EH47 ... 162 B2
Overhailes Farm Cotts EH41 ... 103 A5
Overhaven KY11 ... 45 E3
Overshiel Farm Cotts EH53 ... 145 B6
Overton Cres Denny FK6 ... 36 D1
East Calder EH53 ... 145 A3
Redding FK2 ... 61 B1
Overton Ct
Dunfermline KY11 ... 46 F7
Kirkcaldy KY1 ... 17 E8
Overton Mains KY1 ... 17 E8
Overton Rd
Grangemouth, Bowhouse FK3 ... 61 E6
Grangemouth, Oil Refinery FK3 ... 62 B8
Kirkcaldy KY1 ... 17 D8
Overton Terr FK6 ... 36 C2
Owen Sq EH54 ... 143 F1
Owen Stone St EH48 ... 141 D3
Oxcars Dr KY11 ... 48 B3
Oxcraig St EH5 ... 92 F7
Oxenfoord Ave EH37 ... 176 B5
Oxenfoord Dr EH37 ... 176 A5
Oxford St EH8 ... 229 C1
Oxford Terr EH4 ... 228 A4
Oxgang Rd FK3 ... 61 E7
OXGANGS ... 149 F6
Oxgangs Ave EH13 ... 149 F7
Oxgangs Bank EH13 ... 149 F6
Oxgangs Brae EH13 ... 149 F6
Oxgangs Broadway EH13 ... 149 F6
Oxgang Sch FK3 ... 61 E7
Oxgangs Cres EH13 ... 149 F7
Oxgangs Dr EH13 ... 149 E7
Oxgangs Farm Ave EH13 ... 149 E6
Oxgangs Farm Dr EH13 ... 149 E6
Oxgangs Farm Gdns EH13 ... 149 E6
Oxgangs Farm Gr EH13 ... 149 E6
Oxgangs Farm Loan EH13 ... 149 E6
Oxgangs Farm Terr EH13 ... 149 E6
Oxgangs Gdns EH13 ... 149 E7
Oxgangs Gn EH13 ... 149 F7
Oxgangs Gr EH13 ... 149 F7
Oxgangs Hill EH13 ... 149 F7
Oxgangs Ho EH13 ... 149 F7
Oxgangs Loan EH13 ... 149 F7
Oxgangs Medway EH13 ... 149 F6
Oxgangs Path EH13 ... 149 F6
Oxgangs Path E EH13 ... 149 F6
Oxgangs Pk EH13 ... 149 F6
Oxgangs Pl EH13 ... 149 E7
Oxgangs Prim Sch EH13 ... 149 D7
Oxgangs Rd EH13 ... 150 A5
Oxgangs Rise EH13 ... 149 F7
Oxgangs Road N EH13 ... 149 E6
Oxgangs Row EH13 ... 149 F6
Oxgangs St EH13 ... 149 F6
Oxgangs Terr EH13 ... 149 E6
Oxgangs View EH13 ... 149 F6

P

Paddockhall Cotts EH49 ... 65 C1
Paddockholm The EH12 ... 119 E6
Paddock The Dirleton EH39 ... 53 B5
Gullane EH31 ... 52 A2
Longniddry EH32 ... 98 B3
Musselburgh EH21 ... 124 D7
North Berwick EH39 ... 54 C6
Whitekirk EH42 ... 75 E8
Page St KY5 ... 14 B8
Paisley Ave EH8 ... 122 D7
Paisley Cl EH1 ... 229 B3
Paisley Cres EH8 ... 122 C8
Paisley Dr EH8 ... 122 D7
Paisley Gdns EH8 ... 122 C8
Paisley Gr EH8 ... 122 D7
Paisley Terr EH8 ... 122 C8
Palmer Ct FK3 ... 61 D8
Palmer Pl Currie EH14 ... 147 F4
Kingseat KY12 ... 12 A1
Palmer Rd EH14 ... 147 F4
Palmer Rise EH54 ... 143 E1
Palmerston Pl EH12 ... 228 A3
Palmerston Place La EH12 ... 228 A2
Palmerston Rd EH9 ... 121 D5
Panbrae Rd EH51 ... 63 E7
Pan Ha' KY1 ... 18 A6
PANHALL ... 18 A6
Pankhurst Loan EH22 ... 153 D3
Panmure Pl EH3 ... 228 C1
Pannie Rd KY1 ... 17 D7
Panstead St FK3 ... 61 E7
Panton Gn EH54 ... 143 B8
Papana Cotts EH41 ... 132 D2
Papermill Wynd EH7 ... 93 E3
Papple Farm Cotts EH41 ... 132 D5
Paradise La FK10 ... 23 E3
Paradykes Ave EH20 ... 172 B8
Paradykes Prim Sch EH20 ... 172 B8
Pardovan Cres EH49 ... 86 D7
Pardovan Holdings EH49 ... 86 C7
Pardovan Pl FK1 ... 59 F6
Paris Ave FK6 ... 36 E1
Paris St FK3 ... 61 E8
Parkandarroch Cres ML8 ... 215 A1
Park Ave Bilston EH25 ... 171 E6
Cowdenbeath KY4 ... 13 C3
Denny FK4 ... 57 E6
Dunbar EH42 ... 78 C2
Dunfermline KY12 ... 29 A3
East Calder EH53 ... 144 F4
Edinburgh EH15 ... 123 A7
Gorebridge EH23 ... 174 C1
Grangemouth FK2 ... 82 D8
Laurieston FK2 ... 60 F4
Loanhead EH20 ... 172 B7
Musselburgh EH21 ... 124 E5
Stenhousemuir FK5 ... 38 D1
Stirling FK8 ... 7 A6
Park Cres Alloa FK10 ... 5 C1
Bannockburn FK7 ... 7 D2
Bonnyrigg and Lasswade EH19 ... 173 B7
Easthouses EH22 ... 174 C8
Edinburgh EH16 ... 151 B8
Falkirk FK2 ... 39 A2
Gifford EH41 ... 220 F6
Loanhead EH20 ... 172 B7
Westquarter FK2 ... 61 A3
Park Ct Broxburn EH52 ... 115 B5
Musselburgh EH21 ... 124 E5
Shotts ML7 ... 179 F4
Park Dr Bannockburn FK7 ... 7 D2
Grangemouth FK2 ... 82 D8
Musselburgh EH21 ... 125 A4
Stenhousemuir FK5 ... 38 D2
West Calder EH55 ... 164 A5
Parkdyke FK7 ... 6 E6
Parkend Haddington EH41 ... 129 F3
Penicuik EH26 ... 191 F4
Parkend Cres FK1 ... 81 C6
Parker Ave EH7 ... 94 E1
Parker Rd EH7 ... 94 F1
Parker Terr EH7 ... 94 F1
PARKFOOT ... 57 C4
Parkfoot Ct FK1 ... 60 B3
Parkgate Alva FK12 ... 4 F6
Rosyth KY11 ... 46 F4
Park Gdns Bannockburn FK7 ... 7 D2
Edinburgh EH16 ... 151 B8
4 Grangemouth FK2 ... 82 D8
Musselburgh EH21 ... 124 E5
Park Gr EH16 ... 151 B7
Parkgrove Ave EH4 ... 91 C2
Parkgrove Bank EH4 ... 91 C2
Parkgrove Cres EH4 ... 91 C2
Parkgrove Dr EH4 ... 91 C2
Parkgrove Gdns EH4 ... 91 C2
Parkgrove Gn EH4 ... 91 C2
Parkgrove Loan EH4 ... 91 C2
Parkgrove Neuk EH4 ... 91 C2
Parkgrove Path EH4 ... 91 D2
Parkgrove Pl EH4 ... 91 D2
Park Grove Pl EH21 ... 124 E5
Parkgrove Rd EH4 ... 91 C2
Parkgrove Row EH4 ... 91 C
Parkgrove St EH4 ... 91 D2
Parkgrove Terr EH4 ... 91 C2
Park Grove Terr EH21 ... 124 E5
Parkgrove View EH4 ... 91 C2
Parkhall Dr FK2 ... 83 A

PARKHEAD 119 F2
Parkhead Ave EH11 119 E2
Parkhead Cotts EH55 163 E2
Parkhead Cres
Edinburgh EH11 119 E2
West Calder EH55 163 E3
Parkhead Ct FK10 10 C8
Parkhead Dr EH11 119 E2
Parkhead Gdns
Edinburgh EH11 119 E2
West Calder EH55 163 E3
Parkhead Gr EH11 119 E2
Parkhead Loan EH11 119 F2
Parkhead Pk EH22 174 C8
Parkhead Pl
Easthouses EH22 174 C8
Edinburgh EH11 119 E2
Parkhead Prim Sch EH55 163 E3
Parkhead Rd Alloa FK10 10 C8
Falkirk FK1 60 B1
Linlithgow EH49 84 F8
Parkhead Smallholdings EH49 64 A1
Parkhead St EH11 119 E2
Parkhead Terr EH11 119 F2
Parkhead View EH11 119 E2
Park Hill EH23 174 B1
Park La Aberdour KY3 49 C7
Bo'ness EH51 64 B7
9 Dunfermline KY12 28 F4
Edinburgh EH15 123 A7
Haddington EH41 129 E8
Musselburgh EH21 124 E5
Stirling FK8 7 B8
Parkland Gr Comrie KY12 26 D7
Stoneyburn EH47 161 F1
Parklands EH52 115 D4
Parklands Cres KY11 48 A3
Park Lea KY11 47 A5
PARKNEUK 28 D6
Parkneuk KY12 28 D6
Parkneuk Rd KY12 28 D5
Park Par EH47 181 E6
Park Pl Alloa FK10 10 C7
Clackmannan FK10 11 B4
Cowdenbeath KY4 30 F8
Dunfermline KY12 29 B4
Edinburgh EH6 93 C6
Kinghorn KY3 34 F2
Kirkcaldy KY1 17 B3
Livingston EH54 143 B5
Stirling FK7 6 F6
Park Prim Sch FK10 10 B5
Park Rd Blackridge EH48 138 E3
Bonnyrigg and Lasswade EH19 173 B7
Broxburn EH52 115 E5
Cockenzie & Port Seton EH32 97 D4
Cowdenbeath KY4 13 B3
Dalkeith EH22 152 F2
Edinburgh EH6 93 C6
Falkirk FK2 39 A1
Gifford EH41 220 F6
Gorebridge EH23 174 C1
Grangemouth FK3 61 D8
Harthill ML7 160 A6
Kirkcaldy KY1 17 E8
Menstrie FK11 4 A6
Newtongrange EH22 174 B5
Ormiston EH35 155 D6
Rosyth KY11 46 F5
Shotts ML7 179 D5
Park Road Prim Sch KY11 47 A4
Park Road W KY11 46 D5
Parkside EH28 117 A6
Parkside Ct
10 Dalkeith EH22 153 A3
Plean FK7 20 C3
Parkside Pl EH22 153 A3
Parkside Rd ML7 179 D4
Parkside Sq KY11 47 A4
Parkside St
Edinburgh EH8 229 C1
Rosyth KY11 46 F4
Parkside Terr EH16 229 C1
Park St Alva FK12 5 A7
Bonnybridge FK4 58 C4
Cowdenbeath KY4 13 C3
Cowie FK7 20 E8
Falkirk FK1 60 B5
Lochgelly KY5 14 B7
Park Terr Broxburn EH52 115 B5
Grangemouth FK2 82 D8
Kirknewton EH27 145 E2
Newcraighall EH21 123 E4
Stirling FK8 7 A6
Tullibody FK10 4 B1
Parkvale Pl EH6 94 B4
Park View Broxburn EH52 115 B5
Fauldhouse EH47 181 E7
Grangemouth FK2 82 E8
Kirkcaldy KY2 16 F6
Loanhead EH20 172 B7
Park-View EH32 98 E5
Park View
Musselburgh EH21 124 E5
Newcraighall EH21 123 E4
Pencaitland EH34 156 F7
Prestonpans EH32 97 B1
Stoneyburn EH47 162 C2
Westfield EH48 110 F4
Whitburn EH47 161 A7
Parkview Ave FK1 59 F2
Park View Ct FK1 59 E5
Park View E EH32 97 D4
Park View Terr KY11 47 B2
Park View W EH32 97 D4
Parkville Ct EH48 138 E3
Parkway FK10 10 B7
Parkway Ct FK10 10 A7
Parkwood Cres EH52 115 D4
Parkwood Gdns EH52 115 D5
Parliament Sq EH1 229 A3
Parliament St EH6 93 F5
Parrot La EH23 195 C8
Parrotshot EH15 123 B5
Parsonage The EH21 124 D6
PARSONS GREEN 94 B1
Parsons Green Prim Sch EH8 122 D7
Parsons Green Terr 2 EH8 94 C1
Parsonspool
Bonnyrigg and Lasswade EH19 173 C5
Dunbar EH42 78 D2
Paterson Dr FK1 81 C6
Paterson La KY4 13 D3
Paterson Pl
Bonnybridge FK4 58 C5
Bridge of Allan FK9 2 A6
Paterson's Ct EH52 115 F5
Paterson Twr FK2 60 D4
Paterson Way KY11 29 B1
Path Brae EH29 89 A1
Pathfoot Ave FK9 2 C7
Pathfoot Dr FK9 2 C7
Pathfoot Rd FK9 2 C6
PATHHEAD Kirkcaldy 17 D6
Mayfield 176 B5
Pathhead Ct 1 KY1 17 D6
Pathhead Prim Sch KY1 17 D7
Path The Airth FK2 22 D4
Bannockburn FK7 7 D2
Kirkcaldy KY1 17 D5
Patie's Rd EH14 149 C8
Pat Kelly Ave FK7 6 F4
Paton Ct FK10 10 B7
Paton St Alloa FK10 10 A7
Dunfermline KY12 29 C6
Patrick Dr FK1 81 E7
Patriothall 5 EH3 93 B2
Patterson Pl KY2 17 B6
Patterson St KY2 17 B6
PATTIESMUIR 46 B4
Pattison St EH6 94 A5
Pattle Ct EH39 54 A7
Paul Dr FK2 22 E4
Paul Pl KY4 13 D4
Paul St KY5 14 A6
PAULVILLE 141 A5
Pavilions Bsns Pk FK10 9 E7
Pavilions The FK10 9 E7
Pavilion View FK10 9 F8
Paxstone Cres ML7 159 E5
Paxstone Dr ML7 159 E5
Paxton Cres KY5 14 A8
Paxton Pl KY5 14 B8
Peachdales EH41 129 F8
Peacock Ave EH19 173 E7
Peacock Ct EH6 93 D7
Peacock Parkway EH19 173 E6
Peacock Pl EH19 173 D6
Peacocktail Cl EH15 123 B4
Pearce Ave EH12 119 C7
Pearce Gr EH12 119 C7
Pearce Rd EH12 119 C7
Pearson Ave FK4 57 D5
Pearson Pl FK4 57 D5
Pearson View FK10 10 C8
Peasehill Brae KY11 46 D3
Peasehill Fauld KY11 46 D2
Peasehill Gait KY11 46 D3
Peasehill Rd KY11 46 E3
PEASTONBANK 156 F1
Peathill Rd FK4 58 A6
Peathill Terr FK4 58 A5
Peatville Gdns EH14 120 A1
Peatville Terr EH14 120 A1
Peddie Pl FK3 61 E8
Peden St ML7 159 C5
Peebles Rd Penicuik EH26 191 F3
West Linton EH46 208 F3
Peebles St KY1 35 B8
Peel Pentland Ctr EH20 151 A1
Peel Prim Sch EH54 143 C4
Peel Rdbt EH54 143 C4
Peel Terr EH9 121 F4
Peffer Bank EH16 122 D4
Peffer Ind Est EH16 122 D4
Peffermill Ind Est EH16 122 C4
Peffermill Rd EH16 122 C4
Peffer Pl EH16 122 D4
Peffer's Pl EH41 130 A8
Peffer St EH16 122 D4
Peggy's Mill Rd EH4 91 A4
Peirson Rd KY11 29 F4
Pelstream Ave FK7 7 B4
Pembroke Pl 7 EH12 120 E7
Pembroke St FK5 38 C3
PENCAITLAND 156 D7
Pencaitland Prim Sch EH34 156 E6
Pencraig Brae EH40 103 D6
Pender Gdns FK2 82 E7
Penders La FK1 60 A5
Pendreich Ave EH19 173 C8
Pendreich Dr EH19 173 C8
Pendreich Gr EH19 173 C8
Pendreich Terr EH19 173 C8
Pendreich View EH19 173 C8
Pendreich Way FK9 2 D6
PENICUIK 191 D4
Penicuik Ctr The EH26 191 E5
Penicuik High Sch EH26 191 E5
Penicuik Rd EH25, EH26 171 E3
Pennelton Pl EH51 63 E5
Pennyschool Pl FK10 11 A5
Pennywell Ct EH4 92 B5
Pennywell Gdns EH4 92 B5
Pennywell Gr EH4 92 B5
Pennywell Medway EH4 92 B5
Pennywell Pl EH4 92 B5
Pennywell Rd EH4 92 B5
Pennywell Villas EH4 92 B6
PENSTON 127 F5
Penston Farm Cotts EH33 127 F5
Pentland Ave
Bathgate EH48 141 F5
Currie EH14 147 F4
Edinburgh EH13 149 A7
Gorebridge EH23 174 B3
Penicuik EH26 191 E6
Pentland Cres
Edinburgh EH10 150 A7
Rosewell EH24 172 D3
Pentland Ct Bilston EH25 171 E6
Dalgety Bay KY11 48 C4
Pentland Dr
Edinburgh EH10 149 F6
Whitburn EH47 161 C6
Pentlandfield Bsns Pk EH25 171 C5
Pentland Gait Office Pk EH11 119 B1
Pentland Gr EH10 150 A7
Pentland Hills Regional Pk★ EH14, EH26 189 D7
Pentland Ind Est EH20 172 A7
Pentland Pk
Livingston EH54 144 B4
Loanhead EH20 171 F8
Pentland Pl
Cairneyhill KY12 27 E1
Currie EH14 147 F4
Kirkcaldy KY2 16 F6
Pentland Prim Sch EH13 149 F6
Pentland Rd
Bonnyrigg and Lasswade EH19 173 A7
Edinburgh EH13 149 A7
Edinburgh, Old Pentland EH10.EH20 150 D1
Loanhead EH20 172 A8
Pentland Rise KY11 48 C5
Pentlands Gdns EH10 150 A7
Pentlands Science Pk EH26 171 C3
Pentland Terr
Dunfermline KY11 29 E2
Edinburgh EH10 150 A8
High Valleyfield KY12 26 A1
Penicuik EH26 191 E6
Pentland View
Currie EH14 147 F4
Dalkeith EH22 153 C2
East Whitburn EH47 161 E7
Edinburgh EH10 150 A6
Uphall EH52 115 A5
Pentland View Cres EH25 171 F3
Pentland View Ct
Currie EH14 148 A4
Livingston EH54 143 A6
Pentland View Pl EH25 171 F3
Pentland View Rd
Kirkliston EH29 89 A2
Roslin EH25 171 F3
Pentland View Terr EH25 171 F3
Pentland Way FK3 61 E5
Pentland Wlk EH47 161 C6
People's Story The★ EH8 229 B3
Peploe Ave 3 FK5 38 B2
Peploe Rise KY11 47 A7
Peppercraig Quarry Ind Site EH41 100 F2
Percival St KY2 17 A5
Perdieus Mount KY12 29 A2
Perdrixknowe EH14 120 D3
Persevere Ct EH6 93 F6
Perth Rd KY4 13 D6
Perth's Gr EH32 97 A2
Perth St Edinburgh EH3 93 B2
Livingston EH54 144 A6
Petershill Gdns EH48 141 C7
Petershill Wildlife Reserve★ EH48 141 C8
Peterswell Brae FK7 7 E1
Petrel Way KY11 30 A2
Pettigrew's Cl 6 EH22 153 A3
PETTYCUR 34 F1
Pettycur Bay KY3 34 E1
Pettycur Ho KY3 34 F1
Pettycur Rd KY3 34 F1
Peveril Rise EH54 164 E8
Peveril Terr EH16 151 B8
Phantassie Cotts EH40 103 E7
Phantassie Doocot★ EH40 103 F7
Pheasantry The FK10 10 D5
Philip Ave Bathgate EH48 141 E6
Linlithgow EH49 84 E7
Philip Dr FK5 38 D2
Philip Pl EH26 191 E7
Philip St FK2 60 B7
Philpingstone La EH51 64 C7
Philpingstone Rd EH51 64 C7
PHILPSTOUN 86 D7
Phoenix Ind Est FK7 7 C7
Phoenix La KY12 28 F4
Picardy Pl EH1 229 A4
Pierhead Bldgs KY11 68 C5
Pier Pl EH6 93 D7
Pier Rd EH51 64 C8
Piersfield Gr EH8 94 D1
Piersfield Pl EH8 94 D1
Piersfield Terr EH8 94 D1
PIERSHILL 94 E1
Piershill La 9 EH8 94 C1
Piershill Pl 10 EH8 94 C1
Piershill Square E EH8 94 D1
Piershill Square W EH8 94 C1
Piershill Terr 1 EH8 94 D1
Pike Rd FK7 7 D4
Pilgrims Hill EH49 85 D8
Pilkham Ct KY4 13 C3
Pilmuir St KY12 29 A5
PILRIG 93 E4
Pilrig Gdns EH6 93 E3
Pilrig Glebe 3 EH6 93 F3
Pilrig House Cl EH6 93 E4
Pilrig Hts EH6 93 E3
Pilrig Ind Est EH6 93 E4
Pilrig Park Sch EH6 93 E4
Pilrig St EH6 93 E3
PILTON 92 E5
Pilton Ave EH5 92 E5
Pilton Cres EH5 92 F5
Pilton Dr EH5 92 E5
Pilton Drive N EH5 92 E6
Pilton Gdns EH5 92 F5
Pilton Loan EH5 92 E5
Pilton Pk EH5 92 E5
Pilton Pl EH5 92 E5
Pineapple The★ FK2 22 B6
Pinebank EH54 143 E5
Pine Cres FK11 3 F6
Pinefield Glade EH54 164 C8
Pine Gn EH51 63 D4
Pine Gr Alloa FK10 10 C6
Dunfermline KY11 46 E8
Livingston EH54 144 B5
Penicuik EH26 171 A1
Westquarter FK2 61 B2
Pinegrove Gdns EH4 91 B2
Pine St EH42 78 B1
Pines The EH31 52 B3
Pine Wlk FK5 38 D1
Pinewood Dr KY11 48 B3
Pinewood Pk EH54 142 E7
Pinewood Pl
Blackburn EH47 162 E8
Mayfield EH22 174 E6
Pinewood Rd EH22 174 E6
Pinewood Sch EH47 162 E8
Pinewood View EH22 174 E6
Pinkerton Ave 4 KY11 47 C8
Pinkerton Cresent KY11 47 C7
Pinkerton Gr KY11 47 C8
Pinkerton Pl KY11 46 F5
Pinkerton St 3 KY11 47 C8
Pinkhill EH12 120 A6
Pinkie Ave EH21 124 E5
PINKIE BRAES 125 A6
Pinkie Dr EH21 124 E5
Pinkie Hill Cres EH21 124 E5
Pinkie Pl EH21 124 E5
Pinkie Rd EH21 124 E6
Pinkie St Peter's Prim Sch EH21 124 E6
Pinkie Terr EH21 124 F5
Pinkie Wlk 10 EH33 126 C5
Pinnel Pl KY11 48 C4
Pipe La EH15 95 A1
Piper Cres KY3 33 D2
Pipe St EH15 95 A1
Pirig Cotts EH6 93 F3
Pirleyhill Dr FK1 81 D6
Pirleyhill Gdns FK1 60 A2
Pirnhall Rd
Bannockburn, Chartershall FK7 19 A8
Bannockburn FK7 19 D7
Pirniefield Bank EH6 94 C4
Pirniefield Gdns EH6 94 C4
Pirniefield Gr EH6 94 C4
Pirniefield Pl EH6 94 C4
Pirniefield Terr EH6 94 C4
Pirniehall Prim Sch 2 EH4 92 C5
Pirrie St EH6 93 F4
Pitbauchie Bank KY11 29 C1
Pitcairn Gr EH10 149 F8
Pitcairn St KY11 29 C2
Pitcaple Gdns EH54 164 D6
PITCORTHIE 29 E1
Pitcorthie Dr KY11 46 E8
Pitcorthie Prim Sch KY11 29 E1
Pitcorthie Rd KY11 29 C1
PITCOX 105 C3
Pitcox Cotts EH42 105 C3
Pitdinnie Pl KY12 27 D1
Pitdinnie Rd KY12 27 D2
Pitfairn Rd FK10 5 E3
Pitfirane Pk KY12 28 B1
Pitfour Pl KY2 16 C7
Pitlochry Pl 4 EH7 94 A2
Pitmedden Rd KY11 30 A1
Pit Rd KY4 13 E6
Pitreavie Bsns Pk KY11 46 C7
Pitreavie Cres KY11 46 C8
Pitreavie Ct KY11 46 D6
Pitreavie Dr KY11 46 D6
Pitreavie Ind Est KY11 46 D6
Pitreavie Prim Sch KY11 46 D8
Pitsligo Rd EH10 121 B4
Pittencrieff Ct EH21 124 F6
Pittencrieff House Mus★ KY12 28 F3
Pittencrieff Pk★ KY12 28 F3
Pittencrieff Prim Sch KY12 28 F4
Pittencrieff St KY12 28 F4
Pittsburgh Rd KY11 30 B5
Pitt St EH6 93 E5
Pitt Terr FK8 7 B6
Pittville St EH15 123 C8
Pittville Street La EH15 123 B8
Place Charente EH22 153 C2
Plane Gr KY11 46 F8
Plane St EH42 78 B1
Plantation St KY5 14 B7
Player Dr KY12 12 A1
Player Gn EH54 143 B8
Players Rd FK7 7 C7
PLEAN 20 C3
Pleanbank Cotts FK7 20 B3
Plean Ctry Pk★ FK7 20 B1
Plean Ind Est FK7 20 D1
Pleasance Edinburgh EH8 229 B2
Falkirk FK1 60 B4
Pleasance Brae KY12 27 D1
Pleasance Ct
12 Falkirk FK2 60 B4
Halbeath KY12 30 B7
Pleasance Gdns FK1 60 B4
Pleasance Rd
Dunfermline KY12 29 F6
Falkirk FK1 60 B3
Halbeath KY12 30 A6
Pleasance Row ML11 201 B3
Pleasance Sq 11 FK1 60 B4
Pleasance The EH32 71 C4
Pleasures The FK10 9 E7
Plewlandcroft EH30 68 B1
Plewlands Ave EH10 120 F2
Plewlands Gdns EH10 120 F2
Plewlands Ho EH30 68 B1
Plewlands Pl EH30 89 B8
Plewlands Terr EH10 120 F2
Pleydell Pl 6 EH16 151 B8
Plough La 2 EH33 126 D6
Plover Brae EH54 143 D5
Plover Cres KY11 30 B1
Plummer Ct EH22 153 A4
Pointgarry Rd EH39 54 B7
POLBETH 163 F5
Polbeth Ave EH55 163 F5
Polbeth Cres EH55 163 F5
Polbeth Gdns EH55 163 F5
Polbeth Ind Est EH55 163 E4
Polbeth Pl EH55 163 F5
Polbeth Rd EH55 163 E5
Polbeth West Calder Ind Est EH55 163 E4
Poldrate EH41 130 B8
Polkemmet Bsns Ctr EH47 160 F5
Polkemmet Ctry Pk★ EH47 160 C7
Polkemmet Dr ML7 160 A6
Polkemmet La ML7 159 F5
Polkemmet Prim Sch EH47 161 A5
Polkemmet Rd
Harthill ML7 159 F6
Whitburn EH47 160 E5
Pollard Glebe EH11 120 A4
Pollock Wlk KY12 28 E5
Polmaise Ave FK7 7 B3
Polmaise Cres FK7 8 C5
Polmaise Ct FK7 7 B3
Polmaise Rd
Cambusbarron FK7 6 E3
Stirling FK7 6 F5
POLMONT 61 F2
Polmont House Gdns FK2 61 E1
Polmont Pk FK2 61 E3
Polmont Rd FK2 61 B3
Polmont Sports Ctr FK2 61 D1
Polmont Sta FK2 61 E1
POLMONT STATION 61 E1
Polson Gdns EH33 126 B6
POLTON 172 D6
Polton Avenue Rd EH19 173 A6
Polton Bank EH18 172 E6
Polton Bank Terr EH18 172 E6
Polton Cotts EH18 172 D6
Polton Ct EH19 173 B7
Polton Dr EH19 173 A7
Polton Gdns EH18 173 A7
POLTONHALL 172 F6
Poltonhall Ind Est EH18 172 E7
Polton Pl EH19 173 B7
Polton Rd
Bonnyrigg and Lasswade EH18 173 A8
Loanhead EH20 172 C7
Polton Road W EH18, EH19 172 F6
Polton St EH19 173 B6
Polton Terr EH18 173 A7
Polton Vale EH20 172 C7
Polwarth Ave FK2 82 C8
Polwarth Cres
Edinburgh EH11 121 A5
Prestonpans EH32 97 A1
Polwarth Gdns EH11 120 F5
Polwarth Gr EH11 120 F5
Polwarth Ho FK9 2 D6
Polwarth Pk EH11 120 F5
Polwarth Pl EH11 120 F5

Polwarth Terr
Edinburgh EH10 . . . . 120 F4
Prestonpans EH32 . . . . 97 A1
Polworth Pl KY4 . . . . 13 D4
Pomathorn Bank EH26 . . . . 191 F4
Pomathorn Rd EH26 . . . . 191 F4
Pompee Rd FK10 . . . . 5 B1
Ponton St EH3 . . . . 228 B1
Poolewe Dr FK2 . . . . 61 C2
Poplar Cres KY2 . . . . 17 B7
Poplar Gdns KY2 . . . . 17 A7
Poplar Gr Dunfermline KY11 46 E8
Livingston EH54 . . . . 144 B6
Poplar La EH6 . . . . 94 B5
Poplar Pk EH32 . . . . 97 D3
Poplar St Dunbar EH42 . . . . 78 B1
Grangemouth FK3 . . . . 61 C7
Mayfield EH22 . . . . 174 E6
Poplars The FK10 . . . . 4 B1
Poplar Terr EH19 . . . . 173 B6
Portal Rd FK3 . . . . 61 C5
PORT BRAE 17 C4
Port Buchan EH52 . . . . 115 D5
Port Downie FK1 . . . . 59 D5
PORT EDGAR 67 F1
Port Edgar Marina & Sailing Sch EH30 . . . . 67 F2
Porteous' Pend EH1 . . . . 228 C2
Porter Ave FK9 . . . . 2 B3
Porterfield KY12 . . . . 26 E7
Porterfield Rd EH4 . . . . 92 E3
Portgower Pl EH4 . . . . 93 A2
Port Hamilton EH3 . . . . 228 B2
Port Laing Wynd KY11 . . . . 68 C7
Portland Gdns EH6 . . . . 93 E6
Portland Pl Edinburgh EH6 . . . . 93 E6
Fauldhouse EH47 . . . . 181 C5
Portland Row EH6 . . . . 93 E6
Portland St EH6 . . . . 93 E6
Portland Terr EH6 . . . . 93 E6
PORTOBELLO 123 B8
Portobello High Sch EH15 . . . . 122 F7
Portobello High St EH15 . . . . 95 A1
Portobello L Ctr EH15 . . . . 95 A1
Portobello Rd EH7, EH8 . . . . 94 E1
Portobello Swim Ctr EH15 . . . . 123 C8
PORT OF LEITH 93 E8
Portree Cres FK2 . . . . 62 A1
Portsburgh Sq EH1 . . . . 228 C2
Port St Clackmannan FK10 . . 11 A4
Inverkeithing KY11 . . . . 47 C2
Stirling FK8 . . . . 7 B7
Posthill FK10 . . . . 5 D1
Postings The KY1 . . . . 17 C3
Post Office La KY11 . . . . 68 C6
Potter Pl FK2 . . . . 39 F3
Potterrow EH8 . . . . 229 A2
Potter's Path EH33 . . . . 126 C6
Pottery St KY1 . . . . 17 E8
Pottery The
Edinburgh EH15 . . . . 95 A1
Prestonpans EH32 . . . . 96 E1
Pottishaw Cotts EH47 . . . . 161 E7
Pottishaw Pl EH48 . . . . 141 C1
Pottishaw Rd EH48 . . . . 140 F1
Pottis Rd FK7 . . . . 7 D3
Povert Rd EH19, EH23 . . . . 173 F2
Powderhall Brae EH7 . . . . 93 D4
Powderhall Rd EH7 . . . . 93 D4
Powderhall Rigg EH7 . . . . 93 D4
Powdermill Brae EH23 . . . 195 D6
Powdrake Rd FK3 . . . . 61 F8
Powie's Path EH53 . . . . 144 D4
Pratt St KY1 . . . . 17 A1
President Kennedy Dr FK7 . . . . 20 C3
Pressmennan Wood Forest Trail★ EH42 . . . . 133 E6
PRESTON 97 A2
Preston Ave
Linlithgow EH49 . . . . 84 F6
Prestonpans EH32 . . . . 97 B1
Preston Cres
Inverkeithing KY11 . . . . 47 C2
Linlithgow EH49 . . . . 84 F6
Prestonpans EH32 . . . . 97 B1
Preston Cross Cotts EH32 . 97 A1
Preston Ct Linlithgow EH49 . 84 F6
Prestonpans EH32 . . . . 125 F8
PRESTONFIELD 122 B4
Prestonfield Ave EH16 . . . 122 B4
Prestonfield Bank EH16 . . . 122 A4
Prestonfield Cres EH16 . . . 122 A4
Prestonfield Gdns
Edinburgh EH16 . . . . 122 A4
2 Linlithgow EH49 . . . . 84 E6
Prestonfield Pk EH16 . . . 122 D4
Prestonfield Prim Sch EH16 . . . . 122 B3
Prestonfield Rd EH16 . . . . 122 B4
Prestonfield Terr EH16 . . . 122 A4
Preston Gdns EH32 . . . . 125 F8
Prestongrange (Ind Mus)★ EH32 . . . . 125 C8
Prestongrange Rd EH32 . . . 125 E8
Prestongrange Terr EH32 . 96 E1
Prestonhall Cres EH24 . . . 172 D2
Prestonhall Rd EH24 . . . . 172 D2
Preston House Gdns EH49 84 E4
Prestonkirk Gdns EH40 . . . 103 E8
Preston Lodge High Sch EH32 . . . . 97 A1
Preston Market Cross★ EH32 . . . . 97 A1
Preston Mill★ EH40 . . . . 103 F8
PRESTONPANS 96 E2
Prestonpans Ind Est EH32 . . . . 126 A8
Prestonpans Inf Sch 5 EH32 . . . . 96 F1
Prestonpans Prim Sch EH32 . . . . 126 A8
Prestonpans Sta EH32 . . . 126 A8
Preston Pk EH49 . . . . 84 F6
Preston Pl EH37 . . . . 176 A4
Preston Rd
East Linton EH40 . . . . 103 E8
Linlithgow EH49 . . . . 84 F6
Prestonpans, Cuthill EH32 . 125 F8
Prestonpans, Preston EH32 . 97 A1
Preston St
High Valleyfield KY12 . . . . 26 A2
Rosewell EH24 . . . . 172 D2
Preston Street Prim Sch EH8 . . . . 229 C1
Preston Terr
Inverkeithing KY11 . . . . 47 D1
Linlithgow EH49 . . . . 84 F6
Prestonpans EH32 . . . . 97 B1
Sauchie FK10 . . . . 5 D1
Preston Tower★ EH32 . . . . 97 A1
Preston Twr EH32 . . . . 97 A1
Pretoria Pl
Cowdenbeath KY4 . . . . 13 B4
Polmont FK2 . . . . 61 E1
Pretoria Rd FK5 . . . . 38 B1
Priest Bank EH41 . . . . 132 C2
Priestfield Ave EH16 . . . . 122 B4
Priestfield Cres EH16 . . . . 122 B4
Priestfield Gdns EH16 . . . . 122 B4
Priestfield Gr EH16 . . . . 122 B5
Priestfield Rd EH16 . . . . 122 B5
Priestfield Road N EH16 . . 122 A5
Priesthill Pl EH16 . . . . 151 B6
Priesthill St EH16 . . . . 151 B6
Prime Gilt Box St KY2 . . . . 17 B6
Primmer Pl KY4 . . . . 13 D3
Primrose Ave
Grangemouth FK3 . . . . 61 B6
Rosyth KY11 . . . . 46 D5
Primrose Avenue Ind Est FK3 . . . . 61 B6
Primrose Bank Rd EH5 . . . . 93 B6
Primrose Cres EH22 . . . . 153 C2
Primrose Ct Alloa FK10 . . . . 10 B6
Broxburn EH52 . . . . 115 E5
Rosyth KY11 . . . . 46 D5
Primrose Dr EH30 . . . . 90 D3
Primrose Gdns
Carrington EH23 . . . . 194 D6
Queensferry EH30 . . . . 89 C8
Primrose La
Cowdenbeath KY4 . . . . 13 C5
Kincardine FK10 . . . . 23 E3
Rosyth KY11 . . . . 46 D5
Primrose Lane Ind Est KY11 . . . . 46 D5
Primrose Pl Alloa FK10 . . . . 10 B6
Livingston EH54 . . . . 143 B5
Primrose Rd KY11 . . . . 46 B5
Primrose St Alloa FK10 . . . . 10 B7
Bonnybridge FK4 . . . . 58 B6
Edinburgh EH6 . . . . 94 A4
Primrose Terr
Dalkeith EH22 . . . . 153 C2
Edinburgh EH11 . . . . 120 E5
Prince Regent St EH6 . . . . 93 E6
Princes Mall Sh Ctr EH1 . 229 A3
Princess Alexandra Eye Pavilion EH3 . . . . 228 C2
Princess Mary Pl EH41 . . . 101 A1
Princess Mary Rd EH41 . . . 101 A1
Princess St FK4 . . . . 58 B5
Princes St California FK1 . . . 81 F5
Edinburgh EH2 . . . . 228 C3
Falkirk FK1 . . . . 60 B5
Grangemouth FK3 . . . . 61 E8
Stirling FK8 . . . . 7 B8
Priorscroft EH48 . . . . 111 F6
Priors Grange EH48 . . . . 111 F5
Priorwood Dr KY11 . . . . 30 A1
Priory Ct KY12 . . . . 29 A3
Priory Gate EH39 . . . . 54 B6
Priory Gr EH30 . . . . 89 B8
Priory La KY12 . . . . 29 A3
Priory Pl EH49 . . . . 83 F7
Priory Rd Linlithgow EH49 . . 84 F5
Whitecross EH49 . . . . 83 F6
Priory Sq FK10 . . . . 23 F3
Priory Wlk EH41 . . . . 130 C8
Priory Wynd EH39 . . . . 54 B7
Promenade Edinburgh EH15 94 F3
Limekilns KY11 . . . . 45 C3
Musselburgh EH21 . . . . 124 B7
Promenade The EH32 . . . . 97 D4
Prora Cotts EH39 . . . . 73 D4
Prospect Bank Cres EH6 . . 94 A4
Prospect Bank Gdns EH6 . . 94 B3
Prospect Bank Gr EH6 . . . . 94 C4
Prospect Bank Pl EH6 . . . . 94 C4
Prospect Bank Rd EH6 . . . . 94 C4
Prospect Bank Sch EH6 . . . 94 B4
Prospect Bank Terr EH6 . . . 94 C4
Prospecthill Rd FK1 . . . . 60 A2
Prospect St
Cowdenbeath KY4 . . . . 13 B4
Falkirk FK1 . . . . 59 F5
Providence Brae EH51 . . . . 63 F8
Provost Haugh EH14 . . . . 148 C5
Provost Hunter Ave FK12 . . . 5 C7
Provost Kay Pk KY1 . . . . 17 C6
Provost Milne Gr EH30 . . . . 89 D7
Provost Rd Bo'ness EH51 . . . 63 C6
Linlithgow EH49 . . . . 85 B7
Pryde Ave EH19 . . . . 173 A7
Pryde Terr EH19 . . . . 173 A7
Puir Wife's Brae EH48 . . . . 141 D5
Pullar Ave FK9 . . . . 2 A6
Pullar Ct FK9 . . . . 2 A6
PUMPHERSTON 144 B8
Pumpherston Rd
Mid Calder EH53, EH54 . . . . 144 C5
Pumpherston EH54 . . . . 144 A8
Uphall Station EH54 . . . . 115 A1
Pumpherston & Uphall Station Com Prim Sch EH53 . . . . 144 B7
Pyothall Ct EH52 . . . . 115 D5
Pyothall Rd EH52 . . . . 115 C6
Pypers Wynd EH32 . . . . 96 F2

Q

Quadrant EH39 . . . . 54 D7
Quadrant La EH39 . . . . 54 D7
Quadrant The EH26 . . . . 191 F6
Quakerfield FK7 . . . . 7 E1
Quality St Dysart KY1 . . . . 18 A7
Edinburgh EH4 . . . . 91 F3
North Berwick EH39 . . . . 54 C7
Quality Street Junc EH4 . . . 91 F3
Quality Street La EH4 . . . . 91 F3
Quarrolhall Cres FK2 . . . . 39 B3
Quarrybank
Cousland EH22 . . . . 154 C5
Edinburgh EH14 . . . . 148 C8
Quarry Bank EH14 . . . . 148 C8
Quarrybank Cl EH14 . . . . 148 C8
Quarrybank Ct EH14 . . . . 148 C8
Quarrybank End EH14 . . . . 148 C8
Quarry Brae
Grangemouth FK2 . . . . 82 E8
Kirkcaldy KY1 . . . . 17 F8
Quarry Cl EH8 . . . . 229 B1
Quarry Cotts
Blackridge EH48 . . . . 138 C3
Edinburgh EH15 . . . . 123 B4
Quarry Ct KY4 . . . . 13 B3
Quarryfoot Gdns EH19 . . . . 173 B7
Quarryfoot Gn EH19 . . . . 173 C7
Quarryfoot Pl EH19 . . . . 173 B7
Quarryford Farm Cotts EH41 . . . . 221 C4
QUARRYHEAD 173 B8
QUARRYHOLES 94 A3
Quarry Howe EH14 . . . . 147 C1
Quarry Knowe FK7 . . . . 19 E8
Quarryknowes The EH51 . . 63 E6
Quarry Pl Alloa FK10 . . . . 10 C8
Shotts ML7 . . . . 179 D5
Quarry Rd
Cambusbarron FK7 . . . . 6 C5
Fauldhouse EH47 . . . . 181 F6
Shotts ML7 . . . . 179 D5
Quarryside Ct KY12 . . . . 28 C6
Quarry St ML7 . . . . 179 D5
Quarryview EH14 . . . . 148 C8
Quarrywood Ct EH54 . . . . 143 D3
Quartermile EH3 . . . . 229 A2
Quayside Mills EH6 . . . . 93 F5
Quayside St EH6 . . . . 93 F6
Quebec Ave EH54 . . . . 143 E4
Queen Anne Dr EH28 . . . . 117 B5
Queen Anne High Sch KY12 . . . . 28 F6
Queen Anne Pk EH28 . . . . 117 B5
Queen Anne St KY12 . . . . 29 A4
Queen Charlotte La EH6 . . . 94 A5
Queen Charlotte St EH6 . . . 94 A5
Queen Margaret Cl EH10 150 D5
Queen Margaret Dr
Musselburgh EH21 . . . . 123 F3
South Queensferry EH30 . . . 68 C1
Queen Margaret Fauld KY12 . . . . 29 F6
Queen Margaret Gdns KY12 . . . . 29 F6
Queen Margaret Hospl KY12 . . . . 29 E6
Queen Margaret Pk KY12 . . 29 F6
Queen Margaret's Pl KY11 68 C6
Queen Margaret St KY3 . . . 34 F1
Queen Margaret Univ EH21 . . . . 124 A3
Queen Margaret Univ Way EH21 . . . . 124 A1
Queen Mary Terr KY11 . . . . 47 B2
Queens Ave
Broxburn EH52 . . . . 115 E4
Haddington EH41 . . . . 100 F1
Queen's Ave
Bridge of Allan FK9 . . . . 2 B6
Edinburgh EH4 . . . . 92 B2
Queen's Avenue S 3 EH4 . 92 C2
Queen's Bay Cres EH15 . . 123 D7
Queen's Bldgs KY11 . . . . 46 E5
Queens Cres Kinghorn KY3 . 34 F1
Livingston EH54 . . . . 143 B6
Queen's Cres Carluke ML8 215 A2
Edinburgh EH9 . . . . 121 F4
Falkirk FK1 . . . . 59 F5
Queens Ct FK5 . . . . 38 D3
Queen's Ct
Bridge of Allan FK9 . . . . 1 F7
Dunfermline KY12 . . . . 29 A3
Queens Dr Denny FK6 . . . . 36 E3
Falkirk FK1 . . . . 59 F5
Queens Dr *continued*
Stenhousemuir FK5 . . . . 38 C3
Queen's Dr California FK1 . . 81 F5
Edinburgh, Canongate EH8 229 C2
Edinburgh, Willowbrae EH8 . . . . 122 C6
Pencaitland EH34 . . . . 156 E6
Stenhousemuir FK5 . . . . 38 C2
QUEENSFERRY 89 A7
Queensferry High Sch EH30 . . . . 89 D8
Queensferry Mus★ EH30 . . 68 C1
Queensferry Prim Sch 1 EH30 . . . . 68 C1
Queensferry Rd
Dunfermline KY11 . . . . 46 D7
Edinburgh EH4 . . . . 91 C2
Edinburgh, Orchard Brae EH4 . . . . 92 D1
Kirkliston EH29 . . . . 89 A2
Rosyth KY11 . . . . 46 E5
Queensferry Recn Ctr EH30 . . . . 89 D8
Queensferry St EH2 . . . . 228 A3
Queensferry Street La EH2 . . . . 228 B3
Queensferry Terr EH4 . . . . 92 E1
Queen's Gallery★ EH8 . . 229 C3
Queen's Gall The★ EH8 . . 229 C3
Queens Gdns
Bridge of Allan FK9 . . . . 1 F7
East Calder EH53 . . . . 144 E4
Queen's Gdns EH4 . . . . 92 C2
Queenshaugh KY12 . . . . 27 C7
Queenshaugh Dr FK8 . . . . 2 C1
Queen's La FK9 . . . . 2 A7
Queen's Park Ave EH8 . . . . 94 B1
Queen's Park Ct EH8 . . . . 122 C8
Queen's Pl EH42 . . . . 78 F1
Queen's Rd
Broxburn EH52 . . . . 115 E4
Dunbar EH42 . . . . 78 E2
Edinburgh EH4 . . . . 92 C2
Stirling FK8 . . . . 6 F7
Queen St Alloa FK10 . . . . 10 B7
Alva FK12 . . . . 5 A7
Bannockburn FK7 . . . . 7 C2
Edinburgh EH2 . . . . 228 C4
Falkirk FK2 . . . . 60 C5
Fallin FK7 . . . . 8 C4
Grangemouth FK3 . . . . 61 F8
Inverkeithing KY11 . . . . 47 B2
Stirling FK8 . . . . 7 A8
Queens Terr EH53 . . . . 144 E4
Queen's Terr FK9 . . . . 2 A7
Queenstonbank EH39 . . . . 52 E3
Queen Street Gardens E EH3 . . . . 228 C4
Queen Street Gardens W EH3 . . . . 228 C4
Queensway EH26 . . . . 191 E7
Queens Way KY11 . . . . 46 B2
Queen's Wlk EH16 . . . . 122 E3
Quench Rd FK3 . . . . 62 B5
Quentin Ct EH54 . . . . 143 E1
Quentin Rise EH54 . . . . 143 E1
Quidenham Ct EH39 . . . . 54 A6
Quilts The EH6 . . . . 93 F5
Quilts Wynd EH6 . . . . 93 E5
Quoiters Ct EH47 . . . . 162 C7

R

Race Rd EH48 . . . . 140 E7
Raeburn Cres
Kirkcaldy KY2 . . . . 17 A4
Whitburn EH47 . . . . 161 B5
Raeburn Mews EH4 . . . . 93 A2
Raeburn Pl EH4 . . . . 93 A2
Raeburn Rd FK5 . . . . 38 B2
Raeburn Rigg EH54 . . . . 143 B6
Raeburn St EH4 . . . . 93 A2
Rae Ct FK2 . . . . 39 C3
Rae's Ct EH16 . . . . 151 A5
Raes Gdns EH19 . . . . 173 C8
Rae St Cowdenbeath KY4 . . . . 13 C2
Stenhousemuir FK5 . . . . 38 D3
Rainhill Ave FK2 . . . . 82 E6
Rainhill Ct 1 FK2 . . . . 82 F7
Raith Ave KY4 . . . . 13 C3
Raith Cres KY2 . . . . 17 A4
Raith Ctr KY4 . . . . 13 D4
Raith Dr KY2 . . . . 17 A3
Raith Gdns KY2 . . . . 17 A3
RAITH PARK 16 D5
Raleigh Ct FK1 . . . . 59 E5
Ramage Rd ML8 . . . . 215 B1
Ramillies Ct Carluke ML8 . 215 A1
Penicuik EH26 . . . . 192 A8
Ramsay Ave FK2 . . . . 61 A3
Ramsay Colliery EH20 . . . . 172 C8
Ramsay Cotts EH19 . . . . 173 F3
Ramsay Cres
Bathgate EH48 . . . . 141 C6
Burntisland KY3 . . . . 34 A2
Mayfield EH22 . . . . 174 E5
Ramsay Ct Kincardine FK10 . 23 E4
Livingston EH54 . . . . 144 C5
Ramsay Gdn EH1 . . . . 228 C3
Ramsay La Edinburgh EH1 . 228 C3
Kincardine FK10 . . . . 23 E4
Limekilns KY11 . . . . 45 D3
Ramsay Pl Edinburgh EH15 . . 95 B1
Penicuik EH26 . . . . 191 C6
Stirling FK8 . . . . 2 A2
Ramsay Rd KY1 . . . . 17 B1
Ramsay Terr EH18 . . . . 172 F6
Ramsay Wlk EH22 . . . . 174 E5
Ramsey Pl KY11 . . . . 46 F3
Ramsey Tullis Dr FK10 . . . . 4 C1
Randolph Cliff EH3 . . . . 228 A3
Randolph Cres
Bannockburn FK7 . . . . 7 C1
Dunbar EH42 . . . . 106 D8
Edinburgh EH3 . . . . 228 A3
Grangemouth FK2 . . . . 82 D8
Randolph Ct Kirkcaldy KY1 . . 18 A8
Stirling FK8 . . . . 7 A5
Randolph Gdns FK6 . . . . 36 D1
Randolph Ind Est KY1 . . . . 18 A8
Randolph La EH3 . . . . 228 B3
Randolph Pl
Bannockburn FK7 . . . . 7 C2
Edinburgh EH3 . . . . 228 B3
Kirkcaldy KY1 . . . . 17 F8
Randolph Rd FK8 . . . . 7 B4
Randolph St
Cowdenbeath KY4 . . . . 13 D3
Dunfermline KY12 . . . . 29 A4
Randolph Terr FK7 . . . . 7 A4
Randyford Rd FK2 . . . . 60 D5
Randyford St FK2 . . . . 60 E5
Range Rd EH51 . . . . 62 D8
Rankeillor St EH8 . . . . 229 B1
Rankin Ave EH9 . . . . 121 F2
Rankin Cres FK4 . . . . 57 D5
Rankin Dr EH9 . . . . 121 E2
Rankine Sq EH54 . . . . 142 C5
Rankine Wynd FK10 . . . . 4 C2
Rankin Rd EH9 . . . . 121 F3
Rannoch Ct FK10 . . . . 10 C5
Rannoch Dr Crossford KY12 28 B1
Whitburn EH47 . . . . 161 C7
Rannoch Gr EH4 . . . . 91 D1
Rannoch Pl Edinburgh EH4 . . 91 D1
Shieldhill FK1 . . . . 81 E7
Shotts ML7 . . . . 179 E6
Stenhousemuir FK5 . . . . 38 F4
Rannoch Rd Edinburgh EH4 91 D1
Grangemouth FK3 . . . . 61 D4
Kirkcaldy KY2 . . . . 16 E8
Rosyth KY11 . . . . 46 E2
Whitburn EH47 . . . . 161 C7
Rannoch Terr EH4 . . . . 91 D1
Rannoch Wlk
Livingston EH54 . . . . 144 A4
Whitburn EH47 . . . . 161 C7
Ransome Gdns EH4 . . . . 91 D1
RAPLOCH 1 F2
Raploch Prim Sch 3 FK8 . . 1 F2
Raploch Rd FK8 . . . . 1 F1
Rashiehill ML11 . . . . 201 A1
Rashiehill Cres EH55 . . . . 182 F6
Rashiehill Rd FK1 . . . . 108 A6
Rashiehill Terr EH55 . . . . 182 E6
Rashierigg EH52 . . . . 115 B5
Rashierigg Pl EH47 . . . . 161 B2
Ratcliffe Terr EH9 . . . . 121 E4
Rathbone Pl EH15 . . . . 95 B1
RATHO 117 D1
Ratho Park Rd EH28 . . . . 117 E2
Ratho Pk EH28 . . . . 117 C6
Ratho Pl KY11 . . . . 29 C3
Ratho Prim Sch EH28 . . . 117 D2
RATHO STATION 117 D5
Rattray Cres EH10 . . . . 149 E8
Rattray Dr EH10 . . . . 149 E8
Rattray Gdns EH47 . . . . 162 E7
Rattray Gr EH10 . . . . 149 E8
Rattray Loan EH10 . . . . 149 E8
Rattray St EH51 . . . . 64 B8
Rattray Terr KY5 . . . . 14 A7
Rattray Way EH10 . . . . 149 F8
Ravelrig Dr EH14 . . . . 147 B2
Ravelrig Gait EH14 . . . . 147 B2
Ravelrig Hill EH14 . . . . 147 B2
Ravelrig Pk EH14 . . . . 147 B2
Ravelrig Rd EH14 . . . . 147 B3
Ravelrig Wynd EH14 . . . . 147 C2
RAVELSTON 120 B8
Ravelston Dykes EH12 . . . 120 D8
Ravelston Dykes La EH4 . . 120 A8
Ravelston Dykes Rd EH4 . 120 B8
Ravelston Gdn EH4 . . . . 120 C8
Ravelston Heights EH4 . . . . 92 C1
Ravelston House Gr 3 EH4 . . . . 92 C1
Ravelston House Loan EH4 . . . . 92 C1
Ravelston House Pk EH4 . . 92 C1
Ravelston House Rd EH4 . . 92 C1
Ravelston Pk EH14 . . . . 120 E8
Ravelston Pl EH4 . . . . 120 F8
Ravelston Rise EH4 . . . . 120 C8
Ravelston Terr EH4 . . . . 92 F1
Ravelston Woods Nature Reserve★ EH4 . . . . 92 B1
Ravelsykes Rd EH26 . . . . 191 C5
Ravendean Gdns EH26 . . . . 191 C5
Ravens Craig 10 KY1 . . . . 17 D6
Ravenscraig Castle★ KY1 . 17 E5
Ravenscraig St KY1 . . . . 17 E6
Ravenscraig View KY1 . . . 17 E6
Ravenscroft Gdns EH17 . . . 151 E5
Ravenscroft Pl EH17 . . . . 151 E5
Ravenscroft St EH17 . . . . 151 E5
Ravenshaugh Cres EH21 . 125 A6
Ravenshaugh Rd EH21 . . . 125 A7
Ravenswood ML11 . . . . 217 F6
Ravenswood Ave EH16 . . . 122 C1
Ravenswood Rise EH54 . . 164 E8
Raw Holdings EH53 . . . . 145 B5
Recreation Pk (Alloa Athletic FC) FK10 . . . . 10 C6
Rectory La KY1 . . . . 18 A7

Redbrae Ave EH51........64 A5
Redbrae Rd FK1..........59 D6
Redbraes Gr EH7..........93 D4
Redbraes Pl EH7..........93 D4
Redburn Rd
Blackridge EH48.........138 B2
Prestonpans EH32.........96 E1
Redburn Road N EH32....96 E1
Redburn Wynd KY1.......17 C4
Redcraig Rd EH53.......144 F2
Redcraigs KY2............16 C7
Redcroft Pl EH47........162 A1
Redcroft St EH22........152 A8
Redcroft Terr EH47......162 A1
REDDING...................61 C1
Redding Ind Est FK2......61 A1
REDDINGMUIRHEAD.......82 A8
Redding Rd
Grangemouth FK2.........82 D8
Laurieston FK2...........60 F2
Redding FK2..............61 B1
Reddingrig Ct FK2........82 A8
Reddingrig Pl FK2........82 A8
Redding Road Rdbt FK2...60 F2
Reddoch Rd FK3...........61 F5
Redford Ave EH13.......149 C6
Redford Bank EH13......149 D6
Redford Cres EH13.......149 C6
Redford Dr EH13.........149 B6
Redford Gdns EH13......149 D6
Redford Gr EH13.........149 D6
Redford Loan EH13......149 C6
Redford Neuk EH13......149 D6
Redford Pl EH13.........149 D6
Redford Rd EH13........149 D6
Redford Terr EH13......149 C6
Redford Wlk EH13.......149 C6
Red Fox Cres EH26.......171 A1
Redgauntlet Terr EH16...122 C1
Redhall FK7................8 A4
Redhall Ave EH14........120 B2
Redhall Bank Rd EH14...120 B1
Redhall Cres EH14.......120 B2
Redhall Dr EH14.........120 A2
Redhall Gdns EH14.......120 A2
Redhall Gr EH14.........120 A2
Redhall House Ave EH14.120 C1
Redhall House Dr EH14..120 B1
Redhall Pl EH14.........120 A2
Redhall Rd EH14.........120 A2
Redhall Sch EH14........120 A1
Redhall View EH14.......120 B1
Redhaws Rd ML7.........180 A3
Redheugh Cotts TD13....219 E3
Redheugh Loan EH23....174 C1
Redheughs Ave EH12....119 A4
Redheughs Rigg EH12...119 A4
Redholm EH39..............54 E6
Redholm Pk EH39..........54 E6
Redhouse Cotts EH49.....86 F3
Redhouse Ct EH47.......162 E7
Redhouse Ind Est FK2....82 B8
Redhouse Pl EH47.......141 D1
Redhouse Rd EH47.......163 A8
Redlands Ct EH47.......161 E7
Redlands Rd FK10..........4 A3
Redmill Cotts EH47......161 E7
Redmill Ct EH47.........161 E7
Redmill Ind Est EH47....161 E6
Redmill View EH47.......161 E7
Redmire Cres ML7.......198 B8
Red Moss Wildlife Reserve*
EH14...................168 C4
Redpath Dr FK2............39 A4
Red Row Aberlady EH32....71 C4
Limekilns KY11...........45 D3
Pathhead EH37..........176 C8
Redside EH39...............55 B1
Redwell Pl FK10.............9 F7
Redwing Brae EH54......143 D6
Redwood Gr EH22.......173 F5
Redwood Wlk EH22......174 A5
Reed Dr EH22.............174 B6
Reedlands Dr FK6..........57 D7
Regal Gr ML7.............179 E4
Regal Lodge EH19.......173 B7
Regent Pl EH7..............94 A2
Regent Rd FH7, EH8......229 B4
Regent Sq EH49.............85 B7
Regent St Edinburgh EH15.123 B8
Kincardine FK10...........23 E3
Regent Street La EH15...123 B8
Regents Way KY11.........48 B3
Regent Terr EH7..........229 C4
Regent Terrace Mews
EH7.....................229 C4
Regis Ct EH4...............91 B4
Register Pl EH2..........229 A4
Register St EH51...........63 F8
Reid Ave KY4...............30 E6
Reid Pl FK5.................38 B2
Reid Rd EH48.............141 C4
Reid's Cl EH8.............229 C3
Reid St Dunfermline KY12...29 A3
Lochgelly KY5..............14 B8
Reid Terr EH3...............93 B2
Reilly Gdns FK4............58 B3
Reilly Rd FK4...............58 B3
Relugas Gdns EH9........121 E3
Relugas Pl EH9...........121 E3
Relugas Rd EH9..........121 E3
Rendall Gdns EH52.......115 F5
Rennie Pl EH40...........103 C8
Rennie's Isle EH6..........93 F6
Rennie Sq EH54...........164 C6
Rennie St FK1...............60 A3
Research Avenue 1 EH14 147 F8
Research Avenue N
Hermiston EH14.........118 F1
Riccarton EH14..........147 E8
Research Avenue S EH14 147 F8
RESTALRIG..................94 D2
Restalrig Ave EH7..........94 D1
Restalrig Cir EH7...........94 C3
Restalrig Cres EH7.........94 C3
Restalrig Dr EH7............94 C2
Restalrig Gdns EH7.........94 C2
Restalrig Ho EH7............94 C2
Restalrig Pk EH7............94 B3
Restalrig Rd EH7............94 B3
Restalrig Road S EH7.......94 C1
Restalrig Sq EH7............94 C3
Restalrig Terr EH6..........94 A4
Restondene EH54.........142 E5
Retail Pk Rdbt EH54......143 E1
Retreat Cres EH42..........78 D1
Retreat Gdns EH42..........78 D1
Reveston La EH47.........161 B5
Reynard Gdns EH49.........84 A6
Rhodders Gr FK12............5 B7
Rhodes Cotts EH39..........54 F7
Rhodes Pk EH39.............54 F6
Rhodes Smallholdings
EH39......................55 A6
Rhodes St KY11.............29 B2
RICCARTON...............147 E7
Clackmannan................11 B5
Riccarton Ave EH14.......148 A5
Riccarton Cres EH14......148 A4
Riccarton Dr EH14........148 A5
Riccarton Gr EH14........148 A5
Riccarton Mains Rd
EH14.....................148 A6
Riccarton Rd EH49..........84 F5
Richard Quinn St FK7......20 D8
Richmond Dr FK2............82 C8
Richmond La EH8..........229 B2
Richmond Pl
Edinburgh EH8............229 B2
Lochgelly KY5...............14 B7
Richmond Terr
Bo'ness EH51................63 F7
Edinburgh EH11...........228 A2
Riddochhill Cres EH47....162 C7
Riddochhill Ct EH47.......162 B8
Riddochhill Dr EH47......162 C7
Riddochhill Rd EH47......162 C8
Riddochhill View EH47...162 B8
Ridge Ct EH47.............161 B2
Ridge Way KY11.............48 B5
Riding Pk EH4...............91 B4
Ridley Dr KY11...............46 F3
Riego St EH3...............228 B2
Rifle Rd EH51................62 D8
Riggonhead Ct 4 EH33..126 D7
Riggonhead Gdns 5
EH33.....................126 D7
Rigg Pk EH42.................78 C2
Riggs View KY12.............27 D1
Rigley Terr EH32...........125 E8
Rig Pl EH32...................71 C4
Rig St EH32...................71 C4
Rillbank Cres EH9.........229 A1
Rillbank Terr EH9..........121 D5
Rimmon Cres ML7.........179 E6
Ringans La FK7................6 F3
Ring Rd FK10.................10 B7
Ringwood Pl 2 EH16.....151 B8
Rintoul Ave KY12............26 A8
Rintoul Pl Blairhall KY12...26 A8
Edinburgh EH3...............93 B2
Riselaw Cres EH10.........150 A8
Riselaw Pl EH10............150 A8
Riselaw Rd EH10...........150 A8
Riselaw Terr EH10.........150 A8
Ritchie Ct KY12..............29 A7
Ritchie Pl Bo'ness EH51....64 A5
Edinburgh EH11...........120 F5
Grangemouth FK3............61 C5
Inverkeithing/Dunfermline
KY11......................29 F3
Rivaldsgreen Cres EH49...85 A6
River Almond Wlk EH4......90 F4
Riverbahk View FK8...........2 C1
Riverbank Ct EH47.........161 F7
Riverbank View FK8..........7 C8
River Gore Gr EH23.......195 C8
River Gore Rd EH23.......195 C8
River Gore View EH23.....195 C8
Riversdale Cres EH12.....120 C7
Riversdale Gr EH12.......120 C7
Riversdale Rd EH12.......120 C7
RIVERSIDE.....................2 B1
Riverside Edinburgh EH4....91 B7
Newbridge EH28...........116 F6
Riverside Ct
Linlithgow EH49..............84 C7
Livingston EH54............143 C3
Riverside Dr
Haddington EH41..........101 B1
Stirling FK8....................2 C1
Riverside Gdns EH21......124 B5
Riverside Lea Crofts
EH47......................162 F7
Riverside Pl EH41.........101 C1
Riverside Prim Sch
Livingston EH54...........144 A4
Stirling FK8....................2 B1
Riverside Rd
Edinburgh EH30..............90 E3
Grangemouth FK3............62 B5
Riverside Terr FK10.........23 F3
Riverside View FK10.........10 B4
River St FK2...................39 A1
Riverview FK10...............10 A7
River View KY11..............48 B2
River Wlk KY11...............48 B2
River Wynd FK9................2 A4
R L Stevenson's Birthplace*
EH3.........................93 C3
Road 4a FK3..................62 C6
Road 4b FK3..................62 C6
Road 5a FK3..................62 C7
Road 30b FK3.................62 B6
Road 30c FK3.................62 B6
Road 4 FK3....................62 C6
Road 6 FK3....................62 C6
Road 7 FK3....................62 C7
Road 8 FK3....................62 C7
Road 9 FK3....................62 C7
Road 10 FK3...................62 C7
Road 11 FK3...................62 C6
Road 13 FK3...................62 C6
Road 15 FK3...................62 C6
Road 17 FK3...................62 A6
Road 21 FK3...................62 A6
Road 24 FK3...................62 A6
Road 25 FK3...................62 B6
Road 26 FK3...................62 B6
Road 27 FK3...................62 B6
Road 28 FK3...................62 B6
Road 29 FK3...................62 B6
Road 30 FK3...................62 A6
Road 31 FK3...................62 B6
Road 32 FK3...................62 B6
Road 33 FK2, FK3..............62 B5
Roanhead Terr FK10..........23 E4
Roanshead Rd EH22........174 C8
Robb's Loan EH14..........120 C4
Robb's Loan Gr EH14.......120 C4
Robert Bruce Ct FK5.........38 A2
Robert Burns Dr EH16.....122 A1
Robert Burns Mews
EH22.......................153 D3
Robert De Quincy Pl
EH32.......................125 F8
Robert Dick Ct FK10..........4 C2
Robert Dow Ct KY5...........14 B8
Robert Hardie Ct FK5........38 C2
Robert Kay Pl FK5............38 B3
Robert Kinmond Ave FK10...4 C2
Robert Knox Ave FK10........4 C2
Roberts Ave FK2...............61 D2
Robert Smillie Ave EH22..174 E5
Robert Smith Ct KY4.........13 E6
Robert Smith Pl EH22......152 F4
Robertson Ave
Bathgate EH48.............140 E5
Bonnybridge FK4.............58 B6
Edinburgh EH11............120 D5
Prestonpans EH32............97 A2
Tranent EH33................126 D6
Robertson Ct
Armadale EH48.............139 F4
Stenhousemuir FK5..........38 D2
Robertson Dr EH33.........126 D7
Robertson Gait EH11......120 D5
Robertson Gdns EH48.....140 A4
Robertson Pl FK7...............7 B3
Robertson Rd KY12...........29 D5
Robertsons Bank EH23....195 D7
Robertson's Cl
4 Dalkeith EH22............153 A3
Edinburgh EH1...............229 B2
Robertson's Ct EH8.........229 C4
Robertson St FK12.............5 B7
Robertson Way EH54.......143 D7
Roberts St KY1.................17 E8
Robert St ML7................179 E4
Robert Wilson Gr KY12......29 D8
Robins Neuk EH33...........127 C5
Rocheid Pk EH4................92 F4
Rochester Terr EH10........121 A4
Rocks Rd KY11..................45 B4
Rockville Gr EH49..............85 A6
Rockville Terr EH19.........173 B8
Roddinglaw Cotts EH12....118 C3
Roddinglaw Rd EH12,
EH28.......................118 C3
Rodel Dr FK2....................61 F1
Rodgers St FK6.................36 E1
Rodney St Edinburgh EH7...93 C2
Grangemouth FK3.............61 C6
Roebuck Pk FK5................38 E2
Roebuck Pl EH51...............63 D5
Rolland St KY12................29 A3
Rollock St FK8...................7 A5
Roman Bldgs FK2...............59 D5
Roman Camp EH37..........176 B4
Roman Camp Cotts
EH52.......................115 C2
Roman Camp Way EH37..176 B4
Roman Ct EH37..............176 B4
Roman Dr FK1..................59 D5
Roman Pk EH22.............153 D2
Roman Rd Bonnybridge FK4 58 A4
Inverkeithing KY11...........47 B2
Roman St EH22..............153 D2
Roman Terr EH22...........153 D2
Roman View EH22..........153 D2
Roman Way EH51..............63 D5
Romero Pl EH16.............121 F5
Romyn Rd KY11.................46 C1
Ronades Rd FK2................60 A8
Ronald Cres FK5................38 B1
Ronald Pl FK8.....................7 B8
Ronaldshay Cres FK3.........61 E8
Ronaldson Gr KY12............29 D5
Roodlands Bsns Pk EH41 100 F1
Roodlands Ct EH41..........100 E1
Roodlands Hospl EH41....100 E1
Roods Cres KY11................47 B3
Roods Rd KY11...................47 B2
Roods Sq KY11....................47 C3
Rood Well Cotts EH42.......104 E1
Roomlin Gdns KY1..............17 F7
Roosevelt Rd EH27............145 E3
Rope Wlk EH32...................96 E1
Rosabelle Rd EH25............171 F3
Rosabelle St KY1.................17 E7
Rose Ave EH19..................173 D6
ROSEBANK........................36 D4
Rosebank Alloa FK10...........5 D1
Bridgend EH49...................86 F4
Cowdenbeath KY4..............13 D4
Dunfermline KY11...............29 C2
Rosebank Ave FK1...............59 F5
Rosebank Cotts EH3.........228 A2
Rosebank Gdns Alloa FK10 10 C8
Dunfermline KY12...............28 D6
Edinburgh EH5....................93 A5
Grangemouth FK2................82 B7
Kincardine FK10..................23 F3
Rosebank Gr EH5.................93 A5
Rosebank Pk EH54.............164 A8
Rosebank Pl FK1..................59 F5
Rosebank Rd
Edinburgh EH5....................93 A5
Livingston EH54.................164 A8
Rosebank Rdbt Falkirk FK1. 59 F5
Livingston EH54.................164 B8
Rosebank Way EH54..........164 A8
Rosebay Glade EH54..........164 C7
Roseberry Ct EH30...............89 C8
Roseberry Pk EH54............142 E5
Rosebery Ave EH30..............89 C8
Rosebery Cres
Bathgate EH48..................141 B5
Edinburgh EH12................120 F7
Gorebridge EH23...............195 C6
Rosebery Crescent La
EH12............................120 F7
Rosebery Ct
Dalgety Bay KY11................47 F2
Kirkcaldy KY1......................17 B5
Rosebery Gr KY11................47 F2
Rosebery Pl
Dalgety Bay KY11................47 F2
Gullane EH31......................52 A2
Livingston EH54................143 B5
Stirling FK8..........................2 B1
Rosebery Resr* EH23.......211 B6
Rosebery Terr KY1...............17 B5
Rosebery View KY11.............47 F2
ROSEBURN.......................120 E7
Roseburn Ave EH12...........120 D7
Roseburn Cliff EH12..........120 E7
Roseburn Cres EH12..........120 D7
Roseburn Dr EH12.............120 D7
Roseburn Gdns EH12.........120 D7
Roseburn Maltings EH12...120 E7
Roseburn Pl EH12..............120 D7
Roseburn Prim Sch
EH12............................120 D6
Roseburn St EH12..............120 D6
Roseburn Terr EH12...........120 E7
Rosebush Cres KY11.............29 C3
Rose Cotts EH19................173 D6
Rose Cres KY12....................29 A4
Rose Ct EH4.........................91 E4
Rosedale Ct EH24..............193 D8
Rosedale Gr EH24..............172 D1
Rosedale Neuk EH24..........172 D1
Rosefield Ave EH15............123 A8
Rosefield Avenue La
EH15............................123 A8
Rosefield La EH15..............123 A8
Rosefield Pl EH15...............123 A8
Rosefield St EH15...............123 A8
Rose Gdns
Bonnyrigg and Lasswade
EH19............................173 D6
Cairneyhill KY12..................27 D2
Rose Gr EH19....................173 D6
Rosehall EH41....................129 F8
Rosehall Ct EH41................129 F8
Rosehall Pl EH41................129 F8
Rosehall Rd ML7................179 C3
Rosehall Terr FK1.................60 B4
Rosehall Wlk EH41.............129 F8
Rosehill Cres KY4..................13 B3
Rosehill Pl EH54.................143 B3
Rose La
South Queensferry EH30.......68 B1
Torryburn KY12....................26 E1
Roseland Hall FK3.................61 B7
Roselea Dr FK2.....................82 E8
Rosemalen Pl KY12...............29 C4
Rosemary Ct FK6..................36 D2
Rosemead Terr FK1...............81 F5
Rosemill Ct KY12...................26 C1
Rosemount EH32...................96 F2
Rosemount Ave KY2..............17 A8
Rosemount Bldgs EH3.........228 A2
Rosemount Ct
Bathgate EH48...................141 B6
Carluke ML8.......................215 A2
Rosemount Dr EH52............114 E4
Rosemount Gdns FK1............81 D6
Rosemount Mews EH32.........96 F2
Roseneath Pl EH9................121 D5
Roseneath St EH9................121 D5
Roseneath Terr EH9.............121 D5
Rose Neuk EH19..................173 D6
Rose Path EH19...................173 D6
Rose Pk
Bonnyrigg and Lasswade
EH19............................173 D6
Edinburgh EH5.....................93 B5
Rose Pl EH19......................173 D6
Rose St Alloa FK10..................4 E1
Rose St continued
Bonnybridge FK4..................58 B6
Burntisland KY3....................50 E8
Cowdenbeath KY4................13 C3
Dunfermline KY12................29 B4
Edinburgh EH2..................228 C3
Tullibody FK10......................4 D4
Rose Street North La
EH2..............................228 C3
Rose Street South La
EH2..............................228 C3
Rose's Wlk EH52.................114 F4
Rosetay Ct KY12....................29 C4
Rose Terr
Bonnyrigg and Lasswade
EH19............................173 D6
Denny FK6............................36 D1
Stenhousemuir FK5...............38 F3
Rosethorn Wynd KY12...........29 C3
Rosevale Pl EH6....................94 B4
Rosevale Terr EH6.................94 B4
Roseville Gdns EH5...............93 C6
Rose Way EH19...................173 D6
ROSEWELL........................172 D2
Rosewell Prim Sch EH24 172 E2
Rosewell Rd EH18, EH19,
EH24............................172 F4
Rose Wynd KY2.....................17 B3
Rosin Ct KY1.........................17 C7
ROSLIN.............................171 F3
Roslin Bio Ctr EH25............172 B4
Roslin Glen Ctry Pk*
EH25............................171 F1
Roslin Prim Sch EH25.........171 F3
Roslin Prim Sch (Bilston
Annexe) EH25..................171 E6
Ross Ave KY11.......................48 A2
Ross Cres Falkirk FK1............59 C5
Tranent EH33.....................126 D5
Ross Ct Addiewell EH55.......183 C8
Stirling FK7............................7 B3
Rossend Terr KY3..................50 D8
Ross Gdns Edinburgh EH9...121 F3
Kirkcaldy KY1........................17 E7
Rossglen Ct EH25................172 A3
Ross High Sch EH33............126 C6
Rosshill Terr EH30.................89 D8
Rossie Pl EH7........................94 A2
Ross La KY12.........................28 F4
Rossland Pl KY3.....................34 F2
Rosslyn Chapel* EH25.........172 A3
Rosslyn Cres EH6..................93 E3
Rosslyn Sch KY1....................17 F8
Rosslyn St KY1.......................17 F8
Rosslyn Terr EH6...................93 E3
Rossness Dr KY3....................34 F1
Ross Pl Edinburgh EH9.........121 F3
Kinghorn KY3........................34 F1
Newtongrange EH22............174 B6
Ross Rd EH16......................122 A2
Ross's Cl 12 EH41...............130 B8
Ross St KY12.........................29 B5
Ross Way EH54...................143 C7
ROSYTH...............................46 F4
Rosyth Europarc KY11............46 D1
Rosyth Sta KY11....................46 E6
Rothesay Mews EH4.............120 F8
Rothesay Pl
Edinburgh EH3...................228 A3
Musselburgh EH21..............124 D5
Rothesay Terr EH3..............228 A3
Rothes Dr EH54...................164 F6
Roughburn Rd FK9..................2 A6
Roughlands Cres FK2............39 B3
Roughlands Dr FK2...............39 A3
Roull Gr EH12.....................119 D5
Roull Pl EH12......................119 E5
Roull Rd EH12.....................119 D5
Roundel The FK2...................60 D7
Roundelwood FK10.................5 B1
Roundhouse FK7....................20 D8
Round The KY12.....................29 C3
Rowallan Ct 4 EH12.............119 A7
Rowallan Dr FK7....................19 F8
Rowan Cres Falkirk FK1.........59 A4
Menstrie FK11.......................3 F6
Shotts ML7.........................180 B4
Rowan Ct FK7..........................7 E1
Rowan Dr EH47....................141 E1
Rowanfield Sch EH4................92 C3
Rowan Gdns EH19...............173 B6
Rowan Gr
Dunfermline KY11..................29 D1
Livingston EH54...................144 B5
Rowanhill Cl EH32..................97 D3
Rowanhill Dr EH32..................97 D3
Rowanhill Pk EH32..................97 C3
Rowanhill Way EH32...............97 D3
Rowan La EH47....................141 D1
Rowan Pl EH47....................141 E1
Rowan St Blackburn EH47....141 D1
Dunbar EH42.........................78 B1
Rowans The Alloa FK10...........5 C2
Gullane EH31........................52 B3
Rowan Terr
Blackburn EH47..................162 D8
Cowdenbeath KY4.................13 C3
Rowantree Ave EH14............147 E4
Rowantree Gr EH14.............147 E4
Rowantree Rd EH22.............174 E7
Rowantree Wlk FK5...............38 B4
Roxburghe Ct EH42...............78 F1
Roxburghe Lodge Wynd
EH42...............................78 F1
Roxburghe Pk EH42...............78 F1

Roxburghe Terr EH42 78 F1
Roxburgh Pl
Edinburgh EH8 229 B2
Stenhousemuir FK5 38 F4
Roxburgh St
Edinburgh EH8 229 B2
Grangemouth FK3 61 F8
Royal Blind Sch The
Edinburgh EH10 121 B3
Edinburgh EH16 121 F3
Royal Botanic Garden★
EH3 93 B3
Royal Cir EH3 228 B4
Royal Coll of Physicians
EH2 228 C4
Royal Commonwealth Pool★
EH16 121 A5
Royal Commonwealth Pool
EH16 121 F6
Royal Cres EH3 93 C2
Royal Ct EH26 191 D7
Royal (Dick) Veterinary Coll
EH8 229 B1
Royal Edinburgh Hospl
EH10 121 A3
Royal Garden Apartments
EH1 229 A3
Royal Gdns FK8 7 A8
Royal Highland Ctr (Royal Highland Showground)★
EH28 117 E6
Royal High Prim Sch The
EH8 122 D8
Royal High Sch The EH4 91 D3
Royal Hospl for Sick Children
EH9 121 D5
Royal Infirmary of Edinburgh
EH16 122 E1
Royal Lyceum Theatre The★
EH3 228 B2
Royal Mile Prim Sch
EH8 229 C3
Royal Observatory★ EH9 121 D2
Royal Park Pl 4 EH8 94 B1
Royal Park Terr EH8 94 B1
Royal Scot Ct EH48 141 B6
Royal Scots Medway
EH19 172 F5
Royal Scots Pl EH19 172 F6
Royal Scottish Acad★
EH2 228 C3
Royal Scot Way KY12 29 A5
Royal Stuart Way FK7 7 E7
Royal Terr Edinburgh EH7 229 C4
Linlithgow EH49 84 F6
Royal Victoria Hospl EH4 92 E2
Royal Yacht Britannia The★
EH6 93 F7
Roy Dr EH54 164 F6
Royston Mains Ave EH5 92 E6
Royston Mains Cl EH5 92 E6
Royston Mains Cres EH5 92 D6
Royston Mains Gdns EH5 92 E6
Royston Mains Gn EH5 92 E6
Royston Mains Pl EH5 92 D5
Royston Mains Rd EH5 92 E6
Royston Mains St EH5 92 D6
Royston Prim Sch EH5 92 E6
Royston Rd EH54 142 E7
Royston Rdbt EH54 142 D7
Royston Terr EH3 93 B4
Rulley View FK6 36 C4
Rullion Green Ave EH26 191 D7
Rullion Green Cres EH26 191 D7
Rullion Green Gr EH26 191 D7
Rullion Rd EH26 191 C6
RUMBLINGWELL 28 D5
Rumblingwell KY12 28 D5
RUMFORD 82 E7
Rumlie The FK1 108 A6
Run The EH51 64 C7
Rushbank EH54 143 E6
Ruskie Rd FK9 2 B3
Ruskin Pl EH22 174 E5
Russel Ct KY5 14 B8
Russell Ave EH48 139 F7
Russell Ct KY11 29 F1
Russell Gdns EH12 120 E7
Russell Gr KY3 33 F2
Russell Hill Ct FK5 38 B1
Russell Pl Bathgate EH48 141 A3
Bonnybridge FK4 57 D5
Edinburgh EH5 93 B6
1 Kirkcaldy KY1 17 C5
Oakley KY12 26 F7
Russell Rd Bathgate EH48 141 A3
Edinburgh EH11 120 E6
Russell St
Cowdenbeath KY4 13 B4
Lochgelly KY5 14 B8
Russell Way EH48 141 A3
Russel St FK2 60 B6
Rutherford Ct
Bridge of Allan FK9 2 A8
Kirkcaldy KY1 17 E7
Rutherford Dr EH16 122 B1
Rutherford Gdns EH46 206 B1
Rutherford Sq EH54 164 C6
Ruthven Pl EH16 122 C1
Ruthven Rd EH39 53 A4
Rutland Court La EH3 228 B2
Rutland Pl EH3 228 B3
Rutland Sq EH1 228 B3
Rutland St EH1 228 B3
Ryebank EH54 143 E6
Ryehill Ave EH6 94 B3
Ryehill Gdns EH6 94 B3
Ryehill Gr EH6 94 B3
Ryehill Pl EH6 94 B4
Ryehill Terr EH6 94 B4
Rymalton KY1 17 D6

S

Sacred Heart RC Prim Sch
1 Grangemouth FK3 61 E6
Penicuik EH26 191 E5
Saddletree Loan EH16 122 C2
Sailors' Wlk KY3 50 D8
Sainford Cres FK2 39 A1
St Alban's Rd EH9 121 E3
St Andrew Pl EH6 94 A4
St Andrew's Ct FK5 38 B3
St Andrew's Dr Airth FK2 22 B7
Armadale EH48 139 F7
Uphall EH52 114 F4
St Andrews Pl 10 FK1 60 B4
St Andrew Sq EH2 229 A4
St Andrew's RC High Sch
KY2 17 D8
St Andrew's RC Prim Sch
Falkirk FK1 60 E4
Gorebridge EH23 174 C2
St Andrew St
Dalkeith EH22 153 A3
Dunfermline KY11 29 C2
North Berwick EH39 54 C7
St Andrew's Way EH54 142 E6
St Andrews Way Bsns Units
EH54 142 E5
St Anne's Ave EH18 172 E6
St Anne's Cres FK7 7 E1
St Anne's Ct EH22 174 A5
St Ann's Path EH18 172 E6
St Ann's Pl 10 EH41 130 B8
St Anthony La EH6 93 F5
St Anthony Pl EH6 93 F5
St Anthony's RC Prim Sch 1
EH48 139 F5
St Anthony St EH6 93 F5
St Augustine's High Sch
EH12 119 C4
St Baldred's Cres EH39 54 D7
St Baldred's Ct EH39 54 D7
St Baldred's Rd EH39 54 D6
St Bernadette's RC Prim Sch
FK10 4 A2
St Bernard's Cres EH4 93 A2
St Bernard's Row 1 EH3 93 B2
St Bride's RC Prim Sch
KY4 13 C3
St Bridgets Brae KY11 48 C4
St Brycedale Ave KY1 17 B4
St Brycedale Ct KY1 17 B4
St Brycedale Rd KY1 17 B4
St Catherine FK2 82 F7
St Catherines Cres ML7 179 D6
St Catherine's Gdns
EH12 120 A6
St Catherine's Manor
EH12 120 A6
St Catherine's Pl EH9 121 E5
St Catherine's RC Prim Sch
EH16 151 B5
St Catherine's Wynd KY12 28 F3
St Clair Ave EH6 94 A3
St Clair Cres EH25 172 A3
St Clair Pl EH6 94 A3
St Clair Rd EH6 94 A3
St Clairs Ct KY3 35 A2
St Clairs Entry KY3 35 A2
St Clair St Edinburgh EH6 94 A3
Kirkcaldy KY1 17 E7
St Clair Terr EH10 120 F1
St Clement's Cres EH21 125 B4
St Clement's Gdns N
EH21 125 B4
St Clement's Gdns S
EH21 125 B4
St Clement's Terr EH21 125 B4
St Colme Ave KY3 49 A5
St Colme Cres KY3 49 B7
St Colme Dr KY11 48 D5
St Colme Rd KY11 48 D4
St Colme St EH3 228 B4
St Colm's Abbey★ KY3 49 B2
St Colm's Ed Ctr & Coll
EH3 93 B3
St Columba's RC High Sch
KY11 29 F3
St Columba's RC Prim Sch
EH48 141 E6
St Crispin's Pl FK1 60 B4
St Crispin's Specl Sch
EH16 121 E3
St Cuthbert's RC Prim Sch
EH14 120 D4
St Davids EH22 174 A5
St Davids Ave EH22 153 A2
St David's Bsns Pk KY11 48 A4
St David's Ct
Dalgety Bay KY11 48 A3
Larbert FK5 38 B1
St David's Dr KY11 48 A4
St Davids Gdns EH22 153 A1
St David's Pl EH3 228 A2
St David's RC High Sch
EH22 153 D5
St Davids RC Prim Sch 1
EH4 92 C5
St David's RC Prim Sch
EH22 153 C2
St Davids Terr EH22 153 A2
St David's Terr EH3 228 A2
St Enoch Cres EH54 143 B6
St Fillans Cres KY3 49 C8
St Fillans Gr KY3 49 C8
St Fillans Pl KY2 16 D7
St Fillans Rd KY2 16 D7
St Fillan's Terr EH10 121 A1
St Francis RC Prim Sch
FK2 60 A6
St Francis' RC Prim Sch
EH16 122 E4
St Gabriel's RC Prim Sch 6
EH32 96 F1
St George's Ct FK5 38 B1
St George's Sch EH12 120 E8
St Georges Sch for Girls
EH12 120 D7
St Germains EH32 98 B2
St Germains Cnr EH33 126 D7
St Germains Terr EH33 127 D6
St Giles Cathedral★ EH1 229 A3
St Giles Sq FK1 59 B6
St Giles St EH1 229 A3
St Giles Way FK1 59 B6
St Helen's Pl EH48 139 F5
Sainthill Ct EH39 54 A7
St James' Orch FK9 2 D1
St James Pl Bridgend EH49 86 F4
Kinghorn KY3 35 A2
St James' Pl EH1 229 A4
St James's Gdns EH26 191 E4
St James Sh Ctr EH1 229 A4
St James Sq EH1 229 A4
St James's View EH26 191 E4
St John Ogilvie RC Prim Sch
EH54 142 F6
St John's Ave
Edinburgh EH12 119 E6
Falkirk FK2 60 C6
Linlithgow EH49 84 F6
St John's Cres EH12 119 F6
St Johns Ct EH54 143 E4
St John's Ct Falkirk FK2 60 C6
Inverkeithing KY11 47 D3
St John's Dr KY12 29 C3
St John's Gate FK6 36 C2
St John's Gdns Denny FK6 36 C2
Edinburgh EH12 119 E6
St John's Gr FK6 36 C2
St John's Hill EH8 229 B2
St John's Hospl EH54 143 D4
St John's Pl
Dunfermline KY12 29 D3
Torphichen EH48 111 F5
St John's Prim Sch FK10 9 F6
St John's RC Prim Sch
Edinburgh EH15 123 A7
Rosyth KY11 46 F3
St John's Rd
Broxburn EH52 115 E4
Edinburgh EH12 119 E6
St John St Edinburgh EH8 229 B3
Spott EH42 106 C3
Stirling FK8 7 A8
St John's Terr EH12 119 E6
St John's Way EH51 63 F5
St John the Baptist RC Prim
Sch EH47 181 E6
St John Vianney Prim Sch 3
EH16 122 B1
St Joseph's Cotts EH33 126 D8
St Josephs RC Prim Sch
EH47 160 F5
St Joseph's RC Prim Sch
Bonnybridge FK4 58 B4
Edinburgh EH11 119 F3
Linlithgow EH49 84 F6
St Katharine's Brae EH16 151 A6
St Katharine's Cres EH16 151 A6
St Katharine's Loan
EH16 151 B5
St Kentigern Rd EH26 191 D6
St Kentigerns RC Acad
EH47 162 B7
St Kilda Cres KY2 16 F8
St Laurence Cres FK1 108 B6
St Lawrence EH41 129 E8
St Lawrence St KY11 29 C1
ST LEONARD'S 229 C1
St Leonard's EH8 121 E5
St Leonard's Bank EH8 229 C1
St Leonard's Crag EH8 229 C1
St Leonard's Ct KY3 35 A3
St Leonard's Hill EH8 229 B1
St Leonard's La EH8 229 B1
St Leonard's Pl
Dunfermline KY11 29 B1
Kinghorn KY3 34 F3
St Leonard's Prim Sch
KY11 29 B1
St Leonard's St
Dunfermline KY11 29 B2
Edinburgh EH8 229 B1
St Lukes RC Prim Sch
EH22 174 D5
St Magaret Wynd KY12 29 F6
St Magdalenes EH49 85 B7
St Margaret's Acad EH54 143 D3
St Margaret's Cave Mus★
KY12 28 F4
St Margaret's Cres FK2 61 E2
St Margarets Ct EH39 54 C7
St Margarets Dr KY12 29 B3
St Margaret's Dr EH48 139 E5
St Margarets Gdns FK2 61 D2
St Margaret's Pl EH9 121 C4
St Margaret's Prim Sch
Dunfermline KY11 29 C3
Redding FK2 61 D1
South Queensferry EH30 68 C1
St Margaret's RC Prim Sch
Cowie FK7 20 D7
Loanhead EH20 172 C8
St Margaret's Rd
Edinburgh EH9 121 B4
North Berwick EH39 54 C7
St Margaret's Sch EH16 122 A3
St Margaret St KY12 29 A3
St Margarets Well KY12 29 B5
St Marie's RC Prim Sch
KY2 17 D8
St Mark's La EH15 123 B8
St Mark's Pl EH15 123 B8
St Mark's RC Prim Sch
EH14 149 E7
St Martin's Ct EH41 130 C8
St Martin's Gate EH41 130 B8
St Martins La EH33 126 E6
St Martin's Pl EH41 130 C7
St Martin's RC Prim Sch
EH33 126 D6
St Mary's Cathedral★
EH2 228 A3
St Mary's Church★ EH41 130 B8
St Mary's Glebe KY1 17 C5
St Mary's (Leith) Prim Sch
EH6 94 B5
St Mary's Music Sch
EH12 120 F7
St Marys Pl FK3 61 E8
St Mary's Pl
Bathgate EH48 141 C5
Edinburgh EH15 123 C8
Kirkcaldy KY1 17 C5
St Mary's Place La EH15 123 C8
St Mary's Pleasance & Lady Kitty's Garden★ EH41 130 B8
St Mary's RC Cath★ EH1 229 A4
St Mary's RC Prim Sch
Bannockburn FK7 7 D2
Bathgate EH48 141 A6
Bo'ness EH51 64 A7
Bonnyrigg and Lasswade
EH19 173 B6
9 Edinburgh EH7 93 D2
Haddington EH41 130 A8
Polbeth EH55 163 F5
St Mary's Rd KY1 17 C5
St Mary's St EH1 229 B3
St Mary's Wynd 5 FK8 7 A8
St Matthew's Prim Sch
EH24 172 E2
St Michael's Ave EH21 124 C5
St Michael's Hospl EH49 85 C6
St Michaels La EH49 85 B7
St Michael's Wynd EH49 85 A7
St Modans Ct 13 FK1 60 B4
St Modan's High Sch FK7 7 F8
St Mungo's High Sch FK2 60 A6
St Mungo's RC Prim Sch
FK10 10 C5
St Mungo's View EH26 191 F5
St Mungo's Wynd FK10 10 A6
St Nicholas RC Prim Sch
EH52 115 C4
ST NINIANS 7 B4
St Ninian's Ave EH49 84 E8
St Ninian's Dr EH12 119 D7
St Ninians Prim Sch FK7 7 A4
St Ninian's Prim Sch EH7 94 C2
St Ninian's RC Prim Sch
EH54 144 A1
St Ninians Rd
Cambusbarron FK7 6 E5
Stirling FK8 7 B6
St Ninian's Rd
Edinburgh EH12 119 D7
Linlithgow EH49 84 F7
St Ninian's Row EH1 229 A4
St Ninian's Terr EH10 120 F1
St Ninians Way
Blackness EH49 65 E4
1 Musselburgh EH21 125 A6
St Ninian's Way EH49 84 F7
St Patrick's Prim Sch
ML7 179 F4
St Patrick Sq EH8 229 B1
St Patrick's RC Prim Sch
FK6 36 E3
St Patrick St EH8 229 B1
St Paul's Dr EH48 140 A5
St Paul's RC Prim Sch
EH53 144 F4
St Peter's Bldgs EH11 228 A1
St Peter's Ct KY11 47 D3
St Peter's Pl EH11 228 A1
St Peter's RC Sch EH10 121 B3
St Ronan's Terr EH10 121 A2
St Sarf's Pl KY1 18 A7
St Serfs Gr FK10 11 B4
St Serf's Pl FK10 4 B3
St Serf's Prim Sch FK10 4 B3
St Serf's RC Prim Sch
KY12 26 A2
St Serf's Rd FK10 4 B3
St Serf's Wlk FK12 4 E6
St Stephen Pl EH3 93 B2
St Stephen's Ct EH11 119 C2
St Stephen St EH3 93 B2
St Teresa Pl EH10 120 F4
St Thomas of Aquin's RC
High Sch EH3 228 C1
St Thomas Rd EH9 121 E3
St Thomas's Pl FK7 6 E6
St Thomas's Well FK7 6 D7
St Triduana's Chapel★
EH7 94 C1
St Triduana's Rest EH7 94 C2
St Valery Ct FK7 7 A4
St Valery Dr FK7 7 A4
St Vincent St EH3 93 B2
Salamanca Cres EH26 192 A8
Salamander Pl EH6 94 B5
Salamander St EH6 94 B5
Salamander Yds EH6 94 C5
Salen Loan ML7 180 B3
Salisbury Mews EH9 121 F5
Salisbury Pl EH9 121 E5
Salisbury Rd EH16 121 F5
Salisbury St KY2 17 B5
Salisbury View EH22 174 D6
Salisbury Wlk EH42 78 E1
Salmond Pl 4 EH7 94 A1
Salmon Dr FK1 59 E1
Salmon Inn Pk FK2 61 C2
Salmon Inn Rd FK2 61 D2
Saltcoats Dr FK3 61 E7
Saltcoats Farm Cotts
EH31 52 B1
Saltcoats Gdns EH54 164 E6
Saltcoats Rd
Grangemouth FK3 62 B8
Gullane EH31 52 A2
Saltersgate Sch EH22 153 D5
Salters' Gr EH22 153 C4
Salter's Rd EH22 153 D6
Salters' Rd
Dalkeith, Woodburn
EH22 153 C3
Pathhead EH37 177 A2
Salter's Rd EH21 125 A4
Salters' Terr EH22 153 C3
Saltire Gdns EH39 101 F7
Saltire Rd EH22 153 D4
Saltire St EH5 92 D7
Saltoun Hall EH34 157 C5
Saltoun Prim Sch EH34 157 E5
Saltpans KY11 45 B4
Salt Preston Pl EH32 96 F1
Salvage Rd KY11 46 C1
Salvesen Cres EH4 92 A5
Salvesen Gdns EH4 92 B5
Salvesen Gr EH4 92 B6
Salvesen Terr EH4 92 B6
Samoa Terr EH26 192 A8
SAMUELSTON 129 A2
Samuelston East Mains Cotts
EH41 129 A2
Sancta Maria Abbey★
EH41 132 E1
Sandeman Ct FK10 23 E4
Sanderling Way KY11 30 B5
Sanderson's Gr 2 EH33 126 D7
Sanderson's Wynd 1
EH33 126 D7
Sandersons Wynd Prim Sch
EH33 126 D7
Sanderson Terr KY2 15 B2
Sandford Gate KY1 17 B3
Sandford Gdns EH15 123 A8
Sandiland Dr EH53 144 B2
Sandilands KY11 45 D3
Sandpiper Dr
Dunfermline KY11 30 C2
Edinburgh EH6 93 D7
Sandpiper Gdns KY11 30 B1
Sandpiper Mdw FK10 10 D5
Sandpiper Rd EH6 93 D7
Sandport EH6 94 A6
Sandport Pl EH6 93 F5
Sandport St EH6 93 F6
Sandport Trad Est EH6 93 F6
Sands The EH41 130 B8
Sandwell Cres KY1 35 B6
Sandyford Ave EH49 84 A6
Sandyhill Ave ML7 180 A3
Sandy La EH31 51 F2
Sandyloan FK2 61 B4
Sandy Loan EH31 52 A2
Sandyloan Cres FK2 61 B3
Sandy Rd KY3 32 C5
Sandyvale Pl ML7 180 A3
Sang Pl KY1 17 B4
Sang Rd KY1 17 B4
Sarazen Ct EH54 143 B8
Sarazen Gn EH54 143 B8
Sarti Terr FK5 38 C3
Sauchenbush Rd KY2 16 F5
Sauchenford Smallholdings
FK7 20 A5
SAUCHIE 5 E1
Sauchiebank EH11 120 E6
Sauchie Ct FK7 7 F1
Sauchie St FK7 7 A2
Saughbank EH52 115 B5
Saughland Cotts EH37 197 F7
Saughs The EH22 174 A4
Saughton Ave EH11 120 C4
Saughton Cres EH12 120 B6
Saughton Gdns EH12 120 B6
Saughton Gr EH12 120 B6
SAUGHTONHALL 120 A6
Saughtonhall Ave EH12 120 C6
Saughtonhall Avenue W
EH12 120 B6
Saughtonhall Cir EH12 120 C6
Saughtonhall Cres EH12 120 B6
Saughtonhall Dr EH12 120 B6
Saughtonhall Gdns EH12 120 C6
Saughtonhall Gr EH12 120 C6
Saughtonhall Pl EH12 120 C6
Saughtonhall Terr EH12 120 C6

Saughton Loan EH12 120 B6
Saughton Mains Ave EH11 119 F3
Saughton Mains Bank EH11 120 A4
Saughton Mains Dr EH11 119 F3
Saughton Mains Gdns EH11 119 F4
Saughton Mains Gr EH11 120 A3
Saughton Mains Loan EH11 119 F3
Saughton Mains Pk EH11 119 F4
Saughton Mains Pl EH11 119 F3
Saughton Mains St EH11 120 A4
Saughton Mains Terr EH11 119 F4
Saughton Pk EH12 120 B6
Saughton Rd EH11 119 F3
Saughton Road N EH12 119 E5
Saughton Sports Complex EH11 120 B4
Saunders Ct KY1 17 B2
Saunders St
Edinburgh EH3 228 B4
Kirkcaldy KY1 17 B2
Savile Pl EH9 121 F3
Savile Terr EH9 121 F3
Sawers Ave FK6 36 D1
Saw Mill Gdns EH19 173 C5
Saw Mill Medway EH19 173 C5
Saxe Coburg Pl EH3 93 B2
Saxe Coburg St EH3 93 B2
Scarlett Pk EH21 125 B5
Schaw Ct FK10 5 D1
Schawpark Ave FK10 5 D1
Schaw Rd EH32 97 B1
Schiltron Way FK7 7 D3
Scholars' Brae KY3 50 E8
School Brae Bo'ness EH51 63 F8
Bonnyrigg and Lasswade EH18 152 A1
Dysart KY1 18 A7
Edinburgh EH4 91 B6
West Barns EH42 105 F8
School Gn
Bonnyrigg and Lasswade EH18 152 A1
Longniddry EH32 98 E5
Schoolhouse Ct ML11 201 B3
Schoolhouse Ind Est EH55 162 E2
School House Rd EH54 142 E5
School La Allanton ML7 198 B8
Bathgate EH48 141 B6
Cockenzie & Port Seton EH32 97 C4
Dalgety Bay KY11 47 F4
Menstrie FK11 4 A7
Mid Calder EH53 144 D4
South Queensferry EH30 68 B1
School Mews FK11 4 A7
School Pl EH52 114 F4
School Rd Aberlady EH32 71 C4
Broxburn EH52 115 D5
East Linton EH40 103 E7
Laurieston FK2 61 A3
Longridge EH47 161 C2
North Berwick EH39 54 D7
Redding FK2 61 B2
Tullibody FK10 4 B2
School Row KY12 28 C6
School St
Cowdenbeath KY4 13 D3
Shotts ML7 179 F4
School View Bo'ness EH51 64 A7
Redding FK2 61 C1
School Wlk FK5 38 D3
School Wynd KY1 17 B2
Schoolyard Ct EH25 172 A3
Sciennes EH9 121 E5
Sciennes Gdns EH9 121 E5
Sciennes Hill Pl 4 EH9 121 E5
Sciennes House Pl 3 EH9 121 E5
Sciennes Pl 1 EH9 121 E5
Sciennes Prim Sch EH9 121 D5
Sciennes Rd EH9 121 D5
Scion Ho FK9 2 D5
Sclandersburn Rd FK6 57 C8
Scobie Pl KY12 29 D4
Scollon Ave EH19 173 C8
Scone Gdns EH8 94 C1
Scotch Whisky Experience★ EH1 228 C2
Scotia Pl FK2 60 C5
Scotland Dr KY12 29 E4
Scotland St EH3 93 C2
Scotmill Way KY11 47 C3
Scots Mill Pl KY11 47 E4
Scotstoun Ave EH30 89 C7
Scotstoun Gn EH30 89 B8
Scotstoun Pk EH30 89 C7
Scotstoun Rd FK7 20 E7
Scott Ave FK2 61 E2
Scott Cres FK10 10 B5
Scott Ct Alva FK12 5 B6
Kelty/Cowdenbeath KY4 30 F6
Livingston EH54 144 C5
Scottish Agricultural Science Agency EH12 119 A8
Scottish Fire Service Coll EH31 52 B3
Scottish Korean War Memorial★ EH48 112 D6
Scottish Mining Mus The★ EH22 174 A4
Scottish Nat Gall of Modern Art★ EH4 120 E8
Scottish National Water Ski & Wakeboard Ctr The★ KY12 29 C7
Scottish Parliament The EH8 229 C3
Scottish Pol Coll FK10 23 F5
Scottish Prison Service Coll 6 FK2 82 C8
Scottish Railway Exhibition★ EH51 64 A8
Scottish Seabird Ctr★ EH39 54 C8
Scott Mon★ EH2 229 A3
Scott Pl EH47 181 F6
Scott Rd EH26 191 E7
Scott St Dunfermline KY12 28 E5
Grangemouth FK3 61 D5
Stirling FK8 2 A2
Scott Terr Bathgate EH48 141 C5
Falkirk FK2 39 B1
SCOUGHALL 56 C3
Scoughall Cotts EH39 56 D3
Seabegs Cres FK4 58 A4
Seabegs Pl FK4 57 F4
Seabegs Rd FK4 57 F4
Seabegs Wood Antonine Wall★ FK4 57 E3
SEACLIFF 56 B5
Seacliff EH39 56 A5
Seacot EH6 94 C4
Sea Eagle Cres 2 KY11 29 F2
SEAFIELD Edinburgh 94 D4
Livingston 142 C1
Loanhead 171 D6
Seafield Ave EH6 94 C4
Seafield Cl EH25 171 E6
Seafield Cres
Bilston EH25 171 E6
Dunbar EH42 78 A1
Kirkcaldy KY1 35 B8
Seafield Ct 3 FK1 59 F2
Seafield Gdns KY1 35 B8
Seafield Ind Est EH15 94 F2
Seafield Moor Rd EH10, EH25 171 C6
Seafield Pl
Dalgety Bay KY11 48 A2
Edinburgh EH6 94 C4
Seafield Prim Sch EH47 142 B1
Seafield Rd Bilston EH25 171 E6
Blackburn EH47 162 F8
Edinburgh EH6 94 D4
Kirkcaldy KY1 35 B8
Seafield Road E EH15 94 F3
Seafield Rows EH47 142 B1
Seafield St EH6 94 D4
Seafield Twrs KY1 35 B8
Seafield View
Kinghorn KY3 35 A3
Kirkcaldy KY1 35 B8
Seafield Way EH15 94 E3
Seaforth Dr EH4 92 C2
Seaforth Pl Burntisland KY3 50 D8
Kirkcaldy KY1 17 F8
5 Stirling FK8 7 B8
Seaforth Rd FK2 39 C1
Seaforth Terr
Bonnyrigg and Lasswade EH19 172 F6
4 Edinburgh EH4 92 C2
Sealcar St EH5 92 E7
Sealock Ct FK3 61 D5
Seals Craig View 4 KY3 33 D1
Sealstrand KY11 48 C4
Seamill Gdns 2 KY3 33 D1
Seaport St EH6 94 A5
Sea Rd EH42 77 F1
Seaside Pl KY3 49 C7
Seaton Pl FK1 60 D4
Seaview Cres EH15 123 E7
Seaview Pl EH51 63 F8
Seaview Terr
Edinburgh EH15 123 E7
Maddiston FK2 82 F6
Sea Wynd EH32 71 D5
Second Gait EH14 147 E8
Second St EH22 174 B5
Seco Pl KY4 13 D4
Sedgebank EH54 143 E6
Segal Pl KY12 28 F4
Seggarsdean Cres EH41 130 C7
Seggarsdean Ct EH41 130 C8
Seggarsdean Pk EH41 130 D8
Selkirk Ave KY4 13 C2
Selkirk Rd KY11 67 B8
Selm Pk EH54 144 A3
Selvage Pl KY11 47 A3
Selvage St KY11 47 A3
Semple St EH3 228 B2
SETON 97 E2
Seton Chapel★ EH32 97 F3
Seton Ct
Cockenzie & Port Seton EH32 97 E4
9 Tranent EH33 126 C5
Seton Dr FK7 7 C4
Seton Mains Cotts EH32 98 B3
Seton Pl
Cockenzie & Port Seton EH32 97 D4
Dalgety Bay KY11 48 D5
Edinburgh EH9 121 E5
Kirkcaldy KY2 16 D7
Seton Rd EH32 98 E5
Seton Steading EH32 98 B3
Seton Terr EH51 64 B7
Seton View EH32 97 E3
Seton Wynd EH32 97 E4
Seventh St EH22 174 B5
Shadepark Cres EH22 153 B4
Shadepark Dr EH22 153 B4
Shadepark Gdns EH22 153 B4
Shaftesbury Pk EH11 120 E4
Shaftesbury St FK10 10 A7
Shafto Pl EH51 63 F5
Shamrock St KY12 29 B5
Shandon Cres EH11 120 E4
Shandon Pl EH11 120 E4
Shandon Rd EH11 120 E4
Shandon St EH11 120 E4
Shandon Terr EH11 120 E4
Shandwick Pl EH2 228 A3
Shanks Ave FK6 57 E8
Shanks Rd EH47 161 B7
Shannon Dr FK1 59 F4
Shanter Way 2 EH16 122 A1
Sharpdale Loan EH16 122 B3
Sharp Terr FK3 61 C6
Shaw Ave EH48 139 F6
Shaw Cres KY5 14 B7
Shawfair Farm Cotts EH22 123 D2
Shaw Pl Armadale EH48 139 F6
Grangemouth FK3 61 C5
Mayfield EH22 174 D8
Shaw's Cres EH26 171 A1
Shaws Ct EH26 171 B1
Shaw's Pl EH7 93 E3
Shaw's St EH7 93 E3
Shaw St KY11 29 D2
Shaw's Terr EH7 93 E3
Shearer Sq KY11 29 B1
Shearwater Cres KY11 30 A2
Sheephousehill EH47 181 F6
Sheilings The FK10 4 B1
Sheiling The KY12 27 E1
Shepherd Cres KY3 50 D8
Shepherdlands Gr KY12 26 D7
Sherbrooke Rd KY11 46 D3
Sheriff Bank EH6 93 F5
Sheriff Brae EH6 93 F5
Sheriffhall Junc EH22 152 D5
Sheriffhall Mains Cotts EH22 152 E6
Sheriffmuirlands FK9 2 C3
Sheriffmuir Rd FK9 2 D7
Sheriff Pk EH6 93 F5
Sheriffs Pk EH49 85 E8
Sherriff Hall Cotts EH39 74 E8
Sherriff La FK5 38 F3
Sherwood Ave EH19 173 C6
Sherwood Cres EH19 173 C6
Sherwood Ct EH19 173 C6
Sherwood Dr EH19 173 C6
Sherwood Gr EH19 173 C6
Sherwood Ind Est EH19 173 C7
Sherwood Loan EH19 173 C6
Sherwood Pk EH19 173 C6
Sherwood Pl EH19 173 C6
Sherwood Terr EH19 173 C6
Sherwood View EH19 173 C6
Sherwood Way EH19 173 C6
Sherwood Wlk EH19 173 D5
Shetland Ct FK10 10 B5
Shetland Pl KY1 17 E7
Shiel Ct FK3 61 D4
SHIELDHILL 81 D6
Shieldhill Prim Sch FK1 81 D6
Shieldhill Rd FK2 82 A8
Shields Ct EH52 115 E5
Shields Rd KY11 29 E3
Shiel Gdns Falkirk FK2 39 C1
Shotts ML7 180 A3
Shiel Ho EH54 144 A5
Shiel Wlk EH54 144 A5
Shierlaw Gdns FK2 22 D4
Shillinghill Alloa FK10 10 B6
Humbie EH36 178 C1
Shinwell Pl KY11 46 E3
Shiphaugh Pl FK8 2 C1
Shire Way FK10 9 F6
Shirra's Brae Rd FK7 7 B4
Shoestanes Rd EH38 214 C1
Shoestanes Terr EH38 214 C2
SHORE 7 C8
Shore EH6 93 F5
Shore Pl EH6 94 A5
Shore Rd Aberdour KY3 49 C7
Airth FK2 22 D4
Dysart KY1 18 A6
South Queensferry EH30 68 B1
Stirling FK8 7 C8
Shore St EH42 78 E3
Shore The FK10 10 A5
Shorthope St EH21 124 C6
SHOTTS 179 F5
Shottsburn Rd ML7 158 A3
Shottskirk Rd ML7 179 C6
Shotts Rd
Fauldhouse EH47 181 C4
Harthill ML7 158 E2
Shotts Sta ML7 179 E4
Shrub Mount EH15 95 A1
Shrub Place La EH7 93 E3
Sibbald Pl EH54 143 B5
Sibbalds Brae EH48 140 D5
Sibbald View EH48 140 A5
Sidegate EH41 130 B8
Sidegate Mews EH41 130 B8
Sidehead Rd ML7 159 E5
Sidlaw Pl FK3 61 E5
Sidlaw St KY2 16 F7
Sienna Gdns EH9 121 E5
SIGHTHILL 119 D3
Sighthill Ave EH11 119 E2
Sighthill Bank EH11 119 D2
Sighthill Cres EH11 119 D1
Sighthill Ct EH11 119 D2
Sighthill Dr EH11 119 D1
Sighthill Gdns EH11 119 D2
Sighthill Gn EH11 119 D2
Sighthill Gr EH11 119 E2
Sighthill Ind Est EH11 119 B3
Sighthill Loan EH11 119 D2
Sighthill Neuk EH11 119 D2
Sighthill Pk EH11 119 E2
Sighthill Pl EH11 119 D2
Sighthill Prim Sch EH11 119 C1
Sighthill Rd EH11 119 D1
Sighthill Rise EH11 119 D1
Sighthill Sh Ctr EH11 119 D2
Sighthill St EH11 119 D1
Sighthill Terr EH11 119 D2
Sighthill View EH11 119 D1
Sighthill Wynd EH11 119 D2
Signal Station KY11 68 C5
Silk Ho 1 FK1 60 B5
Silverbarton Terr KY3 33 D1
Silverbirch Glade EH54 164 C7
SILVERBURN 190 E5
Silverburn Dr EH26 191 C6
Silverburn Gdns FK12 5 C7
Silverdale Rd FK2 82 E8
SILVERKNOWES 91 E5
Silverknowes Ave EH4 91 F4
Silverknowes Bank EH4 91 F4
Silverknowes Brae EH4 92 A4
Silverknowes Cres EH4 91 F4
Silverknowes Ct EH4 91 F4
Silverknowes Dell EH4 91 F4
Silverknowes Dr EH4 91 F4
Silverknowes Eastway EH4 91 F4
Silverknowes Gdns EH4 92 A4
Silverknowes Gn EH4 92 A4
Silverknowes Gr EH4 91 F5
Silverknowes Hill EH4 91 F4
Silverknowes Loan EH4 91 F4
Silverknowes Midway EH4 92 A4
Silverknowes Neuk EH4 92 A3
Silverknowes Parkway EH4 91 F5
Silverknowes Pl EH4 91 F5
Silverknowes Rd EH4 91 F5
Silverknowes Road E EH4 92 A4
Silverknowes Road S EH4 91 F3
Silverknowes Southway EH4 92 A4
Silverknowes Terr EH4 91 F4
Silverknowes View EH4 92 A4
Silver St Dunbar EH42 78 D2
Kincardine FK10 23 E3
Simon Sq EH8 229 B2
Simpson Cres EH48 141 C5
Simpson Dr FK2 83 A6
Simpson Parkway EH54 143 B2
Simpson Prim Sch EH48 141 B3
Simpson Rd EH52 116 B6
Simpson St FK1 59 E6
Simpson Wlk KY11 29 F1
Sinclair Cl EH11 120 E4
Sinclair Cres FK6 36 D1
Sinclair Ct Aberlady EH32 71 D4
Bannockburn FK7 7 E1
Sinclair Dr
Cowdenbeath KY4 13 B2
Fallin FK7 8 D4
Sinclair Gdns
Dunfermline KY12 29 B4
Edinburgh EH11 120 E5
Sinclair Pl
Edinburgh EH11 120 D5
Falkirk FK2 39 A1
SINCLAIRTOWN 17 F7
Sinclairtown Prim Sch KY1 17 F7
Sinclair Way EH54 143 D6
Singers Pl FK4 57 E5
Sir George Bruce Rd KY12 26 F7
Sir Harry Lauder Rd EH15 123 B8
Sir James Black Gait KY5 14 A8
Sir John Brown Pl KY11 46 F7
Sir John Graham Ct FK5 38 B1
Sirling Arcade 3 FK8 7 B7
Sir Robert Maule Pl FK10 23 E4
Sir Walter Scott Pend EH32 96 F2
Sir William Fraser Homes EH13 149 A7
Sir William Wallace Ct FK5 38 B3
Sivewright Ct FK10 23 E4
Sixth St EH22 174 B5
Skaithmuir Ave FK2 39 B3
Skaithmuir Cres FK2 39 B3
Skedsbush Cotts EH41 220 D5
Skelmorlie Pl FK5 38 F4
Skeltiemuir Ave EH19 173 A5
Skeltiemuir Ct EH19 173 A5
Skeltiemuir Gr EH19 173 B5
Skene St FK4 58 A6
Skibo Ct KY12 29 A3
Skibo Pl KY2 16 D5
SKINFLATS 39 F3
Skivo Wynd EH54 164 E4
Skye Ct FK3 61 D6
Skye Dr FK2 61 F1
Skye Rd KY11 29 E2
Skylark Rd KY11 47 A7
Skylaw Terr ML11 201 A1
Skythorn Way FK1 59 E2
Slaeside EH14 147 C1
SLAMANNAN 108 A6
Slamannan Prim Sch FK1 108 A7
Slamannan Rd
Avonbridge FK1 109 F6
Falkirk FK1 60 A2
Limerigg FK1 108 B2
SLATEFORD 120 C2
Slateford Gn EH14 120 D4
Slateford Rd EH14 120 D4
Slateford Sta EH14 120 C3
Sleigh Dr EH7 94 C2
Sleigh Gdns EH7 94 C2
Sligo St KY12 26 F7
Sloan St EH6 93 F3
Smallburn Pl FK3 61 E6
Small St KY5 14 A6
Smart Village Bsns Campus FK10 9 E7
SMEATON 17 C8
Smeaton Farm Cotts EH22 153 E8
Smeaton Gdns KY2 17 C6
Smeaton Gr EH21 124 D3
Smeaton Ind Site KY1 17 C7
Smeaton Rd KY1 17 D6
Smiddy Brae FK2 61 F4
Smiddy View FK7 6 D6
Smiddy Wynd Alva FK12 5 A6
East Linton EH40 103 E7
Newmills KY12 26 C1
Smileyknowes Ct EH39 54 A6
Smillie Terr FK9 2 B3
Smith Art Gallery & Mus★ FK8 7 A8
Smith Ave KY4 13 B3
Smithfield Loan FK10 9 E6
Smithfield Mdws FK10 9 E6
Smithfield St EH11 120 D5
Smith Pl FK6 36 D1
Smith's Pl EH6 93 F4
Smith St FK2 60 B7
Smith's Terr 3 KY1 17 C5
Smithy Brae EH27 145 E2
Smithy Green Ave EH22 152 B7
Smithy Row EH39 74 A3
Snab Brae EH51 63 D6
Snab La EH51 63 D7
Sneddon Pl FK2 22 E3
Snowdon Pl FK8 7 A6
Snowdon Place La FK7 7 A6
Society La EH55 163 D3
Society Pl EH55 163 D3
Society Rd EH30 67 F2
Solway Dr FK6 57 D7
Somerset Pl EH6 94 A4
Somers Pk 11 EH33 126 C5
Somerville Ave KY12 28 E4
Somerville Rd KY11 46 C2
Somerville Sq KY3 50 E8
Somerville St KY3 50 E8
Sommers Pk EH53 144 C2
Sommerville Gdns EH30 89 D7
Somnerfield Ave EH41 129 E8
Somnerfield Cres EH41 129 E8
Somnerfield Ct EH41 129 F8
Somnerfield Gr EH41 129 E8
Somnerfield Pk EH41 129 E8
Souillac Dr FK6 36 C1
Souter Way FK5 38 C4
South Acres KY12 27 D1
SOUTH ALLOA 9 F3
South Approach Rd FK2 23 B2
South Ave Blairhall KY12 26 A7
Maddiston FK2 83 B7
Southbank EH4 91 E4
Southbank Ct EH4 91 E4
South Bantaskine Dr FK1 60 A3
South Bantaskine Rd FK1 60 A3
South Barnton Ave EH4 91 E3
South Beechwood EH12 120 A6
South Belton Farm Cotts EH42 105 E7
South Brae FK2 83 A5
South Bridge EH1 229 A3
South Bridge St
Bathgate EH48 141 A6
Grangemouth FK3 40 C1
SOUTH BROOMAGE 38 D1
South Broomage Ave FK5 38 C1
South Castle Dr KY11 46 F6
South Charlotte St EH2 228 B3
South Clerk St EH8 229 B1
South College St EH1 229 A2
South Craigs Rd FK2 82 E7
South Cres
East Saltoun EH34 157 F4
Prestonpans EH32 97 A1
Southcroft FK12 4 F6
South Dewar St KY12 28 E4
South Doors EH32 97 C4
South Dr KY12 29 B3
South East Circus Pl EH3 228 B4
South East Cumberland Street La EH3 93 C2
South East Longridge Crofts EH47 161 E2
South Elixa Pl EH8 122 D8
Southerton Cres KY2 16 F3
Southerton Gdns KY2 16 F3
Southerton Rd KY2 16 F3
South Ettrick Rd EH10 120 F4

South Fergus Pl KY1 ... 17 B3
Southfield KY4 ... 13 C5
Southfield Ave ML7 ... 180 B4
Southfield Bank EH15 ... 122 F6
Southfield Cres
Shotts ML7 ... 180 B4
Stirling FK8 ... 7 A6
Southfield Ct EH42 ... 78 B2
Southfield Dr FK1 ... 108 A6
Southfield Farm Gr EH15 122 E7
Southfield Gardens E
EH15 ... 122 F7
Southfield Gardens W
EH15 ... 122 F6
Southfield Loan EH15 ... 122 F6
Southfield Pl EH15 ... 123 A8
Southfield Rd
Cousland EH22 ... 154 D5
Shotts ML7 ... 180 B4
Southfield Road E EH15 .. 122 F6
Southfield Road W EH15 . 122 E6
Southfield Sq EH15 ... 122 F6
Southfield Terr EH15 ... 122 F6
South Fort St EH6 ... 93 E5
South Gait EH39 ... 53 F7
South Gayfield La 3 EH7 . 93 E2
South Gillsland Rd EH10 . 120 F3
South Grange Ave EH32 ... 96 F1
South Gray's Cl EH1 ... 229 B3
South Gray St EH9 ... 121 F4
South Green Dr FK2 ... 22 E3
South Groathill Ave EH4 .. 92 C2
SOUTH GYLE ... 119 B4
South Gyle Access EH12 .. 119 C4
South Gyle Broadway
EH12 ... 119 B4
South Gyle Cres EH12 ... 119 B4
South Gyle Crescent La
EH12 ... 119 B4
South Gyle Gdns EH12 ... 119 B5
South Gyle Ind Est EH12 . 119 B4
South Gyle Loan EH12 ... 119 B5
South Gyle Mains EH12 ... 119 C5
South Gyle Pk EH12 ... 119 B4
South Gyle Pk EH12 ... 119 B5
South Gyle Rd EH12 ... 119 B5
South Gyle Sta EH12 ... 119 B5
South Gyle Wynd EH12 ... 119 C4
South Hamilton Rd 1
EH39 ... 54 A7
South Hill St KY3 ... 50 E8
South Hirst Rd ML7 ... 158 D3
SOUTHHOUSE ... 151 C5
Southhouse Ave EH17 ... 151 B5
Southhouse Brae EH17 ... 151 C5
Southhouse Broadway
EH17 ... 151 B4
Southhouse Cres EH17 ... 151 C4
Southhouse Dr EH17 ... 151 B5
Southhouse Gdns EH17 ... 151 B4
Southhouse Gr EH17 ... 151 B4
Southhouse Loan EH17 ... 151 B5
Southhouse Pl EH17 ... 151 B5
Southhouse Rd EH17 ... 151 B4
Southhouse Sq EH17 ... 151 B5
Southhouse Terr EH17 ... 151 C5
Southhouse Wlk EH17 ... 151 B5
South Kersebonny Steading
FK8 ... 6 C7
South Knowe KY4 ... 30 E5
South Larch Rd KY11 ... 29 F4
South Lauder Rd EH9 ... 121 E4
South Laverockbank Ave
EH5 ... 93 C6
Southlawn Ct EH4 ... 91 E4
South Learmonth Ave 4
EH4 ... 92 F1
South Learmonth Gdns 2
EH4 ... 92 F1
SOUTH LEITH ... 94 A5
South Loanhead KY11 ... 45 E3
South Loch Pk EH48 ... 141 A6
South Lodge Ave EH53 ... 144 C2
South Lorimer Pl EH32 ... 97 C3
South Lorne Pl 1 EH6 ... 93 F3
South Lumley St FK3 ... 61 D8
South Mains FK7 ... 9 B1
South Marshall St FK3 ... 61 D7
South Maybury EH12 ... 119 A6
South Mellis Pk EH8 ... 122 E8
South Melville La 4 FK1 .. 60 B5
South Middleton EH52 ... 115 A3
South Mid St EH48 ... 141 B6
South Morningside Prim Sch
EH10 ... 121 A1
South Morton St EH15 ... 123 C7
South Oswald Rd EH9 ... 121 D3
Southouse Cl EH17 ... 151 B4
Southouse Crossway
EH17 ... 151 B4
South Overgate KY3 ... 35 A3
South Oxford St EH8 ... 121 F5
Southpark Pl EH54 ... 143 B4
South Parrotshot EH15 ... 123 B5
South Philpingstone La
EH51 ... 64 C7
South Pilmuir Rd FK10 ... 11 A4
South Pk Armadale EH48 .. 139 F4
Edinburgh EH6 ... 93 D6
South Pleasance Ave FK1 . 60 B4
SOUTH QUEENSFERRY ... 68 B2
South Rd
Fauldhouse EH47 ... 181 E7
Grangemouth FK3 ... 62 B5
South Roundall KY11 ... 45 E3
South Row
Charlestown KY11 ... 45 B4
Kirkcaldy KY1 ... 17 E8
South St Andrew St EH2 . 229 A4
South St David St EH2 ... 229 A3
South Scotstoun EH30 ... 89 C7
South Seton Pk EH32 ... 97 D4
South Shore Rd FK3 ... 41 B2
SOUTH SIDE ... 229 A1
South Sloan St EH6 ... 93 F3
South St Armadale EH48 ... 139 F5
Bo'ness EH51 ... 63 F8
Cambus FK10 ... 9 B8
Cowdenbeath KY4 ... 13 C2
Dalkeith EH22 ... 153 A3
Dunbar EH42 ... 78 B2
Lochgelly KY5 ... 14 B6
Musselburgh EH21 ... 124 B6
Stirling FK9 ... 2 D1
South Steil EH11 ... 120 E1
South Trinity Rd EH5 ... 93 B5
South View Burntisland KY3. 50 F8
Prestonpans EH32 ... 97 A1
Stenhousemuir FK5 ... 38 D1
South Village EH53 ... 144 C6
South West Cumberland
Street La EH3 ... 93 C2
Soutra Aisle* EH37 ... 224 D5
Sovereign Ct EH48 ... 140 B5
Spalding Cres EH22 ... 153 B3
Spa Pl EH15 ... 95 B1
Speedwell Ave EH22 ... 152 A8
Spence Ave KY3 ... 33 F2
Spencerfield Rd KY11 ... 47 D2
Spencerfield Steadings
KY11 ... 47 E3
Spencer Pl Edinburgh EH5 .. 93 B6
Kirkcaldy KY1 ... 17 F6
Spence St Bonnybridge FK4 . 58 A6
Edinburgh EH16 ... 121 F5
Spens La KY11 ... 46 C1
Spey Ct Grangemouth FK3 ... 61 D5
Stirling FK7 ... 7 C5
Spey Dr EH54 ... 144 B4
Spey St EH7 ... 93 E3
Spey Street La EH7 ... 93 E3
Spey Terr EH7 ... 93 E3
Spier's Pl EH6 ... 93 F5
Spilmersford View EH34 . 157 A6
Spinkhill FK2 ... 60 F2
Spinnaker Way KY11 ... 47 F2
Spinner's Ct KY12 ... 27 D1
Spinneys The KY11 ... 48 C3
Spinney The EH17 ... 151 D6
Spitfire Way FK3 ... 61 F5
SPITTAL ... 99 D7
Spittalfield Cres
Edinburgh EH8 ... 229 B1
Inverkeithing KY11 ... 47 C2
Spittalfield Rd KY11 ... 47 C2
Spittal Hill FK9 ... 2 C4
Spittal St Edinburgh EH3 ... 228 B2
Stirling FK8 ... 7 A8
SPOTT ... 106 C4
Spott Ave EH42 ... 106 D3
Spottiswoode Gdns
EH53 ... 144 C2
Spottiswoode Rd EH9 ... 121 C5
Spottiswoode St EH9 ... 121 C5
Spott Loan EH42 ... 106 C3
Spott Rd EH42 ... 78 E1
Spott Road Ind Est EH42 .. 78 E1
Sprig Way ML7 ... 159 E5
Springbank Gdns FK2 ... 60 C5
Springbank Rd
Shotts ML7 ... 179 D6
Stirling FK7 ... 7 C6
Springbank Terr KY12 ... 29 A6
Springfield EH6 ... 93 F4
Springfield Cres
3 North Berwick EH39 ... 54 A7
Queensferry EH30 ... 67 F1
Springfield Ct EH49 ... 85 D8
Springfield Dr FK1 ... 59 F5
Springfield Gdns 2 EH39 . 54 A7
Springfield La 3 EH6 ... 93 F4
Springfield Lea EH30 ... 67 F1
Springfield Pl
Gorebridge EH23 ... 195 D7
Queensferry EH30 ... 67 F1
Roslin EH25 ... 172 A4
Springfield Prim Sch
EH49 ... 85 D8
Springfield Rd Alloa FK10 .. 10 C7
Denny FK6 ... 36 F2
Linlithgow EH49 ... 85 C7
Penicuik EH26 ... 208 E6
Queensferry EH30 ... 67 F1
Stirling FK7 ... 7 C5
Springfield St EH6 ... 93 F4
Springfield Terr
Queensferry EH30 ... 67 F1
West Barns EH42 ... 77 F1
Springfield View EH30 ... 68 A1
Spring Gdns EH8 ... 94 A1
Springhead Rd ML7 ... 198 A8
SPRINGHILL ... 180 B2
Springhill Brae KY4 ... 30 F6
Springhill & Leadloch Rd ML7,
EH47 ... 180 E2
Springhill Rd ML7 ... 180 B3
Springhill View ML7 ... 180 B3
Springkerse Bsns Pk FK7 .. 7 E7
Springkerse Ind Est FK7 ... 7 D7
Springkerse Rd FK7 ... 7 D6
Springkerse Rdbt FK7 ... 7 E7
Springkerse Ret Pk FK7 ... 7 E6
Springvalley Gdns EH10 .. 121 A3
Springvalley Terr EH10 ... 121 A3
Springwell Pl EH11 ... 120 F6
Springwood
Dunfermline KY11 ... 47 A7
Stirling FK7 ... 6 F5
Springwood Ave FK8 ... 6 F5
Springwood Pk EH16 ... 151 B8
Sprinty Ave EH35 ... 155 D7
Sprinty Dr EH35 ... 155 D7
Sprotwell Terr FK10 ... 5 D1
Spruce Dr EH47 ... 161 C6
Spruce Gr
Dunfermline KY11 ... 46 D8
Livingston EH54 ... 144 B5
Spylaw Ave EH13 ... 148 F7
Spylaw Bank Rd EH13 ... 149 A7
Spylaw Ho EH13 ... 149 A6
Spylaw Pk EH13 ... 148 F7
Spylaw Rd EH10 ... 120 F4
Spylaw St EH13 ... 149 B7
Square The
Cockburnspath TD13 ... 218 F4
Danderhall EH22 ... 152 B8
East Linton EH40 ... 103 E7
Fallin FK7 ... 8 D4
Gifford EH41 ... 220 F7
Kirkliston EH29 ... 89 B1
Newtongrange EH22 ... 174 B5
Penicuik EH26 ... 191 F4
Spott EH42 ... 106 C3
Torphichen EH48 ... 111 F5
Sraehouse Wynd ML8 ... 215 B1
Stable Ct EH42 ... 78 E2
Stable La Edinburgh EH10 .. 121 A4
West Calder EH55 ... 164 A5
Stable Rd ML7 ... 180 A4
Stables Rd KY11 ... 46 C1
Stables The
Newtongrange EH22 ... 174 A8
Pathhead EH37 ... 175 E8
Stadium House Bsns Ctr
EH54 ... 143 D2
Staffa EH54 ... 142 E5
Staffa Pl FK1 ... 60 B2
Stafford St EH3 ... 228 A3
Stair Pk Edinburgh EH12 ... 120 C7
North Berwick EH39 ... 54 B6
Tranent EH33 ... 126 B7
Stance Pl FK5 ... 38 C4
Standalane FK10 ... 23 E3
STANDBURN ... 82 D2
Standhill Ct EH48 ... 140 F4
Standhill Rd EH48 ... 140 F3
Standingstane Rd EH30 ... 89 E5
Standing Stone Wlk KY11 . 29 E1
Standrigg Ave FK2 ... 82 C7
Standrigg Gdns FK2 ... 82 D7
Standrigg Rd FK2 ... 82 B6
STANE ... 180 A3
Stanedykehead EH16 ... 150 F6
Stane Gr ML7 ... 180 A3
Stane Prim Sch ML7 ... 180 A4
Stane Rd ML7 ... 180 A2
Stanhope Pl EH12 ... 120 E7
Stanhope St EH12 ... 120 E7
Stanistone Rd ML8 ... 215 A2
Stankards Rd EH52 ... 114 F3
Stanley Ave EH25 ... 171 E6
Stanley Dr
Bridge of Allan FK9 ... 2 B7
Harthill ML7 ... 160 A6
Stanley Gdns FK2 ... 82 F6
Stanley Pk KY1 ... 17 B5
Stanley Pl Dunbar EH42 ... 78 C3
Edinburgh EH7 ... 94 A1
Ormiston EH35 ... 155 E7
Stanley Rd Edinburgh EH6 .. 93 D6
Gullane EH31 ... 52 A2
Harthill ML7 ... 160 A6
Stanley St EH15 ... 123 A7
Stanley Terr Alva FK12 ... 5 A6
Oakley KY12 ... 27 A6
Stanton Ave FK10 ... 9 F6
Stanwell St EH6 ... 93 E4
Stapeley Ave EH7 ... 94 E2
Starbank Rd EH5 ... 93 C6
Starch Mill EH41 ... 130 C8
Stark Ave FK1 ... 59 D5
Stark's Brae EH51 ... 64 A7
Stark's Park (Raith Rovers
FC) KY1 ... 17 A1
Starlaw Ave EH48 ... 141 E5
Starlaw Bsns Pk EH54 .. 142 D4
Starlaw Cres EH48 ... 141 F5
Starlaw Gdns EH48 ... 141 F5
Starlaw Rd EH47 ... 142 C3
Starlaw Terr EH48 ... 141 E5
Starlaw West Rdbt EH47 . 142 A3
Starlaw Wlk EH48 ... 141 F5
Starley Hall Sch KY3 ... 50 A8
Starryshaw Rd ML7 ... 179 E6
Station Ave EH41 ... 129 F8
Station Brae
Edinburgh EH15 ... 123 A7
Kinghorn KY3 ... 34 F2
Station Ct Addiewell EH55 . 162 E2
Haddington EH41 ... 129 F8
North Berwick EH39 ... 54 B7
Station Hill EH39 ... 54 B7
Station Loan EH14 ... 147 C3
Station Mews EH27 ... 145 D3
Station Pl KY3 ... 49 C7
Station Rd Addiewell EH55 162 E2
Armadale EH48 ... 139 F3
Bannockburn FK7 ... 7 E1
Blackridge EH48 ... 138 D2
Bridge of Allan FK9 ... 1 F8
Brightons FK2 ... 61 E1
Station Rd *continued*
Broxburn EH52 ... 115 E5
Cambus FK10 ... 4 B1
Cowdenbeath KY4 ... 13 D4
Cowie FK7 ... 20 D6
Dalkeith EH22 ... 152 E2
Dirleton EH39 ... 53 D3
Dunbar EH42 ... 78 E2
Dysart KY1 ... 18 A7
East Linton EH40 ... 103 E7
Edinburgh EH12 ... 119 E6
Gifford EH41 ... 220 F7
Gorebridge EH23 ... 195 C7
Grangemouth FK3 ... 40 D1
Gullane EH31 ... 52 B2
Haddington EH41 ... 130 A8
Kincardine FK10 ... 23 D4
Kirkliston EH29 ... 89 B1
Kirknewton EH27 ... 145 D3
Linlithgow EH49 ... 85 A7
Loanhead EH20 ... 172 C8
Lochgelly KY5 ... 14 B8
Longcroft FK4 ... 57 B4
Musselburgh EH21 ... 124 B5
Newtongrange EH22 ... 174 A5
North Berwick EH39 ... 54 B7
Oakley KY12 ... 26 F6
Prestonpans EH32 ... 126 A8
Ratho Station EH28 ... 117 C5
Roslin EH25 ... 172 A3
Shotts ML7 ... 179 E4
Slamannan FK1 ... 108 B6
South Queensferry EH30 ... 68 C1
Stirling FK8 ... 7 B8
Uphall EH52, EH54 ... 114 F3
West Calder EH55 ... 163 D3
Whitecross EH49 ... 83 F6
Winchburgh EH52 ... 88 A3
Station Row
Macmerry EH33 ... 127 C5
Slamannan FK1 ... 108 B5
Station Terr EH29 ... 89 B1
Station View EH30 ... 89 D8
Station Yd KY3 ... 35 A2
Staunton Rise EH54 ... 164 D8
Steadings Cres EH42 ... 106 D8
Steadings Gdns EH42 ... 106 C8
Steadings The Airth FK2 ... 21 E5
Fallin FK7 ... 8 A4
Whitecross EH49 ... 84 B8
Steading The
Longniddry EH32 ... 98 C2
Mid Calder EH53 ... 144 B3
Steads' Pl EH6 ... 93 F4
Steel Cres FK6 ... 36 F1
Steele Ave EH22 ... 174 F6
Steel Gr KY12 ... 26 D7
Steel's Pl EH10 ... 121 B3
Steelyard The 4 EH48 ... 141 A6
Steeple Cres KY11 ... 48 A3
Steil Gr EH33 ... 126 D5
Steils The EH11 ... 120 E1
Stein's Pl KY4 ... 13 C3
Stein Sq FK7 ... 7 F1
STENHOUSE ... 120 B4
Stenhouse Ave EH11 ... 120 B4
Stenhouse Ave W EH11 .. 120 A4
Stenhouse Cotts EH11 ... 120 A3
Stenhouse Cres EH11 ... 120 B4
Stenhouse Cross EH11 ... 120 A4
Stenhouse Dr
Burntisland KY3 ... 33 C1
Edinburgh EH11 ... 120 A4
Stenhouse Gdns EH11 ... 120 A4
Stenhouse Gdns N EH11 .. 120 A4
Stenhouse Gr EH11 ... 120 A4
Stenhouse Mill Cres
EH11 ... 120 B3
Stenhouse Mill La EH11 .. 120 B3
Stenhouse Mill Wynd
EH11 ... 120 B3
STENHOUSEMUIR ... 38 D3
Stenhousemuir Prim Sch
FK5 ... 38 D3
Stenhouse Pl E EH11 ... 120 A4
Stenhouse Pl W EH11 ... 120 A4
Stenhouse Prim Sch 1
EH11 ... 120 A4
Stenhouse Rd
Edinburgh EH11 ... 120 A3
Stenhousemuir FK2 ... 38 F2
Stenhouse St E EH11 ... 120 A4
Stenhouse St KY4 ... 13 B4
Stenhouse Street W
EH11 ... 119 F4
Stenhouse Terr EH11 ... 120 B4
Stennis Gdns EH17 ... 151 C7
STENTON ... 104 E1
Stenton Loan EH42 ... 133 E8
Stenton Prim Sch EH42 .. 104 E1
Stenton Rd EH42 ... 105 F8
Stephen Pl KY5 ... 14 B8
Stephens Croft FK2 ... 59 F8
Stephen's Dr KY11 ... 47 C3
Steps St FK5 ... 38 E3
Steuart Rd FK9 ... 1 F7
Stevenlaw's Cl EH1 ... 229 A3
Stevenson Ave
Edinburgh EH11 ... 120 C5
Polmont FK2 ... 61 D1
Stevenson Coll EH11 ... 119 C3
Stevenson Ct
Bridge of Allan FK9 ... 2 A5
Falkirk FK2 ... 39 B1
Livingston EH54 ... 144 C5
Longniddry EH32 ... 98 D4
Stevenson Dr EH11 ... 120 B4
Stevenson Gr EH11 ... 120 C5
Stevenson La EH22 ... 174 B4
Stevenson Pk EH32 ... 98 D4
Stevenson Pl EH18 ... 172 D6
Stevenson Rd
Edinburgh EH11 ... 120 C5
Penicuik EH26 ... 171 B1
Stevenson St FK3 ... 61 D5
Stevenson Terr
Bathgate EH48 ... 141 C5
Edinburgh EH11 ... 120 C5
Stevenson Way EH32 ... 98 D4
Stewart Ave Bo'ness EH51 .. 63 F8
Currie EH14 ... 147 E3
Linlithgow EH49 ... 84 E6
Stenhousemuir FK2 ... 39 A2
Stewart Clark Ave EH30 ... 89 C8
Stewart Cres Currie EH14 . 147 E4
Lochgelly KY5 ... 14 A8
Stewart Ct EH55 ... 163 D2
Stewart Dr EH47 ... 160 F7
Stewartfield EH6 ... 93 D4
Stewartfield Cres EH52 ... 115 F5
Stewartfield Rd EH52 ... 115 F6
Stewart Gdns EH14 ... 147 E4
Stewart Gr
Danderhall EH22 ... 152 A8
Harthill ML7 ... 159 F5
Stewart Pk EH22 ... 154 D5
Stewart Pl Currie EH14 ... 147 E3
Kirkliston EH29 ... 89 B2
Stewart Rd Currie EH14 ... 147 E3
Falkirk FK2 ... 60 C5
Stewart's Melville Coll
EH4 ... 92 F1
Stewart Sq FK8 ... 2 A2
Stewart St Bonnybridge FK4 . 57 F5
Cambusbarron FK7 ... 6 D6
Dysart KY1 ... 18 B8
Townhill KY12 ... 29 C7
West Calder EH55 ... 163 D3
Stewart Terr
Edinburgh EH11 ... 120 E5
South Queensferry EH30 ... 68 B1
Stewart Way EH54 ... 143 C6
STIRLING ... 7 C8
Stirling Bridge* FK8 ... 2 B2
Stirling Bsns Ctr FK8 ... 7 B6
Stirling Castle* FK8 ... 7 A8
Stirling Ent Pk FK7 ... 7 C7
Stirling High Sch FK8 ... 7 A4
Stirling Pl FK7 ... 20 C3
Stirling Rd Alloa FK10 ... 9 E8
Alva FK12 ... 4 F7
Edinburgh EH5 ... 93 B6
Fallin FK7 ... 8 C4
Kirkliston EH29 ... 89 A2
Larbert, North Broomage
FK5 ... 38 A3
Larbert, South Broomage FK2,
FK5 ... 59 C8
Torwood FK5 ... 37 E5
Tullibody FK10 ... 4 B3
Stirling Royal Infmy FK8 ... 7 B5
Stirling St Alva FK12 ... 5 A7
Denny, Dunipace FK6 ... 36 D4
Denny FK6 ... 36 E2
Stirling Sta FK8 ... 7 B8
Stobhill Prim Sch EH23 . 195 D8
Stobhill Rd EH23 ... 174 B3
Stobie Pl KY12 ... 26 F7
Stobs Pl KY2 ... 16 C7
STOCKBRIDGE ... 93 A2
Stockbridge Prim sch
EH3 ... 93 B2
Stockbridge Ret Pk EH49 . 84 D6
Stone Ave EH22 ... 174 D6
Stonebank EH54 ... 143 E6
Stone Cres EH22 ... 174 D6
Stonedyke Cres ML8 ... 215 A3
Stonedyke Rd ML8 ... 215 B3
Stoneheap Crofts EH47 .. 182 E8
Stonelaws Cotts EH40 ... 75 A6
Stone Pl EH22 ... 174 D6
STONEYBANK ... 124 B4
Stoneybank Ave EH21 ... 124 B4
Stoneybank Cres EH21 ... 124 B4
Stoneybank Ct EH21 ... 124 A5
Stoneybank Dr EH21 ... 124 A5
Stoneybank Gardens N
EH21 ... 124 B5
Stoneybank Gardens S
EH21 ... 124 B5
Stoneybank Gdns EH21 ... 124 A5
Stoneybank Gr EH21 ... 124 B4
Stoneybank Pl EH21 ... 124 B4
Stoneybank Rd EH21 ... 124 B4
Stoneybank Terr EH21 ... 124 B4
STONEYBURN ... 162 C2
Stoneyburn Prim Sch
EH47 ... 162 C3
Stoneycroft Rd EH30 ... 68 C1
Stoneyflatts EH30 ... 89 A8
Stoneyflatts Cres EH30 ... 89 A8
Stoneyflatts Pk EH30 ... 89 A8
Stoneyhill Ave EH21 ... 124 A5
Stoneyhill Cres EH21 ... 124 A5
Stoneyhill Ct EH21 ... 124 A5
Stoneyhill Dr EH21 ... 124 A5
Stoneyhill Farm Rd EH21 124 B5
Stoneyhill Gdns 3 EH21 . 124 A5
Stoneyhill Gr EH21 ... 124 A5
Stoneyhill Pl EH21 ... 124 A5
Stoneyhill Prim Sch
EH21 ... 124 A5
Stoneyhill Rd EH21 ... 124 A5
Stoneyhill Rise EH21 ... 124 A5
Stoneyhill Steading
EH21 ... 124 B5

Stoneyhill Terr EH21 ... 124 A5
Stoneyhill Wynd 1 EH21 ... 124 A5
Stoneypath Cotts EH42 ... 133 C3
STONEYWOOD ... 36 C2
Stoneywood Pk FK6 ... 36 B2
Stony Brae FK10 ... 24 C2
Stories Pk EH40 ... 103 E7
Strachan Ct EH51 ... 63 D7
Strachan Gdns EH4 ... 92 A2
Strachan Rd EH4 ... 92 A2
Strachan St FK1 ... 59 E4
STRAITON ... 151 A2
Straiton Mains EH20 ... 151 A1
Straiton Park Cvn Site EH20 ... 150 F1
Straiton Park Way EH20 ... 151 A2
Straiton Pk EH20 ... 151 A1
Straiton Pl EH15 ... 123 B8
Straiton Pond Nature Reserve* EH20 ... 151 C2
Straiton Rd
Loanhead EH20 ... 171 F8
Straiton EH20 ... 151 A2
Strand Dr EH48 ... 140 F1
Strang Pl FK5 ... 38 B2
Strang's Pl FK1 ... 81 F5
Strathallan Ct FK9 ... 2 A6
Strathallan Dr KY2 ... 16 E5
Strathallan Prim Sch KY2 16 E4
Strathallan Rd FK9 ... 2 A6
Strathalmond Ct EH4 ... 90 F3
Strathalmond Gn EH4 ... 90 F3
Strathalmond Pk EH4 ... 90 F3
Strathalmond Rd EH4 ... 90 F3
Strathavon Terr EH48 ... 110 F5
Strathbeg Dr KY11 ... 47 F3
Strathbrock Pl
Broxburn EH52 ... 115 E5
Uphall EH52 ... 114 F4
Strathearn Ct
Grangemouth FK3 ... 61 E8
West Barns EH42 ... 77 F1
Strathearn Pl EH9 ... 121 B4
Strathearn Rd
Edinburgh EH9 ... 121 C4
North Berwick EH39 ... 53 F7
Strathesk Gr EH26 ... 192 A6
Strathesk Pl EH26 ... 192 A6
Strathesk Prim Sch EH26 ... 192 A6
Strathesk Rd EH26 ... 192 A6
Strathfillan Rd EH9 ... 121 C4
Strathkinnes Rd KY2 ... 17 A4
Strathlachlan Ave ML8 ... 215 A1
Strathlogie EH48 ... 110 F5
Strathmiglo Pl FK5 ... 38 F4
Strathmore Cres FK9 ... 2 A3
Strathmore Dr
Dunfermline KY12 ... 29 D5
Stirling FK9 ... 2 A3
Strathmore St KY3 ... 34 F3
Strathyre Dr EH47 ... 162 C2
Strathyre Pl Falkirk FK1 ... 60 A1
Stoneyburn EH47 ... 162 C2
Strawberry Bank
Dalkeith EH22 ... 152 E1
Linlithgow EH49 ... 85 A6
Streets Pl KY12 ... 29 D7
Stripehead 3 FK10 ... 10 B6
Striven Dr FK2 ... 39 C1
Striven Pl KY2 ... 16 E8
Stromness Gdns EH54 ... 164 D6
Strowan Rd FK3 ... 61 F7
Strowan Sq FK3 ... 61 F7
Struan Dr KY11 ... 47 B3
Struan Pl KY11 ... 47 B3
Struan Wynd EH32 ... 97 B2
Strude Howe FK12 ... 5 B7
Strude Mill FK12 ... 5 B7
Strude St FK12 ... 5 B7
Stuart Cres EH12 ... 119 B8
Stuart Ct Bathgate EH48 ... 141 C5
Edinburgh EH12 ... 119 B8
Stuart Gn EH12 ... 119 B8
Stuart Gr FK3 ... 61 B6
Stuart Pk EH12 ... 119 B8
Stuart Pl KY4 ... 13 D5
Stuart Rd KY11 ... 46 C2
Stuart Sq EH12 ... 119 B8
Stuart Terr EH48 ... 141 B5
Stuart Wynd EH12 ... 119 B8
Styles Pl FK1 ... 59 F2
Succoth Ave EH12 ... 120 D8
Succoth Ct EH12 ... 120 D8
Succoth Gdns EH12 ... 120 D8
Succoth Pk EH12 ... 120 D8
Succoth Pl EH12 ... 120 D8
Suffolk Rd EH16 ... 121 F3
Suffolk Rd La EH16 ... 122 A3
Suffolk Road La EH16 ... 121 F3
Sugarhouse Cl EH8 ... 229 B3
Suilven Hts FK2 ... 61 A3
Sultery Bldg KY11 ... 45 B4
Summer Bank EH3 ... 93 C2
Summerfield Gdns EH6 ... 94 B4
Summerfield Pk EH42 ... 78 B2
Summerfield Pl EH6 ... 94 B4
Summerfield Rd EH42 ... 78 C1
SUMMERFORD ... 59 D4
Summerford FK1 ... 59 D4
Summerford Gdns FK1 ... 59 D4
Summerford Rd FK1 ... 59 D4
Summerhall EH8 ... 229 B1
Summerhall Cres EH9 ... 229 B1
Summerhall Pl EH9 ... 229 B1
Summerhall Sq EH9 ... 229 B1
Summerlee EH32 ... 96 E1
Summer Pl EH3 ... 93 C3
Summerside Pl EH6 ... 93 D5
Summerside St EH6 ... 93 D5
Summertrees Ct EH16 ... 122 B1
Summerville Ct EH54 ... 144 A8
Suna Path ML7 ... 180 B3
Sunart Pl FK3 ... 61 D5
Sunbury Mews 4 EH4 ... 120 F8
Sunbury Pl EH4 ... 120 F8
Sunbury St EH4 ... 120 F8
Sundew Glade EH54 ... 164 C8
Sunningdale La KY12 ... 28 D6
Sunnybank ML7 ... 179 F6
Sunnybank Pl 3 EH7 ... 94 B1
Sunnybank Rd FK7 ... 7 B3
Sunnybank Terr 2 EH7 ... 94 B1
Sunnybrae ML11 ... 201 A1
Sunnybrae Terr FK2 ... 82 F6
Sunnydale Dr EH48 ... 138 E3
Sunnydale Rd EH48 ... 138 E3
Sunnylaw Pl FK1 ... 59 F3
Sunnylaw Rd FK9 ... 2 A8
Sunnyside Edinburgh EH7 ... 94 A2
Stirling FK7 ... 7 A4
Stoneyburn EH47 ... 162 B2
Sunnyside Ave
Bathgate EH48 ... 141 C7
Grangemouth FK2 ... 82 C7
Sunnyside Cotts
East Linton EH41 ... 103 E4
Grangemouth FK2 ... 82 D7
Sunnyside Ct Alloa FK10 ... 10 B7
Cowdenbeath KY4 ... 13 D4
Grangemouth FK2 ... 82 C8
Sunnyside Dr FK2 ... 82 C7
Sunnyside Pl Lochgelly KY5 14 A6
Stirling FK9 ... 2 A4
Sunnyside Prim Sch FK10 10 B7
Sunnyside Rd Alloa FK10 ... 10 B7
Falkirk FK1 ... 59 F5
Grangemouth FK2 ... 82 D7
Sunnyside St FK1 ... 59 E6
Surcoat Loan FK7 ... 7 E3
Surgeon's Hall Mus* EH1 ... 229 B2
Sutherland Ave Alloa FK10 . 10 C7
Stirling FK8 ... 2 C1
Sutherland Cres EH48 ... 141 B5
Sutherland Dr FK6 ... 57 D8
Sutherland Ho 2 EH3 ... 93 C2
Sutherland Pl KY1 ... 17 F7
Sutherland St EH12 ... 120 F7
Sutherland Way EH54 ... 143 C6
Suthren Yett EH32 ... 125 E7
Suttieslea Cres EH22 ... 174 C6
Suttieslea Dr EH22 ... 174 C6
Suttieslea Pl EH22 ... 174 C6
Suttieslea Rd EH22 ... 174 C6
Suttieslea Terr EH22 ... 174 C6
Suttieslea Wlk EH22 ... 174 C6
Suttie Way FK9 ... 1 F8
Sutton Park Cres FK5 ... 38 E3
Sutton Pl FK2 ... 60 D5
Swallow Brae EH54 ... 143 D6
Swallow Craig KY11 ... 48 B1
Swallowdrum Rd KY12 ... 28 C6
Swallow La EH22 ... 153 D3
Swan Cres EH23 ... 195 D8
Swanfield EH6 ... 93 F5
Swan Pl FK3 ... 61 D5
Swan Rd Kirkcaldy KY1 ... 17 B3
Tranent EH33 ... 126 C5
Swan Spring Ave EH10 ... 150 A7
SWANSTON ... 149 F5
Swanston Ave EH10 ... 150 A5
Swanston Cres EH10 ... 150 A5
Swanston Dr EH10 ... 150 B4
Swanston Gdns EH10 ... 150 A5
Swanston Gn EH10 ... 150 A5
Swanston Gr EH10 ... 150 B4
Swanston Loan EH10 ... 150 A5
Swanston Muir EH10 ... 149 E5
Swanston Pk EH10 ... 150 A5
Swanston Pl EH10 ... 150 A5
Swanston Rd EH10 ... 150 A4
Swanston Row EH10 ... 150 A5
Swanston Terr EH10 ... 150 B5
Swanston View EH10 ... 150 A5
Swanston Way EH10 ... 150 A5
Swift Brae EH54 ... 143 D6
Swinburne Dr FK10 ... 5 B2
Swintons Pl KY4 ... 12 F1
Sword's Way FK2 ... 39 A1
Sycamore Ave
Bo'ness EH51 ... 63 D5
Cockenzie & Port Seton EH32 ... 97 D3
Kirkcaldy KY1 ... 17 C8
Sycamore Cres KY4 ... 13 D6
Sycamore Dr EH47 ... 161 C6
Sycamore Gdns EH12 ... 119 E6
Sycamore Glade EH54 ... 164 D8
Sycamore Gr
Dunfermline KY11 ... 46 C8
Winchburgh EH52 ... 87 F2
Sycamore Pl FK8 ... 6 F5
Sycamore Rd EH22 ... 174 E6
Sycamore Sch KY12 ... 29 B4
Sycamores The FK10 ... 4 B1
Sycamore Terr 3 EH12 ... 119 E6
Sycamore Wlk EH47 ... 162 D8
Sydney Pk EH7 ... 94 E2
Sydney Pl EH7 ... 94 E2
Sydney St EH54 ... 144 A5
Sydney Terr EH7 ... 94 E2
Sylvan Gr EH51 ... 63 C5
Sylvan Pl EH9 ... 121 D5
Sylvan Way EH48 ... 140 F5
Syme Cres EH10 ... 149 E8
Syme Pl Edinburgh EH10 ... 149 E8
Rosyth KY11 ... 46 C5
Syme Rigg EH10 ... 149 E8
Symington Pl FK2 ... 39 B3
Symon Twr FK1 ... 60 D4

T

Tailend Ct EH54 ... 142 D3
Tailend Ind Pk EH54 ... 142 D4
Tailend Rdbt EH54 ... 142 D3
Tait Dr Larbert FK5 ... 59 C8
Penicuik EH26 ... 191 F5
Tait St 3 EH22 ... 153 A3
Talbot St FK3 ... 61 D8
Talisker FK10 ... 4 B2
Talisman Pl EH16 ... 122 B1
Talisman Rise EH54 ... 164 D8
Talman Gdns FK2 ... 61 E3
TAMFOURHILL ... 59 C4
Tamfourhill Ave FK1 ... 59 C4
Tamfourhill Ind Est FK1 ... 59 C4
Tamfourhill Rd FK1 ... 59 C4
Tam O'shanter Dr FK7 ... 20 D7
Tanderlane Cotts EH41 ... 132 C3
Tanera Ct FK1 ... 60 B2
Tanfield EH3 ... 93 C3
Tanhouse Brae KY12 ... 42 D8
Tanners Rd FK1 ... 60 A4
Tannery La
8 Haddington EH41 ... 130 B8
Stirling FK8 ... 2 A1
Tantallon Castle* EH39 ... 55 F7
Tantallon Dr FK2 ... 39 A3
Tantallon Gdns EH54 ... 164 E6
Tantallon Pl EH9 ... 121 D5
Tantallon Rd EH39 ... 54 F6
Tantallon Terr EH39 ... 54 E7
Tapitlaw Gr KY12 ... 26 D7
Tappoch Pl FK5 ... 38 A3
Taransay Dr FK2 ... 61 F1
Tarbert Dr EH54 ... 164 F7
Tarbert Pl Carluke ML8 ... 215 A1
Polmont FK2 ... 61 F1
Tarbert Terr FK10 ... 23 F3
Tarbolton Ct KY2 ... 17 A7
TARBRAX ... 203 F3
Tarbrax Path ML7 ... 180 A3
Tarbrax Rd EH55 ... 203 E2
Tarduff Dr FK2 ... 83 A5
Tarduff Pl FK6 ... 36 B2
Targate Rd KY12 ... 28 C5
Target Rd FK3 ... 62 C8
Targe Wynd FK7 ... 7 E3
Tarmachan Cl KY11 ... 30 B1
Tarmachen Rd KY11 ... 30 B1
Tarrareoch Ct EH48 ... 140 B4
Tartraven Pl EH52 ... 116 A5
Tarvit St EH3 ... 228 C1
Tashieburn Rd ML11 ... 201 E2
Tavern Cotts KY4 ... 30 F8
Ta-Verne La KY11 ... 29 D1
Taxi Way KY11 ... 48 C5
Tay Ct FK10 ... 10 C6
Taylor Ave KY4 ... 13 C4
Taylor Ct Falkirk FK2 ... 60 C7
Grangemouth FK3 ... 40 E1
Taylor Gdns EH6 ... 93 F5
Taylor Gn EH54 ... 143 C8
Taylor Pl Dalkeith EH22 ... 153 C2
8 Edinburgh EH7 ... 94 A1
Taylor Rd EH47 ... 160 F6
Taylor's Rd FK5 ... 38 C1
Taymouth Rd FK2 ... 62 A1
Tay Pl ML7 ... 179 E6
Tay St Edinburgh EH11 ... 120 F5
Falkirk FK2 ... 39 C1
Grangemouth FK3 ... 40 A1
Tay Terr KY11 ... 29 E2
Tay Wlk EH54 ... 144 A4
Teal Pl KY11 ... 30 A1
Tedder St FK3 ... 61 C5
Telferton EH7 ... 94 F1
Telford Ct FK7 ... 7 D1
Telford Dr EH4 ... 92 D3
Telford Gdns EH4 ... 92 D3
Telford Gr EH4 ... 92 D4
Telford Pl Edinburgh EH4 ... 92 D3
Linlithgow EH49 ... 84 C7
Telford Rd EH4 ... 92 D3
Telford Sq Falkirk FK1 ... 59 E6
Livingston EH54 ... 143 F8
Telford View EH49 ... 84 C6
Telny Pl KY3 ... 49 C7
Templar La EH31 ... 52 A2
Templar Pl EH31 ... 52 A2
Templar Rise EH54 ... 164 D8
Templar's Cramond EH4 ... 91 A4
Templars Cres KY3 ... 34 F3
TEMPLE ... 194 D2
Temple Ave EH48 ... 140 A5
Templedean Pk EH41 ... 101 A1
Temple Denny Rd FK6 ... 36 D2
TEMPLEHALL ... 16 F7
Templehall Ave KY2 ... 16 F7
Templeland Gr EH12 ... 119 D7
Templeland Rd EH12 ... 119 D7
Temple Mains Steading EH42 ... 136 F8
Temple Park Cres EH11 ... 120 F5
Temple Pk EH23 ... 194 D1
Ten Acres FK10 ... 5 B1
Tenacres Pl FK3 ... 61 E6
Tenacres Rd FK3 ... 62 B7
Tenant's March EH55 ... 163 C3
Tennant St EH6 ... 93 F4
Tennent Pk EH53 ... 144 C2
Tenterfield Dr EH41 ... 101 B1
Tenterfield Ho EH41 ... 101 B1
Tenth St EH22 ... 174 B6
Tern Brae EH54 ... 143 C6
Tern Rd KY11 ... 30 A1
Terrace Rdbt EH54 ... 143 E1
Terrace St KY1 ... 18 A7
Terrars Croft EH8 ... 229 C1
Terregles EH26 ... 191 D6
Terris Pl KY4 ... 13 D3
Teviotdale Pl EH3 ... 93 B2
Teviot Dr EH54 ... 165 A7
Teviot Gr EH26 ... 191 F7
Teviot Pl EH1 ... 229 A2
Teviot St FK1 ... 59 F4
Thane Pl KY11 ... 29 F1
THE GYLE ... 119 B6
THE NEW TOWN ... 228 C4
Thimblehall Dr KY12 ... 29 D4
Thimblehall Pl KY12 ... 29 D4
Thimblehall Rd KY12 ... 29 E4
Third Gait EH14 ... 147 E7
Third St EH22 ... 174 B5
Thirlestane EH51 ... 64 B8
Thirlestane La EH9 ... 121 C4
Thirlestane Pl EH51 ... 64 B8
Thirlestane Rd EH9 ... 121 C5
Thirlfield Wynd EH54 ... 142 F2
Thistle Ave Denny FK6 ... 36 D3
Grangemouth FK3 ... 61 B5
Thistle Chambers 4 FK8 ... 7 B7
Thistle Ct KY4 ... 30 E5
Thistle Ind Est
Broxburn EH52 ... 116 A5
Cowdenbeath KY4 ... 13 E4
Stirling FK7 ... 7 C6
Thistle Pl Edinburgh EH11 ... 228 A1
Stirling FK8 ... 2 A2
Thistles Sh Ctr The FK8 ... 7 B7
Thistle St Alloa FK10 ... 10 C6
Burntisland KY3 ... 50 E8
Cowdenbeath KY4 ... 13 D3
Dunfermline KY12 ... 29 B5
Edinburgh EH2 ... 228 C4
Falkirk FK2 ... 60 C6
Kirkcaldy KY1 ... 17 C3
Thistles The FK8 ... 7 B7
Thistle Street North East La EH2 ... 228 C4
Thistle Street North West La EH2 ... 228 C4
Thistle Street South East La EH2 ... 228 C4
Thistle Street South West La EH2 ... 228 C4
Thistly Cross EH42 ... 105 E8
Thistly Cross Rdbt EH42 ... 105 E7
Thompson's Ct EH1 ... 228 C2
Thomson Cres
Cockenzie & Port Seton EH32 ... 97 D4
Currie EH14 ... 148 B5
Falkirk FK1 ... 59 E3
Thomson Ct EH52 ... 114 F4
Thomson Dr EH14 ... 148 C5
Thomson Gn EH54 ... 143 B8
Thomson Gr Currie EH14 ... 148 B5
Uphall EH52 ... 114 F4
Thomson Pl
Cambusbarron FK7 ... 6 D5
Limerigg FK1 ... 108 B3
Rosyth KY11 ... 46 F3
Thomson Rd EH14 ... 148 B5
Thomson Terr ML7 ... 179 D6
Thorburn Gr EH13 ... 149 C6
Thorburn Rd EH13 ... 149 B6
Thorburn Terr EH26 ... 191 F4
Thornbridge Gdns FK2 ... 60 E4
Thornbridge Rd FK2 ... 60 E5
Thornbridge Sq FK2 ... 60 E5
Thorndale Gdns FK4 ... 57 B2
Thorndene Ct 2 FK1 ... 59 F2
Thorndene Terr FK1 ... 108 B7
Thorne Ct EH39 ... 54 A7
Thorne Rd FK10 ... 4 E1
Thorn Gr KY11 ... 46 F8
Thornhill Ct FK2 ... 60 C6
Thornhill Dr KY2 ... 17 B6
Thornhill Rd Falkirk FK2 ... 60 C6
Kirkcaldy KY2 ... 17 C6
Thorn Rd ML8 ... 215 E3
THORNTON ... 218 C6
Thornton Ave FK4 ... 58 B6
Thornton Gdns FK4 ... 58 B6
Thorntonloch Cvn Site EH42 ... 218 D7
Thorntonloch Holdings EH42 ... 218 B6
Thornton Pl EH47 ... 181 D5
Thornton Rd EH24 ... 172 D1
Thorntree Cres EH32 ... 97 B1
Thorn Tree Pl KY12 ... 26 F6
Thorntreeside EH6 ... 94 A3
Thorntreeside Ind Est EH6 ... 94 A3
Thorntree St EH6 ... 94 A4
Thornville Terr EH6 ... 94 A3
Thorny Bank EH22 ... 153 C4
Thornybank Ind Est EH22 ... 153 D4
Thornybauk EH3 ... 228 B1
Thornycroft Terr FK7 ... 20 C3
Thornyhall EH22 ... 153 C4
Threave Loan KY11 ... 30 A1
Three Bridges Rdbt FK1 ... 59 A6
THREEMILETOWN ... 86 F4
Threipmuir Ave EH14 ... 168 C8
Threipmuir Gdns EH14 ... 168 C8
Threipmuir Pl EH14 ... 168 C8
THROSK ... 9 A3
Thrums The FK2 ... 61 A4
Thurston Pl EH54 ... 143 B5
Thymebank EH54 ... 143 E6
Tibbies Loan FK7 ... 20 D8
Timber Bush EH6 ... 94 A6
Timmeryetts EH52 ... 115 C6
Timmons Pk KY5 ... 14 A8
Timmons Pl FK6 ... 36 D1
Tinian Cres KY12 ... 26 D1
Tinto Dr FK3 ... 61 E5
Tinto Pl Dunfermline KY11 ... 29 F2
Edinburgh EH6 ... 93 E4
Tinto View ML11 ... 217 F8
Tipperary Pl FK5 ... 38 E2
Tipperlinn Rd EH10 ... 121 A3
Tipperwell Way EH26 ... 192 B1
Tippethill Hospl EH48 ... 140 B1
Tippet Knowes Ct EH52 ... 87 E3
Tippet Knowes Pk EH52 ... 87 E3
Tippet Knowes Rd EH52 ... 87 E2
Tiree Cres FK2 ... 61 D2
Tiree Pl Falkirk FK1 ... 60 B1
Kirkcaldy KY2 ... 16 F8
Tirran Dr KY11 ... 30 B1
Titania FK10 ... 10 A8
Toddricks Wynd EH1 ... 229 B3
Toddshill Rd EH29 ... 89 A1
Todd Sq EH54 ... 114 E1
Tolbooth St 3 Falkirk FK1 ... 60 B4
Kirkcaldy KY1 ... 17 C3
Tolbooth Wynd EH6 ... 94 A5
Tollbraes Rd EH48 ... 141 D4
TOLLCROSS ... 228 B1
Tollcross EH3 ... 228 B1
Tollcross Prim Sch EH3 ... 228 B1
Tollgate KY11 ... 29 B2
Toll House Gdns EH33 ... 126 D4
Toll House Gr EH33 ... 126 D5
Toll House Neuk EH33 ... 126 D4
Toll Rd FK10 ... 23 F3
Toll Rdbt EH54 ... 142 E3
Toll View TD13 ... 218 F4
Tolmount Cres KY12 ... 29 C3
Tolmount Dr KY12 ... 29 C3
Tolsta Cres FK2 ... 61 F1
Tophill Entry FK1 ... 59 F6
Toravon Dr FK2 ... 83 A6
Torbain KY2 ... 16 D8
Torbain Prim Sch KY2 ... 16 D8
Torbain Rd KY2 ... 16 B6
Torbane Ave EH47 ... 161 E7
Torbane Dr EH47 ... 161 E7
Torbeith Gdns
Cowdenbeath KY4 ... 12 F1
Hill Of Beath KY4 ... 13 A1
TORBOTHIE ... 180 B4
Torbothie Rd ML7 ... 180 B4
TORBREX ... 6 F5
Torbrex Farm Rd FK7 ... 7 A4
Torbrex La FK7, FK8 ... 7 A5
Torbrex Rd FK7 ... 6 F4
Torburn Ave FK7 ... 20 D3
Torduff Rd EH13 ... 148 F4
Torlea Pl FK5 ... 38 B3
Toronto Ave EH54 ... 143 E4
Toronto Prim Sch EH54 ... 143 E4
Torosay Ave FK2 ... 82 F6
TORPHICHEN ... 111 E6
Torphichen Ave EH53 ... 144 B2
Torphichen Pl EH3 ... 228 A2
Torphichen Place La EH3 ... 228 A2
Torphichen Preceptory* EH48 ... 111 F6
Torphichen Prim Sch EH48 ... 111 F6
Torphichen Rd EH48 ... 141 B8
Torphichen St
Bathgate EH48 ... 141 B7
Edinburgh EH3 ... 228 A2
TORPHIN ... 148 E4
Torphin Bank EH13 ... 148 F5
Torphin Rd EH13 ... 148 F5
Torrance Pk EH4 ... 91 C1
Torrence Medway EH26 ... 171 A1
Torridon Ave FK2 ... 39 C1
Torridon Ct FK10 ... 10 C5
Torridon Dr KY11 ... 46 E2
Torridon La KY11 ... 46 E2
Torridon Pl Kirkcaldy KY2 ... 16 E8
Rosyth KY11 ... 46 E2
Torridon Rd EH47 ... 161 C7
Torridon Wlk EH54 ... 144 B4
Torrin Loan ML7 ... 180 B3
Torry Bay Nature Reserve* KY12 ... 43 D8
TORRYBURN ... 26 E1
Torryburn Prim Sch KY12 . 26 E1
Torry Dr FK12 ... 4 E7
Torsonce Rd EH22 ... 152 F2
Torvean Pl KY11 ... 29 C2
TORWOOD ... 37 E6
Torwood Ave
Grangemouth FK3 ... 61 E6
Larbert FK5 ... 38 B2
Torwood Pl KY12 ... 29 D5
Tory Bay Ct KY12 ... 26 C1
Toscana Ct EH22 ... 152 A8
TOUCH ... 29 E5
Touchhill Cres FK7 ... 20 C3
Touch Prim Sch KY11 ... 29 E4
Touch Rd FK7, FK8 ... 6 B6

Touch Wards KY12 . . . . 29 E4
Tovey Rd KY11 . . . . 46 D2
Toward Ct 3 EH12 . . . . 119 A7
Towerbank Prim Sch
EH15 . . . . 95 B1
Tower Gdns The EH51 . . . . . 64 C7
Tower Pl Clackmannan FK10 . 10 F5
Edinburgh EH6 . . . . 94 A6
Towers Ct FK2 . . . . 60 B6
Towers Pl FK9 . . . . 2 D4
Tower Sq FK10 . . . . 10 B5
Tower St Alloa FK10 . . . . 10 A7
Edinburgh EH6 . . . . 94 A6
Tower Terr KY1 . . . . 17 F8
Tower View FK10 . . . . 5 E1
Tower Wynd EH6 . . . . 94 A6
Town Burn FK7 . . . . 6 F4
Townhall St KY11 . . . . 47 C2
Townhead Dysart KY1 . . . . . 18 A7
Kinghorn KY3 . . . . 34 F3
Townhead Apartments 9
FK10 . . . . 10 B6
Townhead Gdns EH47 . . . . 161 C6
TOWNHILL 29 C8
Townhill Ctry Pk* KY12 . . . 29 D8
Townhill Prim Sch KY12 . . 29 D8
Townhill Rd KY12 . . . . 29 B5
Town House St FK6 . . . . 36 E2
Townsend Cres KY1 . . . . 17 C4
Townsend Pl KY1 . . . . 17 C4
Town Sq EH54 . . . . 143 E2
Trafalgar La EH6 . . . . 93 E5
Trafalgar St EH6 . . . . 93 E5
Trainers Brae EH39 . . . . 54 B6
Train Terr KY11 . . . . 46 C5
TRANENT 126 E7
Tranent Rd EH33 . . . . 126 B1
Transy Gr KY12 . . . . 29 C4
Transy Pl KY12 . . . . 29 C4
Tranter Cres EH32 . . . . 71 C4
Tranter Rd EH32 . . . . 71 C4
Traprain Cotts HE41 . . . . . 103 E4
Traprain Cres EH48 . . . . . . 140 F7
Traprain Terr
Haddington EH41 . . . . 101 B1
Loanhead EH20 . . . . 172 C7
Traquair Park E EH12 . . . . 119 F6
Traquair Park W EH12 . . . . 119 F6
Traverse Theatre* EH3 . . 228 B2
Trelawney Terr EH26 . . . . . 192 A8
Tremayne Pl KY12 . . . . 28 F6
Trenchard Pl KY12 . . . . 28 F5
Trench Knowe EH10 . . . . . 150 A5
Tressilian Gdns 1 EH16 . . 122 B1
Trevelyan Cres EH34 . . . . 156 E6
Trevelyan Pl EH34 . . . . . . 156 E6
TRINITY 93 C5
Trinity Acad EH6 . . . . 93 C6
Trinity Cres EH5 . . . . 93 B6
Trinity Ct EH5 . . . . 93 B5
Trinity Gr EH5 . . . . 93 B6
Trinity Mains EH5 . . . . 93 B5
Trinity Prim Sch EH6 . . . . . 93 D6
Trinity Rd EH5 . . . . 93 B6
Trinity Way EH5 . . . . 93 B5
Tron Ct FK10 . . . . 10 B6
Trondheim Parkway KY11 . 29 F2
Trondheim Pl KY11 . . . . 29 F2
Trongate KY3 . . . . 35 A3
Tron Sq EH1 . . . . 229 A3
Trotter Haugh EH9 . . . . . . 121 D3
Troup Ct FK3 . . . . 61 D8
Tryst Pk Edinburgh EH10 . . 149 F5
Stenhousemuir FK5 . . . . 38 C5
Tryst Rd FK5 . . . . 38 D3
Tudor Ct FK2 . . . . 61 C2
Tuke St KY12 . . . . 29 A5
Tulliallan Pl FK5 . . . . 39 A4
Tulliallan Prim Sch FK10 . . 23 E4
Tulliallan Terr FK10 . . . . 23 E5
TULLIBODY 4 C3
Tullibody Rd FK10 . . . . 9 F8
Tulligarth Pk FK10 . . . . 10 A7
Tulloch Ct KY4 . . . . 13 C5
Tulloch Rd ML7 . . . . 180 B3
Tummel Ct FK10 . . . . 10 C5
Tummel Dr KY2 . . . . 16 D8
Tummel Pl
Grangemouth FK3 . . . . 61 E4
Stenhousemuir FK5 . . . . 38 E3
Turf Pl EH47 . . . . 162 D7
Turnbull Gr KY11 . . . . 29 F1
Turnbull Way EH54 . . . . . . 143 D6
Turner Ave EH14 . . . . 147 C3
Turner Pk EH14 . . . . 147 C3
Turner St EH48 . . . . 141 A7
Turnhigh Rd EH47 . . . . 161 A6
Turnhouse Farm Rd EH12 . 90 C1
Turnhouse Rd EH12 . . . . . . 118 D8
Turnstone Rd KY11 . . . . 30 B1
Turpie Dr 6 FK5 . . . . 38 B2
Turret Ct FK10 . . . . 10 C6
Turret Dr FK2 . . . . 62 A2
Turret Gdns EH32 . . . . 125 F8
Turret Rd FK3 . . . . 61 D5
Turriff Pl KY2 . . . . 16 E8
Twain Ave FK5 . . . . 39 A3
Tweed Ave KY1 . . . . 17 E8
Tweeddale Ave EH41 . . . . . 220 F7
Tweeddale Cres EH41 . . . . 220 F7
Tweeddale Ct EH1 . . . . 229 B3
Tweeddale Dr KY11 . . . . 29 E1
Tweeddale Gr EH41 . . . . . . 220 F6
Tweed Dr EH54 . . . . 144 B4
Tweed St Dunfermline KY11 . 29 F2
Tweed St *continued*
Grangemouth FK3 . . . . 40 A1
Tygetshaugh Ct FK6 . . . . . . 36 D4
Tyler's Acre Ave EH12 . . . 119 E5
Tyler's Acre Gdns EH12 . . 119 E5
Tyler's Acre Rd EH12 . . . . 119 E5
Tyndrum Pl KY2 . . . . 16 E7
Tynebank Rd EH41 . . . . . . 130 A7
Tynecastle High Sch
EH11 . . . . 120 E6
Tynecastle La EH11 . . . . . 120 E5
Tynecastle Pk (Heart of
Midlothian FC) EH11 . . . 120 E5
Tynecastle Terr EH11 . . . . 120 E5
Tyne Cl East Linton EH40 . . 103 E7
Haddington EH41 . . . . 130 B8
Tyne Ct EH41 . . . . 130 B8
Tynefield Cotts EH42 . . . . 105 A8
Tyne Ho EH41 . . . . 130 B7
Tyneholm Cotts EH34 . . . . 156 E6
Tynemount Ave EH35 . . . . 155 D6
Tynemount Rd EH35 . . . . . 155 D7
Tyne Pk EH34 . . . . 157 A6
Tyneview EH35 . . . . 155 E7
Tynewater Prim Sch
EH37 . . . . 176 A4
TYNINGHAME 76 B3
Tyrie Ave KY1 . . . . 35 B7
Tyrie Ct KY1 . . . . 35 B7
Tyrie Gr KY1 . . . . 35 B7
Tyrie Pl KY1 . . . . 35 B7
Tyrwhitt Pl KY11 . . . . 46 F3
Tytler Ct EH8 . . . . 94 A1
Tytler Gdns EH8 . . . . 94 A1

U

Ugston Cotts EH41 . . . . . . 100 C2
Uig Way ML7 . . . . 180 A3
Ulster Cres EH8 . . . . 122 D8
Ulster Dr EH8 . . . . 122 D8
Ulster Gdns EH8 . . . . 122 D7
Ulster Gr EH8 . . . . 122 D7
Ulster Terr EH8 . . . . 122 D7
Underwood Cotts FK7 . . . . . . 6 D5
Underwood Rd FK7 . . . . 6 D5
Union Ct EH51 . . . . 64 A8
Union Dr EH47 . . . . 161 B6
Union Gdns FK1 . . . . 59 D5
Union Pk EH19 . . . . 173 B6
Union Pl Brightons FK2 . . . . 61 D1
Edinburgh EH1 . . . . 229 B4
Larbert FK5 . . . . 38 B1
Union Rd Bathgate EH48 . . 141 B6
Broxburn EH52 . . . . 115 D5
Falkirk FK1 . . . . 59 D5
Grangemouth FK3 . . . . 40 D1
Linlithgow EH49 . . . . 84 F6
Whitburn EH47 . . . . 161 B6
Union Sq EH55 . . . . 163 D3
Union St 4 Alloa FK10 . . . . . 10 B6
Bo'ness EH51 . . . . 64 A8
Bridge of Allan FK9 . . . . 2 A7
Burntisland KY3 . . . . 50 E8
Cowdenbeath KY4 . . . . 13 D4
Edinburgh EH1 . . . . 93 E2
Falkirk FK2 . . . . 60 B7
Kirkcaldy KY1 . . . . 17 F7
Lochgelly KY5 . . . . 14 B8
Shotts ML7 . . . . 179 D5
Stenhousemuir FK5 . . . . 38 E3
Stirling FK8 . . . . 2 B1
Unity Pk ML7 . . . . 179 D4
Universal Rd FK2 . . . . 60 E7
University of Edinburgh
EH8 . . . . 229 B2
University of Stirling FK9 . . 2 D6
University Road W FK9 . . . . 2 C6
Univ of Dundee Sch of
Nursing & Midwifery Fife
Campus 1 KY2 . . . . 17 A4
Univ of Edinburgh EH8 . . 229 A2
Univ of Edinburgh (King's
Buildings Campus)
EH9 . . . . 121 F2
UPHALL 114 F4
Uphall Prim Sch EH52 . . . 115 A5
Uphall Sta EH54 . . . . 115 A2
UPHALL STATION 115 A1
Uphall Station Rd EH53 . . 144 B7
Upper Bathville EH48 . . . . 139 F4
Upper Bow EH1 . . . . 229 A3
Upper Bridge St FK8 . . . . 2 A1
Upper Broomieknowe
EH18 . . . . 173 A8
Upper Castlehill 2 FK8 . . . . 7 A8
Upper Coltbridge Terr
EH12 . . . . 120 E8
Upper Craigour EH17 . . . . 151 E8
Upper Craigour Way
EH17 . . . . 122 D1
Upper Craigs FK8 . . . . 7 B7
Upper Cramond Ct EH4 . . . 91 B4
Upper Dalhousie Cotts
EH19 . . . . 173 C3
Upper Damside 1 EH4 . . . 120 F8
Upper Dean Terr EH4 . . . . 228 A4
Upper Gilmore Pl EH3 . . . 228 B1
Upper Gilmore Terr EH3 . 228 B1
Upper Gray St EH9 . . . . . . 121 E5
Upper Grove Pl EH3 . . . . . 228 A1
Upper Hermitage EH6 . . . . . 94 A4
Upper Keith EH36 . . . . 178 B2
Upper Millhill St KY11 . . . . 29 B3
Upper Newmarket St 6
FK1 . . . . 60 B5
UPPER TOWN OF
SALTOUN 157 E4
Upper Wellheads KY11 . . . . 45 E3
Ure Cres FK4 . . . . 58 A6
Ure Ct FK3 . . . . 61 D8
URQUHART 28 D2
Urquhart Cres KY12 . . . . . . 28 E3
Urquhart Ct KY2 . . . . 16 D5
Urquhart Cut KY12 . . . . 28 E3
Urquhart Farm Cotts
KY12 . . . . 28 D2
Usher Hall* EH3 . . . . 228 B2

V

Vale Gr FK9 . . . . 1 F5
Vale of Bonny View FK4 . . . 57 F5
Vale Pl FK6 . . . . 36 E3
Valeview FK5 . . . . 38 D2
Valleyfield Ave KY12 . . . . . 26 B2
Valleyfield Pl
Cowdenbeath KY4 . . . . 13 D5
Stirling FK7 . . . . 7 C6
Valleyfield Rd EH26 . . . . . 191 F4
Valleyfield St EH3 . . . . . . 228 C1
Valleyfield View EH26 . . . 191 F4
Valleyfield Woodland Pk*
KY12 . . . . 26 B3
Valley Gdns KY2 . . . . 16 F6
Valley Gdns S KY2 . . . . 16 F6
Valley Prim Sch KY2 . . . . . 17 A7
Valley View KY2 . . . . 16 F6
Valleyview Dr FK2 . . . . 60 A8
Valleyview Pl FK2 . . . . 60 A7
Vanburgh Pl EH6 . . . . 94 A4
Vancouver Ave EH54 . . . . . 143 F4
Vandeleur Ave EH7 . . . . 94 E2
Vandeleur Gr EH7 . . . . 94 F1
Vandeleur Pl EH7 . . . . 94 F2
Vardon Gn EH54 . . . . 143 C8
Vardon Rd EH31 . . . . 52 B3
Vaucluse Pl EH26 . . . . 191 E4
Veere Pk KY12 . . . . 25 E1
Veitch's Sq 2 EH3 . . . . 93 B2
Vellore Rd FK2 . . . . 83 A6
Venachar Pl KY12 . . . . 28 B1
Venachar Rd FK1 . . . . 60 A1
Vennachar St ML7 . . . . 179 E6
Vennel The Denny FK6 . . . . 36 E2
Dunbar EH42 . . . . 78 E2
Linlithgow EH49 . . . . 85 A7
South Queensferry EH30 . . . 68 C1
Ventnor Pl EH9 . . . . 122 A4
Ventnor Terr EH9 . . . . 121 F4
Venturefair Ave KY12 . . . . . 29 A6
Veronica Cres KY1 . . . . 17 C8
Vetch Pk EH41 . . . . 101 A1
Veterane Cotts EH48 . . . . . 141 C6
Vexhim Pk EH15 . . . . 123 B5
Vicar St FK1 . . . . 60 B5
Viceroy St KY2 . . . . 17 B6
Victoria Gdns
Kirkcaldy KY1 . . . . 17 B4
Newtongrange EH22 . . . . . 173 F6
Victoria Hospl KY2 . . . . 17 B7
Victoria Mills Ind Est
EH51 . . . . 64 C8
Victoria Park Neuk EH6 . . . 93 D5
Victoria Pk
Fauldhouse EH47 . . . . 181 F7
Haddington EH41 . . . . 101 A1
Victoria Pl Bo'ness EH51 . . . 64 B7
Brightons FK2 . . . . 61 D1
Dunbar EH42 . . . . 78 D3
Stirling FK8 . . . . 7 A7
Victoria Prim Sch
Edinburgh EH6 . . . . 93 D7
Falkirk FK2 . . . . 60 D6
Victoria Rd Falkirk FK2 . . . . 60 C6
Fauldhouse EH47 . . . . 181 F7
Grangemouth FK3 . . . . 61 E8
Haddington EH41 . . . . 130 A8
Harthill ML7 . . . . 159 E5
Kirkcaldy KY1 . . . . 17 C5
Larbert FK5 . . . . 38 B1
Newtongrange EH22 . . . . . 173 F5
North Berwick EH39 . . . . . . 54 C7
Stirling FK8 . . . . 7 A8
Victoria Sq FK8 . . . . 7 A7
Victoria St Alloa FK10 . . . . . 10 A7
Dunbar EH42 . . . . 78 D3
Dunfermline KY12 . . . . 29 A5
Dysart KY1 . . . . 18 A7
Edinburgh EH1 . . . . 229 A3
Gorebridge EH23 . . . . 174 B1
Harthill ML7 . . . . 159 E5
Livingston EH54 . . . . 144 A4
Rosewell EH24 . . . . 172 D2
Victoria Terr
Dunfermline KY12 . . . . 29 A5
Edinburgh EH1 . . . . 229 A2
Haddington EH41 . . . . 130 B8
Menstrie FK11 . . . . 4 B7
Musselburgh EH21 . . . . . . 124 E6
Victor Park Terr EH12 . . . . 119 D7
Viewbank Dr EH19 . . . . . . 173 C8
Viewbank Rd EH19 . . . . . . 173 B8
Viewbank View EH19 . . . . . 173 C8
Viewcraig Gdns EH8 . . . . . 229 B2
Viewcraig St EH8 . . . . 229 B2
Viewfield EH19 . . . . 173 D8
Viewfield Ave EH19 . . . . . 173 D8
Viewfield Dr FK12 . . . . 4 F6
Viewfield Ho KY12 . . . . 29 B3
Viewfield Pl Harthill ML7 . . 159 F6
3 Stirling FK8 . . . . 7 B8
Viewfield Rd
Edinburgh EH14 . . . . 148 E7
Tarbrax EH55 . . . . 203 F3
Viewfield St Harthill ML7 . . 159 F6
4 Stirling FK8 . . . . 7 B8
Viewfield Terr
Cowdenbeath KY4 . . . . 13 F6
Dunfermline KY12 . . . . 29 B3
VIEWFORTH 228 A1
Viewforth Bo'ness EH51 . . . . 64 A7
Cockenzie & Port Seton
EH32 . . . . 97 D4
Dunbar EH42 . . . . 78 C3
Edinburgh EH10 . . . . 121 A5
North Berwick EH39 . . . . . . 54 C7
Stirling FK8 . . . . 7 B6
Viewforth Ave KY1 . . . . 17 F7
Viewforth Ct KY3 . . . . 34 F2
Viewforth Dr FK2 . . . . 61 B4
Viewforth Gdns
Edinburgh EH10 . . . . 121 B5
Kirkcaldy KY1 . . . . 17 F7
Tranent EH33 . . . . 126 C6
Viewforth High Sch KY1 . . 17 F7
Viewforth Pl Kinghorn KY3 . . 34 F2
Queensferry EH30 . . . . 89 B8
Viewforth Rd EH30 . . . . 89 B8
Viewforth Sq EH10 . . . . . . 121 A5
Viewforth St KY1 . . . . 17 F7
Viewforth Terr
Edinburgh EH10 . . . . 121 A5
Kirkcaldy KY1 . . . . 17 F8
Tranent EH33 . . . . 126 C6
Viewpark Gdns EH19 . . . . . 173 B8
Viking Way KY11 . . . . 46 D2
Villabank FK6 . . . . 36 E2
Villa Dean EH24 . . . . 172 C1
Villa Dean Pk EH24 . . . . . . 172 D1
Village La EH54 . . . . 143 B3
Villa Pl FK10 . . . . 11 A5
Villa Rd EH30 . . . . 68 B1
Vinefields EH34 . . . . 156 F6
Vineyard Bsns Ctr EH37 . . 197 F7
Violet Bank 5 EH48 . . . . . . 141 B6
Violet Terr EH11 . . . . 120 E5
Vivian Terr EH4 . . . . 92 A3
Vogrie Cres S EH23 . . . . . . 195 D8
Vogrie Ctry Pk* EH23 . . . 175 D3
Vogrie Pl EH23 . . . . 195 D8
Vogrie Rd EH23 . . . . 195 D7
Voil Rd FK9 . . . . 2 A3
Volunteer's Gn KY1 . . . . 17 C3
Vorlich Cres EH26 . . . . 192 A7
Vorlich Dr FK1 . . . . 81 E7
Vorlich Pl FK9 . . . . 2 A3
Vorlich Way
Dunfermline KY11 . . . . 30 B1
Inverkeithing/Dunfermline
KY11 . . . . 30 B1
Vrackie Pl KY11 . . . . 30 B1

W

Waddell St FK2 . . . . 39 C2
WADINGBURN 151 F1
Wadingburn La EH18 . . . . . 151 F1
Wadingburn Rd EH18 . . . . 172 E8
Waggon Rd Bo'ness EH51 . . 63 F8
Crossford KY11 . . . . 45 C7
Falkirk FK2 . . . . 60 B7
Grangemouth FK2 . . . . 82 C8
Inverkeithing KY11 . . . . 47 C2
Wakefield Ave EH7 . . . . 94 F2
Walden Dr EH41 . . . . 220 F7
Walden Pl EH41 . . . . 220 F6
Walden Terr EH41 . . . . 220 F6
Waldie Ave EH49 . . . . 85 A5
Walker Cres EH22 . . . . 152 D1
Walker Dr Bonnybridge FK4 . 57 D5
South Queensferry EH30 . . . 68 A1
Walker Pl
Bonnyrigg and Lasswade
EH18 . . . . 172 E6
Dunfermline KY11 . . . . 29 E1
Walker Rd EH47 . . . . 181 D5
Walkers Ct EH14 . . . . 119 E1
Walkers Rigg EH14 . . . . . . 119 E1
Walker St
Alloa/Clackmannan FK10 . . . 23 F2
Cowdenbeath KY4 . . . . 13 B3
Edinburgh EH3 . . . . 228 A3
Kincardine FK10 . . . . 23 E3
Kirkcaldy KY2 . . . . 17 B6
Lochgelly KY5 . . . . 14 A6
Walkers Wynd EH14 . . . . . 119 E1
Walker Terr
East Linton EH40 . . . . 103 D7
Edinburgh EH11 . . . . 228 A2
Walk The KY1 . . . . 18 B7
Wallace Ave EH21 . . . . 125 A4
Wallace Bldgs FK2 . . . . 60 B6
Wallace Brae Ave FK2 . . . . 82 C8
Wallace Brae Bank FK2 . . . 82 C8
Wallace Brae Ct 1 FK2 . . . 82 C8
Wallace Brae Dr FK2 . . . . . 82 C8
Wallace Brae Gdns 4
FK2 . . . . 82 C8
Wallace Brae Gr 2 FK2 . . . 82 C8
Wallace Brae Pl 3 FK2 . . . 82 C8
Wallace Brae Rise FK2 . . . 82 C8
Wallace Cres Denny FK6 . . . 36 C2
Grangemouth FK2 . . . . 82 D8
Musselburgh EH21 . . . . . . 125 A4
Plean FK7 . . . . 20 D3
Roslin EH25 . . . . 172 A3
Wallace Ct
Grangemouth FK3 . . . . 61 D8
Wallace Ct *continued*
Stirling FK8 . . . . 2 B1
Wallace Gate FK8 . . . . 7 B8
Wallace Gdns FK9 . . . . 2 D3
Wallace High Sch FK9 . . . . . 2 C4
Wallacelea FK2 . . . . 82 E7
Wallace Mill Gdns EH53 . . 144 C4
Wallace Monument* FK9 . . 2 E4
Wallace Pl
Cambusbarron FK7 . . . . 6 D5
Falkirk FK2 . . . . 60 C6
Fallin FK7 . . . . 8 C4
Kingseat KY12 . . . . 12 A1
Tranent EH33 . . . . 126 C7
Wallace Rd EH48 . . . . 141 C6
Wallacerig Gdns FK2 . . . . . 82 E8
Wallace St Alloa FK10 . . . . . 10 C7
Bannockburn FK7 . . . . 7 E1
Cowdenbeath KY4 . . . . 13 C3
Dunfermline KY11 . . . . 29 C2
Falkirk FK2 . . . . 60 C6
Grangemouth FK3 . . . . 61 D8
Stirling FK8 . . . . 2 B1
WALLACESTONE 82 B7
Wallacestone Brae FK2 . . . 82 B7
Wallacestone Prim Sch
FK2 . . . . 82 D7
Wallace View
Bo'ness EH51 . . . . 63 D5
Shieldhill FK1 . . . . 81 D7
Tullibody FK10 . . . . 4 D3
Wallace Wlk EH47 . . . . 162 A1
Wall Gdns FK1 . . . . 59 C5
Wallsend Ct KY12 . . . . 28 D5
Walls Pl KY11 . . . . 29 E1
Wall St FK1 . . . . 59 C5
Wallstale Rd FK7 . . . . 7 A3
WALLYFORD 125 C5
Wallyford Ind Est EH21 . . . 125 B4
Wallyford Prim Sch
EH21 . . . . 125 B5
Wallyford Sta EH21 . . . . . . 125 B5
Wallyford Toll EH21 . . . . . . 125 C6
Walmer Dr KY12 . . . . 29 A3
Walnut Gr KY11 . . . . 46 D8
Walter Hay Ct KY11 . . . . . . 46 F3
Walter Scott Ave EH16 . . . 122 B1
Wanless Ct EH21 . . . . 124 D6
Ward Ave FK2 . . . . 61 C2
Warden's Cl EH1 . . . . 229 A2
WARDIE 93 A6
Wardie Ave EH5 . . . . 93 A5
Wardieburn Dr EH5 . . . . . . 92 F6
Wardieburn Place E EH5 . . 92 F6
Wardieburn Place N EH5 . . 92 F6
Wardieburn Place S EH5 . . 92 F6
Wardieburn Place W EH5 . 92 E6
Wardieburn Rd EH5 . . . . . . 92 E6
Wardieburn Street E EH5 . 92 F6
Wardieburn Street W EH5 92 E6
Wardieburn Terr EH5 . . . . . 92 F6
Wardie Cres EH5 . . . . 93 A6
Wardie Dell EH5 . . . . 93 A6
Wardiefield EH5 . . . . 92 F6
Wardie Gr EH5 . . . . 92 F6
Wardie House La EH5 . . . . 93 A6
Wardie Pk EH5 . . . . 93 A5
Wardie Prim Sch EH5 . . . . . 93 A6
Wardie Rd EH5 . . . . 93 A5
Wardie Sq EH5 . . . . 93 A6
Wardie Steps EH5 . . . . 93 A6
Wardlaw Cres KY12 . . . . 26 F7
Wardlaw Pl
Edinburgh EH11 . . . . 120 E5
Falkirk FK2 . . . . 39 C2
Wardlaw St
Cowdenbeath KY4 . . . . 13 C3
Edinburgh EH11 . . . . 120 E5
Wardlaw Terr EH11 . . . . . . 120 E5
Wardlaw Way KY12 . . . . 26 F7
Ward Pl EH54 . . . . 143 C5
Wardrop Cres EH48 . . . . . . 139 E5
Ward St FK10 . . . . 10 A5
Ware Rd Dirleton EH39 . . . . . 53 C6
North Berwick EH39 . . . . . . 54 A7
Warrender Cres EH42 . . . . . 78 E1
Warrender Ct EH39 . . . . 54 A6
Warrender Park Cres
EH9 . . . . 121 C5
Warrender Park Rd EH9 . . 121 C5
Warrender Park Terr
EH9 . . . . 121 C5
Warrender Swim Ctr
EH9 . . . . 121 C4
Warren Hill EH31 . . . . 51 F2
WARRISTON 93 C4
Warriston Ave EH3 . . . . 93 C4
Warriston Cres EH3 . . . . . . 93 C3
Warriston Dr EH3 . . . . 93 C4
Warriston Farm Rd EH14 147 C6
Warriston Gdns EH3 . . . . . . 93 C4
Warriston Gr EH3 . . . . 93 B4
Warriston Pl EH3 . . . . 93 C3
Warriston Rd EH7 . . . . 93 C4
Warriston Terr EH3 . . . . 93 B4
Washington La 3 EH11 . . 120 F6
Waterfall Wlk EH22 . . . . . . 153 B2
Waterfront Ave EH5 . . . . . . 92 D7
Waterfront Broadway
EH5 . . . . 92 D6
Waterfront Gait EH5 . . . . . . 92 B6
Waterfront Pk EH5 . . . . 92 B6
Waterfront Way FK9 . . . . 2 A3
Waterfurs Dr FK2 . . . . 60 A8
Waterlands Gdns ML8 . . . . 215 A3
Waterloo Bank EH26 . . . . . 191 F4
Waterloo Pl
Edinburgh EH1 . . . . 229 A4

Waterloo Pl *continued*
Elphinstone EH33 126 B2
Waterloo Rd RH33 126 D4
Water of Leith Visitor Ctr★
EH14 120 C2
Water of Leith Walkway★
EH14 147 D2
Waters' Cl EH6 94 A5
Waters End FK2 39 B2
Waterside
9 Haddington EH41 130 B8
Linlithgow EH49 84 C7
Water St EH6 94 A5
Watertoun Rd EH9 121 E3
Water Yett EH49 84 F7
Watling Ave FK1 59 C5
Watling Dr FK1 59 D5
Watling Gdns FK1 59 D6
Watling St FK1 59 C5
Watson Cres EH11 120 F5
Watson Ct KY4 12 E8
Watson Gn EH54 143 C8
Watson Pl Armadale EH48 140 A6
Dunfermline KY12 29 B6
Longcroft FK4 57 C4
Watson St
Cowdenbeath KY4 13 D3
Falkirk FK2 60 B5
Penicuik EH26 191 F5
Watt Ave EH48 140 A5
Watters Cres KY5 14 B6
Watt Gdns FK1 59 E6
Watt Gr EH22 174 E5
Watt Pk EH22 174 B4
Watt Rd KY11 46 B2
Watt's Cl EH21 124 B6
Watt St KY1 18 A7
Wauchope Ave EH16 122 E4
Wauchope Cres EH16 122 E4
Wauchope Ho EH16 122 F3
Wauchope Pl EH16 122 E4
Wauchope Terr EH16 122 E4
Waugh Path EH19 173 D8
Waughton Cotts EH40 74 F5
Waughton Steading EH40 74 E5
Waulker Ave FK8 1 F2
Waulkmill Dr EH26 192 A5
Waulkmill Loan EH14 147 E3
Waulkmill Rd EH26 192 A5
Waulkmill View EH26 191 F5
Wavell St FK3 61 C5
Waverley Bridge EH1 229 A3
Waverley Cres
Bonnybridge FK4 58 B3
Bonnyrigg and Lasswade
EH19 173 C7
Grangemouth FK3 61 D5
Livingston EH54 143 B6
Stirling FK8 2 C1
Waverley Ct EH19 173 C7
Waverley Dr EH19 173 C7
Waverley House N EH31 52 A2
Waverley House S EH31 52 A2
Waverley Park Terr EH8 94 A1
Waverley Pk
Bonnyrigg and Lasswade
EH19 173 C7
Edinburgh EH8 94 A1
Mayfield EH22 174 D6
Redding FK2 61 B1
Waverley Pl EH7 94 A2
Waverley Rd
Bonnyrigg and Lasswade
EH19 173 C7
Dalkeith EH22 152 F2
Stenhousemuir FK5 38 C2
Waverley Sh Ctr EH1 229 A3
Waverley St
Bathgate EH48 141 A7
Falkirk FK2 60 B8
Mayfield EH22 174 D6
Waverley Steps EH2 229 A3
Waverley Street Ind Units 1
EH48 141 A7
Waverley Terr
Bonnyrigg and Lasswade
EH19 173 C7
Mayfield EH22 174 D6
Stenhousemuir FK5 38 C2
Wayfarers Dr KY11 47 F3
Wayfarers Pl KY11 47 F3
Wayfarers Way KY11 47 F3
Weaver Pl EH48 141 B7
Weaver Row FK7 7 A4
Weavers Cres KY2 17 B6
Weaver's Knowe Cres
EH14 147 F5
Weavers La EH47 161 A6
Weaver's Terr KY12 27 D1
Weavers Wlk KY12 29 A2
Webster Ave FK2 39 B3
Webster Ct EH52 115 E5
Webster Pl KY11 46 C5
Webster's Land EH1 228 C2
Wedderburn Cres KY11 29 E1
Wedderburn Ct EH21 124 D3
Wedderburn Ho EH21 124 D3
Wedderburn Pl KY11 29 D2
Wedderburn Rd KY2 16 C7
Wedderburn St KY11 29 D2
Wedderburn Terr EH21 124 D4
Wee Brae EH18 152 A1
Wee Cswy KY12 42 D8
Wee Row FK2 60 B6
Weir Ave KY4 13 B2
Weir Cres EH22 152 E2
Weir Ct EH22 152 E2
Weir Dr FK7 8 D4
Weir St Falkirk FK1 60 C5
Stirling FK8 1 F2
Wellbank FK2 61 B2
Well Ct EH3 228 A3
Wellflats Rd EH29 89 B1
Wellgate Dr FK9 2 C7
Wellgreen La 11 FK8 7 B7
Wellgreen Pl FK8 7 B6
Wellgreen Rd FK8 7 B7
Wellhead Cl EH30 89 D8
Wellheads The KY11 45 D3
Wellington Pl EH6 94 A5
Wellington Sch EH26 208 F6
Wellington St EH7 93 F2
Wellmyre FK10 11 A3
Wellpark EH52 114 F8
Wellpark Cres FK7 6 F4
Wellpark Terr FK4 58 A5
Well Rd Bridge of Allan FK9 2 A8
Falkirk FK1 59 F3
Lochgelly KY5 14 B7
Wellside EH41 129 F8
Wellside Ct FK1 60 A5
Wellside Pl FK1 60 A5
Wellview La EH54 164 F5
WELLWOOD 29 A7
Wellwood Prim Sch KY12 29 A7
Well Wynd EH33 126 D6
Welsh Ct FK6 36 E1
Welsh Gdns FK9 2 A8
Welsh Rd EH47 160 F6
Wemyss Ave KY12 26 A8
Wemyss Ct KY11 46 E5
Wemyssfield KY1 17 B3
Wemyss Gdns EH21 125 C5
Wemyss Pl
Cockenzie & Port Seton
EH32 97 C4
Edinburgh EH3 228 B4
Haddington EH41 130 A8
Longniddry EH32 98 E6
Wemyss Place Mews
EH3 228 B4
Wemyss Rd EH32 98 E6
Wemyss St
Cowdenbeath KY4 13 D3
Rosyth KY11 46 F5
Wemyss Terr EH32 98 F5
Werberside Mews EH4 92 E4
Wesley Cres EH19 173 D7
Wesley Pl FK2 82 B8
West Adam St EH8 229 B2
West Adniston Cotts
EH33 127 C6
West Albert Rd KY1 17 B4
West Annandale St EH7 93 D3
West Approach Rd
Edinburgh, Dalry EH11 120 E6
Edinburgh, Fountainbridge EH3,
EH11 228 A2
West Baldridge Rd KY12 28 E5
Westbank Ct EH33 127 D5
Westbank Gdns EH33 127 D5
Westbank Loan EH15 95 A1
Westbank Pl EH15 95 A1
Westbank Rd EH33 127 C5
Westbank St EH15 95 A1
Westbank Terr EH33 127 C5
West Bankton Pl EH54 164 F7
WEST BARNS 77 E1
West Barns Prim Sch
EH42 77 F1
West Bay Ct EH39 54 B7
West Bay Rd EH39 54 B7
WEST BENHAR 159 B4
West Benhar Rd ML7 159 B3
West Boreland Rd FK6 36 D2
West Bow EH1 229 A2
West Bowling Green St
EH6 93 E5
West Bridge St FK1 60 A5
West Brighton Cres
EH15 123 A8
West Broomhill Rd KY3 50 E8
West Bryson Rd EH11 120 F5
Westburn Ave
Cowdenbeath KY4 13 B2
Edinburgh EH14 148 C8
Falkirk FK1 59 F4
Westburn Gr EH14 148 C8
Westburn Middlefield
EH14 148 C8
Westburn Pk EH14 148 D8
West Burnside EH52 115 E5
West Cairn Cres EH26 191 E6
West Caiystane Rd EH10 150 A5
WEST CALDER 163 D2
West Calder High Sch
EH55 164 B5
West Calder Sta EH55 163 D3
West Calder Workspace
EH55 163 C3
West Camus Rd EH10 150 A6
West Carmuirs Loan FK5 58 F6
West Carnethy Ave EH13 149 A5
West Castle Rd EH10 121 A5
West Catherine Pl EH12 120 E7
West Cherrybank EH6 93 C6
West Church Dr FK3 40 B1
Westcliffe Ct FK3 61 F6
West Clifton Farm Cotts
EH53 145 D8
West Coates EH12 120 E7
West Colinton Ho EH13 149 A6
West College St EH1 229 A2
WEST CRAIGS 118 E7
West Craigs Ave EH12 118 F6
West Craigs Cres EH12 119 A6
West Craigs Ind Est
EH12 118 F7
Westcraigs Pk EH48 138 C3
Westcraigs Rd
Blackridge EH48 138 D2
Harthill ML7 159 F6
West Cres EH34 157 E4
West Croft EH28 117 E2
West Cromwell St EH6 93 F6
West Crosscauseway
EH8 229 B1
West Ct
Edinburgh, Niddrie Mains
EH16 122 E3
Edinburgh, Ravelston EH4 92 C1
West Dr Dunfermline KY12 29 B3
Stenhousemuir FK5 38 C1
WEST END 228 B2
West End
Cockburnspath TD13 218 F4
West Calder EH55 163 C2
West End Gdns FK10 10 A6
Westend Pl EH39 54 B7
West End Pl EH11 120 F6
WESTER ABERDOUR 49 B6
Wester Bankton EH54 165 A7
Wester Bogie Rd KY2 16 B7
Wester Broom Ave EH12 119 C5
Wester Broom Dr EH12 119 C5
Wester Broom Gdns
EH12 119 C5
Wester Broom Gr EH12 119 C5
Wester Broomhouse Cotts
EH42 106 B5
Wester Broom Pl EH12 119 C6
Wester Broom Terr
EH12 119 C5
Wester Cl EH6 93 C7
Wester Coates Ave EH12 120 E7
Wester Coates Gdns
EH12 120 E7
Wester Coates Pl EH12 120 E7
Wester Coates Rd EH12 120 E7
Wester Coates Terr
EH12 120 E7
Wester Cowden Cotts
EH22 153 E3
Wester Dalmeny Steading
EH30 89 E8
Wester Drylaw Ave EH4 92 B3
Wester Drylaw Dr EH4 92 B3
Wester Drylaw Pk EH4 92 C3
Wester Drylaw Pl EH4 92 B3
Wester Drylaw Row EH4 92 C2
Westerdunes Ct EH39 53 E7
Westerdunes Pk EH39 53 D7
Westerfield Dr KY12 29 F6
Westerglen Rd FK1 60 A2
WESTER HAILES 148 D8
Wester Hailes Ed Ctr
EH11 119 C1
Wester Hailes Pk EH14 148 E8
Wester Hailes Rd EH14 148 D7
Wester Hailes Sta EH14 148 D8
Wester Hill EH10 149 E8
Wester Inch Bsns Pk
EH48 141 D3
Wester Inch Rdbt EH48 141 D4
Westerlands Dr FK8 7 B5
Westerlea Ct FK9 2 A5
Westerlea Dr FK9 2 A5
Westermains EH48 139 E5
WESTER MILLERHILL 152 E7
Western Ave
Crossford KY12 28 B1
Falkirk FK2 60 B6
Western Cnr EH12 120 B7
Western Gdns EH12 120 C7
Western General Hospl
EH4 92 D3
Western Harbour Breakwater
EH6 93 D8
Western Harbour Dr EH6 93 D8
Western Harbour Midway
EH6 93 D8
Western Harbour Pl EH6 93 D8
Western Harbour Terr
EH6 93 D8
Western Harbour View
EH6 93 D8
Western Harbour Way
EH6 93 D8
Western Pl EH12 120 C7
Western Terr EH12 120 C7
WESTER PENCAITLAND 156 D6
Wester Row EH14 118 E1
Wester Steil EH10 120 E1
Westerton FK7 20 D8
Westerton Dr FK9 2 A7
Westerton Rd
Broxburn EH52 116 B5
Grangemouth FK3 61 F7
Westerton Terr FK2 39 C3
West Fairbrae Cres EH11 119 E3
West Fairbrae Dr EH11 119 E3
West Fenton Cotts EH39 72 E8
West Fenton Ct EH39 72 D8
West Fenton Gait EH31 52 C2
West Fergus Pl KY1 17 B3
West Ferryfield EH5 92 F5
WESTFIELD 110 F5
Westfield FK10 24 B3
Westfield Ave EH11 120 C5
Westfield Bank 6 EH22 152 E1
Westfield Cotts EH41 129 D3
Westfield Ct 4 EH22 152 E1
Westfield Dr 5 EH22 152 E1
Westfield Gr
Crossgates KY4 30 E6
Dalkeith EH22 152 E1
Westfield Pk EH22 152 E1
Westfield Pl FK6 36 E1
Westfield Prim Sch EH48 110 F4
Westfield Rd EH11 120 D5
Westfield Rdbt FK2 60 F6
Westfield St
Edinburgh EH11 120 D5
Falkirk FK2 60 E5
Westfield Trad Est 2 FK6 36 E1
West Fountain Pl EH11 120 F6
West Garleton Holdings
EH41 100 E4
Westgarth Ave EH13 149 B6
Westgate Dunbar EH42 78 D3
Mid Calder EH53 144 B3
North Berwick EH39 54 B7
Westgate Ct 2 EH39 54 B7
West Gate Rd FK3 62 A8
West Glen Ave EH54 142 E6
West Gorgie Pk EH14 120 C4
West Gorgie Pl EH14 120 C3
West Grange Gdns EH9 121 D3
West Granton Access EH5 92 D5
West Granton Rd EH5 92 D6
Westhall Cres KY12 27 D1
Westhall Gdns
Edinburgh EH10 121 B5
Uphall EH52 115 A4
West Hall Rd EH52 115 E4
West Harbour Rd
Charlestown KY11 45 A4
Cockenzie & Port Seton
EH32 97 B4
Edinburgh EH5 92 E7
West Harwood Crofts
EH55 184 C6
Westhaugh Rd FK9 1 F4
West Holmes Gdns EH21 124 B6
West Holmes Pl EH52 115 B4
West Holmes Rd EH52 115 B4
Westhouses Ave EH22 174 E5
Westhouses Dr EH22 174 E5
Westhouses Rd EH22 174 E5
Westhouses St EH22 174 E5
West James St FK12 5 A6
West Johnstone St FK12 5 A6
West La KY4 13 B2
Westland Cotts EH17 151 E5
West Leven St KY3 50 E8
West Link Rd FK9 2 D5
West Links Rd EH31 51 F2
West Loan EH32 96 F1
West Lodge Gdns FK10 9 F8
West Lorimer Pl EH32 97 B3
West Lothian Coll EH54 143 D1
WEST MAINS 121 E2
Westmains Cotts EH41 132 A5
West Mains Cotts EH55 183 F8
West Mains Ind Est
Falkirk FK3 60 F7
Grangemouth FK3 61 A7
West Mains Rd
Edinburgh EH9 121 F2
Falkirk FK3 60 F7
West Main St
Aberlady EH32 71 C4
Armadale EH48 139 E5
Blackburn EH47 162 C7
Broxburn EH52 115 D5
Harthill ML7 159 E5
Uphall EH52 114 F4
Whitburn EH47 160 F6
West Maitland St EH12 228 A2
West March St KY1 17 D7
West Mayfield EH9 121 F4
West Meikle Pinkerton Cotts
EH42 107 C4
West Mill Bank EH13 149 A6
Westmill Ct EH18 173 A8
West Mill La EH4 228 A3
Westmill Rd EH18 173 A8
West Mill Rd EH13 148 F6
Westmill Wynd EH18 173 A8
Westminster Pl FK5 38 E4
West Montgomery Pl 4
EH7 93 F2
Westmost Cl EH6 93 C7
Westmuir Rd EH55 163 D2
West Murrayfield FK7 7 D1
West Nethertown St KY12 29 A2
West Newington Pl 7
EH9 121 E5
West Nicolson St EH8 229 B2
West Norton Pl EH7 229 C4
WESTPANS 125 B7
Westpark Cres FK2 59 F8
Westpark Ct FK2 59 F8
West Park Gr EH52 115 B5
West Park Pl EH11 120 F6
WEST PILTON 92 C5
West Pilton Ave EH4 92 C4
West Pilton Bank EH4 92 C5
West Pilton Brae EH4 92 D5
West Pilton Cres EH4 92 B5
West Pilton Crossway
EH4 92 C5
West Pilton Dr EH4 92 C5
West Pilton Gdns EH4 92 C5
West Pilton Gn EH4 92 C5
West Pilton Gr EH4 92 C5
West Pilton Lea EH4 92 C5
West Pilton Loan EH4 92 C5
West Pilton March EH4 92 D5
West Pilton Pk EH4 92 C5
West Pilton Pl EH4 92 D5
West Pilton Rd EH4 92 D5
West Pilton Rise EH4 92 C5
West Pilton St EH4 92 C5
West Pilton Terr EH4 92 C5
West Pilton View EH4 92 C4
West Pk Carnock KY12 27 C6
Lochgelly KY5 14 A7
Westpoint Dunbar EH42 78 C2
Garvald EH41 132 D2
West Port Dunbar EH42 78 D2
Dysart KY1 18 A7
Edinburgh EH1 228 C2
Linlithgow EH49 84 F7
West Powburn EH9 121 E3
West Preston St EH8 121 E5
West Quality St KY1 18 A7
WESTQUARTER 61 B2
Westquarter Ave FK2 61 B2
Westquarter Dovecot★
FK2 61 A2
Westquarter Prim Sch
FK2 61 A2
Westray Terr FK1 60 C2
West Rd Charlestown KY11 45 A4
Haddington EH41 129 E8
Whitekirk EH42 75 E7
West Register St EH2 229 A4
West Register Street La
EH2 229 A4
West Relugas Rd EH9 121 D3
Westreron Ho
Bridge of Allan FK9 2 A8
Stirling FK9 2 A1
West Richmond St EH8 229 B2
WESTRIGG 138 F3
WEST SALTOUN 157 C3
West Saltoun EH34 157 C3
West Sands KY11 68 C6
West Savile Gdns EH9 121 E3
West Savile Rd EH16 121 F3
West Savile Terr EH9 121 E3
West Scotland Street La 1
EH3 93 C2
West Seaside EH32 96 F1
West Shore Bsns Ctr EH5 92 C7
West Shore Rd EH5 92 C7
West Shore Road Trad Est
EH5 92 C7
Westside Plaza Sh Ctr
EH14 148 D8
West Silvermills La EH3 93 B2
West St EH26 191 E4
West Stanhope Pl 6
EH12 120 E7
West Stirling St FK12 4 F7
West Telferton EH7 94 F1
West Terr Blackness EH49 65 D5
South Queensferry EH30 68 B1
West Tollcross EH3 228 B1
West Torbain KY2 16 D8
West Vennel 6 FK10 10 B6
Westview EH49 84 C7
Westview Cres FK10 4 C2
West Vows Wlk KY1 35 B6
Westwater St KY5 14 B8
West Way KY11 48 B5
West Werberside EH4 92 E4
WEST WINDYGOUL 126 C4
West Windygoul EH33 126 C5
West Windygoul Gdns
EH33 126 C4
West Winnelstrae EH5 92 F4
Westwood Ave KY1 17 E8
Westwood Cres FK9 2 B3
Westwood Pk EH54 142 F7
Westwood Pl KY11 29 E4
West Woods EH4 92 E3
Westwood View EH55 163 D3
West Wynd 12 KY1 17 D6
Wetherby Bsns Coll EH1 229 B3
Whale Brae EH6 93 D6
Wharry Rd FK12 4 E7
Whauphill ML11 217 F8
Whauphill Cres ML11 217 F8
Wheatear Ct 2 KY11 29 F3
Wheatfield Gr EH20 172 A8
Wheatfield Loan EH20 151 B1
Wheatfield Pl EH11 120 D5
Wheatfield Rd
Bo'ness EH51 64 C6
Edinburgh EH11 120 D5
Wheatfield St EH11 120 E5
Wheatfield Terr EH11 120 D5
Wheatfield Wlk EH20 172 B8
Wheatlands Ave FK4 58 A6
Wheatsheaf La EH22 153 A3
Whimbrel Pl KY11 30 C4
Whim Rd EH31 51 F2
Whinbank EH54 143 E6
Whinhill KY11 29 C3
Whinneyknowe KY11 68 C6
Whinniehill Terr KY12 27 C6
Whinnyburn Pl KY11 46 D5
Whinny Hill Cres KY11 47 A1
Whinny View EH32 71 C4
Whin Park Ind Est EH32 97 B3
Whin Pk EH32 97 B3
Whinrig EH52 115 C6
WHINS OF MILTON 7 B2
Whins Pl EH15 95 A1
Whins Rd Alloa FK10 10 C7
Stirling FK7 7 B2
Whinwell Rd FK8 2 A1
Whirlbut Cres KY11 29 B2
Whirlbut St KY11 29 B2

Whitburgh Mains Cotts EH37 176 D4
WHITBURN 161 D5
Whitburn Acad EH47 161 C7
Whitburn Rd
Bathgate EH48 140 E3
Livingston EH54 143 C3
Whitdale Prim Sch EH47 161 C6
White Castle Hillfort* EH14 222 B7
WHITECRAIG 124 E1
Whitecraig Ave EH21 124 E1
Whitecraig Cres EH21 124 E1
Whitecraig Gardens E EH21 124 E1
Whitecraig Gdns EH21 124 E1
Whitecraig Prim Sch EH21 124 E1
Whitecraig Rd EH21 124 E1
Whitecraig Terr EH21 124 E1
WHITECROSS 83 F6
Whitecross Ind Pk EH49 83 E7
Whitecross Prim Sch EH49 83 F6
Whitedalehead Rd EH47 161 C6
Whitedales EH10 150 C5
Whitefield Neuk KY12 29 F6
Whitefield Rd KY12 29 E6
Whitegates Pl FK1 59 C4
Whitehall Ct EH4 92 B2
White Hart St 12 EH22 153 A3
Whitehead Gr EH30 89 D8
Whitehill EH22 153 F2
Whitehill Ave EH21 124 A4
Whitehill Dr
Blackburn EH47 162 C8
Dalkeith EH22 153 D2
Whitehill Farm Rd EH21 124 A4
Whitehill Gdns EH21 124 A4
Whitehill Gr EH22 153 D2
Whitehill Ind Est
Blackburn EH48 141 C2
Dalkeith EH22 153 E2
Whitehill Pl
Rosewell EH24 172 D2
Stirling FK8 7 A5
Whitehill Rd
Blackburn EH47 141 C1
Edinburgh EH15 123 D3
Rosewell EH24 172 E1
Whitehill St EH21 123 E4
Whitehill View EH47 162 C8
White Horse Cl EH8 229 C3
Whitehouse Loan EH9 121 C5
Whitehouse Rd
Edinburgh EH4 91 A4
Stirling FK7 7 D7
Whitehouse Terr EH9 121 C4
WHITEKIRK 75 F8
Whitelaw Cres KY11 29 D2
Whitelaw Dr EH48 141 E6
Whitelaw Pl KY11 29 D2
Whitelaw Rd KY11 29 D2
Whitelaw St EH48 138 D1
Whitelea Cres EH14 168 C8
Whitelea Rd EH14 168 C8
Whiteloch Ct EH33 127 C5
Whiteloch Rd EH33 127 C5
Whitemoss La EH27 145 E2
Whitemoss Rd EH27 145 E2
Whitemyre Ct KY12 28 D5
White Pk EH11 120 E5
Whitequarries Ind Est EH52 87 C7
Whitesands Geology Trail* EH42 107 F7
White's Cl 5 EH22 153 A3
Whiteside EH48 140 F4
Whiteside Cotts EH48 140 F4
Whiteside Ct EH48 140 F4
Whiteside Farm La EH48 140 D4
Whiteside Ind Est EH48 140 E4
Whitesideloan FK2 82 E8
Whites Quay KY11 47 F2
White St EH47 161 A6
Whitestone Pl EH48 141 C1
Whiteyetts Cres FK10 5 D2
Whiteyetts Dr FK10 5 D2
Whiteyetts Pl FK10 5 D2
Whitingford EH6 93 D5
Whitson Cres EH11 120 B5
Whitson Gr EH11 120 B5
Whitson Place E EH11 120 B5
Whitson Place W EH11 120 B5
Whitson Rd EH11 120 B5
Whitson Terr EH11 120 B5
Whitson Way EH11 120 B5
Whitson Wlk EH11 120 A5
Whitten La EH49 84 F7
Whittingehame Dr EH41 130 C8
Whittingehame Mews EH41 130 C8
Whittret Knowe ML11 217 F7
Wholeflats Rd FK2, FK3 62 A4
Wholeflats Rdbt FK3 61 E5
Wholequarter Ave FK2 61 B2
Whytebank Gdns KY2 17 B5
Whytehouse Ave KY1 17 B3
Whyteman's Brae KY1 17 C8
Whytemans Brae Hospl KY1 17 B7
Whyte Melville Rd KY2 17 A4
Whyte Pl 7 EH7 94 A1
Whytescauseway KY1 17 B3
Whyte St Harthill ML7 159 F6
Whyte St *continued*
Lochgelly KY5 14 B8
Whyte Wlk KY11 29 F4
Widows Row EH42 76 B3
Wilderness Rdbt EH54 164 C6
Wilderness The FK2 22 D4
Wilfrid Terr 6 EH8 94 C1
Wilkie Pl FK5 38 B2
WILKIESTON 146 A6
Wilkieston Rd EH28 117 C2
William Black Pl EH30 89 C8
William Booth Pl FK7 7 A3
Williamfield Ave FK7 7 A4
Williamfield Sq 2 EH15 123 A8
William Jameson Pl EH15 95 A1
William Sharp Pl KY4 13 D4
Williamson Ave FK2 39 A1
Williamson Pl FK2 60 C7
Williamson's Quay KY1 17 C4
Williamson St FK1 60 B4
William St
Dunfermline KY12 28 E4
Edinburgh EH3 228 A3
Kirkcaldy KY1 17 B2
Williamstone Ct EH39 54 A6
Williamston Intc EH54 144 A1
Williamston Prim Sch EH54 164 F8
William Street NE La EH3 228 A3
William Street NW La EH3 228 A3
William Street SE La EH3 228 A3
William Street SW La EH3 228 A2
Willow Ave
Bonnyrigg and Lasswade EH19 173 B6
Fauldhouse EH47 181 F5
Willowbank EH54 143 E6
Willowbank Row EH6 93 D6
WILLOWBRAE 122 D7
Willowbrae FK2 82 D8
Willow Brae
Fauldhouse EH47 181 F5
Plean FK7 20 C3
Willowbrae Ave EH8 122 C8
Willowbrae Gdns EH8 122 D8
Willowbrae Rd EH8 122 D8
Willowdean EH49 86 C4
Willow Dell EH51 63 D5
Willow Dr KY1 17 B8
Willow Gr
Dunfermline KY11 46 E8
Fauldhouse EH47 181 F5
Livingston EH54 144 B5
Menstrie FK11 3 E6
Willow Grange FK2 61 C1
Willowgrove House Sch EH54 144 B5
Willow Pk EH47 181 F5
Willow Rd EH22 174 E6
Willows The
Cairneyhill KY12 27 D1
Tullibody FK10 4 B1
Willow Tree Pl EH14 147 D3
Willow View EH47 181 F5
Wilson Ave Dalkeith EH22 153 C3
Denny FK6 36 D2
Falkirk FK1 59 C5
Kirkcaldy KY2 17 B6
Polmont FK2 61 F2
Prestonpans EH32 96 F1
Wilson Bruce Ct KY5 14 C8
Wilson Ct ML11 217 F7
Wilson Dr Bannockburn FK7 7 C2
Falkirk FK1 59 C5
Wilson Gdns FK1 59 C6
Wilson Pl Bonnybridge FK4 58 C4
Dunbar EH42 106 E8
Wilson Rd Allanton ML7 198 A8
Dunbar EH42 106 D8
Falkirk FK1 59 C6
Gorebridge EH23 174 D1
Livingston EH54 142 E3
Wilson's Cl
1 Dunfermline KY12 29 A3
16 Falkirk FK1 60 B4
Wilson's Ct EH1 229 B3
Wilson's Pk EH15 95 B1
Wilson St Blairhall KY12 26 A8
Cowdenbeath KY4 13 C4
Grangemouth FK3 61 C6
Penicuik EH26 191 E5
Townhill KY12 29 D8
Wilson Terr
Broxburn EH52 115 B5
Stoneyburn EH47 162 A2
WILSONTOWN 201 C2
Wilsontown Rd ML11 201 C2
Wilson Way KY11 46 D2
Wilson Wlk 5 EH33 126 C5
Wilton Rd Carluke ML8 215 B1
Edinburgh EH16 121 F3
WINCHBURGH 87 E2
Winchburgh Cotts EH52 87 F2
Winchburgh Prim Sch EH52 87 E2
Winchester Ave FK6 36 E3
Winchester Avenue Ind Est FK6 36 F3
Winchester Ct FK6 36 F3
Winchester Dr FK6 36 F2
Windlebrook KY11 47 A7
Windmill Cl EH8 229 B1
Windmill Gn KY1 17 F8
Windmill Knowe KY4 30 E6
Windmill La EH8 229 B1
Windmill Pl
Edinburgh EH8 229 B1
Kirkcaldy KY1 18 A8
Windmill Rd KY1 17 F8
Windmill St EH8 229 A1
Windmill View FK10 5 D2
Windrush Dr EH6 93 D7
Windsor Ave FK1 59 E4
Windsor Cres Falkirk FK1 59 E4
Maddiston FK2 83 A6
Penicuik EH26 192 A6
Windsor Dr Denny FK6 36 D3
Falkirk FK1 59 F4
Penicuik EH26 192 A6
Windsor Gdns Alloa FK10 9 F8
3 Falkirk FK1 59 F4
Musselburgh EH21 124 E6
Windsor Park Dr EH21 124 F6
Windsor Park Pl EH21 124 F6
Windsor Park Sch FK1 59 E4
Windsor Park Terr EH21 124 F6
Windsor Pk EH21 124 F6
Windsor Pl
Edinburgh EH15 123 B8
Shotts ML7 179 E5
Stirling FK8 7 A7
Windsor Rd Falkirk FK1 59 E4
Penicuik EH26 192 A6
Windsor Sq EH26 192 A6
Windsor St Edinburgh EH7 93 E2
Menstrie FK11 3 F6
Shotts ML7 179 E5
Windsor Street La EH7 93 E2
Windsor Terr EH26 192 A6
Windygate KY2 16 F1
Windygates Rd EH39 54 B6
Windygoul Cres EH33 126 E5
Windygoul Prim Sch EH33 126 D4
Windyhill Ave FK10 23 D6
WINDYKNOWE 140 F5
Windyknowe Cres EH48 140 E6
Windyknowe Pk EH48 140 E6
Windyknowe Prim Sch EH48 140 D6
Windy Mains Farm Cotts EH36 177 D5
Wingate Cres EH42 78 C2
Winifred Cres KY2 17 A6
Winifred St KY2 17 A6
Winterfield Mains EH42 78 A2
Winterfield Pl EH42 78 A2
Winterthur La KY12 29 A4
Winton Cl EH33 126 E4
Winton Ct
Cockenzie & Port Seton EH32 97 C4
New Winton EH33 127 B3
Tranent EH33 126 E4
Winton Dr EH10 150 C4
Winton Gdns EH10 150 C4
Winton Gr Edinburgh EH10 150 B5
Tranent EH33 126 E4
Wintonhill Cotts EH34 127 D2
Winton Ho* EH34 156 D7
Winton Loan
Edinburgh EH10 150 C4
Macmerry EH33 127 A6
Winton Pk
Cockenzie & Port Seton EH32 97 C3
Edinburgh EH10 150 B4
Winton Pl EH33 126 D6
Winton Terr
Edinburgh EH10 150 B5
New Winton EH33 127 B3
Winton Way EH33 126 D4
Wishart Ave
Bonnyrigg and Lasswade EH19 173 D8
North Berwick EH39 54 C6
Wishart Dr FK7 7 D3
Wishart Pl Dalkeith EH22 152 E2
Kirkcaldy KY1 17 F6
Tranent EH35 155 D6
Wishaw Terr EH7 94 B1
Wisp Gn EH15 123 B4
Wisp The Dalkeith EH22 123 B1
Edinburgh EH15, EH16 123 B3
Witchbrae KY12 29 B4
Witholm EH22 153 E2
Wolfe Rd FK1 60 D4
Wolfstar Farm Cotts EH35 155 F6
Wolrige Rd EH16 151 A8
Wolseley Cres EH8 94 C1
Wolseley Pl EH8 94 C1
Wolseley Terr 7 EH8 94 C1
Wolsey Ave EH19 173 C6
Wood Avens FK10 4 B1
Woodbank KY4 13 B2
Woodbank Crofts EH48 110 F2
Woodbank Gr KY12 26 D7
Woodbine Terr EH6 94 A3
WOODBURN 153 C3
Woodburn Ave
Dalkeith EH22 153 C2
Redding FK2 61 B2
Woodburn Bank EH22 153 C3
Woodburn Cres
Bonnybridge FK4 57 F3
Oakley KY12 26 F7
Redding FK2 61 B2
Woodburn Dr Alloa FK10 4 F1
Dalkeith EH22 153 B3
Woodburn Gdns
Dalkeith EH22 153 C3
Woodburn Gdns *continued*
Falkirk FK2 60 E5
Woodburn Gr EH22 153 C2
Woodburn Loan EH22 153 C3
Woodburn Medway EH22 153 C3
Woodburn Pk EH22 153 C3
Woodburn Pl EH22 153 C3
Woodburn Prim Sch EH22 153 C3
Woodburn Rd
Dalkeith EH22 153 C3
Falkirk FK2 60 D5
Woodburn St
Dalkeith EH22 153 C3
Falkirk FK2 60 E5
Woodburn Terr
Dalkeith EH22 153 D3
Edinburgh EH10 121 B3
Woodburn View EH22 153 D3
Woodburn Way FK12 5 A6
Woodbush EH42 78 E2
Woodbush Brae EH42 78 E2
Woodbush Ct EH42 78 E2
Woodbush Pl EH42 78 E2
Wood Dr EH47 160 F6
WOODEND 87 F7
Woodend Bsns Ctr KY4 13 B1
Woodend Gdns KY11 47 F5
Woodend Ind Est KY4 13 B1
Woodend Pk EH25 171 F3
Woodend Pl KY4 13 B1
Woodend Rd ML8 215 A2
Woodend Wlk EH48 139 E6
Woodfield Ave EH13 148 F6
Woodfield Pk
Bilston EH25 171 D6
Edinburgh EH13 148 F6
Woodhall Ave EH14 148 D6
Woodhall Bank EH13 148 F5
Woodhall Cotts EH42 135 F6
Woodhall Dr EH14 148 D6
Woodhall Gr EH13 148 F5
Woodhall Millbrae EH14 148 E6
Woodhall Pl EH34 156 E6
Woodhall Rd
Edinburgh EH13 148 F5
Pencaitland EH34 156 D6
Woodhall Terr EH14 148 D6
Woodhead Farm Rd KY12 25 F2
Woodhead Gr EH48 139 D5
Woodhead Pl EH48 140 E6
Woodhead St KY12 26 A2
Woodhill Ct FK3 61 D6
Woodhill Gr KY12 28 B2
Woodhill Rd EH48 138 B3
WOODLANDS 60 B4
Woodlands FK10 5 E1
Woodlands Bank KY11 48 A3
Woodlands Cotts EH48 140 B5
Woodlands Cres FK1 60 A4
Woodlands Dr
Bo'ness EH51 63 D5
Crossford KY12 28 A2
Grangemouth FK2 82 E8
Woodlands Gr
Armadale EH48 140 B5
Edinburgh EH15 122 E6
Townhill KY12 29 D7
Woodlands Pk EH54 142 F8
Woodlands Rd KY2 16 D6
Woodlands Sch EH14 147 F4
Woodlands Terr KY12 26 B8
Woodlands The KY11 46 F5
Woodland View EH22 153 D4
Woodland Way FK6 57 D7
Wood Lea FK10 23 E5
Woodlea Cotts EH49 65 A3
Woodlea Gdns Alloa FK10 5 A1
Bonnybridge FK4 57 F5
Woodlea Pk Alloa FK10 10 B8
Sauchie FK10 5 A1
Woodmill Cres KY11 29 D3
Woodmill High Sch KY11 29 E3
Woodmill Pl KY11 29 E3
Woodmill Rd KY11 29 D3
Woodmill St KY11 29 B3
Woodmill Terr KY11 29 B3
Woodmuir Pl EH55 182 E6
Woodmuir Prim Sch EH55 182 E6
Woodmuir Rd
Breich EH55 182 E6
Whitburn EH47 161 C6
Wood Pl Livingston EH54 143 C4
Rosyth KY11 46 E5
Wood Rd KY11 46 C2
Woodrow EH23 174 C1
Woodruff Gait KY12 28 F5
Woodrush Glade EH54 164 C8
Wood's Ct EH19 173 B7
Woodside KY4 13 C3
Woodside Ave KY11 46 F5
Woodside Ct
Cambusbarron FK7 6 D5
Falkirk FK1 60 B3
Woodside Dr EH26 191 F5
Woodside Gdns
Grangemouth FK2 82 E8
Musselburgh EH21 124 E6
Woodside Gr FK5 59 D8
Woodside Pl
Bridgend EH49 86 C4
Fallin FK7 8 C4
Woodside Rd Alloa FK10 4 F1
Forrestfield ML6 137 A3
Stirling FK8 2 A3
Tullibody FK10 4 A1
Woodside St KY11 46 F5
Woodside Terr
Bridgend EH49 86 C4
Clackmannan FK10 10 F4
Edinburgh EH15 123 D7
Falkirk FK1 60 B3
Tarbrax EH55 203 F3
Wood St FK3 61 C7
Woodstock Pl EH16 122 B1
Wood Terr EH48 140 A6
Woodville Ct EH52 115 D4
Woodville Terr EH6 94 A3
Wooer St 4 FK1 60 B4
Woolcarders Ct FK7 6 D6
Woolfords Cotts EH55 203 A7
Woolmet Cres EH22 152 B8
Woolmet Pl EH16 122 F3
Wordie Rd FK7 6 F4
World's End Cl EH1 229 B3
Wotherspoon Cres EH48 139 F5
Wotherspoon Dr EH51 63 D6
W Parliament Sq EH1 229 A3
Wright Ave EH48 141 A3
Wright Pl Kirkcaldy KY1 17 D7
Lochgelly KY5 14 A8
Wright St FK2 60 B6
Writers Ct EH42 78 D3
Writers' Mus* EH1 229 A3
Wyckliffe KY12 28 C6
Wymet Ct KY12 29 A3
Wymet Ho KY12 29 A3
Wyndford Ave EH52 115 A5
Wyndford Brae EH49 86 E7
Wyndford Pl EH52 115 A5
Wynd The Alva FK12 5 A7
Dalgety Bay KY11 48 C3
Gifford EH41 220 F6
Ormiston EH35 155 E7
Wyre Hayes Cotts KY4 30 F8
Wyvern Pk EH9 121 D4
Wyvis Pk EH26 192 A7
Wyvis Pl ML7 180 B3

X

Xcite Bathgate Sports Ctr EH48 141 B1

Y

Yardheads EH6 93 F5
Yardley Pl FK2 39 A1
Yarrow Ct EH26 192 A7
Yarrow Pl FK3 61 F6
Yeaman La EH11 120 F6
Yeaman Pl EH11 120 F5
Yellowcraig Trail* EH39 53 B8
Yester Mains Cotts EH41 220 F5
Yester Pl EH41, EH32 100 F1
Yester Prim Sch EH41 220 F6
Yetholm Pk KY12 28 F2
Yetholm Way KY2 17 C6
Yetts The FK7 6 C5
Yew Gr EH54 144 B5
Yewlands Cres EH16 151 B7
Yewlands Gdns EH16 151 B7
Yew Terr FK2 61 A2
YIELDSHIELDS 215 E2
Yieldshields Rd ML8 216 D3
York Arc 4 FK3 40 D1
York Dr FK2 60 D6
York La 2 Edinburgh EH1 229 A4
2 Grangemouth FK3 40 D1
York Pl Dunfermline KY12 29 C6
Edinburgh EH1 229 A4
Kirkcaldy KY1 17 F8
York Rd Edinburgh EH5 93 C6
North Berwick EH39 54 A7
York Sq 3 FK3 40 D1
York St FK2 60 D6
Young Ave EH33 126 D5
Young Cres EH48 140 F5
Young Ct KY4 13 C3
Young Sq EH54 164 B6
Youngs Rd EH52 116 A6
Young St Edinburgh EH2 228 B3
West Calder EH55 163 C2
Young's Terr 2 KY1 17 C5
Young Street North La EH2 228 B3
Young Street South La EH2 228 B3
Young Terr KY4 13 B3
Yule Pl EH47 141 C1
Yule Terr EH47 162 C8

Z

Zealandia Rd KY11 46 B1
Zetland Dr
Grangemouth FK3 61 A8
Laurieston FK2 61 A4
Zetland Pl Edinburgh EH5 93 B6
Lochgelly KY5 14 A7
Skinflats FK2 39 F3
Zetland St FK10 11 B4
Zetland Terr FK2 61 F2